FOOTBALL REGISTER

1989 EDITION

SO-CYE-352

Editors/Football Register
HOWARD BALZER
BARRY SIEGEL

President-Chief Executive Officer
RICHARD WATERS

Book Publisher
GREGORY WILEY

Editorial Director of Books and Periodicals
RON SMITH

Published by

The Sporting News

1212 North Lindbergh Boulevard
P.O. Box 56 — St. Louis, MO 63166

Copyright © 1989
The Sporting News Publishing Company

A Times Mirror
Company

ISBN 0-89204-326-1   ISSN 0071-7258

TABLE
of
CONTENTS

ON THE COVER: Cincinnati quarterback Boomer Esiason, The Sporting News' NFL Player of the Year in 1988, guided the high-powered Bengals to a 12-4 record and a berth in Super Bowl XXIII.

Photo by Richard Pilling

EXPLANATION OF ABBREVIATIONS

AAFC—All America Football Conference. AFL—American Football League. CFL—Canadian Football League. CoFL—Continental Football League. EFL—Eastern Football League. NFL—National Football League. PFLA—Professional Football League of America. USFL—United States Football League. WFL—World Football League.

Att.—Attempts. Avg.—Average. Blk.—Blocked punts. Cmp.—Pass completions. F—Fumbles. FG—Field goals made. FGA—Field goal attempts. G—Games. Gain—Yards gained passing. No.—Number. P.C.—Passes caught. Pct.—Percentage completed. P.I.—Passes intercepted. Pts.—Total points scored. TD—Touchdowns. T.P.—Touchdown passes thrown. XP—Extra points made. XPM—Extra points missed. Yds.—Net yards gained.

Veteran Players

Please note for statistical comparisons: In 1982, only nine of 16 games were played due to the cancellation of games because of players' strike. In 1987, only 15 of 16 games were played due to the cancellation of games during week three because of players' strike. Most NFL players also missed games scheduled during weeks four through six.

*Indicates led league or tied for leadership.

VINCENT STEVEN ABBOTT
(Vince)
Placekicker—San Diego Chargers

Born May 31, 1958, at London, England.
Height, 5.11. Weight, 206.
High School—Tsawwassen, Vancouver, Canada, South Delta.
Attended University of Washington and received bachelor of arts degree in accounting
from California State University at Fullerton in 1981.

Signed as free agent by Los Angeles Rams, June 15, 1981.
Released by Los Angeles Rams, August 7, 1981; signed as free agent by San Francisco 49ers, April 20, 1982.
Released by San Francisco 49ers, August 24, 1982; awarded on waivers to Miami Dolphins, August 25, 1982.
Released by Miami Dolphins, August 31, 1982; signed as free agent by Los Angeles Express, November 1, 1982.
Released by Los Angeles Express, February 21, 1984; signed as free agent by Chicago Bears, April 13, 1984.
Released by Chicago Bears, August 21, 1984; signed as free agent by Tampa Bay Buccaneers for 1985, November 9, 1984.
Released by Tampa Bay Buccaneers, August 19, 1985; signed as free agent by Los Angeles Raiders, June 21, 1986.
Released by Los Angeles Raiders, August 19, 1986; signed as free agent by San Diego Chargers, April 13, 1987.
On injured reserve with knee injury, November 17 through remainder of 1988 season.

		——PLACE KICKING——					
Year	Club	G.	XP.	XPM.	FG.	FGA.	Pts.
1983—Los Angeles USFL...		18	31	3	17	30	82
1987—San Diego NFL		12	22	1	13	22	61
1988—San Diego NFL		11	15	0	8	12	39
Pro Totals—3 Years		41	68	4	38	64	182

WALTER AUGUSTUS ABERCROMBIE
Running Back—Philadelphia Eagles

Born September 26, 1959, at Waco, Tex.
Height, 6.00. Weight, 210.
High School—Waco, Tex., University.
Attended Baylor University.

Selected by Pittsburgh in 1st round (12th player selected) of 1982 NFL draft.
On injured reserve with knee injury, September 7 through November 26, 1982; activated, November 27, 1982.
Released by Pittsburgh Steelers, August 30, 1988; signed as free agent by Philadelphia Eagles, November 9, 1988.

			——RUSHING——				PASS RECEIVING				—TOTAL—		
Year	Club	G.	Att.	Yds.	Avg.	TD.	P.C.	Yds.	Avg.	TD.	TD.	Pts.	F.
1982—Pittsburgh NFL		6	21	100	4.8	2	1	14	14.0	0	2	12	0
1983—Pittsburgh NFL		15	112	446	4.0	4	26	391	15.0	3	7	42	2
1984—Pittsburgh NFL		14	145	610	4.2	1	16	135	8.4	0	1	6	0
1985—Pittsburgh NFL		16	227	851	3.7	7	24	209	8.7	2	9	54	5
1986—Pittsburgh NFL		16	214	877	4.1	6	47	395	8.4	2	8	48	4
1987—Pittsburgh NFL		12	123	459	3.7	2	24	209	8.7	0	2	12	4
1988—Philadelphia NFL		5	5	14	2.8	0	1	—2	—2.0	0	0	0	0
Pro Totals—7 Years		84	847	3357	4.0	22	139	1351	9.7	7	29	174	15

Additional pro statistics: Returned seven kickoffs for 139 yards (19.9 avg.) and recovered two fumbles, 1982; recovered one fumble, 1985; recovered three fumbles for two yards, 1987; returned five kickoffs for 87 yards, 1988.
Played in AFC Championship Game following 1984 season.

CURTIS LADONN ADAMS
Running Back

Born April 30, 1962, at Muskegon, Mich.
Height, 5.11. Weight, 207.
High School—Muskegon, Mich., Orchard View.
Attended Central Michigan University.

Selected by Orlando in 9th round (117th player selected) of 1985 USFL draft.
Selected by San Diego in 8th round (207th player selected) of 1985 NFL draft.
Signed by San Diego Chargers, June 19, 1985.
On injured reserve with knee injury, September 12 through remainder of 1985 season.
On injured reserve with shoulder injury, September 2 through November 7, 1986; activated, November 8, 1986.
On injured reserve with knee injury, October 29 through remainder of 1988 season.
Granted unconditional free agency, February 1, 1989; rights released, May 22, 1989.

			——RUSHING——				PASS RECEIVING				—TOTAL—		
Year	Club	G.	Att.	Yds.	Avg.	TD.	P.C.	Yds.	Avg.	TD.	TD.	Pts.	F.
1985—San Diego NFL		1	16	49	3.1	1	1	12	12.0	0	1	6	0
1986—San Diego NFL		7	118	366	3.1	4	4	26	6.5	0	4	24	3
1987—San Diego NFL		12	90	343	3.8	1	4	38	9.5	0	1	6	1
1988—San Diego NFL		7	38	149	3.9	1		None			1	6	1
Pro Totals—4 Years		27	262	907	3.5	7	9	76	8.4	0	7	42	5

Additional pro statistics: Returned two kickoffs for 50 yards, 1985; returned five kickoffs for 100 yards and recovered one fumble, 1986; returned four kickoffs for 32 yards, 1987; returned one kickoff for 13 yards, 1988.

GEORGE WALLACE ADAMS
Running Back—New York Giants

Born December 22, 1962, at Lexington, Ky.
Height, 6.01. Weight, 225.
High School—Lexington, Ky., Lafayette.
Attended University of Kentucky.
Cousin of Dermontti Dawson, guard-center with Pittsburgh Steelers.

Selected by Orlando in 3rd round (33rd player selected) of 1985 USFL draft.
Selected by New York Giants in 1st round (19th player selected) of 1985 NFL draft.
Signed by New York Giants, July 22, 1985.
On injured reserve with hip injury, September 1 through entire 1986 season.

Year Club	G.	Att.	Yds.	Avg.	TD.	P.C.	Yds.	Avg.	TD.	TD.	Pts.	F.
1985—New York Giants NFL	16	128	498	3.9	2	31	389	12.5	2	4	24	7
1987—New York Giants NFL	12	61	169	2.8	1	35	298	8.5	1	2	12	3
1988—New York Giants NFL	16	29	76	2.6	0	27	174	6.4	0	0	0	0
Pro Totals—3 Years	44	218	743	3.4	3	93	861	9.3	3	6	36	10

(Header spans: RUSHING — Att. Yds. Avg. TD.; PASS RECEIVING — P.C. Yds. Avg. TD.; —TOTAL— TD. Pts. F.)

Year Club	G.	No.	Yds.	Avg.	TD.
1985—N.Y. Giants NFL	16	14	241	17.2	0
1987—N.Y. Giants NFL	12	9	166	18.4	0
1988—N.Y. Giants NFL	16		None		
Pro Totals—3 Years	44	23	407	17.7	0

(Header: KICKOFF RETURNS)

Additional pro statistics: Attempted one pass with no completions and recovered two fumbles, 1985; recovered one fumble, 1987.

MICHAEL ADAMS
Cornerback—Phoenix Cardinals

Born April 5, 1964, at Shelby, Miss.
Height, 5.10. Weight, 195.
High School—Shelby, Miss., Broad Street.
Attended Mississippi Delta Junior College and Arkansas State University.

Selected by New Orleans in 3rd round (67th player selected) of 1987 NFL draft.
Signed by New Orleans Saints, August 3, 1987.
On injured reserve with hamstring injury, September 11 through September 29, 1987; activated, September 30, 1987.
Crossed picket line during player's strike, September 30, 1987.
On injured reserve with knee injury, October 17 through remainder of 1988 season.
Granted unconditional free agency, February 1, 1989; signed by Phoenix Cardinals, March 13, 1989.
New Orleans NFL, 1987 and 1988.
Games: 1987 (7), 1988 (5). Total—12.
Pro statistics: Returned four kickoffs for 52 yards and fumbled once, 1987; recovered two fumbles, 1987 and 1988.

STEFON LEE ADAMS
Safety—Los Angeles Raiders

Born August 11, 1963, at High Point, N. C.
Height, 5.10. Weight, 190.
High School—High Point, N. C., Southwest Guilford.
Attended East Carolina University.

Selected by Baltimore in 4th round (58th player selected) of 1985 USFL draft.
Selected by Los Angeles Raiders in 3rd round (80th player selected) of 1985 NFL draft.
Signed by Los Angeles Raiders, July 17, 1985.
On injured reserve with hamstring injury, September 2 through entire 1985 season.
Released by Los Angeles Raiders, August 26, 1988; re-signed by Raiders, September 14, 1988.

Year Club	G.	No.	Yds.	Avg.	TD.
1986—L.A. Raiders NFL	16	27	573	21.2	0
1987—L.A. Raiders NFL	9	3	61	20.3	0
1988—L.A. Raiders NFL	14	8	132	16.5	0
Pro Totals—3 Years	39	38	766	20.2	0

(Header: KICKOFF RETURNS)

Additional pro statistics: Intercepted one pass for 32 yards and recovered two fumbles, 1986; intercepted one pass for eight yards and returned five punts for 39 yards, 1987; returned six punts for 45 yards and recovered three fumbles for one yard, 1988.

JOHN M. ADICKES

Name pronounced ADD-dix.

Center—Chicago Bears

Born June 29, 1964, at St. Albans, N. Y.
Height, 6.03. Weight, 264.
High School—Killeen, Tex.
Received degree in finance and real estate from Baylor University in 1987.
Brother of Mark Adickes, guard with Kansas City Chiefs.

Selected by Chicago in 6th round (154th player selected) of 1987 NFL draft.
Signed by Chicago Bears, July 30, 1987.
Chicago NFL, 1987 and 1988.
Games: 1987 (6), 1988 (16). Total—22.
Pro statistics: Fumbled once for minus 13 yards, 1988.
Played in NFC Championship Game following 1988 season.

MARK STEPHEN ADICKES
Name pronounced ADD-dix.
Guard—Kansas City Chiefs
Born April 22, 1961, at Badconstadt, West Germany.
Height, 6.04. Weight, 270.
High School—Killeen, Tex.
Attended Baylor University.
Brother of John Adickes, center with Chicago Bears.

Named as offensive tackle on THE SPORTING NEWS College All-America Team, 1983.
Selected by Houston in 1984 USFL territorial draft.
USFL rights traded with rights to center Mike Ruether by Houston Gamblers to Los Angeles Express for 2nd round pick in 1985 and 1986 draft, February 13, 1984.
Signed by Los Angeles Express, February 13, 1984.
Granted roster exemption, February 13, 1984; activated, February 24, 1984.
On injured reserve with knee injury, March 6 through remainder of 1984 season.
Selected by Kansas City in 1st round (5th player selected) of 1984 NFL supplemental draft.
Released by Los Angeles Express, August 1, 1985; re-signed by Express, August 2, 1985.
Released by Los Angeles Express, April 3, 1986; signed by Kansas City Chiefs, June 5, 1986.
On injured reserve with back injury, August 22 through October 14, 1988; activated, October 15, 1988.
Los Angeles USFL, 1984 and 1985; Kansas City NFL, 1986 through 1988.
Games: 1984 (2), 1985 (11), 1986 (15), 1987 (12), 1988 (10). Total USFL—13. Total NFL—37. Total Pro—50.
Pro statistics: Caught one pass for three yards and a touchdown and recovered one fumble, 1987.

TOMMIE LEE AGEE
Fullback—Kansas City Chiefs
Born February 22, 1964, at Chilton, Ala.
Height, 6.00. Weight, 218.
High School—Maplesville, Ala.
Received degree in criminal justice from Auburn University.

Selected by Seattle in 5th round (119th player selected) of 1987 NFL draft.
Signed by Seattle Seahawks, July 21, 1987.
On injured reserve with knee injury, September 1 through entire 1987 season.
Granted unconditional free agency, February 1, 1989; signed by Kansas City Chiefs, February 24, 1989.

| | | ——RUSHING—— | | | | PASS RECEIVING | | | | —TOTAL— | | |
Year Club	G.	Att.	Yds.	Avg.	TD.	P.C.	Yds.	Avg.	TD.	TD.	Pts.	F.
1988—Seattle NFL	16	1	2	2.0	0	3	31	10.3	0	0	0	0

Additional pro statistics: Had only pass attempt intercepted and recovered one fumble, 1988.

DAVID IVER AHRENS
Name pronounced AIR-ens.
(Dave)
Linebacker—Miami Dolphins
Born December 5, 1958, at Cedar Falls, Ia.
Height, 6.04. Weight, 247.
High School—Oregon, Wis.
Attended University of Wisconsin.

Selected by St. Louis in 6th round (143rd player selected) of 1981 NFL draft.
Traded by St. Louis Cardinals to Indianapolis Colts for 10th round pick in 1986 draft, August 27, 1985.
Released by Indianapolis Colts, August 24, 1988; signed as free agent by Detroit Lions, October 20, 1988.
Granted unconditional free agency, February 1, 1989; signed by Miami Dolphins, March 23, 1989.
St. Louis NFL, 1981 through 1984; Indianapolis NFL, 1985 through 1987; Detroit NFL, 1988.
Games: 1981 (16), 1982 (9), 1983 (16), 1984 (16), 1985 (16), 1987 (12), 1988 (8). Total—109.
Pro statistics: Intercepted one pass for 14 yards, 1981; returned one kickoff for five yards, 1982; recovered one fumble, 1982 and 1985; caught one pass for four yards, 1983; returned one punt for no yards and recovered two fumbles, 1987.

VINCE DENADER ALBRITTON
Safety—Dallas Cowboys
Born July 23, 1962, at Oakland, Calif.
Height, 6.02. Weight, 217.
High School—Oakland, Calif., McClymond.
Attended University of Washington.

Selected by Philadelphia in 16th round (326th player selected) of 1984 USFL draft.
Signed as free agent by Dallas Cowboys, May 3, 1984.
On injured reserve with hamstring injury, August 20 through November 7, 1985; activated after clearing procedural waivers, November 9, 1985.
On injured reserve with thigh injury, August 23 through October 28, 1988; activated, October 29, 1988.

Dallas NFL, 1984 through 1988.
Games: 1984 (16), 1985 (7), 1986 (16), 1987 (11), 1988 (6). Total—56.
Pro statistics: Recovered two fumbles, 1984 and 1986.

DAN LAMARR ALEXANDER
Guard—New York Jets
Born June 17, 1955, at Houston, Tex.
Height, 6.04. Weight, 274.
High School—Houston, Tex., Lamar.
Received degree in law enforcement from Louisiana State University.

Selected by New York Jets in 8th round (200th player selected) of 1977 NFL draft.
New York Jets NFL, 1977 through 1988.
Games: 1977 (14), 1978 (16), 1979 (16), 1980 (16), 1981 (16), 1982 (9), 1983 (16), 1984 (16), 1985 (16), 1986 (16), 1987 (12), 1988 (14). Total—177.
Pro statistics: Recovered one fumble, 1978 and 1982; recovered two fumbles, 1987.
Played in AFC Championship Game following 1982 season.

DAVID ALEXANDER
Center-Guard—Philadelphia Eagles
Born July 28, 1964, at Silver Spring, Md.
Height, 6.03. Weight, 275.
High School—Broken Arrow, Okla.
Attended The University of Tulsa.

Selected by Philadelphia in 5th round (121st player selected) of 1987 NFL draft.
Signed by Philadelphia Eagles, August 5, 1987.
Philadelphia NFL, 1987 and 1988.
Games: 1987 (12), 1988 (16). Total—28.
Pro statistics: Recovered one fumble, 1988.

VERNEST RAYNARD ALEXANDER
(Ray)
Wide Receiver—Dallas Cowboys
Born January 8, 1962, at Miami, Fla.
Height, 6.04. Weight, 196.
High School—Mobile, Ala., John S. Shaw.
Attended Florida A&M University.

Selected by Tampa Bay in 1984 USFL territorial draft.
Signed as free agent by Denver Broncos, May 2, 1984.
Released by Denver Broncos, August 27, 1984; re-signed by Broncos, September 27, 1984.
Released by Denver Broncos, August 26, 1985; signed as free agent by Calgary Stampeders, September 8, 1985.
Granted free agency, March 1, 1987; signed as free agent by Dallas Cowboys, March 23, 1987.
On injured reserve with broken wrist, September 1 through entire 1987 season.
Crossed picket line during player's strike, October 14, 1987.

		—PASS RECEIVING—			
Year Club	G.	P.C.	Yds.	Avg.	TD.
1984—Denver NFL	8	8	132	16.5	1
1985—Calgary CFL	8	22	361	16.4	1
1986—Calgary CFL	18	88	1590	18.1	10
1988—Dallas NFL	16	54	788	14.6	6
NFL Totals—2 Years	24	62	920	14.8	7
CFL Totals—2 Years	26	110	1951	17.7	11
Pro Totals—4 Years	50	172	2871	16.7	18

Additional pro statistics: Fumbled once, 1985; scored one 2-point conversion, 1986.

RAUL ENRIQUE ALLEGRE
Placekicker—New York Giants
Born June 15, 1959, at Torreon, Coahuila, Mex.
Height, 5.10. Weight, 167.
High School—Shelton, Wash.
Attended University of Montana and received degree in civil engineering from University of Texas.

Signed as free agent by Dallas Cowboys, April 28, 1983.
Traded by Dallas Cowboys to Baltimore Colts for 9th round pick in 1984 draft, August 29, 1983.
Franchise transferred to Indianapolis, March 31, 1984.
Released by Indianapolis Colts, September 1, 1986; signed as free agent by New York Giants, September 25, 1986.
On injured reserve with groin injury, November 26 through remainder of 1988 season.

		—PLACE KICKING—				
Year Club	G.	XP.	XPM.	FG.	FGA.	Pts.
1983—Baltimore NFL	16	22	2	30	35	112
1984—Indianapolis NFL	12	14	0	11	18	47
1985—Indianapolis NFL	16	36	3	16	26	84
1986—N.Y. Giants NFL	13	33	0	24	32	105
1987—N.Y. Giants NFL	12	25	1	17	27	76
1988—N.Y. Giants NFL	6	14	0	10	11	44
Pro Totals—6 Years	75	144	6	108	149	468

Played in NFC Championship Game following 1986 season.
Played in NFL Championship Game following 1986 season.

ANTHONY DERRICK ALLEN
Wide Receiver—Minnesota Vikings
Born June 29, 1959, at McComb, Miss.
Height, 5.11. Weight, 182.
High School—Seattle, Wash., Garfield.
Attended University of Washington.
Brother of Patrick Allen, cornerback with Houston Oilers.

Selected by Tampa Bay in 3rd round (36th player selected) of 1983 USFL draft.
Selected by Atlanta in 6th round (156th player selected) of 1983 NFL draft.
USFL rights traded by Tampa Bay Bandits to Los Angeles Express for 4th round pick in 1984 draft, May 9, 1983.
Signed by Los Angeles Express, May 9, 1983.
Granted roster exemption, May 9, 1983; activated, May 14, 1983.
Traded by Los Angeles Express to Michigan Panthers for draft pick, April 18, 1984.
Not protected in merger of Michigan Panthers and Oakland Invaders; selected by Baltimore Stars in USFL dispersal draft, December 6, 1984.
Released by Baltimore Stars, February 18, 1985; signed as free agent by Portland Breakers, April 4, 1985.
Released by Portland Breakers, May 14, 1985; signed by Atlanta Falcons, July 18, 1985.
On injured reserve with knee injury, October 8 through remainder of 1986 season.
Released by Atlanta Falcons, September 7, 1987; signed as free agent replacement player by Washington Redskins, October 1, 1987.
Released by Washington Redskins, November 28, 1987; re-signed by Redskins, December 9, 1987.
Released by Washington Redskins, August 29, 1988; re-signed by Redskins, August 30, 1988.
Granted unconditional free agency, February 1, 1989; signed by Minnesota Vikings, March 16, 1989.

Year Club	G.	—RUSHING— Att.	Yds.	Avg.	TD.	PASS RECEIVING P.C.	Yds.	Avg.	TD.	—TOTAL— TD.	Pts.	F.
1983—Los Angeles USFL	8	1	—6	—6.0	0	37	613	16.6	3	3	18	1
1984—Los Angeles (8)-Mich. (10) USFL	18	2	0	0.0	0	34	535	15.7	3	3	18	4
1985—Portland USFL	6		None			9	125	13.9	2	2	12	0
1985—Atlanta NFL	16		None			14	207	14.8	2	2	12	0
1986—Atlanta NFL	5		None			10	156	15.6	2	2	12	1
1987—Washington NFL	3		None			13	337	25.9	3	3	18	0
1988—Washington NFL	14		None			5	48	9.6	1	1	6	2
USFL Totals—3 Years	32	3	—6	—2.0	0	80	1273	15.9	8	8	48	5
NFL Totals—4 Years	38	0	0	0.0	0	42	748	17.8	8	8	48	3
Pro Totals—7 Years	70	3	—6	—2.0	0	122	2021	16.6	16	16	96	8

Year Club	G.	—PUNT RETURNS— No.	Yds.	Avg.	TD.	—KICKOFF RET.— No.	Yds.	Avg.	TD.
1983—Los Angeles USFL	8	15	105	7.0	0	11	211	19.2	0
1984—Los Angeles (8)-Michigan (10) USFL	18	36	233	6.5	0	2	31	15.5	0
1985—Portland USFL	6		None					None	
1985—Atlanta NFL	16	21	141	6.7	0	8	140	17.5	0
1986—Atlanta NFL	5	2	10	5.0	0			None	
1987—Washington NFL	3		None					None	
1988—Washington NFL	14	10	62	6.2	0			None	
USFL Totals—3 Years	32	51	338	6.6	0	13	242	18.6	0
NFL Totals—4 Years	38	33	213	6.5	0	8	140	17.5	0
Pro Totals—7 Years	70	84	551	6.6	0	21	382	18.2	0

Additional USFL statistics: Attempted one pass with no completions and recovered one fumble, 1983.
Additional NFL statistics: Recovered one fumble, 1985 and 1986.
Played in NFC Championship Game following 1987 season.
Member of Washington Redskins for NFL Championship Game following 1987 season; inactive.

ERIC ANDRE ALLEN
Cornerback—Philadelphia Eagles
Born November 22, 1965, at San Diego, Calif.
Height, 5.10. Weight, 181.
High School—San Diego, Calif., Point Loma.
Received degree in broadcasting from Arizona State University in 1988.

Selected by Philadelphia in 2nd round (30th player selected) of 1988 NFL draft.
Signed by Philadelphia Eagles, July 19, 1988.

Year Club	G.	—INTERCEPTIONS— No.	Yds.	Avg.	TD.
1988—Philadelphia NFL	16	5	76	15.2	0

LLOYD PATRICK ALLEN
(Known by middle name.)
Cornerback—Houston Oilers
Born August 26, 1961, at Seattle, Wash.
Height, 5.10. Weight, 179.
High School—Seattle, Wash., Garfield.
Attended Utah State University.
Brother of Anthony Allen, wide receiver with Minnesota Vikings.

Selected by Washington in 2nd round (27th player selected) of 1984 USFL draft.
Selected by Houston in 4th round (100th player selected) of 1984 NFL draft.
Signed by Houston Oilers, July 18, 1984.
Granted free agency, February 1, 1988; re-signed by Oilers, August 29, 1988.
Granted roster exemption, August 29 through September 4, 1988; activated, September 5, 1988.

| Year Club | G. | —INTERCEPTIONS— | | |
		No.	Yds.	Avg.TD.
1984—Houston NFL	16	1	2	2.0 0
1985—Houston NFL	16		None	
1986—Houston NFL	16	3	20	6.7 0
1987—Houston NFL	11	1	37	37.0 0
1988—Houston NFL	15	1	23	23.0 0
Pro Totals—5 Years	74	6	82	13.7 0

Additional pro statistics: Returned 11 kickoffs for 210 yards (19.1 avg.), 1984; recovered two fumbles, 1985; recovered one fumble, 1987; recovered one fumble for seven yards, 1988.

MARCUS ALLEN
Running Back—Los Angeles Raiders
Born March 26, 1960, at San Diego, Calif.
Height, 6.02. Weight, 205.
High School—San Diego, Calif., Lincoln.
Attended University of Southern California.
Brother of Damon Allen, quarterback with Edmonton Eskimos, 1985 through 1988.

Named THE SPORTING NEWS NFL Player of the Year, 1985.
Named to THE SPORTING NEWS NFL All-Star Team, 1985.
Named THE SPORTING NEWS NFL Rookie of the Year, 1982.
Heisman Trophy winner, 1981.
Named THE SPORTING NEWS College Player of the Year, 1981.
Named as running back on THE SPORTING NEWS College All-America Team, 1981.
Established NFL record for most combined yards, season (2,314), 1985.
Tied NFL record for most consecutive games, 100 yards rushing (9), 1985.
Selected by Los Angeles Raiders in 1st round (10th player selected) of 1982 NFL draft.

| Year Club | G. | —RUSHING— | | | | PASS RECEIVING | | | | —TOTAL— | | |
		Att.	Yds.	Avg.	TD.	P.C.	Yds.	Avg.	TD.	TD.	Pts.	F.
1982—Los Angeles Raiders NFL	9	160	697	4.4	*11	38	401	10.6	3	*14	*84	5
1983—Los Angeles Raiders NFL	15	266	1014	3.8	9	68	590	8.7	2	12	72	*14
1984—Los Angeles Raiders NFL	16	275	1168	4.2	13	64	758	11.8	5	*18	108	8
1985—Los Angeles Raiders NFL	16	380	*1759	4.6	11	67	555	8.3	3	14	84	3
1986—Los Angeles Raiders NFL	13	208	759	3.6	5	46	453	9.8	2	7	42	7
1987—Los Angeles Raiders NFL	12	200	754	3.8	5	51	410	8.0	0	5	30	3
1988—Los Angeles Raiders NFL	15	223	831	3.7	7	34	303	8.9	1	8	48	5
Pro Totals—7 Years	96	1712	6982	4.1	61	368	3470	9.4	16	78	468	45

Additional pro statistics: Completed one of four pass attempts for 47 yards, 1982; recovered two fumbles, 1982 and 1985; attempted seven passes with four completions for 111 yards and three touchdowns and recovered two fumbles (including one in end zone for a touchdown), 1983; attempted four passes with one completion for 38 yards and recovered three fumbles, 1984; attempted two passes with one completion for 16 yards, 1985; recovered one fumble, 1986; attempted two passes with one completion for 23 yards, 1987; attempted two passes with one completion for 21 yards, 1988.
Played in AFC Championship Game following 1983 season.
Played in NFL Championship Game following 1983 season.
Played in Pro Bowl (NFL All-Star Game) following 1982, 1984, 1985 and 1987 seasons.
Named to play in Pro Bowl following 1986 season; replaced due to injury by Sammy Winder.

MARVIN RAY ALLEN
Running Back—New England Patriots
Born November 23, 1965, at Wichita Falls, Tex.
Height, 5.10. Weight, 215.
High School—Wichita Falls, Tex., Hirschi.
Attended Tyler Junior College and received degree in sports administration
from Tulane University in 1988.

Selected by New England in 11th round (294th player selected) of 1988 NFL draft.
Signed by New England Patriots, July 13, 1988.
Released by New England Patriots, August 29, 1988; re-signed by Patriots, August 30, 1988.
On injured reserve with fractured shoulder, November 16 through remainder of 1988 season.

| Year Club | G. | —RUSHING— | | | | PASS RECEIVING | | | —TOTAL— | | |
		Att.	Yds.	Avg.	TD.	P.C.	Yds.	Avg. TD.	TD.	Pts.	F.
1988—New England NFL	11	7	40	5.7	0		None		0	0	0

| Year Club | G. | KICKOFF RETURNS | | |
		No.	Yds.	Avg.TD.
1988—New England NFL	11	18	391	21.7 0

Additional pro statistics: Recovered two fumbles, 1988.

TY HUNTER ALLERT
Linebacker—Philadelphia Eagles
Born July 23, 1963, at Rosenberg, Tex.
Height, 6.02. Weight, 233.
High School—Houston, Tex., Northbrook.
Attended University of Texas.

Selected by San Diego in 4th round (95th player selected) of 1986 NFL draft.
Signed by San Diego Chargers, July 25, 1986.
Released by San Diego Chargers, November 3, 1987; awarded on waivers to Philadelphia Eagles, November 4, 1987.
On injured reserve with leg injury, September 23 through November 3, 1988; activated, November 4, 1988.
San Diego NFL, 1986; San Diego (3)-Philadelphia (7) NFL, 1987; Philadelphia NFL, 1988.
Games: 1986 (16), 1987 (10), 1988 (10). Total—36.

O'BRIEN DARWIN ALSTON
Linebacker—Indianapolis Colts
Born December 21, 1965, at New Haven, Conn.
Height, 6.06. Weight, 246.
High School—Oxon Hill, Md.
Attended University of Maryland.

Selected by Indianapolis in 10th round (270th player selected) of 1988 NFL draft.
Signed by Indianapolis Colts, July 13, 1988.
Indianapolis NFL, 1988.
Games: 1988 (15).

JOHN MICHAEL ALT
Offensive Tackle—Kansas City Chiefs
Born May 30, 1962, at Stuttgart, West Germany.
Height, 6.07. Weight, 290.
High School—Columbia Heights, Minn.
Attended University of Iowa.

Selected by Oklahoma in 3rd round (46th player selected) of 1984 USFL draft.
Selected by Kansas City in 1st round (21st player selected) of 1984 NFL draft.
Signed by Kansas City Chiefs, July 18, 1984.
On injured reserve with back injury, December 6 through remainder of 1985 season.
On physically unable to perform/reserve with back injury, August 18 through November 7, 1986; activated, November 8, 1986.
On injured reserve with knee injury, December 9 through remainder of 1987 season.
Kansas City NFL, 1984 through 1988.
Games: 1984 (15), 1985 (13), 1986 (7), 1987 (9), 1988 (14). Total—58.

JIM ALTHOFF
Defensive Lineman—New York Giants
Born September 27, 1961, at McHenry, Ill.
Height, 6.03. Weight, 278.
High School—McHenry, Ill., Community.
Attended Winona State University.

Signed as free agent by Buffalo Bills, July 16, 1987.
Released by Buffalo Bills, August 10, 1987; signed as free agent replacement player by Chicago Bears, September 24, 1987.
On injured reserve with back injury, December 14, 1987 through remainder of season.
Released by Chicago Bears, August 24, 1988; signed as free agent by New York Giants, February 3, 1989.
Chicago NFL, 1987.
Games: 1987 (4).
Pro statistics: Recovered one fumble, 1987.

STEVEN LEE ALVORD
(Steve)
Defensive Tackle—Phoenix Cardinals
Born October 2, 1964, at Bellingham, Wash.
Height, 6.04. Weight, 272.
High School—Bellingham, Wash.
Attended University of Washington.

Selected by St. Louis in 8th round (201st player selected) of 1987 NFL draft.
Signed by St. Louis Cardinals, July 18, 1987.
Franchise transferred to Phoenix, March 15, 1988.
St. Louis NFL, 1987; Phoenix NFL, 1988.
Games: 1987 (12), 1988 (15). Total—27.

—DID YOU KNOW—

That the Chicago Bears did not score in the third period of any game in 1988 until their 10th game of the season?

JOHNNY RAY AMBROSE
(J. R.)
Wide Receiver—Green Bay Packers

Born April 19, 1964, at Monroe, La.
Height, 6.00. Weight, 185.
High Schools—Monroe, La., Neville; and Sweetwater, Tenn.,
Tennessee Military Institute.
Attended University of Mississippi.

Selected by Kansas City in 4th round (96th player selected) of 1988 NFL draft.
Signed by Kansas City Chiefs, July 16, 1988.
Released by Kansas City Chiefs, September 5, 1988; signed as free agent by Green Bay Packers, October 18, 1988.
On injured reserve with thumb and finger injuries, October 27 through remainder of 1988 season.
Active for 1 game with Green Bay Packers in 1988; did not play.
Green Bay NFL, 1988.

MORTEN ANDERSEN
Placekicker—New Orleans Saints

Born August 19, 1960, at Struer, Denmark.
Height, 6.02. Weight, 221.
High School—Indianapolis, Ind., Davis.
Attended Michigan State University.

Named to THE SPORTING NEWS NFL All-Star Team, 1985 through 1987.
Named as placekicker on THE SPORTING NEWS College All-America Team, 1981.
Established NFL record for highest field goal percentage, career (78.2).
Selected by New Orleans in 4th round (86th player selected) of 1982 NFL draft.
On injured reserve with sprained ankle, September 15 through November 19, 1982; activated, November 20, 1982.

		—————PLACE KICKING———					
Year	Club	G.	XP.	XPM.	FG.	FGA.	Pts.
1982—New Orleans NFL...		8	6	0	2	5	12
1983—New Orleans NFL...		16	37	1	18	24	91
1984—New Orleans NFL...		16	34	0	20	27	94
1985—New Orleans NFL...		16	27	2	31	35	120
1986—New Orleans NFL...		16	30	0	26	30	108
1987—New Orleans NFL...		12	37	0	★28	★36	121
1988—New Orleans NFL...		16	32	1	26	36	110
Pro Totals—7 Years.......		100	203	4	151	193	656

Played in Pro Bowl (NFL All-Star Game) following 1985 through 1988 seasons.

ALFRED ANTHONY ANDERSON
Running Back—Minnesota Vikings

Born August 4, 1961, at Waco, Tex.
Height, 6.01. Weight, 220.
High School—Waco, Tex., Richfield.
Attended Baylor University.

Selected by San Antonio in 1984 USFL territorial draft.
Selected by Minnesota in 3rd round (67th player selected) of 1984 NFL draft.
Signed by Minnesota Vikings, May 18, 1984.

			—————RUSHING———				PASS RECEIVING				—TOTAL—		
Year	Club	G.	Att.	Yds.	Avg.	TD.	P.C.	Yds.	Avg.	TD.	TD.	Pts.	F.
1984—Minnesota NFL.........................		16	201	773	3.8	2	17	102	6.0	1	3	18	8
1985—Minnesota NFL.........................		12	50	121	2.4	4	16	175	10.9	1	5	30	0
1986—Minnesota NFL.........................		16	83	347	4.2	2	17	179	10.5	2	4	24	3
1987—Minnesota NFL.........................		10	68	319	4.7	2	7	69	9.9	0	2	12	1
1988—Minnesota NFL.........................		16	87	300	3.4	7	23	242	10.5	1	8	48	3
Pro Totals—5 Years...................................		70	489	1860	3.8	17	80	767	9.6	5	22	132	15

			KICKOFF RETURNS			
Year	Club	G.	No.	Yds.	Avg.	TD.
1984—Minnesota NFL.............		16	30	639	21.3	0
1985—Minnesota NFL.............		12		None		
1986—Minnesota NFL.............		16	3	38	12.7	0
1987—Minnesota NFL.............		10		None		
1988—Minnesota NFL.............		16		None		
Pro Totals—5 Years.............		70	33	677	20.5	0

Additional pro statistics: Attempted seven passes with three completions for 95 yards with two touchdowns and one interception, 1984; recovered two fumbles, 1984 and 1986; attempted two passes with one completion for 17 yards, 1986.
Played in NFC Championship Game following 1987 season.

CHARLES NEAL ANDERSON
(Known by middle name.)
Running Back—Chicago Bears

Born August 14, 1964, at Graceville, Fla.
Height, 5.11. Weight, 210.
High School—Graceville, Fla.
Received degree in public relations from University of Florida in 1986.

Selected by Tampa Bay in 1986 USFL territorial draft.
Selected by Chicago in 1st round (27th player selected) of 1986 NFL draft.
Signed by Chicago Bears, August 15, 1986.

Year Club	G.	Att.	Yds.	Avg.	TD.	P.C.	Yds.	Avg.	TD.	TD.	Pts.	F.
		—RUSHING—				PASS RECEIVING				—TOTAL—		
1986—Chicago NFL	14	35	146	4.2	0	4	80	20.0	1	1	6	1
1987—Chicago NFL	11	129	586	4.5	3	47	467	9.9	3	6	36	2
1988—Chicago NFL	16	249	1106	4.4	12	39	371	9.5	0	12	72	8
Pro Totals—3 Years	41	413	1838	4.5	15	90	918	10.2	4	19	114	11

Additional pro statistics: Returned four kickoffs for 26 yards, 1986; attempted one pass with no completions and recovered two fumbles, 1988.
Played in NFC Championship Game following 1988 season.
Played in Pro Bowl (NFL All-Star Game) following 1988 season.

EDDIE LEE ANDERSON JR.
Safety—Los Angeles Raiders
Born July 22, 1963, at Warner Robins, Ga.
Height, 6.01. Weight, 199.
High School—Warner Robins, Ga.
Attended Fort Valley State College.

Selected by Seattle in 6th round (153rd player selected) of 1986 NFL draft.
Signed by Seattle Seahawks, July 16, 1986.
On injured reserve with back injury, September 11 through November 20, 1986; activated, November 21, 1986.
Released by Seattle Seahawks, September 1, 1987; signed as free agent replacement player by Los Angeles Raiders, September 24, 1987.
Seattle NFL, 1986; Los Angeles Raiders NFL, 1987 and 1988.
Games: 1986 (5), 1987 (13), 1988 (16). Total—34.
Pro statistics: Intercepted one pass for 58 yards and recovered one fumble, 1987; intercepted two passes for minus six yards, 1988.

GARY ALLAN ANDERSON
Placekicker—Pittsburgh Steelers
Born July 16, 1959, at Parys, Orange Free State, South Africa.
Height, 5.11. Weight, 175.
High School—Durban, South Africa, Brettonwood.
Received bachelor of science degree in management and accounting
from Syracuse University in 1982.
Son of Rev. Douglas Anderson, former pro soccer player in England.

Selected by Buffalo in 7th round (171st player selected) of 1982 NFL draft.
Released by Buffalo Bills, September 6, 1982; claimed on waivers by Pittsburgh Steelers, September 7, 1982.

Year Club	G.	XP.	XPM.	FG.	FGA.	Pts.	Year Club	G.	XP.	XPM.	FG.	FGA.	Pts.
	—PLACE KICKING—							—PLACE KICKING—					
1982—Pittsburgh NFL	9	22	0	10	12	52	1987—Pittsburgh NFL	12	21	0	22	27	87
1983—Pittsburgh NFL	16	38	1	27	31	119	1988—Pittsburgh NFL	16	34	1	28	36	118
1984—Pittsburgh NFL	16	45	0	24	32	117	Pro Totals—7 Years	101	232	2	165	212	727
1985—Pittsburgh NFL	16	40	0	*33	*42	139							
1986—Pittsburgh NFL	16	32	0	21	32	95							

Played in AFC Championship Game following 1984 season.
Played in Pro Bowl (NFL All-Star Game) following 1983 and 1985 seasons.

GARY WAYNE ANDERSON
Running Back—San Diego Chargers
Born April 18, 1961, at Columbia, Mo.
Height, 6.00. Weight, 180.
High School—Columbia, Mo., Hickman.
Attended University of Arkansas

Named as running back on THE SPORTING NEWS USFL All-Star Team, 1985.
Selected by New Jersey in 1st round (5th player selected) of 1983 USFL draft.
Selected by San Diego in 1st round (20th player selected) of 1983 NFL draft.
USFL rights traded by New Jersey Generals to Tampa Bay Bandits for 1st round pick in 1984 draft, May 9, 1983.
Signed by Tampa Bay Bandits, May 9, 1983.
Granted roster exemption, May 9 through May 13, 1983; activated, May 14, 1983.
Released by Tampa Bay Bandits, September 27, 1985; signed by San Diego Chargers, September 30, 1985.
Granted roster exemption, September 30 through October 4, 1985; activated, October 5, 1985.

Year Club	G.	Att.	Yds.	Avg.	TD.	P.C.	Yds.	Avg.	TD.	TD.	Pts.	F.
		—RUSHING—				PASS RECEIVING				—TOTAL—		
1983—Tampa Bay USFL	8	97	516	5.3	4	29	347	12.0	0	4	24	7
1984—Tampa Bay USFL	18	268	1008	3.8	*19	66	682	10.3	2	*21	126	8
1985—Tampa Bay USFL	18	276	1207	4.4	16	72	678	9.4	4	20	120	11
1985—San Diego NFL	12	116	429	3.7	4	35	422	12.1	2	7	42	5
1986—San Diego NFL	16	127	442	3.5	1	80	871	10.9	8	9	54	5
1987—San Diego NFL	12	80	260	3.3	3	47	503	10.7	2	5	30	4
1988—San Diego NFL	14	225	1119	5.0	3	32	182	5.7	0	3	18	5
USFL Totals—3 Years	44	641	2731	4.3	39	167	1707	10.2	6	45	270	26
NFL Totals—4 Years	54	548	2250	4.1	11	194	1978	10.2	12	24	144	19
Pro Totals—7 Years	98	1189	4981	4.2	50	361	3685	10.2	18	69	414	45

Year Club	G.	—PUNT RETURNS— No.	Yds.	Avg.	TD.	—KICKOFF RET.— No.	Yds.	Avg.	TD.
1983—Tampa Bay USFL	8	2	—1	—0.5	0	3	47	15.7	0
1984—Tampa Bay USFL	18	4	22	5.5	0		None		
1985—Tampa Bay USFL	18		None			0	2	0.0	0
1985—San Diego NFL	12		None			13	302	23.2	1
1986—San Diego NFL	16	25	227	9.1	0	24	482	20.1	0
1987—San Diego NFL	12		None			22	433	19.7	0
1988—San Diego NFL	14		None				None		
USFL Totals—3 Years	44	6	21	3.5	0	3	49	16.3	0
NFL Totals—4 Years	54	25	227	9.1	0	59	1217	20.6	1
Pro Totals—7 Years	98	31	248	8.0	0	62	1266	20.4	1

Additional USFL statistics: Attempted one pass with no completions and recovered one fumble, 1983; attempted three passes with two completions for 44 yards, one touchdown and one interception and recovered two fumbles, 1984; attempted three passes with two completions for three yards and a touchdown and recovered five fumbles, 1985.

Additional NFL statistics: Recovered three fumbles, 1985 and 1988; attempted one pass with one completion for four yards and a touchdown and recovered two fumbles, 1986; recovered one fumble, 1987.

Played in Pro Bowl (NFL All-Star Game) following 1986 season.

OTTIS JEROME ANDERSON
(O. J.)
Running Back—New York Giants

Born November 19, 1957, at West Palm Beach, Fla.
Height, 6.02. Weight, 225.
High School—West Palm Beach, Fla., Forest Hill.
Received degree in physical education from University of Miami (Fla.).
Step-brother of Mike Taliferro, defensive lineman with Denver Gold, 1985.

Tied NFL record for most 100-yard games by rookie, season (9), 1979.
Named THE SPORTING NEWS NFL Rookie of the Year, 1979.
Named THE SPORTING NEWS NFC Player of the Year, 1979.
Named to THE SPORTING NEWS NFC All-Star Team, 1979.
Selected by St. Louis in 1st round (8th player selected) of 1979 NFL draft.
Traded by St. Louis Cardinals to New York Giants for 2nd and 7th round picks in 1987 draft, October 8, 1986.
Granted unconditional free agency, February 1, 1989; received no qualifying offer, April 15, 1989.
Re-signed by Giants, April 21, 1989.

Year Club	G.	——RUSHING—— Att.	Yds.	Avg.	TD.	PASS RECEIVING P.C.	Yds.	Avg.	TD.	—TOTAL— TD.	Pts.	F.
1979—St. Louis NFL	16	331	1605	4.8	8	41	308	7.5	2	10	60	10
1980—St. Louis NFL	16	301	1352	4.5	9	36	308	8.6	0	9	54	5
1981—St. Louis NFL	16	328	1376	4.2	9	51	387	7.6	0	9	54	13
1982—St. Louis NFL	8	145	587	4.0	3	14	106	7.6	0	3	18	2
1983—St. Louis NFL	15	296	1270	4.3	5	54	459	8.5	1	6	36	10
1984—St. Louis NFL	15	289	1174	4.1	6	70	611	8.7	2	8	48	8
1985—St. Louis NFL	9	117	479	4.1	4	23	225	9.8	0	4	24	3
1986—St. Louis (4)-N.Y. Giants (8) NFL	12	75	237	3.2	3	19	137	7.2	0	3	18	2
1987—New York Giants NFL	4	2	6	3.0	0	2	16	8.0	0	0	0	0
1988—New York Giants NFL	16	65	208	3.2	8	9	57	6.3	0	8	48	0
Pro Totals—10 Years	127	1949	8294	4.3	55	319	2614	8.2	5	60	360	53

Additional pro statistics: Recovered one fumble, 1979, 1982, 1984 and 1985; attempted one pass with no completions, 1979; recovered four fumbles, 1980; recovered three fumbles, 1981 and 1983; recovered one fumble for five yards, 1988.
Played in NFC Championship Game following 1986 season.
Played in NFL Championship Game following 1986 season.
Played in Pro Bowl (NFL All-Star Game) following 1979 and 1980 seasons.

ROGER JOHN ANDERSON
(Known by middle name.)
Linebacker—Green Bay Packers

Born February 14, 1956, at Waukesha, Wis.
Height, 6.03. Weight, 229.
High School—Waukesha, Wis., South.
Received bachelor of arts degree in environmental studies from University
of Michigan in 1978.

Selected by Green Bay in 1st round (26th player selected) of 1978 NFL draft.
On injured reserve with broken arm, December 6 through remainder of 1978 season.
On injured reserve with broken arm, August 28 through October 29, 1979; activated, October 30, 1979.
On injured reserve with broken arm, November 5 through remainder of 1980 season.
On injured reserve with torn ligaments in ankle and fractured fibula, October 1 through remainder of 1986 season.

Year Club	G.	—INTERCEPTIONS— No.	Yds.	Avg.	TD.	Year Club	G.	—INTERCEPTIONS— No.	Yds.	Avg.	TD.
1978—Green Bay NFL	13	5	27	5.4	0	1984—Green Bay NFL	16	3	24	8.0	0
1979—Green Bay NFL	7		None			1985—Green Bay NFL	16	2	2	1.0	0
1980—Green Bay NFL	9		None			1986—Green Bay NFL	4	1	3	3.0	0
1981—Green Bay NFL	16	3	12	4.0	0	1987—Green Bay NFL	12	2	22	11.0	0
1982—Green Bay NFL	9	3	22	7.3	0	1988—Green Bay NFL	14		None		
1983—Green Bay NFL	16	5	54	10.8	1	Pro Totals—11 Years	132	24	166	6.9	1

Additional pro statistics: Recovered one fumble, 1978 through 1980 and 1983 through 1985; scored four points, kicking one field goal on one attempt and one extra point on two attempts, 1979; recovered four fumbles for 22 yards, 1981; recovered two fumbles, 1982; returned one kickoff for 14 yards, 1985; recovered three fumbles, 1987.

WILLIE LEE ANDERSON JR.
Wide Receiver—Los Angeles Rams
Born March 7, 1965, at Philadelphia, Pa.
Height, 6.00. Weight, 169.
High School—Paulsboro, N. J.
Attended University of California at Los Angeles.

Selected by Los Angeles Rams in 2nd round (46th player selected) of 1988 NFL draft.
Signed by Los Angeles Rams, July 17, 1988.

			—PASS RECEIVING—			
Year	Club	G.	P.C.	Yds.	Avg.	TD.
1988—L. A. Rams NFL		16	11	319	29.0	0

ERIC THOMAS ANDOLSEK
Guard—Detroit Lions
Born August 22, 1966, at Thibodaux, La.
Height, 6.02. Weight, 277.
High School—Thibodaux, La.
Attended Louisiana State University.

Selected by Detroit in 5th round (111th player selected) of 1988 NFL draft.
Signed by Detroit Lions, July 16, 1988.
Detroit NFL, 1988.
Games: 1988 (13).
Pro statistics: Returned one kickoff for three yards, 1988.

SAM ANNO
(Last name originally was Aono.)
Linebacker—Tampa Bay Buccaneers
Born January 26, 1965, at Silver Springs, Md.
Height, 6.02. Weight, 230.
High School—Santa Monica, Calif.
Attended University of Southern California.

Signed as free agent by Los Angeles Rams, May 14, 1987.
Released by Los Angeles Rams, September 7, 1987; re-signed by Rams, September 8, 1987.
Crossed picket line during players' strike, October 14, 1987.
Released by Los Angeles Rams, November 3, 1987; signed as free agent by Minnesota Vikings, November 18, 1987.
Released by Minnesota Vikings, August 30, 1988; re-signed by Vikings, September 17, 1988.
Released by Minnesota Vikings, December 17, 1988; re-signed by Vikings, December 21, 1988.
Granted unconditional free agency, February 1, 1989; signed by Tampa Bay Buccaneers, March 27, 1989.
Los Angeles Rams (3)-Minnesota (6) NFL, 1987; Minnesota NFL, 1988.
Games: 1987 (9), 1988 (13). Total—22.
Played in NFC Championship Game following 1987 season.

DAVID ARCHER
(Dave)
Quarterback—San Diego Chargers
Born February 15, 1962, at Fayetteville, N.C.
Height, 6.02. Weight, 208.
High School—Soda Springs, Ida.
Attended Snow College and Iowa State University.

Selected by Denver in 9th round (171st player selected) of 1984 USFL draft.
Signed as free agent by Atlanta Falcons, May 2, 1984.
On injured reserve with separated shoulder, November 17 through remainder of 1986 season.
Granted free agency, February 1, 1988; withdrew qualify offer, April 27, 1988.
Signed by Miami Dolphins, May 27, 1988.
Released by Miami Dolphins, August 30, 1988; signed as free agent by Washington Redskins, September 22, 1988.
Released by Washington Redskins, October 24, 1988; signed as free agent by San Diego Chargers, March 13, 1989.

			—————PASSING—————							—RUSHING—				—TOTAL—		
Year	Club	G.	Att.	Cmp.	Pct.	Gain	T.P.	P.I.	Avg.	Att.	Yds.	Avg.	TD.	TD.	Pts.	F.
1984—Atlanta NFL		2	18	11	61.1	181	1	1	10.06	6	38	6.3	0	0	0	1
1985—Atlanta NFL		16	312	161	51.6	1992	7	17	6.38	70	347	5.0	2	2	12	9
1986—Atlanta NFL		11	294	150	51.0	2007	10	9	6.83	52	298	5.7	0	0	0	8
1987—Atlanta NFL		9	23	9	39.1	95	0	2	4.13	2	8	4.0	0	0	0	0
1988—Washington NFL		1	2	0	0.0	0	0	0	0.00	3	1	0.3	0	0	0	0
Pro Totals—5 Years...........		39	649	331	51.0	4275	18	29	6.59	133	692	5.2	2	2	12	18

Quarterback Rating Points: 1984 (90.3), 1985 (56.5), 1986 (71.6), 1987 (15.7), 1988 (39.6). Total—62.6.
Additional pro statistics: Recovered two fumbles, 1985; recovered one fumble and fumbled eight times for minus three yards, 1986.

WILLIAM DONOVAN ARD
(Billy)
Guard—Green Bay Packers
Born March 12, 1959, at East Orange, N.J.
Height, 6.03. Weight, 270.
High School—Watchung, N.J.
Attended Wake Forest University.

Named as guard on THE SPORTING NEWS College All-America Team, 1980.
Selected by New York Giants in 8th round (221st player selected) of 1981 NFL draft.
On injured reserve with knee injury, December 11 through remainder of 1984 season.
Granted unconditional free agency, February 1, 1989; signed by Green Bay Packers, February 27, 1989.
New York Giants NFL, 1981 through 1988.
Games: 1981 (13), 1982 (9), 1983 (16), 1984 (15), 1985 (16), 1986 (16), 1987 (12), 1988 (16). Total—113.
Pro statistics: Recovered one fumble, 1981; recovered one fumble for one yard, 1986.
Played in NFC Championship Game following 1986 season.
Played in NFL Championship Game following 1986 season.

BRUCE ARMSTRONG
Offensive Tackle—New England Patriots
Born September 7, 1965, at Miami, Fla.
Height, 6.04. Weight, 284.
High School—Miami, Fla., Central.
Attended University of Louisville.

Named to THE SPORTING NEWS NFL All-Star Team, 1988.
Selected by New England in 1st round (23rd player selected) of 1987 NFL draft.
Signed by New England Patriots, July 23, 1987.
New England NFL, 1987 and 1988.
Games: 1987 (12), 1988 (16). Total—28.

HARVEY LEE ARMSTRONG
Nose Tackle—Indianapolis Colts
Born December 29, 1959, at Houston, Tex.
Height, 6.03. Weight, 265.
High School—Houston, Tex., Kashmere.
Received degree in business management from Southern Methodist University.

Selected by Philadelphia in 7th round (190th player selected) of 1982 NFL draft.
Released by Philadelphia Eagles, August 20, 1985; signed as free agent by Indianapolis Colts, May 21, 1986.
Philadelphia NFL, 1982 through 1984; Indianapolis NFL, 1986 through 1988.
Games: 1982 (8), 1983 (16), 1984 (16), 1986 (16), 1987 (11), 1988 (16). Total—83.
Pro statistics: Recovered two fumbles, 1983, 1987 and 1988; intercepted one pass for four yards and recovered three fumbles, 1986.

JAMES EDWARD ARNOLD
(Jim)
Punter—Detroit Lions
Born January 31, 1961, at Dalton, Ga.
Height, 6.03. Weight, 211.
High School—Dalton, Ga.
Attended Vanderbilt University.

Named to THE SPORTING NEWS NFL All-Star Team, 1987.
Named as punter on THE SPORTING NEWS College All-America Team, 1982.
Led NFL in net punting average with 39.6 in 1987.
Led NFL in punting yards with 4,397 in 1984 and 4,110 in 1988.
Selected by Kansas City in 5th round (119th player selected) of 1983 NFL draft.
Released by Kansas City Chiefs, August 26, 1986; signed as free agent by Detroit Lions, November 5, 1986.
Released by Detroit Lions, September 7, 1987; re-signed by Lions, September 14, 1987.

			—PUNTING—		
Year	Club	G.	No.	Avg.	Blk.
1983—Kansas City NFL		16	93	39.9	0
1984—Kansas City NFL		16	*98	*44.9	0
1985—Kansas City NFL		16	*93	41.2	*2
1986—Detroit NFL		7	36	42.6	1
1987—Detroit NFL		11	46	43.6	0
1988—Detroit NFL		16	97	42.4	0
Pro Totals—6 Years		82	463	42.3	3

Additional pro statistics: Rushed once for no yards, recovered two fumbles and fumbled once for minus nine yards, 1984; attempted one pass with no completions, 1988.
Played in Pro Bowl (NFL All-Star Game) following 1987 and 1988 seasons.

DOUGLAS ARONSON
(Doug)
Guard—Cleveland Browns
Born August 14, 1964, at San Francisco, Calif.
Height, 6.03. Weight, 290.
High School—South San Francisco, Calif.
Attended San Diego State University.

Signed as free agent by Cincinnati Bengals, May 1, 1987.
On injured reserve with Achilles heel injury, August 26 through November 13, 1987; activated, November 14, 1987.
Released by Cincinnati Bengals, August 30, 1988; signed as free agent by Cleveland Browns for 1989, November 23, 1988.
Cincinnati NFL, 1987.
Games: 1987 (2).

WALKER LEE ASHLEY
(Walker Lee)
Linebacker—Kansas City Chiefs
Born July 28, 1960, at Bayonne, N.J.
Height, 6.00. Weight, 232.
High School—Jersey City, N.J., Snyder.
Received degree in community development from Penn State University.

Selected by Philadelphia in 1983 USFL territorial draft.
Selected by Minnesota in 3rd round (73rd player selected) of 1983 NFL draft.
Signed by Minnesota Vikings, June 16, 1983.
On injured reserve with ruptured Achilles tendon, August 20 through entire 1985 season.
Granted unconditional free agency, February 1, 1989; signed by Kansas City Chiefs, March 2, 1989.
Minnesota NFL, 1983, 1984 and 1986 through 1988.
Games: 1983 (15), 1984 (15), 1986 (16), 1987 (12), 1988 (16). Total—74.
Pro statistics: Recovered one fumble, 1986; intercepted one pass for 94 yards and a touchdown, 1988.
Played in NFC Championship Game following 1987 season.

GENE REYNARD ATKINS
Defensive Back—New Orleans Saints
Born August 31, 1964, at Tallahassee, Fla.
Height, 6.01. Weight, 200.
High School—Tallahassee, Fla., James S. Rickards.
Attended Florida A&M University.

Selected by New Orleans in 7th round (179th player selected) of 1987 NFL draft.
Signed by New Orleans Saints, July 25, 1987.
On injured reserve with eye injury, September 7 through September 30, 1987; activated, October 1, 1987.
Crossed picket line during players' strike, October 1, 1987.

| | | —INTERCEPTIONS— | | | | —KICKOFF RET.— | | | | —TOTAL— | | |
Year Club	G.	No.	Yds.	Avg.	TD.	No.	Yds.	Avg.	TD.	TD.	Pts.	F.
1987—New Orleans NFL	13	3	12	4.0	0		None			0	0	0
1988—New Orleans NFL	16	4	42	10.5	0	20	424	21.2	0	0	0	1
Pro Totals—2 Years	29	7	54	7.7	0	20	424	21.2	0	0	0	1

Additional pro statistics: Recovered one fumble, 1987; recovered two fumbles, 1988.

ROBERT MITCHELL AWALT
(Name pronounced A-walt.)
Tight End—Phoenix Cardinals
Born April 9, 1964, at Landsthul, West Germany.
Height, 6.05. Weight, 248.
High School—Sacramento, Calif., Valley.
Attended University of Nevada at Reno (did not play football), Sacramento City College
and San Diego State University.

Named THE SPORTING NEWS Rookie of the Year, 1987.
Selected by St. Louis in 3rd round (62nd player selected) of 1987 NFL draft.
Signed by St. Louis Cardinals, July 31, 1987.
Franchise transferred to Phoenix, March 15, 1988.

| | | ——PASS RECEIVING—— | | | |
Year Club	G.	P.C.	Yds.	Avg.	TD.
1987—St. Louis NFL	12	42	526	12.5	6
1988—Phoenix NFL	16	39	454	11.6	4
Pro Totals—2 Years	28	81	980	12.1	10

Additional pro statistics: Rushed twice for minus nine yards and recovered one fumble, 1987; fumbled once, 1988.

MICHEAL JAMES BAAB
(Mike)
Center—New England Patriots
Born December 6, 1959, at Fort Worth, Tex.
Height, 6.04. Weight, 270.
High School—Euless, Tex., Trinity.
Attended Tarrant County Junior College, Austin Community College
and University of Texas.

Selected by Cleveland in 5th round (115th player selected) of 1982 NFL draft.
Traded by Cleveland Browns to New England Patriots for 5th round pick in 1989 draft, August 29, 1988.
Cleveland NFL, 1982 through 1987; New England NFL, 1988.
Games: 1982 (7), 1983 (15), 1984 (16), 1985 (16), 1986 (16), 1987 (12), 1988 (15). Total—97.
Pro statistics: Fumbled once for minus 11 yards, 1984; rushed once for no yards and fumbled once for minus two yards, 1985.
Played in AFC Championship Game following 1986 and 1987 seasons.

STEVEN WILLIAM BAACK

Name pronounced Bock.

(Steve)
Guard—Detroit Lions

Born November 16, 1960, at Ames, Ia.
Height, 6.04. Weight, 265.
High School—John Day, Ore., Grant Union.
Received bachelor of science degree in psychology from University of Oregon in 1984.

Selected by Philadelphia in 9th round (184th player selected) of 1984 USFL draft.
Selected by Detroit in 3rd round (75th player selected) of 1984 NFL draft.
Signed by Detroit Lions, June 20, 1984.
On injured reserve with knee injury, September 11 through October 30, 1987; activated, October 31, 1987.
On injured reserve with hip injury, August 29 through entire 1988 season.
Detroit NFL, 1984 through 1987.
Games: 1984 (16), 1985 (16), 1986 (16), 1987 (7). Total—55.
Pro statistics: Recovered one fumble, 1985.

CHRIS BAHR
Placekicker—San Diego Chargers

Born February 3, 1953, at State College, Pa.
Height, 5.10. Weight, 170.
High School—Langhorne, Pa., Neshaminy Langhorne.
Received bachelor of science degree in biology from Penn State University in 1976, attended Chase Law School at Northern Kentucky University and graduated from Southwestern Law School in 1986.
Brother of Matt Bahr, placekicker with Cleveland Browns.

Named to THE SPORTING NEWS AFC All-Star Team, 1977.
Named as placekicker on THE SPORTING NEWS College All-America Team, 1975.
Selected by Cincinnati in 2nd round (51st player selected) of 1976 NFL draft.
Released by Cincinnati Bengals, August 26, 1980; signed as free agent by Oakland Raiders, September 1, 1980.
Franchise transferred to Los Angeles, May 7, 1982.
Crossed picket line during players' strike, October 14, 1987.
Granted unconditional free agency, February 1, 1989; signed by San Diego Chargers, April 1, 1989.
Played with Philadelphia Atoms of North American Soccer League, 1975 (22 games, 11 goals, 2 assists).

		—PLACE KICKING—						—PLACE KICKING—			
Year Club	G.	XP.	XPM.	FG.	FGA.	Pts.	Year Club	G.	XP.	XPM.	FG.	FGA.	Pts.
1976—Cincinnati NFL........	14	39	3	14	27	81	1983—L.A. Raiders NFL....	16	51	2	21	27	114
1977—Cincinnati NFL........	14	25	1	19	27	82	1984—L.A. Raiders NFL....	16	40	2	20	27	100
1978—Cincinnati NFL........	16	26	3	16	30	74	1985—L.A. Raiders NFL....	16	40	2	20	32	100
1979—Cincinnati NFL........	16	40	2	13	23	79	1986—L.A. Raiders NFL....	16	36	0	21	28	99
1980—Oakland NFL............	16	41	3	19	37	98	1987—L.A. Raiders NFL....	13	27	1	19	29	84
1981—Oakland NFL............	16	27	6	14	24	69	1988—L.A. Raiders NFL....	16	37	2	18	29	91
1982—L.A. Raiders NFL....	9	*32	1	10	16	62	Pro Totals—13 Years.....	194	461	28	224	356	1133

Additional pro statistics: Punted twice for 44.0 average, 1977; punted four times for 27.0 average, 1978; punted twice for 21.5 average, 1981.
Played in AFC Championship Game following 1980 and 1983 seasons.
Played in NFL Championship Game following 1980 and 1983 seasons.

MATTHEW DAVID BAHR
(Matt)
Placekicker—Cleveland Browns

Born July 6, 1956, at Philadelphia, Pa.
Height, 5.10. Weight, 175.
High School—Langhorne, Pa., Neshaminy Langhorne.
Received bachelor of science degree in electrical engineering from Penn State University in 1979; attending Carnegie-Mellon University for master's degree in industrial administration.
Brother of Chris Bahr, placekicker with San Diego Chargers.

Selected by Pittsburgh in 6th round (165th player selected) of 1979 NFL draft.
Released by Pittsburgh Steelers, August 31, 1981; signed as free agent by San Francisco 49ers, September 8, 1981.
Traded by San Francisco 49ers to Cleveland Browns for 9th round pick in 1983 draft, October 6, 1981.
On injured reserve with knee injury, November 26 through remainder of 1986 season.
On physically unable to perform/reserve with knee injury, September 1 through December 11, 1987; activated, December 12, 1987.
Played with Colorado Caribous and Tulsa Roughnecks of North American Soccer League, 1978 (26 games, 3 assists).

		—PLACE KICKING—						—PLACE KICKING—			
Year Club	G.	XP.	XPM.	FG.	FGA.	Pts.	Year Club	G.	XP.	XPM.	FG.	FGA.	Pts.
1979—Pittsburgh NFL........	16	*50	2	18	30	104	1985—Cleveland NFL.........	16	35	0	14	18	77
1980—Pittsburgh NFL........	16	39	3	19	28	96	1986—Cleveland NFL.........	12	30	0	20	26	90
1981—SF (4)-Cle (11) NFL	15	34	0	15	26	79	1987—Cleveland NFL.........	3	9	1	4	5	21
1982—Cleveland NFL........	9	17	0	7	15	38	1988—Cleveland NFL.........	16	32	1	24	29	104
1983—Cleveland NFL........	16	38	2	21	24	101	Pro Totals—10 Years.....	135	309	9	166	233	807
1984—Cleveland NFL........	16	25	0	24	32	97							

Additional pro statistics: Rushed once for minus eight yards, 1988.
Played in AFC Championship Game following 1979 and 1987 seasons.
Played in NFL Championship Game following 1979 season.

CARLTON WILSON BAILEY
Linebacker—Buffalo Bills

Born December 15, 1964, at Baltimore, Md.
Height, 6.02. Weight, 240.
High School—Baltimore, Md., Woodlawn.
Received bachelor of arts degree in sociology from
University of North Carolina in 1988.

Selected by Buffalo in 9th round (235th player selected) of 1988 NFL draft.
Signed by Buffalo Bills, July 15, 1988.
On injured reserve with knee injury, August 30 through November 13, 1988; activated, November 14, 1988.
Buffalo NFL, 1988.
Games: 1988 (6).
Played in AFC Championship Game following 1988 season.

EDWIN RAYMOND BAILEY
Guard—Seattle Seahawks

Born May 15, 1959, at Savannah, Ga.
Height, 6.04. Weight, 270.
High School—Savannah, Ga., Tompkins.
Attended South Carolina State College.

Selected by Seattle in 5th round (114th player selected) of 1981 NFL draft.
On injured reserve with knee injury, November 10 through December 7, 1984; activated, December 8, 1984.
On injured reserve with knee injury, September 11 through October 10, 1986; activated, October 11, 1986.
Seattle NFL, 1981 through 1988.
Games: 1981 (16), 1982 (9), 1983 (16), 1984 (12), 1985 (16), 1986 (12), 1987 (12), 1988 (16). Total—109.
Pro statistics: Recovered one fumble, 1982; caught one pass for three yards, 1986; recovered two fumbles, 1988.
Played in AFC Championship Game following 1983 season.

STACEY DWAYNE BAILEY
Wide Receiver—Atlanta Falcons

Born February 10, 1960, at San Rafael, Calif.
Height, 6.01. Weight, 160.
High School—San Rafael, Calif., Terra Linda.
Attended San Jose State University.

Selected by Atlanta in 3rd round (63rd player selected) of 1982 NFL draft.
On inactive list, September 12 and September 19, 1982.
On injured reserve with hamstring injury, September 2 through October 31, 1986; activated, November 1, 1986.
On injured reserve with shoulder injury, October 29 through December 9, 1988; activated, December 10, 1988.

| | | | —PASS RECEIVING— | | |
Year	Club	G.	P.C.	Yds.	Avg.	TD.
1982—Atlanta NFL		5	2	24	12.0	1
1983—Atlanta NFL		15	55	881	16.0	6
1984—Atlanta NFL		16	67	1138	17.0	6
1985—Atlanta NFL		15	30	364	12.1	0
1986—Atlanta NFL		6	3	39	13.0	0
1987—Atlanta NFL		7	20	325	16.3	3
1988—Atlanta NFL		10	17	437	25.7	2
Pro Totals—7 Years		74	194	3208	16.5	18

Additional pro statistics: Fumbled once, 1982 through 1985 and 1987; rushed twice for minus five yards and recovered one fumble, 1983; rushed once for minus three yards, 1985; rushed once for six yards, 1986.

JAMES ALBERT LONDON BAKER
(Al or Bubba)
Defensive End—Cleveland Browns

Born December 9, 1956, at Jacksonville, Fla.
Height, 6.06. Weight, 280.
High School—Newark, N. J., Weequahic.
Attended Colorado State University.

Named THE SPORTING NEWS NFC Rookie of the Year, 1978.
Selected by Detroit in 2nd round (40th player selected) of 1978 NFL draft.
On reserve-retired list, August 19 through September 10, 1980; activated, September 11, 1980.
On physically unable to perform/active list with groin injury, July 29 through August 30, 1982; activated, August 31, 1982.
Traded by Detroit Lions to St. Louis Cardinals for defensive tackle Mike Dawson and 3rd round pick in 1984 draft, July 18, 1983.
Granted free agency, February 1, 1986; re-signed by Cardinals, August 26, 1986.
Granted roster exemption, August 26 and 27, 1986; activated, August 28, 1986.
Traded by St. Louis Cardinals to Cleveland Browns for 5th round pick in 1988 draft, September 3, 1987.
Released by Cleveland Browns, August 30, 1988; signed as free agent by Minnesota Vikings, September 10, 1988.
On suspended list, September 30 through October 2, 1988; reinstated, October 3, 1988.
Granted unconditional free agency, February 1, 1989; signed by Cleveland Browns, March 31, 1989.
Detroit NFL, 1978 through 1982; St. Louis NFL, 1983 through 1986; Cleveland NFL, 1987; Minnesota NFL, 1988.
Games: 1978 (16), 1979 (16), 1980 (15), 1981 (11), 1982 (9), 1983 (16), 1984 (15), 1985 (16), 1986 (16), 1987 (12), 1988 (14).
Total—156.

Pro statistics: Recovered one fumble, 1978 through 1980, 1982, 1985 and 1987; intercepted one pass for no yards, 1980; intercepted one pass for nine yards, 1981; intercepted two passes for 24 yards and recovered two fumbles, 1983.
Played in AFC Championship Game following 1987 season.
Played in Pro Bowl (NFL All-Star Game) following 1978 through 1980 seasons.

RONALD BAKER
(Ron)
Guard—Philadelphia Eagles
Born November 19, 1954, at Gary, Ind.
Height, 6.04. Weight, 274.
High School—Gary, Ind., Emerson.
Attended Indian Hills Junior College and Oklahoma State University.

Selected by Baltimore in 10th round (277th player selected) of 1977 NFL draft.
On injured reserve with ankle injury entire 1977 season.
Traded by Baltimore Colts to Philadelphia Eagles for 8th round pick in 1981 draft, August 26, 1980.
On injured reserve with knee injury, December 17 through remainder of 1987 season.
On injured reserve with foot injury, August 22 through October 13, 1988; activated, October 14, 1988.
Baltimore NFL, 1978 and 1979; Philadelphia NFL, 1980 through 1988.
Games: 1978 (16), 1979 (16), 1980 (16), 1981 (16), 1982 (9), 1983 (16), 1984 (16), 1985 (15), 1986 (16), 1987 (10), 1988 (9). Total—155.
Pro statistics: Returned one kickoff for six yards, 1980; recovered one fumble, 1982 through 1984 and 1987.
Played in NFC Championship Game following 1980 season.
Played in NFL Championship Game following 1980 season.

STEPHEN BAKER
Wide Receiver—New York Giants
Born August 30, 1964, at San Antonio, Tex.
Height, 5.08. Weight, 160.
High School—Los Angeles, Calif., Hamilton.
Attended West Los Angeles College and Fresno State University.

Selected by New York Giants in 3rd round (83rd player selected) of 1987 NFL draft.
Signed by New York Giants, July 27, 1987.

| | | ——PASS RECEIVING—— | | | |
Year Club	G.	P.C.	Yds.	Avg.	TD.
1987—N.Y. Giants NFL	12	15	277	18.5	2
1988—N.Y. Giants NFL	16	40	656	16.4	7
Pro Totals—2 Years............	28	55	933	17.0	9

Additional pro statistics: Rushed once for 18 yards, returned three punts for 16 yards and fumbled once, 1987; returned five punts for 34 yards and recovered one fumble, 1988.

TONY FERRINO BAKER
Running Back—Cleveland Browns
Born June 11, 1964, at High Point, N.C.
Height, 5.10. Weight, 176.
High School—High Point, N.C., T. Wingate Andrews.
Attended East Carolina University.

Selected by Atlanta in 10th round (252nd player selected) of 1986 NFL draft.
Selected by Memphis in 2nd round (14th player selected) of 1986 USFL draft.
Signed by Atlanta Falcons, July 15, 1986.
Released by Atlanta Falcons, September 9, 1986; re-signed by Falcons, October 9, 1986.
Released by Atlanta Falcons, October 18, 1986; awarded on waivers to Cleveland Browns, October 20, 1986.
Released by Cleveland Browns, November 22, 1986; re-signed by Browns, March 17, 1987.
On injured reserve with wrist injury, September 7 through entire 1987 season.
On injured reserve with knee injury, August 16 through November 11, 1988; activated, November 12, 1988.
Atlanta (2)-Cleveland (2) NFL, 1986; Cleveland NFL, 1988.
Games: 1986 (4), 1988 (4). Total—8.
Pro statistics: Rushed once for three yards, 1986; rushed three times for 19 yards, 1988.

BRIAN D. BALDINGER
Guard—Indianapolis Colts
Born January 7, 1959, at Pittsburgh, Pa.
Height, 6.04. Weight, 268.
High School—Massapequa, N.Y.
Attended Nassau Community College and received bachelor of science degree
in psychology from Duke University in 1982.
Brother of Rich Baldinger, guard-offensive tackle with Kansas City Chiefs; and
Gary Baldinger, nose tackle-defensive end with Atlanta Falcons.

Signed as free agent by Dallas Cowboys, April 30, 1982.
On inactive list, September 13 and September 19, 1982.
On injured reserve with knee injury, August 27 through entire 1985 season.
On injured reserve with knee injury, September 2 through October 23, 1987; activated, October 24, 1987.
Granted free agency with option not exercised, February 1, 1988; signed by Indianapolis Colts, July 19, 1988.
Dallas NFL, 1982 through 1984, 1986 and 1987; Indianapolis NFL, 1988.
Games: 1982 (4), 1983 (16), 1984 (16), 1986 (16), 1987 (3), 1988 (16). Total—71.
Pro statistics: Caught one pass for 37 yards and recovered one fumble, 1988.
Played in NFC Championship Game following 1982 season.

GARY THOMAS BALDINGER
Nose Tackle-Defensive End—Atlanta Falcons
Born October 4, 1963, at Philadelphia, Pa.
Height, 6.03. Weight, 265.
High School—Massapequa, N.Y.
Received degree in history from Wake Forest University in 1986.
Brother of Brian Baldinger, guard with Indianapolis Colts; and Rich Baldinger,
guard-offensive tackle with Kansas City Chiefs.

Selected by Kansas City in 9th round (229th player selected) of 1986 NFL draft.
Signed by Kansas City Chiefs, July 17, 1986.
Released by Kansas City Chiefs, September 1, 1986; re-signed by Chiefs, September 2, 1986.
Released by Kansas City Chiefs, October 10, 1986; re-signed by Chiefs, February 12, 1987.
On injured reserve with back injury, October 30 through December 4, 1987; activated, December 5, 1987.
On injured reserve with broken thumb, November 16 through remainder of 1988 season.
Granted unconditional free agency, February 1, 1989; signed by Atlanta Falcons, March 30, 1989.
Kansas City NFL, 1986 through 1988.
Games: 1986 (5), 1987 (7), 1988 (11). Total—23.

RICHARD L. BALDINGER
(Rich)
Guard-Offensive Tackle—Kansas City Chiefs
Born December 31, 1959, at Camp Le Jeune, N.C.
Height, 6.04. Weight, 285.
High School—Massapequa, N.Y.
Attended Wake Forest University.
Brother of Brian Baldinger, guard with Indianapolis Colts; and Gary Baldinger,
nose tackle-defensive end with Atlanta Falcons.

Selected by New York Giants in 10th round (270th player selected) of 1982 NFL draft.
On inactive list, September 12, 1982.
Released by New York Giants, August 29, 1983; re-signed by Giants, September 8, 1983.
Released by New York Giants, October 7, 1983; signed as free agent by Kansas City Chiefs, October 26, 1983.
New York Giants NFL, 1982; New York Giants (2)-Kansas City (6) NFL, 1983; Kansas City NFL, 1984 through 1988.
Games: 1982 (1), 1983 (8), 1984 (14), 1985 (16), 1986 (16), 1987 (12), 1988 (14). Total—81.
Pro statistics: Recovered one fumble, 1987 and 1988.

KEITH MANNING BALDWIN
Defensive End—Los Angeles Raiders
Born October 13, 1960, at Houston, Tex.
Height, 6.04. Weight, 270.
High School—Houston, Tex., M.B. Smiley.
Attended Texas A&M University.

Selected by Cleveland in 2nd round (31st player selected) of 1982 NFL draft.
On injured reserve with knee injury, August 18 through entire 1986 season.
Granted free agency, February 1, 1987; withdrew qualifying offer, June 25, 1987.
Signed by San Diego Chargers, July 20, 1987.
On injured reserve with knee injury, September 7 through November 20, 1987; activated, November 21, 1987.
Released by San Diego Chargers, October 17, 1988; signed as free agent by Los Angeles Raiders, November 10, 1988.
Inactive for 3 games with Los Angeles Raiders in 1988.
Released by Los Angeles Raiders, November 30, 1988; re-signed by Raiders, February 3, 1989.
Cleveland NFL, 1982 through 1985; San Diego NFL, 1987; Los Angeles Raiders (0)-San Diego (6) NFL, 1988.
Games: 1982 (9), 1983 (16), 1984 (16), 1985 (10), 1987 (6), 1988 (6). Total—63.

THOMAS BURKE BALDWIN
(Tom)
Defensive End-Defensive Tackle—Detroit Lions
Born May 13, 1961, at Evergreen Park, Ill.
Height, 6.04. Weight, 275.
High School—Lansing, Ill., Thornton Fractional South.
Attended University of Wisconsin, Thornton Community College and
and received degree in education from The University of Tulsa.
Brother of Brian Baldwin, pitcher in Los Angeles Dodgers' organization, 1977 through 1979.

Selected by Oklahoma in 1984 USFL territorial draft.
Selected by New York Jets in 9th round (234th player selected) of 1984 NFL draft.
Signed by New York Jets, May 29, 1984.
On injured reserve with stress fracture in foot, September 1 through entire 1987 season.
Granted unconditional free agency, February 1, 1989; signed by Detroit Lions, April 1, 1989.
New York Jets NFL, 1984 through 1986 and 1988.
Games: 1984 (16), 1985 (16), 1986 (16), 1988 (16). Total—64.
Pro statistics: Recovered one fumble for nine yards and a touchdown, 1985; returned two kickoffs for three yards, recovered one fumble and fumbled once, 1986.

JERRY LEE BALL
Nose Tackle—Detroit Lions
Born December 15, 1964, at Beaumont, Tex.
Height, 6.01. Weight, 292.
High School—Westbrook, Tex.
Attended Southern Methodist University.

Selected by Detroit in 3rd round (63rd player selected) of 1987 NFL draft.
Signed by Detroit Lions, July 6, 1987.
Detroit NFL, 1987 and 1988.
Games: 1987 (12), 1988 (16). Total—28.
Pro statistics: Returned two kickoffs for 23 yards, 1987.

MICHAEL BALL JR.
Defensive Back—Indianapolis Colts
Born August 5, 1964, at New Orleans, La.
Height, 6.00. Weight, 216.
High School—New Orleans, La., Booker T. Washington.
Attended Southern University.

Selected by Indianapolis in 4th round (104th player selected) of 1988 NFL draft.
Signed by Indianapolis Colts, July 20, 1988.
Indianapolis NFL, 1988.
Games: 1988 (16).
Pro statistics: Recovered one fumble, 1988.

HOWARD LOUIS BALLARD
Offensive Tackle—Buffalo Bills
Born November 3, 1963, at Ashland, Ala.
Height, 6.06. Weight, 300.
High School—Ashland, Ala., Clay County.
Attended Alabama A&M University.

Selected by Buffalo in 11th round (283rd player selected) of 1987 NFL draft (elected to return to college for final year of eligibility).
Signed by Buffalo Bills, March 30, 1988.
Buffalo NFL, 1988.
Games: 1988 (16).
Played in AFC Championship Game following 1988 season.

TED BANKER
Guard-Center—Cleveland Browns
Born February 17, 1961, at Belleville, Ill.
Height, 6.02. Weight, 275.
High School—Belleville, Ill., Althoff.
Attended Southeast Missouri State University.

Signed as free agent by New York Jets, June 20, 1983.
On injured reserve with knee injury, August 12 through entire 1983 season.
On injured reserve with broken leg, December 24 through remainder of 1985 season playoffs.
Crossed picket line during players' strike, October 14, 1987.
On injured reserve with sprained foot, October 18 through November 18, 1988; activated, November 19, 1988.
Granted unconditional free agency, February 1, 1989; signed by Cleveland Browns, February 24, 1989.
New York Jets NFL, 1984 through 1988.
Games: 1984 (14), 1985 (16), 1986 (15), 1987 (13), 1988 (11). Total—69.
Pro statistics: Returned one kickoff for five yards, 1984; recovered one fumble, 1987.

CARL BANKS
Linebacker—New York Giants
Born August 29, 1962, at Flint, Mich.
Height, 6.04. Weight, 235.
High School—Flint, Mich., Beecher.
Attended Michigan State University.

Named to THE SPORTING NEWS NFL All-Star Team, 1987.
Named as linebacker on THE SPORTING NEWS College All-America Team, 1983.
Selected by Michigan in 1984 USFL territorial draft.
Selected by New York Giants in 1st round (3rd player selected) of 1984 NFL draft.
Signed by New York Giants, July 12, 1984.
On injured reserve with knee injury, October 12 through November 8, 1985; activated, November 9, 1985.
Granted free agency, February 1, 1988; re-signed by Giants, August 29, 1988.
Granted roster exemption, August 29 through September 4, 1988; activated, September 5, 1988.
New York Giants NFL, 1984 through 1988.
Games: 1984 (16), 1985 (12), 1986 (16), 1987 (12), 1988 (14). Total—70.
Pro statistics: Recovered one fumble, 1984 and 1985; recovered two fumbles for five yards, 1986; intercepted one pass for no yards, 1987; intercepted one pass for 15 yards and a touchdown, 1988.
Played in NFC Championship Game following 1986 season.
Played in NFL Championship Game following 1986 season.
Played in Pro Bowl (NFL All-Star Game) following 1987 season.

CHUCK EDWARD BANKS
Running Back—New York Jets
Born January 4, 1964, at Baltimore, Md.
Height, 6.01. Weight, 225.
High School—Hyattsville, Md., Northwestern.
Attended Ferrum College and West Virginia Institute of Technology.

Selected by Houston in 12th round (310th player selected) of 1986 NFL draft.
Selected by Arizona in 9th round (62nd player selected) of 1986 USFL draft.
Signed by Houston Oilers, July 21, 1986.
Released by Houston Oilers, October 31, 1986; re-signed by Oilers, November 12, 1986.
Released by Houston Oilers, September 6, 1987; signed as free agent replacement player by Indianapolis Colts, September 23, 1987.
On injured reserve with knee and ankle injuries, November 6 through remainder of 1987 season.
Released by Indianapolis Colts, August 30, 1988; signed as free agent by New York Jets, January 11, 1989.

		——RUSHING——				PASS RECEIVING				—TOTAL—		
Year Club	G.	Att.	Yds.	Avg.	TD.	P.C.	Yds.	Avg.	TD.	TD.	Pts.	F.
1986—Houston NFL	13	29	80	2.8	0	7	71	10.1	0	0	0	1
1987—Indianapolis NFL	3	50	245	4.9	0	9	50	5.6	0	0	0	1
Pro Totals—2 Years	16	79	325	4.1	0	16	121	7.6	0	0	0	2

FREDERICK RAY BANKS
(Fred)
Wide Receiver—Miami Dolphins
Born May 26, 1962, at Columbus, Ga.
Height, 5.10. Weight, 177.
High School—Columbus, Ga., Baker.
Attended Chowan College and Liberty Baptist College.

Selected by Denver in 8th round (107th player selected) of 1985 USFL draft.
Selected by Cleveland in 8th round (203rd player selected) of 1985 NFL draft.
Signed by Cleveland Browns, July 11, 1985.
On injured reserve with pulled hamstring, October 9 through November 15, 1985; activated, November 16, 1985.
On physically unable to perform/reserve with ankle injury, August 19 through September 15, 1986.
Released by Cleveland Browns, September 16, 1986; signed as free agent by Miami Dolphins for 1987, November 24, 1986.
Released by Miami Dolphins, December 12, 1987; re-signed by Dolphins, December 15, 1987.
On injured reserve with ribs injury, September 2 through September 30, 1988; activated, October 1, 1988.

		——PASS RECEIVING——			
Year Club	G.	P.C.	Yds.	Avg.	TD.
1985—Cleveland NFL	10	5	62	12.4	2
1987—Miami NFL	3	1	10	10.0	1
1988—Miami NFL	11	23	430	18.7	2
Pro Totals—3 Years	24	29	502	17.3	5

ROBERT NATHAN BANKS
Defensive End—Cleveland Browns
Born December 10, 1963, at Williamsburg, Va.
Height, 6.05. Weight, 263.
High Schools—Newport News, Va., Peninsula Catholic; and Hampton, Va.
Attended University of Notre Dame.

Selected by Houston in 7th round (176th player selected) of 1987 NFL draft.
Signed by Houston Oilers, July 12, 1987.
On injured reserve with finger injury, September 6 through entire 1987 season.
Granted unconditional free agency, February 1, 1989; signed by Cleveland Browns, March 16, 1989.
Houston NFL, 1988.
Games: 1988 (14).

ROY F. BANKS
Wide Receiver—Indianapolis Colts
Born February 19, 1965, at Detroit, Mich.
Height, 5.10. Weight, 190.
High School—Detroit, Mich., Martin Luther King.
Attended Eastern Illinois University.

Selected by Indianapolis in 5th round (114th player selected) of NFL draft.
Signed by Indianapolis Colts, July 24, 1987.
On injured reserve with ankle injury, September 7 through December 10, 1987; activated, December 11, 1987.
Indianapolis NFL, 1987 and 1988.
Games: 1987 (1), 1988 (14). Total—15.
Pro statistics: Returned four kickoffs for 56 yards, 1988.

ROLAND ANTHONY BARBAY JR.
Nose Tackle—Seattle Seahawks
Born October 1, 1964, at New Orleans, La.
Height, 6.04. Weight, 260.
High School—New Orleans, La., Holy Cross.
Attended Louisiana State University.

Selected by Seattle in 7th round (184th player selected) of 1987 NFL draft.
Signed by Seattle Seahawks, July 21, 1987.
On injured reserve with back injury, September 7 through November 29, 1987; activated, November 30, 1987.
On injured reserve with knee injury, July 21 through entire 1988 season.
Seattle NFL, 1987.
Games: 1987 (5).

MARION BARBER
Fullback—New York Jets

Born December 6, 1959, at Fort Lauderdale, Fla.
Height, 6.03. Weight, 228.
High School—Detroit, Mich., Chadsey.
Received degree in juvenile behavior from University of Minnesota.

Selected by New York Jets in 2nd round (30th player selected) of 1981 NFL draft.
On injured reserve with concussion, August 17 through entire 1981 season.
On inactive list, September 12 and September 19, 1982.
On injured reserve with cracked rib, November 5 through remainder of 1985 season.
Granted unconditional free agency, February 1, 1989; re-signed by Jets, April 27, 1989.

		—————RUSHING—————				PASS RECEIVING				—TOTAL—		
Year Club	G.	Att.	Yds.	Avg.	TD.	P.C.	Yds.	Avg.	TD.	TD.	Pts.	F.
1982—New York Jets NFL	6	8	24	3.0	0		None			0	0	0
1983—New York Jets NFL	14	15	77	5.1	1	7	48	6.9	1	2	12	0
1984—New York Jets NFL	14	31	148	4.8	2	10	79	7.9	0	2	12	3
1985—New York Jets NFL	8	9	41	4.6	0	3	46	15.3	0	0	0	0
1986—New York Jets NFL	15	11	27	2.5	0	5	36	7.2	0	0	0	1
1987—New York Jets NFL	12		None				None			0	0	0
1988—New York Jets NFL	16		None				None			0	0	0
Pro Totals—7 Years	85	74	317	4.3	3	25	209	8.4	1	4	24	4

Additional pro statistics: Returned one kickoff for nine yards and recovered two fumbles, 1983; recovered one fumble, 1984; returned two kickoffs for five yards, 1987; returned one kickoff for 11 yards, 1988.
Played in AFC Championship Game following 1982 season.

LEO BARKER
Linebacker—Cincinnati Bengals

Born November 7, 1959, at Cristobal, Panama.
Height, 6.02. Weight, 227.
High School—Cristobal, Panama.
Attended New Mexico State University.

Selected by Arizona in 1984 USFL territorial draft.
Selected by Cincinnati in 7th round (177th player selected) of 1984 NFL draft.
Signed by Cincinnati Bengals, June 26, 1984.
Cincinnati NFL, 1984 through 1988.
Games: 1984 (16), 1985 (16), 1986 (16), 1987 (12), 1988 (16). Total—76.
Pro statistics: Intercepted two passes for seven yards, 1986; returned one fumble for 34 yards and a touchdown, 1988.
Played in AFC Championship Game following 1988 season.
Played in NFL Championship Game following 1988 season.

ROD DEAN BARKSDALE
Wide Receiver—Dallas Cowboys

Born September 8, 1962, at Los Angeles, Calif.
Height, 6.01. Weight, 193.
High School—Compton, Calif.
Received bachelor of science degree in political science
from University of Arizona in 1985.
Cousin of Jeremiah Castille, defensive back with Denver Broncos.

Signed as free agent by Los Angeles Raiders, May 11, 1985.
On injured reserve with ankle injury, August 20 through entire 1985 season.
Traded by Los Angeles Raiders to Dallas Cowboys for cornerback Ron Fellows, August 2, 1987.
On injured reserve with knee injury, August 16 through entire 1988 season.

		——PASS RECEIVING——			
Year Club	G.	P.C.	Yds.	Avg.	TD.
1986—L.A. Raiders NFL	16	18	434	24.1	2
1987—Dallas NFL	12	12	165	13.8	1
Pro Totals—2 Years	28	30	599	20.0	3

Additional pro statistics: Recovered one fumble and fumbled once, 1986.

LEW ERIC BARNES
Wide Receiver—Kansas City Chiefs

Born December 27, 1962, at Long Beach, Calif.
Height, 5.08. Weight, 163.
High School—San Diego, Calif., Abraham Lincoln.
Attended San Diego Mesa College and University of Oregon.

Selected by Chicago in 5th round (138th player selected) of 1986 NFL draft.
Signed by Chicago Bears, July 16, 1986.

On injured reserve with broken leg, August 27 through entire 1987 season.
Released by Chicago Bears, August 23, 1988; awarded on waivers to Detroit Lions, August 24, 1988.
Released by Detroit Lions, August 30, 1988; signed as free agent by Atlanta Falcons, September 14, 1988.
Granted unconditional free agency, February 1, 1989; signed by Kansas City Chiefs, March 31, 1989.

Year Club		PASS RECEIVING				–PUNT RETURNS–				—KICKOFF RET.—				—TOTAL—		
	G.	P.C.	Yds.	Avg.	TD.	No.	Yds.	Avg.	TD.	No.	Yds.	Avg.	TD.	TD.	Pts.	F.
1986—Chicago NFL	16	4	54	13.5	0	*57	482	8.5	0	3	94	31.3	*1	1	6	5
1988—Atlanta NFL	13	None				34	307	9.0	0	6	142	23.7	0	0	0	4
Pro Totals—2 Years	29	4	54	13.5	0	91	789	8.7	0	9	236	26.2	1	1	6	9

Additional pro statistics: Recovered three fumbles, 1986.

TOMMY RAY BARNHARDT
Punter—Washington Redskins
Born June 11, 1963, at Salisbury, N.C.
Height, 6.03. Weight, 205.
High School—China Grove, N.C., South Rowan.
Attended East Carolina University and received degree in industrial relations
from University of North Carolina in 1986.

Selected by Baltimore in 1986 USFL territorial draft.
Selected by Tampa Bay in 9th round (223rd player selected) of 1986 NFL draft.
Signed by Tampa Bay Buccaneers, July 16, 1986.
Released by Tampa Bay Buccaneers, August 25, 1986; re-signed by Buccaneers, February 6, 1987.
Released by Tampa Bay Buccaneers, August 5, 1987; signed as free agent replacement player by New Orleans Saints, September 23, 1987.
Released by New Orleans Saints, November 3, 1987; signed as free agent by Chicago Bears, December 16, 1987.
Released by Chicago Bears, August 24, 1988; signed as free agent by Washington Redskins, September 9, 1988.
On injured reserve with pulled quadricep, October 11 through remainder of 1988 season.
Granted unconditional free agency, February 1, 1989; re-signed by Redskins, May 11, 1989.

Year Club	——PUNTING——			
	G.	No.	Avg.	Blk.
1987—N.O. (3)-Chi. (2) NFL	5	17	42.3	0
1988—Washington NFL	4	15	41.9	0
Pro Totals—2 Years	9	32	42.1	0

Additional pro statistics: Rushed once for minus 13 yards, 1987.

SCOTT MARTIN BARROWS
Guard-Center—Detroit Lions
Born March 31, 1963, at Marietta, O.
Height, 6.03. Weight, 278.
High School—Marietta, O.
Attended West Virginia University.

Selected by Tampa Bay in 11th round (150th player selected) of 1985 USFL draft.
Signed as free agent by Detroit Lions, May 9, 1986.
Released by Detroit Lions, August 27, 1986; re-signed by Lions, April 21, 1986.
Detroit NFL, 1986 through 1988.
Games: 1986 (16), 1987 (12), 1988 (16). Total—44.
Pro statistics: Recovered one fumble, 1986 and 1987.

DOUGLAS WILLIAM BARTLETT
(Doug)
Defensive Lineman—Green Bay Packers
Born May 22, 1963, at Springfield, Ill.
Height, 6.02. Weight, 239.
High School—Springfield, Ill., Griffin.
Attended Northern Illinois University.

Selected by Los Angeles Rams in 4th round (91st player selected) of 1987 NFL draft.
Signed by Los Angeles Rams, July 24, 1987.
On injured reserve with hamstring injury, August 31 through entire 1987 season.
On injured reserve with elbow injury, August 29 through September 12, 1988.
Released by Los Angeles Rams, September 13, 1988; signed as free agent by Philadelphia Eagles, September 15, 1988.
On injured reserve with ankle injury, December 2 through remainder of 1988 season.
Granted unconditional free agency, February 1, 1989; signed by Green Bay Packers, February 28, 1989.
Philadelphia NFL, 1988.
Games: 1988 (10).

HARRIS SCOTT BARTON
Offensive Tackle—San Francisco 49ers
Born April 19, 1964, at Atlanta, Ga.
Height, 6.04. Weight, 280.
High School—Dunwoody, Ga.
Received bachelor of science degree from University of North Carolina in 1987.

Selected by San Francisco in 1st round (22nd player selected) of 1987 NFL draft.
Signed by San Francisco 49ers, July 22, 1987.
San Francisco NFL, 1987 and 1988.

Games: 1987 (12), 1988 (16). Total—28.
Pro statistics: Recovered one fumble, 1987.
Played in NFC Championship Game following 1988 season.
Played in NFL Championship Game following 1988 season.

WILLIAM FREDERICK BATES
(Bill)
Safety—Dallas Cowboys
Born June 6, 1961, at Knoxville, Tenn.
Height, 6.01. Weight, 201.
High School—Knoxville, Tenn., Farragut.
Attended University of Tennessee.

Selected by New Jersey in 1983 USFL territorial draft.
Signed as free agent by Dallas Cowboys, April 28, 1983.
On injured reserve with hip injury, September 3 through September 27, 1984; activated, September 28, 1984.

Year Club		-INTERCEPTIONS-				-PUNT RETURNS-				—TOTAL—		
	G.	No.	Yds.	Avg.	TD.	No.	Yds.	Avg.	TD.	TD.	Pts.	F.
1983—Dallas NFL	16	1	29	29.0	0		None			0	0	1
1984—Dallas NFL	12	1	3	3.0	0		None			0	0	0
1985—Dallas NFL	16	4	15	3.8	0	22	152	6.9	0	0	0	0
1986—Dallas NFL	15		None				None			0	0	0
1987—Dallas NFL	12	3	28	9.3	0		None			0	0	0
1988—Dallas NFL	16	1	0	0.0	0		None			0	0	0
Pro Totals—6 Years	87	10	75	7.5	0	22	152	6.9	0	0	0	1

Additional pro statistics: Recovered two fumbles, 1983; recovered one fumble, 1984 and 1988.
Played in Pro Bowl (NFL All-Star Game) following 1984 season.

GREGORY JAMES BATY
(Greg)
Tight End—New York Giants
Born August 28, 1964, at Haistings, Mich.
Height, 6.05. Weight, 241.
High School—Sparta, N.J.
Received bachelor of arts degree in human biology from Stanford University in 1986.

Selected by New England in 8th round (220th player selected) of 1986 NFL draft.
Signed by New England Patriots, July 18, 1986.
Released by New England Patriots, November 12, 1987; awarded on waivers to Los Angeles Rams, November 13, 1987.
Granted free agency, February 1, 1988; withdrew qualifying offer, August 1, 1988.
Signed by San Francisco 49ers, August 4, 1988.
On injured reserve with thigh injury, August 23 through September 19, 1988.
Released by San Francisco 49ers, September 20, 1988; signed as free agent by Phoenix Cardinals, September 30, 1988.
Released by Phoenix Cardinals, October 19, 1988; signed as free agent by New York Giants, April 25, 1989.

Year Club		——PASS RECEIVING——			
	G.	P.C.	Yds.	Avg.	TD.
1986—New England NFL	16	37	331	8.9	2
1987—N.E.(5)-Rams(4) NFL .	9	18	175	9.7	2
1988—Phoenix NFL	1		None		
Pro Totals—3 Years	26	55	506	9.2	4

THOMAS A. BAUGH
(Tom)
Center—Cleveland Browns
Born December 1, 1963, at Chicago, Ill.
Height, 6.03. Weight, 274.
High School—Riverside, Ill., Brookfield.
Received degree in construction management from University of Southern Illinois in 1986.

Selected by Kansas City in 4th round (87th player selected) of 1986 NFL draft.
Signed by Kansas City Chiefs, June 10, 1986.
On injured reserve with broken finger, September 9 through November 27, 1986; activated, November 28, 1986.
On injured reserve with knee injury, November 24 through remainder of 1988 season.
Granted unconditional free agency, February 1, 1989; signed by Cleveland Browns, March 16, 1989.
Kansas City NFL, 1986 through 1988.
Games: 1986 (5), 1987 (12), 1988 (12). Total—29.
Pro statistics: Recovered two fumbles and fumbled once, 1987; fumbled once for minus nine yards, 1988.

MARK BAVARO
Tight End—New York Giants
Born April 28, 1963, at Winthrop, Mass.
Height, 6.04. Weight, 245.
High School—Danvers, Mass.
Received bachelor of arts degree in history from University of Notre Dame in 1985.
Brother of David Bavaro, linebacker at Syracuse University.

Named to THE SPORTING NEWS NFL All-Star Team, 1986 and 1987.
Selected by Orlando in 15th round (212th player selected) of 1985 USFL draft.
Selected by New York Giants in 4th round (100th player selected) of 1985 NFL draft.
Signed by New York Giants, July 7, 1985.
Granted free agency, February 1, 1988; re-signed by Giants, August 23, 1988.

Year Club	G.	P.C.	Yds.	Avg.	TD.
1985—N.Y. Giants NFL	16	37	511	13.8	4
1986—N.Y. Giants NFL	16	66	1001	15.2	4
1987—N.Y. Giants NFL	12	55	867	15.8	8
1988—N.Y. Giants NFL	16	53	672	12.7	4
Pro Totals—4 Years............	60	211	3051	14.5	20

—PASS RECEIVING—

Additional pro statistics: Recovered two fumbles and fumbled three times, 1986; returned one kickoff for 16 yards and fumbled twice, 1987; fumbled once, 1988.
Played in NFC Championship Game following 1986 season.
Played in NFL Championship Game following 1986 season.
Played in Pro Bowl (NFL All-Star Game) following 1986 season.
Named to play in Pro Bowl following 1987 season; replaced due to injury by Hoby Brenner.

MARTIN BAYLESS
Safety—San Diego Chargers
Born October 11, 1962, at Dayton, O.
Height, 6.02. Weight, 212.
High School—Dayton, O., Belmont.
Attended Bowling Green State University.

Selected by Memphis in 1st round (20th player selected) of 1984 USFL draft.
Selected by St. Louis in 4th round (101st player selected) of 1984 NFL draft.
Signed by St. Louis Cardinals, July 20, 1984.
Released by St. Louis Cardinals, September 19, 1984; awarded on waivers to Buffalo Bills, September 20, 1984.
On injured reserve with pinched nerve in neck, December 6 through remainder of 1985 season.
Traded by Buffalo Bills to San Diego Chargers for cornerback Wayne Davis, August 26, 1987.
St. Louis (3)-Buffalo (13) NFL, 1984; Buffalo NFL, 1985 and 1986; San Diego NFL, 1987 and 1988.
Games: 1984 (16), 1985 (12), 1986 (16), 1987 (12), 1988 (15). Total—71.
Pro statistics: Intercepted two passes for 10 yards and recovered one fumble, 1985; intercepted one pass for no yards, 1986.

PATRICK JESSE BEACH
(Pat)
Tight End—Indianapolis Colts
Born December 28, 1959, at Grant's Pass, Ore.
Height, 6.04. Weight, 252.
High School—Pullman, Wash.
Attended Washington State University.

Named as tight end on THE SPORTING NEWS College All-America team, 1981.
Selected by Baltimore in 6th round (140th player selected) of 1982 NFL draft.
Franchise transferred to Indianapolis, March 31, 1984.
On non-football injury list with ankle injury, August 10 through August 21, 1984.
On injured reserve with ankle injury, August 22 through entire 1984 season.

Year Club	G.	P.C.	Yds.	Avg.	TD.
1982—Baltimore NFL	9	4	45	11.3	1
1983—Baltimore NFL	16	5	56	11.2	1
1985—Indianapolis NFL	16	36	376	10.4	6
1986—Indianapolis NFL	16	25	265	10.6	1
1987—Indianapolis NFL	12	28	239	8.5	0
1988—Indianapolis NFL	16	26	235	9.0	0
Pro Totals—6 Years............	85	124	1216	9.8	9

—PASS RECEIVING—

Additional pro statistics: Returned one kickoff for no yards, 1983; recovered one fumble for five yards and fumbled three times, 1985; recovered one fumble and fumbled twice, 1986; returned one kickoff for 35 yards and fumbled once, 1988.

SHAWN BEALS
Wide Receiver-Kick Returner—Washington Redskins
Born August 16, 1966, at Pittsburg, Calif.
Height, 5.10. Weight, 178.
High School—Pittsburg, Calif.
Attended Idaho State University.

Signed as free agent by Miami Dolphins, May 3, 1988.
Released by Miami Dolphins, August 29, 1988; awarded on waivers to Philadelphia Eagles, August 30, 1988.
On reserve list, December 29 through remainder of 1988 season playoffs.
Granted unconditional free agency, February 1, 1989.
Released by Philadelphia Eagles, April 3, 1989; awarded on waivers to Washington Redskins, April 14, 1989.

Year Club	G.	No.	Yds.	Avg.	TD.
1988—Philadelphia NFL	13	34	625	18.4	0

KICKOFF RETURNS

Additional pro statistics: Recovered one fumble and fumbled once, 1988.

KURT FRANK BECKER
Guard—Chicago Bears
Born December 22, 1958, at Aurora, Ill.
Height, 6.05. Weight, 269.
High School—Aurora, Ill., East.
Received bachelor of arts degree in business administration from University of Michigan.
Selected by Chicago in 6th round (146th player selected) of 1982 NFL draft.
On inactive list, September 12 and September 19, 1982.
On injured reserve with knee injury, October 4 through remainder of 1985 season.
Chicago NFL, 1982 through 1988.
Games: 1982 (5), 1983 (16), 1984 (16), 1985 (3), 1986 (14), 1987 (12), 1988 (16). Total—82.
Played in NFC Championship Game following 1984 and 1988 seasons.

BRADLEY SCOTT BECKMAN
(Brad)
Tight End—Atlanta Falcons
Born December 31, 1964, at Lincoln, Neb.
Height, 6.02. Weight, 236.
High School—Omaha, Neb., Northwest.
Attended University of Nebraska at Omaha.
Selected by Minnesota in 7th round (183rd player selected) of 1988 NFL draft.
Signed by Minnesota Vikings, July 19, 1988.
Released by Minnesota Vikings, August 31, 1988; signed as free agent by New York Giants, September 27, 1988.
Granted unconditional free agency, February 1, 1989; signed by Atlanta Falcons, March 13, 1989.
New York Giants NFL, 1988.
Games: 1988 (9).
Pro statistics: Returned one kickoff for seven yards, 1988.

WILLIAM WEIGEL BEECHER
(Willie)
Placekicker—Green Bay Packers
Born April 14, 1963, at El Paso, Tex.
Height, 5.11. Weight, 175.
High School—Logan, Utah.
Received degree in marketing from Utah State University.
Signed as free agent by Miami Dolphins, June 1, 1987.
Released by Miami Dolphins, August 31, 1987; re-signed by Dolphins, September 23, 1987.
Released by Miami Dolphins, October 27, 1987; signed as free agent by Buffalo Bills, December 9, 1987.
Released by Buffalo Bills, August 1, 1988; awarded on waivers to New York Giants, August 2, 1988.
Released by New York Giants, August 16, 1988; signed as free agent by Miami Dolphins, November 26, 1988.
Released by Miami Dolphins, November 30, 1988; signed as free agent by Green Bay Packers, February 3, 1989.
Active for 1 game with Miami Dolphins in 1988; did not play.

| | | ——PLACE KICKING—— | | | | | |
Year	Club	G.	XP.	XPM.	FG.	FGA.	Pts.
1987—Miami NFL		3	12	0	3	4	21

MARK GERALD BEHNING
Name pronounced BEN-ing.
Offensive Tackle—San Diego Chargers
Born September 26, 1961, at Alpena, Mich.
Height, 6.06. Weight, 277.
High School—Denton, Tex.
Attended University of Nebraska.
Selected by Pittsburgh in 2nd round (47th player selected) of 1985 NFL draft.
Signed by Pittsburgh Steelers, July 19, 1985.
On injured reserve with broken arm, August 20 through entire 1985 season.
On injured reserve with torn Achilles tendon, August 31 through entire 1987 season.
Released by Pittsburgh Steelers, August 24, 1988; signed as free agent by San Diego Chargers, February 27, 1989.
Pittsburgh NFL, 1986.
Games: 1986 (16).

ANTHONY DEWITT BELL
Linebacker—Phoenix Cardinals
Born July 2, 1964, at Miami, Fla.
Height, 6.03. Weight, 231.
High School—Fort Lauderdale, Fla., Boyd H. Anderson.
Attended Michigan State University.
Selected by St. Louis in 1st round (5th player selected) of 1986 NFL draft.
Signed by St. Louis Cardinals, August 11, 1986.
Franchise transferred to Phoenix, March 15, 1988.
St. Louis NFL, 1986 and 1987; Phoenix NFL, 1988.
Games: 1986 (16), 1987 (12), 1988 (16). Total—44.
Pro statistics: Intercepted one pass for 13 yards and fumbled once, 1987; recovered three fumbles, 1988.

GREG LEON BELL
Running Back—Los Angeles Rams
Born August 1, 1962, at Columbus, O.
Height, 5.10. Weight, 210.
High School—Columbus, O., South.
Received bachelor of arts degree in economics from University of Notre Dame in 1984.

Selected by Chicago in 1984 USFL territorial draft.
Selected by Buffalo in 1st round (26th player selected) of 1984 NFL draft.
Signed by Buffalo Bills, July 23, 1984.
On injured reserve with groin injury, October 18 through December 12, 1986; activated, December 13, 1986.
On injured reserve with groin injury, December 20 through remainder of 1986 season.
Traded with 1st round pick in 1988 draft and 1st and 2nd round picks in 1989 draft by Buffalo Bills to Los Angeles Rams in exchange for Indianapolis Colts trading rights to linebacker Cornelius Bennett, October 31, 1987; Rams also acquired 1st and 2nd round picks in 1988 draft, 2nd round pick in 1989 draft and running back Owen Gill from Colts for running back Eric Dickerson.
On injured reserve with shoulder injury, December 4 through remainder of 1987 season.

Year Club	G.	Att.	RUSHING Yds.	Avg.	TD.	PASS RECEIVING P.C.	Yds.	Avg.	TD.	—TOTAL— TD.	Pts.	F.
1984—Buffalo NFL	16	262	1100	4.2	7	34	277	8.1	1	8	48	5
1985—Buffalo NFL	16	223	883	4.0	8	58	576	9.9	1	9	54	8
1986—Buffalo NFL	6	90	377	4.2	4	12	142	11.8	2	6	36	2
1987—Buffalo (2)-L.A. Rams (2) NFL	4	22	86	3.9	0	9	96	10.7	1	1	6	1
1988—Los Angeles Rams NFL	16	288	1212	4.2	*16	24	124	5.2	2	*18	108	6
Pro Totals—5 Years	58	885	3658	4.1	35	137	1215	8.9	7	42	252	22

Additional pro statistics: Returned one kickoff for 15 yards and recovered three fumbles, 1984; attempted one pass with no completions, 1985; recovered two fumbles, 1985, 1986 and 1988.
Played in Pro Bowl (NFL All-Star Game) following 1984 season.

KENNETH SHAWN BELL
(Ken)
Running Back—Denver Broncos
Born November 16, 1964, at Greenwich, Conn.
Height, 5.10. Weight, 190.
High School—Greenwich, Conn.
Received bachelor of arts degree from Boston College in 1986.

Signed as free agent by Denver Broncos, May 1, 1986.
Selected by Baltimore in 8th round (57th player selected) of 1986 USFL draft.
Released by Denver Broncos, September 7, 1987; re-signed by Broncos, September 8, 1987.

Year Club	G.	Att.	RUSHING Yds.	Avg.	TD.	PASS RECEIVING P.C.	Yds.	Avg.	TD.	—TOTAL— TD.	Pts.	F.
1986—Denver NFL	16	9	17	1.9	0	2	10	5.0	0	0	0	1
1987—Denver NFL	12	13	43	3.3	0	1	8	8.0	0	0	0	2
1988—Denver NFL	16	9	36	4.0	0	None				0	0	2
Pro Totals—3 Years	44	31	96	3.1	0	3	18	6.0	0	0	0	5

Year Club	G.	KICKOFF RETURNS No.	Yds.	Avg.	TD.
1986—Denver NFL	16	23	531	23.1	0
1987—Denver NFL	12	15	323	21.5	0
1988—Denver NFL	16	36	762	21.2	0
Pro Totals—3 Years	44	74	1616	21.8	0

Pro statistics: Recovered one fumble, 1987 and 1988; returned one punt for four yards, 1988.
Played in AFC Championship Game following 1986 and 1987 seasons.
Played in NFL Championship Game following 1986 and 1987 seasons.

KERWIN DOUGLAS BELL
Quarterback—Tampa Bay Buccaneers
Born June 15, 1965, at Live Oak, Fla.
Height, 6.02. Weight, 205.
High School—Mayo, Fla., Lafayette.
Received bachelor of science degree in psychology from
University of Florida in 1988.

Selected by Miami in 7th round (180th player selected) of 1988 NFL draft.
Signed by Miami Dolphins, July 8, 1988.
Released by Miami Dolphins, August 23, 1988; awarded on waivers to Atlanta Falcons, August 24, 1988.
Released by Atlanta Falcons, August 31, 1988; signed as free agent by Atlanta Falcons, October 19, 1988.
Granted unconditional free agency, February 1, 1989; signed by Tampa Bay Buccaneers, February 16, 1989.
Active for 6 games with Atlanta Falcons in 1988; did not play.
Atlanta NFL, 1988.

LEONARD CHARLES BELL
Safety—Houston Oilers
Born March 14, 1964, at Rockford, Ill.
Height, 5.11. Weight, 201.
High School—Rockford, Ill., Thomas Jefferson.
Attended Indiana University.

Selected by Cincinnati in 3rd round (76th player selected) of 1987 NFL draft.
Signed by Cincinnati Bengals, July 26, 1987.
On injured reserve with strained Achilles heel injury, September 1 through December 25, 1987; activated, December 26, 1987.
Released by Cincinnati Bengals, August 16, 1988; signed as free agent by Dallas Cowboys, January 4, 1989.
Released by Dallas Cowboys, April 14, 1989; signed as free agent by Houston Oilers, May 12, 1989.
Cincinnati NFL, 1987.
Games: 1987 (1).

MIKE J. BELL
Defensive End—Kansas City Chiefs
Born August 30, 1957, at Wichita, Kan.
Height, 6.04. Weight, 260.
High School—Wichita, Kan., Bishop Carroll.
Attended Colorado State University.
Twin brother of Mark E. Bell, tight end with Seattle Seahawks and Baltimore-Indianapolis
Colts, 1979, 1980 and 1982 through 1984.

Named as defensive lineman on THE SPORTING NEWS College All-America Team, 1978.
Selected by Kansas City in 1st round (2nd player selected) of 1979 NFL draft.
On injured reserve with knee injury, October 9 through November 16, 1979; activated, November 17, 1979.
On injured reserve with torn bicep, September 20 through remainder of 1980 season.
On injured reserve with groin injury, December 14 through remainder of 1982 season.
On injured reserve with knee injury, December 13 through remainder of 1984 season.
Granted roster exemption/leave of absence with drug problem, November 20 through remainder of 1985 season.
Placed on reserve/did not report, August 11 through entire 1986 season (included prison term on drug charges, August 11 through December 10, 1986); reinstated, March 25, 1987.
On non-football injury list with substance abuse, October 22 through November 15, 1988; activated, November 16, 1988.
Kansas City NFL, 1979 through 1985, 1987 and 1988.
Games: 1979 (11), 1980 (2), 1981 (16), 1982 (6), 1983 (16), 1984 (15), 1985 (11), 1987 (12), 1988 (12). Total—101.
Pro statistics: Recovered one fumble, 1979, 1981, 1983, 1985 and 1988; recovered two fumbles, 1984 and 1987; fumbled once, 1984.

TODD ANTHONY BELL
Linebacker—Philadelphia Eagles
Born November 28, 1958, at Middletown, O.
Height, 6.01. Weight, 212.
High School—Middletown, O.
Attended Ohio State University.

Named to THE SPORTING NEWS NFL All-Star Team, 1984.
Selected by Chicago in 4th round (95th player selected) of 1981 NFL draft.
Granted free agency, February 1, 1985.
On reserve/unsigned free agency list, August 20 through remainder of 1985 season.
Re-signed by Chicago Bears, August 16, 1986.
Released by Chicago Bears, May 10, 1988; signed as free agent by Philadelphia Eagles, June 14, 1988.

| | | —INTERCEPTIONS— | | | |
Year Club	G.	No.	Yds.	Avg.	TD.
1981—Chicago NFL	16	1	92	92.0	1
1982—Chicago NFL	9		None		
1983—Chicago NFL	15		None		
1984—Chicago NFL	16	4	46	11.5	1
1986—Chicago NFL	15	1	−1	−1.0	0
1987—Chicago NFL	12		None		
1988—Philadelphia NFL	16	0	24	.....	0
Pro Totals—7 Years	99	6	161	26.8	2

Additional pro statistics: Recovered one fumble, 1981 and 1987; returned one kickoff for 14 yards, 1982; returned two kickoffs for 18 yards and recovered one fumble for 10 yards, 1983; returned two kickoffs for 33 yards and recovered two fumbles for four yards, 1984; returned one kickoff for 18 yards and fumbled once, 1987; recovered two fumbles, 1988.
Played in NFC Championship Game following 1984 season.
Played in Pro Bowl (NFL All-Star Game) following 1984 season.

MARK JOSEPH BELLINI
Wide Receiver—Phoenix Cardinals
Born January 19, 1964, at San Leandro, Calif.
Height, 5.11. Weight, 185.
High School—San Leandro, Calif.
Attended Brigham Young University.

Selected by Indianapolis in 7th round (170th player selected) of 1987 NFL draft.
Signed by Indianapolis Colts, July 26, 1987.
Crossed picket line during players' strike, October 14, 1987.
Granted unconditional free agency, February 1, 1989; signed by Phoenix Cardinals, March 13, 1989.

| | | —PASS RECEIVING— | | | |
Year Club	G.	P.C.	Yds.	Avg.	TD.
1987—Indianapolis NFL	10	5	69	13.8	0
1988—Indianapolis NFL	15	5	64	12.8	0
Pro Totals—2 Years	25	10	133	13.3	0

Additional pro statistics: Recovered one fumble, 1988.

DAN BENISH
Defensive Tackle—Washington Redskins
Born November 21, 1961, at Youngstown, O.
Height, 6.05. Weight, 280.
High School—Hubbard, O.
Attended Clemson University.

Selected by Washington in 1983 USFL territorial draft.
Signed as free agent by Atlanta Falcons, May 3, 1983.
Released by Atlanta Falcons, October 9, 1986; signed as free agent by Miami Dolphins, March 9, 1987.
Released by Miami Dolphins after failing physical, May 4, 1987; signed as free agent by Tampa Bay Buccaneers, July 18, 1987.
Released by Tampa Bay Buccaneers, September 7, 1987; signed as free agent replacement player by Washington Redskins, September 23, 1987.
On injured reserve with elbow injury, October 27 through remainder of 1987 season.
On injured reserve with knee injury, August 1 through entire 1988 season.
Atlanta NFL, 1983 through 1986; Washington NFL, 1987.
Games: 1983 (16), 1984 (15), 1985 (16), 1986 (5), 1987 (3). Total—55.
Pro statistics: Recovered one fumble, 1985 and 1987.

CHARLES A. BENNETT
Defensive Tackle—Cleveland Browns
Born February 9, 1963, at Alligator, Miss.
Height, 6.05. Weight, 250.
High School—Clarksdale, Miss., Coahoma County.
Attended Mississippi Delta Junior College and University of Southwestern Louisiana.

Selected by Portland in 5th round (65th player selected) of 1985 USFL draft.
Selected by Chicago in 7th round (190th player selected) of 1985 NFL draft.
Signed by Chicago Bears, July 19, 1985.
Released by Chicago Bears, August 27, 1985; signed as free agent by Saskatchewan Roughriders, November 2, 1985.
Released by Saskatchewan Roughriders, June 12, 1986; signed as free agent by Dallas Cowboys, June 27, 1986.
Released by Dallas Cowboys, August 19, 1986; signed as free agent by Miami Dolphins for 1987, November 30, 1986.
Released by Miami Dolphins, August 31, 1987; re-signed as replacement player by Dolphins, September 24, 1987.
Released by Miami Dolphins, November 3, 1987; re-signed by Dolphins for 1988, December 12, 1987.
Released by Miami Dolphins, August 30, 1988; signed as free agent by Cleveland Browns, April 4, 1989.
Saskatchewan CFL, 1985; Miami NFL, 1987.
Games: 1985 (1), 1987 (3). Total—4.

CORNELIUS O'LANDA BENNETT
Linebacker—Buffalo Bills
Born August 25, 1966, at Birmingham, Ala.
Height, 6.02. Weight, 235.
High School—Birmingham, Ala., Ensley.
Attended University of Alabama.

Named to THE SPORTING NEWS NFL All-Star Team, 1988.
Named as linebacker on THE SPORTING NEWS College All-America Team, 1984 through 1986.
Selected by Indianapolis in 1st round (2nd player selected) of 1987 NFL draft.
Placed on reserve/unsigned list, August 31 through October 30, 1987.
Rights traded by Indianapolis Colts to Buffalo Bills in exchange for Bills trading 1st round pick in 1988 draft, 1st and 2nd round picks in 1989 draft and running back Greg Bell to Los Angeles Rams, October 31, 1987; Rams also traded running back Eric Dickerson to Colts for 1st and 2nd round picks in 1988 draft, 2nd round pick in 1989 draft and running back Owen Gill.
Signed by Buffalo Bills, October 31, 1987.
Granted roster exemption, October 31 through November 6, 1987; activated, November 7, 1987.
Buffalo NFL, 1987 and 1988.
Games: 1987 (8), 1988 (16). Total—24.
Pro statistics: Intercepted two passes for 30 yards and recovered three fumbles, 1988.
Played in AFC Championship Game following 1988 season.
Played in Pro Bowl (NFL All-Star Game) following 1988 season.

ROY BENNETT
Cornerback—San Diego Chargers
Born July 5, 1961, at Birmingham, Ala.
Height, 6.02. Weight, 195.
High School—Birmingham, Ala., West End.
Attended Jackson State University.

Selected by Jacksonville in 15th round (315th player selected) of 1984 USFL draft.
Signed by Jacksonville Bulls, January 6, 1984.
Released by Jacksonville Bulls, January 30, 1984; signed as free agent by Dallas Cowboys, May 15, 1984.
Released by Dallas Cowboys, July 25, 1984; signed as free agent by Winnipeg Blue Bombers, March, 1985.
Granted free agency, March 1, 1988; signed by San Diego Chargers, April 13, 1988.

Year Club	G.	No.	Yds.	Avg.	TD.
1985—Winnipeg CFL	16	5	105	21.0	0
1986—Winnipeg CFL	17	8	204	25.5	2
1987—Winnipeg CFL	18	*13	146	11.2	0
1988—San Diego NFL	16	1	21	21.0	0
CFL Totals—3 Years	51	26	455	17.5	2
NFL Totals—1 Year	16	1	21	21.0	0
Pro Totals—4 Years	67	27	476	17.6	2

Additional CFL statistics: Returned one punt for 10 yards, 1985; recovered one fumble, 1985 and 1987; returned two punts for minus four yards and fumbled once, 1986.

Additional NFL statistics: Recovered blocked punt in end zone for a touchdown, 1988.

CLIFFORD ANTHONY BENSON
(Cliff)
Tight End—Chicago Bears
Born August 28, 1961, at Chicago, Ill.
Height, 6.04. Weight, 238.
High School—Palos Heights, Ill., Alan B. Shepard.
Received bachelor of arts degree in social work from Purdue University in 1984.

Selected by Oakland in 1st round (11th player selected) of 1984 USFL draft.
Selected by Atlanta Falcons in 5th round (132nd player selected) of 1984 NFL draft.
Signed by Atlanta Falcons, July 12, 1984.
Released by Atlanta Falcons, August 26, 1986; signed as free agent by San Francisco 49ers, March 10, 1987.
Released by San Francisco 49ers, August 24, 1987; awarded on waivers to Washington Redskins, August 25, 1987.
Released by Washington Redskins, September 7, 1987; re-signed by Redskins, September 8, 1987.
Released by Washington Redskins, November 3, 1987; awarded on waivers to New Orleans Saints, November 4, 1987.
Released by New Orleans Saints, August 30, 1988; re-signed by Saints, September 14, 1988.
Released by New Orleans Saints, November 1, 1988; signed as free agent by Chicago Bears, April 14, 1989.

			——PASS RECEIVING——			
Year	Club	G.	P.C.	Yds.	Avg.	TD.
1984—Atlanta NFL		16	26	244	9.4	0
1985—Atlanta NFL		16	10	37	3.7	0
1987—Wash.(2)-N.O.(8) NFL		10	2	11	5.5	0
1988—New Orleans NFL		7	1	5	5.0	0
Pro Totals—4 Years		49	39	297	7.6	0

Additional pro statistics: Rushed three times for eight yards, 1984.

THOMAS CARL BENSON
Linebacker—Los Angeles Raiders
Born September 6, 1961, at Ardmore, Okla.
Height, 6.02. Weight, 245.
High School—Ardmore, Okla.
Attended University of Oklahoma.
Cousin of Rich Turner, defensive tackle with Green Bay Packers, 1981 through 1983.

Selected by Oklahoma in 1984 USFL territorial draft.
Selected by Atlanta in 2nd round (36th player selected) of 1984 NFL draft.
Signed by Atlanta Falcons, July 22, 1984.
Traded by Atlanta Falcons to San Diego Chargers for 6th round pick in 1987 draft, July 25, 1986.
Granted free agency, February 1, 1987; re-signed by San Diego Chargers, September 8, 1987.
Granted roster exemption, September 8 through September 18, 1987; activated, September 19, 1987.
On physically unable to perform/active with shoulder injury, July 25 through July 31, 1988; passed physical, August 1, 1988.
Traded by San Diego Chargers to New England Patriots for 7th round pick in 1989 draft, August 22, 1988.
On injured reserve with thigh injury, August 30 through September 29, 1988; activated, Sepember 30, 1988.
Granted unconditional free agency, February 1, 1989; signed by Los Angeles Raiders, April 1, 1989.
Atlanta NFL, 1984 and 1985; San Diego NFL, 1986 and 1987; New England NFL, 1988.
Games: 1984 (16), 1985 (16), 1986 (16), 1987 (11), 1988 (12). Total—71.
Pro statistics: Recovered two fumbles, 1985 and 1986; recovered one fumble, 1987.

TROY B. BENSON
Linebacker—New York Jets
Born July 30, 1963, at Altoona, Pa.
Height, 6.02. Weight, 235.
High School—Altoona, Pa.
Attended University of Pittsburgh.
Brother of Brad Benson, offensive tackle with New York Giants, 1977 through 1987.

Selected by Baltimore in 1985 USFL territorial draft.
Selected by New York Jets in 5th round (120th player selected) of 1985 NFL draft.
Signed by New York Jets, July 22, 1985.
On injured reserve with ankle injury, August 22 through entire 1985 season.
New York Jets NFL, 1986 through 1988.
Games: 1986 (15), 1987 (11), 1988 (16). Total—42.
Pro statistics: Intercepted one pass for two yards and recovered one fumble, 1988.

ALBERT TIMOTHY BENTLEY
Running Back—Indianapolis Colts
Born August 15, 1960, at Naples, Fla.
Height, 5.11. Weight, 214.
High School—Immokalee, Fla.
Attended University of Miami (Fla.).

Selected by Chicago in 1st round (7th player selected) of 1984 USFL draft.
USFL rights traded by Chicago Blitz to Michigan Panthers for safety John Arnaud, April 17, 1984.
Signed by Michigan Panthers, April 17, 1984.

Granted roster exemption, April 17 through May 4, 1984; activated, May 5, 1984.
Selected by Indianapolis in 2nd round (36th player selected) of 1984 NFL supplemental draft.
Not protected in merger of Michigan Panthers and Oakland Invaders; selected by Oakland Invaders in USFL dispersal draft, December 6, 1984.
Released by Oakland Invaders, August 1, 1985; signed by Indianapolis Colts, September 3, 1985.
Granted roster exemption, September 3 through September 11, 1985; activated, September 12, 1985.
On injured reserve with ankle injury, October 20 through November 20, 1986; activated, November 21, 1986.

Year Club	G.	Att.	RUSHING Yds.	Avg.	TD.	P.C.	PASS RECEIVING Yds.	Avg.	TD.	TOTAL TD.	Pts.	F.
1984—Michigan USFL	8	18	60	3.3	0	2	7	3.5	0	0	0	1
1985—Oakland USFL	18	191	1020	5.3	4	42	441	10.5	3	7	42	6
1985—Indianapolis NFL	15	54	288	5.3	2	11	85	7.7	0	2	12	1
1986—Indianapolis NFL	12	73	351	4.8	3	25	230	9.2	0	3	18	2
1987—Indianapolis NFL	12	142	631	4.4	7	34	447	13.1	2	9	54	3
1988—Indianapolis NFL	16	45	230	5.1	2	26	252	9.7	1	3	18	2
USFL Totals—2 Years	26	209	1080	5.2	4	44	448	10.2	3	7	42	7
NFL Totals—4 Years	55	314	1500	4.8	14	96	1014	10.6	3	17	102	8
Pro Totals—6 Years	81	523	2580	4.9	18	140	1462	10.4	6	24	144	15

Year Club	KICKOFF RETURNS G.	No.	Yds.	Avg.	TD.	Year Club	KICKOFF RETURNS G.	No.	Yds.	Avg.	TD.
1984—Michigan USFL	8	19	425	22.4	0	1988—Indianapolis NFL	16	39	775	19.9	0
1985—Oakland USFL	18	7	177	25.3	0	USFL Totals—2 Years	26	26	602	23.2	0
1985—Indianapolis NFL	15	27	674	25.0	0	NFL Totals—4 Years	55	120	2636	22.0	0
1986—Indianapolis NFL	12	32	687	21.5	0	Pro Totals—6 Years	81	146	3238	22.2	0
1987—Indianapolis NFL	12	22	500	22.7	0						

Additional USFL statistics: Recovered two fumbles, 1984 and 1985; attempted one pass with no completions, 1985.
Additional NFL statistics: Attempted one pass with one completion for six yards and recovered one fumble, 1985; recovered one fumble for nine yards, 1986; recovered three fumbles, 1987; attempted one pass with no completions, 1988.
Played in USFL Championship Game following 1985 season.

RAY RUSSELL BENTLEY
Linebacker—Buffalo Bills
Born November 25, 1960, at Grand Rapids, Mich.
Height, 6.02. Weight, 235.
High School—Hudsonville, Mich.
Attended Central Michigan University.

Named as inside linebacker on THE SPORTING NEWS USFL All-Star Team, 1983.
Selected by Michigan in 1983 USFL territorial draft.
Signed by Michigan Panthers, January 24, 1983.
On developmental squad, May 4 through June 4, 1983; activated, June 5, 1983.
Protected in merger of Michigan Panthers and Oakland Invaders, December 6, 1984.
Sold by Oakland Invaders to Arizona Outlaws, August 14, 1985.
Traded by Arizona Outlaws to Memphis Showboats for rights to linebacker Steve Hathaway, September 17, 1985.
Granted free agency when USFL suspended operations, August 7, 1986; signed as free agent by Tampa Bay Buccaneers, August 12, 1986.
Granted roster exemption, August 12 through August 21, 1986; activated, August 22, 1986.
Released by Tampa Bay Buccaneers, August 30, 1986; signed as free agent by Buffalo Bills, September 17, 1986.
Released by Buffalo Bills, October 18, 1986; re-signed by Bills, October 21, 1986.
On developmental squad for 5 games with Michigan Panthers in 1983.
Michigan USFL, 1983 and 1984; Oakland USFL, 1985; Buffalo NFL, 1986 through 1988.
Games: 1983 (14), 1984 (18), 1985 (18), 1986 (13), 1987 (9), 1988 (16). Total USFL—50. Total NFL—38. Total Pro—88.
USFL statistics: Intercepted two passes for 11 yards and credited with one sack for nine yards, 1983; recovered one fumble, 1983 through 1985; intercepted two passes for 10 yards and credited with 1½ sacks for 12½ yards, 1984; credited with two sacks for 20 yards and intercepted two passes for nine yards, 1985.
NFL statistics: Intercepted one pass for no yards and recovered one fumble, 1988.
Played in USFL Championship Game following 1983 and 1985 seasons.
Played in AFC Championship Game following 1988 season.

ROD EARL BERNSTINE
Tight End—San Diego Chargers
Born February 8, 1965, at Fairfield, Calif.
Height, 6.03. Weight, 235.
High School—Bryan, Tex.
Attended Texas A&M University.

Selected by San Diego in 1st round (24th player selected) of 1987 NFL draft.
Signed by San Diego Chargers, August 11, 1987.
On injured reserve with hamstring injury, September 8 through October 23, 1987; activated, October 24, 1987.
On injured reserve with knee injury, December 9 through remainder of 1988 season.

Year Club	PASS RECEIVING G.	P.C.	Yds.	Avg.	TD.
1987—San Diego NFL	10	10	76	7.6	1
1988—San Diego NFL	14	29	340	11.7	0
Pro Totals—2 Years	24	39	416	10.7	1

Additional pro statistics: Rushed once for nine yards, returned one kickoff for 13 yards and recovered one fumble, 1987; rushed twice for seven yards, 1988.

RAYMOND LENN BERRY
(Ray)
Linebacker—Minnesota Vikings
Born October 28, 1963, at Lovington, N. M.
Height, 6.02. Weight, 225.
High School—Abilene, Tex., Cooper.
Received degree in business management and real estate from Baylor University in 1987.

Selected by Minnesota in 2nd round (44th player selected) of 1987 NFL draft.
Signed by Minnesota Vikings, August 10, 1987.
Minnesota NFL, 1987 and 1988.
Games: 1987 (11), 1988 (15). Total—26.
Pro statistics: Recovered one fumble, 1987.
Played in NFC Championship Game following 1987 season.

STEPHEN TAYLOR BEUERLEIN
(Name pronounced BURR-line.)
(Steve)
Quarterback—Los Angeles Raiders
Born March 7, 1965, at Hollywood, Calif.
Height, 6.02. Weight, 205.
High School—Anaheim, Calif., Servite.
Received bachelor of arts degree in American studies from University of Notre Dame in 1987.

Selected by Los Angeles Raiders in 4th round (110th player selected) of 1987 NFL draft.
Signed by Los Angeles Raiders, July 24, 1987.
On injured reserve with elbow and shoulder injuries, September 7 through entire 1987 season.

				—————PASSING—————						——RUSHING——			—TOTAL—		
Year	Club	G.	Att.	Cmp.	Pct.	Gain	T.P.	P.I.	Avg.	Att.	Yds.	Avg.	TD.	TD.	Pts.	F.
1988—L.A. Raiders NFL		10	238	105	44.1	1643	8	7	6.90	30	35	1.2	0	0	0	6

Quarterback Rating Points: 1988 (66.6).
Additional pro statistics: Caught one pass for 21 yards, recovered two fumbles and fumbled six times for minus one yard, 1988.

DEAN BIASUCCI
Placekicker—Indianapolis Colts
Born July 25, 1962, at Niagara Falls, N.Y.
Height, 6.00. Weight, 191.
High School—Miramar, Fla.
Attended Western Carolina University.

Named to THE SPORTING NEWS NFL All-Star Team, 1988.
Established record for most field goals, 50 or more yards, season (6), 1988.
Signed as free agent by Atlanta Falcons, May 16, 1984.
Released by Atlanta Falcons, August 14, 1984; signed as free agent by Indianapolis Colts, September 8, 1984.
Released by Indianapolis Colts, August 27, 1985; re-signed by Indianapolis Colts, April 22, 1986.

		——PLACE KICKING——					
Year	Club	G.	XP.	XPM.	FG.	FGA.	Pts.
1984—Indianapolis NFL		15	13	1	3	5	22
1986—Indianapolis NFL		16	26	1	13	25	65
1987—Indianapolis NFL		12	24	0	24	27	96
1988—Indianapolis NFL		16	39	1	25	32	114
Pro Totals—4 Years		59	102	3	65	89	297

Additional pro statistics: Recovered one fumble, 1988.
Played in Pro Bowl (NFL All-Star Game) following 1987 season.

DUANE CLAIR BICKETT
Name pronounced BIK-ett.
Linebacker—Indianapolis Colts
Born December 1, 1962, at Los Angeles, Calif.
Height, 6.05. Weight, 241.
High School—Glendale, Calif.
Received degree in accounting from University of Southern California in 1986.

Named as linebacker on THE SPORTING NEWS College All-America Team, 1984.
Selected by Los Angeles in 1985 USFL territorial draft.
Selected by Indianapolis in 1st round (5th player selected) of 1985 NFL draft.
Signed by Indianapolis Colts, August 7, 1985.
Indianapolis NFL, 1985 through 1988.
Games: 1985 (16), 1986 (16), 1987 (12), 1988 (16). Total—60.
Pro statistics: Intercepted one pass for no yards and recovered two fumbles, 1985; intercepted two passes for 10 yards, 1986; recovered one fumble, 1986 and 1988; recovered two fumbles for 32 yards and fumbled once, 1987; intercepted three passes for seven yards, 1988.
Played in Pro Bowl (NFL All-Star Game) following 1987 season.

LEWIS KENNETH BILLUPS
Cornerback—Cincinnati Bengals
Born October 10, 1963, at Tampa, Fla.
Height, 5.11. Weight, 190.
High School—Niceville, Fla.
Attended University of North Alabama.

Selected by Birmingham in 1986 USFL territorial draft.
Selected by Cincinnati in 2nd round (38th player selected) of 1986 NFL draft.
Signed by Cincinnati Bengals, August 13, 1986.
On injured reserve with knee injury, October 17 through November 9, 1986; activated, November 10, 1986.
Cincinnati NFL, 1986 through 1988.
Games: 1986 (12), 1987 (11), 1988 (16). Total—39.
Pro statistics: Recovered one fumble for two yards, 1986; recovered one fumble, 1987; intercepted four passes for 47 yards and recovered two fumbles for 26 yards and a touchdown, 1988.
Played in AFC Championship Game following 1988 season.
Played in NFL Championship Game following 1988 season.

GUY RICHARD BINGHAM
Center-Guard—New York Jets
Born February 25, 1958, at Koiaumi Gumma Ken, Japan.
Height, 6.03. Weight, 260.
High School—Aberdeen, Wash., Weatherwax.
Received degree in physical education from University of Montana.

Selected by New York Jets in 10th round of 1980 NFL draft.
On injured reserve with knee injury, September 7 through November 18, 1982; activated, November 19, 1982.
On injured reserve with knee injury, December 16 through remainder of 1988 season.
New York Jets NFL, 1980 through 1988.
Games: 1980 (16), 1981 (16), 1982 (7), 1983 (16), 1984 (16), 1985 (16), 1986 (16), 1987 (12), 1988 (10). Total—125.
Pro statistics: Returned one kickoff for 19 yards, 1980; recovered one fumble, 1984 and 1986.
Played in AFC Championship Game following 1982 season.

KEITH BRYAN BISHOP
Center-Guard—Denver Broncos
Born March 10, 1957, at San Diego, Calif.
Height, 6.03. Weight, 265.
High School—Midland, Tex., Robert E. Lee.
Attended University of Nebraska and Baylor University.

Selected by Denver in 6th round (157th player selected) of 1980 NFL draft.
On injured reserve with ankle injury, August 18 through entire 1981 season.
Denver NFL, 1980 and 1982 through 1988.
Games: 1980 (16), 1982 (9), 1983 (16), 1984 (16), 1985 (14), 1986 (16), 1987 (12), 1988 (16). Total—115.
Pro statistics: Recovered one fumble, 1982, 1983 and 1986; fumbled once for minus five yards, 1988.
Played in AFC Championship Game following 1986 and 1987 seasons.
Played in NFL Championship Game following 1986 and 1987 seasons.
Played in Pro Bowl (NFL All-Star Game) following 1986 and 1987 seasons.

TODD ALAN BLACKLEDGE
Quarterback—Pittsburgh Steelers
Born February 25, 1961, at Canton, O.
Height, 6.03. Weight, 227.
High School—North Canton, O., Hoover.
Received degree in speech communications from Penn State University in 1983.
Son of Ron Blackledge, offensive line coach with Pittsburgh Steelers.

Selected by Kansas City in 1st round (7th player selected) of 1983 NFL draft.
Selected by Philadelphia in 1984 USFL territorial draft.
Granted free agency, February 1, 1988; re-signed by Chiefs and traded to Pittsburgh Steelers for 4th round pick in 1988 draft, March 29, 1988.

| | | | | | PASSING | | | | | | RUSHING | | | | TOTAL | |
Year	Club	G.	Att.	Cmp.	Pct.	Gain	T.P.	P.I.	Avg.	Att.	Yds.	Avg.	TD.	TD.	Pts.	F.
1983—Kansas City NFL		4	34	20	58.8	259	3	0	7.62	1	0	0.0	0	0	0	1
1984—Kansas City NFL		11	294	147	50.0	1707	6	11	5.81	18	102	5.7	1	1	6	8
1985—Kansas City NFL		12	172	86	50.0	1190	6	14	6.92	17	97	5.7	0	0	0	3
1986—Kansas City NFL		10	211	96	45.5	1200	10	6	5.69	23	60	2.6	0	0	0	5
1987—Kansas City NFL		3	31	15	48.4	154	1	1	4.97	5	21	4.2	0	0	0	2
1988—Pittsburgh NFL		3	79	38	48.1	494	2	3	6.25	8	25	3.1	1	1	6	4
Pro Totals—6 Years		43	821	402	49.0	5004	28	35	6.10	72	305	4.2	2	2	12	23

Quarterback Rating Points: 1983 (112.3), 1984 (59.2), 1985 (50.3), 1986 (67.6), 1987 (60.4), 1988 (60.8). Total—61.8.
Additional pro statistics: Recovered four fumbles and fumbled eight times for minus three yards, 1984; recovered one fumble, 1985; recovered two fumbles and fumbled five times for minus six yards, 1986; fumbled twice for minus six yards, 1987; recovered two fumbles and fumbled four times for minus two yards, 1988.

—DID YOU KNOW—
That the Kansas City Chiefs had a league-high three safeties in 1988?

BRIAN KEITH BLADES
Wide Receiver—Seattle Seahawks
Born July 24, 1965, at Fort Lauderdale, Fla.
Height, 5.11. Weight, 182.
High School—Sunrise, Fla., Piper.
Attended University of Miami (Fla.).
Brother of Bennie Blades, defensive back with Detroit Lions.

Selected by Seattle in 2nd round (49th player selected) of 1988 NFL draft.
Signed by Seattle Seahawks, May 19, 1988.

Year Club		——PASS RECEIVING——			
	G.	P.C.	Yds.	Avg.	TD.
1988—Seattle NFL..................	16	40	682	17.1	8

Additional pro statistics: Rushed five times for 24 yards, recovered one fumble and fumbled once, 1988.

HORATIO BENEDICT BLADES
(Bennie)
Defensive Back—Detroit Lions
Born September 3, 1966, at Fort Lauderdale, Fla.
Height, 6.01. Weight, 221.
High School—Sunrise, Fla., Piper.
Attended University of Miami (Fla.).
Brother of Brian Blades, wide receiver with Seattle Seahawks.

Named as defensive back on THE SPORTING NEWS College All-America Team, 1986 and 1987.
Selected by Detroit in 1st round (3rd player selected) of 1988 NFL draft.
Signed by Detroit Lions, July 14, 1988.

Year Club		——INTERCEPTIONS——			
	G.	No.	Yds.	Avg.	TD.
1988—Detroit NFL..................	15	2	12	6.0	0

Additional pro statistics: Recovered four fumbles for 22 yards, 1988.

BRIAN TIMOTHY BLADOS
Guard—Cincinnati Bengals
Born January 11, 1962, at Arlington, Va.
Height, 6.05. Weight, 295.
High School—Arlington, Va., Washington Lee.
Attended University of North Carolina.

Selected by Pittsburgh in 1984 USFL territorial draft.
Selected by Cincinnati in 1st round (28th player selected) of 1984 NFL draft.
Signed by Cincinnati Bengals, June 28, 1984.
Cincinnati NFL, 1984 through 1988.
Games: 1984 (16), 1985 (16), 1986 (16), 1987 (11), 1988 (16). Total—75.
Pro statistics: Caught one pass for four yards, 1985.
Played in AFC Championship Game following 1988 season.
Played in NFL Championship Game following 1988 season.

PAUL KEVIN BLAIR
Offensive Tackle—Denver Broncos
Born August 3, 1963, at Edmond, Okla.
Height, 6.04. Weight, 280.
High School—Edmond, Okla., Memorial.
Received degree in finance from Oklahoma State University in 1987.

Selected by New Jersey in 1986 USFL territorial draft.
Selected by Chicago in 4th round (110th player selected) of 1986 NFL draft.
Signed by Chicago Bears, July 17, 1986.
On injured reserve with knee injury, August 29 through entire 1988 season.
Granted unconditional free agency, February 1, 1989; signed by Denver Broncos, March 31, 1989.
Chicago NFL, 1986 and 1987.
Games: 1986 (14), 1987 (10). Total—24.

CARL NATHANIEL BLAND
Wide Receiver—Green Bay Packers
Born August 17, 1961, at Fluvanna County, Va.
Height, 5.11. Weight, 182.
High School—Richmond, Va., Thomas Jefferson.
Attended Virginia Union University.

Signed as free agent by Detroit Lions, May 3, 1984.
On injured reserve with hamstring injury, August 20 through November 7, 1984; activated after clearing procedural waivers, November 9, 1984.
Released by Detroit Lions, September 3, 1985; re-signed by Lions, October 17, 1985.
Released by Detroit Lions, October 31, 1985; re-signed by Lions, November 4, 1985.
On injured reserve with knee injury, September 7 through October 23, 1987; activated, October 24, 1987.
Granted unconditional free agency, February 1, 1989; signed by Green Bay Packers, March 27, 1989.

Year Club	G.	P.C.	Yds.	Avg.	TD.
1984—Detroit NFL...................	3			None	
1985—Detroit NFL...................	8	12	157	13.1	0
1986—Detroit NFL...................	16	44	511	11.6	2
1987—Detroit NFL...................	10	2	14	7.0	1
1988—Detroit NFL...................	16	21	307	14.6	2
Pro Totals—5 Years............	53	79	989	12.5	5

Additional pro statistics: Returned six kickoffs for 114 yards, recovered two fumbles for eight yards, 1986; fumbled once, 1986 and 1988; returned two kickoffs for 44 yards, 1987; rushed once for four yards, returned five punts for 59 yards and returned eight kickoffs for 179 yards, 1988.

BRIAN PATRICK BLANKENSHIP
Guard-Center—Pittsburgh Steelers
Born April 7, 1963, at Omaha, Neb.
Height, 6.01. Weight, 275.
High School—Omaha, Neb., Daniel J. Gross.
Attended University of Nebraska at Omaha and University of Nebraska at Lincoln.

Selected by Memphis in 1986 USFL territorial draft.
Signed as free agent by Pittsburgh Steelers, May 13, 1986.
Released by Pittsburgh Steelers, September 1, 1986; signed as free agent by Indianapolis Colts, May 11, 1987.
Released by Indianapolis Colts, August 7, 1987; signed as free agent replacement player by Pittsburgh Steelers, September 24, 1987.
Released by Pittsburgh Steelers, August 30, 1988; re-signed by Steelers, September 21, 1988.
Pittsburgh NFL, 1987 and 1988.
Games: 1987 (13), 1988 (13). Total—26.
Pro statistics: Returned one kickoff for five yards and recovered one fumble, 1988.

ANTHONY DARIUS BLAYLOCK
Cornerback—Cleveland Browns
Born February 21, 1965, at Raleigh, N.C.
Height, 5.11. Weight, 190.
High School—Garner, N.C.
Attended Winston-Salem State University.

Selected by Cleveland in 4th round (103rd player selected) of 1988 NFL draft.
Signed by Cleveland Browns, July 17, 1988.
On injured reserve with back injury, December 12 through remainder of 1988 season.
Cleveland NFL, 1988.
Games: 1988 (12).

DWAINE P. BOARD
Defensive End—New Orleans Saints
Born November 29, 1956, at Union Hall, Va.
Height, 6.05. Weight, 248.
High School—Rocky Mount, Va., Franklin County.
Received bachelor of science degree in industrial technology from
North Carolina A&T State University in 1979.

Selected by Pittsburgh in 5th round (137th player selected) of 1979 NFL draft.
Released by Pittsburgh Steelers, August 27, 1979; claimed on waivers by San Francisco 49ers, August 28, 1979.
On injured reserve with knee injury, September 23 through remainder of 1980 season.
On injured reserve with knee injury, September 16 through remainder of 1982 season.
Crossed picket line during players' strike, October 7, 1987.
On injured reserve with ankle injury, September 22 through November 16, 1988.
Released by San Francisco 49ers, November 17, 1988; awarded on waivers to New Orleans Saints, November 18, 1988.
San Francisco NFL, 1979 through 1987; San Francisco (3)-New Orleans (4) NFL, 1988.
Games: 1979 (16), 1980 (3), 1981 (16), 1982 (1), 1983 (16), 1984 (16), 1985 (16), 1986 (16), 1987 (14), 1988 (7). Total—121.
Pro statistics: Recovered five fumbles (including one in end zone for a touchdown), 1983; recovered one fumble, 1984, 1985 and 1987; recovered two fumbles for 16 yards, 1986.
Played in NFC Championship Game following 1981, 1983 and 1984 seasons.
Played in NFL Championship Game following 1981 and 1984 seasons.

RICKEY ALLEN BOLDEN
Offensive Tackle—Cleveland Browns
Born September 8, 1961, at Dallas, Tex.
Height, 6.04. Weight, 280.
High School—Dallas, Tex., Hillcrest.
Attended Southern Methodist University.

Selected by Oakland in 4th round (72nd player selected) of 1984 USFL draft.
Selected by Cleveland in 4th round (96th player selected) of 1984 NFL draft.
Signed by Cleveland Browns, May 17, 1984.
On injured reserve with dislocated shoulder, November 21 through remainder of 1984 season.
On injured reserve with broken arm, October 8 through December 12, 1986; activated, December 13, 1986.
Crossed picket line during players' strike, October 14, 1987.
On injured reserve with fractured ankle, November 3 through remainder of 1987 season.
Cleveland NFL, 1984 through 1988.

Games: 1984 (12), 1985 (16), 1986 (7), 1987 (5), 1988 (16). Total—56.

Pro statistics: Caught one pass for 19 yards and fumbled once, 1984; caught one pass for three yards and a touchdown, 1988.

Played in AFC Championship Game following 1986 season.

SCOTT ALLEN BOLTON
Wide Receiver—Green Bay Packers
Born January 4, 1965, at Mobile, Ala.
Height, 6.00. Weight, 188.
High School—Theodore, Ala.
Attended Auburn University.

Selected by Green Bay in 12th round (312th player selected) of 1988 NFL draft.

Signed by Green Bay Packers, June 27, 1988.

On injured reserve with shoulder and ankle injuries, August 30 through November 23, 1988; activated after clearing procedural waivers, November 25, 1988.

Green Bay NFL, 1988.

Games: 1988 (4).

Pro statistics: Caught two passes for 33 yards, 1988.

JOHN FITZGERALD BOOTY
Defensive Back—New York Jets
Born October 9, 1965, at Deberry, Tex.
Height, 6.00. Weight, 179.
High School—Carthage, Tex.
Attended Cisco Junior College and received bachelor of arts degree in speech communications
from Texas Christian University in 1988.

Selected by New York Jets in 10th round (257th player selected) of 1988 NFL draft.

Signed by New York Jets, June 7, 1988.

New York Jets NFL, 1988.

Games: 1988 (16).

Pro statistics: Intercepted three passes for no yards and recovered two fumbles, 1988.

MARK STEVEN BORTZ
Guard—Chicago Bears
Born February 12, 1961, at Pardeeville, Wis.
Height, 6.06. Weight, 275.
High School—Pardeeville, Wis.
Attended University of Iowa.

Selected by Los Angeles in 4th round (48th player selected) of 1983 USFL draft.

Selected by Chicago in 8th round (219th player selected) of 1983 NFL draft.

Signed by Chicago Bears, June 2, 1983.

Chicago NFL, 1983 through 1988.

Games: 1983 (16), 1984 (15), 1985 (16), 1986 (15), 1987 (12), 1988 (16). Total—90.

Pro statistics: Caught one pass for eight yards, 1986.

Played in NFC Championship Game following 1984, 1985 and 1988 seasons.

Played in NFL Championship Game following 1985 season.

Played in Pro Bowl (NFL All-Star Game) following 1988 season.

JOHN WILFRED BOSA
Defensive End—Miami Dolphins
Born January 10, 1964, at Keene, N. H.
Height, 6.04. Weight, 273.
High School—Keene, N. H.
Received bachelor of science degree in marketing from Boston College in 1987.

Selected by Miami in 1st round (16th player selected) of 1987 NFL draft.

Signed by Miami Dolphins, September 1, 1987.

Granted roster exemption, September 1 and September 2, 1987; activated, September 3, 1987.

On injured reserve with knee injury, October 19 through remainder of 1988 season.

Miami NFL, 1987 and 1988.

Games: 1987 (12), 1988 (6). Total—18.

Pro statistics: Recovered two fumbles, 1987.

CASPER N. BOSO
(Name pronounced BO-sew.)
(Cap)
Tight End—Chicago Bears
Born September 10, 1963, at Kansas City, Mo.
Height, 6.03. Weight, 240.
High School—Indianapolis, Ind., Bishop Chatard.
Attended Joliet Junior College and received liberal arts and sciences degree
in sociology from University of Illinois in 1986.

Selected by Orlando in 1986 USFL territorial draft.

Selected by Pittsburgh in 8th round (207th player selected) of 1986 NFL draft.

Signed by Pittsburgh Steelers, July 18, 1986.

Released by Pittsburgh Steelers, September 1, 1986; signed as free agent by St. Louis Cardinals, December 10, 1986.

Released by St. Louis Cardinals, September 7, 1987; awarded on waivers to Chicago Bears, September 8, 1987.
On injured reserve with neck injury, August 31 through November 10, 1988; activated, November 11, 1988.

Year Club	——PASS RECEIVING——				
	G.	P.C.	Yds.	Avg.	TD.
1986—St. Louis NFL	2	None			
1987—Chicago NFL	12	17	188	11.1	2
1988—Chicago NFL	6	6	50	8.3	0
Pro Totals—3 Years	20	23	238	10.3	2

Member of Chicago Bears for NFC Championship Game following 1988 season; inactive.

JEFF BOSTIC
Center—Washington Redskins
Born September 18, 1958, at Greensboro, N. C.
Height, 6.02. Weight, 260.
High School—Greensboro, N. C., Benjamin L. Smith.
Attended Clemson University.
Brother of Joe Bostic, guard with Phoenix Cardinals.

Signed as free agent by Philadelphia Eagles, May 20, 1980.
Released by Philadelphia Eagles, August 26, 1980; signed as free agent by Washington Redskins, September 1, 1984.
On injured reserve with knee injury, October 23 through remainder of 1984 season.
On injured reserve with knee injury, August 24 through October 18, 1985; activated, October 19, 1985.
Washington NFL, 1980 through 1988.
Games: 1980 (16), 1981 (16), 1982 (9), 1983 (16), 1984 (8), 1985 (10), 1986 (16), 1987 (12), 1988 (13). Total—116.
Pro statistics: Recovered one fumble, 1980 and 1985; caught one pass for minus four yards, 1981; recovered three fumbles, 1983; recovered two fumbles, 1984; recovered one fumble for one yard, 1986.
Played in NFC Championship Game following 1982, 1983, 1986 and 1987 seasons.
Played in NFL Championship Game following 1982, 1983 and 1987 seasons.
Played in Pro Bowl (NFL All-Star Game) following 1983 season.

JOE EARL BOSTIC JR.
Guard—Phoenix Cardinals
Born April 20, 1957, at Greensboro, N.C.
Height, 6.03. Weight, 265.
High School—Greensboro, N.C., Benjamin L. Smith.
Attended Clemson University.
Brother of Jeff Bostic, center with Washington Redskins.

Selected by St. Louis in 3rd round (64th player selected) of 1979 NFL draft.
On injured reserve with knee injury, December 3 through remainer of 1986 season.
On injured reserve with knee injury, December 12 through remainder of 1987 season.
Franchise transferred to Phoenix, March 15, 1988.
On injured reserve with knee injury, November 8 through remainder of 1988 season.
St. Louis NFL, 1979 through 1987; Phoenix NFL, 1988.
Games: 1979 (16), 1980 (16), 1981 (14), 1982 (8), 1983 (14), 1984 (16), 1985 (16), 1986 (13), 1987 (9), 1988 (10). Total—132.
Pro statistics: Recovered one fumble, 1983 and 1988.

KEITH BOSTIC
Safety—Indianapolis Colts
Born January 17, 1961, at Ann Arbor, Mich.
Height, 6.01. Weight, 215.
High School—Ann Arbor, Mich., Pioneer.
Attended University of Michigan.

Selected by Michigan in 1983 USFL territorial draft.
Selected by Houston in 2nd round (42nd player selected) of 1983 NFL draft.
Signed by Houston Oilers, June 27, 1983.
Granted unconditional free agency, February 1, 1989; signed by Indianapolis Colts, March 31, 1989.

Year Club	——INTERCEPTIONS——				
	G.	No.	Yds.	Avg.	TD.
1983—Houston NFL	16	2	0	0.0	0
1984—Houston NFL	16	None			
1985—Houston NFL	16	3	28	9.3	0
1986—Houston NFL	16	1	0	0.0	0
1987—Houston NFL	12	6	—14	—2.3	0
1988—Houston NFL	16	1	7	7.0	0
Pro Totals—6 Years	92	13	21	1.6	0

Additional pro statistics: Recovered two fumbles for 25 yards and a touchdown, 1984; recovered one fumble, 1985 and 1986; recovered one fumble for two yards and fumbled once, 1987; recovered two fumbles for 22 yards, 1988.
Played in Pro Bowl (NFL All-Star Game) following 1987 season.

BRIAN KEITH BOSWORTH
Linebacker—Seattle Seahawks
Born March 9, 1965, at Oklahoma City, Okla.
Height, 6.02. Weight, 248.
High School—Irving, Tex., MacArthur.
Received degree in business from University of Oklahoma in 1987.

Named as linebacker on THE SPORTING NEWS College All-America Team, 1986.
Selected by Seattle in 1st round of 1987 NFL supplemental draft, June 12, 1987.
Signed by Seattle Seahawks, August 14, 1987.
On injured reserve with shoulder injury, December 10 through remainder of 1988 season.
Seattle NFL, 1987 and 1988.
Games: 1987 (12), 1988 (10). Total—22.
Pro statistics: Recovered two fumbles for 38 yards, 1987; recovered one fumble, 1988.

MATTHEW KYLE BOUZA
(Matt)
Wide Receiver—Indianapolis Colts
Born April 8, 1958, at San Jose, Calif.
Height, 6.03. Weight, 211.
High School—Sacramento, Calif., Jesuit.
Received degree in political science from University of California at Berkeley.

Signed as free agent by San Francisco 49ers, May 8, 1981.
Released by San Francisco 49ers, August 31, 1981; re-signed by 49ers, September 1, 1981.
Released by San Francisco 49ers, September 9, 1981; signed as free agent by Baltimore Colts, May 15, 1982.
On injured reserve with separated shoulder, November 18 through remainder of 1983 season.
Franchise transferred to Indianapolis, March 31, 1984.
On injured reserve with knee injury, November 1 through November 28, 1985; activated, November 29, 1985.
Granted free agency, February 1, 1988; re-signed by Colts, August 24, 1988.

Year Club	G.	P.C.	Yds.	Avg.	TD.
1981—San Francisco NFL	1			None	
1982—Baltimore NFL	9	22	287	13.0	2
1983—Baltimore NFL	11	25	385	15.4	0
1984—Indianapolis NFL	16	22	270	12.3	0
1985—Indianapolis NFL	12	27	381	14.1	2
1986—Indianapolis NFL	16	71	830	11.7	5
1987—Indianapolis NFL	12	42	569	13.5	4
1988—Indianapolis NFL	15	25	342	13.7	4
Pro Totals—8 Years ...	92	234	3064	13.1	17

Additional pro statistics: Returned three kickoffs for 31 yards and returned two punts for no yards, 1982; recovered one fumble, 1982 and 1988; fumbled once, 1982 through 1984; returned one kickoff for minus four yards, 1983; returned three punts for 17 yards, 1984; rushed once for 12 yards, 1986; fumbled twice, 1987.

TODD ROBERT BOWLES
Safety—Washington Redskins
Born November 18, 1963, at Elizabeth, N.J.
Height, 6.02. Weight, 203.
High School—Elizabeth, N.J.
Attended Temple University.

Selected by Baltimore in 1986 USFL territorial draft.
Signed as free agent by Washington Redskins, May 6, 1986.

Year Club	G.	No.	Yds.	Avg.	TD.
1986—Washington NFL	15	2	0	0.0	0
1987—Washington NFL	12	4	24	6.0	0
1988—Washington NFL	16	1	20	20.0	0
Pro Totals—3 Years	43	7	44	6.3	0

Additional pro statistics: Recovered one fumble, 1987.
Played in NFC Championship Game following 1986 and 1987 seasons.
Played in NFL Championship Game following 1987 season.

JAMES EDWIN BOWMAN
(Jim)
Safety—New England Patriots
Born October 26, 1963, at Cadillac, Mich.
Height, 6.02. Weight, 210.
High School—Cadillac, Mich.
Attended Central Michigan University.

Selected by Oakland in 11th round (153rd player selected) of 1985 USFL draft.
Selected by New England in 2nd round (52nd player selected) of 1985 NFL draft.
Signed by New England Patriots, July 23, 1985.
New England NFL, 1985 through 1988.
Games: 1985 (16), 1986 (16), 1987 (12), 1988 (16). Total—60.
Pro statistics: Returned one punt for minus three yards, 1985; intercepted two passes for three yards and recovered one fumble for six yards, 1987; intercepted one pass for no yards and recovered one fumble, 1988.
Played in AFC Championship Game following 1985 season.
Played in NFL Championship Game following 1985 season.

WALTER NATHANIEL BOWYER JR.

Name pronounced BOY-er.

(Walt)

Defensive End—Kansas City Chiefs

Born September 8, 1960, at Pittsburgh, Pa.
Height, 6.04. Weight, 260.
High School—Winkinsburg, Pa.
Attended Arizona State University.

Selected by Denver in 10th round (254th player selected) of 1983 NFL draft.
Released by Denver Broncos, August 27, 1985; re-signed by Broncos for 1986, December 14, 1985.
Released by Denver Broncos, September 1, 1986; re-signed by Broncos, August 19, 1987.
Released by Denver Broncos, September 7, 1987; re-signed by Broncos, September 8, 1987.
Crossed picket line during players' strike, October 2, 1987.
Released by Denver Broncos, August 30, 1988; re-signed by Broncos, September 1, 1988.
Granted unconditional free agency, February 1, 1989; signed by Kansas City Chiefs, March 3, 1989.
Denver NFL, 1983, 1984, 1987 and 1988.
Games: 1983 (14), 1984 (16), 1987 (15), 1988 (16). Total—61.
Pro statistics: Recovered one fumble, 1983 and 1984; intercepted one pass for one yard, 1988.
Played in AFC Championship Game following 1987 season.
Played in NFL Championship Game following 1987 season.

GERARD MARK JOSEPH BOYARSKY

Name pronounced Boy-ARE-ski.

(Jerry)

Nose Tackle—Green Bay Packers

Born May 15, 1959, at Scranton, Pa.
Height, 6.03. Weight, 290.
High School—Jermyn, Pa., Lakeland.
Received bachelor of arts degree in political science from University of Pittsburgh in 1981.

Selected by New Orleans in 5th round (128th player selected) of 1981 NFL draft.
On injured reserve with knee injury, September 1 through October 1, 1981; activated, October 2, 1981.
Released by New Orleans Saints, September 6, 1982; signed as free agent by Cincinnati Bengals, December 1, 1982 and 1983.
Released by Cincinnati Bengals, September 3, 1986; signed as free agent by Buffalo Bills, September 10, 1986.
Released by Buffalo Bills, November 21, 1986; signed as free agent by Green Bay Packers, December 2, 1986.
Released by Green Bay Packers, December 15, 1986; re-signed by Packers, February 24, 1987.
On injured reserve with broken arm, September 12 through remainder of 1988 season.
New Orleans NFL, 1981; Cincinnati NFL, 1982 through 1985; Buffalo (10)-Green Bay (2) NFL, 1986; Green Bay NFL, 1987 and 1988.
Games: 1981 (11), 1982 (2), 1983 (15), 1984 (15), 1985 (16), 1986 (12), 1987 (12), 1988 (2). Total—85.

MARK HEARN BOYER

Tight End—Indianapolis Colts

Born September 16, 1962, at Huntington Beach, Calif.
Height, 6.04. Weight, 239.
High School—Huntington Beach, Calif., Edison.
Attended University of Southern California.

Selected by Los Angeles in 1985 USFL territorial draft.
Selected by Indianapolis in 9th round (229th player selected) of 1985 NFL draft.
Signed by Indianapolis Colts, July 18, 1985.
On injured reserve with broken arm, October 26 through December 3, 1987; activated, December 4, 1987.
Granted free agency, February 1, 1988; re-signed by Colts, August 23, 1988.

Year Club	G.	P.C.	Yds.	Avg.	TD.
			—PASS RECEIVING—		
1985—Indianapolis NFL	16	25	274	11.0	0
1986—Indianapolis NFL	16	22	237	10.8	1
1987—Indianapolis NFL	7	10	73	7.3	0
1988—Indianapolis NFL	16	27	256	9.5	2
Pro Totals—4 Years	55	84	840	10.0	3

Additional pro statistics: Recovered one fumble, 1985; fumbled once, 1986.

JAMES ROBERT BOYLE

(Jim)

Guard-Offensive Tackle—Atlanta Falcons

Born July 27, 1962, at Cincinnati, O.
Height, 6.05. Weight, 275.
High School—Cincinnati, O., Western Hills.
Received bachelor of science degree in physical education from Tulane University in 1984.

Selected by New Orleans in 1984 USFL territorial draft.
Franchise transferred to Portland, November 13, 1984.
Selected by Miami in 9th round (250th player selected) of 1984 NFL draft.
Signed by Miami Dolphins, June 26, 1984.
Released by Miami Dolphins, August 27, 1984; signed by Portland Breakers, January 18, 1985.

Released by Portland Breakers, January 25, 1985; signed as free agent replacement player by Pittsburgh Steelers, September 24, 1987.
Released by Pittsburgh Steelers, November 3, 1987; re-signed by Steelers, December 30, 1987.
Released by Pittsburgh Steelers, August 30, 1988; re-signed by Steelers, September 26, 1988.
Released by Pittsburgh Steelers, November 14, 1988; signed as free agent by Atlanta Falcons, February 24, 1989.
Pittsburgh NFL, 1987 and 1988.
Games: 1987 (3), 1988 (6). Total—9.
Pro statistics: Returned one kickoff for 19 yards, 1988.

DONALD CRAIG BRACKEN
(Don)
Punter—Green Bay Packers
Born February 16, 1962, at Coalinga, Calif.
Height, 6.01. Weight, 211.
High School—Thermopolis, Wyo., Hot Springs County.
Received bachelor of science degree in physical education from University of Michigan.

Selected by Michigan in 1984 USFL territorial draft.
Signed by Michigan Panthers, January 8, 1984.
Released by Michigan Panthers, February 16, 1984; signed as free agent by Kansas City Chiefs, May 4, 1984.
Released by Kansas City Chiefs, June 1, 1984; signed as free agent by Indianapolis Colts, June 14, 1984.
Released by Indianapolis Colts, August 6, 1984; signed as free agent by Denver Broncos, January 30, 1985.
Released by Denver Broncos, August 26, 1985; signed as free agent by Green Bay Packers, November 6, 1985.
On injured reserve with dislocated elbow, December 5 through remainder of 1986 season.
Released by Green Bay Packers, September 7, 1987; re-signed by Packers, September 8, 1987.

Year Club		G.	No.	Avg.	Blk.
			—PUNTING—		
1985—Green Bay NFL		7	26	40.5	0
1986—Green Bay NFL		13	55	40.1	2
1987—Green Bay NFL		12	72	40.9	1
1988—Green Bay NFL		16	85	38.7	1
Pro Totals—4 Years		48	238	39.8	4

ED JOHN BRADY
Linebacker—Cincinnnati Bengals
Born June 17, 1960, at Morris, Ill.
Height, 6.02. Weight, 235.
High School—Morris, Ill.
Attended University of Illinois.

Selected by Chicago in 1984 USFL territorial draft.
Selected by Los Angeles Rams in 8th round (215th player selected) of 1984 NFL draft.
Signed by Los Angeles Rams, July 14, 1984.
Released by Los Angeles Rams, August 27, 1984; re-signed by Rams, August 28, 1984.
Released by Los Angeles Rams, September 1, 1986; awarded on waivers to Cincinnati Bengals, September 2, 1986.
Los Angeles Rams NFL, 1984 and 1985; Cincinnati NFL, 1986 through 1988.
Games: 1984 (16), 1985 (16), 1986 (16), 1987 (12), 1988 (16). Total—76.
Pro statistics: Recovered one fumble, 1985 and 1987; fumbled once for minus seven yards, 1986.
Played in NFC Championship Game following 1985 season.
Played in AFC Championship Game following 1988 season.
Played in NFL Championship Game following 1988 season.

KERRY BRADY
Placekicker—Indianapolis Colts
Born August 27, 1963, at Vancouver, Wash.
Height, 6.02. Weight, 195.
High School—Vancouver, Wash., Hudson's Bay.
Attended Portland Community College and University of Hawaii.

Signed as free agent by Dallas Cowboys, March 17, 1987.
Released by Dallas Cowboys, August 25, 1987; re-signed as replacement player by Cowboys, October 17, 1987.
Released by Dallas Cowboys, October 20, 1987; signed as free agent by Buffalo Bills, April 5, 1988.
Released by Buffalo Bills, August 24, 1988; signed as free agent by Indianapolis Colts, September 22, 1988.
Released by Indianapolis Colts, October 5, 1988; re-signed by Colts, April 20, 1989.
Dallas NFL, 1987; Indianapolis NFL, 1988.
Games: 1987 (1), 1988 (2). Total—3.
Pro statistics: Successful on only extra point attempt, 1987.

STEPHEN BRAGGS
Defensive Back—Cleveland Browns
Born August 29, 1965, at Houston, Tex.
Height, 5.10. Weight, 180.
High School—Smiley, Tex.
Attended University of Texas.

Selected by Cleveland in 6th round (165th player selected) of 1987 NFL draft.
Signed by Cleveland Browns, July 26, 1987.
Cleveland NFL, 1987 and 1988.
Games: 1987 (12), 1988 (16). Total—28.
Pro statistics: Returned one kickoff for 27 yards, 1988.
Played in AFC Championship Game following 1987 season.

REGINALD ETOY BRANCH
(Reggie)
Running Back—Washington Redskins

Born October 22, 1962, at Sanford, Fla.
Height, 5.11. Weight, 235.
High School—Sanford, Fla., Seminole.
Attended West Virginia State College and East Carolina University.
Nephew of Tony Collins, running back with New England Patriots, 1981 through 1987.

Signed as free agent by Washington Redskins, May 2, 1985.
Released by Washington Redskins, August 27, 1985; re-signed by Redskins, October 1, 1985.
Released by Washington Redskins, November 12, 1985; re-signed by Redskins, December 11, 1985.
Released by Washington Redskins, August 26, 1986; re-signed by Redskins, December 17, 1986.
On injured reserve with broken wrist, September 13 through November 16, 1988; activated after clearing procedural waivers, November 18, 1988.
Washington NFL, 1985 through 1988.
Games: 1985 (8), 1986 (1), 1987 (12), 1988 (7). Total—28.
Pro statistics: Rushed four times for nine yards and a touchdown and returned four kickoffs for 61 yards, 1987.
Played in NFC Championship Game following 1986 and 1987 seasons.
Played in NFL Championship Game following 1987 season.

JOHN WESLEY BRANDES
Tight End—Indianapolis Colts

Born April 2, 1964, at Fort Riley, Kan.
Height, 6.02. Weight, 255.
High School—Arlington, Tex., Lamar.
Received bachelor of science degree in health from Cameron University.

Signed as free agent by Indianapolis Colts, May 11, 1987.
Crossed picket line during players' strike, October 7, 1987.

Year Club	G.	P.C.	Yds.	Avg.	TD.
1987—Indianapolis NFL	12	5	35	7.0	0
1988—Indianapolis NFL	16		None		
Pro Totals—2 Years	28	5	35	7.0	0

DAVID SHERROD BRANDON
Linebacker—San Diego Chargers

Born February 9, 1965, at Memphis, Tenn.
Height, 6.04. Weight, 230.
High School—Memphis, Tenn., Mitchell.
Attended Memphis State University.

Selected by Buffalo in 3rd round (60th player selected) of 1987 NFL draft.
Signed by Buffalo Bills, July 25, 1987.
Traded with 4th round pick in 1988 draft by Buffalo Bills to San Diego Chargers for Wide Receiver Trumaine Johnson and 7th round pick in 1988 draft, August 31, 1987.
San Diego NFL, 1987 and 1988.
Games: 1987 (8), 1988 (8). Total—16.
Pro statistics: Recovered blocked punt in end zone for a touchdown, 1987.

TYRONE SCOTT BRAXTON
Safety—Denver Broncos

Born December 17, 1964, at Madison, Wis.
Height, 5.11. Weight, 174.
High School—Madison, Wis., James Madison Memorial.
Attended North Dakota State University.
Related to Jim Braxton, fullback with Buffalo Bills and Miami Dolphins, 1971 through 1978.

Selected by Denver in 12th round (334th player selected) of 1987 NFL draft.
Signed by Denver Broncos, July 18, 1987.
On injured reserve with shoulder injury, September 1 through December 17, 1987; activated, December 18, 1987.
Denver NFL, 1987 and 1988.
Games: 1987 (2), 1988 (16). Total—18.
Pro statistics: Intercepted two passes for six yards and recovered one fumble, 1988.
Played in AFC Championship Game following 1987 season.
Played in NFL Championship Game following 1987 season.

JAMES THOMAS BREECH
(Jim)
Placekicker—Cincinnati Bengals

Born April 11, 1956, at Sacramento, Calif.
Height, 5.06. Weight, 161.
High School—Sacramento, Calif.
Attended University of California.

Selected by Detroit in 8th round (206th player selected) of 1978 NFL draft.
Released by Detroit Lions, August 23, 1978; signed as free agent by Oakland Raiders, December 12, 1978.
Released by Oakland Raiders, September 1, 1980; signed as free agent by Cincinnati Bengals, November 25, 1980.
Active for 1 game with Oakland Raiders in 1978; did not play.

Year Club			—PLACE KICKING—					Year Club			—PLACE KICKING—				
		G.	XP.	XPM.	FG.	FGA.	Pts.			G.	XP.	XPM.	FG.	FGA.	Pts.
1979—Oakland NFL		16	41	4	18	27	95	1985—Cincinnati NFL		16	48	2	24	33	120
1980—Cincinnati NFL		4	11	1	4	7	23	1986—Cincinnati NFL		16	50	1	17	32	101
1981—Cincinnati NFL		16	49	2	22	32	115	1987—Cincinnati NFL		12	25	2	24	30	97
1982—Cincinnati NFL		9	25	1	14	18	67	1988—Cincinnati NFL		16	*56	3	11	16	89
1983—Cincinnati NFL		16	39	2	16	23	87	Pro Totals—11 Years		137	381	18	172	249	897
1984—Cincinnati NFL		16	37	0	22	31	103								

Additional pro statistics: Punted twice for 33.5 yard avg., 1980; fumbled once, 1983; punted five times for 30.6 avg., 1985; punted three times for 21.3 avg., 1988.

Played in AFC Championship Game following 1981 and 1988 seasons.

Played in NFL Championship Game following 1981 and 1988 seasons.

JEFFERY BRYAN BREGEL
(Jeff)
Guard—San Francisco 49ers
Born May 1, 1964, at Redondo Beach, Calif.
Height, 6.04. Weight, 280.
High School—Los Angeles, Calif., John F. Kennedy.
Attended University of Southern California.

Named as guard on THE SPORTING NEWS College All-America Team, 1985 and 1986.
Selected by San Francisco in 2nd round (37th player selected) of 1987 NFL draft.
Signed by San Francisco 49ers, July 20, 1987.
On injured reserve with knee injury, September 7 through October 30, 1987; activated, October 31, 1987.
On injured reserve with back injury, December 18 through remainder of 1987 season.
On injured reserve with knee injury, December 9 through remainder of 1988 season.
San Francisco NFL, 1987 and 1988.
Games: 1987 (5), 1988 (13). Total—18.

BRIAN MICHAEL BRENNAN
Wide Receiver—Cleveland Browns
Born February 15, 1962, at Bloomfield, Mich.
Height, 5.09. Weight, 178.
High School—Birmingham, Mich., Brother Rice.
Received bachelor of science degree in finance from Boston College in 1984.

Selected by Denver in 16th round (324th player selected) in 1984 USFL draft.
Selected by Cleveland in 4th round (104th player selected) of 1984 NFL draft.
Signed by Cleveland Browns, May 18, 1984.
On injured reserve with separated shoulder, September 4 through October 1, 1985; activated, October 2, 1985.
Crossed picket line during players' strike, October 14, 1987.

Year Club		G.	-PASS RECEIVING-				-PUNT RETURNS-				—TOTAL—		
			P.C.	Yds.	Avg.	TD.	No.	Yds.	Avg.	TD.	TD.	Pts.	F.
1984—Cleveland NFL		15	35	455	13.0	3	25	199	8.0	0	3	18	1
1985—Cleveland NFL		12	32	487	15.2	0	19	153	8.1	1	1	6	3
1986—Cleveland NFL		16	55	838	15.2	6		None			7	42	0
1987—Cleveland NFL		13	43	607	14.1	6		None			6	36	1
1988—Cleveland NFL		16	46	579	12.6	1		None			1	6	0
Pro Totals—5 Years		72	211	2966	14.1	16	44	352	8.0	1	18	108	5

Additional pro statistics: Attempted one pass with one completion for 33 yards and a touchdown, 1985; recovered fumble in end zone for a touchdown, attempted one pass with one completion for 35 yards and fumbled once, 1986; recovered one fumble, 1987.

Played in AFC Championship Game following 1986 and 1987 seasons.

HOBY F. J. BRENNER
Tight End—New Orleans Saints
Born June 2, 1959, at Linwood, Calif.
Height, 6.04. Weight, 240.
High School—Fullerton, Calif.
Attended University of Southern California.

Selected by New Orleans in 3rd round (71st player selected) of 1981 NFL draft.
On injured reserve with turf toe, September 1 through October 22, 1981; activated, October 23, 1981.
On injured reserve with knee injury, December 31 through remainder of 1982 season.
On injured reserve with separated shoulder, September 27 through October 23, 1987; activated, October 24, 1987.

Year Club		G.	—PASS RECEIVING—			
			P.C.	Yds.	Avg.	TD.
1981—New Orleans NFL		9	7	143	20.4	0
1982—New Orleans NFL		8	16	171	10.7	0
1983—New Orleans NFL		16	41	574	14.0	3
1984—New Orleans NFL		16	28	554	19.8	6
1985—New Orleans NFL		16	42	652	15.5	3
1986—New Orleans NFL		15	18	286	15.9	0
1987—New Orleans NFL		12	20	280	14.0	2
1988—New Orleans NFL		10	5	67	13.4	0
Pro Totals—8 Years		102	177	2727	15.4	14

Additional pro statistics: Fumbled once, 1981, 1982 and 1985; recovered one fumble, 1982.
Played in Pro Bowl (NFL All-Star Game) following 1987 season.

DARRICK JOSEPH BRILZ
Guard-Offensive Tackle—San Diego Chargers
Born February 14, 1964, at Richmond, Calif.
Height, 6.03. Weight, 270.
High School—Pinole, Calif., Pinole Valley.
Attended Oregon State University.

Signed as free agent by Washington Redskins, May 1, 1987.
Released by Washington Redskins, August 31, 1987; re-signed as replacement player by Redskins, September 23, 1987.
On injured reserve with pinched nerve in neck, December 12 through remainder of 1987 season.
Released by Washington Redskins, August 29, 1988; awarded on waivers to San Diego Chargers, August 30, 1988.
Washington NFL, 1987; San Diego NFL, 1988.
Games: 1987 (7), 1988 (14). Total—21.

MICHAEL ANTHONY BRIM
Cornerback—Phoenix Cardinals
Born January 23, 1966, at Danville, Va.
Height, 6.00. Weight, 186.
High School—Danville, Va., George Washington.
Received degree in history from Virginia Union University in 1988.

Selected by Phoenix in 4th round (95th player selected) of 1988 NFL draft.
Signed by Phoenix Cardinals, July 10, 1988.
On injured reserve with cracked ribs, August 29 through November 24, 1988; activated, November 25, 1988.
Phoenix NFL, 1988.
Games: 1988 (4).

WALTER ANDREW BRISTER III
(Bubby)
Quarterback—Pittsburgh Steelers
Born August 15, 1962, at Alexandria, La.
Height, 6.03. Weight, 205.
High School—Monroe, La., Neville.
Attended Tulane University and Northeast Louisiana University.

Selected by Pittsburgh in 3rd round (67th player selected) of 1986 NFL draft.
Selected by New Jersey in 11th round (80th player selected) of 1986 USFL draft.
Signed by Pittsburgh Steelers, July 25, 1986.

Year Club	G.	Att.	Cmp.	Pct.	Gain	T.P.	P.I.	Avg.	Att.	Yds.	Avg.	TD.	TD.	Pts.	F.
1986—Piitsburgh NFL	2	60	21	35.0	291	0	2	4.85	6	10	1.7	1	1	6	1
1987—Pittsburgh NFL	2	12	4	33.3	20	0	3	1.67		None			0	0	0
1988—Pittsburgh NFL	13	370	175	47.3	2634	11	14	7.12	45	209	4.6	6	6	36	8
Pro Totals—3 Years	17	442	200	45.2	2945	11	19	6.66	51	219	4.3	7	7	42	9

Quarterback Rating Points: 1986 (37.6), 1987 (2.8), 1988 (65.3). Total—57.9.
Additional pro statistics: Recovered two fumbles, 1988.

RECORD AS BASEBALL PLAYER

Year Club	League	Pos.	G.	AB.	R.	H.	2B.	3B.	HR.	RBI.	B.A.	PO.	A.	E.	F.A.
1981—Bristol	Appal.	OF-SS	39	111	12	20	7	0	0	10	.180	46	11	9	.864
1982—Bristol†‡	Appal.						(Did not play)								

Selected by Detroit Tigers' organization in 4th round of free-agent draft, June 8, 1981.
†On suspended list, June 22, 1982 through entire season.
‡Placed on restricted list, October 7, 1982.

LOUIS CLARK BROCK JR.
(Lou)
Cornerback—Los Angeles Rams
Born May 8, 1964, at Chicago, Ill.
Height, 5.10. Weight, 175.
High School—St. Louis, Mo., Horton Watkins.
Attended University of Southern California.
Son of Lou Brock Sr., Hall of Fame outfielder with Chicago Cubs
and St. Louis Cardinals, 1961 through 1979.

Selected by San Diego in 2nd round (53rd player selected) of 1987 NFL draft.
Signed by San Diego Chargers, July 25, 1987.
On injured reserve with lymph infection in groin, November 3 through remainder of 1987 season.
Selected by Montreal Expos' organization in 17th round of free-agent draft, June 7, 1982.
Released by San Diego Chargers, August 30, 1988; signed as free agent by Seattle Seahawks, September 6, 1988.
Released by Seattle Seahawks, September 17, 1988; awarded on waivers to Detroit Lions, September 19, 1988.
Released by Detroit Lions, October 12, 1988; signed as free agent by Los Angeles Rams, April 6, 1989.
San Diego NFL, 1987; Seattle (1)-Detroit (2) NFL, 1988.
Games: 1987 (1), 1988 (3). Total—4.

STANLEY JAMES BROCK
(Stan)
Offensive Tackle—New Orleans Saints

Born June 8, 1958, at Portland, Ore.
Height, 6.06. Weight, 292.
High School—Beaverton, Ore., Jesuit.
Attended University of Colorado.
Brother of Pete Brock, center with New England Patriots, 1976 through 1987; and
Willie Brock, center with Detroit Lions, 1978.

Named as offensive tackle on THE SPORTING NEWS College All-America Team, 1979.
Selected by New Orleans in 1st round (12th player selected) of 1980 NFL draft.
On injured reserve with knee injury, December 5 through remainder of 1984 season.
On injured reserve with knee injury, October 22 through remainder of 1988 season.
New Orleans NFL, 1980 through 1988.
Games: 1980 (16), 1981 (16), 1982 (9), 1983 (16), 1984 (14), 1985 (16), 1986 (16), 1987 (12), 1988 (7). Total—122.
Pro statistics: Recovered one fumble, 1980, 1983 and 1985; returned two kickoffs for 18 yards and recovered two fumbles, 1981; returned one kickoff for 15 yards, 1983; returned one kickoff for 11 yards, 1987.

JAMES ROBERT BROOKS
Running Back—Cincinnati Bengals

Born December 28, 1958, at Warner Robins, Ga.
Height, 5.10. Weight, 182.
High School—Warner Robins, Ga.
Attended Auburn University.
Cousin of Kevin Porter, defensive back with Kansas City Chiefs.

Selected by San Diego in 1st round (24th player selected) of 1981 NFL draft.
Traded by San Diego Chargers to Cincinnati Bengals for running back Pete Johnson, May 29, 1984.

Year Club	G.	Att.	Yds.	Avg.	TD.	P.C.	Yds.	Avg.	TD.	TD.	Pts.	F.
1981—San Diego NFL	14	109	525	4.8	3	46	329	7.2	3	6	36	7
1982—San Diego NFL	9	87	430	4.9	6	13	66	5.1	0	6	36	4
1983—San Diego NFL	15	127	516	4.1	3	25	215	8.6	0	3	18	8
1984—Cincinnati NFL	15	103	396	3.8	2	34	268	7.9	2	4	24	4
1985—Cincinnati NFL	16	192	929	4.8	7	55	576	10.5	5	12	72	7
1986—Cincinnati NFL	16	205	1087	*5.3	5	54	686	12.7	4	9	54	2
1987—Cincinnati NFL	9	94	290	3.1	1	22	272	12.4	2	3	18	0
1988—Cincinnati NFL	15	182	931	5.1	8	29	287	9.9	6	14	84	1
Pro Totals—8 Years	109	1099	5104	4.6	35	278	2699	9.7	22	57	342	33

Year Club	G.	No.	Yds.	Avg.	TD.	No.	Yds.	Avg.	TD.
1981—San Diego NFL	14	22	290	13.2	0	40	949	23.7	0
1982—San Diego NFL	9	12	138	11.5	0	*33	*749	22.7	0
1983—San Diego NFL	15	18	137	7.6	0	32	607	19.0	0
1984—Cincinnati NFL	15		None			7	144	20.6	0
1985—Cincinnati NFL	16		None			3	38	12.7	0
1986—Cincinnati NFL	16		None				None		
1987—Cincinnati NFL	9		None			2	42	21.0	0
1988—Cincinnati NFL	15		None			1	—6	—6.0	0
Pro Totals—8 Years	109	52	565	10.9	0	118	2523	21.4	0

Additional pro statistics: Recovered two fumbles, 1981; recovered one fumble, 1982 and 1985; recovered three fumbles, 1983; attempted one pass with one completion for eight yards and a touchdown, 1985; attempted one pass with no completions, 1986.
Played in AFC Championship Game following 1981 and 1988 seasons.
Played in NFL Championship Game following 1988 season.
Played in Pro Bowl (NFL All-Star Game) following 1986 and 1988 seasons.

KEVIN CRAIG BROOKS
Defensive Tackle—Dallas Cowboys

Born February 9, 1963, at Detroit, Mich.
Height, 6.06. Weight, 284.
High School—Detroit, Mich., MacKenzie.
Received bachelor of general studies degree from University of Michigan in 1985.

Selected by Tampa Bay in 10th round (141st player selected) of 1985 USFL draft.
Selected by Dallas in 1st round (17th player selected) of 1985 NFL draft.
Signed by Dallas Cowboys, July 17, 1985.
On injured reserve with knee injury, August 21 through October 24, 1986; activated, October 25, 1986.
Crossed picket line during players' strike, October 7, 1987.
Dallas NFL, 1985 through 1988.
Games: 1985 (11), 1986 (9), 1987 (13), 1988 (15). Total—48.
Pro statistics: Recovered one fumble, 1987.

MICHAEL BROOKS
Linebacker—Denver Broncos

Born October 2, 1964, at Ruston, La.
Height, 6.01. Weight, 235.
High School—Ruston, La.
Attended Louisiana State University.

Selected by Denver in 3rd round (86th player selected) of 1987 NFL draft.
Signed by Denver Broncos, July 24, 1987.
Denver NFL, 1987 and 1988.
Games: 1987 (12), 1988 (16). Total—28.
Pro statistics: Recovered one fumble, 1987.
Played in AFC Championship Game following 1987 season.
Played in NFL Championship Game following 1987 season.

TERRANCE DONNELL BROOKS
(Chet)
Cornerback—San Francisco 49ers
Born January 1, 1966, at Midland, Tex.
Height, 5.11. Weight, 191.
High School—Dallas, Tex., David W. Carter.
Attended Texas A&M University.

Selected by San Francisco in 11th round (303rd player selected) of 1988 NFL draft.
Signed by San Francisco 49ers, July 16, 1988.
On injured reserve with knee injury, November 12 through remainder of 1988 season.
San Francisco NFL, 1988.
Games: 1988 (10).

WILLIAM BROOKS JR.
(Bill)
Wide Receiver—Indianapolis Colts
Born April 6, 1964, at Boston, Mass.
Height, 6.00. Weight, 190.
High School—Framingham, Mass., North.
Received bachelor of science degree in business administration
from Boston University in 1986.

Selected by Indianapolis in 4th round (86th player selected) of 1986 NFL draft.
Signed by Indianapolis Colts, June 23, 1986.

		PASS RECEIVING				-PUNT RETURNS-				—KICKOFF RET.—				—TOTAL—		
Year	Club	G.	P.C.	Yds.	Avg.	TD.	No.	Yds.	Avg.	TD.	No.	Yds.	Avg.	TD.	TD.	Pts.	F.
1986—Indianapolis NFL		16	65	1131	17.4	8	18	141	7.8	0	8	143	17.9	0	8	48	2
1987—Indianapolis NFL		12	51	722	14.2	3	22	136	6.2	0		None			3	18	3
1988—Indianapolis NFL		16	54	867	16.1	3	3	15	5.0	0		None			3	18	1
Pro Totals—3 Years		44	170	2720	16.0	14	43	292	6.8	0	8	143	17.9	0	14	84	6

Additional pro statistics: Rushed four times for five yards and recovered one fumble, 1986; rushed twice for minus two yards, 1987; rushed five times for 62 yards and recovered two fumbles, 1988.

ROBERT JOHN BROTZKI
(Bob)
Offensive Tackle—Atlanta Falcons
Born December 24, 1962, at Sandusky, O.
Height, 6.05. Weight, 280.
High School—Sandusky, O., Saint Mary's Central Catholic.
Received bachelor of science degree in marketing from Syracuse University in 1986.

Selected by New Jersey in 1986 USFL territorial draft.
Selected by Indianapolis in 9th round (228th player selected) of 1986 NFL draft.
Signed by Indianapolis Colts, July 17, 1986.
On injured reserve with back injury, August 30 through November 6, 1986; activated, November 7, 1986.
Placed on reserve/retired list, August 19 through September 21, 1988; reinstated, September 22, 1988.
Released by Indianapolis Colts, September 28, 1988; signed as free agent by Dallas Cowboys, October 19, 1988.
Granted unconditional free agency, February 1, 1989; signed by Atlanta Falcons, February 21, 1989.
Indianapolis NFL, 1986 and 1987; Indianapolis (1)-Dallas (4) NFL, 1988.
Games: 1986 (2), 1987 (11), 1988 (5). Total—18.

WALTER CRAIG BROUGHTON
Wide Receiver—Buffalo Bills
Born October 20, 1962, at Brewton, Ala.
Height, 5.10. Weight, 180.
High School—Brewton, Ala., T.R. Miller.
Attended Jacksonville State University.

Selected by Michigan in 2nd round (35th player selected) of 1984 USFL draft.
Signed by Michigan Panthers, February 6, 1984.
Not protected in merger of Michigan Panthers and Oakland Invaders; selected by Houston Gamblers in USFL dispersal draft, December 6, 1984.
Released by Houston Gamblers, February 18, 1985; awarded on waivers to New Jersey Generals, February 19, 1985.
On developmental squad, February 21 through March 18, 1985; activated, March 19, 1985.
Released by New Jersey Generals, July 31, 1985; awarded on waivers to Baltimore Stars, August 1, 1985.
Released by Baltimore Stars, August 2, 1985; signed as free agent by Buffalo Bills, May 10, 1986.
On injured reserve with thigh injury, November 7 through remainder of 1986 season.
On injured reserve with hamstring injury, September 27 through remainder of 1988 season.
On developmental squad for 2 games with New Jersey Generals in 1985.

Year Club	G.	P.C.	Yds.	Avg.	TD.	No.	Yds.	Avg.	TD.	No.	Yds.	Avg.	TD.	TD.	Pts.	F.
		PASS RECEIVING				-PUNT RETURNS-				—KICKOFF RET.—				—TOTAL—		
1984—Michigan USFL	18	35	593	16.9	5	16	110	6.9	0	11	220	20.0	0	5	30	2
1985—New Jersey USFL	15	21	359	17.1	3	None				1	0	0.0	0	3	18	1
1986—Buffalo NFL	8	3	71	23.7	0	12	53	4.4	0	11	243	22.1	0	0	0	5
1987—Buffalo NFL	9	5	90	18.0	1	None				None				1	6	0
1988—Buffalo NFL	1	None				None				None				0	0	0
USFL Totals—2 Years	33	56	952	17.0	8	16	110	6.9	0	12	220	18.3	0	8	48	3
NFL Totals—3 Years	18	8	161	20.1	1	12	53	4.4	0	11	243	22.1	0	1	6	5
Pro Totals—5 Years	51	64	1113	17.4	9	28	163	5.8	0	23	463	20.1	0	9	54	8

Additional USFL statistics: Recovered one fumble, 1984; recovered one fumble for five yards, 1985.
Additional NFL statistics: Rushed once for minus six yards and recovered one fumble, 1986.

CHARLES LEE BROWN
(Bud)
Safety—Miami Dolphins
Born April 19, 1961, at DeKalb, Miss.
Height, 6.00. Weight, 194.
High School—DeKalb, Miss., West Kemper.
Attended University of Southern Mississippi.

Selected by New Orleans in 1984 USFL territorial draft.
Selected by Miami in 11th round (305th player selected) of 1984 NFL draft.
Signed by Miami Dolphins, June 26, 1984.
Released by Miami Dolphins, August 27, 1984; re-signed by Dolphins, August 28, 1984.
Granted unconditional free agency, February 1, 1989; re-signed by Dolphins, May 1, 1989.

Year Club	G.	No.	Yds.	Avg.	TD.
		—INTERCEPTIONS—			
1984—Miami NFL	16	1	53	53.0	0
1985—Miami NFL	16	2	40	20.0	0
1986—Miami NFL	16	1	3	3.0	0
1987—Miami NFL	9	1	0	0.0	0
1988—Miami NFL	16	None			
Pro Totals—5 Years	73	5	96	19.2	0

Additional pro statistics: Recovered five fumbles for six yards, 1985; recovered two fumbles for six yards, 1986; fumbled once, 1986 and 1987; returned two punts for eight yards and recovered one fumble, 1987.
Played in AFC Championship Game following 1984 and 1985 seasons.
Played in NFL Championship Game following 1984 season.

DAVID STEVEN BROWN
(Dave)
Defensive Back—Green Bay Packers
Born January 16, 1953, at Akron, O.
Height, 6.01. Weight, 195.
High School—Akron, O., Garfield.
Received bachelor of arts degree in speech from University of Michigan.

Tied NFL record for most touchdowns scored by interception, game (2), vs. Kansas City Chiefs, November 4, 1984.
Named as safety on THE SPORTING NEWS College All-America Team, 1974.
Selected by Pittsburgh in 1st round (26th player selected) of 1975 NFL draft.
Selected from Pittsburgh Steelers by Seattle Seahawks in NFL expansion draft, March 30, 1976.
Granted free agency, February 1, 1985; re-signed by Seahawks, August 19, 1985.
Granted roster exemption, August 19 through August 29, 1985; activated, August 30, 1985.
Traded by Seattle Seahawks to Green Bay Packers for 11th round pick in 1988 draft, August 26, 1987.

Year Club	G.	No.	Yds.	Avg.	TD.	No.	Yds.	Avg.	TD.	TD.	Pts.	F.
		-INTERCEPTIONS-				-PUNT RETURNS-				—TOTAL—		
1975—Pittsburgh NFL	13	None				22	217	9.9	0	0	0	1
1976—Seattle NFL	14	4	70	17.5	0	13	74	5.6	0	0	2	0
1977—Seattle NFL	14	4	68	17.0	1	None				1	6	0
1978—Seattle NFL	16	3	44	14.7	0	None				0	0	0
1979—Seattle NFL	16	5	46	9.2	0	None				0	0	0
1980—Seattle NFL	16	6	32	5.3	0	None				0	0	0
1981—Seattle NFL	10	2	2	1.0	0	None				0	0	0
1982—Seattle NFL	9	1	3	3.0	0	None				0	0	0
1983—Seattle NFL	16	6	83	13.8	0	None				0	0	1
1984—Seattle NFL	16	8	179	22.4	*2	None				2	12	0
1985—Seattle NFL	16	6	58	9.7	*1	None				1	6	0
1986—Seattle NFL	16	5	58	11.6	1	None				1	6	0
1987—Green Bay NFL	12	3	16	5.3	0	None				0	0	0
1988—Green Bay NFL	16	3	27	9.0	0	None				0	0	0
Pro Totals—14 Years	200	56	686	12.3	5	35	291	8.3	0	4	26	2

Additional pro statistics: Returned six kickoffs for 126 yards, 1975; scored one safety, 1976; recovered one fumble for eight yards, 1981; recovered two fumbles for 15 yards, 1982; recovered three fumbles, 1983; recovered one fumble, 1984 through 1986.
Played in AFC Championship Game following 1975 and 1983 seasons.
Played in NFL Championship Game following 1975 season.
Played in Pro Bowl (NFL All-Star Game) following 1984 season.

EDDIE LEE BROWN
Wide Receiver—Cincinnati Bengals
Born December 17, 1962, at Miami, Fla.
Height, 6.00. Weight, 185.
High School—Miami, Fla., Senior.
Attended Navarro College and University of Miami (Fla.).

Named THE SPORTING NEWS NFL Rookie of the Year, 1985.
Selected by Orlando in 1985 USFL territorial draft.
Selected by Cincinnati in 1st round (13th player selected) of 1985 NFL draft.
Signed by Cincinnati Bengals, August 7, 1985.

| | | ——RUSHING—— | | | | PASS RECEIVING | | | | —TOTAL— | | |
Year Club	G.	Att.	Yds.	Avg.	TD.	P.C.	Yds.	Avg.	TD.	TD.	Pts.	F.
1985—Cincinnati NFL	16	14	129	9.2	0	53	942	17.8	8	8	48	2
1986—Cincinnati NFL	16	8	32	4.0	0	58	964	16.6	4	4	24	0
1987—Cincinnati NFL	12	1	0	0.0	0	44	608	13.8	3	3	18	3
1988—Cincinnati NFL	16	1	—5	—5.0	0	53	1273	*24.0	9	9	54	1
Pro Totals—4 Years	60	24	156	6.5	0	208	3787	18.2	24	24	144	6

Additional pro statistics: Returned one kickoff for six yards, 1985; recovered one fumble, 1985, 1987 and 1988; recovered two fumbles, 1986; returned 10 punts for 48 yards, 1988.
Played in AFC Championship Game following 1988 season.
Played in NFL Championship Game following 1988 season.
Played in Pro Bowl (NFL All-Star Game) following 1988 season.

GREGORY LEE BROWN
(Greg)
Defensive End—Atlanta Falcons
Born January 5, 1957, at Washington, D.C.
Height, 6.05. Weight, 265.
High School—Washington, D.C., Woodson.
Attended Kansas State University and Eastern Illinois University.

Signed as free agent by Philadelphia Eagles, May 16, 1981.
Traded by Philadelphia Eagles to Atlanta Falcons for defensive end Mike Pitts, September 7, 1987.
Philadelphia NFL, 1981 through 1986; Atlanta NFL, 1987 and 1988.
Games: 1981 (16), 1982 (9), 1983 (16), 1984 (16), 1985 (16), 1986 (16), 1987 (12), 1988 (16). Total—117.
Pro statistics: Recovered two fumbles for seven yards and one touchdown, 1981; recovered two fumbles, one for a touchdown, 1982; recovered one fumble, 1984, recovered two fumbles, 1985; credited with a safety, 1986.

JEROME BROWN
Defensive Tackle—Philadelphia Eagles
Born February 4, 1965, at Brooksville, Fla.
Height, 6.02. Weight, 288.
High School—Brooksville, Fla., Hernando.
Attended University of Miami (Fla.).
Cousin of Maulty Moore, offensive tackle with Miami Dolphins,
Cincinnati Bengals and Tampa Bay Buccaneers, 1972 through 1976.

Named as defensive lineman on THE SPORTING NEWS College All-America Team, 1986.
Selected by Philadelphia in 1st round (9th player selected) of 1987 NFL draft.
Signed by Philadelphia Eagles, August 21, 1987.
Philadelphia NFL, 1987 and 1988.
Games: 1987 (12), 1988 (16). Total—28.
Pro statistics: Intercepted two passes for seven yards and recovered one fumble for 37 yards, 1987; intercepted one pass for minus five yards, 1988.

LEONARD RAY BROWN JR.
(Known by middle name.)
Guard-Offensive Tackle—Washington Redskins
Born December 12, 1962, at West Memphis, Ark.
Height, 6.05. Weight, 280.
High School—Marion, Ark.
Attended Memphis State University, Arizona State University
and Arkansas State University.

Selected by St. Louis in 8th round (201st player selected) of 1986 NFL draft.
Signed by St. Louis Cardinals, July 14, 1986.
On injured reserve with knee injury, October 17 through November 20, 1986; activated, November 21, 1986.
Released by St. Louis Cardinals, September 7, 1987; re-signed as free agent replacement player by Cardinals, September 25, 1987.
On injured reserve with disclosed finger, November 12 through December 11, 1987; activated, December 12, 1987.
Franchise transferred to Phoenix, March 15, 1988.
Granted unconditional free agency, February 1, 1989; signed by Washington Redskins, March 10, 1989.
St. Louis NFL, 1986 and 1987; Phoenix NFL, 1988.
Games: 1986 (11), 1987 (7), 1988 (15). Total—33.

—DID YOU KNOW—
That there were 92 100-yard rushing performances in the NFL in 1988?

LOMAS BROWN JR.
Offensive Tackle—Detroit Lions
Born March 30, 1963, at Miami, Fla.
Height, 6.04. Weight, 275.
High School—Miami Springs, Fla.
Attended University of Florida.
Cousin of Joe Taylor, defensive back with Chicago Bears, 1967 through 1974;
and Guy McIntyre, guard with San Francisco 49ers.

Named as tackle on THE SPORTING NEWS College All-America Team, 1984.
Selected by Orlando in 2nd round (18th player selected) of 1985 USFL draft.
Selected by Detroit in 1st round (6th player selected) of 1985 NFL draft.
Signed by Detroit Lions, August 9, 1985.
Detroit NFL, 1985 through 1988.
Games: 1985 (16), 1986 (16), 1987 (11), 1988 (16). Total—59.

MARK ANTHONY BROWN
Linebacker—Miami Dolphins
Born July 18, 1961, at New Brunswick, N.J.
Height, 6.02. Weight, 235.
High School—Inglewood, Calif.
Attended Los Angeles Southwest Community College and Purdue University.

Selected by Boston in 10th round (115th player selected) of 1983 USFL draft.
Selected by Miami in 9th round (250th player selected) of 1983 NFL draft.
Signed by Miami Dolphins, June 15, 1983.
On suspended list, November 30 through December 4, 1988; reinstated, December 5, 1988.
Miami NFL, 1983 through 1988.
Games: 1983 (14), 1984 (16), 1985 (15), 1986 (14), 1987 (12), 1988 (13). Total—84.
Pro statistics: Intercepted one pass for no yards, returned one kickoff for no yards and recovered one fumble, 1983; intercepted one pass for five yards and recovered two fumbles, 1985; recovered four fumbles for 11 yards, 1986; recovered one fumble for one yard, 1987; intercepted two passes for 13 yards, 1988.
Played in AFC Championship Game following 1984 and 1985 seasons.
Played in NFL Championship Game following 1984 season.

RICHARD SOLOMON BROWN
Linebacker—Los Angeles Rams
Born September 21, 1965, at Western Samoa.
Height, 6.03. Weight, 240.
High School—Westminster, Calif.
Attended San Diego State University.

Signed as free agent by Los Angeles Rams, May 14, 1987.
On injured reserve with hamstring injury, August 31 through November 2, 1987; activated, November 3, 1987.
Released by Los Angeles Rams, August 30, 1988; re-signed by Rams, March 10, 1989.
Los Angeles Rams NFL, 1987.
Games: 1987 (8).

ROBERT LEE BROWN
Defensive End—Green Bay Packers
Born May 21, 1960, at Edenton, N.C.
Height, 6.02. Weight, 267.
High School—Edenton, N.C., John A. Holmes.
Attended Chowan Junior College and Virginia Polytechnic Institute and State University.

Selected by Green Bay in 4th round (98th player selected) of 1982 NFL draft.
On inactive list, September 20, 1982.
Green Bay NFL, 1982 through 1988.
Games: 1982 (8), 1983 (16), 1984 (16), 1985 (16), 1986 (16), 1987 (12), 1988 (16). Total—100.
Pro statistics: Recovered one fumble, 1982 and 1986; intercepted one pass for five yards and a touchdown, 1984; credited with one safety, 1985; recovered four fumbles, 1985 and 1987.

RONALD BROWN
(Ron)
Defensive End—Los Angeles Raiders
Born April 28, 1964, at Oroville, Calif.
Height, 6.04. Weight, 225.
High School—La Puenta, Calif., Bishop Amat.
Received degree in economics from University of Southern California in 1987.

Selected by San Diego in 8th round (204th player selected) of 1987 NFL draft.
Signed by San Diego Chargers, July 25, 1987.
Released by San Diego Chargers, August 29, 1987; signed as free agent replacement player by Los Angeles Raiders, September 24, 1987.
Released by Los Angeles Raiders, October 21, 1987; re-signed by Raiders, April 8, 1988.
Los Angeles Raiders NFL, 1987 and 1988.
Games: 1987 (3), 1988 (16). Total—19.
Pro statistics: Recovered one fumble, 1987.

RONALD JAMES BROWN
(Ron)
Wide Receiver—Los Angeles Rams
Born March 31, 1961, at Los Angeles, Calif.
Height, 5.11. Weight, 181.
High School—Baldwin Park, Calif.
Attended Arizona State University.
Won gold medal in 4x100 relay during 1984 Olympics.

Tied NFL record for most touchdowns scored by kickoff return, game (2), against Green Bay Packers, November 24, 1985.

Named as kick returner to THE SPORTING NEWS NFL All-Star Team, 1985.
Selected by Arizona in 1983 USFL territorial draft.
Selected by Cleveland in 2nd round (41st player selected) of 1983 NFL draft.
NFL rights traded by Cleveland Browns to Los Angeles Rams for 2nd round pick in 1984 draft, April 27, 1984.
Signed by Los Angeles Rams, August 16, 1984.
Crossed picket line during players' strike, October 14, 1987.
Granted free agency, February 1, 1988; re-signed by Rams, October 17, 1988.
Granted roster exemption, October 17 through October 30, 1988; activated, October 31, 1988.

		PASS RECEIVING				—KICKOFF RET.—				—TOTAL—		
Year Club	G.	P.C.	Yds.	Avg.	TD.	No.	Yds.	Avg.	TD.	TD.	Pts.	F.
1984—Los Angeles Rams NFL	16	23	478	20.8	4		None			4	24	0
1985—Los Angeles Rams NFL	13	14	215	15.4	3	28	918	*32.8	*3	6	36	2
1986—Los Angeles Rams NFL	14	25	396	15.8	3	36	794	22.1	0	3	18	1
1987—Los Angeles Rams NFL	12	26	521	20.0	2	27	581	21.5	1	3	18	2
1988—Los Angeles Rams NFL	7	2	16	8.0	0	19	401	21.1	0	0	0	1
Pro Totals—5 Years	62	90	1626	18.1	12	110	2694	24.5	4	16	96	6

Additional pro statistics: Rushed twice for 25 yards, 1984; rushed twice for 13 yards, 1985; rushed four times for five yards and recovered two fumbles, 1986; rushed twice for 22 yards and recovered one fumble, 1987; rushed three times for 24 yards, 1988.

Played in NFC Championship Game following 1985 season.
Played in Pro Bowl (NFL All-Star Game) following 1985 season.

STEVE BROWN
Cornerback—Houston Oilers
Born March 20, 1960, at Sacramento, Calif.
Height, 5.11. Weight, 188.
High School—Sacramento, Calif., C.K. McClatchy.
Attended University of Oregon.

Selected by Arizona in 7th round (74th player selected) of 1983 USFL draft.
Selected by Houston in 3rd round (83rd player selected) of 1983 NFL draft.
Signed by Houston Oilers, June 28, 1983.

		-INTERCEPTIONS-				—KICKOFF RET.—				—TOTAL—		
Year Club	G.	No.	Yds.	Avg.	TD.	No.	Yds.	Avg.	TD.	TD.	Pts.	F.
1983—Houston NFL	16	1	16	16.0	0	31	795	25.6	*1	1	6	2
1984—Houston NFL	16	1	26	26.0	0	3	17	5.7	0	0	0	1
1985—Houston NFL	15	5	41	8.2	0	2	45	22.5	0	0	0	1
1986—Houston NFL	16	2	34	17.0	0		None			0	0	0
1987—Houston NFL	10	2	45	22.5	0		None			0	0	1
1988—Houston NFL	14	2	48	24.0	1		None			1	6	0
Pro Totals—6 Years	87	13	210	16.2	1	36	857	23.8	1	2	12	5

Additional pro statistics: Recovered one fumble, 1984, 1985 and 1987.

THOMAS MARTIN BROWN
(Tom)
Fullback—Miami Dolphins
Born November 20, 1964, at Ridgway, Pa.
Height, 6.01. Weight, 218.
High School—Lower Burrell, Pa., Burrell.
Attended University of Pittsburgh.

Selected by Miami in 7th round (182nd player selected) of 1987 NFL draft.
Signed by Miami Dolphins, July 22, 1987.
On injured reserve with ankle injury, September 8 through October 30, 1987; activated, October 31, 1987.
On injured reserve with knee injury, November 3 through remainder of 1987 season.
On physically unable to perform/active with knee injury, July 12 through August 22, 1988; transferred to physically unable to perform/reserve with knee injury, August 23 through entire 1988 season.
Miami NFL, 1987.
Games: 1987 (1).
Pro statistics: Rushed three times for three yards and caught one pass for six yards, 1987.

TIMOTHY DONELL BROWN
(Tim)
Wide Receiver—Los Angeles Raiders
Born July 22, 1966, at Dallas, Tex.
Height, 6.00. Weight, 195.
High School—Dallas, Tex., Woodrow Wilson.
Received degree from University of Notre Dame.

Established NFL record for most yards gained, rookie, season (2,317), 1988.
Heisman Trophy winner, 1987.
Named as wide receiver on THE SPORTING NEWS College All-America Team, 1986 and 1987.
Named as kick returner to THE SPORTING NEWS NFL All-Star Team, 1988.
Selected by Los Angeles Raiders in 1st round (6th player selected) of 1988 NFL draft.
Signed by Los Angeles Raiders, July 14, 1988.

		—RUSHING—				PASS RECEIVING				—TOTAL—		
Year Club	G.	Att.	Yds.	Avg.	TD.	P.C.	Yds.	Avg.	TD.	TD.	Pts.	F.
1988—Los Angeles Raiders NFL	16	14	50	3.6	1	43	725	16.9	5	7	42	5

		—PUNT RETURNS—				—KICKOFF RET.—		
Year Club	G.	No.	Yds.	Avg.	TD.	No.	Yds.	Avg.TD.
1988—Los Angeles Raiders NFL	16	49	444	9.1	0	*41	*1098	*26.8 *1

Additional pro statistics: Recovered seven fumbles (including one in end zone for a touchdown), 1988.
Played in Pro Bowl (NFL All-Star Game) following 1988 season.

VINCENT BERNARD BROWN
Linebacker—New England Patriots
Born January 9, 1965, at Atlanta, Ga.
Height, 6.02. Weight, 245.
High School—Atlanta, Ga., Walter F. George.
Received degree in criminal justice from Mississippi Valley State University in 1988.

Selected by New England in 2nd round (43rd player selected) of 1988 NFL draft.
Signed by New England Patriots, July 20, 1988.
New England NFL, 1988.
Games: 1988 (16).

JOEY MATTHEW BROWNER
Safety—Minnesota Vikings
Born May 15, 1960, at Warren, O.
Height, 6.02. Weight, 212.
High Schools—Warren, O., Western Reserve; and Atlanta, Ga., Southwest.
Attended University of Southern California.
Brother of Ross Browner, defensive end with Cincinnati Bengals, Houston Gamblers and Green Bay Packers,
1978 through 1988; brother of Jim Browner, defensive back with Cincinnati Bengals,
1979 and 1980; and Keith Browner, linebacker with San Diego Chargers.

Named to THE SPORTING NEWS NFL All-Star Team, 1987 and 1988.
Selected by Los Angeles in 1983 USFL territorial draft.
Selected by Minnesota in 1st round (19th player selected) of 1983 NFL draft.
Signed by Minnesota Vikings, April 30, 1983.

		—INTERCEPTIONS—		
Year Club	G.	No.	Yds.	Avg.TD.
1983—Minnesota NFL	16	2	0	0.0 0
1984—Minnesota NFL	16	1	20	20.0 0
1985—Minnesota NFL	16	2	17	8.5 *1
1986—Minnesota NFL	16	4	62	15.5 1
1987—Minnesota NFL	12	6	67	11.2 0
1988—Minnesota NFL	16	5	29	5.8 0
Pro Totals—6 Years	92	20	195	9.8 2

Additional pro statistics: Recovered four fumbles for four yards, 1983; fumbled once, 1983 and 1985; recovered three fumbles for 63 yards and a touchdown, 1984; returned one kickoff for no yards and recovered three fumbles for five yards, 1985; recovered four fumbles, 1986; recovered one fumble, 1987; recovered two fumbles for nine yards, 1988.
Played in NFC Championship Game following 1987 season.
Played in Pro Bowl (NFL All-Star Game) following 1985 through 1988 seasons.

KEITH TELLUS BROWNER
Linebacker—San Diego Chargers
Born January 24, 1962, at Warren, O.
Height, 6.06. Weight, 266.
High Schools—Atlanta, Ga., Southwest; and Warren, O., Warren Western Reserve.
Attended University of Southern California.
Brother of Ross Browner, defensive end with Cincinnati Bengals, Houston Gamblers and Green Bay Packers,
1978 through 1988; Jim Browner, defensive back with Cincinnati Bengals,
1979 and 1980; and Joey Browner, safety with Minnesota Vikings.

Selected by Los Angeles in 1984 USFL territorial draft.
Selected by Tampa Bay in 2nd round (30th player selected) of 1984 NFL draft.
Signed by Tampa Bay Buccaneers, May 30, 1984.
Placed on suspended list, December 13 through December 16, 1986; reinstated, December 17, 1986.
Traded by Tampa Bay Buccaneers to San Francisco 49ers for 6th round pick in 1988 draft, February 27, 1987.
Released by San Francisco 49ers, September 7, 1987; re-signed as replacement player by 49ers, September 24, 1987.
Traded by San Francisco 49ers to Los Angeles Raiders for cash, October 7, 1987.
On injured reserve with ankle injury, October 19 through November 2, 1987.
Released by Los Angeles Raiders, November 3, 1987; release voided due to injured status and placed on injured reserve with ankle injury, November 9 through November 23, 1987.
Released by Los Angeles Raiders, November 24, 1987; signed as free agent by San Diego Chargers, April 13, 1988.
Tampa Bay NFL, 1984 through 1986; San Francisco (1)-Los Angeles Raiders (1) NFL, 1987; San Diego NFL, 1988.
Games: 1984 (16), 1985 (16), 1986 (15), 1987 (2), 1988 (16). Total—65.

Pro statistics: Recovered one fumble, 1984 and 1985; intercepted one pass for 25 yards and fumbled once, 1985; intercepted one pass for 16 yards and recovered two fumbles, 1986; intercepted two passes for 65 yards and a touchdown and recovered one fumble for 25 yards, 1988.

AUNDRAY BRUCE
Linebacker—Atlanta Falcons

Born April 30, 1966, at Montgomery, Ala.
Height, 6.05. Weight, 245.
High School—Montgomery, Ala., George Washington Carver.
Attended Auburn University.
Uncle of Ricky Shaw, linebacker with New York Giants.

Named as linebcker on THE SPORTING NEWS College All-America Team, 1987.
Signed by Atlanta Falcons, April 6, 1988.
Selected officially by Atlanta in 1st round (1st player selected) of 1988 NFL draft.
Atlanta NFL, 1988.
Games: 1988 (16).
Pro statistics: Intercepted two passes for 10 yards and recovered one fumble, 1988.

ROBERT LOUIS BRUDZINSKI
(Bob)
Linebacker—Miami Dolphins

Born January 1, 1955, at Fremont, O.
Height, 6.04. Weight, 235.
High School—Fremont, O., Ross.
Received bachelor of science degree in business (marketing) from Ohio State University in 1977.

Named as linebacker on THE SPORTING NEWS College All-America Team, 1976.
Selected by Los Angeles in 1st round (23rd player selected) of 1977 NFL draft.
Granted roster exemption when left camp, September 2, 1980; reinstated, September 6, 1980.
Left camp, November 5, 1980; granted roster exemption, November 6, 1980.
On retired-reserve list, November 12 through remainder of 1980 season.
Traded with 2nd round pick in 1981 draft by Los Angeles Rams to Miami Dolphins for 2nd and 3rd round picks in 1981 draft and 2nd round pick in 1982 draft, April 28, 1981.
Granted free agency, February 1, 1985; re-signed by Dolphins, September 21, 1985.
Granted unconditional free agency, February 1, 1989; received no qualifying offer, April 15, 1989.
Re-signed by Dolphins, April 26, 1989.

		—INTERCEPTIONS—						—INTERCEPTIONS—			
Year Club	G.	No.	Yds.	Avg.	TD.	Year Club	G.	No.	Yds.	Avg.	TD.
1977—Los Angeles NFL	14	2	24	12.0	0	1984—Miami NFL	16	1	0	0.0	0
1978—Los Angeles NFL	16	1	31	31.0	1	1985—Miami NFL	14	1	6	6.0	0
1979—Los Angeles NFL	16	1	26	26.0	0	1986—Miami NFL	16		None		
1980—Los Angeles NFL	9		None			1987—Miami NFL	12		None		
1981—Miami NFL	16	2	35	17.5	0	1988—Miami NFL	16		None		
1982—Miami NFL	9	1	5	5.0	0	Pro Totals—12 Years	170	9	127	14.1	1
1983—Miami NFL	16		None								

Additional pro statistics: Recovered one fumble for three yards, 1979; recovered one fumble, 1982, 1983, 1986 and 1988; recovered two fumbles for seven yards and a touchdown, 1985.
Played in NFC Championship Game following 1978 and 1979 seasons.
Played in AFC Championship Game following 1982, 1984 and 1985 seasons.
Played in NFL Championship Game following 1979, 1982 and 1984 seasons.

JOHN GLENN BRUHIN

Name pronounced Bruin.

Guard—Tampa Bay Buccaneers

Born December 9, 1964, at Knoxville, Tenn.
Height, 6.03. Weight, 280.
High School—Powell, Tenn.
Attended University of Tennessee.

Selected by Tampa Bay in 4th round (86th player selected) of 1988 NFL draft.
Signed by Tampa Bay Buccaneers, July 10, 1988.
Tampa Bay NFL, 1988.
Games: 1988 (16).

RICK DON BRYAN
Defensive End—Atlanta Falcons

Born March 20, 1962, at Tulsa, Okla.
Height, 6.04. Weight, 265.
High School—Coweta, Okla.
Attended University of Oklahoma.
Brother of Steve Bryan, linebacker with Denver Broncos.

Named as defensive lineman on THE SPORTING NEWS College All-America Team, 1983.
Selected by Oklahoma in 1984 USFL territorial draft.
Selected by Atlanta in 1st round (9th player selected) of 1984 NFL draft.
Signed by Atlanta Falcons, July 20, 1984.
Granted free agency, February 1, 1988; re-signed by Falcons, August 29, 1988.
Atlanta NFL, 1984 through 1988.

Games: 1984 (16), 1985 (16), 1986 (16), 1987 (9), 1988 (16). Total—73.
Pro statistics: Credited with one safety, 1984; caught extra point and ran four yards with lateral on fumble recovery, 1985; recovered one fumble, 1987 and 1988.

STEVE RAY BRYAN
Linebacker—Denver Broncos
Born May 6, 1964, at Wagoner, Okla.
Height, 6.02. Weight, 256.
High School—Coweta, Okla.
Received bachelor of arts degree in communications from
University of Oklahoma in 1987.
Brother of Rick Bryan, defensive end with Atlanta Falcons.
Selected by Chicago in 5th round (120th player selected) of 1987 NFL draft.
Signed by Chicago Bears, July 31, 1987.
Released by Chicago Bears, September 7, 1987; signed as free agent replacement player by Denver Broncos, September 25, 1987.
On injured reserve with knee injury, August 29 through October 23, 1988; activated, October 24, 1988.
Denver NFL, 1987 and 1988.
Games: 1987 (4), 1988 (8). Total—12.
Pro statistics: Recovered one fumble, 1988.
Played in AFC Championship Game following 1987 season.
Member of Denver Broncos for NFL Championship Game following 1987 season; inactive.

WILLIAM KIRBY BRYAN
(Bill)
Center—Denver Broncos
Born June 21, 1955, at Burlington, N. C.
Height, 6.02. Weight, 258.
High School—Burlington, N. C., Walter Williams.
Received bachelor of arts degree in economics from Duke University in 1977.
Selected by Denver in 4th round (101st player selected) of 1977 NFL draft.
On injured reserve, October 3 through remainder of 1977 season.
Crossed picket line during players' strike, October 1, 1987.
On injured reserve with knee injury, October 20 through remainder of 1987 season.
Denver NFL, 1978 through 1988.
Games: 1978 (13), 1979 (16), 1980 (16), 1981 (14), 1982 (9), 1983 (16), 1984 (16), 1985 (16), 1986 (16), 1987 (4), 1988 (16). Total—152.
Pro statistics: Recovered two fumbles, 1979; recovered one fumble, 1980, 1985, 1987 and 1988; fumbled twice for minus 20 yards, 1980; fumbled once, 1981 and 1984.
Played in AFC Championship Game following 1986 season.
Played in NFL Championship Game following 1986 season.

DOMINGO GARCIA BRYANT
Safety—Houston Oilers
Born December 8, 1963, at Nacagdoches, Tex.
Height, 6.04. Weight, 175.
High School—Garrison, Tex.
Attended Texas A&M University.
Selected by Jacksonville in 1986 USFL territorial draft.
Selected by Pittsburgh in 6th round (148th player selected) of 1986 NFL draft.
Signed by Pittsburgh Steelers, July 10, 1986.
On injured reserve with broken finger, August 19 through September 3, 1986.
Released by Pittsburgh Steelers, September 4, 1986; signed as free agent by Houston Oilers for 1987, November 13, 1986.
Released by Houston Oilers, September 1, 1987; re-signed as replacement player by Oilers, September 23, 1987.
Released by Houston Oilers, October 17, 1988; awarded on waivers to New York Jets, October 18, 1988.
Released by New York Jets, October 24, 1988; signed as free agent by Houston Oilers, November 3, 1988.

| | | | —INTERCEPTIONS— | | |
Year Club	G.	No.	Yds.	Avg.	TD.
1987—Houston NFL	13	4	75	18.8	0
1988—Houston NFL	14	3	56	18.7	1
Pro Totals—2 Years	27	7	131	18.7	1

Additional pro statistics: Recovered one fumble, 1987.

JEFF DWIGHT BRYANT
Defensive End—Seattle Seahawks
Born May 22, 1960, at Atlanta, Ga.
Height, 6.05. Weight, 270.
High School—Decatur, Ga., Gordon.
Attended Clemson University.
Selected by Seattle in 1st round (6th player selected) of 1982 NFL draft.
On injured reserve with ankle injury, November 14 through December 12, 1986; activated, December 13, 1986.
Granted free agency, February 1, 1988; re-signed by Seahawks, August 31, 1988.
Seattle NFL, 1982 through 1988.
Games: 1982 (9), 1983 (16), 1984 (16), 1985 (16), 1986 (12), 1987 (12), 1988 (16). Total—97.

Pro statistics: Recovered one fumble, 1983 and 1987; intercepted one pass for one yard and credited with a safety, 1984; recovered two fumbles, 1984 and 1988; recovered four fumbles, 1985.
Played in AFC Championship Game following 1983 season.

KELVIN LeROY BRYANT
Running Back—Washington Redskins
Born September 26, 1960, at Tarboro, N.C.
Height, 6.02. Weight, 195.
High School—Tarboro, N.C.
Attended University of North Carolina.

Named as running back on THE SPORTING NEWS USFL All-Star Team, 1983 and 1984.
Selected by Philadelphia in 1983 USFL territorial draft.
Signed by Philadelphia Stars, February 8, 1983.
Selected by Washington in 7th round (196th player selected) of 1983 NFL draft.
On developmental squad, July 1 through July 4, 1983; activated, July 5, 1983.
On developmental squad, April 8 through April 25, 1984; activated, April 26, 1984.
Franchise transferred to Baltimore, November 1, 1984.
On developmental squad, March 31 through April 12, 1985; activated, April 13, 1985.
Granted free agency when USFL suspended operations, August 7, 1986; signed by Washington Redskins, August 13, 1986.
Granted roster exemption, August 13 through August 22, 1986; activated, August 23, 1986.
On injured reserve with knee and ankle injuries, September 16 through October 31, 1986; activated, November 1, 1986.
On injured reserve with knee injury, December 9 through remainder of 1988 season.
On developmental squad for 1 game with Philadelphia Stars in 1983.
On developmental squad for 3 games with Philadelphia Stars in 1984.
On developmental squad for 2 games with Baltimore Stars in 1985.

| | | —RUSHING— | | | | PASS RECEIVING | | | | —TOTAL— | | |
Year Club	G.	Att.	Yds.	Avg.	TD.	P.C.	Yds.	Avg.	TD.	TD.	Pts.	F.
1983—Philadelphia USFL	17	318	1442	4.5	16	53	410	7.7	1	17	102	4
1984—Philadelphia USFL	15	*297	1406	4.7	13	48	453	9.4	1	15	90	8
1985—Baltimore USFL	15	238	1207	5.1	12	40	407	10.2	4	16	96	3
1986—Washington NFL	10	69	258	3.7	4	43	449	10.4	3	7	42	2
1987—Washington NFL	11	77	406	5.3	1	43	490	11.4	5	6	36	4
1988—Washington NFL	10	108	498	4.6	1	42	447	10.6	5	6	36	3
USFL Totals—3 Years	47	853	4055	4.8	41	141	1270	9.0	6	48	288	15
NFL Totals—3 Years	31	254	1162	4.6	6	128	1386	10.8	13	19	114	9
Pro Totals—6 Years	78	1107	5217	4.7	47	269	2656	9.9	19	67	402	24

Additional USFL statistics: Recovered two fumbles, 1983; recovered three fumbles for 38 yards and a touchdown, 1984; recovered one fumble and attempted one pass with no completions, 1985.
Additional NFL statistics: Recovered one fumble, 1986 through 1988; attempted one pass with no completions, 1987.
Played in USFL Championship Game following 1983 through 1985 seasons.
Played in NFC Championship Game following 1986 and 1987 seasons.
Played in NFL Championship Game following 1987 season.

CHARLES HARRISON BUCHANAN
Defensive End—Cleveland Browns
Born September 20, 1964, at Memphis, Tenn.
Height, 6.03. Weight, 245.
High School—Memphis, Tenn., Hamilton.
Received bachelor of science degree in health and physcial education
from Tennessee State University in 1987.

Selected by Pittsburgh in 8th round (205th player selected) of 1987 NFL draft.
Signed by Pittsburgh Steelers, July 26, 1987.
Released by Pittsburgh Steelers, September 7, 1987; signed as free agent by Cleveland Browns for 1988, November 5, 1988.
On physically unable to perform/active with back injury, July 23 through August 22, 1988; then transferred to physically unable to perform/reserve with back injury, August 23 through October 13, 1988; activated, October 14, 1988.
On injured reserve with back injury, December 14 through remainder of 1988 season.
Cleveland NFL, 1988.
Games: 1988 (9).
Pro statistics: Credited with a safety, 1988.

JASON OGDEN BUCK
Defensive End—Cincinnati Bengals
Born July 27, 1963, at Moses Lake, Wash.
Height, 6.05. Weight, 264.
High School—St. Anthony, Ida., South Fremont.
Attended Ricks College (Ida.) and Brigham Young University.

Outland Trophy winner, 1986.
Named as defensive lineman on THE SPORTING NEWS College All-America Team, 1986.
Selected by Cincinnati in 1st round (17th player selected) of 1987 NFL draft.
Signed by Cincinnati Bengals, September 8, 1987.
Granted roster exemption, September 8, 1987.
Cincinnati NFL, 1987 and 1988.
Games: 1987 (12), 1988 (16). Total—28.
Played in AFC Championship Game following 1988 season.
Played in NFL Championship Game following 1988 season.

JOHN ROBERT BUCZKOWSKI
(Bob)
Defensive End—San Diego Chargers
Born May 5, 1964, at Pittsburgh, Pa.
Height, 6.05. Weight, 260.
High School—Monroeville, Pa., Gateway.
Attended University of Pittsburgh.

Selected by Los Angeles Raiders in 1st round (24th player selected) of 1986 NFL draft.
Signed by Los Angeles Raiders, July 17, 1986.
On injured reserve with back injury, August 26 through entire 1986 season.
On non-football injury list with hepatitis, September 9 through October 13, 1987; activated, October 14, 1987.
Crossed picket line during player's strike, October 14, 1987.
On injured reserve with ankle injury, November 11 through December 11, 1987; activated, December 12, 1987.
Released by Los Angeles Raiders, August 30, 1988; signed as free agent by San Diego Chargers, May 25, 1989.
Los Angeles Raiders NFL, 1987.
Games: 1987 (2).

MAURY ANTHONY BUFORD
Punter—Green Bay Packers
Born February 18, 1960, at Mount Pleasant, Tex.
Height, 6.01. Weight, 191.
High School—Mount Pleasant, Tex.
Received degree in business administration and marketing from Texas Tech University in 1982.

Selected by San Diego in 8th round (215th player selected) of 1982 NFL draft.
Traded by San Diego Chargers to Chicago Bears for 12th round pick in 1986 draft, August 20, 1985.
Released by Chicago Bears, September 7, 1987; signed as free agent by Denver Broncos, April 28, 1988.
Released by Denver Broncos, July 22, 1988; awarded on waivers to Atlanta Falcons, July 26, 1988.
Released by Atlanta Falcons, August 25, 1988; signed as free agent by New York Giants, September 7, 1988.
Granted unconditional free agency, February 1, 1989; signed by Green Bay Packers, March 30, 1989.

Year Club	—PUNTING—				Year Club	—PUNTING—			
	G.	No.	Avg.	Blk.		G.	No.	Avg.	Blk.
1982—San Diego NFL	9	21	41.3	*2	1986—Chicago NFL	16	69	41.3	1
1983—San Diego NFL	16	63	43.9	0	1988—N.Y. Giants NFL	15	73	41.3	2
1984—San Diego NFL	16	66	42.0	0	Pro Totals—6 Years	88	360	42.0	6
1985—Chicago NFL	16	68	42.2	1					

Additional pro statistics: Attempted one pass with no completions, 1983; attempted one pass with one completion for five yards, 1985; rushed once for minus 13 yards and fumbled once, 1986.
Played in NFC Championship Game following 1985 season.
Played in NFL Championship Game following 1985 season.

CORNELL RODNEY BURBAGE
Wide Receiver—Dallas Cowboys
Born February 22, 1965, at Lexington, Ky.
Height, 5.10. Weight, 180.
High School—Lexington, Ky., Bryan Station.
Received bachelor of science in mathematics from University of Kentucky in 1987.

Signed as free agent by Dallas Cowboys, April 30, 1987.
Released by Dallas Cowboys, September 7, 1987; re-signed as replacement player by Cowboys, September 23, 1987.
Released by Dallas Cowboys, October 26, 1987; re-signed by Cowboys for 1988 season, December 24, 1987.
Released by Dallas Cowboys, August 30, 1988; re-signed by Cowboys, October 11, 1988.

Year Club		PASS RECEIVING				—KICKOFF RET.—			—TOTAL—		
	G.	P.C.	Yds.	Avg.	TD.	No.	Yds.	Avg.	TD.	TD.	Pts.	F.
1987—Dallas NFL	3	7	168	24.0	2		None			0	0	0
1988—Dallas NFL	10	2	50	25.0	0	20	448	22.4	0	0	0	1
Pro Totals—2 Years	13	9	218	24.2	2	20	448	22.4	0	0	0	1

Additional pro statistics: Returned five punts for 29 yards, 1987.

CHRIS BURKETT
Wide Receiver—Buffalo Bills
Born August 21, 1962, at Laurel, Miss.
Height, 6.04. Weight, 210.
High School—Collins, Miss.
Attended Jackson State University.

Selected by Baltimore in 1st round (14th player selected) of 1985 USFL draft.
Selected by Buffalo in 2nd round (42nd player selected) of 1985 NFL draft.
Signed by Buffalo Bills, July 23, 1985.

Year Club	—PASS RECEIVING—				
	G.	P.C.	Yds.	Avg.	TD.
1985—Buffalo NFL	16	21	371	17.7	0
1986—Buffalo NFL	14	34	778	*22.9	4
1987—Buffalo NFL	12	56	765	13.7	4
1988—Buffalo NFL	11	23	354	15.4	1
Pro Totals—4 Years	53	134	2268	16.9	9

Additional pro statistics: Fumbled once, 1986 and 1987.
Played in AFC Championship Game following 1988 season.

DERRICK D. BURROUGHS
Cornerback—Buffalo Bills
Born May 18, 1962, at Mobile, Ala.
Height, 6.01. Weight, 180.
High School—Prichard, Ala., M. T. Blount.
Attended Memphis State University.

Selected by Memphis in 1985 USFL territorial draft.
Selected by Buffalo in 1st round (14th player selected) of 1985 NFL draft.
Signed by Buffalo Bills, May 17, 1985.
On injured reserve with knee injury, December 17 through remainder of 1986 season.

Year Club	G.	No.	Yds.	Avg.	TD.
1985—Buffalo NFL	14	2	7	3.5	0
1986—Buffalo NFL	15	2	49	24.5	0
1987—Buffalo NFL	12	2	11	5.5	0
1988—Buffalo NFL	14			None	
Pro Totals—4 Years	55	6	67	11.2	0

Additional pro statistics: Recovered one fumble, 1987 and 1988.
Played in AFC Championship Game following 1988 season.

CURTIS D. BURROW
Placekicker—Green Bay Packers
Born December 11, 1962, at Brinkley, Ark.
Height, 5.11. Weight, 185.
High School—Brinkley, Ark.
Attended University of Central Arkansas.

Signed as free agent by New Orleans Saints, May 15, 1986.
Released by New Orleans Saints, August 18, 1986; signed as free agent by Cincinnati Bengals, February 5, 1987.
Released by Cincinnati Bengals, May 8, 1987; signed as free agent by Green Bay Packers, August 18, 1988.
Released by Green Bay Packers, August 23, 1988; re-signed by Packers, December 14, 1988.

Year Club	G.	XP.	XPM.	FG.	FGA.	Pts.
1988—Green Bay NFL	1	2	2	0	1	2

LLOYD EARL BURRUSS JR.
Safety—Kansas City Chiefs
Born October 31, 1957, at Charlottesville, Va.
Height, 6.00. Weight, 209.
High School—Charlottesville, Va.
Received bachelor of arts degree in general studies from University of Maryland in 1981.

Selected by Kansas City in 3rd round (78th player selected) of 1981 NFL draft.
On injured reserve with knee injury, December 23 through remainder of 1987 season.

Year Club	G.	No.	Yds.	Avg.	TD.
1981—Kansas City NFL	14	4	75	18.8	1
1982—Kansas City NFL	9	1	25	25.0	0
1983—Kansas City NFL	12	4	46	11.5	0
1984—Kansas City NFL	16	2	16	8.0	0
1985—Kansas City NFL	15	1	0	0.0	0
1986—Kansas City NFL	15	5	*193	38.6	*3
1987—Kansas City NFL	11			None	
1988—Kansas City NFL	10	2	57	28.5	0
Pro Totals—8 Years	102	19	412	21.7	4

Additional pro statistics: Returned five kickoffs for 91 yards, recovered one fumble for four yards and fumbled once, 1981; recovered two fumbles for 26 yards, 1983; recovered one fumble, 1984 and 1986; returned blocked field goal 78 yards for a touchdown, 1986.
Played in Pro Bowl (NFL All-Star Game) following 1986 season.

TONY LEE BURSE
Fullback—Seattle Seahawks
Born April 4, 1965, at Lafayette, Ga.
Height, 6.00. Weight, 220.
High School—Lafayette, Ga.
Attended Middle Tennessee State University.

Selected by Seattle in 12th round (324th player selected) of 1987 NFL draft.
Signed by Seattle Seahawks, July 22, 1987.
Released by Seattle Seahawks, August 30, 1988; signed as free agent by Miami Dolphins, December 16, 1988.
Granted unconditional free agency, February 1, 1989; signed by Seattle Seahawks, April 1, 1989.
Inactive for 1 game with Miami Dolphins in 1988.

Year Club	G.	Att.	Yds.	Avg.	TD.	P.C.	Yds.	Avg.	TD.	TD.	Pts.	F.
		RUSHING				PASS RECEIVING				TOTAL		
1987—Seattle NFL	12	7	36	5.1	0		None			0	0	1

Additional pro statistics: Returned one kickoff for one yard, 1987.

JAMES P. BURT
(Jim)
Nose Tackle—New York Giants
Born June 7, 1959, at Buffalo, N. Y.
Height, 6.01. Weight, 260.
High School—Orchard Park, N. Y.
Attended University of Miami (Fla.).

Signed as free agent by New York Giants, May 4, 1981.
On injured reserve with back injury, December 24 through remainder of 1982 season.
On injured reserve with back injury, November 2 through remainder of 1983 season.
On injured reserve with back injury, December 7 through remainder of 1987 season.
New York Giants NFL, 1981 through 1988.
Games: 1981 (13), 1982 (4), 1983 (7), 1984 (16), 1985 (16), 1986 (13), 1987 (8), 1988 (16). Total—93.
Pro statistics: Recovered one fumble, 1983; recovered two fumbles, 1984 and 1985; recovered three fumbles for one yard, 1986; recovered two fumbles for 39 yards and a touchdown, 1988.
Played in NFC Championship Game following 1986 season.
Played in NFL Championship Game following 1986 season.
Played in Pro Bowl (NFL All-Star Game) following 1986 season.

LEONARD BERNARD BURTON
Offensive Tackle—Buffalo Bills
Born June 18, 1964, at Memphis, Tenn.
Height, 6.03. Weight, 275.
High School—Memphis, Tenn., Oakhaven.
Attended Northwest Mississippi Junior College and University of South Carolina.

Selected by Jacksonville in 1986 USFL territorial draft.
Selected by Buffalo in 3rd round (77th player selected) of 1986 NFL draft.
USFL rights traded with rights to offensive tackle Doug Williams by Jacksonville Bulls to Memphis Showboats for rights to wide receiver Tim McGee, May 6, 1986.
Signed by Buffalo Bills, July 24, 1986.
On injured reserve with knee injury, December 17 through remainder of 1986 season.
Buffalo NFL, 1986 through 1988.
Games: 1986 (14), 1987 (12), 1988 (16). Total—42.
Played in AFC Championship Game following 1988 season.

RONALD LEON BURTON
(Ron)
Linebacker—Dallas Cowboys
Born May 2, 1964, at Richmond, Va.
Height, 6.01. Weight, 245.
High School—Highland Springs, Va.
Received bachelor of industrial relations degree from
University of North Carolina in 1987.

Signed as free agent by Dallas Cowboys, April 30, 1987.
Dallas NFL, 1987 and 1988.
Games: 1987 (12), 1988 (16). Total—28.
Pro statistics: Recovered one fumble, 1988.

BLAIR WALTER BUSH
Center—Green Bay Packers
Born November 25, 1956, at Fort Hood, Tex.
Height, 6.03. Weight, 272.
High School—Palos Verdes, Calif.
Received degree in education from University of Washington.

Selected by Cincinnati in 1st round (16th player selected) of 1978 NFL draft.
Traded by Cincinnati Bengals to Seattle Seahawks for 1st round pick in 1985 draft, June 29, 1983.
On injured reserve with knee injury, October 22 through remainder of 1986 season.
Crossed picket line during players' strike, October 14, 1987.
On injured reserve with broken hand, December 18 through remainder of 1987 season.
Granted unconditional free agency, February 1, 1989; signed by Green Bay Packers, March 10, 1989.
Cincinnati NFL, 1978 through 1982; Seattle, NFL, 1983 through 1988.
Games: 1978 (16), 1979 (12), 1980 (16), 1981 (16), 1982 (8), 1983 (16), 1984 (16), 1985 (16), 1986 (7), 1987 (11), 1988 (16). Total—150.
Pro statistics: Recovered one fumble for 12 yards, 1981; recovered one fumble, 1985.
Played in AFC Championship Game following 1981 and 1983 seasons.
Played in NFL Championship Game following 1981 season.

BARNEY A. BUSSEY
Safety—Cincinnati Bengals
Born May 20, 1962, at Lincolnton, Ga.
Height, 6.00. Weight, 195.
High School—Lincolnton, Ga., Lincoln County.
Attended South Carolina State College.

Named as strong safety on THE SPORTING NEWS USFL All-Star Team, 1985.
Selected by Memphis in 1st round (4th player selected) of 1984 USFL draft.

Selected by Cincinnati in 5th round (119th player selected) of 1984 NFL draft.
Signed by Memphis Showboats, May 8, 1984.
Granted roster exemption, May 8 through May 14, 1984; activated, May 15, 1984.
On developmental squad, March 16 through March 23, 1985; activated, March 24, 1985.
Granted free agency when USFL suspended operations, August 7, 1986; signed by Cincinnati Bengals, August 12, 1986.
On developmental squad for 1 game with Memphis Showboats in 1985.
Memphis USFL, 1984 and 1985; Cincinnati NFL, 1986 through 1988.
Games: 1984 (6), 1985 (17), 1986 (16), 1987 (12), 1988 (16). Total USFL—23. Total NFL—44. Total Pro—67.
USFL statistics: Recovered on fumble, 1984; intercepted three passes for 11 yards, credited with one sack for four yards and recovered one fumble for 12 yards, 1985.
NFL statistics: Intercepted one pass for 19 yards, 1986; intercepted one pass for no yards and returned 21 kickoffs for 406 yards (19.3 avg.), 1987; fumbled once, 1987 and 1988; returned seven kickoffs for 83 yards and recovered one fumble, 1988.
Played in AFC Championship Game following 1988 season.
Played in NFL Championship Game following 1988 season.

PAUL MARTIN BUTCHER
Linebacker—Philadelphia Eagles
Born November 8, 1963, at Detroit, Mich.
Height, 6.00. Weight, 219.
High School—Dearborn, Mich., St. Alphonsus.
Received degree in mechanical engineering from Wayne State University in 1986.

Signed as free agent by Detroit Lions, July 23, 1986.
Released by Detroit Lions, August 18, 1986; re-signed by Lions, October 3, 1986.
Granted unconditional free agency, February 1, 1989; signed by Philadelphia Eagles, March 27, 1989.
Detroit NFL, 1986 through 1988.
Games: 1986 (12), 1987 (12), 1988 (16). Total—40.

KEVIN GREGORY BUTLER
Placekicker—Chicago Bears
Born July 24, 1962, at Savannah, Ga.
Height, 6.01. Weight, 204.
High School—Redan, Ga.
Attended University of Georgia.

Selected by Jacksonville in 1985 USFL territorial draft.
Selected by Chicago in 4th round (105th player selected) of 1985 NFL draft.
Signed by Chicago Bears, July 23, 1985.

Year Club		—PLACE KICKING—				
	G.	XP.	XPM.	FG.	FGA.	Pts.
1985—Chicago NFL	16	51	0	31	37	★144
1986—Chicago NFL	16	36	1	28	★41	120
1987—Chicago NFL	12	28	2	19	28	85
1988—Chicago NFL	16	37	1	15	19	82
Pro Totals—4 Years	60	152	4	93	125	431

Played in NFC Championship Game following 1985 and 1988 seasons.
Played in NFL Championship Game following 1985 season.

RAYMOND LEONARD BUTLER
(Ray)
Wide Receiver—Cleveland Browns
Born June 28, 1956, at Port Lavaca, Tex.
Height, 6.03. Weight, 206.
High School—Sweeny, Tex.
Attended Wharton County Junior College and received
degree in speech from University of Southern California in 1980.

Selected by Baltimore in 4th round (88th player selected) of 1980 NFL draft.
On injured reserve with broken arm, November 28 through remainder of 1983 season.
Franchise transferred to Indianapolis, March 31, 1984.
Released by Indianapolis Colts, November 18, 1985; signed as free agent by Seattle Seahawks, December 4, 1985.
On injured reserve with broken foot, October 6 through November 4, 1988; activated, November 5, 1988.
Granted unconditional free agency, February 1, 1989; signed by Cleveland Browns, February 28, 1989.

Year Club		—PASS RECEIVING—			
	G.	P.C.	Yds.	Avg.	TD.
1980—Baltimore NFL	16	34	574	16.9	2
1981—Baltimore NFL	16	46	832	18.1	9
1982—Baltimore NFL	9	17	268	15.8	2
1983—Baltimore NFL	11	10	207	20.7	3
1984—Indianapolis NFL	16	43	664	15.4	6
1985—Ind.(11)-Sea.(2) NFL	13	19	345	18.2	2
1986—Seattle NFL	16	19	351	18.5	4
1987—Seattle NFL	12	33	465	14.1	5
1988—Seattle NFL	11	18	242	13.4	4
Pro Totals—9 Years	120	239	3948	16.5	37

Additional pro statistics: Rushed three times for 10 yards and recovered one fumble, 1982; rushed once for minus one yard, 1985; fumbled once, 1987.

ROBERT CALVIN BUTLER
(Bobby)
Cornerback—Atlanta Falcons

Born May 28, 1959, at Boynton Beach, Fla.
Height, 5.11. Weight, 175.
High School—Delray Beach, Fla., Atlantic.
Attended Florida State University.
Cousin of James (Cannonball) Butler, running back with Pittsburgh Steelers,
Atlanta Falcons and St. Louis Cardinals, 1965 through 1972.

Selected by Atlanta in 1st round (25th player selected) of 1981 NFL draft.
On injured reserve with broken leg, October 20 through remainder of 1986 season.

Year Club	G.	No.	Yds.	Avg.	TD.
1981—Atlanta NFL	16	5	86	17.2	0
1982—Atlanta NFL	9	2	0	0.0	0
1983—Atlanta NFL	16	4	12	3.0	0
1984—Atlanta NFL	15	2	25	12.5	0
1985—Atlanta NFL	16	5	—4	—0.8	0
1986—Atlanta NFL	7	1	33	22.0	1
1987—Atlanta NFL	12	4	48	12.0	0
1988—Atlanta NFL	16	1	22	22.0	0
Pro Totals—8 Years	107	24	222	9.3	1

Additional pro statistics: Returned one kickoff for 17 yards and recovered one fumble, 1983; recovered one fumble for 10 yards, 1984; recovered three fumbles for 29 yards, 1988.

KEITH BYARS
Running Back—Philadelphia Eagles

Born October 14, 1963, at Dayton, O.
Height, 6.01. Weight, 238.
High School—Dayton, O., Nettie Lee Roth.
Attended Ohio State University.

Named as running back on THE SPORTING NEWS College All-America Team, 1984.
Selected by New Jersey in 1986 USFL territorial draft.
Selected by Philadelphia in 1st round (10th player selected) of 1986 NFL draft.
Signed by Philadelphia Eagles, July 25, 1986.

Year Club	G.	—RUSHING— Att.	Yds.	Avg.	TD.	PASS RECEIVING P.C.	Yds.	Avg.	TD.	—TOTAL— TD.	Pts.	F.
1986—Philadelphia NFL	16	177	577	3.3	1	11	44	4.0	0	1	6	3
1987—Philadelphia NFL	10	116	426	3.7	3	21	177	8.4	1	4	24	3
1988—Philadelphia NFL	16	152	517	3.4	6	72	705	9.8	4	10	60	5
Pro Totals—3 Years	42	445	1520	3.4	10	104	926	8.9	5	15	90	11

Additional pro statistics: Returned two kickoffs for 47 yards, attempted two passes with one completion for 55 yards and one touchdown, 1986; recovered two fumbles, 1986 and 1987; returned two kickoffs for 20 yards, recovered two fumbles for 14 yards and attempted two passes with no completions, 1988.

EARNEST ALEXANDER BYNER
Running Back—Washington Redskins

Born September 15, 1962, at Milledgeville, Ga.
Height, 5.10. Weight, 215.
High School—Milledgeville, Ga., Baldwin.
Attended East Carolina University.

Selected by Cleveland in 10th round (280th player selected) of 1984 NFL draft.
On injured reserve with ankle injury, October 21, 1986 through January 9, 1987; activated, January 10, 1987.
Granted free agency, February 1, 1989; re-signed by Browns and traded to Washington Redskins for running back Mike Oliphant, April 23, 1989.

Year Club	G.	—RUSHING— Att.	Yds.	Avg.	TD.	PASS RECEIVING P.C.	Yds.	Avg.	TD.	—TOTAL— TD.	Pts.	F.
1984—Cleveland NFL	16	72	426	5.9	2	11	118	10.7	0	3	18	3
1985—Cleveland NFL	16	244	1002	4.1	8	45	460	10.2	2	10	60	5
1986—Cleveland NFL	7	94	277	2.9	2	37	328	8.9	2	4	24	1
1987—Cleveland NFL	12	105	432	4.1	8	52	552	10.6	2	10	60	5
1988—Cleveland NFL	16	157	576	3.7	3	59	576	9.8	2	5	30	5
Pro Totals—5 Years	67	672	2713	4.0	23	204	2034	10.0	8	32	192	19

			KICKOFF RETURNS			
Year Club	G.	No.	Yds.	Avg.	TD.	
1984—Cleveland NFL	16	22	415	18.9	0	
1985—Cleveland NFL	16		None			
1986—Cleveland NFL	7		None			
1987—Cleveland NFL	12	1	2	2.0	0	
1988—Cleveland NFL	16		None			
Pro Totals—5 Years	67	23	417	18.1	0	

Additional pro statistics: Recovered two fumbles for 55 yards and a touchdown, 1984; recovered four fumbles, 1985; recovered one fumble, 1987; recovered two fumbles, 1988.
Played in AFC Championship Game following 1986 and 1987 seasons.

GILL ARNETTE BYRD
Defensive Back—San Diego Chargers

Born February 20, 1961, at San Francisco, Calif.
Height, 5.11. Weight, 194.
High School—San Francisco, Calif., Lowell.
Received degree in business administration and finance
from San Jose State University in 1982.
Nephew of MacArthur Byrd, linebacker with Los Angeles Rams, 1965.

Selected by Oakland in 1983 USFL territorial draft.
Selected by San Diego in 1st round (22nd player selected) of 1983 NFL draft.
Signed by San Diego Chargers, May 20, 1983.
On injured reserve with pulled hamstring, December 12 through remainder of 1984 season.

| | | | —INTERCEPTIONS— | | |
Year	Club	G.	No.	Yds.	Avg.	TD.
1983—San Diego NFL		14	1	0	0.0	0
1984—San Diego NFL		13	4	157	39.3	★2
1985—San Diego NFL		16	1	25	25.0	0
1986—San Diego NFL		15	5	45	9.0	0
1987—San Diego NFL		12		None		
1988—San Diego NFL		16	7	82	11.7	0
Pro Totals—6 Years		86	18	309	17.2	2

Additional pro statistics: Recovered one fumble, 1985 and 1987; fumbled once, 1988.

RICHARD BYRD
Nose Tackle—Houston Oilers

Born March 20, 1962, at Natchez, Miss.
Height, 6.04. Weight, 264.
High School—Jackson, Miss., Jim Hill.
Attended University of Southern Mississippi.

Selected by Portland in 1985 USFL territorial draft.
Selected by Houston in 2nd round (36th player selected) of 1985 NFL draft.
Signed by Houston Oilers, July 19, 1985.
Houston NFL, 1985 through 1988.
Games: 1985 (15), 1986 (16), 1987 (12), 1988 (16). Total—59.
Pro statistics: Recovered one fumble, 1985 and 1986; intercepted one pass for one yard, 1988.

CARL EDWARD BYRUM
Fullback—Houston Oilers

Born June 29, 1963, at Olive Branch, Miss.
Height, 6.00. Weight, 232.
High School—Southaven, Miss.
Attended Mississippi Valley State University.

Selected by Buffalo in 5th round (111th player selected) of 1986 NFL draft.
Signed by Buffalo Bills, July 19, 1986.
On injured reserve with knee injury, December 13 through remainder of 1986 season.
Crossed picket line during players' strike, October 7, 1987.
Granted unconditional free agency, February 1, 1989; signed by Houston Oilers, March 31, 1989.

| | | | —RUSHING— | | | | PASS RECEIVING | | | | —TOTAL— | | |
Year	Club	G.	Att.	Yds.	Avg.	TD.	P.C.	Yds.	Avg.	TD.	TD.	Pts.	F.
1986—Buffalo NFL		13	38	156	4.1	0	13	104	8.0	1	1	6	0
1987—Buffalo NFL		13	66	280	4.2	0	3	23	7.7	0	0	0	4
1988—Buffalo NFL		15	28	91	3.3	0	2	0	0.0	0	0	0	1
Pro Totals—3 Years		41	132	527	4.0	0	18	127	7.1	1	1	6	5

Additional pro statistics: Recovered one fumble, 1987; returned two kickoffs for nine yards, 1988.
Played in AFC Championship Game following 1988 season.

DAVE CADIGAN
Offensive Tackle—New York Jets

Born April 6, 1965, at Needham, Mass.
Height, 6.04. Weight, 285.
High School—Newport Beach, Calif., Newport Harbor.
Received degree in communications from University of Southern California in 1988.

Named as offensive tackle on THE SPORTING NEWS College All-America Team, 1987.
Selected by New York Jets in 1st round (8th player selected) of 1988 NFL draft.
Signed by New York Jets, July 26, 1988.
On injured reserve with foot injury, October 17 through remainder of 1988 season.
New York Jets NFL, 1988.
Games: 1988 (5).
Pro statistics: Recovered one fumble, 1988.

—DID YOU KNOW—

That there were 122 100-yard receiving performances in the NFL in 1988?

RAVIN CALDWELL JR.
Linebacker—Washington Redskins
Born August 4, 1963, at Port Arthur, Tex.
Height, 6.03. Weight, 229.
High School—Fort Smith, Ark., Northside.
Attended University of Arkansas.

Selected by Memphis in 1986 USFL territorial draft.
Selected by Washington in 5th round (113th player selected) of 1986 NFL draft.
Signed by Washington Redskins, July 18, 1986.
On injured reserve with knee injury, August 23 through entire 1986 season.
Washington NFL, 1987 and 1988.
Games: 1987 (12), 1988 (16). Total—28.
Pro statistics: Returned one punt for no yards and credited with a safety, 1988.
Played in NFC Championship Game following 1987 season.
Played in NFL Championship Game following 1987 season.

KEVIN BRADLEY CALL
Offensive Tackle—Indianapolis Colts
Born November 13, 1961, at Boulder, Colo.
Height, 6.07. Weight, 302.
High School—Boulder, Colo., Fairview.
Attended Colorado State University.

Selected by Denver in 1984 USFL territorial draft.
Selected by Indianapolis in 5th round (130th player selected) of 1984 NFL draft.
Signed by Indianapolis Colts, July 24, 1984.
Indianapolis NFL, 1984 through 1988.
Games: 1984 (15), 1985 (14), 1986 (16), 1987 (12), 1988 (8). Total—65.

RICHARD JON CAMARILLO
(Rich)
Punter—Phoenix Cardinals
Born November 29, 1959, at Whittier, Calif.
Height, 5.11. Weight, 185.
High School—Pico Rivera, Calif., El Rancho.
Attended Cerritos Junior College and University of Washington.
Nephew of Leo Camarillo, professional on rodeo circuit.

Named to THE SPORTING NEWS NFL All-Star Team, 1983.
Led NFL in punting yards with 3,953 in 1985.
Led NFL in net punting average with 37.1 in 1983.
Signed as free agent by New England Patriots, May 11, 1981.
Released by New England Patriots, August 24, 1981; re-signed by Patriots after clearing procedural waivers, October 20, 1981.
On injured reserve with knee injury, August 28 through November 2, 1984; activated, November 3, 1984.
Released by New England Patriots, August 30, 1988; signed as free agent by Los Angeles Rams, August 31, 1988.
Released by Los Angeles Rams, November 2, 1988; signed as free agent by Phoenix Cardinals, April 7, 1989.

		—PUNTING—		
Year Club	G.	No.	Avg.	Blk.
1981—New England NFL	9	47	41.7	0
1982—New England NFL	9	49	43.7	0
1983—New England NFL	16	81	44.6	0
1984—New England NFL	7	48	42.1	0
1985—New England NFL	16	92	43.0	0
1986—New England NFL	16	89	42.1	∗3
1987—New England NFL	12	62	40.1	1
1988—L.A. Rams NFL	9	40	39.5	0
Pro Totals—8 Years	94	508	42.4	4

Additional pro statistics: Recovered one fumble and fumbled once, 1981; rushed once for no yards, 1987.
Played in AFC Championship Game following 1985 season.
Played in NFL Championship Game following 1985 season.
Played in Pro Bowl (NFL All-Star Game) following 1983 season.

JOSEPH CAMPBELL JR.
(Joe)
Linebacker—San Diego Chargers
Born December 28, 1966, at Chandler, Ariz.
Height, 6.03. Weight, 245.
High Schools—Los Angeles, Calif., Verbum Dei; Inglewood, Calif.,
Morningside; and Tempe, Ariz.
Attended New Mexico State University.
Related to Joe Caldwell, forward with Detroit Pistons, St. Louis-Atlanta Hawks,
Carolina Cougars and St. Louis Spirits, 1964-65 through 1974-75.

Selected by San Diego in 4th round (91st player selected) of 1988 NFL draft.
Signed by San Diego Chargers, July 12, 1988.
San Diego NFL, 1988.
Games: 1988 (16).

ROBERT SCOTT CAMPBELL

(Known by middle name.)

Quarterback—Atlanta Falcons

Born April 15, 1962, at Hershey, Pa.
Height, 6.00. Weight, 195.
High School—Hershey, Pa.
Attended Purdue University.
Son of Ken Campbell, wide receiver with New York Titans of AFL, 1960.

Selected by Philadelphia in 4th round (76th player selected) of 1984 USFL draft.
Selected by Pittsburgh in 7th round (191st player selected) of 1984 NFL draft.
Signed by Pittsburgh Steelers, May 19, 1984.
Released by Pittsburgh Steelers, September 24, 1986; signed as free agent by Atlanta Falcons for 1987, November 7, 1986.
Signed for 1986 season, November 17, 1986.
On injured reserve with knee injury, August 22 through entire 1988 season.

			PASSING						RUSHING				TOTAL		
Year Club	G.	Att.	Cmp.	Pct.	Gain	T.P.	P.I.	Avg.	Att.	Yds.	Avg.	TD.	TD.	Pts.	F.
1984—Pittsburgh NFL	5	15	8	53.3	109	1	1	7.27	3	—5	—1.7	0	0	0	1
1985—Pittsburgh NFL	16	96	43	44.8	612	4	6	6.38	9	28	3.1	0	0	0	3
1986—Pitt.(3)-Atl.(1) NFL	4	7	1	14.3	7	0	0	1.00	1	7	7.0	0	0	0	0
1987—Atlanta NFL	12	260	136	52.3	1728	11	14	6.65	21	102	4.9	2	2	12	4
Pro Totals—4 Years	37	378	188	49.7	2456	16	21	6.50	34	132	3.9	2	2	12	8

Quarterback Rating Points: 1984 (71.3), 1985 (53.8), 1986 (39.6), 1987 (65.0). Total—61.3.
Additional pro statistics: Recovered one fumble, 1984; recovered three fumbles, 1985; recovered two fumbles, 1987.
Member of Pittsburgh Steelers for AFC Championship Game following 1984 season; did not play.

JAMES F. CAMPEN

Center-Guard—Green Bay Packers

Born June 11, 1964, at Sacramento, Calif.
Height, 6.03. Weight, 260.
High School—Shingle Springs, Calif., Ponderosa.
Attended Sacramento City College and Tulane University.

Signed as free agent by New Orleans Saints, May 13, 1986.
Released by New Orleans Saints, August 25, 1986; re-signed by Saints for 1987, October 23, 1986.
On injured reserve with rotator cuff injury, September 7 through September 27, 1987; activated, September 28, 1987.
Crossed picket line during players' strike, September 28, 1987.
Released by New Orleans Saints, August 30, 1988; re-signed by Saints, September 9, 1988.
On injured reserve with back injury, December 10 through remainder of 1988 season.
Granted unconditional free agency, February 1, 1989; signed by Green Bay Packers, February 24, 1989.
New Orleans NFL, 1987 and 1988.
Games: 1987 (3), 1988 (3). Total—6.
Pro statistics: Recovered one fumble, 1987.

JOHN RAYMOND CANNON

Defensive End—Tampa Bay Buccaneers

Born July 30, 1960, at Long Branch, N.J.
Height, 6.05. Weight, 260.
High School—Holmdel, N.J.
Received bachelor of business administration degree from
College of William & Mary in 1982.

Selected by Tampa Bay in 3rd round (83rd player selected) of 1982 NFL draft.
USFL rights traded by Memphis Showboats to Houston Gamblers for rights to defensive end Ray Yakavonis, February 13, 1985.
On injured reserve with leg injury, October 23 through December 11, 1986; activated, December 12, 1986.
Tampa Bay NFL, 1982 through 1988.
Games: 1982 (9), 1983 (14), 1984 (16), 1985 (16), 1986 (9), 1987 (11), 1988 (16). Total—91.
Pro statistics: Recovered one fumble, 1983, 1984, 1987 and 1988; intercepted one pass for no yards, 1984; recovered three fumbles, 1985; recovered two fumbles, 1986.

MARK MAIDA CANNON

Center—Green Bay Packers

Born June 14, 1962, at Whittier, Calif.
Height, 6.03. Weight, 258.
High School—Austin, Tex., S.F. Austin.
Attended University of Texas at Arlington.

Selected by Tampa Bay in 3rd round (62nd player selected) of 1984 USFL draft.
Selected by Green Bay in 11th round (294th player selected) of 1984 NFL draft.
Signed by Green Bay Packers, July 12, 1984.
Granted free agency, February 1, 1986; re-signed by Packers, August 20, 1986.
Granted roster exemption, August 20 through August 28, 1986; activated, August 29, 1986.
On injured reserve with knee injury, October 11 through November 14, 1986; activated, November 15, 1986.
On injured reserve with knee injury, November 26 through remainder of 1986 season.
Granted free agency, February 1, 1988; re-signed by Packers, August 24, 1988.
Green Bay NFL, 1984 through 1988.

Games: 1984 (16), 1985 (16), 1986 (7), 1987 (12), 1988 (16). Total—67.

Pro statistics: Recovered two fumbles, 1985; fumbled once for minus eight yards, 1987; fumbled twice for minus 31 yards, 1988.

WILLIE JAMES CANNON
Running Back—San Francisco 49ers
Born September 28, 1964, at Sarasota, Fla.
Height, 6.02. Weight, 200.
Attended Murray State University.

Signed as free agent by Miami Dolphins, May 3, 1988.

Released by Miami Dolphins, August 24, 1988; signed as free agent by Winnipeg Blue Bombers, September 26, 1988.

Released by Winnipeg Blue Bombers, October 13, 1988; signed as free agent by San Francisco 49ers, March 28, 1989.

			—RUSHING—			PASS RECEIVING				—TOTAL—		
Year	Club	G.	Att.	Yds.	Avg.	TD.	P.C.	Yds.	Avg.	TD.	TD.	Pts.	F.
1988—Winnipeg CFL		2	18	48	2.7	0	2	19	9.5	0	0	0	0

JOSEPH J. CARAVELLO
(Joe)
Tight End—San Diego Chargers
Born June 6, 1963, at Santa Monica, Calif.
Height, 6.03. Weight, 270.
High School—El Segundo, Calif.
Attended Tulane University.

Signed as free agent by Atlanta Falcons, May 2, 1986.

Released by Atlanta Falcons, September 1, 1986; re-signed by Falcons, March 13, 1987.

Released by Atlanta Falcons, September 7, 1987; signed as free agent replacement player by Washington Redskins, September 24, 1987.

On injured reserve with back injury, August 30 through September 30, 1988; activated, October 1, 1988.

Granted unconditional free agency, February 1, 1989; signed by San Diego Chargers, February 27, 1989.

Washington NFL, 1987 and 1988.

Games: 1987 (11), 1988 (12). Total—23.

Pro statistics: Caught two passes for 29 yards, 1987; recovered one fumble, 1987 and 1988; caught two passes for 15 yards, 1988.

Member of Washington Redskins for NFL Championship Game following 1987 season; inactive.

MATTHEW CODY CARLSON
(Known by middle name.)
Quarterback—Houston Oilers
Born November 5, 1963, at Dallas, Tex.
Height, 6.03. Weight, 203.
High School—San Antonio, Tex., Winston Churchill.
Received bachelor of science degree in marketing management
from Baylor University in 1987.

Selected by Houston in 3rd round (64th player selected) of 1987 NFL draft.

Signed by Houston Oilers, June 3, 1987.

Active for 4 games with Houston Oilers in 1987; did not play.

			——PASSING——							——RUSHING——				—TOTAL—		
Year	Club	G.	Att.	Cmp.	Pct.	Gain	T.P.	P.I.	Avg.	Att.	Yds.	Avg.	TD.	TD.	Pts.	F.
1988—Houston NFL		6	112	52	46.4	775	4	6	6.92	12	36	3.0	1	1	6	5

Quarterback Rating Points: 1988 (59.2).

Additional pro statistics: Fumbled five times for minus 12 yards, 1988.

JOHN MICHAEL CARNEY
Placekicker—Tampa Bay Buccaneers
Born April 20, 1964, at Hartford, Conn.
Height, 5.11. Weight, 160.
High School—West Palm Beach, Fla., Cardinal Newman.
Received bachelor of science degree in business from
University of Notre Dame in 1987.

Signed as free agent by Cincinnati Bengals, May 1, 1987.

Released by Cincinnati Bengals, August 10, 1987; signed as free agent replacement player by Tampa Bay Buccaneers, September 24, 1987.

Released by Tampa Bay Buccaneers, October 14, 1987; re-signed by Buccaneers, April 5, 1988.

Released by Tampa Bay Buccaneers, August 23, 1988; re-signed by Buccaneers, November 22, 1988.

Granted unconditional free agency, February 1, 1989; re-signed by Buccaneers, April 13, 1989.

		——PLACE KICKING——					
Year	Club	G.	XP.	XPM.	FG.	FGA.	Pts.
1988—Tampa Bay NFL		4	6	0	2	5	12

GREGG KEVIN CARR
Linebacker—Pittsburgh Steelers
Born March 31, 1962, at Birmingham, Ala.
Height, 6.02. Weight, 224.
High School—Birmingham, Ala., Woodlawn.
Attended Auburn University.

Selected by Birmingham in 1985 USFL territorial draft.
Selected by Pittsburgh in 6th round (160th player selected) of 1985 NFL draft.
Signed by Pittsburgh Steelers, July 19, 1985.
Pittsburgh NFL, 1985 through 1988.
Games: 1985 (16), 1986 (16), 1987 (12), 1988 (13). Total—57.
Pro statistics: Recovered two fumbles, 1985; credited with a safety, 1987; intercepted one pass for 27 yards, 1988.

ALPHONSO CARREKER
Name pronounced CARE-uh-ker.
Defensive End—Denver Broncos
Born May 25, 1962, at Columbus, O.
Height, 6.06. Weight, 271.
High School—Columbus, O., Marion Franklin.
Attended Florida State University.

Selected by Tampa Bay in 1984 USFL territorial draft.
Selected by Green Bay in 1st round (12th player selected) of 1984 NFL draft.
Signed by Green Bay Packers, June 20, 1984.
Granted unconditional free agency, February 1, 1989; signed by Denver Broncos, March 15, 1989.
Green Bay NFL, 1984 through 1988.
Games: 1984 (14), 1985 (16), 1986 (16), 1987 (12), 1988 (14). Total—72.
Pro statistics: Recovered two fumbles, 1986; intercepted one pass for six yards, 1987; recovered one fumble, 1988.

JOHN MARK CARRIER
(Known by middle name.)
Wide Receiver—Tampa Bay Buccaneers
Born October 28, 1965, at Lafayette, La.
Height, 6.00. Weight, 182.
High School—Church Point, La.
Attended Nicholls State University.

Selected by Tampa Bay in 3rd round (57th player selected) of 1987 NFL draft.
Signed by Tampa Bay Buccaneers, July 18, 1987.

		—PASS RECEIVING—			
Year Club	G.	P.C.	Yds.	Avg.	TD.
1987—Tampa Bay NFL	10	26	423	16.3	3
1988—Tampa Bay NFL	16	57	970	17.0	5
Pro Totals—2 Years	26	83	1393	16.8	8

Additional pro statistics: Returned one kickoff for no yards, 1987; fumbled twice, 1988.

PAUL OTT CARRUTH
(Paul Ott)
Running Back—Green Bay Packers
Born July 12, 1961, at Hattiesburg, Miss.
Height, 6.01. Weight, 220.
High School—McComb, Miss., Parklane.
Received bachelor of science degree in communications from University of Alabama.

Selected by Birmingham in 1985 USFL territorial draft.
Signed by Birmingham Stallions, January 28, 1985.
Granted free agency when USFL suspended operations, August 7, 1986; signed as free agent by Green Bay Packers, August 14, 1986.
Granted roster exemption, August 14 through August 21, 1986; activated, August 22, 1986.

		—RUSHING—				PASS RECEIVING				—TOTAL—		
Year Club	G.	Att.	Yds.	Avg.	TD.	P.C.	Yds.	Avg.	TD.	TD.	Pts.	F.
1985—Birmingham USFL	18	57	265	4.7	2	2	11	5.5	0	2	12	2
1986—Green Bay NFL	16	81	308	3.8	2	24	134	5.6	2	4	24	1
1987—Green Bay NFL	12	64	192	3.0	3	10	78	7.8	1	4	24	0
1988—Green Bay NFL	15	49	114	2.3	0	24	211	8.8	0	0	0	4
Pro Totals—4 Years	61	251	879	3.5	7	60	434	7.2	3	10	60	7

		KICKOFF RETURNS			
Year Club	G.	No.	Yds.	Avg.	TD.
1985—Birmingham USFL	18	26	477	18.4	0
1986—Green Bay NFL	16	4	40	10.0	0
1987—Green Bay NFL	12	1	8	8.0	0
1988—Green Bay NFL	15		None		
Pro Totals—4 Years	61	31	525	16.9	0

Additional pro statistics: Attempted one pass with one completion for three yards and a touchdown, 1987; attempted two passes with no completions, 1988.

CARLOS A. CARSON
Wide Receiver—Kansas City Chiefs
Born December 28, 1958, at Lake Worth, Fla.
Height, 5.11. Weight, 190.
High School—Lake Worth, Fla., John I. Leonard.
Attended Louisiana State University.

Cousin of Darrin Nelson, running back with Minnesota Vikings; and Kevin Nelson, running back with Los Angeles Express, 1984 and 1985.

Selected by Kansas City in 5th round (114th player selected) of 1980 NFL draft.
On injured reserve with broken foot, September 23 through December 11, 1981; activated, December 12, 1981.
On injured reserve with foot injury, November 28 through December 26, 1986; activated, December 27, 1986.

Year Club	G.	Att.	—RUSHING— Yds.	Avg.	TD.	PASS RECEIVING P.C.	Yds.	Avg.	TD.	—TOTAL— TD.	Pts.	F.
1980—Kansas City NFL	16	2	41	20.5	0	5	68	13.6	0	0	0	1
1981—Kansas City NFL	5	1	—1	—1.0	0	7	179	25.6	1	1	6	1
1982—Kansas City NFL	9		None			27	494	18.3	2	2	12	1
1983—Kansas City NFL	16	2	20	10.0	0	80	1351	16.9	7	7	42	2
1984—Kansas City NFL	16	1	—8	—8.0	0	57	1078	18.9	4	4	24	0
1985—Kansas City NFL	15	3	25	8.3	0	47	843	17.9	4	4	24	0
1986—Kansas City NFL	10		None			21	497	23.7	4	4	24	1
1987—Kansas City NFL	12	1	—7	—7.0	0	55	1044	19.0	7	7	42	1
1988—Kansas City NFL	14	1	1	1.0	0	46	711	15.5	3	3	18	0
Pro Totals—9 Years	113	11	71	6.5	0	345	6265	18.2	32	32	192	7

Year Club	G.	KICKOFF RETURNS No.	Yds.	Avg.	TD.	Year Club	G.	KICKOFF RETURNS No.	Yds.	Avg.	TD.
1980—Kansas City NFL	16	40	917	22.9	0	1985—Kansas City NFL	15		None		
1981—Kansas City NFL	5	10	227	22.7	0	1986—Kansas City NFL	10	5	88	17.6	0
1982—Kansas City NFL	9		None			1987—Kansas City NFL	12		None		
1983—Kansas City NFL	16	1	12	12.0	0	1988—Kansas City NFL	14		None		
1984—Kansas City NFL	16	1	2	2.0	0	Pro Totals—9 Years	113	57	1246	21.9	0

Additional pro statistics: Recovered one fumble, 1980 and 1981; attempted one pass with one completion for 48 yards and one touchdown, 1983; recovered two fumbles, 1984.
Played in Pro Bowl (NFL All-Star Game) following 1983 and 1987 seasons.

ANTHONY CARTER
Wide Receiver—Minnesota Vikings
Born September 17, 1960, at Riviera Beach, Fla.
Height, 5.11. Weight, 175.
High School—Riviera Beach, Fla., Sun Coast.
Attended University of Michigan.
Cousin of Leonard Coleman, safety with San Diego Chargers.
Named as wide receiver on THE SPORTING NEWS USFL All-Star Team, 1985.
Named as punt returner on THE SPORTING NEWS USFL All-Star Team, 1983.
Named as wide receiver on THE SPORTING NEWS College All-America Team, 1981 and 1982.
Selected by Michigan in 1983 USFL territorial draft.
Signed by Michigan Panthers, February 26, 1983.
Selected by Miami in 12th round (334th player selected) of 1983 NFL draft.
On injured reserve with broken arm, April 5 through remainder of 1984 season.
Protected in merger of Michigan Panthers and Oakland Invaders, December 6, 1984.
On developmental squad, June 24 through June 29, 1985; activated, June 30, 1985.
NFL rights traded by Miami Dolphins to Minnesota Vikings for linebacker Robin Sendlein and 2nd round pick in 1986 NFL draft, August 15, 1985.
Released by Oakland Invaders, August 23, 1985; signed by Minnesota Vikings, August 25, 1985.
Granted roster exemption, August 25 through August 28, 1985; activated, August 29, 1985.
On injured reserve with knee injury, September 5 through October 3, 1986; activated, October 4, 1986.
On developmental squad for 1 game with Oakland Invaders in 1985.

Year Club	G.	-PASS RECEIVING- P.C.	Yds.	Avg.	TD.	-PUNT RETURNS- No.	Yds.	Avg.	TD.	—TOTAL— TD.	Pts.	F.
1983—Michigan USFL	18	60	1181	19.7	9	40	387	9.7	*1	10	60	6
1984—Michigan USFL	6	30	538	17.9	4	5	21	4.2	0	4	24	2
1985—Oakland USFL	17	70	1323	18.9	14		None			15	90	0
1985—Minnesota NFL	16	43	821	19.1	8	9	117	13.0	0	8	48	1
1986—Minnesota NFL	12	38	686	18.1	7		None			7	42	1
1987—Minnesota NFL	12	38	922	*24.3	7	3	40	13.3	0	7	42	0
1988—Minnesota NFL	16	72	1225	17.0	6	1	3	3.0	0	6	36	1
USFL Totals—3 Years	41	160	3042	19.0	27	45	408	9.1	1	29	174	8
NFL Totals—4 Years	56	191	3654	19.1	28	13	160	12.3	0	28	168	3
Pro Totals—7 Years	97	351	6696	19.1	55	58	568	9.8	1	57	342	11

Additional USFL statistics: Rushed three times for one yard and recovered three fumbles, 1983; recovered one fumble, 1984; recovered one fumble in end zone for a touchdown and attempted one pass with no completions, 1985.
Additional NFL statistics: Recovered one fumble, 1985 and 1988; rushed once for 12 yards, 1986; rushed four times for 41 yards and returned one kickoff for no yards, 1988.
Played in NFC Championship Game following 1987 season.
Played in USFL Championship Game following 1983 and 1985 seasons.
Played in Pro Bowl (NFL All-Star Game) following 1987 and 1988 seasons.

CARL ANTHONY CARTER
Cornerback—Phoenix Cardinals
Born March 7, 1964, at Fort Worth, Tex.
Height, 5.11. Weight, 180.
High School—Fort Worth, Tex., O. D. Wyatt.
Attended Texas Tech University.

Selected by St. Louis in 4th round (89th player selected) of 1986 NFL draft.
Signed by St. Louis Cardinals, July 12, 1986.
Franchise transferred to Phoenix, March 15, 1988.

| | | —INTERCEPTIONS— | | | |
Year Club	G.	No.	Yds.	Avg.	TD.
1986—St. Louis NFL	14	2	12	6.0	0
1987—St. Louis NFL	12	1	0	0.0	0
1988—Phoenix NFL	16	3	0	0.0	0
Pro Totals—3 Years	42	6	12	2.0	0

Additional pro statistics: Returned two kickoffs for 21 yards, returned one punt for no yards and fumbled once, 1986; recovered one fumble, 1986 and 1987.

CRIS CARTER
Wide Receiver—Philadelphia Eagles
Born November 25, 1965, at Middletown, O.
Height, 6.03. Weight, 194.
High School—Middletown, O.
Attended Ohio State University.

Selected by Philadelphia in 4th round of 1987 NFL supplemental draft, September 4, 1987.
Signed by Philadelphia Eagles, September 17, 1987.
Granted roster exemption, September 17 through October 25, 1987; activated, October 26, 1987.

| | | PASS RECEIVING | | | | —KICKOFF RET.— | | | | —TOTAL— | | |
Year Club	G.	P.C.	Yds.	Avg.	TD.	No.	Yds.	Avg.	TD.	TD.	Pts.	F.
1987—Philadelphia NFL	9	5	84	16.8	2	12	241	20.1	0	2	12	0
1988—Philadelphia NFL	16	39	761	19.5	6		None			7	42	0
Pro Totals—2 Years	25	44	845	19.2	8	12	241	20.1	0	9	54	0

Additional pro statistics: Attempted one pass with no completions, 1987; rushed once for one yard and recovered one fumble in end zone for a touchdown, 1988.

MICHAEL D'ANDREA CARTER
Nose Tackle—San Francisco 49ers
Born October 29, 1960, at Dallas, Tex.
Height, 6.02. Weight, 285.
High School—Dallas, Tex., Thomas Jefferson.
Received bachelor of science degree in sociology from Southern Methodist University in 1984.
Won silver medal in shot put during 1984 Olympics.

Named to THE SPORTING NEWS NFL All-Star Team, 1987.
Selected by Los Angeles in 10th round (194th player selected) of 1984 USFL draft.
Selected by San Francisco in 5th round (121st player selected) of 1984 NFL draft.
USFL rights traded by Los Angeles Express to New Orleans Breakers for past considerations, June 19, 1984.
Signed by San Francisco 49ers, August 14, 1984.
On injured reserve with torn hamstring, September 28 through October 25, 1985; activated, October 26, 1985.
San Francisco NFL, 1984 through 1988.
Games: 1984 (16), 1985 (12), 1986 (15), 1987 (12), 1988 (16). Total—71.
Pro statistics: Intercepted one pass for no yards, 1988.
Played in NFC Championship Game following 1984 and 1988 seasons.
Played in NFL Championship Game following 1984 and 1988 seasons.
Played in Pro Bowl (NFL All-Star Game) following 1985, 1987 and 1988 seasons.

RODNEY CARL CARTER
Running Back—Pittsburgh Steelers
Born October 30, 1964, at Elizabeth, N.J.
Height, 6.00. Weight, 212.
High School—Elizabeth, N.J.
Received bachelor of social sciences degree in criminology
and criminal justice from Purdue University in 1986.

Selected by Pittsburgh in 7th round (175th player selected) of 1986 NFL draft.
Signed by Pittsburgh Steelers, July 10, 1986.
On injured reserve with knee injury, August 26 through entire 1986 season.
Released by Pittsburgh Steelers, September 7, 1987; re-signed as replacement player by Steelers, September 24, 1987.

| | | —RUSHING— | | | | PASS RECEIVING | | | | —TOTAL— | | |
Year Club	G.	Att.	Yds.	Avg.	TD.	P.C.	Yds.	Avg.	TD.	TD.	Pts.	F.
1987—Pittsburgh NFL	11	5	12	2.4	0	16	180	11.3	3	3	18	0
1988—Pittsburgh NFL	14	36	216	6.0	3	32	363	11.3	2	5	30	0
Pro Totals—2 Years	25	41	228	5.6	3	48	543	11.3	5	8	48	0

Additional pro statistics: Attempted three passes with two completions for 56 yards, 1988.

—DID YOU KNOW—
That last season's AFC championship game between Cincinnati and Buffalo was the first since the NFL-AFL merger in 1970 in which neither team had made the playoffs the year before?

RUSSELL EDMONDS CARTER JR.
Safety—Los Angeles Raiders
Born February 10, 1962, at Philadelphia, Pa.
Height, 6.02. Weight, 200.
High School—Ardmore, Pa., Lower Merion.
Attended Southern Methodist University.

Named as defensive back on THE SPORTING NEWS College All-America Team, 1983.
Selected by Denver in 1st round (9th player selected) of 1984 USFL draft.
Selected by New York Jets in 1st round (10th player selected) of 1984 NFL draft.
Signed by New York Jets, May 25, 1984.
On injured reserve with back injury, November 16 through December 26, 1985; activated, December 27, 1985.
On injured reserve with separated shoulder, December 9 through remainder of 1987 season.
Granted free agency, February 1, 1988; re-signed by Jets and traded to Los Angeles Raiders for 6th round pick in 1989 draft, May 21, 1988.
Released by Los Angeles Raiders, August 30, 1988; re-signed by Raiders, September 8, 1988.
New York Jets NFL, 1984 through 1987; Los Angeles Raiders NFL, 1988.
Games: 1984 (11), 1985 (8), 1986 (13), 1987 (8), 1988 (15). Total—55.
Pro statistics: Intercepted four passes for 26 yards, 1984; recovered one fumble, 1986 through 1988; returned one kickoff for 14 yards, 1988.

WENDELL PATRICK CARTER
(Pat)
Tight End—Detroit Lions
Born August 1, 1966, at Sarasota, Fla.
Height, 6.04. Weight, 250.
High School—Sarasota, Fla., Riverview.
Attended Florida State University.

Named as tight end on THE SPORTING NEWS College All-America Team, 1987.
Selected by Detroit in 2nd round (32nd player selected) of 1988 NFL draft.
Signed by Detroit Lions, June 13, 1988.

		——PASS RECEIVING——			
Year Club	G.	P.C.	Yds.	Avg.	TD.
1988—Detroit NFL..................	15	13	145	11.2	0

MAURICE CARTHON
Running Back—New York Giants
Born April 24, 1961, at Chicago, Ill.
Height, 6.01. Weight, 225.
High School—Osceola, Ark.
Attended Arkansas State University.

Selected by New Jersey in 8th round (94th player selected) of 1983 USFL draft.
Signed by New Jersey Generals, January 19, 1983.
On developmental squad, June 17 through remainder of 1983 season.
Signed by New York Giants, March 7, 1985, for contract to take effect after being granted free agency after 1985 USFL season.
Placed on did not report list, January 21 through January 27, 1985; activated, January 28, 1985.
Granted roster exemption, January 28 through February 3, 1985; activated, February 4, 1985.
On developmental squad for 3 games with New Jersey Generals in 1983.

		——RUSHING——				PASS RECEIVING				—TOTAL—		
Year Club	G.	Att.	Yds.	Avg.	TD.	P.C.	Yds.	Avg.	TD.	TD.	Pts.	F.
1983—New Jersey USFL.....................	11	90	334	3.7	3	20	170	8.5	0	3	†24	4
1984—New Jersey USFL.....................	18	238	1042	4.4	11	26	194	7.5	1	12	72	4
1985—New Jersey USFL.....................	18	175	726	4.2	6	18	154	8.6	0	6	36	3
1985—New York Giants NFL............	16	27	70	2.6	0	8	81	10.1	0	0	0	1
1986—New York Giants NFL............	16	72	260	3.6	0	16	67	4.2	0	0	0	1
1987—New York Giants NFL............	11	26	60	2.3	0	8	71	8.9	0	0	0	1
1988—New York Giants NFL............	16	46	146	3.2	2	19	194	10.2	1	3	18	1
USFL Totals—3 Years................	47	503	2102	4.2	20	64	518	8.1	1	21	132	11
NFL Totals—4 Years................	59	171	536	3.1	2	51	413	8.1	1	3	18	3
Pro Totals—7 Years....................	106	674	2638	3.9	22	115	931	8.1	2	24	150	14

†Includes three 2-point conversions.
Additional pro statistics: Recovered one fumble, 1984.
Played in NFC Championship Game following 1986 season.
Played in NFL Championship Game following 1986 season.

JEFFREY SCOTT CASE
(Known by middle name.)
Cornerback—Atlanta Falcons
Born May 17, 1962, at Waynoka, Okla.
Height, 6.00. Weight, 178.
High Schools—Alva, Okla.; and Edmond, Okla., Memorial.
Attended Northeastern Oklahoma A&M and University of Oklahoma.

Selected by Oklahoma in 1984 USFL territorial draft.
Selected by Atlanta in 2nd round (32nd player selected) of 1984 NFL draft.
Signed by Atlanta Falcons, July 20, 1984.
Granted free agency, February 1, 1988; re-signed by Falcons, August 29, 1988.

Year Club		G.	No.	Yds.	Avg.	TD.
			—INTERCEPTIONS—			
1984—Atlanta NFL	....	16		None		
1985—Atlanta NFL	....	14	4	78	19.5	0
1986—Atlanta NFL	....	16	4	41	10.3	0
1987—Atlanta NFL	....	11	1	12	12.0	0
1988—Atlanta NFL	....	16	★10	47	4.7	0
Pro Totals—5 Years	....	73	19	178	9.4	0

Additional pro statistics: Credited with one safety and recovered one fumble for 13 yards, 1985.
Played in Pro Bowl (NFL All-Star Game) following 1988 season.

TONY STEVEN CASILLAS
Nose Tackle—Atlanta Falcons
Born October 26, 1963, at Tulsa, Okla.
Height, 6.03. Weight, 280.
High School—Tulsa, Okla., East Central.
Received degree from University of Oklahoma in 1986.

Named as defensive lineman on THE SPORTING NEWS College All-America Team, 1984 and 1985.
Selected by Atlanta in 1st round (2nd player selected) of 1986 NFL draft.
Selected by Arizona in 1st round (2nd player selected) of 1986 USFL draft.
Signed by Atlanta Falcons, July 20, 1986.
Atlanta NFL, 1986 through 1988.
Games: 1986 (16), 1987 (9), 1988 (16). Total—41.
Pro statistics: Recovered one fumble, 1986 through 1988.

JEREMIAH CASTILLE
Name pronounced Cass-TEEL.
Defensive Back—Denver Broncos
Born January 15, 1961, at Columbus, Ga.
Height, 5.10. Weight, 175.
High School—Phenix City, Ala., Central.
Received degree in broadcasting from University of Alabama.
Cousin of Rod Barksdale, wide receiver with Dallas Cowboys.

Selected by Birmingham in 1983 USFL territorial draft.
Selected by Tampa Bay in 3rd round (72nd player selected) of 1983 NFL draft.
Signed by Tampa Bay Buccaneers, May 18, 1983.
Released by Tampa Bay Buccaneers, August 24, 1987; awarded on waivers to Denver Broncos, August 25, 1987.

Year Club		G.	No.	Yds.	Avg.	TD.
			—INTERCEPTIONS—			
1983—Tampa Bay NFL	....	15	1	69	69.0	1
1984—Tampa Bay NFL	....	16	3	38	12.7	0
1985—Tampa Bay NFL	....	16	7	49	7.0	0
1986—Tampa Bay NFL	....	13		None		
1987—Denver NFL	....	11		None		
1988—Denver NFL	....	16	3	51	17.0	0
Pro Totals—6 Years	....	87	14	207	14.8	1

Additional pro statistics: Recovered two fumbles for 16 yards, 1984; recovered two fumbles and fumbled once, 1985.
Played in AFC Championship Game following 1987 season.
Played in NFL Championship Game following 1987 season.

SEBASTIAN TOBIAS CASTON
(Toby)
Linebacker—Detroit Lions
Born July 17, 1965, at Monroe, La.
Height, 6.01. Weight, 240.
High School—Monroe, La., Neville.
Attended Louisiana State University.

Selected by Houston in 6th round (159th player selected) of 1987 NFL draft.
Signed by Houston Oilers, July 27, 1987.
On injured reserve with foot and arch injuries, November 24 through remainder of 1987 season.
Granted unconditional free agency, February 1, 1989; signed by Detroit Lions, March 15, 1989.
Houston NFL, 1987 and 1988.
Games: 1987 (6), 1988 (16). Total—22.

MATTHEW ANDREW CAVANAUGH
(Matt)
Quarterback—Philadelphia Eagles
Born October 27, 1956, at Youngstown, O.
Height, 6.02. Weight, 212.
High School—Youngstown, O., Chaney.
Received bachelor of science degree in administration of justice from University of Pittsburgh.

Selected by New England in 2nd round (50th player selected) of 1978 NFL draft.
Traded by New England Patriots to San Francisco 49ers for 7th round pick in 1984 draft, 8th round pick in 1985 draft and 7th round pick in 1986 draft, August 10, 1983.

Traded by San Francisco 49ers to Philadelphia Eagles for 3rd round pick in 1986 draft and 2nd round pick in 1987 draft, April 29, 1986.

Active for 16 games with New England Patriots in 1978; did not play.

Year Club	G.	Att.	Cmp.	Pct.	Gain	T.P.	P.I.	Avg.	Att.	Yds.	Avg.	TD.	TD.	Pts.	F.
				PASSING						RUSHING				TOTAL	
1979—New England NFL	13	1	1	100.0	10	0	0	10.00	1	—2	—2.0	0	0	0	0
1980—New England NFL	16	105	63	60.0	885	9	5	8.43	19	97	5.1	0	0	0	1
1981—New England NFL	16	219	115	52.5	1633	5	13	7.46	17	92	5.4	3	3	18	2
1982—New England NFL	7	60	27	45.0	490	5	5	8.17	2	3	1.5	0	0	0	1
1983—San Francisco NFL	5				None				1	8	8.0	0	0	0	0
1984—San Francisco NFL	8	61	33	54.1	449	4	0	7.36	4	—11	—2.8	0	0	0	0
1985—San Francisco NFL	16	54	28	51.9	334	1	1	6.19	4	5	1.3	0	0	0	0
1986—Philadelphia NFL	10	58	28	48.3	397	2	4	6.84	9	26	2.9	0	0	0	2
1987—Philadelphia NFL	3				None				1	—2	—2.0	0	0	0	0
1988—Philadelphia NFL	5	16	7	43.8	101	1	1	6.31			None		0	0	0
Pro Totals—11 Years	99	574	302	52.6	4299	27	29	7.49	58	216	3.7	3	3	18	6

Quarterback Rating Points: 1979 (108.3), 1980 (95.9), 1981 (60.0), 1982 (66.7), 1984 (99.7), 1985 (69.5), 1986 (53.6), 1988 (59.6). Total—71.6.

Additional pro statistics: Recovered one fumble and fumbled once for minus four yards, 1980; caught one pass for nine yards, 1981.

Played in NFC Championship Game following 1984 season.

Member of San Francisco 49ers for NFC Championship Game following 1983 season; did not play.

Member of San Francisco 49ers for NFL Championship Game following 1984 season; did not play.

CHARLES DOUGLAS CECIL
(Chuck)
Safety—Green Bay Packers

Born November 8, 1964, at Red Bluff, Calif.
Height, 6.00. Weight, 184.
High School—La Mesa, Calif., Helix.
Attended University of Arizona.

Selected by Green Bay in 4th round (89th player selected) of 1988 NFL draft.
Signed by Green Bay Packers, July 17, 1988.

Year Club	G.	No.	Yds.	Avg.	TD.
		INTERCEPTIONS			
1988—Green Bay NFL	16	4	56	14.0	0

Additional pro statistics: Recovered one fumble, 1988.

JEFFREY ALLAN CHADWICK
(Jeff)
Wide Receiver—Detroit Lions

Born December 16, 1960, at Detroit, Mich.
Height, 6.03. Weight, 190.
High School—Dearborn, Mich., Divine Child.
Attended Grand Valley State College.

Signed as free agent by Detroit Lions, May 15, 1983.
On injured reserve with broken collarbone, November 4 through remainder of 1985 season.
On injured reserve with Achilles heal injury, December 17 through remainder of 1986 season.
On injured reserve with broken hand, December 1 through remainder of 1987 season.
On injured reserve with Achilles heel injury, August 23 through October 14, 1988; activated, October 15, 1988.
Granted unconditional free agency, February 1, 1989; re-signed by Lions, April 26, 1989.

Year Club	G.	P.C.	Yds.	Avg.	TD.
		PASS RECEIVING			
1983—Detroit NFL	16	40	617	15.4	4
1984—Detroit NFL	16	37	540	14.6	2
1985—Detroit NFL	7	25	478	19.1	3
1986—Detroit NFL'	15	53	995	18.8	5
1987—Detroit NFL	8	30	416	13.9	0
1988—Detroit NFL	10	20	304	15.2	3
Pro Totals—6 Years	72	205	3350	16.3	17

Additional pro statistics: Rushed once for 12 yards and a touchdown, 1984; fumbled once, 1986; rushed once for minus six yards, 1987.

CHRISTOPHER MARK CHANDLER
(Chris)
Quarterback—Indianapolis Colts

Born October 12, 1965, at Everett, Wash.
Height, 6.04. Weight, 210.
High School—Everett, Wash.
Received degree in economics from University of Washington in 1988.
Brother of Greg Chandler, catcher in San Francisco Giants' organization, 1978.

Selected by Indianapolis in 3rd round (76th player selected) of 1988 NFL draft.
Signed by Indianapolis Colts, July 23, 1988.

Year Club	G.	Att.	Cmp.	Pct.	Gain	T.P.	P.I.	Avg.	Att.	Yds.	Avg.	TD.	TD.	Pts.	F.
1988—Indianapolis NFL	15	233	129	55.4	1619	8	12	6.95	46	139	3.0	3	3	18	8

Quarterback Rating Points: 1988 (67.2).
Additional pro statistics: Recovered five fumbles and fumbled eight times for minus six yards, 1988.

THORNTON GREENE CHANDLER
Tight End—Dallas Cowboys
Born November 27, 1963, at Jacksonville, Fla.
Height, 6.05. Weight, 240.
High School—Jacksonville, Fla., William M. Raines.
Attended Florida A&M University and University of Alabama.

Selected by Dallas in 6th round (140th player selected) of 1986 NFL draft.
Signed by Dallas Cowboys, July 6, 1986.

		—PASS RECEIVING—			
Year Club	G.	P.C.	Yds.	Avg.	TD.
1986—Dallas NFL	15	6	57	9.5	2
1987—Dallas NFL	12	5	25	5.0	1
1988—Dallas NFL	16	18	186	10.3	1
Pro Totals—3 Years............	43	29	268	9.2	4

Additional pro statistics: Fumbled once, 1986; returned one kickoff for seven yards, 1987.

RICHARD HARRY CHAPURA JR.
Name pronounced Sha-POOR-a.
(Dick)
Defensive Tackle—Chicago Bears
Born June 15, 1964, at Sarasota, Fla.
Height, 6.03. Weight, 275.
High School—Sarasota, Fla., Riverview.
Attended University of Missouri.

Selected by Chicago in 10th round (277th player selected) of 1987 NFL draft.
Signed by Chicago Bears, July 27, 1987.
On injured reserve with knee injury, August 27 through November 15, 1987; activated, November 16, 1987.
Chicago NFL, 1987 and 1988.
Games: 1987 (2), 1988 (15). Total—17.
Played in NFC Championship Game following 1988 season.

MICHAEL WILLIAM CHARLES
(Mike)
Nose Tackle—San Diego Chargers
Born September 23, 1962, at Newark, N.J.
Height, 6.04. Weight, 296.
High School—Newark, N.J., Central.
Received bachelor of science degree in speech communications from Syracuse University.

Selected by New Jersey in 1983 USFL territorial draft.
Selected by Miami in 2nd round (55th player selected) of 1983 NFL draft.
Signed by Miami Dolphins, July 12, 1983.
On injured reserve with knee injury, November 17 through December 27, 1984; activated, December 28, 1984.
On suspended list, September 6 through September 25, 1986; activated, September 26, 1986.
On injured reserve with knee injury, October 1 through October 31, 1986; activated, November 1, 1986.
Released by Miami Dolphins, July 31, 1987; awarded on waivers to Tampa Bay Buccaneers, August 3, 1987.
Released by Tampa Bay Buccaneers, August 17, 1987; awarded on waivers to San Diego Chargers, August 18, 1987.
Miami NFL, 1983 through 1986; San Diego NFL, 1987 and 1988.
Games: 1983 (16), 1984 (10), 1985 (16), 1986 (9), 1987 (11), 1988 (16). Total—78.
Pro statistics: Recovered one fumble and credited with one safety, 1983; intercepted one pass for two yards, 1986.
Played in AFC Championship Game following 1984 and 1985 seasons.
Played in NFL Championship Game following 1984 season.

CLIFFORD TYRONE CHARLTON
Linebacker—Cleveland Browns
Born February 16, 1965, at Tallahassee, Fla.
Height, 6.03. Weight, 240.
High School—Tallahassee, Fla., Leon.
Attended University of Florida.

Named as linebacker on THE SPORTING NEWS College All-America Team, 1987.
Selected by Cleveland in 1st round (21st player selected) of 1988 NFL draft.
Signed by Cleveland Browns, July 22, 1988.
Cleveland NFL, 1988.
Games: 1988 (16).

LOUIS RAY CHEEK JR.
Offensive Tackle—Miami Dolphins
Born October 6, 1964, at Galveston, Tex.
Height, 6.06. Weight, 295.
High School—Fairfield, Tex.
Received bachelor of science degree in agricultural economics
from Texas A&M University in 1988.

Selected by Miami in 8th round (220th player selected) of 1988 NFL draft.
Signed by Miami Dolphins, July 15, 1988.
Miami NFL, 1988.
Games: 1988 (15).

DERON LEIGH CHERRY
First name pronounced Da-RON.
Safety—Kansas City Chiefs
Born September 12, 1959, at Riverside, N.J.
Height, 5.11. Weight, 203.
High School—Palmyra, N.J.
Attended Rutgers University.
Related to Raphel Cherry, safety with Detroit Lions.

Named to THE SPORTING NEWS NFL All-Star Team, 1986 and 1988.
Tied NFL record for most interceptions, game (4), against Seattle Seahawks, September 29, 1985.
Signed as free agent by Kansas City Chiefs, May 4, 1981.
Released by Kansas City Chiefs, August 31, 1981; re-signed by Chiefs, September 23, 1981.
On inactive list, September 19, 1982.
On injured reserve with shoulder separation, December 30 through remainder of 1982 season.

Year Club	G.	No.	Yds.	Avg.	TD.
			—INTERCEPTIONS—		
1981—Kansas City NFL	13	1	4	4.0	0
1982—Kansas City NFL	7		None		
1983—Kansas City NFL	16	7	100	14.3	0
1984—Kansas City NFL	16	7	140	20.0	0
1985—Kansas City NFL	16	7	87	12.4	*1
1986—Kansas City NFL	16	9	150	16.7	0
1987—Kansas City NFL	8	3	58	19.3	0
1988—Kansas City NFL	16	7	51	7.3	0
Pro Totals—8 Years	108	41	590	14.4	1

Additional pro statistics: Returned three kickoffs for 52 yards, 1981; returned one kickoff for 39 yards, 1982; returned two kickoffs for 54 yards, recovered two fumbles for four yards and fumbled twice, 1983; returned one kickoff for no yards, 1984; recovered blocked punt in end zone twice for two touchdowns and recovered two fumbles for seven yards, 1986; recovered one fumble, 1987; recovered six fumbles for 10 yards, 1988.
Played in Pro Bowl (NFL All-Star Game) following 1983 through 1988 seasons.

RAPHEL JEROME CHERRY
First name pronounced RA-fehl.
Safety—Detroit Lions
Born December 19, 1961, at Little Rock, Ark.
Height, 6.00. Weight, 194.
High School—Los Angeles, Calif., Washington.
Attended University of Hawaii.
Related to Deron Cherry, safety with Kansas City Chiefs.

Selected by Houston in 1st round (6th player selected) of 1985 USFL draft.
Selected by Washington in 5th round (122nd player selected) of 1985 NFL draft.
Signed by Washington Redskins, July 18, 1985.
Released by Washington Redskins, September 1, 1986; signed as free agent by San Francisco 49ers, December 23, 1986.
Released by San Francisco 49ers, September 7, 1987; signed as free agent by Detroit Lions to begin play after strike is settled, October 5, 1987.

Year Club	G.	No.	Yds.	Avg.	TD.
			—INTERCEPTIONS—		
1985—Washington NFL	16	2	29	14.5	0
1987—Detroit NFL	10	1	2	2.0	0
1988—Detroit NFL	10	2	0	0.0	0
Pro Totals—3 Years	36	5	31	6.2	0

Additional pro statistics: Returned four punts for 22 yards, returned one kickoff for nine yards and caught one pass for 11 yards, 1985.

RAY CHILDRESS
Defensive End—Houston Oilers
Born October 20, 1962, at Memphis, Tenn.
Height, 6.06. Weight, 270.
High School—Richardson, Tex., J.J. Pearce.
Attended Texas A&M University.

Named as defensive lineman on THE SPORTING NEWS College All-America Team, 1984.

Selected by Houston in 1985 USFL territorial draft.
Selected by Houston in 1st round (3rd player selected) of 1985 NFL draft.
Signed by Houston Oilers, August 24, 1985.
Granted roster exemption, August 24 through August 29, 1985; activated, August 30, 1985.
Crossed picket line during players' strike, October 14, 1987.
Granted free agency, February 1, 1989.
Tendered offer sheet by Chicago Bears, March 30, 1989; matched by Houston Oilers, April 3, 1989.
Houston NFL, 1985 through 1988.
Games: 1985 (16), 1986 (16), 1987 (13), 1988 (16). Total—61.
Pro statistics: Recovered one fumble, 1985 and 1986; recovered one fumble for one yard, 1987; recovered seven fumbles, 1988.
Played in Pro Bowl (NFL All-Star Game) following 1988 season.

GENE ALAN CHILTON
Offensive Tackle—Kansas City Chiefs
Born March 27, 1964, at Houston, Tex.
Height, 6.03. Weight, 271.
High School—Houston, Tex., Memorial.
Attended University of Texas.

Selected by St. Louis in 3rd round (59th player selected) of 1986 NFL draft.
Signed by St. Louis Cardinals, July 25, 1986.
Franchise transferred to Phoenix, March 15, 1988.
Released by Phoenix Cardinals, August 30, 1988; signed as free agent by Kansas City Chiefs, March 3, 1989.
St. Louis NFL, 1986 and 1987.
Games: 1986 (16), 1987 (11). Total—27.
Pro statistics: Recovered one fumble, 1986.

JEFFREY BRUCE CHRISTENSEN
(Jeff)
Quarterback—New York Jets
Born January 8, 1961, at Gibson City, Ill.
Height, 6.03. Weight, 195.
High School—Gibson City, Ill.
Attended Eastern Illinois University.

Selected by New Jersey in 17th round (195th player selected) of 1983 USFL draft.
Selected by Cincinnati in 5th round (137th player selected) of 1983 NFL draft.
Signed by Cincinnati Bengals, June 2, 1983.
Traded by Cincinnati Bengals to Los Angeles Rams for draft choice, July 25, 1984.
Released by Los Angeles Rams, August 15, 1984; signed as free agent by Philadelphia Eagles for 1985, October 23, 1984.
Signed for 1984 season, November 27, 1984.
Released by Philadelphia Eagles, September 2, 1985; re-signed by Eagles, November 20, 1985.
Released by Philadelphia Eagles, November 25, 1985; signed as free agent by Cleveland Browns, April 20, 1986.
Released by Cleveland Browns, August 18, 1986; signed as free agent by Denver Broncos, April 21, 1987.
Released by Denver Broncos, July 27, 1987; signed as free agent replacement player by Cleveland Browns, September 23, 1987.
Released by Cleveland Browns, October 19, 1987; signed as free agent by New York Jets, April 20, 1989.
Active for 3 games with Philadelphia Eagles in 1984; did not play.
Active for 1 game with Philadelphia Eagles in 1985; did not play.

Year Club	G.	Att.	Cmp.	Pct.	Gain	T.P.	P.I.	Avg.	Att.	Yds.	Avg.	TD.	TD.	Pts.	F.
				—PASSING—					—RUSHING—				—TOTAL—		
1983—Cincinnati NFL	1				None				1	—2	—2.0	0	0	0	0
1987—Cleveland NFL	3	58	24	41.4	297	1	3	5.12	11	41	3.7	0	0	0	3
Pro Totals—4 Years	4	58	24	41.4	297	1	3	5.12	12	39	3.3	0	0	0	3

Quarterback Rating Points: 1987 (42.1).
Additional pro statistics: Fumbled three times for minus three yards, 1987.

TODD JAY CHRISTENSEN
Tight End—Los Angeles Raiders
Born August 3, 1956, at Bellefonte, Pa.
Height, 6.03. Weight, 230.
High School—Eugene, Ore., Sheldon.
Attended Brigham Young University.

Named to The Sporting News NFL All-Star Team, 1983 and 1985.
Selected by Dallas in 2nd round (56th player selected) of 1978 NFL draft.
On injured reserve with broken foot, August 28 through entire 1978 season.
Released by Dallas Cowboys, August 27, 1979; claimed on waivers by New York Giants, August 28, 1979.
Released by New York Giants, September 4, 1979; signed as free agent by Oakland Raiders, September 26, 1979.
Franchise transferred to Los Angeles, May 7, 1982.
On did not report list, August 14 through August 22, 1984.
Reported and granted roster exemption, August 23 through August 31, 1984; activated, September 1, 1984.
On injured reserve with knee injury, November 10 through December 16, 1988; activated, December 17, 1988.

Year Club		—PASS RECEIVING—		
Year Club	G.	P.C.	Yds.	Avg.	TD.
1979—NYG (1)-Oak (12) NFL	13	None			
1980—Oakland NFL	16	None			
1981—Oakland NFL	16	8	115	14.4	2
1982—L.A. Raiders NFL	9	42	510	12.1	4
1983—L.A. Raiders NFL	16	★92	1247	13.6	12
1984—L.A. Raiders NFL	16	80	1007	12.6	7
1985—L.A. Raiders NFL	16	82	987	12.0	6
1986—L.A. Raiders NFL	16	★95	1153	12.1	8
1987—L.A. Raiders NFL	12	47	663	14.1	2
1988—L.A. Raiders NFL	7	15	190	12.7	0
Pro Totals—10 Years	137	461	5872	12.7	41

Additional pro statistics: Recovered two fumbles for one yard, 1979; recovered one fumble in end zone for a touchdown and returned one kickoff for 10 yards, 1980; returned four kickoffs for 54 yards and credited with one safety, 1981; recovered one fumble, 1981 and 1983 through 1985; rushed once for minus six yards and fumbled three times, 1982; fumbled once, 1983, 1984 and 1986; recovered one fumble for two yards, 1988.
Played in AFC Championship Game following 1980 and 1983 seasons.
Played in NFL Championship Game following 1980 and 1983 seasons.
Played in Pro Bowl (NFL All-Star Game) following 1983 through 1987 seasons.

DARRYL E. CLACK
Running Back—Dallas Cowboys
Born October 29, 1963, at San Antonio, Tex.
Height, 5.10. Weight, 218.
High School—Security, Colo., Widefield.
Attended Arizona State University.

Selected by Arizona in 1986 USFL territorial draft.
Selected by Dallas in 2nd round (33rd player selected) of 1986 NFL draft.
Signed by Dallas Cowboys, July 21, 1986.

Year Club		—RUSHING—				PASS RECEIVING				—TOTAL—		
Year Club	G.	Att.	Yds.	Avg.	TD.	P.C.	Yds.	Avg.	TD.	TD.	Pts.	F.
1986—Dallas NFL	16	4	19	4.8	0	1	18	18.0	0	0	0	3
1987—Dallas NFL	12	None				None				0	0	1
1988—Dallas NFL	15	11	54	4.9	0	17	126	7.4	1	1	6	0
Pro Totals—3 Years	43	15	73	4.9	0	18	144	8.0	1	1	6	4

Year Club		KICKOFF RETURNS		
Year Club	G.	No.	Yds.	Avg.TD.
1986—Dallas NFL	16	19	421	22.2	0
1987—Dallas NFL	12	29	635	21.9	0
1988—Dallas NFL	15	32	690	21.6	0
Pro Totals—3 Years	43	80	1746	21.8	0

SAM CLANCY
Defensive End—Indianapolis Colts
Born May 29, 1958, at Pittsburgh, Pa.
Height, 6.07. Weight, 275.
High School—Pittsburgh, Pa., Brashear.
Attended University of Pittsburgh.

Selected by Phoenix in 3rd round (62nd player selected) of 1981 NBA draft.
Released by Phoenix Suns, October 19, 1981; signed by Billings Volcanos (CBA), November 12, 1981.
Selected by Seattle in 11th round (284th player selected) of 1982 NFL draft.
On injured reserve with knee injury, August 16 through entire 1982 season.
Granted free agency, February 1, 1984; signed by Pittsburgh Maulers, February 10, 1984.
Franchise disbanded, October 25, 1984.
Selected by Memphis Showboats in USFL dispersal draft, December 6, 1984.
Granted free agency, August 1, 1985; re-signed by Seahawks and traded to Cleveland Browns for 7th round pick in 1986 draft, August 27, 1985.
Granted roster exemption, August 27 through September 5, 1985; activated, September 6, 1985.
Crossed picket line during players' strike, October 14, 1987.
Granted unconditional free agency, February 1, 1989; signed by Indianapolis Colts, March 31, 1989.
Seattle NFL, 1983; Pittsburgh USFL, 1984; Memphis USFL, 1985; Cleveland NFL, 1985 through 1988.
Games: 1983 (13), 1984 (18), 1985 USFL (18), 1985 NFL (14), 1986 (16), 1987 (13), 1988 (16). Total NFL—72. Total USFL—36. Total Pro—108.
USFL statistics: Credited with 15 sacks for 136 yards and recovered two fumbles, 1984; credited with four sacks for 28 yards, 1985.
NFL statistics: Recovered one fumble, 1986; recovered two fumbles, 1987.
Played in AFC Championship Game following 1986 and 1987 seasons.

BASKETBALL RECORD AS PLAYER

Year—Team	G	Min.	FGM	FGA	Pct.	FTM	FTA	Pct.	3-pt. Made	3-pt. Att.	Pts.	Avg.	Reb.	Avg.	Ast.	PF	Blk. Shots	Steals
81-82 Billings CBA	41	1170	190	355	53.5	89	128	69.5	1	5	472	11.5	342	8.3	50	144	41	67

PLAYOFF RECORD

Year—Team	G	Min.	FGM	FGA	Pct.	FTM	FTA	Pct.	3-pt. Made	3-pt. Att.	Pts.	Avg.	Reb.	Avg.	Ast.	PF	Blk. Shots	Steals
81-82 Billings CBA	5	167	24	46	52.1	12	19	63.1	1	1	63	12.6	54	10.8	8	23	5	8

BRUCE CLARK
Defensive End—New Orleans Saints
Born March 31, 1958, at New Castle, Pa.
Height, 6.03. Weight, 274.
High School—New Castle, Pa.
Attended Penn State University.

Selected by Green Bay in 1st round (4th player selected) of 1980 NFL draft.
Signed by Toronto Argonauts, May 26, 1980.
Granted free agency, March 1, 1982; traded by Green Bay Packers to New Orleans Saints for 1st round pick in 1983 draft, June 10, 1982.
Crossed picket line during players' strike, September 30, 1987.
Toronto CFL, 1980 and 1981; New Orleans NFL, 1982 through 1988.
Games: 1980 (16), 1981 (16), 1982 (9), 1983 (15), 1984 (15), 1985 (16), 1986 (16), 1987 (15), 1988 (16). Total CFL—32. Total NFL—102. Total Pro—134.
CFL statistics: Intercepted one pass for no yards and recovered four fumbles for six yards, 1980; recovered one fumble, 1981.
NFL statistics: Recovered one fumble, 1983; intercepted one pass for nine yards and recovered two fumbles for five yards, 1984; recovered one fumble for four yards, 1985; recovered three fumbles for 28 yards, 1986; recovered two fumbles and credited with a safety, 1987.
Played in Pro Bowl (NFL All-Star Game) following 1984 season.

GARY C. CLARK
Wide Receiver—Washington Redskins
Born May 1, 1962, at Radford, Va.
Height, 5.09. Weight, 175.
High School—Dublin, Va., Pulaski County.
Attended James Madison University.

Selected by Jacksonville in 1st round (6th player selected) of 1984 USFL draft.
Signed by Jacksonville Bulls, January 16, 1984.
On developmental squad, May 9 through May 15, 1984; activated, May 16, 1984.
On developmental squad, June 4 through June 11, 1984; activated, June 12, 1984.
Selected by Washington in 2nd round (55th player selected) of 1984 NFL supplemental draft.
On developmental squad, March 17 through March 19, 1985; activated, March 20, 1985.
Released by Jacksonville Bulls, May 1, 1985; signed by Washington Redskins, May 13, 1985.
On developmental squad for 2 games with Jacksonville Bulls in 1984.
On developmental squad for 1 game with Jacksonville Bulls in 1985.

		PASS RECEIVING			–PUNT RETURNS–				—KICKOFF RET.—				—TOTAL—		
Year Club	G.	P.C.	Yds.	Avg. TD.	No.	Yds.	Avg.	TD.	No.	Yds.	Avg.	TD.	TD.	Pts.	F.
1984—Jacksonville USFL......	16	56	760	13.6 2	20	84	4.2	0	19	341	18.0	0	2	12	5
1985—Jacksonville USFL......	9	10	61	6.1 1	7	44	6.3	0	3	56	18.7	0	1	6	1
1985—Washington NFL.........	16	72	926	12.9 5		None				None			5	30	0
1986—Washington NFL.........	15	74	1265	17.1 7	1	14	14.0	0		None			7	42	1
1987—Washington NFL.........	12	56	1066	19.0 7		None				None			7	42	3
1988—Washington NFL.........	16	59	892	15.1 7	8	48	6.0	0		None			7	42	2
USFL Totals—2 Years....	25	66	821	12.4 3	27	128	4.7	0	22	397	18.0	0	3	18	6
NFL Totals—4 Years.......	59	261	4149	15.9 26	9	62	6.9	0	0	0	0.0	0	26	156	6
Pro Totals—6 Years.......	84	327	4970	15.2 29	36	190	5.3	0	22	397	18.0	0	29	174	12

Additional USFL statistics: Rushed twice for nine yards and recovered four fumbles, 1984; recovered one fumble, 1985.
Additional NFL statistics: Rushed twice for 10 yards and recovered one fumble, 1986; rushed once for no yards, 1987; rushed twice for six yards, 1988.
Played in NFC Championship Game following 1986 and 1987 seasons.
Played in NFL Championship Game following 1987 season.
Played in Pro Bowl (NFL All-Star Game) following 1986 and 1987 seasons.

GREGORY KLONDIKE CLARK
(Greg)
Linebacker—Miami Dolphins
Born March 5, 1965, at Los Angeles, Calif.
Height, 6.00. Weight, 221.
High School—Torrance, Calif., North.
Attended Arizona State University.

Selected by Chicago in 12th round (329th player selected) of 1988 NFL draft.
Signed by Chicago Bears, July 21, 1988.
Granted unconditional free agency, February 1, 1989; signed by Miami Dolphins, March 16, 1989.
Chicago NFL, 1988.
Games: 1988 (15).
Pro statistics: Recovered one fumble, 1988.
Played in NFC Championship Game following 1988 season.

—DID YOU KNOW—

That the Tampa Bay Buccaneers did not score in the first period of any game in 1988 until their eighth game of the season?

JESSIE L. CLARK
Fullback—Phoenix Cardinals
Born January 3, 1960, at Thebes, Ark.
Height, 6.00. Weight, 233.
High School—Crossett, Ark.
Attended Louisiana Tech University and received bachelor of arts
degree in criminal justice from University of Arkansas in 1983.
Cousin of Dennis Woodberry, cornerback with Denver Broncos.

Selected by Green Bay in 7th round (188th player selected) of 1983 NFL draft.
On injured reserve with muscle tear in elbow, November 16 through remainder of 1984 season.
On injured reserve with elbow injury, November 19 through remainder of 1986 season.
Granted free agency, February 1, 1988; rights relinquished, July 19, 1988.
Signed by Detroit Lions, August 3, 1988.
Released by Detroit Lions, October 5, 1988; signed as free agent by Phoenix Cardinals, November 22, 1988.

Year Club	G.	Att.	Yds.	Avg.	TD.	P.C.	Yds.	Avg.	TD.	TD.	Pts.	F.
			RUSHING				PASS RECEIVING				—TOTAL—	
1983—Green Bay NFL	16	71	328	4.6	0	18	279	15.5	1	1	6	2
1984—Green Bay NFL	11	87	375	4.3	4	29	234	8.1	2	6	36	2
1985—Green Bay NFL	16	147	633	4.3	5	24	252	10.5	2	7	42	4
1986—Green Bay NFL	5	18	41	2.3	0	6	41	6.8	0	0	0	1
1987—Green Bay NFL	12	56	211	3.8	0	22	119	5.4	1	1	6	0
1988—Detroit (5)-Phoenix (4) NFL	9		None				None			0	0	0
Pro Totals—6 Years	69	379	1588	4.2	9	99	925	9.3	6	15	90	9

Additional pro statistics: Recovered one fumble, 1983; recovered two fumbles, 1985; returned two kickoffs for 10 yards, 1988.

KEVIN RANDALL CLARK
(K. C.)
Defensive Back—Dallas Cowboys
Born June 8, 1964, at Sacramento, Calif.
Height, 5.10. Weight, 185.
High School—Sacramento, Calif., K. C. McClatchy.
Attended San Jose State University.

Signed as free agent by Denver Broncos, May 1, 1987.
Released by Denver Broncos, September 7, 1987; re-signed as replacement player by Broncos, September 25, 1987.
Released by Denver Broncos, September 22, 1988; signed as free agent by Dallas Cowboys, February 3, 1989.

Year Club	G.	No.	Yds.	Avg.	TD.	No.	Yds.	Avg.	TD.	No.	Yds.	Avg.	TD.	TD.	Pts.	F.
		INTERCEPTIONS				–PUNT RETURNS–				—KICKOFF RET.—				—TOTAL—		
1987—Denver NFL	11	3	105	35.0	0	18	233	12.9	1	2	33	16.5	0	1	6	1
1988—Denver NFL	3		None			13	115	8.8	0		None			0	0	0
Pro Totals—2 Years	14	3	105	35.0	0	31	348	11.2	1	2	33	16.5	0	1	6	1

Additional pro statistics: Recovered one fumble, 1987.
Played in AFC Championship Game following 1987 season.
Played in NFL Championship Game following 1987 season.

LOUIS STEVEN CLARK
Wide Receiver—Seattle Seahawks
Born July 3, 1964, at Shannon, Miss.
Height, 6.01. Weight, 193.
High School—Shannon, Miss.
Attended Mississippi State University.
Brother of Dave Clark, outfielder in Cleveland Indians' organization.

Selected by Seattle in 10th round (270th player selected) of 1987 NFL draft.
Signed by Seattle Seahawks, July 21, 1987.
On injured reserve with pulled hamstring, November 16 through remainder of 1987 season.
On injured reserve with hamstring injury, August 29 through October 21, 1988; activated, October 22, 1988.
Seattle NFL, 1987 and 1988.
Games: 1987 (2), 1988 (7). Total—9.
Pro statistics: Caught one pass for 20 yards and a touchdown, 1988.

ROBERT CLARK
Wide Receiver—Detroit Lions
Born August 6, 1965, at Brooklyn, N.Y.
Height, 5.11. Weight, 175.
High School—Richmond, Va., Maggie L. Walker.
Attended North Carolina Central University.

Selected by New Orleans in 10th round (263rd player selected) of 1987 NFL draft.
Signed by New Orleans Saints, July 24, 1987.
On injured reserve with stress fracture of leg, October 30 through remainder of 1987 season.
Granted unconditional free agency, February 1, 1989; signed by Detroit Lions, February 27, 1989.

Year Club	G.	P.C.	Yds.	Avg.	TD.
		PASS RECEIVING			
1987—New Orleans NFL	2	3	38	12.7	0
1988—New Orleans NFL	16	19	245	12.9	2
Pro Totals—2 Years	18	22	283	12.9	2

Additional pro statistics: Recovered one fumble and fumbled once, 1988.

KENNETH MAURICE CLARKE
(Ken)
Nose Tackle—Seattle Seahawks
Born August 28, 1956, at Savannah, Ga.
Height, 6.01. Weight 272.
High School—Boston, Mass., English.
Received bachelor of science degree in psychology from Syracuse University in 1978.

Signed as free agent by Philadelphia Eagles, May 4, 1978.
Released by Philadelphia Eagles, May 9, 1988; signed as free agent by Seattle Seahawks, July 18, 1988.
Philadelphia NFL, 1978 through 1987; Seattle NFL, 1988.
Games: 1978 (16), 1979 (16), 1980 (16), 1981 (16), 1982 (9), 1983 (16), 1984 (16), 1985 (16), 1986 (16), 1987 (11), 1988 (16).
Total—164.
Pro statistics: Recovered one fumble, 1978 and 1982; returned one kickoff for no yards, 1980 and 1981; fumbled once, 1980; credited with a safety, 1981; recovered three fumbles for five yards, 1983; recovered two fumbles, 1985.
Played in NFC Championship Game following 1980 season.
Played in NFL Championship Game following 1980 season.

ROBERT JAMES CLASBY
(Bob)
Defensive Tackle—Phoenix Cardinals
Born September 28, 1960, at Detroit, Mich.
Height, 6.05. Weight, 258.
High School—Dorchester, Mass., Boston College.
Received bachelor of business administration degree in finance from Notre Dame University.
Cousin of former President John F. Kennedy, former Senator Robert F. Kennedy
and Senator Edward Kennedy (D-Mass.).

Selected by Chicago in 1983 USFL territorial draft.
Selected by Seattle in 9th round (236th player selected) of 1983 NFL draft.
Signed by Seattle Seahawks, May 8, 1983.
Released by Seattle Seahawks, August 23, 1983; signed by Chicago Blitz, September 24, 1983.
Traded by Chicago Blitz to Arizona Wranglers for rights to offensive tackle Russ Washington, January 24, 1984.
Released by Arizona Wranglers, February 24, 1984; signed as free agent by Chicago Blitz, March 6, 1984.
On developmental squad, March 24 through March 28, 1984; activated, March 29, 1984.
Traded by Chicago Blitz to Jacksonville Bulls for defensive back Kerry Baird, April 17, 1984.
Granted free agency when USFL suspended operations, August 7, 1986; signed as free agent by St. Louis Cardinals, August 15, 1986.
Granted roster exemption, August 15 through August 20, 1986; activated, August 21, 1986.
Franchise transferred to Phoenix, March 15, 1988.
On developmental squad for 1 game with Chicago Blitz in 1984.
Chicago (3)-Jacksonville (10) USFL, 1984; Jacksonville USFL, 1985; St. Louis NFL, 1986 and 1987; Phoenix NFL, 1988.
Games: 1984 (13), 1985 (18), 1986 (16), 1987 (12), 1988 (16). Total USFL—31. Total NFL—44. Total Pro—75.
USFL statistics: Credited with five sacks for 43 yards and recovered two fumbles, 1984; credited with 3½ sacks for 38½ yards and recovered one fumble, 1985.
NFL statistics: Recovered one fumble, 1986 and 1987; intercepted one pass for seven yards, 1988.

JOHN GREGORY CLAY
Offensive Tackle—San Diego Chargers
Born May 1, 1964, at St. Louis, Mo.
Height, 6.05. Weight, 305.
High School—St. Louis, Mo., Northwest.
Attended University of Missouri.

Selected by Los Angeles Raiders in 1st round (15th player selected) of 1987 NFL draft.
Signed by Los Angeles Raiders, July 29, 1987.
Traded with 3rd round pick in 1989 draft and conditional pick in 1990 draft by Los Angeles Raiders to San Diego Chargers for offensive tackle Jim Lachey, July 30, 1988.
On injured reserve with neck injury, September 23 through remainder of 1988 season.
Los Angeles Raiders NFL, 1987; San Diego NFL, 1988.
Games: 1987 (10), 1988 (2). Total—12.
Pro statistics: Recovered one fumble, 1987.

RAYMOND DE WAYNE CLAYBORN
Cornerback—New England Patriots
Born January 2, 1955, at Fort Worth, Tex.
Height, 6.01. Weight, 186.
High School—Fort Worth, Tex., Trimble.
Received degree in communications from University of Texas.

Named as cornerback on THE SPORTING NEWS College All-America Team, 1976.
Named to THE SPORTING NEWS NFL All-Star Team, 1983.
Selected by New England in 1st round (16th player selected) of 1977 NFL draft.
Crossed picket line during players' strike, October 2, 1987.
On injured reserve with knee injury, November 23 through remainder of 1987 season.

Year Club	G.	No.	Yds.	Avg.	TD.	No.	Yds.	Avg.	TD.	TD.	Pts.	F.
			-INTERCEPTIONS-				—KICKOFF RET.—				—TOTAL—	
1977—New England NFL	14		None			28	869	*31.0	*3	3	†20	1
1978—New England NFL	16	4	72	18.0	0	27	636	23.6	0	0	0	0
1979—New England NFL	16	5	56	11.2	0	2	33	16.5	0	0	0	0
1980—New England NFL	16	5	87	17.4	0		None			0	0	0
1981—New England NFL	16	2	39	19.5	0		None			0	0	0
1982—New England NFL	9	1	26	26.0	0		None			0	0	0
1983—New England NFL	16		None				None			0	0	0
1984—New England NFL	16	3	102	34.0	0		None			0	0	0
1985—New England NFL	16	6	80	13.3	*1		None			1	6	0
1986—New England NFL	16	3	4	1.3	0		None			0	0	0
1987—New England NFL	10	2	24	12.0	0		None			1	6	0
1988—New England NFL	16	4	65	16.3	0		None			0	0	0
Pro Totals—12 Years	177	35	555	15.9	1	57	1538	27.0	3	5	32	1

†Includes one safety.
Additional pro statistics: Recovered one fumble, 1978, 1980, 1982 and 1987; recovered two fumbles for four yards, 1981; recovered two fumbles, 1986; returned blocked field goal attempt 71 yards for a touchdown, 1987.
Played in AFC Championship Game following 1985 season.
Played in NFL Championship Game following 1985 season.
Played in Pro Bowl (NFL All-Star Game) following 1983, 1985 and 1986 seasons.

MARK GREGORY CLAYTON
Wide Receiver—Miami Dolphins
Born April 8, 1961, at Indianapolis, Ind.
Height, 5.09. Weight, 184.
High School—Indianapolis, Ind., Cathedral.
Attended University of Louisville.

Selected by Miami in 8th round (223rd player selected) of 1983 NFL draft.

Year Club	G.	P.C.	Yds.	Avg.	TD.	No.	Yds.	Avg.	TD.	TD.	Pts.	F.
			-PASS RECEIVING-				-PUNT RETURNS-				—TOTAL—	
1983—Miami NFL	14	6	114	19.0	1	41	392	9.6	*1	2	12	3
1984—Miami NFL	15	73	1389	19.0	*18	8	79	9.9	0	*18	108	2
1985—Miami NFL	16	70	996	14.2	4	2	14	7.0	0	4	24	2
1986—Miami NFL	15	60	1150	19.2	10	1	0	0.0	0	10	60	1
1987—Miami NFL	12	46	776	16.9	7		None			7	42	0
1988—Miami NFL	16	86	1129	13.1	*14		None			14	84	0
Pro Totals—6 Years	88	341	5554	16.3	54	52	485	9.3	1	55	330	8

Additional pro statistics: Rushed twice for nine yards, returned one kickoff for 25 yards, attempted one pass with one completion for 48 yards and a touchdown, 1983; recovered one fumble, 1983 through 1985; rushed three times for 35 yards, returned two kickoffs for 15 yards and attempted one pass with one interception, 1984; rushed once for 10 yards, 1985; rushed twice for 33 yards, 1986; rushed twice for eight yards, 1987; rushed once for four yards, 1988.
Played in AFC Championship Game following 1984 and 1985 seasons.
Played in NFL Championship Game following 1984 season.
Played in Pro Bowl (NFL All-Star Game) following 1984 through 1986 and 1988 seasons.

STANLEY DAVID CLAYTON
(Stan)
Offensive Tackle-Guard—Atlanta Falcons
Born January 31, 1965, at Philadelphia, Pa.
Height, 6.03. Weight, 265.
High School—Cherry Hill, N.J., East.
Attended Penn State University.

Selected by Atlanta in 10th round (250th player selected) of 1988 NFL draft.
Signed by Atlanta Falcons, July 16, 1988.
On injured reserve with knee injury, August 31 through December 9, 1988; activated, December 10, 1988.
Atlanta NFL, 1988.
Games: 1988 (2).

KYLE CLIFTON
Linebacker—New York Jets
Born August 23, 1962, at Onley, Tex.
Height, 6.04. Weight, 233.
High School—Bridgeport, Tex.
Received degree in business management from Texas Christian University.

Selected by Birmingham in 1st round (12th player selected) of 1984 USFL draft.
Selected by New York Jets in 3rd round (64th player selected) of 1984 NFL draft.
Signed by New York Jets, July 12, 1984.

Year Club	G.	No.	Yds.	Avg.	TD.
			—INTERCEPTIONS—		
1984—N.Y. Jets NFL	16	1	0	0.0	0
1985—N.Y. Jets NFL	16	3	10	3.3	0
1986—N.Y. Jets NFL	16	2	8	4.0	0
1987—N.Y. Jets NFL	12		None		
1988—N.Y. Jets NFL	16		None		
Pro Totals—5 Years	76	6	18	3.0	0

Additional pro statistics: Recovered one fumble, 1984 and 1986; recovered two fumbles, 1985; recovered two fumbles for six yards, 1988.

JACKIE WAYNE CLINE
Defensive End—Miami Dolphins
Born March 13, 1960, at Kansas City, Kan.
Height, 6.05. Weight, 280.
High School—McCalla, Ala., McAdory.
Received bachelor of science degree in advertising from University of Alabama.

Selected by Birmingham in 1983 USFL territorial draft.
Signed by Birmingham Stallions, January 26, 1983.
On developmental squad, April 16 through April 22, 1983; activated, April 23, 1983.
On developmental squad, May 5 through May 25, 1984; activated, May 26, 1984.
Released by Birmingham Stallions, August 7, 1986; signed as free agent by Green Bay Packers, August 14, 1986.
Granted roster exemption, August 14 through August 24, 1986.
Released by Green Bay Packers, August 25, 1986; signed as free agent by Cleveland Browns, July 17, 1987.
Released by Cleveland Browns, September 7, 1987; signed as free agent replacement player by Pittsburgh Steelers, October 8, 1987.
Released by Pittsburgh Steelers, November 7, 1987; awarded on waivers to Miami Dolphins, November 9, 1987.
On developmental squad for 1 game with Birmingham Stallions in 1983.
On developmental squad for 3 games with Birmingham Stallions in 1984.
Birmingham USFL, 1983 through 1985; Pittsburgh (1)-Miami (7) NFL, 1987; Miami NFL, 1988.
Games: 1983 (17), 1984 (15), 1985 (18), 1987 (8), 1988 (14). Total USFL—50. Total NFL—22. Total Pro—72.
Pro statistics: Credited with 5½ sacks for 45 yards and recovered one fumble for two yards, 1983; credited with one safety and four sacks for 37 yards and recovered one fumble, 1984; credited with five sacks for 47 yards, 1985.

WILLIAM JOSEPH CLINKSCALES
(Joey)
Wide Receiver—Indianapolis Colts
Born May 21, 1964, at Asheville, N. C.
Height, 6.00. Weight, 204.
High School—Knoxville, Tenn., Austin-East.
Received bachelor of arts degree in liberal arts from University of Tennessee in 1987.

Selected by Pittsburgh in 9th round (233rd player selected) of 1987 NFL draft.
Signed by Pittsburgh Steelers, July 26, 1987.
Released by Pittsburgh Steelers, August 31, 1987; re-signed as replacement player by Steelers, September 24, 1987.
Released by Pittsburgh Steelers, October 10, 1988; signed as free agent by Tampa Bay Buccaneers, October 18, 1988.
Released by Tampa Bay Buccaneers, November 30, 1988; signed as free agent by Indianapolis Colts, March 29, 1989.

Year Club	G.	P.C.	Yds.	Avg.	TD.
		—PASS RECEIVING—			
1987—Pittsburgh NFL............	7	13	240	18.5	1
1988—Pitt. (4)-T.B. (3) NFL...	7			None	
Pro Totals—2 Years............	14	13	240	18.5	1

GARRY WILBERT COBB
Linebacker—Dallas Cowboys
Born March 16, 1957, at Carthage, N. C.
Height, 6.02. Weight, 233.
High School—Stamford, Conn.
Attended University of Southern California.

Selected by Dallas in 9th round (247th player selected) of 1979 NFL draft.
Released by Dallas Cowboys, August 21, 1979; signed as free agent by Detroit Lions, October 24, 1979.
Granted free agency, February 1, 1985; re-signed by Lions and traded to Philadelphia Eagles for running back Wilbert Montgomery, August 21, 1985.
Released by Philadelphia Eagles, August 24, 1988; signed as free agent by Dallas Cowboys, August 26, 1988.

Year Club	G.	No.	Yds.	Avg.	TD.
		—INTERCEPTIONS—			
1979—Detroit NFL..................	8			None	
1980—Detroit NFL..................	16			None	
1981—Detroit NFL..................	16	3	32	10.7	0
1982—Detroit NFL..................	6	2	12	6.0	0
1983—Detroit NFL..................	15	4	19	4.8	0
1984—Detroit NFL..................	16			None	
1985—Philadelphia NFL	16			None	
1986—Philadelphia NFL	16	1	3	3.0	0
1987—Philadelphia NFL	12			None	
1988—Dallas NFL	16			None	
Pro Totals—10 Years..........	137	10	66	6.6	0

Additional pro statistics: Caught one pass for 19 yards, 1981; recovered three fumbles, 1981 and 1987; caught one pass for 25 yards, 1982; recovered two fumbles, 1983; recovered one fumble, 1986 and 1988.

SHERMAN COCROFT
Safety—Tampa Bay Buccaneers
Born August 29, 1961, at Watsonville, Calif.
Height, 6.01. Weight, 190.
High School—Watsonville, Calif.
Attended Cabrillo College and San Jose State University.

Selected by Oakland in 1984 USFL territorial draft.
Signed as free agent by Seattle Seahawks, May 3, 1984.
Released by Seattle Seahawks, August 21, 1984; signed as free agent by Kansas City Chiefs for 1985, October 15, 1984.
Released by Kansas City Chiefs, August 30, 1988; signed as free agent by Buffalo Bills, September 15, 1988.
Released by Buffalo Bills, September 21, 1988; re-signed by Bills, September 27, 1988.
Granted unconditional free agency, February 1, 1989; signed by Tampa Bay Buccaneers, March 27, 1989.

		—INTERCEPTIONS—			
Year Club	G.	No.	Yds.	Avg.	TD.
1985—Kansas City NFL..........	16	3	27	9.0	0
1986—Kansas City NFL..........	16	3	32	10.7	0
1987—Kansas City NFL..........	12		None		
1988—Buffalo NFL.................	13	1	17	17.0	0
Pro Totals—4 Years............	57	7	76	10.9	0

Additional pro statistics: Recovered two fumbles, 1985; returned one kickoff for 23 yards, 1986; recovered one fumble, 1986 and 1988; returned one punt for no yards, 1987.
Played in AFC Championship Game following 1988 season.

JAMES MICHAEL COFER
(Mike)
Placekicker—San Francisco 49ers
Born February 19, 1964, at Columbia, S.C.
Height, 6.01. Weight, 190.
High School—Charlotte, N.C., Country Day.
Received bachelor of arts degree in business management and
political science from North Carolina State University.

Signed as free agent by Cleveland Browns, May 5, 1987.
Released by Cleveland Browns, September 1, 1987; signed as free agent replacement player by New Orleans Saints, September 24, 1987.
Released by New Orleans Saints, October 16, 1987; signed as free agent by San Francisco 49ers, April 5, 1988.

		—PLACE KICKING—				
Year Club	G.	XP.	XPM.	FG.	FGA.	Pts.
1987—New Orleans NFL...	2	5	2	1	1	8
1988—San Francisco NFL	16	40	1	27	*38	121
Pro Totals—2 Years.......	18	45	3	28	39	129

Played in NFC Championship Game following 1988 season.
Played in NFL Championship Game following 1988 season.

MICHAEL LYNN COFER
Linebacker—Detroit Lions
Born April 7, 1960, at Knoxville, Tenn.
Height, 6.05. Weight, 245.
High School—Knoxville, Tenn., Rule.
Attended University of Tennessee.
Brother of James Cofer, linebacker with Baltimore Stars, 1985.

Selected by New Jersey in 1983 USFL territorial draft.
Selected by Detroit in 3rd round (67th player selected) of 1983 NFL draft.
Signed by Detroit Lions, July 1, 1983.
On injured reserve with hip injury, October 25 through remainder of 1985 season.
Detroit NFL, 1983 through 1988.
Games: 1983 (16), 1984 (16), 1985 (7), 1986 (16), 1987 (11), 1988 (16). Total—82.
Pro statistics: Recovered one fumble, 1983, 1984 and 1987; recovered three fumbles, 1986; recovered two fumbles, 1988.
Played in Pro Bowl (NFL All-Star Game) following 1988 season.

TIMMY LEE COFIELD
(Tim)
Linebacker—New York Jets
Born May 18, 1963, at Murfreesboro, N.C.
Height, 6.02. Weight, 245.
High School—Murfreesboro, N.C.
Attended Elizabeth City State University.

Selected by Baltimore in 6th round (45th player selected) of 1986 USFL draft.
Signed as free agent by Kansas City Chiefs, May 8, 1986.
Granted unconditional free agency, February 1, 1989; signed by New York Jets, March 9, 1989.
Kansas City NFL, 1986 through 1988.
Games: 1986 (15), 1987 (12), 1988 (16). Total—43.
Pro statistics: Recovered one fumble, 1986 through 1988; intercepted one pass for no yards, 1988.

DARRELL RAY COLBERT
Wide Receiver—New Orleans Saints
Born November 16, 1964, at Beaumont, Tex.
Height, 5.10. Weight, 174.
High School—Beaumont, Tex., Westbrook.
Attended Texas Southern University.

Signed as free agent by Kansas City Chiefs, May 13, 1987.
Released by Kansas City Chiefs, August 30, 1988; re-signed by Chiefs, September 3, 1988.
On injured reserve with thigh injury, September 27 through remainder of 1988 season.
Granted unconditional free agency, February 1, 1989; signed by New Orleans Saints, March 24, 1989.
Kansas City NFL, 1987 and 1988.
Games: 1987 (12), 1988 (3). Total—15.
Pro statistics: Caught three passes for 21 yards, returned one punt for 11 yards and returned one kickoff for 18 yards, 1987; caught one pass for minus three yards, recovered one fumble and fumbled once, 1988.

LEWIS WELTON COLBERT
Punter—San Diego Chargers
Born August 23, 1963, at Phenix City, Ala.
Height, 5.11. Weight, 180.
High School—Phenix City, Ala., Glenwood Academy.
Attended Auburn University.

Named as punter on THE SPORTING NEWS College All-America Team, 1985.
Selected by Birmingham in 1986 USFL territorial draft.
Selected by Kansas City in 8th round (196th player selected) of 1986 NFL draft.
Signed by Kansas City Chiefs, July 18, 1986.
On injured reserve with back injury, November 3 through remainder of 1987 season.
Released by Kansas City Chiefs, August 23, 1988; awarded on waivers to Atlanta Falcons, August 24, 1988.
Released by Atlanta Falcons, September 5, 1988; signed as free agent by San Diego Chargers, May 25, 1989.

		——PUNTING——		
Year Club	G.	No.	Avg.	Blk.
1986—Kansas City NFL..................	16	99	40.7	0
1987—Kansas City NFL..................	2	10	37.7	0
Pro Totals—2 Years......................	18	109	40.4	0

LEONARD DAVID COLEMAN
Safety—San Diego Chargers
Born January 30, 1962, at Boynton Beach, Fla.
Height, 6.02. Weight, 202.
High School—Lake Worth, Fla.
Received degree from Vanderbilt University.
Cousin of Anthony Carter, wide receiver with Minnesota Vikings.

Selected by Memphis in 1984 USFL territorial draft.
Selected by Indianapolis in 1st round (8th player selected) of 1984 NFL draft.
Signed by Memphis Showboats, September 13, 1984.
Released by Memphis Showboats, September 18, 1985; signed by Indianapolis Colts, September 18, 1985.
Granted roster exemption, September 18 through September 29, 1985; activated, September 30, 1985.
On injured reserve with broken thumb, December 8 through remainder of 1987 season.
Traded by Indianapolis Colts to San Diego Chargers for future draft choice, July 8, 1988.

		——INTERCEPTIONS——			
Year Club	G.	No.	Yds.	Avg.	TD.
1985—Memphis USFL..............	18	2	6	3.0	0
1985—Indianapolis NFL.........	12		None		
1986—Indianapolis NFL.........	16	4	36	9.0	0
1987—Indianapolis NFL.........	4		None		
1988—San Diego NFL............	16	2	0	0.0	0
USFL Totals—1 Year..........	18	2	6	3.0	0
NFL Totals—4 Years..........	48	6	36	6.0	0
Pro Totals—5 Years............	66	8	42	5.3	0

Additional USFL statistics: Credited with one sack for nine yards and recovered four fumbles for 31 yards and a touchdown, 1985.
Additional NFL statistics: Recovered one fumble, 1986 and 1988.

MONTE COLEMAN
Linebacker—Washington Redskins
Born November 4, 1957, at Pine Bluff, Ark.
Height, 6.02. Weight, 230.
High School—Pine Bluff, Ark.
Attended Central Arkansas University.

Selected by Washington in 11th round (289th player selected) of 1979 NFL draft.
On injured reserve with thigh injury, September 16 through October 16, 1983; activated, October 17, 1983.
On injured reserve with strained hamstring, September 25 through November 8, 1985; activated, November 9, 1985.
On injured reserve with pulled hamstring, October 8 through November 7, 1986; activated, November 8, 1986.

Year Club	G.	—INTERCEPTIONS—			
		No.	Yds.	Avg.	TD.
1979—Washington NFL..........	16	1	13	13.0	0
1980—Washington NFL..........	16	3	92	30.7	0
1981—Washington NFL..........	12	3	52	17.3	1
1982—Washington NFL..........	8		None		
1983—Washington NFL..........	10		None		
1984—Washington NFL..........	16	1	49	49.0	1
1985—Washington NFL..........	10		None		
1986—Washington NFL..........	11		None		
1987—Washington NFL..........	12	2	53	26.5	0
1988—Washington NFL..........	13	1	11	11.0	0
Pro Totals—10 Years..........	124	11	270	24.5	2

Additional pro statistics: Recovered three fumbles, 1979; caught one pass for 12 yards, 1980; recovered two fumbles, 1980 and 1983; recovered one fumble for two yards, 1981; ran 27 yards with lateral on punt return and recovered one fumble, 1984; recovered one fumble for nine yards, 1988.
Played in NFC Championship Game following 1982, 1983, 1986 and 1987 seasons.
Played in NFL Championship Game following 1982, 1983 and 1987 seasons.

SIDNEY COLEMAN
Linebacker—Tampa Bay Buccaneers
Born January 14, 1964, at Gulfport, Miss.
Height, 6.02. Weight, 250.
High School—Gulfport, Miss., Harrison Central.
Attended University of Southern Mississippi.

Signed as free agent by Tampa Bay Buccaneers, April 29, 1988.
Tampa Bay NFL, 1988.
Games: 1988 (16).
Pro statistics: Recovered one fumble, 1988.

BRUCE STOKES COLLIE
Guard-Offensive Tackle—San Francisco 49ers
Born June 27, 1962, at Nuremburg, Germany.
Height, 6.06. Weight, 275.
High School—San Antonio, Tex., Robert E. Lee.
Attended University of Texas at Arlington.

Selected by Baltimore in 6th round (78th player selected) of 1985 USFL draft.
Selected by San Francisco in 5th round (140th player selected) of 1985 NFL draft.
Signed by San Francisco 49ers, June 25, 1985.
San Francisco NFL, 1985 through 1988.
Games: 1985 (16), 1986 (16), 1987 (11), 1988 (15). Total—58.
Played in NFC Championship Game following 1988 season.
Played in NFL Championship Game following 1988 season.

STEVEN ANDRE COLLIER
(Steve)
Offensive Tackle-Nose Tackle—New York Jets
Born April 19, 1963, at Chicago, Ill.
Height, 6.07. Weight, 342.
High School—Chicago, Ill., Whitney-Young.
Attended Garden City Community College, University of Illinois and Bethune-Cookman College.

Signed as free agent by Cleveland Browns, May 6, 1985.
Released by Cleveland Browns, August 21, 1985; signed as free agent by San Diego Chargers, April 15, 1986.
Released by San Diego Chargers, July 19, 1986; signed as free agent replacement player by Green Bay Packers, September 25, 1987.
On injured reserve with knee injury, August 23 through December 16, 1988; activated, December 17, 1988.
Granted unconditional free agency, February 1, 1989; signed by New York Jets, March 8, 1989.
Active for 1 game with Green Bay Packers in 1988; did not play.
Green Bay NFL, 1987 and 1988.
Games: 1987 (10).

JAMES BRIAN COLLINS
(Jim)
Linebacker—San Diego Chargers
Born June 11, 1958, at Orange, N.J.
Height, 6.02. Weight, 230.
High School—Mendham, N.J.
Received bachelor of science degree in psychology from Syracuse University in 1981.

Named to THE SPORTING NEWS NFL All-Star Team, 1985.
Selected by Los Angeles in 2nd round (43rd player selected) of 1981 NFL draft.
On injured reserve with pulled stomach muscle, September 1 through October 2, 1981; activated October 3, 1981.
On injured reserve with knee injury, December 4 through remainder of 1981 season.
On injured reserve with shoulder injury, August 25 through entire 1986 season.
Crossed picket line during players' strike, October 2, 1987.
On injured reserve with knee injury, August 29 through November 24, 1988; activated, November 25, 1988.
Granted unconditional free agency, February 1, 1989; signed by San Diego Chargers, March 31, 1989.

Year Club	G.	No.	Yds.	Avg.	TD.
1981—L.A. Rams NFL............	7		None		
1982—L.A. Rams NFL............	6		None		
1983—L.A. Rams NFL............	16	2	46	23.0	0
1984—L.A. Rams NFL............	16	2	43	21.5	0
1985—L.A. Rams NFL............	16	2	8	4.0	0
1987—L.A. Rams NFL............	15		None		
1988—L.A. Rams NFL............	4		None		
Pro Totals—7 Years............	80	6	97	16.2	0

Additional pro statistics: Recovered one fumble, 1983 and 1985; recovered two fumbles for 17 yards and fumbled once, 1984; recovered two fumbles, 1987.
Played in NFC Championship Game following 1985 season.
Played in Pro Bowl (NFL All-Star Game) following 1985 season.

MARK COLLINS
Cornerback—New York Giants

Born January 16, 1964, at San Bernardino, Calif.
Height, 5.10. Weight, 190.
High School—San Bernardino, Calif., Pacific.
Attended California State University at Fullerton.

Named as defensive back on THE SPORTING NEWS College All-America Team, 1985.
Selected by New York Giants in 2nd round (44th player selected) of 1986 NFL draft.
Signed by New York Giants, July 30, 1986.
On injured reserve with back injury, December 23 through remainder of 1987 season.
On injured reserve with pulled groin, December 3 through remainder of 1988 season.

Year Club	G.	-INTERCEPTIONS- No.	Yds.	Avg.	TD.	—KICKOFF RET.— No.	Yds.	Avg.	TD.	—TOTAL— TD.	Pts.	F.
1986—New York Giants NFL	15	1	0	0.0	0	11	204	18.5	0	0	0	2
1987—New York Giants NFL	11	2	28	14.0	0		None			0	0	0
1988—New York Giants NFL	11	1	13	13.0	0	4	67	16.8	0	0	†2	0
Pro Totals—3 Years.................	37	4	41	10.3	0	15	271	18.1	0	0	2	2

†Credited with a safety.
Additional pro statistics: Returned three punts for 11 yards and recovered three fumbles for five yards, 1986.
Played in NFC Championship Game following 1986 season.
Played in NFL Championship Game following 1986 season.

PATRICK COLLINS
Running Back—Cleveland Browns

Born August 4, 1966, at Tulsa, Okla.
Height, 5.09. Weight, 197.
High School—Tulsa, Okla., Booker T. Washington.
Attended University of Oklahoma.

Selected by Green Bay in 8th round (200th player selected) of 1988 NFL draft.
Signed by Green Bay Packers, July 16, 1988.
On injured reserve with hamstring injury, August 22 through October 20, 1988; activated, October 21, 1988.
Granted unconditional free agency, February 1, 1989; signed by Cleveland Browns, February 13, 1989.

Year Club	G.	——RUSHING—— Att.	Yds.	Avg.	TD.	PASS RECEIVING P.C.	Yds.	Avg.	TD.	—TOTAL— TD.	Pts.	F.
1988—Green Bay NFL.......................	5	2	2	1.0	0	2	17	8.5	0	0	0	0

ANTHONY CRIS COLLINSWORTH
(Known by middle name.)
Wide Receiver—Cincinnati Bengals

Born January 27, 1959, at Dayton, O.
Height, 6.05. Weight, 192.
High School—Titusville, Fla., Astronaut.
Received degree in accounting from University of Florida in 1981.

Selected by Cincinnati in 2nd round (37th player selected) of 1981 NFL draft.
Signed by Tampa Bay Bandits, June 27, 1983, for contract to take effect after being granted free agency, February 1, 1985.
Released by Tampa Bay Bandits, February 18, 1984; re-signed by Bengals, February 21, 1984.

Year Club	G.	P.C.	Yds.	Avg.	TD.
1981—Cincinnati NFL............	16	67	1009	15.1	8
1982—Cincinnati NFL............	9	49	700	14.3	1
1983—Cincinnati NFL............	14	66	1130	17.1	5
1984—Cincinnati NFL............	15	64	989	15.5	6
1985—Cincinnati NFL............	16	65	1125	17.3	5
1986—Cincinnati NFL............	16	62	1024	16.5	10
1987—Cincinnati NFL............	8	31	494	15.9	0
1988—Cincinnati NFL............	13	13	227	17.5	1
Pro Totals—8 Years............	107	417	6698	16.1	36

Additional pro statistics: Recovered one fumble, 1981, 1983 and 1984; fumbled three times, 1981; rushed once for minus 11 yards, 1982; fumbled once, 1982, 1985, 1986 and 1988; rushed twice for two yards and fumbled twice, 1983;

rushed once for seven yards, 1984; rushed once for three yards and attempted one pass with one interception, 1985; rushed twice for minus 16 yards, 1986.
Played in AFC Championship Game following 1981 and 1988 seasons.
Played in NFL Championship Game following 1981 and 1988 seasons.
Played in Pro Bowl (NFL All-Star Game) following 1981 through 1983 seasons.

DARREN COMEAUX
Linebacker—Seattle Seahawks
Born April 15, 1960, at San Diego, Calif.
Height, 6.01. Weight, 227.
High School—San Diego, Calif.
Attended San Diego Mesa College and Arizona State University.
Signed as free agent by Denver Broncos, April 30, 1982.
On injured reserve with broken foot, September 7 through December 15, 1982; activated, December 16, 1982.
Released by Denver Broncos, August 29, 1983; re-signed by Broncos, September 13, 1983.
Released by Denver Broncos, September 2, 1985; re-signed by Broncos, September 3, 1985.
On injured reserve with broken thumb, October 16 through November 21, 1985; activated, November 22, 1985.
Released by Denver Broncos, September 7, 1987; signed as free agent replacement player by San Francisco 49ers, October 8, 1987.
Released by San Francisco 49ers, November 3, 1987; re-signed by 49ers, November 6, 1987.
On injured reserve with knee and hamstring injuries, August 29 through October 12, 1988.
Released by San Francisco 49ers after clearing procedural waivers, October 13, 1988; awarded on waivers to Seattle Seahawks, October 14, 1988.
Denver NFL, 1982 through 1986; San Francisco NFL, 1987; Seattle NFL, 1988.
Games: 1982 (3), 1983 (14), 1984 (16), 1985 (11), 1986 (16), 1987 (8), 1988 (9). Total—77.
Pro statistics: Intercepted one pass for five yards, 1984; recovered one fumble, 1984 and 1986; intercepted one pass for 18 yards and fumbled once, 1988.
Played in AFC Championship Game following 1986 season.
Played in NFL Championship Game following 1986 season.

SHANE PATRICK CONLAN
Linebacker—Buffalo Bills
Born April 3, 1964, at Frewsburg, N.Y.
Height, 6.03. Weight, 235.
High School—Frewsburg, N.Y., Central.
Received degree in administration of justice from Penn State University in 1987.
Brother of Michael Conlan, linebacker at Rutgers University.
Named to THE SPORTING NEWS NFL All-Star Team, 1988.
Selected by Buffalo in 1st round (8th player selected) of 1987 draft.
Signed by Buffalo Bills, August 9, 1987.
Buffalo NFL, 1987 and 1988.
Games: 1987 (12), 1988 (13). Total—25.
Pro statistics: Intercepted one pass for no yards and recovered one fumble, 1988
Played in AFC Championship Game following 1988 season.
Member of Pro Bowl (NFL All-Star Game) following 1988 season; did not play.

CHRISTOPHER HOWARD CONLIN
(Chris)
Guard-Center—Miami Dolphins
Born June 7, 1965, at Philadelphia, Pa.
Height, 6.03. Weight, 280.
High School—Wyncote, Pa., Bishop McDevitt.
Attended Penn State University.
Brother of Craig Conlin, basketball center at LaSalle University.
Selected by Miami in 5th round (132nd player selected) of 1987 NFL draft.
Signed by Miami Dolphins, July 23, 1987.
On injured reserve with knee injury, December 4 through remainder of 1987 season.
On physically unable to perform/active with knee injury, July 12 through August 22, 1988; then transferred to physically unable to perform/reserve with knee injury, August 23 through entire 1988 season.
Miami NFL, 1987.
Games: 1987 (3).

WILLIAM CONTZ
(Bill)
Offensive Tackle—Denver Broncos
Born May 12, 1961, at Belle Vernon, Pa.
Height, 6.05. Weight, 280.
High School—Belle Vernon, Pa.
Received bachelor of science degree in business logistics
from Penn State University in 1983.
Selected by Philadelphia in 1983 USFL territorial draft.
Selected by Cleveland in 5th round (122nd player selected) of 1983 NFL draft.
Signed by Cleveland Browns, May 31, 1983.
On injured reserve with knee injury, December 12 through remainder of 1984 season.
On physically unable to perform/active with knee injury, August 20 through October 18, 1985; activated, October 19, 1985.

Released by Cleveland Browns, September 10, 1986; signed as free agent by New Orleans Saints, September 23, 1986.

On injured reserve with abdominal muscle injury, November 2 through December 9, 1988; activated, December 10, 1988.

Granted unconditional free agency, February 1, 1989; signed by Denver Broncos, March 28, 1989.

Cleveland NFL, 1983 through 1985; Cleveland (1)-New Orleans (13) NFL, 1986; New Orleans NFL, 1987 and 1988.

Games: 1983 (16), 1984 (15), 1985 (4), 1986 (14), 1987 (3), 1988 (11). Total—63.

Pro statistics: Returned one kickoff for three yards, 1983; returned one kickoff for 10 yards, 1984; recovered two fumbles, 1986.

TOI FITZGERALD COOK

(First name pronounced Toy.)

Safety—New Orleans Saints

Born December 3, 1964, at Chicago, Ill.
Height, 5.11. Weight, 188.
High School—Montclair, Calif.
Attended Stanford University.

Selected by New Orleans in 8th round (207th player selected) of 1987 NFL draft.

Signed by New Orleans Saints, July 24, 1987.

Selected by Minnesota Twins' organization in 38th round of free-agent draft, June 2, 1987.

New Orleans NFL, 1987 and 1988.

Games: 1987 (7), 1988 (16). Total—23.

Pro statistics: Returned one punt for three yards, 1987; intercepted one pass for no yards, 1988.

JOHNIE EARL COOKS

Linebacker—New York Giants

Born November 23, 1958, at Leland, Miss.
Height, 6.04. Weight, 251.
High School—Leland, Miss.
Received degree in physical education from Mississippi State University.

Named as linebacker on THE SPORTING NEWS College All-America Team, 1981.

Selected by Baltimore in 1st round (2nd player selected) of 1982 NFL draft.

Franchise transferred to Indianapolis, March 31, 1984.

Released by Indianapolis Colts, September 13, 1988; awarded on waivers to New York Giants, September 15, 1988.

Baltimore NFL, 1982 and 1983; Indianapolis NFL, 1984 through 1987; Indianapolis (1)-New York Giants (13) NFL, 1988.

Games: 1982 (9), 1983 (16), 1984 (16), 1985 (16), 1986 (15), 1987 (10), 1988 (14). Total—96.

Pro statistics: Recovered one fumble, 1982, 1987 and 1988; intercepted one pass for 15 yards and recovered two fumbles for 52 yards and a touchdown, 1983; fumbled once, 1983 and 1987; intercepted one pass for seven yards, 1985; intercepted one pass for one yard, 1986; intercepted one pass for two yards, 1987.

RAYFORD E. COOKS

Defensive End—Phoenix Cardinals

Born August 25, 1962, at Dallas, Tex.
Height, 6.03. Weight, 245.
High School—Dallas, Tex., L.G. Pinkston.
Attended North Texas State University.

Selected by Houston in 15th round (314th player selected) of 1984 USFL draft.

Signed by Houston Gamblers, October 1, 1984.

On developmental squad, February 21 through March 23, 1985; activated, March 24, 1985.

Released by Houston Gamblers, July 31, 1985; awarded on waivers to Jacksonville Bulls, August 1, 1985.

Granted free agency when USFL suspended operations, August 7, 1986; signed by Montreal Alouettes, August 27, 1986.

Granted free agency when Montreal Alouettes suspended operations, June 24, 1987; signed as replacement player by Houston Oilers, September 23, 1987.

Released by Houston Oilers, August 24, 1988; signed as free agent by Phoenix Cardinals, January 4, 1989.

On developmental squad for 4 games with Houston Gamblers in 1985.

Houston USFL, 1985; Montreal CFL, 1986; Houston NFL, 1987.

Games: 1985 (14), 1986 (6), 1987 (10). Total—30.

USFL statistics: Credited with 3½ sacks for 27½ yards and recovered three fumbles, 1985.

CFL statistics: Recovered one fumble, 1986.

ALEXANDER LOUIS COOPER

(Known by middle name.)

Linebacker—Kansas City Chiefs

Born August 5, 1963, at Marion, S.C.
Height, 6.02. Weight, 245.
High School—Marion, S.C.
Attended West Carolina University.

Selected by Orlando in 6th round (76th player selected) of 1985 USFL draft.

Selected by Seattle in 11th round (305th player selected) of 1985 NFL draft.

Signed by Seattle Seahawks, July 17, 1985.

Released by Seattle Seahawks, August 27, 1985; signed as free agent by Kansas City Chiefs, September 17, 1985.

On injured reserve with ankle injury, October 14 through November 20, 1985; activated after clearing procedural waivers, November 22, 1985.

Released by Kansas City Chiefs, August 26, 1986; re-signed by Chiefs, September 2, 1986.
On injured reserve with elbow injury, November 10 through December 11, 1988; activated, December 12, 1988.
Kansas City NFL, 1985 through 1988.
Games: 1985 (8), 1986 (16), 1987 (12), 1988 (11). Total—47.
Pro statistics: Recovered one fumble, 1986; intercepted one pass for no yards, 1987.

EVAN COOPER
Safety-Defensive Back—Atlanta Falcons
Born June 28, 1962, at Miami, Fla.
Height, 5.11. Weight, 194.
High School—Miami, Fla., Killian.
Received bachelor of science degree in communications
from University of Michigan in 1984.

Selected by Michigan in 1984 USFL territorial draft.
Selected by Philadelphia in 4th round (88th player selected) of 1984 NFL draft.
Signed by Philadelphia Eagles, June 11, 1984.
Traded by Philadelphia Eagles to Houston Oilers for conditional future draft choice, July 23, 1988.
Released by Houston Oilers, August 24, 1988; signed as free agent by Atlanta Falcons, October 18, 1988.

Year Club	G.	INTERCEPTIONS No.	Yds.	Avg.	TD.	-PUNT RETURNS- No.	Yds.	Avg.	TD.	—KICKOFF RET.— No.	Yds.	Avg.	TD.	—TOTAL— TD.	Pts.	F.
1984—Philadelphia NFL	16	None				40	250	6.3	0	17	299	17.6	0	0	0	0
1985—Philadelphia NFL	16	2	13	6.5	0	43	364	8.5	0	3	32	10.7	0	0	0	1
1986—Philadelphia NFL	16	3	20	6.7	0	16	139	8.7	0	2	42	21.0	0	0	0	2
1987—Philadelphia NFL	12	2	0	0.0	0	None				5	86	17.2	0	0	0	1
1988—Atlanta NFL	9	None				2	10	5.0	0	16	331	20.7	0	0	0	1
Pro Totals—5 Years	69	7	33	4.7	0	101	763	7.6	0	43	790	18.4	0	0	0	5

Additional pro statistics: Recovered one fumble, 1985 and 1986.

GEORGE JUNIOUS COOPER
Linebacker—Kansas City Chiefs
Born December 24, 1958, at Detroit, Mich.
Height, 6.02. Weight, 225.
High School—Detroit, Mich., Northern.
Received bachelor of arts degree in art and industrial design from Michigan State University in 1982.

Signed as free agent by Pittsburgh Steelers, May 22, 1982.
Released by Pittsburgh Steelers, August 30, 1982.
USFL rights traded with rights to offensive tackles Bob Gruber and Brad Oates, quarterback Dan Kendra and tight end Al Kimichik by Michigan Panthers to Philadelphia Stars for rights to quarterback Dan Feraday, running back Jim Jodat and linebacker Ed O'Neil, September 27, 1982.
Signed by Philadelphia Stars, September 27, 1982.
On developmental squad, April 2 through May 5, 1983; activated, May 6, 1983.
Franchise transferred to Baltimore, November 1, 1984.
Granted free agency when USFL suspended operations, August 7, 1986; signed as free agent by San Francisco 49ers, May 20, 1987.
Crossed picket line during players' strike, October 7, 1987.
On injured reserve with ankle injury, November 21 through December 14, 1987.
Released by San Francisco 49ers, December 15, 1987; re-signed by 49ers after clearing procedural waivers, December 18, 1987.
Released by San Francisco 49ers, August 30, 1988; signed as free agent by Kansas City Chiefs, February 16, 1989.
On developmental squad for 5 games with Philadelphia Stars in 1983.
Philadelphia USFL, 1983 and 1984; Baltimore USFL, 1985; San Francisco NFL, 1987.
Games: 1983 (13), 1984 (18), 1985 (18), 1987 (10). USFL—49. Total Pro—59.
Pro statistics: Intercepted one pass for 16 yards, credited with ½ sack for 5½ yards and recovered one fumble, 1983; credited with six sacks for 52 yards, intercepted two passes for 10 yards and recovered one fumble for four yards, 1984; intercepted two passes for six yards, credited with four sacks for 30 yards and recovered two fumbles, 1985.
Played in USFL Championship Game following 1983 through 1985 seasons.

MARK SAMUEL COOPER
Offensive Tackle—Tampa Bay Buccaneers
Born February 14, 1960, at Camden, N.J.
Height, 6.05. Weight, 280.
High School—Miami, Fla., Killian.
Received bachelor of arts degree in communications
from University of Miami (Fla.) in 1983.

Selected by New Jersey in 5th round (60th player selected) of 1983 USFL draft.
Selected by Denver in 2nd round (31st player selected) of 1983 NFL draft.
Signed by Denver Broncos, June 26, 1983.
On injured reserve with sprained ankle, December 13 through remainder of 1984 season.
On injured reserve with foot injury, October 22 through December 4, 1986; activated, December 5, 1986.
Released by Denver Broncos, November 10, 1987; signed as free agent by Tampa Bay Buccaneers, November 17, 1987.
Denver NFL, 1983 through 1986; Denver (5)-Tampa Bay (4) NFL, 1987; Tampa Bay NFL, 1988.
Games: 1983 (10), 1984 (15), 1985 (15), 1986 (8), 1987 (9), 1988 (15). Total—72.
Pro statistics: Caught one pass for 13 yards, 1985.
Played in AFC Championship Game following 1986 season.
Played in NFC Championship Game following 1986 season.

DOUGLAS DURANT COSBIE
(Doug)
Tight End—Denver Broncos

Born March 27, 1956, at Palo Alto, Calif.
Height, 6.06. Weight, 244.
High School—Mt. View, Calif., St. Francis.
Attended College of the Holy Cross, DeAnza College and received bachelor of science degree
in marketing from University of Santa Clara in 1979.

Selected by Dallas in 3rd round (76th player selected) of 1979 NFL draft.
USFL rights traded by Michigan Panthers to Oakland Invaders for rights to placekicker Wilson Alvarez, September 2, 1982.
On injured reserve with knee injury, November 23 through remainder of 1988 season.
Granted unconditional free agency, February 1, 1989; signed by Denver Broncos, March 30, 1989.

| | —PASS RECEIVING— | | | | | | —PASS RECEIVING— | | | | |
Year Club	G.	P.C.	Yds.	Avg.	TD.	Year Club	G.	P.C.	Yds.	Avg.	TD.
1979—Dallas NFL	16	5	36	7.2	0	1985—Dallas NFL	16	64	793	12.4	6
1980—Dallas NFL	16	2	11	5.5	1	1986—Dallas NFL	16	28	312	11.1	1
1981—Dallas NFL	16	17	225	13.2	5	1987—Dallas NFL	12	36	421	11.7	3
1982—Dallas NFL	9	30	441	14.7	4	1988—Dallas NFL	11	12	112	9.3	0
1983—Dallas NFL	16	46	588	12.8	6	Pro Totals—10 Years	144	300	3728	12.4	30
1984—Dallas NFL	16	60	789	13.2	4						

Additional pro statistics: Fumbled once, 1979, 1981 and 1984; returned one kickoff for 13 yards and recovered two fumbles, 1980; rushed four times for 33 yards and returned one kickoff for no yards, 1981; rushed once for minus two yards and returned one kickoff for four yards, 1982; returned two kickoffs for 17 yards, 1983; fumbled twice, 1985; rushed once for nine yards, 1986; rushed once for minus five yards, 1987.
Played in NFC Championship Game following 1980 through 1982 seasons.
Played in Pro Bowl (NFL All-Star Game) following 1983 through 1985 seasons.

JOSEPH PATRICK COSTELLO JR.
(Joe)
Linebacker—Los Angeles Raiders

Born June 1, 1960, at New York, N.Y.
Height, 6.03. Weight, 244.
High School—Stratford, Conn.
Received bachelor of science degree in accounting from Central Connecticut State University in 1982.

Signed as free agent by Montreal Concordes, March, 1982.
Released by Montreal Concordes, June 30, 1983; signed by Jacksonville Bulls, October 20, 1983.
Released by Jacksonville Bulls, February 28, 1986; signed as free agent by Cleveland Browns, April 21, 1986.
Released by Cleveland Browns, September 3, 1986; signed as free agent by Atlanta Falcons, September 17, 1986.
On injured reserve with broken arm, August 31 through October 30, 1987; activated, October 31, 1987.
Crossed picket line during player's strike, October 2, 1987.
On injured reserve with calf and ankle injuries, October 15 through remainder of 1988 season.
Granted unconditional free agency, February 1, 1989; signed by Los Angeles Raiders, March 14, 1989.
Montreal CFL, 1982; Jacksonville USFL, 1984 and 1985; Atlanta NFL, 1986 through 1988.
Games: 1982 (2), 1984 (18), 1985 (18), 1986 (14), 1987 (9), 1988 (6). Total USFL—36. Total NFL—29. Total Pro—67.
Pro statistics: Credited with 4½ sacks for 40½ yards, 1984; credited with 4½ sacks for 36 yards, 1985.

MARCUS GLENN COTTON
Linebacker—Atlanta Falcons

Born August 11, 1966, at Los Angeles, Calif.
Height, 6.03. Weight, 225.
High School—Oakland, Calif., Castlemont.
Attended University of Southern California.

Selected by Atlanta in 2nd round (28th player selected) of 1988 NFL draft.
Signed by Atlanta Falcons, May 27, 1988.
Atlanta NFL, 1988.
Games: 1988 (11).

VINCENT ERIC COURVILLE
(Vince)
Wide Receiver—Houston Oilers

Born December 5, 1959, at Galveston, Tex.
Height, 5.10. Weight, 165.
High School—Galveston, Tex., Ball.
Attended Ranger Junior College,
Texas Southern University and Rice University.

Signed as free agent by Montreal Concordes, April 29, 1983.
Released by Montreal Concordes, June 2, 1983; signed as free agent by Los Angeles Raiders, June 12, 1983.
Released by Los Angeles Raiders, August 29, 1983; signed by Houston Gamblers, October 24, 1983.
On developmental squad, February 24 through April 5, 1984; activated, April 6, 1984.
On developmental squad, April 14 through May 10, 1984; activated, May 11, 1984.
Granted free agency, August 1, 1986; signed as free agent by Atlanta Falcons, August 7, 1986.
Released by Atlanta Falcons, August 26, 1986; signed as free agent by Dallas Cowboys and placed on reserve/future list, December 19, 1986.
Released by Dallas Cowboys, August 31, 1987; re-signed as replacement player by Cowboys, September 23, 1987.

Released by Dallas Cowboys, October 20, 1987; signed as free agent by New York Knights (Arena Football), April 10, 1988.
Granted free agency, July 17, 1988; signed as free agent by Buffalo Bills, August 1, 1988.
Released by Buffalo Bills, August 16, 1988; signed as free agent by Houston Oilers, April 20, 1989.
On developmental squad for 10 games with Houston Gamblers in 1984.

Year Club	G.	PASS RECEIVING				—KICKOFF RET.—				—TOTAL—		
		P.C.	Yds.	Avg.	TD.	No.	Yds.	Avg.	TD.	TD.	Pts.	F.
1984—Houston USFL	8	4	83	20.8	1	9	171	19.0	0	1	6	1
1985—Houston USFL	18	25	473	18.9	4	18	434	24.1	0	4	24	0
1987—Dallas NFL	2	None				None				0	0	0
1988—New York AF	12	28	313	11.2	3	33	622	18.8	2	5	30	
USFL Totals—2 Years	26	29	556	19.2	5	27	605	22.4	0	5	30	1
NFL Totals—1 Year	2	0	0	0.0	0	0	0	0.0	0	0	0	0
Pro Totals—3 Years	28	29	556	19.2	5	27	605	22.4	0	5	30	1

Additional USFL statistics: Rushed once for 11 yards and recovered one fumble, 1984.
Additional Arena Football statistics: Recovered one fumble, 1988.

JAMES PAUL COVERT
(Jim)
Offensive Tackle—Chicago Bears
Born March 22, 1960, at Conway, Pa.
Height, 6.04. Weight, 275.
High School—Freedom, Pa., Area.
Attended University of Pittsburgh.
Named to THE SPORTING NEWS NFL All-Star Team, 1985 and 1986.
Selected by Tampa Bay in 1st round (12th player selected) of 1983 USFL draft.
Selected by Chicago in 1st round (6th player selected) of 1983 NFL draft.
Signed by Chicago Bears, July 20, 1983.
On injured reserve with back injury, September 30 through November 4, 1988; activated, November 5, 1988.
Chicago NFL, 1983 through 1988.
Games: 1983 (16), 1984 (16), 1985 (15), 1986 (16), 1987 (9), 1988 (9). Total—81.
Pro statistics: Recovered one fumble, 1983, 1986 and 1987; recovered two fumbles, 1984.
Played in NFC Championship Game following 1984, 1985 and 1988 seasons.
Played in NFL Championship Game following 1985 season.
Played in Pro Bowl (NFL All-Star Game) following 1985 and 1986 seasons.

AARON DION COX
Wide Receiver—Los Angeles Rams
Born March 13, 1965, at Los Angeles, Calif.
Height, 5.09. Weight, 174.
High School—Los Angeles, Calif., Dorsey.
Attended Arizona State University.
Selected by Los Angeles Rams in 1st round (20th player selected) of 1988 NFL draft.
Signed by Los Angeles Rams, July 19, 1988.

Year Club	G.	PASS RECEIVING			
		P.C.	Yds.	Avg.	TD.
1988—L.A. Rams NFL	16	28	590	21.1	5

ARTHUR DEAN COX
Tight End—San Diego Chargers
Born February 5, 1961, at Plant City, Fla.
Height, 6.02. Weight, 277.
High School—Plant City, Fla.
Attended Texas Southern University.
Signed as free agent by Atlanta Falcons, May 4, 1983.
Granted free agency, February 1, 1988; withdrew qualifying offer, May 2, 1988.
Signed by San Diego Chargers, May 10, 1988.

Year Club	G.	PASS RECEIVING			
		P.C.	Yds.	Avg.	TD.
1983—Atlanta NFL	15	9	83	9.2	1
1984—Atlanta NFL	16	34	329	9.7	3
1985—Atlanta NFL	16	33	454	13.8	2
1986—Atlanta NFL	16	24	301	12.5	1
1987—Atlanta NFL	12	11	101	9.2	0
1988—San Diego NFL	16	18	144	8.0	0
Pro Totals—6 Years	91	129	1412	10.9	7

Additional pro statistics: Fumbled once, 1983, 1984 and 1986; recovered two fumbles, 1986; fumbled twice and returned one kickoff for 11 yards, 1987.

—DID YOU KNOW—
That there were nine overtime games played in the NFL in 1988?

GREGORY MARK COX
(Greg)
Safety—New York Giants
Born January 6, 1965, at Niagara Falls, N. Y.
Height, 6.00. Weight, 223.
High School—Columbus, O., Walnut Ridge.
Attended Hartnell Community College and San Jose State University.

Signed as free agent by San Francisco 49ers, May 23, 1988.
Granted free agency, February 1, 1989; signed by New York Giants, March 16, 1989.
San Francisco NFL, 1988.
Games: 1988 (15).
Played in NFC Championship Game following 1988 season.
Played in NFL Championship Game following 1988 season.

ROBERT LLOYD COX
Offensive Tackle—Los Angeles Rams
Born December 30, 1963, at San Francisco, Calif.
Height, 6.05. Weight, 270.
High School—Dublin, Calif.
Attended Chabot College and University of California at Los Angeles.

Selected by Arizona in 1986 USFL territorial draft.
Selected by Los Angeles Rams in 6th round (144th player selected) of 1986 NFL draft.
Signed by Los Angeles Rams, July 22, 1986.
On injured reserve with ankle injury, August 27 through entire 1986 season.
Los Angeles Rams NFL, 1987 and 1988.
Games: 1987 (10), 1988 (16). Total—26.
Pro statistics: Returned one kickoff for 12 yards, 1987.

ERIC COYLE
Center—Dallas Cowboys
Born October 26, 1963, at Longmont, Colo.
Height, 6.03. Weight, 260.
High School—Longmont, Colo.
Attended University of Colorado.

Signed as free agent by Washington Redskins, May 4, 1987.
Released by Washington Redskins, August 31, 1987; re-signed as replacement player by Redskins, September 23, 1987.
On injured reserve with back injury, November 3 through remainder of 1987 season.
On injured reserve with neck injury, September 21 through remainder of 1988 season.
Granted unconditional free agency, February 1, 1989; signed by Dallas Cowboys, March 24, 1989.
Active for 1 game with Washington Redskins in 1988; did not play.
Washington NFL, 1987 and 1988.
Games: 1987 (3).

FRANCISCO LUIS CRAIG
(Paco)
Wide Receiver—Atlanta Falcons
Born February 2, 1965, at Santa Maria, Calif.
Height, 5.10. Weight, 170.
High School—Riverside, Calif., Ramona.
Attended University of California at Los Angeles.

Selected by Detroit in 10th round (254th player selected) of 1988 NFL draft.
Signed by Detroit Lions, July 16, 1988.
Released by Detroit Lions, November 10, 1988; signed as free agent by Atlanta Falcons, January 20, 1989.
Detroit NFL, 1988.
Games: 1988 (8).
Pro statistics: Caught two passes for 29 yards, 1988.

ROGER TIMOTHY CRAIG
Running Back—San Francisco 49ers
Born July 10, 1960, at Davenport, Ia.
Height, 6.00. Weight, 222.
High School—Davenport, Ia., Central.
Attended University of Nebraska.

Established NFL record for most pass receptions by running back, season (92), 1985.
Named to THE SPORTING NEWS NFL All-Star Team, 1988.
Selected by Boston in 1983 USFL territorial draft.
Selected by San Francisco in 2nd round (49th player selected) of 1983 NFL draft.
Signed by San Francisco 49ers, June 13, 1983.
Crossed picket line during players' strike, October 7, 1987.

| | | —RUSHING— | | | | PASS RECEIVING | | | | —TOTAL— | | |
Year Club	G.	Att.	Yds.	Avg.	TD.	P.C.	Yds.	Avg.	TD.	TD.	Pts.	F.
1983—San Francisco NFL	16	176	725	4.1	8	48	427	8.9	4	12	72	6
1984—San Francisco NFL	16	155	649	4.2	7	71	675	9.5	3	10	60	3

Year Club	G.	RUSHING Att.	Yds.	Avg.	TD.	PASS RECEIVING P.C.	Yds.	Avg.	TD.	TOTAL TD.	Pts.	F.
1985—San Francisco NFL	16	214	1050	4.9	9	*92	1016	11.0	6	15	90	5
1986—San Francisco NFL	16	204	830	4.1	7	81	624	7.7	0	7	42	4
1987—San Francisco NFL	14	215	815	3.8	3	66	492	7.5	1	4	24	5
1988—San Francisco NFL	16	310	1502	4.8	9	76	534	7.0	1	10	60	8
Pro Totals—6 Years	94	1274	5571	4.4	43	434	3768	8.7	15	58	348	31

Additional pro statistics: Recovered one fumble, 1983, 1984 and 1986; recovered two fumbles, 1987 and 1988; returned two kickoffs for 32 yards, 1988.
Played in NFC Championship Game following 1983, 1984 and 1988 seasons.
Played in NFL Championship Game following 1984 and 1988 seasons.
Played in Pro Bowl (NFL All-Star Game) following 1985, 1987 and 1988 seasons.

DERRICK LORWENZO CRAWFORD
Wide Receiver-Kick Returner—Cleveland Browns
Born September 3, 1960, at Memphis, Tenn.
Height, 5.10. Weight, 185.
High School—Memphis, Tenn., East.
Attended Memphis State University.

Named as kickoff returner on THE SPORTING NEWS USFL All-Star Team, 1984.
Selected by Memphis in 1984 USFL territorial draft.
Signed by Memphis Showboats, January 21, 1984.
Selected by San Francisco in 1st round (24th player selected) of 1984 NFL supplemental draft.
Granted free agency when USFL suspended operations, August 7, 1986; signed by San Francisco 49ers, August 12, 1986.
On injured reserve with shoulder injury, August 26 through October 17, 1986; activated, October 18, 1986.
On injured reserve with foot injury, August 28 through entire 1987 season.
Released by San Francisco 49ers, August 23, 1988; signed as free agent by Cleveland Browns, March 8, 1989.

Year Club	G.	RUSHING Att.	Yds.	Avg.	TD.	PASS RECEIVING P.C.	Yds.	Avg.	TD.	TOTAL TD.	Pts.	F.
1984—Memphis USFL	18	13	27	2.1	0	61	703	11.5	12	13	78	7
1985—Memphis USFL	18	1	6	6.0	0	70	1057	15.1	9	10	60	1
1986—San Francisco NFL	10			None		5	70	14.0	0	0	0	1
USFL Totals—2 Years	36	14	33	2.4	0	131	1760	13.4	21	23	138	8
NFL Totals—1 Year	10	0	0	0.0	0	5	70	14.0	0	0	0	1
Pro Totals—3 Years	46	14	33	2.4	0	136	1830	13.5	21	23	138	9

Year Club	G.	PUNT RETURNS No.	Yds.	Avg.	TD.	KICKOFF RET. No.	Yds.	Avg.	TD.
1984—Memphis USFL	18	3	—1	—0.3	0	*47	*1237	*26.3	*1
1985—Memphis USFL	18	8	184	23.0	1	11	263	23.9	0
1986—San Francisco NFL	10	4	15	3.8	0	15	280	18.7	0
USFL Totals—2 Years	36	11	183	16.6	1	58	1500	25.9	1
NFL Totals—1 Year	10	4	15	3.8	0	15	280	18.7	0
Pro Totals—3 Years	46	15	198	13.2	1	73	1780	24.4	1

Additional USFL statistics: Recovered five fumbles, 1984; recovered three fumbles, 1985.
Additional NFL statistics: Recovered one fumble, 1986.

JEFF CRISWELL
Offensive Tackle-Guard—New York Jets
Born March 7, 1964, at Grinnell, Ia.
Height, 6.07. Weight, 284.
High School—Sully, Ia., Lynnville-Sully.
Received bachelor of arts degree in education
from Graceland College.

Signed as free agent replacement player by Indianapolis Colts, September 26, 1987.
Released by Indianapolis Colts, October 19, 1988; signed as free agent by New York Jets, May 3, 1988.
Indianapolis NFL, 1987; New York Jets NFL, 1988.
Games: 1987 (3), 1988 (15). Total—18.

JEFFREY ALLEN CROSS
(Jeff)
Defensive End—Miami Dolphins
Born March 25, 1966, at Riverside, Calif.
Height, 6.04. Weight, 270.
High School—Blythe, Calif., Palo Verde Valley.
Attended Riverside City College and University of Missouri.

Selected by Miami in 9th round (239th player selected) of 1988 NFL draft.
Signed by Miami Dolphins, July 11, 1988.
Miami NFL, 1988.
Games: 1988 (16).

DAVID CHARLES CROSTON
(Dave)
Offensive Tackle—Green Bay Packers

Born November 10, 1963, at Sioux City, Ia.
Height, 6.05. Weight, 280.
High School—Sioux City, Ia., East.
Received bachelor's degree in business administration from University of Iowa in 1987.
Brother of Jeff Croston, offensive tackle at University of Iowa.

Named as offensive tackle on THE SPORTING NEWS College All-America Team, 1986.
Selected by Green Bay in 3rd round (61st player selected) of 1987 NFL draft.
Signed by Green Bay Packers, July 24, 1987.
On injured reserve with elbow injury, September 7 through entire 1987 season.
Green Bay NFL, 1988.
Games: 1988 (16).

RANDALL CUNNINGHAM
Quarterback—Philadelphia Eagles

Born March 27, 1963, at Santa Barbara, Calif.
Height, 6.04. Weight, 201.
High School—Santa Barbara, Calif.
Attended University of Nevada at Las Vegas.
Brother of Sam Cunningham, running back with New England Patriots,
1973 through 1979, 1981 and 1982.

Named as punter on THE SPORTING NEWS College All-America Team, 1984.
Selected by Arizona in 1985 USFL territorial draft.
Selected by Philadelphia in 2nd round (37th player selected) of 1985 NFL draft.
Signed by Philadelphia Eagles, July 22, 1985.

				PASSING						RUSHING				TOTAL	
Year Club	G.	Att.	Cmp.	Pct.	Gain	T.P.	P.I.	Avg.	Att.	Yds.	Avg.	TD.	TD.	Pts.	F.
1985—Philadelphia NFL	6	81	34	42.0	548	1	8	6.77	29	205	7.1	0	0	0	3
1986—Philadelphia NFL	15	209	111	53.1	1391	8	7	6.66	66	540	8.2	5	5	30	7
1987—Philadelphia NFL	12	406	223	54.9	2786	23	12	6.86	76	505	6.6	3	3	18	*12
1988—Philadelphia NFL	16	560	301	53.8	3808	24	16	6.80	93	624	6.7	6	6	36	*12
Pro Totals—4 Years	49	1256	669	53.3	8533	56	43	6.79	264	1874	7.1	14	14	84	34

Quarterback Rating Points: 1985 (29.8), 1986 (72.9), 1987 (83.0), 1988 (77.6). Total—75.6.
Additional pro statistics: Punted twice for 27.0 avg. and recovered four fumbles, 1986; caught one pass for minus three yards, recovered six fumbles and fumbled 12 times for minus seven yards, 1987; punted three times for 55.7 avg. and recovered six fumbles, 1988.
Played in Pro Bowl (NFL All-Star Game) following 1988 season.

ALSTON SCOTT CURTIS
(Known by middle name.)
Linebacker—Denver Broncos

Born December 26, 1964, at Burlington, Vt.
Height, 6.01. Weight, 230.
High School—Lynnfield, Mass.
Attended University of New Hampshire.

Signed as free agent by Philadelphia Eagles, April 27, 1988.
Granted unconditional free agency, February 1, 1989; signed by Denver Broncos, February 28, 1989.
Philadelphia NFL, 1988.
Games: 1988 (16).

TRAVIS CURTIS
Safety—Minnesota Vikings

Born September 27, 1965, at Potomac, Md.
Height, 5.10. Weight, 180.
High School—Potomac, Md., Winston Churchill.
Attended West Virginia University.

Signed as free agent by St. Louis Cardinals, May 20, 1987.
Released by St. Louis Cardinals, September 7, 1987; re-signed by Cardinals, September 9, 1987.
Crossed picket line during player's strike, October 14, 1987.
Franchise transferred to Phoenix, March 15, 1988.
On injured reserve with ankle injury, November 22 through December 7, 1988; re-signed after clearing procedural waivers, December 8, 1988.
Lost to Washington Redskins in procedural waivers, December 9, 1988.
Granted unconditional free agency, February 1, 1989; signed by Minnesota Vikings, March 16, 1989.

		INTERCEPTIONS		
Year Club	G.	No.	Yds.	Avg.	TD.
1987—St. Louis NFL	13	5	65	13.0	0
1988—Pho.(12)-Was.(1) NFL	13	1	18	18.0	0
Pro Totals—2 Years	26	6	83	13.8	0

KENNETH RAY DALLAFIOR

Name pronounced DAL-uh-for.

(Ken)

Offensive Tackle-Guard—Detroit Lions

Born August 26, 1959, at Royal Oak, Mich.
Height, 6.04. Weight, 277.
High School—Madison Heights, Mich., Madison.
Received bachelor of arts and science degree in business studies
from University of Minnesota in 1982.

Selected by Pittsburgh in 5th round (124th player selected) of 1982 NFL draft.
On injured reserve with sprained neck, September 6 through entire 1982 season.
Released by Pittsburgh Steelers, August 29, 1983; signed as free agent by Michigan Panthers, October 26, 1983.
Not protected in merger of Michigan Panthers and Oakland Invaders; selected by New Jersey Generals, December 6, 1984.
Released by New Jersey Generals, January 28, 1985; signed as free agent by San Diego Chargers, June 21, 1985.
Released by San Diego Chargers, September 2, 1985; re-signed by Chargers, December 4, 1985.
On injured reserve with knee injury, August 26 through October 4, 1986; activated after clearing procedural waivers, October 6, 1986.
Released by San Diego Chargers, August 30, 1988; re-signed by Chargers, September 21, 1988.
Granted unconditional free agency, February 1, 1989; signed by Detroit Lions, April 1, 1989.
Michigan USFL, 1984: San Diego NFL, 1985 through 1988.
Games: 1984 (18), 1985 (3), 1986 (12), 1987 (8), 1988 (13). Total NFL—36. Total Pro—54.
Pro statistics: Recovered two fumbles, 1988.

COACHING RECORD

Assistant coach at Madison High School, Madison Heights, Mich., 1985.

EUGENE DANIEL JR.

Cornerback—Indianapolis Colts

Born May 4, 1961, at Baton Rouge, La.
Height, 5.11. Weight, 179.
High School—Baton Rouge, La., Robert E. Lee.
Received degree in marketing from Louisiana State University.

Selected by New Orleans in 1984 USFL territorial draft.
Selected by Indianapolis in 8th round (205th player selected) of 1984 NFL draft.
Signed by Indianapolis Colts, June 21, 1984.

Year Club	G.	No.	Yds.	Avg.	TD.
1984—Indianapolis NFL	15	6	25	4.2	0
1985—Indianapolis NFL	16	8	53	6.6	0
1986—Indianapolis NFL	15	3	11	3.7	0
1987—Indianapolis NFL	12	2	34	17.0	0
1988—Indianapolis NFL	16	2	44	22.0	1
Pro Totals—5 Years	74	21	167	8.0	1

Additional pro statistics: Returned one punt for six yards, recovered three fumbles for 25 yards and fumbled once, 1985; returned blocked punt 13 yards for a touchdown and recovered one fumble, 1986.

BYRON DARBY

Nose Tackle—Los Angeles Rams

Born June 4, 1960, at Los Angeles, Calif.
Height, 6.04. Weight, 260.
High School—Inglewood, Calif.
Attended University of Southern California.

Selected by Los Angeles in 1983 USFL territorial draft.
Selected by Philadelphia in 5th round (120th player selected) of 1983 NFL draft.
Signed by Philadelphia Eagles, May 25, 1983.
On injured reserve with knee injury, September 25 through November 4, 1985; activated, November 5, 1985.
Granted free agency, February 1, 1987; withdrew qualifying offer, August 1, 1987.
Signed by Indianapolis Colts, August 3, 1987.
Granted unconditional free agency, February 1, 1989; signed by Los Angeles Rams, March 17, 1989.
Philadelphia NFL, 1983 through 1986; Indianapolis NFL, 1987 and 1988.
Games: 1983 (16), 1984 (16), 1985 (10), 1986 (16), 1987 (12), 1988 (16). Total—86.
Pro statistics: Returned two kickoffs for three yards and fumbled once, 1983; caught two passes for 16 yards, 1986.

MATTHEW WAYNE DARWIN

(Matt)

Offensive Tackle—Philadelphia Eagles

Born March 11, 1963, at Houston, Tex.
Height, 6.04. Weight, 275.
High Schools—Colorado Springs, Colo., Cheyenne Mountain;
and Houston, Tex., Klein.
Attended Texas A&M University.

Selected by Houston in 1985 USFL territorial draft.
Selected by Dallas in 5th round (119th player selected) of 1985 NFL draft.

On reserve/did not sign entire 1985 season through April 28, 1986.
Selected by Philadelphia in 4th round (106th player selected) of 1986 NFL draft.
Signed by Philadelphia Eagles, July 31, 1986.
Philadelphia NFL, 1986 through 1988.
Games: 1986 (16), 1987 (12), 1988 (16). Total—44.
Pro statistics: Recovered one fumble, 1987 and 1988.

RONALD DONOVAN DAVENPORT
(Ron)
Fullback—Miami Dolphins

Born December 22, 1962, at Summerset, Bermuda.
Height, 6.02. Weight, 230.
High School—Atlanta, Ga., Walter F. George.
Attended University of Louisville.

Selected by Memphis in 9th round (120th player selected) of 1985 USFL draft.
Selected by Miami in 6th round (167th player selected) of 1985 NFL draft.
Signed by Miami Dolphins, July 15, 1985.

		—RUSHING—				PASS RECEIVING				—TOTAL—		
Year Club	G.	Att.	Yds.	Avg.	TD.	P.C.	Yds.	Avg.	TD.	TD.	Pts.	F.
1985—Miami NFL	16	98	370	3.8	11	13	74	5.7	2	13	78	2
1986—Miami NFL	16	75	314	4.2	0	20	177	8.9	1	1	6	4
1987—Miami NFL	10	32	114	3.6	1	27	249	9.2	1	2	12	0
1988—Miami NFL	16	55	273	5.0	0	30	282	9.4	0	0	0	1
Pro Totals—4 Years	58	260	1071	4.1	12	90	782	8.7	4	16	96	7

		KICKOFF RETURNS			
Year Club	G.	No.	Yds.	Avg.	TD.
1985—Miami NFL	16	None			
1986—Miami NFL	16	16	285	17.8	0
1987—Miami NFL	10	None			
1988—Miami NFL	16	2	41	20.5	0
Pro Totals—4 Years	58	18	326	18.1	0

Additional pro statistics: Recovered one fumble, 1986.
Played in AFC Championship Game following 1985 season.

BRIAN DAVIS
Cornerback—Washington Redskins

Born August 31, 1963, at Phoenix, Ariz.
Height, 6.02. Weight, 190.
High School—Phoenix, Ariz., Cortez.
Attended Glendale Community College and University of Nebraska.

Selected by Washington in 2nd round (30th player selected) of 1987 NFL draft.
Signed by Washington Redskins, July 26, 1987.
On injured reserve with hamstring injury, November 3 through December 4, 1987; activated, December 5, 1987.
On injured reserve with quadricep injury, November 24 through remainder of 1988 season.
Washington NFL, 1987 and 1988.
Games: 1987 (7), 1988 (9). Total—16.
Pro statistics: Recovered one fumble for 11 yards, 1987; intercepted one pass for 11 yards, 1988.
Played in NFC Championship Game following 1987 season.
Played in NFL Championship Game following 1987 season.

BRUCE EDWARD DAVIS
Offensive Tackle—Houston Oilers

Born June 21, 1956, at Rutherfordton, N.C.
Height, 6.06. Weight, 315.
High School—Marbury, Md., Lackey.
Attended University of California at Los Angeles.

Selected by Oakland in 11th round (294th player selected) of 1979 NFL draft.
Franchise transferred to Los Angeles, May 7, 1982.
Traded by Los Angeles Raiders to Houston Oilers for 2nd round pick in 1988 draft, November 3, 1987.
Oakland NFL, 1979 through 1981; Los Angeles Raiders NFL, 1982 through 1986; Los Angeles Raiders (4)-Houston (7)
NFL, 1987; Houston NFL, 1988.
Games: 1979 (12), 1980 (16), 1981 (16), 1982 (9), 1983 (16), 1984 (16), 1985 (16), 1986 (16), 1987 (11), 1988 (16).
Total—144.
Pro statistics: Recovered one fumble, 1982 and 1983.
Played in AFC Championship Game following 1980 and 1983 seasons.
Played in NFL Championship Game following 1980 and 1983 seasons.

C. WAYNE DAVIS
(Known by middle name.)
Linebacker—Los Angeles Rams

Born March 10, 1964, at Tuscaloosa, Ala.
Height, 6.01. Weight, 213.
High School—Gordo, Ala.
Attended University of Alabama.

Selected by St. Louis in 9th round (229th player selected) of 1987 NFL draft.
Signed by St. Louis Cardinals, July 2, 1987.
Franchise transferred to Phoenix, March 15, 1988.
Granted unconditional free agency, February 1, 1989; signed by Los Angeles Rams, February 27, 1989.
St. Louis NFL, 1987; Phoenix NFL, 1988.
Games: 1987 (12), 1988 (16). Total—28.
Pro statistics: Recovered one fumble, 1988.

ELGIN DAVIS
Running Back—Pittsburgh Steelers
Born October 23, 1965, at Jacksonville, Fla.
Height, 5.10. Weight, 192.
High School—Jacksonville, Fla., Ribault.
Attended University of Central Florida.

Selected by New England in 12th round (330th player selected) of 1987 NFL draft.
Signed by New England Patriots, July 17, 1987.
On injured reserve with quadricep injury, September 7 through October 6, 1987; activated, October 7, 1987.
Crossed picket line during players' strike, October 7, 1987.
On injured reserve with hamstring injury, August 23 through November 16, 1988; activated after clearing procedural waivers, November 18, 1988.
Granted unconditional free agency, February 1, 1989; signed by Pittsburgh Steelers, March 23, 1989.
New England NFL, 1987 and 1988.
Games: 1987 (4), 1988 (5). Total—9.
Pro statistics: Rushed nine times for 43 yards and returned five kickoffs for 134 yards (26.8 avg.), 1987; returned six kickoffs for 106 yards and fumbled once, 1988.

GREGORY BRIAN DAVIS
(Greg)
Placekicker-Punter—New England Patriots
Born October 29, 1965, at Rome, Ga.
Height, 5.11. Weight, 197.
High School—Atlanta, Ga., Lakeside.
Received degree in physical education from The Citadel in 1987.

Selected by Tampa Bay in 9th round (246th player selected) of 1987 NFL draft.
Signed by Tampa Bay Buccaneers, July 18, 1987.
Released by Tampa Bay Buccaneers, September 7, 1987; signed as free agent replacement player by Atlanta Falcons, September 24, 1987.
Released by Atlanta Falcons, October 19, 1987; awarded on waivers to Tampa Bay Buccaneers, October 20, 1987.
Released by Tampa Bay Buccaneers, November 2, 1987; signed as free agent by Atlanta Falcons for 1988; December 24, 1987.
Granted unconditional free agency, February 1, 1989; signed by New England Patriots, March 9, 1989.

| | | —PUNTING— | | | ——PLACE KICKING—— | | | | |
Year Club	G.	No.	Avg.	Blk.	XP.	XPM.	FG.	FGA.	Pts.
1987—Atlanta NFL	3	6	31.8	0	6	0	3	4	15
1988—Atlanta NFL	16		None		25	2	19	30	82
Pro Totals—2 Years	19	6	31.8	0	31	2	22	34	97

JOHN HENRY DAVIS
Center-Offensive Tackle—Buffalo Bills
Born August 22, 1965, at Ellijay, Ga.
Height, 6.04. Weight, 304.
High School—Ellijay, Ga., Gilmer.
Attended Georgia Tech.

Selected by Houston in 11th round (287th player selected) of 1987 NFL draft.
Signed by Houston Oilers, July 24, 1987.
On injured reserve with ankle injury, December 19 through remainder of 1987 season.
Granted unconditional free agency, February 1, 1989; signed by Buffalo Bills, March 3, 1989.
Houston NFL, 1987 and 1988.
Games: 1987 (6), 1988 (13). Total—19.

KENNETH EARL DAVIS
Running Back—Buffalo Bills
Born April 16, 1962, at Williamson County, Tex.
Height, 5.10. Weight, 209.
High School—Temple, Tex.
Attended Texas Christian University.

Named as running back on THE SPORTING NEWS College All-America Team, 1984.
Selected by Green Bay in 2nd round (41st player selected) of 1986 NFL draft.
Signed by Green Bay Packers, May 17, 1986.
On injured reserve with ankle injury, October 21 through December 9, 1988; activated, December 10, 1988.
Granted unconditional free agency, February 1, 1989; signed by Buffalo Bills, March 3, 1989.

| | | ——RUSHING—— | | | | PASS RECEIVING | | | | —TOTAL— | | |
Year Club	G.	Att.	Yds.	Avg.	TD.	P.C.	Yds.	Avg.	TD.	TD.	Pts.	F.
1986—Green Bay NFL	16	114	519	4.6	0	21	142	6.8	1	1	6	2
1987—Green Bay NFL	10	109	413	3.8	3	14	110	7.9	0	3	18	2
1988—Green Bay NFL	9	39	121	3.1	1	11	81	7.4	0	1	6	0
Pro Totals—3 Years	35	262	1053	4.0	4	46	333	7.2	1	5	30	4

| | | KICKOFF RETURNS | | | |
Year Club	G.	No.	Yds.	Avg.	TD.
1986—Green Bay NFL............	16	12	231	19.3	0
1987—Green Bay NFL............	10		None		
1988—Green Bay NFL............	9		None		
Pro Totals—3 Years............	35	12	231	19.3	0

REUBEN CORDELL DAVIS
Defensive Lineman—Tampa Bay Buccaneers
Born May 7, 1965, at Greensboro, N.C.
Height, 6.04. Weight, 290.
High School—Greensboro, N.C., Grimsley.
Received degree in journalism and mass communications from University of North Carolina in 1988.

Selected by Tampa Bay in 9th round (225th player selected) of 1988 NFL draft.
Signed by Tampa Bay Buccaneers, July 6, 1988.
Tampa Bay NFL, 1988.
Games: 1988 (16).

SCOTT DAVIS
Defensive End—Los Angeles Raiders
Born August 7, 1965, at Joliet, Ill.
Height, 6.07. Weight, 270.
High School—Plainfield, Ill.
Received degree in marketing from University of Illinois in 1988.

Selected by Los Angeles Raiders in 1st round (25th player selected) of 1988 NFL draft.
Signed by Los Angeles Raiders, July 14, 1988.
Los Angeles Raiders NFL, 1988.
Games: 1988 (15).

WAYNE ELLIOT DAVIS
Cornerback—Buffalo Bills
Born July 17, 1963, at Cincinnati, O.
Height, 5.11. Weight, 180.
High School—Cincinnati, O., Mount Healthy.
Attended Indiana State University.

Selected by Baltimore in 2nd round (21st player selected) of 1985 USFL draft.
Selected by San Diego in 2nd round (39th player selected) of 1985 NFL draft.
Signed by San Diego Chargers, June 14, 1985.
Traded by San Diego Chargers to Buffalo Bills for safety Martin Bayless, August 26, 1987.
On injured reserve with hamstring injury, September 8 through October 22, 1987; activated, October 23, 1987.

| | | —INTERCEPTIONS— | | | |
Year Club	G.	No.	Yds.	Avg.	TD.
1985—San Diego NFL	16	2	29	14.5	0
1986—San Diego NFL	16		None		
1987—Buffalo NFL.................	10	1	0	0.0	0
1988—Buffalo NFL.................	16	1	3	3.0	0
Pro Totals—4 Years............	58	4	32	8.0	0

Additional pro statistics: Recovered one fumble, 1985.
Played in AFC Championship Game following 1988 season.

WENDELL TYRONE DAVIS
Wide Receiver—Chicago Bears
Born January 3, 1966, at Shreveport, La.
Height, 5.11. Weight, 188.
High School—Shreveport, La., Fair Park.
Attended Louisiana State University.

Named as wide receiver on THE SPORTING NEWS College All-America Team, 1986 and 1987.
Selected by Chicago in 1st round (27th player selected) of 1988 NFL draft.
Signed by Chicago Bears, July 20, 1988.

| | | —PASS RECEIVING— | | | |
Year Club	G.	P.C.	Yds.	Avg.	TD.
1988—Chicago NFL	16	15	220	14.7	0

Additional pro statistics: Rushed once for three yards, returned three punts for 17 yards, recovered one fumble and fumbled twice, 1988.
Played in NFC Championship Game following 1988 season.

DERMONTTI FARRA DAWSON
Guard-Center—Pittsburgh Steelers
Born July 17, 1965, at Lexington, Ky.
Height, 6.02. Weight, 271.
High School—Lexington, Ky., Bryan Station.
Received bachelor of science degree in education from University of Kentucky in 1988.
Cousin of George Adams, running back with New York Giants;
and Marc Logan, running back with Miami Dolphins.

Selected by Pittsburgh in 2nd round (44th player selected) of 1988 NFL draft.
Signed by Pittsburgh Steelers, August 1, 1988.
On injured reserve with knee injury, September 26 through November 25, 1988; activated, November 26, 1988.
Pittsburgh NFL, 1988.
Games: 1988 (8).

JAMES LINWOOD DAWSON
(Lin)
Tight End—New England Patriots
Born June 24, 1959, at Norfolk, Va.
Height, 6.03. Weight, 240.
High School—Kinston, N.C.
Attended North Carolina State University.

Selected by New England in 8th round (212th player selected) of 1981 NFL draft.
On inactive list, September 19, 1982.
On injured reserve with knee injury, August 19 through entire 1986 season.
On injured reserve with shoulder injury, August 30 through September 29, 1988; activated, September 30, 1988.
On injured reserve with fractured ankle, November 11 through remainder of 1988 season.

		—PASS RECEIVING—			
Year	Club	G.	P.C.	Yds.	Avg.	TD.
1981—New England NFL.......	15	7	126	18.0	0
1982—New England NFL.......	8	13	160	12.3	1
1983—New England NFL.......	13	9	84	9.3	1
1984—New England NFL.......	16	39	427	10.9	4
1985—New England NFL.......	16	17	148	8.7	0
1987—New England NFL.......	12	12	81	6.8	0
1988—New England NFL.......	6	8	106	13.3	2
Pro Totals—7 Years............	86	105	1132	10.8	8

Additional pro statistics: Recovered one fumble, 1984 and 1985; fumbled once, 1985.
Played in AFC Championship Game following 1985 season.
Played in NFL Championship Game following 1985 season.

KEVIN JAMES DEAN
Linebacker—Cleveland Browns
Born February 5, 1965, at Newton, Tex.
Height, 6.01. Weight, 235.
High School—Newton, Tex.
Attended Texas Christian University.
Related to Ernie Holmes, defensive tackle with Pittsburgh Steelers, 1972 through 1977;
and Fred Dean, defensive end with San Diego Chargers and San Francisco 49ers, 1975 through 1985.

Signed as free agent by San Francisco 49ers, May 12, 1987.
Crossed picket line during players' strike, October 9, 1987.
On injured reserve with ankle injury, November 2 through remainder of 1987 season.
Released by San Francisco 49ers, July 21, 1988; signed by Cleveland Browns for 1989, November 21, 1988.
San Francisco NFL, 1987.
Games: 1987 (4).

STEVEN L. DeBERG
(Steve)
Quarterback—Kansas City Chiefs
Born January 19, 1954, at Oakland, Calif.
Height, 6.03. Weight, 210.
High School—Anaheim, Calif., Savanna.
Attended Fullerton Junior College and received bachelor of science degree
from San Jose State University in 1980.

Selected by Dallas in 10th round (275th player selected) of 1977 NFL draft.
Claimed on waivers from Dallas Cowboys by San Francisco 49ers, September 12, 1977.
Traded by San Francisco 49ers to Denver Broncos for 4th round pick in 1983 draft, August 31, 1981.
USFL rights traded by Oakland Invaders to Denver Gold for rights to tight end John Thompson and offensive tackle Randy Van Divier, October 7, 1983.
On injured reserve with separated shoulder, November 16 through December 21, 1983; activated, December 22, 1983.
Granted free agency, February 1, 1984; re-signed by Broncos and traded to Tampa Bay Buccaneers for 4th round pick in 1984 draft and 2nd round pick in 1985 draft, April 24, 1984.
Granted free agency, February 1, 1988; re-signed by Buccaneers and traded to Kansas City Chiefs for safety Mark Robinson and 4th and 8th round picks in 1988 draft, March 31, 1988.
Active for 5 games with San Francisco 49ers in 1977; did not play.

			—PASSING—							—RUSHING—				—TOTAL—		
Year	Club	G.	Att.	Cmp.	Pct.	Gain	T.P.	P.I.	Avg.	Att.	Yds.	Avg.	TD.	TD.	Pts.	F.
1978—San Francisco NFL	12	302	137	45.4	1570	8	22	5.20	15	20	1.3	1	1	6	9
1979—San Francisco NFL	16	*578	*347	60.0	3652	17	21	6.32	17	10	0.6	0	0	0	6
1980—San Francisco NFL	11	321	186	57.9	1998	12	17	6.22	6	4	0.7	0	0	0	4
1981—Denver NFL	14	108	64	59.3	797	6	6	7.38	9	40	4.4	0	0	0	2
1982—Denver NFL	9	223	131	58.7	1405	7	11	6.30	8	27	3.4	1	1	6	4
1983—Denver NFL	10	215	119	55.3	1617	9	7	7.52	13	28	2.2	1	1	6	5
1984—Tampa Bay NFL	16	509	308	60.5	3554	19	18	6.98	28	59	2.1	2	2	12	15

Year Club	G.	Att.	Cmp.	PASSING Pct.	Gain	T.P.	P.I.	Avg.	RUSHING Att.	Yds.	Avg.	TD.	TOTAL TD.	Pts.	F.
1985—Tampa Bay NFL	11	370	197	53.2	2488	19	18	6.72	9	28	3.1	0	0	0	3
1986—Tampa Bay NFL	16	96	50	52.1	610	5	12	6.35	2	1	0.5	1	1	6	2
1987—Tampa Bay NFL	12	275	159	57.8	1891	14	7	6.88	8	—8	—1.0	0	0	0	7
1988—Kansas City NFL	13	414	224	54.1	2935	16	16	7.09	18	30	1.7	1	1	6	1
Pro Totals—12 Years	140	3411	1922	56.3	22517	132	155	6.60	133	239	1.8	7	7	42	58

Quarterback Rating Points: 1978 (39.8), 1979 (73.1), 1980 (66.5), 1981 (77.6), 1982 (67.2), 1983 (79.9), 1984 (79.3), 1985 (71.3), 1986 (49.7), 1987 (85.3), 1988 (73.5). Total—70.8.

Additional pro statistics: Recovered two fumbles and fumbled nine times for minus five yards, 1978; recovered two fumbles and fumbled six times for minus 17 yards, 1979; fumbled four times for minus six yards, 1980; recovered two fumbles and fumbled 15 times for minus eight yards, 1984; recovered one fumble and fumbled twice for minus five yards, 1986; recovered two fumbles and fumbled seven times for minus two yards, 1987.

DONNIE DEE JR.
Tight End—Indianapolis Colts
Born March 17, 1965, at Kansas City, Mo.
Height, 6.04. Weight, 247.
High School—Kansas City, Mo., Oak Park.
Attended The University of Tulsa.
Son of Don Dee, Sr., member of 1968 U.S. Olympic Gold medal basketball team,
and with Indiana Pacers of ABA, 1968-69.

Selected by Indianapolis in 11th round (297th player selected) of 1988 NFL draft.
Signed by Indianapolis Colts, July 13, 1988.
Indianapolis NFL, 1988.
Games: 1988 (13).

ALBERT LOUIS DEL GRECO JR.
(Al)
Placekicker—Phoenix Cardinals
Born March 2, 1962, at Providence, R. I.
Height, 5.10. Weight, 191.
High School—Coral Gables, Fla.
Attended Auburn University.

Signed as free agent by Miami Dolphins, May 17, 1984.
Released by Miami Dolphins, August 27, 1984; signed as free agent by Green Bay Packers, October 17, 1984.
Released by Green Bay Packers, November 25, 1987; signed as free agent by St. Louis Cardinals, December 8, 1987.
Franchise transferred to Phoenix, March 15, 1988.

Year Club	G.	XP.	XPM.	PLACE KICKING FG.	FGA.	Pts.
1984—Green Bay NFL	9	34	0	9	12	61
1985—Green Bay NFL	16	38	2	19	26	95
1986—Green Bay NFL	16	29	0	17	27	80
1987—G.B.(5)-St.L.(3) NFL	8	19	1	9	15	46
1988—Phoenix NFL	16	42	2	12	21	78
Pro Totals—5 Years	65	162	5	66	101	360

Additional pro statistics: Rushed once for eight yards, 1988.

STEVE BRAUN DeLINE
Placekicker—San Diego Chargers
Born August 19, 1961, at Denver, Colo.
Height, 5.11. Weight, 185.
High Schools—Englewood, Colo., Cherry Creek; and Denver, Colo., Mullen.
Received degree in animal science from Colorado State University.

Selected by San Francisco in 7th round (189th player selected) of 1987 NFL draft.
Signed by San Francisco 49ers, July 21, 1987.
Released by San Francisco 49ers, August 31, 1987; awarded on waivers to Philadelphia Eagles, September 1, 1987.
On injured reserve with shoulder injury, September 6 through October 21, 1987.
Released by Philadelphia Eagles, October 22, 1987; signed as free agent by San Diego Chargers, February 22, 1988.
Released by San Diego Chargers, August 23, 1988; re-signed by Chargers, November 17, 1988.

Year Club	G.	XP.	XPM.	PLACE KICKING FG.	FGA.	Pts.
1988—San Diego NFL	5	12	0	6	8	30

JEFFREY ALAN DELLENBACH
(Jeff)
Center—Miami Dolphins
Born February 14, 1963, at Wausau, Wis.
Height, 6.05. Weight, 280.
High School—Wausau, Wis., East.
Attended University of Wisconsin.

Selected by Jacksonville in 1985 USFL territorial draft.
Selected by Miami in 4th round (111th player selected) of 1985 NFL draft.
Signed by Miami Dolphins, July 15, 1985.

Miami NFL, 1985 through 1988.
Games: 1985 (11), 1986 (13), 1987 (11), 1988 (16). Total—51.
Pro statistics: Fumbled once for minus 13 yards, 1987; fumbled once for minus nine yards, 1988.
Played in AFC Championship Game following 1985 season.

ROBERT LEWIS DELPINO
Fullback—Los Angeles Rams
Born November 2, 1965, at Dodge City, Kan.
Height, 6.00. Weight, 205.
High School—Dodge City, Kan.
Attended Dodge City Community College and University of Missouri.

Selected by Los Angeles Rams in 5th round (117th player selected) of 1988 NFL draft.
Signed by Los Angeles Rams, July 12, 1988.

Year Club	G.	Att.	Yds.	Avg.	TD.	P.C.	Yds.	Avg.	TD.	TD.	Pts.	F.
		——RUSHING——				PASS RECEIVING				—TOTAL—		
1988—Los Angeles Rams NFL	15	34	147	4.3	0	30	312	10.4	2	2	12	2

Year Club	G.	No.	Yds.	Avg.	TD.
		KICKOFF RETURNS			
1988—L.A. Rams NFL	15	14	333	23.8	0

Additional pro statistics: Recovered one fumble, 1988.

JACK DEL RIO
Linebacker—Kansas City Chiefs
Born April 4, 1963, at Castro Valley, Calif.
Height, 6.04. Weight, 235.
High School—Hayward, Calif.
Attended University of Southern California.

Selected by Los Angeles in 1985 USFL territorial draft.
Selected by New Orleans in 3rd round (68th player selected) of 1985 NFL draft.
Signed by New Orleans Saints, July 31, 1985.
Traded by New Orleans Saints to Kansas City Chiefs for 5th round pick in 1988 draft, August 17, 1987.
On injured reserve with knee injury, December 13 through remainder of 1988 season.
Selected by Toronto Blue Jays' organization in 22nd round of free-agent draft, June 8, 1981.
New Orleans NFL, 1985 and 1986; Kansas City NFL, 1987 and 1988.
Games: 1985 (16), 1986 (16), 1987 (10), 1988 (15). Total—57.
Pro statistics: Recovered five fumbles for 22 yards and a touchdown and intercepted two passes for 13 yards, 1985; rushed once for 16 yards, 1986; intercepted one pass for no yards and recovered one fumble, 1988.

MARK FRANCIS DENNIS
Offensive Tackle—Miami Dolphins
Born April 15, 1965, at Junction City, Kan.
Height, 6.06. Weight, 291.
High School—Washington, Ill.
Attended University of Illinois.

Selected by Miami in 8th round (212th player selected) of 1987 NFL draft.
Signed by Miami Dolphins, July 23, 1987.
On injured reserve with knee injury, November 28 through remainder of 1988 season.
Miami NFL, 1987 and 1988.
Games: 1987 (5), 1988 (13). Total—18.

RICK STEVEN DENNISON
Linebacker—Denver Broncos
Born June 22, 1958, at Kalispell, Mont.
Height, 6.03. Weight, 220.
High School—Fort Collins, Colo., Rocky Mountain.
Received bachelor of science degree in civil engineering from Colorado State University in 1980.

Signed as free agent by Buffalo Bills, May 9, 1980.
Released by Buffalo Bills, August 20, 1980; signed as free agent by Denver Broncos, December 29, 1980.
Released by Denver Broncos, August 31, 1981; signed as free agent by Buffalo Bills, February 26, 1982.
Released by Buffalo Bills, August 31, 1982; signed as free agent by Denver Broncos, September 7, 1982.
Denver NFL, 1982 through 1988.
Games: 1982 (9), 1983 (16), 1984 (16), 1985 (15), 1986 (16), 1987 (12), 1988 (16). Total—100.
Pro statistics: Returned two kickoffs for 27 yards and recovered one fumble, 1984; intercepted one pass for five yards, 1986; intercepted one pass for 10 yards, 1987; intercepted one pass for 29 yards and recovered three fumbles, 1988.
Played in AFC Championship Game following 1986 and 1987 seasons.
Played in NFL Championship Game following 1986 and 1987 seasons.

BURNELL JOSEPH DENT
Linebacker—Green Bay Packers
Born March 16, 1963, at New Orleans, La.
Height, 6.01. Weight, 236.
High School—Destrehan, La.
Received bachelor of science degree in physical education from Tulane University in 1986.

Selected by Green Bay in 6th round (143rd player selected) of 1986 NFL draft.
Signed by Green Bay Packers, July 18, 1986.
On injured reserve with knee injury, September 1 through October 23, 1987; activated, October 24, 1987.
On injured reserve with knee injury, October 4 through November 18, 1988; activated, November 19, 1988.
Green Bay NFL, 1986 through 1988.
Games: 1986 (16), 1987 (9), 1988 (10). Total—35.
Pro statistics: Recovered one fumble, 1988.

RICHARD LAMAR DENT
Defensive End—Chicago Bears
Born December 13, 1960, at Atlanta, Ga.
Height, 6.05. Weight, 268.
High School—Atlanta, Ga., Murphy.
Attended Tennessee State University.

Selected by Philadelphia in 8th round (89th player selected) of 1983 USFL draft.
Selected by Chicago in 8th round (203rd player selected) of 1983 NFL draft.
Signed by Chicago Bears, May 12, 1983.
On non-football injury list with substance abuse, September 8, 1988; activated, September 9, 1988.
On injured reserve with fractured fibula, November 29 through remainder of 1988 season.
Chicago NFL, 1983 through 1988.
Games: 1983 (16), 1984 (16), 1985 (16), 1986 (15), 1987 (12), 1988 (13). Total—88.
Pro statistics: Recovered one fumble, 1984 and 1988; intercepted two passes for 10 yards and a touchdown and recovered two fumbles, 1985; recovered two fumbles for 11 yards, 1987.
Played in NFC Championship Game following 1984 and 1985 seasons.
Played in NFL Championship Game following 1985 season.
Played in Pro Bowl (NFL All-Star Game) following 1984 and 1985 seasons.

STEVEN LEONARD DeOSSIE
(Steve)
Linebacker—Dallas Cowboys
Born November 22, 1962, at Tacoma, Wash.
Height, 6.02. Weight, 248.
High School—Boston, Mass., Don Bosco Technical.
Received bachelor of science degree in communications from Boston College in 1984.

Selected by New Jersey in 1st round (14th player selected) of 1984 USFL draft.
Selected by Dallas in 4th round (110th player selected) of 1984 NFL draft.
Signed by Dallas Cowboys, May 3, 1984.
Dallas NFL, 1984 through 1988.
Games: 1984 (16), 1985 (16), 1986 (16), 1987 (11), 1988 (16). Total—75.

JOSEPH DEVLIN
(Joe)
Offensive Tackle—Buffalo Bills
Born February 23, 1954 at Phoenixville, Pa.
Height, 6.05. Weight, 280.
High School—Frazer, Pa., Great Valley.
Attended University of Iowa.

Named as guard on THE SPORTING NEWS College All-America Team, 1975.
Selected by Buffalo in 2nd round (52nd player selected) of 1976 NFL draft.
On injured reserve with knee injury, December 13 through remainder of 1978 season.
On injured reserve with broken ankle, August 22 through entire 1983 season.
Buffalo NFL, 1976 through 1982 and 1984 through 1988.
Games: 1976 (14), 1977 (14), 1978 (14), 1979 (16), 1980 (16), 1981 (16), 1982 (9), 1984 (16), 1985 (16), 1986 (16), 1987 (12), 1988 (16). Total—175.
Pro statistics: Recovered one fumble, 1978, 1982 and 1988; recovered two fumbles, 1979.
Played in AFC Championship Game following 1988 season.

ERIC DEMETRIC DICKERSON
Running Back—Indianapolis Colts
Born September 2, 1960, at Sealy, Tex.
Height, 6.03. Weight, 218.
High School—Sealy, Tex.
Attended Southern Methodist University.
Cousin of Dexter Manley, defensive end with Washington Redskins.

Named as running back on THE SPORTING NEWS College All-America Team, 1982.
Named THE SPORTING NEWS NFL Player of the Year, 1983.
Named to THE SPORTING NEWS NFL All-Star Team, 1983, 1984 and 1986 through 1988.
Established NFL records for most yards rushing by rookie (1,808), 1983; most touchdowns rushing by rookie (18), 1983; most yards rushing, season (2,105), 1984; most games, 100 yards rushing, season (12), 1984; tied NFL record for most seasons, 2,000 yards rushing and receiving combined (4).
Selected by Arizona in 1st round (6th player selected) of 1983 USFL draft.
Selected by Los Angeles Rams in 1st round (2nd player selected) of 1983 NFL draft.
Signed by Los Angeles Rams, July 12, 1983.
On did not report list, August 20 through September 12, 1985.
Reported and granted roster exemption, September 13 through September 19, 1985; activated, September 20, 1985.
Crossed picket line during players' strike, October 14, 1987.

Traded by Los Angeles Rams to Indianapolis Colts for 1st and 2nd round picks in 1988 draft, 2nd round pick in 1989 draft and running back Owen Gill, October 31, 1987; Rams also acquired 1st round pick in 1988 draft, 1st and 2nd round picks in 1989 draft and running back Greg Bell from Buffalo Bills in exchange for Colts trading rights to linebacker Cornelius Bennett to Bills.

		——RUSHING——				PASS RECEIVING				—TOTAL—		
Year—Club	G.	Att.	Yds.	Avg.	TD.	P.C.	Yds.	Avg.	TD.	TD.	Pts.	F.
1983—Los Angeles Rams NFL	16	*390	*1808	4.6	18	51	404	7.9	2	20	120	13
1984—Los Angeles Rams NFL	16	379	*2105	5.6	*14	21	139	6.6	0	14	84	14
1985—Los Angeles Rams NFL	14	292	1234	4.2	12	20	126	6.3	0	12	72	10
1986—Los Angeles Rams NFL	16	*404	*1821	4.5	11	26	205	7.9	0	11	66	12
1987—L.A. Rams (3)-Ind. (9) NFL	12	283	1288	4.6	6	18	171	9.5	0	6	36	7
1988—Indianapolis NFL	16	*388	*1659	4.3	14	36	377	10.5	1	15	90	5
Pro Totals—6 Years	90	2136	9915	4.6	75	172	1422	8.3	3	78	468	61

Additional pro statistics: Recovered one fumble, 1983 and 1988; attempted one pass with one interception and recovered four fumbles, 1984; recovered three fumbles, 1985 and 1987; attempted one pass with one completion for 15 yards and a touchdown and recovered two fumbles, 1986.
Played in NFC Championship Game following 1985 season.
Played in Pro Bowl (NFL All-Star Game) following 1983, 1984 and 1986 through 1988 seasons.

CLINT DIDIER
Tight End—Green Bay Packers
Born April 4, 1959, at Connell, Wash.
Height, 6.05. Weight, 240.
High School—Connell, Wash.
Attended Columbia Basin Junior College and Portland State University.

Selected by Washington in 12th round (314th player selected) of 1981 NFL draft.
On injured reserve with pulled hamstring, August 18 through entire 1981 season.
On injured reserve with fractured leg, August 28 through September 28, 1984; activated, September 29, 1984.
On injured reserve with hamstring injury, September 8 through October 23, 1987; activated, October 24, 1987.
Released by Washington Redskins, August 30, 1988; signed as free agent by Green Bay Packers, September 6, 1988.

		——PASS RECEIVING——			
Year—Club	G.	P.C.	Yds.	Avg.	TD.
1982—Washington NFL	8	2	10	5.0	1
1983—Washington NFL	16	9	153	17.0	4
1984—Washington NFL	11	30	350	11.7	5
1985—Washington NFL	16	41	433	10.6	4
1986—Washington NFL	14	34	691	20.3	4
1987—Washington NFL	9	13	178	13.7	1
1988—Green Bay NFL	15	5	37	7.4	1
Pro Totals—7 Years	89	134	1852	13.8	20

Additional pro statistics: Recovered one fumble in end zone for a touchdown, 1983; fumbled once, 1983 and 1988; recovered one fumble for four yards, 1988.
Played in NFC Championship Game following 1982, 1983, 1986 and 1987 seasons.
Played in NFL Championship Game following 1982, 1983 and 1987 seasons.

GERALD SCOTT DILL
(Known by middle name.)
Guard—Phoenix Cardinals
Born April 5, 1966, at Birmingham, Ala.
Height, 6.05. Weight, 272.
High School—Birmingham, Ala., W.A. Berry.
Attended Memphis State University.

Selected by Phoenix in 9th round (233rd player selected) of 1988 NFL draft.
Signed by Phoenix Cardinals, July 13, 1988.
Phoenix NFL, 1988.
Games: 1988 (13).

ELLIS ARTO DILLAHUNT JR.
Safety—Washington Redskins
Born November 25, 1964, at New Bern, N.C.
Height, 5.11. Weight, 198.
High School—Jacksonville, N.C.
Received bachelor of science degree in criminal justice
from East Carolina University in 1988.

Selected by Cincinnati in 10th round (253rd player selected) of 1988 NFL draft.
Signed by Cincinnnati Bengals, July 10, 1988.
On injured reserve with calf injury, November 11 through remainder of 1988 season.
Granted unconditional free agency, February 1, 1989; signed by Washington Redskins, March 20, 1989.
Cincinnati NFL, 1988.
Games: 1988 (8).

—DID YOU KNOW—
That Indianapolis placekicker Dean Biasucci set an NFL record in 1988 by kicking six field goals from 50 yards or more?

CHARLES LOUIS DIMRY III
Defensive Back—Atlanta Falcons
Born January 31, 1966, at San Diego, Calif.
Height, 6.00. Weight, 175.
High School—Oceanside, Calif.
Attended University of Nevada at Las Vegas.

Selected by Atlanta in 5th round (110th player selected) of 1988 NFL draft.
Signed by Atlanta Falcons, July 16, 1988.
Atlanta NFL, 1988.
Games: 1988 (16).

CRIS EDWARD DISHMAN
Cornerback—Houston Oilers
Born August 13, 1965, at Louisville, Ky.
Height, 6.00. Weight, 180.
High School—Louisville, Ky., DeSales.
Attended Purdue University.

Selected by Houston in 5th round (125th player selected) of 1988 NFL draft.
Signed by Houston Oilers, July 15, 1988.
Houston NFL, 1988.
Games: 1988 (15).
Pro statistics: Returned blocked punt 10 yards for a touchdown and recovered one fumble, 1988.

FLOYD EUGENE DIXON
Wide Receiver—Atlanta Falcons
Born April 9, 1964, at Beaumont, Tex.
Height, 5.09. Weight, 170.
High School—Beaumont, Tex., Hebert.
Received degree from Stephen F. Austin State University in 1987.

Selected by Atlanta in 6th round (154th player selected) of 1986 NFL draft.
Signed by Atlanta Falcons, July 17, 1986.

		—RUSHING—				PASS RECEIVING				—TOTAL—		
Year Club	G.	Att.	Yds.	Avg.	TD.	P.C.	Yds.	Avg.	TD.	TD.	Pts.	F.
1986—Atlanta NFL	16	11	67	6.1	0	42	617	14.7	2	2	12	3
1987—Atlanta NFL	12	3	—3	—1.0	0	36	600	16.7	5	5	30	0
1988—Atlanta NFL	14	7	69	9.9	0	28	368	13.1	2	2	12	1
Pro Totals—3 Years	42	21	133	6.3	0	106	1585	15.0	9	9	54	4

		—PUNT RETURNS—			
Year Club	G.	No.	Yds.	Avg.	TD.
1986—Atlanta NFL	16	26	151	5.8	0
1987—Atlanta NFL	12		None		
1988—Atlanta NFL	14		None		
Pro Totals—3 Years	42	26	151	5.8	0

Additional pro statistics: Returned one kickoff for 13 yards and recovered two fumbles, 1986.

HANFORD DIXON
Cornerback—Cleveland Browns
Born December 25, 1958, at Mobile, Ala.
Height, 5.11. Weight, 195.
High School—Theodore, Ala.
Attended University of Southern Mississippi.

Named to THE SPORTING NEWS NFL All-Star Team, 1986 and 1987.
Named as defensive back on THE SPORTING NEWS College All-America Team, 1980.
Selected by Cleveland in 1st round (22nd player selected) of 1981 NFL draft.

		—INTERCEPTIONS—			
Year Club	G.	No.	Yds.	Avg.	TD.
1981—Cleveland NFL	16		None		
1982—Cleveland NFL	9	4	22	5.5	0
1983—Cleveland NFL	16	3	41	13.7	0
1984—Cleveland NFL	16	5	31	6.2	0
1985—Cleveland NFL	16	3	65	21.7	0
1986—Cleveland NFL	16	5	35	7.0	0
1987—Cleveland NFL	12	3	5	1.7	0
1988—Cleveland NFL	15	2	24	12.0	0
Pro Totals—8 Years	116	25	223	8.9	0

Additional pro statistics: Fumbled once, 1982 and 1986; recovered one fumble, 1984 and 1988; recovered two fumbles, 1986.
Played in AFC Championship Game following 1986 and 1987 seasons.
Played in Pro Bowl (NFL All-Star Game) following 1986 through 1988 seasons.

RANDY C. DIXON
Offensive Tackle—Indianapolis Colts
Born March 12, 1965, at Clewiston, Fla.
Height, 6.03. Weight, 293.
High School—Clewiston, Fla.
Attended University of Pittsburgh.

Named as offensive tackle on THE SPORTING NEWS College All-America Team, 1986.
Selected by Indianapolis in 4th round (85th player selected) of 1987 NFL draft.
Signed by Indianapolis Colts, July 24, 1987.
Indianapolis NFL, 1987 and 1988.
Games: 1987 (3), 1988 (16). Total—19.

RICKEY DIXON
Cornerback—Cincinnati Bengals
Born December 26, 1966, at Dallas, Tex.
Height, 5.11. Weight, 181.
High School—Dallas, Tex., Wilmer-Hutchins.
Attended University of Oklahoma.

Selected by Cincinnati in 1st round (5th player selected) of 1988 NFL draft.
Signed by Cincinnati Bengals, September 3, 1988.
Cincinnati NFL, 1988.
Games: 1988 (15).
Pro statistics: Intercepted one pass for 13 yards, returned one kickoff for 18 yards and recovered one fumble for minus three yards, 1988.
Played in AFC Championship Game following 1988 season.
Played in NFL Championship Game following 1988 season.

KIRK JAMES DODGE
Linebacker—New York Jets
Born June 4, 1962, at Whittier, Calif.
Height, 6.01. Weight, 231.
High School—San Francisco, Calif., Lowell.
Attended Fullerton College and University of Nevada at Las Vegas.

Selected by Los Angeles in 6th round (112th player selected) of 1984 USFL draft.
Selected by Atlanta in 7th round (175th player selected) of 1984 NFL draft.
Signed by Atlanta Falcons, June 10, 1984.
Released by Atlanta Falcons, August 26, 1984; signed as free agent by Detroit Lions, October 2, 1984
On injured reserve with shoulder injury, August 20 through entire 1985 season.
Released by Detroit Lions, August 18, 1986; signed as free agent by Houston Oilers, October 24, 1986.
Released by Houston Oilers, September 3, 1987; signed as free agent replacement player by Denver Broncos, September 25, 1987.
Released by Denver Broncos, October 19, 1987; re-signed by Broncos, April 5, 1988.
Released by Denver Broncos, July 29, 1988; signed as free agent by New York Jets, January 11, 1989.
Detroit NFL, 1984; Houston NFL, 1986; Denver NFL, 1987.
Games: 1984 (11), 1986 (9), 1987 (3). Total—23.
Pro statistics: Recovered one fumble, 1984.

CHRISTOPHER JOHN DOLEMAN
(Chris)
Defensive End—Minnesota Vikings
Born October 16, 1961, at Indianapolis, Ind.
Height, 6.05. Weight, 262.
High Schools—Wayne, Pa., Valley Forge Military Academy;
and York, Pa., William Penn.
Attended University of Pittsburgh.
Brother of Ty Doleman, basketball player at University of Pittsburgh at Johnstown.

Selected by Baltimore in 1985 USFL territorial draft.
Selected by Minnesota in 1st round (4th player selected) of 1985 NFL draft.
Signed by Minnesota Vikings, August 8, 1985.
Minnesota NFL, 1985 through 1988.
Games: 1985 (16), 1986 (16), 1987 (12), 1988 (16). Total—60.
Pro statistics: Intercepted one pass for five yards and recovered three fumbles, 1985; intercepted one pass for 59 yards and a touchdown, 1986.
Played in NFC Championship Game following 1987 season.
Played in Pro Bowl (NFL All-Star Game) following 1987 and 1988 seasons.

JAMES MATTHEW DOMBROWSKI
(Jim)
Offensive Tackle—New Orleans Saints
Born October 19, 1963, at Williamsville, N.Y.
Height, 6.05. Weight, 298.
High School—Williamsville, N.Y., South.
Received bachelor's degree in biology from University of Virginia in 1986.

Named as offensive tackle on THE SPORTING NEWS College All-America Team, 1985.
Selected by Orlando in 1986 USFL territorial draft.

Selected by New Orleans in 1st round (6th player selected) of 1986 NFL draft.
Signed by New Orleans Saints, August 1, 1986.
On injured reserve with broken foot, September 22 through remainder of 1986 season.
New Orleans NFL, 1986 through 1988.
Games: 1986 (3), 1987 (10), 1988 (16). Total—29.
Pro statistics: Recovered one fumble, 1988.

JEFF DONALDSON
Safety—Houston Oilers
Born April 19, 1962, at Fort Collins, Colo.
Height, 6.00. Weight, 193.
High School—Fort Collins, Colo.
Attended University of Colorado.

Selected by Denver in 1984 USFL territorial draft.
Selected by Houston in 9th round (228th player selected) of 1984 NFL draft.
Signed by Houston Oilers, July 17, 1984.

Year Club	G.	No.	Yds.	Avg.	TD.
1984—Houston NFL	16		None		
1985—Houston NFL	16		None		
1986—Houston NFL	16	1	0	0.0	0
1987—Houston NFL	12	4	16	4.0	0
1988—Houston NFL	16	4	29	7.3	0
Pro Totals—5 Years	76	9	45	5.0	0

Additional pro statistics: Returned six punts for 35 yards, returned five kickoffs for 93 yards and fumbled once, 1985; recovered two fumbles, 1985, 1987 and 1988; recovered two fumbles for one yard and a touchdown, 1986; recovered one kickoff for five yards, 1988.

RAYMOND CANUTE DONALDSON
(Ray)
Center—Indianapolis Colts
Born May 18, 1958, at Rome, Ga.
Height, 6.03. Weight, 288.
High School—Rome, Ga., East.
Attended University of Georgia.
Step-brother of John Tutt, outfielder in Baltimore Orioles' and San Diego Padres'
organizations, 1981 through 1986; and Aguas of Mexican League, 1983; and cousin of Robert
Lavette, running back with Atlanta Falcons.

Selected by Baltimore in 2nd round (32nd player selected) of 1980 NFL draft.
Franchise transferred to Indianapolis, March 31, 1984.
Baltimore NFL, 1980 through 1983; Indianapolis NFL, 1984 through 1988.
Games: 1980 (16), 1981 (16), 1982 (9), 1983 (16), 1984 (16), 1985 (16), 1986 (16), 1987 (12), 1988 (16). Total—133.
Pro statistics: Recovered one fumble, 1981, 1982 and 1985; fumbled once, 1983; fumbled twice for minus four yards, 1986; caught one pass for minus three yards, 1988.
Played in Pro Bowl (NFL All-Star Game) following 1986 through 1988 seasons.

RICK DONNELLY
Punter—Atlanta Falcons
Born May 17, 1962, at Miller Place, N.Y.
Height, 6.00. Weight, 190.
High School—Miller Place, N.Y.
Attended University of Wyoming.

Selected by San Antonio in 14th round (192nd player selected) of 1985 USFL draft.
Signed as free agent by New England Patriots, May 8, 1985.
Released by New England Patriots, August 19, 1985; signed as free agent by Atlanta Falcons, August 23, 1985.
On injured reserve with knee injury, November 18 through remainder of 1985 season.
Granted free agency, February 1, 1988; re-signed by Falcons, August 31, 1988.

Year Club	G.	No.	Avg.	Blk.
1985—Atlanta NFL	11	59	43.6	0
1986—Atlanta NFL	16	78	43.9	1
1987—Atlanta NFL	12	61	★44.0	★2
1988—Atlanta NFL	16	★98	40.0	0
Pro Totals—4 Years	55	296	42.5	3

Additional pro statistics: Rushed twice for minus five yards, 1985; recovered one fumble, 1985 and 1987; successful on only extra point attempt, 1986; rushed three times for minus six yards and fumbled twice for minus four yards, 1987.

ANTHONY DREW DORSETT
Name pronounced Dor-SETT.
(Tony)
Running Back—Denver Broncos
Born April 7, 1954, at Rochester, Pa.
Height, 5.11. Weight, 185.
High School—Aliquippa, Pa., Hopewell.
Attended University of Pittsburgh.

Established NFL record for longest run from scrimmage (99 yards), January 3, 1983, against Minnesota Vikings.
Named THE SPORTING NEWS NFC Rookie of the Year, 1977.
Named to THE SPORTING NEWS NFL All-Star Team, 1981.
Named as running back on THE SPORTING NEWS College All-America Team, 1976.
Named THE SPORTING NEWS College Player of the Year, 1976.
Heisman Trophy winner, 1976.
Selected by Dallas in 1st round (2nd player selected) of 1977 NFL draft.
Crossed picket line during players' strike, October 1, 1987.
Traded by Dallas Cowboys to Denver Broncos for 5th round pick in 1989 draft, June 3, 1988.

Year Club	G.	Att.	Yds.	Avg.	TD.	P.C.	Yds.	Avg.	TD.	TD.	Pts.	F.
1977—Dallas NFL	14	208	1007	4.8	12	29	273	9.4	1	13	78	7
1978—Dallas NFL	16	290	1325	4.6	7	37	378	10.2	2	10	60	12
1979—Dallas NFL	14	250	1107	4.4	6	45	375	8.3	1	7	42	9
1980—Dallas NFL	15	278	1185	4.3	11	34	263	7.7	0	11	66	8
1981—Dallas NFL	16	342	1646	4.8	4	32	325	10.2	2	6	36	10
1982—Dallas NFL	9	*177	745	4.2	5	24	179	7.5	0	5	30	6
1983—Dallas NFL	16	289	1321	4.6	8	40	287	7.2	1	9	54	5
1984—Dallas NFL	16	302	1189	3.9	6	51	459	9.0	1	7	42	12
1985—Dallas NFL	16	305	1307	4.3	7	46	449	9.8	3	10	60	7
1986—Dallas NFL	13	184	748	4.1	5	25	267	10.7	1	6	36	5
1987—Dallas NFL	12	130	456	3.5	1	19	177	9.3	1	2	12	3
1988—Denver NFL	16	181	703	3.9	5	16	122	7.6	0	5	30	6
Pro Totals—12 Years	173	2936	12739	4.3	77	398	3554	8.9	13	91	546	90

Additional pro statistics: Attempted one pass with one completion for 34 yards, 1977; recovered four fumbles for 54 yards and one touchdown, 1978; attempted one pass with no completions, 1978, 1980, 1982 and 1983; recovered one fumble, 1979, 1980, 1982, 1983 and 1988; recovered one fumble for minus 21 yards, 1984; recovered two fumbles, 1981 and 1986; attempted one pass with one interception, 1984; recovered three fumbles, 1985; attempted two passes with one completion for seven yards and a touchdown, 1988.
Played in NFC Championship Game following 1977, 1978 and 1980 through 1982 seasons.
Played in NFL Championship Game following 1977 and 1978 seasons.
Played in Pro Bowl (NFL All-Star Game) following 1978 and 1981 through 1983 seasons.

ERIC HALL DORSEY
Defensive End—New York Giants
Born August 5, 1964, at Washington, D.C.
Height, 6.05. Weight, 280.
High School—McLean, Vir.
Received bachelor of business administration degree in marketing from University of Notre Dame in 1988.
Cousin of Allen Pinkett, running back with Houston Oilers.

Selected by Orlando in 1986 USFL territorial draft.
Selected by New York Giants in 1st round (19th player selected) of 1986 NFL draft.
Signed by New York Giants, August 8, 1986.
New York Giants NFL, 1986 through 1988.
Games: 1986 (16), 1987 (12), 1988 (16). Total—44.
Pro statistics: Returned one kickoff for 13 yards, 1987; recovered two fumbles, 1988.
Played in NFC Championship Game following 1986 season.
Played in NFL Championship Game following 1986 season.

JOHN MICHAEL DORSEY
Linebacker—Green Bay Packers
Born August 31, 1960, at Leonardtown, Md.
Height, 6.02. Weight, 243.
High School—Leonardtown, Md., Fort Union.
Attended University of Connecticut.

Selected by Philadelphia in 7th round (142nd player selected) of 1984 USFL draft.
Selected by Green Bay in 4th round (99th player selected) of 1984 NFL draft.
Signed by Green Bay Packers, July 12, 1984.
Green Bay NFL, 1984 through 1988.
Games: 1984 (16), 1985 (16), 1986 (16), 1987 (12), 1988 (16). Total—76.
Pro statistics: Recovered two fumbles, 1985 and 1986.

DAVID GLENN DOUGLAS
Offensive Tackle—New England Patriots
Born March 20, 1963, at Spring City, Tenn.
Height, 6.04. Weight, 280.
High School—Evansville, Tenn., Rhea County.
Attended University of Tennessee.

Selected by Memphis in 1986 USFL territorial draft.
Selected by Cincinnati in 8th round (204th player selected) of 1986 NFL draft.
Signed by Cincinnati Bengals, July 10, 1986.
Granted unconditional free agency, February 1, 1989; signed by New England Patriots, March 18, 1989.
Cincinnati NFL, 1986 through 1988.
Games: 1986 (14), 1987 (12), 1988 (14). Total—40.
Played in AFC Championship Game following 1988 season.
Played in NFL Championship Game following 1988 season.

MAURICE GERRARD DOUGLASS
Defensive Back—Chicago Bears
Born February 12, 1964, at Muncie, Ind.
Height, 5.11. Weight, 200.
High School—Trotwood, O., Madison.
Attended Coffeyville Community College and University of Kentucky.

Selected by Chicago in 8th round (221st player selected) of 1986 NFL draft.
Signed by Chicago Bears, June 22, 1986.
Released by Chicago Bears, September 1, 1986; re-signed by Bears, November 28, 1986.
Chicago NFL, 1986 through 1988.
Games: 1986 (4), 1987 (12), 1988 (15). Total—31.
Pro statistics: Intercepted two passes for no yards and recovered one fumble, 1987; intercepted one pass for 35 yards, recovered three fumbles and fumbled once, 1988.
Played in NFC Championship Game following 1988 season.

MICHAEL LYNN DOWNS
Safety
Born June 9, 1959, at Dallas, Tex.
Height, 6.03. Weight, 212.
High School—Dallas, Tex., South Oak Cliff.
Received degree in business, political science and physical education from Rice University in 1981.

Signed as free agent by Dallas Cowboys, May, 1981.
Released by Dallas Cowboys, May 19, 1989.

		—INTERCEPTIONS—			
Year Club	G.	No.	Yds.	Avg.	TD.
1981—Dallas NFL	15	7	81	11.6	0
1982—Dallas NFL	9	1	22	22.0	0
1983—Dallas NFL	16	4	80	20.0	0
1984—Dallas NFL	16	7	126	18.0	1
1985—Dallas NFL	16	3	11	3.7	0
1986—Dallas NFL	16	6	54	9.0	0
1987—Dallas NFL	12	4	56	14.0	0
1988—Dallas NFL	16	2	3	1.5	0
Pro Totals—8 Years	116	34	433	12.7	1

Additional pro statistics: Recovered one fumble, 1981 and 1987; recovered three fumbles for 87 yards and one touchdown, 1982; recovered two fumbles for 10 yards and a touchdown, 1983; recovered two fumbles for 28 yards, 1984; recovered three fumbles, 1985; recovered one fumble for 17 yards, 1986; recovered one fumble for 11 yards, 1988.
Played in NFC Championship Game following 1981 and 1982 seasons.

WILLIAM HENRY DOZIER JR.
(D. J.)
Running Back—Minnesota Vikings
Born September 21, 1965, at Norfolk, Va.
Height, 6.00. Weight, 208.
High School—Virginia Beach, Va., Kempsville.
Attended Penn State University.

Selected by Minnesota in 1st round (14th player selected) of 1987 NFL draft.
Signed by Minnesota Vikings, July 6, 1987.
On injured reserve with his injury, September 9 through October 21, 1988; activated, October 22, 1988.
Selected by Detroit Tigers' organization in 18th round of free-agent draft, June 6, 1983.

		—RUSHING—				PASS RECEIVING				—TOTAL—		
Year Club	G.	Att.	Yds.	Avg.	TD.	P.C.	Yds.	Avg.	TD.	TD.	Pts.	F.
1987—Minnesota NFL	9	69	257	3.7	5	12	89	7.4	2	7	42	2
1988—Minnesota NFL	8	42	167	4.0	2	5	49	9.8	0	2	12	0
Pro Totals—2 Years	17	111	424	3.8	7	17	138	8.1	2	9	54	2

Additional pro statistics: Returned two kickoffs for 23 yards, 1987; returned five kickoffs for 105 yards, 1988.
Played in NFC Championship Game following 1987 season.

DWIGHT DRANE
Safety—Buffalo Bills
Born May 6, 1962, at Miami, Fla.
Height, 6.02. Weight, 205.
High School—Miami, Fla., Central.
Attended University of Oklahoma.

Selected by Oklahoma in 1984 USFL territorial draft.
Rights traded by Oklahoma Outlaws to Los Angeles Express for rights to running back Andrew Lazarus, February 29, 1984.
Signed by Los Angeles Express, March 2, 1984.
Granted roster exemption, March 2 through March 8, 1984; activated, March 9, 1984.
Selected by Buffalo in 1st round (14th player selected) of 1984 NFL supplemental draft.
On developmental squad, June 9 through remainder of 1985 season.
Traded with running back Mel Gray, guard Wayne Jones, tight end Ken O'Neal, defensive backs John Warren and Troy West and linebacker Howard Carson by Los Angeles Express to Arizona Outlaws for past considerations, August 1, 1985.
Granted free agency when USFL suspended operations, August 7, 1986; signed by Buffalo Bills, September 10, 1986.

Granted roster exemption, September 10 through September 21, 1986; activated, September 22, 1986.
On developmental squad for 3 games with Los Angeles Express in 1985.
Los Angeles USFL, 1984 and 1985; Buffalo NFL, 1986 through 1988.
Games: 1984 (16), 1985 (15), 1986 (13), 1987 (11), 1988 (16). Total USFL—31. Total NFL—40. Total Pro—71.
USFL statistics: Intercepted three passes for 43 yards and a touchdown and recovered one fumble for 50 yards, 1984.
NFL statistics: Recovered one fumble, 1987.
Played in AFC Championship Game following 1988 season.

CHRIS DRESSEL
Tight End—Kansas City Chiefs
Born February 7, 1961, at Placentia, Calif.
Height, 6.04. Weight, 238.
High School—Placentia, Calif., El Dorado.
Attended Stanford University.

Selected by Oakland in 1983 USFL territorial draft.
Selected by Houston in 3rd round (69th player selected) of 1983 NFL draft.
Signed by Houston Oilers, June 22, 1983.
Traded by Houston Oilers to Washington Redskins for conditional 1988 draft choice, June 22, 1987.
Released by Washington Redskins, September 1, 1987; signed as free agent replacement player by San Francisco 49ers, September 24, 1987.
Released by San Francisco 49ers, October 14, 1987; signed as free agent by Cleveland Browns, November 19, 1987.
Released by Cleveland Browns, December 10, 1987; re-signed by Browns, April 30, 1988.
Released by Cleveland Browns, November 14, 1988; signed as free agent by Kansas City Chiefs, April 6, 1989.
Active for 4 games with Cleveland Browns in 1988; did not play.

| | | —PASS RECEIVING— | | | |
Year Club	G.	P.C.	Yds.	Avg.	TD.
1983—Houston NFL	16	32	316	9.9	4
1984—Houston NFL	16	40	378	9.5	2
1985—Houston NFL	16	3	17	5.7	1
1986—Houston NFL	16			None	
1987—San Francisco NFL	1	1	8	8.0	0
Pro Totals—6 Years	65	76	719	9.5	7

Additional pro statistics: Returned four kickoffs for 40 yards and rushed once for three yards, 1983; fumbled once, 1984; recovered one fumble, 1985.

WILLIE DREWREY
Wide Receiver—Tampa Bay Buccaneers
Born April 28, 1963, at Columbus, N.J.
Height, 5.07. Weight, 164.
High School—Columbus, N.J., Northern Burlington.
Attended West Virginia University.

Named as kick returner on THE SPORTING NEWS College All-America Team, 1984.
Selected by Birmingham in 1985 USFL territorial draft.
Selected by Houston in 11th round (281st player selected) of 1985 NFL draft.
Signed by Houston Oilers, July 18, 1985.
On injured reserve with dislocated elbow, December 6 through remainder of 1988 season.
Granted unconditional free agency, February 1, 1989; signed by Tampa Bay Buccaneers, March 27, 1989.

| | | PASS RECEIVING | | | | –PUNT RETURNS– | | | | —KICKOFF RET.— | | | | —TOTAL— | | |
Year Club	G.	P.C.	Yds.	Avg.	TD.	No.	Yds.	Avg.	TD.	No.	Yds.	Avg.	TD.	TD.	Pts.	F.
1985—Houston NFL	14	2	28	14.0	0	24	215	9.0	0	26	642	24.7	0	0	0	2
1986—Houston NFL	15	18	299	16.6	0	34	262	7.7	0	25	500	20.0	0	0	0	3
1987—Houston NFL	12	11	148	13.5	0	3	11	3.7	0	8	136	17.0	0	0	0	0
1988—Houston NFL	14	11	172	15.6	1	2	8	4.0	0	1	10	10.0	0	1	6	0
Pro Totals—4 Years	55	42	647	15.4	1	63	496	7.9	0	60	1288	21.5	0	1	6	5

Additional pro statistics: Rushed twice for minus four yards, 1985; recovered one fumble, 1986.

DAVID RUSSELL DUERSON
(Dave)
Safety—Chicago Bears
Born November 28, 1960, at Muncie, Ind.
Height, 6.01. Weight, 210.
High School—Muncie, Ind., Northside.
Received bachelor of arts degree in economics and communications from University of Notre Dame in 1983.
Cousin of Allen Leavell, guard with Houston Rockets.

Named to THE SPORTING NEWS NFL All-Star Team, 1986.
Selected by Chicago in 1983 USFL territorial draft.
Selected by Chicago in 3rd round (64th player selected) of 1983 NFL draft.
Signed by Chicago Bears, June 25, 1983.

| | | -INTERCEPTIONS- | | | | -PUNT RETURNS- | | | | —TOTAL— | | |
Year Club	G.	No.	Yds.	Avg.	TD.	No.	Yds.	Avg.	TD.	TD.	Pts.	F.
1983—Chicago NFL	16			None				None		0	0	0
1984—Chicago NFL	16	1	9	9.0	0	1	4	4.0	0	0	0	0
1985—Chicago NFL	15	5	53	10.6	0	6	47	7.8	0	0	0	1

Year Club		G.	No.	INTERCEPTIONS Yds.	Avg.	TD.	PUNT RETURNS No.	Yds.	Avg.	TD.	TOTAL TD.	Pts.	F.
1986—Chicago NFL		16	6	139	23.2	0	None				0	0	0
1987—Chicago NFL		12	3	0	0.0	0	1	10	10.0	0	0	0	0
1988—Chicago NFL		15	2	18	9.0	0	None				0	0	0
Pro Totals—6 Years		90	17	219	12.9	0	8	61	7.6	0	0	0	1

Additional pro statistics: Returned three kickoffs for 66 yards, 1983; returned four kickoffs for 95 yards, 1984; recovered one fumble, 1985; recovered two fumbles for six yards, 1986; recovered one fumble for 10 yards, 1987.

Played in NFC Championship Game following 1984, 1985 and 1988 seasons.

Played in NFL Championship Game following 1985 season.

Played in Pro Bowl (NFL All-Star Game) following 1985 through 1988 seasons.

JAMIE DONNELL DUKES
Guard—Atlanta Falcons

Born June 14, 1964, at Schnectady, N.Y.

Height, 6.01. Weight, 278.

High School—Orlando, Fla., Evans.

Attended Florida State University.

Selected by Tampa Bay in 1986 USFL territorial draft.

Signed as free agent by Atlanta Falcons, May 4, 1986.

On injured reserve with toe injury, November 23 through remainder of 1988 season.

Atlanta NFL, 1986 through 1988.

Games: 1986 (14), 1987 (4), 1988 (12). Total—30.

Pro statistics: Recovered one fumble, 1986; returned one kickoff for 13 yards, 1988.

JONATHAN DUMBAULD
(Jon)
Defensive End—New Orleans Saints

Born February 14, 1963, at Anaheim, Calif.

Height, 6.04. Weight, 259.

High School—Troy, O.

Attended University of Kentucky.

Selected by New Orleans in 10th round (253rd player selected) of 1986 NFL draft.

Selected by Memphis in 6th round (41st player selected) of 1986 USFL draft.

Signed by New Orleans Saints, July 19, 1986.

Released by New Orleans Saints, August 27, 1986; re-signed by Saints, October 14, 1986.

Released by New Orleans Saints, September 7, 1987; awarded on waivers to Philadelphia Eagles, September 8, 1987.

On injured reserve with foot fracture, November 27 through remainder of 1987 season.

Released by Philadelphia Eagles, August 29, 1988; re-signed by Eagles, August 30, 1988.

Released by Philadelphia Eagles, September 8, 1988; signed as free agent by New Orleans Saints, December 15, 1988.

New Orleans NFL, 1986; Philadelphia NFL, 1987; Philadelphia (1)-New Orleans (1) NFL, 1988.

Games: 1986 (9), 1987 (6), 1988 (2). Total—17.

CURTIS EVERETT DUNCAN
Wide Receiver—Houston Oilers

Born January 26, 1965, at Detroit, Mich.

Height, 5.11. Weight, 184.

High School—Detroit, Mich., Redford.

Received bachelor of science degree in business/pre-law from Northwestern University in 1987.

Selected by Houston in 10th round (258th player selected) of 1987 NFL draft.

Signed by Houston Oilers, July 30, 1987.

Year Club		G.	PASS RECEIVING P.C.	Yds.	Avg.	TD.	PUNT RETURNS No.	Yds.	Avg.	TD.	KICKOFF RET. No.	Yds.	Avg.	TD.	TOTAL TD.	Pts.	F.
1987—Houston NFL		10	13	237	18.2	5	8	23	2.9	0	28	546	19.5	0	5	30	0
1988—Houston NFL		16	22	302	13.7	1	4	47	11.8	0	1	34	34.0	0	1	6	0
Pro Totals—2 Years		26	35	539	15.4	6	12	70	5.8	0	29	580	20.0	0	6	36	0

KELDRICK A. DUNN
(K. D.)
Tight End—New York Jets

Born April 28, 1963, at Fort Hood, Tex.

Height, 6.02. Weight, 235.

High School—Decatur, Ga., Gordon.

Attended Clemson University.

Selected by Orlando in 1985 USFL territorial draft.

Selected by St. Louis in 5th round (116th player selected) of 1985 NFL draft.

Signed by St. Louis Cardinals, July 3, 1985.

Released by St. Louis Cardinals, August 26, 1985; signed as free agent by Tampa Bay Buccaneers, November 5, 1985.

Released by Tampa Bay Buccaneers, August 22, 1986; re-signed by Buccaneers, November 4, 1986.

Released by Tampa Bay Buccaneers, August 24, 1987; signed as free agent replacement player by Washington Redskins, September 23, 1987.
Released by Washington Redskins, October 20, 1987; signed as free agent by New York Jets, May 3, 1988.
Tampa Bay NFL, 1985 and 1986; Washington NFL, 1987; New York Jets NFL, 1988.
Games: 1985 (7), 1986 (7), 1987 (3), 1988 (15). Total—32.
Pro statistics: Caught three passes for 83 yards and returned one kickoff for no yards, 1986; caught six passes for 67 yards, 1988.

JON REGINALD DUPARD
(Reggie)
Running Back—New England Patriots
Born October 30, 1963, at New Orleans, La.
Height, 5.11. Weight, 205.
High School—River Ridge, La., John Curtis Christian.
Attended Southern Methodist University.
Selected by New England in 1st round (26th player selected) of 1986 NFL draft.
Selected by Birmingham in 1st round (6th player selected) of 1986 USFL draft.
Signed by New England Patriots, August 5, 1986.
On injured reserve with sprained toe, September 1 through November 12, 1986; activated, November 13, 1986.
On injured reserve with hip injury, September 8 through October 30, 1987; activated, October 31, 1987.

		——RUSHING——				PASS RECEIVING				—TOTAL—		
Year Club	G.	Att.	Yds.	Avg.	TD.	P.C.	Yds.	Avg.	TD.	TD.	Pts.	F.
1986—New England NFL	6	15	39	2.6	0		None			0	0	1
1987—New England NFL	8	94	318	3.4	3	3	1	0.3	0	3	18	2
1988—New England NFL	16	52	151	2.9	2	34	232	6.8	0	2	12	1
Pro Totals—3 Years	30	161	508	3.2	5	37	233	6.3	0	5	30	4

Additional pro statistics: Returned three kickoffs for 50 yards, 1986; returned four kickoffs for 61 yards, 1987; recovered one fumble, 1987 and 1988.

MARK SUPER DUPER
(Given name at birth was Mark Kirby Dupas.)
Wide Receiver—Miami Dolphins
Born January 25, 1959, at Pineville, La.
Height, 5.09. Weight, 187.
High School—Moreauville, La.
Attended Northwestern (La.) State University.
Selected by Miami in 2nd round (52nd player selected) of 1982 NFL draft.
On inactive list, September 12 through September 19, 1982.
On injured reserve with broken leg, September 16 through November 8, 1985; activated, November 9, 1985.
Granted free agency, February 1, 1988; re-signed by Dolphins, August 21, 1988.
On non-football injury list with substance abuse, November 30 through remainder of 1988 season.

		——PASS RECEIVING——			
Year Club	G.	P.C.	Yds.	Avg.	TD.
1982—Miami NFL	2		None		
1983—Miami NFL	16	51	1003	19.7	10
1984—Miami NFL	16	71	1306	18.4	8
1985—Miami NFL	9	35	650	18.6	3
1986—Miami NFL	16	67	1313	19.6	11
1987—Miami NFL	11	33	597	18.1	8
1988—Miami NFL	13	39	626	16.1	1
Pro Totals—7 Years	83	296	5495	18.6	41

Additional pro statistics: Recovered one fumble, 1984; recovered one fumble for three yards and fumbled once, 1985; rushed once for minus 10 yards, 1986.
Played in AFC Championship Game following 1984 and 1985 seasons.
Played in NFL Championship Game following 1984 season.
Member of Miami Dolphins for AFC and NFL Championship Game following 1982 season; did not play.
Played in Pro Bowl (NFL All-Star Game) following 1983 and 1984 seasons.
Named to play in Pro Bowl following 1986 season; replaced due to injury by Mark Clayton.

SEAN RENE DYKES
Cornerback—Dallas Cowboys
Born August 8, 1964, at New Orleans, La.
Height, 5.10. Weight, 170.
High School—New Orleans, La., Joseph S. Clark.
Attended Eastern Arizona Junior College and Bowling Green State University.
Signed as free agent by San Diego Chargers, May 15, 1986.
Released by San Diego Chargers, August 11, 1986; signed as free agent by New York Jets, March 26, 1987.
Released by New York Jets, August 20, 1987; re-signed as replacement player by Jets, September 24, 1987.
Released by New York Jets, October 26, 1987; re-signed by Jets, December 2, 1987.
Released by New York Jets, August 2, 1988; signed as free agent by Dallas Cowboys, April 2, 1989.
New York Jets NFL, 1987.
Games: 1987 (6).

QUINN REMAR EARLY
Wide Reciever—San Diego Chargers
Born April 13, 1965, at West Hempstead, N. Y.
Height, 6.00. Weight, 188.
High School—Great Neck, N. Y.
Received degree in art from University of Iowa in 1988.

Selected by San Diego in 3rd round (60th player selected) of 1988 NFL draft.
Signed by San Diego Chargers, July 11, 1988.

Year Club	G.	Att.	Yds.	Avg.	TD.	P.C.	Yds.	Avg.	TD.	TD.	Pts.	F.
		RUSHING				PASS RECEIVING				—TOTAL—		
1988—San Diego NFL	16	7	63	9.0	0	29	375	12.9	4	4	24	1

CHARLES CARROLL EASON IV
(Tony)
Quarterback—New England Patriots
Height, 6.04. Weight, 212.
High School—Clarksburg, Calif., Delta.
Attended American River College and received bachelor of science degree
in physical education from University of Illinois in 1983.
Brother of Bo Eason, safety with Houston Oilers, 1984 through 1987.

Selected by Chicago in 1983 USFL territorial draft.
USFL rights traded with running back Calvin Murray and 1st round pick in 1983 draft by Chicago Blitz to Arizona Wranglers for rights to placekicker Frank Corral and 1st round pick in 1983 draft, January 4, 1983.
Selected by New England in 1st round (15th player selected) of 1983 NFL draft.
Signed by New England Patriots, June 2, 1983.
On injured reserve with separated shoulder, November 3 through remainder of 1987 season.
On injured reserve with nerve damage in elbow, August 30 through December 4, 1988; activated, December 5, 1988.

Year Club	G.	Att.	Cmp.	Pct.	Gain	T.P.	P.I.	Avg.	Att.	Yds.	Avg.	TD.	TD.	Pts.	F.
		PASSING							RUSHING				—TOTAL—		
1983—New England NFL	16	95	46	48.4	557	1	5	5.86	19	39	2.1	0	0	0	5
1984—New England NFL	16	431	259	60.1	3228	23	8	7.49	40	154	3.9	5	5	30	7
1985—New England NFL	16	299	168	56.2	2156	11	17	7.21	22	70	3.2	1	1	6	4
1986—New England NFL	15	448	276	61.6	3328	19	10	7.43	35	170	4.9	0	0	0	4
1987—New England NFL	4	79	42	53.2	453	3	2	5.73	3	25	8.3	0	0	0	0
1988—New England NFL	2	43	28	65.1	249	0	2	5.79	5	18	3.6	0	0	0	0
Pro Totals—6 Years	69	1395	819	58.7	9971	57	44	7.15	124	476	3.8	6	6	36	21

Quarterback Rating Points: 1983 (48.4), 1984 (93.4), 1985 (67.5), 1986 (89.2), 1987 (72.4), 1988 (61.1). Total—81.1.
Additional pro statistics: Recovered one fumble, 1983; recovered two fumbles and fumbled seven times for minus five yards, 1984; recovered one fumble and fumbled four times for minus 19 yards, 1985; recovered three fumbles, 1986; recovered one fumble for two yards, 1988.
Played in AFC Championship Game following 1985 season.
Played in NFL Championship Game following 1985 season.

IRVIN HUMPHREY EATMAN
(Irv)
Offensive Tackle—Kansas City Chiefs
Born January 1, 1961, at Birmingham, Ala.
Height, 6.07. Weight, 293.
High School—Dayton, O., Meadowdale.
Attended University of California at Los Angeles.

Named as offensive tackle on THE SPORTING NEWS USFL All-Star Team, 1983 and 1984.
Selected by Philadelphia in 1st round (8th player selected) of 1983 USFL draft.
Signed by Philadelphia Stars, February 8, 1983.
Selected by Kansas City in 8th round (204th player selected) of 1983 NFL draft.
Franchise transferred to Baltimore, November 1, 1984.
Granted free agency when USFL suspended operations, August 7, 1986; signed by Kansas City Chiefs, August 10, 1986.
Philadelphia USFL, 1983 and 1984; Baltimore USFL, 1985; Kansas City NFL, 1986 through 1988.
Games: 1983 (18), 1984 (18), 1985 (18), 1986 (16), 1987 (12), 1988 (16). Total USFL—54. Total NFL—44. Total Pro—98.
Played in USFL Championship Game following 1983 through 1985 seasons.

TRACEY EATON
Safety—Houston Oilers
Born July 19, 1965, at Medford, Ore.
Height, 6.01. Weight, 190.
High School—Medford, Ore.
Attended Portland State University.
Son of Scott Eaton, defensive back with New York Giants, 1967 through 1971.

Selected by Houston in 7th round (187th player selected) of 1988 NFL draft.
Signed by Houston Oilers, July 18, 1988.
On injured reserve with shoulder injury, August 23 through December 16, 1988; activated, December 17, 1988.
Houston NFL, 1988.
Games: 1988 (1).

BRAD M. EDELMAN
Guard—New Orleans Saints
Born September 3, 1960, at Jacksonville, Fla.
Height, 6.06. Weight, 270.
High School—Creve Coeur, Mo., Parkway North.
Attended University of Missouri.

Named as center on THE SPORTING NEWS College All-America Team, 1981.
Selected by New Orleans on 2nd round (30th player selected) of 1982 NFL draft.
On injured reserve with knee injury, October 9 through November 18, 1984; activated, November 19, 1984.
On injured reserve with knee injury, September 24 through November 15, 1985; activated, November 16, 1985.
New Orleans NFL, 1982 through 1988.
Games: 1982 (9), 1983 (16), 1984 (11), 1985 (8), 1986 (13), 1987 (11), 1988 (14). Total—82.
Pro statistics: Recovered one fumble, 1986.
Played in Pro Bowl (NFL All-Star Game) following 1987 season.

BOBBY JOE EDMONDS JR.
(Bobby Joe)
Running Back—Detroit Lions
Born September 26, 1964, at Nashville, Tenn.
Height, 5.11. Weight, 186.
High School—St. Louis, Mo., Lutheran North.
Attended University of Arkansas.
Son of Bobby Joe Edmonds Sr., player with Indiana Pacers of ABA, 1967-68 and 1969-70.

Named as punt returner to THE SPORTING NEWS NFL All-Star Team, 1986.
Selected by Memphis in 1986 USFL territorial draft.
Selected by Seattle in 5th round (126th player selected) of 1986 NFL draft.
Signed by Seattle Seahawks, July 17, 1986.
Granted unconditional free agency, February 1, 1989; signed by Detroit Lions, March 16, 1989.
Selected by St. Louis (baseball) Cardinals' organization in 12th round of free-agent draft, June 7, 1982.
Selected by St. Louis (baseball) Cardinals' organization in secondary phase of free-agent draft, June 6, 1983.
Signed as free agent by Philadelphia Phillies' organization, February 9, 1989.

Year Club	G.	No.	Yds.	Avg.	TD.	No.	Yds.	Avg.	TD.	TD.	Pts.	F.
			–PUNT RETURNS–			—KICKOFF RET.—				—TOTAL—		
1986—Seattle NFL	15	34	419	*12.3	1	34	764	22.5	0	1	6	4
1987—Seattle NFL	11	20	251	12.6	0	27	564	20.9	0	0	0	1
1988—Seattle NFL	16	35	340	9.7	0	40	900	22.5	0	0	0	2
Pro Totals—3 Years	42	89	1010	11.3	1	101	2228	22.1	0	1	6	7

Additional pro statistics: Rushed once for minus 11 yards, 1986; recovered one fumble, 1986 through 1988.
Played in Pro Bowl (NFL All-Star Game) following 1986 season.

FERRELL EDMUNDS JR.
Tight End—Miami Dolphins
Born April 16, 1965, at South Boston, Va.
Height, 6.06. Weight, 248.
High School—Danville, Va., George Washington.
Attended University of Maryland.

Selected by Miami in 3rd round (73rd player selected) of 1988 NFL draft.
Signed by Miami Dolphins, July 12, 1988.

Year Club	G.	P.C.	Yds.	Avg.	TD.
		——PASS RECEIVING——			
1988—Miami NFL	16	33	575	17.4	3

Additional pro statistics: Rushed once for minus eight yards, returned one kickoff for 20 yards and fumbled four times, 1988.

BRADFORD WAYNE EDWARDS
(Brad)
Safety—Minnesota Vikings
Born February 22, 1966, at Lumberton, N. C.
Height, 6.01. Weight, 200.
High School—Fayetteville, N. C., Douglas Bryd.
Received degree in business management from University of South Carolina in 1988.
Son of Wayne Edwards, infielder in Baltimore Orioles' organization, 1962 through 1965.

Selected by Minnesota in 2nd round (54th player selected) of 1988 NFL draft.
Signed by Minnesota Vikings, July 20, 1988.

Year Club	G.	No.	Yds.	Avg.	TD.
		——INTERCEPTIONS——			
1988—Minnesota NFL	16	2	47	23.5	1

KELVIN EDWARDS
Wide Receiver—Dallas Cowboys
Born July 19, 1964, at Birmingham, Ala.
Height, 6.02. Weight, 205.
High School—Eastpoint, Ga., Russell.
Attended Liberty Baptist College.

Selected by New Orleans in 4th round (88th player selected) of 1986 NFL draft.
Signed by New Orleans Saints, July 16, 1986.
Released by New Orleans Saints, September 7, 1987; signed as free agent replacement player by Dallas Cowboys, September 23, 1987.
On injured reserve with knee injury, December 1 through remainder of 1988 season.

Year Club	G.	PASS RECEIVING				–PUNT RETURNS–				—KICKOFF RET.—				—TOTAL—		
		P.C.	Yds.	Avg.	TD.	No.	Yds.	Avg.	TD.	No.	Yds.	Avg.	TD.	TD.	Pts.	F.
1986—New Orleans NFL........	14	10	132	13.2	0	3	2	0.7	0	None				0	0	2
1987—Dallas NFL	13	34	521	15.3	3	8	75	9.4	0	7	155	22.1	0	4	24	1
1988—Dallas NFL	8	5	93	18.6	0	None				None				0	0	1
Pro Totals—3 Years.......	35	49	746	15.2	3	11	77	7.0	0	7	155	22.1	0	4	24	4

Additional pro statistics: Rushed once for six yards and recovered two fumbles, 1986; rushed twice for 61 yards and a touchdown, 1987; recovered one fumble, 1988.

CHARLES KALEV EHIN

(Middle name is an Estonian name meaning Atlas, or great person.)

(Chuck)

Nose Tackle—Indianapolis Colts

Born July 1, 1961, at Marysville, Calif.
Height, 6.04. Weight, 266.
High School—Layton, Utah.
Attended Brigham Young University.

Selected by Chicago in 17th round (198th player selected) of 1983 USFL draft.
Selected by San Diego in 12th round (329th player selected) of 1983 NFL draft.
Signed by San Diego Chargers, June 6, 1983.
On injured reserve with knee injury, November 24 through remainder of 1986 season.
Released by San Diego Chargers, August 30, 1988; signed as free agent by Indianapolis Colts, March 29, 1989.
San Diego NFL, 1983 through 1987.
Games: 1983 (9), 1984 (16), 1985 (16), 1986 (12), 1987 (12). Total—65.
Pro statistics: Recovered one fumble, 1984 through 1986; recovered one fumble for 27 yards and fumbled once, 1987.

STANLEY EMERSON EISENHOOTH

(Stan)

Center—Indianapolis Colts

Born July 8, 1963, at Harrisburg, Pa.
Height, 6.05. Weight, 274.
High School—Wingate, Pa., Bald Eagle Area.
Attended Arizona Western College and Towson State University.
Brother of John Eisenhooth, defensive tackle with Seattle Seahawks, 1987.

Signed as free agent by Seattle Seahawks, May 8, 1986.
On injured reserve with shoulder injury, September 3 through entire 1986 season.
On injured reserve with broken hand, September 1 through December 17, 1987; activated, December 18, 1987.
Crossed picket line during players' strike, September 28, 1987; returned to picket line, October 1, 1987.
Granted unconditional free agency, February 1, 1989; signed by Indianapolis Colts, March 29, 1989.
Active for 2 games with Seattle Seahawks in 1987; did not play.
Seattle NFL, 1987 and 1988.
Games: 1988 (13).

ONZY WARREN ELAM

(Name pronounced ON-zee EE-lam.)

Linebacker—Washington Redskins

Born December 1, 1964, at Miami, Fla.
Height, 6.02. Weight, 225.
High School—Miami, Fla., Northwestern.
Received degree in criminal justice from Tennessee State University in 1987.

Selected by New York Jets in 3rd round (75th player selected) of 1987 NFL draft.
Signed by New York Jets, July 23, 1987.
On non-football injury list with gastric irritation, October 4 through remainder of 1988 season.
Granted unconditional free agency, February 1, 1989; signed by Washington Redskins, February 22, 1989.
New York Jets NFL, 1987 and 1988.
Games: 1987 (5), 1988 (4). Total—9.

DONALD EUGENE ELDER

(Donnie)

Defensive Back—Tampa Bay Buccaneers

Born December 13, 1963, at Chattanooga, Tenn.
Height, 5.09. Weight, 175.
High School—Chattanooga, Tenn., Brainerd.
Attended Memphis State University.

Selected by Memphis in 1985 USFL territorial draft.
Selected by New York Jets in 3rd round (67th player selected) of 1985 NFL draft.
Signed by New York Jets, July 17, 1985.
On injured reserve with hip injury, November 16 through remainder of 1985 season.

Released by New York Jets, August 25, 1986; awarded on waivers to Pittsburgh Steelers, August 26, 1986.
Released by Pittsburgh Steelers, November 28, 1986; signed as free agent by Detroit Lions, December 3, 1986.
On injured reserve with knee injury, September 7 through November 16, 1987.
Released by Detroit Lions, November 17, 1987; signed as free agent by Tampa Bay Buccaneers, February 18, 1988.

			KICKOFF RETURNS		
Year Club	G.	No.	Yds.	Avg.	TD.
1985—N.Y. Jets NFL	10	3	42	14.0	0
1986—Pitt.(9)-Det.(3) NFL	12	22	435	19.8	0
1988—Tampa Bay NFL	16	34	772	22.7	0
Pro Totals—3 Years	38	59	1249	21.2	0

Additional pro statistics: Fumbled once, 1985, 1986 and 1988; recovered one fumble, 1986; intercepted three passes for nine yards, returned one punt for no yards and recovered one fumble for six yards, 1988.

HENRY ELLARD
Wide Receiver—Los Angeles Rams
Born July 21, 1961, at Fresno, Calif.
Height, 5.11. Weight, 175.
High School—Fresno, Calif., Hoover.
Attended Fresno State University.

Named to THE SPORTING NEWS NFL All-Star Team, 1988.
Named as punt returner to THE SPORTING NEWS NFL All-Star Team, 1984 and 1985.
Selected by Oakland in 1983 USFL territorial draft.
Selected by Los Angeles Rams in 2nd round (32nd player selected) of 1983 NFL draft.
Signed by Los Angeles Rams, July 22, 1983.
Granted free agency, February 1, 1986; re-signed by Rams, October 22, 1986.
Granted roster exemption, October 22 through October 24, 1986; activated, October 25, 1986.

		PASS RECEIVING				–PUNT RETURNS–				—KICKOFF RET.—				—TOTAL—		
Year Club	G.	P.C.	Yds.	Avg.	TD.	No.	Yds.	Avg.	TD.	No.	Yds.	Avg.	TD.	TD.	Pts.	F.
1983—L.A. Rams NFL	12	16	268	16.8	0	16	217	★13.6	★1	15	314	20.9	0	1	6	2
1984—L.A. Rams NFL	16	34	622	18.3	6	30	403	13.4	★2	2	24	12.0	0	8	48	4
1985—L.A. Rams NFL	16	54	811	15.0	5	37	501	13.5	1		None			6	36	5
1986—L.A. Rams NFL	9	34	447	13.1	4	14	127	9.1	0	1	18	18.0	0	4	24	3
1987—L.A. Rams NFL	12	51	799	15.7	3	15	107	7.1	0	1	8	8.0	0	3	18	3
1988—L.A. Rams NFL	16	86	★1414	16.4	10	17	119	7.0	0		None			10	60	3
Pro Totals—6 Years	81	275	4361	15.9	28	129	1474	11.4	4	19	364	19.2	0	32	192	20

Additional pro statistics: Rushed three times for seven yards, 1983; recovered two fumbles, 1983 and 1984; rushed three times for minus five yards, 1984; rushed three times for eight yards and recovered five fumbles, 1985; rushed once for minus 15 yards, 1986; recovered one fumble, 1986 and 1987; rushed once for four yards, 1987; rushed once for seven yards, 1988.
Played in NFC Championship Game following 1985 season.
Played in Pro Bowl (NFL All-Star Game) following 1984 and 1988 seasons.

JOHN ELLIOTT
Offensive Tackle—New York Giants
Born April 1, 1965, at Lake Ronkonkoma, N. Y.
Height, 6.07. Weight, 305.
High School—Lake Ronkonkoma, N. Y., Sachem.
Received degree from University of Michigan in 1988.

Selected by New York Giants in 2nd round (36th player selected) of 1988 NFL draft.
Signed by New York Giants, July 18, 1988.
New York Giants NFL, 1988.
Games: 1988 (16).
Pro statistics: Recovered one fumble, 1988.

RIKI MORGAN ELLISON
(Formerly known as Riki Gray.)
Linebacker—San Francisco 49ers
Born August 15, 1960, at Christchurch, New Zealand.
Height, 6.02. Weight, 225.
High School—Tucson, Ariz., Amphitheater.
Received bachelor of arts degree in international relations, certificate of defense and strategic studies and physical education from University of Southern California in 1983; and attending University of Southern California for master's degree in international relations and foreign policy.

Selected by Los Angeles in 1983 USFL territorial draft.
Selected by San Francisco in 5th round (117th player selected) of 1983 NFL draft.
Signed by San Francisco 49ers, June 1, 1983.
On injured reserve with broken arm, September 14 through December 16, 1987; activated, December 17, 1987.
San Francisco NFL, 1983 through 1988.
Games: 1983 (16), 1984 (16), 1985 (16), 1986 (16), 1987 (3), 1988 (13). Total—80.
Pro statistics: Recovered two fumbles for seven yards, 1985; recovered one fumble, 1986.
Played in NFC Championship Game following 1983 and 1984 seasons.
Member of San Francisco 49ers for NFC Championship Game following 1988 season; inactive.
Played in NFL Championship Game following 1984 and 1988 seasons.

JOHN ALBERT ELWAY
Quarterback—Denver Broncos

Born June 28, 1960, at Port Angeles, Wash.
Height, 6.03. Weight, 210.
High School—Granada Hills, Calif.
Received bachelor of arts degree in economics from Stanford University in 1983.
Son of Jack Elway, head football coach at Stanford University.

Named to THE SPORTING NEWS NFL All-Star Team, 1987.
Named as quarterback on THE SPORTING NEWS College All-America Team, 1980 and 1982.
Selected by Oakland in 1983 USFL territorial draft.
Selected by Baltimore in 1st round (1st player selected) of 1983 NFL draft.
Rights traded by Baltimore Colts to Denver Broncos for quarterback Mark Herrmann, rights to offensive lineman Chris Hinton and 1st round pick in 1984 draft, May 2, 1983.
Signed by Denver Broncos, May 2, 1983.

		—————PASSING—————							—————RUSHING————				—TOTAL—		
Year Club	G.	Att.	Cmp.	Pct.	Gain	T.P.	P.I.	Avg.	Att.	Yds.	Avg.	TD.	TD.	Pts.	F.
1983—Denver NFL	11	259	123	47.5	1663	7	14	6.42	28	146	5.2	1	1	6	6
1984—Denver NFL	15	380	214	56.3	2598	18	15	6.84	56	237	4.2	1	1	6	14
1985—Denver NFL	16	*605	327	54.0	3891	22	23	6.43	51	253	5.0	0	0	0	7
1986—Denver NFL	16	504	280	55.6	3485	19	13	6.91	52	257	4.9	1	2	12	8
1987—Denver NFL	12	410	224	54.6	3198	19	12	7.80	66	304	4.6	4	4	24	2
1988—Denver NFL	15	496	274	55.2	3309	17	19	6.67	54	234	4.3	1	1	6	7
Pro Totals—6 Years	85	2654	1442	54.3	18144	102	96	6.84	307	1431	4.7	8	9	54	44

Quarterback Rating Points: 1983 (54.9), 1984 (76.8), 1985 (70.2), 1986 (79.0), 1987 (83.4), 1988 (71.4). Total—73.5.
Additional pro statistics: Recovered three fumbles, 1983; recovered three fumbles and fumbled 14 times for minus 10 yards, 1984; recovered two fumbles and fumbled seven times for minus 35 yards, 1985; caught one pass for 23 yards and a touchdown, recovered one fumble and fumbled eight times for minus 13 yards, 1986; fumbled twice for minus one yard and punted once for 31 yards, 1987; punted three times for 39.0 avg., recovered five fumbles and fumbled seven times for minus nine yards, 1988.
Played in AFC Championship Game following 1986 and 1987 seasons.
Played in NFL Championship Game following 1986 and 1987 seasons.
Played in Pro Bowl (NFL All-Star Game) following 1986 and 1987 seasons.

RECORD AS BASEBALL PLAYER

Year Club	League	Pos.	G.	AB.	R.	H.	2B.	3B.	HR.	RBI.	B.A.	PO.	A.	E.	F.A.
1982—Oneonta	NYP	OF	42	151	26	48	6	2	4	25	.318	69	8	0	1.000

Selected by Kansas City Royals' organization in 18th round of free-agent draft, June 5, 1979.
Selected by New York Yankees' organization in 2nd round of free-agent draft, June 8, 1981.

JON W. EMBREE
Tight End—Seattle Seahawks

Born October 15, 1965, at Los Angeles, Calif.
Height, 6.02. Weight, 237.
High School—Englewood, Colo., Cherry Creek.
Attended University of Colorado.
Son of John Embree, wide receiver with Denver Broncos, 1969 and 1970.

Selected by Los Angeles Rams in 6th round (166th player selected) of 1987 NFL draft.
Signed by Los Angeles Rams, July 24, 1987.
On injured reserve with elbow injury, November 13 through remainder of 1987 season.
On injured reserve with knee injury, December 7 through remainder of 1988 season.
Granted unconditional free agency, February 1, 1989; signed by Seattle Seahawks, March 9, 1989.
Los Angeles Rams NFL, 1987 and 1988.
Games: 1987 (1), 1988 (12). Total—13.

LARRY G. EMERY JR.
Running Back—Houston Oilers

Born July 13, 1964, at Macon, Ga.
Height, 5.09. Weight, 195.
High School—Macon, Ga., Northeast.
Attended University of Wisconsin.

Selected by Atlanta in 12th round (320th player selected) of 1987 NFL draft.
Signed by Atlanta Falcons, July 26, 1987.
On injured reserve with blood clot in arm, September 11 through November 2, 1987; activated, November 3, 1987.
On injured reserve with back injury, December 18 through remainder of 1987 season.
On injured reserve with knee injury, August 22 through December 12, 1988.
Released by Atlanta Falcons, December 13, 1988; signed as free agent by Houston Oilers, May 17, 1989.

		—————RUSHING————				PASS RECEIVING				—TOTAL—		
Year Club	G.	Att.	Yds.	Avg.	TD.	P.C.	Yds.	Avg.	TD.	TD.	Pts.	F.
1987—Atlanta NFL	5	1	5	5.0	0	5	31	6.2	0	0	0	0

		KICKOFF RETURNS			
Year Club	G.	No.	Yds.	Avg.	TD.
1987—Atlanta NFL	5	21	440	21.0	0

PHILLIP EARL EPPS
(Phil)
Wide Receiver—Green Bay Packers

Born November 11, 1959, at Atlanta, Tex.
Height, 5.10. Weight, 165.
High School—Atlanta, Tex.
Received bachelor of science degree in criminal justice from Texas Christian University.
Cousin of Cedric Mack, cornerback with Phoenix Cardinals.
Selected by Green Bay in 12th round (321st player selected) of 1982 NFL draft.
USFL rights traded with future draft picks by San Antonio Gunslingers to Philadelphia Stars for rights to running back Billy Campfield, March 5, 1984.
Granted free agency, February 1, 1986; re-signed by Packers, August 18, 1986.
Granted roster exemption, August 18 through August 21; activated, August 22, 1986.
On injured reserve with knee injury, November 26 through remainder of 1986 season.
Granted free agency, February 1, 1988; re-signed by Packers, August 30, 1988.
On injured reserve with broken wrist, September 12 through October 14, 1988; activated, October 15, 1988.
On injured reserve with hamstring injury, November 19 through remainder of 1988 season.

Year Club		PASS RECEIVING				–PUNT RETURNS–				—KICKOFF RET.—				—TOTAL—		
	G.	P.C.	Yds.	Avg.	TD.	No.	Yds.	Avg.	TD.	No.	Yds.	Avg.	TD.	TD.	Pts.	F.
1982—Green Bay NFL...........	9	10	226	22.6	2	20	150	7.5	0		None			2	12	1
1983—Green Bay NFL...........	16	18	313	17.4	0	36	324	9.0	*1		None			1	6	2
1984—Green Bay NFL...........	16	26	435	16.7	3	29	199	6.9	0	12	232	19.3	0	3	18	1
1985—Green Bay NFL...........	16	44	683	15.5	3	15	146	9.7	0	12	279	23.3	0	4	24	1
1986—Green Bay NFL...........	12	49	612	12.5	4		None			1	21	21.0	0	4	24	0
1987—Green Bay NFL...........	10	34	516	15.2	2		None				None			2	12	1
1988—Green Bay NFL...........	6	11	99	9.0	0		None				None			0	0	0
Pro Totals—7 Years.......	85	192	2884	15.0	14	100	819	8.2	1	25	532	21.3	0	16	96	6

Additional pro statistics: Recovered one fumble, 1984; rushed five times for 103 yards and a touchdown, 1985; rushed four times for 18 yards, 1986; rushed once for no yards, 1987.

TOM A. ERLANDSON JR.
Linebacker—Buffalo Bills

Born June 19, 1966, at Denver, Colo.
Height, 6.01. Weight, 220.
High School—Denver, Colo., Smoky Hills.
Attended University of Washington.
Son of Tom Erlandson, Sr., linebacker with Denver Broncos, Miami Dolphins and San Diego Chargers, 1962 through 1968.
Selected by Buffalo in 12th round (316th player selected) of 1988 NFL draft.
Signed by Buffalo Bills, July 16, 1988.
On injured reserve with shoulder injury, October 1 through remainder of 1988 season.
Buffalo NFL, 1988.
Games: 1988 (4).

NORMAN JULIUS ESIASON
(Boomer)
Quarterback—Cincinnati Bengals

Born April 17, 1961, at West Islip, N.Y.
Height, 6.05. Weight, 225.
High School—Islip Terrace, N.Y., East Islip.
Attended University of Maryland.
Named THE SPORTING NEWS NFL Player of the Year, 1988.
Named to THE SPORTING NEWS NFL All-Star Team, 1988.
Led NFL quarterbacks in passing with 97.4 points in 1988.
Selected by Washington in 1984 USFL territorial draft.
Selected by Cincinnati in 2nd round (38th player selected) of 1984 NFL draft.
Signed by Cincinnati Bengals, June 19, 1984.

Year Club				PASSING						RUSHING				—TOTAL—		
	G.	Att.	Cmp.	Pct.	Gain	T.P.	P.I.	Avg.	Att.	Yds.	Avg.	TD.	TD.	Pts.	F.
1984—Cincinnati NFL................	10	102	51	50.0	530	3	3	5.20	19	63	3.3	2	2	12	4
1985—Cincinnati NFL................	15	431	251	58.2	3443	27	12	7.99	33	79	2.4	1	1	6	9
1986—Cincinnati NFL................	16	469	273	58.2	3959	24	17	*8.44	44	146	3.3	1	1	6	12
1987—Cincinnati NFL................	12	440	240	54.5	3321	16	19	7.55	52	241	4.6	0	0	0	10
1988—Cincinnati NFL................	16	388	223	57.5	3572	28	14	*9.21	43	248	5.8	1	1	6	5
Pro Totals—5 Years...........	69	1830	1038	56.7	14825	98	65	8.10	191	777	4.1	5	5	30	40

Quarterback Rating Points: 1984 (62.9), 1985 (93.2), 1986 (87.7), 1987 (73.1), 1988 (97.4). Total—86.1.
Additional pro statistics: Recovered two fumbles and fumbled four times for minus two yards, 1984; recovered four fumbles and fumbled nine times for minus five yards, 1985; punted once for 31 yards, recovered five fumbles and fumbled 12 times for minus 10 yards, 1986; punted twice for a 34.0 average, recovered four fumbles and fumbled 10 times for minus eight yards, 1987; punted once for 21.0 avg. and recovered four fumbles, 1988.
Played in AFC Championship Game following 1988 season.
Played in NFL Championship Game following 1988 season.
Played in Pro Bowl (NFL All-Star Game) following 1986 season.
Named to play in Pro Bowl following 1988 season; replaced due to injury by Jim Kelly.

BYRON NELSON EVANS
Linebacker—Philadelphia Eagles
Born February 23, 1964, at Phoenix, Ariz.
Height, 6.02. Weight, 225.
High School—Phoenix, Ariz., South Mountain.
Attended University of Arizona.

Selected by Philadelphia in 4th round (93rd player selected) of 1987 NFL draft.
Signed by Philadelphia Eagles, August 6, 1987.
Philadelphia NFL, 1987 and 1988.
Games: 1987 (12), 1988 (16). Total—28.
Pro statistics: Intercepted one pass for 12 yards and recovered one fumble, 1987; recovered two fumbles, 1988.

DONALD LEE EVANS
Defensive End—Philadelphia Eagles
Born March 14, 1964, at Raleigh, N.C.
Height, 6.02. Weight, 241.
High School—Raleigh, N.C., Athens Drive.
Attended Winston-Salem State University.

Selected by Los Angeles Rams in 2nd round (47th player selected) of 1987 NFL draft.
Signed by Los Angeles Rams, August 1, 1987.
On injured reserve with strained abdomen, September 7 through December 7, 1987; activated, December 8, 1987.
Released by Los Angeles Rams, August 30, 1988; signed as free agent by Philadelphia Eagles, September 8, 1988.
On injured reserve with fractured jaw, October 13 through remainder of 1988 season.
Los Angeles Rams NFL, 1987; Philadelphia NFL, 1988.
Games: 1987 (1), 1988 (5). Total—6.
Pro statistics: Rushed three times for 10 yards, 1987.

VINCENT TOBIAS EVANS
(Vince)
Quarterback—Los Angeles Raiders
Born June 14, 1955, at Greensboro, N.C.
Height, 6.02. Weight, 210.
High School—Greensboro, N.C., Benjamin L. Smith.
Attended Los Angeles City College and University of Southern California.

Selected by Chicago in 6th round (140th player selected) of 1977 NFL draft.
On injured reserve with staph infection, October 12 through remainder of 1979 season.
USFL rights traded by Los Angeles Express to Washington Federals for rights to cornerback Johnny Lynn, November 11, 1983.
Signed by Chicago Blitz, November 14, 1983, for contract to take effect after being granted free agency, February 1, 1984.
USFL rights traded by Washington Federals to Chicago Blitz for linebacker Ben Apuna and rights to wide receiver Waddell Smith, December 27, 1983.
Franchise disbanded, November 20, 1984.
Traded with linebackers Kelvin Atkins, Jay Wilson and Ed Thomas by Chicago Blitz to Denver Gold for past consideration, December 6, 1984.
Contract rights returned to Chicago Blitz, August 2, 1985.
Granted free agency when USFL suspended operations, August 7, 1986; signed as replacement player by Los Angeles Raiders, September 24, 1987.
Released by Los Angeles Raiders, October 10, 1988; re-signed by Raiders, November 30, 1988.
Active for 6 games with Los Angeles Raiders in 1988; did not play.

Year Club	G.	Att.	Cmp.	Pct.	Gain	T.P.	P.I.	Avg.	Att.	Yds.	Avg.	TD.	TD.	Pts.	F.
1977—Chicago NFL	13				None				1	0	0.0	0	0	0	3
1978—Chicago NFL	3	3	1	33.3	38	0	1	12.67	6	23	3.8	0	0	0	0
1979—Chicago NFL	4	63	32	50.8	508	4	5	8.06	12	72	6.0	1	1	6	1
1980—Chicago NFL	13	278	148	53.2	2039	11	16	7.33	60	306	5.1	8	8	48	4
1981—Chicago NFL	16	436	195	44.7	2354	11	20	5.40	43	218	5.1	3	3	18	13
1982—Chicago NFL	4	28	12	42.9	125	0	4	4.46	2	0	0.0	0	0	0	1
1983—Chicago NFL	9	145	76	52.4	1108	5	7	7.64	22	142	6.5	1	1	6	4
1984—Chicago USFL	15	411	200	48.7	2624	14	22	6.38	30	144	4.8	6	6	36	6
1985—Denver USFL	14	325	157	48.3	2259	12	16	6.95	43	283	6.6	7	7	42	3
1987—L.A. Raiders NFL	3	83	39	47.0	630	5	4	7.59	11	144	13.1	1	1	6	0
NFL Totals—9 Years	65	1036	503	48.6	6802	36	57	6.57	157	905	5.8	14	14	84	26
USFL Totals—2 Years	29	736	357	48.5	4883	26	38	6.63	73	427	5.8	13	13	78	9
Pro Totals—11 Years	94	1772	860	48.5	11685	62	95	6.59	230	1332	5.8	27	27	1620	35

NFL Quarterback Rating Points: 1978 (42.3), 1979 (66.1), 1980 (66.1), 1981 (51.0), 1982 (16.8), 1983 (69.0), 1987 (72.9). Total—58.7.
USFL Quarterback Rating Points: 1984 (58.3), 1985 (63.1). Total—60.1.
Additional NFL statistics: Returned 13 kickoffs for 253 yards (19.5 average) and recovered two fumbles, 1977; fumbled once for minus two yards, 1979; fumbled four times for minus three yards, 1980; recovered two fumbles and fumbled 13 times for minus 10 yards, 1981; fumbled once for minus 24 yards, 1982.
Additional USFL statistics: Recovered two fumbles, 1984.

—DID YOU KNOW—
That the Denver Broncos led the NFL in fewest fair catches with five in 1988?

ERIC EUGENE EVERETT
Cornerback—Philadelphia Eagles

Born July 13, 1966, at Daingerfield, Tex.
Height, 5.10. Weight, 161.
High School—Daingerfield, Tex.
Attended Texas Tech University.
Brother of Thomas Everett, safety with Pittsburgh Steelers.

Selected by Philadelphia in 5th round (122nd player selected) of 1988 NFL draft.
Signed by Philadelphia Eagles, July 21, 1988.
Philadelphia NFL, 1988.
Games: 1988 (16).
Pro statistics: Intercepted one pass for no yards, 1988.

JAMES SAMUEL EVERETT III
(Jim)
Quarterback—Los Angeles Rams

Born January 3, 1963, at Emporia, Kan.
Height, 6.05. Weight, 212.
High School—Albuquerque, N.M., Eldorado.
Received degree in finance from Purdue University in 1986.

Selected by Houston in 1st round (3rd player selected) of 1986 NFL draft.
Selected by Memphis in 1st round (4th player selected) of 1986 USFL draft.
NFL rights traded by Houston Oilers to Los Angeles Rams for guard Kent Hill, defensive end William Fuller, 1st and 5th round picks in 1987 draft and 1st round pick in 1988 draft, September 18, 1986.
Signed by Los Angeles Rams, September 25, 1986.
Granted roster exemption, September 25 through September 29, 1986; activated, September 30, 1986.
Crossed picket line during players' strike, October 14, 1987.

			—PASSING—						—RUSHING—				—TOTAL—		
Year Club	G.	Att.	Cmp.	Pct.	Gain	T.P.	P.I.	Avg.	Att.	Yds.	Avg.	TD.	TD.	Pts.	F.
1986—L.A. Rams NFL	6	147	73	49.7	1018	8	8	6.93	16	46	2.9	1	1	6	2
1987—L.A. Rams NFL	11	302	162	53.6	2064	10	13	6.83	18	83	4.6	1	1	6	2
1988—L.A. Rams NFL	16	517	308	59.6	3964	*31	18	7.67	34	104	3.1	0	0	0	7
Pro Totals—3 Years	33	966	543	56.2	7046	49	39	7.29	68	233	3.4	2	2	12	11

Quarterback Rating Points: 1986 (67.8), 1987 (68.4), 1988 (89.2). Total—79.6.
Additional pro statistics: Fumbled twice for minus two yards, 1986; recovered one fumble, 1987; fumbled seven times for minus 17 yards, 1988.

THOMAS GREGORY EVERETT
Safety—Pittsburgh Steelers

Born November 21, 1964, at Daingerfield, Tex.
Height, 5.09. Weight, 179.
High School—Daingerfield, Tex.
Attended Baylor University.
Brother of Eric Everett, cornerback with Philadelphia Eagles.

Named as defensive back on THE SPORTING NEWS College All-America Team, 1986.
Selected by Pittsburgh in 4th round (94th player selected) of 1987 NFL draft.
Signed by Pittsburgh Steelers, July 26, 1987.

		—INTERCEPTIONS—			
Year Club	G.	No.	Yds.	Avg.	TD.
1987—Pittsburgh NFL	12	3	22	7.3	0
1988—Pittsburgh NFL	14	3	31	10.3	0
Pro Totals—2 Years	26	6	53	8.8	0

Additional pro statistics: Returned four punts for 22 yards, recovered two fumbles for seven yards and fumbled once, 1987; recovered two fumbles for 38 yards, 1988.

SINATAUSILINUU FAAOLA
(Name pronounced SEENA-tau-sili-E-NEW-oo Fa-O-la.)
(Nuu)
Running Back—New York Jets

Born January 15, 1964, at Honolulu, Haw.
Height, 5.11. Weight, 220.
High School—Kalihi, Haw., Farrington.
Attended University of Hawaii.

Selected by New York Jets in 9th round (245th player selected) of 1986 NFL draft.
Signed by New York Jets, May 28, 1986.
Released by New York Jets, August 30, 1986; re-signed by Jets, September 30, 1986.

		—RUSHING—				PASS RECEIVING				—TOTAL—		
Year Club	G.	Att.	Yds.	Avg.	TD.	P.C.	Yds.	Avg.	TD.	TD.	Pts.	F.
1986—New York Jets NFL	12	3	5	1.7	0		None			0	0	0
1987—New York Jets NFL	12	14	43	3.1	2	1	16	16.0	0	2	12	0
1988—New York Jets NFL	16	1	13	13.0	0		None			0	0	0
Pro Totals—3 Years	40	18	61	3.4	2	1	16	16.0	0	2	12	0

Additional pro statistics: Returned one kickoff for four yards and recovered one fumble for three yards, 1987; returned two kickoffs for nine yards, 1988.

KEVIN FAGAN
Defensive End—San Francisco 49ers
Born April 25, 1963, at Lake Worth, Fla.
Height, 6.04. Weight, 265.
High School—Lake Worth, Fla., John I. Leonard.
Attended University of Miami (Fla.).

Selected by Orlando in 1986 USFL territorial draft.
Selected by San Francisco in 4th round (102nd player selected) of 1986 NFL draft.
Signed by San Francisco 49ers, July 20, 1986.
On non-football injury list with knee injury, July 22 through entire 1986 season.
San Francisco NFL, 1987 and 1988.
Games: 1987 (7), 1988 (14). Total—21.
Pro statistics: Recovered one fumble for six yards, 1987.
Played in NFC Championship Game following 1988 season.
Played in NFL Championship Game following 1988 season.

JAMES JOHN FAHNHORST
(Jim)
Linebacker—San Francisco 49ers
Born November 8, 1958, at St. Cloud, Minn.
Height, 6.04. Weight, 230.
High School—St. Cloud, Minn., Technical.
Attended University of Minnesota.
Brother of Keith Fahnhorst, offensive tackle with San Francisco 49ers, 1974 through 1987.

Selected by Minnesota in 4th round (92nd player selected) of 1982 NFL draft.
Signed by Chicago Blitz, August 16, 1982.
USFL rights subsequently traded by Los Angeles Express to Chicago Blitz for rights to tight end Mike Sherrod and wide receiver Kris Haines and 6th, 7th and 8th round picks in 1983 draft, November 2, 1982.
Franchise transferred to Arizona, September 30, 1983.
Signed by San Francisco 49ers, June 13, 1984; Minnesota Vikings did not exercise right of first refusal, June 28, 1984.
On injured reserve with knee injury, December 5 through remainder of 1984 season.
Released by San Francisco 49ers, September 7, 1987; re-signed by 49ers, September 14, 1987.
Chicago USFL, 1983; Arizona USFL, 1984; San Francisco NFL, 1984 through 1988.
Games: 1983 (18), 1984 USFL (18), 1984 NFL (14), 1985 (15), 1986 (16), 1987 (11), 1988 (16). Total USFL—36. Total NFL—72. Total Pro—108.
USFL statistics: Intercepted one pass for 19 yards, recovered three fumbles for six yards and credited with one sack for nine yards, 1983; intercepted one pass for no yards, credited with one sack for seven yards and recovered one fumble, 1984.
NFL statistics: Intercepted two passes for nine yards, 1984; intercepted four passes for 52 yards, 1986; intercepted one pass for no yards, 1987.
Played in NFC Championship Game following 1988 season.
Played in NFL Championship Game following 1988 season.
Played in USFL Championship Game following 1984 season.

PAUL JAY FAIRCHILD
Guard—New England Patriots
Born September 14, 1961, at Carroll, Ia.
Height, 6.04. Weight, 270.
High School—Glidden, Ia., Ralston.
Attended Ellsworth Junior College and received bachelor of
general science degree in liberal arts from University of Kansas in 1984.

Selected by Houston in 6th round (124th player selected) of 1984 USFL draft.
Selected by New England in 5th round (124th player selected) of 1984 NFL draft.
Signed by New England Patriots, June 18, 1984.
New England NFL, 1984 through 1988.
Games: 1984 (7), 1985 (16), 1986 (15), 1987 (11), 1988 (16). Total—65.
Played in AFC Championship Game following 1985 season.
Played in NFL Championship Game following 1985 season.

ERIC JEROME FAIRS
Linebacker—Houston Oilers
Born February 17, 1964, at Memphis, Tenn.
Height, 6.03. Weight, 240.
High School—Memphis, Tenn., Northside.
Attended Memphis State University.

Selected by Memphis in 1986 USFL territorial draft.
Signed as free agent by Houston Oilers, May 21, 1986.
Released by Houston Oilers, August 26, 1986; re-signed by Oilers, October 2, 1986.
Houston NFL, 1986 through 1988.
Games: 1986 (12), 1987 (12), 1988 (16). Total—40.
Pro statistics: Credited with a safety and recovered one fumble, 1988.

DONAVA FANN
Offensive Lineman—Cleveland Browns
Born December 12, 1964, at Jacksonville, Fla.
Height, 6.04. Weight, 275.
Attended Bethune-Cookman College.

Signed as free agent by Dallas Cowboys, May 18, 1987.
Released by Dallas Cowboys, August 25, 1987; signed as free agent by Calgary Stampeders, October 12, 1987.
Released by Calgary Stampeders, August 1, 1988; signed as free agent by Cleveland Browns for 1989, December 30, 1988.
Calgary CFL, 1987 and 1988.
Games: 1987 (3), 1988 (1). Total—4.

SEAN WARD FARRELL
Guard—New England Patriots
Born May 25, 1960, at Southampton, N.Y.
Height, 6.03. Weight, 260.
High School—Westhampton Beach, N.Y.
Received bachelor of arts degree in general arts and sciences from Penn State University in 1982.
Named to THE SPORTING NEWS NFL All-Star Team, 1984.
Named as guard on THE SPORTING NEWS College All-America Team, 1981.
Selected by Tampa Bay in 1st round (17th player selected) of 1982 NFL draft.
Granted free agency, February 1, 1987; re-signed by Buccaneers and traded to New England Patriots for 2nd, 7th and 9th round picks in 1987 draft, February 19, 1987.
Crossed picket line during players' strike, October 2, 1987.
Tampa Bay NFL, 1982 through 1986; New England NFL, 1987 and 1988.
Games: 1982 (9), 1983 (10), 1984 (15), 1985 (14), 1986 (16), 1987 (14), 1988 (15). Total—93.
Pro statistics: Recovered one fumble, 1983; recovered two fumbles, 1984; caught one pass for four yards, 1988.

PAUL V. FARREN
Offensive Tackle-Guard—Cleveland Browns
Born December 24, 1960, at Weymouth, Mass.
Height, 6.06. Weight, 280.
High School—Cohasset, Mass.
Received bachelor of arts degree in marketing finance from Boston University in 1983.
Selected by Boston in 1983 USFL territorial draft.
Selected by Cleveland in 12th round (316th player selected) of 1983 NFL draft.
Signed by Cleveland Browns, May 31, 1983.
On injured reserve with knee injury, December 30 through remainder of 1985 season playoffs.
Cleveland NFL, 1983 through 1988.
Games: 1983 (16), 1984 (15), 1985 (13), 1986 (16), 1987 (12), 1988 (15). Total—87.
Pro statistics: Recovered one fumble, 1984 and 1987.
Played in AFC Championship Game following 1986 and 1987 seasons.

BRETT ALLEN FARYNIARZ
(Name pronounced FAIR-in-nezz.)
Linebacker—Los Angeles Rams
Born July 23, 1965, at Carmichael, Calif.
Height, 6.03. Weight, 225.
High School—Rancho Cordova, Calif., Cordova.
Attended San Diego State University.
Signed as free agent by Los Angeles Rams, June 17, 1988.
Los Angeles Rams NFL, 1988.
Games: 1988 (15).

CHARLES FAUCETTE JR.
(Chuck)
Linebacker—San Diego Chargers
Born October 7, 1963, at Levittown, Pa.
Height, 6.03. Weight, 242.
High School—Willingboro, N. J.
Received degree in finance from University of Maryland.
Selected by New York Giants in 10th round (279th player selected) of 1987 NFL draft.
Signed by New York Giants, July 27, 1987.
Released by New York Giants, September 7, 1987; signed as free agent replacement player by San Diego Chargers, September 30, 1987.
On injured reserve with knee injury, October 13 through remainder of 1987 season.
On injured reserve with neck injury, October 28 through remainder of 1988 season.
San Diego NFL, 1987 and 1988.
Games: 1987 (2), 1988 (8). Total—10.
Pro statistics: Intercepted one pass for two yards and recovered one fumble, 1988.

RECORD AS BASEBALL PLAYER

Year	Club	League	Pos.	G.	AB.	R.	H.	2B.	3B.	HR.	RBI.	B.A.	PO.	A.	E.	F.A.
1981—Bradenton Jays....		G. C.	OF	51	156	16	26	5	0	2	8	.167	72	1	7	.913
1982—Florence		S. Atl.	OF	4	7	0	0	0	0	0	2	.000	3	0	1	.750
1982—Medicine Hat........		Pion.	OF	25	69	10	9	3	0	2	6	.130	20	0	3	.870
1983—Medicine Hat†.......		Pion.						(Did not play)								

Selected by Toronto Blue Jays' organization in 12th round of free-agent draft, June 8, 1981.
†On suspended list, June 22, 1983 through entire season.

JEFFREY ALLAN FEAGLES
(Jeff)
Punter—New England Patriots
Born March 7, 1966, at Scottsdale, Ariz.
Height, 6.00. Weight, 198.
High School—Phoenix, Ariz., Gerard Catholic.
Attended Scottsdale Community College and received bachelor of
business administration degree from University of Miami (Fla.) in 1988.

Signed as free agent by New England Patriots, May 1, 1988.

		—PUNTING—		
Year Club	G.	No.	Avg.	Blk.
1988—New England NFL.................	16	91	38.3	0

Additional pro statistics: Rushed once for no yards and recovered one fumble, 1988.

GRANT EARL FEASEL
Center—Seattle Seahawks
Born June 28, 1960, at Barstow, Calif.
Height, 6.07. Weight, 278.
High School—Barstow, Calif.
Received bachelor of science degree in biology from Abilene Christian University in 1983.
Brother of Greg Feasel, offensive tackle with Denver Gold, Green Bay Packers
and San Diego Chargers, 1983 through 1987.

Selected by Baltimore in 6th round (161st player selected) of 1983 NFL draft.
Franchise transferred to Indianapolis, March 31, 1984.
Released by Indianapolis Colts, October 10, 1984; signed as free agent by Minnesota Vikings, October 17, 1984.
On injured reserve with knee injury, August 29 through entire 1985 season.
Granted free agency with option not exercised, February 1, 1986; re-signed by Vikings, June 21, 1986.
On injured reserve with knee injury, August 19 through October 27, 1986.
Released by Minnesota Vikings, October 28, 1986; re-signed by Vikings after clearing procedural waivers, November 20, 1986.
Released by Minnesota Vikings, November 28, 1986; signed as free agent by Seattle Seahawks, February 25, 1987.
Active for 1 game with Minnesota Vikings in 1986; did not play.
Baltimore NFL, 1983; Indianapolis (6)-Minnesota (9) NFL, 1984; Minnesota NFL, 1986; Seattle NFL, 1987 and 1988.
Games: 1983 (11), 1984 (15), 1987 (12), 1988 (16). Total—54.
Additional pro statistics: Recovered one fumble and fumbled once for minus 19 yards, 1987; recovered four fumbles and fumbled once for minus 22 yards, 1988.

GERRY FEEHERY
Name pronounced FEER-ee.
Center—Kansas City Chiefs
Born March 9, 1960, at Philadelphia, Pa.
Height, 6.02. Weight, 268.
High School—Springfield, Pa., Cardinal O'Hara.
Received bachelor of science degree in marketing from Syracuse University.

Selected by New Jersey in 1983 USFL territorial draft.
Signed as free agent by Philadelphia Eagles, May 4, 1983.
On injured reserve with knee injury, November 4 through remainder of 1983 season.
On injured reserve with knee injury, October 14 through remainder of 1986 season.
On physically unable to perform/active with knee injury, July 26 through August 17, 1988; passed physical, August 18, 1988.
On injured reserve with knee injury, August 30 through October 23, 1988.
Released by Philadelphia Eagles, October 24, 1988; awarded on waivers to Kansas City Chiefs, October 25, 1988.
Philadelphia NFL, 1983 through 1987; Kansas City NFL, 1988.
Games: 1983 (2), 1984 (6), 1985 (15), 1986 (6), 1987 (12), 1988 (6). Total—47.

RICKY DALE FENNEY
(Rick)
Running Back—Minnesota Vikings
Born December 7, 1964, at Everett, Wash.
Height, 6.01. Weight, 232.
High School—Snohomish, Wash.
Attended University of Washington.

Selected by Minnesota in 8th round (211th player selected) of 1987 NFL draft.
Signed by Minnesota Vikings, July 30, 1987.

		—RUSHING—				PASS RECEIVING				—TOTAL—		
Year Club	G.	Att.	Yds.	Avg.	TD.	P.C.	Yds.	Avg.	TD.	TD.	Pts.	F.
1987—Minnesota NFL..........................	11	42	174	4.1	2	7	27	3.9	0	2	12	0
1988—Minnesota NFL..........................	13	55	271	4.9	3	15	224	14.9	0	3	18	0
Pro Totals—2 Years....................................	24	97	445	4.6	5	22	251	11.4	0	5	30	0

Played in NFC Championship Game following 1987 season.

JOE CARLTON FERGUSON JR.
Quarterback—Tampa Bay Buccaneers
Born April 23, 1950, at Alvin, Tex.
Height, 6.01. Weight, 190.
High School—Shreveport, La., Woodlawn.
Received bachelor of science degree in physical education from
University of Arkansas in 1973.

Established NFL record for fewest passes intercepted among qualifiers, season (1), 1976.
Tied NFL records for most fumbles and most own fumbles recovered, game (4), September 18, 1977, against Miami Dolphins.
Selected by Buffalo in 3rd round (57th player selected) of 1973 NFL draft.
Traded by Buffalo Bills to Detroit Lions for 7th round pick in 1986 draft, April 30, 1985.
Granted free agency with no qualifying offer, February 1, 1988; signed by Indianapolis Colts, April 22, 1988.
Traded by Indianapolis Colts to Tampa Bay Buccaneers for 12th round pick in 1989 draft, April 29, 1988.
Active for 12 games with Detroit Lions in 1987; did not play.

				PASSING							RUSHING				TOTAL	
Year Club	G.	Att.	Cmp.	Pct.	Gain	T.P.	P.I.	Avg.	Att.	Yds.	Avg.	TD.	TD.	Pts.	F.
1973—Buffalo NFL	14	164	73	44.5	939	4	10	5.73	48	147	3.1	2	2	12	7
1974—Buffalo NFL	14	232	119	51.3	1588	12	12	6.84	54	111	2.1	2	2	12	*14
1975—Buffalo NFL	14	321	169	52.6	2426	*25	17	7.56	23	82	3.6	1	1	6	4
1976—Buffalo NFL	7	151	74	49.0	1086	9	1	7.19	18	81	4.5	0	0	0	2
1977—Buffalo NFL	14	*457	221	48.4	*2803	12	*24	6.13	41	279	6.8	2	2	12	12
1978—Buffalo NFL	16	330	175	53.0	2136	16	15	6.47	27	76	2.8	0	0	0	5
1979—Buffalo NFL	16	458	238	52.0	3572	14	15	7.80	22	68	3.1	1	1	6	5
1980—Buffalo NFL	16	439	251	57.2	2805	20	18	6.39	31	65	2.1	0	0	0	9
1981—Buffalo NFL	16	498	252	50.6	3652	24	20	7.33	20	29	1.5	1	1	6	2
1982—Buffalo NFL	9	264	144	54.5	1597	7	*16	6.05	16	46	2.9	1	2	12	5
1983—Buffalo NFL	16	508	281	55.3	2995	26	25	5.90	20	88	4.4	0	0	0	3
1984—Buffalo NFL	12	344	191	55.5	1991	12	17	5.79	19	102	5.4	0	0	0	8
1985—Detroit NFL	8	54	31	57.4	364	2	3	6.74	4	12	3.0	1	1	6	1
1986—Detroit NFL	6	155	73	47.1	941	7	7	6.07	5	25	5.0	0	0	0	3
1988—Tampa Bay NFL	2	46	31	67.4	368	3	1	8.00	1	0	0.0	0	0	0	1
Pro Totals—16 Years	180	4421	2323	52.5	29263	193	201	6.62	349	1211	3.5	11	12	72	81

Quarterback Rating Points: 1973 (45.6), 1974 (69.0), 1975 (81.3), 1976 (90.0), 1977 (54.6), 1978 (70.5), 1979 (74.5), 1980 (74.6), 1981 (74.1), 1982 (56.3), 1983 (69.3), 1984 (63.5), 1985 (67.2), 1986 (62.9), 1988 (104.3). Total—69.3.
Additional pro statistics: Recovered four fumbles, fumbled seven times for minus three yards and caught one pass for minus three yards, 1973; recovered five fumbles and fumbled 14 times for minus 13 yards, 1974; recovered three fumbles, 1975, 1978, 1979 and 1983; fumbled four times for minus one yard, 1975; recovered seven fumbles and fumbled 12 times for minus seven yards, 1977; fumbled five times for minus three yards and caught one pass for minus six yards, 1978; recovered one fumble and fumbled nine times for minus 12 yards, 1980; recovered two fumbles, one for a touchdown and fumbled five times for minus 10 yards, 1982; recovered two fumbles and fumbled eight times for minus 26 yards, 1984; recovered two fumbles, 1986.

KEITH TYRONE FERGUSON
Defensive End—Detroit Lions
Born April 3, 1959, at Miami, Fla.
Height, 6.05. Weight, 260.
High School—Miami, Fla., Edison.
Attended Ohio State University.

Selected by San Diego in 5th round (131st player selected) of 1981 NFL draft.
Released by San Diego Chargers, November 20, 1985; awarded on waivers to Detroit Lions, November 21, 1985.
San Diego NFL, 1981 through 1984; San Diego (10)-Detroit (5) NFL, 1985; Detroit NFL, 1986 through 1988.
Games: 1981 (16), 1982 (9), 1983 (16), 1984 (16), 1985 (15), 1986 (16), 1987 (12), 1988 (14). Total—114.
Pro statistics: Recovered one fumble, 1982 and 1984 through 1987; recovered two fumbles, 1983; intercepted one pass for seven yards and fumbled once, 1986.
Played in AFC Championship Game following 1981 season.

MERVYN FERNANDEZ
Wide Receiver—Los Angeles Raiders
Born December 29, 1959, at Merced, Calif.
Height, 6.03. Weight, 200.
High School—San Jose, Calif., Andrew Hill.
Attended De Anza College and San Jose State University.

Signed as free agent by British Columbia Lions, March 11, 1982.
Selected by Los Angeles Raiders in 10th round (277th player selected) of 1983 NFL draft.
On injured list, July 1 through September 2, 1986.
Granted free agency, March 1, 1987; signed by Los Angeles Raiders, March 4, 1987.
Crossed picket line during players' strike, October 14, 1987.
On injured reserve with shoulder injury, November 21 through remainder of 1987 season.

		PASS RECEIVING						PASS RECEIVING				
Year Club	G.	P.C.	Yds.	Avg.	TD.	Year Club		G.	P.C.	Yds.	Avg.	TD.
1982—British Columbia CFL	16	64	1046	16.3	8	1988—L.A. Raiders NFL		16	31	805	26.0	4
1983—British Columbia CFL	16	78	1284	16.5	10	CFL Totals—5 Years		74	374	6408	17.1	55
1984—British Columbia CFL	15	89	*1486	16.7	17	NFL Totals—2 Years		23	45	1041	23.1	4
1985—British Columbia CFL	16	95	*1727	18.2	*15							
1986—British Columbia CFL	11	48	865	18.0	5	Pro Totals—7 Years		97	419	7449	17.8	59
1987—L.A. Raiders NFL	7	14	236	16.9	0							

Additional CFL statistics: Scored one two-point conversion, 1982 and 1983; returned 20 punts for 179 yards and one touchdown, returned one kickoff for 32 yards, rushed twice for one yard and fumbled twice, 1982; returned two punts for 19 yards and fumbled twice, 1983; rushed three times for 33 yards, returned one kickoff for three yards, attempted one pass with one completion for 55 yards and fumbled once, 1985; punted 14 times for 34.0 yard average and attempted one pass with one completion for 86 yards, 1986.
Additional NFL statistics: Fumbled once, 1987; rushed once for nine yards, 1988.

EARL THOMAS FERRELL
Fullback—Phoenix Cardinals

Born March 27, 1958, at Halifax, Va.
Height, 6.00. Weight, 240.
High School—South Boston, Va., Halifax County.
Received degree in physical education from East Tennessee State University.

Selected by St. Louis in 5th round (125th player selected) of 1982 NFL draft.
On non-football injury list with drug problems, November 21 through remainder of 1985 season.
Crossed picket line during players' strike, October 2, 1987.
On injured reserve with knee injury, December 5 through remainder of 1987 season.
Franchise transferred to Phoenix, March 15, 1988.

Year Club	G.	Att.	Yds.	Avg.	TD.	P.C.	Yds.	Avg.	TD.	TD.	Pts.	F.
			—RUSHING—			PASS RECEIVING				—TOTAL—		
1982—St. Louis NFL	9		None			None				0	0	0
1983—St. Louis NFL	16	7	53	7.6	1	None				1	6	2
1984—St. Louis NFL	16	41	190	4.6	1	26	218	8.4	1	2	12	3
1985—St. Louis NFL	11	46	208	4.5	2	25	277	11.1	2	4	24	2
1986—St. Louis NFL	16	124	548	4.4	0	56	434	7.8	3	3	18	6
1987—St. Louis NFL	11	113	512	4.5	7	23	262	11.4	0	7	42	0
1988—Phoenix NFL	16	202	924	4.6	7	38	315	8.3	2	9	54	7
Pro Totals—7 Years	95	533	2435	4.6	18	168	1506	9.0	8	26	156	20

Year Club	G.	No.	Yds.	Avg.	TD.
		KICKOFF RETURNS			
1982—St. Louis NFL	9	4	88	22.0	0
1983—St. Louis NFL	16	13	257	19.8	0
1984—St. Louis NFL	16	1	0	0.0	0
1985—St. Louis NFL	11		None		
1986—St. Louis NFL	16	3	41	13.7	0
1987—St. Louis NFL	11	1	10	10.0	0
1988—Phoenix NFL	16	2	25	12.5	0
Pro Totals—7 Years	95	24	421	17.5	0

Additional pro statistics: Returned one punt for six yards, 1982; returned one punt for 17 yards, 1983; recovered one fumble, 1985 and 1987; recovered three fumbles for six yards, 1988.

CEDRIC NOAH FIGARO
Linebacker—San Diego Chargers

Born August 17, 1966, at Lafayette, La.
Height, 6.02. Weight, 255.
High School—Lafayette, La.
Attended University of Notre Dame.

Selected by San Diego in 6th round (152nd player selected) of 1988 NFL draft.
Signed by San Diego Chargers, July 13, 1988.
On injured reserve with back injury, August 29 through November 11, 1988; activated, November 12, 1988.
San Diego NFL, 1988.
Games: 1988 (6).

DAN CLEMENT FIKE JR.
Guard—Cleveland Browns

Born June 16, 1961, at Mobile, Ala.
Height, 6.07. Weight, 280.
High School—Pensacola, Fla., Pine Forest.
Attended University of Florida.

Selected by Tampa Bay in 1984 USFL territorial draft.
Selected by New York Jets in 10th round (274th player selected) of 1983 NFL draft.
Signed by New York Jets, June 10, 1983.
Released by New York Jets, August 29, 1983; signed by Tampa Bay Bandits, November 13, 1983.
Signed by Cleveland Browns, January 20, 1985, to take affect after being granted free agency following 1985 USFL season.
Tampa Bay USFL, 1984 and 1985; Cleveland NFL, 1985 through 1988.
Games: 1984 (18), 1985 USFL (18), 1985 NFL (13), 1986 (16), 1987 (12), 1988 (16). Total USFL—36. Total NFL—57. Total Pro—93.
Pro statistics: Recovered one fumble, 1986.
USFL statistics: Recovered one fumble, 1985.
Played in AFC Championship Game following 1986 and 1987 seasons.

JAMES JOSEPH FitzPATRICK III
Guard-Offensive Tackle—San Diego Chargers

Born February 1, 1964, at Heidelberg, Germany.
Height, 6.07. Weight, 310.
High School—Beaverton, Ore.
Attended University of Southern California.

Selected by New Jersey in 1986 USFL territorial draft.
Selected by San Diego in 1st round (13th player selected) of 1986 NFL draft.
Signed by San Diego Chargers, July 25, 1986.
On injured reserve with back injury, October 6 through remainder of 1986 season.
On injured reserve with back injury, August 30 through October 7, 1988; activated, October 8, 1988.
San Diego NFL, 1986 through 1988.
Games: 1986 (4), 1987 (10), 1988 (11). Total—25.

R. TERRENCE FLAGLER
(Known by middle name.)
Running Back—San Francisco 49ers
Born September 24, 1964, at New York, N.Y.
Height, 6.00. Weight, 200.
High School—Fernandina Beach, Fla.
Attended Clemson University.

Selected by San Francisco in 1st round (25th player selected) of 1987 NFL draft.
Signed by San Francisco 49ers, July 24, 1987.
On injured reserve with foot injury, September 10 through November 4, 1988; activated, November 5, 1988.

Year Club	G.	Att.	RUSHING Yds.	Avg.	TD.	PASS RECEIVING P.C.	Yds.	Avg.	TD.	TOTAL TD.	Pts.	F.
1987—San Francisco NFL	3	6	11	1.8	0	2	28	14.0	0	0	0	2
1988—San Francisco NFL	3	3	5	1.7	0	4	72	18.0	0	0	0	0
Pro Totals—2 Years	6	9	16	1.8	0	6	100	16.7	0	0	0	2

Additional pro statistics: Returned three kickoffs for 31 yards and recovered one fumble, 1987.
Played in NFC Championship Game following 1988 season.
Member of San Francisco 49ers for NFL Championship Game following 1988 season; inactive.

SIMON RAYNARD FLETCHER
Defensive End—Denver Broncos
Born February 18, 1962, at Bay City, Tex.
Height, 6.05. Weight, 240.
High School—Bay City, Tex.
Attended University of Houston.

Related to Pat Franklin, running back with Tampa Bay Buccaneers and Cincinnati Bengals, 1986 and 1987.
Selected by Houston in 1985 USFL territorial draft.
Selected by Denver in 2nd round (54th player selected) of 1985 NFL draft.
Signed by Denver Broncos, July 16, 1985.
Denver NFL, 1985 through 1988.
Games: 1985 (16), 1986 (16), 1987 (12), 1988 (16). Total—60.
Pro statistics: Recovered two fumbles, 1986; recovered one fumble, 1987 and 1988; intercepted one pass for four yards, 1988.
Played in AFC Championship Game following 1986 and 1987 seasons.
Played in NFL Championship Game following 1986 and 1987 seasons.

KENNETH C. FLOWERS
(Kenny)
Running Back—Atlanta Falcons
Born March 14, 1964, at Daytona Beach, Fla.
Height, 6.00. Weight, 210.
High School—Daytona Beach, Fla., Spruce Creek.
Attended Clemson University.

Selected by Atlanta in 2nd round (31st player selected) in 1987 NFL draft.
Signed by Atlanta Falcons, July 31, 1987.
On injured reserve with hamstring injury, November 10 through December 11, 1987; activated, December 12, 1987.
On injured reserve with knee injury, August 22 through entire 1988 season.

Year Club	G.	Att.	RUSHING Yds.	Avg.	TD.	PASS RECEIVING P.C.	Yds.	Avg.	TD.	TOTAL TD.	Pts.	F.
1987—Atlanta NFL	8	14	61	4.4	0	7	50	7.1	0	0	0	1

Year Club	G.	No.	KICKOFF RETURNS Yds.	Avg.	TD.
1987—Atlanta NFL	8	4	72	18.0	0

Additional pro statistics: Recovered one fumble, 1987.

DARREN PAUL FLUTIE
Wide Receiver—San Diego Chargers
Born November 18, 1966, at Baltimore, Md.
Height, 5.10. Weight, 184.
High School—Natick, Mass.
Received bachelor of science degree in speech communication from Boston College in 1988.
Brother of Doug Flutie, quarterback with New England Patriots.

Signed as free agent by San Diego Chargers, May 4, 1988.

Year Club	G.	PASS RECEIVING P.C.	Yds.	Avg.	TD.
1988—San Diego NFL	16	18	208	11.6	2

Additional pro statistics: Returned seven punts for 36 yards, returned one kickoff for 10 yards and fumbled twice, 1988.

DOUG FLUTIE
Quarterback—New England Patriots

Born October 23, 1962, at Manchester, Md.
Height, 5.10. Weight, 176.
High School—Natick, Mass.
Attended Boston College.
Brother of Darren Flutie, wide receiver with San Diego Chargers.

Heisman Trophy winner, 1984.
Named THE SPORTING NEWS College Football Player of the Year, 1984.
Named as quarterback on THE SPORTING NEWS College All-America Team, 1984.
Selected by New Jersey in 1985 USFL territorial draft.
Signed by New Jersey Generals, February 4, 1985.
Granted roster exemption, February 4 through February 14, 1985; activated, February 15, 1985.
Selected by Los Angeles Rams in 11th round (285th player selected) of 1985 NFL draft.
On developmental squad, June 10 through remainder of 1985 season.
NFL rights traded with 4th round pick in 1987 draft by Los Angeles Rams to Chicago Bears for 3rd and 6th round picks in 1987 draft, October 14, 1986.
Signed by Chicago Bears, October 21, 1986.
Granted roster exemption, October 21 through November 3, 1986; activated, November 4, 1986.
Crossed picket line during players' strike, October 13, 1987.
Traded by Chicago Bears to New England Patriots for 8th round pick in 1988 draft, October 13, 1987.
On developmental squad for 3 games with New Jersey Generals in 1985.

Year	Club	G.	Att.	Cmp.	Pct.	Gain	T.P.	P.I.	Avg.	Att.	Yds.	Avg.	TD.	TD.	Pts.	F.
					PASSING						RUSHING			TOTAL		
1985—New Jersey USFL		15	281	134	47.7	2109	13	14	7.51	65	465	7.2	6	6	36	3
1986—Chicago NFL		4	46	23	50.0	361	3	2	7.85	9	36	4.0	1	1	6	3
1987—Chi. (1)-N.E. (1) NFL		2	25	15	60.0	199	1	0	7.96	6	43	7.2	0	0	0	1
1988—New England NFL		11	179	92	51.4	1150	8	10	6.42	38	179	4.7	1	1	6	3
USFL Totals—1 Year		15	281	134	47.7	2109	13	14	7.51	65	465	7.2	6	6	36	3
NFL Totals—3 Years		17	250	130	52.0	1710	12	12	6.84	53	258	4.9	2	2	12	7
Pro Totals—4 Years		32	531	264	49.7	3819	25	26	7.19	118	723	6.1	8	8	48	10

USFL Quarterback Rating Points: 1985 (67.8).
NFL Quarterback Rating Points: 1986 (80.1), 1987 (98.6), 1988 (63.3). Total—69.9.
Additional USFL statistics: Recovered two fumbles, 1985.
Additional NFL statistics: Recovered two fumbles and fumbled three times for minus four yards, 1986; recovered one fumble, 1987.

THOMAS JEFFERY FLYNN
(Tom)
Safety—New York Giants

Born March 24, 1962, at Verona, Pa.
Height, 6.00. Weight, 195.
High School—Pittsburgh, Pa., Penn Hills.
Attended University of Pittsburgh.

Selected by Pittsburgh in 1984 USFL territorial draft.
Selected by Green Bay in 5th round (126th player selected) of 1984 NFL draft.
Signed by Green Bay Packers, July 1, 1984.
Released by Green Bay Packers, October 21, 1986; signed as free agent by New York Giants, December 9, 1986.

Year	Club	G.	No.	Yds.	Avg.	TD.	No.	Yds.	Avg.	TD.	TD.	Pts.	F.
			INTERCEPTIONS				PUNT RETURNS				TOTAL		
1984—Green Bay NFL		16	9	106	11.8	0	15	128	8.5	0	0	0	1
1985—Green Bay NFL		16	1	7	7.0	0	7	41	5.9	0	0	0	0
1986—G.B.(7)-NYG(2) NFL		9	1	0	0.0	0		None			1	6	0
1987—New York Giants NFL		12		None				None			1	6	0
1988—New York Giants NFL		16		None			1	4	4.0	0	1	6	1
Pro Totals—5 Years		69	11	113	10.3	0	23	173	7.5	0	3	18	1

Additional pro statistics: Recovered three fumbles for three yards, 1984; returned one kickoff for 20 yards and recovered one fumble, 1985; returned blocked punt 36 yards for a touchdown, 1986; recovered blocked punt in end zone for a touchdown, 1987; returned blocked punt 27 yards for a touchdown, 1988.
Played in NFC Championship Game following 1986 season.
Played in NFL Championship Game following 1986 season.

STEVE MARK FOLSOM
Tight End—Dallas Cowboys

Born March 21, 1958, at Los Angeles, Calif.
Height, 6.05. Weight, 236.
High School—Santa Fe Springs, Calif.
Attended California State University at Long Beach and received bachelor of science degree in commercial recreation from University of Utah in 1981.

Selected by Miami in 10th round (261st player selected) of 1981 NFL draft.
Released by Miami Dolphins, August 17, 1981; signed as free agent by Philadelphia Eagles, November 25, 1981.
On injured reserve with pulled hamstring, December 26 through remainder of 1981 season playoffs.
On injured reserve with neck injury, September 6, 1982.

Released by Philadelphia Eagles, September 7, 1982; signed as free agent by New York Giants, September 13, 1982.
On inactive list, September 20, 1982.
Released by New York Giants, November 30, 1982.
USFL rights traded by Los Angeles Express to Philadelphia Stars for rights to defensive back Chuck Scicli, September 9, 1982.
Signed by Philadelphia Stars, January 27, 1983.
On developmental squad, June 21 through remainder of 1984 season.
Franchise transferred to Baltimore, November 1, 1984.
On physically unable to perform, February 18 through April 5, 1985; activated, April 6, 1985.
On developmental squad, May 15 through June 13, 1985; activated, June 14, 1985.
Granted free agency when USFL suspended operations, August 7, 1986; signed as free agent by Dallas Cowboys, April 30, 1987.
Released by Dallas Cowboys, September 7, 1987; re-signed by Cowboys, October 20, 1987.
On developmental squad for 1 game with Philadelphia Stars in 1984.
On developmental squad for 4 games with Baltimore Stars in 1985.

| | | | ——PASS RECEIVING—— | | | |
Year Club	G.	P.C.	Yds.	Avg.	TD.	
1981—Philadelphia NFL	3		None			
1983—Philadelphia USFL	18	26	286	11.0	1	
1984—Philadelphia USFL	17	46	485	10.5	6	
1985—Baltimore USFL	8	1	4	4.0	0	
1987—Dallas NFL	9		None			
1988—Dallas NFL	16	9	84	9.3	2	
USFL Totals—3 Years........	43	73	775	10.6	7	
NFL Totals—3 Years..........	28	9	84	9.3	2	
Pro Totals—6 Years............	71	82	859	10.5	9	

Additional pro statistics: Fumbled once, 1983; returned one kickoff for three yards, 1984.
Played in USFL Championship Game following 1983 and 1985 seasons.
On developmental squad for USFL Championship Game following 1984 season.

HERMAN FONTENOT
Running Back—Green Bay Packers
Born September 12, 1963, at St. Elizabeth, Tex.
Height, 6.00. Weight, 206.
High School—Beaumont, Tex., Charlton-Pollard.
Attended Louisiana State University.

Selected by New Jersey in 9th round (127th player selected) of 1985 USFL draft.
Signed as free agent by Cleveland Browns, May 6, 1985.
On injured reserve with broken bone in back, August 27 through October 24, 1985; activated, October 25, 1985.
Granted unconditional free agency, February 1, 1989.
Traded with 3rd and 5th round picks in 1989 draft and 1st round pick in 1990 draft by Cleveland Browns to Green Bay Packers for 2nd and 5th round picks in 1989 draft, April 23, 1989.

| | | ——RUSHING—— | | | | PASS RECEIVING | | | | —TOTAL— | | |
Year Club	G.	Att.	Yds.	Avg.	TD.	P.C.	Yds.	Avg.	TD.	TD.	Pts.	F.
1985—Cleveland NFL...................	9		None			2	19	9.5	0	0	0	1
1986—Cleveland NFL...................	16	25	105	4.2	1	47	559	11.9	1	2	12	2
1987—Cleveland NFL...................	12	15	33	2.2	0	4	40	10.0	0	0	0	0
1988—Cleveland NFL...................	16	28	87	3.1	0	19	170	8.9	1	2	12	0
Pro Totals—4 Years....................	53	68	225	3.3	1	72	788	10.9	2	4	24	3

| | | KICKOFF RETURNS | | | |
Year Club	G.	No.	Yds.	Avg.	TD.
1985—Cleveland NFL.............	9	8	215	26.9	0
1986—Cleveland NFL.............	16	7	99	14.1	0
1987—Cleveland NFL.............	12	9	130	14.4	0
1988—Cleveland NFL.............	16	21	435	20.7	0
Pro Totals—4 Years...........	53	45	879	19.5	0

Additional pro statistics: Attempted one pass with no completions, 1985 and 1988; attempted one pass with one completion for 46 yards and a touchdown and recovered one fumble, 1986; attempted one pass with one completion for 14 yards, 1987; returned blocked punt one yard for a touchdown, 1988.
Played in AFC Championship Game following 1986 and 1987 seasons.

CHRIS D. FOOTE
Center—Minnesota Vikings
Born December 2, 1956, at Louisville, Ky.
Height, 6.04. Weight, 255.
High School—Boulder, Colo., Fairview.
Received bachelor of arts degree in communications from
University of Southern California in 1980.

Selected by Baltimore in 6th round (144th player selected) of 1980 NFL draft.
Released by Baltimore Colts, September 6, 1982; signed as free agent by New York Giants, September 17, 1982.
Traded by New York Giants to New York Jets for future draft pick, August 23, 1983.
Released by New York Jets, August 29, 1983; signed as free agent by New York Giants, September 12, 1983.
Signed by Los Angeles Express, November 13, 1983, for contract to take effect after being granted free agency, February 1, 1984.
Traded by Los Angeles Express to Tampa Bay Bandits for past considerations, March 12, 1984.
On developmental squad, April 5 through April 18, 1985; activated, April 19, 1985.

Granted free agency when USFL suspended operations, August 7, 1986; re-signed by New York Giants and traded to Minnesota Vikings for conditional pick in 1988 draft, May 7, 1987.

On injured reserve with broken hand, September 1 through November 9, 1987.

Released by Minnesota Vikings, November 10, 1987; re-signed by Vikings after clearing procedural waivers, November 17, 1987.

On developmental squad for 2 games with Tampa Bay Bandits in 1985.

Baltimore NFL, 1980 and 1981; New York Giants NFL, 1982 and 1983; Los Angeles (3)-Tampa Bay (15) USFL, 1984; Tampa Bay USFL, 1985; Minnesota NFL, 1987 and 1988.

Games: 1980 (16), 1981 (16), 1982 (7), 1983 (11), 1984 (18), 1985 (16), 1987 (6), 1988 (16). Total NFL—72. Total USFL—34. Total Pro—106.

NFL statistics: Returned one kickoff for nine yards and recovered one fumble, 1980; returned one kickoff for no yards, 1981.

USFL statistics: Recovered one fumble, 1985.

Played in NFC Championship Game following 1987 season.

BRIAN FORDE
Linebacker—New Orleans Saints
Born November 1, 1963, at Montreal, Que., Canada.
Height, 6.02. Weight, 225.
High School—Montreal, Que., Canada, Champlain Regional College Prep.
Attended Washington State University.

Selected by New Orleans in 7th round (190th player selected) of 1988 NFL draft.
Signed by New Orleans Saints, July 17, 1988.
New Orleans NFL, 1988.
Games: 1988 (16).

ROY ALLEN FOSTER
Guard—Miami Dolphins
Born May 24, 1960, at Los Angeles, Calif.
Height, 6.04. Weight, 272.
High Schools—Woodland Hills, Calif., Taft; and Shawnee Mission, Kan., West.
Attended University of Southern California.

Named as guard on THE SPORTING NEWS College All-America Team, 1981.
Selected by Miami in 1st round (24th player selected) of 1982 NFL draft.
Miami NFL, 1982 through 1988.
Games: 1982 (9), 1983 (16), 1984 (16), 1985 (16), 1986 (16), 1987 (12), 1988 (15). Total—100.
Pro statistics: Recovered one fumble, 1984 and 1987; recovered two fumbles, 1986.
Played in AFC Championship Game following 1982, 1984 and 1985 seasons.
Played in NFL Championship Game following 1982 and 1984 seasons.
Played in Pro Bowl (NFL All-Star Game) following 1985 and 1986 seasons.

JOHN CHARLES FOURCADE
Quarterback—New Orleans Saints
Born October 11, 1960, at Gretna, La.
Height, 6.01. Weight, 208.
High School—Marrero, La., Archbishop Shaw.
Received bachelor of science degree in education
and sports marketing from University of Mississippi.

Signed as free agent by Toronto Argonauts, May 5, 1982.
Traded by Toronto Argonauts to British Columbia Lions, May 20, 1982.
Released by British Columbia Lions, July 4, 1982; re-signed by Lions, July 8, 1982.
Released by British Columbia Lions, June 30, 1983; signed by Birmingham Stallions, October 10, 1983.
Released by Birmingham Stallions, February 13, 1984; signed as free agent by Memphis Showboats, May 31, 1984.
On developmental squad, May 31 through remainder of 1984 season.
Released by Memphis Showboats, January 23, 1985; signed as free agent by New York Giants, May 3, 1985.
Released by New York Giants, July 22, 1985; signed as free agent by New Orleans Saints, May 13, 1986.
Released by New Orleans Saints, August 19, 1986; signed as free agent by Denver Dynamite of Arena Football League, July 15, 1987.
Granted free agency, August 15, 1987; re-signed as replacement player by New Orleans Saints, September 24, 1987.
On developmental squad for 4 games with Memphis Showboats in 1984.

				—PASSING—						RUSHING			—TOTAL—		
Year Club	G.	Att.	Cmp.	Pct.	Gain	T.P.	P.I.	Avg.	Att.	Yds.	Avg.	TD.	TD.	Pts.	F.
1982—British Columbia CFL.....	4	14	5	35.7	55	0	3	3.93	2	37	18.5	0	0	0	0
1987—New Orleans NFL............	3	89	48	53.9	597	4	3	6.71	19	134	7.1	0	0	0	1
1988—New Orleans NFL............	1	1	0	0.0	0	0	0	0.00			None		0	0	0
CFL Totals—1 Year..........	4	14	5	35.7	55	0	3	3.93	2	37	18.5	0	0	0	0
NFL Totals—2 Years.........	4	90	48	53.3	597	4	3	6.63	19	134	7.1	0	0	0	1
Pro Totals—3 Years...........	8	104	53	51.0	652	4	6	6.27	21	171	8.1	0	0	0	1

NFL Quarterback Rating Points: 1987 (75.9), 1988 (39.6). Total—75.1.

STEVEN TODD FOWLER
(Known by middle name.)
Fullback—Dallas Cowboys
Born June 9, 1962, at Van, Tex.
Height, 6.03. Weight, 222.
High School—Van, Tex.
Attended Henderson County Junior College and Stephen F. Austin State University.

Selected by Houston in 16th round (329th player selected) of 1984 USFL draft.
Signed by Houston Gamblers, January 20, 1984.
Selected by Dallas in 1st round (25th player selected) of 1984 NFL supplemental draft.
Signed by Dallas Cowboys, September 24, 1984, for contract to take effect after being granted free agency after 1985 USFL season.
On developmental squad, February 21 through March 30, 1985; activated, March 31, 1985.
On injured reserve with knee injury, August 27 through October 28, 1985; activated, October 29, 1985.
On developmental squad for 5 games with Houston Gamblers in 1985.

Year	Club	G.	Att.	Yds.	Avg.	TD.	P.C.	Yds.	Avg.	TD.	TD.	Pts.	F.
				RUSHING			PASS RECEIVING					TOTAL	
1984—Houston USFL		18	170	1003	5.9	11	24	301	12.5	2	13	78	4
1985—Houston USFL		13	92	402	4.4	3	27	239	8.9	1	4	†26	5
1985—Dallas NFL		8	7	25	3.6	0	5	24	4.8	0	0	0	0
1986—Dallas NFL		16	6	5	0.8	0	1	19	19.0	0	0	0	1
1987—Dallas NFL		12		None			1	6	6.0	0	0	0	0
1988—Dallas NFL		16	3	6	2.0	0	10	64	6.4	0	0	0	0
USFL Totals—2 Years		31	262	1405	5.4	14	51	540	10.6	3	17	104	9
NFL Totals—4 Years		52	16	36	2.3	0	17	113	6.6	0	0	0	1
Pro Totals—6 Years		83	278	1441	5.2	14	68	653	9.6	3	17	104	10

†Includes one 2-point conversion.
Additional USFL statistics: Recovered four fumbles, 1984; recovered two fumbles, 1985.
Additional NFL statistics: Returned three kickoffs for 48 yards, 1985; recovered one fumble, 1986.

WILLIAM P. FRALIC JR.
(Bill)
Guard—Atlanta Falcons
Born October 31, 1962, at Penn Hills, Pa.
Height, 6.05. Weight, 280.
High School—Pittsburgh, Pa., Penn Hills.
Attended University of Pittsburgh.

Named to The Sporting News NFL All-Star Team, 1986 and 1987.
Named as offensive tackle on The Sporting News College Football All-America Team, 1983 and 1984.
Selected by Baltimore in 1985 USFL territorial draft.
Selected by Atlanta in 1st round (2nd player selected) of 1985 NFL draft.
Signed by Atlanta Falcons, July 22, 1985.
On injured reserve with knee injury, December 14 through remainder of 1988 season.
Atlanta NFL, 1985 through 1988.
Games: 1985 (15), 1986 (16), 1987 (12), 1988 (14). Total—57.
Played in Pro Bowl (NFL All-Star Team) following 1986 and 1987 seasons.
Named to play in Pro Bowl following 1988 season; replaced due to injury by Mark Bortz.

RONALD BERNARD FRANCIS
(Ron)
Cornerback—Dallas Cowboys
Born April 7, 1964, at LaMarque, Tex.
Height, 5.09. Weight, 199.
High School—LaMarque, Tex.
Attended Baylor University.
Brother of James Francis, linebacker at Baylor University.

Selected by Dallas in 2nd round (39th player selected) of 1987 NFL draft.
Signed by Dallas Cowboys, July 24, 1987.

Year	Club	G.	No.	Yds.	Avg.	TD.
			INTERCEPTIONS			
1987—Dallas NFL		11	2	18	9.0	1
1988—Dallas NFL		13	1	29	29.0	0
Pro Totals—2 Years		24	3	47	15.7	1

Additional pro statistics: Recovered one fumble for two yards, 1987.

RUSSELL ROSS FRANCIS
(Russ)
Tight End
Born April 3, 1953, at Seattle, Wash.
Height, 6.06. Weight, 242.
High Schools—Kailua, Oahu, Hawaii; and Pleasant Hill, Ore.
Attended University of Oregon.
Son of Ed Francis, former part-time scout with New England Patriots.

Selected by New England in 1st round (16th player selected) of 1975 NFL draft.
On did not report list, August 18 through entire 1981 season.
Traded with 2nd round pick in 1982 draft by New England Patriots to San Francisco 49ers for 1st, 4th and two 2nd round picks in 1982 draft, April 27, 1982.
On injured reserve with neck injury, October 23 through December 6, 1984; activated, December 7, 1984.
On injured reserve with Achilles heel injury, September 7 through October 5, 1987; activated, October 6, 1987.
Crossed picket line during players' strike, October 6, 1987.
On injured reserve with back injury, December 4 through December 14, 1987.
Released by San Francisco 49ers, December 15, 1987; signed as free agent by New England Patriots, December 23, 1987.

Granted unconditional free agency, February 1, 1989; did not receive qualifying offer, April 15, 1989.
Selected by Kansas City Royals' organization in 9th round of free-agent draft, June 5, 1974.

Year—Club	G.	P.C.	Yds.	Avg.	TD.	Year—Club	G.	P.C.	Yds.	Avg.	TD.
	\-\-\-PASS RECEIVING\-\-\-						\-\-\-PASS RECEIVING\-\-\-				
1975—New England NFL	14	35	636	18.2	4	1984—San Francisco NFL	10	23	285	12.4	2
1976—New England NFL	13	26	367	14.1	3	1985—San Francisco NFL	16	44	478	10.9	3
1977—New England NFL	10	16	229	14.3	4	1986—San Francisco NFL	16	41	505	12.3	1
1978—New England NFL	15	39	543	13.9	4	1987—S.F. (8)-N.E. (1) NFL	9	22	202	9.2	0
1979—New England NFL	12	39	557	14.3	5	1988—New England NFL	12	11	161	14.6	0
1980—New England NFL	15	41	664	16.2	8	Pro Totals—13 Years	167	393	5203	13.2	40
1982—San Francisco NFL	9	23	278	12.1	2						
1983—San Francisco NFL	16	33	357	10.8	4						

Additional pro statistics: Fumbled once, 1975, 1976, 1978 and 1984; rushed twice for 12 yards and recovered one fumble, 1976 and 1978; recovered one fumble for three yards, 1977; attempted one pass with one completion for 45 yards, 1982; fumbled twice, 1982, 1983 and 1985; recovered two fumbles, 1984.
Played in NFC Championship Game following 1983 and 1984 seasons.
Played in NFL Championship Game following 1984 season.
Played in Pro Bowl (NFL All-Star Game) following 1976 and 1977 seasons.
Named to play in Pro Bowl following 1978 season; replaced due to injury by Riley Odoms.

PAUL MILES FRASE
Named pronounced Fraze.
Defensive End—New York Jets
Born May 5, 1965, at Elmira, N. Y.
Height, 6.05. Weight, 273.
High School—Rochester, N. H., Spaulding.
Attended Syracuse University.

Selected by New York Jets in 6th round (146th player selected) of 1988 NFL draft.
Signed by New York Jets, June 21, 1988.
New York Jets NFL, 1988.
Games: 1988 (16).

LORENZO Z. FREEMAN
Nose Tackle-Defensive Tackle—Pittsburgh Steelers
Born May 23, 1964, at East Camden, N.J.
Height, 6.05. Weight, 298.
High School—Camden, N.J., Woodrow Wilson.
Attended University of Pittsburgh.

Selected by Green Bay in 4th round (89th player selected) of 1987 NFL draft.
Signed by Green Bay Packers, July 25, 1987.
On injured reserve with ankle injury, September 7 through September 21, 1987; activated, September 22, 1987.
Released by Green Bay Packers, November 3, 1987; signed as free agent by Pittsburgh Steelers, November 18, 1987.
Pittsburgh NFL, 1987 and 1988.
Games: 1987 (6), 1988 (13). Total—19.

PAUL MITCHAEL FREROTTE
(Name pronounced Fur-ROT.)
Guard—Buffalo Bills
Born March 30, 1965, at Kittanning, Pa.
Height, 6.03. Weight, 280.
High School—Kittanning, Pa.
Attended Penn State University.

Signed as free agent by Buffalo Bills, July 22, 1987.
Released by Buffalo Bills, August 30, 1988; re-signed by Bills, January 10, 1989.
Buffalo NFL, 1987.
Games: 1987 (12).

WILLIAM JASPER FRIZZELL
Safety—Philadelphia Eagles
Born September 8, 1962, at Greenville, N.C.
Height, 6.03. Weight, 205.
High School—Greenville, N.C., J.H. Rose.
Attended North Carolina Central University.

Selected by Detroit in 10th round (259th player selected) of 1984 NFL draft.
On injured reserve with ankle injury, September 2 through November 1, 1985; activated, November 2, 1985.
Released by Detroit Lions, August 26, 1986; signed as free agent by Philadelphia Eagles, October 8, 1986.
Released by Philadelphia Eagles, November 6, 1986; re-signed by Eagles, November 26, 1986.
Detroit NFL, 1984 and 1985; Philadelphia NFL, 1986 through 1988.
Games: 1984 (16), 1985 (8), 1986 (8), 1987 (12), 1988 (16). Total—60.
Pro statistics: Intercepted one pass for three yards, 1985; recovered one fumble, 1987; intercepted three passes for 19 yards, 1988.

IRVING DALE FRYAR
Wide Receiver-Punt Returner—New England Patriots

Born September 28, 1962, at Mount Holly, N.J.
Height, 6.00. Weight, 200.
High School—Mount Holly, N.J., Rancocas Valley Regional.
Attended University of Nebraska.
Cousin of Charles Fryar, rookie cornerback with Pittsburgh Steelers.

Named as wide receiver on THE SPORTING NEWS College All-America Team, 1983.
Selected by Chicago in 1st round (3rd player selected) of 1984 USFL draft.
Signed by New England Patriots, April 11, 1984.
Selected officially by New England in 1st round (1st player selected) of 1984 NFL draft.

| | | —RUSHING— | | | | PASS RECEIVING | | | | —TOTAL— | | |
Year Club	G.	Att.	Yds.	Avg.	TD.	P.C.	Yds.	Avg.	TD.	TD.	Pts.	F.
1984—New England NFL	14	2	—11	—5.5	0	11	164	14.9	1	1	6	4
1985—New England NFL	16	7	27	3.9	1	39	670	17.2	7	10	60	4
1986—New England NFL	14	4	80	20.0	0	43	737	17.1	6	7	42	4
1987—New England NFL	12	9	52	5.8	0	31	467	15.1	5	5	30	2
1988—New England NFL	15	6	12	2.0	0	33	490	14.8	5	5	30	2
Pro Totals—5 Years	71	28	160	5.7	1	157	2528	16.1	24	28	168	16

| | | —PUNT RETURNS— | | | | —KICKOFF RET.— | | | |
Year Club	G.	No.	Yds.	Avg.	TD.	No.	Yds.	Avg.	TD.
1984—New England NFL	14	36	347	9.6	0	5	95	19.0	0
1985—New England NFL	16	37	520	*14.1	*2	3	39	13.0	0
1986—New England NFL	14	35	366	10.5	1	10	192	19.2	0
1987—New England NFL	12	18	174	9.7	0	6	119	19.8	0
1988—New England NFL	15	38	398	10.5	0	1	3	3.0	0
Pro Totals—5 Years	71	164	1805	11.0	3	25	448	17.9	0

Additional pro statistics: Recovered one fumble, 1984 and 1986.
Played in NFL Championship Game following 1985 season.
Played in Pro Bowl (NFL All-Star Game) following 1985 season.

DAVID FRYE
(Dave)
Linebacker—Miami Dolphins

Born June 21, 1961, at Cincinnati, O.
Height, 6.02. Weight, 227.
High School—Cincinnati, O., Woodward.
Attended Santa Ana College and Purdue University.

Signed as free agent by Atlanta Falcons, May 9, 1983.
On non-football injury list with drug problem, September 27 through October 8, 1985; activated, October 9, 1985.
Released by Atlanta Falcons, August 26, 1986; signed as free agent by Miami Dolphins, October 24, 1986.
On injured reserve with shoulder injury, October 29 through December 2, 1988; activated, December 3, 1988.
Atlanta NFL, 1983 through 1985; Miami NFL, 1986 through 1988.
Games: 1983 (16), 1984 (16), 1985 (14), 1986 (9), 1987 (12), 1988 (8). Total—75.
Pro statistics: Recovered two fumbles, 1983 and 1984; intercepted one pass for 20 yards and recovered one fumble
for 13 yards, 1985; recovered one fumble, 1986.

DAVID DWAYNE FULCHER
Safety—Cincinnati Bengals

Born September 28, 1964, at Los Angeles, Calif.
Height, 6.03. Weight, 228.
High School—Los Angeles, Calif., John C. Fremont.
Attended Arizona State University.

Named as defensive back on THE SPORTING NEWS College All-America Team, 1984 and 1985.
Selected by Cincinnati in 3rd round (78th player selected) of 1986 NFL draft.
Selected by Arizona in 1986 USFL supplemental territorial draft.
Signed by Cincinnati Bengals, July 19, 1986.
On injured reserve with back injury, December 26 through remainder of 1987 season.

| | | —INTERCEPTIONS— | | | |
Year Club	G.	No.	Yds.	Avg.	TD.
1986—Cincinnati NFL	16	4	20	5.0	0
1987—Cincinnati NFL	11	3	30	10.0	0
1988—Cincinnati NFL	16	5	38	7.6	1
Pro Totals—3 Years	43	12	88	7.3	1

Additional pro statistics: Recovered one fumble, 1986 and 1987; returned one kickoff for no yards, 1987; fumbled
once, 1988.
Played in AFC Championship Game following 1988 season.
Played in NFL Championship Game following 1988 season.
Played in Pro Bowl (NFL All-Star Game) following 1988 season.

—DID YOU KNOW—
That there were 54 300-yard passing performances in the NFL in 1988?

SCOTT ALAN FULHAGE
Punter—Cincinnati Bengals

Born November 17, 1961, at Beloit, Kan.
Height, 5.11. Weight, 191.
High School—Beloit, Kan.
Received bachelor of science degree in agricultural economics
from Kansas State University in 1985.

Signed as free agent by Buffalo Bills, June 20, 1985.
Released by Buffalo Bills, August 5, 1985; signed as free agent by Washington Redskins, June 29, 1986.
Released by Washington Redskins, August 18, 1986; signed as free agent by Cincinnati Bengals, February 4, 1987.
Released by Cincinnati Bengals, September 7, 1987; re-signed as replacement player by Bengals, September 25, 1987.
Released by Cincinnati Bengals, October 19, 1987; awarded on waivers to Green Bay Packers, October 20, 1987.
Released by Green Bay Packers, November 3, 1987; signed as free agent by Cincinnati Bengals, November 5, 1987.
On injured reserve with back injury, December 21 through remainder of 1988 season playoffs.

		—PUNTING—			
Year Club	G.	No.	Avg.	Blk.	
1987—Cincinnati NFL	11	52	41.7	0	
1988—Cincnnati NFL	13	44	38.0	2	
Pro Totals—2 Years	24	96	40.0	2	

JEFFERY AVERY FULLER
(Jeff)
Safety—San Francisco 49ers

Born August 8, 1962, at Dallas, Tex.
Height, 6.02. Weight, 216.
High School—Dallas, Tex., Franklin D. Roosevelt.
Attended Texas A&M University.

Selected by Houston in 1984 USFL territorial draft.
Selected by San Francisco in 5th round (139th player selected) of 1984 NFL draft.
Signed by San Francisco 49ers, May 29, 1984.
On injured reserve with knee injury, September 10 through November 21, 1986; activated, November 22, 1986.
Crossed picket line during players' strike, October 7, 1987.

		—INTERCEPTIONS—			
Year Club	G.	No.	Yds.	Avg.	TD.
1984—San Francisco NFL	13	1	38	38.0	0
1985—San Francisco NFL	16	1	4	4.0	0
1986—San Francisco NFL	6	4	44	11.0	0
1987—San Francisco NFL	14		None		
1988—San Francisco NFL	16	4	18	4.5	0
Pro Totals—5 Years	65	10	104	10.4	0

Additional pro statistics: Recovered one fumble, 1986 and 1988; fumbled twice, 1986; credited with a safety and recovered three fumbles, 1987.
Played in NFC Championship Game following 1984 and 1988 seasons.
Played in NFL Championship Game following 1984 and 1988 seasons.

JOE FULLER
Cornerback—Minnesota Vikings

Born September 25, 1964, at Minneapolis, Minn.
Height, 5.11. Weight, 180.
Attended University of Northern Iowa.

Signed as free agent by Saskatchewan Roughriders, March, 1986.
Granted free agency, March 1, 1989; signed as free agent by Minnesota Vikings, March 16, 1989.

		INTERCEPTIONS				–PUNT RETURNS–				—KICKOFF RET.—				—TOTAL—		
Year Club	G.	No.	Yds.	Avg.	TD.	No.	Yds.	Avg.	TD.	No.	Yds.	Avg.	TD.	TD.	Pts.	F.
1986—Saskatchewan CFL	7		None			6	34	5.7	0	5	106	21.2	0	0	0	0
1987—Saskatchewan CFL	18	5	41	8.2	0	52	403	7.8	0	18	289	16.1	0	0	0	2
1988—Saskatchewan CFL	18	7	131	18.7	1	54	426	7.9	0	4	55	13.8	0	1	6	3
CFL Totals—3 Years	43	12	172	14.3	1	112	863	7.7	0	27	450	16.7	0	1	6	5

Additional CFL statistics: Recovered one fumble, 1988.

WILLIAM HENRY FULLER JR.
Defensive End—Houston Oilers

Born March 8, 1962, at Norfolk, Va.
Height, 6.03. Weight, 269.
High School—Chesapeake, Va., Indian River.
Attended University of North Carolina.

Named as defensive tackle on THE SPORTING NEWS College All-America Team, 1983.
Named as defensive end on THE SPORTING NEWS USFL All-Star Team, 1985.
Selected by Philadelphia in 1984 USFL territorial draft.
Signed by Philadelphia Stars, February 6, 1984.
On injured reserve with fractured ankle, May 18 through June 22, 1984; activated, June 23, 1984.
Selected by Los Angeles Rams in 1st round (21st player selected) of 1984 NFL supplemental draft.
Franchise transferred to Baltimore, November 1, 1984.

Granted free agency when USFL suspended operations, August 7, 1986; signed by Los Angeles Rams, September 10, 1986.

Traded with guard Kent Hill, 1st and 5th round picks in 1987 draft and 1st round pick in 1988 draft by Los Angeles Rams to Houston Oilers for rights to quarterback Jim Everett, September 8, 1986.

Granted roster exemption, September 18 through September 21, 1986; activated, September 22, 1986.

Philadelphia USFL, 1984; Baltimore USFL, 1985; Houston NFL, 1986 through 1988.

Games: 1984 (13), 1985 (18), 1986 (13), 1987 (12), 1988 (16). Total USFL—31. Total NFL—41. Total Pro—72.

USFL statistics: Credited with two sacks for 18 yards and recovered one fumble, 1984; credited with 8½ sacks for 102 yards, intercepted one pass for 35 yards and recovered four fumbles for 17 yards, 1985.

NFL statistics: Recovered one fumble and returned one kickoff for no yards, 1987; intercepted one pass for nine yards, 1988.

Played in USFL Championship Game following 1984 and 1985 seasons.

DARRELL FULLINGTON
Safety—Minnesota Vikings
Born April 17, 1964, at New Smyrna Beach, Fla.
Height, 6.01. Weight, 197.
High School—New Smyrna Beach, Fla.
Received degree in business management organization
from University of Miami (Fla.) in 1988.

Selected by Minnesota in 5th round (124th player selected) of 1988 NFL draft.
Signed by Minnesota Vikings, July 19, 1988.

| | | | —INTERCEPTIONS— | | |
Year	Club	G.	No.	Yds.	Avg.TD.
1988—Minnesota NFL		15	3	57	19.0 0

Additional pro statistics: Recovered one fumble, 1988.

BRENT LANARD FULLWOOD
Running Back—Green Bay Packers
Born October 10, 1963, at Kissimmee, Fla.
Height, 5.11. Weight, 209.
High School—St. Cloud, Fla.
Attended Auburn University.

Named as running back on THE SPORTING NEWS College All-America Team, 1986.
Selected by Green Bay Packers in 1st round (4th player selected) of 1987 NFL draft.
Signed by Green Bay Packers, August 4, 1987.

| | | | —RUSHING— | | | | PASS RECEIVING | | | | —TOTAL— | | |
Year	Club	G.	Att.	Yds.	Avg.	TD.	P.C.	Yds.	Avg.	TD.	TD.	Pts.	F.
1987—Green Bay NFL		11	84	274	3.3	5	2	11	5.5	0	5	30	2
1988—Green Bay NFL		14	101	483	4.8	7	20	128	6.4	1	8	48	6
Pro Totals—2 Years		25	185	757	4.1	12	22	139	6.3	1	13	78	8

| | | | KICKOFF RETURNS | | |
Year	Club	G.	No.	Yds.	Avg.TD.
1987—Green Bay NFL		11	24	510	21.3 0
1988—Green Bay NFL		14	21	421	20.0 0
Pro Totals—2 Years		25	45	931	20.7 0

Additional pro statistics: Recovered one fumble, 1987 and 1988.

ANTHONY JOSEPH FURJANIC
(Tony)
Linebacker—Miami Dolphins
Born February 26, 1964, at Chicago, Ill.
Height, 6.01. Weight, 228.
High School—Chicago, Ill., Mt. Carmel.
Received bachelor of business administration degree in marketing from
University of Notre Dame in 1986.

Selected by Orlando in 1986 USFL territorial draft.
Selected by Buffalo in 8th round (202nd player selected) of 1986 NFL draft.
Signed by Buffalo Bills, July 23, 1986.
Released by Buffalo Bills, September 7, 1987; re-signed by Bills, October 20, 1987.
Released by Buffalo Bills, August 30, 1988; signed as free agent by Miami Dolphins, November 9, 1988.
Buffalo NFL, 1986 and 1987; Miami NFL, 1988.
Games: 1986 (14), 1987 (8), 1988 (6). Total—28.

BOBBY LEE FUTRELL
Name pronounced Few-TRELL.
Defensive Back—Tampa Bay Buccaneers
Born August 4, 1962, at Ahoskie, N.C.
Height, 5.11. Weight, 190.
High School—Ahoskie, N.C.
Attended Elizabeth City State University.

Selected by Michigan in 5th round (93rd player selected) of 1984 USFL draft.
Signed by Michigan Panthers, January 23, 1984.
Not protected in merger of Michigan Panthers and Oakland Invaders; selected by Tampa Bay Bandits in USFL dispersal draft, December 6, 1984.

Released by Tampa Bay Bandits, February 18, 1985; re-signed by Bandits, February 19, 1985.
Released by Tampa Bay Bandits, April 19, 1985; awarded on waivers to Oakland Invaders, April 23, 1985.
On developmental squad, May 23 through June 14, 1985; activated, June 15, 1985.
Released by Oakland Invaders, August 2, 1985; signed as free agent by Tampa Bay Buccaneers, April 2, 1986.
On developmental squad for 3 games with Oakland Invaders in 1985.

Year Club	G.	INTERCEPTIONS				-PUNT RETURNS-				—KICKOFF RET.—				—TOTAL—		
		No.	Yds.	Avg.	TD.	No.	Yds.	Avg.	TD.	No.	Yds.	Avg.	TD.	TD.	Pts.	F.
1984—Michigan USFL...........	18	1	29	29.0	0	3	17	5.7	0	27	576	21.3	0	0	0	4
1985—TB (8)-Oak. (6) USFL..	14	None				None				10	199	19.9	0	0	0	0
1986—Tampa Bay NFL.........	16	None				14	67	4.8	0	5	115	23.0	0	0	0	1
1987—Tampa Bay NFL.........	12	2	46	23.0	0	24	213	8.9	0	31	609	19.6	0	0	0	2
1988—Tampa Bay NFL.........	16	1	26	26.0	0	27	283	10.5	0	2	38	19.0	0	0	0	4
USFL Totals—2 Years....	32	1	29	29.0	0	3	17	5.7	0	37	775	20.9	0	0	0	4
NFL Totals—3 Years.....	44	3	72	24.0	0	65	563	8.7	0	38	762	20.1	0	0	0	7
Pro Totals—5 Years.......	76	4	101	25.3	0	68	580	8.5	0	75	1537	20.5	0	0	0	11

Additional USFL statistics: Recovered two fumbles, 1984.
Additional NFL statistics: Recovered one fumble, 1986 and 1988; recovered two fumbles, 1987.
On developmental squad for USFL Championship Game following 1985 season.

DENNIS RICHARD GADBOIS
Wide Receiver—New England Patriots
Born September 18, 1963, at Biddleford, Me.
Height, 6.01. Weight, 185.
High School—Biddleford, Me.
Attended Boston University.

Signed as free agent by New England Patriots, May 5, 1987.
Released by New England Patriots, August 25, 1987; re-signed as replacement player by Patriots, September 24, 1987.
Released by New England Patriots, October 23, 1987; re-signed by Patriots, December 2, 1987.
On injured reserve with knee injury, August 29 through October 12, 1988; re-signed by Patriots after clearing procedural waivers, October 14, 1988.
On injured reserve with neck injury, October 22 through December 14, 1988; re-signed by Patriots after clearing procedural waivers, December 16, 1988.
Granted unconditional free agency, February 1, 1989; did not receive qualifying offer, April 15, 1989.
Re-signed by Patriots, May 18, 1989.
New England NFL, 1987 and 1988.
Games: 1987 (3), 1988 (2). Total—5.
Pro statistics: Caught three passes for 51 yards, 1987.

STEVE GAGE
Safety—Miami Dolphins
Born May 10, 1964, at Claremore, Okla.
Height, 6.03. Weight, 210.
High School—Claremore, Okla.
Attended The University of Tulsa.

Selected by Washington in 6th round (144th player selected) of 1987 NFL draft.
Signed by Washington Redskins, July 26, 1987.
Released by Washington Redskins, September 7, 1987; re-signed as replacement player by Redskins, October 8, 1987.
On injured reserve, January 9, 1988 through remainder of 1987 season playoffs.
Granted unconditional free agency, February 1, 1989; signed by Miami Dolphins, February 13, 1989.
Washington NFL, 1987 and 1988.
Games: 1987 (4), 1988 (16). Total—20.
Pro statistics: Intercepted one pass for seven yards, 1987; returned five kickoffs for 60 yards, 1988.

ROBERT FRANK GAGLIANO
(Bob)
Quarterback—Detroit Lions
Born September 5, 1958, at Los Angeles, Calif.
Height, 6.03. Weight, 195.
High School—Glendale, Calif., Hoover.
Attended Glendale Junior College, U.S. International University and Utah State University.

Selected by Kansas City in 12th round (319th player selected) of 1981 NFL draft.
Released by Kansas City Chiefs, August 25, 1981; re-signed by Chiefs, August 27, 1981.
On inactive list, September 12 and September 19, 1982.
USFL rights traded with rights to wide receiver Dave Dorn by New Jersey Generals to Chicago Blitz for rights to offensive tackle Jeff Weston and linebacker Bobby Leopold, November 23, 1983.
USFL rights traded by Chicago Blitz to San Antonio Gunslingers for defensive tackle Broderick Thompson and 1st round pick in 1984 draft, January 3, 1984.
Signed by San Antonio Gunslingers, January 6, 1984, for contract to take effect after being granted free agency, February 1, 1984.
Traded by San Antonio Gunslingers to Denver Gold or linebacker Putt Choate and 9th round pick in 1985 draft, February 13, 1984.
On developmental squad, February 24 through March 16, 1984; activated, March 17, 1984.
On developmental squad, April 28 through May 24, 1984; activated, May 25, 1984.
On developmental squad, June 2 through June 7, 1984; activated June 8, 1984.

On developmental squad, June 15 through remainder of 1984 season.
Franchise merged with Jacksonville Bulls, February 19, 1986.
Released by Jacksonville Bulls, March 18, 1986; signed as free agent by San Francisco 49ers, October 29, 1986.
Released by San Francisco 49ers, November 7, 1986; re-signed by 49ers for 1987, November 13, 1986.
Released by San Francisco 49ers, September 7, 1987; re-signed as replacement player by 49ers, September 24, 1987.
Released by San Francisco 49ers, August 9, 1988; signed as free agent by Tampa Bay Buccaneers, August 15, 1988.
Released by Tampa Bay Buccaneers, August 29, 1988; signed as free agent by Houston Oilers, September 13, 1988.
Released by Houston Oilers, September 19, 1988; signed as free agent by Indianapolis Colts, October 11, 1988.
Released by Indianapolis Colts, October 26, 1988; signed as free agent by Detroit Lions, March 16, 1989.
On developmental squad for 10 games with Denver Gold in 1984.
Active for 16 games with Kansas City Chiefs in 1981; did not play.
Active for 1 game with San Francisco 49ers in 1986; did not play.
Active for 1 game with Indianapolis Colts in 1988; did not play.

Year Club	G.	PASSING							RUSHING				TOTAL		
		Att.	Cmp.	Pct.	Gain	T.P.	P.I.	Avg.	Att.	Yds.	Avg.	TD.	TD.	Pts.	F.
1982—Kansas City NFL	1	1	1	100.0	7	0	0	7.00		None			0	0	0
1983—Kansas City NFL	1			None						None			0	0	0
1984—Denver USFL	8	31	20	64.5	236	2	1	7.61	1	7	7.0	0	0	†2	2
1985—Denver USFL	18	358	205	57.3	2695	13	17	7.53	34	111	3.3	2	2	12	5
1987—San Francisco NFL	3	29	16	55.2	229	1	1	7.90		None			0	0	0
NFL Totals—6 Years	5	30	17	56.7	236	1	1	7.87	0	0	0.0	0	0	0	0
USFL Totals—2 Years	26	389	225	57.8	2931	15	18	7.53	35	118	3.4	2	2	14	7
Pro Totals—8 Years	31	419	242	57.8	3167	16	19	7.56	35	118	3.4	2	2	14	7

†Includes one 2-point conversion.
Additional pro statistics: Recovered two fumbles, 1984, recovered three fumbles, 1985.
USFL Quarterback Rating Points: 1984 (95.6), 1985 (73.5). Total—75.5.
NFL Quarterback Rating Points: 1987 (78.1).

CHRIS GAINES
Linebacker—Tampa Bay Buccaneers
Born February 3, 1965, at Nashville, Tenn.
Height, 6.00. Weight, 238.
High School—Hermitage, Tenn., DuPont.
Attended Vanderbilt University.
Brother of Greg Gaines, linebacker with Kansas City Chiefs; brother of Brad Gaines, linebacker
at Vanderbilt University; and nephew of Ray Oldham, safety with Baltimore Colts,
Pittsburgh Steelers, New York Giants and Detroit Lions, 1973 through 1982.
Selected by Phoenix in 5th round (120th player selected) of 1988 NFL draft.
Signed by Phoenix Cardinals, July 11, 1988.
Released by Phoenix Cardinals, August 30, 1988; signed as free agent by Miami Dolphins, September 2, 1988.
Released by Miami Dolphins, September 29, 1988; signed as free agent by Tampa Bay Buccaneers, April 10, 1989.
Miami NFL, 1988.
Games: 1988 (4).

GREGORY SCOTT GAINES
(Greg)
Linebacker—Kansas City Chiefs
Born October 16, 1958, at Martinsville, Va.
Height, 6.03. Weight, 229.
High School—Hermitage, Tenn., DuPont.
Attended University of Tennessee.
Nephew of Ray Oldham, safety with Baltimore Colts, Pittsburgh Steelers,
New York Giants and Detroit Lions, 1973 through 1982; and brother of Chris Gaines,
linebacker with Tampa Bay Buccaneers; and brother of Brad Gaines, linebacker at Vanderbilt University.
Signed as free agent by Seattle Seahawks, May 6, 1981.
On injured reserve with knee injury, October 28 through remainder of 1981 season.
On injured reserve with knee injury, August 31 through entire 1982 season.
On active/non-football injury list with back injury, July 21 through August 21, 1988; then transferred to reserve/non-football injury list with back injury, August 22 through October 28, 1988; activated, October 29, 1988.
Granted unconditional free agency, February 1, 1989; signed by Kansas City Chiefs, March 20, 1989.
Seattle NFL, 1981 and 1983 through 1988.
Games: 1981 (8), 1983 (16), 1984 (16), 1985 (16), 1986 (16), 1987 (11), 1988 (6). Total—89.
Pro statistics: Recovered one fumble, 1981, 1986 and 1987; recovered four fumbles, 1983; intercepted one pass for 18 yards, 1984; recovered two fumbles for seven yards, 1985; intercepted one pass for eight yards, 1986.
Played in AFC Championship Game following 1983 season.

HARRY CURTIS GALBREATH
Guard—Miami Dolphins
Born January 1, 1965, at Clarksville, Tenn.
Height, 6.01. Weight, 275.
High School—Clarksville, Tenn.
Received degree from University of Tennessee.
Named as guard on THE SPORTING NEWS College All-America Team, 1987.
Selected by Miami in 8th round (212nd player selected) of 1988 NFL draft.
Signed by Miami Dolphins, July 12, 1988.
Miami NFL, 1988.
Games: 1988 (16).

JIM PATRICK GALLERY
Placekicker—Cincinnati Bengals
Born September 15, 1961, at Morton, Minn.
Height, 6.01. Weight, 190.
High School—Morton, Minn.
Attended University of Minnesota.

Selected by Tampa Bay in 10th round (254th player selected) of 1984 NFL draft.
NFL rights released by Tampa Bay Buccaneers, July 5, 1984; signed as free agent by Buffalo Bills, July 9, 1984.
Released by Buffalo Bills, August 14, 1984; re-signed by Bills, May 10, 1985.
Released by Buffalo Bills, August 5, 1985.
USFL rights traded by Birmingham Stallions to Arizona Outlaws for past considerations, June 23, 1986.
Signed as free agent by New England Patriots, May 9, 1987.
Released by New England Patriots, September 7, 1987; awarded on waivers to St. Louis Cardinals, September 8, 1987.
Crossed picket line during players' strike, October 14, 1987.
Franchise transferred to Phoenix, March 15, 1988.
Released by Phoenix Cardinals, August 24, 1988; signed as free agent by Cincinnati Bengals, February 10, 1989.

		——PLACE KICKING——				
Year	Club	G.	XP.	XPM.	FG.	FGA.	Pts.
1987—St. Louis NFL............		13	30	1	9	19	57

DAVID LAWRENCE GALLOWAY
Defensive End—Phoenix Cardinals
Born February 16, 1959, at Tampa, Fla.
Height, 6.03. Weight, 277.
High School—Brandon, Fla.
Attended University of Florida.

Selected by St. Louis in 2nd round (38th player selected) of 1982 NFL draft.
On injured reserve with dislocated elbow, September 8 through November 30, 1982; activated, December 1, 1982.
On injured reserve with broken arm, September 1 through December 4, 1987; activated, December 5, 1987.
Franchise transferred to Phoenix, March 15, 1988.
On injured reserve with broken thumb, August 30 through October 21, 1988; activated, October 22, 1988.
St. Louis NFL, 1982 through 1987; Phoenix NFL, 1988.
Games: 1982 (5), 1983 (16), 1984 (14), 1985 (16), 1986 (14), 1987 (4), 1988 (8). Total—77.
Pro statistics: Intercepted one pass for 17 yards and credited with one safety, 1983; recovered one fumble, 1983, 1985 and 1988; recovered two fumbles, 1986.

JOHN BLAKE GALVIN JR.
Linebacker—Minnesota Vikings
Born July 9, 1965, at Lowell, Mass.
Height, 6.03. Weight, 226.
High School—Lowell, Mass.
Received degree in speech communications from Boston College in 1988.

Selected by New York Jets in 11th round (287th player selected) of 1988 NFL draft.
Signed by New York Jets, July 12, 1988.
Granted unconditional free agency, February 1, 1989; signed by Minnesota Vikings, March 29, 1989.
New York Jets NFL, 1988.
Games: 1988 (16).
Pro statistics: Recovered one fumble, 1988.

KENNETH PATRICK GAMBLE
(Kenny)
Running Back—Kansas City Chiefs
Born March 8, 1965, at Holyoke, Mass.
Height, 5.10. Weight, 197.
High Schools—Holyoke, Mass.; and Ashburnham, Mass., Cushing Academy.
Received degree in international relations from Colgate University in 1988.

Selected by Kansas City in 10th round (251st player selected) of 1988 NFL draft.
Signed by Kansas City Chiefs, July 12, 1988.

		KICKOFF RETURNS			
Year	Club	G.	No.	Yds.	Avg.TD.
1988—Kansas City NFL..........		16	15	291	19.4	0

Additional pro statistics: Caught one pass for minus seven yards, intercepted one pass for two yards and fumbled once, 1988.

CHRISTOPHER HUGHES GAMBOL
(Chris)
Offensive Tackle—Detroit Lions
Born September 14, 1964, at Pittsburgh, Pa.
Height, 6.06. Weight, 303.
High School—Oxford, Mich.
Received bachelor of business administration degree in finance
from University of Iowa in 1988.

Selected by Indianapolis in 3rd round (58th player selected) of 1987 NFL draft.
Signed by Indianapolis Colts, July 23, 1987.

On injured reserve with back injury, September 7 through entire 1987 season.
Released by Indianapolis Colts, September 22, 1988; awarded on waivers to San Diego Chargers, September 23, 1988.
Granted unconditional free agency, February 1, 1989; signed by Detroit Lions, March 22, 1989.
Indianapolis (1)-San Diego (11) NFL, 1988.
Games: 1988 (12).

MIKE ALAN GANN
Defensive End—Atlanta Falcons
Born October 19, 1963, at Stillwater, Okla.
Height, 6.05. Weight, 275.
High School—Lakewood, Colo.
Received bachelor of business administration degree
from University of Notre Dame in 1985.

Selected by Tampa Bay in 1st round (12th player selected) of 1985 USFL draft.
Selected by Atlanta in 2nd round (45th player selected) of 1985 NFL draft.
Signed by Atlanta Falcons, July 23, 1985.
Atlanta NFL, 1985 through 1988.
Games: 1985 (16), 1986 (16), 1987 (12), 1988 (16). Total—60.
Pro statistics: Recovered one fumble for 42 yards and a touchdown, 1985; credited with a safety and recovered three fumbles for 12 yards, 1986; recovered two fumbles for 36 yards and a touchdown, 1988.

RICHARD JOSEPH GANNON
(Rich)
Quarterback—Minnesota Vikings
Born December 20, 1965, at Philadelphia, Pa.
Height, 6.03. Weight, 197.
High School—Philadelphia, Pa., St. Joseph's Prep.
Received degree in criminal justice from University of Delaware in 1987.

Selected by New England in 4th round (98th player selected) of 1987 NFL draft.
Rights traded by New England Patriots to Minnesota Vikings for 4th and 11th round picks in 1988 draft, May 6, 1987.
Signed by Minnesota Vikings, July 30, 1987.

		—————PASSING—————							——RUSHING——				—TOTAL—		
Year	Club	G.	Att.	Cmp.	Pct.	Gain	T.P.	P.I.	Avg.	Att.	Yds.	Avg.	TD.	TD.	Pts.	F.
1987—Minnesota NFL		4	6	2	33.3	18	0	1	3.00		None			0	0	0
1988—Minnesota NFL		3	15	7	46.7	90	0	0	6.00	4	29	7.3	0	0	0	0
Pro Totals—2 Years		7	21	9	42.9	108	0	1	5.14	4	29	7.3	0	0	0	0

Quarterback Rating Points: 1987 (2.8), 1988 (66.0). Total—39.3.
Member of Minnesota Vikings for NFC Championship Game following 1987 season; did not play.

MARK PATRICK GARALCZYK
(Name pronounced Guh-RAL-chik.)
Defensive Tackle-Defensive End—Houston Oilers
Born August 12, 1965, at Roseville, Mich.
Height, 6.05. Weight, 272.
High School—Fraser, Mich.
Received bachelor of science degree in communications
from Western Michigan University in 1987.

Selected by St. Louis in 6th round (146th player selected) of 1987 NFL draft.
Signed by St. Louis Cardinals, June 9, 1987.
On injured reserve with pulled thigh muscle, September 7 through September 28, 1987; activated, September 29, 1987.
Crossed picket line during players' strike, September 29, 1987.
Franchise transferred to Phoenix, March 15, 1988.
Released by Phoenix Cardinals, October 22, 1988; awarded on waivers to New York Jets, October 24, 1988.
Granted unconditional free agency, February 1, 1989; signed by Houston Oilers, March 27, 1989.
St. Louis NFL, 1987; Phoenix (6)-New York Jets (7) NFL, 1988.
Games: 1987 (11), 1988 (13). Total—24.
Pro statistics: Recovered one fumble, 1987.

ALFONSO TEDDY GARCIA
(Known by middle name.)
Placekicker—Phoenix Cardinals
Born June 4, 1964, at Caddo Parish, La.
Height, 5.10. Weight, 190.
High School—Lewisville, Tex.
Attended Northeast Louisiana University.

Selected by New England in 4th round (100th player selected) of 1988 NFL draft.
Signed by New England Patriots, July 15, 1988.
Granted unconditional free agency, February 1, 1989; signed by Phoenix Cardinals, March 9, 1989.

		——PLACE KICKING——					
Year	Club	G.	XP.	XPM.	FG.	FGA.	Pts.
1988—New England NFL		16	11	*5	6	13	29

HAL E. GARNER JR.
Linebacker—Buffalo Bills
Born January 18, 1962, at New Iberia, La.
Height, 6.04. Weight, 235.
High School—Logan, Utah.
Attended Utah State University.

Selected by Baltimore in 3rd round (44th player selected) of 1985 USFL draft.
Selected by Buffalo in 3rd round (63rd player selected) of 1985 NFL draft.
Signed by Buffalo Bills, July 19, 1985.
On injured reserve with toe injury, December 6 through remainder of 1985 season.
On injured reserve with knee injury, September 1 through entire 1987 season.
On non-football injury list with substance abuse, November 10 through December 6, 1988; reinstated, December 7, 1988.
Buffalo NFL, 1985, 1986 and 1988.
Games: 1985 (13), 1986 (16), 1988 (12). Total—41.
Played in AFC Championship Game following 1988 season.

GREGG DAVID GARRITY
Wide Receiver—Philadelphia Eagles
Born November 24, 1960, at Pittsburgh, Pa.
Height, 5.10. Weight, 171.
High School—Wexford, Pa., North Allegheny.
Received bachelor of science degree in industrial arts education
from Penn State University in 1983.

Selected by Philadelphia in 1983 USFL territorial draft.
Selected by Pittsburgh in 5th round (140th player selected) of 1983 NFL draft.
Signed by Pittsburgh Steelers, May 20, 1983.
Released by Pittsburgh Steelers, October 23, 1984; awarded on waivers to Philadelphia Eagles, October 24, 1984.
On injured reserve with broken finger, August 19 through September 24, 1986; activated after clearing procedural waivers, September 26, 1986.
On injured reserve with knee injury, November 4 through December 28, 1988; activated December 29, 1988.

| | | –PASS RECEIVING– | | | | –PUNT RETURNS– | | | | —TOTAL— | | |
Year Club	G.	P.C.	Yds.	Avg.	TD.	No.	Yds.	Avg.	TD.	TD.	Pts.	F.
1983—Pittsburgh NFL	15	19	279	14.7	1	None				0	0	0
1984—Pitt. (6)-Phi. (4) NFL	10	2	22	11.0	0	None				0	0	0
1985—Philadelphia NFL	12	7	142	20.3	0	None				0	0	0
1986—Philadelphia NFL	12	12	227	18.9	0	17	187	11.0	1	1	6	0
1987—Philadelphia NFL	12	12	242	20.2	2	4	16	4.0	0	2	12	2
1988—Philadelphia NFL	9	17	208	12.2	1	None				1	6	0
Pro Totals—6 Years	70	69	1120	16.2	4	21	203	9.7	1	5	30	3

Additional pro statistics: Recovered one fumble, 1983.

KEITH JERROLD GARY
Defensive End—Pittsburgh Steelers
Born September 14, 1959, at Bethesda, Md.
Height, 6.03. Weight, 268.
High School—Fairfax, Va., Chantilly.
Attended Ferrum Junior College and University of Oklahoma.

Selected by Pittsburgh in 1st round (17th player selected) of 1981 NFL draft.
Signed by Montreal Alouettes, July 7, 1981.
On reserve, August 30 through September 4, 1982.
On injured list, September 5 through remainder of 1982 season.
Granted free agency, March 11, 1983; signed by Pittsburgh Steelers, April 15, 1983.
On injured reserve with hamstring and knee injuries, October 22 through November 22, 1985; activated, November 23, 1985.
Montreal CFL, 1981 and 1982; Pittsburgh NFL, 1983 through 1988.
Games: 1981 (13), 1982 (7), 1983 (16), 1984 (16), 1985 (12), 1986 (16), 1987 (11), 1988 (15). Total CFL—20. Total NFL—86. Total Pro—106.
CFL statistics: Recovered one fumble for 20 yards, 1982.
NFL statistics: Recovered two fumbles for 17 yards, 1983; recovered one fumble for six yards, 1984; recovered one fumble, 1985.
Played in AFC Championship Game following 1984 season.

THANE ALVIN GASH
Safety—Cleveland Browns
Born September 1, 1965, at Hendersonville, N.C.
Height, 6.00. Weight, 200.
High School—Henderson, N.C.
Received bachelor of science degree from East Tennessee State University in 1988.

Selected by Cleveland in 7th round (188th player selected) of 1988 NFL draft.
Signed by Cleveland Browns, July 13, 1988.
Cleveland NFL, 1988.
Games: 1988 (16).

WILLIE JAMES GAULT
Wide Receiver—Los Angeles Raiders
Born September 5, 1960, at Griffin, Ga.
Height, 6.00. Weight, 183.
High School—Griffin, Ga.
Attended University of Tennessee.

Selected by New Jersey in 1983 USFL territorial draft.
Selected by Chicago in 1st round (18th player selected) of 1983 NFL draft.
Signed by Chicago Bears, August 16, 1983.
Granted free agency, February 1, 1988; re-signed by Bears and traded to Los Angeles Raiders for 1st round pick in 1989 draft and conditional 1990 draft pick, July 28, 1988.

		RUSHING				PASS RECEIVING				TOTAL		
Year Club	G.	Att.	Yds.	Avg.	TD.	P.C.	Yds.	Avg.	TD.	TD.	Pts.	F.
1983—Chicago NFL	16	4	31	7.8	0	40	836	20.9	8	8	48	1
1984—Chicago NFL	16		None			34	587	17.3	6	6	36	1
1985—Chicago NFL	16	5	18	3.6	0	33	704	21.3	1	2	12	0
1986—Chicago NFL	16	8	79	9.9	0	42	818	19.5	5	5	30	1
1987—Chicago NFL	12	2	16	8.0	0	35	705	20.1	7	7	42	0
1988—Los Angeles Raiders NFL	15	1	4	4.0	0	16	392	24.5	2	2	12	1
Pro Totals—6 Years	91	20	148	7.4	0	200	4042	20.2	29	30	180	4

		KICKOFF RETURNS			
Year Club	G.	No.	Yds.	Avg.	TD.
1983—Chicago NFL	16	13	276	21.2	0
1984—Chicago NFL	16	1	12	12.0	0
1985—Chicago NFL	16	22	577	26.2	1
1986—Chicago NFL	16	1	20	20.0	0
1987—Chicago NFL	12		None		
1988—L.A. Raiders NFL	15		None		
Pro Totals—6 Years	91	37	885	23.9	1

Additional pro statistics: Returned nine punts for 60 yards, 1983; recovered one fumble, 1983 and 1987.
Played in NFC Championship Game following 1984 and 1985 seasons.
Played in NFL Championship Game following 1985 season.

EVERETT CARLTON GAY
Wide Receiver—Dallas Cowboys
Born October 23, 1964, at Houston, Tex.
Height, 6.02. Weight, 209.
High School—Houston, Tex., Phillis Wheatley.
Attended University of Texas.

Selected by Dallas in 5th round (124th player selected) of 1987 NFL draft.
Signed by Dallas Cowboys, July 19, 1987.
On injured reserve with ankle injury, August 27 through entire 1987 season.

		PASS RECEIVING			
Year Club	G.	P.C.	Yds.	Avg.	TD.
1988—Dallas NFL	16	15	205	13.7	1

Additional pro statistics: Fumbled once, 1988.

SHAUN LaNARD GAYLE
Safety—Chicago Bears
Born March 8, 1962, at Newport News, Va.
Height, 5.11. Weight, 195.
High School—Hampton, Va., Bethel.
Received bachelor of science degree in education from Ohio State University in 1984.

Selected by Michigan in 14th round (288th player selected) of 1984 USFL draft.
Selected by Chicago in 10th round (271st player selected) of 1984 NFL draft.
Signed by Chicago Bears, June 21, 1984.
On injured reserve with broken ankle, December 12 through remainder of 1984 season.
On injured reserve with ankle injury, September 8 through November 5, 1987; activated, November 6, 1987.
On injured reserve with neck injury, October 14 through remainder of 1988 season.
Chicago NFL, 1984 through 1988.
Games: 1984 (15), 1985 (16), 1986 (16), 1987 (8), 1988 (4). Total—59.
Pro statistics: Intercepted one pass for minus one yard, 1984; recovered one fumble, 1985 and 1986; intercepted one pass for 13 yards, 1986; intercepted one pass for 20 yards and a touchdown, 1987; intercepted one pass for no yards, 1988.
Played in NFC Championship Game following 1985 season.
Played in NFL Championship Game following 1985 season.

JAMES GEATHERS
Defensive End—New Orleans Saints
Born June 26, 1960, at Georgetown, S.C.
Height, 6.07. Weight, 290.
High School—Georgetown, S.C., Choppee.
Attended Paducah Community College and Wichita State University.
Brother of Robert Geathers, defensive end with Boston Breakers, 1983.

Selected by Oklahoma in 1984 USFL territorial draft.
Selected by New Orleans in 2nd round (42nd player selected) of 1984 NFL draft.

Signed by New Orleans Saints, May 30, 1984.
On injured reserve with knee injury, September 1 through December 25, 1987; activated, December 26, 1987.
New Orleans NFL, 1984 through 1988.
Games: 1984 (16), 1985 (16), 1986 (16), 1987 (1), 1988 (16). Total—65.
Pro statistics: Recovered one fumble, 1986; recovered three fumbles, 1988.

STANLEY MORRIS GELBAUGH
(Stan)
Quarterback—Buffalo Bills
Born December 4, 1962, at Carlisle, Pa.
Height, 6.03. Weight, 207.
High School—Mechanicsburg, Pa., Cumberland Valley.
Received bachelor of science degree in marketing from University of Maryland in 1986.

Selected by Baltimore in 1986 USFL territorial draft.
Selected by Dallas in 6th round (150th player selected) of 1986 NFL draft.
Signed by Dallas Cowboys, July 5, 1986.
Released by Dallas Cowboys, August 18, 1986; signed as free agent by Saskatchewan Roughriders, August 27, 1986.
Released by Saskatchewan Roughriders, October 7, 1986; signed as free agent by Buffalo Bills, November 18, 1986.
On injured reserve with elbow injury, September 8 through entire 1987 season.
Released by Buffalo Bills, September 16, 1988; re-signed by Bills, September 20, 1988.
Active for 5 games with Buffalo Bills in 1986; did not play.
Active for 3 games with Buffalo Bills in 1988; did not play.
Saskatchewan CFL, 1986; Buffalo NFL, 1986 and 1988.
Games: 1986 CFL (5).
Member of Buffalo Bills for AFC Championship Game following 1988 season; inactive.

DENNIS LOUIS GENTRY
Wide Receiver—Chicago Bears
Born February 10, 1959, at Lubbock, Tex.
Height, 5.08. Weight, 180.
High School—Lubbock, Tex., Dunbar.
Attended Baylor University.

Selected by Chicago in 4th round (89th player selected) of 1982 NFL draft.

			—RUSHING—				PASS RECEIVING				—TOTAL—		
Year Club		G.	Att.	Yds.	Avg.	TD.	P.C.	Yds.	Avg.	TD.	TD.	Pts.	F.
1982—Chicago NFL		9	4	21	5.3	0	1	9	9.0	0	0	0	4
1983—Chicago NFL		15	16	65	4.1	0	2	8	4.0	0	0	0	1
1984—Chicago NFL		16	21	79	3.8	1	4	29	7.3	0	1	6	0
1985—Chicago NFL		16	30	160	5.3	2	5	77	15.4	0	3	18	0
1986—Chicago NFL		15	11	103	9.4	1	19	238	12.5	0	3	18	0
1987—Chicago NFL		12	6	41	6.8	0	17	183	10.8	1	2	12	2
1988—Chicago NFL		16	7	86	12.3	1	33	486	14.7	3	4	24	2
Pro Totals—7 Years		99	95	555	5.8	5	81	1030	12.7	4	13	78	9

		—PUNT RETURNS—				—KICKOFF RET.—			
Year Club	G.	No.	Yds.	Avg.	TD.	No.	Yds.	Avg.	TD.
1982—Chicago NFL	9	17	89	5.2	0	9	161	17.9	0
1983—Chicago NFL	15		None			7	130	18.6	0
1984—Chicago NFL	16		None			11	209	19.0	0
1985—Chicago NFL	16	0	47	....	0	18	466	25.9	1
1986—Chicago NFL	15		None			20	576	*28.8	*1
1987—Chicago NFL	12		None			25	621	24.8	1
1988—Chicago NFL	16		None			27	578	21.4	0
Pro Totals—7 Years	99	17	136	8.0	0	117	2741	23.4	3

Additional pro statistics: Recovered one fumble, 1982; recovered blocked punt in end zone for a touchdown, 1986.
Played in NFC Championship Game following 1984, 1985 and 1988 seasons.
Played in NFL Championship Game following 1985 season.

JOHN CHRISTIAN GESEK JR.
Guard—Los Angeles Raiders
Born February 18, 1963, at San Francisco, Calif.
Height, 6.05. Weight, 275.
High Schools—Danville, Calif., San Ramon Valley; and Bellflower, Calif.
Attended Diablo Valley College (did not play football) and
California State University at Sacramento.

Selected by Los Angeles Raiders in 10th round (265th player selected) of 1987 NFL draft.
Signed by Los Angeles Raiders, July 11, 1987.
On injured reserve with back injury, September 7 through October 13, 1987; activated, October 14, 1987.
Crossed picket line during players' strike, October 13, 1987.
On injured reserve with knee injury, October 19 through December 4, 1987; activated, December 5, 1987.
On injured reserve with knee injury, November 30 through remainder of 1988 season.
Los Angeles Raiders NFL, 1987 and 1988.
Games: 1987 (3), 1988 (12). Total—15.
Pro statistics: Fumbled once, 1988.

ANTONIO MARICE GIBSON
Safety—New Orleans Saints
Born July 5, 1962, at Jackson, Miss.
Height, 6.03. Weight, 206.
High School—Jackson, Miss., Murrah.
Attended Hinds Junior College and University of Cincinnati.

Selected by Philadelphia in 4th round (41st player selected) of 1983 USFL draft.
Signed by Philadelphia Stars, January 7, 1983.
Franchise transferred to Baltimore, November 1, 1984.
On developmental squad, February 24 through February 27, 1985; activated, February 28, 1985.
Granted free agency when USFL suspended operations, August 7, 1986; signed as free agent by New Orleans Saints, August 11, 1986.
Crossed picket line during players' strike, October 1, 1987.
On injured reserve with broken arm, November 25, 1987 through January 1, 1988; activated, January 2, 1988.
On non-football injury list with substance abuse, September 13 through October 11, 1988; activated, October 12, 1988.
Granted roster exemption, October 12 through October 16, 1988; activated, October 17, 1988.
On developmental squad for 1 game with Baltimore Stars in 1985.
Philadelphia USFL, 1983 and 1984; Baltimore USFL, 1985; New Orleans NFL, 1986 through 1988.
Games: 1983 (18), 1984 (18), 1985 (17), 1986 (16), 1987 (10), 1988 (10). Total USFL—53. Total NFL—36. Total Pro—89.
USFL statistics: Recovered one fumble, 1983 and 1985; credited with one sack for one yard and intercepted three passes for no yards, 1983; credited with two sacks for 13 yards, ran four yards with lateral on kickoff return and fumbled once, 1984; credited with two sacks for 12 yards and intercepted one pass for 50 yards and a touchdown, 1985.
NFL statistics: Intercepted two passes for 43 yards and recovered one fumble, 1986; intercepted one pass for 17 yards, 1987; recovered one fumble for seven yards, 1988.
Played in USFL Championship Game following 1983 through 1985 seasons.

DENNIS MICHAEL GIBSON
Linebacker—Detroit Lions
Born February 8, 1964, at Des Moines, Ia.
Height, 6.02. Weight, 240.
High School—Ankeny, Ia.
Attended Iowa State University.

Selected by Detroit in 8th round (203rd player selected) of 1987 NFL draft.
Signed by Detroit Lions, July 25, 1987.
Detroit NFL, 1987 and 1988.
Games: 1987 (12), 1988 (16). Total—28.
Pro statistics: Intercepted one pass for five yards, 1987; recovered one fumble, 1988.

ERNEST GERARD GIBSON
Cornerback—Miami Dolphins
Born October 3, 1961, at Jacksonville, Fla.
Height, 5.10. Weight, 185.
High School—Jacksonville, Fla., Bishop Kenny.
Received bachelor of arts degree in political science from Furman University in 1984.

Selected by Memphis in 3rd round (44th player selected) of 1984 USFL draft.
USFL rights traded by Memphis Showboats to Birmingham Stallions for rights to quarterback Walter Lewis, January 16, 1984.
Selected by New England in 6th round (151st player selected) of 1984 NFL draft.
Signed by New England Patriots, June 6, 1984.
On injured reserve with chest injury, September 2 through October 3, 1985; activated, October 4, 1985.
Granted unconditional free agency, February 1, 1989; signed by Miami Dolphins, February 16, 1989.
New England NFL, 1984 through 1988.
Games: 1984 (15), 1985 (9), 1986 (15), 1987 (12), 1988 (16). Total—67.
Pro statistics: Intercepted two passes for four yards, returned one punt for three yards and recovered one fumble, 1984; intercepted two passes for 17 yards, 1987.
Played in AFC Championship Game following 1985 season.
Played in NFL Championship Game following 1985 season.

JON WILLIAM GIESLER
Name pronounced Geese-ler.
Offensive Tackle—Miami Dolphins
Born December 23, 1956, at Toledo, O.
Height, 6.05. Weight, 272.
High School—Elmore, O., Woodmore.
Received bachelor of science degree in education from University of Michigan in 1979.

Selected by Miami in 1st round (24th player selected) of 1979 NFL draft.
On injured reserve with shoulder injury, September 2 through October 9, 1980; activated, October 10, 1980.
On physically unable to perform/reserve with knee injury, August 18 through October 17, 1986; activated, October 18, 1986.
On injured reserve with knee injury, December 12 through remainder of 1986 season.
On physically unable to perform/reserve with knee injury, August 31 through October 23, 1987; activated, October 24, 1987.
Granted free agency, February 1, 1988; re-signed by Dolphins, September 13, 1988.
Miami NFL, 1979 through 1988.
Games: 1979 (16), 1980 (10), 1981 (16), 1982 (9), 1983 (16), 1984 (16), 1985 (13), 1986 (7), 1987 (10), 1988 (13). Total—126.

Pro statistics: Recovered one fumble, 1981 and 1985.
Played in AFC Championship Game following 1982, 1984 and 1985 seasons.
Played in NFL Championship Game following 1982 and 1984 seasons.

DAREN GILBERT
Offensive Tackle—New Orleans Saints
Born October 3, 1963, at San Diego, Calif.
Height, 6.05. Weight, 280.
High School—Compton, Calif., Dominguez.
Attended California State University at Fullerton.

Selected by Los Angeles in 1985 USFL territorial draft.
Selected by New Orleans in 2nd round (38th player selected) of 1985 NFL draft.
Signed by New Orleans Saints, August 5, 1985.
Crossed picket line during players' strike, October 2, 1987.
New Orleans NFL, 1985 through 1988.
Games: 1985 (16), 1986 (9), 1987 (6), 1988 (11). Total—42.

FREDDIE GENE GILBERT
Defensive End—Denver Broncos
Born April 8, 1962, at Griffin, Ga.
Height, 6.04. Weight, 275.
High School—Griffin, Ga.
Attended University of Georgia.

Selected by Jacksonville in 1984 USFL territorial draft.
USFL rights traded by Jacksonville Bulls to New Jersey Generals for rights to running back Archie Griffin and draft choice, January 16, 1984.
Signed by New Jersey Generals, January 24, 1984.
On injured reserve with knee injury, March 27 through June 14, 1984; activated, June 15, 1984.
Selected by Denver Broncos in 1st round (19th player selected) of 1984 NFL supplemental draft.
On developmental squad, March 23 through March 29, 1985; activated, March 30, 1985.
On developmental squad, May 5 through June 9, 1985; activated, June 10, 1985.
On developmental squad, June 22 through June 30, 1985; activated , July 1, 1985.
Released by New Jersey Generals, July 31, 1985; re-signed by Generals, August 1, 1985.
Granted free agency when USFL suspended operations, August 7, 1986; signed by Denver Broncos, August 24, 1986.
Granted roster exemption, August 24 through September 7, 1986; activated, September 8, 1986.
On developmental squad for 7 games with New Jersey Generals in 1985.
New Jersey USFL, 1984 and 1985; Denver NFL, 1986 through 1988.
Games: 1984 (7), 1985 (11), 1986 (15), 1987 (7), 1988 (13). Total USFL—18. Total NFL—35. Total Pro—53.
USFL statistics: Credited with three fumbles for 14 yards, 1984; credited with 3½ sacks for 41 yards and recovered one fumble for 31 yards and a touchdown, 1985.
NFL statistics: Recovered one fumble, 1987.
Played in AFC Championship Game following 1986 and 1987 seasons.
Played in NFL Championship Game following 1986 and 1987 seasons.

GALE GILBERT
Quarterback—Buffalo Bills
Born December 20, 1961, at Red Bluff, Calif.
Height, 6.03. Weight, 206.
High School—Red Bluff, Calif.
Attended University of California at Berkeley.

Selected by Oakland in 1985 USFL territorial draft.
Signed as free agent by Seattle Seahawks, May 2, 1985.
On injured reserve with knee injury, September 8 through entire 1987 season.
Granted free agency, February 1, 1988; rights relinquished, June 8, 1988.
Signed by Buffalo Bills, May 11, 1989.

Year Club	G.	Att.	Cmp.	Pct.	Gain	T.P.	P.I.	Avg.	Att.	Yds.	Avg.	TD.	TD.	Pts.	F.
				PASSING						RUSHING				TOTAL	
1985—Seattle NFL	9	40	19	47.5	218	1	2	5.45	7	4	0.6	0	0	0	1
1986—Seattle NFL	16	76	42	55.3	485	3	3	6.38	3	8	2.7	0	0	0	1
Pro Totals—2 Years	25	116	61	52.6	703	4	5	6.06	10	12	1.2	0	0	0	2

Quarterback Rating Points: 1985 (51.9), 1986 (71.4). Total—64.6.
Additional pro statistics: Recovered one fumble and fumbled once for minus five yards, 1985.

JIMMIE GILES JR.
Name pronounced Jiles.
Tight End
Born November 8, 1954, at Natchez, Miss.
Height, 6.03. Weight, 240.
High School—Greenville, Miss.
Received bachelor of science degree in business administration from Alcorn State University in 1977.
Related to Sammy White, wide receiver with Minnesota Vikings, 1976 through 1985.

Selected by Houston in 3rd round (70th player selected) of 1977 NFL draft.
Traded with four draft choices (1st and 2nd round in 1978 and 3rd and 5th round in 1979) by Houston Oilers to Tampa Bay Buccaneers for 1st round pick in 1978 draft, April 24, 1978.
On reserve/did not report, August 16 through August 26, 1983.
Reinstated and granted roster exemption, August 27 through September 1, 1983; activated, September 2, 1983.

Released by Tampa Bay Buccaneers, October 20, 1986; signed as free agent by Detroit Lions, October 24, 1986.
Granted free agency, February 1, 1987; re-signed by Lions, September 8, 1987.
Granted roster exemption, September 8 through September 10, 1987; activated, September 11, 1987.
Traded by Detroit Lions to Philadelphia Eagles for 9th round pick in 1988 draft, November 3, 1987.
Released by Philadelphia Eagles, May 16, 1989.

Year Club	G.	P.C.	Yds.	Avg.	TD.	Year Club	G.	P.C.	Yds.	Avg.	TD.
		—PASS RECEIVING—						—PASS RECEIVING—			
1977—Houston NFL	14	17	147	8.6	0	1984—Tampa Bay NFL	14	24	310	12.9	2
1978—Tampa Bay NFL	16	23	324	14.1	2	1985—Tampa Bay NFL	16	43	673	15.7	8
1979—Tampa Bay NFL	16	40	579	14.5	7	1986—T.B. (7)-Det. (9) NFL	16	37	376	10.2	4
1980—Tampa Bay NFL	16	33	602	18.2	4	1987—Det. (4)-Phi. (8) NFL	12	13	157	12.1	1
1981—Tampa Bay NFL	16	45	786	17.5	6	1988—Philadelphia NFL	16	6	57	9.5	1
1982—Tampa Bay NFL	9	28	499	17.8	3	Pro Totals—12 Years	172	334	4859	14.5	39
1983—Tampa Bay NFL	11	25	349	14.0	1						

Additional pro statistics: Rushed once for minus 10 yards, 1977; returned five kickoffs for 60 yards, rushed once for minus one yard, 1978; fumbled once, 1978 and 1983; rushed twice for seven yards, 1979; recovered one fumble, 1979, 1980 and 1982; fumbled twice, 1980 and 1982; rushed once for one yard, 1982; fumbled three times, 1985.
Played in NFC Championship Game following 1979 season.
Played in Pro Bowl (NFL All-Star Game) following 1980 through 1982 and 1985 seasons.

RECORD AS BASEBALL PLAYER
Selected by Los Angeles Dodgers' organization in 12th round of free-agent draft, June 8, 1976.
Placed on restricted list, July 14, 1977.

Year Club	League	Pos.	G.	AB.	R.	H.	2B.	3B.	HR.	RBI.	B.A.	PO.	A.	E.	F.A.
1976—Bellingham	Northw.	O-1-3	29	51	4	4	0	0	0	0	.078	16	5	2	.913

ERNEST P. GIVINS
Wide Receiver—Houston Oilers
Born September 3, 1964, at St. Petersburg, Fla.
Height, 5.09. Weight, 175.
High School—St. Petersburg, Fla., Lakewood.
Attended Northeastern Oklahoma A&M and University of Louisville.
Selected by Houston in 2nd round (34th player selected) of 1986 NFL draft.
Selected by Tampa Bay in 1st round (8th player selected) of 1986 USFL draft.
Signed by Houston Oilers, August 1, 1986.

Year Club	G.	—RUSHING—				PASS RECEIVING				—TOTAL—		
		Att.	Yds.	Avg.	TD.	P.C.	Yds.	Avg.	TD.	TD.	Pts.	F.
1986—Houston NFL	15	9	148	16.4	1	61	1062	17.4	3	4	24	0
1987—Houston NFL	12	1	−13	−13.0	0	53	933	17.6	6	6	36	2
1988—Houston NFL	16	4	26	6.5	0	60	976	16.3	5	5	30	1
Pro Totals—3 Years	43	14	161	11.5	1	174	2971	17.1	14	15	90	3

Additional pro statistics: Attempted two passes with no completions and returned eight punts for 80 yards, 1986.

NESBY LEE GLASGOW
Safety—Seattle Seahawks
Born April 15, 1957, at Los Angeles, Calif.
Height, 5.10. Weight, 188.
High School—Gardena, Calif.
Attended University of Washington.
Tied NFL record for most combined kick returns, game (12), September 2, 1979, vs. Denver Broncos.
Selected by Baltimore in 8th round (207th player selected) of 1979 NFL draft.
Franchise transferred to Indianapolis, March 31, 1984.
Released by Indianapolis Colts, August 4, 1988; signed as free agent by Seattle Seahawks, August 8, 1988.

Year Club	G.	INTERCEPTIONS				–PUNT RETURNS–				—KICKOFF RET.—				—TOTAL—		
		No.	Yds.	Avg.	TD.	No.	Yds.	Avg.	TD.	No.	Yds.	Avg.	TD.	TD.	Pts.	F.
1979—Baltimore NFL	16	1	−1	−1.0	0	44	352	8.0	1	50	1126	22.5	0	1	6	8
1980—Baltimore NFL	16	4	65	16.3	0	23	187	8.1	0	33	743	22.5	0	0	0	5
1981—Baltimore NFL	14	2	35	17.5	0		None			1	35	35.0	0	0	0	0
1982—Baltimore NFL	9		None			4	24	6.0	0		None			0	0	0
1983—Baltimore NFL	16	3	35	11.7	0	1	9	9.0	0		None			0	0	0
1984—Indianapolis NFL	16	1	8	8.0	0	7	79	11.3	0		None			0	0	1
1985—Indianapolis NFL	16		None				None				None			0	0	0
1986—Indianapolis NFL	14		None				None				None			0	0	0
1987—Indianapolis NFL	11	1	0	0.0	0		None				None			0	0	0
1988—Seattle NFL	16	2	19	9.5	0	1	0	0.0	0		None			0	0	1
Pro Totals—10 Years	144	14	161	11.5	0	80	651	8.1	1	84	1904	22.7	0	1	6	15

Additional pro statistics: Recovered two fumbles, 1979 through 1981 and 1986; recovered one fumble, 1984 and 1987.

KERRY R. GLENN
Cornerback—Cleveland Browns
Born March 31, 1962, at St. Louis, Mo.
Height, 5.09. Weight, 175.
High School—East St. Louis, Ill.
Attended University of Minnesota.
Selected by Orlando in 4th round (46th player selected) of 1985 USFL draft.
Selected by New York Jets in 10th round (262nd player selected) of 1985 NFL draft.

Signed by New York Jets, July 26, 1985.
On injured reserve with sprained foot, September 10 through remainder of 1986 season.
On injured reserve with knee injury, December 4 through remainder of 1987 season.
On physically unable to perform/active with knee injury, July 25 through August 21, 1988; then transferred to physically unable to perform/reserve with knee injury, August 22 through entire 1988 season.
Granted unconditional free agency, February 1, 1989; signed by Cleveland Browns, April 1, 1989.
New York Jets NFL, 1985 through 1987.
Games: 1985 (16), 1986 (1), 1987 (8). Total—25.
Pro statistics: Intercepted four passes for 15 yards and a touchdown, returned five kickoffs for 71 yards and recovered two fumbles for 31 yards, 1985; recovered one fumble, 1986.

VENCIE LEONARD GLENN
Safety—San Diego Chargers

Born October 26, 1964, at Grambling, La.
Height, 6.00. Weight, 192.
High School—Silver Springs, Md., John F. Kennedy.
Attended Indiana State University.

Selected by New England in 2nd round (54th player selected) of 1986 NFL draft.
Signed by New England Patriots, July 29, 1986.
Traded by New England Patriots to San Diego Chargers for 5th round pick in 1987 draft and cash, September 29, 1986.

		—INTERCEPTIONS—			
Year Club	G.	No.	Yds.	Avg.	TD.
1986—San Diego NFL	12	2	31	15.5	0
1987—San Diego NFL	12	4	*166	41.5	1
1988—San Diego NFL	16	1	0	0.0	0
Pro Totals—3 Years	40	7	197	28.1	1

Additional pro statistics: Recovered two fumbles for 32 yards, 1986; recovered one fumble, 1987; recovered two fumbles, 1988.

CLYDE M. GLOVER
Defensive End—Los Angeles Raiders

Born July 16, 1960, at New Orleans, La.
Height, 6.06. Weight, 280.
High School—Las Vegas, Nev., Sunset.
Attended Walla Walla Community College and Fresno State University.

Selected by Oakland in 1984 USFL territorial draft.
Signed as free agent by New England Patriots, May 14, 1984.
Released by New England Patriots, August 21, 1984; signed as free agent by Kansas City Chiefs for 1985, October 15, 1984.
Released by Kansas City Chiefs, June 7, 1985; signed as free agent by Toronto Argonauts, June 10, 1985.
Released by Toronto Argonauts, August 4, 1985; signed as free agent by San Francisco 49ers, March 10, 1986.
Released by San Francisco 49ers, August 19, 1986; re-signed for 1987, October 29, 1986.
Released by San Francisco 49ers, September 7, 1987; re-signed as replacement player by 49ers, September 24, 1987.
On injured reserve with groin injury, August 29 through October 3, 1988.
Released by San Francisco 49ers, October 4, 1988; signed as free agent by Los Angeles Raiders, January 10, 1989.
Toronto CFL, 1985; San Francisco NFL, 1987.
Games: 1985 (5), 1987 (13). Total—18.

KEVIN BERNARD GLOVER
Center-Guard—Detroit Lions

Born June 17, 1963, at Washington, D.C.
Height, 6.02. Weight, 275.
High School—Largo, Md.
Attended University of Maryland.

Named as center on THE SPORTING NEWS College All-America Team, 1984.
Selected by Tampa Bay in 1985 USFL territorial draft.
Selected by Detroit in 2nd round (34th player selected) of 1985 NFL draft.
Signed by Detroit Lions, July 23, 1985.
On injured reserve with knee injury, December 7 through remainder of 1985 season.
On injured reserve with knee injury, September 29 through December 19, 1986; activated, December 20, 1986.
Detroit NFL, 1985 through 1988.
Games: 1985 (10), 1986 (4), 1987 (12), 1988 (16). Total—42.
Additional pro statistics: Returned one kickoff for 19 yards, 1987; recovered two fumbles, 1988.

TIMOTHY RAY GOAD
(Name pronounced Gode.)

(Tim)
Nose Tackle—New England Patriots

Born February 28, 1966, at Claudville, Va.
Height, 6.03. Weight, 280.
High School—Stuart, Va., Patrick County.
Attended University of North Carolina.

Selected by New England in 4th round (87th player selected) of 1988 NFL draft.
Signed by New England Patriots, July 15, 1988.
New England NFL, 1988.
Games: 1988 (16).

ROBERT LAMAR GOFF
Defensive Lineman—Tampa Bay Buccaneers
Born October 2, 1965, at Rochester, N.Y.
Height, 6.03. Weight, 270.
High School—Bradenton, Fla., Bayshore.
Attended Butler County Community College and Auburn University.

Selected by Tampa Bay in 4th round (83rd player selected) of 1988 NFL draft.
Signed by Tampa Bay Buccaneers, July 10, 1988.
Tampa Bay NFL, 1988.
Games: 1988 (16).
Pro statistics: Recovered three fumbles, 1988.

KEVIN PATRICK GOGAN
Offensive Tackle—Dallas Cowboys
Born November 2, 1964, at San Francisco, Calif.
Height, 6.07. Weight, 310.
High School—San Francisco, Calif., Sacred Heart.
Received degree in sociology from University of Washington in 1987.

Selected by Dallas in 8th round (206th player selected) of 1987 NFL draft.
Signed by Dallas Cowboys, July 18, 1987.
On non-football injury list with substance abuse August 5 through August 30, 1988; reinstated, August 31, 1988.
Granted roster exemption, August 31 through September 4, 1988; activated, September 5, 1988.
Dallas NFL, 1987 and 1988.
Games: 1987 (11), 1988 (15). Total—26.
Pro Statistics: Recovered one fumble, 1987.

MIKE GOLIC
Name pronounced Go-lick.
Defensive Tackle—Philadelphia Eagles
Born December 12, 1962, at Willowick, O.
Height, 6.05. Weight, 272.
High School—Cleveland, O., St. Joseph.
Received bachelor of business administration degree in management from University of Notre Dame in 1985.
Son of Louis Golic, former player with Montreal Alouettes, Hamilton Tiger-Cats and Saskatchewan Roughriders; and brother of Bob Golic, nose tackle with Los Angeles Raiders.

Selected by Orlando in 15th round (204th player selected) of 1985 USFL draft.
Selected by Houston in 10th round (255th player selected) of 1985 NFL draft.
Signed by Houston Oilers, July 18, 1985.
On injured reserve with ankle injury, August 27 through entire 1985 season.
Released by Houston Oilers, November 3, 1987; signed as free agent by Philadelphia Eagles, November 11, 1987.
On injured reserve with ankle injury, November 4 through December 1, 1988; activated, December 2, 1988.
Houston NFL, 1986; Houston (2)-Philadelphia (6) NFL, 1987; Philadelphia NFL, 1988.
Games: 1986 (16), 1987 (8), 1988 (12). Total—36.
Pro statistics: Recovered two fumbles for four yards, 1986.

ROBERT PERRY GOLIC
Name pronounced Go-lick.
(Bob)
Nose Tackle—Los Angeles Raiders
Born October 26, 1957, at Cleveland, O.
Height, 6.03. Weight, 265.
High School—Cleveland, O., St. Joseph.
Received bachelor of business administration degree in management from University of Notre Dame in 1979.
Son of Louis Golic, former player with Montreal Alouettes, Hamilton Tiger-Cats and Saskatchewan Roughriders; and brother of Mike Golic, defensive tackle with Philadelphia Eagles.

Named to THE SPORTING NEWS NFL All-Star Team, 1985.
Selected by New England in 2nd round (52nd player selected) of 1979 NFL draft.
On injured reserve with shoulder injury, August 28 through December 14, 1979; activated, December 15, 1979.
Released by New England Patriots, August 31, 1982; signed as free agent by Cleveland Browns, September 2, 1982.
On inactive list, September 12, 1982.
On injured reserve with broken arm, December 30 through remainder of 1987 season playoffs.
Granted unconditional free agency, February 1, 1989; signed by Los Angeles Raiders, April 1, 1989.
New England NFL, 1979 through 1982; Cleveland NFL, 1983 through 1988.
Games: 1979 (1), 1980 (16), 1981 (16), 1982 (6), 1983 (16), 1984 (15), 1985 (16), 1986 (16), 1987 (12), 1988 (16). Total—130.
Pro statistics: Recovered one fumble, 1981; intercepted one pass for seven yards and a touchdown, 1983; recovered one fumble for 18 yards, 1984.
Played in AFC Championship Game following 1986 season.
Played in Pro Bowl (NFL All-Star Game) following 1985 and 1986 seasons.
Named to play in Pro Bowl following 1987 season; replaced due to injury by Tim Krumrie.

KELLY JOE GOODBURN
Punter—Kansas City Chiefs

Born April 14, 1962, at Cherokee, Ia.
Height, 6.02. Weight, 195.
High School—Correctionville,Ia., Eastwood Community.
Attended Iowa State University and received degree in physical education
from Emporia State University in 1987.

Signed as free agent by Kansas City Chiefs, May 3, 1986.
Released by Kansas City Chiefs, August 19, 1986; re-signed by Chiefs, April 7, 1987.
Released by Kansas City Chiefs, August 31, 1987; re-signed as replacement player by Chiefs, September 25, 1987.

| | | —PUNTING— | | |
Year Club	G.	No.	Avg.	Blk.
1987—Kansas City NFL....................	13	59	40.9	0
1988—Kansas City NFL....................	16	76	40.3	0
Pro Totals—2 Years.....................	29	135	40.5	0

Additional pro statistics: Rushed once for 16 yards, 1987; rushed once for 15 yards, 1988.

CHRIS K. GOODE
(Name pronounced Good.)
Defensive Back—Indianapolis Colts

Born September 17, 1963, at Town Creek, Ala.
Height, 6.00. Weight, 193.
High School—Town Creek, Ala., Hazelwood.
Attended University of North Alabama and University of Alabama.
Brother of Kerry Goode, running back with Denver Broncos; and Pierre Goode, running back
and Clyde Goode, quarterback, both at University of Alabama; and cousin of Robert Penchion,
offensive lineman with Buffalo Bills, San Francisco 49ers and Seattle Seahawks, 1972 through 1976.

Selected by Indianapolis in 10th round (253rd player selected) of 1987 NFL draft.
Signed by Indianapolis Colts, July 23, 1987.
On injured reserve with strained abdomen, September 7 through November 5, 1987; activated, November 6, 1987.
On injured reserve with knee injury, December 2 through remainder of 1988 season.
Indianapolis NFL, 1987 and 1988.
Games: 1987 (8), 1988 (13). Total—21.
Pro statistics: Intercepted two passes for 53 yards and recovered four fumbles for 16 yards, 1988.

KERRY GOODE
(Name rhymes with Food.)
Running Back—Denver Broncos

Born July 28, 1965, at Town Creek, Ala.
Height, 5.11. Weight, 200.
High School—Town Creek, Ala., Hazelwood.
Received degree in general management and marketing
from University of Alabama in 1988.
Brother of Chris Goode, defensive back with Indianapolis Colts;
and Pierre Goode, running back, and Clyde Goode, quarterback, both at University of
Alabama; and cousin of Robert Penchion, offensive lineman with Buffalo Bills, San Francisco 49ers and
Seattle Seahawks, 1972 through 1976.

Selected by Tampa Bay in 7th round (167th player selected) of 1988 NFL draft.
Signed by Tampa Bay Buccaneers, July 10, 1988.
Granted unconditional free agency, February 1, 1989; signed by Denver Broncos, March 9, 1989.

| | | —RUSHING— | | | | PASS RECEIVING | | | | —TOTAL— | | |
Year Club	G.	Att.	Yds.	Avg.	TD.	P.C.	Yds.	Avg.	TD.	TD.	Pts.	F.
1988—Tampa Bay NFL	14	63	231	3.7	0	7	68	9.7	0	0	†2	0

†Credited with a safety, 1988.

ALEX GRONCIER GORDON
Linebacker—New York Jets

Born September 14, 1964, at Jacksonville, Fla.
Height, 6.05. Weight, 246.
High School—Jacksonville, Fla., Englewood.
Attended University of Cincinnati.

Selected by New York Jets in 2nd round (42nd player selected) of 1987 NFL draft.
Signed by New York Jets, July 22, 1987.
New York Jets NFL, 1987 and 1988.
Games: 1987 (12), 1988 (13). Total—25.
Pro statistics: Recovered one fumble, 1988.

TIM CARVELLE GORDON
Safety—Atlanta Falcons

Born May 7, 1965, at Ardmore, Okla.
Height, 6.00. Weight, 188.
High School—Ardmore, Okla.
Attended University of Tulsa.

Signed as free agent by Atlanta Falcons, May 6, 1987.
Released by Atlanta Falcons, September 1, 1987; re-signed by Falcons, September 16, 1987.

		-INTERCEPTIONS-				—KICKOFF RET.—				—TOTAL—		
Year	Club	G.	No.	Yds.	Avg.	TD.	No.	Yds.	Avg.	TD.	TD.	Pts.	F.
1987—Atlanta NFL		11	2	28	14.0	0		None			0	0	0
1988—Atlanta NFL		16	2	10	5.0	0	14	209	14.9	0	0	0	1
Pro Totals—2 Years		27	4	38	9.5	0	14	209	14.9	0	0	0	1

Additional pro statistics: Recovered one fumble, 1987 and 1988.

JEFFERY ALAN GOSSETT
(Jeff)
Punter—Los Angeles Raiders
Born January 25, 1957, at Charleston, Ill.
Height, 6.02. Weight, 197.
High School—Charleston, Ill.
Received bachelor of science degree in physical education from Eastern Illinois University in 1982.

Signed as free agent by Dallas Cowboys, May, 1980.
Released by Dallas Cowboys, August 25, 1980; signed as free agent by San Diego Chargers, April 6, 1981.
Released by San Diego Chargers, August 31, 1981; signed as free agent by Kansas City Chiefs, November 5, 1981.
Released by Kansas City Chiefs, December 14, 1982; re-signed by Chiefs, December 21, 1982.
Released by Kansas City Chiefs, August 29, 1983; awarded on waivers to Cleveland Browns, August 30, 1983.
Signed by Chicago Blitz, December 20, 1983, for contract to take effect after being granted free agency, February 1, 1984.
USFL rights traded with placekicker Efren Herrera by Pittsburgh Maulers to Chicago Blitz for rights to linebacker Bruce Huther, December 30, 1983.
Franchise disbanded, November 20, 1984; signed as free agent by Portland Breakers, February 4, 1985.
Signed by Cleveland Browns for 1985 season, May 20, 1985.
Released by Portland Breakers, June 26, 1985.
Crossed picket line during players' strike, October 14, 1987.
Released by Cleveland Browns, November 17, 1987; signed as free agent by Houston Oilers, December 3, 1987.
Traded by Houston Oilers to Los Angeles Raiders for past considerations, August 16, 1988.

		——PUNTING——		
Year	Club	G.	No.	Avg.	Blk.
1981—Kansas City NFL	7	29	39.3	0
1982—Kansas City NFL	8	33	41.4	0
1983—Cleveland NFL	16	70	40.8	0
1984—Chicago USFL	18	85	*42.5	....
1985—Portland USFL	18	74	42.2	....
1985—Cleveland NFL	16	81	40.3	0
1986—Cleveland NFL	16	83	41.2	0
1987—Cle. (5)-Hou. (4) NFL	9	44	40.4	1
1988—L.A. Raiders NFL	16	91	41.8	0
NFL Totals—7 Years	88	431	40.9	1
USFL Totals—2 Years	36	159	42.3	....
Pro Totals—9 Years	124	590	41.3	....

Additional NFL statistics. Recovered one fumble, 1982; attempted one pass with no completions, 1985; attempted two passes with one completion for 30 yards and one interception, 1986.
Additional USFL statistics: Rushed once for no yards, 1984; attempted one pass with one interception, rushed once for minus four yards, recovered one fumble and fumbled once, 1985.
Played in AFC Championship Game following 1986 season.

RECORD AS BASEBALL PLAYER
Selected by New York Mets' organization in 5th round of free-agent draft, June 6, 1978.
Placed on restricted list, April 30, 1980.

Year	Club	League	Pos.	G.	AB.	R.	H.	2B.	3B.	HR.	RBI.	B.A.	PO.	A.	E.	F.A.
1978—Lynchburg	Carol.	3B-OF	10	21	1	5	1	0	0	4	.238	6	8	6	.700
1978—Little Falls	NYP	3B-OF	61	233	30	59	12	4	4	36	.253	54	102	19	.891
1979—Lynchburg	Carol.	3B	112	386	56	98	25	2	13	53	.254	71	200	*32	.894

PRESTON GOTHARD
Tight End—Pittsburgh Steelers
Born February 23, 1962, at Montgomery, Ala.
Height, 6.04. Weight, 235.
High School—Montgomery, Ala., Lowndes Academy.
Attended University of Alabama.

Signed as free agent by Pittsburgh Steelers, May 3, 1985.
On injured reserve with knee injury, November 18 through remainder of 1987 season.

		——PASS RECEIVING——			
Year	Club	G.	P.C.	Yds.	Avg.	TD.
1985—Pittsburgh NFL	16	6	83	13.8	0
1986—Pittsburgh NFL	16	21	246	11.7	1
1987—Pittsburgh NFL	2	2	9	4.5	1
1988—Pittsburgh NFL	16	12	121	10.1	1
Pro Totals—4 Years	50	41	459	11.2	3

Additional pro statistics: Recovered one fumble, 1985 and 1988.

KURT KEOLA GOUVEIA
Linebacker—Washington Redskins
Born September 14, 1964, at Honolulu, Haw.
Height, 6.01. Weight, 227.
High School—Waianae, Haw.
Attended Brigham Young University.

Selected by Washington in 8th round (213th player selected) of 1986 NFL draft.
Signed by Washington Redskins, July 18, 1986.
On injured reserve with knee injury, August 25 through entire 1986 season.
Washington NFL, 1987 and 1988.
Games: 1987 (11), 1988 (16). Total—27.
Played in NFC Championship Game following 1987 season.
Played in NFL Championship Game following 1987 season.

CORNELL ANTHONY GOWDY
Safety—Pittsburgh Steelers
Born October 2, 1963, at Washington, D. C.
Height, 6.01. Weight, 202.
High School—Seat Pleasant, Md., Central.
Received bachelor of science degree in business administration
from Morgan State University in 1985.

Signed as free agent by Pittsburgh Steelers, July 15, 1985.
Released by Pittsburgh Steelers, July 30, 1985; signed as free agent by Dallas Cowboys, May 2, 1986.
Released by Dallas Cowboys, September 23, 1986; signed as free agent by New York Giants for 1987, October 27, 1986.
Released by New York Giants, August 31, 1987; signed as free agent replacement player by Pittsburgh Steelers, September 24, 1987.
Dallas NFL, 1986; Pittsburgh NFL, 1987 and 1988.
Games: 1986 (3), 1987 (13), 1988 (16). Total—32.
Pro statistics: Intercepted two passes for 50 yards and a touchdown, recovered two fumbles for one yard and returned one kickoff for no yards, 1987; intercepted one pass for 24 yards, 1988.

SAMUEL LOUIS GRADDY
(Sam)
Wide Receiver—Los Angeles Raiders
Born February 10, 1964, At Gaffney, S. C.
Height, 5.10. Weight, 165.
High School—Atlanta, Ga., Northside.
Received bachelor of arts degree in economics from University of Tennessee in 1987.
Won gold medal in 4x100 relay during 1984 Olympics.

Signed as free agent by Denver Broncos, May 1, 1987.
On injured reserve with hamstring injury, September 1 through December 11, 1987; activated, December 12, 1987.
Released by Denver Broncos, September 8, 1988; re-signed by Broncos, September 12, 1988.
On injured reserve with back injury, October 31 through remainder of 1988 season.
Granted unconditional free agency, February 1, 1989; signed by Los Angeles Raiders, April 1, 1989.
Denver NFL, 1987 and 1988.
Games: 1987 (1), 1988 (7). Total—8.
Pro statistics: Caught one pass for 30 yards, 1988.
Member of Denver Broncos for NFL Championship Game following 1987 season; inactive.

RICHARD GLENN GRAF
(Rick)
Linebacker—Miami Dolphins
Born August 29, 1963, at Iowa City, Ia.
Height, 6.05. Weight, 249.
High School—Madison, Wis., James Madison Memorial.
Received bachelor of arts degree in communication arts from University of Wisconsin in 1987.

Selected by Miami in 2nd round (43rd player selected) of 1987 NFL draft.
Signed by Miami Dolphins, August 1, 1987.
Miami NFL, 1987 and 1988.
Games: 1987 (12), 1988 (16). Total—28.
Pro statistics: Recovered one fumble, 1987; intercepted one pass for 14 yards and recovered three fumbles for five yards, 1988.

DONALD JOHN GRAHAM
(Don)
Linebacker—Washington Redskins
Born January 31, 1964, at Pittsburgh, Pa.
Height, 6.02. Weight, 244.
High School—Pittsburgh, Pa., Brentwood.
Received degree in hotel, restaurant and institutional management
from Penn State University in 1987.

Selected by Tampa Bay in 4th round (84th player selected) of 1987 NFL draft.
Signed by Tampa Bay Buccaneers, July 18, 1987.
On injured reserve with stomach injury, November 7 through remainder of 1987 season.

Released by Tampa Bay Buccaneers, August 29, 1988; signed as free agent by Buffalo Bills, September 27, 1988. Released by Buffalo Bills, December 10, 1988; awarded on waivers to New York Jets, December 12, 1988. Granted unconditional free agency, February 1, 1989; signed by Washington Redskins, March 8, 1989. Inactive for 1 game with New York Jets in 1988. Tampa Bay NFL, 1987; Buffalo (10)-New York Jets (0) NFL, 1988. Games: 1987 (2), 1988 (10). Total—12.

DARRYL GRANT
Defensive Tackle—Washington Redskins
Born November 22, 1959, at San Antonio, Tex.
Height, 6.01. Weight, 275.
High School—San Antonio, Tex., Highlands.
Attended Rice University.

Selected by Washington in 9th round (231st player selected) of 1981 NFL draft.
On injured reserve with knee injury, November 2 through remainder of 1985 season.
Washington NFL, 1981 through 1988.
Games: 1981 (15), 1982 (9), 1983 (15), 1984 (15), 1985 (8), 1986 (16), 1987 (12), 1988 (16). Total—107.
Pro statistics: Returned one kickoff for 20 yards, 1981; recovered two fumbles, 1983; recovered four fumbles for 22 yards and a touchdown, 1984; recovered one fumble, 1987 and 1988.
Played in NFC Championship Game following 1982, 1983, 1986 and 1987 seasons.
Played in NFL Championship Game following 1982, 1983 and 1987 seasons.

DAVID GRANT
Nose Tackle—Cincinnati Bengals
Born September 17, 1965, at Belleville, N.J.
Height, 6.04. Weight, 277.
High School—Belleville, N.J.
Attended West Virginia University.

Selected by Cincinnati in 4th round (84th player selected) of 1988 NFL draft.
Signed by Cincinnati Bengals, July 10, 1988.
Cincinnati NFL, 1988.
Games: 1988 (16).
Pro statistics: Recovered one fumble, 1988.
Played in AFC Championship Game following 1988 season.
Played in NFL Championship Game following 1988 season.

RORY ANTHONY GRAVES
Offensive Tackle—Los Angeles Raiders
Born July 21, 1963, at Atlanta, Ga.
Height, 6.06. Weight, 285.
High School—Decatur, Ga., Columbia.
Attended Ohio State University.

Selected by New Jersey in 1986 USFL territorial draft.
Signed as free agent by Seattle Seahawks, May 12, 1986.
On injured reserve with back injury, August 19 through entire 1986 season.
Released by Seattle Seahawks, September 1, 1987; signed as free agent by Los Angeles Raiders for 1988, November 5, 1987.
Los Angeles Raiders NFL, 1988.
Games: 1988 (16).
Pro statistics: Recovered one fumble, 1988.

JERRY GRAY
Cornerback—Los Angeles Rams
Born December 2, 1962, at Lubbock, Tex.
Height, 6.00. Weight, 185.
High School—Lubbock, Tex., Estacado.
Attended University of Texas.

Named as defensive back on THE SPORTING NEWS College All-America Team, 1984.
Selected by San Antonio in 1985 USFL territorial draft.
Selected by Los Angeles Rams in 1st round (21st player selected) of 1985 NFL draft.
Signed by Los Angeles Rams, August 1, 1985.
Crossed picket line during players' strike, October 14, 1987.

| | | —INTERCEPTIONS— | | | |
Year Club	G.	No.	Yds.	Avg.	TD.
1985—L.A. Rams NFL............	16		None		
1986—L.A. Rams NFL............	16	8	101	12.6	0
1987—L.A. Rams NFL............	12	2	35	17.5	0
1988—L.A. Rams NFL............	16	3	83	27.7	1
Pro Totals—4 Years...........	60	13	219	16.8	1

Additional pro statistics: Recovered one fumble, 1986 through 1988; recovered blocked punt in end zone for a touchdown, 1987; returned one punt for one yard, 1988.
Played in NFC Championship Game following 1985 season.
Played in Pro Bowl (NFL All-Star Game) following 1986 through 1988 seasons.

MEL GRAY
Running Back—Detroit Lions
Born March 16, 1961, at Williamsburg, Va.
Height, 5.09. Weight, 166.
High School—Williamsburg, Va., Lafayette.
Attended Coffeyville Junior College and Purdue University.

Named as punt returner to THE SPORTING NEWS All-Star Team, 1987.
Named as kickoff returner to THE SPORTING NEWS NFL All-Star Team, 1986.
Selected by Chicago in 7th round (132nd player selected) of 1984 USFL draft.
USFL rights traded by Chicago Blitz to Los Angeles Express for wide receiver Kris Haines, February 11, 1984.
Signed by Los Angeles Express, February 16, 1984.
On developmental squad, February 24 through March 8, 1984; activated, March 9, 1984.
On developmental squad, May 26 through June 8, 1984; activated, June 9, 1984.
Selected by New Orleans in 2nd round (42nd player selected) of 1984 NFL supplemental draft.
Traded with defensive backs Dwight Drane, John Warren and Troy West, guard Wayne Jones, linebacker Howard Carson and tight end Ken O'Neal by Los Angeles Express to Arizona Outlaws for past considerations, August 1, 1985.
Granted free agency when USFL suspended operations, August 7, 1986; signed by New Orleans Saints, August 18, 1986.
Granted roster exemption, August 18 through August 28, 1986; activated, August 29, 1986.
Granted unconditional free agency, February 1, 1989; signed by Detroit Lions, March 1, 1989.
On developmental squad for 4 games with Los Angeles Express in 1984

Year Club	G.	—RUSHING— Att.	Yds.	Avg.	TD.	PASS RECEIVING P.C.	Yds.	Avg.	TD.	—TOTAL— TD.	Pts.	F.
1984—Los Angeles USFL	15	133	625	4.7	3	27	288	10.7	1	4	24	10
1985—Los Angeles USFL	16	125	526	4.2	1	20	101	5.1	0	1	6	7
1986—New Orleans NFL	16	6	29	4.8	0	2	45	22.5	0	1	6	0
1987—New Orleans NFL	12	8	37	4.6	1	6	30	5.0	0	1	6	3
1988—New Orleans NFL	14			None				None		0	0	5
USFL Totals—2 Years	31	258	1151	4.5	4	47	389	8.3	1	5	30	17
NFL Totals—3 Years	42	14	66	4.7	1	8	75	9.4	0	2	12	8
Pro Totals—5 Years	73	272	1217	4.5	5	55	464	8.4	1	7	42	25

Year Club	G.	—PUNT RETURNS— No.	Yds.	Avg.	TD.	—KICKOFF RET.— No.	Yds.	Avg.	TD.
1984—Los Angeles USFL	15			None		20	332	16.6	0
1985—Los Angeles USFL	16			None		11	203	18.5	0
1986—New Orleans NFL	16			None		31	866	27.9	*1
1987—New Orleans NFL	12	24	352	*14.7	0	30	636	21.2	0
1988—New Orleans NFL	14	25	305	12.2	1	32	670	20.9	0
USFL Totals—2 Years	31			None		31	535	17.3	0
NFL Totals—3 Years	42	49	657	13.4	1	93	2172	23.4	1
Pro Totals—5 Years	73	49	657	13.4	1	124	2707	21.8	1

Additional USFL statistics: Attempted one pass with one completion for 29 yards and recovered two fumbles, 1984; recovered one fumble, 1985.
Additional NFL statistics: Recovered one fumble, 1987; recovered two fumbles, 1988.

DAVID LEE GRAYSON JR.
(Dave)
Linebacker—Cleveland Browns
Born February 27, 1964, at San Diego, Calif.
Height, 6.02. Weight, 229.
High School—San Diego, Calif., Abraham Lincoln.
Attended California State Poly University and Fresno State University.
Son of Dave Grayson, defensive back with Dallas Texans-Kansas City Chiefs and
Oakland Raiders, 1961 through 1970; and cousin of Mike Davis, outfielder with Los Angeles Dodgers.

Selected by San Francisco in 8th round (217th player selected) of 1987 NFL draft.
Signed by San Francisco 49ers, July 15, 1987.
Released by San Francisco 49ers, August 28, 1987; signed as free agent replacement player by Cleveland Browns, September 23, 1987.
Cleveland NFL, 1987 and 1988.
Games: 1987 (11), 1988 (16). Total—27.
Pro statistics: Recovered one fumble for 17 yards and a touchdown and returned one kickoff for six yards, 1987.
Played in AFC Championship Game following 1987 season.

CURTIS GREEN
Defensive End-Nose Tackle—Detroit Lions
Born June 3, 1957, at Quincy, Fla.
Height, 6.03. Weight, 265.
High School—Quincy, Fla., James A. Shanks.
Attended Alabama State University.

Selected by Detroit in 2nd round (46th player selected) of 1981 NFL draft.
On inactive list, September 19, 1982.
On injured reserve with strained calf muscle, November 18 through remainder of 1988 season.
Detroit NFL, 1981 through 1988.
Games: 1981 (14), 1982 (7), 1983 (16), 1984 (16), 1985 (15), 1986 (16), 1987 (12), 1988 (11). Total—107.
Pro statistics: Recovered one fumble, 1981, 1985 and 1988; returned one kickoff for no yards and fumbled once, 1987.

DARRELL GREEN
Cornerback—Washington Redskins
Born February 15, 1960, at Houston, Tex.
Height, 5.08. Weight, 170.
High School—Houston, Tex., Jesse Jones.
Attended Texas A&I University.
Selected by Denver in 10th round (112th player selected) of 1983 USFL draft.
Selected by Washington in 1st round (28th player selected) of 1983 NFL draft.
Signed by Washington Redskins, June 10, 1983.
On injured reserve with broken hand, December 13 through remainder of 1988 season.

		-INTERCEPTIONS-				-PUNT RETURNS-				—TOTAL		
Year Club	G.	No.	Yds.	Avg.	TD.	No.	Yds.	Avg.	TD.	TD.	Pts.	F.
1983—Washington NFL	16	2	7	3.5	0	4	29	7.3	0	0	0	1
1984—Washington NFL	16	5	91	18.2	1	2	13	6.5	0	1	6	0
1985—WashingtonNFL	16	2	0	0.0	0	16	214	13.4	0	0	0	2
1986—Washington NFL	16	5	9	1.8	0	12	120	10.0	0	0	0	0
1987—Washington NFL	12	3	65	21.7	0	5	53	10.6	0	1	6	0
1988—Washington NFL	15	1	12	12.0	0	9	103	11.4	0	0	0	1
Pro Totals—6 Years	91	18	184	10.2	1	48	532	11.1	0	2	12	4

Additional pro statistics: Recovered one fumble, 1983, 1985, 1986 and 1988; rushed once for six yards, 1985; fumbled once, 1986; recovered one fumble for 26 yards and a touchdown, 1987.
Played in NFC Championship Game following 1983, 1986 and 1987 seasons.
Played in NFL Championship Game following 1983 and 1987 seasons.
Played in Pro Bowl (NFL All-Star Game) following 1984, 1986 and 1987 seasons.

GASTON ALFRED GREEN III
Running Back—Los Angeles Rams
Born August 1, 1966, at Los Angeles, Calif.
Height, 5.10. Weight, 189.
High School—Gardena, Calif.
Attended University of California at Los Angeles.
Selected by Los Angeles Rams in 1st round (14th player selected) of 1988 NFL draft.
Signed by Los Angeles Rams, July 20, 1988.

		——RUSHING——				PASS RECEIVING				—TOTAL—		
Year Club	G.	Att.	Yds.	Avg.	TD.	P.C.	Yds.	Avg.	TD.	TD.	Pts.	F.
1988—Los Angeles Rams NFL	10	35	117	3.3	0	6	57	9.5	0	0	0	1

		KICKOFF RETURNS			
Year Club	G.	No.	Yds.	Avg.	TD.
1988—L.A. Rams NFL	10	17	345	20.3	0

Additional pro statistics: Recovered three fumbles, 1988.

HUGH DONELL GREEN
Linebacker—Miami Dolphins
Born July 27, 1959, at Natchez, Miss.
Height, 6.02. Weight, 225.
High School—Natchez, Miss., North.
Attended University of Pittsburgh.
Named THE SPORTING NEWS College Player of the Year, 1980.
Named as defensive end on THE SPORTING NEWS College All-America Team, 1979 and 1980.
Named to THE SPORTING NEWS NFL All-Star Team, 1983.
Selected by Tampa Bay in 1st round (7th player selected) of 1981 NFL draft.
On non-football injury list with eye and wrist injury, November 1 through November 29, 1984; activated, November 30, 1984.
Traded by Tampa Bay Buccaneers to Miami Dolphins for 1st and 2nd round picks in 1986 draft, October 9, 1985.
On injured reserve with knee injury, September 23 through remainder of 1986 season.
On injured reserve with knee injury, September 7 through October 23, 1987; activated, October 24, 1987.
Granted unconditional free agency, February 1, 1989; received no qualifying offer, April 15, 1989.
Re-signed by Dolphins, May 5, 1989.

		——INTERCEPTIONS——			
Year Club	G.	No.	Yds.	Avg.	TD.
1981—Tampa Bay NFL	16	2	56	28.0	0
1982—Tampa Bay NFL	9	1	31	31.0	0
1983—Tampa Bay NFL	16	2	54	27.0	★2
1984—Tampa Bay NFL	8		None		
1985—T.B.(5)-Mia.(11) NFL	16	1	28	28.0	0
1986—Miami NFL	3		None		
1987—Miami NFL	9		None		
1988—Miami NFL	16		None		
Pro Totals—8 Years	93	6	169	28.2	2

Additional pro statistics: Recovered one fumble, 1981 and 1985; recovered two fumbles for 11 yards and fumbled once, 1983; recovered one fumble for five yards, 1988.
Played in AFC Championship Game following 1985 season.
Played in Pro Bowl (NFL All-Star Game) following 1982 and 1983 seasons.

JACOB CARL GREEN
Defensive End—Seattle Seahawks

Born January 21, 1957, at Pasadena, Tex.
Height, 6.03. Weight, 255.
High School—Houston, Tex., Kashmere.
Attended Texas A&M University.
Cousin of George Small, defensive tackle with New York Giants and
Calgary Stampeders, 1980 through 1983.

Named to THE SPORTING NEWS NFL All-Star Team, 1984.
Selected by Seattle in 1st round (10th player selected) of 1980 NFL draft.
Seattle NFL, 1980 through 1988.
Games: 1980 (14), 1981 (16), 1982 (9), 1983 (16), 1984 (16), 1985 (16), 1986 (16), 1987 (12), 1988 (16). Total—131.
Pro statistics: Recovered one fumble, 1981, 1986 and 1987; intercepted one pass for 73 yards and a touchdown and recovered two fumbles, 1983; recovered four fumbles, 1984; recovered two fumbles for 79 yards and a touchdown and intercepted one pass for 19 yards and a touchdown, 1985; recovered two fumbles (including one in end zone for a touchdown), 1988.
Played in AFC Championship Game following 1983 season.
Played in Pro Bowl (NFL All-Star Game) following 1986 and 1987 seasons.

ROY GREEN
Wide Receiver—Phoenix Cardinals

Born June 30, 1957, at Magnolia, Ark.
Height, 6.00. Weight, 195.
High School—Magnolia, Ark.
Attended Henderson State University

Tied NFL record for longest kickoff return, game (106 yards), against Dallas Cowboys, October 21, 1979.
Named as kick returner to THE SPORTING NEWS NFC All-Star Team, 1979.
Named to THE SPORTING NEWS NFL All-Star Team, 1983 and 1984.
Selected by St. Louis in 4th round (89th player selected) of 1979 NFL draft.
On injured reserve with knee injury, December 15 through remainder of 1980 season.
On injured reserve with ankle injury, September 23 through October 23, 1986; activated, October 24, 1986.
Crossed picket line during players' strike, September 30, 1987.
Franchise transferred to Phoenix, March 15, 1988.

		—RUSHING—				PASS RECEIVING				—TOTAL—		
Year Club	G.	Att.	Yds.	Avg.	TD.	P.C.	Yds.	Avg.	TD.	TD.	Pts.	F.
1979—St. Louis NFL	16		None			1	15	15.0	0	1	6	4
1980—St. Louis NFL	15		None				None			1	6	2
1981—St. Louis NFL	16	3	60	20.0	1	33	708	21.5	4	5	30	2
1982—St. Louis NFL	9	6	8	1.3	0	32	453	14.2	3	3	18	1
1983—St. Louis NFL	16	4	49	12.3	0	78	1227	15.7	*14	14	84	3
1984—St. Louis NFL	16	1	−10	−10.0	0	78	*1555	19.9	12	12	72	1
1985—St. Louis NFL	13	1	2	2.0	0	50	693	13.9	5	5	30	2
1986—St. Louis NFL	11	2	−4	−2.0	0	42	517	12.3	6	6	36	1
1987—St. Louis NFL	12	2	34	17.0	0	43	731	17.0	4	4	24	1
1988—Phoenix NFL	16	4	1	0.3	0	68	1097	16.1	7	7	42	0
Pro Totals—10 Years	140	23	140	6.1	1	425	6996	16.5	55	58	348	17

		—PUNT RETURNS—				—KICKOFF RET.—			
Year Club	G.	No.	Yds.	Avg.	TD.	No.	Yds.	Avg.	TD.
1979—St. Louis NFL	16	8	42	5.3	0	41	1005	24.5	*1
1980—St. Louis NFL	15	16	168	10.5	1	32	745	23.3	0
1981—St. Louis NFL	16		None			8	135	16.9	0
1982—St. Louis NFL	9	3	20	6.7	0		None		
1983—St. Louis NFL	16		None			1	14	14.0	0
1984—St. Louis NFL	16		None			1	18	18.0	0
1985—St. Louis NFL	13		None				None		
1986—St. Louis NFL	11		None				None		
1987—St. Louis NFL	12		None				None		
1988—Phoenix NFL	16		None				None		
Pro Totals—10 Years	140	27	230	8.5	1	83	1917	23.1	1

Additional pro statistics: Recovered two fumbles, 1979; intercepted one pass for 10 yards, 1980; intercepted two passes for 44 yards, 1981; attempted one pass with no completions and recovered one fumble for two yards, 1982; recovered one fumble, 1983.
Played in Pro Bowl (NFL All-Star Game) following 1983 and 1984 seasons.

TIMOTHY JOHN GREEN
(Tim)
Linebacker—Atlanta Falcons

Born December 16, 1963, at Liverpool, N.Y.
Height, 6.02. Weight, 245.
High School—Liverpool, N.Y.
Received degree in English literature from Syracuse University in 1986.

Named as defensive lineman on THE SPORTING NEWS College All-America Team, 1984 and 1985.
Selected by New Jersey in 1986 USFL territorial draft.
Selected by Atlanta in 1st round (17th player selected) of 1986 NFL draft.
Signed by Atlanta Falcons, August 14, 1986.
Granted roster exemption, August 14 through August 21, 1986; activated, August 22, 1986.
On injured reserve with pulled calf, September 6 through October 10, 1986; activated, October 11, 1986.

Crossed picket line during players' strike, October 2, 1987.
On injured reserve with knee injury, November 17 through remainder of 1987 season.
On injured reserve with elbow injury, September 3 through October 14, 1988; activated, October 15, 1988.
Atlanta NFL, 1986 through 1988.
Games: 1986 (11), 1987 (9), 1988 (10). Total—30.
Pro statistics: Recovered two fumbles for 35 yards, 1987.

GEORGE GREENE
(Tiger)
Defensive Back—Green Bay Packers
Born February 15, 1962, at Hendersonville, N.C.
Height, 6.00. Weight, 194.
High School—Flat Rock, N.C., East Henderson.
Attended Western Carolina University.
Brother of A. J. Greene, rookie defensive back with New York Giants.

Selected by Memphis in 14th round (191st player selected) of 1985 USFL draft.
Signed as free agent by Atlanta Falcons, May 3, 1985.
On injured reserve with knee injury, September 16 through October 18, 1985; activated, October 19, 1985.
On injured reserve with ankle injury, December 10 through remainder of 1985 season.
Released by Atlanta Falcons, August 22, 1986; signed as free agent by Green Bay Packers, September 25, 1986.

| | | ——INTERCEPTIONS—— | | | |
Year Club	G.	No.	Yds.	Avg.TD.	
1985—Atlanta NFL	10	2	27	13.5	0
1986—Green Bay NFL............	13	2	0	0.0	0
1987—Green Bay NFL............	11	1	11	11.0	0
1988—Green Bay NFL............	16			None	
Pro Totals—4 Years............	50	5	38	7.6	0

Additional pro statistics: Recovered two fumbles, 1987.

KEVIN DARWIN GREENE
Linebacker—Los Angeles Rams
Born July 31, 1962, at New York, N.Y.
Height, 6.03. Weight, 238.
High School—Granite City, Ill., South.
Attended Auburn University.

Selected by Birmingham in 1985 USFL territorial draft.
Selected by Los Angeles Rams in 5th round (113th player selected) of 1985 NFL draft.
Signed by Los Angeles Rams, July 12, 1985.
Crossed picket line during players' strike, October 14, 1987.
Los Angeles Rams NFL, 1985 through 1988.
Games: 1985 (15), 1986 (16), 1987 (9), 1988 (16). Total—56.
Pro statistics: Recovered one fumble for 13 yards, 1986; intercepted one pass for 25 yards and a touchdown, 1987; intercepted one pass for 10 yards and credited with a safety, 1988.
Played in NFC Championship Game following 1985 season.

CURTIS WILLIAM GREER
Defensive End—Minnesota Vikings
Born November 10, 1957, at Detroit, Mich.
Height, 6.04. Weight, 258.
High School—Detroit, Mich., Cass Tech.
Received bachelor of science degree in speech communication
from University of Michigan in 1979.

Selected by St. Louis in 1st round (6th player selected) of 1980 NFL draft.
On injured reserve with concussion, September 9 through October 9, 1980; activated, October 10, 1980.
On injured reserve with broken thumb, December 15 through remainder of 1980 season.
On injured reserve with knee injury, September 2 through entire 1986 season.
Crossed picket line during players' strike, September 23, 1987.
On injured reserve with back injury, December 5 through remainder of 1987 season.
Franchise transferred to Phoenix, March 15, 1987.
On injured reserve with back injury, August 29 through entire 1988 season.
Granted unconditional free agency, February 1, 1989; signed by Minnesota Vikings, March 16, 1989.
St. Louis NFL, 1980 through 1985 and 1987.
Games: 1980 (11), 1981 (16), 1982 (9), 1983 (16), 1984 (16), 1985 (16), 1987 (10). Total—94.
Pro statistics: Recovered four fumbles for two yards, 1981; recovered three fumbles, 1982; recovered one fumble for five yards, 1983; recovered one fumble, 1985.

TERRY LEE GREER
Wide Receiver—San Francisco 49ers
Born September 27, 1957, at Memphis, Tenn.
Height, 6.01. Weight, 192.
High School—Memphis, Tenn., Messick.
Received bachelor of science degree in business administration from Alabama State University in 1980.

Signed as free agent by Toronto Argonauts, March 21, 1980.
Selected by Los Angeles Rams in 11th round (304th player selected) of 1980 NFL draft.
On injured reserve, August 10 through remainder of 1981 season.

Granted free agency, March 1, 1986.
Los Angeles Rams matched Cleveland Browns offer sheet and traded him to Cleveland Browns for 4th round pick in 1986 draft, April 18, 1986.
On injured reserve with knee injury, October 10 through November 9, 1986; activated, November 10, 1986.
On injured reserve with bruised thumb, December 23 through remainder of 1986 season playoffs.
Released by Cleveland Browns, September 7, 1987; signed as free agent replacement player by San Francisco 49ers, September 30, 1987.
Released by San Francisco 49ers, November 3, 1987; re-signed by 49ers, April 5, 1988.
On injured reserve with shoulder injury, August 29 through October 12, 1988; activated after clearing procedural waivers, October 14, 1988.
Granted unconditional free agency, February 1, 1989; re-signed by 49ers, April 28, 1989.

			—RUSHING—			PASS RECEIVING				—TOTAL—		
Year	Club	G.	Att.	Yds.	Avg.	TD.	P.C.	Yds.	Avg.	TD.	TD.	Pts.	F.
1980—Toronto CFL		14	2	38	19.0	1	37	552	14.9	2	3	18	0
1981—Toronto CFL		6	1	22	22.0	0	21	284	13.5	3	4	24	1
1982—Toronto CFL		15	7	52	7.4	1	85	1466	17.2	11	12	†74	1
1983—Toronto CFL		16	2	15	7.5	0	*113	*2003	17.7	8	8	48	1
1984—Toronto CFL		15	2	13	6.5	0	70	1189	17.0	14	14	84	1
1985—Toronto CFL		16	3	45	15.0	0	78	1323	17.0	9	9	54	0
1986—Cleveland NFL		11	3	51	17.0	0	3	51	17.0	0	0	0	0
1987—San Francisco NFL		3			None		6	111	18.5	1	1	6	0
1988—San Francisco NFL		10			None		8	120	15.0	0	0	0	0
CFL Totals—6 Years		82	17	185	10.9	2	404	6817	16.9	47	50	302	4
NFL Totals—3 Years		24	3	51	17.0	0	17	282	16.6	1	1	6	0
Pro Totals—9 Years		106	20	236	11.8	2	421	7099	16.9	48	51	308	4

KICKOFF RETURNS

Year	Club	G.	No.	Yds.	Avg.	TD.
1980—Toronto CFL		14	23	533	23.2	0
1981—Toronto CFL		6	11	418	38.0	1
1982—Toronto CFL		15	12	285	23.8	0
1983—Toronto CFL		16	1	0	0.0	0
1984—Toronto CFL		15	3	31	10.3	0
1985—Toronto CFL		16			None	
1986—Cleveland NFL		11			None	
1987—San Francisco NFL		3			None	
1988—San Francisco NFL		10			None	
CFL Totals—6 Years		82	50	1267	25.3	1
NFL Totals—3 Years		24	0	0	0.0	0
Pro Totals—9 Years		106	50	1267	25.3	1

†Scored one 2-point conversion.
Additional pro statistics: Attempted one pass with one completion for 39 yards and a touchdown, 1982; attempted two passes with one completion for 39 yards with one touchdown and one interception, 1983; attempted three passes with one completion for 42 yards and a touchdown, 1984; attempted two passes with one completion for minus one yard and recovered one fumble for two yards, 1985.
Played in NFC Championship Game following 1988 season.
Played in NFL Championship Game following 1988 season.
Played in CFL Championship Game following 1982 and 1983 seasons.

THEODORE ANTHONY GREGORY
(Ted)
Nose Tackle—New Orleans Saints
Born February 11, 1965, at Queens, N.Y.
Height, 6.01. Weight, 260.
High School—Islip Terrace, N.Y., East Islip.
Received degree in economics from Syracuse University in 1988.

Named as nose tackle on THE SPORTING NEWS College All-America Team, 1987.
Selected by Denver in 1st round (26th player selected) of 1988 NFL draft.
Signed by Denver Broncos, July 15, 1988.
Traded by Denver Broncos to New Orleans Saints for defensive end Shawn Knight, August 29, 1988.
On injured reserve with knee injury, November 26 through remainder of season.
New Orleans NFL, 1988.
Games: 1988 (3).

DONALD FREDERICK GRIFFIN
(Don)
Cornerback—San Francisco 49ers
Born March 17, 1964, at Pelham, Ga.
Height, 6.00. Weight, 176.
High School—Pelham, Ga., Mitchell-Baker.
Attended Middle Tennessee State University.
Brother of James Griffin, safety with Detroit Lions.

Selected by Memphis in 1986 USFL territorial draft.
Selected by San Francisco in 6th round (162nd player selected) of 1986 NFL draft.
Signed by San Francisco 49ers, July 21, 1986.

Year Club	G.	No.	Yds.	Avg.	TD.	No.	Yds.	Avg.	TD.	TD.	Pts.	F.
		-INTERCEPTIONS-				-PUNT RETURNS-				—TOTAL—		
1986—San Francisco NFL	16	3	0	0.0	0	38	377	9.9	1	1	6	3
1987—San Francisco NFL	12	5	1	0.2	0	9	79	8.8	0	0	0	0
1988—San Francisco NFL	10			None		4	28	7.0	0	0	0	0
Pro Totals—3 Years	38	8	1	0.1	0	51	484	9.5	1	1	6	3

Additional pro statistics: Returned five kickoffs for 97 yards and recovered two fumbles, 1986; recovered one fumble for seven yards, 1987.

Played in NFC Championship Game following 1988 season.
Played in NFL Championship Game following 1988 season.

JAMES VICTOR GRIFFIN
Safety—Detroit Lions
Born September 7, 1961, at Camilla, Ga.
Height, 6.02. Weight, 203.
High School—Camilla, Ga., Mitchell.
Attended Middle Tennessee State University.
Brother of Don Griffin, cornerback with San Francisco 49ers.

Selected by Cincinnati in 7th round (193rd player selected) of 1983 NFL draft.
Released by Cincinnati Bengals, September 1, 1986; signed as free agent by Detroit Lions, September 4, 1986.

Year Club	G.	No.	Yds.	Avg.	TD.
		——INTERCEPTIONS——			
1983—Cincinnati NFL	16	1	41	41.0	1
1984—Cincinnati NFL	16	1	57	57.0	1
1985—Cincinnati NFL	16	7	116	16.6	*1
1986—Detroit NFL	16	2	34	17.0	0
1987—Detroit NFL	12	6	130	21.7	0
1988—Detroit NFL	16	2	31	15.5	0
Pro Totals—6 Years	92	19	409	21.5	3

Additional pro statistics: Recovered two fumbles, 1984; returned one kickoff for no yards and recovered one fumble for 29 yards, 1985; recovered one fumble for seven yards, 1988.

KEITH GRIFFIN
Running Back—Atlanta Falcons
Born October 26, 1961, at Columbus, O.
Height, 5.08. Weight, 185.
High School—Columbus, O., Eastmoor.
Attended University of Miami (Fla.).
Brother of Archie Griffin, running back with Cincinnati Bengals and Jacksonville Bulls,
1976 through 1982 and 1984; and Ray Griffin, defensive back with Cincinnati Bengals, 1978 through 1984.

Selected by Oklahoma in 11th round (212th player selected) of 1984 USFL draft.
Selected by Washington in 10th round (279th player selected) of 1984 NFL draft.
Signed by Washington Redskins, July 13, 1984.
Released by Washington Redskins, August 30, 1988; re-signed by Redskins, September 22, 1988.
Released by Washington Redskins, November 22, 1988; signed as free agent by Atlanta Falcons, December 14, 1988.
Inactive for 1 game with Atlanta Falcons in 1988.

Year Club	G.	Att.	Yds.	Avg.	TD.	P.C.	Yds.	Avg.	TD.	TD.	Pts.	F.
		——RUSHING——				PASS RECEIVING				—TOTAL—		
1984—Washington NFL	16	97	408	4.2	0	8	43	5.4	0	0	0	7
1985—Washington NFL	16	102	473	4.6	3	37	285	7.7	0	3	18	1
1986—Washington NFL	16	62	197	3.2	0	11	110	10.0	0	0	0	0
1987—Washington NFL	9	62	242	3.9	0	3	13	4.3	1	1	6	3
1988—Washington (8)-Atlanta (0) NFL	8	6	23	3.8	0	2	9	4.5	1	1	6	0
Pro Totals—5 Years	65	329	1343	4.1	3	61	460	7.5	2	5	30	11

Year Club	G.	No.	Yds.	Avg.	TD.
		KICKOFF RETURNS			
1984—Washington NFL	16	9	164	18.2	0
1985—Washington NFL	16	7	142	20.3	0
1986—Washington NFL	16	8	156	19.5	0
1987—Washington NFL	9	25	478	19.1	0
1988—Wash. (8)-Atl. (0) NFL	8	3	45	15.0	0
Pro Totals—5 Years	65	52	985	18.9	0

Played in NFC Championship Game following 1986 season.
Played in NFL Championship Game following 1987 season.

LARRY ANTHONY GRIFFIN
Cornerback—Pittsburgh Steelers
Born January 11, 1963, at Chesapeake, Vir.
Height, 6.00. Weight, 197.
High School—Chesapeake, Vir., Great Bridge.
Attended University of North Carolina.

Selected by Baltimore in 1986 USFL territorial draft.
Selected by Houston in 8th round (199th player selected) of 1986 NFL draft.
Signed by Houston Oilers, July 21, 1986.

Released by Houston Oilers, August 25, 1986; re-signed by Oilers, October 1, 1986.
Released by Houston Oilers, October 22, 1986; signed as free agent by Miami Dolphins, February 23, 1987.
Released by Miami Dolphins, September 7, 1987; signed as free agent replacement player by Pittsburgh Steelers, September 28, 1987.
Houston NFL, 1986; Pittsburgh NFL, 1987 and 1988.
Games: 1986 (3), 1987 (7), 1988 (15). Total—25.
Pro statistics: Intercepted two passes for two yards, 1987; intercepted two passes for 63 yards, recovered one fumble and fumbled once, 1988.

LEONARD JAMES GRIFFIN JR.
Defensive End—Kansas City Chiefs
Born September 22, 1962, at Lake Providence, La.
Height, 6.04. Weight, 270.
High School—Lake Providence, La.
Attended Grambling State University.
Brother of Elinor Griffin, member of 1980 U.S. Women's Olympic Basketball team.

Selected by Kansas City in 3rd round (63rd player selected) of 1986 NFL draft.
Signed by Kansas City Chiefs, July 26, 1986.
On injured reserve with ankle injury, September 2 through October 24, 1986; activated, October 25, 1986.
Kansas City NFL, 1986 through 1988.
Games: 1986 (9), 1987 (12), 1988 (15). Total—36.

ANTHONY GRIGGS
Linebacker—Kansas City Chiefs
Born February 12, 1960, at Lawton, Okla.
Height, 6.03. Weight, 230.
High School—Willingboro, N.J., John F. Kennedy.
Attended Ohio State University and received degree in communications from Villanova University.
Cousin of Billy Griggs, tight end with New York Jets; and
David Griggs, rookie linebacker with New Orleans Saints.

Selected by Philadelphia in 4th round (104th player selected) of 1982 NFL draft.
Traded by Philadelphia Eagles to Cleveland Browns for 8th round pick in 1986 draft, April 29, 1986.
Traded by Cleveland Browns to Indianapolis Colts for conditional 12th round pick in 1989 draft, August 30, 1988.
Released by Indianapolis Colts, September 5, 1988; signed as free agent by Cleveland Browns, October 5, 1988.
Released by Cleveland Browns, November 14, 1988; signed as free agent by Kansas City Chiefs, February 16, 1989.
Philadelphia NFL, 1982 through 1985; Cleveland NFL, 1986 through 1988.
Games: 1982 (9), 1983 (16), 1984 (16), 1985 (16), 1986 (16), 1987 (12), 1988 (5). Total—90.
Pro statistics: Recovered one fumble, 1982; intercepted three passes for 61 yards, 1983; recovered one fumble for three yards, 1986.
Played in AFC Championship Game following 1986 and 1987 seasons.

WILLIAM EDWARD GRIGGS
(Billy)
Tight End—New York Jets
Born August 4, 1962, at Camden, N.J.
Height, 6.03. Weight, 230.
High School—Pennsauken, N.J.
Received bachelor of arts degree in sociology from University of Virginia in 1984.
Brother of David Griggs, rookie linebacker with New Orleans Saints; and
cousin of Anthony Griggs, linebacker with Kansas City Chiefs.

Selected by New York Jets in 8th round (203rd player selected) of 1984 NFL draft.
On injured reserve with ankle injury, August 14 through entire 1984 season.

| | | —PASS RECEIVING— | | | |
Year	Club	G.	P.C.	Yds.	Avg.	TD.
1985—New York Jets NFL....		16		None		
1986—New York Jets NFL....		16		None		
1987—New York Jets NFL....		12	2	17	8.5	1
1988—New York Jets NFL....		15	14	133	9.5	0
Pro Totals—4 Years............		59	16	150	9.4	1

Additional pro statistics: Returned one kickoff for 13 yards, 1987; recovered one fumble and fumbled once, 1988.

RANDALL COLLINS GRIMES
(Randy)
Center—Tampa Bay Buccaneers
Born July 20, 1960, at Tyler, Tex.
Height, 6.04. Weight, 275.
High School—Tyler, Tex., Robert E. Lee.
Attended Baylor University.

Selected by New Jersey in 6th round (70th player selected) of 1983 USFL draft.
Selected by Tampa Bay in 2nd round (45th player selected) of 1983 NFL draft.
Signed by Tampa Bay Buccaneers, June 6, 1983.
Tampa Bay NFL, 1983 through 1988.
Games: 1983 (15), 1984 (10), 1985 (16), 1986 (16), 1987 (12), 1988 (16). Total—85.
Pro statistics: Recovered one fumble, 1983.

RUSS GRIMM
Guard—Washington Redskins
Born May 2, 1959, at Scottsdale, Pa.
Height, 6.03. Weight, 275.
High School—Southmoreland, Pa.
Attended University of Pittsburgh.

Named to THE SPORTING NEWS NFL All-Star Team, 1985.
Selected by Washington in 3rd round (69th player selected) of 1981 NFL draft.
On injured reserve with knee injury, November 14 through December 24, 1987; activated, December 25, 1987.
On injured reserve with knee injury, August 30 through November 20, 1988; activated, November 21, 1988.
Washington NFL, 1981 through 1988.
Games: 1981 (14), 1982 (9), 1983 (16), 1984 (16), 1985 (16), 1986 (15), 1987 (6), 1988 (5). Total—97.
Pro statistics: Recovered one fumble, 1981, 1982 and 1988; recovered two fumbles, 1984 and 1986.
Played in NFC Championship Game following 1982, 1983, 1986 and 1987 seasons.
Played in NFL Championship Game following 1982, 1983 and 1987 seasons.
Played in Pro Bowl (NFL All-Star Game) following 1983 through 1986 seasons.

JOHN GLENN GRIMSLEY
Linebacker—Houston Oilers
Born February 25, 1962, at Canton, O.
Height, 6.02. Weight, 238.
High School—Canton, O., McKinley.
Attended University of Kentucky.

Selected by Denver in 3rd round (59th player selected) of 1984 USFL draft.
Selected by Houston in 6th round (141st player selected) of 1984 NFL draft.
Signed by Houston Oilers, July 7, 1984.
Houston NFL, 1984 through 1988.
Games: 1984 (16), 1985 (15), 1986 (16), 1987 (12), 1988 (16). Total—75.
Pro statistics: Recovered one fumble for five yards, 1985; recovered two fumbles, 1986; recovered one fumble, 1987 and 1988; intercepted one pass for nine yards, 1988.
Played in Pro Bowl (NFL All-Star Game) following 1988 season.

STEVEN JAMES GROGAN
(Steve)
Quarterback—New England Patriots
Born July 24, 1953, at San Antonio, Tex.
Height, 6.04. Weight, 210.
High School—Ottawa, Kan.
Received bachelor of science degree in physical education from Kansas State University in 1975.
Son of Jim Grogan, assistant football coach at Ottawa University (Kan.); and brother of Scott Grogan, assistant football coach at University of Nebraska at Omaha.

Selected by New England in 5th round (116th player selected) of 1975 NFL draft.
On injured reserve with broken leg, November 30, 1985 through January 3, 1986; activated, January 4, 1986.

| | | | PASSING | | | | | | RUSHING | | | | TOTAL | |
Year Club	G.	Att.	Cmp.	Pct.	Gain	T.P.	P.I.	Avg.	Att.	Yds.	Avg.	TD.	TD.	Pts.	F.
1975—New England NFL	13	274	139	50.7	1976	11	18	7.21	30	110	3.7	3	3	18	6
1976—New England NFL	14	302	145	48.0	1903	18	20	6.30	60	397	6.6	12	13	78	6
1977—New England NFL	14	305	160	52.5	2162	17	21	7.09	61	324	5.3	1	1	6	7
1978—New England NFL	16	362	181	50.0	2824	15	23	7.80	81	539	*6.7	5	5	30	9
1979—New England NFL	16	423	206	48.7	3286	*28	20	7.77	64	368	5.8	2	2	12	12
1980—New England NFL	12	306	175	57.2	2475	18	22	*8.09	30	112	3.7	1	1	6	4
1981—New England NFL	8	216	117	54.2	1859	7	16	*8.61	12	49	4.1	2	2	12	5
1982—New England NFL	6	122	66	54.1	930	7	4	7.62	9	42	4.7	1	1	6	2
1983—New England NFL	12	303	168	55.4	2411	15	12	7.96	23	108	4.7	2	2	12	4
1984—New England NFL	3	68	32	47.1	444	3	6	6.53	7	12	1.7	0	0	0	4
1985—New England NFL	7	156	85	54.5	1311	7	5	8.40	20	29	1.5	2	2	12	6
1986—New England NFL	4	102	62	60.8	976	9	2	9.57	9	23	2.6	1	1	6	2
1987—New England NFL	7	161	93	57.8	1183	10	9	7.35	20	37	1.9	2	2	12	8
1988—New England NFL	6	140	67	47.9	834	4	13	5.96	6	12	2.0	1	1	6	2
Pro Totals—14 Years	138	3240	1696	52.3	24574	169	191	7.58	432	2162	5.0	35	36	216	77

Quarterback Rating Points: 1975 (60.2), 1976 (60.8), 1977 (65.3), 1978 (63.3), 1979 (77.5), 1980 (73.1), 1981 (63.0), 1982 (84.2), 1983 (81.4), 1984 (46.4), 1985 (84.1), 1986 (113.8), 1987 (78.2), 1988 (37.6). Total—70.0.
Additional pro statistics: Recovered four fumbles and fumbled six times for minus 12 yards, 1975; recovered four fumbles and one touchdown and fumbled six times for minus 18 yards, 1976; recovered two fumbles and fumbled seven times for minus 41 yards, 1977; recovered two fumbles and fumbled nine times for minus 24 yards, 1978; recovered four fumbles and fumbled 12 times for minus 12 yards, 1979; recovered one fumble and fumbled four times for minus 10 yards, 1980; recovered two fumbles, caught two passes for 27 yards and fumbled five times for minus eight yards, 1981; recovered one fumble 1982, 1983, 1986 and 1988; caught one pass for minus eight yards, 1983; recovered two fumbles and fumbled four times for minus three yards, 1984; recovered one fumble and fumbled six times for minus 10 yards, 1985; recovered six fumbles and fumbled eight times for minus six yards, 1987.
Member of New England Patriots for AFC Championship Game following 1985 season; did not play.
Played in NFL Championship Game following 1985 season.

PAUL BLAKE GRUBER
Offensive Tackle—Tampa Bay Buccaneers
Born February 24, 1965, at Madison, Wis.
Height, 6.05. Weight, 290.
High School—Prairie du Sac, Wis., Sauk Prairie.
Received degree in communication arts from University of Wisconsin in 1988.

Named as offensive tackle on THE SPORTING NEWS College All-America Team, 1987.
Selected by Tampa Bay in 1st round (4th player selected) of 1988 NFL draft.
Signed by Tampa Bay Buccaneers, August 7, 1988.
Tampa Bay NFL, 1988.
Games: 1988 (16).
Pro statistics: Recovered two fumbles, 1988.

NEAL E. GUGGEMOS
Safety—Buffalo Bills
Born June 14, 1964, at Winsted, Minn.
Height, 6.01. Weight, 187.
High School—Winsted, Minn., Holy Trinity.
Attended College of St. Thomas.

Signed as free agent by Minnesota Vikings, May 2, 1986.
On injured reserve with broken thumb, August 18 through November 24, 1986; activated after clearing procedural waivers, November 26, 1986.
Released by Minnesota Vikings, August 24, 1988; signed as free agent by New York Giants, October 4, 1988.
Granted unconditional free agency, February 1, 1988; signed by Buffalo Bills, March 29, 1989.

Year Club		G.	No.	Yds.	Avg.	TD.
				KICKOFF RETURNS		
1986—Minnesota NFL		4		None		
1987—Minnesota NFL		12	36	808	22.4	0
1988—N.Y. Giants NFL		11	17	344	20.2	0
Pro Totals—3 Years		27	53	1152	21.7	0

Additional pro statistics: Intercepted one pass for 26 yards and fumbled four times, 1987; recovered three fumbles, 1987 and 1988; fumbled twice, 1988.
Played in NFC Championship Game following 1987 season.

KEVIN DALE GUIDRY
Cornerback—Denver Broncos
Born May 16, 1964, at Lake Charles, La.
Height, 6.00. Weight, 176.
High School—Lake Charles, La.
Attended Louisiana State University.

Selected by Denver in 3rd round (79th player selected) of 1988 NFL draft.
Signed by Denver Broncos, July 14, 1988.
Denver NFL, 1988.
Games: 1988 (14).

JAMES JOEL GUSTAFSON
(Jim)
Wide Receiver—Minnesota Vikings
Born March 16, 1961, at Minneapolis, Minn.
Height, 6.01. Weight, 178.
High School—Bloomington, Minn., Lincoln.
Received degree in finance from St. Thomas College in 1983.

Signed as free agent by Cincinnati Bengals, April 28, 1983.
Released by Cincinnati Bengals, August 29, 1983; signed as free agent by Minnesota Vikings, March 3, 1984.
Released by Minnesota Vikings, August 13, 1984; re-signed by Vikings, April 21, 1985.
On injured reserve with separated shoulder, August 20 through entire 1985 season.

Year Club		G.	P.C.	Yds.	Avg.	TD.
				PASS RECEIVING		
1986—Minnesota NFL		14	5	61	12.2	2
1987—Minnesota NFL		12	4	55	13.8	0
1988—Minnesota NFL		16	15	231	15.4	1
Pro Totals—3 Years		42	24	347	14.5	3

Additional pro statistics: Rushed once for minus two yards, 1987.
Played in NFC Championship Game following 1987 season.

BARRY DEAN HACKETT
(Dino)
Linebacker—Kansas City Chiefs
Born June 28, 1964, at Greensboro, N.C.
Height, 6.03. Weight, 225.
High School—Greensboro, N.C., Southern Guilford.
Received degree in criminal justice from Appalachian State University in 1986.
Brother of Joey Hackett, tight end with San Antonio Gunslingers,
Denver Broncos and Green Bay Packers, 1984 through 1988.

Selected by Kansas City in 2nd round (35th player selected) of 1986 NFL draft.
Signed by Kansas City Chiefs, July 23, 1986.
On injured reserve with knee injury, November 29 through remainder of 1988 season.
Kansas City NFL, 1986 through 1988.
Games: 1986 (16), 1987 (11), 1988 (13). Total—40.
Pro statistics: Intercepted one pass for no yards and recovered two fumbles, 1986; credited with a safety and recovered one fumble, 1988.
Named to play in Pro Bowl (NFL All-Star Game) following 1988 season; replaced due to injury by Matt Millen.

GARY ALLAN HADD
Defensive Tackle-Nose Guard—Phoenix Cardinals
Born October 19, 1965, at St. Paul, Minn.
Height, 6.04. Weight, 270.
High School—Burnsville, Minn.
Attended University of Minnesota.

Selected by Detroit in 8th round (196th player selected) of 1988 NFL draft.
Signed by Detroit Lions, July 15, 1988.
On injured reserve with broken foot, August 29 through November 16, 1988; activated after clearing procedural waivers, November 18, 1988.
Granted unconditional free agency, February 1, 1989; signed by Phoenix Cardinals, March 13, 1989.
Detroit NFL, 1988.
Games: 1988 (5).

MICHAEL HADDIX
Fullback—Green Bay Packers
Born December 27, 1961, at Tippah County, Miss.
Height, 6.02. Weight, 225.
High School—Walnut, Miss.
Attended Mississippi State University.
Cousin of Wayne Haddix, cornerback with New York Giants.

Selected by Denver in 2nd round (16th player selected) of 1983 USFL draft.
Selected by Philadelphia in 1st round (8th player selected) of 1983 NFL draft.
Signed by Philadelphia Eagles, May 13, 1983.
Granted unconditional free agency, February 1, 1989; signed by Green Bay Packers, February 17, 1989.

| | | ——RUSHING—— | | | | PASS RECEIVING | | | | —TOTAL— | | |
Year Club	G.	Att.	Yds.	Avg.	TD.	P.C.	Yds.	Avg.	TD.	TD.	Pts.	F.
1983—Philadelphia NFL	14	91	220	2.4	2	23	254	11.0	0	2	12	4
1984—Philadelphia NFL	14	48	130	2.7	1	33	231	7.0	0	1	6	2
1985—Philadelphia NFL	16	67	213	3.2	0	43	330	7.7	0	0	0	2
1986—Philadelphia NFL	16	79	276	3.5	0	26	150	5.8	0	0	0	1
1987—Philadelphia NFL	12	59	165	2.8	0	7	58	8.3	0	0	0	1
1988—Philadelphia NFL	16	57	185	3.2	0	12	82	6.8	0	0	0	1
Pro Totals—6 Years	88	401	1189	3.0	3	144	1105	7.7	0	3	18	11

Additional pro statistics: Returned three kickoffs for 51 yards, 1983; recovered one fumble, 1986 and 1988; returned two kickoffs for 16 yards, 1987.

WAYNE HADDIX
Cornerback—New York Giants
Born July 23, 1965, at Bolivar, Tenn.
Height, 6.01. Weight, 203.
High School—Middleton, Tenn.
Attended Liberty Baptist.
Cousin of Michael Haddix, fullback with Green Bay Packers.

Signed as free agent by New York Giants, May 11, 1987.
On injured reserve with knee injury, September 7 through November 6, 1987; activated, November 7, 1987.
On injured reserve with bruised heel, September 7 through November 11, 1988; activated, November 12, 1988.
New York Giants NFL, 1987 and 1988.
Games: 1987 (5), 1988 (7). Total—12.
Pro statistics: Returned six kickoffs for 123 yards and fumbled once, 1988.

RONALD ARTHUR HADLEY
(Ron)
Linebacker—San Francisco 49ers
Born November 9, 1963, at Caldwell, Ida.
Height, 6.02. Weight, 240.
High School—Boise, Ida.
Received degree in civil engineering from University of Washington in 1985.

Selected by New York Jets in 5th round (132nd player selected) of 1986 NFL draft.
Selected by Jacksonville in 12th round (85th player selected) of 1986 USFL draft.
Signed by New York Jets, July 20, 1986.
Released by New York Jets, August 25, 1986; signed as free agent by New York Giants, March 29, 1987.
Released by New York Giants, September 7, 1987; signed as free agent replacement player by San Francisco 49ers, September 24, 1987.
On injured reserve, October 20 through remainder of 1987 season.
On injured reserve with broken thumb, August 13 through November 30, 1988; activated after clearing procedural waivers, December 2, 1988.

San Francisco NFL, 1987 and 1988.
Games: 1987 (3), 1988 (3). Total—6.
Pro statistics: Recovered one fumble, 1987.
Played in NFC Championship Game following 1988 season.
Member of San Francisco 49ers for NFL Championship Game following 1988 season; inactive.

JOHN KEVIN HAGY
Safety—Buffalo Bills

Born December 9, 1965, at Okinawa, Japan.
Height, 5.11. Weight, 190.
High School—San Antonio, Tex., John Marshall.
Attended University of Texas.

Selected by Buffalo in 8th round (204th player selected) of 1988 NFL draft.
Signed by Buffalo Bills, June 17, 1988.
On injured reserve with knee injury, September 27 through remainder of 1988 season.
Buffalo NFL, 1988.
Games: 1988 (3).

MICHAEL HAIGHT
(Mike)

Name pronounced Hate.

Guard-Offensive Tackle—New York Jets

Born October 6, 1962, at Manchester, Ia.
Height, 6.04. Weight, 281.
High School—Dyersville, Ia., Beckman.
Attended University of Iowa.
Brother of Dave Haight, rookie nose tackle with San Francisco 49ers.

Selected by New York Jets in 1st round (22nd player selected) of 1986 NFL draft.
Selected by Orlando in 1st round (1st player selected) of 1986 USFL draft.
Signed by New York Jets, July 23, 1986.
On injured reserve with knee injury, September 2 through October 3, 1986; activated, October 4, 1986.
New York Jets NFL, 1986 through 1988.
Games: 1986 (2), 1987 (6), 1988 (14). Total—22.

CARL BLAKE HAIRSTON
Defensive End—Cleveland Browns

Born December 15, 1952, at Martinsville, Va.
Height, 6.02. Weight, 270.
High School—Martinsville, Va.
Received bachelor of arts degree in education from University of Maryland (Eastern Shore) in 1985.

Selected by Philadelphia in 7th round (191st player selected) of 1976 NFL draft.
Traded by Philadelphia Eagles to Cleveland Browns for 9th round pick in 1985 draft, February 9, 1984.
Crossed picket line during players' strike, October 7, 1987.
Granted unconditional free agency, February 1, 1989; re-signed by Browns, April 11, 1989.
Philadelphia NFL, 1976 through 1983; Cleveland NFL, 1984 through 1988.
Games: 1976 (14), 1977 (14), 1978 (16), 1979 (15), 1980 (16), 1981 (16), 1982 (9), 1983 (16), 1984 (16), 1985 (16), 1986 (16), 1987 (14), 1988 (14). Total—192.
Pro statistics: Recovered one fumble, 1977, 1980, 1981 and 1985 through 1987; intercepted one pass for no yards, 1980; recovered two fumbles for 24 yards, 1982; recovered two fumbles, 1983; ran 40 yards with lateral from interception, 1987.
Played in NFC Championship Game following 1980 season.
Played in AFC Championship Game following 1986 and 1987 seasons.
Played in NFL Championship Game following 1980 season.

ALI HAJI-SHEIKH

Name pronounced Hodgie-Sheek.

Placekicker—Detroit Lions

Born January 11, 1961, at Ann Arbor, Mich.
Height, 6.00. Weight, 172.
High School—Arlington, Tex.
Attended University of Michigan.

Established NFL record for most field goals, season (35), 1983.
Named to THE SPORTING NEWS NFL All-Star Team, 1983.
Selected by Michigan in 1983 USFL territorial draft.
Selected by New York Giants in 9th round (237th player selected) of 1983 NFL draft.
Signed by New York Giants, June 13, 1983.
On injured reserve with hamstring injury, September 17 through remainder of 1985 season.
On injured reserve with groin injury, September 1 through September 16, 1986.
Released by New York Giants, September 17, 1986; signed as free agent by Atlanta Falcons, November 12, 1986.
Released by Atlanta Falcons, August 25, 1987; signed as free agent by Washington Redskins, September 16, 1987.
Released by Washington Redskins, August 24, 1988; signed as free agent by Detroit Lions, May 26, 1989.

Year Club			—PLACE KICKING—			
Year Club	G.	XP.	XPM.	FG.	FGA.	Pts.
1983—N.Y. Giants NFL	16	22	1	*35	42	127
1984—N.Y. Giants NFL	16	32	3	17	33	83
1985—N.Y. Giants NFL	2	5	0	2	5	11
1986—Atlanta NFL	6	7	1	9	12	34
1987—Washington NFL	11	29	*3	13	19	68
Pro Totals—5 Years.......	51	95	8	76	111	323

Additional pro statistics: Had only attempted punt blocked, 1984.
Played in NFC Championship Game following 1987 season.
Played in NFL Championship Game following 1987 season.
Played in Pro Bowl (NFL All-Star Game) following 1983 season.

CHARLES LEWIS HALEY
Linebacker-Defensive End—San Francisco 49ers
Born January 6, 1964, at Gladys, Va.
Height, 6.05. Weight, 230.
High School—Naruna, Va., William Campbell.
Attended James Madison University.

Selected by San Francisco in 4th round (96th player selected) of 1986 NFL draft.
Signed by San Francisco 49ers, May 27, 1986.
San Francisco NFL, 1986 through 1988.
Games: 1986 (16), 1987 (12), 1988 (16). Total—44.
Pro statistics: Intercepted one pass for eight yards, recovered two fumbles for three yards and fumbled once, 1986; recovered two fumbles and credited with a safety, 1988.
Played in NFC Championship Game following 1988 season.
Played in NFL Championship Game following 1988 season.
Played in Pro Bowl (NFL All-Star Game) following 1988 season.

DARRYL HALEY
Offensive Tackle—Green Bay Packers
Born February 16, 1961, at Los Angeles, Calif.
Height, 6.05. Weight, 265.
High School—Los Angeles, Calif., Alin Leroy Locke.
Attended University of Utah.
Cousin of Darrell Jackson, pitcher with Minnesota Twins, 1978 through 1982.

Selected by New England in 2nd round (55th player selected) of 1982 NFL draft.
On non-football injury list with colitis, August 28 through entire 1985 season.
Traded by New England Patriots to Tampa Bay Buccaneers for conditional draft pick, July 27, 1987.
Released by Tampa Bay Buccaneers, August 5, 1987; signed as free agent by San Diego Chargers, August 11, 1987.
Released by San Diego Chargers, August 27, 1987; signed as free agent replacement player by Cleveland Browns, October 10, 1987.
Released by Cleveland Browns, September 7, 1988; signed as free agent by Green Bay Packers, September 13, 1988.
Active for 1 game with Cleveland Browns in 1988; did not play.
New England NFL, 1982 through 1984 and 1986; Cleveland NFL, 1987; Cleveland (0)-Green Bay (13) NFL, 1988.
Games: 1982 (9), 1983 (16), 1984 (16), 1986 (16), 1987 (9), 1988 (13). Total—79.
Played in AFC Championship Game following 1987 season.

DELTON DWAYNE HALL
Defensive Back—Pittsburgh Steelers
Born January 16, 1965, at Greensboro, N.C.
Height, 6.01. Weight, 205.
High School—Greensboro, N.C., Grimsley.
Attended Clemson University.

Selected by Pittsburgh in 2nd round (38th player selected) of 1987 NFL draft.
Signed by Pittsburgh Steelers, August 6, 1987.

Year Club		—INTERCEPTIONS—			
Year Club	G.	No.	Yds.	Avg.	TD.
1987—Pittsburgh NFL............	12	3	29	9.7	1
1988—Pittsburgh NFL............	14		None		
Pro Totals—2 Years...........	26	3	29	9.7	1

Additional pro statistics: Recovered two fumbles for 50 yards and a touchdown and fumbled once, 1987.

RONALD A. HALL
(Ron)
Tight End—Tampa Bay Buccaneers
Born March 15, 1964, at Fort Huachuca, Ariz.
Height, 6.04. Weight, 245.
High School—Escondido, Calif., San Pasqual.
Attended California State Poly University and University of Hawaii.

Selected by Tampa Bay in 4th round (87th player selected) of 1987 NFL draft.
Signed by Tampa Bay Buccaneers, July 18, 1987.

Year Club			PASS RECEIVING		
	G.	P.C.	Yds.	Avg.	TD.
1987—Tampa Bay NFL	11	16	169	10.6	1
1988—Tampa Bay NFL	15	39	555	14.2	0
Pro Totals—2 Years............	26	55	724	13.2	1

RONALD DAVID HALLSTROM
(Ron)
Guard—Green Bay Packers
Born June 11, 1959, at Holden, Mass.
Height, 6.06. Weight, 290.
High School—Moline, Ill.
Attended Iowa Central Junior College and University of Iowa.

Selected by Green Bay in 1st round (22nd player selected) of 1982 NFL draft.
On inactive list, September 12 and September 20, 1982.
Granted free agency, February 1, 1988; re-signed by Packers, August 22, 1988.
Green Bay NFL, 1982 through 1988.
Games: 1982 (6), 1983 (16), 1984 (16), 1985 (16), 1986 (16), 1987 (12), 1988 (16). Total—98.
Pro statistics: Recovered two fumbles for one yard, 1984; recovered one fumble, 1985 and 1987.

DEAN HAMEL
Defensive Tackle—Washington Redskins
Born July 7, 1961, at Detroit, Mich.
Height, 6.03. Weight, 280.
High School—Warren, Mich., Mott.
Attended Coffeyville Community College and University of Tulsa.

Selected by Washington in 12th round (309th player selected) in 1985 NFL draft.
Signed by Washington Redskins, June 14, 1985.
Washington NFL, 1985 through 1988.
Games: 1985 (16), 1986 (16), 1987 (12), 1988 (16). Total—60.
Pro statistics: Returned one kickoff for 14 yards, 1985.
Played in NFC Championship Game following 1986 and 1987 seasons.
Played in NFL Championship Game following 1987 season.

HARRY E. HAMILTON
Defensive Back—Tampa Bay Buccaneers
Born November 29, 1962, at Jamaica, N.Y.
Height, 6.00. Weight, 193.
High School—Nanticoke, Pa., John S. Fine.
Received bachelor of arts degree in pre-law and liberal arts from Penn State University in 1984.

Selected by Philadelphia in 1984 USFL territorial draft.
Selected by New York Jets in 7th round (176th player selected) of 1984 NFL draft.
Signed by New York Jets, May 29, 1984.
On injured reserve with knee injury, October 22 through remainder of 1984 season.
On injured reserve with shoulder injury, October 14 through November 15, 1985; activated, November 16, 1985.
Granted free agency, February 1, 1988; rights released, August 8, 1988.
Signed as free agent by Tampa Bay Buccaneers, August 11, 1988.

Year Club		INTERCEPTIONS			
	G.	No.	Yds.	Avg.	TD.
1984—N.Y. Jets NFL	8	None			
1985—N.Y. Jets NFL	11	2	14	7.0	0
1986—N.Y. Jets NFL	15	1	29	29.0	0
1987—N.Y. Jets NFL	12	3	25	8.3	0
1988—Tampa Bay NFL	16	6	123	20.5	0
Pro Totals—5 Years............	62	12	191	15.9	0

Additional pro statistics: Recovered one fumble, 1985 and 1987; recovered two fumbles for 28 yards, 1986; recovered two fumbles and fumbled once, 1988.

STEVEN HAMILTON
(Steve)
Defensive End-Defensive Tackle—Detroit Lions
Born September 28, 1961, at Niagara Falls, N.Y.
Height, 6.04. Weight, 270.
High Schools—Fork Union, Va., Fork Union Military Academy; and Williamsville, N.Y., East.
Attended East Carolina University.

Selected by Michigan in 4th round (79th player selected) of 1984 USFL draft.
Selected by Washington in 2nd round (55th player selected) of 1984 NFL draft.
Signed by Washington Redskins, June 5, 1984.
On injured reserve with fractured ankle, August 20 through entire 1984 season.
On injured reserve with shoulder injury, September 3, through November 1, 1985; activated, November 2, 1985.
On injured reserve with knee injury, December 6, 1986 through January 8, 1987; activated, January 9, 1987.
Granted unconditional free agency, February 1, 1989; signed by Detroit Lions, March 27, 1989.
Washington NFL, 1985 through 1988.
Games: 1985 (7), 1986 (12), 1987 (12), 1988 (15). Total—46.
Pro statistics: Recovered one fumble, 1987; returned one kickoff for seven yards, 1988.
Played in NFC Championship Game following 1986 and 1987 seasons.
Played in NFL Championship Game following 1987 season.

MICHAEL SCOTT HAMMERSTEIN
(Mike)
Defensive End—Cincinnati Bengals
Born March 29, 1963, at Kokomo, Ind.
Height, 6.04. Weight, 270.
High School—Wapakoneta, O.
Received degree from University of Michigan in 1987.

Selected by Baltimore in 1986 USFL territorial draft.
Selected by Cincinnati in 3rd round (65th player selected) of 1986 NFL draft.
Signed by Cincinnati Bengals, July 26, 1986.
On physically unable to perform/active with knee injury, July 11 through July 30, 1988; then transferred to physically unable to perform/reserve with knee injury, August 1 through entire 1988 season.
Cincinnati NFL, 1986 and 1987.
Games: 1986 (15), 1987 (11). Total—26.

STEVEN REED HAMMOND
(Steve)
Linebacker—New York Jets
Born February 5, 1960, at Hartford, Conn.
Height, 6.04. Weight, 225.
High School—Merrick, N.Y., Sanford H. Calhoun.
Attended Wake Forest University.

Selected by New Jersey in 23rd round (267th player selected) of 1983 USFL draft.
Signed by New Jersey Generals, January 19, 1983.
On developmental squad, April 2 through April 22, 1983; activated, April 23, 1983.
Traded with running back Dwight Sullivan by New Jersey Generals to Los Angeles Express for rights to quarterback Brian Sipe, December 27, 1983.
Traded by Los Angeles Express to Memphis Showboats for rights to linebacker Doug West, January 21, 1984.
Granted free agency when USFL suspended operations, August 7, 1986; signed as free agent by Buffalo Bills, May 11, 1987.
On injured reserve with ankle injury, September 8 through entire 1987 season.
Released by Buffalo Bills, August 23, 1988; signed as free agent by New York Jets, August 25, 1988.
Released by New York Jets, August 30, 1988; re-signed by Jets, October 19, 1988.
Released by New York Jets, November 9, 1988; re-signed by Jets, February 24, 1989.
On developmental squad for 3 games with New Jersey Generals in 1983.
New Jersey USFL, 1983; Memphis USFL, 1984 and 1985; New York Jets NFL, 1988.
Games: 1983 (15), 1984 (18), 1985 (17), 1988 (2). Total USFL—50. Total Pro—52.
Pro statistics: Credited with ½ sack for three yards and recovered one fumble for three yards, 1983; credited with one sack for 14 yards and recovered four fumbles, 1984; credited with 2½ sacks for 20½ yards and recovered two fumbles, 1985.

DANIEL OLIVER HAMPTON
(Dan)
Defensive End—Chicago Bears
Born September 19, 1957, at Oklahoma City, Okla.
Height, 6.05. Weight, 270.
High School—Jacksonville, Ark.
Attended University of Arkansas.

Named to THE SPORTING NEWS NFL All-Star Team, 1984.
Selected by Chicago in 1st round (4th player selected) of 1979 NFL draft.
On injured reserve with knee injury, November 16 through December 13, 1987; activated, December 14, 1987.
Chicago NFL, 1979 through 1988.
Games: 1979 (16), 1980 (16), 1981 (16), 1982 (9), 1983 (11), 1984 (15), 1985 (16), 1986 (16), 1987 (8), 1988 (16). Total—139.
Pro statistics: Recovered two fumbles, 1979 and 1986; recovered three fumbles, 1984 and 1985; credited with a safety, 1986.
Played in NFC Championship Game following 1984, 1985 and 1988 seasons.
Played in NFL Championship Game following 1985 season.
Played in Pro Bowl (NFL All-Star Game) following 1980, 1982, 1984 and 1985 seasons.

LORENZO TIMOTHY HAMPTON
Running Back—Miami Dolphins
Born March 12, 1962, at Lake Wales, Fla.
Height, 5.11. Weight, 208.
High School—Lake Wales, Fla.
Attended University of Florida.

Selected by Tampa Bay in 1985 USFL territorial draft.
USFL rights traded with rights to running back Greg Allen by Tampa Bay Bandits to Orlando Renegades for rights to running back Jeff McCall, December 21, 1984.
Selected by Miami in 1st round (27th player selected) of 1985 NFL draft.
Signed by Miami Dolphins, July 19, 1985.

Year Club	G.	Att.	Yds.	Avg.	TD.	P.C.	Yds.	Avg.	TD.	TD.	Pts.	F.
1985—Miami NFL	16	105	369	3.5	3	8	56	7.0	0	3	18	3
1986—Miami NFL	16	186	830	4.5	9	61	446	7.3	3	12	72	4
1987—Miami NFL	12	75	289	3.9	1	23	223	9.7	0	1	6	4
1988—Miami NFL	16	117	414	3.5	9	23	204	8.9	3	12	72	2
Pro Totals—4 Years	60	483	1902	3.9	22	115	929	8.1	6	28	168	13

Year Club		KICKOFF RETURNS			
	G.	No.	Yds.	Avg.	TD.
1985—Miami NFL	16	45	1020	22.7	0
1986—Miami NFL	16	9	182	20.2	0
1987—Miami NFL	12	16	304	19.0	0
1988—Miami NFL	16	9	216	24.0	0
Pro Totals—4 Years	60	79	1722	21.8	0

Additional pro statistics: Recovered one fumble, 1985 through 1988.
Played in AFC Championship Game following 1985 season.

JON THOMAS HAND
Defensive End—Indianapolis Colts

Born November 13, 1963, at Sylacauga, Ala.
Height, 6.07. Weight, 298.
High School—Sylacauga, Ala.
Attended University of Alabama.

Named as defensive lineman of THE SPORTING NEWS College All-America Team, 1985.
Selected by Birmingham in 1986 USFL territorial draft.
Selected by Indianapolis in 1st round (4th player selected) of 1986 NFL draft.
Signed by Indianapolis Colts, August 7, 1986.
Indianapolis NFL, 1986 through 1988.
Games: 1986 (15), 1987 (12), 1988 (15). Total—42.
Pro statistics: Intercepted one pass for eight yards and recovered two fumbles, 1986; recovered one fumble, 1988.

BRIAN HANSEN
Punter—New Orleans Saints

Born October 18, 1960, at Hawarden, Ia.
Height, 6.03. Weight, 209.
High School—Hawarden, Ia., West Sioux Community.
Attended Sioux Falls College.

Selected by New Orleans in 9th round (237th player selected) of 1984 NFL draft.

Year Club		——PUNTING——		
	G.	No.	Avg.	Blk.
1984—New Orleans NFL	16	69	43.8	1
1985—New Orleans NFL	16	89	42.3	0
1986—New Orleans NFL	16	81	42.7	1
1987—New Orleans NFL	12	52	40.5	0
1988—New Orleans NFL	16	72	40.5	1
Pro Totals—5 Years	76	363	42.0	3

Additional pro statistics: Rushed twice for minus 27 yards, 1984; attempted one pass with one completion for eight yards, 1985; rushed once for no yards, recovered one fumble and fumbled once, 1986; rushed twice for minus six yards, 1987; rushed once for 10 yards, 1988.
Played in Pro Bowl (NFL All-Star Game) following 1984 season.

JAMES JOSEPH HARBAUGH
(Jim)
Quarterback—Chicago Bears

Born December 23, 1963, at Toledo, O.
Height, 6.03. Weight, 202.
High Schools—Ann Arbor, Mich., Pioneer; and Palo Alto, Calif.
Received bachelor's degree in communications
from University of Michigan in 1987.
Son of Jack Harbaugh, head coach at Western Kentucky University; and cousin of Mike Gottfried, head coach at University of Pittsburgh.

Selected by Chicago in 1st round (26th player selected) of 1987 NFL draft.
Signed by Chicago Bears, August 3, 1987.

Year Club		————PASSING————							——RUSHING——				—TOTAL—		
	G.	Att.	Cmp.	Pct.	Gain	T.P.	P.I.	Avg.	Att.	Yds.	Avg.	TD.	TD.	Pts.	F.
1987—Chicago NFL	6	11	8	72.7	62	0	0	5.64	4	15	3.8	0	0	0	0
1988—Chicago NFL	10	97	47	48.5	514	0	2	5.30	19	110	5.8	1	1	6	1
Pro Totals—2 Years	16	108	55	50.9	576	0	2	5.33	23	125	5.4	1	1	6	1

Quarterback Rating Points: 1987 (86.2), 1988 (55.9). Total—58.8.
Additional pro statistics: Fumbled once for minus one yard, 1988.
Member of Chicago Bears for NFC Championship Game following 1988 season; did not play.

DAVID LYNN HARBOUR
(Dave)
Center—Washington Redskins

Born October 23, 1965, at Boston, Mass.
Height, 6.04. Weight, 265.
High School—St. Charles, Ill.
Received bachelor of science degree in communications from University of Illinois in 1988.

Signed as free agent by Washington Redskins, May 10, 1988.

Released by Washington Redskins, August 24, 1988; re-signed by Redskins, September 9, 1988.
Washington NFL, 1988.
Games: 1988 (15).
Pro statistics: Returned one kickoff for six yards, 1988.

MICHAEL HARDEN
(Mike)
Defensive Back—Denver Broncos
Born February 16, 1959, at Memphis, Tenn.
Height, 6.01. Weight, 190.
High School—Detroit, Mich., Central.
Received bachelor of arts degree in political science from University of Michigan in 1980.
Selected by Denver in 5th round (131st player selected) of 1980 NFL draft.
On injured reserve with knee injury, December 16 through remainder of 1982 season.
On injured reserve with broken arm, January 16, 1988 through remainder of 1987 season playoffs.

| | | -INTERCEPTIONS- | | | | —KICKOFF RET.— | | | | —TOTAL— | | |
Year	Club	G.	No.	Yds.	Avg.	TD.	No.	Yds.	Avg.	TD.	TD.	Pts.	F.
1980—Denver NFL		16		None			12	214	17.8	0	0	0	1
1981—Denver NFL		16	2	34	17.0	0	11	178	16.2	0	0	0	0
1982—Denver NFL		5	2	3	1.5	0		None			0	0	0
1983—Denver NFL		15	4	127	31.8	0	1	9	9.0	0	0	0	0
1984—Denver NFL		16	6	79	13.2	1	1	4	4.0	0	1	6	1
1985—Denver NFL		16	5	100	20.0	*1		None			1	6	0
1986—Denver NFL		16	6	179	29.8	2		None			3	18	0
1987—Denver NFL		12	4	85	21.3	0	2	11	5.5	0	0	0	0
1988—Denver NFL		16	4	36	9.0	0	1	9	9.0	0	0	0	1
Pro Totals—9 Years		128	33	643	19.5	4	28	425	15.2	0	5	30	3

Additional pro statistics: Returned two punts for 36 yards, 1981; recovered one fumble, 1981 and 1988; recovered one fumble for 13 yards, 1982; recovered three fumbles, 1983; recovered two fumbles, 1984; recovered two fumbles for five yards, 1985; returned one punt for 41 yards and a touchdown, 1986; recovered one fumble for 14 yards, 1987; returned two punts for 14 yards, 1988.
Played in AFC Championship Game following 1986 season.
Played in NFL Championship Game following 1986 season.

BRUCE ALAN HARDY
Tight End—Miami Dolphins
Born June 1, 1956, at Murray, Utah.
Height, 6.04. Weight, 232.
High School—Copperton, Utah, Bingham.
Received bachelor of science degree in business administration
from Arizona State University.
Brother of Bryan Hardy, pitcher in Chicago Cubs' organization, 1979, 1980 and 1982.
Selected by Miami in 9th round (247th player selected) of 1978 NFL draft.
On injured reserve with torn ligaments in ankle, September 17 through remainder of 1988 season.

| | | —PASS RECEIVING— | | | | | | —PASS RECEIVING— | | | |
Year	Club	G.	P.C.	Yds.	Avg.	TD.	Year	Club	G.	P.C.	Yds.	Avg.	TD.
1978—Miami NFL		16	4	32	8.0	2	1984—Miami NFL		16	28	257	9.2	5
1979—Miami NFL		16	30	386	12.9	3	1985—Miami NFL		16	39	409	10.5	4
1980—Miami NFL		16	19	159	8.4	2	1986—Miami NFL		16	54	430	8.0	5
1981—Miami NFL		16	15	174	11.6	0	1987—Miami NFL		12	28	292	10.4	2
1982—Miami NFL		9	12	66	5.5	2	1988—Miami NFL		2	4	46	11.5	0
1983—Miami NFL		15	22	202	9.2	0	Pro Totals—11 Years		150	255	2453	9.6	25

Additional pro statistics: Returned two kickoffs for 27 yards, 1978; attempted one pass with no completions, 1979; fumbled once, 1980, 1981 and 1985; rushed once for two yards, 1983; returned one kickoff for 11 yards, 1985; returned three kickoffs for 39 yards and fumbled twice, 1986; returned five kickoffs for 62 yards and fumbled once for minus seven yards, 1987; returned one kickoff for 17 yards, 1988.
Played in AFC Championship Game following 1982, 1984 and 1985 seasons.
Played in NFL Championship Game following 1982 and 1984 seasons.

KEVIN ANTHONY HARMON
Running Back—Seattle Seahawks
Born October 26, 1965, at Queens, N.Y.
Height, 6.00. Weight, 190.
High School—Queens, N.Y., Bayside.
Attended University of Iowa.
Brother of Ronnie Harmon, running back with Buffalo Bills; and Derrick Harmon,
running back with San Francisco 49ers, 1984 through 1986.
Selected by Seattle in 4th round (101st player selected) of 1988 NFL draft.
Signed by Seattle Seahawks, July 17, 1988.
Seattle NFL, 1988.
Games: 1988 (5).
Pro statistics: Rushed twice for 13 yards and returned three kickoffs for 62 yards, 1988.

RONNIE KEITH HARMON
Running Back—Buffalo Bills

Born May 7, 1964, at Queens, N. Y.
Height, 5.11. Weight, 200.
High School—Queens, N. Y., Bayside.
Attended University of Iowa.
Brother of Derrick Harmon, running back with San Francisco 49ers, 1984 through 1986;
and Kevin Harmon, running back with Seattle Seahawks.

Selected by Buffalo in 1st round (16th player selected) of 1986 NFL draft.
Signed by Buffalo Bills, August 13, 1986.
Granted roster exemption, August 13 through August 24, 1986; activated, August 25, 1986.

			—RUSHING—			PASS RECEIVING				—TOTAL—		
Year	Club	G.	Att.	Yds.	Avg.	TD.	P.C.	Yds.	Avg.	TD.	TD.	Pts.	F.
1986—Buffalo NFL		14	54	172	3.2	0	22	185	8.4	1	1	6	2
1987—Buffalo NFL		12	116	485	4.2	2	56	477	8.5	2	4	24	2
1988—Buffalo NFL		16	57	212	3.7	1	37	427	11.5	3	4	24	2
Pro Totals—3 Years		42	227	869	3.8	3	115	1089	9.5	6	9	54	6

			KICKOFF RETURNS			
Year	Club	G.	No.	Yds.	Avg.	TD.
1986—Buffalo NFL	14	18	321	17.8	0
1987—Buffalo NFL	12	1	30	30.0	0
1988—Buffalo NFL	16	11	249	22.6	0
Pro Totals—3 Years	42	30	600	20.0	0

Played in AFC Championship Game following 1988 season.

DWAYNE ANTHONY HARPER
Cornerback—Seattle Seahawks

Born March 29, 1966, at Orangeburg, S.C.
Height, 5.11. Weight, 165.
High School—Orangeburg, S.C., Orangeburg-Wilkinson.
Attended South Carolina State College.

Selected by Seattle in 11th round (299th player selected) of 1988 NFL draft.
Signed by Seattle Seahawks, July 16, 1988.
Seattle NFL, 1988.
Games: 1988 (16).
Pro statistics: Recovered one fumble, 1988.

GLENN HARPER
Punter—San Francisco 49ers

Born September 12, 1962, at Edmonton, Alta., Canada.
Height, 5.11. Weight, 173.
High School—Edmonton, Alta., Canada, St. Xavier.
Attended Washington State University.

Selected by Saskatchewan in 5th round (43rd player selected) of 1986 CFL draft.
Released by Saskatchewan Roughriders, April, 1986; signed as free agent by Calgary Stampeders, May, 1986.
Granted free agency, March 1, 1989; signed as free agent by San Francisco 49ers, April 27, 1989.

			—PUNTING—		
Year	Club	G.	No.	Avg.	Blk.
1986—Calgary CFL	18	156	41.6	....
1987—Calgary CFL	18	140	*42.8	....
1988—Calgary CFL	18	165	40.5	....
CFL Totals—3 Years	54	461	41.6	....

Additional CFL statistics: Credited with five singles, attempted two passes with two completions for 98 yards and a touchdown and fumbled seven times, 1986; credited with three singles, attempted four passes with three completions for 43 yards, rushed once for three yards, recovered one fumble and fumbled five times, 1987; credited with four singles, attempted one pass with no completions and fumbled twice, 1988.

MARK HARPER
Cornerback—Cleveland Browns

Born November 5, 1961, at Memphis, Tenn.
Height, 5.09. Weight, 185.
High School—Memphis, Tenn., Northside.
Received degree from Alcorn State University in 1982.

Signed by Chicago Blitz, July 31, 1983.
Franchise transferred to Arizona, September 30, 1983.
Traded by Arizona Wranglers to Pittsburgh Maulers for draft choice, February 13, 1984.
On developmental squad, February 24 through March 28, 1984; activated, March 29, 1984.
Franchise disbanded, October 25, 1984.
Selected by Jacksonville Bulls in USFL dispersal draft, December 6, 1984.
On developmental squad, April 25 through June 13, 1985; activated, June 14, 1985.
Released by Jacksonville Bulls, February 28, 1986; signed as free agent by Cleveland Browns, April 7, 1986.
On developmental squad for 5 games with Pittsburgh Maulers in 1984.
On developmental squad for 7 games with Jacksonville Bulls in 1985.

Year Club	G.	INTERCEPTIONS				-PUNT RETURNS-				-KICKOFF RET.-				-TOTAL-		
		No.	Yds.	Avg.	TD.	No.	Yds.	Avg.	TD.	No.	Yds.	Avg.	TD.	TD.	Pts.	F.
1984—Pittsburgh USFL..........	12		None			22	157	7.1	0	7	130	18.6	0	0	0	1
1985—Jacksonville USFL......	11	1	10	10.0	0		None				None			0	0	0
1986—Cleveland NFL.............	16	1	31	31.0	0		None				None			0	0	0
1987—Cleveland NFL.............	12	2	16	8.0	0		None				None			0	0	0
1988—Cleveland NFL.............	13	2	13	6.5	0		None				None			0	0	0
USFL Totals—2 Years....	23	1	10	10.0	0	22	157	7.1	0	7	130	18.6	0	0	0	1
NFL Totals—3 Years......	41	5	60	12.0	0	0	0	0.0	0	0	0	0.0	0	0	0	0
Pro Totals—5 Years.......	64	6	70	11.7	0	22	157	7.1	0	7	130	18.6	0	0	0	1

Additional USFL statistics: Recovered three fumbles, 1984.
Additional NFL statistics: Recovered two fumbles, 1986; recovered one fumble, 1988.
Played in AFC Championship Game following 1986 and 1987 seasons.

MICHAEL HARPER
Wide Receiver-Kick Returner—New York Jets
Born May 11, 1961, at Kansas City, Mo.
Height, 5.10. Weight, 180.
High School—Kansas City, Mo., Hickman Mills.
Received bachelor of arts degree in business from University of Southern California.

Selected by Los Angeles in 1984 USFL territorial draft.
Selected by Los Angeles Rams in 11th round (293rd player selected) of 1984 NFL draft.
Signed by Los Angeles Rams, July 9, 1984.
Released by Los Angeles Rams, August 27, 1984; re-signed by Rams, July 24, 1985.
Released by Los Angeles Rams, September 2, 1985; signed as free agent by New York Jets, April 23, 1986.
Released by New York Jets, September 6, 1987; re-signed as replacement player by Jets, September 24, 1987.
On injured reserve with knee injury, October 20 through remainder of 1987 season.
On injured reserve with knee injury, August 29 through October 16, 1988; activated, October 17, 1988.
Granted unconditional free agency, February 1, 1989; re-signed by Jets, May 19, 1989.

Year Club	G.	PASS RECEIVING				-KICKOFF RET.-				-TOTAL-		
		P.C.	Yds.	Avg.	TD.	No.	Yds.	Avg.	TD.	TD.	Pts.	F.
1986—N. Y. Jets NFL..........................	16		None			7	71	10.1	0	0	0	0
1987—N. Y. Jets NFL..........................	3	18	225	12.5	1	4	75	18.8	0	0	0	0
1988—N. Y. Jets NFL..........................	10		None			7	114	16.3	0	0	0	0
Pro Totals—3 Years...................	29	18	225	12.5	1	18	260	14.4	0	0	0	0

Additional pro statistics: Recovered three fumbles, 1986; returned four punts for 93 yards (23.3 avg.) and a touchdown, 1987.

ALFRED CARL HARRIS
(Al)
Linebacker-Defensive End—Philadelphia Eagles
Born December 31, 1956, at Bangor, Me.
Height, 6.05. Weight, 270.
High School—Wahiawa, Hawaii, Leilehua.
Received bachelor of science degree in communications from Arizona State University.
Cousin of Ricky Bell, running back with Tampa Bay Buccaneers and San Diego Chargers,
1977 through 1982; and Archie Bell, lead singer of Archie Bell and the Drells.

Named as defensive lineman on THE SPORTING NEWS College All-America Team, 1978.
Selected by Chicago in 1st round (9th player selected) of 1979 NFL draft.
On injured reserve with knee injury, August 28 through October 25, 1979; activated, October 26, 1979.
On inactive list, September 19, 1982.
Granted free agency, February 1, 1985.
On reserve/unsigned free agency list, August 20 through entire 1985 season.
Re-signed by Bears, July 16, 1986.
Granted unconditional free agency, February 1, 1989; signed by Philadelphia Eagles, March 30, 1989.
Chicago NFL, 1979 through 1984 and 1986 through 1988.
Games: 1979 (4), 1980 (16), 1981 (16), 1982 (8), 1983 (13), 1984 (16), 1986 (16), 1987 (12), 1988 (16). Total—117.
Pro statistics: Caught one pass for 18 yards, intercepted one pass for 44 yards and a touchdown and recovered three fumbles for five yards, 1981; recovered two fumbles, 1983; intercepted one pass for 34 yards, 1984; recovered three fumbles, 1988.
Played in NFC Championship Game following 1984 and 1988 seasons.

DARRYL LYNN HARRIS
Running Back—Green Bay Packers
Born February 20, 1966, at Jackson, Miss.
Height, 5.10. Weight, 178.
High School—Ponona, Calif., Garey.
Attended Arizona State University.

Signed as free agent by Minnesota Vikings, April 27, 1988.
Granted unconditional free agency, February 1, 1989; signed by Green Bay Packers, March 29, 1989.

Year Club	G.	——RUSHING——				PASS RECEIVING				-TOTAL-		
		Att.	Yds.	Avg.	TD.	P.C.	Yds.	Avg.	TD.	TD.	Pts.	F.
1988—Minnesota NFL..........................	14	34	151	4.4	1	6	30	5.0	0	1	6	1

Year Club	G.	KICKOFF RETURNS		
		No.	Yds.	Avg.TD.
1988—Minnesota NFL.............	14	39	833	21.4 0

LEONARD MILTON HARRIS
Wide Receiver-Kick Returner—Houston Oilers
Born November 27, 1960, at McKinney, Tex.
Height, 5.08. Weight, 162.
High School—McKinney, Tex.
Attended Austin College and Texas Tech University.
Cousin of Judson Flint, defensive back with Cleveland Browns and Buffalo Bills, 1980 through 1983.

Selected by Denver in 1984 USFL territorial draft.
Signed by Denver Gold, January 24, 1984.
Franchise merged with Jacksonville, February 19, 1986.
Granted free agency when USFL suspended operations, August 7, 1986; signed as free agent by Tampa Bay Buccaneers, August 12, 1986.
Granted roster exemption, August 12 through August 21, 1986; activated, August 22, 1986.
On injured reserve with hamstring injury, November 10 through remainder of 1986 season.
Released by Tampa Bay Buccaneers, June 11, 1987; signed as free agent by Washington Redskins, June 26, 1987.
Released by Washington Redskins, August 31, 1987; signed as free agent replacement player by Houston Oilers, September 23, 1987.
On injured reserve with knee injury, October 24 through remainder of 1987 season.

		PASS RECEIVING				—KICKOFF RET.—				—TOTAL—		
Year	Club	G.	P.C.	Yds.	Avg.	TD.	No.	Yds.	Avg.	TD.	TD.	Pts.	F.
1984—Denver USFL		18	35	657	18.8	4	43	1086	25.3	0	4	24	2
1985—Denver USFL		18	101	*1432	14.2	8	4	86	21.5	0	8	48	8
1986—Tampa Bay NFL		6	3	52	17.3	0	4	63	15.8	0	0	0	1
1987—Houston NFL		3	10	164	16.4	0	3	87	29.0	0	0	0	0
1988—Houston NFL		16	10	136	13.6	0	34	678	19.9	0	0	0	1
USFL Totals—2 Years		36	136	2089	15.4	12	47	1172	24.9	0	12	72	10
NFL Totals—3 Years		25	23	352	15.3	0	41	828	20.2	0	0	0	2
Pro Totals—5 Years		61	159	2441	15.4	12	88	2000	22.7	0	12	72	12

Additional USFL statistics: Returned one punt for four yards, 1984; recovered two fumbles, 1984 and 1985; returned seven punts for 35 yards and rushed six times for one yard, 1985.
Additional NFL statistics: Returned three punts for 16 yards, 1986; rushed once for 17 yards, 1987.

ODIE LAZAR HARRIS JR.
Defensive Back—Tampa Bay Buccaneers
Born April 1, 1966, at Bryan, Tex.
Height, 6.00. Weight, 190.
High School—Bryan, Tex.
Attended Sam Houston State University.
Cousin of Gerald Carter, wide receiver with New York Jets
and Tampa Bay Buccaneers, 1980 through 1987.

Signed as free agent by Tampa Bay Buccaneers, April 29, 1988.
Tampa Bay NFL, 1988.
Games: 1988 (16).
Pro statistics: Intercepted two passes for 26 yards and recovered one fumble, 1988.

TIMOTHY DAVID HARRIS
(Tim)
Linebacker—Green Bay Packers
Born September 10, 1964, at Birmingham, Ala.
Height, 6.05. Weight, 235.
High Schools—Birmingham, Ala., Woodlawn; and Memphis, Tenn., Catholic.
Attended Memphis State University.

Selected by Memphis in 1986 USFL territorial draft.
Selected by Green Bay in 4th round (84th player selected) of 1986 NFL draft.
Signed by Green Bay Packers, May 17, 1986.
Green Bay NFL, 1986 through 1988.
Games: 1986 (16), 1987 (12), 1988 (16). Total—44.
Pro statistics: Recovered one fumble, 1986; returned blocked punt 10 yards for a touchdown and credited with two safeties, 1988.

EMILE MICHAEL HARRY
Wide Receiver—Kansas City Chiefs
Born April 5, 1963, at Los Angeles, Calif.
Height, 5.11. Weight, 175.
High School—Fountain Valley, Calif.
Received bachelor of arts degree in political science
from Stanford University in 1985.

Selected by Oakland in 1985 USFL territorial draft.
Selected by Atlanta in 4th round (89th player selected) of 1985 NFL draft.
Signed by Atlanta Falcons, July 19, 1985.
Released by Atlanta Falcons, September 2, 1985; signed as free agent by Kansas City Chiefs, January 18, 1986.
Released by Kansas City Chiefs, September 1, 1986; re-signed by Chiefs, September 30, 1986.
On injured reserve with shoulder injury, August 14 through entire 1987 season.

| | | —PASS RECEIVING— | | | |
Year Club	G.	P.C.	Yds.	Avg.	TD.
1986—Kansas City NFL..........	12	9	211	23.4	1
1988—Kansas City NFL..........	16	26	362	13.9	1
Pro Totals—2 Years..............	28	35	573	16.4	2

Additional pro statistics: Returned six kickoffs for 115 yards, returned six punts for 20 yards and fumbled once, 1986.

ROY HART JR.
Nose Tackle—Seattle Seahawks
Born July 10, 1965, at Tifton, Ga.
Height, 6.01. Weight, 280.
High School—Tifton, Ga., Tift County.
Attended Northwest Mississippi Junior College and
University of South Carolina.

Selected by Seattle in 6th round (158th player selected) of 1988 NFL draft.
Signed by Seattle Seahawks, June 8, 1988.
On injured reserve with hamstring injury, September 9 through remainder of 1988 season.
Active for 1 game with Seattle Seahawks in 1988; did not play.
Seattle NFL, 1988.

JAMES M. HARVEY
Guard—Atlanta Falcons
Born November 27, 1965, at New Orleans, La.
Height, 6.03. Weight, 265.
High School—Columbia, Miss.
Attended Jackson State University.

Signed as free agent by Kansas City Chiefs, May 6, 1987.
Released by Kansas City Chiefs, August 3, 1987; re-signed as replacement player by Chiefs, September 25, 1987.
Released by Kansas City Chiefs, October 20, 1987; re-signed by Chiefs for 1988, November 6, 1987.
Released by Kansas City Chiefs, August 30, 1988; re-signed by Chiefs, September 28, 1988.
Released by Kansas City Chiefs, October 12, 1988; signed as free agent by Atlanta Falcons, February 24, 1989.
Kansas City NFL, 1987 and 1988.
Games: 1987 (3), 1988 (1). Total—4.

KENNETH RAY HARVEY
(Ken)
Linebacker—Phoenix Cardinals
Born May 6, 1965, at Austin, Tex.
Height, 6.02. Weight, 225.
High School—Austin, Tex., Lanier.
Attended Laney College and University of California at Berkeley.

Selected by Phoenix in 1st round (12th player selected) of 1988 NFL draft.
Signed by Phoenix Cardinals, June 17, 1988.
Phoenix NFL, 1988.
Games: 1988 (16).
Pro statistics: Credited with a safety, 1988.

JAMES EDWARD HASTY
Cornerback—New York Jets
Born May 23, 1965, at Seattle, Wash.
Height, 6.00. Weight, 200.
High School—Seattle, Wash., Franklin.
Attended Central Washington University and received degree in communications
from Washington State University in 1988.

Selected by New York Jets in 3rd round (74th player selected) of 1988 NFL draft.
Signed by New York Jets, July 12, 1988.

| | | —INTERCEPTIONS— | | | |
Year Club	G.	No.	Yds.	Avg.	TD.
1988—N.Y. Jets NFL	15	5	20	4.0	0

Additional pro statistics: Recovered three fumbles for 35 yards, 1988.

ROGER DALE HATCHER
(Known by middle name.)
Punter—Los Angeles Rams
Born April 5, 1963, at Cheraw, S.C.
Height, 6.02. Weight, 211.
High School—Cheraw, S.C.
Attended Clemson University.

Named to THE SPORTING NEWS NFL All-Star Team, 1985.
Led NFL in punting yards with 3,140 in 1987.
Led NFL in net punting average with 38.0 in 1985.
Selected by Orlando in 8th round (114th player selected) of 1985 USFL draft.
Selected by Los Angeles Rams in 3rd round (77th player selected) of 1985 NFL draft.

Signed by Los Angeles Rams, July 12, 1985.
Crossed picket line during players' strike, October 2, 1987.
On injured reserve with knee injury, August 31 through November 3, 1988; activated, November 4, 1988.

		—PUNTING—		
Year Club	G.	No.	Avg.	Blk.
1985—L.A. Rams NFL	16	87	43.2	1
1986—L.A. Rams NFL	16	97	38.6	1
1987—L.A. Rams NFL	15	76	41.3	1
1988—L.A. Rams NFL	7	36	39.6	0
Pro Totals—4 Years	54	296	40.8	3

Played in NFC Championship Game following 1985 season.
Played in Pro Bowl (NFL All-Star Game) following 1985 season.

JONATHAN MICHAEL HAYES
Tight End—Kansas City Chiefs
Born August 11, 1962, at South Fayette, Pa.
Height, 6.05. Weight, 240.
High School—McDonald, Pa., South Fayette.
Received degree in criminology from University of Iowa in 1986.
Brother of Jay Hayes, defensive end with Michigan Panthers,
San Antonio Gunslingers and Memphis Showboats, 1984 and 1985.

Selected by Kansas City in 2nd round (41st player selected) of 1985 NFL draft.
Signed by Kansas City Chiefs, June 19, 1985.

		—PASS RECEIVING—			
Year Club	G.	P.C.	Yds.	Avg.	TD.
1985—Kansas City NFL	16	5	39	7.8	1
1986—Kansas City NFL	16	8	69	8.6	0
1987—Kansas City NFL	12	21	272	13.0	2
1988—Kansas City NFL	16	22	233	10.6	1
Pro Totals—4 Years	60	56	613	10.9	4

Additional pro statistics: Returned one kickoff for no yards, 1985; recovered one fumble, 1987.

JAMES HAYNES
Linebacker—New Orleans Saints
Born August 9, 1960, at Tallulah, La.
Height, 6.02. Weight, 233.
High School—Tallulah, La.
Attended Coahoma Junior College and Mississippi Valley State University.

Signed as free agent by New Orleans Saints, June 20, 1984.
On injured reserve with rotator cuff injury, August 27 through October 4, 1984; activated after clearing procedural waivers, October 5, 1984.
On injured reserve with neck injury, August 22 through November 25, 1988; activated, November 26, 1988.
New Orleans NFL, 1984 through 1988.
Games: 1984 (10), 1985 (16), 1986 (16), 1987 (12), 1988 (4). Total—58.
Pro statistics: Caught one pass for eight yards and recovered two fumbles, 1985; intercepted one pass for 17 yards and a touchdown and recovered two fumbles for seven yards, 1986; recovered one fumble, 1988.

MARK HAYNES
Cornerback—Denver Broncos
Born November 6, 1958, at Kansas City, Kan.
Height, 5.11. Weight, 198.
High School—Kansas City, Kan., Harmon.
Attended University of Colorado.

Selected by New York Giants in 1st round (8th player selected) of 1980 NFL draft.
Left camp voluntarily and granted roster exemption, August 21 through August 27, 1984; returned and activated, August 28, 1984.
On injured reserve with knee injury, December 14 through remainder of 1984 season.
Granted free agency, February 1, 1985; re-signed by Giants, October 16, 1985.
Granted roster exemption, October 16 through October 27, 1985; activated, October 28, 1985.
On injured reserve with groin injury, December 14 through remainder of 1985 season.
Traded by New York Giants to Denver Broncos for 2nd and 6th round picks in 1986 draft and 2nd round pick in 1987 draft, April 29, 1986.
On injured reserve with thigh injury, September 2 through October 9, 1986; activated, October 10, 1986.

		—INTERCEPTIONS—						—INTERCEPTIONS—			
Year Club	G.	No.	Yds.	Avg.	TD.	Year Club	G.	No.	Yds.	Avg.	TD.
1980—N.Y. Giants NFL	15	1	6	6.0	0	1985—N.Y. Giants NFL	5		None		
1981—N.Y. Giants NFL	16	1	9	9.0	0	1986—Denver NFL	11		None		
1982—N.Y. Giants NFL	9	1	0	0.0	0	1987—Denver NFL	12	3	39	13.0	1
1983—N.Y. Giants NFL	15	3	18	6.0	0	1988—Denver NFL	15	1	0	0.0	0
1984—N.Y. Giants NFL	15	7	90	12.9	0	Pro Totals—9 Years	113	17	162	9.5	1

Additional pro statistics: Returned two kickoffs for 40 yards, 1980; recovered one fumble, 1981; recovered two fumbles for four yards, 1983; recovered two fumbles for 12 yards, 1984; recovered one fumble for 24 yards, 1987.
Played in AFC Championship Game following 1987 season.
Member of Denver Broncos for AFC Championship Game following 1986 season; did not play.
Played in NFL Championship Game following 1986 and 1987 seasons.

Played in Pro Bowl (NFL All-Star Game) following 1982 and 1983 seasons.
Named to play in Pro Bowl following 1984 season; replaced due to injury by Eric Wright.

MICHAEL DAVID HAYNES
Wide Receiver—Atlanta Falcons
Born December 24, 1965, at New Orleans, La.
Height, 6.00. Weight, 180.
High School—New Orleans, La., Joseph S. Clark.
Attended Eastern Arizona Junior College and Northern Arizona University.

Selected by Atlanta in 7th round (166th player selected) of 1988 NFL draft.
Signed by Atlanta Falcons, July 18, 1988.

		PASS RECEIVING				—KICKOFF RET.—				—TOTAL—		
Year	Club	G.	P.C.	Yds.	Avg.	TD.	No.	Yds.	Avg.	TD.	TD.	Pts.	F.
1988—Atlanta NFL		15	13	232	17.8	4	6	113	18.8	0	4	24	1

MICHAEL JAMES HAYNES
(Mike)
Cornerback—Los Angeles Raiders
Born July 1, 1953, at Denison, Tex.
Height, 6.02. Weight, 190.
High School—Los Angeles, Calif., John Marshall.
Attending Arizona State University.
Brother of Reggie Haynes, tight end with Washington Redskins, 1978.

Named to THE SPORTING NEWS NFL All-Star Team, 1984 and 1985.
Named to THE SPORTING NEWS AFC All-Star Team, 1976, 1978 and 1979.
Named by THE SPORTING NEWS as AFC Rookie of the Year, 1976.
Named as defensive back on THE SPORTING NEWS College All-America Team, 1975.
Selected by New England in 1st round (5th player selected) of 1976 NFL draft.
On did not report list, September 1 through September 22, 1980.
Granted roster exemption, September 23 through September 28, 1980; activated, September 29, 1980.
On injured reserve with collapsed lung, November 6 through December 10, 1981; activated, December 11, 1981.
Granted free agency, February 1, 1983; signed by Los Angeles Raiders, November 2, 1983 (Haynes had sued NFL when trade to Raiders was voided because it was after trading deadline).
Contract awarded to Raiders in settlement, November 10, 1983, with Patriots receiving 1st round pick in 1984 draft and 2nd round pick in 1985 draft and Raiders receiving 7th round pick in 1985 draft.
Granted roster exemption, November 10, 1983; activated, November 18, 1983.

			INTERCEPTIONS				PUNT RETURNS				—TOTAL—		
Year	Club	G.	No.	Yds.	Avg.	TD.	No.	Yds.	Avg.	TD.	TD.	Pts.	F.
1976—New England NFL		14	8	90	11.3	0	45	608	13.5	2	2	12	3
1977—New England NFL		14	5	54	10.8	0	24	200	8.3	0	0	0	4
1978—New England NFL		16	6	123	20.5	1	14	183	13.1	0	1	6	1
1979—New England NFL		16	3	66	22.0	0	5	16	3.2	0	0	0	1
1980—New England NFL		13	1	31	31.0	0	17	140	8.2	0	1	6	2
1981—New England NFL		8	1	3	3.0	0	6	12	2.0	0	0	0	0
1982—New England NFL		9	4	26	6.5	0		None			0	0	0
1983—Los Angeles Raiders NFL		5	1	0	0.0	0		None			0	0	0
1984—Los Angeles Raiders NFL		16	6	★220	36.7	1		None			1	6	0
1985—Los Angeles Raiders NFL		16	4	8	2.0	0	1	9	9.0	0	0	0	0
1986—Los Angeles Raiders NFL		13	2	28	14.0	0		None			0	0	0
1987—Los Angeles Raiders NFL		8	2	9	4.5	0		None			0	0	0
1988—Los Angeles Raiders NFL		16	3	30	10.0	0		None			0	0	0
Pro Totals—13 Years		164	46	688	15.0	2	112	1168	10.4	2	5	30	11

Additional pro statistics: Recovered three fumbles, 1976 and 1979; recovered two fumbles, 1977; returned blocked field goal 65 yards for a touchdown and recovered three fumbles for six yards, 1980; recovered one fumble, 1988.
Played in AFC Championship Game following 1983 season.
Played in NFL Championship Game following 1983 season.
Played in Pro Bowl (NFL All-Star Game) following 1976 through 1980, 1982, 1985 and 1986 seasons.
Member of Pro Bowl following 1984 season; did not play.

HERMAN WILLIE HEARD JR.
Running Back—Kansas City Chiefs
Born November 24, 1961, at Denver, Colo.
Height, 5.10. Weight, 190.
High School—Denver, Colo., South.
Attended Fort Lewis College and University of Southern Colorado.

Selected by Kansas City in 3rd round (61st player selected) of 1984 NFL draft.
On injured reserve with separated shoulder, August 30 through September 30, 1988; activated, October 1, 1988.

			——RUSHING——				PASS RECEIVING				—TOTAL—		
Year	Club	G.	Att.	Yds.	Avg.	TD.	P.C.	Yds.	Avg.	TD.	TD.	Pts.	F.
1984—Kansas City NFL		16	165	684	4.1	4	25	223	8.9	0	4	24	5
1985—Kansas City NFL		16	164	595	3.6	4	31	257	8.3	2	6	36	4
1986—Kansas City NFL		15	71	295	4.2	2	17	83	4.9	0	2	12	4
1987—Kansas City NFL		12	82	466	5.7	3	14	118	8.4	0	3	18	5
1988—Kansas City NFL		12	106	438	4.1	0	20	198	9.9	0	0	0	2
Pro Totals—5 Years		71	588	2478	4.2	13	107	879	8.2	2	15	90	20

Additional pro statistics: Recovered three fumbles, 1984; recovered one fumble, 1985; recovered two fumbles, 1987.

BOBBY JOSEPH HEBERT JR.

Name pronounced A-bear.

Quarterback—New Orleans Saints

Born August 19, 1960, at Baton Rouge, La.
Height, 6.04. Weight, 215.
High School—Galliano, La., South Lafourche.
Received degree in business administration from Northwestern Louisiana State University in 1983.

Named THE SPORTING NEWS USFL Player of the Year, 1983.
Named as quarterback on THE SPORTING NEWS USFL All-Star Team, 1983.
Selected by Michigan in 3rd round (34th player selected) of 1983 USFL draft.
Signed by Michigan Panthers, January 22, 1983.
On reserve/did not report, January 23 through February 15, 1984; activated, February 16, 1984.
Protected in merger of Michigan Panthers and Oakland Invaders, December 6, 1984.
Granted free agency, July 15, 1985; signed by New Orleans Saints, August 7, 1985.
On injured reserve with broken foot, September 22 through November 7, 1986; activated, November 8, 1986.

Year Club	G.	PASSING							RUSHING				TOTAL		
		Att.	Cmp.	Pct.	Gain	T.P.	P.I.	Avg.	Att.	Yds.	Avg.	TD.	TD.	Pts.	F.
1983—Michigan USFL	18	451	257	57.0	3568	*27	17	*7.91	28	35	1.3	3	3	†20	8
1984—Michigan USFL	17	500	272	54.4	3758	24	22	7.52	18	76	4.2	1	1	6	8
1985—Oakland USFL	18	456	244	53.5	3811	30	19	8.36	12	31	2.6	1	1	6	5
1985—New Orleans NFL	6	181	97	53.6	1208	5	4	6.67	12	26	2.2	0	1	6	1
1986—New Orleans NFL	5	79	41	51.9	498	2	8	6.30	5	14	2.8	0	0	0	3
1987—New Orleans NFL	12	294	164	55.8	2119	15	9	7.21	13	95	7.3	0	0	0	4
1988—New Orleans NFL	16	478	280	58.6	3156	20	15	6.60	37	79	2.1	0	0	0	9
USFL Totals—3 Years	53	1407	773	54.9	11137	81	58	7.92	58	142	2.4	5	5	32	21
NFL Totals—4 Years	39	1032	582	56.4	6981	42	36	6.76	67	214	3.2	0	1	6	17
Pro Totals—7 Years	92	2439	1355	55.6	18118	123	94	7.43	125	356	2.8	5	6	38	38

†Includes one 2-point conversion.
USFL Quarterback Rating Points: 1983 (86.7), 1984 (76.4), 1985 (86.1). Total—83.1.
NFL Quarterback Rating Points: 1985 (74.6), 1986 (40.5), 1987 (82.9), 1988 (79.3). Total—76.3.
Additional USFL statistics: Recovered two fumbles, 1983; recovered three fumbles, 1984; recovered three fumbles and fumbled five times for minus two yards, 1985.
Additional NFL statistics: Caught one pass for seven yards and a touchdown, 1985; recovered one fumble, 1985 and 1988; caught one pass for one yard, 1986; recovered two fumbles, 1987; caught two passes for no yards, 1988.
Played in USFL Championship Game following 1983 and 1985 seasons.

JOHNNY LYNDELL HECTOR

Running Back—New York Jets

Born November 26, 1960, at Lafayette, La.
Height, 5.11. Weight, 202.
High School—New Iberia, La.
Attended Texas A&M University.

Selected by Chicago in 2nd round (19th player selected) of 1983 USFL draft.
Selected by New York Jets in 2nd round (51st player selected) of 1983 NFL draft.
Signed by New York Jets, June 9, 1983.

Year Club	G.	RUSHING				PASS RECEIVING				TOTAL		
		Att.	Yds.	Avg.	TD.	P.C.	Yds.	Avg.	TD.	TD.	Pts.	F.
1983—New York Jets NFL	10	16	85	5.3	0	5	61	12.2	1	1	6	2
1984—New York Jets NFL	13	124	531	4.3	1	20	182	9.1	0	1	6	2
1985—New York Jets NFL	14	145	572	3.9	6	17	164	9.6	0	6	36	2
1986—New York Jets NFL	13	164	605	3.7	8	33	302	9.2	0	8	48	2
1987—New York Jets NFL	11	111	435	3.9	*11	32	249	7.8	0	11	66	2
1988—New York Jets NFL	16	137	561	4.1	10	26	237	9.1	0	10	60	3
Pro Totals—6 Years	77	697	2789	4.0	36	133	1195	9.0	1	37	222	13

		KICKOFF RETURNS			
Year Club	G.	No.	Yds.	Avg.	TD.
1983—New York Jets NFL	10	14	274	19.6	0
1984—New York Jets NFL	13	None			
1985—New York Jets NFL	14	11	274	24.9	0
1986—New York Jets NFL	13	None			
1987—New York Jets NFL	11	None			
1988—New York Jets NFL	16	None			
Pro Totals—6 Years	77	25	548	21.9	0

Additional pro statistics: Recovered one fumble, 1985, 1987 and 1988; attempted one pass with no completions, 1988.

RONALD JEFFERY HELLER

(Ron)

Tight End—Atlanta Falcons

Born September 18, 1963, at Gross Valley, Calif.
Height, 6.03. Weight, 235.
High School—Clark Fork, Ida.
Attended Oregon State University.

Signed as free agent by Dallas Cowboys, May 1, 1986.
Released by Dallas Cowboys, July 24, 1986; signed as free agent by San Francisco 49ers, July 29, 1986.
On injured reserve with neck and head injuries, September 1 through entire 1986 season.
Crossed picket line during players' strike, October 7, 1987.

Granted unconditional free agency, February 1, 1989; signed by Atlanta Falcons, March 8, 1989.

		—PASS RECEIVING—				
Year Club	G.	P.C.	Yds.	Avg.	TD.
1987—San Francisco NFL	13	12	165	13.8	3
1988—San Francisco NFL	16	14	140	10.0	0
Pro Totals—2 Years............	29	26	305	11.7	3

Additional pro statistics: Fumbled once, 1987.
Played in NFC Championship Game following 1988 season.
Played in NFL Championship Game following 1988 season.

RONALD RAMON HELLER
(Ron)
Offensive Tackle—Philadelphia Eagles
Born August 25, 1962, at East Meadow, N.Y.
Height, 6.06. Weight, 280.
High School—Farming Dale, N.Y.
Received bachelor of science degree in administration of justice
from Penn State University in 1984.

Selected by Philadelphia in 1984 USFL territorial draft.
Selected by Tampa Bay in 4th round (112th player selected) of 1984 NFL draft.
Signed by Tampa Bay Buccaneers, June 6, 1984.
Granted free agency, February 1, 1988; re-signed by Buccaneers and traded to Seattle Seahawks for defensive end Randy Edwards and 6th round pick in 1989 draft, May 4, 1988.
Traded by Seattle Seahawks to Philadelphia Eagles for 4th round pick in 1989 draft, August 22, 1988.
Tampa Bay NFL, 1984 through 1987; Philadelphia NFL, 1988.
Games: 1984 (14), 1985 (16), 1986 (16), 1987 (12), 1988 (15). Total—73.
Pro statistics: Caught one pass for one yard and a touchdown and recovered one fumble, 1986; recovered two fumbles, 1988.

DALE ROBERT HELLESTRAE
Name pronounced Hellus-TRAY.
Offensive Tackle—Los Angeles Raiders
Born July 11, 1962, at Phoenix, Ariz.
Height, 6.05. Weight, 280.
High School—Scottsdale, Ariz., Saguaro.
Attended Southern Methodist University.

Selected by Houston in 1985 USFL territorial draft.
Selected by Buffalo in 4th round (112th player selected) of 1985 NFL draft.
Signed by Buffalo Bills, July 19, 1985.
On injured reserve with broken thumb, October 4 through remainder of 1985 season.
On injured reserve with broken wrist, September 17 through November 14, 1986; activated, November 15, 1986.
On injured reserve with hip injury, September 1 through entire 1987 season.
Granted unconditional free agency, February 1, 1989; signed by Los Angeles Raiders, February 24, 1989.
Buffalo NFL, 1985, 1986 and 1988.
Games: 1985 (4), 1986 (8), 1988 (16). Total—28.
Pro statistics: Fumbled once for minus 14 yards, 1986.
Played in AFC Championship Game following 1988 season.

BARRY BRET HELTON
Punter—San Francisco 49ers
Born January 2, 1965, at Colorado Springs, Colo.
Height 6.03. Weight, 205.
High School—Simla, Colo.
Received bachelor of science degree in business finance from
University of Colorado in 1988.

Named as punter on THE SPORTING NEWS College All-America Team, 1986.
Selected by San Francisco in 4th round (102nd player selected) of 1988 NFL draft.
Signed by San Francisco 49ers, July 16, 1988.
Released by San Francisco 49ers, August 30, 1988; re-signed by 49ers, September 6, 1988.

		—PUNTING—		
Year Club	G.	No.	Avg.	Blk.
1988—San Francisco NFL	15	78	39.3	1

Additional pro statistics: Rushed once for no yards and recovered one fumble, 1988.
Played in NFC Championship Game following 1988 season.
Played in NFL Championship Game following 1988 season.

WYMON HENDERSON
Defensive Back—Denver Broncos
Born December 15, 1961, at North Miami Beach, Fla.
Height, 5.10. Weight, 186.
High School—Miami Beach, Fla., North.
Attended Hancock Junior College and University of Nevada at Las Vegas.

Selected by Los Angeles in 8th round (96th player selected) of 1983 USFL draft.
Signed by Los Angeles Express, January 20, 1983.
Granted free agency, August 1, 1985; signed by San Francisco 49ers, August 7, 1985.
Released by San Francisco 49ers, August 20, 1985; re-signed by 49ers, February 3, 1986.

On injured reserve with foot injury, August 19 through entire 1986 season.
Granted free agency with option not exercised, February 1, 1987; signed by Minnesota Vikings, April 20, 1987.
Granted unconditional free agency, February 1, 1989; signed by Denver Broncos, March 13, 1989.

			—INTERCEPTIONS—			
Year Club	G.	No.	Yds.	Avg.	TD.	
1983—Los Angeles USFL........	16		None			
1984—Los Angeles USFL........	18	3	23	7.7	0	
1985—Los Angeles USFL........	18	4	44	11.0	0	
1987—Minnesota NFL............	12	4	33	8.3	0	
1988—Minnesota NFL............	16	1	13	13.0	0	
USFL Totals—3 Years........	52	7	67	9.6	0	
NFL Totals—2 Years..........	28	5	46	9.2	0	
Pro Totals—5 Years...........	80	12	113	9.4	0	

Additional USFL statistics: Recovered one fumble for 30 yards and one touchdown, 1983; returned one punt for three yards and recovered two fumbles, 1984; recovered one fumble and fumbled three times, 1985.
Additional NFL statistics: Recovered two fumbles, 1988.
Played in NFC Championship Game following 1987 season.

MANUEL HENDRIX
(Manny)
Cornerback—Dallas Cowboys
Born October 20, 1964, at Phoenix, Ariz.
Height, 5.10. Weight, 178.
High School—Phoenix, Ariz., South Mountain.
Attended University of Utah.

Signed as free agent by Dallas Cowboys, May 1, 1986.
Released by Dallas Cowboys, August 26, 1986; re-signed by Cowboys, September 23, 1986.
Dallas NFL, 1986 through 1988.
Games: 1986 (13), 1987 (12), 1988 (16). Total—41.
Pro statistics: Recovered one fumble, 1986 and 1987; intercepted one pass for no yards, 1988.

OSCAR ANTHONY HENTON
(Known by middle name.)
Linebacker—Seattle Seahawks
Born July 27, 1963, at Bessemer, Ala.
Height, 6.01. Weight, 234.
High School—Bessemer, Ala., Jess Lanier.
Attended Troy State University.

Selected by Birmingham in 1986 USFL territorial draft.
Selected by Pittsburgh in 9th round (234th player selected) of 1986 NFL draft.
Signed by Pittsburgh Steelers, July 14, 1986.
On physically unable to perform/reserve with knee injury, September 1 through entire 1987 season.
Granted unconditional free agency, February 1, 1989; signed by Seattle Seahawks, April 1, 1989.
Pittsburgh NFL, 1986 and 1988.
Games: 1986 (16), 1988 (16). Total—32.
Pro statistics: Recovered one fumble, 1986.

MARK DONALD HERRMANN
Quarterback—Los Angeles Rams
Born January 9, 1959, at Cincinnati, O.
Height, 6.04. Weight, 186.
High School—Carmel, Ind.
Received bachelor of science degree in business
management from Purdue University in 1981.

Selected by Denver in 4th round (98th player selected) of 1981 NFL draft.
On inactive list, September 19, 1982.
Traded with rights to offensive tackle Chris Hinton and 1st round pick in 1984 draft by Denver Broncos to Baltimore Colts for rights to quarterback John Elway, May 2, 1983.
On injured reserve with broken collarbone, August 30 through October 27, 1983; activated, October 28, 1983.
Franchise transferred to Indianapolis, March 31, 1984.
On injured reserve with broken thumb, August 28 through October 19, 1984; activated, October 20, 1984.
Granted free agency, February 1, 1985; re-signed by Colts and traded to San Diego Chargers for 10th round pick in 1986 draft, March 27, 1985.
Traded by San Diego Chargers to Indianapolis Colts for future considerations, April 27, 1988.
Released by Indianapolis Colts, August 23, 1988; signed as free agent by Los Angeles Rams, August 31, 1988.
Active for 16 games with Denver Broncos in 1981; did not play.

		—PASSING—							—RUSHING—				—TOTAL—		
Year Club	G.	Att.	Cmp.	Pct.	Gain	T.P.	P.I.	Avg.	Att.	Yds.	Avg.	TD.	TD.	Pts.	F.
1982—Denver NFL......................	2	60	32	53.3	421	1	4	7.02	3	7	2.3	1	1	6	1
1983—Baltimore NFL.................	2	36	18	50.0	256	0	3	7.11	1	0	0.0	0	0	0	2
1984—Indianapolis NFL.............	3	56	29	51.8	352	1	6	6.29		None			0	0	0
1985—San Diego NFL.................	9	201	132	65.7	1537	10	10	7.65	18	—8	—0.4	0	0	0	8
1986—San Diego NFL.................	6	97	51	52.6	627	2	3	6.46	2	6	3.0	0	0	0	2
1987—San Diego NFL.................	3	57	37	64.9	405	1	5	7.11	4	—1	—0.3	0	0	0	1
1988—L.A. Rams NFL.................	6	5	4	80.0	38	0	0	7.60	1	—1	—1.0	0	0	0	0
Pro Totals—8 Years...........	31	512	303	59.2	3636	15	31	7.10	29	3	0.1	1	1	6	14

Quarterback Rating Points: 1982 (53.5), 1983 (38.7), 1984 (37.8), 1985 (84.5), 1986 (66.8), 1987 (55.1), 1988 (98.3). Total—65.3.

Additional pro statistics: Recovered one fumble, 1983; recovered two fumbles and fumbled eight times for minus 26 yards, 1985; recovered one fumble and fumbled once for minus five yards, 1987.

JEFF SYLVESTER HERROD
Linebacker—Indianapolis Colts
Born July 29, 1966, at Birmingham, Ala.
Height, 6.00. Weight, 243.
High School—Birmingham, Ala., Banks.
Attended University of Mississippi.

Selected by Indianapolis in 9th round (243rd player selected) of 1988 NFL draft.
Signed by Indianapolis Colts, July 13, 1988.
Indianapolis NFL, 1988.
Games: 1988 (16).

JESSIE LEE HESTER
Wide Receiver—Atlanta Falcons
Born January 21, 1963, at Belle Glade, Fla.
Height, 5.11. Weight, 170.
High School—Belle Glade, Fla., Central.
Received degree in social science from Florida State University.

Selected by Tampa Bay in 1985 USFL territorial draft.
Selected by Los Angeles Raiders in 1st round (23rd player selected) of 1985 NFL draft.
Signed by Los Angeles Raiders, July 23, 1985.
Traded by Los Angeles Raiders to Atlanta Falcons for 5th round pick in 1989 draft, August 22, 1988.

		—PASS RECEIVING—				
Year	Club	G.	P.C.	Yds.	Avg.	TD.
1985—L.A. Raiders NFL		16	32	665	20.8	4
1986—L.A. Raiders NFL		13	23	632	27.5	6
1987—L.A. Raiders NFL		10	1	30	30.0	0
1988—Atlanta NFL		16	12	176	14.7	0
Pro Totals—4 Years		55	68	1503	22.1	10

Additional pro statistics: Rushed once for 13 yards and a touchdown and recovered one fumble, 1985; rushed once for three yards and fumbled once, 1988.

CRAIG W. HEYWARD
Fullback—New Orleans Saints
Born September 26, 1966, at Passaic, N.J.
Height, 5.11. Weight, 251.
High School—Passaic, N.J.
Attended University of Pittsburgh.

Named as running back on THE SPORTING NEWS College All-America Team, 1987.
Selected by New Orleans in 1st round (24th player selected) of 1988 NFL draft.
Signed by New Orleans Saints, July 8, 1988.

		—RUSHING—				PASS RECEIVING				—TOTAL—		
Year	Club	G.	Att.	Yds.	Avg.	TD.	P.C.	Yds.	Avg.	TD.	TD.	Pts.	F.
1988—New Orleans NFL		11	74	355	4.8	1	13	105	8.1	0	1	6	0

Additional pro statistics: Recovered one fumble, 1988.

CLIFFORD WENDELL HICKS JR.
(Cliff)
Cornerback—Los Angeles Rams
Born August 18, 1964, at San Diego, Calif.
Height, 5.10. Weight, 188.
High School—San Diego, Calif., Kearny.
Attended San Diego Mesa College and University of Oregon.

Selected by Los Angeles Rams in 3rd round (74th player selected) of 1987 NFL draft.
Signed by Los Angeles Rams, July 23, 1987.
On injured reserve with broken leg, August 29 through November 3, 1988; activated, November 4, 1988.

		—PUNT RETURNS—				
Year	Club	G.	No.	Yds.	Avg.	TD.
1987—L.A. Rams NFL		11	13	110	8.5	0
1988—L.A. Rams NFL		7	25	144	5.8	0
Pro Totals—2 Years		18	38	254	6.7	0

Additional pro statistics: Intercepted one pass for nine yards and returned four kickoffs for 119 yards (29.8 avg.), 1987; fumbled once, 1987 and 1988.

—DID YOU KNOW—

That the Miami Dolphins (1,205 yards) and Detroit Lions (1,243) combined for 262 fewer rushing yards in 1988 than the Cincinnati Bengals, who led the NFL with 2,710?

ALEX HIGDON
Tight End—Atlanta Falcons
Born September 9, 1966, at Cincinnati, O.
Height, 6.05. Weight, 247.
High School—Cincinnati, O., Princeton.
Attended Ohio State University.

Selected by Atlanta in 3rd round (56th player selected) of 1988 NFL draft.
Signed by Atlanta Falcons, July 24, 1988.
On injured reserve with knee injury, September 21 through remainder of 1988 season.

		—PASS RECEIVING—			
Year	Club	G.	P.C.	Yds.	Avg. TD.
1988—Atlanta NFL		3	3	60	20.0 2

MARK DEYON HIGGS
Running Back—Philadelphia Eagles
Born April 11, 1966, at Chicago, Ill.
Height, 5.07. Weight, 196.
High School—Owensboro, Ky.
Attended University of Kentucky.

Selected by Dallas in 8th round (205th player selected) of 1988 NFL draft.
Signed by Dallas Cowboys, July 6, 1988.
Granted unconditional free agency, February 1, 1989; signed by Philadelphia Eagles, March 2, 1989.
Dallas NFL, 1988.
Games: 1988 (5).
Pro statistics: Returned two kickoffs for 31 yards, 1988.

ALONZO WALTER HIGHSMITH
Fullback—Houston Oilers
Born February 26, 1965, at Bartow, Fla.
Height 6.01. Weight, 235.
High School—Miami, Fla., Christopher Columbus.
Received bachelor of science degree in business management from University of Miami (Fla.) in 1987.
Son of Walter Highsmith, offensive lineman with Charleston of Continental Football League,
1965 through 1967; Denver Broncos and Houston Oilers, 1968, 1969 and 1972; with
Montreal Alouettes; and currently head coach at Texas Southern University;
and cousin of Fred Highsmith, rookie running back with Pittsburgh Steelers.

Selected by Houston in 1st round (3rd player selected) of 1987 NFL draft.
Placed on reserve/unsigned list, August 31 through October 27, 1987.
Signed by Houston Oilers, October 28, 1987.
Granted roster exemption, October 28 through November 6, 1987; activated, November 7, 1987.

		——RUSHING——				PASS RECEIVING				—TOTAL—		
Year	Club	G.	Att.	Yds.	Avg. TD.	P.C.	Yds.	Avg. TD.		TD.	Pts.	F.
1987—Houston NFL		8	29	106	3.7 1	4	55	13.8 1		2	12	2
1988—Houston NFL		16	94	466	5.0 2	12	131	10.9 0		2	12	7
Pro Totals—2 Years		24	123	572	4.7 3	16	186	11.6 1		4	24	9

Additional pro statistics: Recovered two fumbles, 1988.

JAY WALTER HILGENBERG
Center—Chicago Bears
Born March 21, 1960, at Iowa City, Ia.
Height, 6.03. Weight, 260.
High School—Iowa City, Ia., City.
Attended University of Iowa.
Brother of Joel Hilgenberg, center-guard with New Orleans Saints; and nephew of Wally Hilgenberg,
linebacker with Detroit Lions and Minnesota Vikings, 1964 through 1979.

Named to THE SPORTING NEWS NFL All-Star Team, 1987 and 1988.
Signed as free agent by Chicago Bears, May 8, 1981.
Chicago NFL, 1981 through 1988.
Games: 1981 (16), 1982 (9), 1983 (16), 1984 (16), 1985 (16), 1986 (16), 1987 (12), 1988 (16). Total—117.
Pro statistics: Recovered one fumble for five yards, 1982; recovered one fumble, 1983, 1985 and 1988; fumbled once
for minus 28 yards, 1986; fumbled once for minus 18 yards, 1988.
Played in NFC Championship Game following 1984, 1985 and 1988 seasons.
Played in NFL Championship Game following 1985 season.
Played in Pro Bowl (NFL All-Star Game) following 1985 through 1988 seasons.

JOEL HILGENBERG
Center-Guard—New Orleans Saints
Born July 10, 1962, at Iowa City, Ia.
Height, 6.02. Weight, 253.
High School—Iowa City, Ia., City.
Attended University of Iowa.
Brother of Jay Hilgenberg, center with Chicago Bears; and nephew of Wally Hilgenberg,
linebacker with Detroit Lions and Minnesota Vikings, 1964 through 1979.

Selected by Washington in 6th round (109th player selected) of 1984 USFL draft.
USFL rights traded with 1st round pick in 1985 draft by Washington Federals to Birmingham Stallions for quarterback Reggie Collier, January 12, 1984.

Selected by New Orleans in 4th round (97th player selected) of 1984 NFL draft.
Signed by New Orleans Saints, July 24, 1984.
On injured reserve with dislocated elbow, October 30 through December 6, 1984; activated, December 7, 1984.
New Orleans NFL, 1984 through 1988.
Games: 1984 (10), 1985 (15), 1986 (16), 1987 (12), 1988 (16). Total—69.
Pro statistics: Recovered one fumble, 1985 and 1987.

RUSSELL TODD HILGER
(Rusty)
Quarterback—Detroit Lions
Born May 9, 1962, at Oklahoma City, Okla.
Height, 6.04. Weight, 205.
High School—Oklahoma City, Okla., Southeast.
Attended Oklahoma State University.

Selected by Denver in 1985 USFL territorial draft.
Selected by Los Angeles Raiders in 6th round (143rd player selected) of 1985 NFL draft.
Signed by Los Angeles Raiders, July 21, 1985.
Crossed picket line during players' strike, October 14, 1987.
Released by Los Angeles Raiders, August 30, 1988; signed by Detroit Lions, October 4, 1988.

| | | | | | —PASSING— | | | | | —RUSHING— | | | —TOTAL— | | |
Year	Club	G.	Att.	Cmp.	Pct.	Gain	T.P.	P.I.	Avg.	Att.	Yds.	Avg.	TD.	TD.	Pts.	F.
1985—L.A. Raiders NFL		4	13	4	30.8	54	1	0	4.15	3	8	2.7	0	0	0	1
1986—L.A. Raiders NFL		2	38	19	50.0	266	1	1	7.00	6	48	8.0	0	0	0	3
1987—L.A. Raiders NFL		5	106	55	51.9	706	2	6	6.66	8	8	1.0	0	0	0	3
1988—Detroit NFL		11	306	126	41.2	1558	7	12	5.09	18	27	1.5	0	0	0	7
Pro Totals—4 Years		22	463	204	44.1	2584	11	19	5.58	35	91	2.6	0	0	0	14

Quarterback Rating Points: 1985 (70.7), 1986 (70.7), 1987 (55.8), 1988 (48.9). Total—53.0.
Additional pro statistics: Recovered one fumble, 1985 and 1987; recovered one fumble and fumbled three times for minus seven yards, 1986; recovered five fumbles and fumbled seven times for minus 19 yards, 1988.

ANDREW HILL
(Drew)
Wide Receiver—Houston Oilers
Born February 5, 1956, at Newman, Ga.
Height, 5.09. Weight, 175.
High School—Newman, Ga.
Received bachelor of arts degree in industrial management from Georgia Tech in 1981.

Established NFL record for most kickoff returns, season (60), 1981.
Selected by Los Angeles in 12th round (328th player selected) of 1979 NFL draft.
On injured reserve with back injury, August 24 through entire 1983 season.
Traded by Los Angeles Rams to Houston Oilers for 7th round pick in 1986 draft and 4th round pick in 1987 draft, July 3, 1985.

| | | | PASS RECEIVING | | | | —KICKOFF RET.— | | | | —TOTAL— | | |
Year	Club	G.	P.C.	Yds.	Avg.	TD.	No.	Yds.	Avg.	TD.	TD.	Pts.	F.
1979—Los Angeles Rams NFL		16	4	94	23.5	1	40	803	20.1	0	1	6	2
1980—Los Angeles Rams NFL		16	19	416	21.9	2	43	880	20.5	*1	3	18	2
1981—Los Angeles Rams NFL		16	16	355	22.2	3	*60	1170	19.5	0	3	18	1
1982—Los Angeles Rams NFL		9	7	92	13.1	0	2	42	21.0	0	0	0	0
1984—Los Angeles Rams NFL		16	14	390	27.9	4	26	543	20.9	0	4	24	0
1985—Houston NFL		16	64	1169	18.3	9	1	22	22.0	0	9	54	0
1986—Houston NFL		16	65	1112	17.1	5		None			5	30	0
1987—Houston NFL		12	49	989	20.2	6		None			6	36	1
1988—Houston NFL		16	72	1141	15.8	10		None			10	60	0
Pro Totals—9 Years		133	310	5758	18.6	40	172	3460	20.1	1	41	246	6

Additional pro statistics: Returned one punt for no yards, 1979; recovered one fumble and rushed once for four yards, 1980; rushed once for 14 yards, returned two punts for 22 yards and recovered one fumble, 1981; attempted one pass with no completions, 1987.
Played in NFC Championship Game following 1979 season.
Played in NFL Championship Game following 1979 season.
Named to play in Pro Bowl (NFL All-Star Game) following 1988 season; replaced due to injury by Andre Reed.

BRUCE EDWARD HILL
Wide Receiver—Tampa Bay Buccaneers
Born February 29, 1964, at Fort Dix, N. J.
Height, 6.00. Weight, 180.
High School—Lancaster, Calif., Antelope Valley.
Attended Arizona State University.

Selected by Tampa Bay in 4th round (106th player selected) of 1987 NFL draft.
Signed by Tampa Bay Buccaneers, July 20, 1987.
On injured reserve with knee injury, September 7 through November 6, 1987; activated, November 7, 1987.

| | | —PASS RECEIVING— | | | | |
Year	Club	G.	P.C.	Yds.	Avg.	TD.
1987—Tampa Bay NFL		8	23	402	17.5	2
1988—Tampa Bay NFL		14	58	1040	17.9	9
Pro Totals—2 Years		22	81	1442	17.8	11

Additional pro statistics: Rushed three times for three yards, returned one kickoff for eight yards and fumbled once, 1987; recovered one fumble, 1987 and 1988; rushed twice for minus 11 yards and fumbled twice, 1988.

GREGORY M. HILL
(Greg)
Cornerback—Kansas City Chiefs
Born February 12, 1961, at Orange, Tex.
Height, 6.01. Weight, 199.
High School—West Orange, Tex., Stark.
Attended Oklahoma State University.

Selected by Philadelphia in 3rd round (32nd player selected) of 1983 USFL draft.
Selected by Houston in 4th round (86th player selected) of 1983 NFL draft.
Signed by Houston Oilers, June 25, 1983.
Released by Houston Oilers, August 27, 1984; awarded on waivers to Kansas City Chiefs, August 28, 1984.
On injured reserve with sprained wrist, December 5 through remainder of 1986 season.
Released by Kansas City Chiefs, August 31, 1987; awarded on waivers to St. Louis Cardinals, September 1, 1987.
Released by St. Louis Cardinals, September 7, 1987; signed as free agent replacement player by Los Angeles Raiders, October 9, 1987.
Released by Los Angeles Raiders, November 3, 1987; signed as free agent by Houston Oilers, November 19, 1987.
Released by Houston Oilers, November 27, 1987; awarded on waivers to Kansas City Chiefs, November 30, 1987.

			—INTERCEPTIONS—			
Year	Club	G.	No.	Yds.	Avg.	TD.
1983—Houston NFL		14		None		
1984—Kansas City NFL		15	2	−1	−0.5	0
1985—Kansas City NFL		16	3	37	12.3	0
1986—Kansas City NFL		13	3	64	21.3	1
1987—Raid. (2)-K.C. (4) NFL		6		None		
1988—Kansas City NFL		15	1	24	24.0	0
Pro Totals—6 Years		79	9	124	13.8	1

Additional pro statistics: Fumbled once, 1984.

KENNETH HILL
(Kenny)
Safety—New York Giants
Born July 25, 1958, at Oak Grove, La.
Height, 6.00. Weight, 195.
High School—Oak Grove, La.
Received bachelor of science degree in molecular biophysics from Yale University in 1980.

Selected by Oakland in 8th round (194th player selected) of 1980 NFL draft.
On injured reserve with hip pointer, August 26 through entire 1980 season.
On injured reserve with pulled hamstring, August 31 through October 18, 1981; activated after clearing procedural waivers, October 20, 1981.
Franchise transferred to Los Angeles, May 7, 1982.
Traded by Los Angeles Raiders to New York Giants for 7th round pick in 1985 draft, August 27, 1984.
On injured reserve with hamstring injury, September 3 through October 3, 1985; activated, October 4, 1985.

			—INTERCEPTIONS—				—KICKOFF RET.—				—TOTAL—		
Year	Club	G.	No.	Yds.	Avg.	TD.	No.	Yds.	Avg.	TD.	TD.	Pts.	F.
1981—Oakland NFL		9		None			1	21	21.0	0	0	0	0
1982—Los Angeles Raiders NFL		9		None			2	20	10.0	0	0	0	1
1983—Los Angeles Raiders NFL		16		None				None			0	0	0
1984—New York Giants NFL		12		None			1	27	27.0	0	0	0	0
1985—New York Giants NFL		12	2	30	15.0	0	11	186	16.9	0	0	0	1
1986—New York Giants NFL		16	3	25	8.3	0	5	61	12.2	0	0	0	1
1987—New York Giants NFL		12	1	1	1.0	0		None			0	0	0
1988—New York Giants NFL		16		None			13	262	20.2	0	0	0	2
Pro Totals—8 Years		102	6	56	9.3	0	33	577	17.5	0	0	0	5

Additional pro statistics: Recovered two fumbles, 1985; recovered three fumbles, 1986; recovered one fumble for six yards, 1987; recovered one fumble, 1988.
Played in AFC Championship Game following 1983 season.
Played in NFC Championship Game following 1986 season.
Played in NFL Championship Game following 1983 and 1986 seasons.

LONZELL RAMON HILL
Wide Receiver—New Orleans Saints
Born September 25, 1965, at Stockton, Calif.
Height, 6.00. Weight, 189.
High School—Stockton, Calif., Amos Alonzo Stagg.
Attended University of Washington.
Son of J. D. Hill, Sr., wide receiver with Buffalo Bills and Detroit Lions,
1971 through 1977; brother of J. D. Hill, Jr., wide receiver at University of Washington;
and cousin of Paul Dunn, former wide receiver with Cincinnati Bengals, Washington Redskins
and Philadelphia Bell (WFL).

Selected by New Orleans in 2nd round (40th player selected) of 1987 NFL draft.
Signed by New Orleans Saints, August 8, 1987.

Year	Club	—PASS RECEIVING—				
		G.	P.C.	Yds.	Avg.	TD.
1987—New Orleans NFL		10	19	322	16.9	2
1988—New Orleans NFL		16	66	703	10.7	7
Pro Totals—2 Years		26	85	1025	12.1	9

Additional pro statistics: Rushed once for minus nine yards and recovered one fumble, 1987; rushed twice for seven yards, returned 10 punts for 108 yards, attempted one pass with no completions and fumbled three times, 1988.

NATHANIAL HILL
(Nate)
Defensive End—Miami Dolphins
Born February 21, 1966, at LaGrange, Ga.
Height, 6.04. Weight, 275.
High School—LaGrange, Ga.
Attended Auburn University.

Selected by Green Bay in 6th round (144th player selected) of 1988 NFL draft.
Signed by Green Bay Packers, July 15, 1988.
Released by Green Bay Packers, September 26, 1988; signed as free agent by Miami Dolphins, December 6, 1988.
Green Bay (3)-Miami (1) NFL, 1988.
Games: 1988 (4).
Pro statistics: Returned one kickoff for one yard, 1988.

WILL J. HILL
Defensive Back—Cleveland Browns
Born March 5, 1963, at Vero Beach, Fla.
Height, 6.00. Weight, 200.
High School—Vero Beach, Fla.
Attended Ranger Junior College and Bishop College.

Signed as free agent by Cleveland Browns, May 4, 1987.
On injured reserve with knee injury, September 1 through entire 1987 season.
Cleveland NFL, 1988.
Games: 1988 (16).
Pro statistics: Recovered one fumble, 1988.

IRA McDONALD HILLARY
Wide Receiver—Cincinnati Bengals
Born November 13, 1962, at Edgefield, S. C.
Height, 5.11. Weight, 190.
High School—Johnston, S. C., Strom Thurmond.
Received bachelor of arts degree in interdisciplinary studies (management)
from University of South Carolina in 1985.

Selected by Los Angeles in 1985 USFL territorial draft.
Selected by Kansas City in 8th round (210th player selected) of 1985 NFL draft.
Signed by Kansas City Chiefs, July 15, 1985.
Released by Kansas City Chiefs, August 26, 1985; signed as free agent by Cincinnati Bengals, February 18, 1986.
On injured reserve with Achilles heel injury, August 26 through entire 1986 season.

Year	Club		PASS RECEIVING				–PUNT RETURNS–				—KICKOFF RET.—				—TOTAL—		
		G.	P.C.	Yds.	Avg.	TD.	No.	Yds.	Avg.	TD.	No.	Yds.	Avg.	TD.	TD.	Pts.	F.
1987—Cincinnati NFL		11	5	65	13.0	0	None				1	15	15.0	0	0	0	0
1988—Cincinnati NFL		16	5	76	15.2	1	17	166	9.8	0	12	195	16.3	0	1	6	0
Pro Totals—2 Years		27	10	141	14.1	1	17	166	9.8	0	13	210	16.2	0	1	6	0

Additional pro statistics: Returned one kickoff for 15 yards, 1987.
Played in AFC Championship Game following 1988 season.
Played in NFL Championship Game following 1988 season.

DALTON HILLIARD
Running Back—New Orleans Saints
Born January 21, 1964, at Patterson, La.
Height, 5.08. Weight, 204.
High School—Patterson, La.
Attended Louisiana State University.

Selected by Tampa Bay in 1986 USFL territorial draft.
Signed by New Orleans in 2nd round (31st player selected) of 1986 NFL draft.
Signed by New Orleans Saints, July 21, 1986.

Year	Club		——RUSHING——				PASS RECEIVING				—TOTAL—		
		G.	Att.	Yds.	Avg.	TD.	P.C.	Yds.	Avg.	TD.	TD.	Pts.	F.
1986—New Orleans NFL		16	121	425	3.5	5	17	107	6.3	0	5	30	3
1987—New Orleans NFL		12	123	508	4.1	7	23	264	11.5	1	8	48	4
1988—New Orleans NFL		16	204	823	4.0	5	34	335	9.9	1	6	36	3
Pro Totals—3 Years		44	448	1756	3.9	17	74	706	9.5	2	19	114	10

Year	Club	KICKOFF RETURNS				
		G.	No.	Yds.	Avg.	TD.
1986—New Orleans NFL		16	None			
1987—New Orleans NFL		12	10	248	24.8	0
1988—New Orleans NFL		16	6	111	18.5	0
Pro Totals—3 Years		44	16	359	22.4	0

Additional pro statistics: Attempted three passes with one completion for 29 yards and a touchdown, 1986; attempted one pass with one completion for 23 yards and a touchdown, 1987; attempted two passes with one completion for 27 yards and a touchdown, 1988.

CARL PATRICK HILTON
Tight End—Minnesota Vikings
Born February 28, 1964, at Galveston, Tex.
Height, 6.03. Weight, 230.
High School—Galveston, Tex., Ball.
Attended University of Houston.

Named as tight end on THE SPORTING NEWS College All-America Team, 1984.
Selected by Minnesota in 7th round (179th player selected) of 1986 NFL draft.
Signed by Minnesota Vikings, July 27, 1986.
On injured reserve with broken wrist, August 16 through October 28, 1988; activated, October 29, 1988.
Minnesota NFL, 1986 through 1988.
Games: 1986 (16), 1987 (11), 1988 (8). Total—35.
Pro statistics: Caught two passes for 16 yards and two touchdowns and returned one kickoff for 13 yards, 1987; caught one pass for one yard and a touchdown, 1988.
Played in NFC Championship Game following 1987 season.

BRYAN ERIC HINKLE
Linebacker—Pittsburgh Steelers
Born June 4, 1959, at Long Beach, Calif.
Height, 6.02. Weight, 222.
High School—Silverdale, Wash., Central Kitsap.
Received degree in business from University of Oregon.

Selected by Pittsburgh in 6th round (156th player selected) of 1981 NFL draft.
On injured reserve with ankle injury and concussion, August 31 through entire 1981 season.
On injured reserve with torn quadricep, January 7 through remainder of 1982 season playoffs.
On injured reserve with dislocated toe, December 1 through remainder of 1988 season.

| | | —INTERCEPTIONS— | | | |
Year Club	G.	No.	Yds.	Avg.	TD.
1982—Pittsburgh NFL	9		None		
1983—Pittsburgh NFL	16	1	14	14.0	1
1984—Pittsburgh NFL	15	3	77	25.7	0
1985—Pittsburgh NFL	14		None		
1986—Pittsburgh NFL	16	3	7	2.3	0
1987—Pittsburgh NFL	12	3	15	5.0	0
1988—Pittsburgh NFL	13	1	1	1.0	0
Pro Totals—7 Years	95	11	114	10.4	1

Additional pro statistics: Recovered two fumbles for four yards, 1983; recovered two fumbles for 21 yards and a touchdown, 1984; recovered one fumble, 1986 and 1987; fumbled once, 1987; recovered one fumble for five yards, 1988.
Played in AFC Championship Game following 1984 season.

GEORGE ALLEN HINKLE JR.
Defensive End—San Diego Chargers
Born March 17, 1965, at St. Louis, Mo.
Height, 6.05. Weight, 267.
High School—Pacific, Mo.
Received degree from University of Arizona in 1988.

Selected by San Diego in 11th round (293rd player selected) of 1988 NFL draft.
Signed by San Diego Chargers, July 13, 1988.
On injured reserve with foot injury, August 29 through December 2, 1988; activated, December 3, 1988.
San Diego NFL, 1988.
Games: 1988 (3).

MICHAEL WESLEY HINNANT
(Mike)
Tight End—Pittsburgh Steelers
Born September 8, 1966, at Washington, D.C.
Height, 6.03. Weight, 258.
High School—Washington, D.C., Spingarn.
Attended Temple University.

Selected by Pittsburgh in 8th round (211th player selected) of 1988 NFL draft.
Signed by Pittsburgh Steelers, July 16, 1988.
Pittsburgh NFL, 1988.
Games: 1988 (16).
Pro statistics: Caught one pass for 23 yards, 1988.

CHRISTOPHER JERROD HINTON
(Chris)
Offensive Tackle—Indianapolis Colts
Born July 31, 1961, at Chicago, Ill.
Height, 6.04. Weight, 295.
High School—Chicago, Ill., Wendell Phillips.
Received degree in sociology from Northwestern University.

Named to THE SPORTING NEWS NFL All-Star Team, 1987.
Named as offensive tackle on THE SPORTING NEWS All-America Team, 1982.
Selected by Chicago in 1983 USFL territorial draft.
Selected by Denver in 1st round (4th player selected) of 1983 NFL draft.
Rights traded with quarterback Mark Herrmann, and 1st round pick in 1984 draft by Denver Broncos to Baltimore Colts for rights to quarterback John Elway, May 2, 1983.
Signed by Baltimore Colts, May 12, 1983.
Franchise transferred to Indianapolis, March 31, 1984.
On injured reserve with fractured fibula, October 8 through remainder of 1984 season.
Baltimore NFL, 1983; Indianapolis NFL, 1984 through 1988.
Games: 1983 (16), 1984 (6), 1985 (16), 1986 (16), 1987 (12), 1988 (14). Total—80.
Pro statistics: Recovered one fumble, 1983 and 1987; recovered two fumbles, 1986; caught one pass for one yard, 1988.
Played in Pro Bowl (NFL All-Star Game) following 1983 and 1985 through 1988 seasons.

ERIC ELLSWORTH HIPPLE
Quarterback—Detroit Lions

Born September 16, 1957, at Lubbock, Tex.
Height, 6.02. Weight, 196.
High School—Downey, Calif., Warren.
Received bachelor of science degree in business administration from
Utah State University in 1980.

Selected by Detroit in 4th round (85th player selected) of 1980 NFL draft.
On injured reserve with knee injury, October 18 through December 13, 1984; activated, December 14, 1984.
On injured reserve with broken thumb, September 8 through entire 1987 season.
On injured reserve with broken ankle, October 4 through remainder of 1988 season.

				PASSING					RUSHING			TOTAL		
Year Club	G.	Att.	Cmp.	Pct.	Gain	T.P.	P.I.	Avg.	Att.	Yds.	Avg. TD.	TD.	Pts.	F.
1980—Detroit NFL	15			None						None		0	0	0
1981—Detroit NFL	16	279	140	50.2	2358	14	15	8.45	41	168	4.1 7	7	42	*14
1982—Detroit NFL	9	86	36	41.9	411	2	4	4.78	10	57	5.7 0	0	0	1
1983—Detroit NFL	16	387	204	52.7	2577	12	18	6.66	41	171	4.2 3	3	18	12
1984—Detroit NFL	8	38	16	42.1	246	1	1	6.47	2	3	1.5 0	0	0	0
1985—Detroit NFL	16	406	223	54.9	2952	17	18	7.27	32	89	2.8 2	2	12	13
1986—Detroit NFL	16	305	192	*63.0	1919	9	11	6.29	16	46	2.9 0	0	0	7
1988—Detroit NFL	5	27	12	44.4	158	0	0	5.85	1	5	5.0 0	0	0	0
Pro Totals—8 Years	101	1528	823	53.9	10621	55	67	6.95	143	539	3.8 12	12	72	47

Quarterback Rating Points: 1981 (73.3), 1982 (66.9), 1983 (64.7), 1984 (62.0), 1985 (73.6), 1986 (75.6), 1988 (63.5). Total—69.6.
Additional pro statistics: Recovered four fumbles and fumbled 14 times for minus 10 yards; recovered six fumbles, 1983; recovered three fumbles and fumbled 13 times for minus three yards, 1985; recovered two fumbles and fumbled seven times for minus two yards, 1986.

RAY HITCHCOCK
Center-Guard—Washington Redskins

Born June 20, 1965, at St. Paul, Minn.
Height, 6.02. Weight, 289.
High School—St. Paul, Minn., Johnson.
Attended University of Minnesota.

Selected by Washington in 12th round (331st player selected) of 1987 NFL draft.
Signed by Washington Redskins, July 26, 1987.
On injured reserve with hamstring injury, September 1 through November 22, 1987; activated, November 23, 1987.
On injured reserve with hamstring injury, December 25 through remainder of 1987 season.
Place on physically unable to perform/active with knee injury, July 18 through August 22, 1988; then transferred to physically unable to perform/reserve with knee injury, August 23 through entire 1988 season.
Washington NFL, 1987.
Games: 1987 (5).

TERRELL LEE HOAGE
(Terry)
Safety—Philadelphia Eagles

Born April 11, 1962, at Ames, Ia.
Height, 6.03. Weight, 199.
High School—Huntsville, Tex.
Received degree in genetics from University of Georgia.

Named as defensive back on THE SPORTING NEWS College All-America Team, 1983.
Selected by Jacksonville in 1984 USFL territorial draft.
Selected by New Orleans in 3rd round (68th player selected) of 1984 NFL draft.
Signed by New Orleans Saints, July 25, 1984.
Released by New Orleans Saints, August 26, 1986; signed as free agent by Philadelphia Eagles, September 3, 1986.

		INTERCEPTIONS			
Year Club	G.	No.	Yds.	Avg.	TD.
1984—New Orleans NFL	14		None		
1985—New Orleans NFL	16	4	79	19.8	*1
1986—Philadelphia NFL	16	1	18	18.0	0
1987—Philadelphia NFL	11	2	3	1.5	0
1988—Philadelphia NFL	16	8	116	14.5	0
Pro Totals—5 Years	73	15	216	14.4	1

Additional pro statistics: Recovered one fumble, 1984; recovered two fumbles, 1985 through 1987; rushed once for 38 yards and a touchdown, 1988.

LIFFORT HOBLEY
Safety—Miami Dolphins
Born May 12, 1962, at Shreveport, La.
Height, 6.00. Weight, 199.
High School—Shreveport, La., C.E. Byrd.
Attended Louisiana State University.

Selected by Portland in 1985 USFL territorial draft.
Selected by Pittsburgh in 3rd round (74th player selected) of 1985 NFL draft.
Signed by Pittsburgh Steelers, June 5, 1985.
Released by Pittsburgh Steelers, August 25, 1985; signed as free agent by San Diego Chargers, August 28, 1985.
Released by San Diego Chargers after failing physical, August 29, 1985; signed as free agent by St. Louis Cardinals, September 11, 1985.
Released by St. Louis Cardinals, October 15, 1985; signed as free agent by Miami Dolphins, March 6, 1986.
Released by Miami Dolphins, August 19, 1986; re-signed by Dolphins, April 21, 1987.
Released by Miami Dolphins, September 7, 1987; re-signed by Dolphins, September 8, 1987.
Crossed picket line during players' strike, October 7, 1987.
St. Louis NFL, 1985; Miami NFL, 1987 and 1988.
Games: 1985 (5), 1987 (14), 1988 (16). Total—35.
Pro statistics: Intercepted two passes for seven yards and recovered four fumbles for 55 yards and a touchdown, 1987; recovered two fumbles for 19 yards and a touchdown, 1988.

MILFORD HODGE
Defensive End—New England Patriots
Born March 11, 1961, at Los Angeles, Calif.
Height, 6.03. Weight, 278.
High School—San Francisco, Calif., South.
Attended Washington State University.

Selected by New England in 8th round (224th player selected) of 1985 NFL draft.
Signed by New England Patriots, July 19, 1985.
Released by New England Patriots, August 28, 1985; re-signed by Patriots, February 24, 1986.
On injured reserve with thumb injury, August 18 through September 29, 1986.
Released by New England Patriots, September 30, 1986; signed as free agent by New Orleans Saints, October 10, 1986.
Released by New Orleans Saints, October 14, 1986; signed as free agent by New England Patriots, November 14, 1986.
Released by New England Patriots, September 7, 1987; re-signed by Patriots, September 8, 1987.
Granted free agency with no qualifying offer, February 1, 1988; re-signed by Patriots, April 26, 1988.
New Orleans (1)-New England (6) NFL, 1986; New England NFL, 1987 and 1988.
Games: 1986 (7), 1987 (12), 1988 (15). Total—34.
Pro statistics: Recovered one fumble for two yards, 1988.

MERRIL D. HOGE
(Name pronounced Hodge.)
Running Back—Pittsburgh Steelers
Born January 26, 1965, at Pocatello, Ida.
Height, 6.02. Weight, 226.
High School—Pocatello, Ida., Highland.
Attended Idaho State University.

Selected by Pittsburgh in 10th round (261st player selected) of 1987 NFL draft.
Signed by Pittsburgh Steelers, July 26, 1987.
Crossed picket line during players' strike, October 13, 1987.

| | | ——RUSHING—— | | | | PASS RECEIVING | | | | —TOTAL— | | |
Year Club	G.	Att.	Yds.	Avg.	TD.	P.C.	Yds.	Avg.	TD.	TD.	Pts.	F.
1987—Pittsburgh NFL	13	3	8	2.7	0	7	97	13.9	1	1	6	0
1988—Pittsburgh NFL	16	170	705	4.1	3	50	487	9.7	3	6	36	8
Pro Totals—2 Years	29	173	713	4.1	3	57	584	10.2	4	7	42	8

Additional pro statistics: Returned one kickoff for 13 yards, 1987; recovered six fumbles, 1988.

GARY KEITH HOGEBOOM
Name pronounced HOAG-ih-boom.
Quarterback—Phoenix Cardinals
Born August 21, 1958, at Grand Rapids, Mich.
Height, 6.04. Weight, 217.
High School—Grand Rapids, Mich., Northview.
Attended Central Michigan University.

Selected by Dallas in 5th round (133rd player selected) of 1980 NFL draft.
Traded with 2nd round pick in 1986 draft by Dallas Cowboys to Indianapolis Colts for 2nd round pick in 1986 draft and conditional 1987 pick, April 28, 1986.
On injured reserve with separated shoulder, September 16 through December 4, 1986; activated, December 5, 1986.
Crossed picket line during players' strike, September 23, 1987.
Granted unconditional free agency, February 1, 1989; signed by Phoenix Cardinals, March 3, 1989.

Year Club	G.	PASSING							RUSHING				TOTAL		
		Att.	Cmp.	Pct.	Gain	T.P.	P.I.	Avg.	Att.	Yds.	Avg.	TD.	TD.	Pts.	F.
1980—Dallas NFL	2	None							None				0	0	0
1981—Dallas NFL	1	None							None				0	0	0
1982—Dallas NFL	4	8	3	37.5	45	0	1	5.63	3	0	0.0	0	0	0	2
1983—Dallas NFL	6	17	11	64.7	161	1	1	9.47	6	—10	—1.7	0	0	0	0
1984—Dallas NFL	16	367	195	53.1	2366	7	14	6.45	15	19	1.3	0	0	0	8
1985—Dallas NFL	16	126	70	55.6	978	5	7	7.76	8	48	6.0	1	1	6	0
1986—Indianapolis NFL	5	144	85	59.0	1154	6	6	8.01	10	20	2.0	1	1	6	3
1987—Indianapolis NFL	6	168	99	58.9	1145	9	5	6.82	3	3	1.0	0	0	0	1
1988—Indianapolis NFL	9	131	76	58.0	996	7	7	7.60	11	—8	—0.7	1	1	6	2
Pro Totals—9 Years	65	961	539	56.1	6845	35	41	7.12	56	72	1.3	3	3	18	16

Quarterback Rating Points: 1982 (17.2), 1983 (90.6), 1984 (63.7), 1985 (70.8), 1986 (81.2), 1987 (85.0), 1988 (77.7). Total—72.6.

Additional pro statistics: Recovered four fumbles and fumbled eight times for minus three yards, 1984; recovered two fumbles and fumbled three times for 50 yards, 1986; recovered one fumble and fumbled once for minus one yard, 1987.

Member of Dallas Cowboys for NFC Championship Game following 1980 and 1981 seasons; did not play.
Played in NFC Championship Game following 1982 season.

JAMIE LORENZA HOLLAND
Wide Receiver—San Diego Chargers
Born February 1, 1964, at Raleigh, N. C.
Height, 6.01. Weight, 195.
High School—Wake Forest, N. C., Rolesville.
Attended Butler County (Kan.) Community College and received bachelor's degree in education from Ohio State University in 1986.

Selected by San Diego in 7th round (173rd player selected) of 1987 NFL draft.
Signed by San Diego Chargers, July 25, 1987.

Year Club	G.	PASS RECEIVING				KICKOFF RET.				TOTAL		
		P.C.	Yds.	Avg.	TD.	No.	Yds.	Avg.	TD.	TD.	Pts.	F.
1987—San Diego NFL	12	6	138	23.0	0	19	410	21.6	0	0	0	0
1988—San Diego NFL	16	39	536	13.7	1	31	810	26.1	★1	2	12	1
Pro Totals—2 Years	28	45	674	15.0	1	50	1220	24.4	1	2	12	1

Additional pro statistics: Rushed once for 17 yards, 1987; rushed three times for 19 yards, 1988.

JOHNNY RAY HOLLAND
Linebacker—Green Bay Packers
Born March 11, 1965, at Bellville, Tex.
Height, 6.02. Weight, 221.
High School—Hempstead, Tex.
Attended Texas A&M University.

Selected by Green Bay in 2nd round (41st player selected) of 1987 NFL draft.
Signed by Green Bay Packers, July 25, 1987.
Green Bay NFL, 1987 and 1988.
Games: 1987 (12), 1988 (13). Total—25.
Pro statistics: Intercepted two passes for four yards, 1987; recovered one fumble, 1987 and 1988.

ERIC W. HOLLE
Defensive Tackle—Houston Oilers
Born September 5, 1960, at Houston, Tex.
Height, 6.05. Weight, 265.
High School—Austin, Tex., LBJ.
Attended University of Texas.

Selected by San Antonio in 1984 USFL territorial draft.
Selected by Kansas City in 5th round (117th player selected) of 1984 NFL draft.
Signed by Kansas City Chiefs, July 12, 1984.
On injured reserve with hip injury, December 5 through remainder of 1987 season.
On injured reserve with back injury, August 22 through October 4, 1988.
Released by Kansas City Chiefs, October 5, 1988; signed as free agent by Houston Oilers, May 16, 1989.
Kansas City NFL, 1984 through 1987.
Games: 1984 (16), 1985 (16), 1986 (16), 1987 (8). Total—56.
Pro statistics: Recovered one fumble for two yards, 1984.

DAVID LANIER HOLLIS
Safety—Seattle Seahawks
Born July 4, 1965, at Harbor City, Calif.
Height, 5.11. Weight, 180.
High School—Gardena, Calif.
Attended University of Nevada at Las Vegas.

Signed as free agent by Seattle Seahawks, May 12, 1987.
Released by Seattle Seahawks, August 30, 1988; re-signed by Seahawks, September 1, 1988.
Released by Seattle Seahawks, September 7, 1988; signed as free agent by Kansas City Chiefs, September 14, 1988.
Released by Kansas City Chiefs, September 28, 1988; signed as free agent by Seattle Seahawks, November 2, 1988.

Year Club	G.	No.	Yds.	Avg.	TD.	No.	Yds.	Avg.	TD.	TD.	Pts.	F.
		—PUNT RETURNS—				—KICKOFF RET.—				—TOTAL—		
1987—Seattle NFL	11	6	33	5.5	0	10	263	26.3	0	0	0	0
1988—Seattle (6)-Kansas City (2) NFL	8	3	28	9.3	0	13	261	20.1	0	0	0	1
Pro Totals—2 Years	19	9	61	6.8	0	23	524	22.8	0	0	0	1

Additional pro statistics: Intercepted two passes for 32 yards, 1988.

STEVE HOLLOWAY
Tight End—New York Jets

Born August 23, 1964, at Montgomery, Ala.
Height, 6.03. Weight, 235.
High School—Montgomery, Ala., Jeff Davis.
Attended Tennessee State University.

Signed as free agent by Tampa Bay Buccaneers, May 11, 1987.
Released by Tampa Bay Buccaneers, September 7, 1987; re-signed as replacement player by Buccaneers, September 24, 1987.
Released by Tampa Bay Buccaneers, November 17, 1987; signed as free agent by Miami Dolphins for 1988, December 17, 1987.
Released by Miami Dolphins, August 24, 1988; signed as free agent by New York Jets, February 24, 1989.

Year Club	G.	P.C.	Yds.	Avg.	TD.
		—PASS RECEIVING—			
1987—Tampa Bay NFL	6	10	127	12.7	0

Additional pro statistics: Recovered one fumble, 1987.

RODNEY A. HOLMAN
Tight End—Cincinnati Bengals

Born April 20, 1960, at Ypsilanti, Mich.
Height, 6.03. Weight, 238.
High School—Ypsilanti, Mich.
Received degree from Tulane University in 1981.
Cousin of Preston Pearson, running back with Baltimore Colts,
Pittsburgh Steelers and Dallas Cowboys, 1967 through 1980.

Selected by Cincinnati in 3rd round (82nd player selected) of 1982 NFL draft.

Year Club	G.	P.C.	Yds.	Avg.	TD.
		—PASS RECEIVING—			
1982—Cincinnati NFL	9	3	18	6.0	1
1983—Cincinnati NFL	16	2	15	7.5	0
1984—Cincinnati NFL	16	21	239	11.4	1
1985—Cincinnati NFL	16	38	479	12.6	7
1986—Cincinnati NFL	16	40	570	14.3	2
1987—Cincinnati NFL	12	28	438	15.6	2
1988—Cincinnati NFL	16	39	527	13.5	3
Pro Totals—7 Years	101	171	2286	13.4	16

Additional pro statistics: Recovered one fumble, 1984, 1985, 1987 and 1988; fumbled once, 1984 through 1986; returned one kickoff for 18 yards, 1986; fumbled twice, 1988.
Played in AFC Championship Game following 1988 season.
Played in NFL Championship Game following 1988 season.
Played in Pro Bowl (NFL All-Star Game) following 1988 season.

DARRYL DeWAYNE HOLMES
Safety—New England Patriots

Born September 6, 1964, at Birmingham, Ala.
Height, 6.02. Weight, 190.
High School—Warner Robins, Ga., Northside.
Attended Fort Valley State College.

Signed as free agent by New England Patriots, May 12, 1987.
Released by New England Patriots, September 7, 1987; re-signed by Patriots, September 8, 1987.
Crossed picket line during players' strike, October 2, 1987.
New England NFL, 1987 and 1988.
Games: 1987 (15), 1988 (16). Total—31.
Pro statistics: Intercepted one pass for four yards, 1987; recovered one fumble, 1987 and 1988.

DON IRA HOLMES
Wide Receiver—Phoenix Cardinals

Born April 1, 1961, at Miami, Fla.
Height, 5.10. Weight, 180.
High School—Miami, Fla., Northwestern.
Attended University of Colorado, Gavilan College and Mesa College (Colo.).

Selected by Oakland in supplemental round (404th player selected) of 1984 USFL draft.
Selected by Atlanta in 12th round (318th player selected) of 1986 NFL draft.
Signed by Atlanta Falcons, April 29, 1985.
Released by Atlanta Falcons, August 23, 1985; signed as free agent by Indianapolis Colts for 1986, December 6, 1985.
On injured reserve with toe injury, August 18 through September 28, 1986.
Released after clearing procedural waivers, September 29, 1986; awarded to St. Louis Cardinals, September 30, 1986.
Franchise transferred to Phoenix, March 15, 1988.

		—PASS RECEIVING—				
Year Club	G.	P.C.	Yds.	Avg.	TD.	
1986—St. Louis NFL	12		None			
1987—St. Louis NFL	11	11	132	12.0	0	
1988—Phoenix NFL	16	1	10	10.0	0	
Pro Totals—3 Years	39	12	142	11.8	0	

Additional pro statistics: Returned one kickoff for two yards, 1986; returned one kickoff for 25 yards, 1987.

JERRY HOLMES
Cornerback—Detroit Lions
Born December 22, 1957, at Newport News, Va.
Height, 6.02. Weight, 175.
High School—Hampton, Va., Bethel.
Attended Chowan Junior College and received degree in
personnel management from University of West Virginia.

Named as cornerback on THE SPORTING NEWS USFL All-Star Team, 1984 and 1985.
Signed as free agent by New York Jets, June 4, 1980.
On injured reserve with knee injury, October 21 through November 21, 1980; activated, November 22, 1980.
Signed by Pittsburgh Maulers, September 2, 1983, for contract to take effect after being granted free agency, February 1, 1984.
Franchise disbanded, October 25, 1984.
Assigned to Baltimore Stars, November 1, 1984.
Assigned by USFL to New Jersey Generals, January 18, 1985.
On developmental squad, February 23 through March 22, 1985; activated, March 23, 1985.
Granted free agency when USFL suspended operations, August 7, 1986; re-signed by New York Jets, August 30, 1986.
Granted roster exemption, August 30 through September 9, 1986; activated, September 10, 1986.
On injured reserve with broken rib, November 16 through December 18, 1987; activated, December 19, 1987.
Released by New York Jets, August 9, 1988; signed as free agent by Detroit Lions, August 17, 1988.
On developmental squad for 4 games when New Jersey Generals in 1985.

		—INTERCEPTIONS—				
Year Club	G.	No.	Yds.	Avg.	TD.	
1980—New York Jets NFL	12		None			
1981—New York Jets NFL	16	1	0	0.0	0	
1982—New York Jets NFL	9	3	2	0.7	0	
1983—New York Jets NFL	16	3	107	35.7	1	
1984—Pittsburgh USFL	18	2	0	0.0	0	
1985—New Jersey USFL	14	3	27	9.0	0	
1986—New York Jets NFL	15	6	29	4.8	0	
1987—New York Jets NFL	8	1	20	20.0	0	
1988—Detroit NFL	16	1	32	32.0	0	
NFL Totals—7 Years	92	15	190	12.7	1	
USFL Totals—2 Years	32	5	27	5.4	0	
Pro Totals—9 Years	124	20	217	10.9	1	

Additional pro statistics: Recovered one fumble, 1981; ran back blocked field goal attempt 57 yards for a touchdown and recovered one fumble for three yards, 1983; recovered three fumbles and fumbled once, 1985.
Played in AFC Championship Game following 1982 season.

RONALD HOLMES
(Ron)
Defensive End—Tampa Bay Buccaneers
Born August 26, 1963, at Fort Benning, Ga.
Height, 6.04. Weight, 265.
High School—Lacey, Wash., Timberline.
Attended University of Washington.

Selected by Portland in 1985 USFL territorial draft.
USFL rights traded with rights to linebacker Tim Meamber by Portland Breakers to Baltimore Stars for rights to defensive end Kenny Neil, February 13, 1985.
Selected by Tampa Bay in 1st round (8th player selected) of 1985 NFL draft.
Signed by Tampa Bay Buccaneers, August 4, 1985.
On injured reserve with knee injury, November 18 through remainder of 1988 season.
Tampa Bay NFL, 1985 through 1988.
Games: 1985 (16), 1986 (14), 1987 (10), 1988 (10). Total—50.
Pro statistics: Recovered two fumbles, 1985; recovered one fumble, 1986 and 1987.

—DID YOU KNOW—

That only four men in NFL history have coached the same team for at least 20 consecutive seasons? Curly Lambeau (Green Bay, 1921-49) and Tom Landry (Dallas, 1960-88) share the record with 29 seasons each while Steve Owen (New York Giants, 1931-53) had 23 and Pittsburgh's Chuck Noll (1969-88) currently has 20. Don Shula enters his 20th consecutive season with the Miami Dolphins in 1989.

TOM HOLMOE
Safety—San Francisco 49ers

Born March 7, 1960, at Los Angeles, Calif.
Height, 6.02. Weight, 195.
High School—La Crescenta, Calif., Valley.
Attended Brigham Young University.

Selected by Boston in 9th round (102nd player selected) of 1983 USFL draft.
Selected by San Francisco in 4th round (90th player selected) of 1983 NFL draft.
Signed by San Francisco 49ers, July 16, 1983.
On injured reserve with separated shoulder, September 1 through entire 1985 season.
Released by San Francisco 49ers, August 19, 1986; re-signed by 49ers, August 25, 1986.
San Francisco NFL, 1983, 1984 and 1986 through 1988.
Games: 1983 (16), 1984 (16), 1986 (16), 1987 (11), 1988 (16). Total—75.
Pro statistics: Recovered one fumble, 1983; intercepted three passes for 149 yards and two touchdowns and recovered three fumbles, 1986; intercepted one pass for no yards, 1987; intercepted two passes for no yards, 1988.
Played in NFC Championship Game following 1983, 1984 and 1988 seasons.
Played in NFL Championship Game following 1984 and 1988 seasons.

PETER JOSEPH HOLOHAN
(Pete)
Tight End—Los Angeles Rams

Born July 25, 1959, at Albany, N.Y.
Height, 6.04. Weight, 232.
High School—Liverpool, N.Y.
Attended University of Notre Dame.

Selected by San Diego in 7th round (189th player selected) of 1981 NFL draft.
Left San Diego Chargers voluntarily and placed on left-camp retired list; October 28, 1981; reinstated, April 30, 1982.
USFL rights traded with wide receiver Neil Balholm, defensive end Bill Purifoy, tight end Mike Hirn and linebacker Orlando Flanagan by Chicago Blitz to Denver Gold for center Glenn Hyde and defensive end Larry White, December 28, 1983.
Traded by San Diego Chargers to Los Angeles Rams for 4th round pick in 1988 draft, April 24, 1988.

| | | —PASS RECEIVING— | | | |
Year Club	G.	P.C.	Yds.	Avg.	TD.
1981—San Diego NFL	7	1	14	14.0	0
1982—San Diego NFL	9		None		
1983—San Diego NFL	16	23	272	11.8	2
1984—San Diego NFL	15	56	734	13.1	1
1985—San Diego NFL	15	42	458	10.9	3
1986—San Diego NFL	16	29	356	12.3	1
1987—San Diego NFL	12	20	239	12.0	0
1988—L.A. Rams NFL	16	59	640	10.8	3
Pro Totals—8 Years	106	230	2713	11.8	10

Additional pro statistics: Recovered one fumble, 1982 and 1987; attempted one pass with no completions, 1983 and 1985; attempted two passes with one completion for 25 yards and a touchdown and recovered two fumbles for 19 yards, 1984; returned one kickoff for no yards, 1985; fumbled once, 1985 and 1988; attempted two passes with one completion for 21 yards, 1986.

ISSIAC HOLT III
Cornerback—Minnesota Vikings

Born October 4, 1962, at Birmingham, Ala.
Height, 6.02. Weight, 202.
High School—Birmingham, Ala., Carver.
Attended Alcorn State University.

Selected by San Antonio in 1st round (3rd player selected) of 1985 USFL draft.
Selected by Minnesota in 2nd round (30th player selected) of 1985 NFL draft.
Signed by Minnesota Vikings, May 24, 1985.

| | | —INTERCEPTIONS— | | | |
Year Club	G.	No.	Yds.	Avg.	TD.
1985—Minnesota NFL	15	1	0	0.0	0
1986—Minnesota NFL	16	8	54	6.8	0
1987—Minnesota NFL	9	2	7	3.5	0
1988—Minnesota NFL	13	2	15	7.5	0
Pro Totals—4 Years	53	13	76	5.8	0

Additional pro statistics: Recovered blocked punt in end zone for a touchdown and fumbled once, 1986; credited with a safety, 1988.
Played in NFC Championship Game following 1987 season.

JOHN STEPHANIE HOLT
Cornerback—Indianapolis Colts

Born May 14, 1959, at Lawton, Okla.
Height, 5.10. Weight, 180.
High School—Enid, Okla.
Attended West Texas State University.

Selected by Tampa Bay in 4th round (89th player selected) of 1981 NFL draft.

USFL rights traded with rights to defensive end Clenzie Pierson by Denver Gold to Houston Gamblers for rights to center George Yarno, September 23, 1983.

Traded by Tampa Bay Buccaneers to Indianapolis Colts for 8th round pick in 1987 draft, August 13, 1986.

On non-football injury/active, July 21 through August 1, 1988; then transferred to non-football injury/reserve, August 2 through October 13, 1988; activated, October 14, 1988.

Granted unconditional free agency, February 1, 1989; re-signed by Colts, May 3, 1989.

		-INTERCEPTIONS-				-PUNT RETURNS-				—TOTAL—		
Year Club	G.	No.	Yds.	Avg.	TD.	No.	Yds.	Avg.	TD.	TD.	Pts.	F.
1981—Tampa Bay NFL	16	1	13	13.0	0	9	100	11.1	0	0	0	1
1982—Tampa Bay NFL	9		None			16	81	5.1	0	0	0	2
1983—Tampa Bay NFL	16	3	43	14.3	0	5	43	8.6	0	0	0	1
1984—Tampa Bay NFL	15	1	25	25.0	0	6	17	2.8	0	0	0	0
1985—Tampa Bay NFL	16	1	3	3.0	0		None			0	0	0
1986—Indianapolis NFL	16	1	80	80.0	0		None			0	0	0
1987—Indianapolis NFL	12		None				None			0	0	0
1988—Indianapolis NFL	9		None				None			0	0	0
Pro Totals—8 Years	109	7	164	23.4	0	36	241	6.7	0	0	0	4

Additional pro statistics: Returned 11 kickoffs for 274 yards (24.9 avg.), 1981; recovered one fumble, 1982 through 1984; recovered two fumbles, 1985; recovered four fumbles, 1986.

PIERCE HOLT
Defensive End—San Francisco 49ers
Born January 1, 1962, at Marlin, Tex.
Height, 6.04. Weight, 280.
High School—Rosenberg, Tex., Lamar.
Received degree in physical education and history from Angelo State University.

Signed by San Francisco in 2nd round (39th player selected) of 1988 NFL draft.
Signed by San Francisco 49ers, July 17, 1988.
On injured reserve with toe injury, August 30 through October 23, 1988; activated, October 24, 1988.
San Francisco NFL, 1988.
Games: 1988 (9).
Pro statistics: Recovered one fumble, 1988.
Played in NFC Championship Game following 1988 season.
Played in NFL Championship Game following 1988 season.

WINFORD DeWAYNE HOOD
Guard—Denver Broncos
Born March 29, 1962, at Atlanta, Ga.
Height, 6.03. Weight, 262.
High School—Atlanta, Ga., Therrell.
Attended University of Georgia.

Selected by Jacksonville in 1984 USFL territorial draft.
Selected by Denver in 8th round (207th player selected) of 1984 NFL draft.
Signed by Denver Broncos, May 21, 1984.
Released by Denver Broncos, August 25, 1986; re-signed by Broncos, September 17, 1986.
Released by Denver Broncos, October 10, 1986; re-signed by Broncos, October 22, 1986.
Released by Denver Broncos, December 5, 1986; re-signed by Broncos, May 1, 1987.
On injured reserve with wrist injury, September 1 through September 30, 1987; activated, October 1, 1987.
Crossed picket line during players' strike, October 1, 1987.
On injured reserve with knee injury, October 21 through remainder of 1987 season.
On injured reserve with hand injury, August 29 through November 25, 1988; activated, November 26, 1988.
Denver NFL, 1984 through 1988.
Games: 1984 (16), 1985 (16), 1986 (9), 1987 (3), 1988 (3). Total—47.

HOUSTON ROOSEVELT HOOVER
Offensive Tackle—Atlanta Falcons
Born June 2, 1965, at Yazoo City, Miss.
Height, 6.02. Weight, 285.
High School—Yazoo City, Miss.
Received degree in business management
from Jackson State University in 1988.

Selected by Atlanta in 6th round (140th player selected) of 1988 NFL draft.
Signed by Atlanta Falcons, June 8, 1988.
Atlanta NFL, 1988.
Games: 1988 (15).
Pro statistics: Recovered two fumbles, 1988.

WES HOPKINS
Safety—Philadelphia Eagles
Born September 26, 1961, at Birmingham, Ala.
Height, 6.01. Weight, 210.
High School—Birmingham, Ala., John Carroll.
Attended Southern Methodist University.

Named to THE SPORTING NEWS NFL All-Star Team, 1985.
Selected by New Jersey in 4th round (46th player selected) of 1983 USFL draft.
Selected by Philadelphia in 2nd round (35th player selected) of 1983 NFL draft.
Signed by Philadelphia Eagles, May 26, 1983.

On injured reserve with knee injury, October 1 through remainder of 1986 season.
On physically unable to perform/reserve with knee injury, September 6 through entire 1987 season.
Crossed picket line during players' strike, October 14, 1987.

		—INTERCEPTIONS—			
Year Club	G.	No.	Yds.	Avg.	TD.
1983—Philadelphia NFL	14			None	
1984—Philadelphia NFL	16	5	107	21.4	0
1985—Philadelphia NFL	15	6	36	6.0	*1
1986—Philadelphia NFL	4			None	
1988—Philadelphia NFL	16	5	21	4.2	0
Pro Totals—5 Years............	65	16	164	10.3	1

Additional pro statistics: Recovered three fumbles, 1984; recovered two fumbles for 42 yards and fumbled once, 1985; recovered one fumble for minus four yards, 1986; recovered one fumble, 1988.
Played in Pro Bowl (NFL All-Star Game) following 1985 season.

MICHAEL WILLIAM HORAN
Name pronounced Hor-RAN.
(Mike)
Punter—Denver Broncos
Born February 1, 1959, at Orange, Calif.
Height, 5.11. Weight, 190.
High School—Fullerton, Calif., Sunny Hills.
Attended Fullerton College and received degree in mechanical engineering
from California State University at Long Beach.

Named to THE SPORTING NEWS NFL All-Star Team, 1988.
Led NFL in net punting average with 37.8 in 1988.
Selected by Atlanta in 9th round (235th player selected) of 1982 NFL draft.
Released by Atlanta Falcons, September 4, 1982; signed as free agent by Green Bay Packers, March 15, 1983.
Released by Green Bay Packers after failing physical, May 6, 1983; signed as free agent by Buffalo Bills, May 25, 1983.
Released by Buffalo Bills, August 22, 1983; signed as free agent by Philadelphia Eagles, May 7, 1984.
Released by Philadelphia Eagles, August 28, 1986; signed as free agent by Minnesota Vikings, October 31, 1986.
Released by Minnesota Vikings, November 3, 1986; signed as free agent by Denver Broncos, November 25, 1986.
Active for 1 game with Minnesota Vikings in 1986; did not play.

		—PUNTING—		
Year Club	G.	No.	Avg.	Blk.
1984—Philadelphia NFL	16	92	42.2	0
1985—Philadelphia NFL	16	91	41.5	0
1986—Minn. (0)-Den. (4) NFL.........	4	21	41.1	0
1987—Denver NFL	12	44	41.1	*2
1988—Denver NFL	16	65	44.0	0
Pro Totals—5 Years..........	64	313	42.2	2

Additional pro statistics: Rushed once for 12 yards, 1985; rushed once for no yards, recovered one fumble and fumbled once for minus 12 yards, 1986.
Played in AFC Championship Game following 1986 and 1987 seasons.
Played in NFL Championship Game following 1986 and 1987 seasons.
Played in Pro Bowl (NFL All-Star Game) following 1988 season.

GREG HORNE
Punter—Washington Redskins
Born November 22, 1964, at Russellville, Ark.
Height, 6.00. Weight, 188.
High School—Russellville, Ark.
Attended University of Arkansas.

Selected by Cincinnati in 5th round (139th player selected) of 1987 NFL draft.
Signed by Cincinnati Bengals, July 23, 1987.
Released by Cincinnati Bengals, November 5, 1987; signed as free agent by St. Louis Cardinals, November 25, 1987.
Franchise transferred to Phoenix, March 15, 1988.
Granted unconditional free agency, February 1, 1989; signed by Washington Redskins, February 21, 1989.

		—PUNTING—		
Year Club	G.	No.	Avg.	Blk.
1987—Cinc. (4)-St.L. (5) NFL..........	9	43	40.2	0
1988—Phoenix NFL..........................	16	79	40.9	1
Pro Totals—2 Years.....................	25	122	40.6	1

Additional pro statistics: Rushed three times for 20 yards, recovered two fumbles and fumbled twice for minus 10 yards, 1988.

ETHAN SHANE HORTON
Running Back—Los Angeles Raiders
Born December 19, 1962, at Kannapolis, N.C.
Height, 6.03. Weight, 228.
High School—Kannapolis, N.C., A.L. Brown.
Attended University of North Carolina.

Selected by Baltimore in 1985 USFL territorial draft.
Selected by Kansas City in 1st round (15th player selected) of 1985 NFL draft.

Signed by Kansas City Chiefs, July 26, 1985.
Released by Kansas City Chiefs, September 1, 1986; signed as free agent by Los Angeles Raiders, May 6, 1987.
Released by Los Angeles Raiders, September 7, 1987; re-signed by Raiders, September 16, 1987.
Crossed picket line during players' strike, October 2, 1987.
Released by Los Angeles Raiders, November 3, 1987; re-signed by Raiders, April 27, 1988.
Released by Los Angeles Raiders, August 23, 1988; re-signed by Raiders, February 24, 1989.

Year Club	G.	Att.	Yds.	Avg.	TD.	P.C.	Yds.	Avg.	TD.	TD.	Pts.	F.
		——RUSHING——				PASS RECEIVING				—TOTAL—		
1985—Kansas City NFL	16	48	146	3.0	3	28	185	6.6	1	4	24	2
1987—Los Angeles Raiders NFL	4	31	95	3.1	0	3	44	14.7	1	1	6	2
Pro Totals—2 Years	20	79	241	3.1	3	31	229	7.4	2	5	30	4

Additional pro statistics: Attempted one pass with no completions, 1985.

RAYMOND ANTHONY HORTON
(Ray)
Cornerback—Dallas Cowboys

Born April 12, 1960, at Tacoma, Wash.
Height, 5.11. Weight, 190.
High School—Tacoma, Wash., Mt. Tahoma.
Received bachelor of arts degree in sociology from University of Washington in 1983.

Selected by Los Angeles in 3rd round (25th player selected) of 1983 USFL draft.
Selected by Cincinnati in 2nd round (53rd player selected) of 1983 NFL draft.
Signed by Cincinnati Bengals, May 21, 1983.
Granted unconditional free agency, February 1, 1989; signed by Dallas Cowboys, March 15, 1989.

Year Club	G.	No.	Yds.	Avg.	TD.	No.	Yds.	Avg.	TD.	TD.	Pts.	F.
		-INTERCEPTIONS-				-PUNT RETURNS-				—TOTAL—		
1983—Cincinnati NFL	16	5	121	24.2	1	1	10	10.0	0	1	6	1
1984—Cincinnati NFL	15	3	48	16.0	1	2	—1	—0.5	0	1	6	0
1985—Cincinnati NFL	16	2	3	1.5	0		None			0	0	1
1986—Cincinnati NFL	16	1	4	4.0	0	11	111	10.1	0	0	0	0
1987—Cincinnati NFL	12		None			1	0	0.0	0	0	0	0
1988—Cincinnati NFL	14	3	13	4.3	0		None			0	0	0
Pro Totals—6 Years	89	14	189	13.5	2	15	120	8.0	0	2	12	2

Additional pro statistics: Returned five kickoffs for 128 yards (25.6 avg.), 1983; recovered one fumble, 1983 and 1984; recovered two fumbles, 1985; fumbled twice, 1986.
Played in AFC Championship Game following 1988 season.
Played in NFL Championship Game following 1988 season.

JEFF W. HOSTETLER
Quarterback—New York Giants

Born April 22, 1961, at Hollsopple, Pa.
Height, 6.03. Weight, 212.
High School—Johnstown, Pa., Conemaugh Valley.
Attended West Virginia University.
Son-in-law of Don Nehlen, head coach at West Virginia University.

Selected by Pittsburgh in 1984 USFL territorial draft.
Selected by New York Giants in 3rd round (59th player selected) of 1984 NFL draft.
USFL rights traded with rights to cornerback Dwayne Woodruff by Pittsburgh Maulers to Arizona Wranglers for draft choice, May 2, 1984.
Signed by New York Giants, June 12, 1984.
On injured reserve with pulled hamstring, December 14 through remainder of 1985 season.
On injured reserve with leg injury, December 6 through remainder of 1986 season.
On injured reserve with kidney injury, September 7 through November 6, 1987; activated, November 7, 1987.
Crossed picket line during players' strike, October 14, 1987.
Active for 16 games with New York Giants in 1984; did not play.
Active for 2 games with New York Giants in 1987; did not play.

Year Club	G.	Att.	Cmp.	Pct.	Gain	T.P.	P.I.	Avg.	Att.	Yds.	Avg.	TD.	TD.	Pts.	F.
		——————PASSING——————							——RUSHING——				—TOTAL—		
1985—New York Giants NFL	5		None							None			0	0	0
1986—New York Giants NFL	13		None						1	1	1.0	0	0	0	0
1988—New York Giants NFL	16	29	16	55.2	244	1	2	8.41	5	—3	—0.6	0	0	0	1
Pro Totals—5 Years	34	29	16	55.2	244	1	2	8.41	6	—2	—0.3	0	0	0	1

Quarterback Rating Points: 1988 (65.9).
Additional pro statistics: Caught one pass for 10 yards and recovered one fumble, 1988.

BOBBY HOWARD
Running Back—Green Bay Packers

Born June 1, 1964, at Pittsburgh, Pa.
Height, 6.00. Weight, 220.
High School—Pittsburgh, Pa., Langley.
Attended Indiana University.

Selected by Philadelphia in 12th round (325th player selected) of 1986 NFL draft.
Selected by Orlando in 6th round (44th player selected) of 1986 USFL draft.
Signed by Philadelphia Eagles, July 16, 1986.
Released by Philadelphia Eagles, August 26, 1986; signed as free agent by Tampa Bay Buccaneers, October 28, 1986.

On injured reserve with knee injury, July 26 through December 15, 1988; activated, December 16, 1988.
Granted unconditional free agency, February 1, 1989; signed by Green Bay Packers, March 8, 1989.

		—RUSHING—				PASS RECEIVING				—TOTAL—		
Year	Club	G.	Att.	Yds.	Avg.	TD.	P.C.	Yds.	Avg.	TD.	TD.	Pts.	F.
1986—Tampa Bay NFL		7	30	110	3.7	1	5	60	12.0	0	1	6	1
1987—Tampa Bay NFL		12	30	100	3.3	1	10	123	12.3	0	1	6	1
1988—Tampa Bay NFL		1		None				None			0	0	0
Pro Totals—3 Years		20	60	210	3.5	2	15	183	12.2	0	2	12	2

Additional pro statistics: Returned four kickoffs for 71 yards, 1986; returned one kickoff for five yards, 1987.

CARL DELANO HOWARD JR.
Defensive Back—New York Jets
Born September 20, 1961, at Newark, N.J.
Height, 6.02. Weight, 190.
High School—Irvington, N.J., Technical.
Received degree in economics from Rutgers University.

Selected by New Jersey in 1984 USFL territorial draft.
Signed as free agent by Dallas Cowboys, May 3, 1984.
On injured reserve with knee injury, November 20 through remainder of 1984 season.
Released by Dallas Cowboys, September 2, 1985; awarded on waivers to Houston Oilers, September 3, 1985.
Released by Houston Oilers, September 7, 1985; signed as free agent by Tampa Bay Buccaneers, October 15, 1985.
Released by Tampa Bay Buccaneers, November 12, 1985; signed as free agent by New York Jets, December 5, 1985.
Released by New York Jets, August 30, 1986; re-signed by Jets, September 14, 1986.
Granted unconditional free agency, February 1, 1989; re-signed by Jets, May 1, 1989.
Dallas NFL, 1984; Tampa Bay (4)-New York Jets (3) NFL, 1985; New York Jets NFL, 1986 through 1988.
Games: 1984 (10), 1985 (7), 1986 (14), 1987 (12), 1988 (16). Total—59.
Pro statistics: Recovered one fumble for four yards, 1986; intercepted three passes for 29 yards, 1987; intercepted two passes for no yards, 1988.

DAVID HOWARD
Linebacker—Minnesota Vikings
Born December 8, 1961, at Enterprise, Ala.
Height, 6.02. Weight, 232.
High School—Long Beach, Calif., Poly.
Attended Oregon State University and California State University at Long Beach.

Selected by Los Angeles in 1984 USFL territorial draft.
Signed by Los Angeles Express, February 10, 1984.
On developmental squad, April 28 through May 10, 1984; activated, May 11, 1984.
Selected by Minnesota in 3rd round (67th player selected) of 1984 NFL supplemental draft.
Released by Los Angeles Express, August 22, 1985; signed by Minnesota Vikings, August 25, 1985.
Granted roster exemption, August 25 through September 6, 1985; activated, September 7, 1985.
On developmental squad for 2 games with Los Angeles Express in 1984.
Los Angeles USFL, 1984 and 1985; Minnesota NFL, 1985 through 1988.
Games: 1984 (15), 1985 USFL (18), 1985 NFL (16), 1986 (14), 1987 (10), 1988 (16). Total USFL—33. Total NFL—56. Total Pro—89.
USFL statistics: Intercepted two passes for 14 yards, credited with 4½ sacks for 39 yards, recovered three fumbles and fumbled once, 1984; intercepted one pass for six yards, recovered four fumbles for 12 yards, credited with three sacks for 30 yards and returned two kickoffs for 10 yards, 1985.
NFL statistics: Intercepted one pass for one yard, 1987; intercepted three passes for 16 yards and recovered two fumbles for 33 yards, 1988.
Played in NFC Championship Game following 1987 season.

ERIK HOWARD
Nose Tackle—New York Giants
Born November 12, 1964, at Pittsfield, Mass.
Height, 6.04. Weight, 268.
High School—San Jose, Calif., Bellarmine College Prep.
Attended Washington State University.

Selected by New York Giants in 2nd round (46th player selected) of 1986 NFL draft.
Selected by Baltimore in 1st round (7th player selected) of 1986 USFL draft.
Signed by New York Giants, July 30, 1986.
On injured reserve with hand injury, October 9 through December 5, 1986; activated, December 6, 1986.
New York Giants NFL, 1986 through 1988.
Games: 1986 (8), 1987 (12), 1988 (16). Total—36.
Pro statistics: Recovered one fumble, 1987; recovered two fumbles, 1988.
Played in NFC Championship Game following 1986 season.
Played in NFL Championship Game following 1986 season.

WALTER LEE HOWARD
(Todd)
Linebacker—Green Bay Packers
Born February 18, 1965, at Bryan, Tex.
Height, 6.02. Weight, 235.
High School—Bryan, Tex.
Attended Texas A&M University.

Selected by Kansas City in 3rd round (73rd player selected) of 1987 NFL draft.
Signed by Kansas City Chiefs, July 22, 1987.
On injured reserve with knee injury, October 21 through remainder of 1988 season.
Granted unconditional free agency, February 1, 1989; signed by Green Bay Packers, March 8, 1989.
Kansas City NFL, 1987 and 1988.
Games: 1987 (12), 1988 (7). Total—19.

WILLIAM DOTSON HOWARD
Fullback—Tampa Bay Buccaneers
Born June 2, 1964, at Lima, O.
Height, 6.00. Weight, 240.
High Schools—Lima, O.; and Sweetwater, Tenn.,
Tennessee Military Academy.
Attended University of Tennessee.

Selected by Tampa Bay in 5th round (113th player selected) of 1988 NFL draft.
Signed by Tampa Bay Buccaneers, July 8, 1988.

| | | —RUSHING— | | | | PASS RECEIVING | | | | —TOTAL— | | |
Year Club	G.	Att.	Yds.	Avg.	TD.	P.C.	Yds.	Avg.	TD.	TD.	Pts.	F.
1988—Tampa Bay NFL	15	115	452	3.9	1	11	97	8.8	0	1	6	2

Additional pro statistics: Returned two kickoffs for 21 yards, 1988.

DAVID LAMBERT HUFFMAN
(Dave)
Offensive Tackle—Minnesota Vikings
Born April 4, 1957, at Canton, O.
Height, 6.06. Weight, 284.
High School—Dallas, Tex., Thomas Jefferson.
Recieved bachelor of arts degree in anthropology from
University of Notre Dame in 1979.
Brother of Tim Huffman, guard with Green Bay Packers, 1981 through 1985.

Named as center on THE SPORTING NEWS College All-America Team, 1978.
Selected by Minnesota in 2nd round (43rd player selected) of 1979 NFL draft.
Signed by Arizona Wranglers, January 6, 1984, for contract to take effect after being granted free agency, February 1, 1984.
Traded by Arizona Wranglers to Memphis Showboats for past consideration, December 6, 1984.
Released by Memphis Showboats, August 20, 1985; re-signed by Minnesota Vikings, September 5, 1985.
Granted roster exemption, September 5 through September 13, 1985; activated, September 14, 1985.
On injured reserve with back injury, September 17 through October 14, 1988; activated, October 15, 1988.
On injured reserve with back injury, October 25 through remainder of 1988 season.
Minnesota NFL, 1979 through 1983 and 1985 through 1988; Arizona USFL, 1984; Memphis USFL, 1985.
Games: 1979 (13), 1980 (16), 1981 (13), 1982 (9), 1983 (15), 1984 (18), 1985 USFL (18), 1985 NFL (15), 1986 (16), 1987 (12), 1988 (2). Total USFL—36. Total NFL—111. Total Pro—147.
NFL statistics: Recovered blocked fumble in end zone for a touchdown, returned three kickoffs for 42 yards and recovered two fumbles, 1983; fumbled once for minus 26 yards, 1985.
USFL statistics: Returned one kickoff for eight yards, 1984; caught one pass for two yards and a touchdown and recovered two fumbles, 1985.
Played in NFC Championship Game following 1987 season.
Played in USFL Championship Game following 1984 season.

JAMES KENT HULL
(Known by middle name.)
Center—Buffalo Bills
Born January 13, 1961, at Ponotoc, Miss.
Height, 6.04. Weight, 275.
High School—Greenwood, Miss.
Received bachelor of arts degree from Mississippi State University.

Named as center on THE SPORTING NEWS USFL All-Star Team, 1985.
Selected by New Jersey in 7th round (75th player selected) of 1983 USFL draft.
Signed by New Jersey Generals, January 19, 1983.
Granted free agency when USFL suspended operations, August 7, 1986; signed as free agent by Buffalo Bills, August 18, 1986.
Granted roster exemption, August 18 through August 21, 1986; activated, August 22, 1986.
New Jersey USFL, 1983 through 1985; Buffalo NFL, 1986 through 1988.
Games: 1983 (18), 1984 (18), 1985 (18), 1986 (16), 1987 (12), 1988 (16). Total USFL—54. Total NFL—44. Total Pro—98.
Played in AFC Championship Game following 1988 season.
Played in Pro Bowl (NFL All-Star Game) following 1988 season.

ROBERT CHARLES HUMPHERY
(Bobby)
Cornerback-Kick Returner—New York Jets
Born August 23, 1961, at Lubbock, Tex.
Height 5.10. Weight, 180.
High School—Lubbock, Tex., Estacado.
Received degree in social work from New Mexico State University.

Named as kick returner to THE SPORTING NEWS NFL All-Star Team, 1984.

Selected by New York Jets in 9th round (247th player selected) of 1983 NFL draft.
On injured reserve with broken finger, August 1 through entire 1983 season.
On injured reserve with fractured wrist, September 3 through October 4, 1985; activated, October 5, 1985.

Year Club	G.	PASS RECEIVING				—KICKOFF RET.—				—TOTAL—		
		P.C.	Yds.	Avg.	TD.	No.	Yds.	Avg.	TD.	TD.	Pts.	F.
1984—New York Jets NFL	16	14	206	14.7	1	22	675	*30.7	*1	2	12	1
1985—New York Jets NFL	12		None			17	363	21.4	0	0	0	2
1986—New York Jets NFL	16		None			28	655	23.4	*1	1	6	1
1987—New York Jets NFL	12		None			18	357	19.8	0	1	6	1
1988—New York Jets NFL	16		None			21	510	24.3	0	0	0	0
Pro Totals—5 Years	72	14	206	14.7	1	106	2560	24.2	2	4	24	6

Additional pro statistics: Recovered two fumbles, 1984 and 1988; returned one punt for no yards, ran once for 10 yards and recovered one fumble, 1985; credited with a safety, 1986; recovered two fumbles for 46 yards and a touchdown, 1987; intercepted one pass for no yards, 1988.

STEFAN GOVAN HUMPHRIES
Guard—Denver Broncos
Born January 20, 1962, at Fort Lauderdale, Fla.
Height, 6.03. Weight, 265.
High School—Fort Lauderdale, Fla., St. Thomas Aquinas.
Received bachelor of science degree in engineering science
from University of Michigan in 1984.

Named as guard on THE SPORTING NEWS College All-America Team, 1983.
Selected by Michigan in 1984 USFL territorial draft.
Selected by Chicago in 3rd round (71st player selected) of 1984 NFL draft.
Signed by Chicago Bears, July 2, 1984.
On injured reserve with knee injury, December 5 through remainder of 1984 season.
On injured reserve with knee injury, September 3 through October 3, 1985; activated, October 4, 1985.
On injured reserve with broken foot, August 26 through November 26, 1986; activated after clearing procedural waivers, November 28, 1986.
Traded by Chicago Bears to Denver Broncos for punter Bryan Wagner and draft pick, August 25, 1987.
On injured reserve with pulled thigh muscle, Sepember 8 through November 9, 1987; activated, November 10, 1987.
On injured reserve with torn triceps, September 6 through remainder of 1988 season.
Chicago NFL, 1984 through 1986; Denver NFL, 1987 and 1988.
Games: 1984 (9), 1985 (11), 1986 (4), 1987 (7), 1988 (1). Total—32.
Played in NFC Championship Game following 1985 season.
Played in AFC Championship Game following 1987 season.
Played in NFL Championship Game following 1985 and 1987 seasons.

RICKY CARDELL HUNLEY
Linebacker—Phoenix Cardinals
Born November 11, 1961, at Petersburg, Va.
Height, 6.02. Weight, 250.
High School—Petersburg, Va.
Received degree in business from University of Arizona in 1984.
Brother of LaMonte Hunley, linebacker with Indianapolis Colts, 1985 and 1986.

Selected by Arizona in 1984 USFL territorial draft.
Selected by Cincinnati in 1st round (7th player selected) in 1984 NFL draft.
NFL rights traded by Cincinnati Bengals to Denver Broncos for 1st and 3rd round picks in 1986 draft and 5th round pick in 1987 draft, October 9, 1984.
Signed by Denver Broncos, October 16, 1984.
Granted roster exemption, October 16 though October 25, 1984; activated, October 26, 1984.
Granted free agency, February 1, 1988; re-signed by Broncos and traded to Phoenix Cardinals for center Mike Ruether, July 19, 1988.
Selected by Pittsburgh Pirates' organization in 26th round of free-agent draft, June 3, 1980.
Denver NFL, 1984 through 1987; Phoenix NFL, 1988.
Games: 1984 (8), 1985 (16), 1986 (16), 1987 (12), 1988 (16). Total—68.
Pro statistics: Intercepted one pass for 22 yards, returned two kickoffs for 11 yards and recovered one fumble, 1986; intercepted two passes for 64 yards and a touchdown, 1987; returned one punt for three yards, 1988.
Played in AFC Championship Game following 1986 and 1987 seasons.
Played in NFL Championship Game following 1986 and 1987 seasons.

BYRON RAY HUNT
Linebacker—Detroit Lions
Born December 17, 1958, at Longview, Tex.
Height, 6.05. Weight, 242.
High School—Longview, Tex., White Oak.
Received degree in political science from Southern Methodist University.
Brother of Sam Hunt, defensive end with New England Patriots
and Green Bay Packers, 1974 through 1980.

Selected by New York Giants in 9th round (224th player selected) of 1981 NFL draft.
Released by New York Giants, September 16, 1988; signed as free agent by Detroit Lions, May 12, 1989.
New York Giants NFL, 1981 through 1988.
Games: 1981 (16), 1982 (9), 1983 (16), 1985 (16), 1986 (16), 1987 (12), 1988 (2). Total—100.
Pro statistics: Intercepted one pass for seven yards, 1981; intercepted one pass for 14 yards and recovered two fumbles, 1984; recovered one fumble, 1985.
Played in NFC Championship Game following 1986 season.
Played in NFL Championship Game following 1986 season.

PATRICK EDWARD HUNTER
Cornerback—Seattle Seahawks
Born October 24, 1964, at San Francisco, Calif.
Height, 5.11. Weight, 185.
High School—South San Francisco, Calif.
Attended University of Nevada at Reno.
Cousin of Louis Wright, cornerback with Denver Broncos, 1975 through 1986.

Selected by Seattle in 3rd round (68th player selected) of 1986 NFL draft.
Signed by Seattle Seahawks, July 16, 1986.
On non-football injury list with lacerated kidney, November 1 through December 9, 1988; activated, December 10, 1988.
Seattle NFL, 1986 through 1988.
Games: 1986 (16), 1987 (11), 1988 (10). Total—37.
Pro statistics: Intercepted one pass for three yards, 1987; returned one punt for no yards and fumbled once, 1988.

TONY WAYNE HUNTER
Tight End—San Diego Chargers
Born May 22, 1960, at Cincinnati, O.
Height, 6.04. Weight, 235.
High School—Cincinnati, O., Moeller.
Received bachelor of science degree in economics from University of Notre Dame in 1984.

Selected by Chicago in 1983 USFL territorial draft.
Selected by Buffalo in 1st round (12th player selected) of 1983 NFL draft.
Signed by Buffalo Bills, June 17, 1983.
On injured reserve with back injury, September 29 through October 25, 1984; activated, October 26, 1984.
Traded by Buffalo Bills to Los Angeles Rams for quarterback Vince Ferragamo and 3rd round pick in 1986 draft, July 18, 1985.
On injured reserve with shin injury, November 21 through remainder of 1986 season.
Released by Los Angeles Rams after failing physical, September 1, 1987; signed as free agent by San Diego Chargers, June 1, 1989.

		——PASS RECEIVING——			
Year Club	G.	P.C.	Yds.	Avg.	TD.
1983—Buffalo NFL..................	13	36	402	11.2	3
1984—Buffalo NFL..................	11	33	331	10.0	2
1985—L.A. Rams NFL............	16	50	562	11.2	4
1986—L.A. Rams NFL.............	7	15	206	13.7	0
Pro Totals—4 Years............	47	134	1501	11.2	9

Additional pro statistics: Rushed twice for 28 yards, 1983; recovered one fumble, 1983 through 1985; fumbled once, 1983 and 1984; rushed once for six yards, 1984; fumbled three times, 1985; rushed once for minus six yards and fumbled twice, 1986.
Played in NFC Championship Game following 1985 season.

JEFFERY TONJA HURD
(Jeff)
Linebacker—Dallas Cowboys
Born May 25, 1964, at Monroe, La.
Height, 6.02. Weight, 245.
High School—Kansas City, Mo., Lincoln Academy.
Attended Kansas State University.

Signed as free agent by Dallas Cowboys, April 30, 1987.
Released by Dallas Cowboys, August 17, 1987; re-signed as replacement player by Cowboys, September 23, 1987.
Released by Dallas Cowboys, October 26, 1987; re-signed by Cowboys for 1988, October 27, 1987.
Signed for 1987 season, December 16, 1987.
On injured reserve with knee injury, August 16 through entire 1988 season.
Dallas NFL, 1987.
Games: 1987 (5).

DONALD AMECHI IGWEBUIKE
Name pronounced Ig-way-BWEE-kay.

(Middle name means "You can't predict tomorrow.")

Placekicker—Tampa Bay Buccaneers
Born December 27, 1960, at Anambra, Nigeria.
Height, 5.09. Weight, 185.
High School—Anambra, Nigeria, Immaculate Conception.
Attended Clemson University.

Selected by Tampa Bay in 10th round (260th player selected) of 1985 NFL draft.
Signed by Tampa Bay Buccaneers, June 6, 1985.
On injured reserve with pulled groin, November 22 through remainder of 1988 season.

		——PLACE KICKING——				
Year Club	G.	XP.	XPM.	FG.	FGA.	Pts.
1985—Tampa Bay NFL.....	16	30	2	22	32	96
1986—Tampa Bay NFL.....	16	26	1	17	24	77
1987—Tampa Bay NFL.....	12	24	2	14	18	66
1988—Tampa Bay NFL.....	12	21	0	19	25	78
Pro Totals—4 Years.......	56	101	5	72	99	317

TUNCH ALI ILKIN

Name pronounced TOON-ch ILL-kin.

Offensive Tackle—Pittsburgh Steelers

Born September 23, 1957, at Istanbul, Turkey.
Height, 6.03. Weight, 265.
High School—Highland Park, Ill.
Received bachelor of science degree in broadcasting from Indiana State University in 1980.

Selected by Pittsburgh in 6th round (165th player selected) of 1980 NFL draft.
Released by Pittsburgh Steelers, August 25, 1980; re-signed by Steelers, October 15, 1983.
On injured reserve with shoulder injury, August 30 through September 29, 1983; activated, September 30, 1983.
Pittsburgh NFL, 1980 through 1988.
Games: 1980 (10), 1981 (16), 1982 (8), 1983 (11), 1984 (16), 1985 (16), 1986 (15), 1987 (11), 1988 (16). Total—119.
Pro statistics: Recovered one fumble, 1981, 1983 and 1985.
Played in AFC Championship Game following 1984 season.
Played in Pro Bowl (NFL All-Star Game) following 1988 season.

TIMOTHY JAMES INGLIS
(Tim)
Linebacker—Green Bay Packers

Born March 10, 1964, at Toledo, O.
Height, 6.03. Weight, 232.
High School—Toledo, O., St. John's.
Received bachelor of business administration degree from University of Toledo in 1987.

Signed as free agent by Cincinnati Bengals, May 1, 1987.
Released by Cincinnati Bengals, August 24, 1987; re-signed as replacement player by Bengals, September 25, 1987.
Released by Cincinnati Bengals, October 19, 1987; re-signed by Bengals, October 29, 1987.
Released by Cincinnati Bengals, August 30, 1988; re-signed by Bengals, September 2, 1988.
On injured reserve with ankle and hamstring injuries, September 23 through October 19, 1988; activated after clearing procedural waivers, October 21, 1988.
Released by Cincinnati Bengals, November 7, 1988; signed as free agent by Green Bay Packers, February 10, 1989.
Cincinnati NFL, 1987 and 1988.
Games: 1987 (8), 1988 (4). Total—12.

BYRON KIMBLE INGRAM
Guard—Kansas City Chiefs

Born November 17, 1964, at Lexington, Ky.
Height, 6.02. Weight, 295.
High School—Lexington, Ky., Henry Clay.
Attended Eastern Kentucky University.

Signed as free agent by Kansas City Chiefs, June 26, 1987.
On injured reserve with neck injury, September 7 through October 29, 1987; activated, October 30, 1987.
On injured reserve, September 28 through October 27, 1988; activated, October 28, 1988.
Kansas City NFL, 1987 and 1988.
Games: 1987 (1), 1988 (12). Total—13.
Pro statistics: Returned two kickoffs for 16 yards, 1988.

MARK INGRAM
Wide Receiver—New York Giants

Born August 23, 1965, at Rockford, Ill.
Height, 5.10. Weight, 188.
High School—Flint, Mich., Northwestern.
Attended Michigan State University.

Selected by New York Giants in 1st round (28th player selected) of 1987 NFL draft.
Signed by New York Giants, July 31, 1987.
On injured reserve with broken collarbone, September 26 through December 2, 1988; activated, December 3, 1988.

Year Club	G.	PASS RECEIVING				—KICKOFF RET.—				—TOTAL—		
		P.C.	Yds.	Avg.	TD.	No.	Yds.	Avg.	TD.	TD.	Pts.	F.
1987—New York Giants NFL	9	2	32	16.0	0	6	114	19.0	0	0	0	0
1988—New York Giants NFL	7	13	158	12.2	1	8	129	16.1	0	1	6	0
Pro Totals—2 Years	16	15	190	12.7	1	14	243	17.4	0	1	6	0

LeROY IRVIN JR.
Cornerback—Los Angeles Rams

Born September 15, 1957, at Fort Dix, N.J.
Height, 5.11. Weight, 184.
High School—Augusta, Ga., Glenn Hills.
Attended University of Kansas.

Established NFL record for most punt return yards, game (207), against Atlanta Falcons, October 11, 1981.
Tied NFL record for most touchdowns, punt returns, game (2), against Atlanta Falcons, October 11, 1981.
Named to The Sporting News NFL All-Star Team, 1986.
Named as punt returner to The Sporting News NFL All-Star Team, 1981.
Selected by Los Angeles in 3rd round (70th player selected) of 1980 NFL draft.
Placed on suspended list, November 4 through November 9, 1987; activated, November 10, 1987.

Year Club	G.	No.	Yds.	Avg.	TD.	No.	Yds.	Avg.	TD.	TD.	Pts.	F.
			—INTERCEPTIONS—				—PUNT RETURNS—				—TOTAL—	
1980—Los Angeles Rams NFL	16	2	80	40.0	0	42	296	7.0	0	0	0	5
1981—Los Angeles Rams NFL	16	3	18	6.0	0	46	*615	*13.4	*3	3	18	3
1982—Los Angeles Rams NFL	9			None		22	242	11.0	1	1	6	4
1983—Los Angeles Rams NFL	15	4	42	10.5	0	25	212	8.5	0	0	0	4
1984—Los Angeles Rams NFL	16	5	166	33.2	*2	9	83	9.2	0	2	12	0
1985—Los Angeles Rams NFL	16	6	83	13.8	*1			None		1	6	0
1986—Los Angeles Rams NFL	16	6	150	25.0	1			None		3	18	1
1987—Los Angeles Rams NFL	10	2	47	23.5	1	1	0	0.0	0	1	6	0
1988—Los Angeles Rams NFL	16	3	25	8.3	0	1	2	2.0	0	0	0	1
Pro Totals—9 Years	130	31	611	19.7	5	146	1450	9.9	4	11	66	18

Additional pro statistics: Returned one kickoff for five yards and recovered three fumbles, 1980; recovered three fumbles for 14 yards, 1981; recovered two fumbles, 1982 and 1983; returned one kickoff for 22 yards, 1983; returned two kickoffs for 33 yards, 1984; returned blocked field goal 65 yards for a touchdown and recovered three fumbles for 55 yards and a touchdown, 1986.

Played in NFC Championship Game following 1985 season.
Played in Pro Bowl (NFL All-Star Game) following 1985 and 1986 seasons.

MICHAEL JEROME IRVIN
Wide Receiver—Dallas Cowboys
Born March 5, 1966, at Fort Lauderdale, Fla.
Height, 6.02. Weight, 202.
High School—Fort Lauderdale, Fla., St. Thomas Aquinas.
Received degree in business management from University of Miami (Fla.) in 1988.

Selected by Dallas in 1st round (11th player selected) of 1988 NFL draft.
Signed by Dallas Cowboys, July 9, 1988.

Year Club	G.	P.C.	Yds.	Avg.	TD.
		—PASS RECEIVING—			
1988—Dallas NFL	14	32	654	20.4	5

Additional pro statistics: Rushed once for two yards, 1988.

TIMOTHY EDWARD IRWIN
(Tim)
Offensive Tackle—Minnesota Vikings
Born December 13, 1958, at Knoxville, Tenn.
Height, 6.07. Weight, 285.
High School—Knoxville, Tenn., Central.
Received degree in political science from University of Tennessee in 1981.

Selected by Minnesota in 3rd round (74th player selected) of 1981 NFL draft.
Minnesota NFL, 1981 through 1988.
Games: 1981 (7), 1982 (9), 1983 (16), 1984 (16), 1985 (16), 1986 (16), 1987 (12), 1988 (16). Total—108.
Pro statistics: Recovered one fumble, 1983; recovered one fumble for two yards, 1984; returned one kickoff for no yards and recovered two fumbles, 1986.
Played in NFC Championship Game following 1987 season.

EARNEST JACKSON
Running Back—Indianapolis Colts
Born December 18, 1959, at Needville, Tex.
Height, 5.09. Weight, 219.
High School—Rosenburg, Tex., Lamar.
Attended Texas A&M University.

Selected by Oakland in 9th round (103rd player selected) of 1983 USFL draft.
USFL rights traded by Oakland Invaders to Michigan Panthers for 8th round pick in 1984 draft, March 24, 1983.
Selected by San Diego in 8th round (202nd player selected) of 1983 NFL draft.
Signed by San Diego Chargers, July 11, 1983.
Traded by San Diego Chargers to Philadelphia Eagles for 4th round pick in 1986 draft and 8th round pick in 1987 draft, September 2, 1985.
Released by Philadelphia Eagles, September 16, 1986; signed as free agent by Pittsburgh Steelers, September 23, 1986.
Crossed picket line during players' strike, September 30, 1987.
Granted unconditional free agency, February 1, 1989; released by Pittsburgh Steelers, April 25, 1989.
Signed by Indianapolis Colts, May 12, 1989.
Active for 2 games with Philadelphia Eagles in 1986; did not play.

Year Club	G.	Att.	Yds.	Avg.	TD.	P.C.	Yds.	Avg.	TD.	TD.	Pts.	F.
		—RUSHING—				PASS RECEIVING				—TOTAL—	
1983—San Diego NFL	12	11	39	3.5	0	5	42	8.4	0	0	0	1
1984—San Diego NFL	16	296	1179	4.0	8	39	222	5.7	1	9	54	3
1985—Philadelphia NFL	16	282	1028	3.6	5	10	126	12.6	1	6	36	3
1986—Phi. (0)-Pitt. (13) NFL	13	216	910	4.2	5	17	169	9.9	0	5	30	3
1987—Pittsburgh NFL	12	180	696	3.9	1	7	52	7.4	0	1	6	2
1988—Pittsburgh NFL	12	74	315	4.3	3	9	84	9.3	0	3	18	3
Pro Totals—6 Years	81	1059	4167	3.9	22	87	695	8.0	2	24	144	15

Year Club	G.	No.	Yds.	Avg.TD.	
			KICKOFF RETURNS		
1983—San Diego NFL	12	11	201	18.3	0
1984—San Diego NFL	16	1	10	10.0	0
1985—Philadelphia NFL	16		None		
1986—Phi. (0)-Pitt. (13) NFL.	13		None		
1987—Pittsburgh NFL............	12		None		
1988—Pittsburgh NFL............	12		None		
Pro Totals—6 Years............	81	12	211	17.6	0

Additional pro statistics: Recovered one fumble, 1983 and 1986; recovered two fumbles, 1984; recovered three fumbles, 1987.

Played in Pro Bowl (NFL All-Star Game) following 1984 and 1986 seasons.

JEFFERY PAUL JACKSON
(Jeff)
Linebacker—San Diego Chargers
Born October 9, 1961, at Shreveport, Ga.
Height, 6.01. Weight, 242.
High School—Griffin, Ga.
Attended Auburn University.

Selected by Birmingham in 1984 USFL territorial draft.
Selected by Atlanta in 8th round (206th player selected) of 1984 NFL draft.
Signed by Atlanta Falcons, June 10, 1984.
Released by Atlanta Falcons, November 21, 1985; re-signed by Falcons, January 21, 1986.
Released by Atlanta Falcons, August 18, 1986; signed as free agent by San Diego Chargers, April 22, 1987.
Released by San Diego Chargers, September 7, 1987; re-signed as replacement player by Chargers, September 24, 1987.
Released by San Diego Chargers, November 9, 1988; re-signed by Chargers, November 23, 1988.
Atlanta NFL, 1984 and 1985; San Diego NFL, 1987 and 1988.
Games: 1984 (16), 1985 (11), 1987 (11), 1988 (14). Total—52.
Pro statistics: Intercepted one pass for 35 yards and a touchdown, 1984; recovered one fumble, 1984 and 1987.

JOHN JACKSON
Offensive Tackle—Pittsburgh Steelers
Born January 4, 1965, at Camp Kwe, Okinawa, Japan.
Height, 6.06. Weight, 282.
High School—Cincinnati, O., Woodward.
Attended Eastern Kentucky University.

Selected by Pittsburgh in 10th round (252nd player selected) of 1988 NFL draft.
Signed by Pittsburgh Steelers, May 17, 1988.
Pittsburgh NFL, 1988.
Games: 1988 (16).
Pro statistics: Returned one kickoff for 10 yards, 1988.

KEITH JEROME JACKSON
Tight End—Philadelphia Eagles
Born April 19, 1965, at Little Rock, Ark.
Height, 6.02. Weight, 250.
High School—Little Rock, Ark., Parkview.
Received degree in communications from University of Oklahoma in 1988.

Named to THE SPORTING NEWS NFL All-Star Team, 1988.
Named THE SPORTING NEWS NFL Rookie of the Year, 1988.
Named as tight end on THE SPORTING NEWS College All-America Team, 1986.
Selected by Philadelphia in 1st round (13th player selected) of 1988 NFL draft.
Signed by Philadelphia Eagles, August 10, 1988.

Year Club	G.	P.C.	Yds.	Avg.	TD.
		—PASS RECEIVING—			
1988—Philadelphia NFL	16	81	869	10.7	6

Additional pro statistics: Fumbled three times, 1988.
Played in Pro Bowl (NFL All-Star Game) following 1988 season.

KENNY JACKSON
Wide Receiver—Houston Oilers
Born February 15, 1962, at Neptune, N.J.
Height, 6.00. Weight, 180.
High School—South River, N.J.
Received degree in finance from Penn State University.
Cousin of Tony Collins, running back with New England Patriots, 1981 through 1987.

Selected by Philadelphia in 1984 USFL territorial draft.
Selected by Philadelphia in 1st round (4th player selected) of 1984 NFL draft.
Signed by Philadelphia Eagles, May 1, 1984.
On injured reserve with separated shoulder, October 22 through November 22, 1984; activated, November 23, 1984.
Granted free agency, February 1, 1988; re-signed by Eagles, October 31, 1988.
Granted roster exemption, October 31 through November 3, 1988; activated, November 4, 1988.
Granted unconditional free agency, February 1, 1989; signed by Houston Oilers, April 1, 1989.

Year Club	G.	P.C.	Yds.	Avg.	TD.
			—PASS RECEIVING—		
1984—Philadelphia NFL	11	26	398	15.3	1
1985—Philadelphia NFL	16	40	692	17.3	1
1986—Philadelphia NFL	16	30	506	16.9	6
1987—Philadelphia NFL	12	21	471	22.4	3
1988—Philadelphia NFL	7			None	
Pro Totals—5 Years............	62	117	2067	17.7	11

Additional pro statistics: Rushed once for six yards, 1986; rushed six times for 27 yards, recovered one fumble and fumbled once, 1987.

KIRBY JACKSON
Cornerback—Buffalo Bills

Born February 2, 1965, at Sturgis, Miss.
Height, 5.10. Weight, 180.
High School—Sturgis, Miss.
Attended Mississippi State University.

Selected by New York Jets in 5th round (129th player selected) of 1987 NFL draft.
Signed by New York Jets, July 24, 1987.
Released by New York Jets, September 6, 1987; signed as free agent replacement player by Los Angeles Rams, September 23, 1987.
Released by Los Angeles Rams, November 16, 1987; signed as free agent by Buffalo Bills, November 27, 1987.
On injured reserve with hamstring injury, August 17 through October 28, 1988; activated, October 29, 1988.
Los Angeles Rams NFL, 1987; Buffalo NFL, 1988.
Games: 1987 (5), 1988 (8). Total—13.
Pro statistics: Intercepted one pass for 36 yards and recovered blocked punt in end zone for a touchdown, 1987.
Played in AFC Championship Game following 1988 season.

MARK ANTHONY JACKSON
Wide Receiver—Denver Broncos

Born July 23, 1963, at Chicago, Ill.
Height, 5.10. Weight, 180.
High School—Terre Haute, Ind., South Vigo.
Received bachelor's degree in public relations from Purdue University in 1986.

Selected by Denver in 6th round (161st player selected) of 1986 NFL draft.
Selected by New Jersey in 2nd round (11th player selected) of 1986 USFL draft.
Signed by Denver Broncos, July 16, 1986.
On injured reserve with broken collarbone, September 12 through October 9, 1988; activated, October 10, 1988.

Year Club	G.	P.C.	Yds.	Avg.	TD.
			—PASS RECEIVING—		
1986—Denver NFL	16	38	738	19.4	1
1987—Denver NFL	12	26	436	16.8	2
1988—Denver NFL	12	46	852	18.5	6
Pro Totals—3 Years............	40	110	2026	18.4	9

Additional pro statistics: Rushed twice for six yards, returned two punts for seven yards, returned one kickoff for 16 yards and fumbled three times, 1986; rushed once for five yards, recovered one fumble and fumbled once, 1988.
Played in AFC Championship Game following 1986 and 1987 seasons.
Played in NFL Championship Game following 1986 and 1987 seasons.

RICKEY ANDERSON JACKSON
Linebacker—New Orleans Saints

Born March 20, 1958, at Pahokee, Fla.
Height, 6.02. Weight, 243.
High School—Pahokee, Fla.
Attended University of Pittsburgh.

Named to THE SPORTING NEWS NFL All-Star Team, 1987.
Selected by New Orleans in 2nd round (51st player selected) of 1981 NFL draft.
New Orleans NFL, 1981.
Games: 1981 (16), 1982 (9), 1983 (16), 1984 (16), 1985 (16), 1986 (16), 1987 (12), 1988 (16). Total—117.
Pro statistics: Recovered one fumble, 1981 and 1986; intercepted one pass for 32 yards and recovered two fumbles, 1982; intercepted one pass for no yards and recovered two fumbles for minus two yards, 1983; fumbled once, 1983 and 1984; recovered four fumbles for four yards and intercepted one pass for 14 yards, 1984; intercepted one pass for one yard, 1986; intercepted two passes for four yards, 1987; intercepted one pass for 16 yards and credited with a safety, 1988.
Played in Pro Bowl (NFL All-Star Game) following 1983 through 1986 seasons.

ROBERT MICHAEL JACKSON
Safety—Cincinnati Bengals

Born October 10, 1958, at Grand Rapids, Mich.
Height, 5.10. Weight, 186.
High School—Allendale, Mich.
Attended Central Michigan University.

Selected by Cincinnati in 11th round (285th player selected) of 1981 NFL draft.
On injured reserve with knee injury, August 10 through entire 1981 season.
On injured reserve with elbow injury, September 16 through November 9, 1986; activated, November 10, 1986.

Granted free agency, February 1, 1988; rights relinquished, August 29, 1988.
Signed by Cincinnati Bengals, March 29, 1989.

Year Club	G.	No.	Yds.	Avg.TD.		Year Club	G.	No.	Yds.	Avg.TD.
1982—Cincinnati NFL.............	9			None		1986—Cincinnati NFL.............	7			None
1983—Cincinnati NFL.............	16	2	21	10.5	0	1987—Cincinnati NFL.............	12	3	49	16.3	0
1984—Cincinnati NFL.............	16	4	32	8.0	1	Pro Totals—6 Years............	76	15	202	13.5	2
1985—Cincinnati NFL.............	16	6	100	16.7	*1						

Both INTERCEPTIONS headers span their respective No./Yds./Avg./TD columns.

Additional pro statistics: Recovered one fumble, 1982, 1985 and 1987; recovered three fumbles, 1984.

VESTEE JACKSON II
Cornerback—Chicago Bears
Born August 14, 1963, at Fresno, Calif.
Height, 6.00. Weight, 186.
High School—Fresno, Calif., McLane.
Attended University of Washington.

Selected by Chicago in 2nd round (55th player selected) of 1986 NFL draft.
Signed by Chicago Bears, July 24, 1986.

		—INTERCEPTIONS—			
Year Club	G.	No.	Yds.	Avg.	TD.
1986—Chicago NFL................	16	3	0	0.0	0
1987—Chicago NFL................	12	1	0	0.0	0
1988—Chicago NFL................	16	8	94	11.8	0
Pro Totals—3 Years...........	44	12	94	7.8	0

Additional pro statistics: Recovered two fumbles for minus seven yards, 1986.
Played in NFC Championship Game following 1988 season.

VINCENT EDWARD JACKSON
(Bo)
Running Back—Los Angeles Raiders
Born November 30, 1962, at Bessemer, Ala.
Height, 6.01. Weight, 225.
High School—McCalla, Ala., McAdory.
Attended Auburn University, Auburn, Ala.

Heisman Trophy winner, 1985.
Named college football Player of the Year by THE SPORTING NEWS, 1985.
Named as running back on THE SPORTING NEWS College All-America Team, 1985.
Selected by Tampa Bay in 1st round (1st player selected) of 1986 NFL draft.
Selected by Birmingham in 1986 USFL territorial draft.
On reserve/did not sign entire 1986 football season through April 27, 1987.
Selected by Los Angeles Raiders in 7th round (183rd player selected) of 1987 NFL draft.
Signed by Los Angeles Raiders, July 17, 1987.
On reserve/did not report, August 27 through October 23, 1987; activated, October 24, 1987.
On reserve/did not report, August 22 through October 11, 1988; reported, October 12, 1988.
Activated from reserve/did not report, October 15, 1988.

		—RUSHING—				PASS RECEIVING				—TOTAL—		
Year Club	G.	Att.	Yds.	Avg.	TD.	P.C.	Yds.	Avg.	TD.	TD.	Pts.	F.
1987—Los Angeles Raiders NFL	7	81	554	6.8	4	16	136	8.5	2	6	36	2
1988—Los Angeles Raiders NFL	10	136	580	4.3	3	9	79	8.8	0	3	18	5
Pro Totals—2 Years.................................	17	217	1134	5.2	7	25	215	8.6	2	9	54	7

Additional pro statistics: Recovered one fumble, 1987; recovered two fumbles, 1988.

RECORD AS BASEBALL PLAYER

Tied major league records for most strikeouts, nine-inning game (5), April 18, 1987; most strikeouts, inning (2), April 8, 1987, fourth inning.
Major League stolen bases: 1986 (3), 1987 (10), 1988 (27). Total—40.

Year Club	League	Pos.	G.	AB.	R.	H.	2B.	3B.	HR.	RBI.	B.A.	PO.	A.	E.	F.A.
1986—Memphis†	South.	OF	53	184	30	51	9	3	7	25	.277	116	8	7	.947
1986—Kansas City	Amer.	OF	25	82	9	17	2	1	2	9	.207	29	2	4	.886
1987—Kansas City	Amer.	OF	116	396	46	93	17	2	22	53	.235	180	9	9	.955
1988—Kansas City‡	Amer.	OF	124	439	63	108	16	4	25	68	.246	246	11	7	.973
Major League Totals—3 Years................			265	917	118	218	35	7	49	130	.238	455	22	20	.960

Selected by New York Yankees' organization in 2nd round of free-agent draft, June 7, 1982.
Selected by California Angels' organization in 20th round of free-agent draft, June 3, 1985.
Selected by Kansas City Royals' organization in 4th round of free-agent draft, June 2, 1986.
†On temporary inactive list, June 20 to June 30, 1986.
‡On disabled list, June 1 to July 2, 1988.

JOE JACOBY
Offensive Tackle—Washington Redskins
Born July 6, 1959, at Louisville, Ky.
Height, 6.07. Weight, 305.
High School—Louisville, Ky., Western.
Attended University of Louisville.

Named to THE SPORTING NEWS NFL All-Star Team, 1983 and 1984.
Signed as free agent by Washington Redskins, May 1, 1981.
Washington NFL, 1981 through 1988.
Games: 1981 (14), 1982 (9), 1983 (16), 1984 (16), 1985 (11), 1986 (16), 1987 (12), 1988 (16). Total—110.
Pro statistics: Recovered one fumble, 1981, 1982 and 1988; recovered fumble in end zone for a touchdown, 1984.
Played in NFC Championship Game following 1982, 1983, 1986 and 1987 seasons.
Played in NFL Championship Game following 1982, 1983 and 1987 seasons.
Played in Pro Bowl (NFL All-Star Game) following 1983 through 1986 seasons.

JEFF TODD JAEGER
(Name pronounced JAY-ger.)
Placekicker—Los Angeles Raiders
Born November 26, 1964, at Tacoma, Wash.
Height, 5.11. Weight, 189.
High School—Kent, Wash., Kent-Meridian.
Attended University of Washington.

Selected by Cleveland in 3rd round (82nd player selected) of 1987 NFL draft.
Signed by Cleveland Browns, July 26, 1987.
Crossed picket line during players' strike, October 14, 1987.
On injured reserve with foot injury, August 26 through entire 1988 season.
Granted unconditional free agency, February 1, 1989; signed by Los Angeles Raiders, March 20, 1989.

		——PLACE KICKING——				
Year	Club	G.	XP.	XPM.	FG.	FGA.	Pts.
1987—Cleveland NFL.........	10	33	0	14	22	75

Additional pro statistics: Attempted one pass with no completions and recovered one fumble, 1987.

VAN JAKES
Cornerback—Green Bay Packers
Born May 10, 1961, at Phenix City, Ala.
Height, 6.00. Weight, 190.
High School—Buffalo, N.Y., Seneca Vocational.
Attended Kent State University.

Signed as free agent by Kansas City Chiefs, May 5, 1983.
On injured reserve with ankle injury, October 16 through November 27, 1984.
Released by Kansas City Chiefs, November 28, 1984; re-signed by Chiefs, December 11, 1984.
Signed by Jacksonville Bulls, December 31, 1984, to contract to take effect after being granted free agency, February 1, 1985.
Released by Jacksonville Bulls, August 28, 1985; signed as free agent by New Orleans Saints, July 11, 1986.
On injured reserve with knee injury, December 3 through remainder of 1986 season.
Granted unconditional free agency, February 1, 1989; signed by Green Bay Packers, March 2, 1989.

	——INTERCEPTIONS——				
Year	Club	G.	No.	Yds.	Avg.	TD.
1983—Kansas City NFL..........	14		None		
1984—Kansas City NFL..........	7		None		
1985—Jacksonville USFL......	18	3	13	4.3	0
1986—New Orleans NFL........	12	2	6	3.0	0
1987—New Orleans NFL........	12	3	32	10.7	0
1988—New Orleans NFL........	16	3	61	20.3	0
NFL Totals—5 Years..........	61	8	99	12.4	0
USFL Totals—1 Year..........	18	3	13	4.3	0
Pro Totals—6 Years............	79	11	112	10.2	0

Additional USFL statistics: Credited with one sack for 18 yards and recovered one fumble, 1985.
Additional NFL statistics: Recovered one fumble for 30 yards, 1987.

GARRY MALCOM JAMES
Running Back—Detroit Lions
Born September 4, 1963, at Marrero, La.
Height, 5.10. Weight, 214.
High School—Harvey, La., West Jefferson.
Attended Louisiana State University.
Cousin of Louis Lipps, wide receiver with Pittsburgh Steelers.

Selected by Tampa Bay in 1986 USFL territorial draft.
Selected by Detroit in 2nd round (29th player selected) of 1986 NFL draft.
Signed by Detroit Lions, July 23, 1986.

		——RUSHING——				PASS RECEIVING				—TOTAL—		
Year	Club	G.	Att.	Yds.	Avg.	TD.	P.C.	Yds.	Avg.	TD.	TD.	Pts.	F.
1986—Detroit NFL................................	16	159	688	4.3	3	34	219	6.4	0	3	18	3
1987—Detroit NFL................................	8	82	270	3.3	4	16	215	13.4	0	4	24	3
1988—Detroit NFL................................	16	182	552	3.0	5	39	382	9.8	2	7	42	3
Pro Totals—3 Years...................	40	423	1510	3.6	12	89	816	9.2	2	14	84	9

Additional pro statistics: Recovered one fumble, 1986 and 1987.

JESSE CRAIG JAMES

(Known by middle name.)

Fullback—New England Patriots

Born January 2, 1961, at Jacksonville, Tex.
Height, 6.00. Weight, 215.
High School—Houston, Tex., Stratford.
Received degree in history from Southern Methodist University.
Brother of Chris James, outfielder with San Diego Padres.

Selected by Washington in 1st round (4th player selected) of 1983 USFL draft.
Signed by Washington Federals, January 12, 1983.
Selected by New England in 7th round (187th player selected) of 1983 NFL draft.
On developmental squad, March 19 through April 14, 1983; activated, April 15, 1983.
On developmental squad, March 9 through April 11, 1984.
Released with knee injury by Washington Federals, April 12, 1984; signed by New England Patriots, April 20, 1984.
On injured reserve with knee injury, October 26 through remainder of 1987 season.
On injured reserve with shoulder injury, October 14 through remainder of 1988 season.
On developmental squad for 4 games with Washington Federals in 1983.
On developmental squad for 5 games with Washington Federals in 1984.

		—————RUSHING—————				PASS RECEIVING				—TOTAL—		
Year Club	G.	Att.	Yds.	Avg.	TD.	P.C.	Yds.	Avg.	TD.	TD.	Pts.	F.
1983—Washington USFL	14	202	823	4.1	4	40	342	8.6	2	6	36	6
1984—Washington USFL	2	16	61	3.8	0	1	13	13.0	0	0	0	0
1984—New England NFL	15	160	790	4.9	1	22	159	7.2	0	1	6	4
1985—New England NFL	16	263	1227	4.7	5	27	360	13.3	2	7	42	8
1986—New England NFL	13	154	427	2.8	4	18	129	7.2	0	4	24	5
1987—New England NFL	2	4	10	2.5	0		None			0	0	0
1988—New England NFL	6	4	15	3.8	1	14	171	12.2	0	1	6	0
USFL Totals—2 Years	16	218	884	4.1	4	41	355	8.7	2	6	36	6
NFL Totals—5 Years	52	585	2469	4.2	11	81	819	10.1	2	13	78	17
Pro Totals—7 Years	68	803	3353	4.2	15	122	1174	9.6	4	19	114	23

Additional pro statistics: Returned one kickoff for no yards, attempted two passes with two completions for 16 yards and two touchdowns and recovered four fumbles, 1985; attempted four passes with one completion for 10 yards with one touchdown and one interception and recovered one fumble, 1986.
Played in AFC Championship Game following 1985 season.
Played in NFL Championship Game following 1985 season.
Played in Pro Bowl (NFL All-Star Game) following 1985 season.

LIONEL JAMES

Running Back—San Diego Chargers

Born May 25, 1962, at Albany, Ga.
Height, 5.06. Weight, 172.
High School—Albany, Ga., Dougherty.
Received degree in math education from Auburn University in 1989.

Established NFL records for most combined yards gained, season (2,535), 1985; most 300-yard combined yardage games, season (2), 1985; most pass reception yards by running back, season (1,027), 1985.
Selected by Birmingham in 1984 USFL territorial draft.
Selected by San Diego in 5th round (118th player selected) of 1984 NFL draft.
Signed by San Diego Chargers, June 8, 1984.
On injured reserve with foot injury, October 24 through remainder of 1986 season.

		—————RUSHING—————				PASS RECEIVING				—TOTAL—		
Year Club	G.	Att.	Yds.	Avg.	TD.	P.C.	Yds.	Avg.	TD.	TD.	Pts.	F.
1984—San Diego NFL	16	25	115	4.6	0	23	206	9.0	0	1	6	9
1985—San Diego NFL	16	105	516	4.9	2	86	1027	11.9	6	8	48	9
1986—San Diego NFL	7	51	224	4.4	0	23	173	7.5	0	0	0	5
1987—San Diego NFL	12	27	102	3.8	2	41	593	14.5	3	6	36	6
1988—San Diego NFL	16	23	105	4.6	0	36	279	7.8	1	1	6	3
Pro Totals—5 Years	67	231	1062	4.6	4	209	2278	10.9	10	16	96	32

		—PUNT RETURNS—				—KICKOFF RET.—		
Year Club	G.	No.	Yds.	Avg.	TD.	No.	Yds.	Avg.TD.
1984—San Diego NFL	16	30	208	6.9	1	★43	★959	22.3 0
1985—San Diego NFL	16	25	213	8.5	0	36	779	21.6 0
1986—San Diego NFL	7	9	94	10.4	0	18	315	17.5 0
1987—San Diego NFL	12	32	400	12.5	1	2	41	20.5 0
1988—San Diego NFL	16	28	278	9.9	0		None	
Pro Totals—5 Years	67	124	1193	9.6	2	99	2094	21.2 0

Additional pro statistics: Attempted two passes with no completions and one interception and recovered four fumbles, 1984; recovered one fumble, 1985 and 1986; fumbled six times for minus eight yards, 1987.

ROLAND ORLANDO JAMES

Safety—New England Patriots

Born February 18, 1958, at Xenia, O.
Height, 6.02. Weight, 191.
High School—Jamestown, O., Greenview.
Attended University of Tennessee.

Named as cornerback on THE SPORTING NEWS College All-America Team, 1979.

Selected by New England in 1st round (14th player selected) of 1980 NFL draft.
On injured reserve with knee injury, January 6, 1983 through remainder of 1982 season playoffs.
On injured reserve with knee injury, September 8 through October 22, 1987; activated, October 23, 1987.

Year Club	G.	-INTERCEPTIONS-				-PUNT RETURNS-				-TOTAL-		
		No.	Yds.	Avg.	TD.	No.	Yds.	Avg.	TD.	TD.	Pts.	F.
1980—New England NFL	16	4	32	8.0	0	33	331	10.0	1	1	6	2
1981—New England NFL	16	2	29	14.5	0	7	56	8.0	0	0	0	1
1982—New England NFL	7	3	12	4.0	0	None				0	0	1
1983—New England NFL	16	5	99	19.8	0	None				0	0	0
1984—New England NFL	15	2	14	7.0	0	None				0	0	0
1985—New England NFL	16	4	51	12.8	0	2	13	6.5	0	0	0	1
1986—New England NFL	15	2	39	19.5	0	None				0	0	0
1987—New England NFL	9	1	27	27.0	0	None				0	0	0
1988—New England NFL	15	4	30	7.5	0	None				0	0	0
Pro Totals—9 Years	125	27	333	12.3	0	42	400	9.5	1	1	6	5

Additional pro statistics: Recovered one fumble, 1980, 1981, 1984 and 1988; recovered four fumbles, 1983; credited with one safety, 1984.
Played in AFC Championship Game following 1985 season.
Played in NFL Championship Game following 1985 season.

GEORGE R. JAMISON
Linebacker—Detroit Lions
Born September 30, 1962, at Bridgeton, N.J.
Height, 6.01. Weight, 228.
High School—Bridgeton, N.J.
Attended University of Cincinnati.
Cousin of Anthony (Bubba) Green, defensive tackle with Baltimore Colts, 1981;
and Larry Milbourne, infielder with Houston Astros, Seattle Mariners, New York Yankees,
Minnesota Twins, Cleveland Indians and Philadelphia Phillies, 1975 through 1984.

Selected by Philadelphia in 2nd round (34th player selected) of 1984 USFL draft.
Signed by Philadelphia Stars, January 17, 1984.
On developmental squad, February 24 through March 1, 1984; activated, March 2, 1984.
On developmental squad, June 21 through remainder of 1984 season.
Selected by Detroit in 2nd round (47th player selected) of 1984 NFL supplemental draft.
Franchise transferred to Baltimore, November 1, 1984.
On developmental squad, May 3 through May 9, 1985; activated, May 10, 1985.
Granted free agency when USFL suspended operations, August 7, 1986; signed by Detroit Lions, August 17, 1986.
On injured reserve with Achilles tendon injury, August 30 through entire 1986 season.
On developmental squad for 2 games with Philadelphia Stars in 1984.
On developmental squad for 1 game with Baltimore Stars in 1985.
Philadelphia USFL, 1984; Baltimore USFL, 1985; Detroit NFL, 1987 and 1988.
Games: 1984 (15), 1985 (17), 1987 (12), 1988 (16). Total USFL—32. Total NFL—28. Total Pro—60.
USFL statistics: Credited with four sacks for 37 yards, 1984; intercepted one pass for 16 yards and credited with five sacks for 40½ yards, 1985.
NFL statistics: Credited with a safety, 1987; intercepted three passes for 56 yards and a touchdown and recovered three fumbles for four yards and a touchdown, 1988.
Played in USFL Championship Game following 1984 and 1985 seasons.

ILIA JAROSTCHUK
(Name pronounced ILL-ee-uh Jur-ROST-chuk.)
Linebacker—Phoenix Cardinals
Born August 1, 1964, at Utica, N. Y.
Height, 6.03. Weight, 231.
High School—Whitesboro, N. Y., Central.
Received bachelor of science degree in civil engineering
from University of New Hampshire in 1987.

Selected by St. Louis in 5th round (127th player selected) of 1987 NFL draft.
Signed by St. Louis Cardinals, July 20, 1987.
Franchise transferred to Phoenix, March 15, 1988.
Released by Phoenix Cardinals, August 30, 1988; signed as free agent by San Francisco 49ers, September 13, 1988.
Released by San Francisco 49ers, September 16, 1988; signed as free agent by Miami Dolphins, September 28, 1988.
Released by Miami Dolphins, November 10, 1988; signed as free agent by Phoenix Cardinals, February 10, 1989.
St. Louis NFL, 1987; Miami NFL, 1988.
Games: 1987 (12), 1988 (6). Total—18.

CURTIS JARVIS JR.
(Curt)
Nose Tackle—Tampa Bay Buccaneers
Born January 28, 1965, at Birmingham, Ala.
Height, 6.02. Weight, 266.
High School—Gardendale, Ala.
Attended University of Alabama.

Selected by Tampa Bay in 7th round (169th player selected) of 1987 NFL draft.
Signed by Tampa Bay Buccaneers, July 16, 1987.
On injured reserve with knee injury, August 31 through November 27, 1987; activated, November 28, 1987.
Tampa Bay NFL, 1987 and 1988.
Games: 1987 (2), 1988 (15). Total—17.

RALPH A. JARVIS
Defensive End—New York Jets
Born June 1, 1965, at Philadelphia, Pa.
Height, 6.04. Weight, 255.
High School—Glen Mills, Pa.
Attended Temple University.

Selected by Chicago in 3rd round (78th player selected) of 1988 NFL draft.
Signed by Chicago Bears, May 17, 1988.
Released by Chicago Bears, August 29, 1988; awarded on waivers to New York Jets, August 30, 1988.
Released by New York Jets, September 14, 1988; re-signed by Jets for 1989; November 21, 1988.
Inactive for 2 games with New York Jets in 1988.
New York Jets NFL, 1988.

RONALD VINCENT JAWORSKI
(Ron)
Quarterback—Kansas City Chiefs
Born March 23, 1951, at Lackawanna, N. Y.
Height, 6.01. Weight, 205.
High School—Lackawanna, N. Y.
Attended Youngstown State University.

Tied NFL record for longest completed passing play from scrimmage when he threw a 99-yard touchdown pass to wide receiver Mike Quick against Atlanta Falcons, November 10, 1985.
Selected by Los Angeles in 2nd round (37th player selected) of 1973 NFL draft.
Member of Los Angeles Rams' taxi squad, 1973.
Traded by Los Angeles Rams to Philadelphia Eagles for tight end Charle Young, March 10, 1977.
On injured reserve with broken fibula, November 27 through remainder of 1984 season.
On injured reserve with torn tendon in finger, November 13 through remainder of 1986 season.
Granted free agency, March 1, 1987; signed by Miami Dolphins, August 18, 1987.
Granted unconditional free agency, February 1, 1989; signed by Kansas City Chiefs, April 1, 1989.
Active for 2 games with Miami Dolphins in 1987; did not play.

Year	Club	G.	Att.	Cmp.	Pct.	Gain	T.P.	P.I.	Avg.	Att.	Yds.	Avg.	TD.	TD.	Pts.	F.
					PASSING						RUSHING			TOTAL		
1974—Los Angeles NFL		5	24	10	41.7	144	0	1	6.00	7	34	4.9	1	1	6	1
1975—Los Angeles NFL		14	48	24	50.0	302	0	2	6.29	12	33	2.8	2	2	12	1
1976—Los Angeles NFL		5	52	20	38.5	273	1	5	5.25	2	15	7.5	1	1	6	0
1977—Philadelphia NFL		14	346	166	48.0	2183	18	21	6.31	40	124	3.1	5	5	30	6
1978—Philadelphia NFL		16	398	206	51.8	2487	16	16	6.25	30	79	2.6	0	0	0	7
1979—Philadelphia NFL		16	374	190	50.8	2669	18	12	7.14	43	119	2.8	2	2	12	12
1980—Philadelphia NFL		16	451	257	57.0	3529	27	12	7.82	27	95	3.5	1	1	6	6
1981—Philadelphia NFL		16	461	250	54.2	3095	23	20	6.71	22	128	5.8	0	0	0	3
1982—Philadelphia NFL		9	286	167	58.4	2076	12	12	7.26	10	9	0.9	0	0	0	9
1983—Philadelphia NFL		16	446	235	52.7	3315	20	18	7.43	25	129	5.2	1	1	6	11
1984—Philadelphia NFL		13	427	234	54.8	2754	16	14	6.45	5	18	3.6	1	1	6	5
1985—Philadelphia NFL		16	484	255	52.7	3450	17	20	7.13	17	35	2.1	2	2	12	5
1986—Philadelphia NFL		10	245	128	52.2	1405	8	6	5.73	13	33	2.5	0	0	0	4
1988—Miami NFL		16	14	9	64.3	123	1	0	8.79			None		0	0	0
Pro Totals—15 Years		182	4056	2151	53.0	27805	177	159	6.86	253	851	3.4	16	16	96	70

Quarterback Rating Points: 1974 (44.3), 1975 (52.5), 1976 (22.8), 1977 (60.3), 1978 (68.0), 1979 (76.8), 1980 (90.9), 1981 (74.0), 1982 (77.5), 1983 (75.1), 1984 (73.5), 1985 (70.2), 1986 (70.2), 1988 (116.1). Total—73.3.
Additional pro statistics: Recovered two fumbles and fumbled once for minus three yards, 1975; recovered three fumbles and fumbled six times for minus four yards, 1977; recovered three fumbles and fumbled seven times for minus one yard, 1978; recovered five fumbles and fumbled 12 times for minus 23 yards, 1979; recovered four fumbles, 1980 and 1983; recovered three fumbles and fumbled three times for minus two yards, 1981; recovered four fumbles and fumbled nine times for minus 11 yards, 1982; recovered two fumbles, 1984 and 1985; recovered one fumble, 1986.
Played in NFC Championship Game following 1975 and 1980 seasons.
Member of Los Angeles Rams for NFC Championship Game following 1974 and 1976 seasons; did not play.
Played in NFL Championship Game following 1980 season.
Played in Pro Bowl (NFL All-Star Game) following 1980 season.

JAMES GARTH JAX
(Known by middle name.)
Linebacker—Phoenix Cardinals
Born September 16, 1963, at Houston, Tex.
Height, 6.02. Weight, 230.
High School—Houston, Tex., Strake Jesuit Preparatory.
Received bachelor of science degree in criminology from
Florida State University in 1986.

Selected by Tampa Bay in 1986 USFL territorial draft.
Selected by Dallas in 11th round (296th player selected) of 1986 NFL draft.
Signed by Dallas Cowboys, July 1, 1986.
Released by Dallas Cowboys, September 1, 1986; re-signed by Cowboys, September 8, 1986.
On injured reserve with fractured wrist, November 2 through remainder of 1987 season.
Granted unconditional free agency, February 1, 1989; signed by Phoenix Cardinals, April 1, 1989.
Dallas NFL, 1986 through 1988.
Games: 1986 (16), 1987 (3), 1988 (16). Total—35.
Pro statistics: Recovered one fumble, 1988.

JAMES WILSON JEFFCOAT JR.
(Jim)
Defensive End—Dallas Cowboys

Born April 1, 1961, at Long Branch, N.J.
Height, 6.05. Weight, 263.
High School—Matawan, N.J., Regional.
Received bachelor of arts degree in communications
from Arizona State University in 1983.

Selected by Arizona in 1983 USFL territorial draft.
Selected by Dallas in 1st round (23rd player selected) of 1983 NFL draft.
Signed by Dallas Cowboys, May 24, 1983.
Dallas NFL, 1983 through 1988.
Games: 1983 (16), 1984 (16), 1985 (16), 1986 (16), 1987 (12), 1988 (16). Total—92.
Pro statistics: Recovered fumble in end zone for a touchdown, 1984; intercepted one pass for 65 yards and a touchdown and recovered two fumbles, 1985; recovered two fumbles for eight yards, 1986 and 1987; intercepted one pass for 26 yards and a touchdown, 1987.

JAMES ANDREW JEFFERSON III
Defensive Back—Seattle Seahawks

Born November 18, 1963, at Portsmouth, Va.
Height, 6.01. Weight, 195.
High School—Kingsville, Tex., H.M. King.
Attended Texas A&I University.

Signed as free agent by Winnipeg Blue Bombers, March 10, 1986.
Granted free agency, March 1, 1989; signed by Seattle Seahawks, March 21, 1989.

Year Club	G.	INTERCEPTIONS				–PUNT RETURNS–				—KICKOFF RET.—				—TOTAL—		
		No.	Yds.	Avg.	TD.	No.	Yds.	Avg.	TD.	No.	Yds.	Avg.	TD.	TD.	Pts.	F.
1986—Winnipeg CFL	14	2	38	19.0	0	44	415	9.4	1	4	91	22.8	0	1	6	1
1987—Winnipeg CFL	17	8	99	12.4	2	4	73	18.3	1	0	26	......	0	4	24	0
1988—Winnipeg CFL	18	2	56	28.0	0	71	650	9.2	1	28	666	23.8	1	2	12	5
CFL Totals—3 Years	49	12	193	16.1	2	119	1138	9.6	3	32	783	24.5	1	7	42	6

Additional CFL statistics: Recovered one fumble for minus 17 yards, 1986; recovered three fumbles for 26 yards and a touchdown, 1987; recovered one fumble, 1988.
Played in CFL Championship Game following 1988 season.

NORMAN JEFFERSON JR.
Defensive Back—Green Bay Packers

Born August 7, 1964, at Marrero, La.
Height, 5.10. Weight, 183.
High School—Marrero, La., John Ehret.
Attended Louisiana State University.

Selected by Green Bay in 12th round (335th player selected) of 1987 NFL draft.
Signed by Green Bay Packers, July 23, 1987.
On injured reserve with knee injury, September 15 through remainder of 1988 season.
Green Bay NFL, 1987 and 1988.
Games: 1987 (12), 1988 (2). Total—14.
Pro statistics: Returned two kickoffs for 30 yards, 1987; returned five punts for 15 yards, four kickoffs for 116 yards (29.0 avg.), recovered one fumble and fumbled three times, 1988.

TONY LORENZO JEFFERY
Running Back—Phoenix Cardinals

Born July 8, 1964, at Gladewater, Tex.
Height, 5.11. Weight, 208.
High School—Gladewater, Tex.
Attended Texas Christian University.

Selected by Phoenix in 2nd round (38th player selected) of 1988 NFL draft.
Signed by Phoenix Cardinals, July 11, 1988.
Phoenix NFL, 1988.
Games: 1988 (3).
Pro statistics: Rushed three times for eight yards and returned one kickoff for 11 yards, 1988.

HAYWOOD FRANKLIN JEFFIRES
Wide Receiver—Houston Oilers

Born December 12, 1964, at Greensboro, N. C.
Height, 6.02. Weight, 198.
High School—Greensboro, N. C., Page.
Received bachelor of arts degree in recreation administration
from North Carolina State University in 1987.

Selected by Houston in 1st round (20th player selected) of 1987 NFL draft.
Signed by Houston Oilers, July 22, 1987.
Crossed picket line during players' strike, October 14, 1987.
On injured reserve with ankle injury, August 29 through December 9, 1988; activated, December 10, 1988.

Year Club		PASS RECEIVING			
	G.	P.C.	Yds.	Avg.	TD.
1987—Houston NFL	9	7	89	12.7	0
1988—Houston NFL	2	2	49	24.5	1
Pro Totals—2 Years	11	9	138	15.3	1

IZEL JENKINS JR.

First name pronounced Eye-ZELL.

Cornerback—Philadelphia Eagles

Born May 27, 1964, at Wilson, N.C.
Height, 5.10. Weight, 191.
High School—Wilson, N.C., R.L. Fike.
Attended Taft College and North Carolina State University.

Selected by Philadelphia in 11th round (288th player selected) of 1988 NFL draft.
Signed by Philadelphia Eagles, July 18, 1988.
Philadelphia NFL, 1988.
Games: 1988 (16).
Pro statistics: Credited with a safety and returned one kickoff for 20 yards, 1988.

MELVIN JENKINS

Cornerback—Seattle Seahawks

Born March 16, 1962, at Jackson, Miss.
Height, 5.10. Weight, 170.
High School—Jackson, Miss., Wingfield.
Attended University of Cincinnati.

Signed as free agent by Calgary Stampeders, April 17, 1984.
Granted free agency, March 1, 1987; signed as free agent by Seattle Seahawks, April 22, 1987.

		INTERCEPTIONS				PUNT RETURNS				KICKOFF RET.				TOTAL		
Year Club	G.	No.	Yds.	Avg.	TD.	No.	Yds.	Avg.	TD.	No.	Yds.	Avg.	TD.	TD.	Pts.	F.
1984—Calgary CFL	13	3	50	16.7	1	41	349	8.5	0	15	312	20.8	0	1	6	4
1985—Calgary CFL	9	1	—5	—5.0	0	7	74	10.6	0	6	110	18.3	0	0	0	1
1986—Calgary CFL	18	7	139	19.9	1	1	10	10.0	0			None		1	6	0
1987—Seattle NFL	12	3	46	15.3	0			None				None		0	0	1
1988—Seattle NFL	16	3	41	13.7	0			None				None		0	0	1
CFL Totals—3 Years	40	11	184	16.7	2	49	433	8.8	0	21	422	20.1	0	2	12	5
NFL Totals—2 Years	28	6	87	14.5	0	0	0	0.0	0	0	0	0.0	0	0	0	2
Pro Totals—5 Years	68	17	271	15.9	2	49	433	8.8	0	21	422	20.1	0	2	12	7

Additional CFL statistics: Recovered three fumbles, 1984; recovered one fumble, 1985 and 1986.
Additional NFL statistics: Recovered one fumble for 50 yards, 1988.

STANFORD JAMISON JENNINGS

Running Back—Cincinnati Bengals

Born March 12, 1962, at Summerville, S.C.
Height, 6.01. Weight, 205.
High School—Summerville, S.C.
Attended Furman University.
Brother of Keith Jennings, rookie tight end with Dallas Cowboys.

Selected by Michigan in 1st round (17th player selected) of 1984 USFL draft.
Selected by Cincinnati in 3rd round (65th player selected) of 1984 NFL draft.
Signed by Cincinnati Bengals, July 2, 1984.

		RUSHING				PASS RECEIVING				TOTAL		
Year Club	G.	Att.	Yds.	Avg.	TD.	P.C.	Yds.	Avg.	TD.	TD.	Pts.	F.
1984—Cincinnati NFL	15	79	379	4.8	2	35	346	9.9	3	5	30	3
1985—Cincinnati NFL	16	31	92	3.0	1	12	101	8.4	3	4	24	1
1986—Cincinnati NFL	16	16	54	3.4	1	6	86	14.3	0	1	6	0
1987—Cincinnati NFL	12	70	314	4.5	1	35	277	7.9	2	3	18	0
1988—Cincinnati NFL	16	17	47	2.8	1	5	75	15.0	0	2	12	1
Pro Totals—5 Years	75	213	886	4.2	6	93	885	9.5	8	15	90	5

		KICKOFF RETURNS			
Year Club	G.	No.	Yds.	Avg.	TD.
1984—Cincinnati NFL	15	22	452	20.5	0
1985—Cincinnati NFL	16	13	218	16.8	0
1986—Cincinnati NFL	16	12	257	21.4	0
1987—Cincinnati NFL	12	2	32	16.0	0
1988—Cincinnati NFL	16	32	684	21.4	*1
Pro Totals—5 Years	75	81	1643	20.3	1

Additional pro statistics: Recovered two fumbles, 1984; recovered one fumble, 1985 and 1987.
Played in AFC Championship Game following 1988 season.
Played in NFL Championship Game following 1988 season.

JAMES CHRISTOPHER JENSEN
(Jim)
Wide Receiver—Miami Dolphins
Born November 14, 1958, at Abington, Pa.
Height, 6.04. Weight, 220.
High School—Doylestown, Pa., Central Bucks.
Received bachelor of science degree in special education from Boston University in 1981.
Selected by Miami in 11th round (291st player selected) of 1981 NFL draft.
On Inactive list, September 12 and September 19, 1982.
Granted free agency, February 1, 1985; re-signed by Dolphins, August 31, 1985.
Granted roster exemption, August 31 through September 6, 1985; activated, September 7, 1985.

Year Club	G.	P.C.	Yds.	Avg.	TD.	Year Club	G.	P.C.	Yds.	Avg.	TD.
1981—Miami NFL	16		None			1986—Miami NFL	16	5	50	10.0	1
1982—Miami NFL	6		None			1987—Miami NFL	12	26	221	8.5	1
1983—Miami NFL	16		None			1988—Miami NFL	16	58	652	11.2	5
1984—Miami NFL	16	13	139	10.7	2	Pro Totals—8 Years	114	103	1066	10.3	10
1985—Miami NFL	16	1	4	4.0	1						

Additional pro statistics: Attempted one pass with no completions, 1982; attempted one pass with one completion for 35 yards and a touchdown, 1984; attempted two passes with no completions, 1986; rushed four times for 18 yards, recovered three fumbles for two yards and fumbled once, 1987; rushed 10 times for 68 yards, recovered two fumbles and fumbled twice, 1988.
Played in AFC Championship Game following 1982, 1984 and 1985 seasons.
Played in NFL Championship Game following 1982 and 1984 seasons.

MARK DARRELL JERUE
Linebacker—Los Angeles Rams
Born January 15, 1960, at Seattle, Wash.
Height, 6.03. Weight, 234.
High School—Mercer Island, Wash.
Attended University of Washington.
Selected by New York Jets in 5th round (135th player selected) of 1982 NFL draft.
On injured reserve with heart irregularity, August 24 through entire 1982 season.
Released by New York Jets, August 29, 1983; awarded on waivers to Baltimore Colts, August 30, 1983.
Traded by Baltimore Colts to Los Angeles Rams for quarterback Mark Reed, August 30, 1983.
USFL rights traded with rights to running back Ted McKnight and 1st and 5th round picks in 1984 draft by Jacksonville Bulls to Oakland Invaders for rights to quarterback Turk Schonert, October 24, 1983.
On injured reserve with knee injury, September 8 through October 23, 1987; activated, October 24, 1987.
On injured reserve with knee injury, November 16 through remainder of 1987 season.
On injured reserve with knee injury, December 17 through remainder of 1988 season.
Los Angeles Rams NFL, 1983 through 1988.
Games: 1983 (16), 1984 (16), 1985 (16), 1986 (16), 1987 (4), 1988 (12). Total—80.
Pro statistics: Recovered one fumble, 1985; intercepted two passes for 23 yards and a touchdown and fumbled once, 1986; intercepted one pass for no yards, 1988.
Played in NFC Championship Game following 1985 season.

GARY MICHAEL JETER
Defensive End—New England Patriots
Born January 24, 1955, at Weirton, W. Va.
Height, 6.04. Weight, 260.
High School—Cleveland, O., Cathedral Latin.
Attended University of Southern California.
Nephew of Bob Jeter, back with Green Bay Packers and Chicago Bears, 1963 through 1973;
and Tony Jeter, end with Pittsburgh Steelers, 1966 and 1968.
Selected by New York Giants in 1st round (5th player selected) of 1977 NFL draft.
On injured reserve with knee injury, December 8 through remainder of 1978 season.
On injured reserve with knee injury, September 1 through October 1, 1981; activated, October 2, 1981.
On inactive list, September 20, 1982.
On injured reserve with knee injury, November 24 through December 23, 1982; activated, December 24, 1982.
Traded by New York Giants to Los Angeles Rams for 3rd and 6th round picks in 1983 draft, April 13, 1983.
On injured reserve with herniated disc, August 28 through November 8, 1984; activated, November 9, 1984.
Granted unconditional free agency, February 1, 1989; signed by New England Patriots, March 14, 1989.
New York Giants NFL, 1977 through 1982; Los Angeles Rams NFL, 1983 through 1988.
Games: 1977 (14), 1978 (13), 1979 (16), 1980 (16), 1981 (12), 1982 (4), 1983 (16), 1984 (5), 1985 (16), 1986 (15), 1987 (12), 1988 (15). Total—154.
Pro statistics: Recovered one fumble, 1978, 1979 and 1985; recovered three fumbles for seven yards, 1980; credited with a safety, 1986.
Played in NFC Championship Game following 1985 season.

DWAYNE JILES
Linebacker—Philadelphia Eagles
Born November 23, 1961, at Linden, Tex.
Height, 6.04. Weight, 250.
High School—Linden, Tex., Kildare.
Attended Texas Tech University.
Selected by Denver in 1985 USFL territorial draft.

Selected by Philadelphia in 5th round (121st player selected) of 1985 NFL draft.
Signed by Philadelphia Eagles, July 23, 1985.
On injured reserve with cracked vertebra, August 27 through October 17, 1985; activated, October 18, 1985.
Philadelphia NFL, 1985 through 1988.
Games: 1985 (10), 1986 (16), 1987 (9), 1988 (16). Total—51.
Pro statistics: Recovered one fumble, 1986.

DAMIAN JOHNSON
Offensive Tackle—New York Giants
Born December 18, 1962, at Great Bend, Kan.
Height, 6.05. Weight, 290.
High School—Great Bend, Kan.
Attended Kansas State University.

Selected by Jacksonville in 15th round (205th player selected) of 1985 USFL draft.
Signed as free agent by New York Giants, May 7, 1985.
On injured reserve with knee injury, September 2 through entire 1985 season.
On injured reserve with neck injury, October 22 through remainder of 1988 season.
New York Giants NFL, 1986 through 1988.
Games: 1986 (16), 1987 (12), 1988 (6). Total—34.
Played in NFC Championship Game following 1986 season.
Played in NFL Championship Game following 1986 season.

DAMONE JOHNSON
Tight End—Los Angeles Rams
Born March 2, 1962, at Los Angeles, Calif.
Height, 6.04. Weight, 230.
High School—Santa Monica, Calif.
Attended California Poly State University (SLO).

Selected by Oakland in 1985 USFL territorial draft.
Selected by Los Angeles Rams in 6th round (162nd player selected) of 1985 NFL draft.
Signed by Los Angeles Rams, July 9, 1985.
Released by Los Angeles Rams, August 10, 1985; re-signed by Rams, March 21, 1986.
On injured reserve with knee injury, September 2 through November 20, 1986, activated, November 21, 1986.

Year Club	G.	P.C.	Yds.	Avg.	TD.
1986—L. A. Rams NFL	5		None		
1987—L. A. Rams NFL	12	21	198	9.4	2
1988—L.A. Rams NFL	16	42	350	8.3	6
Pro Totals—3 Years	33	63	548	8.7	8

EDDIE JOHNSON
Linebacker—Cleveland Browns
Born February 3, 1959, at Albany, Ga.
Height, 6.01. Weight, 225.
High School—Albany, Ga., Daughtery.
Attended University of Louisville.

Selected by Cleveland in 7th round (187th player selected) of 1981 NFL draft.
Cleveland NFL, 1981 through 1988.
Games: 1981 (16), 1982 (9), 1983 (16), 1984 (16), 1985 (16), 1986 (16), 1987 (12), 1988 (15). Total—116.
Pro statistics: Returned one kickoff for seven yards, 1981; recovered one fumble, 1981 and 1987; intercepted two passes for three yards, 1984; intercepted one pass for six yards, 1985; intercepted one pass for 11 yards, 1987; intercepted two passes for no yards and recovered three fumbles, 1988.
Played in AFC Championship Game following 1986 and 1987 seasons.

EZRA RAY JOHNSON
Defensive End—Indianapolis Colts
Born October 2, 1955, at Shreveport, La.
Height, 6.04. Weight, 250.
High School—Shreveport, La., Green Oaks.
Attended Morris Brown College.

Selected by Green Bay in 1st round (28th player selected) of 1977 NFL draft.
On injured reserve with knee injury, December 14 through remainder of 1984 season.
On injured reserve with knee injury, September 11 through November 6, 1987; activated, November 7, 1987.
Granted free agency with no qualifying offer, February 1, 1988; signed by Indianapolis Colts, April 27, 1988.
Green Bay NFL, 1977 through 1987; Indianapolis NFL, 1988.
Games: 1977 (14), 1978 (16), 1979 (11), 1980 (15), 1981 (16), 1982 (9), 1983 (16), 1984 (13), 1985 (16), 1986 (16), 1987 (6), 1988 (10). Total—158.
Pro statistics: Recovered one fumble, 1977; recovered two fumbles, 1978 and 1985; returned one kickoff for 14 yards, 1978; recovered two fumbles, 1983.
Played in Pro Bowl (NFL All-Star Game) following 1978 season.

FULTON JOHNSON
(Flip)
Wide Receiver—Buffalo Bills
Born July 13, 1963, at Cheek, Tex.
Height, 5.10. Weight, 185.
High School—Hamshire, Tex., Hamshire Fannett.
Attended McNeese State University.

Signed as free agent by Buffalo Bills, May 2, 1987.
On injured reserve with thigh injury, September 1 through entire 1987 season.
On injured reserve with hamstring injury, August 30 through September 30, 1988; activated, October 1, 1988.

		PASS RECEIVING				-PUNT RETURNS-				—KICKOFF RET.—				—TOTAL—		
Year	Club	G.	P.C.	Yds.	Avg.	TD.	No.	Yds.	Avg.	TD.	No.	Yds.	Avg.	TD.	TD.	Pts.	F.
1988—Buffalo NFL	11	9	170	18.9	1	16	72	4.5	0	14	250	17.9	0	1	6	1

Played in AFC Championship Game following 1988 season.

GREGORY KENT JOHNSON
(Greg)
Guard—Miami Dolphins
Born December 19, 1964, at Oklahoma City, Okla.
Height, 6.04. Weight, 295.
High School—Moore, Okla.
Received bachelor of arts degree in business administration from University of Oklahoma in 1988.

Selected by Miami in 4th round (99th player selected) of 1988 NFL draft.
Signed by Miami Dolphins, July 12, 1988.
Miami NFL, 1988.
Games: 1988 (2).

JAMES L. JOHNSON
Linebacker—New York Jets
Born June 21, 1962, at Los Angeles, Calif.
Height, 6.02. Weight, 235.
High School—Lake Elsinore, Calif.
Attended Orange Coast College and San Diego State University.

Selected by Portland in 4th round (50th player selected) of 1985 USFL draft.
Selected by Detroit in 3rd round (62nd player selected) of 1985 NFL draft.
Signed by Detroit Lions, July 26, 1985.
On injured reserve with back injury, September 2 through entire 1985 season.
Released by Detroit Lions, October 11, 1986; re-signed by Lions, November 11, 1986.
Released by Detroit Lions, September 1, 1987; signed as free agent replacement player by San Francisco 49ers, September 24, 1987.
Traded by San Francisco 49ers to San Diego Chargers for past considerations, October 13, 1987.
Released by San Diego Chargers, October 20, 1987; signed as free agent by Los Angeles Raiders, April 22, 1988.
Released by Los Angeles Raiders, August 3, 1988; signed as free agent by New York Jets, April 4, 1989.
Detroit NFL, 1986; San Francisco (1)-San Diego (1) NFL, 1987.
Games: 1986 (11), 1987 (2). Total—13.

JASON MANSFIELD JOHNSON
Wide Receiver—Pittsburgh Steelers
Born November 8, 1965, at Gary, Ind.
Height, 5.10. Weight, 178.
High School—Gary, Ind., West Side.
Attended Illinois State University.

Signed as free agent by Denver Broncos, April 27, 1988.
On injured reserve with back injury, August 22 through October 26, 1988; activated, October 27, 1988.
Granted unconditional free agency, February 1, 1989; signed by Pittsburgh Steelers, March 16, 1989.

		PASS RECEIVING				—KICKOFF RET.—				—TOTAL—		
Year	Club	G.	P.C.	Yds.	Avg.	TD.	No.	Yds.	Avg.	TD.	TD.	Pts.	F.
1988—Denver NFL	8	1	6	6.0	0	14	292	20.9	0	0	0	1

Additional pro statistics: Returned one punt for five yards, rushed once for three yards and recovered one fumble, 1988.

JOHNNIE JOHNSON JR.
Safety—Seattle Seahawks
Born October 8, 1956, at La Grange, Tex.
Height, 6.01. Weight, 183.
High School—La Grange, Tex.
Attended University of Texas.
Brother of Bobby Johnson, defensive back with New Orleans Saints
and St. Louis Cardinals, 1983 through 1986.

Named as safety on THE SPORTING NEWS College All-America Team, 1980.
Selected by Los Angeles in 1st round (17th player selected) of 1980 NFL draft.
On injured reserve with broken ankle, August 28 through October 16, 1984; activated, October 17, 1984.
On injured reserve with broken arm, November 25 through remainder of 1987 season.
Granted unconditional free agency, February 1, 1989; signed by Seattle Seahawks, March 23, 1989.

Year	Club	G.	—INTERCEPTIONS— No.	Yds.	Avg.	TD.
1980—L.A. Rams NFL............		16	3	102	34.0	1
1981—L.A. Rams NFL............		16		None		
1982—L.A. Rams NFL............		9	1	7	7.0	0
1983—L.A. Rams NFL............		16	4	115	28.8	*2
1984—L.A. Rams NFL............		9	2	21	10.5	0
1985—L.A. Rams NFL............		16	5	96	19.2	*1
1986—L.A. Rams NFL............		16	1	13	13.0	0
1987—L.A. Rams NFL............		7	1	0	0.0	0
1988—L.A. Rams NFL............		16	4	18	4.5	0
Pro Totals—9 Years............		121	21	372	17.7	4

Additional pro statistics: Returned one punt for three yards, 1980 and 1984; recovered five fumbles for 16 yards, 1980; returned one punt for 39 yards and recovered five fumbles for five yards, 1981; recovered two fumbles for nine yards, 1982; returned 14 punts for 109 yards and recovered two fumbles for four yards, 1983; fumbled once, 1983 and 1988; recovered one fumble, 1985; recovered two fumbles, 1986.; returned blocked punt 20 yards for a touchdown and returned one punt for five yards, 1987; returned two punts for four yards and recovered three fumbles, 1988.

Played in NFC Championship Game following 1985 season.

KELLEY ANTONIO JOHNSON
Wide Receiver—Detroit Lions
Born June 3, 1962, at Carlsbad, N.M.
Height, 5.08. Weight, 155.
High School—Carlsbad, N.M.
Attended Los Angeles Valley College and University of Colorado.

Selected by Denver in 1985 USFL territorial draft.
Signed by Denver Gold, January 3, 1985.
On developmental squad, February 21 through March 1, 1985; activated, March 2, 1985.
Released by Denver Gold, July 31, 1985; re-signed by Gold, August 22, 1985.
Franchise merged with Jacksonville, February 19, 1986.
Granted free agency when USFL suspended operations, August 7, 1986; signed by Ottawa Rough Riders, August 27, 1986.
Released by Ottawa Rough Riders, June 20, 1987; signed as free agent by Houston Oilers, August 6, 1987.
Released by Houston Oilers, September 1, 1987; signed as free agent replacement player by Indianapolis Colts, September 24, 1987.
Released by Indianapolis Colts, October 20, 1987; re-signed by Colts, April 27, 1988.
Released by Indianapolis Colts, August 24, 1988; signed as free agent by Detroit Lions, March 15, 1989.
On developmental squad for 1 game with Denver Gold in 1985.

Year	Club	G.	—PASS RECEIVING— P.C.	Yds.	Avg.	TD.
1985—Denver USFL		13	10	149	14.9	1
1986—Ottawa CFL		4	5	158	31.6	1
1987—Indianapolis NFL		3	1	15	15.0	0
Pro Totals—3 Years...........		20	16	322	20.1	2

Additional USFL statistics: Rushed once for 28 yards, 1985.
Additional CFL statistics: Returned 13 punts for 29 yards, returned one kickoff for 10 yards and rushed once for minus eight yards, 1987.
Additional NFL statistics: Returned six kickoffs for 98 yards, returned nine punts for 42 yards and fumbled once, 1987.

KENNETH RAY JOHNSON
(Kenny)
Safety—Houston Oilers
Born January 7, 1958, at Columbia, Miss.
Height, 5.10. Weight, 172.
High School—Moss Point, Miss.
Attended Mississippi State University.

Selected by Atlanta in 5th round (137th player selected) of 1980 NFL draft.
Tied NFL record for most touchdowns scored by interception, game (2), against Green Bay Packers, November 27, 1983.
On injured reserve with fractured shoulder blade, September 16 through December 6, 1985; activated, December 7, 1985.
On non-football injury list with chicken pox, October 24 through December 17, 1986; awarded on procedural waivers to Houston Oilers, December 19, 1986.
Released by Houston Oilers, September 7, 1987; re-signed as replacement player by Oilers, September 30, 1987.
On injured reserve with broken arm, November 28 through remainder of 1988 season.

Year	Club	G.	INTERCEPTIONS No.	Yds.	Avg.	TD.	-PUNT RETURNS- No.	Yds.	Avg.	TD.	—KICKOFF RET.— No.	Yds.	Avg.	TD.	—TOTAL— TD.	Pts.	F.
1980—Atlanta NFL		16	4	49	12.3	0	23	281	12.2	0		None			0	0	2
1981—Atlanta NFL		16	3	35	11.7	0	4	6	1.5	0		None			2	12	1
1982—Atlanta NFL		9	2	30	15.0	0		None				None			0	0	0
1983—Atlanta NFL		16	2	57	28.5	*2		None			11	224	20.4	0	2	12	1
1984—Atlanta NFL		16	5	75	15.0	0	10	79	7.9	0	19	359	18.9	0	0	0	2
1985—Atlanta NFL		5		None				None			1	20	20.0	0	0	0	0
1986—Atl. (7)-Hou. (1) NFL...		8		None				None				None			0	0	0
1987—Houston NFL................		12		None			24	196	8.2	0	2	24	12.0	0	0	0	3
1988—Houston NFL................		13	1	51	51.0	0	30	170	5.7	0	6	157	26.2	0	0	0	1
Pro Totals—9 Years.......		111	17	297	17.5	2	91	732	8.0	0	39	784	20.1	0	4	24	10

Additional pro statistics: Recovered four fumbles for seven yards, 1980; recovered two fumbles for 55 yards and two touchdowns, 1981; recovered one fumble, 1983 and 1987.

LEE JOHNSON
Punter—Cincinnati Bengals
Born November 27, 1961, at Dallas, Tex.
Height, 6.02. Weight, 199.
High School—The Woodlands, Tex., McCullough.
Attended Brigham Young University.

Selected by Houston in 9th round (125th player selected) of 1985 USFL draft.
Selected by Houston in 5th round (138th player selected) of 1985 NFL draft.
Signed by Houston Oilers, June 25, 1985.
Crossed picket line during players' strike, October 14, 1987.
Released by Houston Oilers, December 1, 1987; awarded on waivers to Buffalo Bills, December 2, 1987.
Released by Buffalo Bills, December 9, 1987; awarded on waivers to Cleveland Browns, December 10, 1987.
Released by Cleveland Browns, September 22, 1988; awarded on waivers to Cincinnati Bengals, September 23, 1988.

| | | —PUNTING— | | |
Year	Club	G.	No.	Avg.	Blk.
1985—Houston NFL		16	83	41.7	0
1986—Houston NFL		16	88	41.2	0
1987—Hou. (9)-Cle. (3) NFL		12	50	39.4	0
1988—Cle.(3)-Cinc.(12) NFL		15	31	39.9	0
Pro Totals—4 Years		59	252	40.8	0

Additional pro statistics: Rushed once for no yards, recovered one fumble for seven yards and fumbled twice, 1985; made one of two field goal attempts, 1988.
Played in AFC Championship Game following 1987 and 1988 seasons.
Played in NFL Championship Game following 1988 season.

MICHAEL JOHNSON
(Mike)
Linebacker—Cleveland Browns
Born November 26, 1962, at Southport, N.C.
Height, 6.01. Weight, 228.
High School—Hyattsville, Md., DeMatha.
Attended Virginia Tech.

Selected by Pittsburgh in 1984 USFL territorial draft.
USFL rights traded with defensive end Mark Buben, rights to linebacker Al Chesley and draft choice by Pittsburgh Maulers to Philadelphia Stars for rights to linebacker Ron Crosby, February 1, 1984.
Signed by Philadelphia Stars, February 20, 1984.
Granted roster exemption, February 20 through March 1, 1984; activated, March 2, 1984.
Selected by Cleveland in 1st round (18th player selected) of 1984 NFL supplemental draft.
Franchise transferred to Baltimore, November 1, 1984.
Granted free agency when USFL suspended operations, August 7, 1986; signed by Cleveland Browns, August 12, 1986.
Granted roster exemption, August 12 through August 21, 1986; activated, August 22, 1986.
Philadelphia USFL, 1984; Baltimore USFL, 1985; Cleveland NFL, 1986 through 1988.
Games: 1984 (17), 1985 (18), 1986 (16), 1987 (11), 1988 (16). Total USFL—35. Total NFL—43. Total Pro—78.
USFL statistics: Credited with two sacks for four yards and recovered one fumble for eight yards, 1984; credited with 3½ sacks for 25½ yards and recovered two fumbles, 1985.
NFL statistics: Recovered two fumbles, 1986; intercepted one pass for three yards and recovered one fumble, 1987; intercepted two passes for 36 yards, 1988.
Played in USFL Championship Game following 1984 and 1985 seasons.
Played in AFC Championship Game following 1986 and 1987 seasons.

MICHAEL LAMAR JOHNSON
(M. L.)
Linebacker—Seattle Seahawks
Born January 24, 1964, at New York, N. Y.
Height, 6.03. Weight, 225.
High School—Los Angeles, Calif., Thomas Jefferson.
Attended University of Hawaii.

Selected by Seattle in 9th round (243rd selected) of 1987 NFL draft.
Signed by Seattle Seahawks, July 21, 1987.
Seattle NFL, 1987 and 1988.
Games: 1987 (8), 1988 (16). Total—24.

NORM JOHNSON
Placekicker—Seattle Seahawks
Born May 31, 1960, at Inglewood, Calif.
Height, 6.02. Weight, 198.
High School—Garden Grove, Calif., Pacifica.
Attended University of California at Los Angeles.

Named to THE SPORTING NEWS NFL All-Star Team, 1984.
Signed as free agent by Seattle Seahawks, May 4, 1982.
Crossed picket line during players' strike, October 14, 1987.

Year Club	PLACE KICKING					
	G.	XP.	XPM.	FG.	FGA.	Pts.
1982—Seattle NFL	9	13	1	10	14	43
1983—Seattle NFL	16	49	1	18	25	103
1984—Seattle NFL	16	50	1	20	24	110
1985—Seattle NFL	16	40	1	14	25	82
1986—Seattle NFL	16	42	0	22	35	108
1987—Seattle NFL	13	40	0	15	20	85
1988—Seattle NFL	16	39	0	22	28	105
Pro Totals—7 Years	102	273	4	121	171	636

Additional pro statistics: Attempted one pass with one completion for 27 yards, 1982.
Played in AFC Championship Game following 1983 season.
Played in Pro Bowl (NFL All-Star Game) following 1984 season.

RICHARD JOHNSON
Cornerback—Houston Oilers
Born September 16, 1963, at Harvey, Ill.
Height, 6.01. Weight, 190.
High School—Harvey, Ill., Thornton.
Attended University of Wisconsin.

Named as defensive back on THE SPORTING NEWS College All-America Team, 1984.
Selected by Jacksonville in 1985 USFL territorial draft.
Selected by Houston in 1st round (11th player selected) of 1985 NFL draft.
Signed by Houston Oilers, August 22, 1985.
Granted roster exemption, August 22 through August 29, 1985; activated, August 30, 1985.
On injured reserve with knee injury, November 14 through remainder of 1987 season.
Houston NFL, 1985 through 1988.
Games: 1985 (16), 1986 (16), 1987 (5), 1988 (16). Total—53.
Pro statistics: Recovered one fumble, 1985; intercepted two passes for six yards, 1986; intercepted one pass for no yards, 1987; intercepted three passes for no yards and returned one kickoff for two yards, 1988.

RICHARD JOHNSON
Wide Receiver—Detroit Lions
Born October 19, 1961, at Los Angeles, Calif.
Height, 5.09. Weight, 195.
High School—San Pedro, Calif.
Attended Los Angeles Harbor Junior College and received
bachelor of arts degree from University of Colorado.

Named as wide receiver on THE SPORTING NEWS USFL All-Star Team, 1985.
Selected by Denver in 1983 USFL territorial draft.
Signed by Denver Gold, January 28, 1983.
Released by Denver Gold, February 14, 1983; re-signed by Gold, April 27, 1983.
On developmental squad, April 27 through May 9, 1983; activated, May 10, 1983.
On developmental squad, May 20 through May 26, 1983; activated, May 27, 1983.
On developmental squad, June 3 through remainder of 1983 season.
Selected by Houston Gamblers in 10th round (59th player selected) of USFL expansion draft, September 6, 1983.
Traded with defensive backs Luther Bradley, Will Lewis, Mike Mitchell and Durwood Roquemore, defensive end Pete Catan, quarterbacks Jim Kelly and Todd Dillon, defensive tackles Tony Fitzpatrick, Van Hughes and Hosea Taylor, running back Sam Harrell, linebackers Andy Hawkins and Ladell Wills, wide receivers Scott McGhee, Gerald McNeil, Ricky Sanders and Clarence Verdin, guard Rich Kehr, center Billy Kidd and offensive tackles Chris Riehm and Tommy Robison by Houston Gamblers to New Jersey Generals for past considerations, March 7, 1986.
Granted free agency when USFL suspended operations, August 7, 1986; signed as free agent by New York Jets, April 19, 1987.
Released by New York Jets, August 10, 1987; signed as free agent replacement player by Washington Redskins, September 23, 1987.
Released by Washington Redskins, October 6, 1987; signed as free agent by Buffalo Bills, October 9, 1987.
Released by Buffalo Bills, October 19, 1987; signed as free agent by Detroit Lions, March 15, 1989.
On developmental squad for 8 games with Denver Gold in 1983.

Year Club		RUSHING				PASS RECEIVING				TOTAL		
	G.	Att.	Yds.	Avg.	TD.	P.C.	Yds.	Avg.	TD.	TD.	Pts.	F.
1983—Denver USFL	1		None				None			0	0	0
1984—Houston USFL	18	4	19	4.8	0	*115	1455	12.7	*15	15	90	3
1985—Houston USFL	17	2	15	7.5	0	*103	1384	13.4	14	14	84	2
1987—Washington NFL	1		None			1	5	5.0	0	0	0	0
USFL Totals—3 Years	36	6	34	5.7	0	218	2839	13.0	29	29	174	5
NFL Totals—1 Year	1	0	0	0.0	0	1	5	5.0	0	0	0	0
Pro Totals—4 Years	37	6	34	5.7	0	219	2844	13.0	29	29	174	5

Year Club	KICKOFF RETURNS				
	G.	No.	Yds.	Avg.	TD.
1983—Denver USFL	1		None		
1984—Houston USFL	18	6	109	18.2	0
1985—Houston USFL	17		None		
1987—Washington NFL	1		None		
USFL Totals—3 Years	36	6	109	18.2	0
NFL Totals—1 Year	1	0	0	0.0	0
Pro Totals—4 Years	37	6	109	18.2	0

Additional pro statistics: Recovered one fumble, 1983 and 1984; recovered two fumbles, 1985.

RON JOHNSON
Wide Receiver—Philadelphia Eagles
Born September 21, 1958, at Monterey, Calif.
Height, 6.03. Weight, 186.
High School—Monterey, Calif.
Attended California State University at Long Beach.

Selected by Seattle in 7th round (170th player selected) of 1981 NFL draft.
Released by Seattle Seahawks, August 17, 1981; claimed on waivers by Baltimore Colts, August 19, 1981.
Released by Baltimore Colts, August 25, 1981; signed as free agent by Hamilton Tiger-Cats, March 10, 1982.
Granted free agency, March 1, 1985.
USFL rights traded by Los Angeles Express to Portland Breakers for past considerations, May 15, 1985.
Signed by Portland Breakers, May 15, 1985.
Released by Portland Breakers, June 26, 1985; signed as free agent by Philadelphia Eagles, July 22, 1985.
Released by Philadelphia Eagles, August 30, 1988; re-signed by Eagles, October 5, 1988.
Granted unconditional free agency, February 1, 1989; re-signed by Eagles, May 1, 1989.
On injured reserve with dislocated shoulder, November 19 through remainder of 1985 season.
On injured reserve with concussion, October 29 through November 23, 1986; activated, November 24, 1986.

Year Club	G.	P.C.	—PASS RECEIVING— Yds.	Avg.	TD.
1982—Hamilton CFL	11	37	505	13.6	5
1983—Hamilton CFL	16	53	914	17.2	6
1984—Hamilton CFL	15	50	684	13.6	2
1985—Portland USFL	6	22	476	21.6	2
1985—Philadelphia NFL	8	11	186	16.9	0
1986—Philadelphia NFL	12	11	207	18.8	1
1987—Philadelphia NFL	3		None		
1988—Philadelphia NFL	10	19	417	21.9	2
CFL Totals—3 Years	42	140	2103	15.0	13
USFL Totals—1 Year	6	22	476	21.6	2
NFL Totals—4 Years	33	41	810	19.8	3
Pro Totals—8 Years	81	203	3389	16.7	18

Additional CFL statistics: Rushed once for minus three yards, 1982; fumbled once, 1982 and 1983.
Additonal USFL statistics: Rushed four times for 15 yards, 1985.
Additional NFL statistics: Recovered one fumble, 1986.

SIDNEY JOHNSON
Cornerback—Kansas City Chiefs
Born March 7, 1965, at Los Angeles, Calif.
Height, 5.09. Weight, 175.
High School—Cerritos, Calif.
Attended Cerritos College and University of California at Berkeley.

Signed as free agent by Kansas City Chiefs, May 14, 1987.
On injured reserve with knee injury, August 31 through entire 1987 season.
Kansas City NFL, 1988.
Games: 1988 (13).

STEVEN EMIL JOHNSON
(Steve)
Tight End—New England Patriots
Born June 22, 1965, at Huntsville, Ala.
Height, 6.06. Weight, 245.
High School—Oneonta, Ala.
Attended Virginia Tech.
Received bachelor of science degree in sports management from Virginia Tech in 1988.

Selected by New England in 6th round (154th player selected) of 1988 NFL draft.
Signed by New England Patriots, June 13, 1988.
New England NFL, 1988.
Games: 1988 (14).
Pro statistics: Caught one pass for five yards, 1988.

THOMAS JOHNSON
(Pepper)
Linebacker—New York Giants
Born July 29, 1964, at Detroit, Mich.
Height, 6.03. Weight, 248.
High School—Detroit, Mich., Mackenzie.
Attended Ohio State University.

Selected by New Jersey in 1986 USFL territorial draft.
Selected by New York Giants in 2nd round (51st player selected) of 1986 NFL draft.
Signed by New York Giants, July 30, 1986.
New York Giants NFL, 1986 through 1988.
Games: 1986 (16), 1987 (12), 1988 (16). Total—44.
Pro statistics: Intercepted one pass for 13 yards, 1986; recovered one fumble, 1987 and 1988; intercepted one pass for 33 yards and a touchdown, 1988.
Played in NFC Championship Game following 1986 season.
Played in NFL Championship Game following 1986 season.

TIMOTHY JOHNSON
(Tim)
Defensive End-Defensive Tackle—Pittsburgh Steelers
Born January 29, 1965, at Sarasota, Fla.
Height, 6.03. Weight, 260.
High School—Sarasota, Fla.
Received bachelor of arts degree in hotel, restaurant and institutional management
from Penn State University in 1987.

Selected by Pittsburgh in 6th round (141st player selected) of 1987 NFL draft.
Signed by Pittsburgh Steelers, July 26, 1987.
Pittsburgh NFL, 1987 and 1988.
Games: 1987 (12), 1988 (15). Total—27.

TROY ANTWAIN JOHNSON
Linebacker—Chicago Bears
Born November 10, 1964, at Houston, Tex.
Height, 6.00. Weight, 236.
High School—Alief, Tex., Hastings.
Attended University of Oklahoma.
Cousin of David Lewis, linebacker with Tampa Bay Buccaneers,
San Diego Chargers and Los Angeles Rams, 1977 through 1983.

Selected by Chicago in 5th round (133rd player selected) of 1988 NFL draft.
Signed by Chicago Bears, July 21, 1988.
Chicago NFL, 1988.
Games: 1988 (16).
Played in NFC Championship Game following 1988 season.

TROY DWAN JOHNSON
Wide Receiver—Pittsburgh Steelers
Born October 20, 1962, at New Orleans, La.
Height, 6.01. Weight, 185.
High School—Bourg, La., South Terrebonne.
Attended Southeastern Louisiana University and Southern University.

Signed as free agent by Denver Gold, January 29, 1985.
On developmental squad, February 21 through March 15, 1985; activated, March 16, 1985.
Released by Denver Gold, July 31, 1985; awarded on waivers to Arizona Outlaws, August 1, 1985.
Granted free agency when USFL suspended operations, August 7, 1986; signed as free agent by Dallas Cowboys,
August 19, 1986.
Released by Dallas Cowboys, August 23, 1986; signed as free agent by St. Louis Cardinals, September 25, 1986.
Crossed picket line during players' strike, October 2, 1987.
Franchise transferred to Phoenix, March 15, 1988.
Released by Phoenix Cardinals, August 30, 1988; signed as free agent by Pittsburgh Steelers, September 7, 1988.
On developmental squad for 3 games with Denver Gold in 1985.

| | | —PASS RECEIVING— | | | |
Year Club	G.	P.C.	Yds.	Avg.	TD.
1985—Denver USFL	14	14	167	11.9	0
1986—St. Louis NFL	13	14	203	14.5	0
1987—St. Louis NFL	14	15	308	20.5	2
1988—Pittsburgh NFL	14	10	237	23.7	0
USFL Totals—1 Year	14	14	167	11.9	0
NFL Totals—3 Years	41	39	748	19.2	2
Pro Totals—4 Years	55	53	915	17.3	2

Additional USFL statistics: Returned five kickoffs for 97 yards, rushed twice for 11 yards, recovered one fumble and fumbled once, 1985.
Additional NFL statistics: Returned three kickoffs for 46 yards, 1986; rushed once for nine yards, 1987.

TRUMAINE JOHNSON
Wide Receiver—Buffalo Bills
Born January 16, 1960, at Bogaloosa, La.
Height, 6.01. Weight, 196.
High School—Baker, La.
Attended Grambling State University.

Named as wide receiver on THE SPORTING NEWS USFL All-Star Team, 1983 and 1984.
Selected by Chicago in 1st round (11th player selected) of 1983 USFL draft.
Signed by Chicago Blitz, January 14, 1983.
Selected by San Diego in 6th round (141st player selected) of 1983 NFL draft.
Franchise transferred to Arizona, September 30, 1983.
Protected in merger of Arizona Wranglers and Oklahoma Outlaws, December 6, 1984.
Left Arizona Outlaws camp voluntarily, January 23, 1985.
On suspended list, February 22 through entire 1985 season.
Released by Arizona Outlaws, July 10, 1985; signed by San Diego Chargers, July 12, 1985.
Traded with 7th round pick in 1988 draft by San Diego Chargers to Buffalo Bills for linebacker David Brandon and 4th round pick in 1988 draft, August 31, 1987.

Year Club	G.	P.C.	Yds.	Avg.	TD.
		PASS RECEIVING			
1983—Chicago USFL	18	*81	*1322	16.3	10
1984—Arizona USFL	18	90	1268	14.1	13
1985—San Diego NFL	11	4	51	12.8	1
1986—San Diego NFL	16	30	399	13.3	1
1987—Buffalo NFL	12	15	186	12.4	2
1988—Buffalo NFL	16	37	514	13.9	0
USFL Totals—2 Years....	36	171	2590	15.1	23
NFL Totals—4 Years......	55	86	1150	13.4	4
Pro Totals—6 Years........	91	257	3740	14.6	27

Additional USFL statistics: Rushed seven times for 40 yards, returned one punt for 26 yards, recovered two fumbles and attempted one pass with no completions, 1983; fumbled three times, 1983 and 1984; rushed once for three yards, recovered one fumble and returned two punts for four yards, 1984.

Additional NFL statistics: Returned three kickoffs for 48 yards, 1986; fumbled once, 1986 and 1988.

Played in AFC Championship Game following 1988 season.

Played in USFL Championship Game following 1984 season.

VANCE EDWARD JOHNSON
Wide Receiver—Denver Broncos
Born March 13, 1963, at Trenton, N.J.
Height, 5.11. Weight, 185.
High School—Tucson, Ariz., Cholla.
Attended University of Arizona.

Selected by Arizona in 1985 USFL territorial draft.
Selected by Denver in 2nd round (31st player selected) of 1985 NFL draft.
Signed by Denver Broncos, July 16, 1985.
On injured reserve with knee injury, September 9 through October 9, 1986; activated, October 10, 1986.

Year Club	G.	RUSHING				PASS RECEIVING				TOTAL		
		Att.	Yds.	Avg.	TD.	P.C.	Yds.	Avg.	TD.	TD.	Pts.	F.
1985—Denver NFL	16	10	36	3.6	0	51	721	14.1	3	3	18	5
1986—Denver NFL	12	5	15	3.0	0	31	363	11.7	2	2	12	1
1987—Denver NFL	11	1	—8	—8.0	0	42	684	16.3	7	7	42	1
1988—Denver NFL	16	1	1	1.0	0	68	896	13.2	5	5	30	0
Pro Totals—4 Years	55	17	44	2.6	0	192	2664	13.9	17	17	102	7

Year Club	G.	PUNT RETURNS				KICKOFF RET.		
		No.	Yds.	Avg.	TD.	No.	Yds.	Avg.TD.
1985—Denver NFL	16	30	260	8.7	0	30	740	24.7 0
1986—Denver NFL	12	3	36	12.0	0	2	21	10.5 0
1987—Denver NFL	11	1	9	9.0	0	7	140	20.0 0
1988—Denver NFL	16		None				None	
Pro Totals—4 Years	55	34	305	9.0	0	39	901	23.1 0

Additional pro statistics: Attempted one pass with no completions, 1985 through 1987; recovered two fumbles, 1985.

Played in AFC Championship Game following 1986 season.

Played in NFL Championship Game following 1986 and 1987 seasons.

VAUGHAN MONROE JOHNSON
Linebacker—New Orleans Saints
Born March 24, 1962, at Morehead City, N.C.
Height, 6.03. Weight, 235.
High School—Morehead City, N.C., West Carteret.
Attended North Carolina State University.

Named as linebacker on THE SPORTING NEWS College All-America Team, 1983.
Selected by Jacksonville in 1984 USFL territorial draft.
Signed by Jacksonville Bulls, January 17, 1984.
On developmental squad, April 6 through April 12, 1984; activated, April 13, 1984.
Selected by New Orleans in 1st round (15th player selected) of 1984 NFL supplemental draft.
Granted free agency when USFL suspended operations, August 7, 1986; signed by New Orleans Saints, August 12, 1986.
Granted roster exemption, August 12 through August 24, 1986; activated, August 25, 1986.
On developmental squad for 1 game with Jacksonville Bulls in 1984.
Jacksonville USFL, 1984 and 1985; New Orleans NFL, 1986 through 1988.
Games: 1984 (17), 1985 (18), 1986 (16), 1987 (12), 1988 (16). Total USFL—35. Total NFL—44. Total Pro—79.
USFL statistics: Credited with one sack for 13 yards, intercepted one pass for four yards and recovered blocked kick in end zone for a touchdown, 1984; credited with three sacks for 18 yards and recovered one fumble for three yards, 1985.
NFL statistics: Intercepted one pass for 15 yards, 1986; recovered one fumble, 1986 and 1987; intercepted one pass for no yards, 1987; intercepted one pass for 34 yards, 1988.

WALTER ULYSSES JOHNSON
Linebacker—New Orleans Saints
Born November 13, 1963, at Monroe, La.
Height, 6.00. Weight, 241.
High School—Ferriday, La.
Attended Louisiana Tech University.

Selected by Houston in 2nd round (46th player selected) of 1987 NFL draft.

Signed by Houston Oilers, July 31, 1987.
Crossed picket line during players' strike, October 14, 1987.
Granted unconditional free agency, February 1, 1989; signed by New Orleans Saints, March 28, 1989.
Houston NFL, 1987 and 1988.
Games: 1987 (10), 1988 (16). Total—26.

WILLIAM ALEXANDER JOHNSON
(Will)
Linebacker—New Orleans Saints

Born December 4, 1964, at Monroe, La.
Height, 6.04. Weight, 245.
High School—Monroe, La., Neville.
Attended Northeast Louisiana University.

Selected by Chicago in 5th round (138th player selected) of 1987 NFL draft.
Signed by Chicago Bears, July 30, 1987.
Released by Chicago Bears, August 24, 1988; signed as free agent by New Orleans Saints, March 6, 1989.
Chicago NFL, 1987.
Games: 1987 (11).

AARON DELMAS JONES II
Defensive End-Linebacker—Pittsburgh Steelers

Born December 18, 1966, at Orlando, Fla.
Height, 6.05. Weight, 257.
High School—Apopka, Fla.
Attended Eastern Kentucky University.

Selected by Pittsburgh in 1st round (18th player selected) of 1988 NFL draft.
Signed by Pittsburgh Steelers, July 15, 1988.
On injured reserve with knee injury, December 16 through remainder of 1988 season.
Pittsburgh NFL, 1988.
Games: 1988 (15).

ANTHONY JONES
Tight End—Dallas Cowboys

Born May 16, 1960, at Baltimore, Md.
Height, 6.03. Weight, 248.
High School—Baltimore, Md., Patterson.
Attended University of Maryland (Eastern Shore) and Wichita State University.

Selected by Oklahoma in 1984 USFL territorial draft.
Selected by Washington in 11th round (306th player selected) of 1984 NFL draft.
Signed by Washington Redskins, June 21, 1984.
On injured reserve with neck injury, December 21 through remainder of 1984 season.
On injured reserve with knee injury, December 16 through remainder of 1986 season.
On physically unable to perform/reserve with knee injury, September 1 through December 18, 1987; activated, December 19, 1987.
Released by Washington Redskins, November 21, 1988; awarded on waivers to San Diego Chargers, November 22, 1988.
Granted unconditional free agency, February 1, 1989; signed by Dallas Cowboys, March 13, 1989.
Washington NFL, 1984 through 1987; Washington (8)-San Diego (4) NFL, 1988.
Games: 1984 (16), 1985 (16), 1986 (15), 1987 (2), 1988 (12). Total—61.
Pro statistics: Caught one pass for six yards, 1984; returned one kickoff for no yards, 1985; recovered one fumble, 1986; caught three passes for 21 yards and returned one kickoff for 13 yards, 1988.
Played in NFC Championship Game following 1987 season.
Played in NFL Championship Game following 1987 season.

BRENT MICHAEL JONES
Tight End—San Francisco 49ers

Born February 12, 1963, at Santa Clara, Calif.
Height, 6.04. Weight, 230.
High School—San Jose, Calif., Leland.
Received bachelor of science degree in economics from University of Santa Clara in 1986.
Son of Mike Jones, selected by Oakland Raiders in 21st round of 1961 AFL draft
and by Pittsburgh Steelers in 20th round of 1961 NFL draft.

Selected by Pittsburgh in 5th round (135th player selected) of 1986 NFL draft.
Signed by Pittsburgh Steelers, July 30, 1986.
On injured reserve with neck injury, August 19 through September 23, 1986.
Released by Pittsburgh Steelers, September 24, 1986; signed as free agent by San Francisco 49ers for 1987, December 24, 1986.
On injured reserve with neck injury, September 1 through December 4, 1987, activated, December 5, 1987.
Crossed picket line during players' strike, October 14, 1987.
On injured reserve with knee injury, August 29 through October 5, 1988; re-signed by 49ers after clearing procedural waivers, October 7, 1988.
Granted unconditional free agency, February 1, 1989; re-signed by 49ers, April 28, 1989.

| | | ——PASS RECEIVING—— | | | |
Year Club	G.	P.C.	Yds.	Avg.	TD.
1987—San Francisco NFL	4	2	35	17.5	0
1988—San Francisco NFL	11	8	57	7.1	2
Pro Totals—2 Years............	15	10	92	9.2	2

Played in NFC Championship Game following 1988 season.
Played in NFL Championship Game following 1988 season.

CEDRIC DECORRUS JONES

First name pronounced SEED-rick.

Wide Receiver—New England Patriots

Born June 1, 1960, at Norfolk, Va.
Height, 6.01. Weight, 184.
High School—Weldon, N.C.
Received bachelor of arts degree in history and political science from
Duke University in 1982.

Selected by New England in 3rd round (56th player selected) of 1982 NFL draft.
On inactive list, September 19, 1982.

			—PASS RECEIVING—			
Year	Club	G.	P.C.	Yds.	Avg.	TD.
1982—New England NFL.......		2	1	5	5.0	0
1983—New England NFL.......		15	20	323	16.2	1
1984—New England NFL.......		14	19	244	12.8	2
1985—New England NFL.......		16	21	237	11.3	2
1986—New England NFL.......		16	14	222	15.9	1
1987—New England NFL.......		12	25	388	15.5	3
1988—New England NFL.......		16	22	313	14.2	1
Pro Totals—7 Years...........		91	122	1732	14.2	10

Additional pro statistics: Returned four kickoffs for 63 yards, 1983; fumbled once, 1983, 1984, 1986 and 1988; returned one kickoff for 20 yards and recovered fumble in end zone for a touchdown, 1984; returned three kickoffs for 37 yards and recovered one fumble for 15 yards and a touchdown, 1985; returned four kickoffs for 63 yards and rushed once for minus seven yards, 1986; attempted one pass with no completions, 1987.
Played in AFC Championship Game following 1985 season.
Played in NFL Championship Game following 1985 season.

DANTE DELANEO JONES

Linebacker—Chicago Bears

Born March 23, 1965, at Dallas, Tex.
Height, 6.01. Weight, 236.
High School—Dallas, Tex., Skyline.
Received bachelor of science degree in political science at University of Oklahoma in 1988.

Selected by Chicago in 2nd round (51st player selected) of 1988 NFL draft.
Signed by Chicago Bears, July 21, 1988.
Chicago NFL, 1988.
Games: 1988 (15).
Played in NFC Championship Game following 1988 season.

DWIGHT SEAN JONES

(Known by middle name.)

Defensive End—Houston Oilers

Born December 19, 1962, at Kingston, Jamaica.
Height, 6.07. Weight, 273.
High School—Montclair, N.J., Kimberly Academy.
Attended Northeastern University.
Brother of Max Jones, linebacker with Birmingham Stallions, 1984.

Selected by Washington in 5th round (91st player selected) of 1984 USFL draft.
Selected by Los Angeles Raiders in 2nd round (51st player selected) of 1984 NFL draft.
Signed by Los Angeles Raiders, July 12, 1984.
Traded with 2nd and 3rd round picks in 1988 draft by Los Angeles Raiders to Houston Oilers for 1st, 3rd and 4th round picks in 1988 draft, April 21, 1988.
Los Angeles Raiders NFL, 1984 through 1987; Houston NFL, 1988.
Games: 1984 (16), 1985 (15), 1986 (16), 1987 (12), 1988 (16). Total—75.
Pro statistics: Recovered one fumble, 1985; recovered two fumbles, 1987.

EDWARD LEE JONES

(Ed or Too Tall)

Defensive End—Dallas Cowboys

Born February 23, 1951, at Jackson, Tenn.
Height, 6.09. Weight, 278.
High School—Jackson, Tenn., Central-Merry.
Received degree in health and physical education from Tennessee State University.

Named as defensive end on THE SPORTING NEWS College All-America Team, 1973.
Placed on retired reserve, June 19, 1979.
Selected by Dallas in 1st round (1st player selected) of 1974 NFL draft.
Crossed picket line during players' strike, October 2, 1987.
Dallas NFL, 1974 through 1978 and 1980 through 1988.
Games: 1974 (14), 1975 (14), 1976 (14), 1977 (14), 1978 (16), 1980 (16), 1981 (16), 1982 (9), 1983 (16), 1984 (16), 1985 (16), 1986 (16), 1987 (15), 1988 (16). Total—208.
Pro statistics: Intercepted one pass for two yards, 1975; recovered one fumble, 1975, 1976, 1982 and 1987; recovered

three fumbles, 1980, 1981 and 1986; intercepted one pass for no yards, 1982; intercepted one pass for 12 yards, 1983; recovered two fumbles, 1983, 1984 and 1988.

Played in NFC Championship Game following 1975, 1977, 1978 and 1980 through 1982 seasons.
Played in NFL Championship Game following 1975, 1977 and 1978 seasons.
Played in Pro Bowl (NFL All-Star Game) following 1981 through 1983 seasons.

ERNEST LEE JONES
(Ernie)
Wide Receiver—Phoenix Cardinals
Born December 13, 1964, at Elkhart, Ind.
Height, 5.11. Weight, 186.
High School—Elkhart, Ind., Memorial.
Received degree in general studies from Indiana University in 1988.

Selected by Phoenix in 7th round (179th player selected) of 1988 NFL draft.
Signed by Phoenix Cardinals, July 11, 1988.

		PASS RECEIVING				—KICKOFF RET.—				—TOTAL—		
Year	Club	G.	P.C.	Yds.	Avg.	TD.	No.	Yds.	Avg.	TD.	TD.	Pts.	F.
1988—Phoenix NFL		16	23	496	21.6	3	11	147	13.4	0	3	18	1

HASSAN AMEER JONES
Wide Receiver—Minnesota Vikings
Born July 2, 1964, at Clearwater, Fla.
Height, 6.00. Weight, 195.
High School—Clearwater, Fla.
Attended Florida State University.

Selected by Tampa Bay in 1986 USFL territorial draft.
Selected by Minnesota in 5th round (120th player selected) of 1986 NFL draft.
Signed by Minnesota Vikings, July 9, 1986.

		PASS RECEIVING				
Year	Club	G.	P.C.	Yds.	Avg.	TD.
1986—Minnesota NFL		16	28	570	20.4	4
1987—Minnesota NFL		12	7	189	27.0	2
1988—Minnesota NFL		16	40	778	19.5	5
Pro Totals—3 Years		44	75	1537	20.5	11

Additional pro statistics: Rushed once for 14 yards and fumbled once, 1986; rushed once for seven yards, 1988.
Played in NFC Championship Game following 1987 season.

JAMES ROOSEVELT JONES
Fullback—Detroit Lions
Born March 21, 1961, at Pompano Beach, Fla.
Height, 6.02. Weight, 228.
High School—Pompano Beach, Fla., Ely.
Attended University of Florida.

Selected by Tampa Bay in 1983 USFL territorial draft.
Selected by Detroit in 1st round (13th player selected) of 1983 NFL draft.
Signed by Detroit Lions, May 12, 1983.

		RUSHING				PASS RECEIVING				—TOTAL—		
Year	Club	G.	Att.	Yds.	Avg.	TD.	P.C.	Yds.	Avg.	TD.	TD.	Pts.	F.
1983—Detroit NFL		14	135	475	3.5	6	46	467	10.2	1	7	42	4
1984—Detroit NFL		16	137	532	3.9	3	77	662	8.6	5	8	48	6
1985—Detroit NFL		14	244	886	3.6	6	45	334	7.4	3	9	54	7
1986—Detroit NFL		16	252	903	3.6	8	54	334	6.2	1	9	54	6
1987—Detroit NFL		11	96	342	3.6	0	34	262	7.7	0	0	0	2
1988—Detroit NFL		14	96	314	3.3	0	29	259	8.9	0	0	0	2
Pro Totals—6 Years		85	960	3452	3.6	23	285	2318	8.1	10	33	198	27

Additional pro statistics: Recovered one fumble, 1983 and 1985; attempted two passes with no completions, 1983; attempted five passes with three completions for 62 yards and a touchdown and recovered three fumbles, 1984; attempted one pass with no completions, 1985 and 1988; recovered two fumbles, 1986; attempted one pass with one interception, 1987.

MARLON JONES
Defensive End—Cleveland Browns
Born July 1, 1964, at Baltimore, Md.
Height, 6.04. Weight, 260.
High School—Baltimore, Md., Milford Mill.
Attended Central State University (O.).

Signed as free agent by Toronto Argonauts, February, 1986.
Released by Toronto Argonauts, October 19, 1987; signed by Cleveland Browns, November 19, 1987.
On injured reserve with back injury, December 21 through remainder of 1988 season playoffs.
Toronto CFL, 1986 and 1987; Cleveland NFL, 1987 and 1988.
Games: 1986 CFL (14), 1987 CFL (10), 1987 NFL (1), 1988 (16). Total CFL—24. Total NFL—17. Total Pro—41.
CFL statistics: Intercepted one pass for 35 yards, recovered one fumble and credited with nine sacks, 1986; credited with three sacks, 1987.

MICHAEL ANTHONY JONES
(Mike)
Wide Receiver—New England Patriots
Born April 14, 1960, at Chattanooga, Tenn.
Height, 5.11. Weight, 180.
High School—Chattanooga, Tenn., Riverside.
Attended Tennessee State University.

Selected by Minnesota in 6th round (159th player selected) of 1983 NFL draft.
Traded by Minnesota Vikings to New Orleans Saints for fullback Wayne Wilson, September 2, 1986.
Released by New Orleans Saints, August 30, 1988; signed as free agent by Kansas City Chiefs, September 28, 1988.
Released by Kansas City Chiefs, October 17, 1988; re-signed by Chiefs, December 14, 1988.
Granted unconditional free agency, February 1, 1989; signed by New England Patriots, February 27, 1989.
Active for 1 game with Kansas City Chiefs in 1988; did not play.

Year Club	G.	P.C.	Yds.	Avg.	TD.
1983—Minnesota NFL............	16	6	95	15.8	0
1984—Minnesota NFL............	16	38	591	15.6	1
1985—Minnesota NFL............	16	46	641	13.9	4
1986—New Orleans NFL........	16	48	625	13.0	3
1987—New Orleans NFL........	12	27	420	15.6	3
Pro Totals—6 Years............	76	165	2372	14.4	11

Additional pro statistics: Rushed once for nine yards and returned two kickoffs for 31 yards, 1983; rushed four times for 45 yards and recovered two fumbles, 1984; fumbled once, 1984 and 1987; rushed twice for six yards, 1985; recovered one fumble and fumbled twice, 1986.

QUINTIN MAURICE JONES
Safety—Houston Oilers
Born July 28, 1966, at Miami, Fla.
Height, 5.11. Weight, 194.
High School—Pompono Beach, Fla., Ely.
Attended University of Pittsburgh.

Selected by Houston in 2nd round (48th player selected) of 1988 NFL draft.
Signed by Houston Oilers, October 3, 1988.
Granted roster exemption, October 3 through October 16, 1988; activated, October 17, 1988.
On injured reserve with quadricep injury, November 2 through December 2, 1988; activated, December 3, 1988.
On injured reserve with knee injury, December 17 through remainder of 1988 season.
Houston NFL, 1988.
Games: 1988 (4).

RODERICK EARL JONES
(Rod)
Tight End—San Francisco 49ers
Born March 3, 1964, at Richmond, Calif.
Height, 6.04. Weight, 241.
High School—El Cerrito, Calif.
Attended University of Washington.

Selected by New York Giants in 8th round (223rd player selected) of 1987 NFL draft.
Signed by New York Giants, July 5, 1987.
Released by New York Giants, September 7, 1987; signed as free agent replacement player by Kansas City Chiefs, September 25, 1987.
Released by Kansas City Chiefs, November 3, 1987; re-signed by Chiefs for 1988, November 5, 1987.
Released by Kansas City Chiefs, September 28, 1988; signed as free agent by San Francisco 49ers for 1989, December 9, 1988.

Year Club	G.	P.C.	Yds.	Avg.	TD.
1987—Kansas City NFL..........	3	8	76	9.5	1
1988—Kansas City NFL..........	2		None		
Pro Totals—2 Years............	5	8	76	9.5	1

Additional pro statistics: Fumbled once, 1987.

RODERICK WAYNE JONES
(Rod)
Defensive Back—Tampa Bay Buccaneers
Born March 31, 1964, at Dallas, Tex.
Height, 6.00. Weight, 185.
High School—Dallas, Tex., South Oak Cliff.
Attended Southern Methodist University.

Selected by Tampa Bay in 1st round (25th player selected) of 1986 NFL draft.
Signed by Tampa Bay Buccaneers, June 19, 1986.

Year Club	G.	No.	Yds.	Avg.	TD.
1986—Tampa Bay NFL	16	1	0	0.0	0
1987—Tampa Bay NFL	11	2	9	4.5	0
1988—Tampa Bay NFL	14	1	0	0.0	0
Pro Totals—3 Years............	41	4	9	2.3	0

Additional pro statistics: Recovered one fumble, 1986; recovered one fumble for eight yards, 1987.

RULON KENT JONES
Defensive End—Denver Broncos
Born March 25, 1958, at Salt Lake City, Utah.
Height, 6.06. Weight, 260.
High School—Ogden, Utah, Weber.
Attended Utah State University.

Named to THE SPORTING NEWS NFL All-Star Team, 1985 and 1986.
Named as defensive tackle on THE SPORTING NEWS College All-America Team, 1979.
Selected by Denver in 2nd round (42nd player selected) of 1980 NFL draft.
On injured reserve with knee injury, September 21 through October 20, 1983; activated, October 21, 1983.
Denver NFL, 1980 through 1988.
Games: 1980 (16), 1981 (16), 1982 (9), 1983 (12), 1984 (16), 1985 (16), 1986 (16), 1987 (12), 1988 (16). Total—129.
Pro statistics: Credited with a safety, 1980, 1983 and 1986; recovered one fumble, 1980, 1981 and 1986; recovered two fumbles for four yards, 1983, recovered two fumbles for five yards and a touchdown, 1984; recovered three fumbles, 1985.
Played in AFC Championship Game following 1986 and 1987 seasons.
Played in NFL Championship Game following 1986 and 1987 seasons.
Played in Pro Bowl (NFL All-Star Game) following 1985 and 1986 seasons.

TONY EDWARD JONES
Offensive Tackle—Cleveland Browns
Born May 24, 1966, at Royston, Ga.
Height, 6.05. Weight, 280.
High School—Carnesville, Ga., Franklin County.
Received bachelor of science degree in management from
Western Carolina University in 1989.

Signed as free agent by Cleveland Browns, May 2, 1988.
On injured reserve with toe injury, August 29 through October 21, 1988; activated, October 22, 1988.
Cleveland NFL, 1988.
Games: 1988 (4).

TYRONE JONES
Linebacker—Phoenix Cardinals
Born August 3, 1961, at St. Marys, Ga.
Height, 6.00. Weight, 220.
High School—St. Marys, Ga., Camden.
Attended Southern University & A&M.

Signed as free agent by Winnipeg Blue Bombers, April 12, 1983.
Granted free agency, March 1, 1988; signed by Phoenix Cardinals, April 6, 1988.
On injured reserve with ankle injury, August 23 through December 15, 1988; activated, December 16, 1988.

| | | | —INTERCEPTIONS— | | |
Year Club	G.	No.	Yds.	Avg.	TD.
1983—Winnipeg CFL	16	1	22	22.0	0
1984—Winnipeg CFL	16	3	10	3.3	0
1985—Winnipeg CFL	16	1	5	5.0	0
1986—Winnipeg CFL	16	1	2	2.0	0
1987—Winnipeg CFL	18	1	0	0.0	0
1988—Phoenix NFL	1			None	
CFL Totals—5 Years	82	7	39	5.6	0
NFL Totals—1 Year	1	0	0	0.0	0
Pro Totals—6 Years	83	7	39	5.6	0

Additional CFL statistics: Credited with 17½ sacks, 1983; credited with 20½ sacks and returned one punt for 23 yards, 1984; credited with 11 sacks, 1985; credited with 10 sacks, caught one pass for seven yards and recovered two fumbles, 1986; credited with 15 sacks, caught one pass for one yard and a touchdown and recovered two fumbles for 92 yards and a touchdown, 1987.
Played in CFL Championship Game following 1984 season.

VICTOR PERNELL JONES
Linebacker—Detroit Lions
Born October 10, 1966, at Rockville, Md.
Height, 6.02. Weight, 250.
High School—Rockville, Md., Robert E. Peary.
Attended Virginia Tech.

Selected by Tampa Bay in 12th round (310th player selected) of 1988 NFL draft.
Signed by Tampa Bay Buccaneers, July 6, 1988.
On injured reserve with back injury, August 22 through October 12, 1988; activated after clearing procedural waivers, October 14, 1988.
Granted unconditional free agency, February 1, 1989; signed by Detroit Lions, February 24, 1989.
Tampa Bay NFL, 1988.
Games: 1988 (8).

ANTHONY T. JORDAN
(Tony)
Running Back—Phoenix Cardinals
Born May 8, 1965, at Rochester, N. Y.
Height, 6.02. Weight, 220.
High School—Rochester, N. Y., East.
Received degree in social science from Kansas State University in 1988.

Selected by Phoenix in 5th round (132nd player selected) of 1988 NFL draft.
Signed by Phoenix Cardinals, July 7, 1988.
On injured reserve with stress fracture in back, November 16 through remainder of 1988 season.

			—RUSHING—			PASS RECEIVING				—TOTAL—		
Year	Club	G.	Att.	Yds.	Avg.	TD.	P.C.	Yds.	Avg.	TD.	TD.	Pts.	F.
1988—Phoenix NFL	9	61	160	2.6	3	4	24	6.0	0	3	18	1

DARIN GODFREY JORDAN
Linebacker-Defensive End—Pittsburgh Steelers
Born December 4, 1964, at Boston, Mass.
Height, 6.01. Weight, 235.
High School—Stoughton, Mass.
Received bachelor of arts degree in speech communications
from Northeastern University in 1988.

Selected by Pittsburgh in 5th round (121st player selected) of 1988 NFL draft.
Signed by Pittsburgh Steelers, July 16, 1988.
Pittsburgh NFL, 1988.
Games: 1988 (15).
Pro statistics: Intercepted one pass for 28 yards and a touchdown and recovered four fumbles, 1988.

DAVID TURNER JORDAN
Guard—Los Angeles Raiders
Born July 14, 1962, at Birmingham, Ala.
Height, 6.06. Weight, 276.
High School—Vestavia Hills, Ala.
Attended Auburn University.

Selected by Birmingham in 1984 USFL territorial draft.
Selected by New York Giants in 10th round (255th player selected) of 1984 NFL draft.
Signed by New York Giants, June 3, 1984.
On injured reserve with sprained foot, September 2 through entire 1986 season.
Released by New York Giants, September 7, 1987; signed as free agent replacement player by Tampa Bay Buccaneers, September 24, 1987.
Released by Tampa Bay Buccaneers, November 3, 1987; signed as free agent by Denver Broncos, April 5, 1988.
Released by Denver Broncos, August 23, 1988; signed as free agent by Los Angeles Raiders, April 4, 1989.
New York Giants NFL, 1984 and 1985; Tampa Bay NFL, 1987.
Games: 1984 (14), 1985 (16), 1987 (3). Total—33.
Pro statistics: Recovered one fumble, 1987.

PAUL BUFORD JORDAN
(Known by middle name.)
Fullback—New Orleans Saints
Born June 26, 1962, at Lafayette, La.
Height, 6.00. Weight, 222.
High School—Iota, La.
Attended McNeese State University.

Selected by New Orleans in 1st round (13th player selected) of 1984 USFL draft.
Signed by New Orleans Breakers, January 9, 1984.
Selected by Green Bay in 1st round (12th player selected) of 1984 NFL supplemental draft.
Franchise transferred to Portland, November 13, 1984.
On developmental squad, April 6 through April 20, 1985; activated, April 21, 1985.
Released, July 31, 1985; signed by Green Bay Packers, September 2, 1985.
Granted roster exemption, September 2 through September 15, 1985.
Released by Green Bay Packers, September 16, 1985; signed as free agent by New Orleans Saints, March 6, 1986.
On injured reserve with knee injury, August 23 through September 12, 1988.
Released by New Orleans Saints, September 13, 1988; re-signed by Saints, September 14, 1988.
On developmental squad for 2 games with Portland Breakers in 1985.

			—RUSHING—			PASS RECEIVING				—TOTAL—		
Year	Club	G.	Att.	Yds.	Avg.	TD.	P.C.	Yds.	Avg.	TD.	TD.	Pts.	F.
1984—New Orleans USFL	18	214	1276	*6.0	8	45	427	9.5	4	12	72	9
1985—Portland USFL	15	165	817	5.0	5	12	192	16.0	1	6	†38	11
1986—New Orleans NFL	16	68	207	3.0	1	11	127	11.5	0	1	6	2
1987—New Orleans NFL	12	12	36	3.0	2	2	13	6.5	0	2	12	0
1988—New Orleans NFL	14	19	115	6.1	0	5	70	14.0	0	1	6	1
USFL Totals—2 Years	33	379	2093	5.5	13	57	619	10.9	5	18	110	20
NFL Totals—3 Years	42	99	358	3.6	3	18	210	11.7	0	4	24	3
Pro Totals—5 Years	75	478	2451	5.1	16	75	829	11.1	5	22	134	23

†Includes one 2-point conversion.
Additional USFL statistics: Recovered four fumbles, 1984 and 1985.
Additional NFL statistics: Returned one punt for 13 yards and returned two kickoffs for 28 yards, 1987; recovered one fumble for seven yards and a touchdown, 1988.

STEVEN RUSSELL JORDAN
(Steve)
Tight End—Minnesota Vikings

Born January 10, 1961, at Phoenix, Ariz.
Height, 6.03. Weight, 235.
High School—Phoenix, Ariz., South Mountain.
Received bachelor of science degree in civil engineering from Brown University in 1982.
Selected by Minnesota in 7th round (179th player selected) of 1982 NFL draft.

			—PASS RECEIVING—			
Year	Club	G.	P.C.	Yds.	Avg.	TD.
1982—Minnesota NFL............		9	3	42	14.0	0
1983—Minnesota NFL............		13	15	212	14.1	2
1984—Minnesota NFL............		14	38	414	10.9	2
1985—Minnesota NFL............		16	68	795	11.7	0
1986—Minnesota NFL............		16	58	859	14.8	6
1987—Minnesota NFL............		12	35	490	14.0	2
1988—Minnesota NFL............		16	57	756	13.3	5
Pro Totals—7 Years............		96	274	3568	13.0	17

Additional pro statistics: Rushed once for four yards and a touchdown, 1984; recovered one fumble, 1984 and 1986; fumbled twice, 1985 and 1988; fumbled once, 1987.
Played in NFC Championship Game following 1987 season.
Played in Pro Bowl (NFL All-Star Game) following 1986 through 1988 seasons.

TIMOTHY JORDAN
(Tim)
Linebacker—New England Patriots

Born April 26, 1964, at Madison, Wis.
Height, 6.03. Weight, 226.
High School—Madison, Wis., Robert M. LaFollette.
Attended University of Wisconsin.

Selected by New England in 4th round (107th player selected) of 1987 NFL draft.
Signed by New England Patriots, July 24, 1987.
On injured reserve with hamstring injury, September 1 through November 6, 1987; activated, November 7, 1987.
New England NFL, 1987 and 1988.
Games: 1987 (5), 1988 (16). Total—21.
Pro statistics: Intercepted one pass for 31 yards and recovered one fumble, 1988.

SETH JOYNER
Linebacker—Philadelphia Eagles

Born November 18, 1964, at Spring Valley, N. Y.
Height, 6.02. Weight, 248.
High School—Spring Valley, N. Y.
Attended University of Texas at El Paso.

Selected by Philadelphia in 8th round (208th player selected) of 1986 NFL draft.
Signed by Philadelphia Eagles, July 17, 1986.
Released by Philadelphia Eagles, September 1, 1986; re-signed by Eagles, September 17, 1986.

			—INTERCEPTIONS—			
Year	Club	G.	No.	Yds.	Avg.	TD.
1986—Philadelphia NFL		14	1	4	4.0	0
1987—Philadelphia NFL		12	2	42	21.0	0
1988—Philadelphia NFL		16	4	96	24.0	0
Pro Totals—3 Years............		42	7	142	20.3	0

Additional pro statistics: Recovered two fumbles for 18 yards and a touchdown, 1987; recovered one fumble and fumbled once, 1988.

WILLIAM THADIUS JUDSON
Cornerback—Miami Dolphins

Born March 26, 1959, at Detroit, Mich.
Height, 6.01. Weight, 192.
High School—Atlanta, Ga., Sylvan Hills.
Received bachelor of science degree in business administration
from South Carolina State College in 1981.

Selected by Miami in 8th round (208th player selected) of 1981 NFL draft.
On injured reserve with hamstring injury, August 31 through entire 1981 season.

			—INTERCEPTIONS—			
Year	Club	G.	No.	Yds.	Avg.	TD.
1982—Miami NFL		9		None		
1983—Miami NFL		16	6	60	10.0	0
1984—Miami NFL		16	4	121	30.3	1
1985—Miami NFL		16	4	88	22.0	*1
1986—Miami NFL		16	2	0	0.0	0
1987—Miami NFL		12	2	11	5.5	0
1988—Miami NFL		16	4	57	14.3	0
Pro Totals—7 Years............		101	22	337	15.3	2

Additional pro statistics: Recovered two fumbles for 37 yards, 1984; recovered one fumble, 1988.
Played in AFC Championship Game following 1982, 1984 and 1985 seasons.
Played in NFL Championship Game following 1982 and 1984 seasons.

ESTER JAMES JUNIOR III
(E.J.)
Linebacker—Miami Dolphins
Born December 8, 1959, at Sallsburg, N.C.
Height, 6.03. Weight, 235.
High School—Nashville, Tenn., Maplewood.
Received degree in public relations from University of Alabama.

Named as defensive end on THE SPORTING NEWS College All-America Team, 1980.
Selected by St. Louis in 1st round (5th player selected) of 1981 NFL draft.
On suspended list for drug use, July 25 through September 25, 1983; reinstated, September 26, 1983.
Crossed picket line during players' strike, October 2, 1987.
Franchise transferred to Phoenix, March 15, 1988.
Granted unconditional free agency, February 1, 1989; signed by Miami Dolphins, February 24, 1989.

| | | ——INTERCEPTIONS—— | | | |
Year Club	G.	No.	Yds.	Avg.	TD.
1981—St. Louis NFL	16	1	5	5.0	0
1982—St. Louis NFL	9		None		
1983—St. Louis NFL	12	3	27	9.0	0
1984—St. Louis NFL	16	1	18	18.0	0
1985—St. Louis NFL	16	5	109	21.8	0
1986—St. Louis NFL	13		None		
1987—St. Louis NFL	13	1	25	25.0	0
1988—Phoenix NFL	16	1	2	2.0	0
Pro Totals—8 Years	111	12	186	15.5	0

Additional pro statistics: Recovered one fumble, 1982 and 1986; recovered one fumble for one yard, 1983; recovered two fumbles for five yards and fumbled once, 1987; recovered one fumble for 36 yards and a touchdown, 1988.
Played in Pro Bowl (NFL All-Star Game) following 1984 and 1985 seasons.

ABNER KIRK JUNKIN
(Trey)
Tight End—Los Angeles Raiders
Born January 23, 1961, at Conway, Ark.
Height, 6.02. Weight, 230.
High School—North Little Rock, Ark., Northeast.
Attended Louisiana Tech University.
Brother of Mike Junkin, linebacker with Kansas City Chiefs.

Selected by Buffalo in 4th round (93rd player selected) of 1983 NFL draft.
Released by Buffalo Bills, September 12, 1984; signed as free agent by Washington Redskins, September 25, 1984.
Granted free agency after not receiving qualifying offer, February 1, 1985; signed by Los Angeles Raiders, March 10, 1985.
On injured reserve with knee injury, September 24 through remainder of 1986 season.
Buffalo NFL, 1983; Buffalo (2)-Washington (12) NFL, 1984; Los Angeles Raiders NFL, 1985 through 1988.
Games: 1983 (16), 1984 (14), 1985 (16), 1986 (3), 1987 (12), 1988 (16). Total—77.
Pro statistics: Recovered one fumble, 1983 and 1984; caught two passes for eight yards and a touchdown, 1985; caught two passes for 38 yards, 1986; caught two passes for 15 yards, 1987; caught four passes for 25 yards and two touchdowns, 1988.

MICHAEL WAYNE JUNKIN
(Mike)
Linebacker—Kansas City Chiefs
Born November 21, 1964, at North Little Rock, Ark.
Height, 6.03. Weight, 238.
High School—Belvidere, Ill.
Attended Duke University.
Brother of Trey Junkin, tight end with Los Angeles Raiders.

Selected by Cleveland in 1st round (5th player selected) of 1987 NFL draft.
Signed by Cleveland Browns, August 11, 1987.
On injured reserve with fractured wrist, November 13 through remainder of 1987 season.
On injured reserve with knee injury, October 5 through November 11, 1988; activated, November 12, 1988.
Traded by Cleveland Browns to Kansas City Chiefs for 5th round pick in 1989 draft, April 23, 1989.
Cleveland NFL, 1987 and 1988.
Games: 1987 (4), 1988 (11). Total—15.

JAMES ALLEN JURIGA
(Jim)
Guard-Offensive Tackle—Denver Broncos
Born September 12, 1964, at Fort Wayne, Ind.
Height, 6.06. Weight, 269.
High School—Wheaton, Ill., North.
Attended University of Illinois.

Selected by Orlando in 1986 USFL territorial draft.

Selected by Denver in 4th round (104th player selected) of 1986 NFL draft.
Signed by Denver Broncos, July 16, 1988.
On injured reserve with knee injury, September 1 through entire 1986 season.
On injured reserve with knee injury, September 8 through entire 1987 season.
Denver NFL, 1988.
Games: 1988 (16).

TODD ALEXANDER KALIS
(Name pronounced KA-lis.)
Guard—Minnesota Vikings
Born May 10, 1965, at Stillwater, Minn.
Height, 6.05. Weight, 284.
High School—Phoenix, Ariz., Thunderbird.
Attended Arizona State University.

Selected by Minnesota in 4th round (108th player selected) of 1988 NFL draft.
Signed by Minnesota Vikings, July 21, 1988.
Minnesota NFL, 1988.
Games: 1988 (14).

TOMMY HENRY KANE
Wide Receiver—Seattle Seahawks
Born January 14, 1964, at Montreal, Que., Can.
Height, 5.11. Weight, 180.
High School—Montreal, Que., Can., Dawson.
Received bachelor of science degree in retailing from
Syracuse University in 1988.

Selected by Seattle in 3rd round (75th player selected) of 1988 NFL draft.
Signed by Seattle Seahawks, July 11, 1988.
On injured reserve with groin injury, November 5 through remainder of 1988 season.

		—PASS RECEIVING—			
Year	Club	G.	P.C.	Yds.	Avg. TD.
1988—Seattle NFL		9	6	32	5.3 0

KENNETH PAUL KARCHER
(Ken)
Quarterback—Denver Broncos
Born July 1, 1963, at Pittsburgh, Pa.
Height, 6.03. Weight, 205.
High School—Glenshaw, Pa., Shaler Area.
Attended University of Notre Dame, Delgado College and received bachelor of
general studies degree from Tulane University in 1986.

Signed as free agent by Denver Broncos, May 1, 1986.
Released by Denver Broncos, August 25, 1986; signed as free agent by New Orleans Saints, January 10, 1987.
Released by New Orleans Saints, September 7, 1987; signed as free agent replacement player by Denver Broncos,
September 25, 1987.

			—————PASSING—————						—RUSHING—				—TOTAL—		
Year	Club	G.	Att.	Cmp.	Pct.	Gain	T.P.	P.I.	Avg.	Att.	Yds.	Avg.	TD.	TD.	Pts.	F.
1987—Denver NFL		3	102	56	54.9	628	5	4	6.16	9	3	0.3	0	0	0	2
1988—Denver NFL		1	12	6	50.0	128	1	0	10.67	—	—	None	—	0	0	0
Pro Totals—2 Years		4	114	62	54.4	756	6	4	6.63	9	3	0.3	0	0	0	0

Quarterback Rating Points: 1987 (73.5), 1988 (116.0). Total—78.1.
Additional pro statistics: Recovered three fumbles and fumbled twice for minus 11 yards, 1987.
Member of Denver Broncos for NFL Championship Game following 1987 season; inactive.

RICHARD JOHN KARLIS
(Rich)
Placekicker—Denver Broncos
Born May 23, 1959, at Salem, O.
Height, 6.00. Weight, 180.
High School—Salem, O.
Received degree in economics from University of Cincinnati.

Signed as free agent by Houston Oilers, June 5, 1981.
Released by Houston Oilers, July 31, 1981; signed as free agent by Denver Broncos, June 4, 1982.

		—PLACE KICKING—					
Year	Club	G.	XP.	XPM.	FG.	FGA.	Pts.
1982—Denver NFL		9	15	1	11	13	48
1983—Denver NFL		16	33	1	21	25	96
1984—Denver NFL		16	38	3	21	28	101
1985—Denver NFL		16	41	3	23	38	110
1986—Denver NFL		16	44	1	20	28	104
1987—Denver NFL		12	37	0	18	25	91
1988—Denver NFL		16	36	1	23	36	105
Pro Totals—7 Years		101	244	10	137	193	655

Played in AFC Championship Game following 1986 and 1987 seasons.
Played in NFL Championship Game following 1986 and 1987 seasons.

KEITH LEONARD KARTZ
Offensive Tackle—Denver Broncos
Born May 5, 1963, at Las Vegas, Nev.
Height, 6.04. Weight, 270.
High School—Encinitas, Calif., San Dieguito.
Received bachelor of science degree in social science
from University of California at Berkeley in 1986.

Signed as free agent by Seattle Seahawks, May 9, 1986.
Released by Seattle Seahawks, August 18, 1986; signed as free agent by Denver Broncos, May 1, 1987.
On injured reserve with back injury, September 7 through September 29, 1987; activated, September 30, 1987.
Crossed picket line during players' strike, September 30, 1987.
Denver NFL, 1987 and 1988.
Games: 1987 (12), 1988 (13). Total—25.
Played in AFC Championship Game following 1987 season.
Played in NFL Championship Game following 1987 season.

JOHN ERIC KATTUS
(Known by middle name.)
Tight End—Cincinnati Bengals
Born March 4, 1963, at Cincinnati, O.
Height, 6.05. Weight, 235.
High School—Cincinnati, O., Colerain.
Attended University of Michigan.

Selected by Baltimore in 1986 USFL territorial draft.
Selected by Cincinnati in 4th round (91st player selected) of 1986 NFL draft.
Signed by Cincinnati Bengals, July 18, 1986.
On injured reserve with knee injury, October 1 through remainder of 1988 season.

| | | —PASS RECEIVING— | | | |
Year Club	G.	P.C.	Yds.	Avg.	TD.
1986—Cincinnati NFL	16	11	99	9.0	1
1987—Cincinnati NFL	11	18	217	12.1	2
1988—Cincinnati NFL	4	2	8	4.0	0
Pro Totals—3 Years	31	31	324	10.5	3

Additional pro statistics: Returned two kickoffs for 22 yards, 1987; fumbled once, 1988.

DANIEL KANI KAUAHI
Name pronounced Ka-WAH-he.
(Known by middle name.)
Center—Phoenix Cardinals
Born September 6, 1959, at Kekaha, Haw.
Height, 6.02. Weight, 271.
High School—Honolulu, Haw., Kamehameha.
Attended Arizona State University and University of Hawaii.

Signed as free agent by Seattle Seahawks, April 30, 1982.
Released by Seattle Seahawks, August 22, 1986; re-signed by Seahawks, September 3, 1986.
Released by Seattle Seahawks, September 1, 1987; signed as free agent by Green Bay Packers, June 24, 1988.
Granted unconditional free agency, February 1, 1989; signed by Phoenix Cardinals, March 31, 1989.
Seattle NFL, 1982 through 1986; Green Bay NFL, 1988.
Games: 1982 (2), 1983 (10), 1984 (16), 1985 (16), 1986 (16), 1988 (16). Total—76.
Pro statistics: Recovered two fumbles, 1984.
Member of Seattle Seahawks for AFC Championship Game following 1983 season; did not play.

MEL KAUFMAN
Linebacker—Washington Redskins
Born February 24, 1958, at Los Angeles, Calif.
Height, 6.02. Weight, 230.
High School—Santa Monica, Calif.
Attended California Poly State University at San Luis Obispo.
Son-in-law of Billie Matthews, assistant coach with University of Kansas, 1970;
University of California at Los Angeles, 1971 through 1978; San Francisco 49ers,
1979 through 1982; Philadelphia Eagles, 1983 and 1984; Indianapolis
Colts, 1985 and 1986; Kansas City Chiefs, 1987 and 1988;
and with Detroit Lions since 1989.

Signed as free agent by Washington Redskins, May 6, 1981.
On injured reserve with shoulder injury, November 19 through remainder of 1981 season.
On injured reserve with torn Achilles tendon, September 16 through remainder of 1986 season.

Year Club	—INTERCEPTIONS— G.	No.	Yds.	Avg.TD.		Year Club	—INTERCEPTIONS— G.	No.	Yds.	Avg.TD.
1981—Washington NFL	11	2	25	12.5	0	1986—Washington NFL	2		None	
1982—Washington NFL	9		None			1987—Washington NFL	12		None	
1983—Washington NFL	16	2	93	46.5	1	1988—Washington NFL	11		None	
1984—Washington NFL	15		None			Pro Totals—8 Years	91	7	128	18.3 1
1985—Washington NFL	15	3	10	3.3	0					

Additional pro statistics: Recovered one fumble, 1982 and 1984; recovered one fumble for 30 yards and a touchdown, 1983; recovered two fumbles, 1985.
Played in NFC Championship Game following 1982, 1983 and 1987 seasons.
Played in NFL Championship Game following 1982, 1983 and 1987 seasons.

CLARENCE HUBERT KAY
Tight End—Denver Broncos
Born July 30, 1961, at Seneca, S.C.
Height, 6.02. Weight, 237.
High School—Seneca, S.C.
Attended University of Georgia.

Selected by Jacksonville in 1984 USFL territorial draft.
Selected by Denver in 7th round (186th player selected) of 1984 NFL draft.
Signed by Denver Broncos, May 17, 1984.
On suspended list, November 15 through November 18, 1986; activated, November 19, 1986.
On suspended list, December 12, 1986 through January 9, 1987; activated, January 10, 1987.

			—PASS RECEIVING—		
Year	Club	G.	P.C.	Yds.	Avg.	TD.
1984—Denver NFL	16	16	136	8.5	3
1985—Denver NFL	16	29	339	11.7	3
1986—Denver NFL	13	15	195	13.0	1
1987—Denver NFL	12	31	440	14.2	0
1988—Denver NFL	14	34	352	10.4	4
Pro Totals—5 Years	71	125	1462	11.7	11

Additional pro statistics: Fumbled once, 1984, 1985 and 1988; recovered one fumble, 1985; fumbled three times, 1987.
Played in AFC Championship Game following 1986 and 1987 seasons.
Played in NFL Championship Game following 1986 and 1987 seasons.

MARK ANTHONY KEEL
Tight End—Green Bay Packers
Born October 1, 1961, at Fort Worth, Tex.
Height, 6.04. Weight, 228.
High School—Tacoma, Wash., Clover Park.
Attended Olympic College and University of Arizona.

Selected by Arizona in 1983 USFL territorial draft.
Signed by Arizona Wranglers, February 25, 1983.
Selected by New England in 9th round (240th player selected) of 1983 NFL draft.
Franchise transferred to Chicago, September 30, 1983.
On developmental squad, June 15 through remainder of 1984 season.
Franchise disbanded, November 20, 1984.
Selected by Jacksonville Bulls in USFL dispersal draft, December 6, 1984.
On developmental squad, June 14 through remainder of 1985 season.
Traded by Jacksonville Bulls to Arizona Outlaws for draft choice, February 28, 1986.
Granted free agency when USFL suspended operations, August 7, 1986; signed by New England Patriots, September 8, 1986.
On non-football injury list, September 8 through remainder of 1986 season.
Released by New England Patriots, September 7, 1987; signed as free agent replacement player by Seattle Seahawks, September 29, 1987.
Released by Seattle Seahawks, October 20, 1987; signed as free agent by Kansas City Chiefs, October 30, 1987.
On injured reserve with ankle injury, August 22 through September 14, 1988.
Released by Kansas City Chiefs, September 15, 1988; signed as free agent by Green Bay Packers, January 4, 1989.
On developmental squad for 2 games with Chicago Blitz in 1984.
On developmental squad for 2 games with Jacksonville Bulls in 1985.

			—PASS RECEIVING—		
Year	Club	G.	P.C.	Yds.	Avg.	TD.
1983—Arizona USFL	18	65	802	12.3	2
1984—Chicago USFL	16	23	263	11.4	2
1985—Jacksonville USFL	16	53	585	11.0	0
1987—Sea. (3)-K.C. (7) NFL	10	8	97	12.1	1
USFL Totals—3 Years	50	141	1650	11.7	4
NFL Totals—1 Year	10	8	97	12.1	1
Pro Totals—4 Years	60	149	1747	11.7	5

Additional USFL statistics: Fumbled once, recovered one fumble and credited with one 2-point conversion, 1983; scored one 2-point conversion, 1984; fumbled three times, 1985.
Additional NFL statistics: Recovered two fumbles, 1987.

SCOTT JEFFERY KELLAR
Nose Tackle—Green Bay Packers
Born December 31, 1963, at Elgin, Ill.
Height, 6.03. Weight, 278.
High School—Roselle, Ill., Lake Park.
Attended Northern Illinois University.
Brother of Mark Kellar, running back with Chicago Fire (WFL),
San Antonio Wings (WFL) and Minnesota Vikings, 1974 through 1978.

Selected by Indianapolis in 5th round (117th player selected) of 1986 NFL draft.
Signed by Indianapolis Colts, July 17, 1986.

Crossed picket line during players' strike, October 7, 1987.
On injured reserve with knee injury, November 2 through remainder of 1987 season.
Released by Indianapolis Colts, August 24, 1988; signed as free agent by Green Bay Packers for 1989, November 23, 1988.
Indianapolis NFL, 1986 and 1987.
Games: 1986 (14), 1987 (3). Total—17.

JAMES EDWARD KELLY
(Jim)
Quarterback—Buffalo Bills

Born February 14, 1960, at Pittsburgh, Pa.
Height, 6.03. Weight, 215.
High School—East Brady, Pa.
Received bachelor of business management degree from University of Miami (Fla.) in 1982.
Brother of Pat Kelly, linebacker with Birmingham Vulcans (WFL), 1975.

Named THE SPORTING NEWS USFL Rookie of the Year, 1984.
Named as quarterback on THE SPORTING NEWS USFL All-Star Team, 1985.
Led USFL quarterbacks in passing with 97.9 points in 1985.
Selected by Chicago in 14th round (163rd player selected) of 1983 USFL draft.
Selected by Buffalo in 1st round (14th player selected) of 1983 NFL draft.
USFL rights traded with running back Mark Rush by Chicago Blitz to Houston Gamblers for 1st, 3rd, 8th and 10th round picks in 1984 draft, June 9, 1983.
Signed by Houston Gamblers, June 9, 1983.
On developmental squad, June 1 through June 28, 1985; activated, June 29, 1985.
Traded with defensive backs Luther Bradley, Will Lewis, Mike Mitchell and Durwood Roquemore, defensive end Pete Catan, quarterback Todd Dillon, defensive tackles Tony Fitzpatrick, Van Hughes and Hosea Taylor, running back Sam Harrell, linebackers Andy Hawkins and Ladell Wills, wide receivers Richard Johnson, Scott McGhee, Gerald McNeil, Ricky Sanders and Clarence Verdin, guard Rich Kehr, center Billy Kidd and offensive tackles Chris Riehm and Tommy Robison by Houston Gamblers to New Jersey Generals for past considerations, March 7, 1986.
Granted free agency when USFL suspended operations, August 7, 1986; signed by Buffalo Bills, August 18, 1986.
Granted roster exemption, August 18 through August 28, 1986; activated, August 29, 1986.
On developmental squad for 4 games with Houston Gamblers in 1985.

Year Club	G.	Att.	Cmp.	Pct.	Gain	T.P.	P.I.	Avg.	Att.	Yds.	Avg.	TD.	TD.	Pts.	F.
				PASSING						RUSHING				TOTAL	
1984—Houston USFL	18	★587	★370	63.0	★5219	★44	★26	★8.89	85	493	5.8	5	5	†32	9
1985—Houston USFL	14	★567	★360	★63.5	★4623	★39	19	8.15	28	170	6.1	1	1	6	10
1986—Buffalo NFL	16	480	285	59.4	3593	22	17	7.49	41	199	4.9	0	0	0	7
1987—Buffalo NFL	12	419	250	59.7	2798	19	11	6.68	29	133	4.6	0	0	0	6
1988—Buffalo NFL	16	452	269	59.5	3380	15	17	7.48	35	154	4.4	0	0	0	5
USFL Totals—2 Years	32	1154	730	63.3	9842	83	45	8.53	113	663	5.9	6	6	38	19
NFL Totals—3 Years	44	1351	804	59.5	9771	56	45	7.23	105	486	4.6	0	0	0	18
Pro Totals—5 Years	76	2505	1534	61.2	19613	139	90	7.83	218	1149	5.3	6	6	38	37

†Includes one 2-point conversion.
USFL Quarterback Rating Points: 1984 (98.2), 1985 (97.9). Total—98.1.
NFL Quarterback Rating Points: 1986 (83.3), 1987 (83.8), 1988 (78.2). Total—81.7.
Additional USFL statistics: Caught one pass for minus 13 yards and recovered four fumbles, 1984; caught one pass for three yards and recovered three fumbles, 1985.
Additional NFL statistics: Recovered two fumbles, 1986 and 1987; caught one pass for 35 yards, 1987; caught one pass for five yards, 1988.
Played in AFC Championship Game following 1988 season.
Played in Pro Bowl (NFL All-Star Game) following 1987 season.
Named to play in Pro Bowl following 1988 season; replaced due to injury by Dave Krieg.

JOSEPH WINSTON KELLY
(Joe)
Linebacker—Cincinnati Bengals

Born December 11, 1964, at Sun Valley, Calif.
Height, 6.02. Weight, 227.
High School—Los Angeles, Calif., Jefferson.
Received degree from University of Washington in 1986.
Son of Joe Kelly Sr., former player with Montreal Argonauts (CFL); and nephew of Bob Kelly, tackle with Houston Oilers, Kansas City Chiefs, Cincinnati Bengals and Atlanta Falcons, 1961 through 1964 and 1967 through 1969.

Selected by Cincinnati in 1st round (11th player selected) of 1986 NFL draft.
Signed by Cincinnati Bengals, August 29, 1986.
Granted roster exemption, August 29 through September 2, 1986; activated, September 3, 1986.
Cincinnati NFL, 1986 through 1988.
Games: 1986 (16), 1987 (10), 1988 (16). Total—42.
Pro statistics: Intercepted one pass for six yards and recovered one fumble, 1986.
Played in AFC Championship Game following 1988 season.
Played in NFL Championship Game following 1988 season.

—DID YOU KNOW—

That when the Philadelphia Eagles selected only four players in the 1989 NFL draft, it marked the fewest players taken by one team in any draft in league history?

PATRICK JOSEPH KELLY
(Pat)
Tight End—Denver Broncos

Born October 29, 1965, at Rochester, N.Y.
Height, 6.06. Weight, 252.
High School—Webster, N.Y., R.L. Thomas.
Received bachelor of science degree in speech communications and
public relations from Syracuse University in 1988.

Selected by Denver in 7th round (174th player selected) of 1988 NFL draft.
Signed by Denver Broncos, June 17, 1988.
Denver NFL, 1988.
Games: 1988 (16).
Pro statistics: Caught one pass for four yards and fumbled once, 1988.

LARRY DEAN KELM
Linebacker—Los Angeles Rams

Born November 29, 1964, at Corpus Christi, Tex.
Height, 6.04. Weight, 226.
High School—Corpus Christi, Tex., Richard King.
Attended Texas A&M University.

Selected by Los Angeles Rams in 4th round (108th player selected) of 1987 NFL draft.
Signed by Los Angeles Rams, July 23, 1987.
Crossed picket line during players' strike, October 14, 1987.
Los Angeles Rams NFL, 1987 and 1988.
Games: 1987 (12), 1988 (16). Total—28.
Pro statistics: Intercepted two passes for 15 yards, 1988.

MARK ALAN KELSO
Safety—Buffalo Bills

Born July 23, 1963, at Pittsburgh, Pa.
Height, 5.11. Weight, 185.
High School—Pittsburgh, Pa., North Hills.
Attended College of William & Mary.

Selected by Baltimore in 6th round (84th player selected) of 1985 USFL draft.
Selected by Philadelphia in 10th round (261st player selected) of 1985 NFL draft.
Signed by Philadelphia Eagles, July 19, 1985.
Released by Philadelphia Eagles, August 27, 1985; signed as free agent by Buffalo Bills, April 17, 1986.
On injured reserve with knee injury, September 22 through remainder of 1986 season.

			—INTERCEPTIONS—		
Year Club	G.	No.	Yds.	Avg.	TD.
1986—Buffalo NFL	3		None		
1987—Buffalo NFL	12	6	25	4.2	0
1988—Buffalo NFL	16	7	*180	25.7	1
Pro Totals—3 Years	31	13	205	15.8	1

Additional pro statistics: Recovered two fumbles for 56 yards and a touchdown, 1987.
Played in AFC Championship Game following 1988 season.

JEFFREY ALLAN KEMP
(Jeff)
Quarterback—Seattle Seahawks

Born July 11, 1959, at Santa Ana, Calif.
Height, 6.00. Weight, 201.
High School—Potomac, Md., Winston Churchill.
Received bachelor of arts degree in economics from Dartmouth College in 1981;
and received master's in business administration degree from Pepperdine University in 1986.
Son of Jack Kemp, quarterback with Pittsburgh Steelers, Los Angeles-San Diego Chargers and
Buffalo Bills, 1957, 1960 through 1967 and 1969; and currently Republican Congressman from New York
and Secretary of Housing and Urban Development.

Signed as free agent by Los Angeles Rams, May 11, 1981.
Released by Los Angeles Rams, August 31, 1981; re-signed by Rams, September 1, 1981.
On injured reserve with back injury, October 3 through December 1, 1981; activated, December 2, 1981.
On inactive list, September 12 and September 19, 1982.
Granted free agency, February 1, 1986; re-signed by Rams and traded to San Francisco 49ers, May 26, 1986. (This
completed deal of April 29, 1986 in which 49ers traded 3rd round pick in 1986 draft to Rams for two 4th round picks in
1986 draft.)
Traded by San Francisco 49ers to Seattle Seahawks for 5th round pick in 1988 draft, May 19, 1987.
Crossed picket line during players' strike, October 14, 1987.
Active for 7 games with Los Angeles Rams in 1982; did not play.

Year Club	G.	—PASSING—							—RUSHING—				—TOTAL—		
		Att.	Cmp.	Pct.	Gain	T.P.	P.I.	Avg.	Att.	Yds.	Avg.	TD.	TD.	Pts.	F.
1981—L.A. Rams NFL	1	6	2	33.3	25	0	1	4.17	2	9	4.5	0	0	0	0
1983—L.A. Rams NFL	4	25	12	48.0	135	1	0	5.40	3	—2	—0.7	0	0	0	2
1984—L.A. Rams NFL	14	284	143	50.4	2021	13	7	7.12	34	153	4.5	1	1	6	8
1985—L.A. Rams NFL	5	38	16	42.1	214	0	1	5.63	5	0	0.0	0	0	0	2
1986—San Francisco NFL	10	200	119	59.5	1554	11	8	7.77	15	49	3.3	0	0	0	3

			—PASSING—					—RUSHING—			—TOTAL—		
Year Club	G.	Att.	Cmp.	Pct.	Gain	T.P.	P.I.	Avg.	Att.	Yds.	Avg. TD.	TD.	Pts.	F.
1987—Seattle NFL	13	33	23	69.7	396	5	1	12.00	5	9	1.8 0	0	0	2
1988—Seattle NFL	11	35	13	37.1	132	0	5	3.77	6	51	8.5 0	0	0	0
Pro Totals—8 Years	58	621	328	52.8	4477	30	23	7.21	70	269	3.8 1	1	6	17

Quarterback Rating Points: 1981 (7.6), 1983 (77.9), 1984 (78.7), 1985 (49.7), 1986 (85.7), 1987 (137.1), 1988 (9.2). Total—76.7.

Additional pro statistics: Recovered three fumbles and fumbled eight times for minus 16 yards, 1984; recovered one fumble and fumbled three times for minus three yards, 1986; recovered one fumble and fumbled twice for minus eight yards, 1987.

Member of Los Angeles Rams for 1985 Championship Game following 1985 season; did not play.

PERRY COMMODORE KEMP
Wide Receiver—Green Bay Packers
Born December 31, 1961, at Canonsburg, Pa.
Height, 5.11. Weight, 170.
High School—McDonald, Pa., Fort Cherry.
Attended California State College (Pa.).

Selected by Jacksonville in 11th round (208th player selected) of 1984 USFL draft.
Signed by Jacksonville Bulls, January 21, 1984.
Released by Jacksonville Bulls, February 20, 1986; awarded on waivers to Memphis Showboats, February 21, 1986.
Granted free agency when USFL suspended operations, August 7, 1986; signed as free agent by Dallas Cowboys, August 12, 1986.
Granted roster exemption, August 12 through August 22, 1986; activated, August 23, 1986.
Released by Dallas Cowboys, August 26, 1986; signed as free agent by Cleveland Browns, April 22, 1987.
Released by Cleveland Browns, August 25, 1987; signed as free agent replacement player by Cleveland Browns, October 1, 1987.
Released by Cleveland Browns, November 3, 1987; signed as free agent by Green Bay Packers, April 15, 1988.

		—PASS RECEIVING—				-PUNT RETURNS-				—TOTAL—		
Year Club	G.	P.C.	Yds.	Avg.	TD.	No.	Yds.	Avg.	TD.	TD.	Pts.	F.
1984—Jacksonville USFL	18	44	730	16.6	2	3	7	2.3	0	2	12	1
1985—Jacksonville USFL	18	59	915	15.5	4	13	116	8.9	0	4	†26	2
1987—Cleveland NFL	3	12	224	18.7	2		None			2	12	0
1988—Green Bay NFL	16	48	620	12.9	0		None			0	0	3
USFL Totals—2 Years	36	103	1645	16.0	6	16	123	7.7	0	6	38	3
NFL Totals—2 Years	19	60	844	14.1	2	0	0	0.0	0	2	12	3
Pro Totals—4 Years	55	163	2489	15.3	8	16	123	7.7	0	8	50	6

†Includes one 2-point conversion.

Additional pro statistics: Returned four kickoffs for 84 yards, 1984; recovered one fumble, 1984 and 1985; rushed once for minus one yard, 1985.

MICHAEL LEE KENN
(Mike)
Offensive Tackle—Atlanta Falcons
Born February 9, 1956, at Evanston, Ill.
Height, 6.07. Weight, 277.
High School—Evanston, Ill.
Received bachelor of arts degree in general studies from University of Michigan in 1978.

Named to THE SPORTING NEWS NFL All-Star Team, 1980.
Selected by Atlanta in 1st round (13th player selected) of 1978 NFL draft.
On injured reserve with knee injury, November 18 through remainder of 1985 season.
Atlanta NFL, 1978 through 1988.
Games: 1978 (16), 1979 (16), 1980 (16), 1981 (16), 1982 (9), 1983 (16), 1984 (14), 1985 (11), 1986 (16), 1987 (12), 1988 (16). Total—158.
Pro statistics: Recovered two fumbles, 1978 and 1979; recovered three fumbles, 1980; recovered one fumble, 1981 through 1983.
Played in Pro Bowl (NFL All-Star Game) following 1980 through 1984 seasons.

DEREK KENNARD
Center-Guard—Phoenix Cardinals
Born September 9, 1962, at Stockton, Calif.
Height, 6.03. Weight, 285.
High School—Stockton, Calif., Edison.
Attended University of Nevada at Reno.

Selected by Los Angeles in 3rd round (52nd player selected) of 1984 USFL draft.
Signed by Los Angeles Express, March 22, 1984.
Granted roster exemption, March 22, 1984; activated, April 13, 1984.
On developmental squad, April 13 through April 27, 1984; activated, April 28, 1984.
Selected by St. Louis in 2nd round (45th player selected) of 1984 NFL supplemental draft.
On developmental squad, March 15 through April 12, 1985; activated, April 13, 1985.
Released by Los Angeles Express, August 1, 1985; re-signed by Express, August 2, 1985.
Released by Los Angeles Express, April 26, 1986; signed by St. Louis Cardinals, May 29, 1986.
Franchise transferred to Phoenix, March 15, 1988.
On developmental squad for 2 games with Los Angeles Express in 1984.
On developmental squad for 4 games with Los Angeles Express in 1985.
Los Angeles USFL, 1984 and 1985; St. Louis NFL, 1986 and 1987; Phoenix NFL, 1988.
Games: 1984 (6), 1985 (14), 1986 (15), 1987 (12), 1988 (16). Total USFL—20. Total NFL—43. Total Pro—63.

USFL statistics: Returned one kickoff for no yards and recovered one fumble, 1985.
NFL statistics: Fumbled twice for minus four yards, 1987.

SAMUEL EDWARD KENNEDY
(Sam)
Linebacker—San Francisco 49ers

Born July 10, 1964, at San Mateo, Calif.
Height, 6.03. Weight, 235.
High School—Aptos, Calif.
Attended Cabrillo College and received bachelor of science degree in
industrial engineering from San Jose State University in 1987.

Signed as free agent by San Francisco 49ers, May 12, 1987.
On injured reserve with wrist injury, August 28 through October 25, 1987.
Released by San Francisco 49ers, October 26, 1987; re-signed by 49ers, April 12, 1988.
San Francisco NFL, 1988.
Games: 1988 (16).
Pro statistics: Recovered two fumbles, 1988.
Played in NFC Championship Game following 1988 season.
Played in NFL Championship Game following 1988 season.

WILLIAM PATRICK KENNEY
(Bill)
Quarterback—Kansas City Chiefs

Born January 20, 1955, at San Francisco, Calif.
Height, 6.04. Weight, 217.
High School—San Clemente, Calif.
Attended Arizona State University, Saddleback Community College and received bachelor of science degree
in business management from University of Northern Colorado in 1978.
Son of Charles Kenney, guard with San Francisco 49ers, 1947.

Selected by Miami in 12th round (333rd player selected) of 1978 NFL draft.
Traded by Miami Dolphins to Washington Redskins for 6th round pick in 1979 draft, August 1, 1978.
Released by Washington Redskins, August 21, 1978; signed as free agent by Kansas City Chiefs, January 19, 1979.
On injured reserve with broken thumb, August 28 through October 5, 1984; activated, October 6, 1984.
Active for 16 games with Kansas City Chiefs in 1979; did not play.

Year Club	G.	Att.	Cmp.	Pct.	Gain	T.P.	P.I.	Avg.	Att.	Yds.	Avg.	TD.	TD.	Pts.	F.
		PASSING							*RUSHING*				*TOTAL*		
1980—Kansas City NFL	3	69	37	53.6	542	5	2	7.86	8	8	1.0	0	0	0	1
1981—Kansas City NFL	13	274	147	53.6	1983	9	16	7.24	24	89	3.7	1	1	6	4
1982—Kansas City NFL	7	169	95	56.2	1192	7	6	7.05	13	40	3.1	0	0	0	3
1983—Kansas City NFL	16	*603	*346	57.4	4348	24	18	7.21	23	59	2.6	3	3	18	7
1984—Kansas City NFL	9	282	151	53.5	2098	15	10	7.44	9	—8	—0.9	0	0	0	8
1985—Kansas City NFL	16	338	181	53.6	2536	17	9	7.50	14	1	0.1	1	1	6	6
1986—Kansas City NFL	15	308	161	52.3	1922	13	11	6.24	18	0	0.0	0	0	0	5
1987—Kansas City NFL	11	273	154	56.4	2107	15	9	7.72	12	—2	—0.2	0	0	0	8
1988—Kansas City NFL	16	114	58	50.9	549	0	5	4.82	2	4	2.0	0	0	0	1
Pro Totals—10 Years	106	2430	1330	54.7	17277	105	86	7.11	123	191	1.6	5	5	30	43

Quarterback Rating Points: 1980 (91.4), 1981 (63.8), 1982 (77.0), 1983 (80.8), 1984 (80.7), 1985 (83.6), 1986 (70.8), 1987
(85.8), 1988 (46.3). Total—77.1.
Additional pro statistics: Fumbled once for minus six yards, 1980; fumbled four times for minus two yards, 1981;
recovered two fumbles, 1982; caught one pass for no yards, 1983 and 1986; recovered four fumbles, 1983; recovered
three fumbles and fumbled eight times for minus 34 yards, 1984; recovered five fumbles and fumbled six times for
minus 18 yards, 1985; recovered one fumble and fumbled five times for minus six yards, 1986; recovered two fumbles
and fumbled eight times for minus eight yards, 1987.
Played in Pro Bowl (NFL All-Star Game) following 1983 season.

CRAWFORD FRANCIS KER
Guard—Dallas Cowboys

Born May 5, 1962, at Philadelphia, Pa.
Height, 6.03. Weight, 290.
High School—Dunedin, Fla.
Attended Arizona Western College and University of Florida.

Selected by Tampa Bay in 1985 USFL territorial draft.
Selected by Dallas in 3rd round (76th player selected) of 1985 NFL draft.
Signed by Dallas Cowboys, July 12, 1985.
On injured reserve with back injury, October 23 through remainder of 1985 season.
Dallas NFL, 1985 through 1988.
Games: 1985 (5), 1986 (16), 1987 (12), 1988 (16). Total—49.

—DID YOU KNOW—

That the Bengals had a blocked field goal attempt returned against them for touchdowns in consecutive games in 1987? On November 29, Rich Miano of the Jets returned one
67 yards for a score. Kevin Ross of the Chiefs returned a blocked kick 65 yards for a
touchdown one week later.

TYRONE P. KEYS
Defensive End—San Diego Chargers
Born October 24, 1960, at Jackson, Miss.
Height, 6.07. Weight, 291.
High School—Jackson, Miss., Callaway.
Received bachelor of science degree in physical education from Mississippi State University.
Related to Lee Calhoun, gold medal winner in 1956 and 1960 110-meter hurdles.

Selected by New York Jets in 5th round (113th player selected) of 1981 NFL draft.
Signed as free agent by British Columbia Lions, May 20, 1981.
On reserve list, July 12 through July 18, 1981; activated, July 19, 1981.
On reserve list, July 25 through August 2, 1981; activated, August 3, 1981.
On reserve list, August 16 through September 12, 1981; activated, September 13, 1981.
On reserve list, September 21 through remainder of 1981 season.
On reserve list, July 2 through July 17, 1982; activated, July 18, 1982.
On reserve list, August 15 through August 31, 1982; activated, September 1, 1982.
On reserve list, September 12 through September 18, 1982; activated, September 19, 1982.
On reserve list, October 17 through October 23, 1982; activated, October 24, 1982.
Traded by British Columbia Lions to Toronto Argonauts for defensive back Jo Jo Heath, April 25, 1983.
Released by Toronto Argonauts, July 2, 1983.
NFL rights traded by New York Jets to Chicago Bears for 5th round pick in 1985 draft, July 13, 1983.
Signed by Chicago Bears, July 10, 1983.
Released by Chicago Bears, September 1, 1986; awarded on waivers to Tampa Bay Buccaneers, September 2, 1986.
On injured reserve with abdomen injury, December 12 through remainder of 1986 season.
On injured reserve with back injury, November 3 through November 9, 1987.
Released by Tampa Bay Buccaneers, November 10, 1987; signed as free agent by Miami Dolphins, March 10, 1988.
Released by Miami Dolphins, March 23, 1988; signed as free agent by San Diego Chargers, May 12, 1988.
On injured reserve with herniated disc in back, December 3 through remainder of 1988 season.
British Columbia CFL, 1981 and 1982; Chicago NFL, 1983 through 1985; Tampa Bay NFL, 1986 and 1987; San Diego NFL, 1988.
Games: 1981 (5), 1982 (10), 1983 (14), 1984 (15), 1985 (16), 1986 (14), 1987 (3), 1988 (13). Total CFL—15. Total NFL—75. Total Pro—90.
Pro statistics: Recovered one fumble for two yards, 1988.
Played in NFC Championship Game following 1984 and 1985 seasons.
Played in NFL Championship Game following 1985 season.

MAX JOHN KIDD
(Known by middle name.)
Punter—Buffalo Bills
Born August 22, 1961, at Springfield, Ill.
Height, 6.03. Weight, 208.
High School—Findlay, O.
Received bachelor of science degree in industrial engineering and
management science from Northwestern University in 1984.

Selected by Chicago in 1984 USFL territorial draft.
Selected by Buffalo in 5th round (128th player selected) of 1984 NFL draft.
Signed by Buffalo Bills, June 1, 1984.

Year Club	G.	—PUNTING— No.	Avg.	Blk.	Year Club	G.	—PUNTING— No.	Avg.	Blk.
1984—Buffalo NFL	16	88	42.0	2	1987—Buffalo NFL	12	64	39.0	0
1985—Buffalo NFL	16	92	41.5	0	1988—Buffalo NFL	16	62	39.5	0
1986—Buffalo NFL	16	75	40.4	0	Pro Totals—5 Years	76	381	40.6	2

Additional pro statistics: Rushed once for no yards and recovered one fumble, 1986; attempted one pass with no completions, 1987.
Played in AFC Championship Game following 1988 season.

BLAIR ARMSTRONG KIEL
Quarterback-Punter—Green Bay Packers
Born November 29, 1961, at Columbus, Ind.
Height, 6.00. Weight, 214.
High School—Columbus, Ind., East.
Received degree in marketing from University of Notre Dame in 1984.

Selected by Chicago in 1984 USFL territorial draft.
Selected by Tampa Bay in 11th round (281st player selected) of 1984 NFL draft.
Signed by Tampa Bay Buccaneers, June 5, 1984.
On non-football injury list with ulcerative colitis, November 13 through remainder of 1984 season.
On non-football injury with Crohn's Disease, August 12 through September 30, 1985.
Released by Tampa Bay Buccaneers, October 1, 1985; signed as free agent by Indianapolis Colts, February 13, 1986.
Released by Indianapolis Colts, September 1, 1986; re-signed by Colts, September 16, 1986.
Crossed picket line during players' strike, October 7, 1987.
Released by Indianapolis Colts, November 24, 1987; signed as free agent by Green Bay Packers, May 10, 1988.

Year Club	G.	—PASSING— Att.	Cmp.	Pct.	Gain	T.P.	P.I.	Avg.	—RUSHING— Att.	Yds.	Avg.	TD.	—TOTAL— TD.	Pts.	F.
1984—Tampa Bay NFL	10	None							None				0	0	0
1986—Indianapolis NFL	3	25	11	44.0	236	2	0	9.44	3	20	6.7	0	0	0	0
1987—Indianapolis NFL	4	33	17	51.5	195	1	3	5.91	4	30	7.5	0	0	0	0
1988—Green Bay NFL	1	None							None				0	0	0
Pro Totals—4 Years	18	58	28	48.3	431	3	3	7.43	7	50	7.1	0	0	0	0

Quarterback Rating Points: 1986 (104.8), 1987 (41.9). Total—69.0.
Additional pro statistics: Punted five times for 38.0 average, 1986; punted 12 times for a 36.7 average, 1987.

JAMIE KIMMEL
Linebacker—Los Angeles Raiders
Born March 28, 1962, at Johnson City, N.Y.
Height, 6.03. Weight, 235.
High School—Conklin, N.Y., Susquehanna Valley.
Attended Syracuse University.

Selected by New Jersey in 1985 USFL territorial draft.
Selected by Los Angeles Raiders in 4th round (107th player selected) of 1985 NFL draft.
Signed by Los Angeles Raiders, July 22, 1985.
On injured reserve with hamstring injury, August 27 through entire 1985 season.
Crossed picket line during players' strike, October 2, 1987.
On injured reserve with knee injury, July 27 through entire 1988 season.
Los Angeles Raiders NFL, 1986 and 1987.
Games: 1986 (16), 1987 (15). Total—31.
Pro statistics: Recovered one fumble, 1987.

ALFRED TERANCE KINARD
(Terry)
Safety—New York Giants
Born November 24, 1959, at Bitburg, West Germany.
Height, 6.01. Weight, 200.
High School—Sumter, S.C.
Attended Clemson University.

Named as defensive back on THE SPORTING NEWS College All-America Team, 1982.
Selected by Washington in 1983 USFL territorial draft.
Selected by New York Giants in 1st round (10th player selected) of 1983 NFL draft.
Signed by New York Giants, May 17, 1983.
On injured reserve with knee injury, December 9 through remainder of 1986 season.

| | | | —INTERCEPTIONS— | | |
Year Club	G.	No.	Yds.	Avg.	TD.
1983—N.Y. Giants NFL	16	3	49	16.3	0
1984—N.Y. Giants NFL	15	2	29	14.5	0
1985—N.Y. Giants NFL	16	5	100	20.0	0
1986—N.Y. Giants NFL	14	4	52	13.0	0
1987—N.Y. Giants NFL	12	5	163	32.6	1
1988—N.Y. Giants NFL	16	3	46	15.3	0
Pro Totals—6 Years............	89	22	439	20.0	1

Additional pro statistics: Recovered one fumble for 10 yards, 1983; returned one punt for no yards and fumbled once, 1984; recovered one fumble, 1984 and 1985; recovered two fumbles, 1986; returned one punt for eight yards, 1988.
Played in Pro Bowl (NFL All-Star Game) following 1988 season.

BRIAN DOUGLAS KINCHEN
Tight End—Miami Dolphins
Born August 6, 1965, at Baton Rouge, La.
Height, 6.02. Weight, 238.
High School—Baton Rouge, La., University.
Attended Louisiana State University.

Selected by Miami in 12th round (320th player selected) of 1988 NFL draft.
Signed by Miami Dolphins, June 6, 1988.
Miami NFL, 1988.
Games: 1988 (16).
Pro statistics: Caught one pass for three yards, 1988.

DAVID JOEL KING
Cornerback—Houston Oilers
Born May 19, 1963, at Mobile, Ala.
Height, 5.08. Weight, 176.
High School—Fairhope, Ala.
Attended Auburn University.

Selected by Birmingham in 1985 USFL territorial draft.
Selected by San Diego in 10th round (264th player selected) of 1985 NFL draft.
Signed by San Diego Chargers, July 10, 1985.
On injured reserve with ankle injury, September 10 through remainder of 1985 season.
Released by San Diego Chargers, August 15, 1986; signed as free agent by Denver Broncos, May 1, 1987.
Released by Denver Broncos, August 1, 1987; signed as free agent replacement player by Green Bay Packers, September 25, 1987.
Released by Green Bay Packers, October 20, 1987; signed as free agent by Houston Oilers, May 4, 1989.
San Diego NFL, 1985; Green Bay NFL, 1987.
Games: 1985 (1), 1987 (3). Total—4.

EMANUEL KING
Linebacker—Los Angeles Raiders
Born August 15, 1963, at Leroy, Ala.
Height, 6.04. Weight, 251.
High School—Leroy, Ala.
Attended University of Alabama.

Selected by Birmingham in 1985 USFL territorial draft.
Selected by Cincinnati in 1st round (25th player selected) of 1985 NFL draft.
Signed by Cincinnati Bengals, May 30, 1985.
On non-football injury list with substance abuse, September 1 through September 27, 1988; activated, September 28, 1988.
On injured reserve with back injury, October 1 through November 4, 1988; activated, November 5, 1988.
Granted unconditional free agency, February 1, 1989; signed by Los Angeles Raiders, March 23, 1989.
Cincinnati NFL, 1985 through 1988.
Games: 1985 (16), 1986 (16), 1987 (12), 1988 (7). Total—51.
Pro statistics: Recovered one fumble, 1985; recovered one fumble for one yard, 1986.
Played in AFC Championship Game following 1988 season.
Played in NFL Championship Game following 1988 season.

LINDEN KEITH KING
Linebacker—Los Angeles Raiders
Born June 28, 1955, at Memphis, Tenn.
Height, 6.04. Weight, 245.
High School—Colorado Springs, Colo., Air Academy.
Attended Colorado State University.

Selected by San Diego in 3rd round (77th player selected) of 1977 NFL draft.
On injured reserve, September 12 through 1977 season.
On injured reserve with ankle injury, November 5, 1980, through January 9, 1981; activated, January 10, 1981.
Released by San Diego Chargers, July 25, 1986; signed as free agent by Los Angeles Raiders, August 2, 1986.
San Diego NFL, 1978 through 1985; Los Angeles Raiders NFL, 1986 through 1988.
Games: 1978 (14), 1979 (16), 1980 (5), 1981 (16), 1982 (9), 1983 (16), 1984 (16), 1985 (16), 1986 (16), 1987 (12), 1988 (14). Total—150.
Pro statistics: Intercepted one pass for three yards and recovered one fumble for 14 yards, 1978; recovered two fumbles, 1979, 1983 and 1984; intercepted one pass for 28 yards, 1981; recovered one fumble, 1982 and 1987; intercepted one pass for 19 yards, 1983; intercepted two passes for 52 yards and fumbled once, 1984; intercepted two passes for eight yards, 1985; intercepted one pass for eight yards, 1987.
Played in AFC Championship Game following 1980 and 1981 seasons.

LARRY D. KINNEBREW
Running Back—Buffalo Bills
Born June 11, 1959, at Rome, Ga.
Height, 6.01. Weight, 258.
High School—Rome, Ga., East.
Attended Tennessee State University.

Selected by Cincinnati in 6th round (165th player selected) of 1983 NFL draft.
On injured reserve with broken hand, September 24 through October 25, 1985; activated, October 26, 1985.
Granted free agency, February 1, 1988; rights relinquished, August 29, 1988.
Signed as free agent by Buffalo Bills, January 10, 1989.

Year Club	G.	Att.	Yds.	Avg.	TD.	P.C.	Yds.	Avg.	TD.	TD.	Pts.	F.
			—RUSHING—			PASS RECEIVING				—TOTAL—		
1983—Cincinnati NFL	16	39	156	4.0	3	2	4	2.0	0	3	18	3
1984—Cincinnati NFL	16	154	623	4.0	9	19	159	8.4	1	10	60	4
1985—Cincinnati NFL	12	170	714	4.2	9	22	187	8.5	1	10	60	4
1986—Cincinnati NFL	16	131	519	4.0	8	13	136	10.5	1	9	54	6
1987—Cincinnati NFL	11	145	570	3.9	8	9	114	12.7	0	8	48	1
Pro Totals—5 Years	71	639	2582	4.0	37	65	600	9.2	3	40	240	18

Additional pro statistics: Recovered one fumble, 1983, 1985 and 1986; returned one kickoff for seven yards, 1984.

RANDALL SCOTT KIRK
(Randy)
Linebacker—Phoenix Cardinals
Born December 27, 1964, at San Jose, Calif.
Height, 6.02. Weight, 227.
High School—San Jose, Calif., Bellarmine College Prep.
Attended De Anza College and San Diego State University.

Signed as free agent by New York Giants, May 10, 1987.
Released by New York Giants, August 31, 1987; signed as free agent replacement player by San Diego Chargers, September 24, 1987.
Granted unconditional free agency, February 1, 1989; signed by Phoenix Cardinals, March 31, 1989.
San Diego NFL, 1987 and 1988.
Games: 1987 (13), 1988 (16). Total—29.
Pro statistics: Recovered one fumble, 1988.

JOHN KLINGEL
Defensive End—Philadelphia Eagles
Born December 21, 1963, at Marion, O.
Height, 6.03. Weight, 267.
High School—Cardington, O., Lincoln.
Attended Eastern Kentucky University.

Signed as free agent by Philadelphia Eagles, May 1, 1987.
On injured reserve with ankle and back injuries, September 6 through November 26, 1987; activated, November 27, 1987.
Philadelphia NFL, 1987 and 1988.
Games: 1987 (5), 1988 (16). Total—21.
Pro statistics: Recovered one fumble, 1987.

BRUCE DONALD KLOSTERMANN
Linebacker—Denver Broncos
Born April 17, 1963, at Dubuque, Ia.
Height, 6.04. Weight, 232.
High School—Dyersville, Ia., Beckman.
Attended Waldorf College, University of Iowa and received bachelor of science degree
in agricultural business from South Dakota State University in 1986.

Selected by Denver in 8th round (217th player selected) of 1986 NFL draft.
Signed by Denver Broncos, July 14, 1986.
On injured reserve with knee injury, August 25 through entire 1986 season.
On injured reserve with back injury, November 23 through remainder of 1988 season.
Denver NFL, 1987 and 1988.
Games: 1987 (9), 1988 (12). Total—21.
Played in AFC Championship Game following 1987 season.
Played in NFL Championship Game following 1987 season.

LEANDER KNIGHT
Defensive Back—New York Jets
Born February 16, 1963, at East Orange, N. J.
Height, 6.01. Weight, 193.
High School—East Orange, N. J.
Attended Montclair State College.

Signed as free agent by New Jersey Generals, May 30, 1986.
Granted free agency when USFL suspended operations, August 7, 1986; signed by San Diego Chargers, May 8, 1987.
Released by San Diego Chargers, August 24, 1987; signed as free agent replacement player by Atlanta Falcons, September 24, 1987.
Released by Atlanta Falcons, October 19, 1987; re-signed by Falcons for 1988, November 13, 1987.
Released by Atlanta Falcons, August 30, 1988; re-signed by Falcons, September 21, 1988.
Released by Atlanta Falcons, September 28, 1988; re-signed by Falcons, October 14, 1988.
Released by Atlanta Falcons, October 19, 1988; signed as free agent by New York Jets, April 10, 1989.
Played with Connecticut Giants of Continental International Football League.
Atlanta NFL, 1987 and 1988.
Games: 1987 (1), 1988 (2). Total—3.

COACHING RECORD
Assistant coach at Montclair State College, 1988.

SHAWN MATT KNIGHT
Defensive End—Denver Broncos
Born June 4, 1964, at Provo, Utah.
Height, 6.06. Weight, 290.
High School—Sparks, Nev., Edward C. Reed.
Attended Brigham Young University.

Selected by New Orleans in 1st round (11th player selected) of 1987 NFL draft.
Signed by New Orleans Saints, August 31, 1987.
Granted roster exemption, August 31 and September 1, 1987; activated, September 2, 1987.
On injured reserve with ankle injury, December 26 through remainder of 1987 season.
Traded by New Orleans Saints to Denver Broncos for nose tackle Ted Gregory, August 29, 1988.
New Orleans NFL, 1987; Denver NFL, 1988.
Games: 1987 (10), 1988 (14). Total—24.

STEVEN PAUL KNIGHT
(Steve)
Offensive Tackle—Indianapolis Colts
Born March 13, 1962, at Abingdon, Va.
Height, 6.03. Weight, 283.
High School—Abingdon, Va.
Received degree in criminal justice from University of Tennessee.

Selected by Memphis in 1984 USFL territorial draft.
Signed as free agent by Dallas Cowboys, May 3, 1984.
Released by Dallas Cowboys, August 9, 1984; signed by Memphis Showboats, November 1, 1984.
Left Memphis Showboats camp voluntarily and released, January 21, 1985; signed as free agent by San Diego Chargers, April 12, 1985.

Released by San Diego Chargers, August 19, 1985; re-signed by Chargers, May 10, 1987.
Released by San Diego Chargers, August 24, 1987; signed as free agent replacement player by Indianapolis Colts, September 23, 1987.
Released by Indianapolis Colts, October 20, 1987; re-signed by Colts, March 30, 1988.
Released by Indianapolis Colts, August 30, 1988; re-signed by Colts, September 14, 1988.
Released by Indianapolis Colts, September 21, 1988; re-signed by Colts, January 6, 1989.
Active for 1 game with Indianapolis Colts in 1988; did not play.
Indianapolis NFL, 1987 and 1988.
Games: 1987 (3).

MARKUS KOCH
Defensive End—Washington Redskins
Born February 13, 1963, at Niedermarsberg, W. Germany.
Height, 6.05. Weight, 275.
High School—Kitchener, Ontario, Can., Eastwood Collegiate.
Attended Boise State University.

Selected by Washington in 2nd round (30th player selected) of 1986 NFL draft.
Signed by Washington Redskins, July 22, 1986.
On injured reserve with stress fracture in back, November 17 through remainder of 1988 season.
Washington NFL, 1986 through 1988.
Games: 1986 (16), 1987 (12), 1988 (11). Total—39.
Played in NFC Championship Game following 1986 and 1987 seasons.
Played in NFL Championship Game following 1987 season.

PETER ALAN KOCH
(Pete)
Defensive End—Los Angeles Raiders
Born January 23, 1962, at Nassau County, N.Y.
Height, 6.06. Weight, 275.
High School—New Hyde Park, N.Y., Memorial.
Attended University of Maryland.
Brother of Larry Koch, pitcher in St. Louis Cardinals' organization, 1967, 1968, 1970 and 1971.

Selected by Washington in 1984 USFL territorial draft.
Selected by Cincinnati in 1st round (16th player selected) of 1984 NFL draft.
Signed by Cincinnati Bengals, July 30, 1984.
Released by Cincinnati Bengals, September 2, 1985; awarded on waivers to Kansas City Chiefs, September 3, 1985.
On injured reserve with knee injury, November 18 through remainder of 1987 season.
On physically unable to perform/active with wrist injury, July 22 through August 21, 1988; then transferred to physically unable to perform/reserve with wrist injury, August 22 through entire 1988 season.
Granted unconditional free agency, February 1, 1989; signed by Los Angeles Raiders, March 1, 1989.
Cincinnati NFL, 1984; Kansas City NFL, 1985 through 1987.
Games: 1984 (16), 1985 (16), 1986 (16), 1987 (6). Total—54.

JOE KOHLBRAND
Linebacker—New Orleans Saints
Born March 18, 1963, at Merritt Island, Fla.
Height, 6.04. Weight, 242.
High School—Merritt Island, Fla.
Attended University of Miami (Fla.).

Selected by New Orleans in 8th round (206th player selected) of 1985 NFL draft.
Signed by New Orleans Saints, July 25, 1985.
On injured reserve with knee injury, August 28 through October 3, 1985; activated after clearing procedural waivers, October 4, 1985.
New Orleans NFL, 1985 through 1988.
Games: 1985 (12), 1986 (16), 1987 (12), 1988 (16). Total—56.

MARK WILLIAM KONECNY
Running Back-Punt Returner—New York Jets
Born April 2, 1963, at Chicago, Ill.
Height, 6.00. Weight, 200.
High School—Muskegon, Mich., Mona Shores.
Received bachelor of arts degree in business from Alma College and
attended Central Michigan University (did not play college football there).

Signed as free agent by Toronto Argonauts, February 17, 1985.
Released by Toronto Argonauts, June 29, 1985; signed as free agent by Ottawa Rough Riders, March 6, 1986.
Released by Ottawa Rough Riders, June 16, 1986; signed as free agent by Miami Dolphins, March 31, 1987.
Released by Miami Dolphins, September 3, 1987; re-signed as replacement player by Dolphins, September 23, 1987.
On injured reserve, October 20 through November 9, 1987.
Released by Miami Dolphins, November 10, 1987; signed as free agent by New York Jets, February 29, 1988.
Released by New York Jets, August 22, 1988; awarded on waivers to Philadelphia Eagles, August 23, 1988.
Released by Philadelphia Eagles, August 29, 1988; re-signed by Eagles, August 30, 1988.
Granted unconditional free agency, February 1, 1989; signed by New York Jets, February 27, 1989.

		——RUSHING——				PASS RECEIVING				—TOTAL—		
Year Club	G.	Att.	Yds.	Avg.	TD.	P.C.	Yds.	Avg.	TD.	TD.	Pts.	F.
1987—Miami NFL	3	6	46	7.7	0	6	26	4.3	0	0	0	0
1988—Philadelphia NFL	16		None			1	18	18.0	0	0	0	3
Pro Totals—2 Years	19	6	46	7.7	0	7	44	6.3	0	0	0	3

Year Club	G.	No.	Yds.	Avg.	TD.	No.	Yds.	Avg.TD.
1987—Miami NFL	3			None				None
1988—Philadelphia NFL	16	33	233	7.1	0	17	276	16.2 0
Pro Totals—2 Years	19	33	233	7.1	0	17	276	16.2 0

Additional pro statistics: Recovered one fumble, 1987; recovered two fumbles, 1988.

STEVE KORTE

Name pronounced Court.

Center—New Orleans Saints

Born January 15, 1960, at Denver, Colo.
Height, 6.02. Weight, 260.
High School—Littleton, Colo., Arapahoe.
Received degree in physical education from University of Arkansas.

Named as guard on THE SPORTING NEWS College All-America Team, 1982.
Selected by Birmingham in 2nd round (20th player selected) of 1983 USFL draft.
Selected by New Orleans in 2nd round (38th player selected) of 1983 NFL draft.
Signed by New Orleans Saints, June 20, 1983.
USFL rights traded by Birmingham Stallions to Memphis Showboats for offensive tackle Phil McKinnely, January 22, 1985.
On injured reserve with knee injury, September 25 through October 24, 1985; activated, October 25, 1985.
Crossed picket line during players' strike, September 23, 1987.
On injured reserve with shoulder injury, September 7 through November 27, 1987; activated, November 28, 1987.
New Orleans NFL, 1983 through 1988.
Games: 1983 (16), 1984 (15), 1985 (12), 1986 (16), 1987 (3), 1988 (16). Total—78.
Pro statistics: Recovered one fumble in end zone for a touchdown, 1983; recovered one fumble, 1984 and 1986; fumbled once for minus 18 yards, 1985.

BERNIE KOSAR

Quarterback—Cleveland Browns

Born November 25, 1963, at Boardman, O.
Height, 6.05. Weight, 210.
High School—Boardman, O.
Received degree in finance and economics from University of Miami (Fla.) in 1985.

Selected by Cleveland in 1st round of NFL supplemental draft, July 2, 1985.
Signed by Cleveland Browns, July 2, 1985.
On injured reserve with elbow injury, September 10 through October 20, 1988; activated, October 21, 1988.

Year Club	G.	Att.	Cmp.	Pct.	Gain	T.P.	P.I.	Avg.	Att.	Yds.	Avg.	TD.	TD.	Pts.	F.
				PASSING						RUSHING			TOTAL		
1985—Cleveland NFL	12	248	124	50.0	1578	8	7	6.36	26	—12	—0.5	1	1	6	14
1986—Cleveland NFL	16	531	310	58.4	3854	17	10	7.26	24	19	0.8	0	0	0	7
1987—Cleveland NFL	12	389	241	62.0	3033	22	9	7.80	15	22	1.5	1	1	6	2
1988—Cleveland NFL	9	259	156	60.2	1890	10	7	7.30	12	—1	—0.1	1	1	6	0
Pro Totals—4 Years	49	1427	831	58.2	10355	57	33	7.26	77	28	0.4	3	3	18	23

Quarterback Rating Points: 1985 (69.3), 1986 (83.8), 1987 (95.4), 1988 (84.3). Total—84.6.
Additional pro statistics: Recovered two fumbles and fumbled 14 times for minus 25 yards, 1985; caught one pass for one yard, recovered three fumbles and fumbled seven times for minus 15 yards, 1986; recovered one fumble and fumbled twice for minus three yards, 1987; recovered two fumbles, 1988.
Played in AFC Championship Game following 1986 and 1987 seasons.
Played in Pro Bowl (NFL All-Star Game) following 1987 season.

GARY STUART KOWALSKI

Guard-Offensive Tackle—San Diego Chargers

Born July 2, 1960, at New Haven, Conn.
Height, 6.06. Weight, 288.
High School—Clinton, Conn., Morgan.
Attended Boston College.

Selected by Boston in 1983 USFL territorial draft.
Selected by Los Angeles Rams in 6th round (144th player selected) of 1983 NFL draft.
Signed by Los Angeles Rams, June 3, 1983.
On injured reserve with knee injury, August 28 through entire 1984 season.
Traded with 5th round pick in 1986 draft by Los Angeles Rams to San Diego Chargers for wide receiver Bobby Duckworth, September 3, 1985.
On injured reserve with knee injury, December 7 through remainder of 1985 season.
On injured reserve with neck injury, September 21 through remainder of 1988 season.
Los Angeles Rams NFL, 1983; San Diego NFL, 1985 through 1988.
Games: 1983 (15), 1985 (13), 1986 (16), 1987 (12), 1988 (2). Total—58.
Pro statistics: Recovered one fumble, 1987.

BRUCE KOZERSKI

Center-Guard—Cincinnati Bengals

Born April 2, 1962, at Plains, Pa.
Height, 6.04. Weight, 275.
High School—Wilkes-Barre, Pa., James M. Coughlin.
Attended Holy Cross College.

Selected by Houston in 12th round (245th player selected) of 1984 USFL draft.
Selected by Cincinnati in 9th round (231st player selected) of 1984 NFL draft.
Signed by Cincinnati Bengals, June 10, 1984.
On injured reserve with pinched neck, November 14 through December 10, 1987; activated, December 11, 1987.
Cincinnati NFL, 1984 through 1988.
Games: 1984 (16), 1985 (14), 1986 (16), 1987 (8), 1988 (16). Total—70.
Pro statistics: Recovered one fumble, 1987.
Played in AFC Championship Game following 1988 season.
Played in NFL Championship Game following 1988 season.

GLEN ALLEN KOZLOWSKI
Wide Receiver—Chicago Bears
Born December 31, 1962, at Honolulu, Haw.
Height, 6.01. Weight, 205.
High School—Carlsbad, N.M.
Attended Brigham Young University.
Brother of Mike Kozlowski, safety with Miami Dolphins,
1979 and 1981 through 1986.

Selected by Chicago in 11th round (305th player selected) of 1986 NFL draft.
Selected by Memphis in 10th round (73rd player selected) of 1986 USFL draft.
Signed by Chicago Bears, July 15, 1986.
On non-football injury list with knee injury, August 14 through entire 1986 season.
Released by Chicago Bears, September 7, 1987; re-signed as replacement player by Bears, October 3, 1987.
On injured reserve with broken ankle, October 19 through remainder of 1987 season.

		—PASS RECEIVING—			
Year Club	G.	P.C.	Yds.	Avg.	TD.
1987—Chicago NFL	3	15	199	13.3	3
1988—Chicago NFL	16	3	92	30.7	0
Pro Totals—2 Years	19	18	291	16.2	3

Additional pro statistics: Returned three kickoffs for 72 yards, 1987; returned two kickoffs for 37 yards, rushed once for three yards, returned one punt for no yards and fumbled once, 1988.
Played in NFC Championship Game following 1988 season.

GREG JOHN KRAGEN
Nose Tackle—Denver Broncos
Born March 4, 1962, at Chicago, Ill.
Height, 6.03. Weight, 260.
High School—Pleasanton, Calif., Amador.
Attended Utah State University.

Selected by Oklahoma in 15th round (296th player selected) of 1984 USFL draft.
Signed as free agent by Denver Broncos, May 2, 1984.
Released by Denver Broncos, August 27, 1984; re-signed by Broncos, January 20, 1985.
Denver NFL, 1985 through 1988.
Games: 1985 (16), 1986 (16), 1987 (12), 1988 (16). Total—60.
Pro statistics: Recovered three fumbles, 1986; recovered one fumble, 1987 and 1988.
Played in AFC Championship Game following 1986 and 1987 seasons.
Played in NFL Championship Game following 1986 and 1987 seasons.

THOMAS FRANCIS KRAMER
(Tommy)
Quarterback—Minnesota Vikings
Born March 7, 1955, at San Antonio, Tex.
Height, 6.02. Weight, 202.
High School—San Antonio, Tex., Robert E. Lee.
Received bachelor of business administration degree from Rice University.
Son of Colonel John J. Kramer, head coach at Texas Lutheran College, 1953 through 1958.

Led NFL quarterback in passing with 92.6 points in 1986.
Selected by Minnesota in 1st round (27th player selected) of 1977 NFL draft.
On injured reserve with knee injury, September 20 through remainder of 1983 season.

		—————PASSING—————							—RUSHING—				—TOTAL—		
Year Club	G.	Att.	Cmp.	Pct.	Gain	T.P.	P.I.	Avg.	Att.	Yds.	Avg.	TD.	TD.	Pts.	F.
1977—Minnesota NFL	6	57	30	52.6	425	5	4	7.46	10	3	0.3	0	0	0	3
1978—Minnesota NFL	4	16	5	31.3	50	0	1	3.13	1	10	10.0	0	0	0	0
1979—Minnesota NFL	16	566	315	55.7	3397	23	24	6.00	32	138	4.3	1	1	6	9
1980—Minnesota NFL	15	522	299	57.3	3582	19	23	6.86	31	115	3.7	1	1	6	2
1981—Minnesota NFL	14	593	322	54.3	3912	26	24	6.60	10	13	1.3	0	0	0	8
1982—Minnesota NFL	9	308	176	57.1	2037	15	12	6.61	21	77	3.7	3	3	18	3
1983—Minnesota NFL	3	82	55	67.1	550	3	4	6.71	8	3	0.4	0	0	0	2
1984—Minnesota NFL	9	236	124	52.5	1678	9	10	7.11	15	9	0.6	0	1	6	10
1985—Minnesota NFL	15	506	277	54.7	3522	19	★26	6.96	27	54	2.0	0	0	0	9
1986—Minnesota NFL	13	372	208	55.9	3000	24	10	8.06	23	48	2.1	1	1	6	7
1987—Minnesota NFL	6	81	40	49.4	452	4	3	5.58	10	44	4.4	2	2	12	2
1988—Minnesota NFL	10	173	83	48.0	1264	5	9	7.31	14	8	0.6	0	0	0	3
Pro Totals—12 Years	120	3512	1934	55.1	23869	152	150	6.80	202	522	2.6	8	9	54	58

Quarterback Rating Points: 1977 (77.2), 1978 (15.0), 1979 (69.7), 1980 (72.1), 1981 (72.8), 1982 (77.3), 1983 (77.8), 1984 (70.6), 1985 (67.8), 1986 (92.6), 1987 (67.5), 1988 (60.5). Total—72.8.

Additional pro statistics: Fumbled three times for minus three yards, 1977; ran three yards with lateral on pass reception and fumbled nine times for minus six yards, 1979; recovered two fumbles, 1979 and 1980; recovered three fumbles, 1981; recovered one fumble and fumbled three times for minus 21 yards, 1982; recovered one fumble, 1983; caught one pass for 20 yards and a touchdown, recovered three fumbles and fumbled 10 times for minus five yards, 1984; fumbled nine times for minus 16 yards, 1985; recovered three fumbles and fumbled seven times for minus three yards, 1986; fumbled three times for minus 12 yards, 1988.

Member of Minnesota Vikings for NFC Championship Game following 1977 and 1987 seasons; did not play.

Played in Pro Bowl (NFL All-Star Game) following 1986 season.

RICHARD BARRY KRAUSS

(Known by middle name.)

Linebacker—Cleveland Browns

Born March 17, 1957, at Pompano Beach, Fla.
Height, 6.03. Weight, 248.
High School—Pompano Beach, Fla.
Received bachelor of science degree in education from University of Alabama.

Named as linebacker on THE SPORTING NEWS College All-America Team, 1978.
Selected by Baltimore in 1st round (6th player selected) of 1979 NFL draft.
Franchise transferred to Indianapolis, March 31, 1984.
On injured reserve with knee injury, September 29 through remainder of 1986 season.
Granted unconditional free agency, February 1, 1989; signed by Cleveland Browns, March 8, 1989.
Baltimore NFL, 1979 through 1983; Indianapolis NFL, 1984 through 1988.
Games: 1979 (15), 1980 (16), 1981 (16), 1982 (9), 1983 (16), 1984 (16), 1985 (16), 1986 (4), 1987 (12), 1988 (16). Total—136.

Pro statistics: Recovered two fumbles, 1979, 1981, 1983, 1985, 1987 and 1988; recovered one fumble, 1980 and 1986; intercepted one pass for 10 yards, 1981; caught one pass for five yards and a touchdown, 1982; rushed once for minus one yard, 1983; intercepted three passes for 20 yards, recovered two fumbles for minus five yards and fumbled once, 1984; intercepted one pass for no yards, 1985; intercepted one pass for three yards, 1988.

RICH KRAYNAK

Linebacker—Indianapolis Colts

Born January 20, 1961, at Phoenixville, Pa.
Height, 6.01. Weight, 230.
High School—Phoenixville, Pa.
Attended University of Pittsburgh.

Selected by Philadelphia in 8th round (93rd player selected) of 1983 USFL draft.
Selected by Philadelphia in 8th round (201st player selected) of 1983 NFL draft.
Signed by Philadelphia Eagles, May 25, 1983.
On injured reserve with finger injury, October 15 through remainder of 1986 season.
Released by Philadelphia Eagles, September 6, 1987; signed as free agent replacement player by Atlanta Falcons, October 1, 1987.
On injured reserve with ankle injury, October 19 through November 16, 1987; activated, November 17, 1987.
Granted free agency, February 1, 1988; rights relinquished, June 20, 1988.
Signed as free agent by Indianapolis Colts, May 1, 1989.
Philadelphia NFL, 1983 through 1986; Atlanta NFL, 1987.
Games: 1983 (16), 1984 (14), 1985 (16), 1986 (6), 1987 (9). Total—61.

Pro statistics: Recovered one fumble, 1983; returned blocked punt eight yards for a touchdown, 1984; intercepted one pass for 26 yards, 1985.

DAVID M. KRIEG

Name pronounced Craig.

(Dave)

Quarterback—Seattle Seahawks

Born October 20, 1958, at Iola, Wis.
Height, 6.01. Weight, 196.
High School—Schofield, Wis., D.C. Everest.
Received bachelor of science degree in marketing management from Milton College in 1980.

Signed as free agent by Seattle Seahawks, May 6, 1980.
On injured reserve with separated shoulder, September 19 through November 11, 1988; activated, November 12, 1988.

Year Club	G.	Att.	Cmp.	Pct.	Gain	T.P.	P.I.	Avg.	Att.	Yds.	Avg.	TD.	TD.	Pts.	F.
1980—Seattle NFL	1	2	0	0.0	0	0	0	0.00	None				0	0	0
1981—Seattle NFL	7	112	64	57.1	843	7	5	7.53	11	56	5.1	1	1	6	4
1982—Seattle NFL	3	78	49	62.8	501	2	2	6.42	6	—3	—0.5	0	0	0	5
1983—Seattle NFL	9	243	147	60.5	2139	18	11	8.80	16	55	3.4	2	2	12	10
1984—Seattle NFL	16	480	276	57.5	3671	32	*24	7.65	46	186	4.0	3	3	18	11
1985—Seattle NFL	16	532	285	53.6	3602	27	20	6.77	35	121	3.5	1	1	6	11
1986—Seattle NFL	15	375	225	60.0	2921	21	11	7.79	35	122	3.5	1	1	6	10
1987—Seattle NFL	12	294	178	60.5	2131	23	15	7.25	36	155	4.3	2	2	12	11
1988—Seattle NFL	9	228	134	58.8	1741	18	8	7.64	24	64	2.7	0	0	0	6
Pro Totals—9 Years	88	2344	1358	57.9	17549	148	96	7.49	209	756	3.6	10	10	60	68

Quarterback Rating Points: 1980 (39.6), 1981 (83.3), 1982 (79.0), 1983 (95.0), 1984 (83.3), 1985 (76.2), 1986 (91.0), 1987 (87.6), 1988 (94.6). Total—85.5.

Additional pro statistics: Recovered one fumble and fumbled twice for minus 14 yards, 1982; caught one pass for 11 yards and recovered two fumbles, 1983; recovered three fumbles and fumbled 11 times for minus 24 yards, 1984;

recovered three fumbles and fumbled 11 times for minus two yards, 1985; recovered one fumble and fumbled 10 times for minus five yards, 1986; recovered five fumbles and fumbled 11 times for minus two yards, 1987.

Played in AFC Championship Game following 1983 season.

Played in Pro Bowl (NFL All-Star Game) following 1984 and 1988 seasons.

TODD ALAN KRUMM
Safety—Chicago Bears
Born December 18, 1965, at Royal Oak, Mich.
Height, 6.00. Weight, 189.
High School—West Bloomfield, Mich.
Attended Michigan State University.

Signed as free agent by Washington Redskins, May 3, 1988.

Released by Washington Redskins, August 24, 1988; signed as free agent by Chicago Bears, September 1, 1988.

Selected by New York Mets' organization in 15th round of free-agent draft, June 2, 1987.

Selected by Seattle Mariners' organization in 24th round of free-agent draft, June 1, 1988.

Chicago NFL, 1988.

Games: 1988 (15).

Pro statistics: Intercepted two passes for 14 yards, 1988.

TIMOTHY A. KRUMRIE
Name pronounced KRUM-RYE.
(Tim)
Nose Tackle—Cincinnati Bengals
Born May 20, 1960, at Eau Claire, Wis.
Height, 6.02. Weight, 268.
High School—Mondovi, Wis.
Attended University of Wisconsin.

Named to THE SPORTING NEWS NFL All-Star Team, 1988.

Selected by Tampa Bay in 7th round (84th player selected) of 1983 USFL draft.

Selected by Cincinnati in 10th round (276th player selected) of 1983 NFL draft.

Signed by Cincinnati Bengals, May 19, 1983.

Cincinnati NFL, 1983 through 1988.

Games: 1983 (16), 1984 (16), 1985 (16), 1986 (16), 1987 (12), 1988 (16). Total—92.

Pro statistics: Recovered one fumble, 1983; recovered one fumble for eight yards, 1984; recovered two fumbles, 1985; recovered two fumbles for 18 yards, 1986; recovered three fumbles, 1988.

Played in AFC Championship Game following 1988 season.

Played in NFL Championship Game following 1988 season.

Played in Pro Bowl (NFL All-Star Game) following 1987 season.

Named to play in Pro Bowl following 1988 season; replaced due to injury by Brian Sochia.

GARY WAYNE KUBIAK
Quarterback—Denver Broncos
Born August 15, 1961, at Houston, Tex.
Height, 6.00. Weight, 192.
High School—Houston, Tex., Saint Pius X.
Received degree in physical education from Texas A&M University.

Selected by Denver in 8th round (197th player selected) of 1983 NFL draft.

Year Club	G.	Att.	Cmp.	Pct.	Gain	T.P.	P.I.	Avg.	Att.	Yds.	Avg.	TD.	TD.	Pts.	F.
1983—Denver NFL	4	22	12	54.5	186	1	1	8.45	4	17	4.3	1	1	6	0
1984—Denver NFL	7	75	44	58.7	440	4	1	5.87	9	27	3.0	1	1	6	1
1985—Denver NFL	16	5	2	40.0	61	1	0	12.20	1	6	6.0	0	0	0	0
1986—Denver NFL	16	38	23	60.5	249	1	3	6.55	6	22	3.7	0	0	0	0
1987—Denver NFL	12	7	3	42.9	25	0	2	3.57	1	3	3.0	0	0	0	0
1988—Denver NFL	16	69	43	62.3	497	5	3	7.20	17	65	3.8	0	0	0	3
Pro Totals—6 Years	71	216	127	58.8	1458	12	10	6.75	38	140	3.7	2	2	12	4

Quarterback Rating Points: 1983 (78.9), 1984 (87.6), 1985 (125.8), 1986 (55.7), 1987 (13.1), 1988 (90.1). Total—78.7.

Additional pro statistics: Caught one pass for 20 yards, 1984; recovered three fumbles and fumbled three times for minus nine yards, 1988.

Played in AFC Championship Game following 1986 and 1987 seasons.

Played in NFL Championship Game following 1986 and 1987 seasons.

PETE DAVID KUGLER
Defensive End—San Francisco 49ers
Born August 9, 1959, at Philadelphia, Pa.
Height, 6.04. Weight, 255.
High School—Cherry Hill, N.J.
Received degree from Penn State University.

Selected by San Francisco in 6th round (147th player selected) of 1981 NFL draft.

On injured reserve with pulled hamstring, December 3 through remainder of 1981 season.

On inactive list, September 12, 1982.

Granted free agency, February 1, 1984; signed by Philadelphia Stars, February 16, 1984.

On developmental squad, March 23 through March 30, 1984; activated, March 31, 1984.

On developmental squad, May 18 through May 24, 1984; activated, May 25, 1984.

Franchise transferred to Baltimore, November 1, 1984.

On developmental squad, April 6 through April 12, 1985; activated, April 13, 1985.
On developmental squad, May 15 through June 27, 1985; activated, June 28, 1985.
Granted free agency when USFL suspended operations, August 7, 1986; re-signed by San Francisco 49ers, September 4, 1986.
Granted roster exemption, September 4 through September 14, 1986; activated, September 15, 1986.
On injured reserve with rib injury, October 18, 1986 through January 1, 1987; activated, January 2, 1987.
Crossed picket line during players' strike, October 7, 1987.
On injured reserve with ankle injury, August 23 through November 11, 1988; activated, November 12, 1988.
On developmental squad for 2 games with Philadelphia Stars in 1984.
On developmental squad for 7 games with Baltimore Stars in 1985.
San Francisco NFL, 1981 through 1983 and 1986 through 1988; Philadelphia USFL, 1984; Baltimore USFL, 1985.
Games: 1981 (13), 1982 (7), 1983 (16), 1984 (16), 1985 (11), 1986 (3), 1987 (11), 1988 (6). Total NFL—56. Total USFL—27. Total Pro—83.
Pro statistics: Credited with three sacks for 21 yards and recovered two fumbles, 1984; credited with two sacks for 12 yards, 1985.
Played in NFC Championship Game following 1983 and 1988 seasons.
Played in NFL Championship Game following 1988 season.
Played in USFL Championship Game following 1984 and 1985 seasons.

ERIC PALMER KUMEROW
Linebacker—Miami Dolphins
Born April 17, 1965, at Chicago, Ill.
Height, 6.07. Weight, 260.
High School—Oak Park, Ill., River Forest.
Received bachelor of arts degree in education from Ohio University in 1988.
Son of Palmer Pyle, guard with Baltimore Colts, Minnesota Vikings and Oakland Raiders, 1960 through 1964 and 1966; and step-son of Ernie Kumerow, minor league pitcher, 1961 and 1962.

Selected by Miami in 1st round (16th player selected) of 1988 NFL draft.
Signed by Miami Dolphins, July 13, 1988.
On injured reserve with pulled groin, December 15 through remainder of 1988 season.
Miami NFL, 1988.
Games: 1988 (14).

JAMES MICHAEL LACHEY
Name pronounced Luh-SHAY.
(Jim)
Offensive Tackle—Washington Redskins
Born June 4, 1963, at St. Henry, O.
Height, 6.06. Weight, 288.
High School—St. Henry, O.
Received degree in marketing from Ohio State University in 1985.

Selected by New Jersey in 1985 USFL territorial draft.
Selected by San Diego in 1st round (12th player selected) of 1985 NFL draft.
Signed by San Diego Chargers, July 28, 1985.
Traded by San Diego Chargers to Los Angeles Raiders for offensive tackle John Clay and 3rd round pick in 1989 draft and conditional pick in 1990 draft, July 30, 1988.
Traded with 2nd, 4th and 5th round picks in 1989 draft and conditional pick in 1990 draft by Los Angeles Raiders to Washington Redskins for quarterback Jay Schroeder and 2nd round pick in 1989 draft, September 7, 1988.
San Diego NFL, 1985 through 1987; Los Angeles Raiders (1)-Washington (15) NFL, 1988.
Games: 1985 (16), 1986 (16), 1987 (12), 1988 (16). Total—60.
Pro statistics: Recovered one fumble, 1988.
Played in Pro Bowl (NFL All-Star Game) following 1987 season.

MICHAEL JAMES LAMBRECHT
(Mike)
Nose Tackle—New York Giants
Born May 2, 1963, at Watertown, Minn.
Height, 6.01. Weight, 271.
High School—Watertown, Minn.
Attended St. Cloud State University.

Signed as free agent by Miami Dolphins, March 31, 1987.
Released by Miami Dolphins, September 7, 1987; re-signed as replacement player by Dolphins, September 23, 1987.
On injured reserve with sprained ankle, November 9 through remainder of 1987 season.
Released by Miami Dolphins, September 8, 1988; re-signed by Dolphins, September 17, 1988.
Released by Miami Dolphins, September 26, 1988; re-signed by Dolphins, October 19, 1988.
Granted unconditional free agency, February 1, 1989; signed by New York Giants, March 10, 1989.
Miami NFL, 1987 and 1988.
Games: 1987 (5), 1988 (8). Total—13.

SEAN EDWARD LANDETA
Punter—New York Giants
Born January 6, 1962, at Baltimore, Md.
Height, 6.00. Weight, 200.
High School—Baltimore, Md., Loch Raven.
Attended Towson State University.

Named to THE SPORTING NEWS NFL All-Star Team, 1986.

Named as punter on THE SPORTING NEWS USFL All-Star Team, 1983 and 1984.
Led USFL in net punting average with 38.1 in 1984.
Selected by Philadelphia in 14th round (161st player selected) of 1983 USFL draft.
Signed by Philadelphia Stars, January 24, 1983.
Franchise transferred to Baltimore, November 1, 1984.
Granted free agency, August 1, 1985; signed by New York Giants, August 5, 1985.
On injured reserve with back injury, September 7 through remainder of 1988 season.

			—PUNTING—		
Year Club	G.	No.	Avg.	Blk.	
1983—Philadelphia USFL	18	86	41.9	....	
1984—Philadelphia USFL	18	53	41.0	....	
1985—Baltimore USFL	18	65	41.8	....	
1985—New York Giants NFL	16	81	42.9	0	
1986—New York Giants NFL	16	79	44.8	0	
1987—New York Giants NFL	12	65	42.7	1	
1988—New York Giants NFL	1	6	37.0	0	
USFL Totals—3 Years	54	204	41.6	....	
NFL Totals—4 Years	45	231	43.3	1	
Pro Totals—7 Years	99	435	42.5	....	

Additional USFL statistics: Rushed once for minus five yards and fumbled once, 1983; recovered one fumble, 1983 and 1984.
Additional NFL statistics: Attempted one pass with no completions, 1985.
Played in NFC Championship Game following 1986 season.
Played in NFL Championship Game following 1986 season.
Played in USFL Championship Game following 1983 through 1985 seasons.
Played in Pro Bowl (NFL All-Star Game) following 1986 season.

GENE ERIC LANG
Running Back—Atlanta Falcons
Born March 15, 1962, at Pass Christian, Miss.
Height, 5.10. Weight, 206.
High School—Pass Christian, Miss.
Attended Louisiana State University.

Selected by Denver in 11th round (298th player selected) of 1984 NFL draft.
On injured reserve with broken hand, December 3 through remainder of 1985 season.
Released by Denver Broncos, August 29, 1988; awarded on waivers to Atlanta Falcons, August 31, 1988.

		—RUSHING—				PASS RECEIVING				—TOTAL—		
Year Club	G.	Att.	Yds.	Avg.	TD.	P.C.	Yds.	Avg.	TD.	TD.	Pts.	F.
1984—Denver NFL	16	8	42	5.3	2	4	24	6.0	1	3	18	0
1985—Denver NFL	12	84	318	3.8	5	23	180	7.8	2	7	42	3
1986—Denver NFL	15	29	94	3.2	1	13	105	8.1	2	3	18	0
1987—Denver NFL	12	89	303	3.4	2	17	130	7.6	2	4	24	0
1988—Atlanta NFL	16	53	191	3.6	0	37	398	10.8	1	1	6	3
Pro Totals—5 Years	71	263	948	3.6	10	94	837	8.9	8	18	108	6

		KICKOFF RETURNS			
Year Club	G.	No.	Yds.	Avg.	TD.
1984—Denver NFL	16	19	404	21.3	0
1985—Denver NFL	12	17	361	21.2	0
1986—Denver NFL	15	21	480	22.9	0
1987—Denver NFL	12	4	78	19.5	0
1988—Atlanta NFL	16	1	12	12.0	0
Pro Totals—5 Years	71	62	1335	21.5	0

Additional pro statistics: Recovered one fumble for six yards, 1984; recovered one fumble, 1985; attempted one pass with no completions, 1987.
Played in AFC Championship Game following 1986 and 1987 seasons.
Played in NFL Championship Game following 1986 and 1987 seasons.

REGINALD DEVAN LANGHORNE
(Reggie)
Wide Receiver—Cleveland Browns
Born April 7, 1963, at Suffolk, Va.
Height, 6.02. Weight, 200.
High School—Smithfield, Va.
Attended Elizabeth City State University.

Selected by Oakland in 4th round (52nd player selected) of 1985 USFL draft.
Selected by Cleveland in 7th round (175th player selected) of 1985 NFL draft.
Signed by Cleveland Browns, July 15, 1985.

		—PASS RECEIVING—			
Year Club	G.	P.C.	Yds.	Avg.	TD.
1985—Cleveland NFL	16	1	12	12.0	0
1986—Cleveland NFL	16	39	678	17.4	1
1987—Cleveland NFL	12	20	288	14.4	1
1988—Cleveland NFL	16	57	780	13.7	7
Pro Totals—4 Years	60	117	1758	15.0	9

Additional pro statistics: Returned three kickoffs for 46 yards and fumbled once, 1985; recovered one fumble, 1985

and 1988; rushed once for minus 11 yards, returned four kickoffs for 57 yards and fumbled twice, 1986; returned one kickoff for eight yards, 1987; rushed twice for 26 yards and a touchdown and fumbled three times, 1988.
Played in AFC Championship Game following 1986 and 1987 seasons.

KENNETH WAYNE LANIER
(Ken)
Offensive Tackle—Denver Broncos
Born July 8, 1959, at Columbus, O.
Height, 6.03. Weight, 269.
High School—Columbus, O., Marion Franklin.
Received degree in industrial arts from Florida State University in 1981.

Selected by Denver in 5th round (125th player selected) of 1981 NFL draft.
Denver NFL, 1981 through 1988.
Games: 1981 (8), 1982 (9), 1983 (16), 1984 (16), 1985 (16), 1986 (16), 1987 (12), 1988 (16). Total—109.
Pro statistics: Recovered one fumble, 1982 and 1984.
Played in AFC Championship Game following 1986 and 1987 seasons.
Played in NFL Championship Game following 1986 and 1987 seasons.

PAUL JAY LANKFORD
Cornerback—Miami Dolphins
Born June 15, 1958, at New York, N.Y.
Height, 6.01. Weight, 190.
High School—Farmingdale, N.Y.
Received bachelor of science degree in health planning and administration
from Penn State University in 1982.

Selected by Miami in 3rd round (80th player selected) of 1982 NFL draft.
On inactive list, September 12 and September 19, 1982.
On injured reserve with cracked tibia, November 28 through remainder of 1986 season.

		—INTERCEPTIONS—			
Year Club	G.	No.	Yds.	Avg.TD.	
1982—Miami NFL	7		None		
1983—Miami NFL	16	1	10	10.0	0
1984—Miami NFL	16	3	25	8.3	0
1985—Miami NFL	16	4	10	2.5	0
1986—Miami NFL	12		None		
1987—Miami NFL	12	3	44	14.7	0
1988—Miami NFL	13	1	0	0.0	0
Pro Totals—7 Years	92	12	89	7.4	0

Additional pro statistics: Recovered one fumble, 1984 and 1986; recovered one fumble for four yards, 1987.
Played in AFC Championship Game following 1982, 1984 and 1985 seasons.
Played in NFL Championship Game following 1982 and 1984 seasons.

MICHAEL JOHN LANSFORD
(Mike)
Placekicker—Los Angeles Rams
Born July 20, 1958, at Monterrey Park, Calif.
Height, 6.00. Weight, 183.
High School—Arcadia, Calif.
Attended Pasadena City College and University of Washington.

Selected by New York Giants in 12th round (312th player selected) of 1980 NFL draft.
Released by New York Giants, August 3, 1980; claimed on waivers by San Francisco 49ers, August 5, 1980.
Released by San Francisco 49ers, August 18, 1980; signed as free agent by Oakland Raiders, June, 1981.
Released by Oakland Raiders, August 18, 1981; signed as free agent by Los Angeles Rams, July 1, 1982.
On injured reserve with knee injury, August 24 through November 23, 1983; activated after clearing procedural waivers, November 25, 1983.
Crossed picket line during players' strike, October 2, 1987.

		—PLACE KICKING—				
Year Club	G.	XP.	XPM.	FG.	FGA.	Pts.
1982—L.A. Rams NFL	9	23	1	9	15	50
1983—L.A. Rams NFL	4	9	0	6	9	27
1984—L.A. Rams NFL	16	37	1	25	33	112
1985—L.A. Rams NFL	16	38	1	22	29	104
1986—L.A. Rams NFL	16	34	1	17	24	85
1987—L.A. Rams NFL	15	36	2	17	21	87
1988—L.A. Rams NFL	16	45	3	24	32	117
Pro Totals—7 Years	92	222	9	120	163	582

Played in NFC Championship Game following 1985 season.

CHARLES LOUIS LANZA
(Chuck)
Center—Pittsburgh Steelers
Born September 20, 1964, at Coraopolis, Pa.
Height, 6.02. Weight, 263.
High School—Memphis, Tenn., Christian Brothers.
Received bachelor of arts degree in sociology from University of Notre Dame in 1988.

Selected by Pittsburgh in 3rd round (70th player selected) of 1988 NFL draft.
Signed by Pittsburgh Steelers, July 28, 1988.
Pittsburgh NFL, 1988.
Games: 1988 (16).

STEVE M. LARGENT
Wide Receiver—Seattle Seahawks
Born September 28, 1954, at Tulsa, Okla.
Height, 5.11. Weight, 191.
High School—Oklahoma City, Okla., Putnam.
Received bachelor of science degree in biology from University of Tulsa in 1976.

Establish NFL records for most pass receptions, career (791); most consecutive games, pass reception (167); most yards gained, career (12,686); most seasons, 50 or more pass receptions (10); most seasons, 1,000 or more yards in pass receptions (8).
Named to THE SPORTING NEWS NFL All-Star Team, 1983.
Named to THE SPORTING NEWS AFC All-Star Team, 1978.
Selected by Houston in 4th round (117th player selected) of 1976 NFL draft.
Traded by Houston Oilers to Seattle Seahawks for 8th round pick in 1977 draft, August 26, 1976.
On injured reserve with broken wrist, December 16 through remainder of 1979 season.
Crossed picket line during players' strike, October 14, 1987.
Granted free agency, February 1, 1989; re-signed by Seahawks, May 3, 1989.

			—————RUSHING—————				PASS RECEIVING				—TOTAL—		
Year Club	G.	Att.	Yds.	Avg.	TD.	P.C.	Yds.	Avg.	TD.	TD.	Pts.	F.
1976—Seattle NFL	14	4	—14	—3.5	0	54	705	13.0	4	4	24	2
1977—Seattle NFL	14		None			33	643	19.5	10	10	60	0
1978—Seattle NFL	16		None			71	1168	16.5	8	8	48	0
1979—Seattle NFL	15		None			66	1237	18.7	9	9	54	0
1980—Seattle NFL	16	1	2	2.0	0	66	1064	16.1	6	6	36	1
1981—Seattle NFL	16	6	47	7.8	1	75	1224	16.3	9	10	60	2
1982—Seattle NFL	8	1	8	8.0	0	34	493	14.5	3	3	18	0
1983—Seattle NFL	15		None			72	1074	14.9	11	11	66	3
1984—Seattle NFL	16	2	10	5.0	0	74	1164	15.7	12	12	72	1
1985—Seattle NFL	16		None			79	*1287	16.3	6	6	†37	0
1986—Seattle NFL	16		None			70	1070	15.3	9	9	54	3
1987—Seattle NFL	13	2	33	16.5	0	58	912	15.7	8	8	48	2
1988—Seattle NFL	15	1	—3	—3.0	0	39	645	16.5	2	2	12	3
Pro Totals—13 Years	190	17	83	4.9	1	791	12686	16.0	97	98	589	17

†Scored an extra point.
Additional pro statistics: Returned eight kickoffs for 156 yards and returned four punts for 36 yards, 1976; returned four punts for 32 yards, 1977; recovered one fumble, 1978; recovered two fumbles, 1980; attempted one pass with no completions, 1981 and 1985; attempted one pass with one completion for 11 yards, 1983; attemped one pass with one completion for 18 yards, 1986; attempted two passes with no completions, 1987.
Played in AFC Championship Game following 1983 season.
Played in Pro Bowl (NFL All-Star Game) following 1978, 1981 and 1984 through 1987 seasons.
Named in Pro Bowl following 1979 season; replaced due to wrist injury.

BRANDON HUGH LAUFENBERG
(Babe or The Babe)
Quarterback—Dallas Cowboys
Born December 5, 1959, at Burbank, Calif.
Height, 6.03. Weight, 205.
High School—Encino, Calif., Crespi Carmelite.
Attended Stanford University, University of Missouri, Los Angeles Pierce College
and received degree in business administration and marketing from Indiana University.

Selected by Chicago in 20th round (235th player selected) of 1983 USFL draft.
Selected by Washington in 6th round (168th player selected) of 1983 NFL draft.
Signed by Washington Redskins, June 17, 1983.
On injured reserve with rotator cuff injury, August 27 through entire 1984 season.
Released by Washington Redskins, September 2, 1985; signed as free agent by San Diego Chargers, September 30, 1985.
Released by San Diego Chargers, October 15, 1985.
USFL rights traded by Arizona Outlaws to Memphis Showboats for quarterback John Conner, November 1, 1985.
Signed as free agent by Washington Redskins, November 20, 1985.
Released by Washington Redskins, August 26, 1986; awarded on waivers to New Orleans Saints, August 27, 1986.
Released by New Orleans Saints, September 1, 1986; re-signed by Saints, September 23, 1986.
Released by New Orleans Saints, November 8, 1986; signed as free agent by Kansas City Chiefs, May 28, 1987.
Released by Kansas City Chiefs, August 31, 1987; signed as free agent by Washington Redskins, September 16, 1987.
Released by Washington Redskins, October 27, 1987; signed as free agent by San Diego Chargers, March 24, 1988.
Granted unconditional free agency, February 1, 1989; did not receive qualifying offer, April 15, 1989.
Signed by Dallas Cowboys, May 17, 1989.
Active for 16 games with Washington Redskins in 1983; did not play.
Active for 2 games with San Diego Chargers and 5 games with Washington Redskins in 1985; did not play.
Active for 1 game with Washington Redskins in 1987; did not play.

		————PASSING————							——RUSHING——				—TOTAL—		
Year Club	G.	Att.	Cmp.	Pct.	Gain	T.P.	P.I.	Avg.	Att.	Yds.	Avg.	TD.	TD.	Pts.	F.
1986—New Orleans NFL	1		None							None			0	0	0
1988—San Diego NFL	8	144	69	47.9	778	4	5	5.40	31	120	3.9	0	0	0	2
Pro Totals—5 Years	9	144	69	47.9	778	4	5	5.40	31	120	3.9	0	0	0	2

Quarterback Rating Points: 1988 (59.3).
Additional pro statistics: Recovered three fumbles and fumbled twice for minus 10 yards, 1988.
Member of Washington Redskins for NFC and NFL Championship Games following 1983 season; did not play.

ROBERT L. LAVETTE
Running Back—San Diego Chargers
Born September 8, 1963, at Cartersville, Ga.
Height, 5.11. Weight, 190.
High School—Cartersville, Ga.
Attended Georgia Tech.
Cousin of Ray Donaldson, center with Indianapolis Colts.

Selected by Jacksonville in 1985 USFL territorial draft.
Selected by Dallas in 4th round (103rd player selected) of 1985 NFL draft.
Signed by Dallas Cowboys, July 14, 1985.
On injured reserve with knee injury, December 5 through remainder of 1985 season.
Crossed picket line during players' strike, October 7, 1987.
Released by Dallas Cowboys, November 3, 1987; awarded on waivers to Philadelphia Eagles, November 4, 1987.
Released by Philadelphia Eagles, December 11, 1987; signed as free agent by Atlanta Falcons, March 21, 1988.
Released by Atlanta Falcons, August 30, 1988; signed as free agent by San Diego Chargers, May 9, 1989.

		—RUSHING—				PASS RECEIVING				—TOTAL—		
Year Club	G.	Att.	Yds.	Avg.	TD.	P.C.	Yds.	Avg.	TD.	TD.	Pts.	F.
1985—Dallas NFL	12	13	34	2.6	0	1	8	8.0	0	0	0	0
1986—Dallas NFL	16	10	6	0.6	0	5	31	6.2	1	1	6	3
1987—Dallas (4)-Philadelphia (1) NFL	5			None		1	6	6.0	0	0	0	0
Pro Totals—3 Years	33	23	40	1.7	0	7	45	6.4	1	1	6	3

		—PUNT RETURNS—				—KICKOFF RET.—			
Year Club	G.	No.	Yds.	Avg.	TD.	No.	Yds.	Avg.	TD.
1985—Dallas NFL	12		None			34	682	20.1	0
1986—Dallas NFL	16	18	92	5.1	0	36	699	19.4	0
1987—Dallas (4)-Philadelphia (1) NFL	5		None			6	109	18.2	0
Pro Totals—3 Years	33	18	92	5.1	0	76	1490	19.6	0

Additional pro statistics: Recovered three fumbles, 1986.

PATRICK JOSEPH LEAHY
(Pat)
Placekicker—New York Jets
Born March 19, 1951, at St. Louis, Mo.
Height, 6.00. Weight, 193.
High School—St. Louis, Mo., Augustinian Academy.
Received degree in marketing and business administration from St. Louis University
(did not play college football).

Named to THE SPORTING NEWS AFC All-Star Team, 1978.
Signed as free agent by St. Louis Cardinals, 1974.
Released by St. Louis Cardinals and signed as free agent by New York Jets, November 8, 1974.
On injured reserve with knee injury, October 13 through remainder of 1979 season.

		—PLACE KICKING—				
Year Club	G.	XP.	XPM.	FG.	FGA.	Pts.
1974—N.Y. Jets NFL	6	18	1	6	11	36
1975—N.Y. Jets NFL	14	27	3	13	21	66
1976—N.Y. Jets NFL	14	16	4	11	16	49
1977—N.Y. Jets NFL	14	18	3	15	25	63
1978—N.Y. Jets NFL	16	41	1	22	30	107
1979—N.Y. Jets NFL	6	12	3	8	13	36
1980—N.Y. Jets NFL	16	36	0	14	22	78
1981—N.Y. Jets NFL	16	38	1	25	36	113
1982—N.Y. Jets NFL	9	26	*5	11	17	59
1983—N.Y. Jets NFL	16	36	1	16	24	84
1984—N.Y. Jets NFL	16	38	1	17	24	89
1985—N.Y. Jets NFL	16	43	2	26	34	121
1986—N.Y. Jets NFL	16	44	0	16	19	92
1987—N.Y. Jets NFL	12	31	0	18	22	85
1988—N.Y. Jets NFL	16	43	0	23	28	112
Pro Totals—15 Years	203	467	25	241	342	1190

Additional pro statistics: Recovered one fumble, 1975; rushed once for 10 yards, 1988.
Played in AFC Championship Game following 1982 season.

—DID YOU KNOW—
That every intradivisional series in the NFC Central in 1988 was a sweep? The Bears swept the Buccaneers, Lions and Packers; the Vikings swept the Bears, Buccaneers and Lions; the Buccaneers swept the Lions and Packers; the Lions swept the Packers and the Packers swept the Vikings.

CARL LEE III
Defensive Back—Minnesota Vikings
Born April 6, 1961, at South Charleston, W. Va.
Height, 5.11. Weight, 185.
High School—South Charleston, W. Va.
Attended Marshall University.

Named to THE SPORTING NEWS NFL All-Star Team, 1988.
Selected by Minnesota in 7th round (186th player selected) of 1983 NFL draft.
Released by Minnesota Vikings, August 27, 1985; re-signed by Vikings, September 2, 1985.

| | | —INTERCEPTIONS— | | | |
Year Club	G.	No.	Yds.	Avg.	TD.
1983—Minnesota NFL	16	1	31	31.0	0
1984—Minnesota NFL	16	1	0	0.0	0
1985—Minnesota NFL	15	3	68	22.7	0
1986—Minnesota NFL	16	3	10	3.3	0
1987—Minnesota NFL	12	3	53	17.7	0
1988—Minnesota NFL	16	8	118	14.8	*2
Pro Totals—6 Years	91	19	280	14.7	2

Additional pro statistics: Recovered one fumble, 1984 and 1988.
Played in NFC Championship Game following 1987 season.
Played in Pro Bowl (NFL All-Star Game) following 1988 season.

DANZELL IVAN LEE
Tight End—Atlanta Falcons
Born March 16, 1963, at Corsicana, Tex.
Height, 6.02. Weight, 237.
High School—Corsicana, Tex.
Attended Lamar University.

Selected by Washington in 6th round (163rd player selected) of 1985 NFL draft.
Signed by Washington Redskins, July 18, 1985.
On injured reserve with sprained back, August 27 through entire 1985 season.
Released by Washington Redskins, August 19, 1986; signed as free agent by Pittsburgh Steelers, March 29, 1987.
Released by Pittsburgh Steelers, September 7, 1987; re-signed as replacement player by Steelers, September 24, 1987.
On injured reserve with toe injury, August 29 through September 7, 1988.
Released by Pittsburgh Steelers, September 8, 1988; signed as free agent by Atlanta Falcons, September 28, 1988.
Released by Atlanta Falcons, October 17, 1988; re-signed by Falcons, November 23, 1988.
Released by Atlanta Falcons, December 12, 1988; re-signed by Falcons, December 14, 1988.

| | | —PASS RECEIVING— | | | |
Year Club	G.	P.C.	Yds.	Avg.	TD.
1987—Pittsburgh NFL	13	12	124	10.3	0
1988—Atlanta NFL	5		None		
Pro Totals—2 Years	18	12	124	10.3	0

Additional pro statistics: Recovered one fumble, 1987.

GARY DeWAYNE LEE
Wide Receiver-Kick Returner—Detroit Lions
Born February 12, 1965, at Albany, Ga.
Height, 6.01. Weight, 202.
High School—Albany, Ga., Westover.
Attended Georgia Tech.

Selected by Detroit in 12th round (315th player selected) of 1987 NFL draft.
Signed by Detroit Lions, July 25, 1987.

| | | PASS RECEIVING | | | | —KICKOFF RET.— | | | | —TOTAL— | | |
Year Club	G.	P.C.	Yds.	Avg.	TD.	No.	Yds.	Avg.	TD.	TD.	Pts.	F.
1987—Detroit NFL	12	19	308	16.2	0	32	719	22.5	0	0	0	1
1988—Detroit NFL	14	22	261	11.9	1	18	355	19.7	0	1	6	2
Pro Totals—2 Years	26	41	569	13.9	1	50	1074	21.5	0	1	6	3

Additional pro statistics: Recovered one fumble, 1988.

GREGORY LAMONT LEE
(Greg)
Cornerback—Pittsburgh Steelers
Born January 15, 1965, at Pine Bluff, Ark.
Height, 6.01. Weight, 207.
High School—Pine Bluff, Ark., Dollarway.
Attended Arkansas State University.

Signed as free agent by Pittsburgh Steelers, April 29, 1988.
Released by Pittsburgh Steelers, August 29, 1988; re-signed by Steelers, August 30, 1988.
Pittsburgh NFL, 1988.
Games: 1988 (16).

LARRY DWAYNE LEE
Guard—Los Angeles Raiders
Born September 10, 1959, at Dayton, O.
Height, 6.02. Weight, 270.
High School—Dayton, O., Roth.
Attended University of California at Los Angeles.
Cousin of Rick Porter, running back with Detroit Lions, Baltimore Colts
and Memphis Showboats, 1982, 1983 and 1985.

Selected by Detroit in 5th round (129th player selected) of 1981 NFL draft.
Released by Detroit Lions, September 2, 1985; re-signed by Lions, September 10, 1985.
Released by Detroit Lions, November 16, 1985; awarded on waivers to Miami Dolphins, November 18, 1985.
Left Miami Dolphins camp voluntarily and retired, August 12, 1987.
Rights traded by Miami Dolphins to Denver Broncos for 8th round pick in 1988 draft, August 19, 1987.
Released by Denver Broncos, August 30, 1988; re-signed by Broncos, September 6, 1988.
Released by Denver Broncos, October 12, 1988; signed as free agent by Los Angeles Raiders, April 4, 1989.
Detroit NFL, 1981 through 1984; Detroit (6)-Miami (5) NFL, 1985; Miami NFL, 1986; Denver NFL, 1987 and 1988.
Games: 1981 (16), 1982 (9), 1983 (16), 1984 (15), 1985 (11), 1986 (16), 1987 (9), 1988 (4). Total—96.
Pro statistics: Returned one kickoff for no yards, 1981; returned one kickoff for 14 yards, 1982; returned one kickoff for 11 yards, 1983; recovered one fumble, 1984 and 1987; fumbled twice for minus 24 yards, 1984; returned one kickoff for five yards and fumbled once, 1986.
Played in AFC Championship Game following 1985 season.
Member of Denver Broncos for AFC and NFL Championship Games following 1987 season; did not play.

MARK ANTHONY LEE
Defensive Back—Green Bay Packers
Born March 20, 1958, at Hanford, Calif.
Height, 5.11. Weight, 187.
High School—Hanford, Calif.
Attended University of Washington.

Selected by Green Bay in 2nd round (34th player selected) of 1980 NFL draft.

Year Club	G.	INTERCEPTIONS No.	Yds.	Avg.	TD.	PUNT RETURNS No.	Yds.	Avg.	TD.	KICKOFF RET. No.	Yds.	Avg.	TD.	TOTAL TD.	Pts.	F.
1980—Green Bay NFL	15	None				5	32	6.4	0	30	589	19.6	0	0	0	1
1981—Green Bay NFL	16	6	50	8.3	0	20	187	9.4	1	14	270	19.3	0	1	6	0
1982—Green Bay NFL	9	1	40	40.0	0	None				None				0	0	0
1983—Green Bay NFL	16	4	23	5.8	0	1	−4	−4.0	0	1	0	0	0	0	0	1
1984—Green Bay NFL	16	3	33	11.0	0	None				None				0	0	0
1985—Green Bay NFL	14	1	23	23.0	0	None				None				0	0	0
1986—Green Bay NFL	16	9	33	3.7	0	None				None				0	0	0
1987—Green Bay NFL	12	1	0	0.0	0	None				None				0	0	0
1988—Green Bay NFL	15	3	37	12.3	0	None				None				0	0	0
Pro Totals—9 Years	129	28	239	8.5	0	26	215	8.3	1	45	859	19.1	0	1	6	2

Additional pro statistics: Recovered one fumble, 1981, 1986 and 1988; recovered one fumble for 15 yards, 1983; recovered two fumbles, 1984.

RONALD VAN LEE
(Ronnie)
Offensive Tackle—Miami Dolphins
Born December 24, 1956, at Pine Bluff, Ark.
Height, 6.03. Weight, 275.
High School—Tyler, Tex.
Attended Baylor University.

Selected by Miami in 3rd round (65th player selected) of 1979 NFL draft.
Released by Miami Dolphins, August 29, 1983; signed as free agent by Atlanta Falcons, September 14, 1983.
Traded with 6th round pick in 1985 draft by Atlanta Falcons to Miami Dolphins for cornerback Gerald Small, August 26, 1984.
On injured reserve with groin injury, October 18 through November 23, 1986; activated, November 24, 1986.

Year Club	G.	PASS RECEIVING P.C.	Yds.	Avg.	TD.	Year Club	G.	PASS RECEIVING P.C.	Yds.	Avg.	TD.
1979—Miami NFL	16	2	14	7.0	0	1985—Miami NFL	15	None			
1980—Miami NFL	16	7	83	11.9	2	1986—Miami NFL	10	None			
1981—Miami NFL	16	14	64	4.6	1	1987—Miami NFL	9	None			
1982—Miami NFL	9	2	6	3.0	0	1988—Miami NFL	16	None			
1983—Atlanta NFL	14	None				Pro Totals—10 Years	137	25	167	6.7	3
1984—Miami NFL	16	None									

Played in AFC Championship Game following 1982, 1984 and 1985 seasons.
Played in NFL Championship Game following 1982 and 1984 seasons.

SHAWN SWABODA LEE
Nose Tackle—Tampa Bay Buccaneers
Born October 24, 1966, at Brooklyn, N.Y.
Height, 6.02. Weight, 290.
High School—Brooklyn, N. Y., Erasmus Hall.
Attended University of North Alabama.

Selected by Tampa Bay in 6th round (163rd player selected) of 1988 NFL draft.

Signed by Tampa Bay Buccaneers, July 10, 1988.
Tampa Bay NFL, 1988.
Games: 1988 (15).

ZEPHRINI LEE
(First name pronounced Zef-ren-EYE.)
(Zeph)
Safety—Los Angeles Raiders
Born June 17, 1963, at San Francisco, Calif.
Height, 6.03. Weight, 205.
High School—San Francisco, Calif., Abraham Lincoln.
Received bachelor of science degree in exercise science
from University of Southern California in 1986.
Cousin of Ricky Bell, running back with Tampa Bay Buccaneers and San Diego Chargers,
1977 through 1982; and Archie Bell, lead singer of Archie Bell and the Drells.
Selected by New Jersey in 1986 USFL territorial draft.
Selected by Los Angeles Raiders in 9th round (246th player selected) of 1986 NFL draft.
Signed by Los Angeles Raiders, July 14, 1986.
On injured reserve with groin injury, August 26 through entire 1986 season.
Released by Los Angeles Raiders, September 1, 1987; signed as free agent replacement player by Denver Broncos,
September 25, 1987.
Released by Denver Broncos, October 6, 1987; signed as free agent replacement player by Los Angeles Raiders,
October 10, 1987.
Released by Los Angeles Raiders, November 3, 1987; re-signed by Raiders, November 9, 1987.
On injured reserve with groin injury, November 9 through December 18, 1987; activated, December 19, 1987.
On injured reserve with neck injury, October 29 through remainder of 1988 season.
Denver (1)-Los Angeles Raiders (2) NFL, 1987; Los Angeles Raiders NFL, 1988.
Games: 1987 (3), 1988 (8). Total—11.
Pro statistics: Intercepted one pass for 30 yards and returned one kickoff for no yards, 1988.

ALBERT RAY LEWIS
Cornerback—Kansas City Chiefs
Born October 6, 1960, at Mansfield, La.
Height, 6.02. Weight, 198.
High School—Mansfield, La., DeSoto.
Attended Grambling State University.
Selected by Philadelphia in 15th round (175th player selected) of 1983 USFL draft.
Selected by Kansas City in 3rd round (61st player selected) of 1983 NFL draft.
Signed by Kansas City Chiefs, May 19, 1983.
On injured reserve with knee injury, December 10 through remainder of 1984 season.

Year Club	G.	No.	Yds.	Avg.	TD.
1983—Kansas City NFL	16	4	42	10.5	0
1984—Kansas City NFL	15	4	57	14.3	0
1985—Kansas City NFL	16	8	59	7.4	0
1986—Kansas City NFL	15	4	18	4.5	0
1987—Kansas City NFL	12	1	0	0.0	0
1988—Kansas City NFL	14	1	19	19.0	0
Pro Totals—6 Years	88	22	195	8.9	0

Additional pro statistics: Recovered two fumbles, 1983 and 1986; recovered one fumble in end zone for a touchdown, 1985; recovered one fumble, 1987 and 1988; credited with a safety, 1988.
Played in Pro Bowl (NFL All-Star Game) following 1987 season.
Named to play in Pro Bowl following 1988 season; replaced due to injury by Eric Thomas.

LEO E. LEWIS III
Wide Receiver—Minnesota Vikings
Born September 17, 1956, at Columbia, Mo.
Height, 5.08. Weight, 170.
High School—Columbia, Mo., Hickman.
Received degree in education from University of Missouri, received master's degree from
University of Tennessee and accepted at University of Minnesota for doctorate in physical education.
Son of Leo Lewis, member of Canadian Football League Hall of Fame and
running back with Winnipeg Blue Bombers, 1955 through 1966; brother of
Marc Lewis, wide receiver with Oakland Invaders and Denver Gold, 1983 through 1985;
and related to Mickey Pruitt, linebacker-safety with Chicago Bears.
Signed as free agent by St. Louis Cardinals, May 21, 1979.
On injured reserve with ankle injury, August 21 through November 15, 1979.
Released by St. Louis Cardinals, November 16, 1979; signed as free agent by Calgary Stampeders, March, 1980.
Released by Calgary Stampeders, August 7, 1980; signed as free agent by Hamilton Tiger-Cats, August 13, 1980.
Released by Hamilton Tiger-Cats, August 20, 1980; signed as free agent by Minnesota Vikings, May 10, 1981.
Released by Minnesota Vikings, August 25, 1981; re-signed after clearing procedural waivers, November 11, 1981.

Year Club		RUSHING				PASS RECEIVING				—TOTAL—		
	G.	Att.	Yds.	Avg.	TD.	P.C.	Yds.	Avg.	TD.	TD.	Pts.	F.
1980—Calgary (5)-Hamilton (1) CFL	6	1	62	62.0	1	8	91	11.4	1	2	12	0
1981—Minnesota NFL	4	1	16	16.0	0	2	58	29.0	0	0	0	0
1982—Minnesota NFL	9		None			8	150	18.8	3	3	18	0

Year Club	G.	Att.	Yds.	Avg.	TD.	P.C.	Yds.	Avg.	TD.	TD.	Pts.	F.
		RUSHING				PASS RECEIVING				TOTAL		
1983—Minnesota NFL	14	1	2	2.0	0	12	127	10.6	0	0	0	0
1984—Minnesota NFL	16	2	11	5.5	0	47	830	17.7	4	4	24	1
1985—Minnesota NFL	10	1	2	2.0	0	29	442	15.2	3	3	18	1
1986—Minnesota NFL	16	3	—16	—5.3	0	32	600	18.8	2	2	12	3
1987—Minnesota NFL	12	5	—7	—1.4	0	24	383	16.0	2	3	18	1
1988—Minnesota NFL	16			None		11	141	12.8	1	1	6	2
CFL Totals—1 Year	6	1	62	62.0	1	8	91	11.4	1	2	12	0
NFL Totals—8 Years	97	13	8	0.6	0	165	2731	16.6	15	16	96	8
Pro Totals—9 Years	103	14	70	5.0	1	173	2822	16.3	16	18	108	8

Year Club	G.	No.	Yds.	Avg.	TD.	No.	Yds.	Avg.	TD.
		PUNT RETURNS				KICKOFF RET.			
1980—Calgary (5)-Hamilton (1) CFL	6	22	163	7.4	0	15	345	23.0	0
1981—Minnesota NFL	4			None				None	
1982—Minnesota NFL	9			None				None	
1983—Minnesota NFL	14	3	52	17.3	0	1	25	25.0	0
1984—Minnesota NFL	16	4	31	7.8	0	1	31	31.0	0
1985—Minnesota NFL	10			None				None	
1986—Minnesota NFL	16	7	53	7.6	0			None	
1987—Minnesota NFL	12	22	275	12.5	1			None	
1988—Minnesota NFL	16	*58	550	9.5	0	1	12	12.0	0
CFL Totals—1 Year	6	22	163	7.4	0	15	345	23.0	0
NFL Totals—8 Years	97	94	961	10.2	1	3	68	22.7	0
Pro Totals—9 Years	103	116	1124	9.7	1	18	413	22.9	0

Additional pro statistics: Recovered three fumbles, 1984; recovered one fumble, 1985 and 1986; recovered two fumbles, 1987.

Played in NFC Championship Game following 1987 season.

MARK JOSEPH LEWIS
Tight End—Detroit Lions
Born May 5, 1961, at Houston, Tex.
Height, 6.02. Weight, 250.
High School—Houston, Tex., Kashmere.
Attended Texas A&M University.

Selected by Houston in 1985 USFL territorial draft.
Selected by Green Bay in 6th round (155th player selected) of 1985 NFL draft.
Signed by Green Bay Packers, July 19, 1985.
On injured reserve with knee injury, August 27 through December 20, 1985; activated, December 21, 1985.
Released by Green Bay Packers, September 15, 1987; signed as free agent replacement player by Detroit Lions, October 16, 1987.
Released by Detroit Lions, September 21, 1988; re-signed by Lions, April 11, 1989.
Green Bay NFL, 1985 and 1986; Green Bay (1)-Detroit (9) NFL, 1987; Detroit NFL, 1988.
Games: 1985 (1), 1986 (16), 1987 (10), 1988 (3). Total—30.
Pro statistics: Caught two passes for seven yards and two touchdowns, 1986; caught three passes for 32 yards and a touchdown, 1988.

WILLIAM GLENN LEWIS
(Bill)
Center—Los Angeles Raiders
Born July 12, 1963, at Sioux City, Ia.
Height, 6.07. Weight, 275.
High School—Sioux City, Ia., East.
Attended University of Nebraska.

Selected by Memphis in 1986 USFL territorial draft.
Selected by Los Angeles Raiders in 7th round (191st player selected) of 1986 NFL draft.
Signed by Los Angeles Raiders, July 14, 1986.
On non-football injury list with appendectomy, September 22 through October 23, 1987; activated, October 24, 1987.
Los Angeles Raiders NFL, 1986 through 1988.
Games: 1986 (4), 1987 (8), 1988 (14). Total—26.

GEORGE VINCENT LILJA
Center—Los Angeles Raiders
Born March 3, 1958, at Evergreen Park, Ill.
Height, 6.04. Weight, 282.
High School—Orland Park, Ill., Carl Sandburg.
Received bachelor of arts degree in general studies from University of Michigan in 1981.
Brother of Larry Lilja, strength coach at Northwestern University.

Selected by Los Angeles in 4th round (104th player selected) of 1981 NFL draft.
On injured reserve with ankle injury, August 31 through entire 1981 season.
Released by Los Angeles Rams, September 8, 1983; signed as free agent by New York Jets, September 27, 1983.
Released by New York Jets, November 15, 1984; signed as free agent by Cleveland Browns, November 21, 1984.
Released by Cleveland Browns, September 7, 1987; signed as free agent replacement player by Dallas Cowboys, October 14, 1987.
On injured reserve with broken hand, August 23 through September 27, 1988.

Released by Dallas Cowboys, September 28, 1988; signed as free agent by Los Angeles Raiders, February 24, 1989.
Active for 1 game with Los Angeles Rams in 1983; did not play.
Los Angeles Rams NFL, 1982; Los Angeles Rams (0)-New York Jets (1) NFL, 1983; New York Jets (3)-Cleveland (4) NFL, 1984; Cleveland NFL, 1985 and 1986; Dallas NFL, 1987.
Games: 1982 (9), 1983 (1), 1984 (7), 1985 (16), 1986 (16), 1987 (5). Total—54.
Pro statistics: Recovered one fumble, 1985; fumbled once, 1987.
Played in AFC Championship Game following 1986 season.

KEVIN PASCHAL LILLY
Nose Tackle—San Francisco 49ers
Born May 14, 1963, at Tulsa, Okla.
Height, 6.04. Weight, 265.
High School—Tulsa, Okla., Memorial.
Received degree from The University of Tulsa.

Signed as free agent by San Diego Chargers, May 15, 1986.
Released by San Diego Chargers after failing physical, July 20, 1986; re-signed by Chargers, August 11, 1986.
Released by San Diego Chargers, August 25, 1986; signed as free agent by San Francisco 49ers, April 8, 1987.
On injured reserve with foot injury, August 28 through entire 1987 season.
Released by San Francisco 49ers, August 29, 1988; re-signed by 49ers, August 30, 1988.
Released by San Francisco 49ers, November 14, 1988; re-signed by 49ers, November 19, 1988.
Released by San Francisco 49ers, December 5, 1988; re-signed by 49ers, December 9, 1988.
Released by San Francisco 49ers, December 14, 1988; re-signed by 49ers, March 28, 1989.
San Francisco NFL, 1988.
Games: 1988 (9).

ADAM JAMES LINGNER
Offensive Lineman—Buffalo Bills
Born November 2, 1960, at Indianapolis, Ind.
Height, 6.04. Weight, 265.
High School—Rock Island, Ill., Alleman.
Attended University of Illinois.

Selected by Chicago in 1983 USFL territorial draft.
Selected by Kansas City in 9th round (231st player selected) of 1983 NFL draft.
Signed by Kansas City Chiefs, June 1, 1983.
Released by Kansas City Chiefs, November 24, 1986; signed as free agent by New England Patriots, November 28, 1986.
Released by New England Patriots, December 2, 1986; signed as free agent by Denver Broncos, May 1, 1987.
Released by Denver Broncos, August 26, 1987; awarded on waivers to Buffalo Bills, August 27, 1987.
Released by Buffalo Bills, August 22, 1988; awarded on waivers to Kansas City Chiefs, August 23, 1988.
Granted unconditional free agency, February 1, 1989; signed as free agent by Buffalo Bills, March 16, 1989.
Active for 1 game with New England Patriots in 1986; did not play.
Kansas City NFL, 1983 through 1985 and 1988; Kansas City (12)-New England (0) NFL, 1986; Buffalo NFL, 1987.
Games: 1983 (16), 1984 (16), 1985 (16), 1986 (12), 1987 (12), 1988 (16). Total—88.
Pro statistics: Recovered one fumble, 1987.

RONNIE LEON LIPPETT
Name pronounced Lip-PET.
Cornerback—New England Patriots
Born December 10, 1960, at Melborne, Fla.
Height, 5.11. Weight, 180.
High School—Sebring, Fla.
Attended University of Miami (Fla.).

Selected by New England in 8th round (214th player selected) of 1983 NFL draft.

Year Club	G.	No.	Yds.	Avg.	TD.
			—INTERCEPTIONS—		
1983—New England NFL.......	16			None	
1984—New England NFL.......	16	3	23	7.7	0
1985—New England NFL.......	16	3	93	31.0	0
1986—New England NFL.......	15	8	76	9.5	0
1987—New England NFL.......	12	3	103	34.3	*2
1988—New England NFL.......	15	1	4	4.0	0
Pro Totals—6 Years...........	90	18	299	16.6	2

Additional pro statistics: Recovered one fumble, 1983, 1984 and 1988; fumbled once, 1984.
Played in AFC Championship Game following 1985 season.
Played in NFL Championship Game following 1985 season.

LOUIS ADAM LIPPS
Wide Receiver-Punt Returner—Pittsburgh Steelers
Born August 9, 1962, at New Orleans, La.
Height, 5.10. Weight, 190.
High School—Reserve, La., East St. John's.
Attended University of Southern Mississippi.
Cousin of Garry James, running back with Detroit Lions.

Named THE SPORTING NEWS NFL Rookie of the Year, 1984.
Selected by Arizona in 8th round (155th player selected) of 1984 USFL draft.
Selected by Pittsburgh in 1st round (23rd player selected) of 1984 NFL draft.

Signed by Pittsburgh Steelers, May 19, 1984.
On injured reserve with hamstring injury, November 21 through December 18, 1987; activated, December 19, 1987.

		——RUSHING——				PASS RECEIVING				—TOTAL—		
Year Club	G.	Att.	Yds.	Avg.	TD.	P.C.	Yds.	Avg.	TD.	TD.	Pts.	F.
1984—Pittsburgh NFL	14	3	71	23.7	1	45	860	19.1	9	11	66	8
1985—Pittsburgh NFL	16	2	16	8.0	1	59	1134	19.2	12	15	90	5
1986—Pittsburgh NFL	13	4	−3	−0.8	0	38	590	15.5	3	3	18	2
1987—Pittsburgh NFL	4			None		11	164	14.9	0	0	0	0
1988—Pittsburgh NFL	16	6	129	21.5	1	50	973	19.5	5	6	36	2
Pro Totals—5 Years	63	15	213	14.2	3	203	3721	18.3	29	35	210	17

		—PUNT RETURNS—				—KICKOFF RET.—			
Year Club	G.	No.	Yds.	Avg.	TD.	No.	Yds.	Avg.	TD.
1984—Pittsburgh NFL	14	53	*656	12.4	1			None	
1985—Pittsburgh NFL	16	36	437	12.1	*2	13	237	18.2	0
1986—Pittsburgh NFL	13	3	16	5.3	0			None	
1987—Pittsburgh NFL	4	7	46	6.6	0			None	
1988—Pittsburgh NFL	16	4	30	7.5	0			None	
Pro Totals—5 Years	63	103	1185	11.5	3	13	237	18.2	0

Additional pro statistics: Recovered two fumbles, 1984; recovered four fumbles for three yards, 1985; recovered one fumble, 1986; attempted two passes with one completion for 13 yards and a touchdown and one interception, 1988.
Played in AFC Championship Game following 1984 season.
Played in Pro Bowl (NFL All-Star Game) following 1984 and 1985 seasons.

DAVID GENE LITTLE
(Dave)
Tight End—Philadelphia Eagles
Born April 18, 1961, at Selma, Calif.
Height, 6.02. Weight, 226.
High School—Fresno, Calif., Roosevelt.
Attended Kings River College and Middle Tennessee State University.

Signed as free agent by Memphis Showboats, January 11, 1984.
Released by Memphis Showboats, February 20, 1984; signed as free agent by Kansas City Chiefs, June 21, 1984.
On injured reserve with knee injury, November 6 through remainder of 1984 season.
Released by Kansas City Chiefs, August 19, 1985; signed as free agent by Philadelphia Eagles, September 11, 1985.
On injured reserve with knee injury, September 15 through October 10, 1988; activated, October 11, 1988.

		——PASS RECEIVING——			
Year Club	G.	P.C.	Yds.	Avg.	TD.
1984—Kansas City NFL	10	1	13	13.0	0
1985—Philadelphia NFL	15	7	82	11.7	0
1986—Philadelphia NFL	16	14	132	9.4	0
1987—Philadelphia NFL	12	1	8	8.0	0
1988—Philadelphia NFL	10			None	
Pro Totals—5 Years	63	23	235	10.2	0

Additional pro statistics: Recovered fumble in end zone for a touchdown, 1985; fumbled once, 1986.

DAVID LAMAR LITTLE
Linebacker—Pittsburgh Steelers
Born January 3, 1959, at Miami, Fla.
Height, 6.01. Weight, 230.
High School—Miami, Fla., Jackson.
Received degree in sociology from University of Florida.
Brother of Larry Little, guard with San Diego Chargers
and Miami Dolphins, 1967 through 1980; and currently head coach at Bethune-Cookman College.

Selected by Pittsburgh in 7th round (183rd player selected) of 1981 NFL draft.
Pittsburgh NFL, 1981 through 1988.
Games: 1981 (16), 1982 (9), 1983 (16), 1984 (16), 1985 (16), 1986 (16), 1987 (12), 1988 (16). Total—117.
Pro statistics: Recovered one fumble 1981 and 1987; recovered one fumble for two yards, 1982; intercepted two passes for no yards and recovered two fumbles for 11 yards, 1985; intercepted one pass for no yards and recovered two fumbles for two yards, 1988.
Played in AFC Championship Game following 1984 season.

GREGORY LENARD LLOYD
(Greg)
Linebacker—Pittsburgh Steelers
Born May 26, 1965, at Miami, Fla.
Height, 6.02. Weight, 224.
High School—Peach County, Ga.
Attended Fort Valley State College.

Selected by Pittsburgh in 6th round (150th player selected) of 1987 NFL draft.
Signed by Pittsburgh Steelers, May 19, 1987.
On injured reserve with knee injury, August 31 through entire 1987 season.
On injured reserve with knee injury, August 30 through October 21, 1988; activated, October 22, 1988.
Pittsburgh NFL, 1988.
Games: 1988 (9).
Pro statistics: Recovered one fumble, 1988.

CHARLES EDWARD LOCKETT
Wide Receiver—Pittsburgh Steelers
Born October 1, 1965, at Los Angeles, Calif.
Height, 6.00. Weight, 179.
High School—Los Angeles, Calif., Crenshaw.
Attended California State University at Long Beach.

Selected by Pittsburgh in 3rd round (66th player selected) of 1987 NFL draft.
Signed by Pittsburgh Steelers, July 20, 1987.
Crossed picket line during players' strike, October 14, 1987.

			———PASS RECEIVING———			
Year	Club	G.	P.C.	Yds.	Avg.	TD.
1987—Pittsburgh NFL		11	7	116	16.6	1
1988—Pittsburgh NFL		16	22	365	16.6	1
Pro Totals—2 Years		27	29	481	16.6	2

Additional pro statistics: Returned two punts for three yards, recovered one fumble and fumbled once, 1987.

DANNY KEY LOCKETT
Linebacker—Detroit Lions
Born July 11, 1964, at Fort Valley, Ga.
Height, 6.02. Weight, 250.
High School—Fort Valley, Ga., Peach County.
Attended College of the Sequoias and University of Arizona.

Selected by Detroit in 6th round (148th player selected) of 1987 NFL draft.
Signed by Detroit Lions, July 25, 1987.
Crossed picket line during players' strike, October 14, 1987.
Detroit NFL, 1987 and 1988.
Games: 1987 (13), 1988 (16). Total—29.
Pro statistics: Recovered one fumble, 1987 and 1988.

EUGENE LOCKHART JR.
Linebacker—Dallas Cowboys
Born March 8, 1961, at Crockett, Tex.
Height, 6.02. Weight, 233.
High School—Crockett, Tex.
Received bachelor of arts degree in marketing from University of Houston in 1983.

Selected by Houston in 1984 USFL territorial draft.
Selected by Dallas in 6th round (152nd player selected) of 1984 NFL draft.
Signed by Dallas Cowboys, May 8, 1984.
On injured reserve with broken leg, December 8 through remainder of 1987 season.
Dallas NFL, 1984 through 1988.
Games: 1984 (15), 1985 (16), 1986 (16), 1987 (9), 1988 (16). Total—72.
Pro statistics: Intercepted one pass for 32 yards, 1984; recovered one fumble, 1984, 1986 and 1987; intercepted one pass for 19 yards and a touchdown and recovered four fumbles for 17 yards, 1985; intercepted one pass for five yards, 1986; intercepted one pass for 13 yards, 1987.

JAMES DAVID LOFTON
Wide Receiver—Los Angeles Raiders
Born July 5, 1956, at Fort Ord, Calif.
Height, 6.03. Weight, 190.
High School—Los Angeles, Calif., Washington.
Received bachelor of science degree in industrial engineering from
Stanford University in 1978.
Cousin of Kevin Bass, outfielder with Houston Astros.

Named to THE SPORTING NEWS NFL All-Star Team, 1980 and 1981.
Selected by Green Bay in 1st round (6th player selected) of 1978 NFL draft.
On suspended list, December 18 through remainder of 1986 season.
Traded by Green Bay Packers to Los Angeles Raiders for 3rd round pick in 1987 draft and 4th round pick in 1988 draft, April 13, 1987.

			———RUSHING———				PASS RECEIVING				—TOTAL—		
Year	Club	G.	Att.	Yds.	Avg.	TD.	P.C.	Yds.	Avg.	TD.		TD.	Pts.	F.
1978—Green Bay NFL		16	3	13	4.3	0	46	818	17.8	6		6	36	2
1979—Green Bay NFL		15	1	—1	—1.0	0	54	968	17.9	4		4	24	5
1980—Green Bay NFL		16			None		71	1226	17.3	4		4	24	0
1981—Green Bay NFL		16			None		71	1294	18.2	8		8	48	0
1982—Green Bay NFL		9	4	101	25.3	1	35	696	19.9	4		5	30	0
1983—Green Bay NFL		16	9	36	4.0	0	58	1300	⋆22.4	8		8	48	0
1984—Green Bay NFL		16	10	82	8.2	0	62	1361	⋆22.0	7		7	42	1
1985—Green Bay NFL		16	4	14	3.5	0	69	1153	16.7	4		4	24	3
1986—Green Bay NFL		15			None		64	840	13.1	4		4	24	3
1987—Los Angeles Raiders NFL		12	1	1	1.0	0	41	880	21.5	5		5	30	0
1988—Los Angeles Raiders NFL		16			None		28	549	19.6	0		0	0	0
Pro Totals—11 Years		163	32	246	7.7	1	599	11085	18.5	54		55	330	14

Additional pro statistics: Returned one kickoff for no yards and attempted two passes with no completions, 1978; attempted one pass with no completions, 1979 and 1986; recovered one fumble, 1981; attempted one pass with one completion for 43 yards, 1982; recovered two fumbles for eight yards, 1986; recovered one fumble for 19 yards, 1988.
Played in Pro Bowl (NFL All-Star Game) following 1978 and 1980 through 1985 seasons.

MARC ANTHONY LOGAN
Fullback—Miami Dolphins
Born May 9, 1965, at Lexington, Ky.
Height, 5.11. Weight, 225.
High School—Lexington, Ky., Bryan Station.
Received bachelor of arts degree in political science from University of Kentucky in 1987.
Cousin of Dermontti Dawson, guard-center with Pittsburgh Steelers.

Selected by Cincinnati in 5th round (130th player selected) of 1987 NFL draft.
Signed by Cincinnati Bengals, July 7, 1987.
Released by Cincinnati Bengals, September 7, 1987; re-signed as replacement player by Bengals, September 25, 1987.
Released by Cincinnati Bengals, October 19, 1987; awarded on waivers to Cleveland Browns, October 20, 1987.
Released by Cleveland Browns, November 5, 1987; re-signed by Browns for 1988, November 7, 1987.
Released by Cleveland Browns, August 24, 1988; signed as free agent by Cincinnati Bengals, October 4, 1988.
Granted unconditional free agency, February 1, 1989; signed by Miami Dolphins, February 16, 1989.

		—RUSHING—				PASS RECEIVING				—TOTAL—		
Year	Club	G.	Att.	Yds.	Avg.	TD.	P.C.	Yds.	Avg.	TD.	TD.	Pts.	F.
1987—Cincinnati NFL		3	37	203	5.5	1	3	14	4.7	0	1	6	0
1988—Cincinnati NFL		9	2	10	5.0	0	2	20	10.0	0	0	0	1
Pro Totals—2 Years		12	39	213	5.5	1	5	34	6.8	0	1	6	1

Additional pro statistics: Returned three kickoffs for 31 yards, 1987; returned four kickoffs for 80 yards, 1988.
Member of Cincinnati Bengals for AFC Championship Game following 1988 season; inactive.
Played in NFL Championship Game following 1988 season.

JOHN M. LOHMILLER
(Chip)
Placekicker—Washington Redskins
Born July 16, 1966, at Woodbury, Minn.
Height, 6.03. Weight, 213.
High School—Woodbury, Minn.
Attended University of Minnesota.

Selected by Washington in 2nd round (55th player selected) of 1988 NFL draft.
Signed by Washington Redskins, July 17, 1988.

		—PLACE KICKING—					
Year	Club	G.	XP.	XPM.	FG.	FGA.	Pts.
1988—Washington NFL		16	40	1	19	26	97

Additional pro statistics: Punted six times for a 34.7 avg., 1988.

NEIL VINCENT LOMAX
Quarterback—Phoenix Cardinals
Born February 17, 1959, at Portland, Ore.
Height, 6.03. Weight, 215.
High School—Lake Oswego, Ore.
Received degree in communications from Portland State University.

Selected by St. Louis in 2nd round (33rd player selected) of 1981 NFL draft.
Franchise transferred to Phoenix, March 15, 1988.

			—————PASSING—————							—RUSHING—				—TOTAL—		
Year	Club	G.	Att.	Cmp.	Pct.	Gain	T.P.	P.I.	Avg.	Att.	Yds.	Avg.	TD.	TD.	Pts.	F.
1981—St. Louis NFL		14	236	119	50.4	1575	4	10	6.67	19	104	5.5	2	2	12	4
1982—St. Louis NFL		9	205	109	53.2	1367	5	6	6.67	28	119	4.3	1	1	6	8
1983—St. Louis NFL		13	354	209	59.0	2636	24	11	7.45	27	127	4.7	2	2	12	9
1984—St. Louis NFL		16	560	345	61.6	4614	28	16	8.24	35	184	5.3	3	3	18	11
1985—St. Louis NFL		16	471	265	56.3	3214	18	12	6.82	32	125	3.9	0	0	0	10
1986—St. Louis NFL		14	421	240	57.0	2583	13	12	6.14	35	148	4.2	1	1	6	7
1987—St. Louis NFL		12	★463	★275	59.4	★3387	24	12	7.32	29	107	3.7	0	0	0	7
1988—Phoenix NFL		14	443	255	57.6	3395	20	11	7.66	17	55	3.2	1	1	6	5
Pro Totals—8 Years		108	3153	1817	57.6	22771	136	90	7.22	222	969	4.4	10	10	60	63

Quarterback Rating Points: 1981 (60.1), 1982 (70.1), 1983 (92.0), 1984 (92.5), 1985 (79.5), 1986 (73.6), 1987 (88.5), 1988 (86.7). Total—82.4.

Additional pro statistics: Caught one pass for 10 yards, recovered one fumble and fumbled eight times for minus one yard, 1982; recovered three fumbles, 1983; recovered two fumbles and fumbled 11 times for minus five yards, 1984; recovered four fumbles and fumbled 10 times for minus one yard, 1985; recovered six fumbles, 1986; recovered three fumbles and fumbled seven times for minus three yards, 1987; recovered two fumbles and fumbled five times for minus nine yards, 1988.

Played in Pro Bowl (NFL All-Star Game) following 1984 and 1987 seasons.

CHARLES FRANKLIN LONG II
(Chuck)
Quarterback—Detroit Lions
Born February 18, 1963, at Norman, Okla.
Height, 6.04. Weight, 221.
High School—Wheaton, Ill., North.
Received degree in marketing from University of Iowa in 1985.

Named as quarterback on THE SPORTING NEWS College All-America Team, 1985.

Selected by Detroit in 1st round (12th player selected) of 1986 NFL draft.
Selected by Baltimore in 10th round (75th player selected) of 1986 USFL draft.
Signed by Detroit Lions, August 18, 1986.
Granted roster exemption, August 18 through August 29, 1986; activated, August 30, 1986.
On injured reserve with knee injury, October 11 through November 18, 1988; activated, November 19, 1988.

Year Club	G.	Att.	Cmp.	Pct.	Gain	T.P.	P.I.	Avg.	Att.	Yds.	Avg.	TD.	TD.	Pts.	F.
				PASSING						RUSHING			TOTAL		
1986—Detroit NFL	3	40	21	52.5	247	2	2	6.18	2	0	0.0	0	0	0	1
1987—Detroit NFL	12	416	232	55.8	2598	11	*20	6.25	22	64	2.9	0	0	0	8
1988—Detroit NFL	7	141	75	53.2	856	6	6	6.07	7	22	3.1	0	0	0	4
Pro Totals—3 Years	22	597	328	54.9	3701	19	28	6.20	31	86	2.8	0	0	0	13

Quarterback Rating Points: 1986 (67.4), 1987 (63.4), 1988 (68.2). Total—64.8.
Additional pro statistics: Recovered three fumbles and fumbled eight times for minus eight yards, 1987; recovered two fumbles and fumbled four times for minus three yards, 1988.

HOWARD M. LONG
(Howie)
Defensive End—Los Angeles Raiders
Born January 6, 1960, at Somerville, Mass.
Height, 6.05. Weight, 265.
High School—Milford, Mass.
Received bachelor of arts degree in communications from Villanova University in 1981.

Named to THE SPORTING NEWS NFL All-Star Team, 1983.
Selected by Oakland in 2nd round (48th player selected) of 1981 NFL draft.
Franchise transferred to Los Angeles, May 7, 1982.
Left Los Angeles Raiders camp voluntarily, July 30 through August 2, 1984; returned, August 3, 1984.
Crossed picket line during players' strike, October 6, 1987.
Oakland NFL, 1981; Los Angeles Raiders NFL, 1982 through 1988.
Games: 1981 (16), 1982 (9), 1983 (16), 1984 (16), 1985 (16), 1986 (13), 1987 (14), 1988 (7). Total—107.
Pro statistics: Recovered two fumbles, 1983, 1986 and 1987; recovered two fumbles for four yards, 1984; intercepted one pass for 73 yards, 1988.
Played in AFC Championship Game following 1983 season.
Played in NFL Championship Game following 1983 season.
Played in Pro Bowl (NFL All-Star Game) following 1983 through 1987 seasons.

TERRY LUTHER LONG
Guard—Pittsburgh Steelers
Born July 21, 1959, at Columbia, S.C.
Height, 5.11. Weight, 275.
High School—Columbia, S.C., Eau Claire.
Attended East Carolina University.
Spent two years in Army before entering college.

Selected by Washington in 4th round (76th player selected) of 1984 USFL draft.
Selected by Pittsburgh in 4th round (111th player selected) of 1984 NFL draft.
Signed by Pittsburgh Steelers, July 10, 1984.
Crossed picket line during players' strike, October 14, 1987.
Pittsburgh NFL, 1984 through 1988.
Games: 1984 (12), 1985 (15), 1986 (16), 1987 (13), 1988 (12). Total—68.
Pro statistics: Returned one punt for no yards and fumbled once, 1984; recovered one fumble, 1986 and 1988.
Played in AFC Championship Game following 1984 season.

RONALD MANDEL LOTT
(Ronnie)
Safety—San Francisco 49ers
Born May 8, 1959, at Albuquerque, N.M.
Height, 6.00. Weight, 199.
High School—Rialto, Calif., Eisenhower.
Received bachelor of science degree in public administration
from University of Southern California in 1981.

Named as defensive back on THE SPORTING NEWS College All-America Team, 1980.
Named to THE SPORTING NEWS NFL All-Star Team, 1981 and 1987.
Selected by San Francisco in 1st round (8th player selected) of 1981 NFL draft.

Year Club	G.	No.	Yds.	Avg.	TD.
		INTERCEPTIONS			
1981—San Francisco NFL	16	7	117	16.7	*3
1982—San Francisco NFL	9	2	95	47.5	■1
1983—San Francisco NFL	15	4	22	5.5	0
1984—San Francisco NFL	12	4	26	6.5	0
1985—San Francisco NFL	16	6	68	11.3	0
1986—San Francisco NFL	14	*10	134	13.4	1
1987—San Francisco NFL	12	5	62	12.4	0
1988—San Francisco NFL	13	5	59	11.8	0
Pro Totals—8 Years	107	43	583	13.6	5

Additional pro statistics: Returned seven kickoffs for 111 yards and fumbled once, 1981; recovered two fumbles, 1981 and 1985; recovered one fumble, 1983; returned one kickoff for two yards, 1985; recovered two fumbles for 33 yards, 1987; recovered four fumbles for three yards, 1988.

Played in NFC Championship Game following 1981, 1983, 1984 and 1988 seasons.
Played in NFL Championship Game following 1981, 1984 and 1988 seasons.
Played in Pro Bowl (NFL All-Star Game) following 1981 through 1984 and 1986 through 1988 seasons.

DUVAL LEE LOVE
Guard—Los Angeles Rams
Born June 24, 1963, at Los Angeles, Calif.
Height, 6.03. Weight, 280.
High School—Fountain Valley, Calif.
Attended University of California at Los Angeles.

Selected by Memphis in 1985 USFL territorial draft.
Selected by Los Angeles Rams in 10th round (274th player selected) of 1985 NFL draft.
Signed by Los Angeles Rams, July 16, 1985.
On injured reserve with shoulder injury, September 2 through October 3, 1985; activated, October 4, 1985.
On injured reserve with pinched nerve in neck, November 15 through remainder of 1985 season.
On injured reserve with knee injury, September 8 through October 23, 1987; activated, October 24, 1987.
Crossed picket line during players' strike, October 14, 1987.
Los Angeles Rams NFL, 1985 through 1988.
Games: 1985 (6), 1986 (16), 1987 (10), 1988 (15). Total—47.
Pro statistics: Returned one kickoff for minus six yards and fumbled once, 1986; recovered one fumble, 1988.

CALVIN E. LOVEALL
Defensive Back—Kansas City Chiefs
Born July 23, 1962, at Kennewick, Wash.
Height, 5.09. Weight, 182.
High School—Kennewick, Wash.
Attended University of Idaho.

Selected by Denver in 4th round (51st player selected) of 1985 USFL draft.
Signed by Denver Gold, January 21, 1985.
Franchise merged with Jacksonville, February 19, 1986.
Granted free agency when USFL suspended operations, August 7, 1986; signed as free agent by Ottawa Rough Riders, August 26, 1986.
Released by Ottawa Rough Riders, November 5, 1987; signed as free agent by Houston Oilers, May 18, 1988.
Released by Houston Oilers, September 14, 1988; re-signed by Oilers, September 16, 1988.
Released by Houston Oilers, October 12, 1988; signed as free agent by Kansas City Chiefs, October 19, 1988.
Released by Kansas City Chiefs, November 21, 1988; signed as free agent by Atlanta Falcons, November 23, 1988.
Granted unconditional free agency, February 1, 1989; signed by Kansas City Chiefs, April 1, 1989.
Denver USFL, 1985; Ottawa CFL, 1986 and 1987; Houston (3)-Kansas City (4)-Atlanta (4) NFL, 1988.
Games: 1985 (18), 1986 (10), 1987 (18), 1988 (11). Total CFL—28. Total Pro—57.
USFL statistics: Caught two passes for 57 yards and returned one punt for no yards, 1985.
CFL statistics: Intercepted two passes for 18 yards, 1986; intercepted five passes for 45 yards, recovered one fumble for six yards and credited with one sack, 1987.
NFL statistics: Recovered one fumble, 1988.

ROBERT KIRK LOWDERMILK
(Known by middle name.)
Center—Minnesota Vikings
Born April 10, 1963, at Canton, O.
Height, 6.03. Weight, 265.
High School—Salem, O.
Attended Ohio State University.

Selected by New Jersey in 1985 USFL territorial draft.
Selected by Minnesota in 3rd round (59th player selected) of 1985 NFL draft.
Signed by Minnesota Vikings, August 12, 1985.
On injured reserve with knee injury, September 2 through October 10, 1986; activated, October 11, 1986.
Granted free agency, February 1, 1988; re-signed by Vikings, August 23, 1988.
On injured reserve with fractured thumb, September 27 through October 28, 1988; activated, October 29, 1988.
Minnesota NFL, 1985 through 1988.
Games: 1985 (16), 1986 (11), 1987 (12), 1988 (12). Total—51.
Played in NFC Championship Game following 1987 season.

DOMINIC GERALD LOWERY
(Nick)
Placekicker—Kansas City Chiefs
Born May 27, 1956, at Munich, Germany
Height, 6.04. Weight, 189.
High School—Washington, D. C., St. Albans.
Received bachelor of arts degree in government from Dartmouth College in 1978.

Signed as free agent by New York Jets, May 17, 1978.
Released by New York Jets, August 21, 1978; signed as free agent by New England Patriots, September 19, 1978.
Released by New England Patriots, October 6, 1978; signed as free agent by Cincinnati Bengals, July 2, 1979.
Released by Cincinnati Bengals, August 13, 1979; signed as free agent by Washington Redskins, August 18, 1979.
Released by Washington Redskins, August 20, 1979; re-signed by Redskins, August 25, 1979.
Released by Washington Redskins, August 27, 1979; signed as free agent by Kansas City Chiefs, February 16, 1980.

Year	Club		PLACE KICKING				
		G.	XP.	XPM.	FG.	FGA.	Pts.
1978—New England NFL..		2	7	0	0	1	7
1980—Kansas City NFL.....		16	37	0	20	26	97
1981—Kansas City NFL.....		16	37	1	26	36	115
1982—Kansas City NFL.....		9	17	0	19	*24	74
1983—Kansas City NFL.....		16	44	1	24	30	116
1984—Kansas City NFL.....		16	35	0	23	33	104
1985—Kansas City NFL.....		16	35	0	24	27	107
1986—Kansas City NFL.....		16	43	0	19	26	100
1987—Kansas City NFL.....		12	26	0	19	23	83
1988—Kansas City NFL.....		16	23	0	27	32	104
Pro Totals—10 Years.....		135	304	2	201	258	907

Additional pro statistics: Recovered one fumble, 1981.
Played in Pro Bowl (NFL All-Star Game) following 1981 season.

ORLANDO DEWEY LOWRY
Linebacker—Kansas City Chiefs
Born August 14, 1961, at Cleveland, O.
Height, 6.04. Weight, 234.
High School—Shaker Heights, O.
Attended Ohio State University.
Brother of Quentin Lowry, linebacker with Washington Redskins
and Tampa Bay Buccaneers, 1981 through 1983.

Selected by New Jersey in 1984 USFL territorial draft.
USFL rights traded with rights to defensive back Garcia Lane by New Jersey Generals to Philadelphia Stars for past considerations involving linebacker Lawrence Taylor, January 9, 1984.
Signed as free agent by Washington Redskins, May 3, 1984.
Released by Washington Redskins, August 27, 1984; signed as free agent by Indianapolis Colts, March 20, 1985.
On injured reserve with finger injury, October 26 through November 26, 1987; activated, November 27, 1987.
Released by Indianapolis Colts, August 31, 1988; re-signed by Colts, September 2, 1988.
Granted unconditional free agency, February 1, 1989; signed by Kansas City Chiefs, February 22, 1989.
Indianapolis NFL, 1985 through 1988.
Games: 1985 (16), 1986 (16), 1987 (8), 1988 (16). Total—56.
Pro statistics: Returned one punt for no yards, 1985; recovered one fumble, 1987.

TIMOTHY BRIAN LUCAS
(Tim)
Linebacker—Denver Broncos
Born April 3, 1961, at Stockton, Calif.
Height, 6.03. Weight, 230.
High School—Rio Vista, Calif.
Received bachelor of arts degree in economics from University of California.

Selected by Oakland in 1983 USFL territorial draft.
Selected by St. Louis in 10th round (269th player selected) of 1983 NFL draft.
Signed by Oakland Invaders, May 6, 1983.
On developmental squad, May 6 through May 28, 1983; activated, May 29, 1983.
Protected in merger of Oakland Invaders and Michigan Panthers, December 6, 1984.
On developmental squad, April 6 through remainder of 1985 season.
Granted free agency, August 1, 1985; signed by St. Louis Cardinals, July 22, 1986.
Left St. Louis Cardinals camp and placed on reserve/left camp, July 30, 1986.
Traded by St. Louis Cardinals to San Diego Chargers for draft pick, July 18, 1987.
Released by San Diego Chargers, August 29, 1987; signed as free agent replacement player by Denver Broncos, September 25, 1987.
Released by Denver Broncos, August 29, 1988; re-signed by Broncos, August 30, 1988.
On developmental squad for 3 games with Oakland Invaders in 1983.
On developmental squad for 12 games with Oakland Invaders in 1985.
Oakland USFL, 1983 through 1985; Denver NFL, 1987 and 1988.
Games: 1983 (6), 1984 (18), 1985 (6), 1987 (11), 1988 (16). Total USFL—30. Total NFL—27. Total Pro—57.
USFL statistics: Credited with 5½ sacks for 47½ yards, 1984; intercepted one pass for 18 yards and credited with two sacks for six yards, 1985.
NFL statistics: Intercepted one pass for 11 yards and recovered one fumble, 1987.
On developmental squad for USFL Championship Game following 1985 season.
Played in AFC Championship Game following 1987 season.
Played in NFL Championship Game following 1987 season.

DAVID GRAHAM LUTZ
Name pronounced Loots.
Offensive Tackle—Kansas City Chiefs
Born December 30, 1959, at Monroe, N.C.
Height, 6.06. Weight, 290.
High School—Wadesboro, N.C., Bowman.
Attended Georgia Tech.

Selected by Oakland in 3rd round (31st player selected) of 1983 USFL draft.
Selected by Kansas City in 2nd round (34th player selected) of 1983 NFL draft.
Signed by Kansas City Chiefs, June 1, 1983.
On injured reserve with knee injury, September 4 through November 8, 1984; activated, November 9, 1984.

On injured reserve with knee injury, October 7 through November 27, 1986; activated, November 28, 1986.
Kansas City NFL, 1983 through 1988.
Games: 1983 (16), 1984 (7), 1985 (16), 1986 (9), 1987 (12), 1988 (15). Total—75.
Pro statistics: Recovered one fumble, 1985.

LESTER EVERETT LYLES
Safety—San Diego Chargers
Born December 27, 1962, at Washington, D.C.
Height, 6.03. Weight, 200.
High School—Washington, D.C., St. Albans.
Attended University of Virginia.

Selected by Orlando in 1985 USFL territorial draft.
Selected by New York Jets in 2nd round (40th player selected) of 1985 NFL draft.
Signed by New York Jets, July 3, 1985.
On injured reserve with hip injury, August 27 through November 15, 1985; activated, November 16, 1985.
On injured reserve with knee injury, September 14 through November 8, 1987; activated, November 9, 1987.
On injured reserve with ankle injury, November 27 through remainder of 1987 season.
Released by New York Jets, August 30, 1988; signed as free agent by Phoenix Cardinals, November 8, 1988.
Granted unconditional free agency, February 1, 1989; signed by San Diego Chargers, March 31, 1989.

| | | ——INTERCEPTIONS—— | | | |
Year Club	G.	No.	Yds.	Avg.	TD.
1985—N.Y. Jets NFL	6		None		
1986—N.Y. Jets NFL	16	5	36	7.2	0
1987—N.Y. Jets NFL	4		None		
1988—Phoenix NFL	6	2	0	0.0	0
Pro Totals—4 Years	32	7	36	5.1	0

Additional pro statistics: Recovered one fumble for 13 yards, 1985; recovered one fumble for 16 yards, 1986.

ROBERT LYLES
Linebacker—Houston Oilers
Born March 21, 1961, at Los Angeles, Calif.
Height, 6.01. Weight, 230.
High School—Los Angeles, Calif., Belmont.
Attended Texas Christian University.

Selected by Houston in 5th round (114th player selected) of 1984 NFL draft.
On injured reserve with knee injury, September 25 through December 6, 1984; activated, December 7, 1984.
Houston NFL, 1984 through 1988.
Games: 1984 (6), 1985 (16), 1986 (16), 1987 (12), 1988 (16). Total—66.
Pro statistics: Recovered one fumble for 93 yards and a touchdown and intercepted two passes for no yards, 1986;
intercepted two passes for 42 yards and recovered three fumbles for 55 yards and a touchdown, 1987; intercepted two
passes for three yards and recovered two fumbles for five yards, 1988.

LORENZO LYNCH
Defensive Back—Chicago Bears
Born April 6, 1963, at Oakland, Calif.
Height, 5.09. Weight, 199.
High School—Oakland, Calif.
Attended California State University at Sacramento.

Signed as free agent by Dallas Cowboys, April 30, 1987.
Released by Dallas Cowboys, July 27, 1987; signed as free agent by Chicago Bears, July 31, 1987.
Released by Chicago Bears, September 1, 1987; re-signed as replacement player by Bears, September 24, 1987.
On injured reserve with dislocated shoulder, October 16 through remainder of 1987 season.
On injured reserve with hamstring injury, August 29 to October 12, 1988; activated after clearing procedural
waivers, October 14, 1988.
Chicago NFL, 1987 and 1988.
Games: 1987 (2), 1988 (9). Total—11.
Played in NFC Championship Game following 1988 season.

MARTY LYONS
Defensive End-Defensive Tackle—New York Jets
Born January 15, 1957, at Tokoma Park, Md.
Height, 6.05. Weight, 269.
High School—St. Petersburg, Fla., Catholic.
Attended University of Alabama.

Named as defensive lineman on THE SPORTING NEWS College All-America Team, 1978.
Selected by New York Jets in 1st round (14th player selected) of 1979 NFL draft.
On injured reserve with shoulder injury, November 12 through December 11, 1986; activated, December 12, 1986.
Crossed picket line during players' strike, October 2, 1987.
New York Jets NFL, 1979 through 1988.
Games: 1979 (16), 1980 (16), 1981 (12), 1982 (7), 1983 (16), 1984 (13), 1985 (16), 1986 (12), 1987 (13), 1988 (16).
Total—137.
Pro statistics: Recovered three fumbles, 1979; recovered one fumble, 1981 and 1986; recovered one fumble for 10
yards, 1982; credited with a safety, 1987 and 1988; recovered two fumbles, 1988.
Played in AFC Championship Game following 1982 season.

JOHN DAVID MAARLEVELD
(Name pronounced MARLEY-veld.)
(J. D.)
Offensive Tackle—Houston Oilers
Born October 24, 1961, at Jersey City, N.J.
Height, 6.06. Weight, 280.
High School—West New York, N.J., Saint Joseph's of the Palisades.
Attended University of Notre Dame and University of Maryland.

Selected by Baltimore in 1986 USFL territorial draft.
Selected by Tampa Bay in 5th round (112th player selected) of 1986 NFL draft.
Signed by Tampa Bay Buccaneers, July 25, 1986.
Released by Tampa Bay Buccaneers, August 29, 1988; signed as free agent by Houston Oilers, January 6, 1989.
Tampa Bay NFL, 1986 and 1987.
Games: 1986 (14), 1987 (11). Total—25.

WILLIAM THOMAS MAAS
(Bill)
Nose Tackle—Kansas City Chiefs
Born March 2, 1962, at Newton Square, Pa.
Height, 6.05. Weight, 268.
High School—Newton Square, Pa., Marple Newtown.
Attended University of Pittsburgh.
Brother-in-law of Dan Marino, quarterback with Miami Dolphins.

Selected by Pittsburgh in 1984 USFL territorial draft.
Selected by Kansas City in 1st round (5th player selected) of 1984 NFL draft.
Signed by Kansas City Chiefs, July 13, 1984.
On injured reserve with knee injury, October 28 through remainder of 1988 season.
Kansas City NFL, 1984 through 1988.
Games: 1984 (14), 1985 (16), 1986 (16), 1987 (11), 1988 (8). Total—65.
Pro statistics: Recovered one fumble, 1985; recovered two fumbles, 1986; recovered one fumble for six yards and a touchdown, 1987; credited with a safety, 1988.
Played in Pro Bowl (NFL All-Star Game) following 1986 and 1987 seasons.

MARK GOODWIN MacDONALD
Guard-Center—Phoenix Cardinals
Born April 30, 1961, at West Roxbury, Mass.
Height, 6.04. Weight, 267.
High School—Boston, Mass., Catholic Memorial.
Attended Boston College.

Selected by Pittsburgh in 4th round (84th player selected) of 1984 USFL draft (elected to return to college for final year of eligibility).
Selected by Minnesota in 5th round (115th player selected) of 1985 NFL draft.
Signed by Minnesota Vikings, July 25, 1985.
On injured reserve with knee injury, November 12 through remainder of 1986 season.
Released by Minnesota Vikings, September 2, 1988; awarded on waivers to New Orleans Saints, September 5, 1988.
Released by New Orleans Saints, September 12, 1988; signed as free agent by Minnesota Vikings, September 28, 1988.
Released by Minnesota Vikings, November 1, 1988; signed as free agent by Phoenix Cardinals, December 13, 1988.
Minnesota NFL, 1985 through 1987; Minnesota (5)-Phoenix (1) NFL, 1988.
Games: 1985 (16), 1986 (10), 1987 (12), 1988 (6). Total—44.
Played in NFC Championship Game following 1987 season.

DONALD MATTHEW MACEK
Name pronounced MAY-sick.
(Don)
Center—San Diego Chargers
Born July 2, 1954, at Manchester, N. H.
Height, 6.02. Weight, 278.
High School—Manchester, N. H., Central.
Received bachelor of science degree in marketing from Boston College and attending National University for master's degree in marketing.

Selected by San Diego in 2nd round (31st player selected) of 1976 NFL draft.
On injured reserve with neck injury, December 7 through remainder of 1979 season.
Left San Diego Chargers camp voluntarily, August 7 through August 21, 1984; returned, August 22, 1984.
On injured reserve with shoulder injury, October 8 through remainder of 1988 season.
San Diego NFL, 1976 through 1988.
Games: 1976 (14), 1977 (14), 1978 (14), 1979 (10), 1980 (16), 1981 (15), 1982 (9), 1983 (11), 1984 (13), 1985 (15), 1986 (13), 1987 (11), 1988 (5). Total—160.
Pro statistics: Recovered one fumble, 1976, 1977, 1980, 1981, 1983, 1986 and 1987; returned one kickoff for six yards, 1978; fumbled once, 1978, 1982, 1987 and 1988; fumbled twice for minus 23 yards, 1980.
Played in AFC Championship Game following 1980 and 1981 seasons.

CEDRIC MANUEL MACK
Cornerback—Phoenix Cardinals
Born September 14, 1960, at Freeport, Tex.
Height, 6.00. Weight, 194.
High School—Freeport, Tex., Brazosport.
Attended Baylor University.
Cousin of Phillip Epps, wide receiver with Green Bay Packers; and Milton Mack, cornerback with New Orleans Saints.

Selected by Oakland in 12th round (138th player selected) of 1983 USFL draft.
Selected by St. Louis in 2nd round (44th player selected) of 1983 NFL draft.
Signed by St. Louis Cardinals, July 11, 1983.
On injured reserve with dislocated shoulder, September 28 through October 25, 1984; activated, October 26, 1984.
Franchise transferred to Phoenix, March 15, 1988.
Selected by New York Yankees' organization in 22nd round of free-agent draft, June 5, 1979.

			—INTERCEPTIONS—		
Year Club	G.	No.	Yds.	Avg.	TD.
1983—St. Louis NFL	16	3	25	8.3	0
1984—St. Louis NFL	12		None		
1985—St. Louis NFL	16	2	10	5.0	0
1986—St. Louis NFL	15	4	42	10.5	0
1987—St. Louis NFL	10	2	0	0.0	0
1988—Phoenix NFL	16	3	33	11.0	0
Pro Totals—6 Years	85	14	110	7.9	0

Additional pro statistics: Caught five passes for 61 yards, 1984; recovered two fumbles, 1985 and 1987; caught one pass for 16 yards, 1985; recovered one fumble, 1986; recovered one fumble for 45 yards and a touchdown, 1988.

KEVIN MACK
Fullback—Cleveland Browns
Born August 9, 1962, at Kings Mountain, N.C.
Height, 6.00. Weight, 255.
High School—Kings Mountain, N.C.
Attended Clemson University.

Selected by Washington in 1984 USFL territorial draft.
Rights traded with rights to defensive tackle James Robinson by Washington Federals to Los Angeles Express for draft choices, March 16, 1984.
Signed by Los Angeles Express, March 16, 1984.
Granted roster exemption, March 16, 1984; activated, March 23, 1984.
On developmental squad, March 30 through April 6, 1984; activated, April 7, 1984.
On developmental squad, April 28 through May 10, 1984; activated, May 11, 1984.
Selected by Cleveland in 1st round (11th player selected) of 1984 NFL supplemental draft.
Released by Los Angeles Express, January 31, 1985; signed by Cleveland Browns, February 1, 1985.
On developmental squad for 3 games with Los Angeles Express in 1984.

		—RUSHING—				PASS RECEIVING				—TOTAL—		
Year Club	G.	Att.	Yds.	Avg.	TD.	P.C.	Yds.	Avg.	TD.	TD.	Pts.	F.
1984—Los Angeles USFL	12	73	330	4.5	4	6	38	6.3	0	4	24	3
1985—Cleveland NFL	16	222	1104	5.0	7	29	297	10.2	3	10	60	4
1986—Cleveland NFL	12	174	665	3.8	10	28	292	10.4	0	10	60	6
1987—Cleveland NFL	12	201	735	3.7	5	32	223	7.0	1	6	36	6
1988—Cleveland NFL	11	123	485	3.9	3	11	87	7.9	0	3	18	5
USFL Totals—1 Year	12	73	330	4.5	4	6	38	6.3	0	4	24	3
NFL Totals—4 Years	51	720	2989	4.2	25	100	899	9.0	4	29	174	21
Pro Totals—5 Years	63	793	3319	4.2	29	106	937	8.8	4	33	198	24

Additional USFL statistics: Returned three kickoffs for 20 yards and recovered four fumbles, 1984.
Additional NFL statistics: Recovered three fumbles, 1985; recovered one fumble, 1986 through 1988.
Played in AFC Championship Game following 1986 and 1987 seasons.
Played in Pro Bowl (NFL All-Star Game) following 1985 and 1987 seasons.

MILTON JEROME MACK
Cornerback—New Orleans Saints
Born September 20, 1963, at Jackson, Miss.
Height, 5.11. Weight, 182.
High School—Jackson, Miss., Callaway.
Attended Alcorn State University.
Cousin of Cedric Mack, cornerback with Phoenix Cardinals.

Selected by New Orleans in 5th round (123rd player selected) of 1987 NFL draft.
Signed by New Orleans Saints, July 24, 1987.
Crossed picket line during players' strike, October 14, 1987.

			—INTERCEPTIONS—		
Year Club	G.	No.	Yds.	Avg.	TD.
1987—New Orleans NFL	13	4	32	8.0	0
1988—New Orleans NFL	14	1	19	19.0	0
Pro Totals—2 Years	27	5	51	10.2	0

KYLE ERICKSON MACKEY
Quarterback—New York Jets

Born March 2, 1962, at Alpine, Tex.
Height, 6.03. Weight, 220.
High School—Alpine, Tex.
Attended East Texas State University.
Son of Dee Mackey, tight end with San Francisco 49ers, Baltimore Colts
and New York Jets, 1960 through 1965.

Selected by Washington in 11th round (215th player selected) of 1984 USFL draft.
Selected by St. Louis in 11th round (296th player selected) of 1984 NFL draft.
Signed by St. Louis Cardinals, July 16, 1984.
Released by St. Louis Cardinals, August 26, 1985; signed as free agent by Philadelphia Eagles, March 10, 1986.
Released by Philadelphia Eagles, August 19, 1986; re-signed by Eagles, December 8, 1986.
Released by Philadelphia Eagles, April 15, 1987; signed as free agent by New Orleans Saints, May 7, 1987.
Released by New Orleans Saints, August 3, 1987; signed as free agent replacement player by Miami Dolphins, September 23, 1987.
On injured reserve with mouth injury, October 20 through November 2, 1987.
Released by Miami Dolphins, November 3, 1987; signed as free agent by New York Jets, April 29, 1988.
On injured reserve with shoulder injury, August 29 through entire 1988 season.
Active for 16 games with St. Louis Cardinals in 1984; did not play.
Active for 2 games with Philadelphia Eagles in 1986; did not play.

		—PASSING—							—RUSHING—				—TOTAL—		
Year Club	G.	Att.	Cmp.	Pct.	Gain	T.P.	P.I.	Avg.	Att.	Yds.	Avg.	TD.	TD.	Pts.	F.
1987—Miami NFL	3	109	57	52.3	604	3	5	5.54	17	98	5.8	2	2	12	3

Quarterback Rating Points: 1987 (58.8).
Additional pro statistics: Fumbled three times for minus six yards, 1987.

CALVIN MAGEE
Tight End—Houston Oilers

Born April 23, 1963, at New Orleans, La.
Height, 6.03. Weight, 255.
High School—New Orleans, La., Booker T. Washington.
Attended Southern University.

Selected by Portland in 1985 USFL territorial draft.
Signed as free agent by Tampa Bay Buccaneers, May 9, 1985.
On injured reserve with knee injury, November 30 through remainder of 1988 season.
Granted unconditional free agency, February 1, 1989; signed by Houston Oilers, March 20, 1989.

		—PASS RECEIVING—			
Year Club	G.	P.C.	Yds.	Avg.	TD.
1985—Tampa Bay NFL	16	26	288	11.1	3
1986—Tampa Bay NFL	16	45	564	12.5	5
1987—Tampa Bay NFL	11	34	424	12.5	3
1988—Tampa Bay NFL	13	9	103	11.4	0
Pro Totals—4 Years	56	114	1379	12.1	11

Additional pro statistics: Returned two kickoffs for 20 yards, 1985; fumbled once, 1985 and 1986; returned two kickoffs for 21 yards, 1986.

DONALD JAMES MAGGS
(Don)
Offensive Tackle-Guard—Houston Oilers

Born November 1, 1961, at Youngstown, O.
Height, 6.05. Weight, 285.
High School—Youngstown, O., Cardinal Mooney.
Attended Tulane University.

Selected by Pittsburgh in 2nd round (28th player selected) of 1984 USFL draft.
Signed by Pittsburgh Maulers, January 10, 1984.
On developmental squad, March 3 through March 17, 1984; activated, March 18, 1984.
Selected by Houston in 2nd round (29th player selected) of 1984 NFL supplemental draft.
Franchise disbanded, October 25, 1984.
Selected by New Jersey Generals in USFL dispersal draft, December 6, 1984.
Granted free agency when USFL suspended operations, August 7, 1986; signed by Houston Oilers, August 13, 1986.
Granted roster exemption, August 13 through August 24, 1986; activated, August 25, 1986.
On injured reserve with knee injury, August 31 through December 18, 1987; activated, December 19, 1987.
Active for 1 game with Houston Oilers in 1987; did not play.
Pittsburgh USFL, 1984; New Jersey USFL, 1985; Houston NFL, 1986 through 1988.
Games: 1984 (16), 1985 (18), 1986 (14), 1988 (16). Total USFL—34. Total NFL—30. Total Pro—64.
Pro statistics: Recovered one fumble, 1984.

—DID YOU KNOW—

That the Buffalo Bills had zero net yards rushing in a 24-3 loss to the Chicago Bears last October 2? Thurman Thomas rushed for 12 yards, Jamie Mueller eight and Jim Kelly four. That total was wiped out when Ronnie Harmon lost 24 yards on a sweep.

DONALD VINCENT MAJKOWSKI
(Name pronounced Muh-KOW-skee.)
(Don)
Quarterback—Green Bay Packers
Born February 25, 1964, at Buffalo, N.Y.
Height, 6.02. Weight, 197.
High Schools—Depew, N.Y.; and Fork Union, Vir., Military Academy.
Received degree in sports management from University of Virginia in 1987.
Grandson of Edward Majkowski, minor league pitcher, 1931 and 1940.

Selected by Green Bay in 10th round (255th player selected) of 1987 NFL draft.
Signed by Green Bay Packers, July 25, 1987.

| | | | | PASSING | | | | | | RUSHING | | | | TOTAL | |
Year Club	G.	Att.	Cmp.	Pct.	Gain	T.P.	P.I.	Avg.	Att.	Yds.	Avg.	TD.	TD.	Pts.	F.
1987—Green Bay NFL	7	127	55	43.3	875	5	3	6.89	15	127	8.5	0	0	0	5
1988—Green Bay NFL	13	336	178	53.0	2119	9	11	6.31	47	225	4.8	1	1	6	8
Pro Totals—2 Years	20	463	233	50.3	2994	14	14	6.47	62	352	5.7	1	1	6	13

Quarterback Rating Points: 1987 (70.2), 1988 (67.8). Total—68.5.
Additional pro statistics: Recovered three fumbles, 1988.

RICK LEROY MALLORY
Guard—Tampa Bay Buccaneers
Born October 21, 1960, at Seattle, Wash.
Height, 6.02. Weight, 265.
High School—Renton, Wash., Lindbergh.
Attended University of Washington.

Selected by Arizona in 11th round (221st player selected) of 1984 USFL draft.
Selected by Tampa Bay in 9th round (225th player selected) of 1984 NFL draft.
Signed by Tampa Bay Buccaneers, June 21, 1984.
On injured reserve with ankle injury, August 27 through entire 1984 season.
Tampa Bay NFL, 1985 through 1988.
Games: 1985 (13), 1986 (16), 1987 (12), 1988 (16). Total—57.
Pro statistics: Caught one pass for nine yards, 1986.

MARK M. MALONE
Quarterback—San Diego Chargers
Born November 22, 1958, at El Cajon, Calif.
Height, 6.04. Weight, 222.
High School—El Cajon, Calif., Valley.
Attended Arizona State University.

Selected by Pittsburgh in 1st round (28th player selected) of 1980 NFL draft.
On physically unable to perform/active with knee injury, July 29 through August 23, 1982.
On reserve, August 24 through December 13, 1982; activated, December 14, 1982.
Traded by Pittsburgh Steelers to San Diego Chargers for 8th round pick in 1988 draft and conditional future considerations, April 12, 1988.
Active for 3 games with Pittsburgh Steelers in 1982; did not play.

| | | | | PASSING | | | | | | RUSHING | | | | TOTAL | |
Year Club	G.	Att.	Cmp.	Pct.	Gain	T.P.	P.I.	Avg.	Att.	Yds.	Avg.	TD.	TD.	Pts.	F.
1980—Pittsburgh NFL	1				None						None		0	0	0
1981—Pittsburgh NFL	8	88	45	51.1	553	3	5	6.28	16	68	4.3	2	3	18	2
1983—Pittsburgh NFL	2	20	9	45.0	124	1	2	6.20			None		0	0	0
1984—Pittsburgh NFL	13	272	147	54.0	2137	16	17	7.86	25	42	1.7	3	3	18	4
1985—Pittsburgh NFL	10	233	117	50.2	1428	13	7	6.13	15	80	5.3	1	1	6	3
1986—Pittsburgh NFL	14	425	216	50.8	2444	15	18	5.75	31	107	3.5	5	5	30	7
1987—Pittsburgh NFL	12	336	156	46.4	1896	6	19	5.64	34	162	4.8	3	3	18	10
1988—San Diego NFL	12	272	147	54.0	1580	6	13	5.81	37	169	4.6	4	4	24	6
Pro Totals—9 Years	72	1646	837	50.9	10162	60	81	6.17	158	628	4.0	18	19	114	32

Quarterback Rating Points: 1981 (58.4), 1983 (42.5), 1984 (73.4), 1985 (75.5), 1986 (62.5), 1987 (46.7), 1988 (58.8). Total—61.8.
Additional pro statistics: Caught one pass for 90 yards and a touchdown and returned one kickoff for three yards, 1981; recovered one fumble, 1983; recovered two fumbles, 1984; recovered three fumbles and fumbled three times for minus five yards, 1985; recovered one fumble and fumbled seven times for minus eight yards, 1986; recovered five fumbles and fumbled 10 times for minus three yards, 1987; recovered one fumble and fumbled six times for minus two yards, 1988.
Played in AFC Championship Game following 1984 season.

CHRIS SCOTT MANDEVILLE
Safety—Washington Redskins
Born February 1, 1965, at Santa Barbara, Calif.
Height, 6.01. Weight, 213.
High School—Irvine, Calif.
Attended University of California at Davis.

Signed as free agent by Green Bay Packers, May 18, 1987.
On injured reserve with thigh injury, November 17 through December 25, 1987; activated, December 26, 1987.
Released by Green Bay Packers, August 30, 1988; re-signed by Packers, December 8, 1988.
Granted unconditional free agency, February 1, 1989; signed by Washington Redskins, April 1, 1989.

Green Bay NFL, 1987 and 1988.
Games: 1987 (4), 1988 (2). Total—6.

WILLIAM H. MANDLEY
(Pete)
Wide Receiver-Punt Returner—Detroit Lions
Born July 29, 1961, at Mesa, Ariz.
Height, 5.10. Weight, 191.
High School—Mesa, Ariz., Westwood.
Attended Northern Arizona University.

Selected by Arizona in 1984 USFL territorial draft.
Selected by Detroit in 2nd round (47th player selected) of 1984 NFL draft.
Signed by Detroit Lions, July 10, 1984.

		PASS RECEIVING			-PUNT RETURNS-				—KICKOFF RET.—				—TOTAL—		
Year Club	G.	P.C.	Yds.	Avg.	TD.	No.	Yds.	Avg.	TD.	No.	Yds.	Avg.	TD.	TD.	Pts.	F.
1984—Detroit NFL..............	15	3	38	12.7	0	2	0	0.0	0	22	390	17.7	0	0	0	2
1985—Detroit NFL..............	16	18	316	17.6	0	38	403	10.6	1	6	152	25.3	0	1	6	3
1986—Detroit NFL..............	16	7	106	15.1	0	43	420	9.8	1	2	37	18.5	0	1	6	3
1987—Detroit NFL..............	12	58	720	12.4	7	23	250	10.9	0		None			7	42	0
1988—Detroit NFL..............	15	44	617	14.0	4	37	287	7.8	0		None			5	30	3
Pro Totals—5 Years.......	74	130	1797	13.8	11	143	1360	9.5	2	30	579	19.3	0	14	84	11

Additional pro statistics: Recovered two fumbles, 1984 and 1985; recovered one fumble, 1986 and 1987; rushed once for three yards, 1987; rushed six times for 44 yards and a touchdown and recovered one fumble for minus two yards, 1988.

DEXTER MANLEY
Defensive End—Washington Redskins
Born February 2, 1959, at Houston, Tex.
Height, 6.03. Weight, 257.
High School—Houston, Tex., Yates.
Attended Oklahoma State University.
Cousin of Eric Dickerson, running back with Indianapolis Colts.

Named to THE SPORTING NEWS NFL All-Star Team, 1986.
Selected by Washington in 5th round (119th player selected) of 1981 NFL draft.
Granted free agency, February 1, 1986; re-signed by Redskins, August 27, 1986.
Granted roster exemption, August 27 through September 4, 1986; activated, Septmber 5, 1986.
On non-football injury/reserve with drug problem, July 28 through August 28, 1988; activated, August 29, 1988.
Washington NFL, 1981 through 1988.
Games: 1981 (16), 1982 (9), 1983 (16), 1984 (15), 1985 (16), 1986 (16), 1987 (11), 1988 (16). Total—115.
Pro statistics: Intercepted one pass for minus two yards and recovered three fumbles for three yards, 1982; intercepted one pass for one yard, 1983; recovered one fumble, 1984; recovered one fumble for 26 yards and a touchdown, 1986.
Played in NFC Championship Game following 1982, 1983, 1986 and 1987 seasons.
Played in NFL Championship Game following 1982, 1983 and 1987 seasons.
Played in Pro Bowl (NFL All-Star Game) following 1986 season.

CHARLES MANN
Defensive End—Washington Redskins
Born April 12, 1961, at Sacramento, Calif.
Height, 6.06. Weight, 270.
High School—Sacramento, Calif., Valley.
Attended University of Nevada at Reno.

Selected by Oakland in 18th round (210th player selected) of 1983 USFL draft.
Selected by Washington in 3rd round (84th player selected) of 1983 NFL draft.
Signed by Washington Redskins, May 9, 1983.
Washington NFL, 1983 through 1988.
Games: 1983 (16), 1984 (16), 1985 (16), 1986 (15), 1987 (12), 1988 (14). Total—89.
Pro statistics: Credited with one safety, 1983; recovered one fumble, 1984, 1985 and 1987.
Played in NFC Championship Game following 1983, 1986 and 1987 seasons.
Played in NFL Championship Game following 1983 and 1987 seasons.
Played in Pro Bowl (NFL All-Star Game) following 1987 and 1988 seasons.

TIM MANOA
Fullback—Cleveland Browns
Born September 9, 1964, at Tonga.
Height, 6.01. Weight, 227.
High Schools—Kahuka, Haw.; and Wexford, Pa., North Allegheny.
Attended Penn State University.

Selected by Cleveland in 3rd round (80th player selected) of 1987 NFL draft.
Signed by Cleveland Browns, July 26, 1987.

		——RUSHING——				PASS RECEIVING				—TOTAL—		
Year Club	G.	Att.	Yds.	Avg.	TD.	P.C.	Yds.	Avg.	TD.	TD.	Pts.	F.
1987—Cleveland NFL............................	12	23	116	5.0	0	1	8	8.0	0	0	0	1
1988—Cleveland NFL............................	16	99	389	3.9	2	10	54	5.4	0	2	12	4
Pro Totals—2 Years..................................	28	122	505	4.1	2	11	62	5.6	0	2	12	5

Additional pro statistics: Returned two kickoffs for 14 yards and recovered one fumble, 1987.
Played in AFC Championship Game following 1987 season.

LIONEL MANUEL JR.
Wide Receiver—New York Giants
Born April 13, 1962, at Rancho Cucamonga, Calif.
Height, 5.11. Weight, 180.
High School—La Puente, Calif., Bassett.
Attended Citrus College and University of The Pacific.

Selected by Los Angeles in 1984 USFL territorial draft.
Selected by New York Giants in 7th round (171st player selected) of 1984 NFL draft.
Signed by New York Giants, June 4, 1984.
On injured reserve with pulled hamstring, November 30 through December 27, 1985; activated, December 28, 1985.
On injured reserve with knee injury, September 29, 1986 through January 2, 1987; activated, January 3, 1987.
On injured reserve with thumb injury, September 21 through October 23, 1987; activated, October 24, 1987.

| | | —PASS RECEIVING— | | | | —PUNT RETURNS— | | | | —TOTAL— | | |
Year Club	G.	P.C.	Yds.	Avg.	TD.	No.	Yds.	Avg.	TD.	TD.	Pts.	F.
1984—New York Giants NFL	16	33	619	18.8	4	8	62	7.8	0	4	24	2
1985—New York Giants NFL	12	49	859	17.5	5		None			5	30	1
1986—New York Giants NFL	4	11	181	16.5	3	3	22	7.3	0	3	18	0
1987—New York Giants NFL	12	30	545	18.2	6		None			6	36	1
1988—New York Giants NFL	16	65	1029	15.8	4		None			4	24	1
Pro Totals—5 Years	60	188	3233	17.2	22	11	84	7.6	0	22	132	5

Additional pro statistics: Rushed three times for two yards, 1984; rushed once for 25 yards, 1986; rushed once for minus 10 yards, 1987; rushed four times for 27 yards and recovered one fumble, 1988.
Played in NFC Championship Game following 1986 season.
Played in NFL Championship Game following 1986 season.

GREGORY MANUSKY
(Greg)
Linebacker—Washington Redskins
Born August 12, 1966, at Wilkes-Barre, Pa.
Height, 6.01. Weight, 242.
High School—Dallas, Pa.
Received bachelor of arts degree in education from Colgate University in 1988.

Signed as free agent by Washington Redskins, May 3, 1988.
On injured reserve with thigh injury, August 29 through November 2, 1988; activated after clearing procedural waivers, November 4, 1988.
Washington NFL, 1988.
Games: 1988 (7).

DANIEL CONSTANTINE MARINO JR.
(Dan)
Quarterback—Miami Dolphins
Born September 15, 1961, at Pittsburgh, Pa.
Height, 6.04. Weight, 222.
High School—Pittsburgh, Pa., Central Catholic.
Received bachelor of arts degree in communications from University of Pittsburgh.
Brother-in-law of Bill Maas, nose tackle with Kansas City Chiefs.

Named THE SPORTING NEWS NFL Player of the Year, 1984.
Named to THE SPORTING NEWS NFL All-Star Team, 1984 through 1986.
Named THE SPORTING NEWS NFL Rookie of the Year, 1983.
Named as quarterback on THE SPORTING NEWS College All-America Team, 1981.
Established NFL records for completion percentage by rookie (58.45), 1983; most touchdowns passing, season (48), 1984; most passing yards gained, season (5,084), 1984; most passes completed, season (378), 1984; most games, 300 yards passing, season (9), 1984; most games, 400 yards passing, season (4), 1984; most passes attempted, season (623), 1986; most 400-yard passing games, career (9); most 4,000-yard seasons (4).
Tied NFL record for most consecutive games, 400 yards passing (2), 1984; most consecutive seasons leading league in completions (3).
Led NFL quarterbacks in passing with 108.9 points in 1984.
Selected by Los Angeles in 1st round (1st player selected) of 1983 USFL draft.
Selected by Miami in 1st round (27th player selected) of 1983 NFL draft.
Signed by Miami Dolphins, July 9, 1983.
Left Miami Dolphins camp voluntarily, July 25 through August 31, 1985.
Reported and granted roster exemption, September 1 through September 4, 1985; activated, September 5, 1985.
Selected by Kansas City Royals' organization in 4th round of free-agent draft, June 5, 1979.

| | | —————PASSING————— | | | | | | | ——RUSHING—— | | | | —TOTAL— | | |
Year Club	G.	Att.	Cmp.	Pct.	Gain	T.P.	P.I.	Avg.	Att.	Yds.	Avg.	TD.	TD.	Pts.	F.
1983—Miami NFL	11	296	173	58.4	2210	20	6	7.47	28	45	1.6	2	2	12	5
1984—Miami NFL	16	∗564	∗362	64.2	∗5084	∗48	17	∗9.01	28	—7	—0.3	0	0	0	6
1985—Miami NFL	16	567	∗336	59.3	∗4137	∗30	21	7.30	26	—24	—0.9	0	0	0	9
1986—Miami NFL	16	∗623	∗378	60.7	∗4746	∗44	23	7.62	12	—3	—0.3	0	0	0	8
1987—Miami NFL	12	444	263	59.2	3245	26	13	7.31	12	—5	—0.4	1	1	6	5
1988—Miami NFL	16	∗606	∗354	58.4	∗4434	28	23	7.32	20	—17	—0.9	0	0	0	10
Pro Totals—6 Years	87	3100	1866	60.2	23856	196	103	7.70	126	—11	—0.1	3	3	18	43

Quarterback Rating Points: 1983 (96.0), 1984 (108.9), 1985 (84.1), 1986 (92.5), 1987 (89.2), 1988 (80.8). Total—91.6.

Additional pro statistics: Recovered two fumbles, 1983; recovered two fumbles and fumbled six times for minus three yards, 1984; recovered two fumbles and fumbled nine times for minus four yards, 1985; recovered four fumbles and fumbled eight times for minus 12 yards, 1986; recovered four fumbles and fumbled five times for minus 25 yards, 1987; recovered eight fumbles and fumbled 10 times for minus 31 yards, 1988.

Played in AFC Championship Game following 1984 and 1985 seasons.
Played in NFL Championship Game following 1984 season.
Played in Pro Bowl (NFL All-Star Game) following 1984 season.
Named to play in Pro Bowl following 1983 season; replaced due to injury by Bill Kenney.
Named to play in Pro Bowl following 1985 season; replaced due to injury by Ken O'Brien.
Named to play in Pro Bowl following 1986 season; replaced due to injury by Boomer Esiason.
Named to play in Pro Bowl following 1987 season; replaced due to injury by Jim Kelly.

FRED D. MARION
Safety—New England Patriots

Born January 2, 1959, at Gainesville, Fla.
Height, 6.02. Weight, 191.
High School—Gainesville, Fla., Buchholz.
Attended University of Miami (Fla.).
Brother of Frank Marion, linebacker with Memphis Southmen (WFL) and New York Giants,
1975 and 1977 through 1983.

Selected by New England in 5th round (112th player selected) of 1982 NFL draft.

| | | | —INTERCEPTIONS— | | |
Year	Club	G.	No.	Yds.	Avg.	TD.
1982—New England NFL		9		None		
1983—New England NFL		16	2	4	2.0	0
1984—New England NFL		16	2	39	19.5	0
1985—New England NFL		16	7	*189	27.0	0
1986—New England NFL		16	2	56	28.0	1
1987—New England NFL		12	4	53	13.3	0
1988—New England NFL		16	4	47	11.8	0
Pro Totals—7 Years		101	21	388	18.5	1

Additional pro statistics: Recovered one fumble, 1982, 1984 and 1987; recovered three fumbles for nine yards, 1985; returned one punt for 12 yards, 1986; returned one punt for no yards, 1987; recovered two fumbles for 16 yards, 1988.

Played in AFC Championship Game following 1985 season.
Played in NFL Championship Game following 1985 season.
Played in Pro Bowl (NFL All-Star Game) following 1985 season.

JEFFREY STUART MARKLAND
(Jeff)
Tight End—Miami Dolphins

Born November 16, 1965, at Los Angeles, Calif.
Height, 6.03. Weight, 245.
High School—Burbank, Calif., John Burroughs.
Attended Los Angeles Pierce Junior College and received
bachelor of arts degree in communications from University of Illinois in 1988.

Signed as free agent by Pittsburgh Steelers, April 26, 1988.
On injured reserve with knee injury, August 23 through December 15, 1988; activated, December 16, 1988.
Granted unconditional free agency, February 1, 1989; signed by Miami Dolphins, April 1, 1989.
Pittsburgh NFL, 1988.
Games: 1988 (1).

DOUGLAS CHARLES MARRONE
(Doug)
Offensive Lineman—Dallas Cowboys

Born July 25, 1964, at Bronx, N.Y.
Height, 6.05. Weight, 295.
High School—Bronx, N.Y., Herbert H. Lehman.
Attended Syracuse University.

Selected by New Jersey in 1986 USFL territorial draft.
Selected by Los Angeles Raiders in 6th round (164th player selected) of 1986 NFL draft.
Signed by Los Angeles Raiders, July 14, 1986.
Released by Los Angeles Raiders, August 19, 1986; signed as free agent by Miami Dolphins for 1987, October 16, 1986.
Released by Miami Dolphins, September 7, 1987; re-signed by Dolphins, September 8, 1987.
On injured reserve with thigh injury, September 19 through December 11, 1987; activated, December 12, 1987.
Left Miami Dolphins camp voluntarily, August 16, 1988.
Released by Miami Dolphins, August 24, 1988; signed as free agent by Dallas Cowboys, February 3, 1989.
Miami NFL, 1987.
Games: 1987 (4).

—DID YOU KNOW—

That Ray Criswell, then with Tampa Bay, was the only qualifying punter in 1988 who did not have any touchbacks?

LEONARD ALLEN MARSHALL
Defensive End—New York Giants
Born October 22, 1961, at Franklin, La.
Height, 6.03. Weight, 285.
High School—Franklin, La.
Attended Louisiana State University.
Related to Eddie Robinson, head coach at Grambling State University; Ernie Ladd, defensive lineman with San Diego Chargers, Houston Oilers and Kansas City Chiefs, 1961 through 1968; and Warren Wells, wide receiver with Detroit Lions and Oakland Raiders, 1964 and 1967 through 1970.
Selected by Tampa Bay in 10th round (109th player selected) of 1983 USFL draft.
Selected by New York Giants in 2nd round (37th player selected) of 1983 NFL draft.
Signed by New York Giants, June 13, 1983.
On injured reserve with dislocated wrist, December 15 through remainder of 1987 season.
New York Giants NFL, 1983 through 1988.
Games: 1983 (14), 1984 (16), 1985 (16), 1986 (16), 1987 (10), 1988 (15). Total—87.
Pro statistics: Credited with one safety, 1983; intercepted one pass for three yards, 1985; intercepted one pass for no yards and recovered three fumbles, 1986.
Played in NFC Championship Game following 1986 season.
Played in NFL Championship Game following 1986 season.
Played in Pro Bowl (NFL All-Star Game) following 1985 and 1986 seasons.

WARREN KEITH MARSHALL
Running Back—Phoenix Cardinals
Born July 24, 1964, at High Point, N.C.
Height, 6.00. Weight, 216.
High School—High Point, N.C., T. Wingate Andrews.
Received bachelor of science degree in education from James Madison University in 1987.
Selected by Denver in 6th round (167th player selected) of 1987 NFL draft.
Signed by Denver Broncos, July 21, 1987.
On injured reserve with eye injury, September 1 through November 27, 1987; activated, November 28, 1987.
On injured reserve with knee injury, January 16, 1988 through remainder of 1987 season playoffs.
Released by Denver Broncos, August 30, 1988; signed as free agent by Phoenix Cardinals, February 28, 1989.
Denver NFL, 1987.
Games: 1987 (1).

WILBER BUDDYHIA MARSHALL
Linebacker—Washington Redskins
Born April 18, 1962, at Titusville, Fla.
Height, 6.01. Weight, 230.
High School—Titusville, Fla., Astronaut.
Attended University of Florida.
Named to THE SPORTING NEWS NFL All-Star Team, 1986.
Selected by Tampa Bay in 1984 USFL territorial draft.
Selected by Chicago in 1st round (11th player selected) of 1984 NFL draft.
Signed by Chicago Bears, June 19, 1984.
Granted free agency, February 1, 1988; signed by Washington Redskins, March 15, 1988 when Chicago Bears elected not to match offer; Chicago received 1st round picks in 1988 and 1989 drafts in compensation.

Year Club	G.	No.	Yds.	Avg.	TD.
			INTERCEPTIONS		
1984—Chicago NFL	15		None		
1985—Chicago NFL	16	4	23	5.8	0
1986—Chicago NFL	16	5	68	13.6	1
1987—Chicago NFL	12		None		
1988—Washington NFL	16	3	61	20.3	0
Pro Totals—5 Years	75	12	152	12.7	1

Additional pro statistics: Ran two yards with lateral on kickoff return and recovered one fumble for eight yards, 1985; recovered three fumbles for 12 yards and a touchdown, 1986; ran once for one yard and recovered one fumble, 1987.
Played in NFC Championship Game following 1984 and 1985 seasons.
Played in NFL Championship Game following 1985 season.
Played in Pro Bowl (NFL All-Star Team) following 1986 and 1987 seasons.

CHARLES M. MARTIN
Nose Tackle—Atlanta Falcons
Born August 31, 1959, at Canton, Ga.
Height, 6.04. Weight, 280.
High School—Canton, Ga., Cherokee.
Attended Livingston University.
Selected by Birmingham in 15th round (173rd player selected) of 1983 USFL draft.
Signed by Birmingham Stallions, January 22, 1983.
On developmental squad, March 26 through April 9, 1983; activated, April 10, 1983.
On developmental squad, June 17 through July 1, 1983; activated, July 2, 1983.
Released by Birmingham Stallions, February 13, 1984; signed as free agent by Green Bay Packers, July 7, 1984.
On suspended list, December 2 through December 14, 1986; activated, December 15, 1986.
Released by Green Bay Packers, September 22, 1987; awarded on waivers to Houston Oilers, September 23, 1987.

Crossed picket line during players' strike, October 8, 1987.
Released by Houston Oilers, August 29, 1988; awarded on waivers to Atlanta Falcons, August 31, 1988.
On developmental squad for 4 games with Birmingham Stallions in 1983.
Birmingham USFL, 1983; Green Bay NFL, 1984 through 1986; Green Bay (2)-Houston (12) NFL, 1987; Atlanta NFL, 1988.
Games: 1983 (14), 1984 (16), 1985 (16), 1986 (14), 1987 (14), 1988 (16). Total NFL—76. Total Pro—90.
USFL statistics: Recovered one fumble, 1983.
NFL statistics: Recovered one fumble, 1985 through 1987.

CHRISTOPHER MARTIN
(Chris)
Linebacker—Kansas City Chiefs
Born December 19, 1960, at Huntsville, Ala.
Height, 6.02. Weight, 231.
High School—Huntsville, Ala., J. O. Johnson.
Attended Auburn University.

Selected by Birmingham in 1983 USFL territorial draft.
Signed as free agent by New Orleans Saints, May 5, 1983.
On injured reserve with ankle injury, December 17 through remainder of 1983 season.
Released by New Orleans Saints, August 27, 1984; awarded on waivers to Minnesota Vikings, August 28, 1984.
Released by Minnesota Vikings, November 2, 1988; signed as free agent by Kansas City Chiefs, November 9, 1988.
New Orleans NFL, 1983; Minnesota NFL, 1984 through 1987; Minnesota (9)-Kansas City (6) NFL, 1988.
Games: 1983 (15), 1984 (16), 1985 (12), 1986 (16), 1987 (12), 1988 (15). Total—86.
Pro statistics: Recovered one fumble for eight yards and a touchdown, 1984; recovered one fumble, 1986 and 1987; recovered one fumble in end zone for a touchdown, 1988.
Played in NFC Championship Game following 1987 season.

DOUG MARTIN
Defensive End—Minnesota Vikings
Born May 22, 1957, at Fairfield, Calif.
Height, 6.03. Weight, 258.
High School—Fairfield, Calif., Armijo.
Attended University of Washington.
Brother of George Martin, defensive end with New York Giants, 1975 through 1988.

Selected by Minnesota in 1st round (9th player selected) of 1980 NFL draft.
Placed on did not report list, August 15, 1980; activated, September 13, 1980.
Granted free agency, February 1, 1984.
Placed on did not report list, August 14 through August 17, 1984; re-signed by Vikings, August 18, 1984.
Granted roster exemption, August 21 through August 31, 1984; activated, September 1, 1984.
Granted free agency, February 1, 1988; re-signed by Vikings, September 10, 1988.
Granted roster exemptions, September 13 through September 23, 1988; activated, September 24, 1988.
On injured reserve with knee injury, December 6 through remainder of 1988 season.
Minnesota NFL, 1980 through 1988.
Games: 1980 (11), 1981 (16), 1982 (9), 1983 (16), 1984 (13), 1985 (16), 1986 (15), 1987 (12), 1988 (11). Total—119.
Pro statistics: Recovered one fumble, 1981; intercepted one pass for no yards, 1982; recovered two fumbles, 1983 and 1986; recovered two fumbles for 29 yards, 1985.
Played in NFC Championship Game following 1987 season.

ERIC MARTIN
Wide Receiver—New Orleans Saints
Born November 8, 1961, at Van Vleck, Tex.
Height, 6.01. Weight, 207.
High School—Van Vleck, Tex.
Attended Louisiana State University.

Named as wide receiver on THE SPORTING NEWS College All-America Team, 1983.
Selected by Portland in 1985 USFL territorial draft.
Selected by New Orleans in 7th round (179th player selected) of 1985 NFL draft.
Signed by New Orleans Saints, June 21, 1985.
Crossed picket line during players' strike, September 30, 1987.

| | | PASS RECEIVING | | | -PUNT RETURNS- | | | —KICKOFF RET.— | | | —TOTAL— | | |
Year Club	G.	P.C.	Yds.	Avg.	TD.	No.	Yds.	Avg.	TD.	No.	Yds.	Avg.	TD.	TD.	Pts.	F.
1985—New Orleans NFL	16	35	522	14.9	4	8	53	6.6	0	15	384	25.6	0	4	24	1
1986—New Orleans NFL	16	37	675	18.2	5	24	227	9.5	0	3	64	21.3	0	5	30	5
1987—New Orleans NFL	15	44	778	17.7	7	14	88	6.3	0	1	15	15.0	0	7	42	3
1988—New Orleans NFL	16	85	1083	12.7	7		None			3	32	10.7	0	7	42	2
Pro Totals—4 Years	63	201	3058	15.2	23	46	368	8.0	0	22	495	22.5	0	23	138	11

Additional pro statistics: Rushed twice for minus one yard, 1985; recovered one fumble, 1987; rushed twice for 12 yards, 1988.
Played in Pro Bowl (NFL All-Star Game) following 1988 season.

KELVIN BRIAN MARTIN
Wide Receiver—Dallas Cowboys
Born May 14, 1965, at San Diego, Calif.
Height, 5.09. Weight, 163.
High School—Jacksonville, Fla., Ribault.
Received bachelor of arts degree in speech communication from Boston College in 1987.

Named as wide receiver on THE SPORTING NEWS College All-America Team, 1985.
Selected by Dallas in 4th round (95th player selected) of 1987 NFL draft.
Signed by Dallas Cowboys, July 13, 1987.
On injured reserve with leg injury, September 15 through November 13, 1987; activated, November 14, 1987.
Crossed picket line during players' strike, October 14, 1987.

| | | PASS RECEIVING | | | | –PUNT RETURNS– | | | | —KICKOFF RET.— | | | | —TOTAL— | | |
Year Club	G.	P.C.	Yds.	Avg.	TD.	No.	Yds.	Avg.	TD.	No.	Yds.	Avg.	TD.	TD.	Pts.	F.
1987—Dallas NFL	7	5	103	20.6	0	22	216	9.8	0	12	237	19.8	0	0	0	1
1988—Dallas NFL	16	49	622	12.7	3	44	360	8.2	0	12	210	17.5	0	3	18	2
Pro Totals—2 Years	23	54	725	13.4	3	66	576	8.7	0	24	447	18.6	0	3	18	3

Additional pro statistics: Rushed four times for minus four yards, 1988.

MICHAEL MARTIN
(Mike)
Wide Receiver—Cincinnati Bengals
Born November 18, 1960, at Washington, D.C.
Height, 5.10. Weight, 186.
High School—Washington, D.C., Eastern.
Attended University of Illinois.

Selected by Chicago in 1983 USFL territorial draft.
Selected by Cincinnati in 8th round (221st player selected) of 1983 NFL draft.
Signed by Cincinnati Bengals, May 19, 1983.
On injured reserve with broken fibula, November 17 through remainder of 1983 season.
On injured reserve with hamstring injury, October 13 through December 18, 1986; activated, December 19, 1986.
On injured reserve with torn Achilles tendon, October 10 through remainder of 1988 season.

| | | PASS RECEIVING | | | | –PUNT RETURNS– | | | | —KICKOFF RET.— | | | | —TOTAL— | | |
Year Club	G.	P.C.	Yds.	Avg.	TD.	No.	Yds.	Avg.	TD.	No.	Yds.	Avg.	TD.	TD.	Pts.	F.
1983—Cincinnati NFL	10	2	22	11.0	0	23	227	9.9	0	1	19	19.0	0	0	0	2
1984—Cincinnati NFL	15	11	164	14.9	0	24	376	*15.7	0	19	386	20.3	0	0	0	4
1985—Cincinnati NFL	16	14	187	13.4	0	32	268	8.4	0	48	1104	23.0	0	0	0	4
1986—Cincinnati NFL	7	3	68	22.7	0	13	96	7.4	0	4	83	20.8	0	0	0	0
1987—Cincinnati NFL	12	20	394	19.7	3	28	277	9.9	0	3	51	17.0	0	3	18	1
1988—Cincinnati NFL	4	2	22	11.0	1	5	30	6.0	0		None			1	6	0
Pro Totals—6 Years	64	52	857	16.5	4	125	1274	10.2	0	75	1643	21.9	0	4	24	11

Additional pro statistics: Rushed twice for 21 yards, 1983; rushed once for three yards and recovered two fumbles, 1984.

ROD MARTIN
Linebacker
Born April 7, 1954, at Welch, W. Va.
Height, 6.02. Weight, 225.
High School—Los Angeles, Calif., Hamilton.
Attended Los Angeles City College and University of Southern California.
Brother of Ricky Martin, wide receiver with Winnipeg Blue Bombers
and Pittsburgh Maulers, 1982 through 1984.

Named to THE SPORTING NEWS NFL All-Star Team, 1983.
Selected by Oakland in 12th round (317th player selected) of 1977 NFL draft.
Traded with defensive back Steve Jackson by Oakland Raiders to San Francisco 49ers for future considerations, August 30, 1977.
Released by San Francisco 49ers, September 14, 1977; signed as free agent by Oakland Raiders, November 7, 1977.
Franchise transferred to Los Angeles, May 7, 1982.
Granted unconditional free agency, February 1, 1989; released by Los Angeles Raiders, May 15, 1989.

| | —INTERCEPTIONS— | | | | | | —INTERCEPTIONS— | | | |
Year Club	G.	No.	Yds.	Avg.TD.	Year Club	G.	No.	Yds.	Avg.TD.
1977—Oakland NFL	1		None		1984—L.A. Raiders NFL	16	2	31	15.5	1
1978—Oakland NFL	15		None		1985—L.A. Raiders NFL	16	1	16	16.0	0
1979—Oakland NFL	16		None		1986—L.A. Raiders NFL	16	1	15	15.0	0
1980—Oakland NFL	16	2	15	7.5	0	1987—L.A. Raiders NFL	12		None	
1981—Oakland NFL	16	1	7	7.0	0	1988—L.A. Raiders NFL	16		None	
1982—L.A. Raiders NFL	9	3	60	20.0	*1	Pro Totals—12 Years	165	14	225	16.1	4
1983—L.A. Raiders NFL	16	4	81	20.3	*2					

Additional pro statistics: Recovered one fumble, 1979; recovered two fumbles for 42 yards and a touchdown, 1980; recovered three fumbles, 1981; returned one kickoff for no yards, 1983; recovered one fumble for 77 yards and a touchdown and credited with one safety, 1984; recovered three fumbles for three yards and fumbled once, 1985.
Played in AFC Championship Game following 1977, 1980 and 1983 seasons.
Played in NFL Championship Game following 1980 and 1983 seasons.
Played in Pro Bowl (NFL All-Star Team) following 1983 and 1984 seasons.

SAMMY MARTIN
Wide Receiver-Kick Returner—New England Patriots
Born August 21, 1965, at Gretna, La.
Height, 5.11. Weight, 175.
High School—New Orleans, La., De La Salle.
Attended Louisiana State University.

Selected by New England in 4th round (97th player selected) of 1988 NFL draft.
Signed by New England Patriots, July 17, 1988.
On non-football injury/active with hamstring injury, July 18 through July 31, 1988; passed physical, August 1, 1988.

Year Club	PASS RECEIVING				—KICKOFF RET.—				—TOTAL—		
	G.	P.C.	Yds.	Avg.	TD.	No.	Yds.	Avg.	TD.	TD.	Pts.	F.
1988—New England NFL	16	4	51	12.8	0	31	735	23.7	*1	1	6	0

TRACY MARTIN
Wide Receiver—Pittsburgh Steelers
Born December 4, 1964, at Minneapolis, Minn.
Height, 6.03. Weight, 205.
High School—Brooklyn Center, Minn.
Attended University of North Dakota.
Son of Bill Lordan, former drummer for Sly and The Family Stone, Jimi Hendrix and James Brown.
Selected by New York Jets in 6th round (161st player selected) of 1987 NFL draft.
Signed by New York Jets, July 24, 1987.
On injured reserve with quadricep injury, August 22 through entire 1988 season.
Granted unconditional free agency, February 1, 1989; signed by Pittsburgh Steelers, March 31, 1989.

KICKOFF RETURNS

Year Club	G.	No.	Yds.	Avg.	TD.
1987—New York Jets NFL	12	8	180	22.5	0

EUGENE RAYMOND MARVE
Linebacker—Tampa Bay Buccaneers
Born August 14, 1960, at Flint, Mich.
Height, 6.02. Weight, 240.
High School—Flint, Mich., Northern.
Attended Saginaw Valley State College.
Selected by Buffalo in 3rd round (59th player selected) of 1982 NFL draft.
On injured reserve with dislocated elbow, November 14 through remainder of 1987 season.
Traded by Buffalo Bills to Tampa Bay Buccaneers for 7th round pick in 1989 draft, June 13, 1988.
Buffalo NFL, 1982 through 1987; Tampa Bay NFL, 1988.
Games: 1982 (9), 1983 (16), 1984 (16), 1985 (14), 1986 (16), 1987 (5), 1988 (16). Total—92.
Pro statistics: Intercepted one pass for no yards, 1982; recovered one fumble, 1982 and 1985; recovered three fumbles, 1984; intercepted one pass for 29 yards, 1988.

LARRY DARNELL MASON
Running Back—Green Bay Packers
Born March 21, 1961, at Birmingham, Ala.
Height, 5.11. Weight, 205.
High School—McAlla, Ala., McAdory.
Attended University of Southern Mississippi and Troy State University.
Signed as free agent by Miami Dolphins, May 27, 1983.
Released by Miami Dolphins, August 16, 1983; signed by Jacksonville Bulls, October 7, 1983.
Granted free agency, August 1, 1985; signed as free agent by Cleveland Browns, July 17, 1987.
On injured reserve with hamstring injury, September 7 through September 15, 1987.
Released by Cleveland Browns, September 16, 1987; re-signed as replacement player by Browns, October 2, 1987.
Released by Cleveland Browns, October 27, 1987; signed as free agent by Green Bay Packers, July 21, 1988.
Released by Green Bay Packers, September 7, 1988; re-signed by Packers, September 14, 1988.

Year Club		——RUSHING——				PASS RECEIVING				—TOTAL—		
	G.	Att.	Yds.	Avg.	TD.	P.C.	Yds.	Avg.	TD.	TD.	Pts.	F.
1984—Jacksonville USFL	18	130	495	3.8	7	31	281	9.1	2	9	†56	5
1985—Jacksonville USFL	18	64	331	5.2	5	38	302	8.0	3	8	48	1
1987—Cleveland NFL	3	56	207	3.7	2	5	26	5.2	1	3	18	4
1988—Green Bay NFL	15	48	194	4.0	0	8	84	10.5	1	1	6	0
USFL Totals—2 Years	36	194	826	4.3	12	69	583	8.4	5	17	104	6
NFL Totals—2 Years	18	104	401	3.9	2	13	110	8.5	2	4	24	4
Pro Totals—5 Years	54	298	1227	4.1	14	82	693	8.5	7	21	128	10

†Includes one 2-point conversion.
Additional USFL statistics: Returned two kickoffs for 45 yards and recovered two fumbles for minue one yard, 1984; returned one kickoff for 15 yards, 1985.
Additional NFL statistics: Returned one kickoff for no yards and recovered one fumble, 1987.

RICHARD RAY MASSIE
(Rick)
Wide Receiver—Denver Broncos
Born January 16, 1960, at Paris, Ky.
Height, 6.01. Weight, 190.
High School—Paris, Ky., Bourbon County.
Received bachelor of arts degree in education from University of Kentucky in 1983.
Signed as free agent by Calgary Stampeders, March 27, 1984.
Selected by Denver in 2nd round (46th player selected) of 1984 NFL supplemental draft.
Released by Calgary Stampeders, August 18, 1984; re-signed by Stampeders, September 16, 1984.
On injured reserve, October 14 through remainder of 1984 season.
Released by Calgary Stampeders, June 20, 1985; signed by Denver Broncos, February 6, 1986.
Released by Denver Broncos, August 4, 1986; re-signed by Broncos, May 1, 1987.
Released by Denver Broncos, August 26, 1987; re-signed as replacement player by Broncos, September 25, 1987.
On injured reserve with broken leg, December 18 through remainder of 1987 season.

Released by Denver Broncos, August 30, 1988; re-signed by Broncos, September 7, 1988.
On non-football injury list with claustophobia, October 8 through remainder of 1988 season.

Year	Club		G.	P.C.	Yds.	Avg.	TD.
1984—Calgary CFL	....		9	15	233	15.5	0
1987—Denver NFL	....		9	13	244	18.8	4
1988—Denver NFL	....		4	3	39	13.0	0
Pro Totals—3 Years	....		22	31	516	16.6	4

BRUCE MARTIN MATHISON
Quarterback—Seattle Seahawks
Born April 25, 1959, at Superior, Wis.
Height, 6.03. Weight, 203.
High School—Superior, Wis.
Attended University of Nebraska.

Selected by Boston in 1983 USFL territorial draft.
Selected by San Diego in 10th round (272nd player selected) of 1983 NFL draft.
Signed by San Diego Chargers, May 26, 1983.
Released by San Diego Chargers, September 2, 1985; signed as free agent by Buffalo Bills, September 10, 1985.
Released by Buffalo Bills, August 26, 1986; signed as free agent by San Diego Chargers, October 28, 1986.
Released by San Diego Chargers, November 12, 1986; signed as free agent by Los Angeles Raiders, March 4, 1987.
Released by Los Angeles Raiders, July 31, 1987; signed as free agent replacement player by Houston Oilers, September 23, 1987.
Left Houston Oilers camp voluntarily and released, September 25, 1987; signed as free agent replacement player by Seattle Seahawks, September 30, 1987.
On injured reserve with back injury, December 4 through remainder of 1987 season.
On physically unable to perform/active with back injury, July 18 through July 26, 1988; passed physical, July 27, 1988.
Released by Seattle Seahawks, August 30, 1988; re-signed by Seahawks, September 20, 1988.
On injured reserve with back injury, October 29 through remainder of 1988 season.
Inactive for 5 games with Seattle Seahawks in 1988.

Year	Club		G.	Att.	Cmp.	Pct.	Gain	T.P.	P.I.	Avg.	Att.	Yds.	Avg.	TD.	TD.	Pts.	F.
						PASSING						RUSHING				TOTAL	
1983—San Diego NFL	....		1	5	3	60.0	41	0	1	8.20	1	0	0.0	0	0	0	1
1984—San Diego NFL	....		2			None							None		0	0	0
1985—Buffalo NFL	....		10	228	113	49.6	1635	4	14	7.17	27	231	8.6	1	1	6	8
1986—San Diego NFL	....		2			None					1	—1	—1.0	0	0	0	0
1987—Seattle NFL	....		3	76	36	47.4	501	3	5	6.59	5	15	3.0	0	0	0	0
Pro Totals—5 Years	....		18	309	152	49.2	2177	7	20	7.05	34	245	7.2	1	1	6	9

Quarterback Rating Points: 1985 (53.5), 1987 (54.8). Total—53.1.
Additional pro statistics: Recovered two fumbles and fumbled eight times for minus nine yards, 1985.

TREVOR ANTHONY MATICH
Center—New England Patriots
Born October 9, 1961, at Sacramento, Calif.
Height, 6.04. Weight, 270.
High School—Sacramento, Calif., Rio Americano.
Attended Brigham Young University.

Selected by Houston in 10th round (139th player selected) of 1985 USFL draft.
Selected by New England in 1st round (28th player selected) of 1985 NFL draft.
Signed by New England Patriots, July 30, 1985.
On injured reserve with ankle injury, October 12 through remainder of 1985 season.
On injured reserve with broken foot, September 7 through November 6, 1987; activated, November 7, 1987.
New England NFL, 1985 through 1988.
Games: 1985 (1), 1986 (11), 1987 (6), 1988 (8). Total—26.

RONALD ANTHONY MATTES
(Ron)
Offensive Tackle—Seattle Seahawks
Born August 8, 1963, at Shenandoah, Pa.
Height, 6.06. Weight, 306.
High School—Ashland, Pa., North Schuylkill.
Attended University of Virginia.

Selected by Orlando in 1985 USFL territorial draft.
Selected by Seattle in 7th round (193rd player selected) of 1985 NFL draft.
Signed by Seattle Seahawks, July 19, 1985.
On injured reserve with back injury, August 27 through entire 1985 season.
Seattle NFL, 1986 through 1988.
Games: 1986 (16), 1987 (12), 1988 (16). Total—44.

AUBREY DERRON MATTHEWS
Wide Receiver—Green Bay Packers
Born September 15, 1962, at Pasaqoula, Miss.
Height, 5.07. Weight, 165.
High School—Moss Point, Miss.
Attended Gulf Coast Junior College and Delta State University.

Signed by Jacksonville Bulls, January 10, 1984.
On developmental squad, April 10 through April 24, 1984; activated, April 25, 1984.
On developmental squad, June 10 through June 14, 1985; activated, June 15, 1985.
Granted free agency when USFL suspended operations, August 7, 1986; signed as free agent by Atlanta Falcons, August 18, 1986.
Granted roster exemption, August 18 through August 21, 1986; activated, August 22, 1986.
On injured reserve with hamstring injury, August 26 through November 26, 1986; activated after clearing procedural waivers, November 28, 1986.
Released by Atlanta Falcons, September 29, 1988; signed as free agent by Green Bay Packers, November 2, 1988.
On developmental squad for 2 games with Jacksonville Bulls in 1984.
On developmental squad for 1 game with Jacksonville Bulls in 1985.

		PASS RECEIVING				—KICKOFF RET.—				—TOTAL—		
Year Club	G.	P.C.	Yds.	Avg.	TD.	No.	Yds.	Avg.	TD.	TD.	Pts.	F.
1984—Jacksonville USFL	16	27	406	15.0	1	29	623	21.5	0	1	6	5
1985—Jacksonville USFL	16	25	271	10.8	5	19	366	19.3	0	5	30	2
1986—Atlanta NFL	4	1	25	25.0	0	3	42	14.0	0	0	0	0
1987—Atlanta NFL	12	32	537	16.8	3		None			3	18	2
1988—Atl. (4)-G.B. (7) NFL	11	20	231	11.6	2		None			2	12	2
USFL Totals—2 Years	32	52	677	13.0	6	48	989	20.6	0	6	36	7
NFL Totals—3 Years	27	53	793	15.0	5	3	42	14.0	0	5	30	4
Pro Totals—5 Years	59	105	1470	14.0	11	51	1031	20.2	0	11	66	11

Additional USFL statistics: Rushed three times for five yards and recovered four fumbles, 1984; recovered two fumbles, 1985.
Additional NFL statistics: Rushed once for 12 yards, 1986; rushed once for minus four yards and recovered one fumble, 1987; returned six punts for 26 yards and rushed three times for three yards, 1988.

BRUCE MATTHEWS
Guard—Houston Oilers
Born August 8, 1961, at Arcadia, Calif.
Height, 6.05. Weight, 293.
High School—Arcadia, Calif.
Received degree in industrial engineering from University of Southern California in 1983.
Son of Clay Matthews Sr., end with San Francisco 49ers, 1950 and 1953 through 1955;
brother of Clay Matthews Jr., linebacker with Cleveland Browns.
Named to THE SPORTING NEWS NFL All-Star Team, 1988.
Named as guard on THE SPORTING NEWS College All-America Team, 1982.
Selected by Los Angeles in 1983 USFL territorial draft.
Selected by Houston in 1st round (9th player selected) of 1983 NFL draft.
Signed by Houston Oilers, July 24, 1983.
Granted free agency, February 1, 1987.
Placed on reserve/unsigned list, August 31 through November 3, 1987.
Re-signed by Houston Oilers, November 4, 1987.
Granted roster exemption, November 4 through November 6, 1987; activated, November 7, 1987.
Houston NFL, 1983 through 1988.
Games: 1983 (16); 1984 (16), 1985 (16), 1986 (16), 1987 (8), 1988 (16). Total—88.
Pro statistics: Recovered three fumbles, 1985; recovered one fumble for seven yards, 1986.
Played in Pro Bowl (NFL All-Star Game) following 1988 season.

WILLIAM CLAY MATTHEWS JR.
(Known by middle name.)
Linebacker—Cleveland Browns
Born March 15, 1956, at Palo Alto, Calif.
Height, 6.02. Weight, 245.
High Schools—Arcadia, Calif.; and Winnetka, Ill., New Trier East.
Received bachelor of science degree in business administration from University of Southern California
in 1978; and attending Southern California for master's in business administration.
Son of Clay Matthews Sr., end with San Francisco 49ers, 1950 and 1953 through 1955;
brother of Bruce Matthews, guard with Houston Oilers.
Named to THE SPORTING NEWS NFL All-Star Team, 1984.
Named as linebacker on THE SPORTING NEWS College All-America Team, 1977.
Selected by Cleveland in 1st round (12th player selected) of 1978 NFL draft.
On injured reserve with broken ankle, September 16 through December 30, 1982; activated, December 31, 1982.

		—INTERCEPTIONS—			
Year Club	G.	No.	Yds.	Avg.	TD.
1978—Cleveland NFL	15	1	5	5.0	0
1979—Cleveland NFL	16	1	30	30.0	0
1980—Cleveland NFL	14	1	6	6.0	0
1981—Cleveland NFL	16	2	14	7.0	0
1982—Cleveland NFL	2		None		
1983—Cleveland NFL	16		None		
1984—Cleveland NFL	16		None		
1985—Cleveland NFL	14		None		
1986—Cleveland NFL	16	2	12	6.0	0
1987—Cleveland NFL	12	3	62	20.7	1
1988—Cleveland NFL	16		None		
Pro Totals—11 Years	153	10	129	12.9	1

Additional pro statistics: Recovered two fumbles, 1979, 1987 and 1988; recovered one fumble, 1980 and 1984; recovered two fumbles for 16 yards, 1981; recovered one fumble for 15 yards, 1985.

Played in AFC Championship Game following 1986 and 1987 seasons.
Played in Pro Bowl (NFL All-Star Game) following 1985, 1987 and 1988 seasons.

CURTIS MAXEY
Defensive Tackle—Washington Redskins
Born June 28, 1965, at Indianapolis, Ind.
Height, 6.03. Weight, 298.
High School—Indianapolis, Ind., Broad Ripple.
Received bachelor's defree in criminal justice from Grambling State University in 1988.

Selected by Cincinnati in 8th round (195th player selected) of 1988 NFL draft.
Signed by Cincinnati Bengals, May 5, 1988.
On injured reserve with knee injury, August 29 through November 25, 1988; activated, November 26, 1988.
Granted unconditional free agency, February 1, 1989; signed by Washington Redskins, April 1, 1989.
Cincinnati NFL, 1988.
Games: 1988 (3).
Played in AFC Championship Game following 1988 season.
Member of Cincinnati Bengals for NFL Championship Game following 1988 season; inactive.

BRETT DERRELL MAXIE
Safety—New Orleans Saints
Born January 13, 1962, at Dallas, Tex.
Height, 6.02. Weight, 194.
High School—Dallas, Tex., James Madison.
Attended Texas Southern University.

Signed as free agent by New Orleans Saints, June 21, 1985.
Released by New Orleans Saints, September 2, 1985; re-signed by Saints, September 3, 1985.
New Orleans NFL, 1985 through 1988.
Games: 1985 (16), 1986 (15), 1987 (12), 1988 (16). Total—59.
Pro statistics: Recovered one fumble, 1985 and 1986; intercepted two passes for 15 yards, 1986; intercepted three passes for 17 yards, returned one punt for 12 yards and credited with a safety, 1987.

MARK MAY
Guard-Offensive Tackle—Washington Redskins
Born November 2, 1959, at Oneonta, N.Y.
Height, 6.06. Weight, 295.
High School—Oneonta, N.Y.
Attended University of Pittsburgh.

Outland Trophy winner, 1980.
Named as offensive tackle on THE SPORTING NEWS College All-America Team, 1980.
Selected by Washington in 1st round (20th player selected) of 1981 NFL draft.
On injured reserve with knee injury, September 8 through October 23, 1987; activated, October 24, 1987.
Washington NFL, 1981 through 1988.
Games: 1981 (16), 1982 (9), 1983 (15), 1984 (16), 1985 (16), 1986 (16), 1987 (10), 1988 (16). Total—114.
Pro statistics: Recovered one fumble, 1983 and 1985 through 1987.
Played in NFC Championship Game following 1982, 1983, 1986 and 1987 seasons.
Played in NFL Championship Game following 1982, 1983 and 1987 seasons.
Played in Pro Bowl (NFL All-Star Game) following 1988 season.

RUEBEN MAYES
Running Back—New Orleans Saints
Born June 16, 1963, at North Battleford, Saskatchewan, Can.
Height, 5.11. Weight, 200.
High School—North Battleford, Saskatchewan, Can., Comprehensive.
Attended Washington State University.

Named THE SPORTING NEWS Rookie of the Year, 1986.
Selected by Memphis in 1986 USFL territorial draft.
Selected by New Orleans in 3rd round (57th player selected) of 1986 NFL draft.
Signed by New Orleans Saints, June 20, 1986.

		—RUSHING—			PASS RECEIVING			—TOTAL—		
Year Club	G.	Att.	Yds.	Avg.	TD.	P.C.	Yds.	Avg.	TD.	TD. Pts. F.
1986—New Orleans NFL	16	286	1353	4.7	8	17	96	5.6	0	8 48 4
1987—New Orleans NFL	12	243	917	3.8	5	15	68	4.5	0	5 30 8
1988—New Orleans NFL	16	170	628	3.7	3	11	103	9.4	0	3 18 1
Pro Totals—3 Years	44	699	2898	4.1	16	43	267	6.2	0	16 96 13

Additional pro statistics: Returned 10 kickoffs for 213 yards (21.3 avg.), 1986; recovered one fumble, 1987; returned seven kickoffs for 132 yards (18.9 avg.), 1988.
Named to play in Pro Bowl (NFL All-Star Game) following 1986 season; replaced due to injury by Gerald Riggs.
Named to play in Pro Bowl following 1987 season; replaced due to injury by Gerald Riggs.

KEVIN LEE McARTHUR
Linebacker—New York Jets
Born May 11, 1963, at Cameron, La.
Height, 6.02. Weight, 250.
High School—Lake Charles, La.
Attended Lamar University.

Signed as free agent by Los Angeles Raiders, May 20, 1984.
Released by Los Angeles Raiders, July 22, 1984; awarded on waivers to New York Jets, July 23, 1984.
Released by New York Jets, August 20, 1984; re-signed by Jets, May 7, 1985.
Released by New York Jets, August 27, 1985; re-signed by Jets, March 21, 1986.
Released by New York Jets, August 19, 1986; re-signed by Jets, October 29, 1986.
New York Jets NFL, 1986 through 1988.
Games: 1986 (8), 1987 (12), 1988 (16). Total—36.
Pro statistics: Intercepted one pass for three yards, 1988.

JEROME FRANCIS McCABE
(Jerry)
Linebacker—Kansas City Chiefs
Born January 25, 1965, at Detroit, Mich.
Height, 6.01. Weight, 225.
High School—Detroit, Mich., De La Salle Collegiate.
Received degree from Holy Cross College.

Signed as free agent by New England Patriots, May 5, 1987.
Released by New England Patriots, August 25, 1987; re-signed as replacement player by Patriots, September 24, 1987.
On injured reserve with foot and ankle injuries, October 26 through remainder of 1987 season.
Released by New England Patriots, August 30, 1988; signed as free agent by Kansas City Chiefs, December 1, 1988.
New England NFL, 1987; Kansas City NFL, 1988.
Games: 1987 (3), 1988 (3). Total—6.

NAPOLEON ARDEL McCALLUM
Running Back—San Diego Chargers
Born October 6, 1963, at Milford, O.
Height, 6.02. Weight, 215.
High School—Milford, O.
Attended U.S. Naval Academy.

Selected by Los Angeles Raiders in 4th round (108th player selected) of 1986 NFL draft.
Selected by Baltimore in 3rd round (21st player selected) of 1986 NFL draft.
Signed by Los Angeles Raiders, June 29, 1986.
Placed on reserve/military list, August 27 through entire 1987 and 1988 seasons.
Traded by Los Angeles Raiders to San Diego Chargers for 3rd round pick in 1989 draft, October 11, 1988.

		——RUSHING——				PASS RECEIVING				—TOTAL—		
Year Club	G.	Att.	Yds.	Avg.	TD.	P.C.	Yds.	Avg.	TD.	TD.	Pts.	F.
1986—Los Angeles Raiders NFL	15	142	536	3.8	1	13	103	7.9	0	1	6	5

Additional pro statistics: Returned eight kickoffs for 183 yards (22.9 avg.), returned seven punts for 44 yards and recovered one fumble, 1986.

KENNETH CHRISTOPHER McCLENDON
(Skip)
Defensive End—Cincinnati Bengals
Born April 9, 1964, at Detroit, Mich.
Height, 6.07. Weight, 275.
High School—Detroit, Mich., Redford.
Attended Northwestern University, Butler County Community College
and Arizona State University.

Selected by Cincinnati in 3rd round (77th player selected) of 1987 NFL draft.
Signed by Cincinnati Bengals, May 29, 1987.
Cincinnati NFL, 1987 and 1988.
Games: 1987 (12), 1988 (16). Total—28.
Played in AFC Championship Game following 1988 season.
Played in NFL Championship Game following 1988 season.

PHILIP JOSEPH McCONKEY
(Phil)
Wide Receiver—New York Giants
Born February 24, 1957, at Buffalo, N.Y.
Height, 5.10. Weight, 170.
High School—Buffalo, N.Y., Caniaius.
Attended U.S. Naval Academy. (Spent five years in Navy after college.)

Signed as free agent by New York Giants, May 6, 1983.
On military reserve, August 29 through entire 1983 season.
On injured reserve with broken ribs, November 26 through remainder of 1984 season.
Released by New York Giants, September 1, 1986; awarded on waivers to Green Bay Packers, September 2, 1986.
Traded by Green Bay Packers to New York Giants for 12th round pick in 1987 draft, September 30, 1986.

		PASS RECEIVING				-PUNT RETURNS-				—KICKOFF RET.—				—TOTAL—		
Year Club	G.	P.C.	Yds.	Avg.	TD.	No.	Yds.	Avg.	TD.	No.	Yds.	Avg.	TD.	TD.	Pts.	F.
1984—N.Y. Giants NFL	13	8	154	19.3	0	46	306	6.7	0	28	541	19.3	0	1	6	2
1985—N.Y. Giants NFL	16	25	404	16.2	1	53	442	8.3	0	12	234	19.5	0	1	6	1
1986—GB (4)-NYG (12) NFL.	16	16	279	17.4	1	32	253	7.9	0	24	471	19.6	0	1	6	1
1987—N.Y. Giants NFL	12	11	186	16.9	0	42	394	9.4	0	1	8	8.0	0	0	0	2
1988—N.Y. Giants NFL	16	5	72	14.4	0	40	313	7.8	0	2	30	15.0	0	0	0	2
Pro Totals—5 Years.......	73	65	1095	16.8	2	213	1708	8.0	0	67	1284	19.2	0	3	18	8

Additional pro statistics: Recovered kickoff in end zone for a touchdown, 1984; recovered one fumble, 1984, 1986 and 1987; recovered two fumbles, 1985.
Played in NFC Championship Game following 1986 season.
Played in NFL Championship Game following 1986 season.

RANDALL CORNELL McDANIEL
Guard—Minnesota Vikings
Born December 19, 1964, at Phoenix, Ariz.
Height, 6.03. Weight, 271.
High School—Avondale, Ariz., Agua Fria Union.
Received degree in physical education from Arizona State University in 1988.
Brother of Kerry McDaniel, safety at Arizona State University.

Selected by Minnesota in 1st round (19th player selected) of 1988 NFL draft.
Signed by Minnesota Vikings, July 22, 1988.
Minnesota NFL, 1988.
Games: 1988 (16).

TERENCE LEE McDANIEL
(Terry)
Cornerback—Los Angeles Raiders
Born February 8, 1965, at Saginaw, Mich.
Height, 5.10. Weight, 175.
High School—Saginaw, Mich.
Attended University of Tennessee.

Selected by Los Angeles Raiders in 1st round (9th player selected) of 1988 NFL draft.
Signed by Los Angeles Raiders, July 13, 1988.
On injured reserve with broken leg, September 14 through remainder of 1988 season.
Los Angeles Raiders NFL, 1988.
Games: 1988 (2).

MIKE McDONALD
Linebacker—Los Angeles Rams
Born June 22, 1958, at North Hollywood, Calif.
Height, 6.01. Weight, 235.
High School—Burbank, Calif., John Burroughs.
Attended University of Southern California.

Signed as free agent by Los Angeles Rams, December 21, 1983.
Released by Los Angeles Rams, August 27, 1984; re-signed by Rams, August 28, 1984.
Released by Los Angeles Rams, August 17, 1986; re-signed by Rams, September 24, 1986.
Released by Los Angeles Rams, February 1, 1987; signed as free agent by Kansas City Chiefs, August 28, 1987.
Released by Kansas City Chiefs, August 31, 1987; signed as free agent replacement player by Los Angeles Rams, October 15, 1987.
Los Angeles Rams NFL, 1984 and 1986 through 1988.
Games: 1984 (16), 1986 (13), 1987 (10), 1988 (16). Total—55.
Pro statistics: Returned three kickoffs for 34 yards and fumbled once, 1988.

COACHING RECORD
Graduate assistant coach at University of Southern California, 1980 and 1981.
Assistant coach at Burroughs (Calif.) High School, 1982, 1983 and 1985.

TIM McDONALD
Defensive Back—Phoenix Cardinals
Born January 6, 1965, at Fresno, Calif.
Height, 6.02. Weight, 207.
High School—Edison, Calif.
Attended University of Southern California.

Named as defensive back on THE SPORTING NEWS College All-America Team, 1985.
Selected by St. Louis in 2nd round (34th player selected) of 1987 NFL draft.
Signed by St. Louis Cardinals, August 2, 1987.
On injured reserve with broken ankle, September 1 through December 11, 1987; activated, December 12, 1987.
Franchise transferred to Phoenix, March 15, 1988.
St. Louis NFL, 1987; Phoenix NFL, 1988.
Games: 1987 (3), 1988 (16). Total—19.
Pro statistics: Intercepted two passes for 11 yards and recovered one fumble for nine yards, 1988.

REGINALD LEE McELROY
(Reggie)
Offensive Tackle—New York Jets
Born March 4, 1960, at Beaumont, Tex.
Height, 6.06. Weight, 275.
High School—Beaumont, Tex., Charlton Pollard.
Received degree in physical education from West Texas State University.

Selected by New York Jets in 2nd round (51st player selected) of 1982 NFL draft.
On injured reserve with knee injury, August 24 through entire 1982 season.

Granted free agency, February 1, 1985; re-signed by Jets, September 10, 1985.
Granted roster exemption, September 10 through September 13, 1985; activated, September 14, 1985.
On injured reserve with knee injury, October 22 through December 11, 1986; activated, December 12, 1986.
On injured reserve with knee injury, December 17 through remainder of 1986 season.
On physically unable to perform/reserve with knee injury, September 6 through November 8, 1987; activated, November 9, 1987.
New York Jets NFL, 1983 through 1988.
Games: 1983 (16), 1984 (16), 1985 (13), 1986 (8), 1987 (8), 1988 (16). Total—77.
Pro statistics: Returned one kickoff for seven yards, 1983; recovered one fumble for minus two yards, 1986; recovered one fumble, 1988.

VANN WILLIAM McELROY
Safety—Los Angeles Raiders
Born January 13, 1960, at Birmingham, Ala.
Height, 6.02. Weight, 195.
High School—Uvalde, Tex.
Received bachelor of business administration degree in marketing management
from Baylor University in 1983.

Selected by Los Angeles Raiders in 3rd round (64th player selected) of 1982 NFL draft.
On inactive list, September 12 and September 19, 1982.
On injured reserve with knee injury, September 8 through October 7, 1988; activated, October 8, 1988.

Year Club	G.	No.	Yds.	Avg.	TD.
1982—L.A. Raiders NFL.........	7		None		
1983—L.A. Raiders NFL.........	16	8	68	8.5	0
1984—L.A. Raiders NFL.........	16	4	42	10.5	0
1985—L.A. Raiders NFL.........	12	2	23	11.5	0
1986—L.A. Raiders NFL.........	16	7	105	15.0	0
1987—L.A. Raiders NFL.........	12	4	41	10.3	1
1988—L.A. Raiders NFL.........	12	3	17	5.7	0
Pro Totals—7 Years............	91	28	296	10.6	1

Additional pro statistics: Intercepted one pass for no yards, 1982; recovered three fumbles for five yards, 1983; recovered four fumbles for 12 yards, 1984; recovered one fumble, 1985 and 1988.
Played in AFC Championship Game following 1983 season.
Played in NFL Championship Game following 1983 season.
Played in Pro Bowl (NFL All-Star Game) following 1983 and 1984 seasons.

CRAIG McEWEN
Tight End—Washington Redskins
Born December 16, 1965, at Northport, N.Y.
Height, 6.01. Weight, 220.
High School—Northport, N.Y.
Attended University of Utah.

Signed as free agent by Washington Redskins, May 4, 1987.
Released by Washington Redskins, September 7, 1987; re-signed as replacement player by Redskins, September 23, 1987.
On injured reserve with back injury, November 3 through remainder of 1987 season.

Year Club	G.	P.C.	Yds.	Avg.	TD.
1987—Washington NFL..........	4	12	164	13.7	0
1988—Washington NFL..........	14	23	323	14.0	0
Pro Totals—2 Years............	18	35	487	13.9	0

PAUL McFADDEN
Placekicker—Atlanta Falcons
Born September 24, 1961, at Cleveland, O.
Height, 5.11. Weight, 163.
High School—Euclid, O.
Received bachelor of science degree in general administration
from Youngstown State University in 1984.

Selected by Chicago in 9th round (174th player selected) of 1984 USFL draft.
Selected by Philadelphia in 12th round (312th player selected) of 1984 NFL draft.
Signed by Philadelphia Eagles, July 15, 1984.
Released by Philadelphia Eagles, August 30, 1988; signed as free agent by New York Giants, September 27, 1988.
Granted unconditional free agency, February 1, 1989; signed by Atlanta Falcons, March 10, 1989.

Year Club	G.	XP.	XPM.	FG.	FGA.	Pts.
1984—Philadelphia NFL ...	16	26	1	*30	*37	116
1985—Philadelphia NFL ...	16	29	0	25	30	104
1986—Philadelphia NFL ...	16	26	1	20	31	86
1987—Philadelphia NFL ...	12	36	0	16	26	84
1988—N.Y. Giants NFL	10	25	2	14	19	67
Pro Totals—5 Years.......	70	142	4	105	143	457

BUFORD LAMAR McGEE
Running Back—Los Angeles Rams
Born August 16, 1960, at Durant, Miss.
Height, 6.00. Weight, 206.
High School—Durant, Miss.
Received bachelor of science degree in business from University of Mississippi in 1984.

Selected by Birmingham in 1984 USFL territorial draft.
Selected by San Diego in 11th round (286th player selected) of 1984 NFL draft.
Signed by San Diego Chargers, June 2, 1984.
On injured reserve with hamstring injury, September 3 through October 4, 1985; activated, October 5, 1985.
On injured reserve with knee injury, November 8 through remainder of 1986 season.
Granted free agency, February 1, 1987; re-signed by Chargers and traded with 2nd round pick in 1988 draft and 6th round pick in 1989 draft to Los Angeles Rams for running back Doug Redden, June 9, 1987.
On injured reserve with ruptured Achilles tendon, October 28 through remainder of 1987 season.

		—RUSHING—				PASS RECEIVING				—TOTAL—		
Year Club	G.	Att.	Yds.	Avg.	TD.	P.C.	Yds.	Avg.	TD.	TD.	Pts.	F.
1984—San Diego NFL	16	67	226	3.4	4	9	76	8.4	2	6	36	1
1985—San Diego NFL	11	42	181	4.3	3	3	15	5.0	0	3	18	4
1986—San Diego NFL	9	63	187	3.0	7	10	105	10.5	0	7	42	4
1987—Los Angeles Rams NFL	3	3	6	2.0	1	7	40	5.7	0	1	6	0
1988—Los Angeles Rams NFL	16	22	69	3.1	0	16	117	7.3	3	3	18	0
Pro Totals—5 Years	55	197	669	3.4	15	45	353	7.8	5	20	120	9

		KICKOFF RETURNS			
Year Club	G.	No.	Yds.	Avg.	TD.
1984—San Diego NFL	16	14	315	22.5	0
1985—San Diego NFL	11	7	135	19.3	0
1986—San Diego NFL	9	1	15	15.0	0
1987—L.A. Rams NFL	3		None		
1988—L.A. Rams NFL	16	1	0	0.0	0
Pro Totals—5 Years	55	23	465	20.2	0

Additional pro statistics: Recovered one fumble, 1984; recovered two fumbles, 1985; attempted one pass with one completion for one yard, 1986.

TIMOTHY DWANYE McGEE
(Tim)
Wide Receiver—Cincinnati Bengals
Born August 7, 1964, at Cleveland, O.
Height, 5.10. Weight, 175.
High School—Cleveland, O., John Hay.
Attended University of Tennessee.

Selected by Memphis in 1986 USFL territorial draft.
Selected by Cincinnati in 1st round (21st player selected) of 1986 NFL draft.
USFL rights traded by Memphis Showboats to Jacksonville Bulls for rights to center Leonard Burton and offensive tackle Doug Williams, May 6, 1986.
Signed by Cincinnati Bengals, July 26, 1986.
On injured reserve with hamstring injury, September 19 through October 20, 1987; activated, October 21, 1987.

		PASS RECEIVING				—KICKOFF RET.—				—TOTAL—		
Year Club	G.	P.C.	Yds.	Avg.	TD.	No.	Yds.	Avg.	TD.	TD.	Pts.	F.
1986—Cincinnati NFL	16	16	276	17.3	1	43	★1007	23.4	0	1	6	0
1987—Cincinnati NFL	11	23	408	17.7	1	15	242	16.1	0	1	6	0
1988—Cincinnati NFL	16	36	686	19.1	6		None			6	36	0
Pro Totals—3 Years	43	75	1370	18.3	8	58	1249	21.5	0	8	48	0

Additional pro statistics: Rushed four times for 10 yards and returned three punts for 21 yards, 1986; recovered one fumble, 1986 and 1988; rushed once for minus 10 yards, 1987.
Played in AFC Championship Game following 1988 season.
Played in NFL Championship Game following 1988 season.

LAWRENCE McGREW
Linebacker—New England Patriots
Born July 23, 1957, at Berkeley, Calif.
Height, 6.05. Weight, 233.
High School—Berkeley, Calif.
Attended Contra Costa Junior College and received degree in speech communications from University of Southern California in 1980.

Selected by New England in 2nd round (45th player selected) of 1980 NFL draft.
On injured reserve with knee and elbow injuries, December 19 through remainder of 1980 season.
On injured reserve with knee injury, August 31 through entire 1981 season.
New England NFL, 1980 and 1982 through 1988.
Games: 1980 (11), 1982 (8), 1983 (16), 1984 (16), 1985 (13), 1986 (14), 1987 (12), 1988 (16). Total—106.
Pro statistics: Intercepted one pass for three yards, 1983; recovered one fumble, 1983 and 1987; intercepted one pass for no yards and recovered two fumbles, 1985; intercepted two passes for 44 yards, 1986; intercepted one pass for six yards, 1988.
Played in AFC Championship Game following 1985 season.
Played in NFL Championship Game following 1985 season.

MIKE McGRUDER
Defensive Back—Green Bay Packers
Born May 6, 1962, at Cleveland Heights, O.
Height, 5.11. Weight, 180.
Attended Kent State University.

Signed as free agent by Ottawa Rough Riders, May, 1985.
Released by Ottawa Rough Riders, July, 1985; signed as free agent by Saskatchewan Roughriders, April, 1986.
Granted free agency, March 1, 1989; signed as free agent by Green Bay Packers, April 26, 1989.

			—INTERCEPTIONS—		
Year Club	G.	No.	Yds.	Avg.TD.	
1986—Saskatchewan CFL......	14	5	35	7.0	0
1987—Saskatchewan CFL......	14	5	26	5.2	0
1988—Saskatchewan CFL......	18	7	89	12.7	0
CFL Totals—3 Years	46	17	150	8.8	0

Additional CFL statistics: Recovered one fumble and lost four yards on lateral of punt return, 1986; recovered four fumbles for 26 yards, 1987; recovered two fumbles for 20 yards and a touchdown, 1988.

THOMAS McHALE
(Tom)
Guard—Tampa Bay Buccaneers
Born February 25, 1963, at Gaithersburg, Md.
Height, 6.04. Weight, 275.
High School—Gaithersburg, Md.
Attended Cornell University.

Signed as free agent by Tampa Bay Buccaneers, May 4, 1987.
On injured reserve with back injury, September 7 through November 27, 1987; activated, November 28, 1987.
Tampa Bay NFL, 1987 and 1988.
Games: 1987 (3), 1988 (10). Total—13.
Pro statistics: Recovered one fumble, 1987; fumbled once for minus four yards, 1988.

GUY MAURICE McINTYRE
Guard—San Francisco 49ers
Born Feburary 17, 1961, at Thomasville, Ga.
Height, 6.03. Weight, 264.
High School—Thomasville, Ga.
Attended University of Georgia.
Cousin of Lomas Brown, offensive tackle with Detroit Lions.

Selected by Jacksonville in 1984 USFL territorial draft.
Selected by San Francisco in 3rd round (73rd player selected) of 1984 NFL draft.
Signed by San Francisco 49ers, May 8, 1984.
On injured reserve with foot injury, October 31 through remainder of 1987 season.
San Francisco NFL, 1984 through 1988.
Games: 1984 (15), 1985 (15), 1986 (16), 1987 (3), 1988 (16). Total—65.
Pro statistics: Returned one kickoff for no yards, 1984; recovered one fumble in end zone for a touchdown, 1985; caught one pass for 17 yards and a touchdown, 1988.
Played in NFC Championship Game following 1984 and 1988 seasons.
Played in NFL Championship Game following 1984 and 1988 seasons.

KEITH McKELLER
Tight End—Buffalo Bills
Born July 9, 1964, at Fairfield, Ala.
Height, 6.06. Weight, 245.
High School—Fairfield, Ala.
Attended Jacksonville State University.

Selected by Buffalo in 9th round (227th player selected) of 1987 NFL draft.
Signed by Buffalo Bills, July 16, 1987.
On injured reserve with back injury, September 1 through entire 1987 season.
Buffalo NFL, 1988.
Games: 1988 (12).
Member of Buffalo Bills for AFC Championship Game following 1988 season; inactive.

RALEIGH McKENZIE
Center-Guard—Washington Redskins
Born February 8, 1963, at Knoxville, Tenn.
Height, 6.02. Weight, 270.
High School—Knoxville, Tenn., Austin-East.
Twin brother of Reggie McKenzie, linebacker with Phoenix Cardinals.

Selected by Washington in 11th round (290th player selected) of 1985 NFL draft.
Signed by Washington Redskins, June 20, 1985.
Washington NFL, 1985 through 1988.
Games: 1985 (6), 1986 (15), 1987 (12), 1988 (16). Total—49.
Played in NFC Championship Game following 1986 and 1987 seasons.
Played in NFL Championship Game following 1987 season.

REGINALD McKENZIE
(Reggie)
Linebacker—Phoenix Cardinals

Born February 8, 1963, at Knoxville, Tenn.
Height, 6.01. Weight, 235.
High School—Knoxville, Tenn., Austin-East.
Attended University of Tennessee.
Twin brother of Raleigh McKenzie, center-guard with Washington Redskins.

Selected by Los Angeles Raiders in 10th round (275th player selected) of 1985 NFL draft.
Signed by Los Angeles Raiders, June 26, 1985.
Granted unconditional free agency, February 1, 1989; signed by Phoenix Cardinals, March 13, 1989.
Los Angeles Raiders NFL, 1985 through 1988.
Games: 1985 (16), 1986 (16), 1987 (10), 1988 (16). Total—58.
Pro statistics: Recovered one fumble, 1985; intercepted one pass for nine yards, 1986; intercepted one pass for 26 yards, 1988.

DENNIS LEWIS McKINNON
Wide Receiver—Chicago Bears

Born August 22, 1961, at Quitman, Ga.
Height, 6.01. Weight, 177.
High School—Miami, Fla., South Miami Senior.
Received bachelor of arts degree in criminology from Florida State University in 1983.

Signed as free agent by Chicago Bears, May 4, 1983.
On physically unable to perform/reserve with knee injury, August 18 through entire 1986 season.

		PASS RECEIVING			-PUNT RETURNS-				—KICKOFF RET.—				—TOTAL—		
Year Club	G.	P.C.	Yds.	Avg. TD.	No.	Yds.	Avg.	TD.	No.	Yds.	Avg.	TD.	TD.	Pts.	F.
1983—Chicago NFL	16	20	326	16.3 4	34	316	9.3	*1	2	42	21.0	0	5	30	2
1984—Chicago NFL	12	29	431	14.9 3	5	62	12.4	0		None			3	18	1
1985—Chicago NFL	14	31	555	17.9 7	4	44	11.0	0	1	16	16.0	0	7	42	1
1987—Chicago NFL	12	27	406	15.0 1	40	405	10.1	*2		None			3	18	6
1988—Chicago NFL	15	45	704	15.6 3	34	277	8.1	0		None			4	24	3
Pro Totals—5 Years	69	152	2422	15.9 18	117	1104	9.4	3	3	58	19.3	0	22	132	13

Additional pro statistics: Recovered one fumble, 1983 and 1988; rushed twice for 12 yards, 1984; rushed once for no yards, 1985; recovered three fumbles, 1987; rushed three times for 25 yards and a touchdown, 1988.
Played in NFC Championship Game following 1984, 1985 and 1988 seasons.
Played in NFL Championship Game following 1985 season.

DENNIS N. McKNIGHT
Center-Guard—San Diego Chargers

Born September 12, 1959, at Dallas, Tex.
Height, 6.03. Weight, 280.
High School—Staten Island, N.Y., Wagner.
Received degree from Drake University in 1981.

Signed as free agent by Cleveland Browns, May 3, 1981.
Released by Cleveland Browns, August 18, 1981; signed as free agent by San Diego Chargers, March 30, 1982.
On inactive list, September 12 and September 19, 1982.
San Diego NFL, 1982 through 1988.
Games: 1982 (7), 1983 (16), 1984 (16), 1985 (16), 1986 (16), 1987 (12), 1988 (16). Total—99.
Pro statistics: Recovered two fumbles, 1983 and 1984.

TIM B. McKYER
Cornerback—San Francisco 49ers

Born September 5, 1963, at Orlando, Fla.
Height, 6.00. Weight, 174.
High School—Port Arthur, Tex., Lincoln.
Attended University of Texas at Arlington.

Selected by San Francisco in 3rd round (64th player selected) of 1986 NFL draft.
Signed by San Francisco 49ers, July 20, 1986.

		——INTERCEPTIONS——			
Year Club	G.	No.	Yds.	Avg.	TD.
1986—San Francisco NFL	16	6	33	5.5	1
1987—San Francisco NFL	12	2	0	0.0	0
1988—San Francisco NFL	16	7	11	1.6	0
Pro Totals—3 Years	44	15	44	2.9	1

Additional pro statistics: Returned one kickoff for 15 yards and returned one punt for five yards, 1986.
Played in NFC Championship Game following 1988 season.
Played in NFL Championship Game following 1988 season.

—DID YOU KNOW—

That the Miami Dolphins enter the 1989 season without having allowed a sack in their last 12 games, an NFL record?

CHRIS McLEMORE
Fullback—Seattle Seahawks
Born December 31, 1963, at Las Vegas, Nev.
Height, 6.01. Weight, 230.
High School—Las Vegas, Nev., Valley.
Attended University of Colorado and University of Arizona.

Selected by Los Angeles Raiders in 11th round (288th player selected) of 1987 NFL draft.
Signed by Los Angeles Raiders, July 10, 1987.
Released by Los Angeles Raiders, September 7, 1987; signed as free agent replacement player by Indianapolis Colts, September 23, 1987.
Released by Indianapolis Colts, October 27, 1987; signed as free agent by Los Angeles Raiders, November 11, 1987.
On injured reserve with elbow injury, December 26 through remainder of 1987 season.
On injured reserve with elbow injury, August 29 through October 25, 1988; re-signed by Raiders after clearing procedural waivers, October 27, 1988.
On injured reserve with elbow injury, December 17 through remainder of 1988 season.
Granted unconditional free agency, February 1, 1989; signed by Seattle Seahawks, March 21, 1989.

| | | RUSHING | | | | PASS RECEIVING | | | | —TOTAL— | | |
Year Club	G.	Att.	Yds.	Avg.	TD.	P.C.	Yds.	Avg.	TD.	TD.	Pts.	F.
1987—Ind.(2)-L.A. Raid.(3) NFL	5	17	58	3.4	0	2	9	4.5	0	0	0	1
1988—Los Angeles Raiders NFL	7			None				None		0	0	0
Pro Totals—2 Years	12	17	58	3.4	0	2	9	4.5	0	0	0	1

JAMES ROBERT McMAHON
(Jim)
Quarterback—Chicago Bears
Born August 21, 1959, at Jersey City, N.J.
Height, 6.01. Weight, 198.
High School—Roy, Utah.
Attended Brigham Young University.

Selected by Chicago in 1st round (5th player selected) of 1982 NFL draft.
On injured reserve with lacerated kidney, November 9 through remainder of 1984 season.
On injured reserve with shoulder injury, November 28 through remainder of 1986 season.
On injured reserve with shoulder injury, September 7 through October 21, 1987; activated, October 22, 1987.
On injured reserve with knee injury, November 5 through December 8, 1988; activated, December 9, 1988.

| | | PASSING | | | | | | | RUSHING | | | | —TOTAL— | | |
Year Club	G.	Att.	Cmp.	Pct.	Gain	T.P.	P.I.	Avg.	Att.	Yds.	Avg.	TD.	TD.	Pts.	F.
1982—Chicago NFL	8	210	120	57.1	1501	9	7	7.15	24	105	4.4	1	1	6	1
1983—Chicago NFL	14	295	175	59.3	2184	12	13	7.40	55	307	5.6	2	3	18	4
1984—Chicago NFL	9	143	85	59.4	1146	8	2	8.01	39	276	7.1	2	2	12	1
1985—Chicago NFL	13	313	178	56.9	2392	15	11	7.64	47	252	5.4	3	4	24	4
1986—Chicago NFL	6	150	77	51.3	995	5	8	6.63	22	152	6.9	1	1	6	1
1987—Chicago NFL	7	210	125	59.5	1639	12	8	7.80	22	88	4.0	2	2	12	2
1988—Chicago NFL	9	192	114	59.4	1346	6	7	7.01	26	104	4.0	4	4	24	6
Pro Totals—7 Years	66	1513	874	57.8	11203	67	56	7.40	235	1284	5.5	15	17	102	19

Quarterback Rating Points: 1982 (80.1), 1983 (77.6), 1984 (97.8), 1985 (82.6), 1986 (61.4), 1987 (87.4), 1988 (76.0). Total—80.3.

Additional pro statistics: Punted once for 59 yards, 1982; caught one pass for 18 yards and a touchdown and punted once for 36 yards, 1983; recovered three fumbles, 1983 and 1988; caught one pass for 42 yards, 1984; caught one pass for 13 yards and a touchdown, 1985.
Played in NFC Championship Game following 1985 and 1988 seasons.
Played in NFL Championship Game following 1985 season.
Played in Pro Bowl (NFL All-Star Game) following 1985 season.

DANNY McMANUS
Quarterback—Kansas City Chiefs
Born June 17, 1965, at Dania, Fla.
Height, 6.00. Weight, 200.
High School—Hollywood, Fla., South Broward.
Received degree in sports management from Florida State University.

Selected by Kansas City in 11th round (282nd player selected) of 1988 NFL draft.
Signed by Kansas City Chiefs, July 14, 1988.
Active for 7 games with Kansas City Chiefs in 1988; did not play.
Kansas City NFL, 1988.

STEVE DOUGLAS McMICHAEL
Defensive Tackle—Chicago Bears
Born October 17, 1957, at Houston, Tex.
Height, 6.02. Weight, 265.
High School—Freer, Tex.
Attended University of Texas.

Named to THE SPORTING NEWS NFL All-Star Team, 1986 and 1987.
Selected by New England in 3rd round (73rd player selected) of 1980 NFL draft.
On injured reserve with back injury, November 3 through remainder of 1980 season.
Released by New England Patriots, August 24, 1981; signed as free agent by Chicago Bears, October 15, 1981.

New England NFL, 1980; Chicago NFL, 1981 through 1988.
Games: 1980 (6), 1981 (10), 1982 (9), 1983 (16), 1984 (16), 1985 (16), 1986 (16), 1987 (12), 1988 (16). Total—117.
Pro statistics: Recovered one fumble, 1981 and 1985; recovered one fumble for 64 yards, 1982; recovered two fumbles, 1983 and 1986; credited with one safety, 1985, 1986 and 1988; intercepted one pass for five yards, 1986; recovered two fumbles for one yard, 1988.
Played in NFC Championship Game following 1984 and 1985 seasons.
Played in NFL Championship Game following 1985 and 1988 seasons.
Played in Pro Bowl (NFL All-Star Team) following 1986 and 1987 seasons.

ERIK McMILLAN
Safety—New York Jets
Born May 3, 1965, at St. Louis, Mo.
Height, 6.02. Weight, 197.
High School—Silver Springs, Md., John F. Kennedy.
Received degree in business management from University of Missouri in 1988.
Son of Ernie McMillan, offensive tackle with St. Louis Cardinals and Green Bay Packers,
1961 through 1975; assistant coach with Green Bay Packers, 1979 through 1983; and assistant coach
with St. Louis Cardinals, 1985; and cousin of Howard Richards, offensive lineman with
Dallas Cowboys and Seattle Seahawks, 1981 through 1987.

Selected by New York Jets in 3rd round (63rd player selected) of 1988 NFL draft.
Signed by New York Jets, July 6, 1988.
On injured reserve with sprained arch, December 17 through remainder of 1988 season.

| | | —INTERCEPTIONS— | | | |
Year Club	G.	No.	Yds.	Avg.	TD.
1988—N.Y. Jets NFL	13	8	168	21.0	*2

Additional pro statistics: Fumbled once, 1988.
Played in Pro Bowl (NFL All-Star Game) following 1988 season.

AUDREY GLENN McMILLIAN
Cornerback—Minnesota Vikings
Born August 13, 1962, at Carthage, Tex.
Height, 6.00. Weight, 190.
High School—Carthage, Tex.
Received bachelor of science degree in industrial distribution
from Purdue University in 1985.

Selected by Houston in 1985 USFL territorial draft.
Selected by New England in 3rd round (84th player selected) of 1985 NFL draft.
Signed by New England Patriots, July 1, 1985.
Released by New England Patriots, September 2, 1985; awarded on waivers to Houston Oilers, September 3, 1985.
Released by Houston Oilers, September 22, 1986; re-signed by Oilers, September 24, 1986.
On injured reserve with knee injury, August 29 through entire 1988 season.
Granted unconditional free agency, February 1, 1989; signed by Minnesota Vikings, March 16, 1989.
Houston NFL, 1985 through 1987.
Games: 1985 (16), 1986 (16), 1987 (12). Total—44.
Pro statistics: Recovered two fumbles for four yards, 1986.

SEAN McNANIE
Defensive End—Phoenix Cardinals
Born September 9, 1961, at Mundelein, Ill.
Height, 6.05. Weight, 270.
High School—Mundelein, Ill.
Attended Arizona State University and San Diego State University.

Selected by Oakland in 2nd round (30th player selected) of 1984 USFL draft.
Selected by Buffalo in 3rd round (79th player selected) of 1984 NFL draft.
Signed by Buffalo Bills, June 1, 1984.
Traded by Buffalo Bills to Phoenix Cardinals for 6th round pick in 1989 draft, August 23, 1988.
Buffalo NFL, 1984 through 1988.
Games: 1984 (15), 1985 (16), 1986 (16), 1987 (12), 1988 (12). Total—71.
Pro statistics: Recovered one fumble, 1986; recovered one fumble for 14 yards and a touchdown, 1987.

DONALD McNEAL
(Don)
Cornerback—Miami Dolphins
Born May 6, 1958, at Atmore, Ala.
Height, 6.00. Weight, 192.
High School—Atmore, Ala., Escambia County.
Received bachelor of science degree in social welfare from University of Alabama.
Cousin of Mike Williams, running back with Philadelphia Eagles, 1983 and 1984.

Named as cornerback on THE SPORTING NEWS College All-America Team, 1979.
Selected by Miami in 1st round (21st player selected) of 1980 NFL draft.
On injured reserve with wrist injury, December 11 through remainder of 1980 season.
On injured reserve with Achilles tendon injury, August 29 through entire 1983 season.
On injured reserve with knee injury, August 19 through October 18, 1985; activated, October 19, 1985.
Granted unconditional free agency, February 1, 1989; re-signed by Dolphins, May 2, 1989.

Year Club	G.	No.	Yds.	Avg.	TD.
		——INTERCEPTIONS——			
1980—Miami NFL	13	5	17	3.4	0
1981—Miami NFL	12		None		
1982—Miami NFL	9	4	42	10.5	*1
1984—Miami NFL	11	3	41	13.7	1
1985—Miami NFL	10		None		
1986—Miami NFL	15	2	46	23.0	0
1987—Miami NFL	12		None		
1988—Miami NFL	16	1	23	23.0	0
Pro Totals—8 Years	98	15	169	11.3	2

Additional pro statistics: Recovered one fumble, 1980, 1981 and 1988; recovered two fumbles for five yards, 1984.
Played in AFC Championship Game following 1982, 1984 and 1985 seasons.
Played in NFL Championship Game following 1982 and 1984 seasons.

FREEMAN McNEIL
Running Back—New York Jets

Born April 22, 1959, at Jackson, Miss.
Height, 5.11. Weight, 212.
High School—Wilmington, Calif., Banning.
Attended University of California at Los Angeles.

Selected by New York Jets in 1st round (3rd player selected) of 1981 NFL draft.
On injured reserve with foot injury, October 10 through November 13, 1981; activated, November 14, 1981.
On injured reserve with separated shoulder, September 27 through November 10, 1983; activated, November 11, 1983.
On injured reserve with broken ribs, December 6 through remainder of 1984 season.
On injured reserve with dislocated elbow, September 14 through October 19, 1986; activated, October 20, 1986.

		——RUSHING——				PASS RECEIVING				—TOTAL—		
Year Club	G.	Att.	Yds.	Avg.	TD.	P.C.	Yds.	Avg.	TD.	TD.	Pts.	F.
1981—New York Jets NFL	11	137	623	4.5	2	18	171	9.5	1	3	18	5
1982—New York Jets NFL	9	151	*786	*5.2	6	16	187	11.7	1	7	42	7
1983—New York Jets NFL	9	160	654	4.1	1	21	172	8.2	3	4	24	4
1984—New York Jets NFL	12	229	1070	4.7	5	25	294	11.8	1	6	36	4
1985—New York Jets NFL	14	294	1331	4.5	3	38	427	11.2	2	5	30	9
1986—New York Jets NFL	12	214	856	4.0	5	49	410	8.4	1	6	36	8
1987—New York Jets NFL	9	121	530	4.4	0	24	262	10.9	1	1	6	1
1988—New York Jets NFL	16	219	944	4.3	6	34	288	8.5	1	7	42	3
Pro Totals—8 Years	92	1525	6794	4.5	28	225	2211	9.8	11	39	234	41

Additional pro statistics: Attempted one pass with one completion for five yards and a touchdown, 1983; recovered one fumble, 1983 and 1984.
Played in AFC Championship Game following 1982 season.
Played in Pro Bowl (NFL All-Star Game) following 1982 and 1985 seasons.
Named to play in Pro Bowl following 1984 season; replaced due to injury by Greg Bell.

GERALD LYNN McNEIL
Wide Receiver-Punt Returner—Cleveland Browns

Born March 27, 1962, at Frankfurt, West Germany.
Height, 5.07. Weight, 147.
High School—Killeen, Tex.
Attended Baylor University.

Named as punt returner on THE SPORTING NEWS USFL All-Star Team, 1985.
Selected by San Antonio in 1984 USFL territorial draft.
Signed by Houston Gamblers, February 16, 1984.
USFL rights traded by San Antonio Gunslingers to Houston Gamblers for 2nd round pick in 1985 draft, February 23, 1984.
On developmental squad, March 23 through April 13, 1984; activated, April 14, 1984.
Selected by Cleveland in 2nd round (44th player selected) of 1984 NFL supplemental draft.
Traded with defensive backs Luther Bradley, Will Lewis, Mike Mitchell and Durwood Roquemore, defensive end Pete Catan, quarterbacks Jim Kelly and Todd Dillon, defensive tackles Tony Fitzpatrick, Van Hughes and Hosea Taylor, running back Sam Harrell, linebackers Andy Hawkins and Ladell Wills, wide receivers Richard Johnson, Scott McGhee, Ricky Sanders and Clarence Verdin, guard Rich Kehr, center Billy Kidd and offensive tackles Chris Riehm and Tommy Robison by Houston Gamblers to New Jersey Generals for past considerations, March 7, 1986.
Granted free agency when USFL suspended operations, August 7, 1986; signed by Cleveland Browns, August 12, 1986.
Granted roster exemption, August 12 through August 21, 1986; activated, August 22, 1986.
On developmental squad for 3 games with Houston Gamblers in 1984.

		PASS RECEIVING				-PUNT RETURNS-				—KICKOFF RET.—				—TOTAL—		
Year Club	G.	P.C.	Yds.	Avg.	TD.	No.	Yds.	Avg.	TD.	No.	Yds.	Avg.	TD.	TD.	Pts.	F.
1984—Houston USFL	15	33	501	15.2	1	31	323	10.4	*1		None			2	12	4
1985—Houston USFL	18	58	1017	17.5	6	39	*505	*13.0	*2	2	62	31.0	0	8	48	4
1986—Cleveland NFL	16	1	9	9.0	0	40	348	8.7	1	47	997	21.2	*1	2	12	3
1987—Cleveland NFL	12	8	120	15.0	0	34	386	11.4	0	11	205	18.6	0	2	12	2
1988—Cleveland NFL	16	5	74	14.8	0	38	315	8.3	0	2	38	19.0	0	0	0	3
USFL Totals—2 Years	33	91	1518	16.7	7	70	828	11.8	3	2	62	31.0	0	10	60	8
NFL Totals—3 Years	44	14	203	14.5	2	112	1049	9.4	1	60	1240	20.7	1	4	24	8
Pro Totals—5 Years	77	105	1721	16.4	9	182	1877	10.3	4	62	1302	21.0	1	14	84	16

Additional USFL statistics: Rushed once for 11 yards and recovered two fumbles, 1984; recovered one fumble, 1985.

Additional NFL statistics: Rushed once for 12 yards, 1986; rushed once for 17 yards, 1987; recovered one fumble, 1988.

Played in AFC Championship Game following 1986 and 1987 seasons.
Played in Pro Bowl (NFL All-Star Game) following 1987 season.

BRUCE EDWARD McNORTON
Cornerback—Detroit Lions

Born February 28, 1959, at Daytona Beach, Fla.
Height, 5.11. Weight, 175.
High School—Daytona Beach, Fla., Spruce Creek.
Received bachelor of arts degree in social work from Georgetown (Ky.) College in 1982.

Selected by Detroit in 4th round (96th player selected) of 1982 NFL draft.
On injured reserve with knuckle injury, September 10 through December 10, 1982; activated, December 11, 1982.

| | | —INTERCEPTIONS— | | | |
Year Club	G.	No.	Yds.	Avg.	TD.
1982—Detroit NFL	4		None		
1983—Detroit NFL	16	7	30	4.3	0
1984—Detroit NFL	16	2	0	0.0	0
1985—Detroit NFL	16	2	14	7.0	0
1986—Detroit NFL	16	4	10	2.5	0
1987—Detroit NFL	12	3	20	6.7	0
1988—Detroit NFL	16	1	4	4.0	0
Pro Totals—7 Years	96	19	78	4.1	0

Additional pro statistics: Recovered two fumbles, 1986; recovered four fumbles for 36 yards, 1988.

DONALD GLENN McPHERSON
(Don)
Quarterback—Philadelphia Eagles

Born April 2, 1965, at Brooklyn, N. Y.
Height, 6.01. Weight, 193.
High School—Hempstead, N.Y.
Received degree in psychology from Syracuse University in 1988
Brother of Miles McPherson, safety with San Diego Chargers, 1982 through 1985.

Named as quarterback on THE SPORTING NEWS College All-America Team, 1987.
Selected by Philadelphia in 6th round (149th player selected) of 1988 NFL draft.
Signed by Philadelphia Eagles, July 27, 1988.
Active for 2 games with Philadelphia Eagles in 1988; did not play.
Philadelphia NFL, 1988.

DAN McQUAID
Offensive Lineman—Indianapolis Colts

Born October 4, 1960, at Cortland, Calif.
Height, 6.07. Weight, 278.
High School—Clarksburg, Calif., Delta.
Attended University of Nevada at Las Vegas.

Selected by New Jersey in 16th round (318th player selected) of 1984 USFL draft.
Signed as free agent by Los Angeles Rams, May 4, 1984.
On injured reserve with back injury, August 21 through entire 1984 season.
Traded by Los Angeles Rams to Washington Redskins for 4th round pick in 1986 draft, August 24, 1985.
On injured reserve with ankle injury, October 27 through remainder of 1987 season.
Released by Washington Redskins, May 9, 1988; awarded on waivers to Minnesota Vikings, May 24, 1988.
Released by Minnesota Vikings, September 21, 1988; awarded on waivers to Indianapolis Colts, September 22, 1988.
Granted unconditional free agency, February 1, 1989; re-signed by Colts, May 3, 1989.
Washington NFL, 1985 through 1987; Minnesota (3)-Indianapolis (1) NFL, 1988.
Games: 1985 (16), 1986 (13), 1987 (1), 1988 (4). Total—34.
Played in NFC Championship Game following 1986 season.

RODNEY McSWAIN
(Rod)
Cornerback—New England Patriots

Born January 28, 1962, at Caroleen, N.C.
Height, 6.01. Weight, 198.
High School—Forest City, N.C., Chase.
Attended Clemson University.
Brother of Chuck McSwain, running back with Dallas Cowboys
and New England Patriots, 1983, 1984 and 1987.

Selected by Washington in 1984 USFL territorial draft.
Selected by Atlanta in 3rd round (63rd player selected) of 1984 NFL draft.
Signed by Atlanta Falcons, May 16, 1984.
Traded by Atlanta Falcons to New England Patriots for 8th round pick in 1985 draft, August 27, 1984.
On injured reserve with shoulder separation, September 2 through October 2, 1986; activated, October 3, 1986.
New England NFL, 1984 through 1988.
Games: 1984 (15), 1985 (16), 1986 (9), 1987 (12), 1988 (16). Total—68.
Pro statistics: Recovered one fumble, 1984; intercepted one pass for no yards, 1985; returned blocked punt 31 yards

for a touchdown and intercepted one pass for three yards, 1986; intercepted one pass for 17 yards, 1987; intercepted two passes for 51 yards, 1988.
Played in AFC Championship Game following 1985 season.
Played in NFL Championship Game following 1985 season.

JOHNNY MEADS
Linebacker—Houston Oilers
Born June 25, 1961, at Labadieville, La.
Height, 6.02. Weight, 235.
High School—Napoleonville, La., Assumption.
Attended Nicholls State University.

Selected by New Orleans in 3rd round (55th player selected) of 1984 USFL draft.
Selected by Houston in 3rd round (58th player selected) of 1984 NFL draft.
Signed by Houston Oilers, July 17, 1984.
On injured reserve with knee injury, October 8 through remainder of 1985 season.
Houston NFL, 1984 through 1988.
Games: 1984 (16), 1985 (5), 1986 (16), 1987 (12), 1988 (16). Total—65.
Pro statistics: Recovered one fumble, 1986.

KARL BERNARD MECKLENBURG
Linebacker—Denver Broncos
Born September 1, 1960, at Seattle, Wash.
Height, 6.03. Weight, 230.
High School—Edina, Minn., West.
Attended Augustana College (S.D.) and received bachelor of
science degree in biology from University of Minnesota in 1983.

Named to THE SPORTING NEWS NFL All-Star Team, 1986.
Selected by Chicago in 21st round (246th player selected) of 1983 USFL draft.
Selected by Denver in 12th round (310th player selected) of 1983 NFL draft.
Signed by Denver Broncos, May 14, 1983.
On injured reserve with broken thumb, October 28 through December 9, 1988; activated, December 10, 1988.
Denver NFL, 1983 through 1988.
Games: 1983 (16), 1984 (16), 1985 (16), 1986 (16), 1987 (12), 1988 (9). Total—85.
Pro statistics: Intercepted two passes for 105 yards, 1984; recovered one fumble, 1984 through 1987; intercepted three passes for 23 yards, 1987.
Played in AFC Championship Game following 1986 and 1987 seasons.
Played in NFL Championship Game following 1986 and 1987 seasons.
Played in Pro Bowl (NFL All-Star Game) following 1985 through 1987 seasons.

GREGORY PAUL MEISNER
(Greg)
Nose Tackle—Kansas City Chiefs
Born April 23, 1959, at New Kensington, Pa.
Height, 6.03. Weight, 265.
High School—New Kensington, Pa., Valley.
Received bachelor of arts degree in psychology from University of Pittsburgh in 1981.

Selected by Los Angeles in 3rd round (63rd player selected) of 1981 NFL draft.
On non-football injury list with head injuries suffered in bar fight, August 18 through October 23, 1981; activated, October 24, 1981.
On injured reserve with knee injury, December 16 through remainder of 1982 season.
Granted free agency, February 1, 1985; re-signed by Rams, September 18, 1985.
Granted roster exemption, September 18 and September 19, 1985; activated, September 20, 1985.
Crossed picket line during players' strike, October 2, 1987.
Granted unconditional free agency, February 1, 1989; signed by Kansas City Chiefs, March 14, 1989.
Los Angeles Rams NFL, 1981 through 1988.
Games: 1981 (9), 1982 (6), 1983 (16), 1984 (16), 1985 (14), 1986 (15), 1987 (15), 1988 (12). Total—103.
Pro statistics: Returned one kickoff for 17 yards, 1981; recovered one fumble, 1984; recovered one fumble for 15 yards, 1986; intercepted one pass for 20 yards, 1988.
Played in NFC Championship Game following 1985 season.

MICHAEL LAMAR MERRIWEATHER
(Mike)
Linebacker—Minnesota Vikings
Born November 26, 1960, at Albans, N.Y.
Height, 6.02. Weight, 221.
High School—Vallejo, Calif.
Received bachelor of arts degree in history from University of the Pacific in 1982.

Selected by Pittsburgh in 3rd round (70th player selected) of 1982 NFL draft.
On reserve/did not report, August 29 through entire 1988 season.
Traded by Pittsburgh Steelers to Minnesota Vikings for 1st round pick in 1989 draft, April 23, 1989.

Year Club	G.	No.	Yds.	Avg.TD.		Year Club	G.	No.	Yds.	Avg.TD.
1982—Pittsburgh NFL............	9			None		1986—Pittsburgh NFL............	16	2	14	7.0 0
1983—Pittsburgh NFL............	16	3	55	18.3 1		1987—Pittsburgh NFL............	12	2	26	13.0 0
1984—Pittsburgh NFL............	16	2	9	4.5 0		Pro Totals—6 Years............	85	11	140	12.7 2
1985—Pittsburgh NFL............	16	2	36	18.0 *1						

The INTERCEPTIONS header spans No., Yds., Avg.TD. columns on both sides.

Additional pro statistics: Returned one punt for three yards, 1982; recovered two fumbles, 1983; recovered one fumble, 1984; fumbled once, 1985; returned one kickoff for 27 yards and recovered two fumbles for 18 yards, 1986; recovered four fumbles for four yards, 1987.

Played in AFC Championship Game following 1984 season.

Played in Pro Bowl (NFL All-Star Game) following 1984 through 1986 seasons.

SCOTT MERSEREAU
Defensive Tackle-Defensive End—New York Jets
Born April 8, 1965, at Riverhead, N.Y.
Height, 6.03. Weight, 273.
High School—Riverhead, N.Y.
Attended Southern Connecticut State University.

Selected by Los Angeles Rams in 5th round (136th player selected) of 1987 NFL draft.

Signed by Los Angeles Rams, July 25, 1987.

Released by Los Angeles Rams, September 7, 1987; signed as replacement player by New York Jets, September 24, 1987.

New York Jets NFL, 1987 and 1988.

Games: 1987 (13), 1988 (16). Total—29.

Pro statistics: Recovered one fumble, 1987 and 1988.

BRUCE M. MESNER
Nose Tackle—Buffalo Bills
Born March 21, 1964, at New York, N.Y.
Height, 6.05. Weight, 280.
High School—Harrison, N.Y.
Attended University of Maryland.

Selected by Buffalo in 8th round (209th player selected) of 1987 NFL draft.

Signed by Buffalo Bills, July 24, 1987.

On injured reserve with ankle injury, August 30 through entire 1988 season.

Buffalo NFL, 1987.

Games: 1987 (11).

PETER HENRY METZELAARS
(Pete)
Tight End—Buffalo Bills
Born May 24, 1960, at Three Rivers, Mich.
Height, 6.07. Weight, 250.
High School—Portage, Mich., Central.
Received bachelor of science degree in economics from Wabash College in 1982.

Selected by Seattle in 3rd round (75th player selected) of 1982 NFL draft.

On injured reserve with knee injury, October 17 through November 30, 1984; activated, December 1, 1984.

Traded by Seattle Seahawks to Buffalo Bills for wide receiver Byron Franklin, August 20, 1985.

Year Club	G.	P.C.	Yds.	Avg.	TD.
1982—Seattle NFL	9	15	152	10.1	0
1983—Seattle NFL	16	7	72	10.3	1
1984—Seattle NFL	9	5	80	16.0	0
1985—Buffalo NFL	16	12	80	6.7	1
1986—Buffalo NFL	16	49	485	9.9	3
1987—Buffalo NFL	12	28	290	10.4	0
1988—Buffalo NFL	16	33	438	13.3	1
Pro Totals—7 Years	94	149	1597	10.7	6

Additional pro statistics: Recovered one fumble, 1982, 1987 and 1988; fumbled twice, 1982 and 1986; returned one kickoff for no yards, 1983; fumbled once, 1984; recovered one fumble for two yards, 1985; recovered one fumble in end zone for a touchdown, 1986; fumbled three times, 1987.

Played in AFC Championship Game following 1983 and 1988 seasons.

RICHARD JAMES MIANO
Name pronounced Mee-AN-oh.
(Rich)
Safety—New York Jets
Born September 3, 1962, at Newton, Mass.
Height, 6.00. Weight, 200.
High School—Honolulu, Haw., Kaiser.
Attended University of Hawaii.

Selected by Denver in 9th round (132nd player selected) of 1985 USFL draft.

Selected by New York Jets in 6th round (166th player selected) of 1985 NFL draft.

Signed by New York Jets, July 16, 1985.

Released by New York Jets, September 2, 1985; re-signed by Jets, September 3, 1985.

Year Club		——INTERCEPTIONS——			
	G.	No.	Yds.	Avg.	TD.
1985—N.Y. Jets NFL	16	2	9	4.5	0
1986—N.Y. Jets NFL	14			None	
1987—N.Y. Jets NFL	12	3	24	8.0	0
1988—N.Y. Jets NFL	16	2	0	0.0	0
Pro Totals—4 Years	58	7	33	4.7	0

Additional pro statistics: Returned blocked field goal attempt 67 yards for a touchdown, 1987.

RONALD ALLEN MIDDLETON
(Ron)
Tight End—Washington Redskins
Born July 17, 1965, at Atmore, Ala.
Height, 6.02. Weight, 252.
High School—Atmore, Ala., Escambia County.
Attended Auburn University.

Selected by Birmingham in 1986 USFL territorial draft.
Signed as free agent by Atlanta Falcons, May 3, 1986.
Released by Atlanta Falcons, August 30, 1988; signed as free agent by Washington Redskins, September 13, 1988.
Released by Washington Redskins, October 3, 1988; re-signed by Redskins, November 14, 1988.
Released by Washington Redskins, December 12, 1988; re-signed by Redskins, December 13, 1988.

Year Club		——PASS RECEIVING——			
	G.	P.C.	Yds.	Avg.	TD.
1986—Atlanta NFL	16	6	31	5.2	0
1987—Atlanta NFL	12	1	1	1.0	0
1988—Washington NFL	2			None	
Pro Totals—3 Years	30	7	32	4.6	0

DOUG ADOLPH MIKOLAS
Nose Tackle—Atlanta Falcons
Born June 7, 1962, at Manteca, Calif.
Height, 6.01. Weight, 270.
High School—Scio, Ore.
Attended Portland State University and Oregon Tech.

Selected by Denver in 7th round (94th player selected) of 1985 USFL draft.
Signed by Denver Gold, January 21, 1985.
On developmental squad, April 20 through May 2, 1985; activated, May 3, 1985.
Franchise merged with Jacksonville, February 19, 1986.
Granted free agency when USFL suspended operations, August 7, 1986; signed as free agent by Toronto Argonauts, August 26, 1986.
Released by Toronto Argonauts, September 22, 1986; signed as free agent by San Francisco 49ers, April 8, 1987.
Released by San Francisco 49ers, September 7, 1987; re-signed by 49ers, September 8, 1987.
Released by San Francisco 49ers, September 12, 1987; re-signed as replacement player by 49ers, September 30, 1987.
Released by San Francisco 49ers, August 30, 1988; re-signed by 49ers, September 22, 1988.
Released by San Francisco 49ers, October 25, 1988; signed as free agent by Houston Oilers, November 11, 1988.
Released by Houston Oilers, December 7, 1988; signed as free agent by Atlanta Falcons, April 26, 1989.
On developmental squad for 2 games with Denver Gold in 1985.
Denver USFL, 1985; Toronto CFL, 1986; San Francisco NFL, 1987; San Francisco (1)-Houston (1) NFL, 1988.
Games: 1985 (16), 1986 (3), 1987 (8), 1988 (2). Total NFL—10. Total Pro—29.
Pro statistics: Credited with 4½ sacks for 27½ yards and recovered one fumble, 1985.

JOSEPH MICHAEL MILINICHIK
(Joe)
(Name pronounced Mah-lynn-check.)
Guard-Offensive Tackle—Detroit Lions
Born March 30, 1963, at Allentown, Pa.
Height, 6.05. Weight, 275.
High School—Emmaus, Pa.
Received bachelor of science degree in vocational industrial education
from North Carolina State University in 1985.

Selected by Jacksonville in 1986 USFL territorial draft.
Selected by Detroit in 3rd round (69th player selected) of 1986 NFL draft.
Signed by Detroit Lions, July 15, 1986.
On injured reserve with dislocated elbow, September 2 through entire 1986 season.
Detroit NFL, 1987 and 1988.
Games: 1987 (11), 1988 (15). Total—26.

BRYAN MILLARD
Name pronounced Mill-ARD.
Guard—Seattle Seahawks
Born December 2, 1960, at Sioux City, Ia.
Height, 6.05. Weight, 282.
High School—Dumas, Tex.
Attended University of Texas.

Selected by New Jersey in 12th round (142nd player selected) of 1983 USFL draft.
Signed by New Jersey Generals, February 4, 1983.
On injured reserve with knee injury, April 18 through remainder of 1983 season.
On developmental squad, May 6 through May 10, 1984; activated, May 11, 1984.
Granted free agency, July 15, 1984; signed as free agent by Seattle Seahawks, July 31, 1984.
On injured reserve with knee injury, December 8 through remainder of 1984 season.
On developmental squad for 1 game with New Jersey Generals in 1984.
New Jersey USFL, 1983 and 1984; Seattle NFL, 1984 through 1988.
Games: 1983 (7), 1984 USFL (17), 1984 NFL (14), 1985 (16), 1986 (16), 1987 (12), 1988 (15). Total USFL—24. Total NFL—73. Total Pro—97.
Pro statistics: Recovered one fumble, 1986; caught one pass for minus five yards and recovered two fumbles, 1987.

KEITH MILLARD
Name pronounced Mill-ARD.
Defensive Tackle—Minnesota Vikings
Born March 18, 1962, at Pleasanton, Calif.
Height, 6.05. Weight, 260.
High School—Pleasanton, Calif., Foothill.
Attended Washington State University.

Named to THE SPORTING NEWS NFL All-Star Team, 1988.
Selected by Arizona in 1st round (5th player selected) of 1984 USFL draft.
Selected by Minnesota in 1st round (13th player selected) of 1984 NFL draft.
USFL rights traded by Arizona Wranglers to Jacksonville Bulls for 1st round pick in 1985 draft, July 5, 1984.
Signed by Jacksonville Bulls, July 5, 1984.
On developmental squad, March 2 through March 8, 1985; activated, March 9, 1985.
On suspended list, May 23 through May 29, 1985; reinstated, May 30, 1985.
Released by Jacksonville Bulls, August 5, 1985; signed by Minnesota Vikings, August 6, 1985.
On developmental squad for 1 game with Jacksonville Bulls in 1985.
Jacksonville USFL, 1985; Minnesota NFL, 1985 through 1988.
Games: 1985 USFL (17), 1985 NFL (16), 1986 (15), 1987 (9), 1988 (15). Total NFL—55. Total Pro—72.
USFL statistics: Credited with 12 sacks for 86½ yards and recovered one fumble, 1985.
NFL statistics: Recovered one fumble, 1985; intercepted one pass for 17 yards and recovered one fumble for three yards, 1986; recovered two fumbles for eight yards, 1987; recovered two fumbles for five yards, 1988.
Played in NFC Championship Game following 1987 season.
Played in Pro Bowl (NFL All-Star Game) following 1988 season.

HUGH MILLEN
Quarterback—Atlanta Falcons
Born November 22, 1963, at Des Moines, Ia.
Height, 6.05. Weight, 216.
High School—Seattle, Wash., Roosevelt.
Attended Santa Rosa Junior College and University of Washington.

Selected by Los Angeles Rams in 3rd round (71st player selected) of 1986 NFL draft.
Signed by Los Angeles Rams, July 17, 1986.
On injured reserve with broken ankle, August 19 through entire 1986 season.
On injured reserve with knee injury, September 7 through December 3, 1987; activated, December 4, 1987.
Released by Los Angeles Rams, August 29, 1988; awarded on waivers to Atlanta Falcons, August 30, 1988.

| | | | | —PASSING— | | | | | —RUSHING— | | | | —TOTAL— | |
Year Club	G.	Att.	Cmp.	Pct.	Gain	T.P.	P.I.	Avg.	Att.	Yds.	Avg.	TD.	TD.	Pts.	F.
1987—L.A. Rams NFL	1	1	1	100.0	0	0	0	0.00	None				0	0	0
1988—Atlanta NFL	3	31	17	54.8	215	0	2	6.94	1	7	7.0	0	0	0	1
Pro Totals—2 Years	4	32	18	56.3	215	0	2	6.72	1	7	7.0	0	0	0	1

Quarterback Rating Points: 1987 (79.2), 1988 (49.8). Total—50.8.

MATT G. MILLEN
Linebacker—Los Angeles Raiders
Born March 12, 1958, at Hokendauqua, Pa.
Height, 6.02. Weight, 250.
High School—Whitehall, Pa.
Received bachelor of business administration degree in marketing from
Pennsylvania State University in 1980.
Nephew of Andy Tomasic, back with Pittsburgh Steelers, 1942 and 1946 and
pitcher with New York Giants, 1949.

Selected by Oakland in 2nd round (43rd player selected) of 1980 NFL draft.
Franchise transferred to Los Angeles, May 7, 1982.
Granted free agency, February 1, 1988; re-signed by Raiders, August 23, 1988.

| | | —INTERCEPTIONS— | | | |
Year Club	G.	No.	Yds.	Avg.	TD.
1980—Oakland NFL	16	2	17	8.5	0
1981—Oakland NFL	16		None		
1982—L.A. Raiders NFL	9	3	77	25.7	0
1983—L.A. Raiders NFL	16	1	14	14.0	0
1984—L.A. Raiders NFL	16		None		
1985—L.A. Raiders NFL	16		None		
1986—L.A. Raiders NFL	16		None		
1987—L.A. Raiders NFL	12	1	6	6.0	0
1988—L.A. Raiders NFL	16		None		
Pro Totals—9 Years	133	7	114	16.3	0

Additional pro statistics: Recovered one fumble, 1981 and 1988; returned one kickoff for 13 yards and recovered two fumbles, 1982; returned two kickoffs for 19 yards, 1983; returned three kickoffs for 40 yards, 1986; returned one kickoff for no yards and fumbled once, 1987.

Played in AFC Championship Game following 1980 and 1983 seasons.
Played in NFL Championship Game following 1980 and 1983 seasons.
Played in Pro Bowl (NFL All-Star Game) following 1988 season.

BRETT MILLER
Offensive Tackle—San Diego Chargers
Born October 2, 1958 at Lynwood, Calif.
Height, 6.07. Weight, 300.
High School—Glendale, Calif.
Attended Glendale Community College and University of Iowa.

Selected by Washington in 5th round (57th player selected) of 1983 USFL draft.
Selected by Atlanta in 5th round (129th player selected) of 1983 NFL draft.
Signed by Atlanta Falcons, May 25, 1983.
On injured reserve with sprained ankle, November 12 through December 9, 1985; activated, December 10, 1985.
On injured reserve with knee injury, October 16 through November 14, 1986; activated, November 15, 1986.
On injury reserve with knee injury, November 28 through remainder of 1986 season.
On injured reserve with injured arch in foot, September 8 through October 30, 1987; activated, October 31, 1987.
Granted unconditional free agency, February 1, 1989; signed by San Diego Chargers, March 13, 1989.
Atlanta NFL, 1983 through 1988.
Games: 1983 (16), 1984 (15), 1985 (12), 1986 (8), 1987 (2), 1988 (15). Total—68.
Pro statistics: Recovered one fumble, 1986.

CHARLES ELLIOT MILLER
(Chuckie)
Defensive Back—Indianapolis Colts
Born May 9, 1965, at Anniston, Ala.
Height, 5.10. Weight, 180.
High School—Long Beach, Calif., Polytechnic.
Attended University of California at Los Angeles.

Selected by Indianapolis in 8th round (200th player selected) of 1987 NFL draft.
Signed by Indianapolis Colts, July 23, 1987.
On injured reserve with leg injury, September 7 through entire 1987 season.
On injured reserve with shoulder injury, September 2 through December 1, 1988; activated, December 2, 1988.
Indianapolis NFL, 1988.
Games: 1988 (3).

CHRISTOPHER JAMES MILLER
(Chris)
Quarterback—Atlanta Falcons
Born August 9, 1965, at Pomona, Calif.
Height, 6.02. Weight, 200.
High School—Eugene, Ore., Sheldon.
Attended University of Oregon.

Selected by Atlanta in 1st round (13th player selected) of 1987 NFL draft.
Signed by Atlanta Falcons, October 30, 1987.
Granted roster exemption, October 30 through November 8, 1987; activated, November 9, 1987.

			PASSING							RUSHING				TOTAL		
Year	Club	G.	Att.	Cmp.	Pct.	Gain	T.P.	P.I.	Avg.	Att.	Yds.	Avg.	TD.	TD.	Pts.	F.
1987—Atlanta NFL		3	92	39	42.4	552	1	9	6.00	4	21	5.3	0	0	0	0
1988—Atlanta NFL		13	351	184	52.4	2133	11	12	6.08	31	138	4.5	1	1	6	2
Pro Totals—2 Years		16	443	223	50.3	2685	12	21	6.06	35	159	4.5	1	1	6	2

Quarterback Rating Points: 1987 (26.4), 1988 (67.3). Total—58.7.
Additional pro statistics: Recovered one fumble, 1988.

RECORD AS BASEBALL PLAYER

Year	Club	League	Pos.	G.	AB.	R.	H.	2B.	3B.	HR.	RBI.	B.A.	PO.	A.	E.	F.A.
1985—Bellingham†		N'west					(Did not play)									
1986—Bellingham		N'west	SS	3	9	5	5	0	1	0	1	.556	5	5	1	.909
1986—Salinas		Calif.	SS	27	79	8	8	2	1	0	3	.101	38	74	8	.933

Selected by Toronto Blue Jays' organization in 17th round of free-agent draft, June 6, 1983.
Selected by Toronto Blue Jays' organization in secondary phase of free-agent draft, January 17, 1984.
Selected by Seattle Mariners' organization in 5th round of free-agent draft, January 9, 1985.
†On disabled list, June 1, 1985 through entire season.

—DID YOU KNOW—
That New Orleans quarterback Bobby Hebert completed a two-yard pass to himself in the Saints' 42-0 romp over Denver on November 20? Hebert threw a pass that was batted back into his hands by Broncos nose tackle Greg Kragen.

DARRIN JAMES MILLER
Linebacker—Seattle Seahawks
Born March 24, 1965, at Flemington, N. J.
Height, 6.01. Weight, 227.
High School—Flemington, N. J., Hunterdon Central.
Received bachelor of science degree in business from
University of Tennessee in 1988.

Signed as free agent by Seattle Seahawks, July 18, 1988.
Seattle NFL, 1988.
Games: 1988 (16).
Pro statistics: Intercepted one pass for seven yards and recovered one fumble, 1988.

LAWRENCE ANTHONY MILLER
(Known by middle name.)
Wide Receiver—San Diego Chargers
Born April 15, 1965, at Los Angeles, Calif.
Height, 5.11. Weight, 185.
High School—Pasadena, Calif., John Muir.
Attended San Diego State University, Pasadena City College and University of Tennessee.

Selected by San Diego in 1st round (15th player selected) of 1988 NFL draft.
Signed by San Diego Chargers, July 12, 1988.

Year Club	G.	Att.	Yds.	Avg.	TD.	P.C.	Yds.	Avg.	TD.	TD.	Pts.	F.
		—RUSHING—				PASS RECEIVING				—TOTAL—		
1988—San Diego NFL	16	7	45	6.4	0	36	526	14.6	3	4	24	1

Year Club	G.	No.	Yds.	Avg.TD.
		KICKOFF RETURNS		
1988—San Diego NFL	16	25	648	25.9 *1

LEON PATRICK MILLER
(Pat)
Safety—San Diego Chargers
Born June 24, 1964, at Panama City, Fla.
Height, 6.01. Weight, 206.
High School—Panama City, Fla., A. Crawford Mosley.
Attended University of Florida.

Selected by San Francisco in 5th round (131st player selected) of 1986 NFL draft.
Selected by New Jersey in 4th round (26th player selected) of 1986 USFL draft.
Signed by San Francisco 49ers, July 19, 1986.
Released by San Francisco 49ers, August 26, 1986; signed as free agent by Los Angeles Raiders, April 11, 1987.
Released by Los Angeles Raiders, September 7, 1987; signed as free agent replacement player by San Diego Chargers, October 14, 1987.
Released by San Diego Chargers, October 27, 1987; re-signed by Chargers for 1988, November 21, 1987.
On injured reserve with knee injury, September 14 through November 11, 1988; activated, November 12, 1988.
San Diego NFL, 1987 and 1988.
Games: 1987 (1), 1988 (8). Total—9.

LES P. MILLER
Defensive End—San Diego Chargers
Born March 1, 1965, at Arkansas City, Kan.
Height, 6.07. Weight, 293.
High School—Arkansas City, Kan.
Attended Fort Hays Kansas State University.

Signed as free agent by New Orleans Saints, May 11, 1987.
Released by New Orleans Saints, September 7, 1987; signed as free agent replacement player by San Diego Chargers, September 24, 1987.
San Diego NFL, 1987 and 1988.
Games: 1987 (9), 1988 (13). Total—22.
Pro statistics: Recovered two fumbles (including one in end zone for a touchdown), 1987.

SHAWN MILLER
Defensive End—Los Angeles Rams
Born March 14, 1961, at Ogden, Utah.
Height, 6.04. Weight, 255.
High School—Ogden, Utah, Weber.
Attended Utah State University.

Signed as free agent by Los Angeles Rams, May 5, 1984.
Released by Los Angeles Rams, August 27, 1984; re-signed by Rams, August 28, 1984.
On injured reserve with back injury, November 9 through remainder of 1984 season.
Crossed picket line during players' strike, October 2, 1987.
Los Angeles Rams NFL, 1984 through 1988.
Games: 1984 (8), 1985 (16), 1986 (16), 1987 (6), 1988 (16). Total—62.
Pro statistics: Returned one kickoff for 10 yards, 1985; recovered two fumbles for 29 yards, 1986.
Played in NFC Championship Game following 1985 season.

JAMES THOMAS MILLING JR.
Wide Receiver—Atlanta Falcons
Born February 14, 1965, at Winnsboro, S. C.
Height, 5.09. Weight, 156.
High School—Oxon Hill, Md., Potomac.
Attended University of Maryland.

Selected by Atlanta in 11th round (278th player selected) of 1988 NFL draft.
Signed by Atlanta Falcons, July 16, 1988.
On injured reserve with ankle injury, September 1 through October 28, 1988; activated, October 29, 1988.

		—PASS RECEIVING—				
Year Club		G.	P.C.	Yds.	Avg.	TD.
1988—Atlanta NFL		6	5	66	13.2	0

SAMUEL DAVIS MILLS JR.
(Sam)
Linebacker—New Orleans Saints
Born June 3, 1959, Neptune, N.J.
Height, 5.09. Weight, 225.
High School—Long Branch, N.J.
Attended Montclair State College.

Named as inside linebacker on THE SPORTING NEWS USFL All-Star Team, 1983 and 1985.
Signed as free agent by Cleveland Browns, May 3, 1981.
Released by Cleveland Browns, August 24, 1981; signed as free agent by Toronto Argonauts, March, 1982.
Released by Toronto Argonauts, June 30, 1982; signed by Philadelphia Stars, October 21, 1982.
Franchise transferred to Baltimore, November 1, 1984.
Granted free agency, August 1, 1985; re-signed by Stars, August 7, 1985.
Granted free agency when USFL suspended operations, August 7, 1986; signed as free agent by New Orleans Saints, August 12, 1986.
Granted roster exemption, August 12 through August 21, 1986; activated, August 22, 1986.

	—INTERCEPTIONS—						—INTERCEPTIONS—				
Year Club	G.	No.	Yds.	Avg.	TD.	Year Club	G.	No.	Yds.	Avg.	TD.
1983—Philadelphia USFL	18	3	13	4.3	0	1988—New Orleans NFL........	16		None		
1984—Philadelphia USFL	18	3	24	8.0	0	USFL Totals—3 Years........	54	9	69	7.7	1
1985—Baltimore USFL	18	3	32	10.7	*1	NFL Totals—3 Years..........	44	0	0	0.0	0
1986—New Orleans NFL........	16		None								
1987—New Orleans NFL........	12		None			Pro Totals—6 Years...........	98	9	69	7.7	1

Additional USFL statistics: Credited with 3½ sacks for 37 yards and recovered five fumbles for eight yards, 1983; credited with five sacks for 39 yards and recovered three fumbles for two yards, 1984; credited with 5½ sacks for 41 yards and recovered two fumbles, 1985.
Additional NFL statistics: Recovered one fumble, 1986; recovered three fumbles, 1987; recovered four fumbles, 1988.
Played in USFL Championship Game following 1983 through 1985 seasons.
Played in Pro Bowl (NFL All-Star Game) following 1987 and 1988 seasons.

FRANKY LyDALE MINNIFIELD
(Frank)
Cornerback—Cleveland Browns
Born January 1, 1960, at Lexington, Ky.
Height, 5.09. Weight, 185.
High School—Lexington, Ky., Henry Clay.
Attended University of Louisville.
Cousin of Dirk Minniefield, guard with Cleveland Cavaliers, Houston Rockets,
Golden State Warriors and Boston Celtics, 1985-86 through 1987-88.

Named to THE SPORTING NEWS NFL All-Star Team, 1987 and 1988.
Selected by Chicago in 3rd round (30th player selected) of 1983 USFL draft.
Signed by Chicago Blitz, January 28, 1983.
On injured reserve with knee injury, March 8 through remainder of 1983 season.
Franchise transferred to Arizona, September 30, 1983.
On developmental squad, March 4 through March 21, 1984; activated, March 22, 1984.
On developmental squad, April 27 through May 6, 1984; activated, May 7, 1984.
Signed by Cleveland Browns, May 20, 1984.
Released by Arizona Wranglers, August 23, 1984.
Cleveland Browns contract approved by NFL, August 25, 1984.
Granted roster exemption, August 25 through August 30, 1984; activated, August 31, 1984.
On developmental squad for 3 games with Arizona Wranglers in 1984.

	—INTERCEPTIONS—						—INTERCEPTIONS—				
Year Club	G.	No.	Yds.	Avg.	TD.	Year Club	G.	No.	Yds.	Avg.	TD.
1983—Chicago USFL	1		None			1988—Cleveland NFL.............	15	4	16	4.0	0
1984—Arizona USFL...............	15	4	74	18.5	1	USFL Totals—2 Years........	16	4	74	18.5	1
1984—Cleveland NFL.............	15	1	26	26.0	0	NFL Totals—5 Years..........	73	13	89	6.8	0
1985—Cleveland NFL.............	16	1	3	3.0	0						
1986—Cleveland NFL.............	15	3	20	6.7	0	Pro Totals—7 Years...........	89	17	163	9.6	1
1987—Cleveland NFL.............	12	4	24	6.0	0						

Additional USFL statistics: Recovered two fumbles for minus six yards, 1984.
Additional NFL statistics: Recovered two fumbles for 10 yards, 1984; recovered one fumble for six yards, 1985;

recovered blocked punt in end zone for a touchdown and recovered two fumbles, 1986; returned blocked punt 11 yards for a touchdown, 1988.

Played in USFL Championship Game following 1984 season.
Played in AFC Championship Game following 1986 and 1987 seasons.
Played in Pro Bowl (NFL All-Star Game) following 1986 through 1988 seasons.

DEVON D. MITCHELL
Safety—Detroit Lions
Born December 30, 1962, at Kingston, Jamaica.
Height, 6.01. Weight, 194.
High School—Brooklyn, N.Y., Samuel J. Tilden.
Attended University of Iowa.

Selected by Detroit in 4th round (92nd player selected) of 1986 NFL draft.
Signed by Detroit Lions, June 17, 1986.
On injured reserve with knee injury, September 7 through entire 1987 season.
Crossed picket line during players' strike, October 14, 1987.
On physically unable to perform/active with knee injury, July 18 through August 21, 1988; then transferred to physically unable to perform/reserve with knee injury, August 22 through October 14, 1988; activated, October 15, 1988.

| | | ——INTERCEPTIONS—— | | | |
Year Club	G.	No.	Yds.	Avg.	TD.
1986—Detroit NFL	16	5	41	8.2	0
1988—Detroit NFL	10	3	107	35.7	1
Pro Totals—2 Years	26	8	148	18.5	1

LYVONIA ALBERT MITCHELL
(Stump)
Running Back—Phoenix Cardinals
Born March 15, 1959, at St. Mary's, Ga.
Height, 5.09. Weight, 188.
High School—St. Mary's, Ga., Camden County.
Attended The Citadel.

Established NFL record for most yards, combined kick returns, season (1,737), 1981; most kickoff returns, rookie season (55), 1981; most combined kick returns, game, 13 vs. Atlanta Falcons, October 10, 1981.
Selected by St. Louis in 9th round (226th player selected) of 1981 NFL draft.
Franchise transferred to Phoenix, March 15, 1988.

| | | ——RUSHING—— | | | | PASS RECEIVING | | | | —TOTAL— | | |
Year Club	G.	Att.	Yds.	Avg.	TD.	P.C.	Yds.	Avg.	TD.	TD.	Pts.	F.
1981—St. Louis NFL	16	31	175	5.6	0	6	35	5.8	1	2	12	3
1982—St. Louis NFL	9	39	189	4.8	1	11	149	13.5	0	1	6	3
1983—St. Louis NFL	15	68	373	5.5	3	7	54	7.7	0	3	18	5
1984—St. Louis NFL	16	81	434	5.4	9	26	318	12.2	2	11	66	6
1985—St. Louis NFL	16	183	1006	*5.5	7	47	502	10.7	3	10	60	6
1986—St. Louis NFL	15	174	800	4.6	5	41	276	6.7	0	5	30	4
1987—St. Louis NFL	12	203	781	3.8	3	45	397	8.8	2	5	30	3
1988—Phoenix NFL	14	164	726	4.4	4	25	214	8.6	1	5	30	6
Pro Totals—8 Years	113	943	4484	4.8	32	208	1945	9.4	9	42	252	36

| | | —PUNT RETURNS— | | | | —KICKOFF RET.— | | |
Year Club	G.	No.	Yds.	Avg.	TD.	No.	Yds.	Avg.	TD.
1981—St. Louis NFL	16	42	445	10.6	1	55	*1292	23.5	0
1982—St. Louis NFL	9	27	165	6.1	0	16	364	22.8	0
1983—St. Louis NFL	15	38	337	8.9	0	36	778	21.6	0
1984—St. Louis NFL	16	38	333	8.8	0	35	804	23.0	0
1985—St. Louis NFL	16	11	97	8.8	0	19	345	18.2	0
1986—St. Louis NFL	15		None			6	203	33.8	0
1987—St. Louis NFL	12		None				None		
1988—Phoenix NFL	14		None			10	221	22.1	0
Pro Totals—8 Years	113	156	1377	8.8	1	177	4007	22.6	0

Additional pro statistics: Recovered one fumble, 1982, 1983, 1986 and 1987; recovered two fumbles, 1984 and 1985; attempted one pass with one completion for 20 yards, 1984; attempted two passes with one completion for 31 yards, 1985; attempted three passes with one completion for 15 yards and a touchdown, 1986; attempted three passes with one completion for 17 yards, 1987; recovered three fumbles for minus three yards, 1988.

MICHAEL G. MITCHELL
Cornerback—New York Jets
Born October 18, 1961, at Waco, Tex.
Height, 5.09. Weight, 192.
High School—Waco, Tex., Richfield.
Attended Howard Payne University.

Signed as free agent by Houston Oilers, June 2, 1983.
Released by Houston Oilers, July 27, 1983.
USFL rights traded by San Antonio Gunslingers to Houston Gamblers for rights to wide receiver Glenn Starks, August 26, 1983.
Signed by Houston Gamblers, September 5, 1983.
Traded with defensive backs Luther Bradley, Will Lewis and Durwood Roquemore, defensive end Pete Catan,

quarterbacks Jim Kelly and Todd Dillon, defensive tackles Tony Fitzpatrick, Van Hughes and Hosea Taylor, running back Sam Harrell, linebackers Andy Hawkins and Ladell Wills, wide receivers Richard Johnson, Scott McGhee, Gerald McNeil, Ricky Sanders and Clarence Verdin, guard Rich Kehr, center Billy Kidd and offensive tackles Chris Riehm and Tommy Robison by Houston Gamblers to New Jersey Generals for past considerations, March 7, 1986.

Granted free agency when USFL suspended operations, August 7, 1986; signed as free agent by Washington Redskins, April 30, 1987.

Released by Washington Redskins, August 17, 1987; re-signed as replacement player by Redskins, September 23, 1987.

Released by Washington Redskins, October 20, 1987; signed as free agent by New York Jets, April 8, 1988.

On injured reserve with groin injury, August 22 through entire 1988 season.

			—INTERCEPTIONS—			
Year Club	G.	No.	Yds.	Avg.	TD.
1984—Houston USFL	18	4	43	10.8	0
1985—Houston USFL	18	3	37	12.3	0
1987—Washington NFL	3	1	17	17.0	0
USFL Totals—2 Years	36	7	80	11.4	0
NFL Totals—1 Year	3	1	17	17.0	0
Pro Totals—3 Years	39	8	97	12.1	0

Additional pro statistics: Credited with one sack for four yards and recovered one fumble, 1984.

ROLAND EARL MITCHELL
Cornerback—Phoenix Cardinals
Born March 15, 1964, at Columbus, Tex.
Height, 5.11. Weight, 180.
High School—Bay City, Tex.
Attended Texas Tech University.

Selected by Buffalo in 2nd round (33rd player selected) of 1987 NFL draft.
Signed by Buffalo Bills, July 24, 1987.
Traded with 6th round pick in 1989 draft by Buffalo Bills to Phoenix Cardinals for safety Leonard Smith, September 21, 1988.
Buffalo NFL, 1987; Buffalo (3)-Phoenix (11) NFL, 1988.
Games: 1987 (11), 1988 (14). Total—25.
Pro statistics: Intercepted one pass for no yards, 1988.

ALONZO MITZ
Defensive End—Seattle Seahawks
Born June 5, 1963, at Henderson, N. C.
Height, 6.03. Weight, 275.
High School—Fort Pierce, Fla., Central.
Attended University of Florida.

Selected by Tampa Bay in 1986 USFL territorial draft.
Selected by Seattle in 8th round (211th player selected) of 1986 NFL draft.
Signed by Seattle Seahawks, June 15, 1986.
On injured reserve with shoulder injury, September 1 through November 13, 1986; activated, November 14, 1986.
On injured reserve with elbow injury, September 7 through October 23, 1987; activated, October 24, 1987.
Seattle NFL, 1986 through 1988.
Games: 1986 (6), 1987 (6), 1988 (16). Total—28.

ORSON ODELL MOBLEY
Tight End—Denver Broncos
Born March 4, 1963, at Brookeville, Fla.
Height, 6.05. Weight, 256.
High School—Miami, Fla., Palmetto.
Attended Florida State University and Salem College.

Selected by Denver in 6th round (151st player selected) of 1986 NFL draft.
Signed by Denver Broncos, July 17, 1986.

		—PASS RECEIVING—			
Year Club	G.	P.C.	Yds.	Avg.	TD.
1986—Denver NFL	14	22	332	15.1	1
1987—Denver NFL	10	16	228	14.3	1
1988—Denver NFL	16	21	218	10.4	2
Pro Totals—3 Years	40	59	778	13.2	4

Additional pro statistics: Rushed once for minus one yard, 1986; fumbled once, 1986 through 1988; recovered one fumble, 1988.

Played in AFC Championship Game following 1986 and 1987 seasons.
Played in NFL Championship Game following 1986 and 1987 seasons.

RALF MOJSIEJENKO
Name pronounced Mose-YEN-ko.
Punter—San Diego Chargers
Born January 28, 1963, at Salzgitter Lebenstadt, West Germany.
Height, 6.03. Weight, 210.
High School—Bridgman, Mich.
Attended Michigan State University.

Named as punter on THE SPORTING NEWS College All-America Team, 1983.

Selected by Jacksonville in 9th round (118th player selected) of 1985 USFL draft.
Selected by San Diego in 4th round (96th player selected) of 1985 NFL draft.
Signed by San Diego Chargers, July 23, 1985.

		—PUNTING—			
Year	Club	G.	No.	Avg.	Blk.
1985—San Diego NFL		16	68	42.4	0
1986—San Diego NFL		16	72	42.0	2
1987—San Diego NFL		12	67	42.9	0
1988—San Diego NFL		16	85	44.1	1
Pro Totals—4 Years		60	292	42.9	3

Additional pro statistics: Rushed once for no yards and fumbled once for 13-yard loss, 1985.
Played in Pro Bowl (NFL All-Star Game) following 1987 season.

MATTHEW L. MONGER
(Matt)
Linebacker—Houston Oilers
Born November 15, 1961, at Denver, Colo.
Height, 6.01. Weight, 235.
High School—Miami, Okla.
Received bachelor of science degree in marketing
from Oklahoma State University in 1985.

Selected by New York Jets in 8th round (208th player selected) of 1985 NFL draft.
Signed by New York Jets, July 23, 1985.
On injured reserve with broken arm, August 15 through entire 1988 season.
Granted unconditional free agency, February 1, 1989; signed by Houston Oilers, March 28, 1989.
New York Jets NFL, 1985 through 1987.
Games: 1985 (15), 1986 (16), 1987 (12). Total—43.
Pro statistics: Recovered two fumbles, 1985; recovered one fumble, 1986.

ART MONK
Wide Receiver—Washington Redskins
Born December 5, 1957, at White Plains, N.Y.
Height, 6.03. Weight, 209.
High School—White Plains, N.Y.
Attended Syracuse University.

Established NFL record for most pass receptions, season (106), 1984.
Named to THE SPORTING NEWS NFL All-Star Team, 1984 and 1985.
Selected by Washington in 1st round (18th player selected) of 1980 NFL draft.
On injured reserve with broken foot, January 7, 1983 through remainder of 1982 season playoffs.
On injured reserve with knee injury, September 2 through September 29, 1983; activated, September 30, 1983.
On injured reserve with knee injury, December 9, 1987 through January 29, 1988; activated, January 30, 1988.

			—RUSHING—				PASS RECEIVING				—TOTAL—		
Year	Club	G.	Att.	Yds.	Avg.	TD.	P.C.	Yds.	Avg.	TD.	TD.	Pts.	F.
1980—Washington NFL		16		None			58	797	13.7	3	3	18	0
1981—Washington NFL		16	1	—5	—5.0	0	56	894	16.0	6	6	36	0
1982—Washington NFL		9	7	21	3.0	0	35	447	12.8	1	1	6	3
1983—Washington NFL		12	3	—19	—6.3	0	47	746	15.9	5	5	30	0
1984—Washington NFL		16	2	18	9.0	0	*106	1372	12.9	7	7	42	1
1985—Washington NFL		15	7	51	7.3	0	91	1226	13.5	2	2	12	2
1986—Washington NFL		16	4	27	6.8	0	73	1068	14.6	4	4	24	2
1987—Washington NFL		9	6	63	10.5	0	38	483	12.7	6	6	36	0
1988—Washington NFL		16	7	46	6.6	0	72	946	13.1	5	5	30	0
Pro Totals—9 Years		125	37	202	5.5	0	576	7979	13.9	39	39	234	8

Additional pro statistics: Returned one kickoff for 10 yards, 1980; attempted one pass with one completion for 46 yards, 1983; recovered two fumbles, 1986; attempted one pass with no completions and recovered one fumble, 1988.
Played in NFC Championship Game following 1983 and 1986 seasons.
Played in NFL Championship Game following 1983 and 1987 seasons.
Played in Pro Bowl (NFL All-Star Game) following 1984 through 1986 seasons.

JOSEPH C. MONTANA
(Joe)
Quarterback—San Francisco 49ers
Born June 11, 1956, at Monongahela, Pa.
Height, 6.02. Weight, 195.
High School—Monongahela, Pa., Ringgold.
Received bachelor of business administration degree in marketing from
University of Notre Dame in 1978.

Established NFL records for highest completion percentage, career (63.22); most consecutive 300-yard games, season (5), 1982.
Led NFL quarterbacks in passing with 102.1 points in 1987.
Selected by San Francisco in 3rd round (82nd player selected) of 1979 NFL draft.
On injured reserve with back injury, September 15 through November 5, 1986; activated, November 6, 1986.
Crossed picket line during players' strike, October 7, 1987.

		PASSING							RUSHING				TOTAL		
Year Club	G.	Att.	Cmp.	Pct.	Gain	T.P.	P.I.	Avg.	Att.	Yds.	Avg.	TD.	TD.	Pts.	F.
1979—San Francisco NFL	16	23	13	56.5	96	1	0	4.17	3	22	7.3	0	0	0	1
1980—San Francisco NFL	15	273	176	*64.5	1795	15	9	6.58	32	77	2.4	2	2	12	4
1981—San Francisco NFL	16	488	311	*63.7	3565	19	12	7.31	25	95	3.8	2	2	12	2
1982—San Francisco NFL	9	*346	213	61.6	2613	*17	11	7.55	30	118	3.9	1	1	6	4
1983—San Francisco NFL	16	515	332	64.5	3910	26	12	7.59	61	284	4.7	2	2	12	3
1984—San Francisco NFL	16	432	279	64.6	3630	28	10	8.40	39	118	3.0	2	2	12	4
1985—San Francisco NFL	15	494	303	*61.3	3653	27	13	7.39	42	153	3.6	3	3	18	5
1986—San Francisco NFL	8	307	191	62.2	2236	8	9	7.28	17	38	2.2	0	0	0	3
1987—San Francisco NFL	13	398	266	*66.8	3054	*31	13	7.67	35	141	4.0	1	1	6	3
1988—San Francisco NFL	14	397	238	59.9	2981	18	10	7.51	38	132	3.5	3	3	18	3
Pro Totals—10 Years	138	3673	2322	63.2	27533	190	99	7.50	322	1178	3.7	16	16	96	32

Quarterback Rating Points: 1979 (80.9), 1980 (87.8), 1981 (88.2), 1982 (87.9), 1983 (94.6), 1984 (102.9), 1985 (91.3), 1986 (80.7), 1987 (102.1), 1988 (87.9). Total—92.1.

Additional pro statistics: Recovered one fumble, 1979 and 1980; recovered two fumbles and fumbled four times for minus two yards, 1982; recovered two fumbles and fumbled four times for minus three yards, 1984; recovered two fumbles and fumbled five times for minus 11 yards, 1985; recovered two fumbles and fumbled three times for minus five yards, 1987; recovered one fumble and fumbled three times for minus three yards, 1988.

Played in NFC Championship Game following 1981, 1983, 1984 and 1988 seasons.

Played in NFL Championship Game following 1981, 1984 and 1988 seasons.

Played in Pro Bowl (NFL All-Star Game) following 1981, 1983, 1984 and 1987 seasons.

Named to play in Pro Bowl following 1985 season; replaced due to injury by Jim McMahon.

GREGORY HUGH MONTGOMERY JR.
(Greg)
Punter—Houston Oilers

Born October 29, 1964, at Morristown, N. J.
Height, 6.03. Weight, 213.
High School—Little Silver, N. J., Red Bank Regional.
Attended Penn State University and received bachelor of arts degree in communications/sales
from Michigan State University in 1988.

Selected by Houston in 3rd round (72nd player selected) of 1988 NFL draft.
Signed by Houston Oilers, August 3, 1988.

		PUNTING		
Year Club	G.	No.	Avg.	Blk.
1988—Houston NFL	16	65	38.8	0

MAX MONTOYA JR.
Guard—Cincinnati Bengals

Born May 12, 1956, at Montebello, Calif.
Height, 6.05. Weight, 275.
High School—La Puente, Calif.
Attended Mt. San Jacinto Junior College and University of California at Los Angeles.

Selected by Cincinnati in 7th round (168th player selected) of 1979 NFL draft.
Cincinnati NFL, 1979 through 1988.
Games: 1979 (11), 1980 (16), 1981 (16), 1982 (9), 1983 (16), 1984 (16), 1985 (16), 1986 (16), 1987 (10), 1988 (15). Total—141.
Pro statistics: Recovered one fumble, 1981 and 1986.
Played in AFC Championship Game following 1981 and 1988 seasons.
Played in NFL Championship Game following 1981 and 1988 seasons.
Played in Pro Bowl (NFL All-Star Game) following 1986 and 1988 seasons.

WARREN MOON
Quarterback—Houston Oilers

Born November 18, 1956, at Los Angeles, Calif.
Height, 6.03. Weight, 210.
High School—Los Angeles, Calif., Hamilton.
Attended University of Washington.

Tied NFL record for most fumbles, season (17), 1984.
Signed as free agent by Edmonton Eskimos, March, 1978.
USFL rights traded by Memphis Showboats to Los Angeles Express for future draft pick, August 30, 1983.
Granted free agency, March 1, 1984; signed by Houston Oilers, March 1, 1984.
On injured reserve with fractured scapula, September 5 through October 14, 1988; activated, October 15, 1988.

		PASSING							RUSHING				TOTAL		
Year Club	G.	Att.	Cmp.	Pct.	Gain	T.P.	P.I.	Avg.	Att.	Yds.	Avg.	TD.	TD.	Pts.	F.
1978—Edmonton CFL	15	173	89	51.4	1112	5	7	6.43	30	114	3.8	1	1	6	1
1979—Edmonton CFL	16	274	149	54.4	2382	20	12	8.69	56	150	2.7	2	2	12	1
1980—Edmonton CFL	16	331	181	54.7	3127	25	11	9.45	55	352	6.4	3	3	18	0
1981—Edmonton CFL	15	378	237	62.7	3959	27	12	10.47	50	298	6.0	3	3	18	1
1982—Edmonton CFL	16	562	333	59.3	5000	36	16	8.90	54	259	4.8	4	4	24	1
1983—Edmonton CFL	16	664	380	57.2	5648	31	19	8.51	85	527	6.2	3	3	18	7
1984—Houston NFL	16	450	259	57.6	3338	12	14	7.42	58	211	3.6	1	1	6	*17
1985—Houston NFL	14	377	200	53.1	2709	15	19	7.19	39	130	3.3	0	0	0	12
1986—Houston NFL	15	488	256	52.5	3489	13	*26	7.15	42	157	3.7	2	2	12	11

Year Club	G.	Att.	Cmp.	Pct.	Gain	T.P.	P.I.	Avg.	Att.	Yds.	Avg.	TD.	TD.	Pts.	F.
				PASSING						RUSHING				TOTAL	
1987—Houston NFL	12	368	184	50.0	2806	21	18	7.63	34	112	3.3	3	3	18	8
1988—Houston NFL	11	294	160	54.4	2327	17	8	7.91	33	88	2.7	5	5	30	8
CFL Totals—6 Years	94	2382	1369	57.5	21228	144	77	8.91	330	1700	5.2	16	16	96	11
NFL Totals—5 Years	68	1977	1059	53.6	14669	78	85	7.42	206	698	3.4	11	11	66	56
Pro Totals—11 Years	162	4359	2428	55.7	35897	222	162	8.24	536	2398	4.5	27	27	162	67

Quarterback Rating Points: 1984 (76.9), 1985 (68.5), 1986 (62.3), 1987 (74.2), 1988 (88.4). Total—72.8.

Additional CFL statistics: Recovered one fumble, 1982.

Additional NFL statistics: Recovered seven fumbles and fumbled 17 times for minus one yard, 1984; recovered five fumbles and fumbled 12 times for minus eight yards, 1985; recovered three fumbles and fumbled 11 times for minus four yards, 1986; recovered six fumbles and fumbled eight times for minus seven yards, 1987; recovered four fumbles and fumbled eight times for minus 12 yards, 1988.

Played in CFL Championship Game following 1978 through 1982 seasons.

Played in Pro Bowl (NFL All-Star Game) following 1988 season.

BRENT ALLEN MOORE
Linebacker—Green Bay Packers
Born January 9, 1963, at Novato, Calif.
Height, 6.05. Weight, 242.
High School—Novato, Calif., San Marin.
Received bachelor of science degree in business administration
from University of Southern California in 1986.

Selected by Green Bay in 9th round (236th player selected) of 1986 NFL draft.
Signed by Green Bay Packers, July 17, 1986.
On injured reserve with toe injury, August 19 through entire 1986 season.
On injured reserve with foot injury, September 1 through October 30, 1987; activated, October 31, 1987.
On injured reserve with knee injury, August 22 through entire 1988 season.
Green Bay NFL, 1987.
Games: 1987 (4).

ERIC PATRICK MOORE
Offensive Tackle—New York Giants
Born January 21, 1965, at Berkeley, Mo.
Height, 6.05. Weight, 290.
High School—Berkeley, Mo.
Attended Northeastern Oklahoma A&M and received degree in general studies
and criminal justice from Indiana University in 1988.
Cousin of Dwight Scales, wide receiver with Los Angeles Rams, New York Giants,
San Diego Chargers and Seattle Seahawks, 1976 through 1979 and 1981 through 1984.

Selected by New York Giants in 1st round (10th player selected) of 1988 NFL draft.
Signed by New York Giants, August 1, 1988.
New York Giants NFL, 1988.
Games: 1988 (11).

MARK QUENTIN MOORE
Safety—San Diego Chargers
Born September 3, 1964, at Nacogdoches, Tex.
Height, 6.00. Weight, 194.
High School—Nacogdoches, Tex.
Attended Oklahoma State University.

Selected by Seattle in 4th round (104th player selected) of 1987 NFL draft.
Signed by Seattle Seahawks, July 22, 1987.
On injured reserve with hamstring injury, September 7 through October 23, 1987; activated, October 24, 1987.
On injured reserve with hamstring injury, October 31 through November 29, 1987; activated, November 30, 1987.
Released by Seattle Seahawks, August 30, 1988; signed as free agent by San Diego Chargers, February 27, 1989.
Seattle NFL, 1987.
Games: 1987 (5).

ROBERT ANTHONY MOORE
Safety—Atlanta Falcons
Born August 15, 1964, at Shreveport, La.
Height, 5.11. Weight, 190.
High School—Shreveport, La., Captain Shreve.
Attended Northwestern State University.

Signed as free agent by Atlanta Falcons, June 30, 1986.
Released by Atlanta Falcons, September 1, 1986; re-signed by Falcons, September 2, 1986.

Year Club	G.	No.	Yds.	Avg.	TD.
		INTERCEPTIONS			
1986—Atlanta NFL	16	1	0	0.0	0
1987—Atlanta NFL	12	2	23	11.5	0
1988—Atlanta NFL	16	5	56	11.2	1
Pro Totals—3 Years	44	8	79	9.9	1

Additional pro statistics: Recovered two fumbles for 20 yards and a touchdown, 1987.

RICHARD JAMES MORAN
(Rich)
Center-Guard—Green Bay Packers
Born March 19, 1962, at Boise, Ida.
Height, 6.02. Weight, 272.
High School—Pleasanton, Calif., Foothill.
Received degree in marketing from San Diego State University in 1985.
Son of Jim Moran, defensive tackle with New York Giants, 1964 through 1967; and brother of Eric Moran, offensive tackle-guard with Los Angeles Express and Houston Oilers, 1983 through 1986.

Selected by Arizona in 4th round (57th player selected) of 1985 USFL draft.
Selected by Green Bay in 3rd round (71st player selected) of 1985 NFL draft.
Signed by Green Bay Packers, July 24, 1985.
On injured reserve with knee injury, September 10 through November 25, 1986; activated, November 26, 1986.
Green Bay NFL, 1985 through 1988.
Games: 1985 (16), 1986 (5), 1987 (12), 1988 (16). Total—49.
Pro statistics: Recovered one fumble and fumbled once for three yards, 1987.

STANLEY DOUGLAS MORGAN
Wide Receiver—New England Patriots
Born February 17, 1955, at Easley, S. C.
Height, 5.11. Weight, 181.
High School—Easley, S. C.
Received bachelor of science degree in education from University of Tennessee in 1979.

Named to THE SPORTING NEWS NFL All-Star Team, 1986.
Selected by New England in 1st round (25th player selected) of 1977 NFL draft.

Year Club	G.	—RUSHING— Att.	Yds.	Avg.	TD.	PASS RECEIVING P.C.	Yds.	Avg.	TD.	—TOTAL— TD.	Pts.	F.
1977—New England NFL	14	1	10	10.0	0	21	443	*21.1	3	3	18	0
1978—New England NFL	16	2	11	5.5	0	34	820	24.1	5	5	30	6
1979—New England NFL	16	7	39	5.6	0	44	1002	*22.8	*12	13	78	1
1980—New England NFL	16	4	36	9.0	0	45	991	*22.0	6	6	36	0
1981—New England NFL	13	2	21	10.5	0	44	1029	*23.4	6	6	36	2
1982—New England NFL	9	2	3	1.5	0	28	584	20.9	3	3	18	0
1983—New England NFL	16	1	13	13.0	0	58	863	14.9	2	2	12	5
1984—New England NFL	13			None		38	709	18.7	5	5	30	0
1985—New England NFL	15	1	0	0.0	0	39	760	19.5	5	5	30	1
1986—New England NFL	16			None		84	1491	17.8	10	10	60	0
1987—New England NFL	10			None		40	672	16.8	3	3	18	0
1988—New England NFL	16	1	—6	—6.0	0	31	502	16.2	4	4	24	1
Pro Totals—12 Years	170	21	127	6.0	0	506	9866	19.5	64	65	390	16

Year Club	G.	—PUNT RETURNS— No.	Yds.	Avg.	TD.
1977—New England NFL	14	16	220	13.8	0
1978—New England NFL	16	32	335	10.5	0
1979—New England NFL	16	29	289	10.0	1
1980—New England NFL	16		None		
1981—New England NFL	13	15	116	7.7	0
1982—New England NFL	9		None		
1983—New England NFL	16		None		
1984—New England NFL	13		None		
1985—New England NFL	15		None		
1986—New England NFL	16		None		
1987—New England NFL	10		None		
1988—New England NFL	16		None		
Pro Totals—12 Years	170	92	960	10.4	1

Additional pro statistics: Returned one kickoff for 17 yards, 1978; returned one kickoff for 12 yards, 1979; recovered one fumble for three yards, 1980; recovered two fumbles, 1981 and 1983; recovered one fumble, 1988.
Played in AFC Championship Game following 1985 season.
Played in NFL Championship Game following 1985 season.
Played in Pro Bowl (NFL All-Star Game) following 1979, 1980, 1986 and 1987 seasons.

JAMES ROBERT MORRIS
(Jim Bob)
Defensive Back—Houston Oilers
Born May 17, 1961, at Burbank, Calif.
Height, 6.03. Weight, 211.
High School—Hamilton, Kan.
Attended Coffeyville Junior College and Kansas State University.

Signed as free agent by Kansas City Chiefs, May 5, 1983.
Released by Kansas City Chiefs, August 1, 1983.
USFL rights traded by Oklahoma Outlaws to San Antonio Gunslingers for past consideration, January 31, 1984.
Signed by San Antonio Gunslingers, January 31, 1984.
On developmental squad, April 26 through May 2, 1984; activated, May 3, 1984.
On developmental squad, May 17 through May 30, 1984; activated, May 31, 1984.
On developmental squad, June 22 through remainder of 1985 season.
Released by San Antonio Gunslingers, July 23, 1985; signed as free agent by Memphis Showboats, June 27, 1986.

Granted free agency when USFL suspended operations, August 7, 1986; signed as replacement player by Green Bay Packers, September 25, 1987.
On injured reserve with knee injury, December 26 through remainder of 1987 season.
Released by Green Bay Packers, August 16, 1988; signed as free agent by Houston Oilers, May 19, 1989.
On developmental squad for 3 games with San Antonio Gunslingers in 1984.
On developmental squad for 1 game with San Antonio Gunslingers in 1985.

| | | —INTERCEPTIONS— | | | |
Year Club	G.	No.	Yds.	Avg.	TD.
1984—San Antonio USFL........	15	3	19	6.3	0
1985—San Antonio USFL........	17	2	37	18.5	0
1987—Green Bay NFL............	11	3	135	45.0	0
USFL Totals—2 Years........	32	5	56	11.2	0
NFL Totals—1 Year............	11	3	135	45.0	0
Pro Totals—3 Years............	43	8	191	23.9	0

Additional pro statistics: Credited with four sacks for 39 yards, 1984; credited with four sacks for 45 yards, recovered two fumbles and fumbled once, 1985.

JAMES WALTER MORRIS
(Jamie)
Running Back—Washington Redskins
Born June 6, 1965, at Southern Pines, N. C.
Height, 5.07. Weight, 188.
High School—Ayer, Mass.
Attended University of Michigan.
Brother of Joe Morris, running back with New York Giants.

Selected by Washington in 4th round (109th player selected) of 1988 NFL draft.
Signed by Washington Redskins, June 13, 1988.

| | | —RUSHING— | | | | PASS RECEIVING | | | | —TOTAL— | | |
Year Club	G.	Att.	Yds.	Avg.	TD.	P.C.	Yds.	Avg.	TD.	TD.	Pts.	F.
1988—Washington NFL......................	16	126	437	3.5	2	1	3	3.0	0	2	12	3

| | | KICKOFF RETURNS | | | |
Year Club	G.	No.	Yds.	Avg.	TD.
1988—Washington NFL..........	16	21	413	19.7	0

JOSEPH MORRIS
(Joe)
Running Back—New York Giants
Born September 15, 1960, at Fort Bragg, N.C.
Height, 5.07. Weight, 195.
High Schools—Southern Pines, N.C.; and Ayer, Mass.
Attended Syracuse University.
Brother of Jamie Morris, running back with Washington Redskins.

Named to THE SPORTING NEWS NFL All-Star Team, 1986.
Selected by New York Giants in 2nd round (45th player selected) of 1982 NFL draft.
Granted roster exemption, August 26 through August 28, 1986; activated, August 29, 1986.

| | | —RUSHING— | | | | PASS RECEIVING | | | | —TOTAL— | | |
Year Club	G.	Att.	Yds.	Avg.	TD.	P.C.	Yds.	Avg.	TD.	TD.	Pts.	F.
1982—New York Giants NFL	5	15	48	3.2	1	8	34	4.3	0	1	6	1
1983—New York Giants NFL	15	35	145	4.1	0	2	1	0.5	1	1	6	2
1984—New York Giants NFL	16	133	510	3.8	4	12	124	10.3	0	4	24	1
1985—New York Giants NFL	16	294	1336	4.5	*21	22	212	9.6	0	*21	126	6
1986—New York Giants NFL	15	341	1516	4.4	14	21	233	11.1	1	15	90	6
1987—New York Giants NFL	11	193	658	3.4	3	11	114	10.4	0	3	18	2
1988—New York Giants NFL	16	307	1083	3.5	5	22	166	7.5	0	5	30	7
Pro Totals—7 Years..................	94	1318	5296	4.0	48	98	884	9.0	2	50	300	25

| | | KICKOFF RETURNS | | | |
Year Club	G.	No.	Yds.	Avg.	TD.
1982—N. Y. Giants NFL	5		None		
1983—N. Y. Giants NFL	15	14	255	18.2	0
1984—N. Y. Giants NFL	16	6	69	11.5	0
1985—N. Y. Giants NFL	16	2	25	12.5	0
1986—N. Y. Giants NFL	15		None		
1987—N. Y. Giants NFL	11		None		
1988—N. Y. Giants NFL	16		None		
Pro Totals—7 Years...........	94	22	349	15.9	0

Additional pro statistics: Recovered one fumble, 1982, 1983 and 1988; recovered two fumbles, 1985 and 1986.
Played in NFC Championship Game following 1986 season.
Played in NFL Championship Game following 1986 season.
Played in Pro Bowl (NFL All-Star Game) following 1985 and 1986 seasons.

MICHAEL STEPHEN MORRIS
(Mike)
Center-Guard—Washington Redskins

Born February 22, 1961, at Centerville, Ia.
Height, 6.05. Weight, 275.
High School—Centerville, Ia.
Received degree in psychology and physical education
from Northeast Missouri State University.

Signed as free agent by Arizona Outlaws, November 1, 1984.
Released by Arizona Outlaws, February 11, 1985; signed as free agent by Denver Broncos, May 8, 1986.
Released by Denver Broncos, July 21, 1986, signed as free agent by St. Louis Cardinals, May 20, 1987.
Crossed picket line during players' strike, October 7, 1987.
Franchise transferred to Phoenix, March 15, 1988.
On injured reserve with knee injury, August 23 through entire 1988 season.
Granted unconditional free agency, February 1, 1989; signed by Washington Redskins, March 20, 1989.
St. Louis NFL, 1987.
Games: 1987 (14).

RANDALL MORRIS
Running Back—Detroit Lions

Born April 22, 1961, at Anniston, Ala.
Height, 6.00. Weight, 200.
High School—Long Beach, Calif., Polytechnic.
Attended University of Tennessee.
Brother of Thomas Morris, safety with Tampa Bay Buccaneers, 1982 and 1983.

Selected by Memphis in 1984 USFL territorial draft.
Selected by Seattle in 10th round (270th player selected) of 1984 NFL draft.
Signed by Seattle Seahawks, May 18, 1984.
On injured reserve with neck injury, August 28 through September 27, 1984; activated, September 28, 1984.
Released by Seattle Seahawks, November 8, 1988; awarded on waivers to Detroit Lions, November 9, 1988.

| | | —RUSHING— | | | | PASS RECEIVING | | | | —TOTAL— | | |
Year Club	G.	Att.	Yds.	Avg.	TD.	P.C.	Yds.	Avg.	TD.	TD.	Pts.	F.
1984—Seattle NFL	10	58	189	3.3	0	9	61	6.8	0	0	0	2
1985—Seattle NFL	16	55	236	4.3	0	6	14	2.3	0	0	0	4
1986—Seattle NFL	16	19	149	7.8	1		None			1	6	2
1987—Seattle NFL	10	21	71	3.4	0		None			0	0	0
1988—Seattle (9)-Detroit (3) NFL	12	3	6	2.0	0		None			0	0	0
Pro Totals—5 Years	64	156	651	4.2	1	15	75	5.0	0	1	6	8

| | | KICKOFF RETURNS | | |
Year Club	G.	No.	Yds.	Avg.TD.
1984—Seattle NFL	10	8	153	19.1 0
1985—Seattle NFL	16	31	636	20.5 0
1986—Seattle NFL	16	23	465	20.2 0
1987—Seattle NFL	10	9	149	16.6 0
1988—Sea. (9)-Det. (3) NFL	12	13	259	19.9 0
Pro Totals—5 Years	64	84	1662	19.8 0

Additional pro statistics: Recovered one fumble, 1984; attempted one pass with no completions, 1985 and 1986.

RONALD WAYNE MORRIS
(Ron)
Wide Receiver—Chicago Bears

Born November 14, 1964, at Cooper, Tex.
Height, 6.01. Weight, 195.
High School—Cooper, Tex.
Attended Southern Methodist University.

Selected by Chicago in 2nd round (54th player selected) of 1987 NFL draft.
Signed by Chicago Bears, July 31, 1987.

| | | —PASS RECEIVING— | | |
Year Club	G.	P.C.	Yds.	Avg. TD.
1987—Chicago NFL	12	20	379	19.0 1
1988—Chicago NFL	16	28	498	17.8 4
Pro Totals—2 Years	28	48	877	18.3 5

Additional pro statistics: Rushed three times for 40 yards, 1988.
Played in NFC Championship Game following 1988 season.

JAMES MORRISSEY
(Jim)
Linebacker—Chicago Bears

Born December 24, 1962, at Flint, Mich.
Height, 6.03. Weight, 227.
High School—Flint, Mich., Powers.
Attended Michigan State University.

Selected by Baltimore in 8th round (106th player selected) of 1985 USFL draft.

Selected by Chicago in 11th round (302nd player selected) of 1985 NFL draft.
Signed by Chicago Bears, June 26, 1985.
Released by Chicago Bears, September 2, 1985; re-signed by Bears, September 10, 1985.
On injured reserve with knee injury, September 30 through November 4, 1988; activated, November 5, 1988.
Chicago NFL, 1985 through 1988.
Games: 1985 (15), 1986 (16), 1987 (10), 1988 (11). Total—52.
Pro statistics: Intercepted three passes for 13 yards and recovered one fumble, 1988.
Played in NFC Championship Game following 1985 and 1988 seasons.
Played in NFL Championship Game following 1985 season.

BOBBY MORSE
Running Back—New Orleans Saints
Born October 3, 1965, at Muskegon, Mich.
Height, 5.10. Weight, 213.
High School—Muskegon, Mich., Catholic Central.
Received degree in advertising from Michigan State University in 1987.

Selected by Philadelphia in 12th round (316th player selected) of 1987 NFL draft.
Signed by Philadelphia Eagles, August 6, 1987.
Left Philadelphia Eagles camp voluntarily, July 28 through August 21, 1988; then transferred to left camp/reserve, August 22 through entire 1988 season.
Traded by Philadelphia Eagles to New Orleans Saints for conditional 11th round pick in 1990 draft, April 24, 1989.

		—RUSHING—				PASS RECEIVING				—TOTAL—		
Year	Club	G.	Att.	Yds.	Avg.	TD.	P.C.	Yds.	Avg.	TD.	TD. Pts.	F.
1987—Philadelphia NFL		11	6	14	2.3	0	1	8	8.0	0	0 0	1

			—PUNT RETURNS—				—KICKOFF RET.—		
Year	Club	G.	No.	Yds.	Avg.	TD.	No.	Yds.	Avg.TD.
1987—Philadelphia NFL		11	20	121	6.1	0	24	386	16.1 0

Additional pro statistics: Recovered one fumble, 1987.

DONALD HOWARD MOSEBAR
(Don)
Center-Offensive Tackle—Los Angeles Raiders
Born September 11, 1961, at Yakima, Calif.
Height, 6.06. Weight, 275.
High School—Visalia, Calif., Mount Whitney.
Attended University of Southern California.

Selected by Los Angeles in 1983 USFL territorial draft.
Selected by Los Angeles Raiders in 1st round (26th player selected) of 1983 NFL draft.
Signed by Los Angeles Raiders, August 29, 1983.
Granted roster exemption, August 29, 1983; activated, September 9, 1983.
On injured reserve with back injury, November 8 through remainder of 1984 season.
Los Angeles Raiders NFL, 1983 through 1988.
Games: 1983 (14), 1984 (10), 1985 (16), 1986 (16), 1987 (12), 1988 (13). Total—81.
Pro statistics: Recovered one fumble and fumbled once, 1986.
Played in AFC Championship Game following 1983 season.
Played in NFL Championship Game following 1983 season.

WINSTON N. MOSS
Linebacker—Tampa Bay Buccaneers
Born December 24, 1965, at Miami, Fla.
Height, 6.03. Weight, 235.
High School—Miami, Fla., Southridge.
Attended University of Miami (Fla.).

Selected by Tampa Bay in 2nd round (50th player selected) of 1987 NFL draft.
Signed by Tampa Bay Buccaneers, July 18, 1987.
Tampa Bay NFL, 1987 and 1988.
Games: 1987 (12), 1988 (16). Total—28.
Pro statistics: Recovered one fumble in end zone for a touchdown, 1987.

WALTER STEPHEN MOTT III
(Steve)
Center—Detroit Lions
Born March 24, 1961, at New Orleans, La.
Height, 6.03. Weight, 265.
High School—Marrero, La., Archbishop Shaw.
Attended University of Alabama.

Selected by Birmingham in 1983 USFL territorial draft.
Selected by Detroit in 5th round (121st player selected) of 1983 NFL draft.
Signed by Detroit Lions, June 1, 1983.
On physically unable to perform/active with knee injury, July 22 through August 8, 1984; activated, August 9, 1984.
On injured reserve with dislocated ankle, October 8 through remainder of 1984 season.
Detroit NFL, 1983 through 1988.
Games: 1983 (13), 1984 (6), 1985 (16), 1986 (14), 1987 (11), 1988 (16). Total—76.
Pro statistics: Fumbled once, 1983; recovered one fumble, 1985; fumbled three times for minus 23 yards, 1988.

ZEKE MOWATT
Tight End—New York Giants

Born March 5, 1961, at Wauchula, Fla.
Height, 6.03. Weight, 238.
High School—Wauchula, Fla., Hardee County.
Attended Florida State University.

Selected by Tampa Bay in 1983 USFL territorial draft.
Signed as free agent by New York Giants, June 1, 1983.
On injured reserve with knee injury, August 31 through entire 1985 season.

Year Club	G.	P.C.	Yds.	Avg.	TD.
1983—N.Y. Giants NFL	16	21	280	13.3	1
1984—N.Y. Giants NFL	16	48	698	14.5	6
1986—N.Y. Giants NFL	16	10	119	11.9	2
1987—N.Y. Giants NFL	12	3	39	13.0	1
1988—N.Y. Giants NFL	16	15	196	13.1	1
Pro Totals—5 Years	76	97	1332	13.7	11

Additional pro statistics: Recovered one fumble and fumbled once, 1986; fumbled twice, 1988.
Played in NFC Championship Game following 1986 season.
Played in NFL Championship Game following 1986 season.

PAUL STEWART MOYER
Safety—Seattle Seahawks

Born July 26, 1961, at Villa Park, Calif.
Height, 6.01. Weight, 196.
High School—Villa Park, Calif.
Attended Fullerton College and Arizona State University.

Signed as free agent by Seattle Seahawks, April 28, 1983.
On injured reserve with shoulder injury, September 11 through October 17, 1985; activated, October 18, 1985.

Year Club	G.	No.	Yds.	Avg.	TD.
1983—Seattle NFL	16	1	19	19.0	1
1984—Seattle NFL	16		None		
1985—Seattle NFL	11		None		
1986—Seattle NFL	16	3	38	12.7	0
1987—Seattle NFL	12	1	0	0.0	0
1988—Seattle NFL	16	6	79	13.2	0
Pro Totals—6 Years	87	11	136	12.4	1

Additional pro statistics: Recovered three fumbles, 1983; recovered blocked punt in end zone for a touchdown, 1986; recovered three fumbles for 10 yards, 1987; recovered two fumbles, 1988.
Played in AFC Championship Game following 1983 season.

MARK DAVID MRAZ
Defensive End—Los Angeles Raiders

Born February 9, 1965, at Glendale, Calif.
Height, 6.04. Weight, 260.
High School—Glendora, Calif.
Attended Utah State University.

Selected by Atlanta in 5th round (125th player selected) of 1987 NFL draft.
Signed by Atlanta Falcons, July 26, 1987.
Released by Atlanta Falcons, August 31, 1988; signed as free agent by Los Angeles Raiders, April 4, 1989.
Atlanta NFL, 1987.
Games: 1987 (11).

JAMIE F. MUELLER
(Name pronounced MEW-ler.)
Fullback—Buffalo Bills

Born October 4, 1964, at Cleveland, O.
Height, 6.01. Weight, 225.
High School—Fairview Park, O., Fairview.
Attended Bendictine College.

Selected by Buffalo in 3rd round (78th player selected) of 1987 NFL draft.
Signed by Buffalo Bills, July 25, 1987.

Year Club		RUSHING				PASS RECEIVING				TOTAL		
	G.	Att.	Yds.	Avg.	TD.	P.C.	Yds.	Avg.	TD.	TD.	Pts.	F.
1987—Buffalo NFL	12	82	354	4.3	2	3	13	4.3	0	2	12	5
1988—Buffalo NFL	15	81	296	3.7	0	8	42	5.3	0	0	0	2
Pro Totals—2 Years	27	163	650	4.0	2	11	55	5.0	0	2	12	7

Additional pro statistics: Returned five kickoffs for 74 yards, 1987; recovered one fumble, 1987 and 1988.
Played in AFC Championship Game following 1988 season.

VANCE ALAN MUELLER
Running Back—Los Angeles Raiders
Born May 5, 1964, at Tucson, Ariz.
Height, 6.00. Weight, 215.
High School—Jackson, Calif.
Received bachelor of science degree in psychology and physiology from Occidental College in 1986.
Selected by Los Angeles Raiders in 4th round (103rd player selected) of 1986 NFL draft.
Signed by Los Angeles Raiders, July 15, 1986.

		—RUSHING—				PASS RECEIVING				—TOTAL—		
Year Club	G.	Att.	Yds.	Avg.	TD.	P.C.	Yds.	Avg.	TD.	TD.	Pts.	F.
1986—Los Angeles Raiders NFL	15	13	30	2.3	0	6	54	9.0	0	0	0	1
1987—Los Angeles Raiders NFL	12	37	175	4.7	1	11	95	8.6	0	1	6	3
1988—Los Angeles Raiders NFL	14	17	60	3.5	0	5	63	12.6	0	0	0	1
Pro Totals—3 Years	41	67	265	4.0	1	22	212	9.6	0	1	6	5

		KICKOFF RETURNS		
Year Club	G.	No.	Yds.	Avg.TD.
1986—L. A. Raiders NFL	15	2	73	36.5 0
1987—L. A. Raiders NFL	12	27	588	21.8 0
1988—L. A. Raiders NFL	14	5	97	19.4 0
Pro Totals—3 Years	41	34	758	22.3 0

Additional pro statistics: Recovered one fumble, 1987 and 1988.

MICHAEL RENE MULARKEY
(Mike)
Tight End—Pittsburgh Steelers
Born November 19, 1961, at Miami, Fla.
Height, 6.04. Weight, 240.
High School—Fort Lauderdale, Fla., Northeast.
Attended University of Florida.
Selected by Tampa Bay in 1983 USFL territorial draft.
Selected by San Francisco in 9th round (229th player selected) of 1983 NFL draft.
Signed by San Francisco 49ers, June 1, 1983.
Released by San Francisco 49ers, August 29, 1983; awarded on waivers to Minnesota Vikings, August 30, 1983.
On injured reserve with ankle injury, September 30 through remainder of 1983 season.
On injured reserve with knee injury, September 8 through October 30, 1987; activated, October 31, 1987.
Crossed picket line during players' strike, October 7, 1987; returned to picket line, October 12, 1987.
Granted unconditional free agency, February 1, 1989; signed by Pittsburgh Steelers, March 31, 1989.

		—PASS RECEIVING—		
Year Club	G.	P.C.	Yds.	Avg. TD.
1983—Minnesota NFL	3		None	
1984—Minnesota NFL	16	14	134	9.6 2
1985—Minnesota NFL	15	13	196	15.1 1
1986—Minnesota NFL	16	11	89	8.1 2
1987—Minnesota NFL	9	1	6	6.0 0
1988—Minnesota NFL	16	3	39	13.0 0
Pro Totals—6 Years	75	42	464	11.0 5

Additional pro statistics: Recovered one fumble and fumbled once, 1984; ran nine yards with lateral on kickoff return, 1985; returned one kickoff for 16 yards, 1987; rushed once for minus six yards, 1988.

MIKE MUNCHAK
Guard—Houston Oilers
Born March 5, 1960, at Scranton, Pa.
Height, 6.03. Weight, 280.
High School—Scranton, Pa., Central.
Received bachelor of business administration degree from Penn State University in 1982.
Named to THE SPORTING NEWS NFL All-Star Team, 1987.
Selected by Houston in 1st round (8th player selected) of 1982 NFL draft.
On injured reserve with broken ankle, November 24 through December 23, 1982; activated, December 24, 1982.
On injured reserve with knee injury, October 14 through remainder of 1986 season.
Houston NFL, 1982 through 1988.
Games: 1982 (4), 1983 (16), 1984 (16), 1985 (16), 1986 (6), 1987 (12), 1988 (16). Total—86.
Pro statistics: Recovered two fumbles for three yards, 1985, recovered one fumble in end zone for a touchdown, 1986; recovered one fumble, 1987 and 1988.
Played in Pro Bowl (NFL All-Star Game) following 1984, 1985, 1987 and 1988 seasons.

MARC CHRISTOPHER MUNFORD
Linebacker—Denver Broncos
Born February 14, 1965, at Lincoln, Neb.
Height, 6.02. Weight, 231.
High School—Littleton, Colo., Heritage.
Attended University of Nebraska.
Selected by Denver in 4th round (111th player selected) of 1987 NFL draft.
Signed by Denver Broncos, July 19, 1987.

On injured reserve with back injury, January 9, 1988 through remainder of 1987 season playoffs.
Released by Denver Broncos, August 30, 1988; re-signed by Broncos, September 21, 1988.
On injured reserve with knee injury, October 10 through November 21, 1988; re-signed by Broncos after clearing procedural waivers, November 23, 1988.
Denver NFL, 1987 and 1988.
Games: 1987 (12), 1988 (7). Total—19.
Pro statistics: Recovered two fumbles, 1987.

MICHAEL ANTHONY MUNOZ
(Known by middle name.)
Offensive Tackle—Cincinnati Bengals
Born August 19, 1958, at Ontario, Calif.
Height, 6.06. Weight, 278.
High School—Ontario, Calif., Chaffey.
Received bachelor of science degree in public administration from
University of Southern California in 1980.

Named to THE SPORTING NEWS NFL All-Star Team, 1981, 1984 through 1986 and 1988.
Selected by Cincinnati in 1st round (3rd player selected) of 1980 NFL draft.
Granted free agency, February 1, 1987; re-signed by Bengals, September 12, 1987.
Granted roster exemption, September 12 through September 18, 1987; activated, September 19, 1987.
Cincinnati NFL, 1980 through 1988.
Games: 1980 (16), 1981 (16), 1982 (9), 1983 (16), 1984 (16), 1985 (16), 1986 (16), 1987 (11), 1988 (16). Total—132.
Pro statistics: Caught one pass for minus six yards, 1980; caught one pass for one yard and a touchdown and recovered one fumble, 1984; caught one pass for one yard, 1985; caught two passes for seven yards and two touchdowns, 1986; caught two passes for 15 yards and a touchdown, 1987; recovered two fumbles, 1988.
Played in AFC Championship Game following 1981 and 1988 seasons.
Played in NFL Championship Game following 1981 and 1988 seasons.
Played in Pro Bowl (NFL All-Star Game) following 1981, 1983 through 1986 and 1988 seasons.
Named to play in Pro Bowl following 1987 season; replaced due to injury by Jim Lachey.

KEVIN DION MURPHY
Linebacker—Tampa Bay Buccaneers
Born September 8, 1963, at Plano, Tex.
Height, 6.02. Weight, 235.
High School—Richardson, Tex., L. V. Berkner.
Received degree in marketing from University of Oklahoma in 1986.

Named as linebacker on THE SPORTING NEWS College All-America Team, 1985.
Selected by Los Angeles in 11th round (154th player selected) of 1985 NFL USFL draft (elected to return to college for final year of eligibility).
Selected by Tampa Bay in 2nd round (40th player selected) of 1986 NFL draft.
Signed by Tampa Bay Buccaneers, July 22, 1986.
Tampa Bay NFL, 1986 through 1988.
Games: 1986 (16), 1987 (9), 1988 (16). Total—41.
Pro statistics: Recovered one fumble, 1986; intercepted one pass for 35 yards and a touchdown and recovered one fumble for four yards, 1988.

MARK STEVEN MURPHY
Safety—Green Bay Packers
Born April 22, 1958, at Canton, O.
Height, 6.02. Weight, 199.
High School—Canton, O., Glen Oaks.
Received bachelor of science degree in business administration from West Liberty State College.

Signed as free agent by Green Bay Packers, April 25, 1980.
On injured reserve with broken hand, August 14 through December 17, 1980; activated after clearing procedural waivers, December 19, 1980.
On injured reserve with ankle injury, September 2 through entire 1986 season.

| | | | —INTERCEPTIONS— | | |
Year	Club	G.	No.	Yds.	Avg.TD.
1980—Green Bay NFL		1		None	
1981—Green Bay NFL		16	3	57	19.0 0
1982—Green Bay NFL		9		None	
1983—Green Bay NFL		16		None	
1984—Green Bay NFL		16	1	4	4.0 0
1985—Green Bay NFL		15	2	50	25.0 ⋆1
1987—Green Bay NFL		12		None	
1988—Green Bay NFL		14	5	19	3.8 0
Pro Totals—8 Years		99	11	130	11.8 1

Additional pro statistics: Recovered two fumbles, 1981 and 1987; recovered one fumble, 1983 and 1985; recovered one fumble for two yards and fumbled once, 1984; returned one punt for four yards, 1985; recovered four fumbles, 1988.

—DID YOU KNOW—
That Eric Dickerson rushed for 38 yards in both his final game with the Los Angeles Rams on October 26, 1987, and his first with the Indianapolis Colts on November 1, 1987?

EDWARD PETER MURRAY
(Eddie)
Placekicker—Detroit Lions

Born August 29, 1956, at Halifax, Nova Scotia.
Height, 5.10. Weight, 180.
High School—Victoria, British Columbia, Spectrum.
Received bachelor of science degree in education from Tulane University in 1980.
Cousin of Mike Rogers, center with Edmonton Oilers, New England-Hartford Whalers and
New York Rangers, 1974-75 through 1985-86.

Selected by Detroit in 7th round (166th player selected) of 1980 NFL draft.
On suspended list, September 10 through November 19, 1982; reinstated, November 20, 1982.

		——PLACE KICKING——					
Year	Club	G.	XP.	XPM.	FG.	FGA.	Pts.
1980—Detroit NFL		16	35	1	★27	★42	116
1981—Detroit NFL		16	46	0	25	35	★121
1982—Detroit NFL		7	16	0	11	12	49
1983—Detroit NFL		16	38	0	25	32	113
1984—Detroit NFL		16	31	0	20	27	91
1985—Detroit NFL		16	31	2	26	31	109
1986—Detroit NFL		16	31	1	18	25	85
1987—Detroit NFL		12	21	0	20	32	81
1988—Detroit NFL		16	22	1	20	21	82
Pro Totals—9 Years		131	271	5	192	257	847

Additional pro statistics: Punted once for 37 yards, 1986; punted four times for a 38.8 average, 1987.
Played in Pro Bowl (NFL All-Star Game) following 1980 season.

WALTER C. MURRAY
Wide Receiver—San Francisco 49ers

Born December 13, 1962, at Berkeley, Calif.
Height, 6.04. Weight, 200.
High School—Berkeley, Calif.
Received bachelor of arts and science degree from University of Hawaii in 1986.
Related to Phil Smith, guard with Golden State Warriors, San Diego Clippers
and Seattle Supersonics, 1974-75 through 1982-83.

Selected by Washington in 2nd round (45th player selected) of 1986 NFL draft.
NFL rights traded by Washington Redskins to Indianapolis Colts for 2nd round pick in 1987 draft, October 7, 1986.
Signed by Indianapolis Colts, October 7, 1986.
Granted roster exemption, October 7 through October 16, 1986; activated, October 17, 1986.
Crossed picket line during players' strike, September 28, 1987; returned to picket line, October 1, 1987.
Crossed picket line during players' strike, October 2, 1987.
Released by Indianapolis Colts, August 30, 1988; signed as free agent by San Francisco 49ers for 1989, December 13, 1988.

		——PASS RECEIVING——			
Year	Club	G.	P.C.	Yds.	Avg. TD.
1986—Indianapolis NFL		5	2	34	17.0 0
1987—Indianapolis NFL		14	20	339	17.0 3
Pro Totals—2 Years		19	22	373	17.0 3

BRAD WILLIAM MUSTER
Fullback—Chicago Bears

Born April 11, 1965, at Novato, Calif.
Height, 6.03. Weight, 231.
High School—Novato, Calif., San Marin.
Received bachelor of arts degree in economics from Stanford University in 1988.

Selected by Chicago in 1st round (23rd player selected) of 1988 NFL draft.
Signed by Chicago Bears, July 20, 1988.

		——RUSHING——				PASS RECEIVING				—TOTAL—		
Year	Club	G.	Att.	Yds.	Avg. TD.	P.C.	Yds.	Avg. TD.		TD.	Pts.	F.
1988—Chicago NFL		16	44	197	4.5 0	21	236	11.2 1		1	6	1

Additional pro statistics: Returned three kickoffs for 33 yards and recovered one fumble, 1988.
Played in NFC Championship Game following 1988 season.

PETER MICHAEL NAJARIAN
(Pete)
Linebacker—Tampa Bay Buccaneers

Born December 22, 1963, at San Francisco, Calif.
Height, 6.02. Weight, 230.
High School—Minneapolis, Minn., Central.
Attended University of Minnesota.

Signed as free agent by Seattle Seahawks, May 2, 1986.
Released by Seattle Seahawks, August 1, 1986; signed as free agent by Minnesota Vikings, August 5, 1986.
Released by Minnesota Vikings, August 26, 1986; re-signed by Vikings, April 8, 1987.
Released by Minnesota Vikings, September 7, 1987; re-signed as replacement player by Vikings, October 1, 1987.
Released by Minnesota Vikings, October 19, 1987; re-signed by Vikings, November 5, 1987.

Released by Minnesota Vikings, November 25, 1987; re-signed by Vikings, December 2, 1987.
Released by Minnesota Vikings, December 8, 1987; signed as free agent by Tampa Bay Buccaneers, February 18, 1988.
Released by Tampa Bay Buccaneers, August 23, 1988; re-signed by Buccaneers, October 4, 1988.
On injured reserve with knee injury, October 14 through remainder of 1988 season.
Minnesota NFL, 1987; Tampa Bay NFL, 1988.
Games: 1987 (5), 1988 (1). Total—6.

ERIC ANDREW NAPOSKI
Linebacker—Dallas Cowboys
Born December 20, 1966, at Manhattan, N.Y.
Height, 6.01. Weight, 197.
High School—Eastchester, N.Y.
Attended University of Connecticut.

Signed as free agent by New England Patriots, April 29, 1988. (signing later voided.)
Signed as free agent by New England Patriots, July 13, 1988.
Released by New England Patriots, August 29, 1988; re-signed by Patriots, August 30, 1988.
On injured reserve with broken ribs, September 29 through remainder of 1988 season.
Granted unconditional free agency, February 1, 1989; signed by Dallas Cowboys, March 1, 1989.
New England NFL, 1988.
Games: 1988 (3).

JOSEPH ANDREW NASH
(Joe)
Nose Tackle—Seattle Seahawks
Born October 11, 1960, at Boston, Mass.
Height, 6.02. Weight, 269.
High School—Dorchester, Mass., Boston College High.
Received bachelor of arts degree in sociology from Boston College in 1982.

Signed as free agent by Seattle Seahawks, April 30, 1982.
On inactive list, September 12 and September 19, 1982.
Seattle NFL, 1982 through 1988.
Games: 1982 (7), 1983 (16), 1984 (16), 1985 (16), 1986 (16), 1987 (12), 1988 (15). Total—98.
Pro statistics: Recovered three fumbles (including one in end zone for a touchdown), 1984; recovered two fumbles, 1986; recovered one fumble, 1988.
Played in AFC Championship Game following 1983 season.
Played in Pro Bowl (NFL All-Star Game) following 1984 season.

RICKY RENNARD NATTIEL
(Name pronounced Na-TEEL.)
Wide Receiver—Denver Broncos
Born January 25, 1966, at Gainesville, Fla.
Height, 5.09. Weight, 180.
High School—Newberry, Fla.
Received degree in rehabilitation counseling from University of Florida in 1987.

Selected by Denver in 1st round (27th player selected) of 1987 NFL draft.
Signed by Denver Broncos, July 23, 1987.

| | | PASS RECEIVING | | | –PUNT RETURNS– | | | | —KICKOFF RET.— | | | | —TOTAL— | | |
Year Club	G.	P.C.	Yds.	Avg.	TD.	No.	Yds.	Avg.	TD.	No.	Yds.	Avg.	TD.	TD.	Pts.	F.
1987—Denver NFL	12	31	630	20.3	2	12	73	6.1	0	4	78	19.5	0	2	12	2
1988—Denver NFL	15	46	574	12.5	1	23	223	9.7	0	6	124	20.7	0	1	6	3
Pro Totals—2 Years	27	77	1204	15.6	3	35	296	8.5	0	10	202	20.2	0	3	18	5

Additional pro statistics: Rushed twice for 13 yards, 1987; recovered one fumble, 1987 and 1988; atttempted one pass with no completions and rushed five times for 51 yards, 1988.
Played in AFC Championship Game following 1987 season.
Played in NFL Championship Game following 1987 season.

CHARLES LaVERNE NELSON
(Chuck)
Placekicker—Minnesota Vikings
Born February 23, 1960, at Seattle, Wash.
Height, 5.11. Weight, 175.
High School—Everett, Wash.
Attended University of Washington.

Named as placekicker on THE SPORTING NEWS College All-America Team, 1982.
Selected by Chicago in 23rd round (270th player selected) of 1983 USFL draft.
Selected by Los Angeles Rams in 4th round (87th player selected) of 1983 NFL draft.
Signed by Los Angeles Rams, July 13, 1983.
Released by Los Angeles Rams, August 27, 1984; signed as free agent by Buffalo Bills, October 30, 1984.
Released by Buffalo Bills, August 19, 1985; signed as free agent by Minnesota Vikings, March 18, 1986.
Released by Minnesota Vikings, September 1, 1986; re-signed by Vikings, September 2, 1986.

			—PLACE KICKING—				
Year Club	G.	XP.	XPM.	FG.	FGA.	Pts.
1983—L. A. Rams NFL	12	33	*4	5	11	48
1984—Buffalo NFL..............	7	14	0	3	5	23
1986—Minnesota NFL........	16	44	3	22	28	110
1987—Minnesota NFL........	12	36	1	13	24	75
1988—Minnesota NFL........	16	48	1	20	25	108
Pro Totals—5 Years.......	63	175	9	63	93	364

Additional pro statistics: Recovered one fumble, 1983; punted three times for a 24.0 avg., 1986.
Played in NFC Championship Game following 1987 season.

DARRIN MILO NELSON
Running Back—Minnesota Vikings

Born January 2, 1959, at Sacramento, Calif.
Height, 5.09. Weight, 185.
High School—Downey, Calif., Pius X.
Received bachelor of science degree in urban and environmental planning
from Stanford University in 1981.
Brother of Kevin Nelson, running back with Los Angeles Express, 1984 and 1985; cousin of
Ozzie Newsome, tight end with Cleveland Browns; Carlos Carson, wide receiver with
Kansas City Chiefs; and Charles Alexander, running back with Cincinnati Bengals, 1979 through 1985.

Selected by Minnesota in 1st round (7th player selected) of 1982 NFL draft.

		—RUSHING—				PASS RECEIVING				—TOTAL—		
Year Club	G.	Att.	Yds.	Avg.	TD.	P.C.	Yds.	Avg.	TD.	TD.	Pts.	F.
1982—Minnesota NFL..	7	44	136	3.1	0	9	100	11.1	0	0	0	2
1983—Minnesota NFL..	15	154	642	4.2	1	51	618	12.1	0	1	6	5
1984—Minnesota NFL..	15	80	406	5.1	3	27	162	6.0	1	4	24	4
1985—Minnesota NFL..	16	200	893	4.5	5	43	301	7.0	1	6	36	7
1986—Minnesota NFL..	16	191	793	4.2	4	53	593	11.2	3	7	42	3
1987—Minnesota NFL..	10	131	642	*4.9	2	26	129	5.0	0	2	12	2
1988—Minnesota NFL..	13	112	380	3.4	1	16	105	6.6	0	1	6	3
Pro Totals—7 Years...................................	92	912	3892	4.3	16	225	2008	8.9	5	21	126	26

		—PUNT RETURNS—				—KICKOFF RET.—		
Year Club	G.	No.	Yds.	Avg.	TD.	No.	Yds.	Avg.	TD.
1982—Minnesota NFL..	7		None			6	132	22.0	0
1983—Minnesota NFL..	15		None			18	445	24.7	0
1984—Minnesota NFL..	15	23	180	7.8	0	39	891	22.8	0
1985—Minnesota NFL..	16	16	133	8.3	0	3	51	17.0	0
1986—Minnesota NFL..	16		None			3	105	35.0	0
1987—Minnesota NFL..	10		None			7	164	23.4	0
1988—Minnesota NFL..	13		None			9	210	23.3	0
Pro Totals—7 Years.................................	92	39	313	8.0	0	85	1998	23.5	0

Additional pro statistics: Recovered one fumble, 1983; recovered three fumbles, 1984; recovered two fumbles for 16 yards, 1985; recovered two fumbles, 1988.
Played in NFC Championship Game following 1987 season.

ROBERT WILLIAM NELSON
(Bob)
Nose Tackle—Green Bay Packers

Born March 3, 1959, at Baltimore, Md.
Height, 6.04. Weight, 275.
High School—Baltimore, Md., Patapsco.
Attended University of Miami (Fla.).

Selected by Miami in 5th round (120th player selected) of 1982 NFL draft.
Released by Miami Dolphins, September 6, 1982; signed by Chicago Blitz, November 30, 1983.
Traded with running back Kevin McLee and 12th round picks in 1984 and 1985 drafts by Chicago Blitz to Arizona Wranglers for rights to guard Bruce Branch, January 13, 1983.
Franchise transferred to Chicago, September 30, 1983.
Traded by Chicago Blitz to Oklahoma Outlaws for guard Terry Crouch, January 19, 1984.
Not protected in merger of Oklahoma Outlaws and Arizona Wranglers; selected by Jacksonville Bulls in USFL dispersal draft, December 6, 1984.
Granted free agency, August 1, 1985; signed by Tampa Bay Buccaneers, August 6, 1985.
Released by Tampa Bay Buccaneers, September 2, 1985; re-signed by Buccaneers, March 21, 1986.
Released by Tampa Bay Buccaneers, September 7, 1987; signed as free agent by Green Bay Packers, May 5, 1988.
Released by Green Bay Packers, August 30, 1988; re-signed by Packers, September 13, 1988.
Arizona USFL, 1983; Oklahoma USFL, 1984; Jacksonville USFL, 1985; Tampa Bay NFL, 1986; Green Bay NFL, 1988.
Games: 1983 (18), 1984 (18), 1985 (18), 1986 (16), 1988 (14). Total USFL—54. Total NFL—30. Total Pro—84.
USFL statistics: Credited with six sacks for 44 yards, 1983; recovered two fumbles and credited with 6½ sacks for 43 yards, 1984; credited with 5½ sacks for 37 yards, 1985.
NFL statistics: Recovered one fumble, 1986.

KEITH ROBERT NEUBERT
Tight End—New York Jets

Born September 13, 1964, at Fort Atkinson, Wis.
Height, 6.05. Weight, 250.
High School—Fort Atkinson, Wis.
Received degree in speech communications from University of Nebraska in 1988.

Selected by New York Jets in 8th round (203rd player selected) of 1988 NFL draft.
Signed by New York Jets, June 2, 1988.
On injured reserve with ribs injury, August 29 through December 15, 1988; activated, December 16, 1988.
New York Jets NFL, 1988.
Games: 1988 (1).

TOM G. NEWBERRY
Guard—Los Angeles Rams
Born December 20, 1962, at Onalaska, Wis.
Height, 6.02. Weight, 279.
High School—Onalaska, Wis.
Received degree in geography from University of Wisconsin at La Crosse in 1986.

Named to THE SPORTING NEWS NFL All-Star Team, 1988.
Selected by Los Angeles Rams in 2nd round (50th player selected) of 1986 NFL draft.
Signed by Los Angeles Rams, July 18, 1986.
On did not report/reserve, August 22, 1988; reported, August 23, 1988.
Los Angeles Rams NFL, 1986 through 1988.
Games: 1986 (16), 1987 (12), 1988 (16). Total—44.
Pro statistics: Recovered one fumble in end zone for a touchdown, 1986.
Played in Pro Bowl (NFL All-Star Game) following 1988 season.

ANTHONY Q. NEWMAN
Cornerback—Los Angeles Rams
Born November 21, 1965, at Bellingham, Wash.
Height, 6.00. Weight, 199.
High School—Beaverton, Ore.
Attended University of Oregon.

Selected by Los Angeles Rams in 2nd round (35th player selected) of 1988 NFL draft.
Signed by Los Angeles Rams, July 11, 1988.
Selected by Toronto Blue Jays' organization in 26th round of free-agent draft, June 4, 1984.
Selected by Cleveland Indians' organization in secondary phase of free-agent draft, January 9, 1985.
Selected by Texas Rangers' organization in secondary phase of free-agent draft, June 3, 1985.
Los Angeles Rams NFL, 1988.
Games: 1988 (16).
Pro statistics: Intercepted two passes for 27 yards and recovered one fumble, 1988.

HARRY KENT NEWSOME JR.
Punter—Pittsburgh Steelers
Born January 25, 1963, at Cheraw, S.C.
Height, 6.00. Weight, 187.
High School—Cheraw, S.C.
Attended Wake Forest University.

Established NFL record for having most punts blocked, season (6), 1988.
Selected by New Jersey in 15th round (213th player selected) of 1985 USFL draft.
Selected by Pittsburgh in 8th round (214th player selected) of 1985 NFL draft.
Signed by Pittsburgh Steelers, July 26, 1985.

| | | ——PUNTING—— | | |
Year Club	G.	No.	Avg.	Blk.
1985—Pittsburgh NFL	16	78	39.6	1
1986—Pittsburgh NFL	16	86	40.1	*3
1987—Pittsburgh NFL	12	64	41.8	1
1988—Pittsburgh NFL	16	65	*45.4	*6
Pro Totals—4 Years	60	293	41.5	11

Additional pro statistics: Attempted two passes with one completion for 12 yards and a touchdown, 1986; rushed twice for 16 yards and fumbled once for minus 17 yards, 1987; recovered one fumble, 1987 and 1988; rushed twice for no yards, 1988.

OZZIE NEWSOME
Tight End—Cleveland Browns
Born March 16, 1956, at Muscle Shoals, Ala.
Height, 6.02. Weight, 232.
High School—Leighton, Ala., Colbert County.
Received bachelor of science degree in recreation and park management from University of Alabama.
Cousin of Darrin Nelson, running back with Minnesota Vikings; and Kevin Nelson,
running back with Los Angeles Express, 1984 and 1985.

Established NFL record for most pass receptions by tight end, career (610).
Named to THE SPORTING NEWS NFL All-Star Team, 1984.
Named to THE SPORTING NEWS AFC All-Star Team, 1979.
Named as wide receiver on THE SPORTING NEWS College All-America Team, 1977.
Selected by Cleveland in 1st round (23rd player selected) of 1978 NFL draft.
Crossed picket line during players' strike, October 14, 1987.
Granted unconditional free agency, February 1, 1989; did not receive qualifying offer, April 15, 1989.
Re-signed by Cleveland Browns, May 24, 1989.

Year Club	G.	P.C.	Yds.	Avg.	TD.
1978—Cleveland NFL............	16	38	589	15.5	2
1979—Cleveland NFL............	16	55	781	14.2	9
1980—Cleveland NFL............	16	51	594	11.6	3
1981—Cleveland NFL............	16	69	1002	14.5	6
1982—Cleveland NFL............	8	49	633	12.9	3
1983—Cleveland NFL............	16	89	970	10.9	6
1984—Cleveland NFL............	16	89	1001	11.2	5
1985—Cleveland NFL............	16	62	711	11.5	5
1986—Cleveland NFL............	16	39	417	10.7	3
1987—Cleveland NFL............	13	34	375	11.0	0
1988—Cleveland NFL............	16	35	343	9.8	2
Pro Totals—11 Years..........	165	610	7416	12.2	44

Additional pro statistics: Returned two punts for 29 yards, rushed 13 times for 96 yards and two touchdowns and fumbled once, 1978; rushed once for six yards, 1979; rushed twice for 13 yards and fumbled twice, 1980; rushed twice for 20 yards, 1981; recovered one fumble, 1985.

Played in AFC Championship Game following 1986 and 1987 seasons.
Played in Pro Bowl (NFL All-Star Game) following 1981, 1984 and 1985 seasons.

TIMOTHY ARTHUR NEWSOME
(Timmy)
Fullback—Dallas Cowboys

Born May 17, 1958, at Ahoskie, N. C.
Height, 6.01. Weight, 235.
High School—Ahoskie, N. C.
Received bachelor of arts degree in business administration from
Winston-Salem State University in 1980.

Selected by Dallas in 6th round (162nd player selected) of 1980 NFL draft.

Year Club	G.	RUSHING Att.	Yds.	Avg.	TD.	PASS RECEIVING P.C.	Yds.	Avg.	TD.	TOTAL TD.	Pts.	F.
1980—Dallas NFL	16	25	79	3.2	2	4	43	10.8	0	2	12	0
1981—Dallas NFL	15	13	38	2.9	0	None				0	0	1
1982—Dallas NFL	9	15	98	6.5	1	6	118	19.7	1	2	12	1
1983—Dallas NFL	16	44	185	4.2	2	18	250	13.9	4	6	36	0
1984—Dallas NFL	15	66	268	4.1	5	26	263	10.1	0	5	30	3
1985—Dallas NFL	14	88	252	2.9	2	46	361	7.8	1	3	18	2
1986—Dallas NFL	16	34	110	3.2	2	48	421	8.8	3	5	30	2
1987—Dallas NFL	11	25	121	4.8	2	34	274	8.1	2	4	24	1
1988—Dallas NFL	9	32	75	2.3	3	30	236	7.9	0	3	18	1
Pro Totals—9 Years...................	121	342	1226	3.6	19	212	1966	9.3	11	30	180	11

Year Club	G.	KICKOFF RETURNS No.	Yds.	Avg.	TD.
1980—Dallas NFL	16	12	293	24.4	0
1981—Dallas NFL	15	12	228	19.0	0
1982—Dallas NFL	9	5	74	14.8	0
1983—Dallas NFL	16	1	28	28.0	0
1984—Dallas NFL	15	None			
1985—Dallas NFL	14	None			
1986—Dallas NFL	16	2	32	16.0	0
1987—Dallas NFL	11	2	22	11.0	0
1988—Dallas NFL	9	None			
Pro Totals—9 Years............	121	34	677	19.9	0

Additional pro statistics: Recovered two fumbles, 1980; recovered one fumble, 1982, 1986 and 1988.
Played in NFC Championship Game following 1980 through 1982 seasons.

VINCENT KARL NEWSOME
(Vince)
Safety—Los Angeles Rams

Born January 22, 1961, at Braintree, Wash.
Height, 6.01. Weight, 179.
High School—Vacaville, Calif.
Attended University of Washington.

Selected by Oakland in 4th round (42nd player selected) of 1983 USFL draft.
Selected by Los Angeles Rams in 4th round (97th player selected) of 1983 NFL draft.
Signed by Los Angeles Rams, May 22, 1983.
On injured reserve with knee injury, December 8 through remainder of 1987 season.
On injured reserve with herniated disc, October 20 through remainder of 1988 season.

Year Club	G.	INTERCEPTIONS No.	Yds.	Avg.	TD.
1983—L.A. Rams NFL............	16	None			
1984—L.A. Rams NFL............	16	1	31	31.0	0
1985—L.A. Rams NFL............	16	3	20	6.7	0
1986—L.A. Rams NFL............	16	3	45	15.0	0
1987—L.A. Rams NFL............	8	None			
1988—L.A. Rams NFL............	6	0	3	....	0
Pro Totals—6 Years............	78	7	99	14.1	0

— 297 —

Additional pro statistics: Recovered one fumble, 1985, 1986 and 1988; recovered one fumble for seven yards, 1987. Played in NFC Championship Game following 1985 season.

NATHANIEL NEWTON JR.
(Nate)
Guard—Dallas Cowboys
Born December 20, 1961, at Orlando, Fla.
Height, 6.03. Weight, 317.
High School—Orlando, Fla., Jones.
Attended Florida A&M University.
Brother of Tim Newton, defensive tackle with Minnesota Vikings.

Selected by Tampa Bay in 1983 USFL territorial draft.
Signed as free agent by Washington Redskins, May 5, 1983.
Released by Washington Redskins, August 29, 1983; signed by Tampa Bay Bandits, November 6, 1983.
Granted free agency when USFL suspended operations, August 7, 1986; signed as free agent by Dallas Cowboys, August 14, 1986.
Granted roster exemption, August 14 through August 20, 1986; activated, August 21, 1986.
Crossed picket line during players' strike, October 24, 1987.
Tampa Bay USFL, 1984 and 1985; Dallas NFL, 1986 through 1988.
Games: 1984 (18), 1985 (18), 1986 (11), 1987 (11), 1988 (15). Total USFL—36. Total NFL—37. Total Pro—73.
Pro statistics: Caught one pass for two yards, 1988.

TIMOTHY REGINALD NEWTON
(Tim)
Defensive Tackle—Minnesota Vikings
Born March 23, 1963, at Orlando, Fla.
Height, 6.00. Weight, 277.
High School—Orlando, Fla., Jones.
Attended University of Florida.
Brother of Nate Newton, guard with Dallas Cowboys.

Selected by Tampa Bay in 1985 USFL territorial draft.
Selected by Minnesota in 6th round (164th player selected) of 1985 NFL draft.
Signed by Minnesota Vikings, June 17, 1985.
On injured reserve with knee injury, December 24 through remainder of 1988 season playoffs.
Minnesota NFL, 1985 through 1988.
Games: 1985 (16), 1986 (14), 1987 (9), 1988 (14). Total—53.
Pro statistics: Intercepted two passes for 63 yards and fumbled once, 1985; recovered one fumble, 1985, 1986 and 1988.
Played in NFC Championship Game following 1987 season.

CALVIN LEWIS NICHOLAS
Wide Receiver—Green Bay Packers
Born June 11, 1964, at Baton Rouge, La.
Height, 6.04. Weight, 208.
High School—Baton Rouge, La., McKinley.
Attended Grambling State University.

Selected by San Francisco in 11th round (301st player selected) in 1987 NFL draft.
Signed by San Francisco 49ers, July 22, 1987.
On injured reserve with torn tendon in finger, August 31 through entire 1987 season.
Released by San Francisco 49ers, November 22, 1988; signed as free agent by Green Bay Packers, May 31, 1989.
San Francisco NFL, 1988.
Games: 1988 (6).
Pro statistics: Caught one pass for 14 yards, 1988.

GERALD W. NICHOLS
Defensive Tackle—New York Jets
Born February 10, 1964, at St. Louis, Mo.
Height, 6.02. Weight, 267.
High School—St. Louis, Mo., Hazelwood East.
Received degree in psychology from Florida State University in 1987.

Selected by New York Jets in 7th round (187th player selected) of 1987 NFL draft.
Signed by New York Jets, July 20, 1987.
Crossed picket line during players' strike, October 12, 1987.
New York Jets NFL, 1987 and 1988.
Games: 1987 (13), 1988 (16). Totals—29.

MARK STEPHEN NICHOLS
Wide Receiver—Detroit Lions
Born October 29, 1959, at Bakersfield, Calif.
Height, 6.02. Weight, 208.
High School—Bakersfield, Calif.
Attended Bakersfield Junior College and San Jose State University.

Selected by Detroit in 1st round (16th player selected) of 1981 NFL draft.
On injured reserve with broken foot, December 25 through remainder of 1982 season.
On injured reserve with knee injury, December 21 through remainder of 1985 season.

On physically unable to perform/reserve with knee injury, July 21 through entire 1986 season.
Released by Detroit Lions, August 29, 1988; re-signed by Lions, March 15, 1989.

Year Club	G.	P.C.	Yds.	Avg.	TD.
1981—Detroit NFL	12	10	222	22.2	1
1982—Detroit NFL	7	8	146	18.3	2
1983—Detroit NFL	16	29	437	15.1	1
1984—Detroit NFL	15	34	744	21.9	1
1985—Detroit NFL	14	36	592	16.4	4
1987—Detroit NFL	12	7	87	12.4	0
Pro Totals—6 Years	76	124	2228	18.0	9

Additional pro statistics: Rushed three times for 50 yards and returned four kickoffs for 74 yards, 1981; fumbled once, 1981 and 1985; rushed once for three yards, 1982; rushed once for 13 yards and fumbled twice, 1983; rushed three times for 27 yards and recovered one fumble, 1984; rushed once for 15 yards, 1985.

HARDY OTTO NICKERSON
Linebacker—Pittsburgh Steelers
Born September 1, 1965, at Los Angeles, Calif.
Height, 6.02. Weight, 229.
High School—Los Angeles, Calif., Verbum Dei.
Attended University of California at Berkeley.

Selected by Pittsburgh in 5th round (122nd player selected) of 1987 NFL draft.
Signed by Pittsburgh Steelers, July 26, 1987.
Pittsburgh NFL, 1987 and 1988.
Games: 1987 (12), 1988 (15). Total—27.
Pro statistics: Recovered one fumble, 1987 and 1988; intercepted one pass for no yards, 1988.

TORRAN BLAKE NIXON
(Tory)
Cornerback—San Francisco 49ers
Born February 24, 1962, at Eugene, Ore.
Height, 5.11. Weight, 186.
High School—Phoenix, Ariz., Shadow Mountain.
Attended Univeristy of Arizona, Phoenix College and San Diego State University.

Selected by Arizona in 1st round (2nd player selected) of 1985 USFL draft.
Selected by Washington in 2nd round (33rd player selected) of 1985 NFL draft.
Signed by Washington Redskins, August 1, 1985.
Traded by Washington Redskins to San Francisco 49ers for 6th round pick in 1986 draft, September 2, 1985.
On injured reserve with knee injury, August 23 through November 11, 1988; activated, November 12, 1988.
On injured reserve with hamstring injury, January 20 through remainder of 1988 season playoffs.

Year Club	G.	No.	Yds.	Avg.	TD.
1985—San Francisco NFL	16		None		
1986—San Francisco NFL	16	2	106	53.0	1
1987—San Francisco NFL	12	1	5	5.0	0
1988—San Francisco NFL	6		None		
Pro Totals—4 Years	50	3	111	37.0	1

Additional pro statistics: Recovered two fumbles, 1986.
Member of San Francisco 49ers for NFC Championship Game following 1988 season; inactive.

BRIAN DAVID NOBLE
Linebacker—Green Bay Packers
Born September 6, 1962, at Anaheim, Calif.
Height, 6.03. Weight, 252.
High School—Anaheim, Calif.
Attended Fullerton College and Arizona State University.

Selected by Arizona in 1985 USFL territorial draft.
Selected by Green Bay in 5th round (125th player selected) of 1985 NFL draft.
Signed by Green Bay Packers, July 19, 1985.
Granted free agency, February 1, 1988; re-signed by Packers, September 27, 1988.
Green Bay NFL, 1985 through 1988.
Games: 1985 (16), 1986 (16), 1987 (12), 1988 (12). Total—56.
Pro statistics: Returned one kickoff for one yard, 1986; intercepted one pass for 10 yards and recovered five fumbles, 1987; recovered one fumble, 1988.

ALAPATI NOGA
(Al)
Defensive Tackle—Minnesota Vikings
Born September 16, 1965, at American Somoa.
Height, 6.01. Weight, 261.
High School—Honolulu, Haw., Farrington.
Attended University of Hawaii.
Brother of Niko Noga, defensive end with Phoenix Cardinals;
and Pete Noga, linebacker with St. Louis Cardinals, 1987.

Selected by Minnesota in 3rd round (71st player selected) of 1988 NFL draft.
Signed by Minnesota Vikings, July 29, 1988.
On suspended list, September 10 through September 12, 1988; reinstated, September 13, 1988.
On non-football injury list with viral infection, October 5 through November 18, 1988; activated, November 19, 1988.
Minnesota NFL, 1988.
Games: 1988 (9).

FALANIKO NOGA
First name pronounced Fah-lah-NEE-koh.
(Niko)
Defensive End—Phoenix Cardinals
Born March 2, 1962, at American Samoa.
Height, 6.01. Weight, 235.
High School—Honolulu, Haw., Farrington.
Attended University of Hawaii.
Brother of Pete Noga, linebacker with St. Louis Cardinals, 1987;
and Al Noga, defensive tackle with Minnesota Vikings.

Selected by Oakland in 10th round (192nd player selected) of 1984 USFL draft.
Selected by St. Louis in 8th round (201st player selected) of 1984 NFL draft.
Signed by St. Louis Cardinals, July 16, 1984.
Franchise transferred to Phoenix, March 15, 1988.
St. Louis NFL, 1984 through 1987; Phoenix NFL, 1988.
Games: 1984 (16), 1985 (16), 1986 (16), 1987 (12), 1988 (16). Total—76.
Pro statistics: Recovered one fumble, 1984; recovered two fumbles, 1985 and 1986; recovered one fumble for 23 yards and a touchdown, 1987.

DANIEL NICHOLAS NOONAN
(Danny)
Defensive Tackle—Dallas Cowboys
Born July 14, 1965, at Lincoln, Neb.
Height, 6.04. Weight, 270.
High School—Lincoln, Neb., Northeast.
Attended University of Nebraska.

Selected by Dallas in 1st round (12th player selected) of 1987 NFL draft.
Signed by Dallas Cowboys, August 30, 1987.
Granted roster exemption, August 30 through September 13, 1987; activated, September 14, 1987.
Dallas NFL, 1987 and 1988.
Games: 1987 (11), 1988 (16). Total—27.
Pro statistics: Intercepted one pass for 17 yards and a touchdown and credited with a safety, 1988.

MICHAEL ADAM NORSETH
(Mike)
Quarterback—Cleveland Browns
Born August 22, 1964, at Hollywood, Calif.
Height, 6.02. Weight, 200.
High School—LaCrescenta, Calif., Valley.
Attended Snow College and Kansas University.

Selected by Cleveland in 7th round (174th player selected) of 1986 NFL draft.
Signed by Cleveland Browns, July 18, 1986.
On injured reserve with stomach injury, August 28 through entire 1986 season.
Released by Cleveland Browns, September 7, 1987; awarded on waivers to Cincinnati Bengals, September 8, 1987.
Granted unconditional free agency, February 1, 1989; signed by Cleveland Browns, February 24, 1989.
Active for 3 games with Cincinnati Bengals in 1987; did not play.
Cincinnati NFL, 1987 and 1988.
Games: 1988 (1).
Pro statistics: Rushed once for five yards, 1988.
Member of Cincinnati Bengals for AFC and NFL Championship Games following 1988 season; did not play.

KENNETH HOWARD NORTON JR.
(Ken)
Linebacker—Dallas Cowboys
Born September 29, 1966, at Jacksonville, Ill.
Height, 6.02. Weight, 236.
High School—Los Angeles, Calif., Westchester.
Attended University of California at Los Angeles.
Son of Ken Norton Sr., former world heavyweight boxing champion.

Named as linebacker on THE SPORTING NEWS College All-America Team, 1987.
Selected by Dallas in 2nd round (41st player selected) of 1988 NFL draft.
Signed by Dallas Cowboys, July 13, 1988.
On injured reserve with broken arm, August 23 through December 2, 1988; activated, December 3, 1988.
Dallas NFL, 1988.
Games: 1988 (3).
Pro statistics: Recovered one fumble, 1988.

SCOTT ALLAN NORWOOD
Placekicker—Buffalo Bills
Born July 17, 1960, at Alexandria, Va.
Height, 6.00. Weight, 206.
High School—Alexandria, Va., Thomas Jefferson.
Received bachelor of business administration degree in management from James Madison University.

Signed as free agent by Atlanta Falcons, May 5, 1982.
Released by Atlanta Falcons, August 30, 1982; signed by Birmingham Stallions, January 4, 1983.
On developmental squad, March 15 through March 25, 1984.
On injured reserve with knee injury. March 26 through remainder of 1984 season.
Released by Birmingham Stallions, February 18, 1985; signed as free agent by Buffalo Bills, March 22, 1985.
Released by Buffalo Bills, September 1, 1986; re-signed by Bills, September 2, 1986.
On developmental squad for 2 games with Birmingham Stallions in 1984.

| | | | ——PLACE KICKING—— | | | |
Year Club	G.	XP.	XPM.	FG.	FGA.	Pts.
1983—Birmingham USFL .	18	34	1	25	34	109
1984—Birmingham USFL .	3	4	0	3	4	13
1985—Buffalo NFL	16	23	0	13	17	62
1986—Buffalo NFL	16	32	2	17	27	83
1987—Buffalo NFL	12	31	0	10	15	61
1988—Buffalo NFL	16	33	0	*32	37	*129
USFL Totals—2 Years...	21	38	1	28	38	122
NFL Totals—4 Years.....	60	119	2	72	96	335
Pro Totals—6 Years.......	81	157	3	100	134	457

Additional pro statistics: Caught one pass for no yards and recovered one fumble, 1983.
Played in AFC Championship Game following 1988 season.
Played in Pro Bowl (NFL All-Star Game) following 1988 season.

JAY McKINLEY NOVACEK
Tight End—Phoenix Cardinals
Born October 24, 1962, at Martin, S.D.
Height, 6.04. Weight, 235.
High School—Gothenburg, Neb.
Received bachelor of science degree in industrial education
from University of Wyoming in 1986.

Selected by Houston in 5th round (69th player selected) of 1985 USFL draft.
Selected by St. Louis in 6th round (158th player selected) of 1985 NFL draft.
Signed by St. Louis Cardinals, July 21, 1985.
On injured reserve with broken thumb, August 19 through October 16, 1986; activated, October 17, 1986.
On injured reserve with knee injury, December 10 through remainder of 1986 season.
On injured reserve with broken bone in elbow, November 3 through December 4, 1987; activated, December 5, 1987.
Franchise transferred to Phoenix, March 15, 1988.

| | | ——PASS RECEIVING—— | | | |
Year Club	G.	P.C.	Yds.	Avg.	TD.
1985—St. Louis NFL	16	1	4	4.0	0
1986—St. Louis NFL	8	1	2	2.0	0
1987—St. Louis NFL	7	20	254	12.7	3
1988—Phoenix NFL	16	38	569	15.0	4
Pro Totals—4 Years	47	60	829	13.8	7

Additional pro statistics: Returned one kickoff for 20 yards, 1985; fumbled once, 1987; rushed once for 10 yards and recovered one fumble, 1988.

BRENT HOWARD NOVOSELSKY
Tight End—Green Bay Packers
Born January 8, 1966, at Skokie, Ill.
Height, 6.03. Weight, 232.
High School—Skokie, Ill., Niles North.
Received bachelor of science degree in economics from University of Pennsylvania in 1988.

Signed as free agent by Chicago Bears, May 16, 1988.
Released by Chicago Bears, August 24, 1988; re-signed by Bears, September 20, 1988.
On injured reserve with ankle injury, November 11 through December 8, 1988.
Released by Chicago Bears, December 9, 1988; re-signed by Bears, December 14, 1988.
Granted unconditional free agency, February 1, 1989; signed by Green Bay Packers, March 15, 1989.
Chicago NFL, 1988.
Games: 1988 (8).
Played in NFC Championship Game following 1988 season.

FREDDIE JOE NUNN
(Freddie Joe)
Defensive End—Phoenix Cardinals
Born April 9, 1962, at Noxubee County, Miss.
Height, 6.04. Weight, 255.
High School—Louisville, Miss., Nanih Waiya.
Attended University of Mississippi.

Selected by Birmingham in 1985 USFL territorial draft.
Selected by St. Louis in 1st round (18th player selected) of 1985 NFL draft.
Signed by St. Louis Cardinals, August 5, 1985.
Franchise transferred to Phoenix, March 15, 1988.
St. Louis NFL, 1985 through 1987; Phoenix NFL, 1988.
Games: 1985 (16), 1986 (16), 1987 (12), 1988 (16). Total—60.
Pro statistics: Recovered two fumbles, 1985; recovered one fumble, 1986; recovered two fumbles for eight yards, 1988.

BART STEVEN OATES
Center—New York Giants
Born December 16, 1958, at Mesa, Ariz.
Height, 6.03. Weight, 267.
High School—Albany, Ga.
Received bachelor's degree in accounting from Brigham Young University;
and attending Seton Hall Law School.
Brother of Brad Oates, offensive tackle with St. Louis Cardinals, Detroit Lions,
Kansas City Chiefs, Cincinnati Bengals, Green Bay Packers and Philadelphia Stars,
1976 through 1981, 1983 and 1984.
Named as center on THE SPORTING NEWS USFL All-Star Team, 1983.
Selected by Philadelphia in 2nd round (17th player selected) of 1983 USFL draft.
Signed by Philadelphia Stars, January 24, 1983.
On developmental squad, April 28 through May 5, 1983; activated, May 6, 1983.
Franchise transferred to Baltimore, November 1, 1984.
Released by Baltimore Stars, August 27, 1985; signed as free agent by New York Giants, August 28, 1985.
On developmental squad for 1 game with Philadelphia Stars in 1983.
Philadelphia USFL, 1983 and 1984; Baltimore USFL, 1985; New York Giants NFL, 1985 through 1988.
Games: 1983 (17), 1984 (17), 1985 USFL (18), 1985 NFL (16), 1986 (16), 1987 (12), 1988 (16). Total USFL—52. Total NFL—60. Total Pro—112.
USFL statistics: Rushed once for five yards and recovered two fumbles, 1984; recovered one fumble for four yards, 1985.
NFL statistics: Recovered two fumbles, 1985; fumbled once for minus four yards, 1986; recovered one fumble, 1987; fumbled once for minus 10 yards, 1988.
Played in NFC Championship Game following 1986 season.
Played in NFL Championship Game following 1986 season.
Played in USFL Championship Game following 1983 through 1985 seasons.

KENNETH JOHN O'BRIEN JR.
(Ken)
Quarterback—New York Jets
Born November 27, 1960, at Long Island, N.Y.
Height, 6.04. Weight, 200.
High School—Sacramento, Calif., Jesuit.
Attended California State University at Sacramento and received degree in
political science from University of California at Davis in 1983.
Established NFL record for lowest interception percentage, career (2.51).
Led NFL quarterbacks in passing with 96.2 points in 1985.
Selected by Oakland in 6th round (66th player selected) of 1983 USFL draft.
Selected by New York Jets in 1st round (24th player selected) of 1983 NFL draft.
Signed by New York Jets, July 21, 1983.
Active for 16 games with New York Jets in 1983; did not play.

Year Club	G.	Att.	Cmp.	Pct.	Gain	T.P.	P.I.	Avg.	Att.	Yds.	Avg.	TD.	TD.	Pts.	F.
				PASSING						RUSHING			TOTAL		
1984—N.Y. Jets NFL	10	203	116	57.1	1402	6	7	6.91	16	29	1.8	0	0	0	4
1985—N.Y. Jets NFL	16	488	297	60.9	3888	25	8	7.97	25	58	2.3	0	0	0	14
1986—N.Y. Jets NFL	15	482	300	62.2	3690	25	20	7.66	17	46	2.7	0	0	0	10
1987—N.Y. Jets NFL	12	393	234	59.5	2696	13	8	6.86	30	61	2.0	0	0	0	8
1988—N.Y. Jets NFL	14	424	236	55.7	2567	15	7	6.05	21	25	1.2	0	0	0	11
Pro Totals—6 Years	67	1990	1183	59.4	14243	84	50	7.16	109	219	2.0	0	0	0	47

Quarterback Rating Points: 1984 (74.0), 1985 (96.2), 1986 (85.8), 1987 (82.8), 1988 (78.6). Total—85.0.
Additional pro statistics: Recovered two fumbles, 1984; recovered four fumbles, 1985; recovered five fumbles and fumbled 10 times for minus three yards, 1986; recovered one fumble and fumbled eight times for minus 10 yards, 1987; recovered five fumbles and fumbled 11 times for minus 14 yards, 1988.
Played in Pro Bowl (NFL All-Star Game) following 1985 season.

CLIFTON LOUIS ODOM
(Cliff)
Linebacker—Indianapolis Colts
Born August 15, 1958, at Beaumont, Tex.
Height, 6.02. Weight, 245.
High School—Beaumont, Tex., French.
Attended University of Texas at Arlington.
Selected by Cleveland in 3rd round (72nd player selected) of 1980 NFL draft.
On injured reserve with knee injury, November 3 through remainder of 1980 season.
Released by Cleveland Browns, August 18, 1981; signed as free agent by Oakland Raiders, March 1, 1982.
Franchise transferred to Los Angeles, May 7, 1982.
Released by Los Angeles Raiders, August 10, 1982; signed as free agent by Baltimore Colts, August 12, 1982.

Released by Baltimore Colts, September 6, 1982; re-signed by Colts, September 7, 1982.
Franchise transferred to Indianapolis, March 31, 1984.
Granted free agency, February 1, 1986; re-signed by Colts, August 17, 1986.
Granted roster exemption, August 17 through August 21, 1986; activated, August 22, 1986.
Cleveland NFL, 1980; Baltimore NFL, 1982 and 1983; Indianapolis NFL, 1984 through 1988.
Games: 1980 (8), 1982 (8), 1983 (15), 1984 (16), 1985 (16), 1986 (16), 1987 (12), 1988 (13). Total—104.
Pro statistics: Recovered one fumble, 1984 and 1988; recovered two fumbles, 1985 and 1986; recovered three fumbles for eight yards, 1987.

NATHANIEL BERNARD ODOMES
(Nate)
Cornerback—Buffalo Bills
Born August 25, 1965, at Columbus, Ga.
Height, 5.10. Weight, 188.
High School—Columbus, Ga., Carver.
Attended University of Wisconsin.

Selected by Buffalo in 2nd round (29th player selected) of 1987 NFL draft.
Signed by Buffalo Bills, July 22, 1987.
Buffalo NFL, 1987 and 1988.
Games: 1987 (12), 1988 (16). Total—28.
Pro statistics: Recovered two fumbles, 1987; intercepted one pass for no yards, 1988.
Played in AFC Championship Game following 1988 season.

JOHN ARNOLD OFFERDAHL
Linebacker—Miami Dolphins
Born August 17, 1964, at Wisconsin Rapids, Wis.
Height, 6.03. Weight, 237.
High School—Fort Atkinson, Wis.
Attended Western Michigan University.

Selected by Miami in 2nd round (52nd player selected) of 1986 NFL draft.
Signed by Miami Dolphins, July 29, 1986.
On injured reserve with torn bicep, September 8 through October 30, 1987; activated, October 31, 1987.
Miami NFL, 1986 through 1988.
Games: 1986 (15), 1987 (9), 1988 (16). Total—40.
Pro statistics: Intercepted one pass for 14 yards, 1986; intercepted two passes for two yards and recovered one fumble, 1988.
Played in Pro Bowl (NFL All-Star Game) following 1986 and 1987 seasons.
Named to play in Pro Bowl following 1988 season; replaced due to injury by Johnny Rembert.

CHRISTIAN E. OKOYE
(Name pronounced Oh-KOY-yea.)
Running Back—Kansas City Chiefs
Born August 16, 1961, at Enugu, Nigeria.
Height, 6.01. Weight, 253.
High School—Enugu, Nigeria, Uwani Secondary School.
Received degree in physcial education from Azusa Pacific University in 1987.

Selected by Kansas City in 2nd round (35th player selected) of 1987 NFL draft.
Signed by Kansas City Chiefs, July 21, 1987.
On injured reserve with broken thumb, August 30 through September 30, 1988; activated, October 1, 1988.
On injured reserve with broken hand, December 14 through remainder of 1988 season.

		—RUSHING—				PASS RECEIVING				—TOTAL—		
Year Club	G.	Att.	Yds.	Avg.	TD.	P.C.	Yds.	Avg.	TD.	TD.	Pts.	F.
1987—Kansas City NFL	12	157	660	4.2	3	24	169	7.0	0	3	18	5
1988—Kansas City NFL	9	105	473	4.5	3	8	51	6.4	0	3	18	1
Pro Totals—2 Years	21	262	1133	4.3	6	32	220	6.9	0	6	36	6

MICHAEL NETHANIEL OLIPHANT
(Mike)
Running Back—Cleveland Browns
Born May 19, 1963, at Jacksonville, Fla.
Height, 5.10. Weight, 183.
High School—Federal Way, Wash.
Received degree in physical education from University of Puget Sound in 1988.

Selected by Washington in 3rd round (66th player selected) of 1988 NFL draft.
Signed by Washington Redskins, July 18, 1988.
On injured reserve with hamstring injury, September 30 through November 20, 1988; activated, November 21, 1988.
Traded by Washington Redskins to Cleveland Browns for running back Earnest Byner, April 23, 1989.
Played semi-pro football for Auburn (Wash.) Panthers.

		—RUSHING—				PASS RECEIVING				—TOTAL—		
Year Club	G.	Att.	Yds.	Avg.	TD.	P.C.	Yds.	Avg.	TD.	TD.	Pts.	F.
1988—Washington NFL	8	8	30	3.8	0	15	111	7.4	0	0	0	2

		—PUNT RETURNS—				—KICKOFF RET.—			
Year Club	G.	No.	Yds.	Avg.	TD.	No.	Yds.	Avg.TD.	
1988—Washington NFL	8	7	24	3.4	0	7	127	18.1	0

Additional pro statistics: Recovered one fumble, 1988.

NEAL OLKEWICZ
Linebacker—Washington Redskins
Born January 30, 1957, at Phoenixville, Pa.
Height, 6.00. Weight, 233.
High School—Phoenixville, Pa.
Received bachelor of arts degree in law enforcement from University of Maryland in 1979.

Signed as free agent by Washington Redskins, May 7, 1979.
On injured reserve with knee injury, December 10 through remainder of 1981 season.
On injured reserve with knee injury, September 7 through October 23, 1987; activated, October 24, 1987.

			—INTERCEPTIONS—			
Year	Club	G.	No.	Yds.	Avg.	TD.
1979—Washington NFL		16	1	4	4.0	0
1980—Washington NFL		12		None		
1981—Washington NFL		14	2	22	11.0	1
1982—Washington NFL		9		None		
1983—Washington NFL		16	1	14	14.0	0
1984—Washington NFL		16		None		
1985—Washington NFL		16	1	21	21.0	0
1986—Washington NFL		16	1	15	15.0	0
1987—Washington NFL		10		None		
1988—Washington NFL		16		None		
Pro Totals—10 Years		141	6	76	12.7	1

Additional pro statistics: Recovered one fumble, 1980 and 1985; recovered three fumbles, 1982 and 1986; recovered two fumbles, 1983 and 1984; recovered three fumbles for eight yards, 1988.
Played in NFC Championship Game following 1982, 1983, 1986 and 1987 seasons.
Played in NFL Championship Game following 1982, 1983 and 1987 seasons.

LESLIE CORNELIUS O'NEAL
Defensive End—San Diego Chargers
Born May 7, 1964, at Pulaski County, Ark.
Height, 6.04. Weight, 255.
High School—Little Rock, Ark., Hall.
Attended Oklahoma State University.

Named as defensive lineman on THE SPORTING NEWS College All-America Team, 1984 and 1985.
Selected by New Jersey in 1986 USFL territorial draft.
Selected by San Diego in 1st round (8th player selected) of 1986 NFL draft.
Signed by San Diego Chargers, August 5, 1986.
On injured reserve with knee injury, December 4 through remainder of 1986 season.
On physically unable to perform/reserve with knee injury, August 30 through entire 1987 season.
On physically unable to perform/active with knee injury, July 23 through August 21, 1988; then transferred to physically unable to perform/reserve with knee injury, August 22 through October 14, 1988; activated, October 15, 1988.
San Diego NFL, 1986 and 1988.
Games: 1986 (13), 1988 (9). Total—22.
Pro statistics: Intercepted two passes for 22 yards and a touchdown and recovered two fumbles, 1986.

TERRY ORR
Tight End—Washington Redskins
Born September 27, 1961, at Savannah, Ga.
Height, 6.03. Weight, 227.
High School—Abilene, Tex., Cooper.
Received bachelor of science degree in speech communications
from University of Texas in 1985.

Selected by San Antonio in 1985 USFL territorial draft.
Selected by Washington in 10th round (263rd player selected) of 1985 NFL draft.
Signed by Washington Redskins, July 18, 1985.
On injured reserve with ankle injury, August 20 through entire 1985 season.
On injured reserve with shoulder injury, September 7 through October 23, 1987; activated, October 24, 1987.
Released by Washington Redskins, August 29, 1988; re-signed by Redskins, August 30, 1988.
Granted unconditional free agency, February 1, 1989; re-signed by Redskins, May 11, 1989.

			—PASS RECEIVING—			
Year	Club	G.	P.C.	Yds.	Avg.	TD.
1986—Washington NFL		16	3	45	15.0	1
1987—Washington NFL		10	3	35	11.7	0
1988—Washington NFL		16	11	222	20.2	2
Pro Totals—3 Years		42	17	302	17.8	3

Additional pro statistics: Returned two kickoffs for 31 yards, 1986; returned four kickoffs for 62 yards, 1987; returned two punts for 10 yards, returned one kickoff for six yards and recovered two fumbles, 1988.
Played in NFC Championship Game following 1986 and 1987 seasons.
Played in NFL Championship Game following 1987 season.

—DID YOU KNOW—

That the 1988 Cincinnati Bengals, including playoffs, were 10-0 at home? In 1987, their home record was 1-7.

PAUL EUGENE OSWALD
Guard—Atlanta Falcons
Born April 9, 1964, at Topeka, Kan.
Height, 6.04. Weight, 273.
High School—Topeka, Kan., Hayden.
Attended University of Kansas.

Selected by Pittsburgh in 11th round (289th player selected) of 1987 NFL draft.
Signed by Pittsburgh Steelers, July 24, 1987.
Released by Pittsburgh Steelers, November 3, 1987; signed as free agent by Dallas Cowboys, April 28, 1988.
Released by Dallas Cowboys, September 6, 1988; signed as free agent by Atlanta Falcons, September 15, 1988.
Released by Atlanta Falcons, October 17, 1988; re-signed by Falcons, November 9, 1988.
Pittsburgh NFL, 1987; Atlanta NFL, 1988.
Games: 1987 (2), 1988 (3). Total—5.

BILLY JOE OWENS JR.
Safety—Dallas Cowboys
Born December 2, 1965, at Syracuse, N.Y.
Height, 6.01. Weight, 207.
High School—Syracuse, N.Y., Christian Brothers Academy.
Received degree in information science from University of Pittsburgh in 1987.

Selected by Dallas in 10th round (263rd player selected) of 1988 NFL draft.
Signed by Dallas Cowboys, July 2, 1988.
Dallas NFL, 1988.
Games: 1988 (16).

MEL TYRAE OWENS
Linebacker—Los Angeles Rams
Born December 7, 1958, at Detroit, Mich.
Height, 6.02. Weight, 224.
High School—DeKalb, Ill.
Received bachelor of arts degree in political science from University of Michigan in 1981.

Selected by Los Angeles in 1st round (9th player selected) of 1981 NFL draft.
Crossed picket line during players' strike, October 14, 1987.
On injured reserve with ankle injury, November 25 through remainder of 1988 season.
Los Angeles Rams NFL, 1981 through 1988.
Games: 1981 (16), 1982 (7), 1983 (16), 1984 (16), 1985 (16), 1986 (16), 1987 (12), 1988 (7). Total—106.
Pro statistics: Recovered two fumbles, 1983 and 1984; intercepted one pass for minus four yards, 1984; recovered two fumbles for 14 yards, 1985; recovered one fumble, 1986 through 1988; intercepted one pass for 26 yards, 1987; intercepted one pass for 11 yards, 1988.
Played in NFC Championship Game following 1985 season.

MICHAEL JONATHAN PAGEL
(Mike)
Quarterback—Cleveland Browns
Born September 13, 1960, at Douglas, Ariz.
Height, 6.02. Weight, 211.
High School—Phoenix, Ariz., Washington.
Attended Arizona State University.

Brother of Karl Pagel, outfielder-first baseman with Chicago Cubs and Cleveland Indians, 1978, 1979 and 1981 through 1983; and minor league coach, Cleveland Indians' organization, 1984.

Selected by Baltimore in 4th round (84th player selected) of 1982 NFL draft.
Franchise transferred to Indianapolis, March 31, 1984.
Granted free agency, February 1, 1986; re-signed by Colts and traded to Cleveland Browns for 9th round pick in 1987 draft, May 22, 1986.
On injured reserve with separated shoulder, October 14 through December 22, 1988; activated, December 23, 1988.

| | | —————PASSING————— | | | | | | | ——RUSHING—— | | | | —TOTAL— | | |
Year Club	G.	Att.	Cmp.	Pct.	Gain	T.P.	P.I.	Avg.	Att.	Yds.	Avg.	TD.	TD.	Pts.	F.
1982—Baltimore NFL	9	221	111	50.2	1281	5	7	5.80	19	82	4.3	1	1	6	9
1983—Baltimore NFL	15	328	163	49.7	2353	12	17	7.17	54	441	8.2	0	0	0	4
1984—Indianapolis NFL	11	212	114	53.8	1426	8	8	6.73	26	149	5.7	1	1	6	4
1985—Indianapolis NFL	16	393	199	50.6	2414	14	15	6.14	25	160	6.4	2	2	12	6
1986—Cleveland NFL	1	3	2	66.7	53	0	0	17.67	2	0	0.0	0	0	0	2
1987—Cleveland NFL	4				None						None		0	0	0
1988—Cleveland NFL	5	134	71	53.0	736	3	4	5.49	4	1	0.3	0	0	0	0
Pro Totals—7 Years	61	1291	660	51.1	8263	42	51	6.40	130	833	6.4	4	4	24	25

Quarterback Rating Points: 1982 (62.4), 1983 (64.0), 1984 (71.8), 1985 (65.8), 1986 (109.7), 1988 (64.1). Total—65.7.
Additional pro statistics: Recovered three fumbles and fumbled nine times for minus four yards, 1982; recovered one fumble, 1984 and 1988; recovered two fumbles and caught one pass for six yards, 1985; recovered one fumble and fumbled twice for minus four yards, 1986.
Played in AFC Championship Game following 1987 season.
Member of Cleveland Browns for AFC Championship Game following 1986 season; did not play.

ANTHONY R. PAIGE
(Tony)
Fullback—Detroit Lions

Born October 14, 1962, at Washington, D.C.
Height, 5.10. Weight, 235.
High School—Hyattsville, Md., DeMatha Catholic.
Received degree in broadcasting from Virginia Tech.
Selected by Pittsburgh in 1984 USFL territorial draft.
Selected by New York Jets in 6th round (149th player selected) of 1984 NFL draft.
Signed by New York Jets, May 29, 1984.
Granted free agency, February 1, 1987; withdrew qualifying offer, August 25, 1987.
Signed by Detroit Lions, November 19, 1987.
Released by Detroit Lions, August 29, 1988; re-signed by Lions, August 30, 1988.

		—————RUSHING—————				PASS RECEIVING				—TOTAL—		
Year Club	G.	Att.	Yds.	Avg.	TD.	P.C.	Yds.	Avg.	TD.	TD.	Pts.	F.
1984—New York Jets NFL	16	35	130	3.7	7	6	31	5.2	1	8	48	1
1985—New York Jets NFL	16	55	158	2.9	8	18	120	6.7	2	10	60	1
1986—New York Jets NFL	16	47	109	2.3	2	18	121	6.7	0	2	12	2
1987—Detroit NFL	5	4	13	3.3	0	2	1	0.5	0	0	0	0
1988—Detroit NFL	16	52	207	4.0	0	11	100	9.1	0	0	0	1
Pro Totals—5 Years	69	193	617	3.2	17	55	373	6.8	3	20	120	5

Additional pro statistics: Returned three kickoffs for seven yards, 1984; recovered one fumble, 1985 and 1987.

STEPHONE PAIGE
Wide Receiver—Kansas City Chiefs

Born October 15, 1961, at Long Beach, Calif.
Height, 6.02. Weight, 183.
High School—Long Beach, Calif., Polytechnic.
Attended Saddleback College and Fresno State University.
Established NFL record for pass reception yards, game (309), against San Diego Chargers, December 22, 1985.
Selected by Oakland in 1983 USFL territorial draft.
Signed as free agent by Kansas City Chiefs, May 9, 1983.

		PASS RECEIVING				—KICKOFF RET.—				—TOTAL—		
Year Club	G.	P.C.	Yds.	Avg.	TD.	No.	Yds.	Avg.	TD.	TD.	Pts.	F.
1983—Kansas City NFL	16	30	528	17.6	6		None			6	36	1
1984—Kansas City NFL	16	30	541	18.0	4	27	544	20.1	0	4	24	0
1985—Kansas City NFL	16	43	943	*21.9	10	2	36	18.0	0	10	60	0
1986—Kansas City NFL	16	52	829	15.9	11		None			11	66	0
1987—Kansas City NFL	12	43	707	16.4	4		None			4	24	0
1988—Kansas City NFL	16	61	902	14.8	7		None			7	42	2
Pro Totals—6 Years	92	259	4450	17.2	42	29	580	20.0	0	42	252	3

Additional pro statistics: Recovered one fumble, 1983; rushed three times for 19 yards, 1984; rushed once for 15 yards, 1985; rushed twice for minus two yards, 1986; recovered two fumbles, 1988.

CARL DREW PAINTER
Running Back—Detroit Lions

Born May 10, 1964, at Norfolk, Va.
Height, 5.09. Weight, 185.
High School—Norfolk, Va., Booker T. Washington.
Attended Hampton University.
Selected by Detroit in 6th round (142nd player selected) of 1988 NFL draft.
Signed by Detroit Lions, July 16, 1988.
On injured reserve with ankle injury, November 4 through December 2, 1988; activated, December 3, 1988.

		—————RUSHING—————				PASS RECEIVING				—TOTAL—		
Year Club	G.	Att.	Yds.	Avg.	TD.	P.C.	Yds.	Avg.	TD.	TD.	Pts.	F.
1988—Detroit NFL	12	17	42	2.5	0	1	1	1.0	0	0	0	1

		KICKOFF RETURNS			
Year Club	G.	No.	Yds.	Avg.	TD.
1988—Detroit NFL	12	17	347	20.4	0

Additional pro statistics: Recovered one fumble, 1988.

PAUL WOODROW PALMER
Running Back-Kick Returner—Kansas City Chiefs

Born October 14, 1964, at Bethesda, Md.
Height, 5.09. Weight, 184.
High School—Potomac, Md., Winston Churchill.
Attended Temple University.
Named as running back on THE SPORTING NEWS College All-America Team, 1986.
Selected by Kansas City in 1st round (19th player selected) of 1987 NFL draft.
Signed by Kansas City Chiefs, July 17, 1987.
On suspended list, November 27 through November 29, 1988; reinstated, November 30, 1988.

Year Club	G.	Att.	Yds.	Avg.	TD.	P.C.	Yds.	Avg.	TD.	TD.	Pts.	F.
			RUSHING			PASS RECEIVING				TOTAL		
1987—Kansas City NFL	12	24	155	6.5	0	4	27	6.8	0	2	12	2
1988—Kansas City NFL	15	134	452	3.4	2	53	611	11.5	4	6	36	7
Pro Totals—2 Years	27	158	607	3.8	2	57	638	11.2	4	8	48	9

KICKOFF RETURNS

Year Club	G.	No.	Yds.	Avg.	TD.
1987—Kansas City NFL	12	*38	*923	24.3	*2
1988—Kansas City NFL	15	23	364	15.8	0
Pro Totals—2 Years	27	61	1287	21.1	2

Additional pro statistics: Attempted one pass with no completions, 1987; recovered one fumble, 1988.

IRVIN LEE PANKEY
(Irv)
Offensive Tackle—Los Angeles Rams
Born February 15, 1958, at Aberdeen, Md.
Height, 6.06. Weight, 287.
High School—Aberdeen, Md.
Attended Pennsylvania State University.

Selected by Los Angeles in 2nd round (50th player selected) of 1980 NFL draft.
On injured reserve with torn Achilles tendon, August 16 through entire 1983 season.
Los Angeles Rams NFL, 1980 through 1988.
Games: 1980 (16), 1981 (13), 1982 (9), 1984 (16), 1985 (16), 1986 (16), 1987 (12), 1988 (16). Total—114.
Pro statistics: Recovered two fumbles and returned one kickoff for no yards, 1981; recovered one fumble, 1985, 1986 and 1988.
Played in NFC Championship Game following 1985 season.

WILLIAM PARIS
(Bubba)
Offensive Tackle—San Francisco 49ers
Born October 6, 1960, at Louisville, Ky.
Height, 6.06. Weight, 306.
High School—Louisville, Ky., DeSales.
Received degree from University of Michigan in 1982.

Selected by San Francisco in 2nd round (29th player selected) of 1982 NFL draft.
On injured reserve with knee injury, September 6 through entire 1982 season.
San Francisco NFL, 1983 through 1988.
Games: 1983 (16), 1984 (16), 1985 (16), 1986 (10), 1987 (11), 1988 (16). Total—85.
Pro statistics: Recovered one fumble, 1984 and 1986.
Played in NFC Championship Game following 1983, 1984 and 1988 seasons.
Played in NFL Championship Game following 1984 and 1988 seasons.

ANDREW JAMES PARKER
(Andy)
Tight End—San Diego Chargers
Born September 8, 1961, at Redlands, Calif.
Height, 6.05. Weight, 245.
High Schools—Dana Point, Calif., Dana Hills; and Encinitas, Calif., San Dieguito.
Received bachelor of science degree in physical education
from University of Utah in 1984.

Selected by Philadelphia in 5th round (100th player selected) of 1984 USFL draft.
Selected by Los Angeles Raiders in 5th round (127th player selected) of 1984 NFL draft.
Signed by Los Angeles Raiders, June 19, 1984.
On injured reserve with back injury, November 3 through remainder of 1984 season.
On injured reserve with foot injury, December 19 through remainder of 1986 season.
Granted unconditional free agency, February 1, 1989; signed by San Diego Chargers, April 1, 1989.
Los Angeles Raiders NFL, 1984 through 1988.
Games: 1984 (9), 1985 (16), 1986 (13), 1987 (12), 1988 (16). Total—66.
Pro statistics: Caught two passes for eight yards and a touchdown, 1986; recovered one fumble, 1987; caught four passes for 33 yards, 1988.

CARL PARKER
Wide Receiver—Cincinnati Bengals
Born February 5, 1965, at Columbus, Ga.
Height, 6.02. Weight, 201.
High School—Valdosta, Ga., Lowndes County.
Attended Vanderbilt University.

Selected by Cincinnati in 12th round (307th player selected) of 1988 NFL draft.
Signed by Cincinnati Bengals, June 6, 1988.
On injured reserve with foot injury, August 29 through November 25, 1988; activated, November 26, 1988.
Cincinnati NFL, 1988.
Games: 1988 (3).
Played in AFC Championship Game following 1988 season.
Played in NFL Championship Game following 1988 season.

JEFFREY DUPREE PARKS
(Jeff)
Tight End—Tampa Bay Buccaneers
Born September 14, 1964, at Columbia, S.C.
Height, 6.04. Weight, 240.
High School—Gardendale, Ala.
Attended Auburn University.

Selected by Birmingham in 1986 USFL territorial draft.
Selected by Houston in 5th round (114th player selected) of 1986 NFL draft.
Signed by Houston Oilers, July 23, 1986.
On injured reserve with pulled hamstring, October 8 through remainder of 1986 season.
On injured reserve with foot injury, September 6 through November 13, 1987; activated, November 14, 1987.
Released by Houston Oilers, August 30, 1988; signed as free agent by Green Bay Packers, September 6, 1988.
On injured reserve with hamstring injury, September 6 through September 25, 1988.
Released by Green Bay Packers, September 26, 1988; signed as free agent by Tampa Bay Buccaneers, November 30, 1988.
Houston NFL, 1986 and 1987; Tampa Bay NFL, 1988.
Games: 1986 (5), 1987 (7), 1988 (3). Total—15.
Pro statistics: Caught one pass for 22 yards, 1988.

JOEL PATTEN
Offensive Tackle—San Diego Chargers
Born February 7, 1958, at Augsburg, Germany.
Height, 6.07. Weight, 307.
High School—Fairfax, Va., Robinson.
Received bachelor of arts degree in history education from Duke University.

Signed as free agent by Cleveland Browns, May 7, 1980.
On injured reserve with groin injury, September 6 through November 6, 1980; activated, November 7, 1980.
On injured reserve with knee injury, August 24 through entire 1981 season.
Released by Cleveland Browns, September 8, 1982.
USFL rights traded by Michigan Panthers to Washington Federals for past consideration, February 8, 1983.
Signed by Washington Federals, February 8, 1983.
On developmental squad, May 4 through June 2, 1984; activated, June 3, 1984.
Franchise transferred to Orlando, October 12, 1984.
Released by Orlando Renegades, August 26, 1985; signed as free agent by Dallas Cowboys, March 21, 1986.
Released by Dallas Cowboys, August 21, 1986; signed as free agent by Indianapolis Colts, May 11, 1987.
Granted unconditional free agency, February 1, 1989; signed by San Diego Chargers, February 15, 1989.
On developmental squad for 4 games with Washington Federals in 1984.
Cleveland NFL, 1980; Washington USFL, 1983 and 1984; Orlando USFL, 1985; Indianapolis NFL, 1987 and 1988.
Games: 1980 (16), 1983 (18), 1984 (14), 1985 (18), 1987 (12), 1988 (15). Total NFL—43. Total USFL—50. Total Pro—93.
Pro statistics: Recovered two fumbles, 1983.

ELVIS VERNELL PATTERSON
Cornerback—San Diego Chargers
Born October 21, 1960, at Bryan, Tex.
Height, 5.11. Weight, 198.
High School—Houston, Tex., Jack Yates.
Attended University of Kansas.

Selected by Jacksonville in 10th round (207th player selected) of 1984 USFL draft.
Signed as free agent by New York Giants, May 3, 1984.
Released by New York Giants, September 16, 1987; signed as free agent replacement player by San Diego Chargers, September 24, 1987.

Year Club	G.	No.	Yds.	Avg.	TD.
1984—N.Y. Giants NFL	15	None			
1985—N.Y. Giants NFL	16	6	88	14.7	*1
1986—N.Y. Giants NFL	15	2	26	13.0	0
1987—NYG (1)-SD (13) NFL	14	1	75	75.0	1
1988—San Diego NFL	14	1	0	0.0	0
Pro Totals—5 Years	74	10	189	18.9	2

Additional pro statistics: Recovered one fumble, 1985, 1987 and 1988.
Played in NFC Championship Game following 1986 season.
Played in NFL Championship Game following 1986 season.

KENNETH SHAWN PATTERSON
(Known by middle name.)
Defensive Tackle-Defensive End—Green Bay Packers
Born June 13, 1964, at Tempe, Ariz.
Height, 6.05. Weight, 261.
High School—Tempe, Ariz., McClintock.
Attended Arizona State University.

Selected by Green Bay in 2nd round (34th player selected) of 1988 NFL draft.
Signed by Green Bay Packers, July 17, 1988.
Green Bay NFL, 1988.
Games: 1988 (15).
Pro statistics: Recovered one fumble, 1988.

MARK LESTER PATTISON
Wide Receiver—Seattle Seahawks
Born December 13, 1961, at Seattle, Wash.
Height, 6.02. Weight, 190.
High School—Seattle, Wash., Roosevelt.
Received degree in political science from University of Washington.

Selected by Portland in 1985 USFL territorial draft.
Selected by Los Angeles Raiders in 7th round (199th player selected) of 1985 NFL draft.
Signed by Los Angeles Raiders, June 29, 1985.
On injured reserve with hamstring injury, August 27 through entire 1985 season.
Released by Los Angeles Raiders, September 1, 1986; signed as free agent by Los Angeles Rams, September 18, 1986.
Released by Los Angeles Rams, September 24, 1986; signed as free agent by Los Angeles Raiders, December 10, 1986.
Released by Los Angeles Raiders, September 9, 1987; awarded on waivers to New Orleans Saints, September 10, 1987.
On injured reserve with ankle injury, August 29 through November 8, 1988; activated after clearing procedural waivers, November 10, 1988.
Granted unconditional free agency, February 1, 1989; signed by Seattle Seahawks, April 1, 1989.

		—PASS RECEIVING—			
Year Club	G.	P.C.	Yds.	Avg.	TD.
1986—Ram (1)-Raid (2) NFL	3	2	12	6.0	0
1987—New Orleans NFL........	9	9	132	14.7	0
1988—New Orleans NFL........	6	1	8	8.0	0
Pro Totals—3 Years............	18	12	152	12.7	0

JOHN ANTHONY PAYE
Quarterback—San Francisco 49ers
Born March 30, 1965, at Stanford, Calif.
Height, 6.03. Weight, 195.
High School—Menlo Park, Calif., Menlo School.
Received degree in economics from Stanford University in 1987.

Selected by San Francisco in 10th round (275th player selected) of 1987 NFL draft.
Signed by San Francisco 49ers, July 20, 1987.
On injured reserve with shoulder injury, August 31 through entire 1987 season.
On injured reserve with shoulder injury, October 14 through remainder of 1988 season.
Active for 3 games with San Francisco 49ers in 1988; did not play.
San Francisco NFL, 1988.

AARON DANTIANTO PEARSON
Linebacker—Kansas City Chiefs
Born August 22, 1964, at Gadsden, Ala.
Height, 6.00. Weight, 236.
High School—Gadsden, Ala.
Attended Itawamba Junior College and Mississippi State University.

Selected by Kansas City in 11th round (285th player selected) of 1986 NFL draft.
Signed by Kansas City Chiefs, July 23, 1986.
Kansas City NFL, 1986 through 1988.
Games: 1986 (15), 1987 (12), 1988 (16). Total—43.
Pro statistics: Returned one kickoff for no yards, 1986; returned two kickoffs for four yards and fumbled twice, 1987.

JAYICE PEARSON
(J. C.)
Cornerback—Kansas City Chiefs
Born August 17, 1963, at Japan.
Height, 5.11. Weight, 190.
High School—Oceanside, Calif., El Camino.
Attended California State Poly University, Fullerton College and University of Washington.

Signed as free agent by Washington Redskins, May 13, 1985.
Released by Washington Redskins, August 27, 1985; signed as free agent by Kansas City Chiefs, April 14, 1986.
On injured reserve with sprained ankle, August 18 through October 29, 1986; activated after clearing procedural waivers, October 31, 1986.
Kansas City NFL, 1986 through 1988.
Games: 1986 (8), 1987 (12), 1988 (16). Total—36.
Pro statistics: Intercepted two passes for eight yards, 1988.

BRENT RICHARD PEASE
Quarterback—Miami Dolphins
Born October 8, 1964, at Moscow, Ida.
Height, 6.02. Weight, 200.
High School—Mountain Home, Ida.
Attended Walla Walla Community College and University of Montana.

Selected by Minnesota in 11th round (295th player selected) of 1987 NFL draft.
Signed by Minnesota Vikings, July 27, 1987.

Released by Minnesota Vikings, September 4, 1987; signed as free agent replacement player by Houston Oilers, September 24, 1987.
Granted unconditional free agency, February 1, 1989; signed by Miami Dolphins, March 21, 1989.

Year	Club	G.	Att.	Cmp.	Pct.	Gain	T.P.	P.I.	Avg.	Att.	Yds.	Avg.	TD.	TD.	Pts.	F.
						PASSING						RUSHING			TOTAL	
1987—Houston NFL		6	113	56	49.6	728	3	5	6.44	15	33	2.2	1	1	6	2
1988—Houston NFL		13	22	6	27.3	64	0	4	2.91	8	—2	—0.3	1	1	6	0
Pro Totals—2 Years		19	135	62	45.9	792	3	9	5.87	23	31	1.3	2	2	12	2

Quarterback Rating Points: 1987 (60.6), 1988 (0.0). Total—44.2.
Additional pro statistics: Recovered two fumbles, 1987.

MARION TODD PEAT
(Known by middle name.)
Guard—Phoenix Cardinals
Born May 20, 1964, at Champaign, Ill.
Height, 6.02. Weight, 294.
High School—Champaign, Ill., Central.
Received degree in criminal justice from Northern Illinois University in 1987.
Selected by St. Louis in 11th round (285th player selected) of 1987 NFL draft.
Signed by St. Louis Cardinals, July 14, 1987.
Franchise transferred to Phoenix, March 15, 1988.
St. Louis NFL, 1987; Phoenix NFL, 1988.
Games: 1987 (12), 1988 (15). Total—27.

STEVEN CARL PELLUER
Name pronounced Puh-LURE.
(Steve)
Quarterback—Dallas Cowboys
Born July 29, 1962, at Yakima, Wash.
Height, 6.04. Weight, 210.
High School—Bellevue, Wash., Interlake.
Attended University of Washington.
Brother of Scott Pelluer, linebacker with New Orleans Saints, 1981 through 1985.
Selected by Oakland in 6th round (110th player selected) of 1984 USFL draft.
Selected by Dallas in 5th round (113th player selected) of 1984 NFL draft.
Signed by Dallas Cowboys, July 7, 1984.

Year	Club	G.	Att.	Cmp.	Pct.	Gain	T.P.	P.I.	Avg.	Att.	Yds.	Avg.	TD.	TD.	Pts.	F.
						PASSING						RUSHING			TOTAL	
1984—Dallas NFL		1				None						None		0	0	0
1985—Dallas NFL		2	8	5	62.5	47	0	0	5.88	3	—2	—0.7	0	0	0	0
1986—Dallas NFL		16	378	215	56.9	2727	8	17	7.21	41	255	6.2	1	1	6	9
1987—Dallas NFL		12	101	55	54.5	642	3	2	6.36	25	142	5.7	1	1	6	0
1988—Dallas NFL		16	435	245	56.3	3139	17	19	7.22	51	314	6.2	2	2	12	6
Pro Totals—5 Years		47	922	520	56.4	6555	28	38	7.11	120	709	5.9	4	4	24	15

Quarterback Rating Points: 1985 (78.6), 1986 (67.9), 1987 (75.6), 1988 (73.9). Total—71.6.
Additional pro statistics: Recovered three fumbles, 1986; recovered two fumbles and fumbled six times for minus 18 yards, 1988.

JAY LESLIE PENNISON
Center—Houston Oilers
Born September 9, 1961, at Houma, La.
Height, 6.01. Weight, 282.
High School—Houma, La., Terrebonne.
Attended Nicholls State University.
Selected by Jacksonville in 13th round (267th player selected) of 1984 USFL draft.
Signed by Jacksonville Bulls, January 19, 1984.
Released injured by Jacksonville Bulls, February 20, 1984; signed as free agent by Washington Redskins, May 2, 1984.
Released by Washington Redskins, August 21, 1984; re-signed by Jacksonville Bulls, October 9, 1984.
Released by Jacksonville Bulls, August 7, 1986; signed as free agent by Houston Oilers, August 12, 1986.
Jacksonville USFL, 1985; Houston NFL, 1986 through 1988.
Games: 1985 (18), 1986 (16), 1987 (12), 1988 (16). Total NFL—44. Total Pro—62.
USFL statistics: Recovered two fumbles, 1985.
NFL statistics: Fumbled once, 1986 and 1988; recovered one fumble, 1987 and 1988; fumbled once for minus 12 yards, 1987.

BRETT PERRIMAN
Wide Receiver—New Orleans Saints
Born October 10, 1965, at Miami, Fla.
Height, 5.09. Weight, 180.
High School—Miami, Fla., Northwestern.
Attended University of Miami (Fla.).
Selected by New Orleans in 2nd round (52nd player selected) of 1988 NFL draft.
Signed by New Orleans Saints, May 19, 1988.

Year Club	G.	P.C.	Yds.	Avg.	TD.
1988—New Orleans NFL........	16	16	215	13.4	2

Additional pro statistics: Rushed three times for 17 yards and fumbled once, 1988.

GERALD PERRY
Offensive Tackle—Denver Broncos
Born November 12, 1964, at Columbia, S.C.
Height, 6.06. Weight, 305.
High School—Columbia, S.C., Dreher.
Attended Northwest Mississippi Junior College and Southern University A&M.

Selected by Denver in 2nd round (45th player selected) of 1988 NFL draft.
Signed by Denver Broncos, July 15, 1988.
Denver NFL, 1988.
Games: 1988 (16).

MICHAEL DEAN PERRY
(Michael Dean)
Defensive End—Cleveland Browns
Born August 27, 1965, at Aiken, S.C.
Height, 6.00. Weight, 285.
High School—Aiken, S.C., South Aiken.
Attended Clemson University.
Brother of William Perry, defensive tackle with Chicago Bears.

Selected by Cleveland in 2nd round (50th player selected) of 1988 NFL draft.
Signed by Cleveland Browns, July 23, 1988.
Cleveland NFL, 1988.
Games: 1988 (16).
Pro statistics: Returned one kickoff for 13 yards and recovered two fumbles for 10 yards and a touchdown, 1988.

WILLIAM PERRY
Defensive Tackle—Chicago Bears
Born December 16, 1962, at Aiken, S.C.
Height, 6.02. Weight, 320.
High School—Aiken, S.C.
Attended Clemson University.
Brother of Michael Dean Perry, defensive end with Cleveland Browns.

Selected by Orlando in 1985 USFL territorial draft.
Selected by Chicago in 1st round (22nd player selected) of 1985 NFL draft.
Signed by Chicago Bears, August 5, 1985.
On non-football injury list with eating disorder, July 23 through August 22, 1988; activated, August 23, 1988.
On injured reserve with broken arm, September 20 through remainder of 1988 season.
Chicago NFL, 1985 through 1988.
Games: 1985 (16), 1986 (16), 1987 (12), 1988 (3). Total—47.
Pro statistics: Rushed five times for seven yards and two touchdowns, caught one pass for four yards and a touchdown and recovered two fumbles for 66 yards, 1985; rushed once for minus one yard and fumbled once, 1986; rushed once for no yards and fumbled once, 1987.
Played in NFC Championship Game following 1985 season.
Played in NFL Championship Game following 1985 season.

ROBERT PERRYMAN
(Bob)
Running Back—New England Patriots
Born October 16, 1964, at Raleigh, N. C.
Height, 6.01. Weight, 233.
High School—Bourne, Mass.
Received degree from University of Michigan in 1987.
Brother of Ron Perryman, linebacker at Boston College.

Selected by New England in 3rd round (79th player selected) of 1987 NFL draft.
Signed by New England Patriots, July 26, 1987.

Year Club		——RUSHING——				PASS RECEIVING				—TOTAL—		
	G.	Att.	Yds.	Avg.	TD.	P.C.	Yds.	Avg.	TD.	TD.	Pts.	F.
1987—New England NFL..................	9	41	187	4.6	0	3	13	4.3	0	0	0	1
1988—New England NFL..................	16	146	448	3.1	6	17	134	7.9	0	6	36	4
Pro Totals—2 Years...................	25	187	635	3.4	6	20	147	7.4	0	6	36	5

Additional pro statistics: Returned three kickoffs for 43 yards and recovered two fumbles, 1987.

BARRY G. PETTYJOHN
Offensive Tackle—Miami Dolphins
Born March 29, 1964, at Cincinnati, O.
Height, 6.05. Weight, 280.
High School—Cincinnati, O., Deer Park.
Attended University of Pittsburgh.

Signed as free agent by Tampa Bay Buccaneers, May 1, 1986.
Released by Tampa Bay Buccaneers, August 30, 1986; signed as free agent by Houston Oilers, March 25, 1987.
Released by Houston Oilers, November 3, 1987; signed as free agent by Atlanta Falcons, March 17, 1988.
Released by Atlanta Falcons, May 17, 1988; signed as free agent by Tampa Bay Buccaneers, July 18, 1988.
Released by Tampa Bay Buccaneers, July 27, 1988; signed as free agent by Miami Dolphins, February 24, 1989.
Houston NFL, 1987.
Games: 1987 (2).

JOSEPH GORDON PHILLIPS
(Joe)
Defensive End—San Diego Chargers
Born July 15, 1963, at Portland, Ore.
Height, 6.05. Weight, 278.
High School—Vancouver, Wash., Columbia River.
Attended Oregon State University, Chemeketa Community College and received bachelor of
arts degree in economics from Southern Methodist University of 1986.

Selected by Minnesota in 4th round (93rd player selected) of 1986 NFL draft.
Signed by Minnesota Vikings, July 28, 1986.
Released by Minnesota Vikings, September 7, 1987; signed as free agent replacement player by San Diego Chargers, September 24, 1987.
Granted free agency, February 1, 1988; re-signed by Chargers, August 29, 1988.
Minnesota NFL, 1986; San Diego NFL, 1987 and 1988.
Games: 1986 (16), 1987 (13), 1988 (16). Total—45.
Pro statistics: Recovered one fumble, 1986.

REGGIE PHILLIPS
Cornerback—Phoenix Cardinals
Born December 29, 1960, at Houston, Tex.
Height, 5.10. Weight, 175.
High School—Houston, Tex., Jack Yates.
Attended Southern Methodist University.

Selected by Houston in 1985 USFL territorial draft.
Selected by Chicago in 2nd round (49th player selected) of 1985 NFL draft.
Signed by Chicago Bears, July 9, 1985.
Released by Chicago Bears, August 29, 1988; awarded on waivers to Phoenix Cardinals, August 30, 1988.
Chicago NFL, 1985 through 1987; Phoenix NFL, 1988.
Games: 1985 (16), 1986 (16), 1987 (12), 1988 (16). Total—60.
Pro statistics: Recovered one fumble, 1985; intercepted one pass for six yards, 1986; intercepted two passes for one yard, 1987; returned one kickoff for four yards, 1988.
Played in NFC Championship Game following 1985 season.
Played in NFL Championship Game following 1985 season.

BILL PICKEL
Name pronounced Pick-ELL.
Defensive Tackle—Los Angeles Raiders
Born November 5, 1959, at Queens, N.Y.
Height, 6.05. Weight, 265.
High Schools—Milford, Conn.; and Brooklyn, N.Y., St. Francis.
Attended Rutgers University.
Brother of Chris Pickel, linebacker at Rutgers University.

Named to THE SPORTING NEWS NFL All-Star Team, 1986.
Selected by New Jersey in 1983 USFL territorial draft.
Selected by Los Angeles Raiders in 2nd round (54th player selected) of 1983 NFL draft.
Signed by Los Angeles Raiders, May 26, 1983.
Crossed picket line during players' strike, October 6, 1987.
Los Angeles Raiders NFL, 1983 through 1988.
Games: 1983 (16), 1984 (16), 1985 (16), 1986 (15), 1987 (12), 1988 (16). Total—91.
Pro statistics: Recovered one fumble, 1983 and 1988; recovered two fumbles, 1986 and 1987.
Played in AFC Championship Game following 1983 season.
Played in NFL Championship Game following 1983 season.

MARK HAROLD PIKE
Defensive End—Buffalo Bills
Born December 27, 1963, at Elizabethtown, Ky.
Height, 6.04. Weight, 272.
High School—Edgewood, Ky., Dixie Heights.
Attended Georgia Tech.

Selected by Jacksonville in 1986 USFL territorial draft.
Selected by Buffalo in 7th round (178th player selected) of 1986 NFL draft.
Signed by Buffalo Bills, July 20, 1986.
On injured reserve with shoulder injury, August 26 through entire 1986 season.
On injured reserve with leg injury, September 16 through November 13, 1987; activated, November 14, 1987.
On injured reserve with foot injury, December 8 through remainder of 1987 season.
Buffalo NFL, 1987 and 1988.
Games: 1987 (3), 1988 (16). Total—19.
Pro statistics: Returned one kickoff for five yards, 1988.
Played in AFC Championship Game following 1988 season.

WILLIAM FRANK PILLOW JR.
(Known by middle name.)
Wide Receiver—Tampa Bay Buccaneers
Born March 11, 1965, at Nashville, Tenn.
Height, 5.10. Weight, 170.
High School—Nashville, Tenn., Whites Creek.
Attended Tennessee State University.
Selected by Tampa Bay in 11th round (279th player selected) of 1988 NFL draft.
Signed by Tampa Bay Buccaneers, July 10, 1988.

		——PASS RECEIVING——			
Year Club	G.	P.C.	Yds.	Avg.	TD.
1988—Tampa Bay NFL	15	15	206	13.7	1

Additional pro statistics: Returned three kickoffs for 38 yards, 1988.

ALLEN JEROME PINKETT
Running Back—Houston Oilers
Born January 25, 1964, at Washington, D.C.
Height, 5.09. Weight, 192.
High School—South Hill, Va., Parkview.
Received bachelor of business administration degree in marketing from
University of Notre Dame in 1986.
Cousin of Eric Dorsey, defensive end with New York Giants.
Selected by Orlando in 1986 USFL territorial draft.
Selected by Houston in 3rd round (61st player selected) of 1986 NFL draft.
Signed by Houston Oilers, July 31, 1986.
On injured reserve with shoulder injury, October 27 through November 27, 1987; activated, November 28, 1987.

Year Club	G.	——RUSHING—— Att.	Yds.	Avg.	TD.	PASS RECEIVING P.C.	Yds.	Avg.	TD.	—TOTAL— TD.	Pts.	F.
1986—Houston NFL..............................	16	77	225	2.9	2	35	248	7.1	1	3	18	2
1987—Houston NFL..............................	8	31	149	4.8	2	1	7	7.0	0	2	12	1
1988—Houston NFL..............................	16	122	513	4.2	7	12	114	9.5	2	9	54	2
Pro Totals—3 Years....................	40	230	887	3.9	11	48	369	7.7	3	14	84	5

		KICKOFF RETURNS			
Year Club	G.	No.	Yds.	Avg.	TD.
1986—Houston NFL.................	16	26	519	20.0	0
1987—Houston NFL.................	8	17	322	18.9	0
1988—Houston NFL.................	16	7	137	19.6	0
Pro Totals—3 Years............	40	50	978	19.6	0

Additional pro statistics: Returned one punt for minus one yard and recovered one fumble, 1986.

MIKE PITTS
Defensive Tackle—Philadelphia Eagles
Born September 25, 1960, at Baltimore, Md.
Height, 6.05. Weight, 277.
High School—Baltimore, Md., Polytechnic.
Attended University of Alabama.
Cousin of Rick Porter, running back with Detroit Lions, Baltimore Colts
and Memphis Showboats, 1982, 1983 and 1985.
Named as defensive end on THE SPORTING NEWS College All-America Team, 1982.
Selected by Birmingham in 1983 USFL territorial draft.
Selected by Atlanta in 1st round (16th player selected) of 1983 NFL draft.
Signed by Atlanta Falcons, July 16, 1983.
On injured reserve with knee injury, December 6 through remainder of 1984 season.
Granted free agency, February 1, 1987; re-signed by Falcons and traded to Philadelphia Eagles for defensive end
Greg Brown, September 7, 1987.
Granted roster exemption, September 7 through September 10, 1987; activated, September 11, 1987.
Atlanta NFL, 1983 through 1986; Philadelphia NFL, 1987 and 1988.
Games: 1983 (16), 1984 (14), 1985 (16), 1986 (16), 1987 (12), 1988 (16). Total—90.
Pro statistics: Recovered one fumble for 26 yards, 1983; recovered two fumbles, 1984; intercepted one pass for one
yard, recovered one fumble for six yards and fumbled once, 1985; recovered two fumbles for 22 yards and a touchdown,
1986; recovered four fumbles for 21 yards, 1987.

RONALD DWAYNE PITTS
(Ron)
Cornerback-Safety—Green Bay Packers
Born October 14, 1962, at Detroit, Mich.
Height, 5.10. Weight, 175.
High School—Orchard Park, N.Y.
Received degree in communications from University of California at Los Angeles in 1985.
Son of Elijah Pitts, running back with Green Bay Packers, Los Angeles Rams and New Orleans Saints,
1961 through 1971; scout, Green Bay Packers, 1972; and assistant coach with Los Angeles Rams,
1973 through 1977; Houston Oilers, 1981 through 1983; Hamilton Tiger-Cats,
1984 and Buffalo Bills, 1978 through 1980 and since 1985.

Selected by Buffalo in 7th round (169th player selected) of 1985 NFL draft.
Signed by Buffalo Bills, July 30, 1985.
On injured reserve with foot injury, August 19 through entire 1985 season.
On injured reserve with foot injury, September 2 through October 17, 1986; activated, October 18, 1986.
Released by Buffalo Bills, August 30, 1988; signed as free agent by Green Bay Packers, September 15, 1988.

		—INTERCEPTIONS-			–PUNT RETURNS–				—TOTAL—		
Year Club	G.	No.	Yds.	Avg.	TD.	No.	Yds.	Avg.	TD.	TD.	Pts.	F.
1986—Buffalo NFL	10		None			18	194	10.8	1	1	6	2
1987—Buffalo NFL	12	3	19	6.3	0	23	149	6.5	0	0	0	3
1988—Green Bay NFL	14	2	56	28.0	0	9	93	10.3	1	1	6	1
Pro Totals—3 Years	36	5	75	15.0	0	50	436	8.7	2	2	12	6

Additional pro statistics: Returned one kickoff for seven yards and recovered two fumbles, 1986; recovered one fumble, 1987; returned one kickoff for 17 yards and recovered four fumbles, 1988.

WILLIE PLESS
Linebacker—New Orleans Saints
Born February 21, 1964, at Anniston, Ala.
Height, 5.10. Weight, 221.
High School—Anniston, Ala.
Attended University of Kansas.

Signed as free agent by Toronto Argonauts, May 6, 1986.
Granted free agency, March 1, 1989; signed by San Francisco 49ers, April 12, 1989.
Released by San Francisco 49ers, April 18, 1989; awarded on waivers to New Orleans Saints, May 1, 1989.

		——INTERCEPTIONS——			
Year Club	G.	No.	Yds.	Avg.	TD.
1986—Toronto CFL	12	3	8	2.7	0
1987—Toronto CFL	16	5	22	4.4	0
1988—Toronto CFL	18	2	22	11.0	0
CFL Totals—3 Years	46	10	52	5.2	0

Additional CFL statistics: Recovered three fumbles for five yards, 1986; recovered three fumbles, 1987; recovered three fumbles for 20 yards, 1988.
Played in CFL Championship Game following 1987 season.

BRUCE ELLIOTT PLUMMER
Defensive Back—Indianapolis Colts
Born September 1, 1964, at Bogalusa, La.
Height, 6.01. Weight, 197.
High School—Bogalusa, La.
Attended Mississippi State University.

Selected by Denver in 9th round (250th player selected) of 1987 NFL draft.
Signed by Denver Broncos, July 19, 1987.
Released by Denver Broncos, November 26, 1988; awarded on waivers to Miami Dolphins, November 28, 1988.
Granted unconditional free agency, February 1, 1989; signed by Indianapolis Colts, March 8, 1989.
Dallas NFL, 1987; Denver (8)-Miami (3) NFL, 1988.
Games: 1987 (11), 1988 (11). Total—22.
Played in AFC Championship Game following 1987 season.
Played in NFL Championship Game following 1987 season.

GARY LEE PLUMMER
Linebacker—San Diego Chargers
Born January 26, 1960, at Fremont, Calif.
Height, 6.02. Weight, 240.
High School—Mission San Jose, Calif.
Attended Ohlone Junior College and University of California at Berkeley.

Selected by Oakland in 1983 USFL territorial draft.
Signed by Oakland Invaders, January 26, 1983.
On developmental squad, March 30 through April 5, 1984; activated, April 6, 1984.
Protected in merger of Oakland Invaders and Michigan Panthers, December 6, 1984.
Released by Oakland Invaders, August 2, 1985; awarded on waivers to Tampa Bay Bandits, August 3, 1985.
Granted free agency when USFL suspended operations, August 7, 1986; signed as free agent by San Diego Chargers, August 18, 1986.
Granted roster exemption, August 18 through August 21, 1986; activated, August 22, 1986.
On injured reserve with broken wrist, October 27 through November 27, 1987; activated, November 28, 1987.
On developmental squad for 1 game with Oakland Invaders in 1984.
Oakland USFL, 1983 through 1985; San Diego NFL, 1986 through 1988.
Games: 1983 (18), 1984 (17), 1985 (18), 1986 (15), 1987 (8), 1988 (16). Total USFL—53. Total NFL—39. Total Pro—92.
USFL statistics: Intercepted three passes for 20 yards, 1983; recovered one fumble, 1983 through 1985; credited with one sack for eight yards and intercepted two passes for 11 yards, 1984; credited with one sack for seven yards, intercepted one pass for 46 yards and returned three kickoffs for 31 yards, 1985.
NFL statistics: Returned one kickoff for no yards and recovered two fumbles, 1986; intercepted one pass for two yards, 1987.
Played in USFL Championship Game following 1985 season.

CEDRIC DARRYL POLLARD
(Known by middle name.)
Cornerback—San Francisco 49ers
Born May 11, 1965, at Ellsworth, Me.
Height, 5.11. Weight, 187.
High School—Colorado Springs, Colo., General William Mitchell.
Attended Weber State College.

Signed as free agent by Seattle Seahawks, May 3, 1986.
Released by Seattle Seahawks, August 19, 1986; signed as free agent by San Francisco 49ers, April 10, 1987.
Released by San Francisco 49ers, August 31, 1987; re-signed as replacement player by 49ers, September 24, 1987.
Released by San Francisco 49ers, October 24, 1987; re-signed by 49ers, August 3, 1988.
Released by San Francisco 49ers, August 23, 1988; re-signed by 49ers, August 25, 1988.
Released by San Francisco 49ers, August 30, 1988; re-signed by 49ers, September 15, 1988.
San Francisco NFL, 1987 and 1988.
Games: 1987 (3), 1988 (14). Total—17.
Pro statistics: Returned one punt for no yards, 1987.
Played in NFC Championship Game following 1988 season.
Played in NFL Championship Game following 1988 season.

KERRY PORTER
Running Back—Los Angeles Raiders
Born September 23, 1964, at Vicenza, Italy.
Height, 6.01. Weight, 210.
High School—Great Falls, Mont.
Attended Washington State University.

Selected by Buffalo in 7th round (171st player selected) of 1987 NFL draft.
Signed by Buffalo Bills, July 23, 1987.
On injured reserve with shoulder injury, September 7 through October 22, 1987, activated, October 23, 1987.
Released by Buffalo Bills, August 30, 1988; signed as free agent by Los Angeles Raiders, May 10, 1989.
Buffalo NFL, 1987.
Games: 1987 (6).
Pro statistics: Rushed twice for no yards, 1987.

KEVIN JAMES PORTER
Defensive Back—Kansas City Chiefs
Born April 11, 1966, at Bronx, N. Y.
Height, 5.10. Weight, 215.
High School—Warner Robins, Ga.
Attended Auburn University.
Cousin of James Brooks, running back with Cincinnati Bengals.

Selected by Kansas City in 3rd round (59th player selected) of 1988 NFL draft.
Signed by Kansas City Chiefs, May 25, 1988.
Kansas City NFL, 1988.
Games: 1988 (15).
Pro statistics: Returned one kickoff for 16 yards, recovered two fumbles and fumbled once, 1988.

RUFUS PORTER
Linebacker—Seattle Seahawks
Born May 18, 1965, at Amite, La.
Height, 6.01. Weight, 207.
High School—Baton Rouge, La., Capitol.
Attended Southern University.

Signed as free agent by Seattle Seahawks, May 11, 1988.
Seattle NFL, 1988.
Games: 1988 (16).
Pro statistics: Recovered one fumble, 1988.
Played in Pro Bowl (NFL All-Star Game) following 1988 season.

DENNIS SEAN PRICE
Cornerback—Los Angeles Raiders
Born June 14, 1965, at Los Angeles, Calif.
Height, 6.01. Weight, 175.
High School—Long Beach, Calif., Polytechnic.
Received degree in economics from University of California
at Los Angeles in 1988.

Selected by Los Angeles Raiders in 5th round (131st player selected) of 1988 USFL draft.
Signed by Los Angeles Raiders, July 13, 1988.
Los Angeles Raiders NFL, 1988.
Games: 1988 (12).
Pro statistics: Intercepted two passes for 18 yards, 1988.

JAMES DEWITT PRIMUS
Running Back—Atlanta Falcons
Born May 18, 1964, at Yuma, Ariz.
Height, 5.11. Weight, 196.
High School—National City, Calif., Sweetwater.
Attended University of California at Los Angeles.
Related to Ron Jessie, wide receiver with Detroit Lions,
Los Angeles Rams and Buffalo Bills, 1971 through 1981.

Selected by Atlanta in 9th round (222nd player selected) of 1988 NFL draft.
Signed by Atlanta Falcons, July 16, 1988.

		—RUSHING—			PASS RECEIVING			—TOTAL—		
Year Club	G.	Att.	Yds.	Avg.	TD.	P.C.	Yds.	Avg.	TD.	TD.	Pts.	F.
1988—Atlanta NFL	16	35	95	2.7	1	8	42	5.3	0	1	6	0

Additional pro statistics: Returned one kickoff for 13 yards and recovered one fumble, 1988.

MICHAEL ROBERT PRIOR
(Mike)
Defensive Back—Indianapolis Colts
Born November 14, 1963, at Chicago Heights, Ill.
Height, 6.00. Weight, 200.
High School—Chicago Heights, Ill., Marian Catholic.
Received bachelor of science degree in business administration
from Illinois State University in 1985.

Selected by Memphis in 4th round (60th player selected) of 1985 USFL draft.
Selected by Tampa Bay in 7th round (176th player selected) of 1985 NFL draft.
Signed by Tampa Bay Buccaneers, June 10, 1985.
On injured reserve with fractured wrist, August 25 through September 28, 1986.
Released by Tampa Bay Buccaneers, September 29, 1986; signed as free agent by Indianapolis Colts, May 11, 1987.
Released by Indianapolis Colts, August 31, 1987; re-signed as replacement player by Colts, September 23, 1987.
Selected by Baltimore Orioles' organization in 18th round of free-agent draft, June 4, 1984.
Selected by Los Angeles Dodgers' organization in 4th round of free-agent draft, June 3, 1985.

		INTERCEPTIONS				–PUNT RETURNS-				—KICKOFF RET.—				—TOTAL—		
Year Club	G.	No.	Yds.	Avg.	TD.	No.	Yds.	Avg.	TD.	No.	Yds.	Avg.	TD.	TD.	Pts.	F.
1985—Tampa Bay NFL	16		None			13	105	8.1	0	10	131	13.1	0	0	0	4
1987—Indianapolis NFL	13	6	57	9.5	0		None			3	47	15.7	0	0	0	0
1988—Indianapolis NFL	16	3	46	15.3	0	1	0	0.0	0		None			0	0	1
Pro Totals—3 Years	45	9	103	11.4	0	14	105	7.5	0	13	178	13.7	0	0	0	5

Additional pro statistics: Recovered three fumbles, 1985 and 1987; recovered one fumble for 12 yards, 1988.

EUGENE ANTHONY PROFIT
Cornerback—Washington Redskins
Born November 11, 1964, at Baton Rouge, La.
Height, 5.10. Weight, 175.
High School—Gardena, Calif., Junipero Serra.
Received bachelor of arts degree in economics from Yale University in 1986.

Selected by New Jersey in 11th round (83rd player selected) of 1986 USFL draft.
Signed as free agent by New England Patriots, May 10, 1986.
On injured reserve with thumb injury, August 18 through November 26, 1986; activated after clearing procedural waivers, November 28, 1986.
On injured reserve with dislocated elbow, August 23 through October 21, 1988; activated, October 22, 1988.
Granted unconditional free agency, February 1, 1989; signed by Washington Redskins, March 10, 1989.
New England NFL, 1986 through 1988.
Games: 1986 (4), 1987 (7), 1988 (1). Total—12.

JOE PROKOP
Punter—New York Jets
Born July 7, 1960, at St. Paul, Minn.
Height, 6.02. Weight, 225.
High School—White Bear Lake, Minn.
Attended California State Poly University at Pomona.

Signed as free agent by Los Angeles Rams, June 20, 1984.
Released by Los Angeles Rams, July 16, 1984.
USFL rights traded by Los Angeles Express to Houston Gamblers for past considerations, November 12, 1984.
Signed by Houston Gamblers, November 12, 1984.
Released by Houston Gamblers, January 28, 1985; signed as free agent by San Antonio Gunslingers, February 5, 1985.
Released by San Antonio Gunslingers, February 12, 1985; signed as free agent by New York Giants, June 21, 1985.
Released by New York Giants, August 26, 1985; signed as free agent by Green Bay Packers, September 4, 1985.
Released by Green Bay Packers, November 5, 1985; signed as free agent by New York Jets, March 25, 1986.
Released by New York Jets, August 25, 1986; signed as free agent by San Diego Chargers, April 13, 1987.
On injured reserve with quadricep injury, September 1 through September 14, 1987.
Released by San Diego Chargers, September 15, 1987; re-signed as replacement player by Chargers, September 24, 1987.
Released by San Diego Chargers, October 21, 1987; signed as free agent by New York Jets, April 8, 1988.

Year Club		PUNTING		
	G.	No.	Avg.	Blk.
1985—Green Bay NFL	9	56	39.5	0
1987—San Diego NFL	3	17	38.5	0
1988—N.Y. Jets NFL	16	85	38.9	0
Pro Total—3 Years	28	158	39.1	0

ANDREW PROVENCE
Nose Tackle—Denver Broncos
Born March 8, 1961, at Savannah, Ga.
Height, 6.03. Weight, 267.
High School—Savannah, Ga., Benedictine.
Attended University of South Carolina.

Selected by Washington in 1983 USFL territorial draft.
Selected by Atlanta in 3rd round (75th player selected) of 1983 NFL draft.
Signed by Atlanta Falcons, May 30, 1983.
On injured reserve with fractured finger, September 7 through November 27, 1987; activated, November 28, 1987.
Granted free agency, February 1, 1988; re-signed by Falcons and traded to Denver Broncos for conditional 10th round pick in 1989 draft, May 10, 1988.
On injured reserve with foot injury, September 1 through entire 1988 season.
Atlanta NFL, 1983 through 1987.
Games: 1983 (16), 1984 (16), 1985 (16), 1986 (16), 1987 (5). Total—69.
Pro statistics: Recovered one fumble for 26 yards, 1983; recovered one fumble, 1984.

JAMES BOUBIAS PRUITT
Wide Receiver—Indianapolis Colts
Born January 29, 1964, at Los Angeles, Calif.
Height, 6.03. Weight, 199.
High School—Los Angeles, Calif., Thomas Jefferson.
Attended California State University at Fullerton.

Selected by Miami in 4th round (107th player selected) of 1986 NFL draft.
Selected by New Jersey in 1st round (5th player selected) of 1986 USFL draft.
Signed by Miami Dolphins, July 24, 1986.
Released by Miami Dolphins, November 19, 1988; awarded on waivers to Indianapolis Colts, November 21, 1988.

Year Club		PASS RECEIVING				PUNT RETURNS				TOTAL		
	G.	P.C.	Yds.	Avg.	TD.	No.	Yds.	Avg.	TD.	TD.	Pts.	F.
1986—Miami NFL	16	15	235	15.7	2	11	150	13.6	1	3	18	4
1987—Miami NFL	12	26	404	15.5	3		None			3	18	1
1988—Miami (11)-Indianapolis (1) NFL	12	2	38	19.0	0		None			0	0	1
Pro Totals—3 Years	40	43	677	15.7	5	11	150	13.6	1	6	36	6

Additional pro statistics: Recovered two fumbles, 1986.

MICKEY AARON PRUITT
Linebacker-Safety—Chicago Bears
Born January 10, 1965, at Bamberg, S.C.
Height, 6.01. Weight, 206.
High School—Chicago, Ill., Paul Robeson.
Received bachelor of arts degree in communications
from University of Colorado in 1988.
Related to Leo Lewis, wide receiver with Minnesota Vikings.

Named as defensive back on THE SPORTING NEWS College All-America team, 1987.
Signed as free agent by Chicago Bears, May 4, 1988.
Chicago NFL, 1988.
Games: 1988 (14).
Played in NFC Championship Game following 1988 season.

ROLLIN W. PUTZIER
Defensive Tackle—Pittsburgh Steelers
Born December 10, 1965, at Coeur d'Alene, Ida.
Height, 6.04. Weight, 281.
High School—Post Falls, Ida.
Attended University of Oregon.

Selected by Green Bay in 4th round (88th player selected) of 1988 NFL draft.
Signed by Green Bay Packers, July 17, 1988.
Released by Green Bay Packers, August 30, 1988; signed as free agent by Pittsburgh Steelers, September 7, 1988.
Released by Pittsburgh Steelers after failing physical, September 9, 1988; re-signed by Steelers, November 2, 1988.
Pittsburgh NFL, 1988.
Games: 1988 (5).

—DID YOU KNOW—
That the Saints' 20-17 victory over Dallas on October 3, 1988 was their first against the Cowboys since October 17, 1971 and just their second over the Cowboys in club history?

PHILLIP DAVID PUZZUOLI

Name pronounced Pa-ZOOL-ee.

(Dave)

Nose Tackle—Indianapolis Colts

Born January 12, 1961, at Greenwich, Conn.
Height, 6.03. Weight, 270.
High School—Stamford, Conn., Catholic.
Attended University of Pittsburgh.

Selected by Tampa Bay in 8th round (85th player selected) of 1983 USFL draft.
Selected by Cleveland in 6th round (149th player selected) of 1983 NFL draft.
Signed by Cleveland Browns, May 31, 1983.
Released by Cleveland Browns, August 30, 1988; signed as free agent by Indianapolis Colts, April 2, 1989.
Cleveland NFL, 1983 through 1987.
Games: 1983 (16), 1984 (16), 1985 (16), 1986 (16), 1987 (12). Total—76.
Pro statistics: Recovered one fumble for two yards, 1983; recovered one fumble, 1984; returned two kickoffs for eight yards, 1985; returned one kickoff for 32 yards, 1986.
Played in AFC Championship Game following 1986 and 1987 seasons.

MICHAEL ANTHONY QUICK

(Mike)

Wide Receiver—Philadelphia Eagles

Born May 14, 1959, at Hamlet, N.C.
Height, 6.02. Weight, 190.
High School—Rockingham, N.C., Richmond.
Attended Fork Union Military Academy and North Carolina State University.

Named to THE SPORTING NEWS NFL All-Star Team, 1985.
Tied NFL record for longest passing play from scrimmage when he caught a 99-yard touchdown pass from quarterback Ron Jaworski against Atlanta Falcons, November 10, 1985.
Selected by Philadelphia in 1st round (20th player selected) of 1982 NFL draft.
On did not report list, August 20 through September 1, 1985.
Reported and granted roster exemption, September 2 through September 4, 1985; activated, September 5, 1985.
On injured reserve with broken leg, October 3 through December 1, 1988; activated, December 2, 1988.

		——PASS RECEIVING——			
Year Club	G.	P.C.	Yds.	Avg.	TD.
1982—Philadelphia NFL	9	10	156	15.6	1
1983—Philadelphia NFL	16	69	*1409	20.4	13
1984—Philadelphia NFL	14	61	1052	17.2	9
1985—Philadelphia NFL	16	73	1247	17.1	11
1986—Philadelphia NFL	16	60	939	15.7	9
1987—Philadelphia NFL	12	46	790	17.2	11
1988—Philadelphia NFL	8	22	508	23.1	4
Pro Totals—7 Years	91	341	6101	17.9	58

Additional pro statistics: Recovered one fumble, 1982 and 1985 through 1987; fumbled once, 1983, 1985 and 1986; rushed once for minus five yards, 1984; returned two kickoffs for six yards, 1986; fumbled three times, 1987.
Played in Pro Bowl (NFL All-Star Game) following 1983 through 1985 and 1987 seasons.
Member of Pro Bowl following 1986 season; did not play.

GEORGE JOSEPH RADACHOWSKY JR.

Safety—New York Jets

Born September 7, 1962, at Danbury, Conn.
Height, 5.11. Weight, 190.
High School—Danbury, Conn.
Attended Boston College.

Selected by Philadelphia in 5th round (84th player selected) of 1984 USFL draft.
Selected by Los Angeles Rams in 7th round (188th player selected) of 1984 NFL draft.
Signed by Los Angeles Rams, July 9, 1984.
Traded by Los Angeles Rams to Indianapolis Colts for 11th round pick in 1985 draft, August 27, 1984.
Released by Indianapolis Colts, September 30, 1985; re-signed by Colts, April 1, 1986.
Released by Indianapolis Colts, August 18, 1986; signed as free agent by New York Jets, May 10, 1987.
Released by New York Jets, August 31, 1987; re-signed as replacement player by Jets, September 24, 1987.
Released by New York Jets, October 26, 1987; re-signed by Jets, October 28, 1987.
Released by New York Jets, November 3, 1987; re-signed by Jets, November 27, 1987.
On injured reserve with knee injury, August 22 through October 19, 1988; activated after clearing procedural waivers, October 21, 1988.
Indianapolis NFL, 1984 and 1985; New York Jets NFL, 1987 and 1988.
Games: 1984 (16), 1985 (3), 1987 (8), 1988 (9). Total—36.
Pro statistics: Returned one kickoff for no yards and fumbled once, 1984; intercepted two passes for 45 yards, 1987.

JOHN RADE

Name pronounced RAY-dee.

Linebacker—Atlanta Falcons

Born August 31, 1960, at Ceres, Calif.
Height, 6.01. Weight, 240.
High School—Sierra Vista, Ariz., Buena.
Attended Modesto Junior College and Boise State University.

Signed as free agent by Boston Breakers, February 10, 1983.
Released by Boston Breakers, February 12, 1983.
Selected by Atlanta in 8th round (215th player selected) of 1983 NFL draft.
Signed by Atlanta Falcons, May 16, 1983.
On injured reserve with pinched nerve in neck, October 24 through remainder of 1984 season.
On injured reserve with ankle injury, December 18 through remainder of 1986 season.
Granted free agency, February 1, 1988; re-signed by Falcons, August 29, 1988.
On injured reserve with knee injury, December 14 through remainder of 1988 season.
Atlanta NFL, 1983 through 1988.
Games: 1983 (16), 1984 (7), 1985 (16), 1986 (15), 1987 (11), 1988 (15). Total—80.
Pro statistics: Recovered two fumbles for 16 yards and a touchdown, 1983; recovered one fumble, 1984; intercepted two passes for 42 yards and a touchdown, 1985; intercepted one pass for six yards, 1986.

J. SCOTT RADECIC

Name pronounced RADD-ah-seck.

(Known by middle name.)

Linebacker—Buffalo Bills

Born June 14, 1962, at Pittsburgh, Pa.
Height, 6.03. Weight, 242.
High School—Pittsburgh, Pa., Brentwood.
Attended Penn State University.
Brother of Keith Radecic, center with St. Louis Cardinals, 1987.

Selected by Philadelphia in 1984 USFL territorial draft.
Selected by Kansas City in 2nd round (34th player selected) of 1984 NFL draft.
Signed by Kansas City Chiefs, July 12, 1984.
Released by Kansas City Chiefs, September 7, 1987; awarded on waivers to Buffalo Bills, September 8, 1987.

| | | ——INTERCEPTIONS—— | | | | |
Year	Club	G.	No.	Yds.	Avg.	TD.
1984—Kansas City NFL		16	2	54	27.0	1
1985—Kansas City NFL		16	1	21	21.0	0
1986—Kansas City NFL		16	1	20	20.0	0
1987—Buffalo NFL		12	2	4	2.0	0
1988—Buffalo NFL		16		None		
Pro Totals—5 Years		76	6	99	16.5	1

Additional pro statistics: Recovered one fumble, 1985 and 1986; returned one kickoff for 14 yards, 1987; recovered two fumbles, 1987 and 1988.
Played in AFC Championship Game following 1988 season.

WAYNE R. RADLOFF

Center—Atlanta Falcons

Born May 17, 1961, at London, England.
Height, 6.05. Weight, 277.
High School—Winter Park, Fla.
Attended University of Georgia.

Named center on THE SPORTING NEWS USFL All-Star Team, 1984.
Selected by Michigan in 2nd round (15th player selected) of 1983 USFL draft.
Signed by Michigan Panthers, January 22, 1983.
On developmental squad, April 4 through April 9, 1983; activated, April 10, 1983.
Not protected an merger of Michigan Panthers and Oakland Invaders; not selected in USFL dispersal draft, December 6, 1984.
Signed as free agent by Atlanta Falcons, March 1, 1985.
On developmental squad for 1 game with Michigan Panthers in 1983.
Michigan USFL, 1983 and 1984; Atlanta NFL, 1985 through 1988.
Games: 1983 (17), 1984 (18), 1985 (16), 1986 (16), 1987 (12), 1988 (10). Total USFL—35. Total NFL—54. Total Pro—89.
USFL statistics: Recovered one fumble, 1983.
NFL statistics: Recovered one fumble for minus three yards, 1986; recovered one fumble, 1988.
Played in USFL Championship Game following 1983 season.

THOMAS MICHAEL RAFFERTY

(Tom)

Center—Dallas Cowboys

Born August 2, 1954, at Syracuse, N. Y.
Height, 6.03. Weight, 264.
High School—Manlius, N. Y.
Received bachelor of science degree in physical education from Penn State University;
attending University of Dallas for master's degree.

Selected by Dallas in 4th round (119th player selected) of 1976 NFL draft.
Dallas NFL, 1976 through 1988.
Games: 1976 (13), 1977 (14), 1978 (16), 1979 (16), 1980 (16), 1981 (16), 1982 (9), 1983 (16), 1984 (16), 1985 (16), 1986 (16), 1987 (12), 1988 (15). Total—191.
Pro statistics: Fumbled once, 1977; recovered one fumble, 1979, 1981, 1986 and 1987; recovered one fumble for six yards, 1980; fumbled twice for minus 30 yards, 1981; recovered two fumbles, 1982, 1984 and 1985; caught one pass for eight yards, 1983.
Played in NFC Championship Game following 1977, 1978 and 1980 through 1982 seasons.
Played in NFL Championship Game following 1977 and 1978 seasons.

GREGG ADAM RAKOCZY
(Name pronounced Ra-KOZE-e.)
Center—Cleveland Browns
Born May 18, 1965, at Medford Lakes, N.J.
Height, 6.06. Weight, 290.
High School—Medford, N.J., Shawnee.
Attended University of Miami (Fla.).

Selected by Cleveland in 2nd round (32nd player selected) of 1987 NFL draft.
Signed by Cleveland Browns, July 29, 1987.
Cleveland NFL, 1987 and 1988.
Games: 1987 (12), 1988 (16). Total—28.
Pro statistics: Fumbled twice for minus 16 yards, 1988.
Played in AFC Championship Game following 1987 season.

THOMAS LLOYD RAMSEY
(Tom)
Quarterback—Indianapolis Colts
Born July 9, 1961, at Encino, Calif.
Height, 6.01. Weight, 188.
High School—Granada Hills, Calif., Kennedy.
Received bachelor of science degree in sociology
from University of California at Los Angeles in 1983.

Selected by Los Angeles in 5th round (49th player selected) of 1983 USFL draft.
Signed by Los Angeles Express, February 10, 1983.
Selected by New England in 10th round (267th player selected) of 1983 NFL draft.
On developmental squad, July 2 through remainder of 1983 season.
Traded by Los Angeles Express to Oakland Invaders for 3rd round pick in 1985 draft, March 29, 1984.
On developmental squad, March 30 through April 28, 1984; activated, April 29, 1984.
Released by Oakland Invaders, July 17, 1984; signed by New England Patriots, July 25, 1984.
On injured reserve with thumb injury, August 21 through entire 1984 season.
Released by New England Patriots, September 11, 1985; re-signed by Patriots, October 17, 1985.
Released by New England Patriots, October 18, 1988; signed as free agent by Indianapolis Colts, March 6, 1989.
On developmental squad for 1 game with Los Angeles Express in 1983.
On developmental squad for 4 games with Oakland Invaders in 1984.
Active for 11 games with New England Patriots in 1985; did not play.

			PASSING						RUSHING				TOTAL	
Year Club	G.	Att.	Cmp.	Pct.	Gain	T.P.	P.I.	Avg.	Att.	Yds.	Avg.	TD.	TD.	Pts.	F.
1983—Los Angeles USFL............	17	307	160	52.1	1975	13	14	6.43	28	80	2.9	1	1	6	4
1984—L.A. (5)-Oak. (5) USFL	10	91	54	59.3	512	2	7	5.63	8	38	4.8	0	0	0	1
1986—New England NFL..........	5	3	1	33.3	7	0	0	2.33	1	—6	—6.0	0	0	0	0
1987—New England NFL..........	9	134	71	53.0	898	6	6	6.70	13	75	5.8	1	1	6	4
1988—New England NFL..........	7	27	12	44.4	100	0	3	3.70	3	8	2.7	0	0	0	0
USFL Totals—2 Years......	27	398	214	53.8	2487	15	21	6.25	36	118	3.3	1	1	6	5
NFL Totals—4 Years........	21	164	84	51.2	1005	6	9	6.13	17	77	4.5	1	1	6	4
Pro Totals—6 Years..........	48	562	298	53.0	3492	21	30	6.21	53	195	3.7	2	2	12	9

USFL Quarterback Rating Points: 1983 (67.1), 1984 (50.3). Total—63.6.
NFL Quarterback Rating Points: 1986 (42.4), 1987 (70.4), 1988 (15.0). Total—59.7.
Additional pro statistics: Recovered one fumble, 1987.
Member of New England Patriots for AFC and NFL Championship Games following 1985 season; did not play.

ERVIN RANDLE
Linebacker—Tampa Bay Buccaneers
Born October 12, 1962, at Hearne, Tex.
Height, 6.01. Weight, 250.
High School—Hearne, Tex.
Attended Baylor University.

Selected by San Antonio in 1985 USFL territorial draft.
Selected by Tampa Bay in 3rd round (64th player selected) of 1985 NFL draft.
Signed by Tampa Bay Buccaneers, July 18, 1985.
On injured reserve with shoulder injury, September 30 through November 3, 1988; activated, November 4, 1988.
Tampa Bay NFL, 1985 through 1988.
Games: 1985 (16), 1986 (16), 1987 (12), 1988 (9). Total—53.
Pro statistics: Intercepted one pass for no yards and recovered two fumbles, 1985; recovered one fumble, 1987.

RANDY ROBERT RASMUSSEN
Center-Guard—Minnesota Vikings
Born September 27, 1960, at Minneapolis, Minn.
Height, 6.01. Weight, 253.
High School—St. Paul, Minn., Irondale.
Received bachelor of applied studies degree in business and marketing from
University of Minnesota in 1984.

Selected by Chicago in 12th round (241st player selected) of 1984 USFL draft.
Selected by Pittsburgh in 8th round (220th player selected) of 1984 NFL draft.
Signed by Pittsburgh Steelers, June 18, 1984.

On injured reserve with knee injury, August 20 through October 2, 1985; activated after clearing procedural waivers, October 4, 1985.

On injured reserve with knee injury, October 24 through remainder of 1986 season.

Released by Pittsburgh Steelers, September 7, 1987; signed as free agent by Minnesota Vikings, October 20, 1987.

Released by Minnesota Vikings, October 21, 1987; re-signed by Vikings, November 16, 1987.

Released by Minnesota Vikings, August 30, 1988; re-signed by Vikings, September 20, 1988.

On injured reserve with knee injury, October 15 through November 1, 1988; activated after clearing procedural waivers, November 3, 1988.

Pittsburgh NFL, 1984 through 1986; Minnesota NFL, 1987 and 1988.

Games: 1984 (16), 1985 (11), 1986 (4), 1987 (5), 1988 (7). Total—43.

Played in AFC Championship Game following 1984 season.

Played in NFC Championship Game following 1987 season.

THOMAS DEAN RATHMAN
(Tom)
Fullback—San Francisco 49ers
Born October 7, 1962, at Grand Island, Neb.
Height, 6.01. Weight, 232.
High School—Grand Island, Neb.
Attended University of Nebraska.

Selected by Memphis in 1986 USFL territorial draft.
Selected by San Francisco in 3rd round (56th player selected) of 1986 NFL draft.
Signed by San Francisco 49ers, July 16, 1986.

Year Club	G.	Att.	Yds.	Avg.	TD.	P.C.	Yds.	Avg.	TD.	TD.	Pts.	F.
1986—San Francisco NFL	16	33	138	4.2	1	13	121	9.3	0	1	6	0
1987—San Francisco NFL	12	62	257	4.1	1	30	329	11.0	3	4	24	1
1988—San Francisco NFL	16	102	427	4.2	2	42	382	9.1	0	2	12	0
Pro Totals—3 Years	44	197	822	4.2	4	85	832	9.8	3	7	42	1

Additional pro statistics: Returned three kickoffs for 66 yards, 1986; returned two kickoffs for 37 yards, 1987; recovered one fumble, 1988.

Played in NFC Championship Game following 1988 season.

Played in NFL Championship Game following 1988 season.

GARY PHILLIP REASONS
Linebacker—New York Giants
Born February 18, 1962, at Crowley, Tex.
Height, 6.04. Weight, 234.
High School—Crowley, Tex.
Received bachelor of science degree in business administration
from Northwestern State University.

Selected by New Jersey in 2nd round (26th player selected) of 1984 USFL draft.
USFL rights traded by New Jersey Generals to Tampa Bay Bandits for rights to linebacker Jim LeClair, January 30, 1984.
Selected by New York Giants in 4th round (105th player selected) of 1984 NFL draft.
Signed by New York Giants, July 12, 1984.
Granted free agency, February 1, 1987; re-signed by Giants, September 10, 1987.
Granted roster exemption, September 10 through September 20, 1987; activated, September 21, 1987.

Year Club	G.	No.	Yds.	Avg. TD.
1984—N.Y. Giants NFL	16	2	26	13.0 0
1985—N.Y. Giants NFL	16	1	10	10.0 0
1986—N.Y. Giants NFL	16	2	28	14.0 0
1987—N.Y. Giants NFL	10		None	
1988—N.Y. Giants NFL	16	1	20	20.0 0
Pro Totals—5 Years	74	6	84	14.0 0

Additional pro statistics: Recovered three fumbles, 1984; recovered two fumbles for five yards, 1988.

Played in NFC Championship Game following 1986 season.

Played in NFL Championship Game following 1986 season.

WILLARD SHELDON REAVES
Running Back—Washington Redskins
Born August 17, 1959, at Flagstaff, Ariz.
Height, 5.11. Weight, 200.
High School—Flagstaff, Ariz., Coconino.
Attended University of Northern Arizona.

Signed as free agent by Green Bay Packers, May 5, 1981.
On injured reserve with sciatic nerve injury, August 18 through entire 1981 season.
Released by Green Bay Packers, August 30, 1982; signed as free agent by Edmonton Eskimos, March, 1983.
Traded with running backs Sean Kehoe and Scott Stauch and defensive back Steven Hall by Edmonton Eskimos to Winnipeg Blue Bombers for 1st round pick in 1984 CFL draft and future considerations, June, 1983.
Released by Winnipeg Blue Bombers, July 9, 1988; signed as free agent by Washington Redskins, July 20, 1988.
On injured reserve with ankle injury, August 29 through entire 1988 season.

Year Club	G.	Att.	Yds.	Avg.	TD.	P.C.	Yds.	Avg.	TD.	TD.	Pts.	F.
			RUSHING			PASS RECEIVING				TOTAL		
1983—Winnipeg CFL	9	164	898	5.5	9	16	185	11.6	0	9	†56	2
1984—Winnipeg CFL	16	304	*1733	5.7	14	40	407	10.2	4	18	108	6
1985—Winnipeg CFL	16	267	*1323	5.0	9	20	289	14.5	1	10	60	6
1986—Winnipeg CFL	6	104	498	4.8	3	10	68	6.8	0	3	18	2
1987—Winnipeg CFL	15	*271	*1471	5.4	9	27	253	9.4	4	13	78	2
CFL Totals—5 Years	62	1110	5923	5.3	44	113	1202	10.6	9	53	320	18

Year Club	G.	No.	Yds.	Avg.	TD.
		KICKOFF RETURNS			
1983—Winnipeg CFL	9	5	164	32.8	0
1984—Winnipeg CFL	16	6	143	23.8	0
1985—Winnipeg CFL	16	1	7	7.0	0
1986—Winnipeg CFL	6		None		
1987—Winnipeg CFL	15		None		
CFL Totals—5 Years	62	12	314	26.2	0

†Credited with one 2-point conversion.
Additional CFL statistics: Attempted two passes with two completions for 78 yards, 1985; recovered two fumbles, 1984, 1985 and 1987.
Played in CFL Championship Game following 1984 season.

BARRY REDDEN
Running Back—San Diego Chargers
Born July 21, 1960, at Sarasota, Fla.
Height, 5.10. Weight, 219.
High School—Sarasota, Fla.
Received degree in psychology from University of Richmond in 1982.

Selected by Los Angeles Rams in 1st round (14th player selected) of 1982 NFL draft.
Granted free agency, February 1, 1987; re-signed by Rams and traded to San Diego Chargers for running back Buford McGee, 2nd round pick in 1988 draft and 6th round pick in 1989 draft, June 9, 1987.
On physically unable to perform/active with hamstring injury, July 23 through August 3, 1988; passed physical, August 4, 1988.
On injured reserve with broken hand, August 30 through October 28, 1988; activated, October 29, 1988.

Year Club	G.	Att.	Yds.	Avg.	TD.	P.C.	Yds.	Avg.	TD.	TD.	Pts.	F.
			RUSHING			PASS RECEIVING				TOTAL		
1982—Los Angeles Rams NFL	9	8	24	3.0	0	4	16	4.0	0	0	0	2
1983—Los Angeles Rams NFL	15	75	372	5.0	2	4	30	7.5	0	2	12	2
1984—Los Angeles Rams NFL	14	45	247	5.5	0	4	39	9.8	0	0	0	0
1985—Los Angeles Rams NFL	14	87	380	4.4	0	16	162	10.1	0	0	0	1
1986—Los Angeles Rams NFL	15	110	467	4.2	4	28	217	7.8	1	5	30	1
1987—San Diego NFL	12	11	36	3.3	0	7	46	6.6	0	0	0	0
1988—San Diego NFL	8	19	30	1.6	3	1	11	11.0	0	3	18	0
Pro Totals—7 Years	87	355	1556	4.4	9	64	521	8.1	1	10	60	6

Year Club	G.	No.	Yds.	Avg.	TD.
		KICKOFF RETURNS			
1982—L.A. Rams NFL	9	22	502	22.8	0
1983—L.A. Rams NFL	15	19	358	18.8	0
1984—L.A. Rams NFL	14	23	530	23.0	0
1985—L.A. Rams NFL	14		None		
1986—L.A. Rams NFL	15		None		
1987—San Diego NFL	12		None		
1988—San Diego NFL	8		None		
Pro Totals—7 Years	87	64	1390	21.7	0

Additional pro statistics: Recovered one fumble, 1982.
Played in NFC Championship Game following 1985 season.

ANDRE DARNELL REED
Wide Receiver—Buffalo Bills
Born January 29, 1964, at Allentown, Pa.
Height, 6.00. Weight, 190.
High School—Allentown Pa., Louis E. Dieruff.
Attended Kutztown State College.

Selected by Orlando in 3rd round (39th player selected) of 1985 USFL draft.
Selected by Buffalo in 4th round (86th player selected) of 1985 NFL draft.
Signed by Buffalo Bills, July 19, 1985.

Year Club	G.	P.C.	Yds.	Avg.	TD.
		PASS RECEIVING			
1985—Buffalo NFL	16	48	637	13.3	4
1986—Buffalo NFL	15	53	739	13.9	7
1987—Buffalo NFL	12	57	752	13.2	5
1988—Buffalo NFL	15	71	968	13.6	6
Pro Totals—4 Years	58	229	3096	13.5	22

Additional pro statistics: Rushed three times for minus one yard and a touchdown, returned five punts for 12 yards and recovered two fumbles, 1985; fumbled once, 1985 and 1988; rushed three times for minus eight yards, recovered two fumbles for two yards and fumbled twice, 1986; rushed once for one yard, 1987; rushed six times for 64 yards, 1988.
Played in AFC Championship Game following 1988 season.
Played in Pro Bowl (NFL All-Star Game) following 1988 season.

DOUG REED
Defensive End—Los Angeles Rams
Born July 16, 1960, at San Diego, Calif.
Height, 6.03. Weight, 250.
High School—San Diego, Calif., Abraham Lincoln.
Attended San Diego City College and San Diego State University.

Selected by Los Angeles in 17th round (193rd player selected) of 1983 USFL draft.
Selected by Los Angeles Rams in 4th round (111th player selected) of 1983 NFL draft.
Signed by Los Angeles Rams, June 3, 1983.
On injured reserve with leg injury, August 29 through entire 1983 season.
Los Angeles Rams NFL, 1984 through 1988.
Games: 1984 (9), 1985 (16), 1986 (16), 1987 (12), 1988 (16). Total—69.
Pro statistics: Recovered one fumble for two yards, 1984; recovered one fumble, 1988.
Played in NFC Championship Game following 1985 season.

JERRY REESE
Defensive End—Pittsburgh Steelers
Born July 11, 1964, at Hopkinsville, Ky.
Height, 6.02. Weight, 267.
High School—Hopkinsville, Ky., Christian County.
Attended University of Kentucky.

Selected by Pittsburgh in 5th round (128th player selected) of 1988 NFL draft.
Signed by Pittsburgh Steelers, July 17, 1988.
Pittsburgh NFL, 1988.
Games: 1988 (15).

KEN REEVES
Offensive Tackle-Guard—Philadelphia Eagles
Born October 4, 1961, at Pittsburg, Tex.
Height, 6.05. Weight, 270.
High School—Pittsburg, Tex.
Attended Texas A&M University.

Selected by Houston in 1985 USFL territorial draft.
Selected by Philadelphia in 6th round (156th player selected) of 1985 NFL draft.
Signed by Philadelphia Eagles, July 23, 1985.
Philadelphia NFL, 1985 through 1988.
Games: 1985 (15), 1986 (15), 1987 (10), 1988 (15). Total—55.
Pro statistics: Recovered one fumble, 1985 and 1986; ran one yard with lateral on kickoff return, 1987.

THOMAS BERNARD REHDER II
(Name pronounced RAY-der.)
(Tom)
Offensive Tackle—New England Patriots
Born January 27, 1965, at Sacramento, Calif.
Height, 6.07. Weight, 280.
High School—Santa Maria, Calif., St. Joseph.
Received degree in economics from University of Notre Dame in 1987.

Selected by New England in 3rd round (69th player selected) of 1988 NFL draft.
Signed by New England Patriots, July 15, 1988.
New England NFL, 1988.
Games: 1988 (16).

FRANK MICHAEL REICH
Name pronounced Rike.
Quarterback—Buffalo Bills
Born December 4, 1961, at Freeport, N.Y.
Height, 6.04. Weight, 208.
High School—Lebanon, Pa., Cedar Crest.
Received bachelor of science degree in finance from University of Maryland in 1984.

Selected by Tampa Bay in 1985 USFL territorial draft.
Selected by Buffalo in 3rd round (57th player selected) of 1985 NFL draft.
Signed by Buffalo Bills, August 1, 1985.
On injured reserve with Achilles heel injury, September 3 to December 5, 1985; activated, December 6, 1985.
Active for 12 games with Buffalo Bills in 1987; did not play.

				—PASSING—					—RUSHING—			—TOTAL—		
Year Club	G.	Att.	Cmp.	Pct.	Gain	T.P.	P.I.	Avg.	Att.	Yds.	Avg. TD.	TD.	Pts.	F.
1985—Buffalo NFL	1	1	1	100.0	19	0	0	19.00		None		0	0	0
1986—Buffalo NFL	3	19	9	47.4	104	0	2	5.47	1	0	0.0 0	0	0	1
1988—Buffalo NFL	3			None					3	—3	—1.0 0	0	0	0
Pro Totals—4 Years	7	20	10	50.0	123	0	2	6.15	4	—3	—0.8 0	0	0	1

Quarterback Rating Points: 1985 (118.8), 1986 (24.8). Total—29.8
Member of Buffalo Bills for AFC Championship Game following 1988 season; did not play.

MIKE REICHENBACH
Linebacker—Philadelphia Eagles
Born September 14, 1961, at Fort Meade, Md.
Height, 6.02. Weight, 235.
High School—Bethlehem, Pa., Liberty.
Attended East Stroudsburg University.

Signed as free agent by Philadelphia Eagles, June 18, 1984.
Released by Philadelphia Eagles, August 27, 1984; re-signed by Eagles, September 25, 1984.
Philadelphia NFL, 1984 through 1988.
Games: 1984 (12), 1985 (16), 1986 (16), 1987 (11), 1988 (16). Total—71.
Pro statistics: Recovered two fumbles, 1984; intercepted one pass for 10 yards, 1985.

MICHAEL EDWARD REID
Linebacker—Atlanta Falcons
Born June 25, 1964, at Albany, Ga.
Height, 6.02. Weight, 226.
High School—Albany, Ga., Dougherty.
Attended University of Wisconsin.

Selected by Atlanta in 7th round (181st player selected) of 1987 NFL draft.
Signed by Atlanta Falcons, July 26, 1987.
Atlanta NFL, 1987 and 1988.
Games: 1987 (11), 1988 (16). Total—27.

BRUCE MICHAEL REIMERS
Offensive Tackle—Cincinnati Bengals
Born September 18, 1960, at Algona, Ia.
Height, 6.07. Weight, 280.
High School—Humboldt, Ia.
Attended Iowa State University.

Selected by Los Angeles in 7th round (136th player selected) of 1984 USFL draft.
Selected by Cincinnati in 8th round (204th player selected) of 1984 NFL draft.
Signed by Cincinnati Bengals, June 20, 1984.
Cincinnati NFL, 1984 through 1988.
Games: 1984 (15), 1985 (14), 1986 (16), 1987 (10), 1988 (16). Total—71.
Pro statistics: Recovered one fumble, 1987.
Played in AFC Championship Game following 1988 season.
Played in NFL Championship Game following 1988 season.

JOHNNY REMBERT
Linebacker—New England Patriots
Born January 19, 1961, at Hollandale, Miss.
Height, 6.03. Weight, 234.
High School—Arcadia, Fla., DeSoto.
Attended Cowley County Community College and Clemson University.

Selected by Washington in 1983 USFL territorial draft.
Selected by New England in 4th round (101st player selected) of 1983 NFL draft.
Signed by New England Patriots, May 16, 1983.
On injured reserve with knee injury, August 28 through November 2, 1984; activated, November 3, 1984.
New England NFL, 1983 through 1988.
Games: 1983 (15), 1984 (7), 1985 (16), 1986 (16), 1987 (11), 1988 (16). Total—81.
Pro statistics: Recovered one fumble, 1983; recovered three fumbles for nine yards (including one in end zone for a touchdown), 1985; intercepted one pass for 37 yards, recovered three fumbles (including one in end zone for a touchdown) and returned three kickoffs for 27 yards, 1986; intercepted one pass for one yard, 1987; intercepted two passes for 10 yards and recovered three fumbles for 10 yards, 1988.
Played in AFC Championship Game following 1985 season.
Played in NFL Championship Game following 1985 season.
Played in Pro Bowl (NFL All-Star Game) following 1988 season.

CAESAR HARRIS RENTIE
Name pronounced RENT-ay.
Offensive Lineman—Buffalo Bills
Born November 10, 1964, at Hartshorne, Okla.
Height, 6.03. Weight, 291.
High School—Hartshorne, Okla.
Received bachelor of science degree in communications
from University of Oklahoma in 1988.

Selected by Chicago in 7th round (189th player selected) of 1988 NFL draft.
Signed by Chicago Bears, July 20, 1988.
Granted unconditional free agency, February 1, 1989; signed by Buffalo Bills, March 2, 1989.
Chicago NFL, 1988.
Games: 1988 (5).
Member of Chicago Bears for NFC Championship Game following 1988 season; inactive.

FUAD REVEIZ
Placekicker—Miami Dolphins
Born February 24, 1963, at Bogota, Columbia.
Height, 5.11. Weight, 217.
High School—Miami, Fla., Sunset.
Attended University of Tennessee.

Selected by Memphis in 1985 USFL territorial draft.
Selected by Miami in 7th round (195th player selected) of 1985 NFL draft.
Signed by Miami Dolphins, July 20, 1985.
On injured reserve with pulled thigh, October 19 through November 25, 1988; activated, November 26, 1988.

		——PLACE KICKING——				
Year Club	G.	XP.	XPM.	FG.	FGA.	Pts.
1985—Miami NFL	16	50	2	22	27	116
1986—Miami NFL	16	*52	3	14	22	94
1987—Miami NFL	11	28	2	9	11	55
1988—Miami NFL	11	31	1	8	12	55
Pro Totals—4 Years	54	161	8	53	72	320

Played in AFC Championship Game following 1985 season.

DERRICK SCOTT REYNOLDS
(Ricky)
Defensive Back—Tampa Bay Buccaneers
Born January 19, 1965, at Sacramento, Calif.
Height, 5.11. Weight, 190.
High School—Sacramento, Calif., Luther Burbank.
Attended Washington State University.
Cousin of Jerry Royster, infielder with Los Angeles Dodgers, Atlanta Braves, San Diego Padres,
Chicago White Sox and New York Yankees, 1973 through 1988.

Selected by Tampa Bay in 2nd round (36th player selected) of 1987 NFL draft.
Signed by Tampa Bay Buccaneers, July 18, 1987.
Tampa Bay NFL, 1987 and 1988.
Games. 1987 (12), 1988 (16). Total—28.
Pro statistics: Intercepted four passes for seven yards and recovered two fumbles, 1988.

EDWARD RANNELL REYNOLDS
(Ed)
Linebacker—New England Patriots
Born September 23, 1961, at Stuttgart, West Germany.
Height, 6.05. Weight, 242.
High School—Ridgeway, Va., Drewry Mason.
Received bachelor of science degree in elementary education from University of Virginia in 1983.

Signed as free agent by New England Patriots, May 10, 1983.
Released by New England Patriots, August 29, 1983; re-signed by Patriots, September 28, 1983.
Released by New England Patriots, August 27, 1984; re-signed by Patriots, August 28, 1984.
On injured reserve with knee injury, September 11 through October 11, 1985; activated, October 12, 1985.
New England NFL, 1983 through 1988.
Games: 1983 (12), 1984 (16), 1985 (12), 1986 (16), 1987 (12), 1988 (14). Total—82.
Pro statistics: Recovered two fumbles, 1983; recovered one fumble, 1986.
Played in AFC Championship Game following 1985 season.
Played in NFL Championship Game following 1985 season.

ALLEN TROY RICE
Running Back—Minnesota Vikings
Born April 5, 1962, at Houston, Tex.
Height, 5.10. Weight, 204.
High School—Houston, Tex., Klein.
Attended Wharton County Junior College, Ranger Junior College and Baylor University.

Selected by Houston in 1984 USFL territorial draft.
Selected by Minnesota in 5th round (140th player selected) of 1984 NFL draft.
Signed by Minnesota Vikings, July 20, 1984.

		——RUSHING——				PASS RECEIVING				—TOTAL—		
Year Club	G.	Att.	Yds.	Avg.	TD.	P.C.	Yds.	Avg.	TD.	TD.	Pts.	F.
1984—Minnesota NFL	14	14	58	4.1	1	4	59	14.8	1	2	12	1
1985—Minnesota NFL	14	31	104	3.4	3	9	61	6.8	1	4	24	0
1986—Minnesota NFL	14	73	220	3.0	2	30	391	13.0	3	5	30	5
1987—Minnesota NFL	12	51	131	2.6	1	19	201	10.6	1	2	12	1
1988—Minnesota NFL	16	110	322	2.9	6	30	279	9.3	0	6	36	1
Pro Totals—5 Years	70	279	835	3.0	13	92	991	10.8	6	19	114	8

Additional pro statistics: Returned three kickoffs for 34 yards, 1984; recovered two fumbles, 1984 and 1986; returned four kickoffs for 70 yards, 1985; recovered one fumble, 1985, 1987 and 1988; returned five kickoffs for 88 yards, returned one punt for no yards and attempted one pass with no completions, 1986; returned two kickoffs for 29 yards, 1987; returned one kickoff for no yards, 1988.
Played in NFC Championship Game following 1987 season.

JERRY LEE RICE
Wide Receiver—San Francisco 49ers

Born October 13, 1962, at Starkville, Miss.
Height, 6.02. Weight, 200.
High School—Crawford, Miss., B.L. Moor.
Attended Mississippi Valley State University.

Established NFL record for most touchdown receptions, season (22), 1987.
Named THE SPORTING NEWS NFL Player of the Year, 1987.
Named to THE SPORTING NEWS NFL All-Star Team, 1986 through 1988.
Named as wide receiver on THE SPORTING NEWS College All-America Team, 1984.
Selected by Birmingham in 1st round (1st player selected) of 1985 USFL draft.
Selected by San Francisco in 1st round (16th player selected) of 1985 NFL draft.
Signed by San Francisco 49ers, July 23, 1985.

| | | ——RUSHING—— | | | | PASS RECEIVING | | | | —TOTAL— | | |
Year Club	G.	Att.	Yds.	Avg.	TD.	P.C.	Yds.	Avg.	TD.	TD.	Pts.	F.
1985—San Francisco NFL	16	6	26	4.3	1	49	927	18.9	3	4	24	1
1986—San Francisco NFL	16	10	72	7.2	1	86	★1570	18.3	★15	16	96	2
1987—San Francisco NFL	12	8	51	6.4	1	65	1078	16.6	★22	★23	★138	2
1988—San Francisco NFL	16	13	107	8.2	1	64	1306	20.4	9	10	60	2
Pro Totals—4 Years	60	37	256	6.9	4	264	4881	18.5	49	53	318	7

Additional pro statistics: Returned one kickoff for six yards, 1985; attempted two passes with one completion for 16 yards and recovered three fumbles, 1986; recovered one fumble, 1987 and 1988; attempted three passes with one completion for 14 yards and one interception, 1988.
Played in NFC Championship Game following 1988 season.
Played in NFL Championship Game following 1988 season.
Played in Pro Bowl (NFL All-Star Game) following 1986 and 1987 seasons.
Named to play in Pro Bowl following 1988 season; replaced due to injury by J. T. Smith.

GARY ROSS RICHARD
Cornerback—Pittsburgh Steelers

Born October 9, 1965, at Denver, Colo.
Height, 5.10. Weight, 176.
High School—Denver, Colo., East.
Attended Bakersfield College and University of Pittsburgh.

Selected by Green Bay in 7th round (173rd player selected) of 1988 NFL draft.
Signed by Green Bay Packers, July 18, 1988.
On injured reserve with ankle injury, December 16 through remainder of 1988 season.
Granted unconditional free agency, February 1, 1989; signed by Pittsburgh Steelers, April 1, 1989.
Green Bay NFL, 1988.
Games: 1988 (10).

DAVID REED RICHARDS
Offensive Tackle—San Diego Chargers

Born April 11, 1966, at Staten Island, N. Y.
Height, 6.04. Weight, 310.
High School—Dallas, Tex., Highland Park.
Attended Southern Methodist University and University of California at Los Angeles.

Selected by San Diego in 4th round (98th player selected) of 1988 NFL draft.
Signed by San Diego Chargers, July 13, 1988.
San Diego NFL, 1988.
Games: 1988 (16).
Pro statistics: Recovered one fumble, 1988.

GREGORY LAMAR RICHARDSON
(Greg)
Wide Receiver—Tampa Bay Buccaneers

Born October 6, 1964, at Mobile, Ala.
Height, 5.07. Weight, 172.
High School—Mobile, Ala., Williamson.
Attended University of Alabama.

Selected by Minnesota in 6th round (156th player selected) of 1987 NFL draft.
Signed by Minnesota Vikings, July 30, 1987.
Released by Minnesota Vikings, August 29, 1988; re-signed by Vikings, October 5, 1988.
Released by Minnesota Vikings, October 24, 1988; signed as free agent by Tampa Bay Buccaneers, December 2, 1988.
Inactive for 2 games with Minnesota Vikings in 1988.
Minnesota NFL, 1987; Minnesota (0)-Tampa Bay (2) NFL, 1988.
Games: 1987 (2), 1988 (2). Total—4.
Pro statistics: Returned four kickoffs for 76 yards, returned four punts for 19 yards and fumbled once, 1987.

MICHAEL CALVIN RICHARDSON
(Mike)
Cornerback—Los Angeles Raiders

Born May 23, 1961, at Compton, Calif.
Height, 6.00. Weight, 188.
High School—Compton, Calif.
Attended Arizona State University.

Named as defensive back on THE SPORTING NEWS College All-America Team, 1981 and 1982.
Selected by Arizona in 1983 USFL territorial draft.
Selected by Chicago in 2nd round (33rd player selected) of 1983 NFL draft.
Signed by Chicago Bears, July 20, 1983.
Granted unconditional free agency, February 1, 1989; signed by Los Angeles Raiders, April 1, 1989.

			—INTERCEPTIONS—		
Year Club	G.	No.	Yds.	Avg.	TD.
1983—Chicago NFL	16	5	9	1.8	0
1984—Chicago NFL	15	2	7	3.5	0
1985—Chicago NFL	14	4	174	43.5	*1
1986—Chicago NFL	16	7	69	9.9	0
1987—Chicago NFL	11		None		
1988—Chicago NFL	16	2	15	7.5	0
Pro Totals—6 Years	88	20	274	13.7	1

Additional pro statistics: Returned one kickoff for 17 yards and recovered two fumbles for seven yards, 1983; recovered one fumble, 1984; recovered one fumble for four yards and fumbled once, 1985; fumbled three times for minus five yards, 1986.
Played in NFC Championship Game following 1984, 1985 and 1988 seasons.
Played in NFL Championship Game following 1985 season.

ROBBERT LEE RIDDICK
(Robb)
Running Back—Buffalo Bills

Born April 26, 1957, at Quakertown, Pa.
Height, 6.00. Weight, 195.
High School—Perkasie, Pa., Pennridge.
Attended Millersville State College.
Cousin of Will Lewis, cornerback with Seattle Seahawks, Kansas City Chiefs,
Denver Gold and Houston Gamblers, 1980, 1981, 1983 and 1984;
and Tim Lewis, defensive back with Green Bay Packers, 1983 through 1986.

Selected by Buffalo in 9th round (241st player selected) of 1981 NFL draft.
On injured reserve with ankle injury, September 3 through October 16, 1981; activated, October 17, 1981.
On injured reserve with knee injury, September 7 through entire 1982 season.
On injured reserve with knee injury, August 19 through entire 1985 season.
Crossed picket line during players' strike, October 14, 1987.
On injured reserve with broken collarbone, November 13 through remainder of 1987 season.
On non-football injury list with substance abuse, August 5 through August 30, 1988; reinstated, August 31, 1988.

		—RUSHING—				PASS RECEIVING				—TOTAL—		
Year Club	G.	Att.	Yds.	Avg.	TD.	P.C.	Yds.	Avg.	TD.	TD.	Pts.	F.
1981—Buffalo NFL	10	3	29	9.7	0		None			0	0	0
1983—Buffalo NFL	16	4	18	4.5	0	3	43	14.3	0	0	0	7
1984—Buffalo NFL	16	3	3	1.0	0	23	276	12.0	0	0	0	1
1986—Buffalo NFL	15	150	632	4.2	4	49	468	9.6	1	5	30	8
1987—Buffalo NFL	6	59	221	3.7	5	15	96	6.4	3	8	†50	2
1988—Buffalo NFL	15	111	438	3.9	12	30	282	9.4	1	14	84	3
Pro Totals—6 Years	78	330	1341	4.1	21	120	1165	9.7	5	27	164	22

		—PUNT RETURNS—				—KICKOFF RET.—			
Year Club	G.	No.	Yds.	Avg.	TD.	No.	Yds.	Avg.	TD.
1981—Buffalo NFL	10	4	48	12.0	0	14	257	18.4	0
1983—Buffalo NFL	16	42	241	5.7	0	28	568	20.3	0
1984—Buffalo NFL	16		None				None		
1986—Buffalo NFL	15		None			8	200	25.0	0
1987—Buffalo NFL	6		None			7	151	21.6	0
1988—Buffalo NFL	15		None			6	100	16.7	0
Pro Totals—6 Years	78	46	289	6.3	0	63	1276	20.3	0

†Includes one safety.
Additional pro statistics: Recovered one fumble, 1983 and 1987; attempted one pass with one completion for 35 yards, 1987; attempted two passes with two completions for 31 yards, returned blocked punt five yards for a touchdown and recovered four fumbles, 1988.
Played in AFC Championship Game following 1988 season.

CHRISTOPHER ALAN RIEHM
(Chris)
Guard—Los Angeles Raiders

Born April 14, 1961, at Columbus, O.
Height, 6.06. Weight, 280.
High School—Medina, O., Highland.
Attended Ohio State University.

Signed as free agent by Kansas City Chiefs, May 5, 1983.
Released by Kansas City Chiefs after failing physical, May 12, 1983; signed as free agent by Baltimore Colts, July 1, 1983.
Left Baltimore Colts camp voluntarily and released, August 2, 1983.
USFL rights traded by Washington Federals to Oakland Invaders for rights to linebacker Bernard West, October 26, 1983.
Signed by Oakland Invaders, November 6, 1983.
Released by Oakland Invaders, February 13, 1984; re-signed by Invaders, March 30, 1984.

On developmental squad, April 21 through May 3, 1984; activated, May 4, 1984.
Not protected in merger of Oakland Invaders and Michigan Panthers; selected by Houston Gamblers in USFL dispersal draft, December 6, 1984.
On developmental squad, March 3 through March 30, 1985; activated, March 31, 1985.
On developmental squad, June 3 through remainder of 1985 season.
Traded with defensive backs Luther Bradley, Will Lewis, Mike Mitchell and Durwood Roquemore, defensive end Pete Catan, quarterbacks Jim Kelly and Todd Dillon, defensive tackles Tony Fitzpatrick, Van Hughes and Hosea Taylor, running back Sam Harrell, linebackers Andy Hawkins and Ladell Wills, wide receivers Richard Johnson, Scott McGhee, Gerald McNeil, Ricky Sanders and Clarence Verdin, guard Rich Kehr, center Billy Kidd and offensive tackle Tommy Robison by Houston Gamblers to New Jersey Generals for past considerations, March 7, 1986.
Granted free agency when USFL suspended operations, August 7, 1986; signed as free agent by Los Angeles Raiders, August 12, 1986.
On injured reserve with pinched nerve in neck, September 1 through November 29, 1987; activated, November 30, 1987.
Crossed picket line during players' strike, September 24, 1987.
On injured reserve with knee injury, December 3 through remainder of 1987 season.
On injured reserve with shoulder injury, August 29 through October 23, 1988; activated, October 24, 1988.
On developmental squad for 2 games with Oakland Invaders in 1984.
On developmental squad for 8 games with Houston Gamblers in 1985.
Oakland USFL, 1984; Houston USFL, 1985; Los Angeles Raiders NFL, 1986 through 1988.
Games: 1984 (7), 1985 (8), 1986 (12), 1987 (1), 1988 (8). Total USFL—15. Total NFL—21. Total Pro—36.
Pro statistics: Caught one pass for eight yards, 1985.

JOHN WILLIAM RIENSTRA
Name pronounced REEN-struh.
Guard—Pittsburgh Steelers
Born March 22, 1963, at Grand Rapids, Mich.
Height, 6.05. Weight, 269.
High School—Bryn Athyn, Pa., Academy of the New Church.
Attended Temple University.
Selected by Baltimore in 1986 USFL territorial draft.
Selected by Pittsburgh in 1st round (9th player selected) of 1986 NFL draft.
Signed by Pittsburgh Steelers, August 12, 1986.
On injured reserve with broken foot, October 9 through remainder of 1986 season.
On non-football injury/active with ucler, July 22 through July 31, 1988; passed physical, August 1, 1988.
On injured reserve with broken fibula, September 20 through November 11, 1988; activated, November 12, 1988.
On injured reserve with shoulder injury, November 26 through remainder of 1988 season.
Pittsburgh NFL, 1986 through 1988.
Games: 1986 (4), 1987 (12), 1988 (5). Total—21.
Pro statistics: Recovered one fumble, 1988.

DOUG RIESENBERG
Offensive Tackle—New York Giants
Born July 22, 1965, at Moscow, Ida.
Height, 6.05. Weight, 275.
High School—Moscow, Ida.
Attended University of California at Berkeley.
Selected by New York Giants in 6th round (168th player selected) of 1987 NFL draft.
Signed by New York Giants, July 27, 1987.
New York Giants NFL, 1987 and 1988.
Games: 1987 (8), 1988 (16). Total—24.
Pro statistics: Recovered one fumble, 1988.

GERALD ANTONIO RIGGS
Running Back—Washington Redskins
Born November 6, 1960, at Tullos, La.
Height, 6.01. Weight, 230.
High School—Las Vegas, Nev., Bonanza.
Attended Arizona State University.
Selected by Atlanta in 1st round (9th player selected) of 1982 NFL draft.
On did not report list, August 19 through September 1, 1986.
Granted roster exemption, September 2 through September 5, 1986; activated, September 6, 1986.
Traded with 5th round pick in 1990 draft by Atlanta Falcons to Washington Redskins for 2nd round pick in 1989 draft and 1st round pick in 1990 draft, April 23, 1989.

Year Club	G.	Att.	Yds.	Avg.	TD.	P.C.	Yds.	Avg.	TD.	TD.	Pts.	F.
			—RUSHING—				PASS RECEIVING				—TOTAL—	
1982—Atlanta NFL	9	78	299	3.8	5	23	185	8.0	0	5	30	1
1983—Atlanta NFL	14	100	437	4.4	8	17	149	8.8	0	8	48	7
1984—Atlanta NFL	15	353	1486	4.2	13	42	277	6.6	0	13	78	11
1985—Atlanta NFL	16	*397	1719	4.3	10	33	267	8.1	0	10	60	0
1986—Atlanta NFL	16	343	1327	3.9	9	24	136	5.7	0	9	54	6
1987—Atlanta NFL	12	203	875	4.3	2	25	199	8.0	0	2	12	4
1988—Atlanta NFL	9	113	488	4.3	1	22	171	7.8	0	1	6	3
Pro Totals—7 Years	91	1587	6631	4.2	48	186	1384	7.4	0	48	288	32

Year Club	G.	No.	Yds.	Avg.	TD.
1982—Atlanta NFL	9		None		
1983—Atlanta NFL	14	17	330	19.4	0
1984—Atlanta NFL	15		None		
1985—Atlanta NFL	16		None		
1986—Atlanta NFL	16		None		
1987—Atlanta NFL	12		None		
1988—Atlanta NFL	9		None		
Pro Totals—7 Years............	91	17	330	19.4	0

Additional pro statistics: Recovered one fumble, 1983, 1986 and 1987; recovered two fumbles, 1984; attempted one pass with no completions, 1986.
Played in Pro Bowl (NFL All-Star Game) following 1985 through 1987 seasons.

JIM THOMAS RIGGS
Tight End—Cincinnati Bengals
Born September 29, 1963, at Fort Knox, Ky.
Height, 6.05. Weight, 245.
High School—Laurinburg, N.C., Scotland.
Received bachelor of science degree in economics and marketing
from Clemson University in 1987.

Selected by Cincinnati in 4th round (103rd player selected) of 1987 NFL draft.
Signed by Cincinnati Bengals, July 26, 1987.

Year Club	G.	P.C.	Yds.	Avg.	TD.
1987—Cincinnati NFL............	9		None		
1988—Cincinnati NFL............	16	9	82	9.1	0
Pro Totals—2 Years............	25	9	82	9.1	0

Additional pro statistics: Recovered one fumble and fumbled twice, 1988.
Played in AFC Championship Game following 1988 season.
Played in NFL Championship Game following 1988 season.

DAVE BRIAN RIMINGTON
Center—Philadelphia Eagles
Born May 22, 1960, at Omaha, Neb.
Height, 6.03. Weight, 288.
High School—Omaha, Neb., South.
Received degree from University of Nebraska.

Outland Trophy winner, 1981 and 1982.
Named as center on THE SPORTING NEWS College All-America Team, 1982.
Selected by Boston in 1983 USFL territorial draft.
Selected by Cincinnati in 1st round (25th player selected) of 1983 NFL draft.
Signed by Cincinnati Bengals, June 6, 1983.
Granted free agency, February 1, 1988; rights released, August 22, 1988.
Signed by Philadelphia Eagles, August 25, 1988.
Cincinnati NFL, 1983 through 1987; Philadelphia NFL, 1988.
Games: 1983 (12), 1984 (16), 1985 (16), 1986 (12), 1987 (8), 1988 (16). Total—80.
Pro statistics: Recovered one fumble and fumbled once, 1983; recovered three fumbles, 1985; fumbled twice for minus 23 yards, 1986; fumbled twice for minus 18 yards, 1987; recovered two fumbles, 1988.

CODY LEWIS RISIEN
Name pronounced RISE-un.
Offensive Tackle—Cleveland Browns
Born March 22, 1957, at Bryan, Tex.
Height, 6.07. Weight, 280.
High School—Houston, Tex., Cypress Fairbanks.
Received bachelor of science degree in building construction from Texas A&M University in 1982.

Selected by Cleveland in 7th round (183rd player selected) of 1979 NFL draft.
On injured reserve with knee injury, August 27 through entire 1984 season.
On injured reserve with knee injury, September 27 through October 22, 1985; activated, October 23, 1985.
Granted free agency, February 1, 1987; re-signed by Browns, August 31, 1987.
Granted roster exemption, August 31 through September 4, 1987; activated, September 5, 1987.
Crossed picket line during players' strike, October 14, 1987.
Cleveland NFL, 1979 through 1983 and 1985 through 1988.
Games: 1979 (15), 1980 (16), 1981 (16), 1982 (9), 1983 (16), 1985 (12), 1986 (16), 1987 (13), 1988 (16). Total—129.
Pro statistics: Recovered two fumbles, 1986.
Played in AFC Championship Game following 1986 and 1987 seasons.
Played in Pro Bowl (NFL All-Star Game) following 1986 and 1987 seasons.

JAMES ALEXANDER RITCHER
(Jim)
Guard—Buffalo Bills
Born May 21, 1958, at Berea, O.
Height, 6.03. Weight, 265.
High School—Granger, O., Highland.
Attended North Carolina State University.

Named as center on THE SPORTING NEWS College All-America Team, 1979.
Outland Trophy winner, 1979.
Selected by Buffalo in 1st round of (16th player selected) 1980 NFL draft.
Buffalo NFL, 1980 through 1988.
Games: 1980, (14), 1981 (14), 1982 (9), 1983 (16), 1984 (14), 1985 (16), 1986 (16), 1987 (12), 1988 (16). Total—127.
Pro statistics: Recovered one fumble, 1986.
Played in AFC Championship Game following 1988 season.

RONALD EUGENE RIVERA
(Ron)
Linebacker—Chicago Bears
Born January 7, 1962, at Fort Ord, Calif.
Height, 6.03. Weight, 240.
High School—Seaside, Calif.
Attended University of California at Berkeley.

Named as linebacker on THE SPORTING NEWS College All-America Team, 1983.
Selected by Oakland in 1984 USFL territorial draft.
Selected by Chicago in 2nd round (44th player selected) of 1984 NFL draft.
Signed by Chicago Bears, July 2, 1984.
Chicago NFL, 1984 through 1988.
Games: 1984 (15), 1985 (16), 1986 (16), 1987 (12), 1988 (16). Total—75.
Pro statistics: Intercepted one pass for four yards and recovered one fumble for five yards and a touchdown, 1985; intercepted two passes for 19 yards, 1987; intercepted two passes for no yards and fumbled once, 1988.
Played in NFC Championship Game following 1984, 1985 and 1988 seasons.
Played in NFL Championship Game following 1985 season.

JAMES ELBERT ROBBINS
(Tootie)
Offensive Tackle—Phoenix Cardinals
Born June 2, 1958, at Windsor, N.C.
Height, 6.05. Weight, 302.
High School—Bertie County, N.C.
Attended East Carolina University.

Selected by St. Louis in 4th round (90th player selected) of 1982 NFL draft.
Granted free agency, February 1, 1986; re-signed by Cardinals, September 4, 1986.
Granted roster exemption, September 4 through September 11, 1986; activated, September 12, 1986.
Crossed picket line during players' strike, October 7, 1987.
Franchise transferred to Phoenix, March 15, 1988.
On injured reserve with groin and shoulder injuries, December 16 through remainder of 1988 season.
St. Louis NFL, 1982 through 1987; Phoenix NFL, 1988.
Games: 1982 (9), 1983 (13), 1984 (16), 1985 (12), 1986 (12), 1987 (14), 1988 (15). Total—91.
Pro statistics: Recovered one fumble, 1983 and 1985.

RANDY ROBBINS
Safety—Denver Broncos
Born September 14, 1962, at Casa Grande, Ariz.
Height, 6.02. Weight, 189.
High School—Casa Grande, Ariz., Union.
Attended University of Arizona.

Selected by Arizona in 1984 USFL territorial draft.
Selected by Denver in 4th round (89th player selected) of 1984 NFL draft.
Signed by Denver Broncos, July 6, 1984.
On injured reserve with fractured forearm, August 20 through October 15, 1985; activated, October 16, 1985.
On injured reserve with knee injury, December 18, 1987 through January 15, 1988; activated, January 16, 1988.

| | | —INTERCEPTIONS— | | | |
Year Club	G.	No.	Yds.	Avg.	TD.
1984—Denver NFL	16	2	62	31.0	1
1985—Denver NFL	10	1	3	3.0	0
1986—Denver NFL	16		None		
1987—Denver NFL	10	3	9	3.0	0
1988—Denver NFL	16	2	66	33.0	0
Pro Totals—5 Years............	68	8	140	17.5	1

Additional pro statistics: Recovered one fumble, 1984; recovered two fumbles, 1986 and 1988; fumbled once, 1988.
Played in AFC Championship Game following 1986 season.
Played in NFL Championship Game following 1986 and 1987 seasons.

ALFREDO ROBERTS
Tight End—Kansas City Chiefs
Born March 17, 1965, at Fort Lauderdale, Fla.
Height, 6.03. Weight, 250.
High School—Plantation, Fla., South Plantation.
Received degree in criminal justice from University of Miami (Fla.) in 1988.

Selected by Kansas City in 8th round (197th player selected) of 1988 NFL draft.
Signed by Kansas City Chiefs, July 16, 1988.

		—PASS RECEIVING—				
Year	Club	G.	P.C.	Yds.	Avg.	TD.
1988—Kansas City NFL..........		16	10	104	10.4	0

LARRY ROBERTS
Defensive End—San Francisco 49ers
Born June 2, 1963, at Dothan, Ala.
Height, 6.03. Weight, 275.
High School—Dothan, Ala., Northview.
Attended University of Alabama.

Selected by Birmingham in 1986 USFL territorial draft.
Selected by San Francisco in 2nd round (39th player selected) of 1986 NFL draft.
Signed by San Francisco 49ers, August 5, 1986.
San Franciso NFL, 1986 through 1988.
Games: 1986 (16), 1987 (11), 1988 (16). Total—43.
Pro statistics: Recovered one fumble, 1986.
Played in NFC Championship Game following 1988 season.
Played in NFL Championship Game following 1988 season.

WILLIAM HAROLD ROBERTS
Offensive Tackle—New York Giants
Born August 5, 1962, at Miami, Fla.
Height, 6.05. Weight, 280.
High School—Miami, Fla., Carol City.
Attended Ohio State University.
Cousin of Reggie Sandilands, wide receiver with Memphis Showboats, 1984.

Selected by New Jersey in 1984 USFL territorial draft.
Selected by New York Giants in 1st round (27th player selected) of 1984 NFL draft.
Signed by New York Giants, June 4, 1984.
On injured reserve with knee injury, July 20 through entire 1985 season.
New York Giants NFL, 1984 and 1986 through 1988.
Games: 1984 (11), 1986 (16), 1987 (12), 1988 (16). Total—55.
Pro statistics: Recovered one fumble, 1984; recovered two fumbles, 1988.
Played in NFC Championship Game following 1986 season.
Played in NFL Championship Game following 1986 season.

EUGENE ROBINSON
Safety—Seattle Seahawks
Born May 28, 1963, at Hartford, Conn.
Height, 6.00. Weight, 186.
High School—Hartford, Conn., Weaver.
Attended Colgate University.

Selected by New Jersey in 1985 USFL territorial draft.
Signed as free agent by Seattle Seahawks, May 15, 1985.

		—INTERCEPTIONS—			
Year	Club	G.	No.	Yds.	Avg.TD.
1985—Seattle NFL....................	16	2	47	23.5	0
1986—Seattle NFL....................	16	3	39	13.0	0
1987—Seattle NFL....................	12	3	75	25.0	0
1988—Seattle NFL....................	16	1	0	0.0	0
Pro Totals—4 Years............	60	9	161	17.9	0

Additional pro statistics: Returned one kickoff for 10 yards, 1985; recovered three fumbles for six yards, 1986; returned blocked punt eight yards for a touchdown and recovered one fumble, 1987.

JERRY DEWAYNE ROBINSON
Linebacker—Los Angeles Raiders
Born December 18, 1956, at San Francisco, Calif.
Height, 6.02. Weight, 230.
High School—Santa Rosa, Calif., Cardinal Newman.
Attended University of California at Los Angeles.

Named as linebacker on THE SPORTING NEWS College All-America Team, 1978.
Selected by Philadelphia in 1st round (21st player selected) of 1979 NFL draft.
On did not report list, August 20 through September 25, 1985.
Reported and granted roster exemption, September 26 through October 7, 1985; activated, October 8, 1985.
Traded by Philadelphia Eagles to Los Angeles Raiders for 2nd round pick in 1986 draft, September 30, 1985.
Crossed picket line during players' strike, October 14, 1987.

		—INTERCEPTIONS—						—INTERCEPTIONS—			
Year	Club	G.	No.	Yds.	Avg.TD.	Year	Club	G.	No.	Yds.	Avg.TD.
1979—Philadelphia NFL	16		None			1985—L.A. Raiders NFL.........	11		None		
1980—Philadelphia NFL	16	2	13	6.5	0	1986—L.A. Raiders NFL.........	16	4	42	10.5	1
1981—Philadelphia NFL	15	1	3	3.0	0	1987—L.A. Raiders NFL.........	12		None		
1982—Philadelphia NFL	9	3	19	6.3	0	1988—L.A. Raiders NFL.........	15		None		
1983—Philadelphia NFL	16		None			Pro Totals—10 Years..........	141	10	77	7.7	1
1984—Philadelphia NFL	15		None								

Pro statistics: Recovered two fumbles, 1979, 1981, 1983 and 1986; recovered four fumbles for 59 yards and one touchdown and fumbled once, 1980; recovered one fumble, 1984 and 1988; returned blocked punt two yards for a touchdown, 1986.

Played in NFC Championship Game following 1980 season.

Played in NFL Championship Game following 1980 season.

Played in Pro Bowl (NFL All-Star Game) following 1981 season.

MARK LEON ROBINSON
Defensive Back—Tampa Bay Buccaneers
Born September 13, 1962, at Washington, D.C.
Height, 5.11. Weight, 200.
High School—Silver Spring, Md., John F. Kennedy.
Received degree in business administration from Penn State University in 1988.
Brother of Eric Robinson, running back with Washington Federal, 1983 and 1984.

Selected by Philadelphia in 1984 USFL territorial draft.

Selected by Kansas City in 4th round (90th player selected) of 1984 NFL draft.

Signed by Kansas City Chiefs, July 12, 1984.

On injured reserve with sprained ankle, September 3 through October 11, 1985; activated, October 12, 1985.

On injured reserve with thigh injury, October 24 through December 4, 1986; activated, December 5, 1986.

Traded with 4th and 8th round picks in 1988 draft by Kansas City Chiefs to Tampa Bay Buccaneers for quarterback Steve DeBerg, March 30, 1988.

On injured reserve with groin injury, October 28 through November 24, 1988; activated, November 25, 1988.

Year Club	G.	No.	Yds.	Avg.	TD.
1984—Kansas City NFL	16		None		
1985—Kansas City NFL	11	1	20	20.0	0
1986—Kansas City NFL	9		None		
1987—Kansas City NFL	12	2	42	21.0	0
1988—Tampa Bay NFL	9	2	28	14.0	0
Pro Totals—5 Years	57	5	90	18.0	0

Additional pro statistics: Recovered one fumble, 1985; returned five kickoffs for 97 yards and recovered two fumbles, 1987.

SHELTON ROBINSON
Linebacker—Detroit Lions
Born September 14, 1960, at Goldsboro, N.C.
Height, 6.02. Weight, 233.
High School—Pikeville, N.C., Aycock.
Received bachelor of science degree in industrial relations from
University of North Carolina in 1982.

Signed as free agent by Seattle Seahawks, April 30, 1982.

Traded by Seattle Seahawks to Detroit Lions for 5th round pick in 1987 draft, September 1, 1986.

On injured reserve with knee injury, December 3 through remainder of 1988 season.

Seattle NFL, 1982 through 1985; Detroit NFL, 1986 through 1988.

Games: 1982 (9), 1983 (16), 1984 (16), 1985 (15), 1986 (16), 1987 (12), 1988 (12). Total—96.

Pro statistics: Intercepted one pass for 18 yards and recovered four fumbles for 21 yards and two touchdowns, 1983; recovered four fumbles for three yards, 1984; recovered one fumble for six yards, 1985; recovered two fumbles, 1987.

Played in AFC Championship Game following 1983 season.

STACY ROBINSON
Wide Receiver—New York Giants
Born February 19, 1962, at St. Paul, Minn.
Height, 5.11. Weight, 186.
High School—St. Paul, Minn., Central.
Attended Prairie View A&M University and North Dakota State University.

Selected by Portland in 3rd round (34th player selected) of 1985 USFL draft.

Selected by New York Giants in 2nd round (46th player selected) of 1985 NFL draft.

Signed by New York Giants, July 17, 1985.

On injured reserve with broken hand, September 4 through November 29, 1985; activated, November 30, 1985.

On injured reserve with ankle injury, October 18 through November 14, 1986; activated, November 15, 1986.

On injured reserve with hairline fracture in leg, December 1 through remainder of 1987 season.

Released by New York Giants, August 30, 1988; re-signed by Giants, September 26, 1988.

Year Club	G.	P.C.	Yds.	Avg.	TD.
1985—N.Y. Giants NFL	4		None		
1986—N.Y. Giants NFL	12	29	494	17.0	2
1987—N.Y. Giants NFL	5	6	58	9.7	2
1988—N.Y. Giants NFL	11	7	143	20.4	3
Pro Totals—4 Years	32	42	695	16.5	7

Additional pro statistics: Fumbled once, 1986.

Played in NFC Championship Game following 1986 season.

Played in NFL Championship Game following 1986 season.

TOMMY L. ROBISON
Guard—Atlanta Falcons

Born November 17, 1961, at Merkle, Tex.
Height, 6.04. Weight, 290.
High School—Gregory, Tex., Gregory-Portland.
Received bachelor of science degree in business management from Texas A&M University.

Selected by Houston in 1984 USFL territorial draft.
Signed by Houston Gamblers, January 22, 1984.
On developmental squad, June 10 through June 17, 1984; activated, June 18, 1984.
Selected by Cleveland in 2nd round (50th player selected) of 1984 NFL supplemental draft.
Traded with defensive backs Luther Bradley, Will Lewis, Mike Mitchell and Durwood Roquemore, defensive end Pete Catan, quarterbacks Jim Kelly and Todd Dillon, defensive tackles Tony Fitzpatrick, Van Hughes and Hosea Taylor, running back Sam Harrell, linebackers Andy Hawkins and Ladell Wills, wide receivers Richard Johnson, Scott McGhee, Gerald McNeil, Ricky Sanders and Clarence Verdin, guard Rich Kehr, center Billy Kidd and offensive tackle Chris Riehm by Houston Gamblers to New Jersey Generals for past considerations, March 7, 1986.
NFL rights traded with 7th round pick in 1987 draft by Cleveland Browns to Green Bay Packers for wide receiver John Jefferson, September 19, 1985.
Granted free agency when USFL suspended operations, August 7, 1986; signed by Green Bay Packers, April 13, 1987.
On injured reserve with groin injury, August 22 through entire 1988 season.
Granted unconditional free agency, February 1, 1989; signed by Atlanta Falcons, March 31, 1989.
On developmental squad for 1 game with Houston Gamblers in 1984.
Houston USFL, 1984 and 1985; Green Bay NFL, 1987.
Games: 1984 (17), 1985 (18), 1987 (3). Total USFL—35. Total Pro—38.

REGINALD HENRY ROBY
(Reggie)
Punter—Miami Dolphins

Born July 30, 1961, at Waterloo, Ia.
Height, 6.02. Weight, 243.
High School—Waterloo, Ia., East.
Attended University of Iowa.
Brother of Mike Roby, first baseman-outfielder in San Francisco Giants' organization, 1967 and 1968.

Named to THE SPORTING NEWS NFL All-Star Team, 1984.
Led NFL in net punting average with 38.1 in 1984 and 37.4 in 1986.
Selected by Chicago in 16th round (187th player selected) of 1983 USFL draft.
Selected by Miami in 6th round (167th player selected) of 1983 NFL draft.
Signed by Miami Dolphins, July 9, 1983.
On injured reserve with knee, ankle and groin injuries, September 16 through October 30, 1987; activated, October 31, 1987.
Crossed picket line during players' strike, October 14, 1987.

| | | ——PUNTING—— | | |
Year Club	G.	No.	Avg.	Blk.
1983—Miami NFL	16	74	43.1	1
1984—Miami NFL	16	51	44.7	0
1985—Miami NFL	16	59	43.7	0
1986—Miami NFL	15	56	44.2	0
1987—Miami NFL	10	32	42.8	0
1988—Miami NFL	15	64	43.0	0
Pro Totals—6 Years	88	336	43.7	1

Additional pro statistics: Rushed twice for minus eight yards, recovered two fumbles and fumbled twice for minus 11 yards, 1986; rushed once for no yards and recovered one fumble, 1987.
Played in AFC Championship Game following 1984 and 1985 seasons.
Played in NFL Championship Game following 1984 season.
Played in Pro Bowl (NFL All-Star Game) following 1984 season.

MARK RODENHAUSER
Center—Minnesota Vikings

Born June 1, 1961, at Addision, Ill.
Height, 6.05. Weight, 252.
High School—Addison, Ill., Addison Trail.
Attended Illinois State University.

Signed as free agent by Michigan Panthers, January 15, 1984.
Released by Michigan Panthers, February 13, 1984; signed as free agent by Memphis Showboats, December 3, 1984.
Released by Memphis Showboats, January 22, 1985; signed as free agent by Chicago Bruisers of Arena Football League, June 29, 1987.
Granted free agency, August 15, 1987; signed as replacement player by Chicago Bears, September 24, 1987.
Left Chicago Bears camp voluntarily, August 16, 1988.
Released by Chicago Bears, August 17, 1988; signed as free agent by Minnesota Vikings, March 16, 1989.
Chicago Bruisers Arena Football, 1987; Chicago NFL, 1987.
Games: 1987 Chicago Arena Football (4), 1987 NFL (9). Total Pro—9.

RUBEN ANGEL RODRIGUEZ
Punter—Seattle Seahawks
Born March 3, 1965, at Visalia, Calif.
Height, 6.02. Weight, 214.
High School—Woodlake, Calif.
Attended College of the Sequoias and University of Arizona.

Selected by Seattle in 5th round (131st player selected) of 1987 NFL draft.
Signed by Seattle Seahawks, July 21, 1987.
Released by Seattle Seahawks, September 7, 1987; re-signed by Seahawks, September 8, 1987.

		—PUNTING—		
Year Club	G.	No.	Avg.	Blk.
1987—Seattle NFL	12	47	40.0	0
1988—Seattle NFL	16	70	40.8	0
Pro Totals—2 Years	28	117	40.5	0

Additional pro statistics: Rushed once for no yards, 1987 and 1988; recovered one fumble and fumbled once, 1988.

REGINALD O'KEITH ROGERS
(Reggie)
Defensive End—Detroit Lions
Born January 21, 1964, at Sacramento, Calif.
Height, 6.06. Weight, 280.
High School—Sacramento, Calif., Norte Del Rio.
Attended University of Washington.
Brother of Don Rogers, safety with Cleveland Browns, 1984 and 1985.

Selected by Detroit in 1st round (7th player selected) of 1987 NFL draft.
Signed by Detroit Lions, July 24, 1987.
On non-football injury list, November 6 through December 6, 1987; activated, December 7, 1987.
On injured reserve with ankle injury, October 8 through remainder of 1988 season.
Detroit NFL, 1987 and 1988.
Games: 1987 (6), 1988 (5). Total—11.

JEFFREY CHARLES ROHRER
(Jeff)
Linebacker—Dallas Cowboys
Born December 25, 1958, at Inglewood, Calif.
Height, 6.02. Weight, 222.
High School—Manhattan Beach, Calif., Mira Costa.
Received bachelor of science degree in administrative sciences from
Yale University in 1982.

Selected by Dallas in 2nd round (53rd player selected) of 1982 NFL draft.
On injured reserve with back injury, August 16 through entire 1988 season.
Dallas NFL, 1982 through 1987.
Games: 1982 (8), 1983 (16), 1984 (16), 1985 (15), 1986 (16), 1987 (12). Total—83.
Pro statistics: Recovered one fumble for five yards and fumbled once, 1984; recovered one fumble, 1986; recovered two fumbles, 1987.
Played in NFC Championship Game following 1982 season.

DONALD DEMETRIUS ROLLE
(Butch)
Tight End—Buffalo Bills
Born August 19, 1964, at Miami, Fla.
Height, 6.03. Weight, 242.
High School—Hallandale, Fla.
Attended Michigan State University.

Selected by Buffalo in 7th round (180th player selected) of 1986 NFL draft.
Signed by Buffalo Bills, July 23, 1986.

		—PASS RECEIVING—			
Year Club	G.	P.C.	Yds.	Avg.	TD.
1986—Buffalo NFL	16	4	56	14.0	0
1987—Buffalo NFL	12	2	6	3.0	2
1988—Buffalo NFL	16	2	3	1.5	2
Pro Totals—3 Years	44	8	65	8.1	4

Additional pro statistics: Returned one kickoff for six yards, 1987; returned one kickoff for 12 yards, 1988.
Played in AFC Championship Game following 1988 season.

HENRY LEE ROLLING
Linebacker—Tampa Bay Buccaneers
Born September 8, 1965, at Fort Eustis, Va.
Height, 6.02. Weight, 225.
High School—Henderson, Nev., Basic.
Received degree in electrical engineering from University of Nevada at Reno in 1987.

Selected by Tampa Bay in 5th round (135th player selected) of 1987 NFL draft.
Signed by Tampa Bay Buccaneers, July 18, 1987.

On injured reserve with hamstring injury, August 10 through entire 1987 season.
Tampa Bay NFL, 1988.
Games: 1988 (15).
Pro statistics: Recovered two fumbles, 1988.

WILLIAM THOMAS ROMANOWSKI
(Bill)
Linebacker—San Francisco 49ers
Born April 2, 1966, at Vernon, Conn.
Height, 6.04. Weight, 231.
High School—Vernon, Conn., Rockville.
Received degree from Boston College in 1988.

Selected by San Francisco in 3rd round (80th player selected) of 1988 NFL draft.
Signed by San Francisco 49ers, July 15, 1988.
San Francisco NFL, 1988.
Games: 1988 (16).
Pro statistics: Recovered one fumble, 1988.
Played in NFC Championship Game following 1988 season.
Played in NFL Championship Game following 1988 season.

RICH ROMER
Linebacker—Cincinnati Bengals
Born February 27, 1966, at East Greenbush, N. Y.
Height, 6.03. Weight, 224.
High School—East Greenbush, N. Y., Columbia.
Attended Union (N.Y.) College.

Selected by Cincinnati in 7th round (168th player selected) of 1988 NFL draft.
Signed by Cincinnati Bengals, July 10, 1988.
On injured reserve with dislocated finger, August 29 through October 12, 1988; activated after clearing procedural waivers, October 14, 1988.
On injured reserve with hamstring injury, November 26 through remainder of 1988 season.
Cincinnati NFL, 1988.
Games: 1988 (4).

DANIEL PETER ROSADO
(Dan)
Center-Guard—San Diego Chargers
Born July 6, 1959, at Lawton, Okla.
Height, 6.03. Weight, 280.
High School—Canton, Ga., Cherokee.
Attended Northern Illinois University.

Signed as free agent by Houston Gamblers, October 21, 1984.
On developmental squad, April 12 through May 3, 1985; activated, May 4, 1985.
On developmental squad, May 12 through May 17, 1985; activated, May 18, 1985.
Released by Houston Gamblers, July 31, 1985; awarded on waivers to Arizona Outlaws, August 1, 1985.
Granted free agency when USFL suspended operations, August 7, 1986; signed as free agent by Miami Dolphins, August 12, 1986.
Released by Miami Dolphins, September 1, 1986; re-signed by Dolphins for 1987, November 7, 1986.
Released by Miami Dolphins, September 7, 1987; signed as free agent replacement player by San Diego Chargers, September 24, 1987.
On injured reserve with pinched nerve in neck, November 3 through remainder of 1987 season.
On developmental squad for 4 games with Houston Gamblers in 1985.
Houston USFL, 1985; San Diego NFL, 1987 and 1988.
Games: 1985 (14), 1987 (4), 1988 (12). Total NFL—16. Total Pro—30.
USFL statistics: Caught one pass for no yards and recovered one fumble, 1985.
NFL statistics: Recovered one fumble and fumbled once for minus 18 yards, 1988.

KENNY FRANK ROSE
(Ken)
Linebacker—New York Jets
Born June 9, 1962, at Sacramento, Calif.
Height, 6.01. Weight, 204.
High School—Sacramento, Calif., Christian Brothers.
Attended University of Nevada at Las Vegas.

Signed as free agent by Saskatchewan Roughriders, May 5, 1985.
Released by Saskatchewan Roughriders, June 16, 1985; re-signed by Roughriders, June 23, 1985.
Released by Saskatchewan Roughriders, July 3, 1985; signed as free agent by Los Angeles Raiders, July 10, 1985.
Released by Los Angeles Raiders, August 13, 1985; re-signed by Raiders, August 16, 1985.
Released by Los Angeles Raiders, August 20, 1985.
USFL rights traded by Oakland Invaders to Tampa Bay Bandits for past considerations, September 6, 1985.
Signed by Tampa Bay Bandits, May 21, 1986.
Granted free agency when USFL suspended operations, August 7, 1986; signed as free agent by New York Jets, April 8, 1987.
Released by New York Jets, September 6, 1987; re-signed as replacement player by Jets, September 24, 1987.
On injured reserve with dislocated elbow, August 30 through September 30, 1988; activated, October 1, 1988.
New York Jets NFL, 1987 and 1988.

Games: 1987 (10), 1988 (12). Total—22.

Pro statistics: Intercepted one pass for one yard, 1987; returned one kickoff for no yards and recovered one fumble, 1988.

KEVIN LESLEY ROSS
Cornerback—Kansas City Chiefs

Born January 16, 1962, at Camden, N.J.
Height, 5.09. Weight, 180.
High School—Paulsboro, N.J.
Attended Temple University.

Selected by Philadelphia in 1984 USFL territorial draft.
Selected by Kansas City in 7th round (173rd player selected) of 1984 NFL draft.
Signed by Kansas City Chiefs, June 21, 1984.
Crossed picket line during players' strike, October 14, 1987.

		—INTERCEPTIONS—			
Year Club	G.	No.	Yds.	Avg.	TD.
1984—Kansas City NFL..........	16	6	124	20.7	1
1985—Kansas City NFL..........	16	3	47	15.7	0
1986—Kansas City NFL..........	16	4	66	16.5	0
1987—Kansas City NFL..........	12	3	40	13.3	0
1988—Kansas City NFL..........	15	1	0	0.0	0
Pro Totals—5 Years............	75	17	277	16.3	1

Additional pro statistics: Recovered one fumble, 1984 and 1985; recovered three fumbles for 33 yards and a touchdown, 1986; returned blocked field goal attempt 65 yards for a touchdown, 1987.

RAYMOND ANTHONY ROUNDTREE
(Ray)
Wide Receiver—Detroit Lions

Born April 19, 1966, at Aiken, S. C.
Height, 6.00. Weight, 182.
High School—Aiken, S. C., South.
Received bachelor of science degree in finance from Penn State University in 1988.

Selected by Detroit in 3rd round (58th player selected) of 1988 NFL draft.
Signed by Detroit Lions, July 17, 1988.
On injured reserve with back injury, October 20 through remainder of 1988 season.
Detroit NFL, 1988.
Games: 1988 (4).

LEE ROUSON
Running Back—New York Giants

Born October 18, 1962, at Elizabeth City, N.C.
Height, 6.01. Weight, 222.
High School—Greensboro, N.C., Page.
Attended Colorado University.
Cousin of Johnny Walton, quarterback with San Antonio Wings (WFL), Philadelphia Eagles and Boston-New Orleans Breakers, 1975, 1976, 1978, 1979, 1983 and 1984; and head coach at Elizabeth City State University, 1980 through 1982.

Selected by New Jersey in 1st round (11th player selected) of 1985 USFL draft.
Selected by New York Giants in 8th round (213th player selected) of 1985 NFL draft.
Signed by New York Giants, July 2, 1985.
On injured reserve with hamstring injury, September 2 through December 13, 1985; activated, December 14, 1985.

		—RUSHING—				PASS RECEIVING				—TOTAL—		
Year Club	G.	Att.	Yds.	Avg.	TD.	P.C.	Yds.	Avg.	TD.	TD.	Pts.	F.
1985—New York Giants NFL	2	1	1	1.0	0		None			0	0	0
1986—New York Giants NFL	14	54	179	3.3	2	8	121	15.1	1	3	18	0
1987—New York Giants NFL	12	41	155	3.8	0	11	129	11.7	1	1	6	3
1988—New York Giants NFL	16	1	1	1.0	0	4	61	15.3	0	0	0	2
Pro Totals—4 Years....................	44	97	336	3.5	2	23	311	13.5	2	4	24	5

		KICKOFF RETURNS			
Year Club	G.	No.	Yds.	Avg.	TD.
1985—N. Y. Giants NFL	2	2	35	17.5	0
1986—N. Y. Giants NFL	14	2	21	10.5	0
1987—N. Y. Giants NFL	12	22	497	22.6	0
1988—N. Y. Giants NFL	16	8	130	16.3	0
Pro Totals—4 Years............	44	34	683	20.1	0

Additional pro statistics: Recovered one fumble, 1987; recovered two fumbles, 1988.
Played in NFC Championship Game following 1986 season.
Played in NFL Championship Game following 1986 season.

MIKE ROZIER
Running Back—Houston Oilers

Born March 1, 1961, at Camden, N.J.
Height, 5.10. Weight, 211.
High School—Camden, N.J., Wilson.
Attended Coffeyville Community College and University of Nebraska.

Named THE SPORTING NEWS College Football Player of the Year, 1983.
Heisman Trophy winner, 1983.
Named as running back on THE SPORTING NEWS College All-America Team, 1983.
Selected by Pittsburgh in 1st round (1st player selected) of 1984 USFL draft.
Signed by Pittsburgh Maulers, January 3, 1984.
On developmental squad, May 18 through June 15, 1984; activated, June 16, 1984.
Selected by Houston in 1st round (2nd player selected) of 1984 NFL supplemental draft.
Franchise disbanded, October 25, 1984.
Personal services contract assigned to Baltimore Stars, November 1, 1984.
Signed as free agent with Jacksonville Bulls, February 1, 1985.
Granted roster exemption, February 1 through February 13, 1985; activated, February 14, 1985.
Granted free agency, July 1, 1985; signed by Houston Oilers, July 1, 1985.
On injured reserve with knee injury, December 2 through remainder of 1986 season.
On developmental squad for 4 games with Pittsburgh Maulers in 1984.

Year Club	G.	RUSHING				PASS RECEIVING				TOTAL		
		Att.	Yds.	Avg.	TD.	P.C.	Yds.	Avg.	TD.	TD.	Pts.	F.
1984—Pittsburgh USFL	14	223	792	3.6	3	32	259	8.1	0	3	18	8
1985—Jacksonville USFL	18	320	1361	4.3	12	50	366	7.3	3	15	90	10
1985—Houston NFL	14	133	462	3.5	8	9	96	10.7	0	8	48	3
1986—Houston NFL	13	199	662	3.3	4	24	180	7.5	0	4	24	6
1987—Houston NFL	11	229	957	4.2	3	27	192	7.1	0	3	18	5
1988—Houston NFL	15	251	1002	4.0	10	11	99	9.0	1	11	66	7
USFL Totals—2 Years	32	543	2153	4.0	15	82	625	7.6	3	18	108	18
NFL Totals—4 Years	53	812	3083	3.8	25	71	567	8.0	1	26	156	21
Pro Totals—6 Years	85	1355	5236	3.9	40	153	1192	7.8	4	44	264	39

Additional USFL statistics: Recovered eight fumbles, 1984; recovered four fumbles, 1985.
Additional NFL statistics: Recovered three fumbles, 1985 and 1988; attempted one pass with one completion for 13 yards, 1986; recovered two fumbles, 1986 and 1987.
Played in Pro Bowl (NFL All-Star Game) following 1987 and 1988 seasons.

ROBIN JAMES RUBICK
(Rob)
Tight End—Detroit Lions
Born September 27, 1960, at Newberry, Mich.
Height, 6.03. Weight, 234.
High School—Newberry, Mich.
Received degree in physical educaton from Grand Valley State College.
Nephew of Tom Villemure, head basketball coach at Grand Valley State College.

Selected by Detroit in 12th round (326th player selected) of 1982 NFL draft.
On physically unable to perform/active with back injury, July 27 through October 16, 1985; activated, October 17, 1985.
Released by Detroit Lions, September 16, 1988; re-signed by Lions, September 20, 1988.

Year Club	G.	PASS RECEIVING			
		P.C.	Yds.	Avg.	TD.
1982—Detroit NFL	7	None			
1983—Detroit NFL	16	10	81	8.1	1
1984—Detroit NFL	16	14	188	13.4	1
1985—Detroit NFL	9	2	33	16.5	0
1986—Detroit NFL	16	5	62	12.4	0
1987—Detroit NFL	9	13	147	11.3	1
1988—Detroit NFL	15	None			
Pro Totals—7 Years	88	44	511	11.6	3

Additional pro statistics: Rushed once for one yard and a touchdown, 1982.

MIKE ALAN RUETHER
Center—Denver Broncos
Born September 20, 1962, at Inglewood, Calif.
Height, 6.04. Weight, 275.
High School—Shawnee Mission, Kan., Bishop Miege.
Attended University of Texas.

Selected by Houston in 1984 USFL territorial draft.
USFL rights traded with rights to offensive tackle Mark Adickes by Houston Gamblers to Los Angeles Express for 2nd round pick in 1985 and 1986 drafts, February 13, 1984.
Signed by Los Angeles Express, February 13, 1984.
Granted roster exemption, February 13 through February 23, 1984; activated, February 24, 1984.
Selected by St. Louis in 1st round (17th player selected) of 1984 NFL supplemental draft.
On developmental squad, February 21 through March 7, 1985; activated, March 8, 1985.
Granted free agency when USFL suspended operations, August 7, 1986; signed by St. Louis Cardinals, September 30, 1986.
Franchise transferred to Phoenix, March 15, 1988.
Traded by Phoenix Cardinals to Denver Broncos for linebacker Ricky Hunley, July 19, 1988.
On developmental squad for 2 games with Los Angeles Express in 1985.
Los Angeles USFL, 1984 and 1985; St. Louis NFL, 1986 and 1987; Denver NFL, 1988.
Games: 1984 (17), 1985 (17), 1986 (10), 1987 (12), 1988 (14). Total USFL—34. Total NFL—36. Total Pro—70.
Pro statistics: Recovered two fumbles, 1984.

KENNETH F. RUETTGERS

Name pronounced RUTT-gers.

(Ken)

Offensive Tackle—Green Bay Packers

Born August 20, 1962, at Bakersfield, Calif.
Height, 6.05. Weight, 280.
High School—Bakersfield, Calif., Garces Memorial.
Received bachelor of business administration degree from University of Southern California in 1985.

Selected by Green Bay in 1st round (7th player selected) of 1985 NFL draft.
Signed by Green Bay Packers, August 12, 1985.
Green Bay NFL, 1985 through 1988.
Games: 1985 (15), 1986 (16), 1987 (12), 1988 (15). Total—58.
Pro statistics: Recovered one fumble, 1986 and 1988.

MAX CULP RUNAGER

Punter—Kansas City Chiefs

Born March 24, 1956, at Greenwood, S.C.
Height, 6.01. Weight, 189.
High School—Orangeburg, S.C., Wilkinson.
Received bachelor of science degree in health and physical education from University of South Carolina.

Selected by Philadelphia in 8th round (211th player selected) of 1979 NFL draft.
Released by Philadelphia Eagles, September 28, 1983; re-signed by Eagles, October 26, 1983.
Released by Philadelphia Eagles, August 27, 1984; signed as free agent by San Francisco 49ers, September 12, 1984.
Released by San Francisco 49ers, September 7, 1988; signed as free agent by Cleveland Browns, September 22, 1988.
Granted unconditional free agency, February 1, 1989; signed by Kansas City Chiefs, March 27, 1989.

Year Club	G.	No.	Avg.	Blk.
1979—Philadelphia NFL	16	74	39.6	1
1980—Philadelphia NFL	16	75	39.3	1
1981—Philadelphia NFL	15	63	40.7	0
1982—Philadelphia NFL	9	44	40.5	0
1983—Philadelphia NFL	12	59	41.7	0
1984—San Francisco NFL	14	56	41.8	1
1985—San Francisco NFL	16	86	39.8	1
1986—San Francisco NFL	16	83	41.6	2
1987—San Francisco NFL	12	55	39.2	1
1988—S.F. (1)-Cleve. (13) NFL	14	49	40.0	2
Pro Totals—10 Years	140	644	40.5	9

Additional pro statistics: Recovered one fumble, 1979 and 1988; fumbled once, 1979; rushed once for six yards, 1983; rushed once for minus five yards, 1984; rushed once for no yards and fumbled once for minus 16 yards, 1988.
Played in NFC Championship Game following 1980 and 1984 seasons.
Played in NFL Championship Game following 1980 and 1984 seasons.

MICHAEL JOSEPH RUTH

(Mike)

Nose Tackle—Houston Oilers

Born June 25, 1964, at Norristown, Pa.
Height, 6.02. Weight, 275.
High School—Fairview Village, Pa., Methacton.
Attended Boston College.

Outland Trophy winner, 1985.
Selected by New England in 2nd round (42nd player selected) of 1986 NFL draft.
Signed by New England Patriots, August 4, 1986.
On injured reserve with hip injury, October 24, 1986 through January 1, 1987; activated, January 2, 1987.
On injured reserve with knee injury, September 1 through November 20, 1987; activated, November 21, 1987.
Released by New England Patriots, August 30, 1988; signed as free agent by Houston Oilers, March 27, 1989.
New England NFL, 1986 and 1987.
Games: 1986 (6), 1987 (2). Total—8.
Pro statistics: Recovered one fumble, 1986.

REGINALD BERNARD RUTLAND

(Reggie)

Safety—Minnesota Vikings

Born June 20, 1964, at East Point, Ga.
Height, 6.01. Weight, 195.
High School—East Point, Ga., Russell.
Attended Georgia Tech.

Selected by Minnesota in 4th round (100th player selected) of 1987 NFL draft.
Signed by Minnesota Vikings, July 17, 1987.
On injured reserve with ankle injury, November 18 through December 24, 1987; activated, December 25, 1987.
Minnesota NFL, 1987 and 1988.
Games: 1987 (7), 1988 (16). Total—23.
Pro statistics: Intercepted three passes for 63 yards, recovered two fumbles for 17 yards and fumbled once, 1988.
Played in NFC Championship Game following 1987 season.

JEFFREY RONALD RUTLEDGE
(Jeff)
Quarterback—New York Giants

Born January 22, 1957, at Birmingham, Ala.
Height, 6.01. Weight, 195.
High School—Birmingham, Ala., Banks.
Received degree in business education from University of Alabama.
Son of Paul E. (Jack) Rutledge, minor league infielder, 1950 through 1952.

Selected by Los Angeles in 9th round (246th player selected) of 1979 NFL draft.
On injured reserve with mononucleosis, October 22 through remainder of 1980 season.
On injured reserve with broken thumb, November 2 through remainder of 1981 season.
Traded by Los Angeles Rams to New York Giants for 4th round pick in 1983 draft, September 5, 1982.
Crossed picket line during players' strike, October 14, 1987.
On injured reserve with knee injury, August 29 through November 25, 1988; activated, November 26, 1988.
Granted unconditional free agency, February 1, 1989; did not receive qualifying offer, April 15, 1989.
Re-signed by New York Giants, May 1, 1989.
Active for 9 games with New York Giants in 1982; did not play.

| | | | | —PASSING— | | | | | | —RUSHING— | | | | —TOTAL— | | |
Year Club	G.	Att.	Cmp.	Pct.	Gain	T.P.	P.I.	Avg.	Att.	Yds.	Avg.	TD.	TD.	Pts.	F.
1979—Los Angeles NFL............	3	32	13	40.6	125	1	4	3.91	5	27	5.4	0	0	0	0
1980—Los Angeles NFL............	1	4	1	25.0	26	0	0	6.50		None			0	0	0
1981—Los Angeles NFL............	4	50	30	60.0	442	3	4	8.84	5	—3	—0.6	0	0	0	0
1983—New York Giants NFL....	4	174	87	50.0	1208	3	8	6.94	7	27	3.9	0	0	0	6
1984—New York Giants NFL....	16	1	1	100.0	9	0	0	9.00		None			0	0	0
1985—New York Giants NFL....	16			None					2	—6	—3.0	0	0	0	1
1986—New York Giants NFL....	16	3	1	33.3	13	1	0	4.33	3	19	6.3	0	0	0	0
1987—New York Giants NFL....	13	155	79	51.0	1048	5	11	6.76	15	31	2.1	0	0	0	7
1988—New York Giants NFL....	1	17	11	64.7	113	0	1	6.65	3	—1	—0.3	0	0	0	2
Pro Totals—10 Years.........	74	436	223	51.1	2984	13	28	6.84	40	94	2.4	0	0	0	16

Quarterback Rating Points: 1979 (23.0), 1980 (54.2), 1981 (75.6), 1983 (59.3), 1984 (104.2), 1986 (87.5), 1987 (53.9), 1988 (59.2). Total—56.5.
Additional pro statistics: Recovered three fumbles and fumbled seven times for minus three yards, 1987.
Played in NFC Championship Game following 1986 season.
Played in NFL Championship Game following 1986 season.
Member of Los Angeles Rams for NFC and NFL Championship Game following 1979 season; did not play.

ROGER BRIAN RUZEK
Placekicker—Dallas Cowboys

Born December 17, 1960, at San Francisco, Calif.
Height, 6.01. Weight, 195.
High School—San Francisco, Calif., El Camino.
Received degree from Weber State College.

Signed as free agent by Cleveland Browns, May 5, 1983.
Released by Cleveland Browns, August 16, 1983; signed by Pittsburgh Maulers, October 10, 1983.
Released by Pittsburgh Maulers, December 16, 1983; signed as free agent by New Jersey Generals, January 7, 1984.
Released by New Jersey Generals, July 31, 1985; awarded on waivers to Memphis Showboats, August 1, 1985.
Granted free agency when USFL suspended operations, August 7, 1986; signed as free agent by Dallas Cowboys, April 10, 1987.
Released by Dallas Cowboys, August 6, 1987; re-signed by Cowboys, August 20, 1987.
On did not report/reserve, August 23 through August 28, 1988; reported, August 29, 1988.
Granted roster exemption, August 29 through September 12, 1988; activated, September 13, 1988.

| | | —PLACE KICKING— | | | | |
Year Club	G.	XP.	XPM.	FG.	FGA.	Pts.
1984—New Jersey USFL...	18	51	2	17	23	102
1985—New Jersey USFL...	18	49	3	17	25	100
1987—Dallas NFL	12	26	0	22	25	92
1988—Dallas NFL	14	27	0	12	22	63
USFL Totals—2 Years...	36	100	5	34	48	202
NFL Totals—2 Years.....	26	53	0	34	47	155
Pro Totals—4 Years.......	62	153	5	68	95	357

Additional pro statistics: Punted once for 36 yards, 1985.

JAMES JOSEPH RYAN
(Jim)
Linebacker—Denver Broncos

Born May 18, 1957, at Camden, N.J.
Height, 6.01. Weight, 225.
High School—Pennsauken, N.J., Bishop Eustace.
Received bachelor of administration degree in management from College of William & Mary in 1979
and received master's degree in business administration from University of Denver.

Signed as free agent by Denver Broncos, May 12, 1979.
Crossed picket line during players' strike, October 2, 1987.
Denver NFL, 1979 through 1988.
Games: 1979 (16), 1980 (16), 1981 (16), 1982 (9), 1983 (15), 1984 (16), 1985 (16), 1986 (16), 1987 (14), 1988 (16). Total—150.
Pro statistics: Recovered one fumble, 1979, 1983, 1984, 1985 and 1988; intercepted one pass for 21 yards, 1980;

returned one kickoff for no yards, 1980 and 1986; returned one kickoff for two yards, 1981; intercepted one pass for 13 yards, 1984; intercepted three passes for seven yards, returned two kickoffs for nine yards, credited with a safety, recovered two fumbles and fumbled once, 1987.

Played in AFC Championship Game following 1986 and 1987 seasons.

Played in NFL Championship Game following 1986 and 1987 seasons.

PATRICK LEE RYAN
(Pat)
Quarterback—New York Jets

Born September 16, 1955, at Hutchinson, Kan.
Height, 6.03. Weight, 210.
High School—Oklahoma City, Okla., Putnam.
Received degree in transportation from University of Tennessee in 1978.

Selected by New York Jets in 11th round (281st player selected) of 1978 NFL draft.
Crossed picket line during players' strike, October 14, 1987.

Year Club	G.	Att.	Cmp.	Pct.	Gain	T.P.	P.I.	Avg.	Att.	Yds.	Avg.	TD.	TD.	Pts.	F.
				PASSING						RUSHING			TOTAL		
1978—New York Jets NFL........	2	14	9	64.3	106	0	2	7.57		None			0	0	0
1979—New York Jets NFL........	1	4	2	50.0	13	0	1	3.25		None			0	0	1
1980—New York Jets NFL........	14			None						None			0	0	0
1981—New York Jets NFL........	15	10	4	40.0	48	1	1	4.80	3	—5	—1.7	0	0	0	0
1982—New York Jets NFL........	9	18	12	66.7	146	2	1	8.11	1	—1	—1.0	0	0	0	0
1983—New York Jets NFL........	16	40	21	52.5	259	2	2	6.48	4	23	5.8	0	0	†1	2
1984—New York Jets NFL........	16	285	156	54.7	1939	14	14	6.80	23	92	4.0	0	0	†1	4
1985—New York Jets NFL........	16	9	6	66.7	95	0	0	10.56	3	—5	—1.7	0	0	0	0
1986—New York Jets NFL........	16	55	34	61.8	342	2	1	6.22	8	28	3.5	0	0	0	0
1987—New York Jets NFL........	13	53	32	60.4	314	4	2	5.92	4	5	1.3	1	1	6	0
1988—New York Jets NFL........	16	113	63	55.8	807	5	4	7.14	5	22	4.4	0	0	0	1
Pro Totals—11 Years.........	134	601	339	56.4	4069	30	28	6.77	51	159	3.1	1	1	8	8

†Scored one extra point.

Quarterback Rating Points: 1978 (47.6), 1979 (17.7), 1981 (49.2), 1982 (105.1), 1983 (68.6), 1984 (72.0), 1985 (101.6), 1986 (84.1), 1987 (86.5), 1988 (78.3). Total—74.4.

Additional pro statistics: Recovered one fumble, 1983 and 1984.

Member of New York Jets for AFC Championship Game following 1982 season; did not play.

MARK ROBERT RYPIEN
Name pronounced Rip-in.
Quarterback—Washington Redskins

Born October 2, 1962, at Calgary, Alberta, Can.
Height, 6.04. Weight, 234.
High School—Spokane, Wash., Shadle Park.
Attended Washington State University.
Brother of Tim Rypien, catcher in Toronto Blue Jays' organization, 1984 through 1986;
and cousin of Shane Churla, forward with Minnesota North Stars.

Selected by Washington in 6th round (146th player selected) of 1986 NFL draft.
Signed by Washington Redskins, July 18, 1986.
On injured reserve with knee injury, September 5 through entire 1986 season.
On injured reserve with back injury, September 7 through November 27, 1987; activated, November 28, 1987.
Active for 1 game with Washington Redskins in 1987; did not play.

Year Club	G.	Att.	Cmp.	Pct.	Gain	T.P.	P.I.	Avg.	Att.	Yds.	Avg.	TD.	TD.	Pts.	F.
				PASSING						RUSHING			TOTAL		
1988—Washington NFL..............	9	208	114	54.8	1730	18	13	8.32	9	31	3.4	1	1	6	6

Quarterback Rating Points: 1988 (85.2).

Member of Washington Redskins for NFL Championship Game following 1987 season; inactive.

RODERICK SADDLER
(Rod)
Defensive End—Phoenix Cardinals

Born September 26, 1965, at Atlanta, Ga.
Height, 6.05. Weight, 276.
High School—Decatur, Ga., Columbia.
Attended Texas A&M University.
Cousin of Clark Gaines, running back with New York Jets and Kansas City Chiefs, 1976 though 1982.

Selected by St. Louis in 4th round (90th player selected) of 1987 NFL draft.
Signed by St. Louis Cardinals, July 21, 1987.
Franchise transferred to Phoenix, March 15, 1988.
St. Louis NFL, 1987; Phoenix NFL, 1988.
Games: 1987 (12), 1988 (16). Total—28.
Pro statistics: Intercepted one pass for no yards, 1987; recovered one fumble for 16 yards and a touchdown, 1988.

—DID YOU KNOW—

That either the Raiders or Broncos have swept their season series every year since 1978? They met only once in the strike-shortened 1982 season.

RAYMOND DANIEL SALEAUMUA
(Name pronounced SAL-uh-MOO-uh.)
(Dan)
Nose Tackle—Kansas City Chiefs
Born November 11, 1964, at San Diego, Calif.
Height, 6.00. Weight, 285.
High School—National City, Calif., Sweetwater.
Attended Arizona State University.

Selected by Detroit in 7th round (175th player selected) of 1987 NFL draft.
Signed by Detroit Lions, July 25, 1987.
On injured reserve with hamstring injury, September 7 through October 30, 1987; activated, October 31, 1987.
Granted unconditional free agency, February 1, 1989; signed by Kansas City Chiefs, March 20, 1989.
Detroit NFL, 1987 and 1988.
Games: 1987 (9), 1988 (16). Total—25.
Pro statistics: Returned three kickoffs for 57 yards, 1987; returned one kickoff for no yards and fumbled once, 1988.

HARVEY SALEM
Offensive Tackle-Guard—Detroit Lions
Born January 15, 1961, at Berkeley, Calif.
Height, 6.06. Weight, 285.
High School—El Cerrito, Calif.
Received degree from University of California at Berkeley.

Named as offensive tackle on THE SPORTING NEWS College All-America Team, 1982.
Selected by Oakland in 1983 USFL territorial draft.
Selected by Houston in 2nd round (30th player selected) of 1983 NFL draft.
Signed by Houston Oilers, July 14, 1983.
On did not report list, August 19 through September 7, 1986.
Granted roster exemption, September 8 through September 18, 1986; activated, September 19, 1986.
Traded by Houston Oilers to Detroit Lions for 2nd round pick in 1987 draft, September 23, 1986.
Granted free agency, February 1, 1987; re-signed by Lions, September 12, 1987.
Granted roster exemption, September 12 through September 18, 1987; activated, September 19, 1987.
Houston NFL, 1983 through 1985; Houston (1)-Detroit (13) NFL, 1986; Detroit NFL, 1987 and 1988.
Games: 1983 (16), 1984 (16), 1985 (14), 1986 (14), 1987 (11), 1988 (16). Total—87.
Pro statistics: Recovered one fumble, 1988.

JEROME ELI SALLY
Nose Tackle—Kansas City Chiefs
Born February 24, 1959, at Chicago, Ill.
Height, 6.03. Weight, 270.
High School—Maywood, Ill., Proviso East.
Received bachelor of science degree in industrial engineering from University of Missouri.

Signed as free agent by New Orleans Saints, May 27, 1982.
Released by New Orleans Saints, August 31, 1982; signed as free agent by New York Giants, December 1, 1982.
Traded by New York Giants to Indianapolis Colts for 7th round pick in 1988 draft, September 2, 1987.
Released by Indianapolis Colts, August 30, 1988; signed as free agent by Kansas City Chiefs, November 29, 1988.
New York Giants NFL, 1982 through 1986; Indianapolis NFL, 1987; Kansas City NFL, 1988.
Games: 1982 (4), 1983 (16), 1984 (16), 1985 (16), 1986 (16), 1987 (12), 1988 (3). Total—83.
Pro statistics: Recovered one fumble, 1983 and 1988; returned one kickoff for four yards, 1985.
Played in NFC Championship Game following 1986 season.
Played in NFL Championship Game following 1986 season.

CLINTON BERNARD SAMPSON
(Clint)
Wide Receiver—San Diego Chargers
Born January 4, 1961, at Los Angeles, Calif.
Height, 6.00. Weight, 188.
High School—Los Angeles, Calif., Crenshaw.
Attended Mt. San Antonio College and received degree in public administration
and business management from San Diego State University in 1983.

Selected by Boston in 3rd round (35th player selected) of 1983 USFL draft.
Selected by Denver in 3rd round (60th player selected) of 1983 NFL draft.
Signed by Denver Broncos, July 13, 1983.
On injured reserve with concussion, October 26 through November 19, 1984; activated, November 20, 1984.
Traded by Denver Broncos to Buffalo Bills for conditional 7th round pick in 1988 draft, July 14, 1987.
On injured reserve with knee injury, September 1 through entire 1987 season.
Released by Buffalo Bills, August 3, 1988; signed as free agent by San Diego Chargers, April 28, 1989.

| | | —PASS RECEIVING— | | | |
Year Club	G.	P.C.	Yds.	Avg.	TD.
1983—Denver NFL	16	10	200	20.0	3
1984—Denver NFL	12	9	123	13.7	1
1985—Denver NFL	16	26	432	16.6	4
1986—Denver NFL	15	21	259	12.3	0
Pro Totals—4 Years	59	66	1014	15.4	8

Additional pro statistics: Fumbled once, 1984 and 1986.
Played in AFC Championship Game following 1986 season.
Played in NFL Championship Game following 1986 season.

ERIC DOWNER SANDERS
Offensive Tackle-Guard—Detroit Lions
Born October 22, 1958, at Reno, Nev.
Height, 6.07. Weight, 280.
High School—Reno, Nev., Wooster.
Attended University of Nevada at Reno.

Selected by Atlanta in 5th round (136th player selected) of 1981 NFL draft.
On injured reserve with knee injury, November 10 through remainder of 1984 season.
On injured reserve with back injury, October 31 through November 26, 1986; awarded on procedural waivers to Detroit Lions, November 28, 1986.
Atlanta NFL, 1981 through 1985; Atlanta (8)-Detroit (3) NFL, 1986; Detroit NFL, 1987 and 1988.
Games: 1981 (16), 1982 (9), 1983 (15), 1984 (10), 1985 (16), 1986 (11), 1987 (12), 1988 (16). Total—105.
Pro statistics: Recovered one fumble, 1982 and 1988; recovered one fumble for minus 23 yards, 1985; fumbled once for minus 17 yards, 1988.

RICKY WAYNE SANDERS
Wide Receiver—Washington Redskins
Born August 30, 1962, at Temple, Tex.
Height, 5.11. Weight, 180.
High School—Belton, Tex.
Attended Southwest Texas State University.

Selected by Houston in 1984 USFL territorial draft.
Signed by Houston Gamblers, January 26, 1984.
Selected by New England in 1st round (16th player selected) of 1984 NFL supplemental draft.
On developmental squad, March 7 through May 5, 1985; activated, May 6, 1985.
Traded with defensive backs Luther Bradley, Will Lewis, Mike Mitchell and Durwood Roquemore, defensive end Pete Catan, quarterbacks Jim Kelly and Todd Dillon, defensive tackles Tony Fitzpatrick, Van Hughes and Hosea Taylor, running back Sam Harrell, linebackers Andy Hawkins and Ladell Wills, wide receivers Richard Johnson, Scott McGhee, Gerald McNeil and Clarence Verdin, guard Rich Kehr, center Billy Kidd and offensive tackles Chris Riehm and Tommy Robison by Houston Gamblers to New Jersey Generals for past considerations, March 7, 1986.
Granted free agency when USFL suspended operations, August 7, 1986.
NFL rights traded by New England Patriots to Washington Redskins for 3rd round pick in 1987 draft, August 11, 1986.
Signed by Washington Redskins, August 13, 1986.
Granted roster exemption, August 13 through August 24, 1986; activated, August 25, 1986.
On injured reserve with pulled calf and hamstring, September 2 through October 10, 1986; activated, October 11, 1986.
On developmental squad for 8 games with Houston Gamblers in 1985.

		—RUSHING—				PASS RECEIVING				—TOTAL—		
Year Club	G.	Att.	Yds.	Avg.	TD.	P.C.	Yds.	Avg.	TD.	TD.	Pts.	F.
1984—Houston USFL	18	10	58	5.8	0	101	1378	13.6	11	11	66	3
1985—Houston USFL	10	5	32	6.4	0	48	538	11.2	7	7	†44	0
1986—Washington NFL	10		None			14	286	20.4	2	2	12	0
1987—Washington NFL	12	1	—4	—4.0	0	37	630	17.0	3	3	18	0
1988—Washington NFL	16	2	14	7.0	0	73	1148	15.7	12	12	72	0
USFL Totals—2 Years	28	15	90	6.0	0	149	1916	12.9	18	18	110	3
NFL Totals—3 Years	38	3	10	3.3	0	124	2064	16.6	17	17	102	0
Pro Totals—5 Years	66	18	100	5.6	0	273	3980	14.6	35	35	212	3

		—PUNT RETURNS—				—KICKOFF RET.—			
Year Club	G.	No.	Yds.	Avg.	TD.	No.	Yds.	Avg.	TD.
1984—Houston USFL	18	19	148	7.8	0	2	28	14.0	0
1985—Houston USFL	10		None				None		
1986—Washington NFL	10		None				None		
1987—Washington NFL	12		None			4	118	29.5	0
1988—Washington NFL	16		None			19	362	19.1	0
USFL Totals—2 Years	28	19	148	7.8	0	2	28	14.0	0
NFL Totals—3 Years	38	0	0	0.0	0	23	480	20.9	0
Pro Totals—5 Years	66	19	148	7.8	0	25	508	20.3	0

†Includes one 2-point conversion.
Additional pro statistics: Recovered two fumbles, 1984; attempted one pass with no completions, 1985.
Played in NFC Championship Game following 1986 and 1987 seasons.
Played in NFL Championship Game following 1987 season.

THOMAS SANDERS
Running Back—Chicago Bears
Born January 4, 1962, at Giddings, Tex.
Height, 5.11. Weight, 203.
High School—Giddings, Tex.
Attended Texas A&M University.

Selected by Houston in 1985 USFL territorial draft.
Selected by Chicago in 9th round (250th player selected) of 1985 NFL draft.
Signed by Chicago Bears, July 10, 1985.

		—RUSHING—				PASS RECEIVING				—TOTAL—		
Year Club	G.	Att.	Yds.	Avg.	TD.	P.C.	Yds.	Avg.	TD.	TD.	Pts.	F.
1985—Chicago NFL	15	25	104	4.2	1	1	9	9.0	0	1	6	1
1986—Chicago NFL	16	27	224	8.3	5	2	18	9.0	0	5	30	2

Year	Club		G.	Att.	Yds.	RUSHING Avg.	TD.	PASS RECEIVING P.C.	Yds.	Avg.	TD.	TD.	TOTAL Pts.	F.
1987—Chicago NFL			12	23	122	5.3	1	3	53	17.7	0	1	6	1
1988—Chicago NFL			16	95	332	3.5	3	9	94	10.4	0	3	18	5
Pro Totals—4 Years			59	170	782	4.6	10	15	174	11.6	0	10	60	9

		KICKOFF RETURNS				
Year	Club	G.	No.	Yds.	Avg.	TD.
1985—Chicago NFL		15	1	10	10.0	0
1986—Chicago NFL		16	22	399	18.1	0
1987—Chicago NFL		12	20	349	17.5	0
1988—Chicago NFL		16	13	248	19.1	0
Pro Totals—4 Years		59	56	1006	18.0	0

Played in NFC Championship Game following 1985 and 1988 seasons.
Played in NFL Championship Game following 1985 season.

JIM SANDUSKY
Wide Receiver—Seattle Seahawks
Born September 9, 1961, at Othello, Wash.
Height, 5.10. Weight, 182.
High School—Othello, Wash.
Attended Walla Walla Community College, University of Nevada
at Las Vegas and San Diego State University.

Selected by Philadelphia in 4th round (74th player selected) of 1984 USFL draft.
Signed by British Columbia Lions, February 13, 1984.
Selected by New York Jets in 2nd round (38th player selected) of 1984 NFL supplemental draft.
NFL rights released by New York Jets, June, 1987.
Traded with future considerations by British Columbia Lions to Edmonton Eskimos for quarterback Matt Dunigan, June, 1988; traded completed when British Columbia traded linebackers Jeff Braswell and Greg Stumon, running back Reggie Taylor, defensive back Andre Francis and 1st round pick in 1989 draft to Edmonton.
Granted free agency, March 1, 1989; signed by Seattle Seahawks, April 4, 1989.

Year	Club		G.	PASS RECEIVING P.C.	Yds.	Avg.	TD.	PUNT RETURNS No.	Yds.	Avg.	TD.	TD.	TOTAL Pts.	F.
1984—British Columbia CFL			9	27	406	12.6	2	13	137	10.5	0	2	12	1
1985—British Columbia CFL			16	58	1073	18.5	7	21	210	10.0	0	7	42	4
1986—British Columbia CFL			15	60	858	14.3	1	42	459	10.9	0	1	6	0
1987—British Columbia CFL			18	80	1437	18.0	12	58	492	85	1	13	78	1
1988—Edmonton CFL			17	55	1089	19.8	8	9	82	9.1	0	8	48	1
CFL Totals—5 Years			75	280	4863	17.3	30	143	1380	9.7	1	31	186	7

Additional CFL statistics: Rushed once for 12 yards, returned two kickoffs for 41 yards and attempted two passes with two completions for 42 yards, 1985; recovered one fumble, 1985 and 1986; rushed once for one yard, returned one kickoff for 23 yards and attempted one pass with no completions, 1986; returned nine kickoffs for 125 yards and attempted four passes with two completions for 65 yards, 1987; recovered two fumbles, 1988.
Played in CFL Championship Game following 1985 season.

TODD DERRICK SANTOS
Quarterback—New Orleans Saints
Born February 12, 1964, at Fresno, Calif.
Height, 6.02. Weight, 210.
High School—Selma, Calif.
Attended San Diego State University.

Selected by New Orleans in 10th round (274th player selected) of 1988 NFL draft.
Signed by New Orleans Saints, July 17, 1988.
Released by New Orleans Saints, August 23, 1988; signed as free agent by San Francisco 49ers, October 18, 1988.
Released by San Francisco 49ers, October 25, 1988; re-signed by 49ers, October 29, 1988.
Released by San Francisco 49ers, November 7, 1988; re-signed by 49ers, March 3, 1989.
Released by San Francisco 49ers, April 26, 1989; awarded on waivers to New Orleans Saints, May 9, 1989.
Active for 1 game with San Francisco 49ers in 1988; did not play.
San Francisco NFL, 1988.

JESSE SAPOLU
Name pronounced SA-pole-low.
Center-Guard—San Francisco 49ers
Born March 10, 1961, at Laie, Western Samoa.
Height, 6.04. Weight, 260.
High School—Honolulu, Haw., Farrington.
Attended University of Hawaii.

Selected by Oakland in 17th round (199th player selected) of 1983 USFL draft.
Selected by San Francisco in 11th round (289th player selected) of 1983 NFL draft.
Signed by San Francisco 49ers, July 10, 1983.
On physically unable to perform/active with fractured foot, July 19 through August 12, 1984.
On physically unable to perform/reserve with fractured foot, August 13 through November 7, 1984; activated, November 8, 1984.
On injured reserve with fractured foot, November 16 through remainder of 1984 season.
On injured reserve with broken foot, August 12 through entire 1985 season.
On injured reserve with broken leg, July 30 through entire 1986 season.
San Francisco NFL, 1983, 1984, 1987 and 1988.

Games: 1983 (16), 1984 (1), 1987 (12), 1988 (16). Total—45.
Played in NFC Championship Game following 1983 and 1988 seasons.
Played in NFL Championship Game following 1988 season.

BRODERICK LAWRENCE SARGENT
Fullback—Dallas Cowboys
Born September 16, 1962, at Waxahachie, Tex.
Height, 5.11. Weight, 215.
High School—Waxahachie, Tex.
Attended Baylor University.

Signed as free agent by St. Louis Cardinals, May 13, 1986.
Crossed picket line during players' strike, October 1, 1987.
Franchise transferred to Phoenix, March 15, 1988.
Released by Phoenix Cardinals, August 24, 1988; signed as free agent by Dallas Cowboys, February 3, 1989.

				——RUSHING——			PASS RECEIVING				—TOTAL—		
Year	Club		G.	Att.	Yds.	Avg.	TD.	P.C.	Yds.	Avg.	TD.	TD.	Pts.	F.
1986—St. Louis NFL			16		None			1	8	8.0	0	0	0	0
1987—St. Louis NFL			15	18	90	5.0	0	2	19	9.5	0	0	0	1
Pro Totals—2 Years			31	18	90	5.0	0	3	27	9.0	0	0	0	1

Additional pro statistics: Returned two kickoffs for 27 yards, 1986; returned three kickoffs for 37 yards, 1987.

JAMES ELIJAH SAXON
Running Back—Kansas City Chiefs
Born March 23, 1966, at Buford, S. C.
Height, 5.11. Weight, 215.
High School—Burton, S. C., Battery Creek.
Attended American River College and San Jose State University.

Selected by Kansas City in 6th round (139th player selected) of 1988 NFL draft.
Signed by Kansas City Chiefs, July 19, 1988.

			——RUSHING——				PASS RECEIVING				—TOTAL—		
Year	Club	G.	Att.	Yds.	Avg.	TD.	P.C.	Yds.	Avg.	TD.	TD.	Pts.	F.
1988—Kansas City NFL		16	60	236	3.9	2	19	177	9.3	0	2	12	0

Additional pro statitics: Returned two kickoffs for 40 yards and recovered one fumble, 1988.

MIKE SAXON
Punter—Dallas Cowboys
Born July 10, 1962, at Arcadia, Calif.
Height, 6.03. Weight, 198.
High School—Arcadia, Calif.
Attended Pasadena City College and San Diego State University.

Selected by Arizona in 13th round (265th player selected) of 1984 USFL draft.
Selected by Detroit in 11th round (300th player selected) of 1984 NFL draft.
Signed by Detroit Lions, May 29, 1984.
Released by Detroit Lions, August 27, 1984; signed by Arizona Wranglers, November 7, 1984.
Released by Arizona Wranglers, February 11, 1985; signed as free agent by Dallas Cowboys, March 27, 1985.

		——PUNTING——		
Year	Club	G.	No.	Avg.	Blk.
1985—Dallas NFL	16	81	41.9	1
1986—Dallas NFL	16	86	40.7	1
1987—Dallas NFL	12	68	39.5	0
1988—Dallas NFL	16	80	40.9	0
Pro Totals—4 Years	60	315	40.8	2

GREG SCALES
Tight End—New Orleans Saints
Born May 9, 1966, at Winston-Salem, N. C.
Height, 6.04. Weight, 253.
High School—Winston-Salem, N. C., East Forsyth.
Attended Wake Forest University.

Selected by New Orleans in 5th round (112th player selected) of 1988 NFL draft.
Signed by New Orleans Saints, July 17, 1988.
New Orleans NFL, 1988.
Games: 1988 (12).
Pro statistics: Caught two passes for 20 yards and a touchdown, 1988.

MIKE SCHAD
Guard—Philadelphia Eagles
Born October 2, 1963, at Trenton, Ontario, Can.
Height, 6.05. Weight, 290.
High School—Bellville, Ontario, Can., Moira Secondary.
Received degrees in geography and physiology from Queens College (Canada) in 1986.

Selected by Los Angeles Rams in 1st round (23rd player selected) of 1986 NFL draft.
Signed by Los Angeles Rams, August 4, 1986.
On injured reserve with back injury, September 4 through entire 1986 season.

On injured reserve with pinched nerve in neck, September 7 through December 3, 1987; activated, December 4, 1987.

Granted unconditional free agency, February 1, 1989; signed by Philadelphia Eagles, March 28, 1989.

Los Angeles Rams NFL, 1987 and 1988.

Games: 1987 (1), 1988 (6). Total—7.

ANDREW C. SCHILLINGER
(Andy)
Wide Receiver—Phoenix Cardinals
Born November 22, 1964, at Lakewood, O.
Height, 5.11. Weight, 179.
High School—Avon Lake, O.
Received degree in finance from Miami University (Ohio) in 1988.

Selected by Phoenix in 10th round (260th player selected) of 1988 NFL draft.

Signed by Phoenix Cardinals, July 11, 1988.

Phoenix NFL, 1988.

Games: 1988 (3).

Pro statistics: Returned one kickoff for 10 yards, 1988.

BRUCE DANIEL SCHOLTZ
Linebacker—Seattle Seahawks
Born September 26, 1958, at La Grange, Tex.
Height, 6.06. Weight, 240.
High School—Austin, Tex., Crockett.
Attended University of Texas.

Selected by Seattle in 2nd round (33rd player selected) of 1982 NFL draft.

On injured reserve with sprained ankle, November 3 through December 4, 1987; activated, December 5, 1987.

		—INTERCEPTIONS—			
Year Club	G.	No.	Yds.	Avg.	TD.
1982—Seattle NFL	9	1	31	31.0	1
1983—Seattle NFL	16	1	8	8.0	0
1984—Seattle NFL	16	1	15	15.0	0
1985—Seattle NFL	16		None		
1986—Seattle NFL	16	2	10	5.0	0
1987—Seattle NFL	8		None		
1988—Seattle NFL	15		None		
Pro Totals—7 Years	96	5	64	12.8	1

Additional pro statistics: Recovered one fumble, 1982 through 1985; returned three kickoffs for 39 yards, 1986; returned one kickoff for 11 yards, 1987.

Played in AFC Championship Game following 1983 season.

TURK LEROY SCHONERT
Quarterback—Cincinnati Bengals
Born January 15, 1957, at Torrance, Calif.
Height, 6.01. Weight, 196.
High School—Anaheim, Calif., Servite.
Attended Stanford University.

Selected by Chicago in 9th round (242nd player selected) of 1980 NFL draft.

Released by Chicago Bears, August 25, 1980; claimed on waivers by Cincinnati Bengals, August 26, 1980.

USFL rights traded by Oakland Invaders to Jacksonville Bulls for rights to running back Ted McKnight, linebacker Mark Jerue and 1st and 5th round picks in 1984 draft, October 24, 1983.

On injured reserve with separated shoulder, December 5 through remainder of 1984 season.

Granted free agency, February 1, 1985; re-signed by Bengals, April 4, 1985.

Traded by Cincinnati Bengals to Atlanta Falcons for 3rd round pick in 1986 draft, April 4, 1986.

Released by Atlanta Falcons, September 8, 1987; signed as free agent by Cincinnati Bengals, September 10, 1987.

Active for 16 games with Cincinnati Bengals in 1980; did not play.

Year Club	G.	—————PASSING—————							——RUSHING——				—TOTAL—		
		Att.	Cmp.	Pct.	Gain	T.P.	P.I.	Avg.	Att.	Yds.	Avg.	TD.	TD.	Pts.	F.
1981—Cincinnati NFL	4	19	10	52.6	166	0	0	8.74	7	41	5.9	0	0	0	1
1982—Cincinnati NFL	2	1	1	100.0	6	0	0	6.00	3	—8	—2.7	0	0	0	1
1983—Cincinnati NFL	9	156	92	59.0	1159	2	5	7.43	29	117	4.0	2	2	12	6
1984—Cincinnati NFL	8	117	78	66.7	945	4	7	8.08	13	77	5.9	1	1	6	2
1985—Cincinnati NFL	7	51	33	64.7	460	1	0	9.02	8	39	4.9	0	0	0	3
1986—Atlanta NFL	8	154	95	61.7	1032	4	8	6.70	11	12	1.1	1	1	6	5
1987—Cincinnati NFL	11			None							None		0	0	0
1988—Cincinnati NFL	16	4	2	50.0	20	0	0	5.00	2	10	5.0	0	0	0	0
Pro Totals—9 Years	65	502	311	62.0	3788	11	20	7.55	73	288	3.9	4	4	24	18

Quarterback Rating Points: 1981 (82.3), 1982 (91.7), 1983 (73.1), 1984 (77.8), 1985 (100.1), 1986 (68.4), 1988 (64.6). Total—75.9.

Additional pro statistics: Recovered one fumble, 1982; recovered four fumbles, 1983; recovered two fumbles and fumbled three times for minus two yards, 1985; recovered one fumble and fumbled five times for minus two yards, 1986.

Played in AFC Championship Game following 1988 season.

Played in NFL Championship Game following 1988 season.

Member of Cincinnati Bengals for AFC and NFL Championship Games following 1981 season; did not play.

ADAM SCHREIBER
Guard—New York Jets
Born February 20, 1962, at Galveston, Tex.
Height, 6.04. Weight, 277.
High School—Huntsville, Ala., Butler.
Attended University of Texas.

Selected by Houston in 1984 USFL territorial draft.
Selected by Seattle in 9th round (243rd player selected) of 1984 NFL draft.
Signed by Seattle Seahawks, June 20, 1984.
Released by Seattle Seahawks, August 27, 1984; re-signed by Seahawks, October 10, 1984.
Released by Seattle Seahawks, August 29, 1985; signed as free agent by New Orleans Saints, November 20, 1985.
Released by New Orleans Saints, September 1, 1986; signed as free agent by Philadelphia Eagles, October 16, 1986.
Released by Philadelphia Eagles, October 18, 1988; awarded on waivers to New York Jets, October 19, 1988.
Seattle NFL, 1984; New Orleans NFL, 1985; Philadelphia NFL, 1986 and 1987; Philadelphia (6)-New York Jets (7) NFL, 1988.
Games: 1984 (6), 1985 (1), 1986 (9), 1987 (12), 1988 (13). Total—41.

JAY BRIAN SCHROEDER
Name pronounced SCHRAY-der.
Quarterback—Los Angeles Raiders
Born June 28, 1961, at Milwaukee, Wis.
Height, 6.04. Weight, 215.
High School—Pacific Palisades, Calif.
Attended University of California at Los Angeles.

Selected by Washington in 3rd round (83rd player selected) of 1984 NFL draft.
Traded with 2nd round pick in 1989 draft by Washington Redskins to Los Angeles Raiders for offensive tackle Jim Lachey, 2nd, 4th and 5th round picks in 1989 draft and conditional pick in 1990 draft, September 7, 1988.
Inactive for 1 game with Washington Redskins in 1988.
Acitve for 16 games with Washington Redskins in 1984; did not play.

				PASSING						RUSHING				TOTAL	
Year Club	G.	Att.	Cmp.	Pct.	Gain	T.P.	P.I.	Avg.	Att.	Yds.	Avg.	TD.	TD.	Pts.	F.
1985—Washington NFL	9	209	112	53.6	1458	5	5	6.98	17	30	1.8	0	0	0	5
1986—Washington NFL	16	541	276	51.0	4109	22	22	7.60	36	47	1.3	1	1	6	9
1987—Washington NFL	11	267	129	48.3	1878	12	10	7.03	26	120	4.6	3	3	18	5
1988—Wash. (0)-Raid. (9) NFL..	9	256	113	44.1	1839	13	13	7.18	29	109	3.8	1	1	6	6
Pro Totals—5 Years	45	1273	630	49.5	9284	52	50	7.29	108	306	2.8	5	5	30	25

Quarterback Rating Points: 1985 (73.8), 1986 (72.9), 1987 (71.0), 1988 (64.6). Total—71.1.
Additional pro statistics: Punted four times for 33.0 average, recovered one fumble and fumbled five times for minus three yards, 1985; recovered five fumbles and fumbled nine times for minus 19 yards, 1986; recovered three fumbles and fumbled six times for minus four yards, 1988.
Played in NFC Championship Game following 1986 and 1987 seasons.
Played in NFL Championship Game following 1987 season.
Played in Pro Bowl (NFL All-Star Game) following 1986 season.

RECORD AS BASEBALL PLAYER

Led Carolina League batters in strikeouts with 172 in 1982.
Led South Atlantic League batters in strikeouts with 142 in 1981.
Received reported $100,000 bonus to sign with Toronto Blue Jays, 1979.

Year Club	League	Pos.	G.	AB.	R.	H.	2B.	3B.	HR.	RBI.	B.A.	PO.	A.	E.	F.A.
1979—Utica†	NYP				(Did not play)										
1980—Medicine Hat‡	Pion.	OF	52	171	27	40	6	2	2	21	.234	93	6	5	.952
1981—Florence	S. Atl.	3B-OF	131	417	51	85	17	1	10	47	.204	112	101	28	.884
1982—Kinston	Carol.	OF	132	435	59	95	17	1	15	55	.218	178	17	15	.929
1983—Kinston§	Carol.	C-OF-1B	92	281	30	58	9	2	9	43	.206	519	53	20	.966

Selected by Toronto Blue Jays' organization in 1st round (third player selected) of free-agent draft, June 5, 1979.
†On temporary inactive list, June 30, 1979 through remainder of season.
‡On temporary inactive list, August 14 to September 3, 1980.
§Released, February 28, 1984.

SCOTT ANDREW SCHWEDES
Wide Receiver—Miami Dolphins
Born June 30, 1965, at Syracuse, N. Y.
Height, 6.00. Weight, 182.
High School—Dewitt, N. Y., Jamesville-DeWitt.
Received bachelor of science degree in marketing
from Syracuse University in 1987.

Selected by Miami in 2nd round (56th player selected) of 1987 NFL draft.
Signed by Miami Dolphins, August 4, 1987.

		PASS RECEIVING				PUNT RETURNS				KICKOFF RET.				TOTAL	
Year Club	G.	P.C.	Yds.	Avg.	TD.	No.	Yds.	Avg.	TD.	No.	Yds.	Avg.	TD.	TD.	Pts.	F.
1987—Miami NFL	12		None			24	203	8.5	0	9	177	19.7	0	0	0	7
1988—Miami NFL	16	6	130	21.7	0	24	230	9.6	0	3	49	16.3	0	0	0	1
Pro Totals—2 Years	28	6	130	21.7	0	48	433	9.0	0	12	226	18.8	0	0	0	8

Additional pro statistics: Recovered three fumbles, 1987.

KEVIN BERNARD SCOTT
Running Back—Dallas Cowboys

Born October 24, 1963, at Fort Bragg, N.C.
Height, 5.09. Weight, 181.
High School—Puyallup, Wash., Gov. John R. Rogers.
Received degree in engineering from Stanford University in 1987.

Signed as free agent by San Diego Chargers, May 10, 1987.
On injured reserve with hamstring injury, September 1 through entire 1987 season.
On injured reserve with toe injury, August 20 through December 6, 1988.
Released by San Diego Chargers, December 7, 1988; re-signed by Chargers, December 9, 1988.
Granted unconditional free agency, February 1, 1989; signed by Dallas Cowboys, April 1, 1989.
San Diego NFL, 1988.
Games: 1988 (1).

PATRICK S. SCOTT
Wide Receiver—Green Bay Packers

Born September 13, 1964, at Shreveport, La.
Height, 5.10. Weight, 170.
High School—Ringgold, La.
Received bachelor of science degree from Grambling State University in 1987.

Selected by Green Bay in 11th round (282nd player selected) of 1987 NFL draft.
Signed by Green Bay Packers, July 28, 1987.
Released by Green Bay Packers, September 7, 1987; re-signed as replacement by Packers, September 25, 1987.

		PASS RECEIVING				—KICKOFF RET.—				—TOTAL—		
Year	Club	G.	P.C.	Yds.	Avg.	TD.	No.	Yds.	Avg.	TD.	TD.	Pts.	F.
1987—Green Bay NFL		8	8	79	9.9	0	2	32	16.0	0	0	0	2
1988—Green Bay NFL		16	20	275	13.8	1	12	207	17.3	0	1	6	0
Pro Totals—2 Years		24	28	354	12.6	1	14	239	17.1	0	1	6	2

Additional pro statistics: Rushed once for two yards, returned six punts for 71 yards and recovered two fumbles, 1987.

COLIN ROBERT SCOTTS
Nose Tackle—Houston Oilers

Born April 26, 1963, at Sydney, Australia.
Height, 6.06. Weight, 263.
High School—Sydney, Australia, Scots College.
Attended University of Hawaii.

Selected by St. Louis in 3rd round (70th player selected) of 1987 NFL draft.
Signed by St. Louis Cardinals, July 18, 1987.
Franchise transferred to Phoenix, March 15, 1988.
On injured reserve with shoulder injury, August 29 through entire 1988 season.
Granted unconditional free agency, February 1, 1989; signed by Houston Oilers, March 31, 1989.
St. Louis NFL, 1987.
Games: 1987 (7).

WILLIAM CHARLES SCRIBNER
(Bucky)
Punter—Minnesota Vikings

Born July 11, 1960, at Lawrence, Kan.
Height, 6.00. Weight, 213.
High School—Lawrence, Kan.
Attended Pratt Community College and received bachelor of
arts degree in personnel administration from Kansas University.

Selected by Green Bay in 11th round (299th player selected) of 1983 NFL draft.
Released by Green Bay Packers, September 2, 1985; signed as free agent by Seattle Seahawks, May 14, 1986.
Released by Seattle Seahawks, August 11, 1986; signed as free agent replacement player by Minnesota Vikings, October 14, 1987.
Released by Minnesota Vikings, October 19, 1987; re-signed by Vikings, November 4, 1987.
Released by Minnesota Vikings, November 10, 1987; re-signed by Vikings for 1988, November 13, 1987.
Signed for 1987 season, December 8, 1987.

			——PUNTING——		
Year	Club	G.	No.	Avg.	Blk.
1983—Green Bay NFL		16	69	41.6	1
1984—Green Bay NFL		16	85	42.3	0
1987—Minnesota NFL		4	20	41.3	0
1988—Minnesota NFL		16	84	40.3	2
Pro Totals—4 Years		52	258	41.4	3

Additional pro statistics: Attemped one pass with no completions, 1984; rushed once for minus seven yards, 1987; fumbled once, 1987 and 1988; rushed once for no yards, 1988.
Played in NFC Championship Game following 1987 season.

—DID YOU KNOW—

That Buffalo tight end Butch Rolle has caught four passes in the last two seasons, all for touchdowns?

JOHN SCULLY
Guard—Atlanta Falcons
Born August 2, 1958, at Huntington, N.Y.
Height, 6.06. Weight, 270.
High School—Huntington, N.Y., Holy Family.
Received bachelor of arts degree in sociology from University of Notre Dame in 1980.
Brother-in-law of Tom Thayer, guard with Chicago Bears.

Named as center on THE SPORTING NEWS College All-America Team, 1980.
Selected by Atlanta in 4th round (109th player selected) of 1981 NFL draft.
On injured reserve with broken leg, October 29 through remainder of 1985 season.
On injured reserve with broken leg, December 13 through remainder of 1986 season.
On injured reserve with hamstring injury, September 12 through October 14, 1988; activated, October 15, 1988.
Atlanta NFL, 1981 through 1988.
Games: 1981 (16), 1982 (9), 1983 (16), 1984 (16), 1985 (8), 1986 (14), 1987 (12), 1988 (11). Total—102.
Pro statistics: Returned one kickoff for no yards, 1982; recovered one fumble, 1984; recovered two fumbles, 1986.

MICHAEL JOHN SCULLY
(Mike)
Center-Guard—Kansas City Chiefs
Born November 1, 1965, at Chicago, Ill.
Height, 6.05. Weight, 280.
High School—Buffalo Grove, Ill.
Attended University of Illinois.

Signed as free agent by Washington Redskins, May 10, 1988.
Released by Washington Redskins, August 30, 1988; re-signed by Redskins, September 3, 1988.
Released by Washington Redskins, September 7, 1988; signed as free agent by Kansas City Chiefs, December 29, 1988.
Washington NFL, 1988.
Games: 1988 (1).

EUGENE SEALE
Linebacker—Houston Oilers
Born June 3, 1964, at Jasper, Tex.
Height, 5.10. Weight, 240.
High School—Jasper, Tex.
Attended Lamar University.

Selected by New Jersey in 5th round (34th player selected) of 1986 USFL draft.
Signed by New Jersey Generals, May 28, 1986.
Granted free agency when USFL suspended operations, August 7, 1986; signed as replacement player by Houston Oilers, September 23, 1987.
Released by Houston Oilers, November 3, 1987; re-signed by Oilers, November 24, 1987.
Houston NFL, 1987 and 1988.
Games: 1987 (9), 1988 (16). Total—25.
Pro statistics: Intercepted one pass for 73 yards and a touchdown, 1987; intercepted one pass for 46 yards and credited with a safety, 1988.

SAMUEL RICARDO SEALE
(Sam)
Cornerback—San Diego Chargers
Born October 6, 1962, at Barbados, West Indies.
Height, 5.09. Weight, 185.
High School—Orange, N.J.
Attended Western State College.

Selected by Memphis in 15th round (309th player selected) of 1984 USFL draft.
Selected by Los Angeles Raiders in 8th round (224th player selected) of 1984 NFL draft.
Signed by Los Angeles Raiders, June 6, 1984.
Released by Los Angeles Raiders, September 2, 1988; signed as free agent by San Diego Chargers, September 14, 1988.

| | | –INTERCEPTIONS– | | | | —KICKOFF RET.— | | | | —TOTAL— | | |
Year Club	G.	No.	Yds.	Avg.	TD.	No.	Yds.	Avg.	TD.	TD.	Pts.	F.
1984—Los Angeles Raiders NFL	12		None				None			0	0	0
1985—Los Angeles Raiders NFL	16	1	38	38.0	1	23	482	21.0	0	1	6	0
1986—Los Angeles Raiders NFL	16	4	2	0.5	0		None			0	0	0
1987—Los Angeles Raiders NFL	12		None				None			0	0	0
1988—San Diego NFL	14		None				None			1	6	0
Pro Totals—5 Years	70	5	40	8.0	1	23	482	21.0	0	2	12	0

Additional pro statistics: Recovered one fumble, 1986; recovered one fumble for minus nine yards, 1987; recovered two fumbles and ran 50 yards with a lateral from a fumble for a touchdown, 1988.

LEON SEALS
Defensive End—Buffalo Bills
Born January 30, 1964, at New Orleans, La.
Height, 6.04. Weight, 265.
High School—Baton Rouge, La., Scotlandville.
Attended Jackson State University.

Selected by Buffalo in 4th round (109th player selected) of 1987 NFL draft.
Signed by Buffalo Bills, July 26, 1987.
Crossed picket line during players' strike, October 14, 1987.
Buffalo NFL, 1987 and 1988.
Games: 1987 (13), 1988 (16). Total—29.
Pro statistics: Recovered three fumbles for seven yards and a touchdown, 1988.
Played in AFC Championship Game following 1988 season.

BOB SEBRING
Linebacker—San Diego Chargers
Born April 10, 1963, at Pittsburgh, Pa.
Height, 6.03. Weight, 235.
High School—Orange, Calif., El Modena.
Attended Saddleback Community College and University of Illinois.

Selected by Houston in 9th round (225th player selected) of 1986 NFL draft.
Signed by Houston Oilers, July 21, 1986.
Released by Houston Oilers, August 25, 1986; signed as free agent by Detroit Lions, March 4, 1987.
Left Detroit Lions camp voluntarily and released, August 20, 1987; signed as free agent by Ottawa Rough Riders, September 16, 1987.
Released by Ottawa Rough Raiders, June 21, 1988; signed as free agent by San Diego Chargers, May 2, 1989.
Ottawa CFL, 1987.
Games: 1987 (7).
Pro statistics: Intercepted one pass for no yards, 1987.

THOMAS WESCOTT SECULES
(Name pronounced SEE-kyools.)
(Scott)
Quarterback—Dallas Cowboys
Born November 8, 1964, at Newport News, Va.
Height, 6.03. Weight, 219.
High School—Chantilly, Va.
Received degree in economics from University of Virginia in 1988.

Selected by Dallas in 6th round (151st player selected) of 1988 NFL draft.
Signed by Dallas Cowboys, July 8, 1988.
Active for 13 games with Dallas Cowboys in 1988; did not play.
Dallas NFL, 1988.

JOHN R. SETTLE
Running Back—Atlanta Falcons
Born June 2, 1965, at Reidsville, N.C.
Height, 5.09. Weight, 207.
High School—Ruffin, N.C., Rockingham County.
Attended Appalachian State University.

Signed as free agent by Atlanta Falcons, May 1, 1987.

		—RUSHING—				PASS RECEIVING				—TOTAL—		
Year Club	G.	Att.	Yds.	Avg.	TD.	P.C.	Yds.	Avg.	TD.	TD.	Pts.	F.
1987—Atlanta NFL	9	19	72	3.8	0	11	153	13.9	0	0	0	2
1988—Atlanta NFL	16	232	1024	4.4	7	68	570	8.4	1	8	48	3
Pro Totals—2 Years	25	251	1096	4.4	7	79	723	9.2	1	8	48	5

Additional pro statistics: Returned 10 kickoffs for 158 yards, 1987; recovered one fumble, 1987 and 1988.
Played in Pro Bowl (NFL All-Star Game) following 1988 season.

STEVEN EDWARD SEWELL
(Steve)
Running Back—Denver Broncos
Born April 2, 1963, at San Francisco, Calif.
Height, 6.03. Weight, 210.
High School—San Francisco, Calif., Riordan.
Attended University of Oklahoma.

Selected by Los Angeles in 1st round (16th player selected) of 1985 USFL draft.
Selected by Denver in 1st round (26th player selected) of 1985 NFL draft.
Signed by Denver Broncos, July 22, 1985.
On injured reserve with separated shoulder, November 14 through December 16, 1986; activated, December 17, 1986.
On injured reserve with broken jaw, November 24, 1987 through January 8, 1988; activated, January 9, 1988.

		—RUSHING—				PASS RECEIVING				—TOTAL—		
Year Club	G.	Att.	Yds.	Avg.	TD.	P.C.	Yds.	Avg.	TD.	TD.	Pts.	F.
1985—Denver NFL	16	81	275	3.4	4	24	224	9.3	1	5	30	0
1986—Denver NFL	11	23	123	5.3	1	23	294	12.8	1	2	12	0
1987—Denver NFL	7	19	83	4.4	2	13	209	16.1	1	3	18	1
1988—Denver NFL	16	32	135	4.2	1	38	507	13.3	5	6	36	2
Pro Totals—4 Years	50	155	616	4.0	8	98	1234	12.6	8	16	96	3

Additional pro statistics: Returned one kickoff for 29 yards and recovered one fumble, 1985; attempted one pass with no completions, 1985 and 1988; attempted one pass with one completion for 23 yards and a touchdown, 1986; recovered three fumbles for four yards, 1988.

Played in AFC Championship Game following 1986 and 1987 seasons.

Played in NFL Championship Game following 1986 and 1987 seasons.

JOHN BYRON SHANNON
Defensive Tackle—Chicago Bears
Born January 18, 1965, at Lexington, Ky.
Height, 6.03. Weight, 269.
High School—Florence, Ky., Boone County.
Received bachelor of science degree in communications from University of Kentucky in 1988.

Signed as free agent by Chicago Bears, May 17, 1988.

Released by Chicago Bears, August 30, 1988; re-signed by Bears, September 8, 1988.

Chicago NFL, 1988.

Games: 1988 (13).

Played in NFC Championship Game following 1988 season.

LUIS ERNESTO SHARPE JR.
Offensive Tackle—Phoenix Cardinals
Born June 16, 1960, at Havana, Cuba.
Height, 6.04. Weight, 260.
High School—Detroit, Mich., Southwestern.
Attended University of California at Los Angeles.

Named as offensive tackle on THE SPORTING NEWS College All-America Team, 1981.

Selected by St. Louis in 1st round (16th player selected) of 1982 NFL draft.

Granted free agency, February 1, 1985.

USFL rights traded by Houston Gamblers to Memphis Showboats for draft picks, April 18, 1985.

Signed by Memphis Showboats, April 18, 1985.

Released by Memphis Showboats, August 25, 1985; re-signed by St. Louis Cardinals, August 31, 1985.

Granted roster exemption, August 31 through September 2, 1985; activated, September 3, 1985.

Franchise transferred to Phoenix, March 15, 1988.

St. Louis NFL, 1982 through 1987; Memphis USFL, 1985; Phoenix NFL, 1988.

Games: 1982 (9), 1983 (16), 1984 (16), 1985 USFL (10), 1985 NFL (16), 1986 (16), 1987 (12), 1988 (16). Total NFL—101. Total Pro—111.

Pro statistics: Recovered one fumble, 1982, 1984 and 1987; rushed once for 11 yards and recovered two fumbles, 1983.

Played in Pro Bowl (NFL All-Star Game) following 1987 and 1988 seasons.

STERLING SHARPE
Wide Receiver-Kick Returner—Green Bay Packers
Born April 6, 1965, at Chicago, Ill.
Height, 5.11. Weight, 202.
High School—Glennville, Ga.
Received bachelor's degree in interdisciplinary studies from University of South Carolina in 1987.

Named as wide receiver on THE SPORTING NEWS College All-America Team, 1987.

Selected by Green Bay in 1st round (7th player selected) of 1988 NFL draft.

Signed by Green Bay Packers, July 31, 1988.

		—————RUSHING—————				PASS RECEIVING				—TOTAL—		
Year Club	G.	Att.	Yds.	Avg.	TD.	P.C.	Yds.	Avg.	TD.	TD.	Pts.	F.
1988—Green Bay NFL	16	4	—2	—0.5	0	55	791	14.4	1	1	6	3

		—PUNT RETURNS—				—KICKOFF RET.—		
Year Club	G.	No.	Yds.	Avg.	TD.	No.	Yds.	Avg.TD.
1988—Green Bay NFL	16	9	48	5.3	0	1	17	17.0 0

Additional pro statistics: Recovered one fumble, 1988.

RICKY ANDREW SHAW
Linebacker—New York Giants
Born July 28, 1965, at Westchester, N.Y.
Height, 6.04. Weight, 240.
High School—Fayetteville, N.C., Douglas Byrd.
Attended Oklahoma State University.
Nephew of Aundray Bruce, linebacker with Atlanta Falcons.

Selected by New York Giants in 4th round (92nd player selected) of 1988 NFL draft.

Signed by New York Giants, July 18, 1988.

New York Giants NFL, 1988.

Games: 1988 (14).

Pro statistics: Recovered one fumble, 1988.

ELBERT VERNELL SHELLEY
Safety—Atlanta Falcons
Born December 24, 1964, at Tyronza, Ark.
Height, 5.11. Weight, 180.
High School—Trumann, Ark.
Attended Arkansas State University.

Selected by Atlanta in 11th round (292nd player selected) of 1987 NFL draft.
Signed by Atlanta Falcons, July 27, 1987.
On injured reserve with neck injury, September 2 through November 27, 1987; activated, November 28, 1987.
On injured reserve with wrist injury, September 15 through October 12, 1988; activated after clearing procedural waivers, October 14, 1988.
Atlanta NFL, 1987 and 1988.
Games: 1987 (4), 1988 (12). Total—16.
Pro statistics: Returned two kickoffs for five yards and fumbled once, 1988.

DERRICK LATHELL SHEPARD
Wide Receiver—New Orleans Saints
Born January 22, 1964, at Odessa, Tex.
Height, 5.10. Weight, 187.
High School—Odessa, Tex.
Attended University of Oklahoma.

Signed as free agent by Washington Redskins, May 4, 1987.
Released by Washington Redskins, August 17, 1987; re-signed as replacement player by Redskins, September 23, 1987.
Released by Washington Redskins, November 28, 1987; re-signed by Redskins, April 15, 1988.
On injured reserve with hip injury, August 29 through Sepgember 30, 1988; activated after clearing procedural waivers, October 1, 1988.
On injured reserve with concussion, November 4 through December 8, 1988; activated after clearing procedural waivers, December 9, 1988.
Granted unconditional free agency, February 1, 1989; signed by New Orleans Saints, March 8, 1989.

		–PUNT RETURNS–				—KICKOFF RET.—				—TOTAL—		
Year Club	G.	No.	Yds.	Avg.	TD.	No.	Yds.	Avg.	TD.	TD.	Pts.	F.
1987—Washington NFL	2	6	146	24.3	0	1	20	20.0	0	0	0	0
1988—Washington NFL	5	12	104	8.7	0	16	329	20.6	0	0	0	3
Pro Totals—2 Years	7	18	250	13.9	0	17	349	20.5	0	0	0	3

MICHAEL WATSON SHERRARD
(Mike)
Wide Receiver—San Francisco 49ers
Born June 21, 1963, at Oakland, Calif.
Height, 6.02. Weight, 187.
High School—Chino, Calif.
Received bachelor of arts degree in history from University of California at Los Angeles in 1986.
Son of Cherrie Sherrard, sprinter in 100-meter hurdles for 1964 U.S. Olympic Team.

Selected by Arizona in 1986 USFL territorial draft.
Selected by Dallas in 1st round (18th player selected) of 1986 NFL draft.
Signed by Dallas Cowboys, August 7, 1986.
On injured reserve with broken leg, September 1 through entire 1987 season.
On physically unable to perform/reserve with leg injury, July 25 through entire 1988 season.
Granted unconditional free agency, February 1, 1989; signed by San Francisco 49ers, March 30, 1989.

		—PASS RECEIVING—			
Year Club	G.	P.C.	Yds.	Avg.	TD.
1986—Dallas NFL	16	41	744	18.1	5

Additional pro statistics: Rushed twice for 11 yards, 1986.

JACKIE RENARDO SHIPP
Linebacker—Los Angeles Raiders
Born March 19, 1962, at Muskogee, Okla.
Height, 6.02. Weight, 236.
High School—Stillwater, Okla., C.E. Donart.
Attended Oklahoma University.

Selected by Oklahoma in 1984 USFL territorial draft.
Selected by Miami in 1st round (14th player selected) of 1984 NFL draft.
Signed by Miami Dolphins, July 14, 1984.
On injured reserve with ankle injury, December 6 through remainder of 1988 season.
Granted unconditional free agency, February 1, 1989; signed by Los Angeles Raiders, March 23, 1989.
Miami NFL, 1984 through 1988.
Games: 1984 (16), 1985 (16), 1986 (16), 1987 (12), 1988 (11). Total—71.
Pro statistics: Intercepted one pass for seven yards and recovered two fumbles, 1985; recovered one fumble, 1986.
Played in AFC Championship Game following 1984 and 1985 seasons.
Played in NFL Championship Game following 1984 season.

MICKEY CHARLES SHULER
Tight End—New York Jets
Born August 21, 1956, at Harrisburg, Pa.
Height, 6.03. Weight, 231.
High School—Enola, Pa., East Pennsboro.
Received degree in health and physical education from Pennsylvania State University.

Selected by New York Jets in 3rd round (61st player selected) of 1978 NFL draft.
On injured reserve with shoulder separation, September 1 through November 13, 1981; activated, November 14, 1981.

Year	Club		G.	P.C.	Yds.	Avg.	TD.
				——PASS RECEIVING——			
1978—N.Y. Jets NFL	....		16	11	67	6.1	3
1979—N.Y. Jets NFL	....		16	16	225	14.1	3
1980—N.Y. Jets NFL	....		16	22	226	10.3	2
1981—N.Y. Jets NFL	....		6		None		
1982—N.Y. Jets NFL	....		9	8	132	16.5	3
1983—N.Y. Jets NFL	....		16	26	272	10.5	1
1984—N.Y. Jets NFL	....		16	68	782	11.5	6
1985—N.Y. Jets NFL	....		16	76	879	11.6	7
1986—N.Y. Jets NFL	....		16	69	675	9.8	4
1987—N.Y. Jets NFL	....		11	43	434	10.1	3
1988—N.Y. Jets NFL	....		15	70	805	11.5	5
Pro Totals—11 Years	....		153	409	4497	11.0	37

Additional pro statistics: Fumbled once, 1978 through 1980, 1984, 1985 and 1988; returned one kickoff for 12 yards, 1978; returned one kickoff for 15 yards, 1979; returned two kickoffs for 25 yards, 1980; returned one kickoff for three yards, 1983; returned one kickoff for no yards, 1984; recovered one fumble, 1985 and 1986; returned two kickoffs for minus three yards, 1986; fumbled twice, 1987; recovered two fumbles, 1988.

Played in AFC Championship Game following 1982 season.
Played in Pro Bowl (NFL All-Star Game) following 1986 and 1988 seasons.

ERIC SCOTT SIEVERS
Tight End—New England Patriots
Born November 9, 1958, at Urbana, Ill.
Height, 6.04. Weight, 230.
High School—Arlington, Va., Washington & Lee.
Attended University of Maryland.

Selected by San Diego in 4th round (107th player selected) of 1981 NFL draft.
On injured reserve with knee injury, November 19 through remainder of 1986 season.
On injured reserve with neck injury, October 13 through December 6, 1988.
Lost through procedural waivers to Los Angeles Rams, December 7, 1988.
Granted unconditional free agency, February 1, 1989; signed by New England Patriots, April 1, 1989.

Year	Club		G.	P.C.	Yds.	Avg.	TD.
				——PASS RECEIVING——			
1981—San Diego NFL	....		16	22	276	12.5	3
1982—San Diego NFL	....		9	12	173	14.4	1
1983—San Diego NFL	....		16	33	452	13.7	3
1984—San Diego NFL	....		14	41	438	10.7	3
1985—San Diego NFL	....		16	41	438	10.7	6
1986—San Diego NFL	....		9	2	14	7.0	0
1987—San Diego NFL	....		12		None		
1988—S.D. (5)-Rams (1) NFL			6	1	2	2.0	0
Pro Totals—8 Years	....		98	152	1793	11.8	16

Additional pro statistics: Returned two kickoffs for four yards, 1981; recovered one fumble and fumbled once, 1981 and 1984; returned one kickoff for 17 yards, 1982; returned one kickoff for six yards and rushed once for minus seven yards, 1983; returned one kickoff for three yards, 1985.

Played in AFC Championship Game following 1981 season.

VAI SIKAHEMA
Running Back-Kick Returner—Phoenix Cardinals
Born August 29, 1962, at Nuku'Alofa, Tonga.
Height, 5.09. Weight, 191.
High School—Mesa, Ariz.
Attended Brigham Young University.

Tied NFL record for most touchdowns, punt returns, game (2), against Tampa Bay Buccaneers, December 21, 1986.

Selected by St. Louis in 10th round (254th player selected) of 1986 NFL draft.
Selected by Arizona in 7th round (47th player selected) of 1986 USFL draft.
Signed by St. Louis Cardinals, July 11, 1986.
Crossed picket line during players' strike, October 2, 1987.
Franchise transferred to Phoenix, March 15, 1988.
On injured reserve with knee injury, November 1 through December 1, 1988; activated, December 2, 1988.

Year	Club	G.	Att.	Yds.	Avg.	TD.	P.C.	Yds.	Avg.	TD.	TD.	Pts.	F.
			——RUSHING——				PASS RECEIVING				—TOTAL—		
1986—St. Louis NFL	16	16	62	3.9	0	10	99	9.9	1	3	18	2
1987—St. Louis NFL	15		None				None			1	6	0
1988—Phoenix NFL	12		None				None			0	0	2
Pro Totals—3 Years	43	16	62	3.9	0	10	99	9.9	1	4	24	4

Year	Club	G.	No.	Yds.	Avg.	TD.	No.	Yds.	Avg.	TD.
			—PUNT RETURNS—				—KICKOFF RET.—			
1986—St. Louis NFL	16	43	*522	12.1	*2	37	847	22.9	0
1987—St. Louis NFL	15	*44	*550	12.5	1	34	761	22.4	0
1988—Phoenix NFL	12	33	341	10.3	0	23	475	20.7	0
Pro Totals—3 Years	43	120	1413	11.8	3	94	2083	22.2	0

Addtional pro statistics: Recovered one fumble, 1988.
Played in Pro Bowl (NFL All-Star Game) following 1986 and 1987 seasons.

DANIEL WILLIAM SILEO
(Dan)
Defensive Tackle—Dallas Cowboys
Born January 3, 1964, at Stamford, Conn.
Height, 6.02. Weight, 291.
High School—Stamford, Conn., Stamford Catholic.
Attended University of Maryland, University of Cincinnati and University of Miami (Fla.).

Signed as free agent by Tampa Bay Bucaneers, September 6, 1987.
Contract voided by NFL, September 11, 1987.
Selected by Tampa Bay in 3rd round of 1987 NFL supplemental draft, September 16, 1987.
Signed by Tampa Bay Bucaneers, September 16, 1987.
Granted roster exemption, September 16 through October 23, 1987; activated, October 24, 1987.
Released by Tampa Bay Buccaneers, August 29, 1988; signed as free agent by Dallas Cowboys, February 3, 1989.
Tampa Bay NFL, 1987.
Games: 1987 (10).

CLYDE SIMMONS
Defensive End—Philadelphia Eagles
Born August 4, 1964, at Lanes, S. C.
Height, 6.06. Weight, 276.
High School—Wilmington, N. C., New Hanover.
Attended Western Carolina University.

Selected by Philadelphia in 9th round (233rd player selected) of 1986 NFL draft.
Signed by Philadelphia Eagles, July 3, 1986.
Philadelphia NFL, 1986 through 1988.
Games: 1986 (16), 1987 (12), 1988 (16). Total—44.
Pro statistics: Returned one kickoff for no yards, 1986; recovered one fumble, 1987; ran 15 yards with blocked field goal attempt, credited with a safety and recovered three fumbles, 1988.

ED SIMMONS
Offensive Tackle—Washington Redskins
Born December 31, 1963, at Seattle, Wash.
Height, 6.05. Weight, 280.
High School—Seattle, Wash., Nathan Hale.
Attended Eastern Washington University.

Selected by Washington in 6th round (164th player selected) of 1987 NFL draft.
Signed by Washington Redskins, July 24, 1987.
On injured reserve with knee injury, November 23 through remainder of 1987 season.
Washington NFL, 1987 and 1988.
Games: 1987 (5), 1988 (16). Total—21.

PHILLIP SIMMS
(Phil)
Quarterback—New York Giants
Born November 3, 1956, at Lebanon, Ky.
Height, 6.03. Weight, 216.
High School—Louisville, Ky., Southern.
Attended Morehead State University.

Selected by New York Giants in 1st round (7th player selected) of 1979 NFL draft.
On injured reserve with separated shoulder, November 18 through December 25, 1981; activated, December 26, 1981.
On injured reserve with knee injury, August 30 through entire 1982 season.
On injured reserve with dislocated thumb, October 13 through remainder of 1983 season.

| | | —————PASSING————— | | | | | | | ——RUSHING—— | | | —TOTAL— | | |
Year Club	G.	Att.	Cmp.	Pct.	Gain	T.P.	P.I.	Avg.	Att.	Yds.	Avg.	TD.	TD.	Pts.	F.
1979—N.Y. Giants NFL	12	265	134	50.6	1743	13	14	6.58	29	166	5.7	1	1	6	9
1980—N.Y. Giants NFL	13	402	193	48.0	2321	15	19	5.77	36	190	5.3	1	1	6	6
1981—N.Y. Giants NFL	10	316	172	54.4	2031	11	9	6.43	19	42	2.2	0	0	0	7
1983—N.Y. Giants NFL	2	13	7	53.8	130	0	1	10.00		None			0	0	0
1984—N.Y. Giants NFL	16	533	286	53.7	4044	22	18	7.59	42	162	3.9	0	0	0	8
1985—N.Y. Giants NFL	16	495	275	55.6	3829	22	20	7.74	37	132	3.6	0	0	0	*16
1986—N.Y. Giants NFL	16	468	259	55.3	3487	21	22	7.45	43	72	1.7	1	1	6	9
1987—N.Y. Giants NFL	9	282	163	57.8	2230	17	9	7.91	14	44	3.1	0	0	0	4
1988—N.Y. Giants NFL	15	479	263	54.9	3359	21	11	7.01	33	152	4.6	0	0	0	7
Pro Totals—9 Years	109	3253	1752	53.9	23174	142	123	7.12	253	960	3.8	3	3	18	66

Quarterback Rating Points: 1979 (65.9), 1980 (58.9), 1981 (74.2), 1983 (56.6), 1984 (78.1), 1985 (78.6), 1986 (74.6), 1987 (90.0), 1988 (82.1). Total—75.5.

Additional pro statistics: Fumbled nine times for minus two yards, 1979; recovered two fumbles, 1980 and 1981; fumbled six times for minus five yards, 1980; fumbled seven times for minus 15 yards, 1981; caught one pass for 13 yards, recovered four fumbles and fumbled eight times for minus five yards, 1984; recovered five fumbles and fumbled 16 times for minus 22 yards, 1985; recovered three fumbles and fumbled nine times for minus two yards, 1986; recovered one fumble, 1987 and 1988.

Played in NFC Championship Game following 1986 season.
Played in NFL Championship Game following 1986 season.
Played in Pro Bowl (NFL All-Star Game) following 1985 season.

DARRYL LEON SIMS
Defensive End—Cleveland Browns
Born July 23, 1961, at Winston-Salem, N.C.
Height, 6.03. Weight, 290.
High School—Bridgeport, Conn., Basick.
Attended University of Wisconsin.

Selected by Jacksonville in 1985 USFL territorial draft.
Selected by Pittsburgh in 1st round (20th player selected) of 1985 NFL draft.
Signed by Pittsburgh Steelers, July 18, 1985.
Released by Pittsburgh Steelers, September 7, 1987; signed as free agent replacement player by Cleveland Browns, September 23, 1987.
Pittsburgh NFL, 1985 and 1986; Cleveland NFL, 1987 and 1988.
Games: 1985 (16), 1986 (16), 1987 (10), 1988 (16). Total—58.
Pro statistics: Recovered one fumble for two yards, 1986.
Played in AFC Championship Game following 1987 season.

KENNETH W. SIMS
(Ken)
Defensive End—New England Patriots
Born October 31, 1959, at Kosse, Tex.
Height, 6.05. Weight, 271.
High School—Groesbeck, Tex.
Attended University of Texas.

Named as defensive end on THE SPORTING NEWS College All-America Team, 1981.
Selected by New England in 1st round (1st player selected) of 1982 NFL draft.
On injured reserve with broken leg, December 3 through remainder of 1985 season.
On injured reserve with back and hip injuries, September 2 through October 16, 1986; activated, October 17, 1986.
On injured reserve with back injury, November 26 through remainder of 1986 season.
On injured reserve with ruptured Achilles tendon, September 6 through remainder of 1988 season.
New England NFL, 1982 through 1988.
Games: 1982 (9), 1983 (5), 1984 (16), 1985 (13), 1986 (3), 1987 (12), 1988 (1). Total—59.
Pro statistics: Recovered two fumbles, 1985; recovered one fumble for six yards, 1986; recovered one fumble, 1987 and 1988.

CURT EDWARD SINGER
Offensive Tackle—Detroit Lions
Born November 4, 1961, at Aliquippa, Pa.
Height, 6.05. Weight, 279.
High School—Aliquippa, Pa., Hopewell.
Attended University of Tennessee.

Selected by Memphis in 1984 USFL territorial draft.
Selected by Washington in 6th round (167th player selected) of 1984 NFL draft.
Signed by Washington Redskins, June 26, 1984.
Released by Washington Redskins, August 27, 1984; re-signed by Redskins, August 28, 1984.
On injured reserve with back injury, August 30 through entire 1984 season.
Released by Washington Redskins, August 20, 1985; signed as free agent by Seattle Seahawks, April 15, 1986.
On injured reserve with ankle injury, September 8 through entire 1987 season.
Released by Seattle Seahawks, August 30, 1988; signed as free agent by Detroit Lions, September 15, 1988.
Seattle NFL, 1986; Detroit NFL, 1988.
Games: 1986 (11), 1988 (3). Total—14.

MICHAEL SINGLETARY
(Mike)
Linebacker—Chicago Bears
Born October 9, 1958, at Houston, Tex.
Height, 6.00. Weight, 230.
High School—Houston, Tex., Evan E. Worthing.
Received bachelor of arts degree in management from Baylor University.
Uncle of Broderick Thomas, rookie linebacker with Tampa Bay Buccaneers;
and William Thomas, defensive back at University of Nebraska.

Named to THE SPORTING NEWS NFL All-Star Team, 1984 through 1988.
Named as linebacker on THE SPORTING NEWS College All-America Team, 1980.
Selected by Chicago in 2nd round (38th player selected) of 1981 NFL draft.
Placed on did not report list, August 19 and August 20, 1985.
Granted roster exemption, August 21 through August 25, 1985; activated, August 26, 1985.
Chicago NFL, 1981 through 1988.
Games: 1981 (16), 1982 (9), 1983 (16), 1984 (16), 1985 (16), 1986 (14), 1987 (12), 1988 (16). Total—115.
Pro statistics: Intercepted one pass for minus three yards, 1981; recovered one fumble, 1982, 1984 and 1987; intercepted one pass for no yards and recovered four fumbles for 15 yards, 1983; intercepted one pass for four yards, 1984; intercepted one pass for 23 yards and recovered three fumbles for 11 yards, 1985; intercepted one pass for three yards, 1986; intercepted one pass for 13 yards and recovered one fumble for four yards, 1988.
Played in NFC Championship Game following 1984, 1985 and 1988 seasons.
Played in NFL Championship Game following 1985 season.
Played in Pro Bowl (NFL All-Star Game) following 1983 through 1988 seasons.

REGGIE SINGLETARY
Guard-Offensive Tackle—Philadelphia Eagles
Born January 17, 1964, at Whiteville, N. C.
Height, 6.03. Weight, 285.
High School—Cerro Gordo, N. C., West Columbus.
Attended North Carolina State University.

Selected by Jacksonville in 1986 USFL territorial draft.
Selected by Philadelphia in 12th round (315th player selected) of 1986 NFL draft.
Signed by Philadelphia Eagles, May 27, 1986.
Philadelphia NFL, 1986 through 1988.
Games: 1986 (16), 1987 (12), 1988 (16). Total—44.
Pro statistics: Recovered one fumble, 1986; caught one pass for minus 11 yards, 1987.

PAUL ANTHONY SKANSI
Wide Receiver—Seattle Seahawks
Born January 11, 1961, at Tacoma, Wash.
Height, 5.11. Weight, 183.
High School—Gig Harbor, Wash., Peninsula.
Attended University of Washington.

Selected by Michigan in 4th round (39th player selected) of 1983 USFL draft.
Selected by Pittsburgh in 5th round (133rd player selected) of 1983 NFL draft.
Signed by Pittsburgh Steelers, June 5, 1983.
Released by Pittsburgh Steelers, August 27, 1984; signed as free agent by Seattle Seahawks, October 25, 1984.
Released by Seattle Seahawks, September 2, 1985; re-signed by Seahawks, October 2, 1985.

		PASS RECEIVING				-PUNT RETURNS-				—KICKOFF RET.—				—TOTAL—		
Year Club	G.	P.C.	Yds.	Avg.	TD.	No.	Yds.	Avg.	TD.	No.	Yds.	Avg.	TD.	TD.	Pts.	F.
1983—Pittsburgh NFL...........	15	3	39	13.0	0	43	363	8.4	0		None			0	0	5
1984—Seattle NFL..................	7	7	85	12.1	0	16	145	9.1	0		None			0	0	0
1985—Seattle NFL..................	12	21	269	12.8	1	31	312	10.1	0	19	358	18.8	0	1	6	1
1986—Seattle NFL..................	16	22	271	12.3	0	5	38	7.6	0	1	21	21.0	0	0	0	1
1987—Seattle NFL..................	12	19	207	10.9	1		None				None			1	6	1
1988—Seattle NFL..................	16	24	238	9.9	1		None				None			1	6	0
Pro Totals—6 Years.......	78	96	1109	11.6	3	95	858	9.0	0	20	379	19.0	0	3	18	8

Additional pro statistics: Recovered two fumbles, 1983; recovered one fumble, 1985.

JAMES JEFFREY SKOW
(Jim)
Defensive End—Cincinnati Bengals
Born June 29, 1963, at Omaha, Neb.
Height, 6.03. Weight, 255.
High School—Omaha, Neb., Roncalli.
Received degree from University of Nebraska in 1987.

Selected by Cincinnati in 3rd round (58th player selected) of 1986 NFL draft.
Signed by Cincinnati Bengals, August 9, 1986.
Cincinnati NFL, 1986 through 1988.
Games: 1986 (16), 1987 (12), 1988 (16). Total—44.
Played in AFC Championship Game following 1988 season.
Played in NFL Championship Game following 1988 season.

JACKIE RAY SLATER
Offensive Tackle—Los Angeles Rams
Born May 27, 1954, at Jackson, Miss.
Height, 6.04. Weight, 275.
High School—Jackson, Miss., Wingfield.
Received bachelor of arts degree from Jackson State University;
attending Livingston University for master's degree in physical education.

Selected by Los Angeles in 3rd round (86th player selected) of 1976 NFL draft.
On injured reserve with knee injury, October 17 through remainder of 1984 season.
Crossed picket line during players' strike, October 14, 1987.
Los Angeles Rams NFL, 1976 through 1988.
Games: 1976 (14), 1977 (14), 1978 (16), 1979 (16), 1980 (15), 1981 (11), 1982 (9), 1983 (16), 1984 (7), 1985 (16), 1986 (16), 1987 (12), 1988 (16). Total—178.
Pro statistics: Recovered one fumble, 1978, 1980 and 1985; recovered one fumble for 13 yards, 1983.
Played in NFC Championship Game following 1976, 1978, 1979 and 1985 seasons.
Played in NFL Championship Game following 1979 season.
Played in Pro Bowl (NFL All-Star Game) following 1983 and 1985 through 1988 seasons.

TONY TYRONE SLATON
Center-Guard—Los Angeles Rams
Born April 12, 1961, at Merced, Calif.
Height, 6.03. Weight, 265.
High School—Merced, Calif.
Received bachelor of science degree from University of Southern California in 1984.

Selected by Los Angeles in 1984 USFL territorial draft.

Selected by Buffalo in 6th round (155th player selected) of 1984 NFL draft.
Signed by Buffalo Bills, June 1, 1984.
Released by Buffalo Bills, August 20, 1984; signed as free agent by Los Angeles Rams, August 23, 1984.
On injured reserve with strained abdominal muscles, September 21 through remainder of 1984 season.
Released by Los Angeles Rams, August 20, 1985; re-signed by Rams, September 19, 1985.
Active for 3 games with Los Angeles Rams in 1984; did not play.
Los Angeles Rams NFL, 1984 through 1988.
Games: 1985 (13), 1986 (14), 1987 (11), 1988 (15). Total—53.
Pro statistics: Returned one kickoff for 18 yards and recovered one fumble, 1985.
Played in NFC Championship Game following 1985 season.

WEBSTER M. SLAUGHTER
Wide Receiver—Cleveland Browns
Born October 19, 1964, at Stockton, Calif.
Height, 6.00. Weight, 170.
High School—Stockton, Calif., Franklin.
Attended San Diego State University.

Selected by Cleveland in 2nd round (43rd player selected) of 1986 NFL draft.
Signed by Cleveland Browns, July 24, 1986.
On injured reserve with broken arm, October 21 through December 11, 1988; activated, December 12, 1988.

| | | —PASS RECEIVING— | | | |
Year Club	G.	P.C.	Yds.	Avg.	TD.
1986—Cleveland NFL..............	16	40	577	14.4	4
1987—Cleveland NFL..............	12	47	806	17.1	7
1988—Cleveland NFL..............	8	30	462	15.4	3
Pro Totals—3 Years............	36	117	1845	15.8	14

Additional pro statistics: Rushed once for one yard, returned one punt for two yards, recovered fumble in end zone for a touchdown, 1986; fumbled once, 1986 through 1988.
Played in AFC Championship Game following 1986 and 1987 seasons.

STEPHEN KAY SLAYDEN
(Steve)
Quarterback—Kansas City Chiefs
Born January 22, 1966, at Huntsville, Ala.
Height, 6.01. Weight, 185.
High School—Atlanta, Ga., Westminister.
Received bachelor of arts degree in political science
from Duke University in 1988.

Selected by Cleveland in 12th round (328th player selected) of 1988 NFL draft.
Signed by Cleveland Browns, July 19, 1988.
Released by Cleveland Browns, August 30, 1988; re-signed by Browns, September 12, 1988.
Released by Cleveland Browns, October 24, 1988; re-signed by Browns and placed on injured reserve with stomach injury, October 25 through December 11, 1988.
Released by Cleveland Browns, December 12, 1988; re-signed by Browns, December 14, 1988.
On reserve list, December 23 through remainder of 1988 playoffs.
Granted unconditional free agency, February 1, 1989; signed by Kansas City Chiefs, March 2, 1989.
Active for 3 games with Cleveland Browns in 1988; did not play.
Cleveland NFL, 1988.

FREDERICK C. SMERLAS
(Fred)
Nose Tackle—Buffalo Bills
Born April 8, 1957, at Waltham, Mass.
Height, 6.03. Weight, 280.
High School—Waltham, Mass.
Attended Boston College.

Selected by Buffalo in 2nd round (32nd player selected) of 1979 NFL draft.
On injured reserve with knee injury, November 29 through remainder of 1979 season.
Buffalo NFL, 1979 through 1988.
Games: 1979 (13), 1980 (16), 1981 (16), 1982 (9), 1983 (16), 1984 (16), 1985 (16), 1986 (16), 1987 (12), 1988 (16). Total—146.
Pro statistics: Recovered three fumbles for 23 yards and one touchdown, 1979; recovered one fumble for 17 yards, 1981; recovered two fumbles, 1982 and 1984; intercepted one pass for 25 yards, 1984; recovered one fumble, 1985; intercepted one pass for three yards, 1986; recovered one fumble for four yards, 1988.
Played in AFC Championship Game following 1988 season.
Played in Pro Bowl (NFL All-Star Game) following 1980 through 1983 and 1988 seasons.

AL FREDRICK SMITH
Linebacker—Houston Oilers
Born November 26, 1964, at Los Angeles, Calif.
Height, 6.01. Weight, 236.
High School—Playa Del Rey, Calif., St. Bernard.
Attended California State Poly University and received bachelor of science degree
in sociology from Utah State University in 1987.
Brother of Aaron Smith, linebacker with Denver Broncos, 1984.

Selected by Houston in 6th round (147th player selected) of 1987 NFL draft.
Signed by Houston Oilers, July 31, 1987.
Houston NFL, 1987 and 1988.
Games: 1987 (12), 1988 (16). Total—28.
Pro statistics: Recovered one fumble, 1988.

BILLY RAY SMITH JR.
(Billy Ray)
Linebacker—San Diego Chargers
Born August 10, 1961, at Fayetteville, Ark.
Height, 6.03. Weight, 236.
High School—Plano, Tex.
Attended University of Arkansas.
Son of Billy Ray Smith, Sr., defensive tackle with Los Angeles Rams, Pittsburgh
Steelers and Baltimore Colts, 1957 through 1962 and 1964 through 1970.

Named as defensive end on THE SPORTING NEWS College All-America Team, 1981 and 1982.
Selected by Oakland in 1st round (7th player selected) of 1983 USFL draft.
Selected by San Diego in 1st round (5th player selected) of 1983 NFL draft.
Signed by San Diego Chargers, May 19, 1983.
On injured reserve with back injury, December 20 through remainder of 1985 season.
On injured reserve with broken leg, November 23 through remainder of 1988 season.

| | | —INTERCEPTIONS— | | | |
Year Club	G.	No.	Yds.	Avg.TD.	
1983—San Diego NFL	16		None		
1984—San Diego NFL	16	3	41	13.7	0
1985—San Diego NFL	15	1	0	0.0	0
1986—San Diego NFL	16		None		
1987—San Diego NFL	12	5	28	5.6	0
1988—San Diego NFL	9	1	9	9.0	0
Pro Totals—6 Years............	84	10	78	7.8	0

Additional pro statistics: Returned one kickoff for 10 yards, 1983; recovered one fumble, 1983 and 1986; recovered three fumbles, 1984, 1985 and 1987; had only pass attempt intercepted, 1987.

BRUCE BERNARD SMITH
Defensive End—Buffalo Bills
Born June 18, 1963, at Norfolk, Va.
Height, 6.04. Weight, 285.
High School—Norfolk, Va., Booker T. Washington.
Attended Virginia Tech.

Named to THE SPORTING NEWS NFL All-Star Team, 1987 and 1988.
Outland Trophy winner, 1984.
Selected by Baltimore in 1985 USFL territorial draft.
Signed by Buffalo Bills, February 28, 1985.
Selected officially by Buffalo in 1st round (1st player selected) of 1985 NFL draft.
On non-football injury list with substance abuse, September 2 through September 27, 1988; activated, September 28, 1988.
Granted free agency, February 1, 1989.
Tendered offer sheet by Denver Broncos, March 23, 1989; matched by Buffalo Bills, March 29, 1989.
Buffalo NFL, 1985 through 1988.
Games: 1985 (16), 1986 (16), 1987 (12), 1988 (12). Total—56.
Pro statistics: Rushed once for no yards and recovered four fumbles, 1985; recovered two fumbles for 15 yards and a touchdown, 1987; credited with a safety, 1988.
Played in AFC Championship Game following 1988 season.
Played in Pro Bowl (NFL All-Star Game) following 1987 and 1988 seasons.

CARL DOUGLAS SMITH
(Doug)
Center—Los Angeles Rams
Born November 25, 1956, at Columbus, O.
Height, 6.03. Weight, 260.
High School—Columbus, O., Northland.
Received bachelor of science degree in education from Bowling Green State University in 1978
and attending California State University at Fullerton for master's degree in exercise physiology.

Signed as free agent by Los Angeles Rams, May 16, 1978.
On injured reserve with knee injury, September 28 through remainder of 1979 season.
On injured reserve with knee injury, October 30 through remainder of 1980 season.
On injured reserve with concussion, December 14 through remainder of 1985 season.
Los Angeles Rams NFL, 1978 through 1988.
Games: 1978 (16), 1979 (4), 1980 (8), 1981 (16), 1982 (9), 1983 (14), 1984 (16), 1985 (13), 1986 (16), 1987 (12), 1988 (16). Total—140.
Pro statistics: Recovered one fumble, 1978 and 1985; returned one kickoff for eight yards, 1978; fumbled once, 1981 and 1983; recovered two fumbles, 1982.
Played in NFC Championship Game following 1978 season.
Played in Pro Bowl (NFL All-Star Game) following 1984 and 1986 through 1988 seasons.
Named to play in Pro Bowl following 1985 season; replaced due to injury by Fred Quillan.

DARYL DIMITRI SMITH
Cornerback—Minnesota Vikings
Born May 8, 1963, at Opelika, Ala.
Height, 5.09. Weight, 185.
High School—Opelika, Ala.
Attended University of North Alabama.

Selected by Portland in 2nd round (22nd player selected) of 1985 USFL draft.
Selected by Denver in 9th round (249th player selected) of 1985 NFL draft.
Signed by Denver Broncos, July 11, 1985.
Released by Denver Broncos, August 20, 1985; signed as free agent by Edmonton Eskimos, March 22, 1986.
Released by Edmonton Eskimos, June 21, 1986; signed as free agent by Cincinnati Bengals, May 1, 1987.
Released by Cincinnati Bengals, September 7, 1987; re-signed as replacement player by Bengals, September 25, 1987.
Released by Cincinnati Bengals, October 19, 1987; re-signed by Bengals, October 30, 1987.
On injured reserved with pulled hamstring, December 11 through remainder of 1987 season.
On non-football injury list with substance abuse, September 1 through September 27, 1988; activated, September 28, 1988.
On injured reserve with Achilles heel injury, October 4 through November 11, 1988; activated, November 12, 1988.
Granted unconditional free agency, February 1, 1989; signed by Minnesota Vikings, March 16, 1989.
Cincinnati NFL, 1987 and 1988.
Games: 1987 (3), 1988 (7). Total—10.
Pro statistics: Intercepted two passes for no yards, 1987.
Played in AFC Championship Game following 1988 season.
Played in NFL Championship Game following 1988 season.

DARYLE RAY SMITH
Offensive Tackle—Dallas Cowboys
Born January 18, 1964, at Knoxville, Tenn.
Height, 6.05. Weight, 278.
High School—Knoxville, Tenn., Powell.
Attended University of Tennessee.

Signed as free agent by Seattle Seahawks, May 5, 1987.
Released by Seattle Seahawks, September 7, 1987; signed as free agent replacement player by Dallas Cowboys, September 23, 1987.
Dallas NFL, 1987 and 1988.
Games: 1987 (9), 1988 (14). Total—23.
Pro statistics: Returned two kickoffs for 24 yards, 1988.

DAVID ALLAN SMITH
(Dave)
Offensive Tackle—Kansas City Chiefs
Born December 12, 1964, at Hammond, Ind.
Height, 6.06. Weight, 290.
High School—Lansing, Ill., Thornton Fractional South.
Received bachelor of science degree in business management
from University of Southern Illinois in 1988.

Signed as free agent by Cincinnati Bengals, April 28, 1988.
Granted unconditional free agency, February 1, 1989; signed by Kansas City Chiefs, March 27, 1989.
Cincinnati NFL, 1988.
Games: 1988 (14).
Played in AFC Championship Game following 1988 season.
Played in NFL Championship Game following 1988 season.

DENNIS SMITH
Safety—Denver Broncos
Born February 3, 1959, at Santa Monica, Calif.
Height, 6.03. Weight, 200.
High School—Santa Monica, Calif.
Attended University of Southern California.

Selected by Denver in 1st round (15th player selected) of 1981 NFL draft.
On injured reserve with broken arm, November 24, 1987 through January 15, 1988; activated, January 16, 1988.
On injured reserve with hamstring injury, September 28 through October 30, 1988; activated, October 31, 1988.

Year Club	G.	No.	Yds.	Avg.	TD.
1981—Denver NFL	16	1	65	65.0	0
1982—Denver NFL	8	1	29	29.0	0
1983—Denver NFL	14	4	39	9.8	0
1984—Denver NFL	15	3	13	4.3	0
1985—Denver NFL	13	3	46	15.3	0
1986—Denver NFL	14	1	0	0.0	0
1987—Denver NFL	6	2	21	10.5	0
1988—Denver NFL	11		None		
Pro Totals—8 Years	97	15	213	14.2	0

Additional pro statistics: Recovered two fumbles, 1981, 1987 and 1988; recovered one fumble for 64 yards and a touchdown, 1984; recovered one fumble, 1986.
Played in AFC Championship Game following 1986 and 1987 seasons.

Played in NFL Championship Game following 1986 and 1987 seasons.
Played in Pro Bowl (NFL All-Star Game) following 1985 and 1986 seasons.

DONALD MICHAEL SMITH
(Don)
Running Back—Tampa Bay Buccaneers
Born October 30, 1963, at Hamilton, Miss.
Height, 5.11. Weight, 195.
High School—Hamilton, Miss.
Attended Mississippi State University.

Selected by Tampa Bay in 2nd round (51st player selected) of 1987 NFL draft.
Signed by Tampa Bay Buccaneers, July 18, 1987.
On injured reserve with leg injury, September 8 through November 12, 1987; then transferred to non-football injury list with back injury, November 13 through remainder of 1987 season.
On injured reserve with knee injury, August 22 through October 13, 1988; activated, October 14, 1988.

		——RUSHING——				PASS RECEIVING				—TOTAL—		
Year Club	G.	Att.	Yds.	Avg.	TD.	P.C.	Yds.	Avg.	TD.	TD.	Pts.	F.
1988—Tampa Bay NFL	10	13	46	3.5	1	12	138	11.5	0	1	6	0

Additional pro statistics: Returned nine kickoffs for 188 yards (20.9 avg.), 1988.

DOUGLAS ARTHUR SMITH
(Doug)
Nose Tackle—Houston Oilers
Born June 13, 1959, at Mesic, N.C.
Height, 6.05. Weight, 285.
High School—Bayboro, N.C., Pamlico Central.
Attended Auburn University.

Named as defensive tackle on THE SPORTING NEWS USFL All-Star Team, 1985.
Selected by Birmingham in 1984 USFL territorial draft.
Selected by Houston in 2nd round (29th player selected) of 1984 NFL draft.
Signed by Birmingham Stallions, August 2, 1984.
On developmental squad, March 2 through March 7, 1985; activated, March 8, 1985.
Released by Birmingham Stallions, October 7, 1985; signed by Houston Oilers, October 10, 1985.
Granted roster exemption, October 10, 1985.
On injured reserve with hamstring injury, December 16 through remainder of 1986 season.
Crossed picket line during players' strike, September 29, 1987.
On non-football injury list with substance abuse, November 10 through December 6, 1988; activated, December 7, 1988.
On developmental squad for 1 game with Birmingham Stallions in 1985.
Birmingham USFL, 1985; Houston NFL, 1985 through 1988.
Games: 1985 USFL (17), 1985 NFL (11), 1986 (13), 1987 (14), 1988 (12). Total NFL—50. Total Pro—67.
USFL statistics: Credited with five sacks and recovered one fumble, 1985.
NFL statistics: Intercepted one pass for 20 yards and recovered two fumbles for three yards, 1988.

JEFF K. SMITH
Running Back—Green Bay Packers
Born March 22, 1962, at Wichita, Kan.
Height, 5.09. Weight, 201.
High School—Wichita, Kan., Southeast.
Attended University of Nebraska.

Selected by Baltimore in 7th round (101st player selected) of 1985 USFL draft.
Selected by Kansas City in 10th round (267th player selected) of 1985 NFL draft.
Signed by Kansas City Chiefs, July 18, 1985.
On injured reserve with sprained ankle, December 4 through remainder of 1985 season.
Traded by Kansas City Chiefs to Tampa Bay Buccaneers for 8th round pick in 1988 draft, September 3, 1987.
Granted unconditional free agency, February 1, 1989; signed by Green Bay Packers, March 30, 1989.

		——RUSHING——				PASS RECEIVING				—TOTAL—		
Year Club	G.	Att.	Yds.	Avg.	TD.	P.C.	Yds.	Avg.	TD.	TD.	Pts.	F.
1985—Kansas City NFL	13	30	118	3.9	0	18	157	8.7	2	2	12	1
1986—Kansas City NFL	15	54	238	4.4	3	33	230	7.0	3	6	36	4
1987—Tampa Bay NFL	12	100	309	3.1	2	20	197	9.9	2	4	24	2
1988—Tampa Bay NFL	16	20	87	4.4	0	16	134	8.4	0	0	0	0
Pro Totals—4 Years	56	204	752	3.7	5	87	718	8.3	7	12	72	7

		—PUNT RETURNS—				—KICKOFF RET.—			
Year Club	G.	No.	Yds.	Avg.	TD.	No.	Yds.	Avg.	TD.
1985—Kansas City NFL	13		None			33	654	19.8	0
1986—Kansas City NFL	15	29	245	8.4	0	29	557	19.2	0
1987—Tampa Bay NFL	12		None			5	84	16.8	0
1988—Tampa Bay NFL	16	8	45	5.6	0	10	180	18.0	0
Pro Totals—4 Years	56	37	290	7.8	0	77	1475	19.2	0

Additional pro statistics: Recovered one fumble, 1985.

JOHN THOMAS SMITH
(J. T.)
Wide Receiver—Phoenix Cardinals

Born October 29, 1955, at Leonard, Tex.
Height, 6.02. Weight, 185.
High School—Leonard, Tex., Big Spring.
Attended North Texas State University.

Named to THE SPORTING NEWS NFL All-Star Team, 1987.
Named as punt returner on THE SPORTING NEWS NFL All-Star Team, 1980.
Signed as free agent by Washington Redskins, May, 1978.
Released by Washington Redskins, September 21, 1978; signed as free agent by Kansas City Chiefs, November 7, 1978.
On inactive list, September 19, 1982.
On injured reserve with knee injury, August 30 through October 13, 1983; activated, October 14, 1983.
On injured reserve with separated shoulder, December 10 through remainder of 1984 season.
Released by Kansas City Chiefs, August 26, 1985; signed as free agent by St. Louis Cardinals, September 17, 1985.
Crossed picket line during players' strike, October 2, 1987.
Franchise transferred to Phoenix, March 15, 1988.

		PASS RECEIVING				–PUNT RETURNS–				—KICKOFF RET.—				—TOTAL—		
Year Club	G.	P.C.	Yds.	Avg.	TD.	No.	Yds.	Avg.	TD.	No.	Yds.	Avg.	TD.	TD.	Pts.	F.
1978—Wash(6)-KC(6) NFL	12		None			4	33	8.3	0	1	18	18.0	0	0	0	0
1979—Kansas City NFL.........	16	33	444	13.5	3	58	*612	10.6	2		None			5	30	3
1980—Kansas City NFL.........	16	46	655	14.2	2	40	*581	*14.5	*2		None			4	24	1
1981—Kansas City NFL.........	16	63	852	13.5	2	50	528	10.6	0		None			2	12	2
1982—Kansas City NFL.........	5	10	168	16.8	1	3	26	8.7	0		None			1	6	0
1983—Kansas City NFL.........	9	7	85	12.1	0	26	210	8.1	0	1	5	5.0	0	0	0	0
1984—Kansas City NFL.........	15	8	69	8.6	0	39	332	8.5	0	19	391	20.6	0	0	0	1
1985—St. Louis NFL..............	14	43	581	13.5	1	26	283	10.9	0	4	59	14.8	0	1	6	3
1986—St. Louis NFL..............	16	80	1014	12.7	6	1	6	6.0	0		None			6	36	1
1987—St. Louis NFL..............	15	*91	*1117	12.3	8		None				None			8	48	2
1988—Phoenix NFL................	16	83	986	11.9	5	17	119	7.0	0		None			5	30	4
Pro Totals—11 Years.....	150	464	5971	12.9	28	264	2730	10.3	4	25	473	18.9	0	32	192	17

Additional pro statistics: Recovered one fumble for one yard, 1979; recovered two fumbles, 1980; recovered fumble for 19 yards, 1981; rushed three times for 36 yards, 1985; recovered three fumbles, 1986; rushed once for 15 yards and recovered one fumble, 1988.
Played in Pro Bowl (NFL All-Star Game) following 1980 and 1988 seasons.

LANCE SMITH
Offensive Tackle-Guard—Phoenix Cardinals

Born January 1, 1963, at Kannapolis, N.C.
Height, 6.02. Weight, 262.
High School—Kannapolis, N.C., A.L. Brown.
Attended Louisiana State University.

Selected by Portland in 1985 USFL territorial draft.
Selected by St. Louis in 3rd round (72nd player selected) of 1985 NFL draft.
Signed by St. Louis Cardinals, July 21, 1985.
Crossed picket line during players' strike, October 2, 1987.
Franchise transferred to Phoenix, March 15, 1988.
St. Louis NFL, 1985 through 1987; Phoenix NFL, 1988.
Games: 1985 (14), 1986 (15), 1987 (15), 1988 (16). Total—60.
Pro statistics: Recovered one fumble, 1985.

LEONARD PHILLIP SMITH
Safety—Buffalo Bills

Born September 2, 1960, at New Orleans, La.
Height, 5.11. Weight, 202.
High School—Baton Rouge, La., Robert E. Lee.
Attended McNeese State University.

Selected by Boston in 2nd round (14th player selected) of 1983 USFL draft.
Selected by St. Louis in 1st round (17th player selected) of 1983 NFL draft.
Signed by St. Louis Cardinals, May 3, 1983.
Crossed picket line during players' strike, September 23, 1987.
Franchise transferred to Phoenix, March 15, 1988.
Traded by Phoenix Cardinals to Buffalo Bills for cornerback Roland Mitchell and 6th round pick in 1989 draft, September 21, 1988.

		—INTERCEPTIONS—						—INTERCEPTIONS—			
Year Club	G.	No.	Yds.	Avg.	TD.	Year Club	G.	No.	Yds.	Avg.	TD.
1983—St. Louis NFL................	16		None			1987—St. Louis NFL................	15		None		
1984—St. Louis NFL................	12	2	31	15.5	1	1988—Pho.(3)-Buf.(13) NFL...	16	2	29	14.5	0
1985—St. Louis NFL................	16	2	73	36.5	0	Pro Totals—6 Years...........	91	7	146	20.9	1
1986—St. Louis NFL................	16	1	13	13.0	0						

Additional pro statistics: Returned one kickoff for 19 yards, 1983; recovered one fumble, 1984; returned five kickoffs for 68 yards and recovered three fumbles and fumbled once, 1985; recoveed one fumble for 29 yards and a touchdown, 1987.
Played in AFC Championship Game following 1988 season.

NEIL SMITH
Defensive End—Kansas City Chiefs
Born April 10, 1966, at New Orleans, La.
Height, 6.04. Weight, 270.
High School—New Orleans, La., McDonogh 35.
Attended University of Nebraska.

Named as defensive lineman on THE SPORTING NEWS College All-America Team, 1987.
Selected by Kansas City in 1st round (2nd player selected) of 1988 NFL draft.
Signed by Kansas City Chiefs, July 19, 1988.
Kansas City NFL, 1988.
Games: 1988 (13).

ROBERT BENJAMIN SMITH
Defensive End—Tampa Bay Buccaneers
Born December 3, 1962, at Bogalusa, La.
Height, 6.07. Weight, 270.
High School—Bogalusa, La.
Received degree in accounting from Grambling State University.
Brother of Sean Smith, defensive tackle with Chicago Bears.

Selected by New Orleans in 1984 USFL territorial draft.
USFL rights traded by New Orleans Breakers to Arizona Wranglers for defensive end Junior Ah You and past considerations, January 9, 1984.
Signed by Arizona Wranglers, January 9, 1984.
On developmental squad, February 24 through April 20, 1984.
On injured reserve with knee injury, April 21 through June 25, 1984; activated, June 26, 1984.
Selected by Minnesota in 2nd round (40th player selected) of 1984 NFL supplemental draft.
Not protected in merger of Arizona Wranglers and Oklahoma Outlaws, December 6, 1984; signed by Minnesota Vikings, March 21, 1985.
Released by Minnesota Vikings, August 26, 1986; signed as free agent by Dallas Cowboys, April 30, 1987.
On injured reserve with broken arm, September 7 through entire 1987 season.
Crossed picket line during players' strike, October 1, 1987.
Released by Dallas Cowboys, August 30, 1988; signed as free agent by Tampa Bay Buccaneers, February 16, 1989.
On developmental squad for 8 games with Arizona Wranglers in 1984.
Minnesota NFL, 1985.
Games: 1985 (16).
On developmental squad for USFL Championship Game following 1984 season.

SEAN LAMAR SMITH
Defensive Tackle—Chicago Bears
Born March 27, 1965, at Bogalusa, La.
Height, 6.04. Weight, 290.
High School—Bogalusa, La.
Attended Grambling State University.
Brother of Robert Smith, defensive end with Tampa Bay Buccaneers.

Selected by Chicago in 4th round (101st player selected) of 1987 NFL draft.
Signed by Chicago Bears, August 3, 1987.
On injured reserve with knee injury, August 29 through October 13, 1988; activated, October 14, 1988.
Chicago NFL, 1987 and 1988.
Games: 1987 (10), 1988 (9). Total—19.
Pro statistics: Recovered one fumble, 1987.
Played in NFC Championship Game following 1988 season.

STEVEN ANTHONY SMITH
(Steve)
Running Back—Los Angeles Raiders
Born August 30, 1964, at Washington, D. C.
Height, 6.01. Weight, 235.
High School—Hyattsville, Md., DeMatha Catholic.
Received degree in hotel, restaurant and institutional management
from Penn State University in 1987.

Selected by Los Angeles Raiders in 3rd round (81st player selected) of 1987 NFL draft.
Signed by Los Angeles Raiders, July 22, 1987.
On injured reserve with knee injury, September 16 through October 23, 1987; activated, October 24, 1987.
On injured reserve with knee and ankle injuries, December 3 through remainder of 1987 season.

Year Club	G.	RUSHING Att.	Yds.	Avg.	TD.	PASS RECEIVING P.C.	Yds.	Avg.	TD.	TOTAL TD.	Pts.	F.
1987—Los Angeles Raiders NFL	7	5	18	3.6	0	3	46	15.3	0	0	0	0
1988—Los Angeles Raiders NFL	16	38	162	4.3	3	26	299	11.5	6	9	54	1
Pro Totals—2 Years	23	43	180	4.2	3	29	345	11.9	6	9	54	1

Additional pro statistics: Recovered one fumble, 1987 and 1988; returned three kickoffs for 46 yards, 1988.

TIMMY SMITH
Running Back—San Diego Chargers
Born January 21, 1964, at Hobbs, N. M.
Height, 5.11. Weight, 216.
High School—Hobbs, N. M.
Attended Texas Tech University.

Selected by Washington in 5th round (117th player selected) of 1987 NFL draft.
Signed by Washington Redskins, July 24, 1987.
Granted unconditional free agency, February 1, 1989; signed by San Diego Chargers, April 1, 1989.

Year	Club	G.	Att.	Yds.	Avg.	TD.	P.C.	Yds.	Avg.	TD.	TD.	Pts.	F.
			——RUSHING——				PASS RECEIVING				—TOTAL—		
1987—Washington NFL		7	29	126	4.3	0	1	—2	—2.0	0	0	0	0
1988—Washington NFL		14	155	470	3.0	3	8	53	6.6	0	3	18	4
Pro Totals—2 Years		21	184	596	3.2	3	9	51	5.7	0	3	18	4

Additional pro statistics: Recovered one fumble, 1988.
Played in NFC Championship Game following 1987 season.
Played in NFL Championship Game following 1987 season.

VINSON ROBERT SMITH
Linebacker—Pittsburgh Steelers
Born July 3, 1965, at Statesville, N. C.
Height, 6.02. Weight, 230.
High School—Statesville, N. C.
Received degree from East Carolina University in 1989.

Signed as free agent by Atlanta Falcons, May 2, 1988.
On injured reserve with elbow injury, August 29 through November 2, 1988; activated after clearing procedural waivers, November 4, 1988.
On injured reserve with knee injury, December 10 through remainder of 1988 season.
Granted unconditional free agency, February 1, 1989; signed by Pittsburgh Steelers, February 28, 1989.
Atlanta NFL, 1988.
Games: 1988 (3).

ANGELO BERNARD SNIPES
Linebacker—Kansas City Chiefs
Born January 11, 1963, at Atlanta, Ga.
Height, 6.00. Weight, 227.
High School—Atlanta, Ga., Walker.
Attended West Georgia College.

Selected by Oakland in 14th round (196th player selected) of 1985 USFL draft.
Signed by Oakland Invaders, Jaunary 23, 1985.
Traded with guard Reggie Irving and defensive tackle Bob Standifer by Oakland Invaders to Memphis Showboats for past considerations, February 28, 1986.
Granted free agency when USFL suspended operations, August 7, 1986; signed as free agent by Washington Redskins, August 11, 1986.
Granted roster exemption, August 11 through August 22, 1986; activated, Augut 23, 1986.
Released by Washington Redskins, November 11, 1986; awarded on waivers to San Diego Chargers, November 12, 1986.
Released by San Diego Chargers, October 27, 1987; signed as free agent by Kansas City Chiefs, December 2, 1987.
Oakland USFL, 1985; Washington (10)-San Diego (6) NFL, 1986; San Diego (2)-Kansas City (4) NFL, 1987; Kansas City NFL, 1988.
Games: 1985 (18), 1986 (16), 1987 (6), 1988 (15). Total NFL—37. Total Pro—55.
USFL statistics: Credited with 11½ sacks for 93 yards, returned one kickoff for 10 yards and recovered one fumble, 1985.
NFL statistics: Recovered one fumble, 1986 and 1988.
Played in USFL Championship Game following 1985 season.

BRYAN SOCHIA
Name pronounced So-SHAY.
Nose Tackle—Miami Dolphins
Born July 21, 1961, at Massena, N.Y.
Height, 6.03. Weight, 274.
High School—Brasher Falls, N.Y., St. Lawrence Central.
Attended Northwestern Oklahoma State University.

Signed as free agent by Houston Oilers, June 2, 1983.
On injured reserve with knee and ankle injuries, August 29 through September 26, 1983; activated after clearing procedural waivers, September 27, 1983.
Granted free agency, February 1, 1986; re-signed by Oilers, October 21, 1986.
Granted roster exemption, October 21 through November 2, 1986.
Released by Houston Oilers, November 3, 1986; signed as free agent by Miami Dolphins, November 12, 1986.
Houston NFL, 1983 through 1985; Miami NFL, 1986 through 1988.
Games: 1983 (12), 1984 (16), 1985 (16), 1986 (6), 1987 (12), 1988 (16). Total—78.
Pro statistics: Recovered two fumbles, 1988.
Played in Pro Bowl (NFL All-Star Game) following 1988 season.

JESSE WILLIAM SOLOMON
Linebacker—Minnesota Vikings
Born November 4, 1963, at Madison, Fla.
Height, 6.00. Weight, 235.
High School—Madison, Fla.
Attended North Florida Junior College and received bachelor of science degree
in political science from Florida State University in 1986.

Selected by Tampa Bay in 1986 USFL territorial draft.

Selected by Minnesota in 12th round (318th player selected) of 1986 NFL draft.
Signed by Minnesota Vikings, July 27, 1986.

			—INTERCEPTIONS—			
Year	Club	G.	No.	Yds.	Avg.	TD.
1986—Minnesota NFL............		13	2	34	17.0	0
1987—Minnesota NFL............		12	1	30	30.0	0
1988—Minnesota NFL............		16	4	84	21.0	1
Pro Totals—3 Years............		41	7	148	21.1	1

Additional pro statistics: Recovered two fumbles, 1986; recovered one fumble for 33 yards, 1987; recovered two fumbles for three yards, 1988.
Played in NFC Championship Game following 1987 season.

RONALD MATTHEW SOLT
(Ron)
Guard—Philadelphia Eagles
Born May 19, 1962, at Bainebridge, Md.
Height, 6.03. Weight, 285.
High School—Wilkes-Barre, Pa., James M. Coughlin.
Attended University of Maryland.

Selected by Washington in 1984 USFL territorial draft.
Selected by Indianapolis in 1st round (19th player selected) of 1984 NFL draft.
Signed by Indianapolis Colts, August 11, 1984.
On injured reserve with knee injury, December 17 through remainder of 1985 season.
Granted free agency, February 1, 1988; re-signed by Colts, September 28, 1988.
Traded by Indianapolis Colts to Philadelphia Eagles for 1st round pick in 1989 draft and 4th round pick in 1990 draft, October 5, 1988.
On injured reserve with knee injury, November 12 through remainder of 1988 season.
Indianapolis NFL, 1984 through 1987; Indianapolis (1)-Philadelphia (1) NFL, 1988.
Games: 1984 (16), 1985 (15), 1986 (16), 1987 (12), 1988 (2). Total—61.
Pro statistics: Recovered one fumble, 1984.
Played in Pro Bowl (NFL All-Star Game) following 1987 season.

JOHN STEPHEN SPAGNOLA
Tight End—Green Bay Packers
Born August 1, 1957, at Bethlehem, Pa.
Height, 6.04. Weight, 240.
High School—Bethlehem, Pa., Catholic.
Received bachelor of arts degree in political science from Yale University in 1980.

Selected by New England in 9th round (245th player selected) of 1979 NFL draft.
Released by New England Patriots, August 20, 1979; signed as free agent by Philadelphia Eagles, August 27, 1979.
On injured reserve with back injury, August 30 through entire 1983 season.
Released by Philadelphia Eagles, August 24, 1988; signed as free agent by Seattle Seahawks, August 29, 1988.
Granted unconditional free agency, February 1, 1989; signed by Green Bay Packers, March 31, 1989.

			—PASS RECEIVING—			
Year	Club	G.	P.C.	Yds.	Avg.	TD.
1979—Philadelphia NFL		16	2	24	12.0	0
1980—Philadelphia NFL		16	18	193	10.7	3
1981—Philadelphia NFL		11	6	83	13.8	0
1982—Philadelphia NFL		9	26	313	12.0	2
1984—Philadelphia NFL		16	65	701	10.8	1
1985—Philadelphia NFL		16	64	772	12.1	5
1986—Philadelphia NFL		15	39	397	10.2	1
1987—Philadelphia NFL		12	36	350	9.7	2
1988—Seattle NFL..................		16	5	40	8.0	1
Pro Totals—9 Years............		127	261	2873	11.0	15

Additional pro statistics: Recovered one fumble, 1979 through 1981 and 1986; returned one kickoff for no yards, 1980; fumbled twice, 1980, 1984, 1986 and 1987; fumbled once, 1985.
Played in NFC Championship Game following 1980 season.
Played in NFL Championship Game following 1980 season.

TIM SPENCER
Running Back—San Diego Chargers
Born December 10, 1960, at Martins Ferry, O.
Height, 6.01. Weight, 227.
High School—St. Clairsville, O., Richland.
Attended Ohio State University.

Selected by Chicago in 1st round (2nd player selected) of 1983 USFL draft.
Signed by Chicago Blitz, January 7, 1983.
Selected by San Diego in 11th round (307th player selected) of 1983 NFL draft.
Franchise transferred to Arizona, September 30, 1983.
Not protected in merger of Arizona Wranglers and Oklahoma Outlaws; selected by Memphis Showboats in USFL dispersal draft, December 6, 1984.
On developmental squad, February 21 through March 8, 1985; activated, March 9, 1985.
Granted free agency, August 1, 1985; signed by San Diego Chargers, August 2, 1985.
On developmental squad for 2 games with Memphis Showboats in 1985.

Year Club	G.	Att.	Yds.	Avg.	TD.	P.C.	Yds.	Avg.	TD.	TD.	Pts.	F.
			—RUSHING—				PASS RECEIVING				—TOTAL—	
1983—Chicago USFL	18	300	1157	3.9	6	38	362	9.5	2	8	48	2
1984—Arizona USFL	18	227	1212	5.3	17	46	589	12.8	2	19	114	3
1985—Memphis USFL	16	198	789	4.0	3	14	96	6.9	0	3	18	3
1985—San Diego NFL	16	124	478	3.9	10	11	135	12.3	0	10	60	1
1986—San Diego NFL	14	99	350	3.5	6	6	48	8.0	0	6	36	2
1987—San Diego NFL	12	73	228	3.1	0	17	123	7.2	0	0	0	1
1988—San Diego NFL	16	44	215	4.9	0	1	14	14.0	0	0	0	0
USFL Totals—3 Years	52	725	3158	4.4	26	98	1047	10.7	4	30	180	8
NFL Totals—4 Years	58	340	1271	3.7	16	35	320	9.1	0	16	96	4
Pro Totals—7 Years	110	1065	4429	4.2	42	133	1367	10.3	4	46	276	12

Additional USFL statistics: Attempted one pass with no completions, 1983; recovered one fumble, 1983 and 1985.

Additional NFL statistics: Returned five kickoffs for 81 yards and recovered one fumble, 1986; returned one kickoff for 16 yards, 1988.

Played in USFL Championship Game following 1984 season.

CHRIS SPIELMAN
Linebacker—Detroit Lions
Born October 11, 1965, at Canton, O.
Height, 6.00. Weight, 247.
High School—Massillon, O., Washington.
Attended Ohio State University.

Named as linebacker on THE SPORTING NEWS College All-America Team, 1986 and 1987.
Selected by Detroit in 2nd round (29th player selected) of 1988 NFL draft.
Signed by Detroit Lions, July 15, 1988.
Detroit NFL, 1988.
Games: 1988 (16).
Pro statistics: Recovered one fumble, 1988.

SYLVESTER STAMPS
Running Back—Tampa Bay Buccaneers
Born February 24, 1961, at Vicksburg, Miss.
Height, 5.07. Weight, 185.
High School—Vicksburg, Miss.
Attended Jackson State University.

Named as kickoff returner to THE SPORTING NEWS NFL All-Star Team, 1987.
Selected by Birmingham in 18th round (370th player selected) of 1984 USFL draft.
Signed by Birmingham Stallions, January 12, 1984.
Released by Birmingham Stallions, February 8, 1984; signed as free agent by Atlanta Falcons, May 2, 1984.
On injured reserve with hamstring injury, November 29 through remainder of 1984 season.
Released by Atlanta Falcons, September 2, 1985; re-signed by Falcons, December 6, 1985.
Released by Atlanta Falcons, December 7, 1985; re-signed by Falcons, December 10, 1985.
On injured reserve with hamstring injury, December 13 through remainder of 1986 season.
On injured reserve with foot injury, November 9 through December 11, 1987; activated, December 12, 1987.
On injured reserve with hamstring injury, November 4 through remainder of 1988 season.
Granted unconditional free agency, February 1, 1989; signed by Tampa Bay Buccaneers, February 23, 1989.

Year Club	G.	Att.	Yds.	Avg.	TD.	P.C.	Yds.	Avg.	TD.	TD.	Pts.	F.
			—RUSHING—				PASS RECEIVING				—TOTAL—	
1984—Atlanta NFL	10	3	15	5.0	0	4	48	12.0	0	0	0	2
1985—Atlanta NFL	2		None				None			0	0	0
1986—Atlanta NFL	14	30	220	7.3	0	20	221	11.1	1	1	6	4
1987—Atlanta NFL	7	1	6	6.0	0	4	40	10.0	0	1	6	1
1988—Atlanta NFL	4	3	0	0.0	0	5	22	4.4	0	0	0	1
Pro Totals—5 Years	37	37	241	6.5	0	33	331	10.0	1	2	12	8

		KICKOFF RETURNS			
Year Club	G.	No.	Yds.	Avg.TD.	
1984—Atlanta NFL	10	19	452	23.8	0
1985—Atlanta NFL	2	4	89	22.3	0
1986—Atlanta NFL	14	24	514	21.4	0
1987—Atlanta NFL	7	24	660	★27.5	1
1988—Atlanta NFL	4	12	219	18.3	0
Pro Totals—5 Years	37	83	1934	23.3	1

Additional pro statistics: Returned one punt for eight yards, 1986; recovered one fumble, 1986 and 1987.

BOB EUGENE STANDIFER
Defensive Tackle—Kansas City Chiefs
Born June 3, 1963, at Chattanooga, Tenn.
Height, 6.05. Weight, 277.
High School—Chattanooga, Tenn., Central.
Received bachelor of science degree in business management
from University of Tennessee at Chattanooga.

Selected by Oakland in 1st round (7th player selected) of 1985 USFL draft.
Signed by Oakland Invaders, January 23, 1985.
Released by Oakland Invaders, February 11, 1985; re-signed by Invaders, February 21, 1985.

On developmental squad, February 21 through May 10, 1985; activated, May 11, 1985.
On developmental squad, May 23 through June 14, 1985; activated, June 15, 1985.
Traded with guard Reggie Irving and linebacker Angelo Snipes by Oakland Invaders to Memphis Showboats for past considerations, February 28, 1986.
Granted free agency when USFL suspended operations, August 7, 1986; signed as free agent by San Francisco 49ers, March 17, 1987.
Released by San Francisco 49ers, August 24, 1987; re-signed by 49ers, September 24, 1987.
On injured reserve with pulled abdomen muscle, October 12 through December 14, 1987.
Released by San Francisco 49ers, December 15, 1987; signed as free agent by Kansas City Chiefs, March 28, 1988.
On reserve/retired list, August 11 through entire 1988 season.
Reinstated by Kansas City Chiefs, May 10, 1989.
On developmental squad for 14 games with Oakland Invaders in 1985.
Oakland USFL, 1985.
Games: 1985 (4).
On developmental squad for USFL Championship Game following 1985 season.

WALTER STANLEY
Wide Receiver-Punt Returner—Green Bay Packers
Born November 5, 1962, at Chicago, Ill.
Height, 5.09. Weight, 180.
High School—Chicago, Ill., South Shore.
Attended University of Colorado and Mesa College (Colo.).

Selected by Memphis in 4th round (54th player selected) of 1985 USFL draft.
Selected by Green Bay in 4th round (98th player selected) of 1985 NFL draft.
Signed by Green Bay Packers, July 19, 1985.
On injured reserve with separated shoulder, October 18 through remainder of 1988 season.

| | | | PASS RECEIVING | | | | –PUNT RETURNS– | | | | —KICKOFF RET.— | | | | —TOTAL— | | |
Year	Club	G.	P.C.	Yds.	Avg.	TD.	No.	Yds.	Avg.	TD.	No.	Yds.	Avg.	TD.	TD.	Pts.	F.
1985—Green Bay NFL		13			None		14	179	12.8	0	9	212	23.6	0	0	0	2
1986—Green Bay NFL		16	35	723	20.7	2	33	316	9.6	1	28	559	20.0	0	3	18	1
1987—Green Bay NFL		12	38	672	17.7	3	28	173	6.2	0	3	47	15.7	0	3	18	5
1988—Green Bay NFL		7	28	436	15.6	0	12	52	4.3	0	2	39	19.5	0	0	0	3
Pro Totals—4 Years		48	101	1831	18.1	5	87	720	8.3	1	42	857	20.4	0	6	36	11

Additional pro statistics: Rushed once for 19 yards, 1986; rushed four times for 38 yards and recovered three fumbles, 1987; rushed once for one yard and recovered one fumble, 1988.

ROHN TAYLOR STARK
(First name pronounced Ron).
Punter—Indianapolis Colts
Born May 4, 1959, at Minneapolis, Minn.
Height, 6.03. Weight, 204.
High School—Pine River, Minn.
Attended United States Air Force Academy Prep School and received degree in finance from Florida State University.

Named as punter on THE SPORTING NEWS College All-America Team, 1981.
Led NFL in punting yards with 4,124 in 1983.
Selected by Baltimore in 2nd round (34th player selected) of 1982 NFL draft.
Franchise transferred to Indianapolis, March 31, 1984.

| | | ——PUNTING—— | | | |
Year	Club	G.	No.	Avg.	Blk.
1982—Baltimore NFL		9	46	44.4	0
1983—Baltimore NFL		16	91	*45.3	0
1984—Indianapolis NFL		16	*98	44.7	0
1985—Indianapolis NFL		16	78	*45.9	*2
1986—Indianapolis NFL		16	76	*45.2	0
1987—Indianapolis NFL		12	61	40.0	*2
1988—Indianapolis NFL		16	64	43.5	0
Pro Totals—7 Years		101	514	44.4	4

Additional pro statistics: Rushed once for eight yards, 1982 and 1983; attempted one pass with no completions, 1982, 1983 and 1985; fumbled once, 1982 and 1986; rushed twice for no yards and attempted one pass with one interception, 1984; recovered one fumble, 1984 through 1986.
Played in Pro Bowl (NFL All-Star Game) following 1985 and 1986 seasons.

STEPHEN DALE STARRING
First name pronounced Steff-in.
Wide Receiver—Detroit Lions
Born July 30, 1961, at Baton Rouge, La.
Height, 5.10. Weight, 172.
High School—Vinton, La.
Received degree in physical education from McNeese State University in 1985.

Selected by Washington in 3rd round (28th player selected) of 1983 USFL draft.
Selected by New England in 3rd round (74th player selected) of 1983 NFL draft.
Signed by New England Patriots, May 16, 1983.
Granted free agency, February 1, 1988; re-signed by Patriots and traded to Tampa Bay Buccaneers for 3rd round pick in 1989 draft, August 26, 1988.

On injured reserve with shoulder injury, October 18 through November 7, 1988.
Released by Tampa Bay Buccaneers, November 8, 1988; awarded on waivers to Detroit Lions, November 9, 1988.

Year Club	G.	-PASS RECEIVING-				-PUNT RETURNS-				—TOTAL—		
		P.C.	Yds.	Avg.	TD.	No.	Yds.	Avg.	TD.	TD.	Pts.	F.
1983—New England NFL	15	17	389	22.9	2		None			2	12	1
1984—New England NFL	16	46	657	14.3	4	10	73	7.3	0	4	24	1
1985—New England NFL	16	16	235	14.7	0	2	0	0.0	0	0	0	4
1986—New England NFL	14	16	295	18.4	2	6	18	3.0	0	2	12	4
1987—New England NFL	11	17	289	17.0	3	1	17	17.0	0	3	18	2
1988—Tampa Bay (6)-Detroit (6) NFL	12	8	164	20.5	0		None			0	0	0
Pro Totals—6 Years	84	120	2029	16.9	11	19	108	5.7	0	11	66	12

Year Club	G.	KICKOFF RETURNS			
		No.	Yds.	Avg.	TD.
1983—New England NFL	15		None		
1984—New England NFL	16		None		
1985—New England NFL	16	48	1012	21.1	0
1986—New England NFL	14	36	802	22.3	0
1987—New England NFL	11	23	445	19.3	0
1988—T.B. (6)-Det. (6) NFL	12	8	130	16.3	0
Pro Totals—6 Years	84	115	2389	20.8	0

Additional pro statistics: Recovered one fumble for eight yards and rushed twice for minus 16 yards, 1984; recovered one fumble, 1985 and 1987; rushed once for no yards and recovered two fumbles for minus five yards, 1986; rushed twice for 13 yards, 1987.
Played in AFC Championship Game following 1985 season.
Played in NFL Championship Game following 1985 season.

JASON CHARLES STAUROVSKY

(Named pronounced Star-OFF-ski.)

Placekicker—New England Patriots

Born March 23, 1963, at Tulsa, Okla.
Height, 5.09. Weight, 170.
High School—Tulsa, Okla., Bishop Kelley.
Received bachelor of science degree in finance from
The University of Tulsa.

Signed as free agent by Buffalo Bills, May 6, 1986.
Released by Buffalo Bills, August 18, 1986; signed as free agent by New Orleans Saints, June 26, 1987.
Released by New Orleans Saints, August 9, 1987; signed as free agent by St. Louis Cardinals, September 4, 1987.
Released by St. Louis Cardinals, September 7, 1987; re-signed as replacement player by Cardinals, September 25, 1987.
Released by St. Louis Cardinals, October 20, 1987; signed as free agent by New England Patriots, April 20, 1988.
Released by New England Patriots, August 17, 1988; re-signed by Patriots, October 27, 1988.
Granted unconditional free agency, February 1, 1989; did not receive qualifying offer, April 15, 1989.
Re-signed by New England Patriots, May 25, 1989.

Year Club	G.	——PLACE KICKING——				
		XP.	XPM.	FG.	FGA.	Pts.
1987—St. Louis NFL	2	6	0	1	3	9
1988—New England NFL	8	14	1	7	11	35
Pro Totals—2 Years	10	20	1	8	14	44

TROY M. STEDMAN

Linebacker—Pittsburgh Steelers

Born May 19, 1965, at Cedar Falls, Ia.
Height, 6.03. Weight, 243.
High School—Cedar Falls, Ia.
Attended Kirkwood Community College (did not play football),
Iowa Central Community College and Washburn University.

Selected by Kansas City in 7th round (170th player selected) of 1988 NFL draft.
Signed by Kansas City Chiefs, July 12, 1988.
Released by Kansas City Chiefs, August 30, 1988; re-signed by Chiefs, November 16, 1988.
Granted unconditional free agency, February 1, 1989; signed by Pittsburgh Steelers, March 13, 1989.
Kansas City NFL, 1988.
Games: 1988 (5).

DEAN STEINKUHLER

Name pronounced Stine-cooler.

Offensive Tackle—Houston Oilers

Born January 27, 1961, at Burr, Neb.
Height, 6.03. Weight, 291.
High School—Sterling, Neb.
Attended University of Nebraska.

Outland Trophy winner, 1983.
Named as guard on THE SPORTING NEWS College All-America Team, 1983.
Selected by Arizona in 6th round (116th player selected) of 1984 USFL draft.
Signed by Houston Oilers, April 30, 1984.

Selected officially by Houston in 1st round (2nd player selected) of 1984 NFL draft.
On injured reserve with knee injury, November 5 through remainder of 1984 season.
On injured reserve with knee injury, October 11 through December 19, 1985; activated, December 20, 1985.
Active for 6 games with Houston Oilers in 1985; did not play.
Houston NFL, 1984 through 1988.
Games: 1984 (10), 1986 (16), 1987 (11), 1988 (16). Total—53.
Pro statistics: Recovered two fumbles, 1986 and 1988.

MICHAEL IVER STENSRUD
Name pronounced STENS-rude.
(Mike)
Nose Tackle—Kansas City Chiefs
Born February 19, 1956, at Forest City, Ia.
Height, 6.05. Weight, 280.
High School—Lake Mills, Ia.
Received degree in agricultural administration from Iowa State University.

Selected by Houston in 2nd round (31st player selected) of 1979 NFL draft.
On injured reserve with knee injury, September 21 through November 16, 1979; activated, November 17, 1979.
Released by Houston Oilers, September 1, 1986; signed as free agent by Minnesota Vikings, October 1, 1986.
Released by Minnesota Vikings, September 1, 1987; signed as free agent by Tampa Bay Buccaneers, September 3, 1987.
Granted free agency, February 1, 1988; withdrew qualifying offer, May 9, 1988.
Signed by Kansas City Chiefs, July 7, 1988.
On injured reserve with pulled hamstring, November 30 through remainder of 1988 season.
Houston NFL, 1979 through 1985; Minnesota NFL, 1986; Tampa Bay NFL, 1987; Kansas City NFL, 1988.
Games: 1979 (6), 1980 (16), 1981 (16), 1982 (9), 1983 (16), 1984 (16), 1985 (16), 1986 (11), 1987 (12), 1988 (13). Total—131.
Pro statistics: Recovered one fumble, 1981 through 1985; intercepted one pass for no yards, 1985; intercepted one pass for five yards, 1988.
Played in AFC Championship Game following 1979 season.

SCOTT STEPHEN
Linebacker—Green Bay Packers
Born June 18, 1964, at Los Angeles, Calif.
Height, 6.02. Weight, 232.
High School—Los Angeles, Calif., Manual Arts.
Attended Arizona State University.

Selected by Green Bay in 3rd round (69th player selected) of 1987 NFL draft.
Signed by Green Bay Packers, July 29, 1987.
Green Bay NFL, 1987 and 1988.
Games: 1987 (8), 1988 (16). Total—24.

JOHN MILTON STEPHENS
Running Back—New England Patriots
Born February 23, 1966, at Shreveport, La.
Height, 6.01. Weight, 220.
High School—Springhill, La.
Attended Northwestern State University.

Selected by New England in 1st round (17th player selected) of 1988 NFL draft.
Signed by New England Patriots, July 29, 1988.

| | | ——RUSHING—— | | | | PASS RECEIVING | | | | —TOTAL— | | |
Year Club	G.	Att.	Yds.	Avg.	TD.	P.C.	Yds.	Avg.	TD.	TD.	Pts.	F.
1988—New England NFL	16	297	1168	3.9	4	14	98	7.0	0	5	30	3

Additional pro statistics: Recovered three fumbles for four yards (including one in end zone for a touchdown), 1988.
Played in Pro Bowl (NFL All-Star Game) following 1988 season.

MICHAEL STEWART
Safety—Los Angeles Rams
Born July 12, 1965, at Atascadero, Calif.
Height, 5.11. Weight, 195.
High School—Bakersfield, Calif.
Attended Bakersfield College and Fresno State University.

Selected by Los Angeles Rams in 8th round (213th player selected) of 1987 NFL draft.
Signed by Los Angeles Rams, July 6, 1987.
Selected by Milwaukee Brewers' organization in 29th round of free-agent draft, June 4, 1984.
Selected by Minnesota Twins' organization in 26th round of free-agent draft, June 2, 1986.
Selected by Toronto Blue Jays' organization in 49th round of free-agent draft, June 2, 1987.
Los Angeles Rams NFL, 1987 and 1988.
Games: 1987 (12), 1988 (16). Total—28.
Pro statistics: Credited with a safety, 1987; intercepted two passes for 61 yards, returned one kickoff for no yards and recovered two fumbles for 24 yards, 1988.

ARTHUR BARRY STILL
(Art)
Defensive End—Buffalo Bills

Born December 5, 1955, at Camden, N.J.
Height, 6.07. Weight, 257.
High School—Camden, N.J.
Received bachelor of arts degree in general studies from University of Kentucky in 1978.

Named as defensive end on THE SPORTING NEWS College All-America Team, 1977.
Named to THE SPORTING NEWS NFL All-Star Team, 1980.
Selected by Kansas City in 1st round (2nd player selected) of 1978 NFL draft.
On injured reserve with knee injury, September 23 through October 30, 1981; activated, October 31, 1981.
On injured reserve with knee injury, November 5 through remainder of 1985 season.
Traded by Kansas City Chiefs to Buffalo Bills for 8th round pick in 1989 draft, June 23, 1988.
Kansas City NFL, 1978 through 1987; Buffalo NFL, 1988.
Games: 1978 (16), 1979 (16), 1980 (16), 1981 (11), 1982 (9), 1983 (15), 1984 (16), 1985 (9), 1986 (16), 1987 (12), 1988 (15). Total—151.
Pro statistics: Recovered one fumble, 1978, 1980, 1981, 1983 and 1988; recovered one fumble for 13 yards, 1979; recovered one fumble for four yards, 1982; recovered one fumble for three yards, 1984; recovered two fumbles, 1985 and 1986.
Played in AFC Championship Game following 1988 season.
Played in Pro Bowl (NFL All-Star Game) following 1980 through 1982 and 1984 seasons.

KENNETH LEE STILLS
(Ken)
Defensive Back—Green Bay Packers

Born September 6, 1963, at Oceanside, Calif.
Height, 5.10. Weight, 185.
High School—Oceanside, Calif., El Camino.
Attended El Camino College and University of Wisconsin.

Selected by Jacksonville in 1985 USFL territorial draft.
Selected by Green Bay in 8th round (209th player selected) of 1985 NFL draft.
Signed by Green Bay Packers, July 19, 1985.
Released by Green Bay Packers, September 2, 1985; re-signed by Packers, October 30, 1985.
On injured reserve with bruised thigh, December 10 through remainder of 1988 season.

| | | KICKOFF RETURNS | | | |
Year Club	G.	No.	Yds.	Avg.	TD.
1985—Green Bay NFL	8	1	14	14.0	0
1986—Green Bay NFL	16	10	209	20.9	0
1987—Green Bay NFL	11			None	
1988—Green Bay NFL	14	3	29	9.7	0
Pro Totals—4 Years	49	14	252	18.0	0

Additional pro statistics: Intercepted one pass for 58 yards and a touchdown and fumbled once, 1986; recovered one fumble, 1987; returned one kickoff for four yards and returned three fumbles for four yards, 1988.

LEMUEL DALE STINSON
Defensive Back—Chicago Bears

Born May 10, 1966, at Houston, Tex.
Height, 5.09. Weight, 159.
High School—Houston, Tex., Evan E. Worthing.
Attended Texas Tech University.

Selected by Chicago in 6th round (161st player selected) of 1988 NFL draft.
Signed by Chicago Bears, June 30, 1988.
Chicago NFL, 1988.
Games: 1988 (15).
Played in NFC Championship Game following 1988 season.

LOUIS FRED STOKES
(Known by middle name.)
Defensive End—Washington Redskins

Born March 14, 1964, at Vidalia, Ga.
Height, 6.03. Weight, 262.
High School—Vidalia, Ga.
Attended Georgia Southern College.

Selected by Los Angeles Rams in 12th round (332nd player selected) of 1987 NFL draft.
Signed by Los Angeles Rams, July 18, 1987.
On injured reserve with shoulder injury, September 7 through November 6, 1987; activated, November 7, 1987.
On injured reserve with ankle injury, October 8 through remainder of 1988 season.
Granted unconditional free agency, February 1, 1989; signed by Washington Redskins, March 20, 1989.
Los Angeles Rams NFL, 1987 and 1988.
Games: 1987 (8), 1988 (5). Total—13.
Pro statistics: Recovered two fumbles, 1988.

DWIGHT STONE
Running Back-Kick Returner—Pittsburgh Steelers
Born January 28, 1964, at Florala, Ala.
Height, 6.00. Weight, 188.
High Schools—Florala, Ala.; and Marion, Ala., Marion Military Institute.
Attended Middle Tennessee State University.

Signed as free agent by Pittsburgh Steelers, May 19, 1987.
Crossed picket line during players' strike, October 7, 1987.

		—RUSHING—				PASS RECEIVING				—TOTAL—		
Year Club	G.	Att.	Yds.	Avg.	TD.	P.C.	Yds.	Avg.	TD.	TD.	Pts.	F.
1987—Pittsburgh NFL	14	17	135	7.9	0	1	22	22.0	0	0	0	0
1988—Pittsburgh NFL	16	40	127	3.2	0	11	196	17.8	1	2	12	5
Pro Totals—2 Years	30	57	262	4.6	0	12	218	18.2	1	2	12	5

		KICKOFF RETURNS			
Year Club	G.	No.	Yds.	Avg.	TD.
1987—Pittsburgh NFL	14	28	568	20.3	0
1988—Pittsburgh NFL	16	29	610	21.0	*1
Pro Totals—2 Years	30	57	1178	20.7	1

Additional pro statistics: Recovered one fumble, 1987.

CLIFFORD LEWIS STOUDT
(Cliff)
Quarterback—Miami Dolphins
Born March 27, 1955, at Oberlin, O.
Height, 6.04. Weight, 218.
High School—Oberlin, O.
Attended Youngstown State University.

Selected by Pittsburgh in 5th round (121st player selected) of 1977 NFL draft.
On injured reserve with broken arm, November 12 through remainder of 1981 season.
On inactive list, September 13, 1982.
Signed by Birmingham Stallions, January 10, 1984, for contract to take effect after being granted free agency, February 1, 1984.
Granted free agency when USFL suspended operations, August 7, 1986; re-signed by Pittsburgh Steelers and traded to St. Louis Cardinals for 5th round pick in 1988 draft, September 2, 1986.
Franchise transferred to Phoenix, March 15, 1988.
Granted free agency, February 1, 1989; rights released, March 14, 1989.
Signed by Miami Dolphins, April 14, 1989.
Active for 11 games with Pittsburgh Steelers in 1977; did not play.
Active for 16 games with Pittsburgh Steelers in 1978 and 1979; did not play.

		—PASSING—							—RUSHING—				—TOTAL—		
Year Club	G.	Att.	Cmp.	Pct.	Gain	T.P.	P.I.	Avg.	Att.	Yds.	Avg.	TD.	TD.	Pts.	F.
1980—Pittsburgh NFL	6	60	32	53.3	493	2	2	8.22	9	35	3.9	0	0	0	1
1981—Pittsburgh NFL	2	3	1	33.3	17	0	0	5.67	3	11	3.7	0	0	0	0
1982—Pittsburgh NFL	6	35	14	40.0	154	0	5	4.40	11	28	2.5	0	0	0	0
1983—Pittsburgh NFL	16	381	197	51.7	2553	12	21	6.70	77	479	6.2	4	4	24	10
1984—Birmingham USFL	17	366	212	57.9	3121	26	7	8.53	68	440	6.5	9	9	†56	1
1985—Birmingham USFL	18	444	266	59.9	3358	34	19	7.56	80	437	5.5	5	5	30	9
1986—St. Louis NFL	5	91	52	57.1	542	3	7	5.96	7	53	7.6	0	0	0	1
1987—St. Louis NFL	12	1	0	0.0	0	0	0	0.00	1	—2	—2.0	0	0	0	0
1988—Phoenix NFL	16	113	63	55.8	747	6	8	6.61	14	57	4.1	0	0	0	4
NFL Totals—10 Years	63	684	359	52.5	4506	23	43	6.59	122	661	5.4	4	4	24	17
USFL Totals— 2 Years	35	810	478	59.0	6479	60	26	8.00	148	877	5.9	14	14	86	10
Pro Totals—12 Years	98	1494	837	56.0	10985	83	69	7.35	270	1538	5.7	18	18	110	27

†Includes one 2-point conversion.
NFL Quarterback Rating Points: 1980 (78.0), 1981 (53.5), 1982 (14.2), 1983 (60.6), 1986 (53.5), 1987 (39.6), 1988 (64.3). Total—58.4.
USFL Quarterback Rating Points: 1984 (101.6), 1985 (91.2). Total—95.9.
Additional NFL statistics: Recovered one fumble and fumbled once for minus two yards, 1980; recovered two fumbles, 1983 and 1988.
Additional USFL statistics: Recovered two fumbles, 1985.
Member of Pittsburgh Steelers for AFC and NFL Championship Game following 1978 and 1979 seasons; did not play.

KELLY WAYNE STOUFFER
Name pronounced STOFF-er.
Quarterback—Seattle Seahawks
. Born July 6, 1964, at Scottsbluff, Neb.
Height, 6.03. Weight, 210.
High School—Rushville, Neb.
Attended Garden City Community College and received bachelor of science degree in biology from Colorado State University.

Selected by St. Louis in 1st round (6th player selected) of 1987 NFL draft.
Placed on reserve/unsigned through entire 1987 season.
Franchise transferred to Phoenix, March 15, 1988.

Rights traded by Phoenix Cardinals to Seattle Seahawks for 5th round pick in 1988 draft and 1st and 5th round picks in 1989 draft, April 22, 1988.

Signed by Seattle Seahawks, April 22, 1988.

Year Club	G.	Att.	Cmp.	Pct.	Gain	T.P.	P.I.	Avg.	Att.	Yds.	Avg.	TD.	TD.	Pts.	F.
				PASSING						RUSHING				TOTAL	
1988—Seattle NFL	8	173	98	56.6	1106	4	6	6.39	19	27	1.4	0	0	0	5

Quarterback Rating Points: 1988 (69.2).

Additional pro statistics: Recovered one fumble and fumbled five times for minus 17 yards, 1988.

JEFF OWEN STOVER
Defensive End—San Francisco 49ers
Born May 22, 1958, at Corning, Calif.
Height, 6.05. Weight, 275.
High School—Corning, Calif., Union.
Attended University of Oregon.

Signed as free agent by San Francisco 49ers, April 20, 1982.
On injured reserve with knee injury, September 4 through November 15, 1984; activated, November 16, 1984.
Granted free agency, February 1, 1987; re-signed by 49ers, September 9, 1987.
Granted roster exemption, September 9 through September 11, 1987; activated, September 12, 1987.
On physically unable to perform/active with elbow injury, July 19 through August 15, 1988; passed physical, August 16, 1988.
On injured reserve with knee injury, October 18, 1988 through January 19, 1989; activated, January 20, 1989.
San Francisco NFL, 1982 through 1988.
Games: 1982 (9), 1983 (16), 1984 (1) 1985 (16), 1986 (15), 1987 (12), 1988 (7). Total—81.
Pro statistics: Recovered one fumble, 1982, 1983 and 1985.
Played in NFC Championship Game following 1983 and 1984 seasons.
Played in NFL Championship Game following 1984 and 1988 seasons.

TYRONNE KEVIN STOWE
Linebacker—Pittsburgh Steelers
Born May 30, 1965, at Passaic, N.J.
Height, 6.01. Weight, 232.
High School—Passaic, N.J.
Attended Rutgers University.

Signed as free agent by San Diego Chargers, April 30, 1987.
Released by San Diego Chargers, September 7, 1987; signed as replacement player by Pittsburgh Steelers, September 24, 1987.
Released by Pittsburgh Steelers, October 20, 1988; re-signed by Steelers, December 1, 1988.
Pittsburgh NFL, 1987 and 1988.
Games: 1987 (13), 1988 (10). Total—23.

STEPHEN MICHAEL STRACHAN
(Steve)
Running Back—Los Angeles Raiders
Born March 22, 1963, at Everett, Mass.
Height, 6.01. Weight, 250.
High School—Burlington, Mass.
Received bachelor of science degree in finance from Boston College in 1985.

Selected by Los Angeles Raiders in 11th round (303rd player selected) of 1985 NFL draft.
Signed by Los Angeles Raiders, June 28, 1985.
Released by Los Angeles Raiders, August 27, 1985; re-signed by Raiders, September 23, 1985.
On injured reserve with hamstring injury, October 23 through remainder of 1985 season.
Crossed picket line during players' strike, October 14, 1987.

Year Club	G.	Att.	Yds.	Avg.	TD.	P.C.	Yds.	Avg.	TD.	TD.	Pts.	F.
			RUSHING				PASS RECEIVING				TOTAL	
1985—Los Angeles Raiders NFL	4	2	1	0.5	0		None			0	0	0
1986—Los Angeles Raiders NFL	16	18	53	2.9	0		None			0	0	0
1987—Los Angeles Raiders NFL	11	28	108	3.9	0	4	42	10.5	0	0	0	1
1988—Los Angeles Raiders NFL	16	4	.12	3.0	0	3	19	6.3	1	1	6	2
Pro Totals—4 Years	47	52	174	3.3	0	7	61	8.7	1	1	6	3

Additional pro statistics: Recovered three fumbles, 1988.

TROY EDWIN STRADFORD
Running Back—Miami Dolphins
Born September 11, 1964, at Elizabeth, N.J.
Height, 5.09. Weight, 191.
High School—Linden, N.J.
Received bachelor of arts degree in communications from Boston College in 1987.

Selected by Miami in 4th round (99th player selected) of 1987 NFL draft.
Signed by Miami Dolphins, July 24, 1987.

Year Club	G.	Att.	Yds.	Avg.	TD.	P.C.	Yds.	Avg.	TD.	TD.	Pts.	F.
			RUSHING				PASS RECEIVING				TOTAL	
1987—Miami NFL	12	145	619	4.3	6	48	457	9.5	1	7	42	6
1988—Miami NFL	15	95	335	3.5	2	56	426	7.6	1	3	18	2
Pro Totals—2 Years	27	240	954	4.0	8	104	883	8.5	2	10	60	8

Year Club	G.	No.	Yds.	Avg.TD.	
1987—Miami NFL	12	14	258	18.4	0
1988—Miami NFL	15			None	
Pro Totals—2 Years............	27	14	258	18.4	0

Additional pro statistics: Attempted one pass with one completion for six yards and recovered two fumbles, 1987; attempted one pass with no completions, 1988.

THOMAS STRAUTHERS
(Tom)
Defensive End—Minnesota Vikings
Born April 6, 1961, at Wesson, Miss.
Height, 6.04. Weight, 265.
High School—Brookhaven, Miss.
Attended Jackson State University.

Selected by Oakland in 21st round (247th player selected) of 1983 USFL draft.
Selected by Philadelphia in 10th round (258th player selected) of 1983 NFL draft.
Signed by Philadelphia Eagles, June 15, 1983.
On injured reserve with broken hand, August 16 through November 23, 1983; activated by Philadelphia Eagles after clearing procedural waivers, November 25, 1983.
Granted free agency, Feburary 1, 1987; re-signed by Eagles, August 11, 1987.
Released by Philadelphia Eagles after failing physical, August 12, 1987; signed as free agent by Miami Dolphins, August 21, 1987.
Released by Miami Dolphins, September 7, 1987; signed as free agent by Atlanta Falcons, February 22, 1988.
Released by Atlanta Falcons, September 2, 1988; signed as free agent by Detroit Lions, October 5, 1988.
Granted unconditional free agency, February 1, 1989; signed by Minnesota Vikings, March 16, 1989.
Philadelphia NFL, 1983 through 1986; Detroit NFL, 1988.
Games: 1983 (4), 1984 (16), 1985 (16), 1986 (11), 1988 (10). Total—57.
Pro statistics: Returned one kickoff for 12 yards, 1984.

RICHARD GENE STRENGER
(Rich)
Offensive Tackle—Buffalo Bills
Born March 10, 1960, at Port Washington, Wis.
Height, 6.07. Weight, 285.
High School—Grafton, Wis.
Received bachelor of science degree in literature science and art from University of Michigan in 1983.

Selected by Michigan in 1983 USFL territorial draft.
Selected by Detroit in 2nd round (40th player selected) of 1983 NFL draft.
Signed by Detroit Lions, July 4, 1983.
On injured reserve with knee injury, September 4 through remainder of 1984 season.
On injured reserve with knee injury, October 31 through remainder of 1987 season.
Granted free agency with no qualifying offer, February 1, 1988; signed by Buffalo Bills, May 27, 1988.
On physically unable to perform/active with knee injury, July 21 through August 21, 1988; then transferred to physically unable to perform/reserve with knee injury, August 22 through entire 1988 season.
Detroit NFL, 1983 through 1987.
Games: 1983 (16), 1984 (1), 1985 (13), 1986 (16), 1987 (3). Total—49.

FREDRICK WILLIAM STRICKLAND JR.
(Fred)
Linebacker—Los Angeles Rams
Born August 15, 1966, at Ringwood, N.J.
Height, 6.02. Weight, 224.
High School—Wanaque, N.J., Lakeland Regional.
Attended Purdue University.

Selected by Los Angeles Rams in 2nd round (47th player selected) of 1988 NFL draft.
Signed by Los Angeles Rams, July 10, 1988.
Los Angeles Rams NFL, 1988.
Games: 1988 (16).
Pro statistics: Recovered two fumbles, 1988.

DONALD JOSEPH STROCK
(Don)
Quarterback
Born November 27, 1950, at Pottstown, Pa.
Height, 6.05. Weight, 220.
High School—Pottstown, Pa., Owen J. Roberts.
Received bachelor of science degree in distributive direction from
Virginia Technical University in 1973.
Brother of Dave Strock, placekicker with Florida Blazers (WFL), 1974.

Selected by Miami in 5th round (111th player selected) of 1973 NFL draft.
On did not report list, August 16 through September 4, 1983.
Reported and granted roster exemption, September 5, 1983; activated, September 9, 1983.
Granted free agency, February 1, 1988; rights released, August 8, 1988.

Signed by Cleveland Browns, September 13, 1988.
Granted unconditional free agency, February 1, 1989; did not receive qualifying offer, April 15, 1989.
Member of Miami Dolphins' taxi squad, 1973.

Year Club	G.	Att.	Cmp.	Pct.	Gain	T.P.	P.I.	Avg.	Att.	Yds.	Avg.	TD.	TD.	Pts.	F.
					PASSING					RUSHING				TOTAL	
1974—Miami NFL	1				None				1	—7	—7.0	0	0	0	0
1975—Miami NFL	6	45	26	57.8	230	2	2	5.11	6	38	6.3	1	1	6	1
1976—Miami NFL	4	47	21	44.7	359	3	2	7.64	2	13	6.5	1	1	6	1
1977—Miami NFL	4	4	2	50.0	12	0	1	3.00		None			0	0	0
1978—Miami NFL	16	135	72	53.3	825	12	6	6.11	10	23	2.3	0	0	0	4
1979—Miami NFL	16	100	56	56.0	830	6	6	8.30	3	18	6.0	0	0	0	3
1980—Miami NFL	16	62	30	48.4	313	1	5	5.05	1	—3	—3.0	0	0	0	1
1981—Miami NFL	16	130	79	60.8	901	6	8	6.93	14	—26	—1.9	0	0	0	0
1982—Miami NFL	9	55	30	54.5	306	2	5	5.56	3	—9	—3.0	0	0	0	1
1983—Miami NFL	15	52	34	65.4	403	4	1	7.75	6	—16	—2.7	0	0	0	0
1984—Miami NFL	16	6	4	66.7	27	0	0	4.50	2	—5	—2.5	0	0	0	1
1985—Miami NFL	16	9	7	77.8	141	1	0	15.67	2	—6	—3.0	0	0	0	0
1986—Miami NFL	16	20	14	70.0	152	2	0	7.60	1	0	0.0	0	0	0	1
1987—Miami NFL	12	23	13	56.5	114	0	1	4.96		None			0	0	0
1988—Cleveland NFL	4	91	55	60.4	736	6	5	8.09	6	—2	—0.3	0	0	0	4
Pro Totals—15 Years	167	779	443	56.9	5349	45	42	6.87	57	18	0.3	2	2	12	17

Quarterback Rating Points: 1975 (67.9), 1976 (74.6), 1977 (16.7), 1978 (83.3), 1979 (78.3), 1980 (35.1), 1981 (71.1), 1982 (44.8), 1983 (106.5), 1984 (76.4), 1985 (155.8), 1986 (125.4), 1987 (51.7), 1988 (85.2). Total—75.0.
Additional pro statistics: Recovered one fumble, 1975 and 1983; recovered one fumble and fumbled four times for minus five yards, 1978; fumbled once for minus three yards, 1982; fumbled once for minus two yards, 1984; recovered one fumble and fumbled once for minus four yards, 1986; punted nine times for a 30.8 average, 1987; recovered two fumbles and fumbled four times for minus two yards, 1988.
Played in AFC Championship Game following 1982, 1984 and 1985 seasons.
Played in NFL Championship Game following 1982 and 1984 seasons.

VINCE M. STROTH
Offensive Tackle—Houston Oilers
Born November 25, 1960, at San Jose, Calif.
Height, 6.04. Weight, 275.
High School—San Jose, Calif., Bellarmine.
Received degree in art history from Brigham Young University.
Selected by Arizona in 13th round (146th player selected) of 1983 USFL draft.
Signed by Arizona Wranglers, January 27, 1983.
On developmental squad, March 4 through March 31, 1983; activated, April 1, 1983.
Franchise transferred to Chicago, September 30, 1983.
Franchise disbanded, November 20, 1984.
Selected by New Jersey Generals in USFL dispersal draft, December 6, 1984.
Granted free agency, August 1, 1985; signed by San Francisco 49ers, December 18, 1985.
Released by San Francisco 49ers, August 19, 1986; signed as free agent by Kansas City Chiefs, April 27, 1987.
Released by Kansas City Chiefs, August 31, 1987; signed as free agent replacement player by Houston Oilers, October 1, 1987.
On injured reserve with knee injury, December 2 through remainder of 1987 season.
Granted free agency with no qualifying offer, February 1, 1988; signed by New York Jets, May 23, 1988.
Released by New York Jets, August 8, 1988; awarded on waivers to Houston Oilers, August 9, 1988.
On developmental squad for 4 games with Arizona Wranglers in 1983.
Arizona USFL 1983; Chicago USFL, 1984; New Jersey USFL, 1985; San Francisco NFL, 1985; Houston NFL, 1987 and 1988.
Games: 1983 (14), 1984 (6), 1985 USFL (18), 1985 NFL (1), 1987 (9), 1988 (6). Total USFL—38. Total NFL—16. Total Pro—54.
Pro statistics: Returned two kickoffs for 25 yards and recovered one fumble for four yards, 1984.

WILBUR LAMAR STROZIER
Tight End—Cleveland Browns
Born November 12, 1964, at LaGrange, Ga.
Height, 6.04. Weight, 255.
High School—LaGrange, Ga.
Attended University of Georgia.
Selected by Denver in 7th round (194th player selected) of 1987 NFL draft.
Signed by Denver Broncos, July 18, 1987.
Released by Denver Broncos, September 1, 1987; signed as free agent by Seattle Seahawks, September 8, 1987.
Released by Seattle Seahawks, August 30, 1988; signed as free agent by San Diego Chargers, October 13, 1988.
Released by San Diego Chargers, November 23, 1988; signed as free agent by Cleveland Browns, January 18, 1989.
Seattle NFL, 1987; San Diego NFL, 1988.
Games: 1987 (12), 1988 (6). Total—18.

DANIEL STUBBS II
Defensive End—San Francisco 49ers
Born January 3, 1965, at Long Branch, N.J.
Height, 6.04. Weight, 260.
High School—Little Silver, N.J., Red Bank Regional.
Received degree in criminal justice from University of Miami (Fla.) in 1988.

Named as defensive lineman on THE SPORTING NEWS College All-America Team, 1987.
Selected by San Francisco in 2nd round (33rd player selected) of 1988 NFL draft.
Signed by San Francisco 49ers, July 19, 1988.
San Francisco NFL, 1988.
Games: 1988 (16).
Pro statistics: Recovered one fumble, 1988.
Played in NFC Championship Game following 1988 season.
Played in NFL Championship Game following 1988 season.

DAVID DERALD STUDDARD
(Dave)
Offensive Tackle—Denver Broncos
Born November 22, 1955, at San Antonio, Tex.
Height, 6.04. Weight, 260.
High School—Pearsall, Tex.
Received degree in physical education from University of Texas.
Brother of Les Studdard, center with Kansas City Chiefs and Houston Oilers, 1982 and 1983; and
nephew of Howard Fest, guard with Cincinnati Bengals and Tampa Bay Buccaneers, 1968 through 1976.
Selected by Baltimore in 9th round (245th player selected) of 1978 NFL draft.
Released by Baltimore Colts, August 30, 1978; signed as free agent by Denver Broncos, January 31, 1979.
Crossed picket line during players' strike, October 1, 1987.
On physically unable to perform/active with knee injury, July 18 through August 28, 1988; passed physical, August 29, 1988.
On injured reserve with knee injury, August 30 through October 7, 1988; activated, October 8, 1988.
Denver NFL, 1979 through 1988.
Games: 1979 (16), 1980 (16), 1981 (16), 1982 (9), 1983 (16), 1984 (16), 1985 (16), 1986 (15), 1987 (14), 1988 (11). Total—145.
Pro statistics: Caught one pass for two yards and a touchdown, 1979 and 1986; recovered one fumble, 1980, 1983 and 1986; caught one pass for 10 yards, 1981; returned two kickoffs for eight yards, 1983; caught one pass for minus four yards, 1984; recovered two fumbles, 1985.
Played in AFC Championship Game following 1986 and 1987 seasons.
Played in NFL Championship Game following 1986 and 1987 seasons.

JOHN SCOTT STUDWELL
(Known by middle name.)
Linebacker—Minnesota Vikings
Born August 27, 1954, at Evansville, Ind.
Height, 6.02. Weight, 230.
High School—Evansville, Ind., Harrison.
Attended University of Illinois.
Selected by Minnesota in 9th round (250th player selected) of 1977 NFL draft.

			—INTERCEPTIONS—			
Year	Club	G.	No.	Yds.	Avg.	TD.
1977—Minnesota NFL		14	1	4	4.0	0
1978—Minnesota NFL		13		None		
1979—Minnesota NFL		14	1	18	18.0	0
1980—Minnesota NFL		16	1	4	4.0	0
1981—Minnesota NFL		16		None		
1982—Minnesota NFL		8	1	3	3.0	0
1983—Minnesota NFL		16		None		
1984—Minnesota NFL		16	1	20	20.0	0
1985—Minnesota NFL		14	2	20	10.0	0
1986—Minnesota NFL		15	1	2	2.0	0
1987—Minnesota NFL		12	2	26	13.0	0
1988—Minnesota NFL		16		None		
Pro Totals—12 Years		170	10	97	9.7	0

Additional pro statistics: Recovered one fumble for six yards and returned one kickoff for no yards, 1979; recovered one fumble, 1980, 1982, 1983 and 1987; recovered three fumbles, 1981; recovered four fumbles, 1986; recovered two fumbles, 1988.
Played in NFC Championship Game following 1977 and 1987 seasons.
Played in Pro Bowl (NFL All-Star Game) following 1987 and 1988 seasons.

MATTHEW JEROME SUHEY
(Matt)
Fullback—Chicago Bears
Born July 7, 1958, at Bellefonte, Pa.
Height, 5.11. Weight, 217.
High School—State College, Pa.
Received bachelor of science degree in marketing from Penn State University in 1980.
Grandson of Bob Higgins, end with Canton Bulldogs, 1920 and 1921; and son of Steve Suhey, guard with Pittsburgh Steelers, 1948 and 1949.
Selected by Chicago in 2nd round (46th player selected) of 1980 NFL draft.
Granted unconditional free agency, February 1, 1989; did not receive qualifying offer, April 15, 1989.
Re-signed by Chicago Bears, May 22, 1989.

Year Club	G.	RUSHING				PASS RECEIVING				TOTAL		
		Att.	Yds.	Avg.	TD.	P.C.	Yds.	Avg.	TD.	TD.	Pts.	F.
1980—Chicago NFL	16	22	45	2.0	0	7	60	8.6	0	0	0	1
1981—Chicago NFL	15	150	521	3.5	3	33	168	5.1	0	3	18	3
1982—Chicago NFL	9	70	206	2.9	3	36	333	9.3	0	3	18	2
1983—Chicago NFL	16	149	681	4.6	4	49	429	8.8	1	5	30	5
1984—Chicago NFL	16	124	424	3.4	4	42	312	7.4	2	6	36	6
1985—Chicago NFL	16	115	471	4.1	1	33	295	8.9	1	2	12	2
1986—Chicago NFL	16	84	270	3.2	2	24	235	9.8	0	2	12	1
1987—Chicago NFL	12	7	24	3.4	0	7	54	7.7	0	0	0	0
1988—Chicago NFL	16	87	253	2.9	2	20	154	7.7	0	2	12	1
Pro Totals—9 Years	132	808	2895	3.6	19	251	2040	8.1	4	23	138	21

Additional pro statistics: Returned 19 kickoffs for 406 yards (21.4 avg.) and returned one punt for four yards, 1980; recovered three fumbles, 1981; recovered one fumble, 1982, 1985 and 1988; attempted one pass with one completion for 74 yards and a touchdown, 1983; attempted one pass with no completions and recovered two fumbles, 1984; returned one kickoff for nine yards, 1987.

Played in NFC Championship Game following 1984, 1985 and 1988 seasons.

Played in NFL Championship Game following 1985 season.

WILLIAM SUTTON
(Mickey)
Cornerback—Green Bay Packers
Born August 28, 1960, at Greenville, Miss.
Height, 5.09. Weight, 172.
High School—Union City, Calif., Logan.
Attended University of Montana.

Signed as free agent by Hamilton Tiger-Cats, April 15, 1983.
Released by Hamilton Tiger-Cats, July 25, 1983; signed by Pittsburgh Maulers, September 2, 1983.
Franchise disbanded, October 25, 1984.
Selected by Birmingham Stallions in USFL dispersal draft, December 6, 1984.
Granted free agency, August 1, 1985; signed by Los Angeles Rams, May 17, 1986.
Crossed picket line during players' strike, October 14, 1987.
Granted unconditional free agency, February 1, 1989; signed by Green Bay Packers, March 21, 1989.

Year Club	G.	INTERCEPTIONS				PUNT RETURNS				KICKOFF RET.				TOTAL		
		No.	Yds.	Avg.	TD.	No.	Yds.	Avg.	TD.	No.	Yds.	Avg.	TD.	TD.	Pts.	F.
1983—Hamilton CFL	1	None				None				None				0	0	0
1984—Pittsburgh USFL	17	1	16	16.0	0	None				9	232	25.8	0	1	6	0
1985—Birmingham USFL	17	2	30	15.0	0	1	0	0.0	0	15	244	16.3	0	0	0	2
1986—L.A. Rams NFL	16	2	25	12.5	0	28	234	8.4	0	5	91	18.2	0	0	0	0
1987—L.A. Rams NFL	12	1	4	4.0	0	None				2	37	18.5	0	0	0	0
1988—L.A. Rams NFL	15	1	1	1.0	0	3	52	17.3	0	2	41	20.5	0	0	0	0
CFL Totals—1 Year	1	0	0	0.0	0	0	0	0.0	0	0	0	0.0	0	0	0	0
USFL Totals—2 Years	34	3	46	15.3	0	1	0	0.0	0	24	476	19.8	0	1	6	2
NFL Totals—3 Years	43	4	30	7.5	0	31	286	9.2	0	9	169	18.8	0	0	0	0
Pro Totals—6 Years	78	7	76	10.9	0	32	286	8.9	0	33	645	19.5	0	1	6	2

Additional CFL statistics: Recovered one fumble, 1983.
Additional USFL statistics: Recovered one fumble for 44 yards and a touchdown, 1984; recovered four fumbles, 1985.
Additional NFL statistics: Recovered one fumble, 1986; recovered two fumbles, 1987.

GEORGE SWARN
Running Back—Cleveland Browns
Born February 15, 1964, at Cincinnati, O.
Height, 5.11. Weight, 220.
High School—Mansfield, O., Malabar.
Attended Miami University (O.).

Selected by St. Louis in 5th round (118th player selected) of 1987 NFL draft.
Signed by St. Louis Cardinals, July 24, 1987.
Released by St. Louis Cardinals, September 7, 1987; signed as free agent replacement player by Cleveland Browns, October 15, 1987.
On injured reserve with ankle injury, December 25 through remainder of season.
On injured reserve with ankle injury, August 29 through entire 1988 season.
Cleveland NFL, 1987.
Games: 1987 (1).

HARRY SWAYNE
Defensive End—Tampa Bay Buccaneers
Born February 2, 1965, at Philadelphia, Pa.
Height, 6.05. Weight, 268.
High School—Philadelphia, Pa., Cardinal Dougherty.
Attended Rutgers University.

Selected by Tampa Bay in 7th round (190th player selected) of 1987 NFL draft.
Signed by Tampa Bay Buccaneers, July 18, 1987.
On injured reserve with fractured hand, September 8 through October 30, 1987; activated, October 31, 1987.
On injured reserve with neck injury, November 18 through remainder of 1988 season.
Tampa Bay NFL, 1987 and 1988.
Games: 1987 (8), 1988 (10). Total—18.

JAMES JOSEPH SWEENEY
(Jim)
Offensive Lineman—New York Jets
Born August 8, 1962, at Pittsburgh, Pa.
Height, 6.04. Weight, 270.
High School—Pittsburgh, Pa., Seton LaSalle.
Attended University of Pittsburgh.

Selected by Pittsburgh in 1984 USFL territorial draft.
Selected by New York Jets in 2nd round (37th player selected) of 1984 NFL draft.
Signed by New York Jets, July 12, 1984.
New York Jets NFL, 1984 through 1988.
Games: 1984 (10), 1985 (16), 1986 (16), 1987 (12), 1988 (16). Total—70.

KEVIN JOSEPH SWEENEY
Quarterback—San Francisco 49ers
Born November 16, 1963, at Bozeman, Mont.
Height, 6.00. Weight, 193.
High School—Fresno, Calif., Bullard.
Received bachelor of science degree in business finance from
Fresno State University in 1987.
Son of Bill Sweeney, head coach at Fresno State University.

Selected by Dallas in 7th round (180th player selected) of 1987 NFL draft.
Signed by Dallas Cowboys, July 19, 1987.
Released by Dallas Cowboys, September 7, 1987; re-signed as replacement player by Cowboys, September 23, 1987.
Granted unconditional free agency, February 1, 1989; signed by San Francisco 49ers, March 14, 1989.

				—PASSING—						—RUSHING—		—TOTAL—		
Year	Club	G.	Att.	Cmp.	Pct.	Gain	T.P.	P.I.	Avg.	Att.	Yds.	Avg.	TD.	TD. Pts. F.
1987—Dallas NFL		3	28	14	50.0	291	4	1	10.39	5	8	1.6	0	0 0 0
1988—Dallas NFL		3	78	33	42.3	314	3	5	4.03	6	34	5.7	0	0 0 3
Pro Totals—2 Years		6	106	47	44.3	605	7	6	5.71	11	42	3.8	0	0 0 3

Quarterback Rating Points: 1987 (111.8), 1988 (40.2). Total—61.1
Additional pro statistics: Recovered one fumble, 1987.

PAT SWILLING
Linebacker—New Orleans Saints
Born October 25, 1964, at Toccoa, Ga.
Height, 6.03. Weight, 242.
High School—Toccoa, Ga., Stephens County.
Attended Georgia Tech.

Selected by Jacksonville in 1986 USFL territorial draft.
Selected by New Orleans in 3rd round (60th player selected) of 1986 NFL draft.
Signed by New Orleans Saints, July 21, 1986.
New Orleans NFL, 1986 through 1988.
Games: 1986 (16), 1987 (12), 1988 (15). Total—43.
Pro statistics: Intercepted one pass for 10 yards and recovered three fumbles for one yard, 1987; recovered one fumble, 1988.

CRAIG AVERY SWOOPE
(Name pronounced Swope.)
Defensive Back—Indianapolis Colts
Born February 3, 1964, at Fort Pierce, Fla.
Height, 6.01. Weight, 214.
High School—Fort Pierce, Fla., Westwood.
Attended University of Illinois.

Selected by Orlando in 1986 USFL territorial draft.
Selected by Tampa Bay in 4th round (83rd player selected) of 1986 NFL draft.
Signed by Tampa Bay Buccaneers, June 27, 1986.
On injured reserve with hamstring injury, September 19 through November 2, 1987.
Released by Tampa Bay Buccaneers, November 3, 1987; awarded on waivers to Indianapolis Colts, November 4, 1987.
On injured reserve with dislocated elbow, September 6 through October 9, 1988; activated, October 10, 1988.
Tampa Bay NFL, 1986; Indianapolis NFL, 1987 and 1988.
Games: 1986 (15), 1987 (3), 1988 (11). Total—29.
Pro statistics: Intercepted one pass for 23 yards and recovered two fumbles, 1986; recovered one fumble for 15 yards, 1988.

PATRICK ROAMAN SWOOPES
Nose Tackle—New Orleans Saints
Born March 4, 1964, at Florence, Ala.
Height, 6.03. Weight, 280.
High School—Florence, Ala., Bradshaw.
Attended Mississippi State University.

Selected by New Jersey in 1986 USFL territorial draft.
Selected by New Orleans in 11th round (284th player selected) of 1986 NFL draft.

Signed by New Orleans Saints, July 14, 1986.
Released by New Orleans Saints, August 18, 1986; re-signed as replacement player by Saints, September 23, 1987.
Released by New Orleans Saints, August 30, 1988; signed as free agent by Hamilton Tiger-Cats, September 26, 1988.
Released by Hamilton Tiger-Cats, October 22, 1988; re-signed by New Orleans Saints, March 16, 1989.
New Orleans NFL, 1987; Hamilton CFL, 1988.
Games: 1987 (9), 1988 (4). Total—13.

HARRY FLANROY SYDNEY III
Fullback—San Francisco 49ers
Born June 26, 1959, at Petersburg, Va.
Height, 6.00. Weight, 215.
High School—Fayetteville, N.C., 71st.
Received bachelor of general studies degree in criminal justice from University of Kansas in 1982.

Signed as free agent by Seattle Seahawks, April 30, 1981.
Released by Seattle Seahawks, August 25, 1981; signed as free agent by Cincinnati Bengals, February 2, 1982.
Released by Cincinnati Bengals, September 6, 1982; signed by Denver Gold, November 23, 1982.
Traded with 4th round pick in 1985 draft by Denver Gold to Memphis Showboats for right of first refusal to free agent defensive back Terry Love and 1st round pick in 1985 draft, January 3, 1985.
On developmental squad, April 14 through April 18, 1985; activated, April 19, 1985.
On developmental squad, May 18 through May 31, 1985; activated, June 1, 1985.
On developmental squad, June 7 through remainder of 1985 season.
Granted free agency when USFL suspended operations, August 7, 1986; signed as free agent by Montreal Alouettes, August 19, 1986.
Released by Montreal Alouettes, September 16, 1986; signed as free agent by San Francisco 49ers, April 8, 1987.
Crossed picket line during players' strike, October 7, 1987.
On developmental squad for 6 games with Memphis Showboats in 1985.

Year Club	G.	Att.	RUSHING Yds.	Avg.	TD.	PASS RECEIVING P.C.	Yds.	Avg.	TD.	TOTAL TD.	Pts.	F.
1983—Denver USFL	18	176	801	4.6	9	31	306	9.9	2	11	66	9
1984—Denver USFL	18	230	961	4.2	10	44	354	8.1	2	12	72	5
1985—Memphis USFL	13	76	341	4.5	4	10	79	7.9	0	4	24	2
1986—Montreal CFL	4	38	115	3.0	2	18	162	9.0	0	2	†14	1
1987—San Francisco NFL	14	29	125	4.3	0	1	3	3.0	0	0	0	2
1988—San Francisco NFL	16	9	50	5.6	0	2	18	9.0	0	0	0	0
USFL Totals—3 Years	49	482	2103	4.4	23	85	739	8.7	4	27	162	16
CFL Totals—1 Year	4	38	115	3.0	2	18	162	9.0	0	2	14	1
NFL Totals—2 Years	30	38	175	4.6	0	3	21	7.0	0	0	0	2
Pro Totals—6 Years	83	558	2393	4.3	25	106	922	8.7	4	29	176	19

Year Club	G.	KICKOFF RETURNS No.	Yds.	Avg.	TD.
1983—Denver USFL	18	1	13	13.0	0
1984—Denver USFL	18	3	24	8.0	0
1985—Memphis USFL	13	3	25	8.3	0
1986—Montreal CFL	4		None		
1987—San Francisco NFL	14	12	243	20.3	0
1988—San Francisco NFL	16	1	8	8.0	0
USFL Totals—3 Years	49	7	62	8.9	0
CFL Totals—1 Year	4	0	0	0.0	0
NFL Totals—2 Years	30	13	251	19.3	0
Pro Totals—6 Years	83	20	313	15.7	0

†Scored one 2-point conversion.
Additional USFL statistics: Attempted three passes with one completion for 46 yards and one interception, 1983; recovered two fumbles, 1983 through 1985; attempted four passes with no completions and one interception, 1984.
Additional NFL statistics: Attempted one pass with one completion for 50 yards and a touchdown, 1987; attempted one pass with no completions, 1988.
Played in NFC Championship Game following 1988 season.
Played in NFL Championship Game following 1988 season.

DARRYL VICTOR TALLEY
Linebacker—Buffalo Bills
Born July 10, 1960, at Cleveland, O.
Height, 6.04. Weight, 235.
High School—East Cleveland, O., Shaw.
Received degree in physical education from West Virginia University.
Brother of John Talley, tight end with Cleveland Browns.

Named as linebacker on THE SPORTING NEWS College All-America Team, 1982.
Selected by New Jersey in 2nd round (24th player selected) of 1983 USFL draft.
Selected by Buffalo in 2nd round (39th player selected) of 1983 NFL draft.
Signed by Buffalo Bills, June 14, 1983.
Buffalo NFL, 1983 through 1988.
Games: 1983 (16), 1984 (16), 1985 (16), 1986 (16), 1987 (12), 1988 (16). Total—92.
Pro statistics: Returned two kickoffs for nine yards and recovered two fumbles for six yards, 1983; recovered one fumble, 1984 and 1988; intercepted one pass for no yards, 1984; recovered one fumble for 47 yards, 1986; recovered one fumble for one yard, 1987.
Played in AFC Championship Game following 1988 season.

BEN ALLEN TAMBURELLO JR.

(Name pronounced TAM-bur-RELL-o.)

Guard-Center—Philadelphia Eagles

Born September 9, 1964, at Birmingham, Ala.
Height, 6.03. Weight, 278.
High Schools—Birmingham, Ala., Shades Valley; and Sweetwater, Tenn.,
Tennessee Military Institute.
Attended Auburn University.

Named as center on THE SPORTING NEWS College All-America Team, 1986.
Selected by Philadelphia in 3rd round (65th player selected) of 1987 NFL draft.
Signed by Philadelphia Eagles, August 6, 1987.
On injured reserve with broken wrist, August 25 through December 16, 1987; activated, December 17, 1987.
Philadelphia NFL, 1987 and 1988.
Games: 1987 (2), 1988 (16). Total—18.
Pro statistics: Recovered one fumble, 1987.

STEVE TASKER

Wide Receiver-Kick Returner—Buffalo Bills

Born April 10, 1962, at Leoti, Kan.
Height, 5.09. Weight, 185.
High School—Leoti, Kan., Wichita County.
Attended Dodge City Community College and Northwestern University.

Selected by Houston in 9th round (226th player selected) of 1985 NFL draft.
Signed by Houston Oilers, June 14, 1985.
On injured reserve with knee injury, October 23 through remainder of 1985 season.
On injured reserve with knee injury, September 15 through November 5, 1986.
Released by Houston Oilers, November 6, 1986; awarded on waivers to Buffalo Bills, November 7, 1986.

		KICKOFF RETURNS		
Year Club	G.	No.	Yds.	Avg.TD.
1985—Houston NFL................	7	17	447	26.3 0
1986—Hou. (2)-Buff. (7) NFL.	9	12	213	17.8 0
1987—Buffalo NFL..................	12	11	197	17.9 0
1988—Buffalo NFL..................	14		None	
Pro Totals—4 Years............	42	40	857	21.4 0

Additional pro statistics: Rushed twice for 16 yards and caught two passes for 19 yards, 1985; credited with a safety and fumbled twice, 1987.
Played in AFC Championship Game following 1988 season.
Played in Pro Bowl (NFL All-Star Game) following 1987 season.

DAVID TATE

Defensive Back—Chicago Bears

Born November 22, 1964, at Denver, Colo.
Height, 6.00. Weight, 177.
High School—Denver, Colo., Mullen.
Attended University of Colorado.

Selected by Chicago in 8th round (208th player selected) of 1988 NFL draft.
Signed by Chicago Bears, July 6, 1988.

		——INTERCEPTIONS——		
Year Club	G.	No.	Yds.	Avg.TD.
1988—Chicago NFL................	16	4	35	8.8 0

Played in NFC Championship Game following 1988 season.

LARS JAMEL TATE

Running Back—Tampa Bay Buccaneers

Born February 2, 1966, at Indianapolis, Ind.
Height, 6.02. Weight, 215.
High School—Indianapolis, Ind., North Central.
Attended University of Georgia.

Selected by Tampa Bay in 2nd round (53rd player selected) of 1988 NFL draft.
Signed by Tampa Bay Buccaneers, July 15, 1988.

		——RUSHING——			PASS RECEIVING			—TOTAL—		
Year Club	G.	Att.	Yds.	Avg. TD.	P.C.	Yds.	Avg. TD.	TD.	Pts.	F.
1988—Tampa Bay NFL	15	122	467	3.8 7	5	23	4.6 1	8	48	2

MOSIULA TATUPU

(Mosi)

Running Back—New England Patriots

Born April 26, 1955, at Pago Pago, American Samoa.
Height, 6.00. Weight, 227.
High School—Honolulu, Haw., Punahou.
Attended University of Southern California.

Son of Mosi Tatupu, former Samoan boxing champ; and cousin of Terry Tautolo,
linebacker with Philadelphia Eagles, San Francisco 49ers, Detroit Lions and Miami Dolphins,
1976 through 1984; and John Tautolo, guard with New York Giants,
Portland Breakers and Los Angeles Raiders, 1982, 1983, 1985 and 1987.
Selected by New England in 8th round (215th player selected) of 1978 NFL draft.

Year Club	G.	Att.	Yds.	Avg.	TD.	P.C.	Yds.	Avg.	TD.	TD.	Pts.	F.
			—RUSHING—			PASS RECEIVING				—TOTAL—		
1978—New England NFL	16	3	6	2.0	0	None				0	0	0
1979—New England NFL	16	23	71	3.1	0	2	9	4.5	0	0	0	0
1980—New England NFL	16	33	97	2.9	3	4	27	6.8	0	3	18	0
1981—New England NFL	16	38	201	5.3	2	12	132	11.0	1	3	18	2
1982—New England NFL	9	30	168	5.6	0	None				0	0	0
1983—New England NFL	16	106	578	5.5	4	10	97	9.7	1	5	30	1
1984—New England NFL	16	133	553	4.2	4	16	159	9.9	0	4	24	4
1985—New England NFL	16	47	152	3.2	2	2	16	8.0	0	2	12	1
1986—New England NFL	16	71	172	2.4	1	15	145	9.7	0	2	12	1
1987—New England NFL	12	79	248	3.1	0	15	136	9.1	0	0	0	1
1988—New England NFL	16	22	75	3.4	2	8	58	7.3	0	2	12	0
Pro Totals—11 Years	165	585	2321	4.0	18	84	779	9.3	2	21	126	10

Additional pro statistics: Returned one kickoff for 17 yards, 1978; returned three kickoffs for 15 yards, 1979;
recovered three fumbles, 1981; recovered one fumble, 1983 through 1985; returned one kickoff for nine yards, 1984;
returned blocked punt 17 yards for a touchdown, 1986; attempted one pass with one completion for 15 yards and a
touchdown, 1987; returned one kickoff for 13 yards, 1988.
Played in AFC Championship Game following 1985 season.
Played in NFL Championship Game following 1985 season.
Played in Pro Bowl (NFL All-Star Game) following 1986 season.

TERRY WAYNE TAUSCH
Guard—San Francisco 49ers
Born February 5, 1959, at New Braunfels, Tex.
Height, 6.05. Weight, 276.
High School—New Braunfels, Tex.
Received bachelor of business administration degree in marketing from
University of Texas in 1981.

Named as offensive tackle on THE SPORTING NEWS College All-America Team, 1981.
Selected by Minnesota in 2nd round (39th player selected) of 1982 NFL draft.
On injured reserve with torn ankle tendon, November 14 through remainder of 1987 season.
Granted unconditional free agency, February 1, 1989; signed by San Francisco 49ers, February 28, 1989.
Minnesota NFL, 1982 through 1988.
Games: 1982 (2), 1983 (10), 1984 (16), 1985 (16), 1986 (16), 1987 (5), 1988 (16). Total—81.

TAIVALE TAUTALATASI JR.
(Name pronounced TIE-volley TAUGHT-a-la-TOSS-ee.)
(Junior)
Running Back—Dallas Cowboys
Born March 24, 1962, at Oakland, Calif.
Height, 5.11. Weight, 210.
High School—Alameda, Calif., Encinal.
Attended Chabot College and Washington State University.

Selected by Philadelphia in 10th round (261st player selected) of 1986 NFL draft.
Selected by Baltimore in 8th round (60th player selected) of 1986 USFL draft.
Signed by Philadelphia Eagles, July 16, 1986.
Released by Philadelphia Eagles, November 10, 1988; signed as free agent by Dallas Cowboys, February 3, 1989.

Year Club	G.	Att.	Yds.	Avg.	TD.	P.C.	Yds.	Avg.	TD.	TD.	Pts.	F.
			—RUSHING—			PASS RECEIVING				—TOTAL—		
1986—Philadelphia NFL	16	51	163	3.2	0	41	325	7.9	2	2	12	6
1987—Philadelphia NFL	12	26	69	2.7	0	25	176	7.0	0	0	0	1
1988—Philadelphia NFL	10	14	28	2.0	0	5	48	9.6	0	0	0	0
Pro Totals—3 Years	38	91	260	2.9	0	71	549	7.7	2	2	12	7

		KICKOFF RETURNS			
Year Club	G.	No.	Yds.	Avg.	TD.
1986—Philadelphia NFL	16	18	344	19.1	0
1987—Philadelphia NFL	12	3	53	17.7	0
1988—Philadelphia NFL	10		None		
Pro Totals—3 Years	38	21	397	18.9	0

Additional pro statistics: Recovered one fumble, 1986.

EUGENE TAYLOR
(Gene)
Wide Receiver—San Francisco 49ers
Born November 12, 1962, at Oakland, Calif.
Height, 6.03. Weight, 189.
High School—Richmond, Calif., Salesian.
Attended Contra Costa College and Fresno State University.

Selected by New England in 6th round (163rd player selected) of 1987 NFL draft.
Signed by New England Patriots, July 26, 1987.
Released by New England Patriots, August 31, 1987; awarded on waivers to Tampa Bay Buccaneers, September 1, 1987.
Released by Tampa Bay Buccaneers, September 7, 1987; re-signed by Buccaneers, September 8, 1987.
Released by Tampa Bay Buccaneers, September 14, 1988; re-signed by Buccaneers, October 18, 1988.
Released by Tampa Bay Buccaneers, November 9, 1988; signed as free agent by San Francisco 49ers, February 27, 1989.

Year Club	G.	P.C.	Yds.	Avg.	TD.
		—PASS RECEIVING—			
1987—Tampa Bay NFL	7	2	21	10.5	0
1988—Tampa Bay NFL	4	5	53	10.6	0
Pro Totals—2 Years............	11	7	74	10.6	0

JOHN GREGORY TAYLOR
Wide Receiver—San Francisco 49ers
Born March 31, 1962, at Pennsauken, N. J.
Height, 6.01. Weight, 185.
High School—Pennsauken, N. J.
Attended Delaware State College.

Named as punt returner to THE SPORTING NEWS NFL All-Star Team, 1988.
Selected by San Francisco in 3rd round (76th player selected) of 1986 NFL draft.
Selected by Baltimore in 2nd round (13th player selected) of 1986 USFL draft.
Signed by San Francisco 49ers, July 21, 1986.
On injured reserve with back injury, August 26 through entire 1986 season.
On non-football injury list with substance abuse, September 2 through September 27, 1988; activated, September 28, 1988.

Year Club	G.	PASS RECEIVING				-PUNT RETURNS-				—KICKOFF RET.—				—TOTAL—		
		P.C.	Yds.	Avg.	TD.	No.	Yds.	Avg.	TD.	No.	Yds.	Avg.	TD.	TD.	Pts.	F.
1987—San Francisco NFL	12	9	151	16.8	0	1	9	9.0	0	None				0	0	0
1988—San Francisco NFL	12	14	325	23.2	2	44	*556	*12.6	*2	12	225	18.8	0	4	24	6
Pro Totals—2 Years.......	24	23	476	20.7	2	45	565	12.6	2	12	225	18.8	0	4	24	6

Additional pro statistics: Recovered one fumble for 26 yards and a touchdown, 1987; recovered two fumbles, 1988.
Played in NFC Championship Game following 1988 season.
Played in NFL Championship Game following 1988 season.
Played in Pro Bowl (NFL All-Star Game) following 1988 season.

KEITH GERARD TAYLOR
Defensive Back—Indianapolis Colts
Born December 21, 1964, at Pennsauken, N.J.
Height, 5.11. Weight, 193.
High School—Pennsauken, N.J.
Attended University of Illinois.

Selected by New Orleans in 5th round (134th player selected) of 1988 NFL draft.
Signed by New Orleans Saints, June 24, 1988.
Released by New Orleans Saints, August 30, 1988; signed as free agent by Indianapolis Colts, November 30, 1988.
Indianapolis NFL, 1988.
Games: 1988 (3).

KITRICK LAVELL TAYLOR
Wide Receiver-Kick Returner—Atlanta Falcons
Born July 22, 1964, at Los Angeles, Calif.
Height, 5.10. Weight, 190.
High School—Pomona, Calif.
Received degree in social welfare from Washington State University in 1987.

Selected by Kansas City in 5th round (128th player selected) of 1987 NFL draft.
Signed by Kansas City Chiefs, July 19, 1987.
On injured reserve with pulled groin, September 7 through entire 1987 season.
Granted unconditional free agency, February 1, 1989; signed by Atlanta Falcons, March 28, 1989.

Year Club	G.	PASS RECEIVING				-PUNT RETURNS-				—KICKOFF RET.—				—TOTAL—		
		P.C.	Yds.	Avg.	TD.	No.	Yds.	Avg.	TD.	No.	Yds.	Avg.	TD.	TD.	Pts.	F.
1988—Kansas City NFL	16	9	105	11.7	0	29	187	6.4	0	5	80	16.0	0	0	0	1

Additional pro statistics: Rushed once for two yards, 1988.

LAWRENCE TAYLOR
Linebacker—New York Giants
Born February 4, 1959, at Williamsburg, Va.
Height, 6.03. Weight, 243.
High School—Williamsburg, Va., Lafayette.
Attended University of North Carolina.

Named THE SPORTING NEWS NFL Player of the Year, 1986.
Named to THE SPORTING NEWS NFL All-Star Team, 1981, 1983 through 1986 and 1988.
Named as linebacker on THE SPORTING NEWS College All-America Team, 1980.
Selected by New York Giants in 1st round (2nd player selected) of 1981 NFL draft.
Crossed picket line during players' strike, October 14, 1987.
On non-football injury list with substance abuse, August 29 through September 27, 1988; activated, September 28, 1988.

Year Club	G.	No.	Yds.	Avg.TD.	
			——INTERCEPTIONS——		
1981—N.Y. Giants NFL	16	1	1	1.0	0
1982—N.Y. Giants NFL	9	1	97	97.0	*1
1983—N.Y. Giants NFL	16	2	10	5.0	0
1984—N.Y. Giants NFL	16	1	—1	—1.0	0
1985—N.Y. Giants NFL	16		None		
1986—N.Y. Giants NFL	16		None		
1987—N.Y. Giants NFL	12	3	16	5.3	0
1988—N.Y. Giants NFL	12		None		
Pro Totals—8 Years............	113	8	123	15.4	1

Additional pro statistics: Recovered one fumble for four yards, 1981; fumbled once, 1981 and 1983; recovered two fumbles for three yards, 1983; recovered two fumbles for 25 yards, 1985; recovered one fumble, 1988.
Played in NFC Championship Game following 1986 season.
Played in NFL Championship Game following 1986 season.
Played in Pro Bowl (NFL All-Star Game) following 1981 through 1988 seasons.

MALCOLM TAYLOR
Defensive Tackle—Los Angeles Raiders
Born June 20, 1960, at Crystal Springs, Miss.
Height, 6.06. Weight, 280.
High School—Crystal Springs, Miss.
Attended Tennessee State University.

Selected by Houston in 5th round (121st player selected) of 1982 NFL draft.
Signed by Chicago Blitz, January 4, 1984, for contract to take effect after being granted free agency, February 1, 1984.
USFL rights traded by Memphis Showboats to Chicago Blitz for past considerations, January 9, 1984.
On developmental squad, April 28 through May 17, 1984; activated, May 18, 1984.
On developmental squad, June 24 through remainder of 1984 season.
Franchise disbanded, November 20, 1984.
Selected by Houston Gamblers in USFL dispersal draft, December 6, 1984.
Traded by Houston Gamblers to Birmingham Stallions for offensive tackle Rob Taylor, February 12, 1985.
On developmental squad, March 16 through March 29, 1985; activated, March 30, 1985.
Granted free agency when USFL suspended operations, August 7, 1986; signed by Houston Oilers, August 24, 1986.
Granted roster exemption, August 24 through August 28, 1986; activated, August 29, 1986.
Released by Houston Oilers, October 2, 1986; signed as free agent by Los Angeles Raiders, April 17, 1987.
On developmental squad for 4 games with Chicago Blitz in 1984.
On developmental squad for 2 games with Birmingham Stallions in 1985.
Houston NFL, 1982, 1983 and 1986; Chicago USFL, 1984; Birmingham USFL, 1985; Los Angeles Raiders NFL, 1987 and 1988.
Games: 1982 (9), 1983 (16), 1984 (14), 1985 (15), 1986 (3), 1987 (12), 1988 (15). Total NFL—55. Total USFL—29. Total Pro—84.
NFL statistics: Recovered one fumble, 1982.
USFL statistics: Credited with six sacks for 47½ yards, 1984; credited with four sacks for 33 yards and recovered one fumble, 1985.

ROBERT EARL TAYLOR
(Rob)
Offensive Tackle—Tampa Bay Buccaneers
Born November 14, 1960, at St. Charles, Ill.
Height, 6.06. Weight, 295.
High School—Kettering, O., Fairmont East.
Received degree in electrical engineering from Northwestern University.

Selected by Philadelphia in 12th round (328th player selected) of 1982 NFL draft.
Released by Philadelphia Eagles, August 23, 1982; claimed on waivers by Baltimore Colts, August 25, 1982.
Released by Baltimore Colts, September 6, 1982; signed as free agent by Chicago Blitz, October 4, 1982.
Franchise transferred to Arizona, September 30, 1983.
Protected in merger of Arizona Wranglers and Oklahoma Outlaws, December 6, 1984.
Granted free agency, November 30, 1984; signed by Birmingham Stallions, January 23, 1985 (Arizona did not exercise right of first refusal).
Traded by Birmingham Stallions to Houston Gamblers for defensive end Malcolm Taylor, February 12, 1985.
On developmental squad, February 21 through March 2, 1985; activated, March 3, 1985.
Released by Houston Gamblers, July 31, 1985; awaded on waivers to Baltimore Stars, August 1, 1985.
Released by Baltimore Stars, August 2, 1985; signed as free agent by Tampa Bay Buccaneers, March 26, 1986.
On injured reserve with knee injury, November 11 through remainder of 1987 season.
On developmental squad for 1 game with Houston Gamblers in 1985.
Chicago USFL, 1983 and 1984; Houston USFL, 1985; Tampa Bay NFL, 1986 through 1988.
Games: 1983 (18), 1984 (18), 1985 (16), 1986 (16), 1987 (5), 1988 (16). Total USFL—52. Total NFL—37. Total Pro—89.
Pro statistics: Recovered one fumble, 1983.
Played in USFL Championship Game following 1984 season.

TERRY TAYLOR
Cornerback—Seattle Seahawks
Born July 18, 1961, at Warren, O.
Height, 5.10. Weight, 181.
High School—Youngstown, O., Rayen.
Attended Southern Illinois University.
Cousin of Walter Poole, running back with Chicago Blitz
and Houston Gamblers, 1983 and 1984.

Selected by Chicago in 2nd round (25th player selected) of 1984 USFL draft.
Selected by Seattle in 1st round (22nd player selected) of 1984 NFL draft.
Signed by Seattle Seahawks, July 10, 1984.
On non-football injury with substance abuse, August 31 through September 16, 1988; activated, September 17, 1988.

Year	Club	G.	—INTERCEPTIONS—			
			No.	Yds.	Avg.	TD.
1984—Seattle NFL		16	3	63	21.0	0
1985—Seattle NFL		16	4	75	18.8	*1
1986—Seattle NFL		16	2	0	0.0	0
1987—Seattle NFL		12	1	11	11.0	0
1988—Seattle NFL		14	5	53	10.6	1
Pro Totals—5 Years		74	15	202	13.5	2

Additional pro statistics: Returned blocked punt for 15 yards and a touchdown, 1985.

JIMMY DEWAYNE TEAL
Wide Receiver—Miami Dolphins
Born August 18, 1962, at Lufkin, Tex.
Height, 5.11. Weight, 175.
High School—Diboll, Tex.
Attended Texas A&M University.

Selected by Houston in 1985 USFL territorial draft.
Selected by Buffalo in 5th round (130th player selected) of 1985 NFL draft.
Signed by Buffalo Bills, July 19, 1985.
On injured reserve with hamstring injury, September 3 through December 5, 1985; activated, December 6, 1985.
On injured reserve with shoulder injury, September 2 through November 20, 1986; activated, November 21, 1986.
Released by Buffalo Bills, August 10, 1987; awarded on waivers to New Orleans Saints, August 11, 1987.
On injured reserve, September 1 through September 6, 1987.
Released by New Orleans Saints, September 7, 1987; signed as free agent replacement player by Seattle Seahawks, September 24, 1987.
Released by Seattle Seahawks, August 30, 1988; re-signed by Seahawks, October 6, 1988.
Released by Seattle Seahawks, October 19, 1988; signed as free agent by Miami Dolphins, November 30, 1988.
Active for 3 games with Miami Dolphins in 1988; did not play.

Year	Club	G.	—PASS RECEIVING—			
			P.C.	Yds.	Avg.	TD.
1985—Buffalo NFL		3	1	24	24.0	0
1986—Buffalo NFL		5	6	60	10.0	1
1987—Seattle NFL		4	14	198	14.1	2
1988—Sea. (2) - Mia. (0) NFL		2			None	
Pro Totals—4 Years		14	21	282	13.4	3

Additional pro statistics: Returned one kickoff for 20 yards, 1985; returned six punts for 38 yards, returned six kickoffs for 95 yards and fumbled once, 1987.

JOHN ROBERT TELTSCHIK
Punter—Philadelphia Eagles
Born March 8, 1964, at Floresville, Tex.
Height, 6.02. Weight, 209.
High School—Kerrville, Tex., Tivy.
Received degree in business administration from University of Texas in 1986.
Related to Fritz Connally, third baseman with Chicago Cubs and Baltimore Orioles, 1983 and 1985.

Led NFL in punting yards with 4,493 in 1986.
Selected by Chicago in 9th round (249th player selected) of 1986 NFL draft.
Selected by New Jersey in 8th round (55th player selected) of 1986 USFL draft.
Signed by Chicago Bears, July 15, 1986.
Released by Chicago Bears, August 26, 1986; signed as free agent by Philadelphia Eagles, August 28, 1986.

Year	Club	G.	—PUNTING—		
			No.	Avg.	Blk.
1986—Philadelphia NFL		16	*108	41.6	1
1987—Philadelphia NFL		12	*82	38.2	1
1988—Philadelphia NFL		16	*98	40.4	3
Pro Totals—3 Years		44	288	40.2	5

Additional pro statistics: Rushed once for no yards, 1986; recovered one fumble, 1986 and 1988; rushed three times for 32 yards, 1987; rushed twice for 36 yards, attempted three passes with one completion for 18 yards and fumbled once, 1988.

DEREK WAYNE TENNELL
(Name pronounced Te-NELL.)
Tight End—Cleveland Browns
Born February 12, 1964, at Los Angeles, Calif.
Height, 6.05. Weight, 245.
High School—West Covina, Calif.
Attended University of California at Los Angeles.

Selected by Seattle in 7th round (185th player selected) of 1987 NFL draft.
Signed by Seattle Seahawks, July 21, 1987.
Released by Seattle Seahawks, September 7, 1987; signed as free agent replacement player by Cleveland Browns, September 24, 1987.

Year Club		—PASS RECEIVING—			
	G.	P.C.	Yds.	Avg.	TD.
1987—Cleveland NFL..............	11	9	102	11.3	3
1988—Cleveland NFL..............	16	9	88	9.8	1
Pro Totals—2 Years............	27	18	190	10.6	4

Additional pro statistics: Returned one kickoff for 11 yards, 1988.
Played in AFC Championship Game following 1987 season.

VINCENT FRANK TESTAVERDE
(Vinny)
Quarterback—Tampa Bay Buccaneers
Born November 13, 1963, at Brooklyn, N. Y.
Height, 6.05. Weight, 215.
High Schools—Floral Park, N.Y., Sewanhaka;
and Fort Union, Vir., Fork Union Military.
Attended University of Miami (Fla.).

Heisman Trophy winner, 1986.
Named college football Player of the Year by THE SPORTING NEWS, 1986.
Named as quarterback on THE SPORTING NEWS College All-America Team, 1986.
Signed by Tampa Bay Buccaneers, April 3, 1987.
Selected officially by Tampa Bay in 1st round (1st player selected) of 1987 NFL draft.

Year Club		—————PASSING—————							—————RUSHING———				—TOTAL—		
	G.	Att.	Cmp.	Pct.	Gain	T.P.	P.I.	Avg.	Att.	Yds.	Avg.	TD.	TD.	Pts.	F.
1987—Tampa Bay NFL	6	165	71	43.0	1081	5	6	6.55	13	50	3.8	1	1	6	7
1988—Tampa Bay NFL	15	466	222	47.6	3240	13	*35	6.95	28	138	4.9	1	1	6	8
Pro Totals—2 Years...........	21	631	293	46.4	4321	18	41	6.85	41	188	4.6	2	2	12	15

Quarterback Rating Points: 1987 (60.2), 1988 (48.8). Total—51.9.
Additional pro statistics: Recovered four fumbles and fumbled seven times for minus three yards, 1987; recovered two fumbles, 1988.

THOMAS ALLEN THAYER
(Tom)
Guard—Chicago Bears
Born August 16, 1961, at Joliet, Ill.
Height, 6.04. Weight, 270.
High School—Joliet, Ill., Catholic.
Received bachelor of arts degree in communications and public relations
from University of Notre Dame.
Brother-in-law of John Scully, guard with Atlanta Falcons.

Selected by Chicago in 1983 USFL territorial draft.
Signed by Chicago Blitz, April 26, 1983.
Selected by Chicago in 4th round (91st player selected) of 1983 NFL draft.
Franchise transferred to Arizona, September 30, 1983.
Protected in merger of Arizona Wranglers and Oklahoma Outlaws, December 6, 1984.
On developmental squad, March 3 through March 10, 1985; activated, March 11, 1985.
Granted free agency, July 15, 1985; signed by Chicago Bears, July 19, 1985.
On developmental squad for 1 game with Arizona Outlaws in 1985.
Chicago USFL, 1983 and 1984; Arizona USFL, 1985; Chicago NFL, 1985 through 1988.
Games 1983 (10), 1984 (18), 1985 USFL (17), 1985 NFL (16), 1986 (16), 1987 (11), 1988 (16). Total USFL—45. Total NFL—59. Total Pro—104.
USFL statistics: Recovered two fumbles, 1985.
Played in USFL Championship Game following 1984 season.
Played in NFC Championship Game following 1985 and 1988 seasons.
Played in NFL Championship Game following 1985 season.

RAY CHARLES THIELEMANN
Name pronounced TEEL-munn.
(R. C.)
Guard
Born August 12, 1955, at Houston, Tex.
Height, 6.04. Weight, 272.
High School—Houston, Tex., Spring Woods.
Attended University of Arkansas.

Selected by Atlanta in 2nd round (36th player selected) of 1977 NFL draft.
On injured reserve with shoulder separation, September 13 through October 12, 1979; activated, October 13, 1979.
On injured reserve with shoulder injury, December 13 through remainder of 1979 season.
On did not report list, August 16 through August 24, 1983.
Reported and granted exemption, August 25, 1983; activated, September 1, 1983.
Granted free agency, February 1, 1985; re-signed by Falcons and traded to Washington Redskins for wide receiver Charlie Brown, August 24, 1985.
Granted roster exemption, August 26 through August 29, 1985; activated, August 30, 1985.
On injured reserve with knee injury, October 2 through remainder of 1985 season.
Granted unconditional free agency, February 1, 1989; did not receive qualifying offer, April 15, 1989.
Atlanta NFL, 1977 through 1984; Washington NFL, 1985 through 1988.

Games: 1977 (14), 1978 (16), 1979 (11), 1980 (16), 1981 (16), 1982 (9), 1983 (16), 1984 (16), 1985 (3), 1986 (14), 1987 (12), 1988 (14). Total—157.
Pro statistics: Recovered one fumble, 1977, 1983 and 1984; recovered two fumbles, 1978 through 1981.
Played in NFC Championship Game following 1986 and 1987 seasons.
Played in NFL Championship Game following 1987 season.
Played in Pro Bowl (NFL All-Star Game) following 1981 through 1983 seasons.

BENJAMIN THOMAS JR.
(Ben)
Defensive Tackle—Atlanta Falcons
Born July 2, 1961, at Ashburn, Ga.
Height, 6.03. Weight, 275.
High School—Ashburn, Ga., Turner County.
Attended Auburn University.

Selected by Birmingham in 1985 USFL territorial draft.
Selected by New England in 2nd round (56th player selected) of 1985 NFL draft.
Signed by New England Patriots, July 24, 1985.
Released by New England Patriots, October 17, 1986; awarded on waivers to Green Bay Packers, October 20, 1986.
On injured reserve with knee injury, September 1 through entire 1987 season.
Crossed picket line during players' strike, October 14, 1987.
Released by Green Bay Packers, August 9, 1988; signed as free agent by Pittsburgh Steelers, August 11, 1988.
Released by Pittsburgh Steelers, November 2, 1988; signed as free agent by Atlanta Falcons, May 2, 1989.
New England NFL, 1985; New England (4)-Green Bay (9) NFL, 1986; Pittsburgh NFL, 1988.
Games: 1985 (15), 1986 (13), 1988 (8). Total—36.
Played in AFC Championship Game following 1985 season.
Played in NFL Championship Game following 1985 season.

CHUCK THOMAS
Center-Guard—San Francisco 49ers
Born December 24, 1960, at Houston, Tex.
Height, 6.03. Weight, 277.
High School—Houston, Tex., Stratford.
Attended University of Oklahoma.

Selected by San Antonio in 1985 USFL territorial draft.
Selected by Houston in 8th round (199th player selected) of 1985 NFL draft.
Signed by Houston Oilers, July 13, 1985.
Released by Houston Oilers, September 2, 1985; signed as free agent by Atlanta Falcons, November 22, 1985.
Released by Atlanta Falcons, August 12, 1986; signed as free agent by San Francisco 49ers, December 22, 1986.
On injured reserve with thigh injury, August 28 through September 6, 1987.
Released by San Francisco 49ers, September 7, 1987; re-signed as replacement player by 49ers, September 24, 1987.
Atlanta NFL, 1985; San Francisco NFL, 1987 and 1988.
Games: 1985 (4), 1987 (7), 1988 (16). Total—27.
Pro statistics: Returned one kickoff for five yards and fumbled once for minus 12 yards, 1988.
Played in NFC Championship Game following 1988 season.
Played in NFL Championship Game following 1988 season.

ERIC JASON THOMAS
Cornerback—Cincinnati Bengals
Born September 11, 1964, at Tucson, Ariz.
Height, 5.11. Weight, 181.
High School—Sacramento, Calif., Norte Del Rio.
Attended Pasadena City College and Tulane University.

Selected by Cincinnati in 2nd round (49th player selected) of 1987 NFL draft.
Signed by Cincinnati Bengals, July 27, 1987.

| | | —INTERCEPTIONS— | | | |
Year Club	G.	No.	Yds.	Avg.	TD.
1987—Cincinnati NFL	12	1	3	3.0	0
1988—Cincinnati NFL	16	7	61	8.7	0
Pro Totals—2 Years	28	8	64	8.0	0

Played in AFC Championship Game following 1988 season.
Played in NFL Championship Game following 1988 season.
Played in Pro Bowl (NFL All-Star Game) following 1988 season.

HENRY LEE THOMAS JR.
Nose Tackle—Minnesota Vikings
Born January 12, 1965, at Houston, Tex.
Height, 6.02. Weight, 268.
High School—Houston, Tex., Dwight D. Eisenhower.
Attended Louisiana State University.

Selected by Minnesota in 3rd round (72nd player selected) of 1987 NFL draft.
Signed by Minnesota Vikings, July 14, 1987.
Minnesota NFL, 1987 and 1988.
Games: 1987 (12), 1988 (15). Total—27.
Pro statistics: Intercepted one pass for no yards and recovered one fumble, 1987; intercepted one pass for seven yards and recovered one fumble for two yards and a touchdown, 1988.
Played in NFC Championship Game following 1987 season.

JOHNNY THOMAS JR.
Cornerback—San Diego Chargers
Born August 3, 1964, at Houston, Tex.
Height, 5.09. Weight, 185.
High School—Houston, Tex., Sterling.
Attended Baylor University.

Selected by Washington in 7th round (192nd player selected) of 1987 NFL draft.
Signed by Washington Redskins, July 24, 1987.
On injured reserve with ankle injury, August 31 through entire 1987 season.
On injured reserve with knee injury, September 30 through remainder of 1988 season.
Granted unconditonal free agency, February 1, 1989; signed by San Diego Chargers, March 30, 1989.
Washington NFL, 1988.
Games: 1988 (4).

KEVIN ALAN THOMAS
Center—Seattle Seahawks
Born July 27, 1964, at Tucson, Ariz.
Height, 6.02. Weight, 268.
High School—Tucson, Ariz., Canyon del Oro.
Attended Arizona State University.

Signed as free agent by Tampa Bay Buccaneers, May 4, 1987.
On injured reserve with knee injury, July 27 through entire 1987 season.
Released by Tampa Bay Buccaneers, October 5, 1988; re-signed by Buccaneers, October 18, 1988.
Granted unconditional free agency, February 1, 1989; signed by Seattle Seahawks, March 29, 1989.
Tampa Bay NFL, 1988.
Games: 1988 (10).

LAVALE ALVIN THOMAS
Running Back—Green Bay Packers
Born December 12, 1963, at Los Angeles, Calif.
Height, 6.00. Weight, 205.
High School—Tulare, Calif., Western.
Attended Fresno State University.

Cousin of Jewerl Thomas, running back with Los Angeles Rams, Kansas City Chiefs and San Diego
Chargers, 1980 through 1984; and Ken Thomas, running back with Kansas City Chiefs, 1983.

Signed as free agent by Kansas City Chiefs, May 6, 1986.
Released by Kansas City Chiefs, August 18, 1986; signed as free agent by Green Bay Packers, April 29, 1987.
Released by Green Bay Packers, September 7, 1987; re-signed as replacement player by Packers, September 25,
1987.
On injured reserve with knee injury, October 15 through remainder of 1987 season.
On injured reserve with knee injury, August 22 through December 14, 1988; activated after clearing procedural
waivers, December 16, 1988.
Green Bay NFL, 1987 and 1988.
Games: 1987 (1), 1988 (1). Total—2.
Pro statistics: Rushed five times for 19 yards, caught two passes for 52 yards and a touchdown and recovered two
fumbles for three yards, 1987.

RODNEY LAMAR THOMAS
Cornerback—Miami Dolphins
Born December 21, 1965, at Los Angeles, Calif.
Height, 5.10. Weight, 190.
High School—Ontario, Calif., Chaffey.
Attended Brigham Young University.

Selected by Miami in 5th round (126th player selected) of 1988 NFL draft.
Signed by Miami Dolphins, July 12, 1988.
On injured reserve with knee injury, November 26 through remainder of 1988 season.
Miami NFL, 1988.
Games: 1988 (12).
Pro statistics: Intercepted one pass for 48 yards, 1988.

THURMAN L. THOMAS
Running Back—Buffalo Bills
Born May 16, 1966, at Houston, Tex.
Height, 5.10. Weight, 198.
High School—Missouri City, Tex., Willow Ridge.
Attended Oklahoma State University.

Selected by Buffalo in 2nd round (40th player selected) of 1988 NFL draft.
Signed by Buffalo Bills, July 14, 1988.

		—RUSHING—				PASS RECEIVING				—TOTAL—		
Year Club	G.	Att.	Yds.	Avg.	TD.	P.C.	Yds.	Avg.	TD.	TD.	Pts.	F.
1988—Buffalo NFL	15	207	881	4.3	2	18	208	11.6	0	2	12	9

Additional pro statistics: Recovered one fumble, 1988.
Played in AFC Championship Game following 1988 season.

BENNIE THOMPSON
Defensive Back—New Orleans Saints
Born February 10, 1963, at New Orleans, La.
Height, 6.00. Weight, 200.
High School—New Orleans, La., John McDonough.
Attended Grambling State University.
Signed as free agent by Kansas City Chiefs, May 9, 1985.
Released by Kansas City Chiefs, August 5, 1985; signed by Winnipeg Blue Bombers, April 21, 1986.
Granted free agency, March 1, 1989; signed by New Orleans Saints, April 12, 1989.

| | | | —INTERCEPTIONS— | | |
Year Club	G.	No.	Yds.	Avg.	TD.
1986—Winnipeg CFL............	9	2	49	24.5	0
1987—Winnipeg CFL............	8	1	0	0.0	0
1988—Winnipeg CFL............	18	4	58	14.5	0
CFL Totals—3 Years	35	7	107	15.3	0

Additional pro statistics: Recovered one fumble, 1987; recovered two fumbles for two yards and fumbled once, 1988.

BRODERICK THOMPSON
Guard-Offensive Tackle—San Diego Chargers
Born August 14, 1960, at Birmingham, Ala.
Height, 6.04. Weight, 295.
High School—Cerritos, Calif., Richard Gahr.
Attended Cerritos College and University of Kansas.
Signed as free agent by Dallas Cowboys, April 28, 1983.
Released by Dallas Cowboys, August 2, 1983; signed as free agent by San Antonio Gunslingers, November 12, 1983.
Traded with 1st round pick in 1984 draft by San Antonio Gunslingers to Chicago Blitz for rights to quarterback Bob Gagliano, January 3, 1984.
Released by Chicago Blitz, January 31, 1984; signed as free agent by Los Angeles Express, February 10, 1984.
Released by Los Angeles Express, February 13, 1984; signed as free agent by Los Angeles Rams, May 4, 1984.
Released by Los Angeles Rams, August 21, 1984; signed as free agent by Portland Breakers, January 23, 1985.
Released by Portland Breakers, July 31, 1985; awarded on waivers to Memphis Showboats, August 1, 1985.
Released by Memphis Showboats, August 2, 1985; signed as free agent by Dallas Cowboys, August 3, 1985.
Released by Dallas Cowboys, August 26, 1986; signed as free agent by San Diego Chargers, April 13, 1987.
Released by San Diego Chargers, September 7, 1987; re-signed by Chargers, September 8, 1987.
Portland USFL, 1985; Dallas NFL, 1985; San Diego NFL, 1987 and 1988.
Games: 1985 USFL (18), 1985 NFL (11), 1987 (8), 1988 (16). Total NFL—35. Total Pro—53.

LAWRENCE DONNELL THOMPSON
(Known by middle name.)
Defensive End—Indianapolis Colts
Born October 27, 1958, at Lumberton, N.C.
Height, 6.04. Weight, 272.
High School—Lumberton, N. C.
Received bachelor of arts and science degree from University of North Carolina.
Selected by Baltimore in 1st round (18th player selected) of 1981 NFL draft.
On physically unable to perform/active with shoulder injury, July 24 through August 22, 1982; activated, August 23, 1982.
Franchise transferred to Indianapolis, March 31, 1984.
Placed on suspended list, August 12 through September 11, 1984.
On non-football injury list with shoulder and back injuries, September 12 through October 11, 1984; activated, October 12, 1984.
Baltimore NFL, 1981 through 1983; Indianapolis NFL, 1984 through 1988.
Games: 1981 (13), 1982 (9), 1983 (14), 1984 (10), 1985 (15), 1986 (16), 1987 (12), 1988 (16). Total—105.
Pro statistics: Recovered one fumble, 1981; credited with one safety, 1983; recovered one fumble for nine yards, 1985; recovered one fumble for 28 yards and a touchdown, 1987; recovered two fumbles, 1988.

REYNA ONALD THOMPSON
First name pronounced Renee.
Cornerback—New York Giants
Born August 28, 1963, at Dallas, Tex.
Height, 6.00. Weight, 194.
High School—Dallas, Tex., Thomas Jefferson.
Received bachelor of arts degree in communications from Baylor University in 1986.
Selected by Miami in 9th round (247th player selected) of 1986 NFL draft.
Signed by Miami Dolphins, July 17, 1986.
Released by Miami Dolphins, August 17, 1986; re-signed by Dolphins, August 18, 1986.
On injured reserve with shoulder injury, September 8 through October 23, 1987; activated, October 24, 1987.
Granted unconditional free agency, February 1, 1989; signed by New York Giants, March 31, 1989.
Miami NFL, 1986 through 1988.
Games: 1986 (16), 1987 (9), 1988 (16). Total—41.
Pro statistics: Returned one punt for no yards and fumbled once, 1986.

WILLIS HOPE THOMPSON
(Weegie)
Wide Receiver—Pittsburgh Steelers

Born March 21, 1961, at Pensacola, Fla.
Height, 6.06. Weight, 216.
High School—Midlothian, Va.
Received bachelor of science degree in management from Florida State University in 1984.

Selected by Tampa Bay in 1984 USFL territorial draft.
USFL rights traded with rights to quarterback Kelly Lowrey by Tampa Bay Bandits to Jacksonville Bulls for rights to wide receiver Mark Militello and running back Mike Grayson, January 4, 1984.
Selected by Pittsburgh in 4th round (108th player selected) of 1984 NFL draft.
Signed by Pittsburgh Steelers, July 22, 1984.
Granted free agency, February 1, 1989; did not receive qualifying offer, April 15, 1989.
Re-signed by Pittsburgh Steelers, May 29, 1989.

| | | | ——PASS RECEIVING | | |
Year Club	G.	P.C.	Yds.	Avg.	TD.
1984—Pittsburgh NFL.............	16	17	291	17.1	3
1985—Pittsburgh NFL.............	16	8	138	17.3	1
1986—Pittsburgh NFL.............	16	17	191	11.2	5
1987—Pittsburgh NFL.............	12	17	313	18.4	1
1988—Pittsburgh NFL.............	16	16	370	23.1	1
Pro Totals—5 Years............	76	75	1303	17.4	11

Additional pro statistics: Fumbled once, 1984; recovered one fumble, 1987.
Played in AFC Championship Game following 1984 season.

JAMES MICHAEL THORNTON
Tight End—Chicago Bears

Born February 8, 1965, at Santa Rosa, Calif.
Height, 6.02. Weight, 242.
High School—Sebastopol, Calif., Analy.
Attended California State University at Fullerton.

Selected by Chicago in 4th round (105th player selected) of 1988 NFL draft.
Signed by Chicago Bears, July 21, 1988.

| | | | ——PASS RECEIVING—— | | |
Year Club	G.	P.C.	Yds.	Avg.	TD.
1988—Chicago NFL	16	15	135	9.0	0

Additional pro statistics: Fumbled once, 1988.
Played in NFC Championship Game following 1988 season.

DONALD KEVIN THORP
(Don)
Defensive End—Miami Dolphins

Born July 10, 1962, at Chicago, Ill.
Height, 6.04. Weight, 260.
High School—Buffalo Grove, Ill.
Received bachelor of arts degree in finance from University of Illinois.

Named as defensive lineman on THE SPORTING NEWS College All-America Team, 1983.
Selected by Chicago in 1984 USFL territorial draft.
Selected by New Orleans in 6th round (156th player selected) of 1984 NFL draft.
Signed by New Orleans Saints, June 21, 1984.
On injured reserve with neck injury, October 9 through remainder of 1984 season.
Released by New Orleans Saints, August 26, 1985; signed as free agent by Chicago Bears, February 12, 1986.
Released by Chicago Bears, August 25, 1986; signed as free agent by New York Jets, March 16, 1987.
Released by New York Jets, September 6, 1987; signed as free agent replacement player by Indianapolis Colts, September 28, 1987.
Released by Indianapolis Colts, August 23, 1988; re-signed by Colts, November 8, 1988.
Released by Indianapolis Colts, November 22, 1988; signed as free agent by Kansas City Chiefs, November 30, 1988.
Granted unconditional free agency, February 1, 1989; signed by Miami Dolphins, April 1, 1989.
New Orleans NFL, 1984; Indianapolis NFL, 1987; Indianapolis (1)-Kansas City (3) NFL, 1988.
Games: 1984 (5), 1987 (5), 1988 (4). Total—14.

JOHN TICE
Tight End—New Orleans Saints

Born June 22, 1960, at Bayshore, N.Y.
Height, 6.05. Weight, 249.
High School—Central Islip, N.Y.
Attended University of Maryland.
Brother of Mike Tice, tight end with Washington Redskins.

Selected by Washington in 1983 USFL territorial draft.
Selected by New Orleans in 3rd round (65th player selected) of 1983 NFL draft.
Signed by New Orleans Saints, July 6, 1983.
On injured reserve with ankle injury, November 19 through remainder of 1984 season.

Year Club	G.	P.C.	Yds.	Avg.	TD.
1983—New Orleans NFL........	16	7	33	4.7	1
1984—New Orleans NFL........	10	6	55	9.2	1
1985—New Orleans NFL........	16	24	266	11.1	2
1986—New Orleans NFL........	16	37	330	8.9	3
1987—New Orleans NFL........	12	16	181	11.3	6
1988—New Orleans NFL........	15	26	297	11.4	1
Pro Totals—6 Years............	85	116	1162	10.0	14

Additional pro statistics: Recovered two fumbles, 1983; recovered one fumble, 1985 and 1986; fumbled once, 1986.

MICHAEL PETER TICE
(Mike)
Tight End—Washington Redskins
Born February 2, 1959, at Bayshore, N.Y.
Height, 6.07. Weight, 244.
High School—Central Islip, N.Y.
Attended University of Maryland.
Brother of John Tice, tight end with New Orleans Saints.

Signed as free agent by Seattle Seahawks, April 30, 1981.
On injured reserve with fractured ankle, October 15 through December 6, 1985; activated, December 7, 1985.
Granted unconditional free agency, February 1, 1989; signed by Washington Redskins, February 20, 1989.

Year Club	G.	P.C.	Yds.	Avg.	TD.
1981—Seattle NFL..................	16	5	47	9.4	0
1982—Seattle NFL..................	9	9	46	5.1	0
1983—Seattle NFL..................	15		None		
1984—Seattle NFL..................	16	8	90	11.3	3
1985—Seattle NFL..................	9	2	13	6.5	0
1986—Seattle NFL..................	16	15	150	10.0	0
1987—Seattle NFL..................	12	14	106	7.6	2
1988—Seattle NFL..................	16	29	244	8.4	0
Pro Totals—8 Years............	109	82	696	8.5	5

Additional pro statistics: Recovered one fumble, 1982, 1983 and 1986; returned two kickoffs for 28 yards, 1983; returned one kickoff for 17 yards, 1985, 1986 and 1988; fumbled once, 1988.
Played in AFC Championship Game following 1983 season.

SPENCER ALLEN TILLMAN
Running Back—Houston Oilers
Born April 21, 1964, at Tulsa, Okla.
Height, 5.11. Weight, 206.
High School—Tulsa, Okla., Thomas Edison.
Received bachelor of science degree in radio and television communications
from University of Oklahoma in 1987.

Selected by Houston in 5th round (133rd player selected) of 1987 NFL draft.
Signed by Houston Oilers, July 28, 1987.

Year Club	G.	RUSHING Att.	Yds.	Avg.	TD.	PASS RECEIVING P.C.	Yds.	Avg.	TD.	TOTAL TD.	Pts.	F.
1987—Houston NFL.............................	5	12	29	2.4	1	None				1	6	1
1988—Houston NFL.............................	16	3	5	1.7	0	None				0	0	0
Pro Totals—2 Years....................	21	15	34	2.3	1	0	0	0.0	0	1	6	1

Additional pro statistics: Returned one kickoff for no yards, 1987; returned one kickoff for 13 yards, 1988.

ANDRE BERNARD TIPPETT
Linebacker—New England Patriots
Born December 27, 1959, at Birmingham, Ala.
Height, 6.03. Weight, 241.
High School—Newark, N.J., Barringer.
Attended Ellsworth Community College and received bachelor of liberal arts degree from
University of Iowa in 1983.

Named to THE SPORTING NEWS NFL All-Star Team, 1985.
Selected by New England in 2nd round (41st player selected) of 1982 NFL draft.
Crossed picket line during players' strike, October 14, 1987.
New England NFL, 1982 through 1988.
Games: 1982 (9), 1983 (15), 1984 (16), 1985 (16), 1986 (11), 1987 (13), 1988 (12). Total—92.
Pro statistics: Recovered one fumble, 1982, 1983 and 1986; recovered four fumbles for 25 yards and a touchdown, 1985; ran 32 yards with lateral from interception, 1986; recovered three fumbles for 29 yards and a touchdown, 1987.
Played in AFC Championship Game following 1985 season.
Played in NFL Championship Game following 1985 season.
Played in Pro Bowl (NFL All-Star Game) following 1984 through 1988 seasons.

GLEN WESTON TITENSOR

Name pronounced TIGHT-en-sir.

Guard—Dallas Cowboys

Born February 21, 1958, at Bellflower, Calif.
Height, 6.04. Weight, 270.
High School—Garden Grove, Calif., Bolsa Grande.
Attended University of California at Los Angeles and Brigham Young University.

Selected by Dallas in 3rd round (81st player selected) of 1981 NFL draft.
On injured reserve with knee injury, September 7 through entire 1987 season.
Released by Dallas Cowboys, August 30, 1988; re-signed by Cowboys, September 23, 1988.
Dallas NFL, 1981 through 1986 and 1988.
Games: 1981 (16), 1982 (4), 1983 (15), 1984 (15), 1985 (16), 1986 (16), 1988 (10). Total—92.
Pro statistics: Recovered one fumble, 1981 and 1986.
Played in NFC Championship Game following 1981 season.
Member of Dallas Cowboys for NFC Championship Game following 1982 season; did not play.

ALVIN TOLES

Linebacker—New Orleans Saints

Born March 23, 1963, at Barnesville, Ga.
Height, 6.01. Weight, 227.
High School—Forsyth, Ga., Mary Persons.
Attended University of Tennessee.

Selected by Memphis in 1985 USFL territorial draft.
Selected by New Orleans in 1st round (24th player selected) of 1985 NFL draft.
Signed by New Orleans Saints, July 10, 1985.
On injured reserve with knee injury, November 17 through remainder of 1988 season.
New Orleans NFL, 1985 through 1988.
Games: 1985 (16), 1986 (16), 1987 (12), 1988 (11). Total—55.
Pro statistics: Recovered one fumble, 1986; returned blocked punt 11 yards for a touchdown, 1987.

MIKE TOMCZAK

Name pronounced Tom-zak.

Quarterback—Chicago Bears

Born October 23, 1962, at Calumet City, Ill.
Height, 6.01. Weight, 195.
High School—Calumet City, Ill., Thornton Fractional North.
Attended Ohio State University.

Selected by New Jersey in 1985 USFL territorial draft.
Signed as free agent by Chicago Bears, May 9, 1985.

Year Club	G.	Att.	Cmp.	Pct.	Gain	T.P.	P.I.	Avg.	Att.	Yds.	Avg.	TD.	TD.	Pts.	F.
1985—Chicago NFL	6	6	2	33.3	33	0	0	5.50	2	3	1.5	0	0	0	1
1986—Chicago NFL	13	151	74	49.0	1105	2	10	7.32	23	117	5.1	3	3	18	2
1987—Chicago NFL	12	178	97	54.5	1220	5	10	6.85	18	54	3.0	1	1	6	6
1988—Chicago NFL	14	170	86	50.6	1310	7	6	7.71	13	40	3.1	1	1	6	1
Pro Totals—4 Years	45	505	259	51.3	3668	14	26	7.26	56	214	3.8	5	5	30	10

Quarterback Rating Points: 1985 (52.8), 1986 (50.2), 1987 (62.0), 1988 (75.4). Total—63.2.
Additional pro statistics: Recovered one fumble, 1985 and 1987; fumbled once for minus 13 yards, 1985, fumbled once for minus three yards, 1988.
Played in NFC Championship Game following 1988 season.
Member of Chicago Bears for NFC Championship Game following 1985 season; did not play.
Played in NFL Championship Game following 1985 season.

ANTHONY TONEY

Fullback—Philadelphia Eagles

Born September 23, 1962, at Salinas, Calif.
Height, 6.00. Weight, 227.
High School—Salinas, Calif., North Salinas.
Attended Hartnell Community College and Texas A&M University.
Cousin of Del Rodgers, running back with Green Bay Packers
and San Francisco 49ers, 1982, 1984, 1987 and 1988.

Selected by Jacksonville in 1986 USFL territorial draft.
Selected by Philadelphia in 2nd round (37th player selected) of 1986 NFL draft.
Signed by Philadelphia Eagles, July 25, 1986.
On injured reserve with sprained ankle, September 2 through September 30, 1986; activated, October 1, 1986.

Year Club	G.	Att.	Yds.	Avg.	TD.	P.C.	Yds.	Avg.	TD.	TD.	Pts.	F.
1986—Philadelphia NFL	12	69	285	4.1	1	13	177	13.6	0	1	6	0
1987—Philadelphia NFL	11	127	473	3.7	5	39	341	8.7	1	6	36	5
1988—Philadelphia NFL	15	139	502	3.6	4	34	256	7.5	1	5	30	2
Pro Totals—3 Years	38	335	1260	3.8	10	86	774	9.0	2	12	72	7

Additional pro statistics: Attempted one pass with no completions and recovered three fumbles, 1987.

AL LEE TOON JR.
Wide Receiver—New York Jets
Born April 30, 1963, at Newport News, Va.
Height, 6.04. Weight, 205.
High School—Newport News, Va., Menchville.
Attended University of Wisconsin.

Selected by Jacksonville in 1985 USFL territorial draft.
Selected by New York Jets in 1st round (10th player selected) of 1985 NFL draft.
Signed by New York Jets, September 11, 1985.
Granted roster exemption, September 11 through September 13, 1985; activated, September 14, 1985.

			—PASS RECEIVING—		
Year Club	G.	P.C.	Yds.	Avg.	TD.
1985—N.Y. Jets NFL	15	46	662	14.4	3
1986—N.Y. Jets NFL	16	85	1176	13.8	8
1987—N.Y. Jets NFL	12	68	976	14.4	5
1988—N.Y. Jets NFL	15	*93	1067	11.5	5
Pro Totals—4 Years............	58	292	3881	13.3	21

Additional pro statistics: Rushed once for five yards, 1985 and 1988; rushed twice for minus three yards, recovered one fumble and fumbled three times, 1986; fumbled twice, 1988.
Played in Pro Bowl (NFL All-Star Game) following 1986 through 1988 seasons.

STACEY J. TORAN
Safety—Los Angeles Raiders
Born November 10, 1961, at Indianapolis, Ind.
Height, 6.03. Weight, 200.
High School—Indianapolis, Ind., Broad Ripple.
Received degree from University of Notre Dame in 1984.

Selected by Chicago in 1984 USFL territorial draft.
Selected by Los Angeles Raiders in 6th round (168th player selected) of 1984 NFL draft.
Signed by Los Angeles Raiders, June 2, 1984.
Granted free agency, February 1, 1988; re-signed by Raiders, August 29, 1988.

			—INTERCEPTIONS—		
Year Club	G.	No.	Yds.	Avg.	TD.
1984—L. A. Raiders NFL........	16		None		
1985—L. A. Raiders NFL........	16	1	76	76.0	1
1986—L. A. Raiders NFL........	16	2	28	14.0	0
1987—L. A. Raiders NFL........	12	3	48	16.0	1
1988—L. A. Raiders NFL........	12		None		
Pro Totals—5 Years............	72	6	152	25.3	2

Additional pro statistics: Recovered one fumble, 1986 and 1987; returned two kickoffs for no yards, 1988.

THOMAS JEFFREY TOTH
(Tom)
Guard—Miami Dolphins
Born May 23, 1962, at Chicago, Ill.
Height, 6.05. Weight, 282.
High School—Orland Park, Ill., Carl Sandberg.
Attended Western Michigan University.

Selected by Oakland in 7th round (95th player selected) of 1985 USFL draft.
Selected by New England in 4th round (102nd player selected) of 1985 NFL draft.
Signed by New England Patriots, July 19, 1985.
On injured reserve with ankle injury, August 15 through entire 1985 season.
Released by New England Patriots, September 1, 1986; signed as free agent by Miami Dolphins, September 9, 1986.
On injured reserve with knee injury, September 28 through November 18, 1988; activated, November 19, 1988.
Miami NFL, 1986 through 1988.
Games: 1986 (13), 1987 (12), 1988 (9). Total—34.
Pro statistics: Returned one kickoff for no yards and fumbled once, 1986.

JOSEPH RAY TOWNSELL
(Jojo)
Wide Receiver-Kick Returner—New York Jets
Born November 4, 1960, at Reno, Nev.
Height, 5.09. Weight, 180.
High School—Reno, Nev., Hug.
Received degree in sociology from University of California at Los Angeles in 1982.

Selected by Los Angeles in 6th round (72nd player selected) of 1983 USFL draft.
Selected by New York Jets in 3rd round (78th player selected) of 1983 NFL draft.
Signed by Los Angeles Express, June 3, 1983.
Released by Los Angeles Express, August 1, 1985; signed by New York Jets, August 5, 1985.

		PASS RECEIVING				-PUNT RETURNS-				—KICKOFF RET.—				—TOTAL—		
Year Club	G.	P.C.	Yds.	Avg.	TD.	No.	Yds.	Avg.	TD.	No.	Yds.	Avg.	TD.	TD.	Pts.	F.
1983—Los Angeles USFL.......	5	21	326	15.5	3		None			1	8	8.0	0	3	18	0
1984—Los Angeles USFL.......	18	58	889	15.3	7		None				None			7	42	2
1985—Los Angeles USFL.......	16	47	777	16.5	6	8	33	4.1	0		None			6	36	2

Year Club	G.	PASS RECEIVING				-PUNT RETURNS-				—KICKOFF RET.—				—TOTAL—		
		P.C.	Yds.	Avg.	TD.	No.	Yds.	Avg.	TD.	No.	Yds.	Avg.	TD.	TD.	Pts.	F.
1985—N.Y. Jets NFL	16	12	187	15.6	0	6	65	10.8	0	2	42	21.0	0	0	0	1
1986—N.Y. Jets NFL	14	1	11	11.0	0	4	52	13.0	0	13	322	24.8	*1	1	6	0
1987—N.Y. Jets NFL	12	4	37	9.3	0	32	381	11.9	1	11	272	24.7	0	1	6	3
1988—N.Y. Jets NFL	16	4	40	10.0	0	35	409	11.7	1	31	601	19.4	0	1	6	3
USFL Totals—3 Years	39	126	1992	15.8	16	8	33	4.1	0	1	8	8.0	0	16	96	5
NFL Totals—4 Years	58	21	275	13.1	0	77	907	11.8	2	57	1237	21.7	1	3	18	6
Pro Totals—7 Years	97	147	2267	15.4	16	85	940	11.1	2	58	1245	21.5	1	19	114	11

Additional USFL statistics: Rushed eight times for 19 yards, 1984; rushed twice for nine yards and recovered one fumble, 1985.

Additional NFL statistics: Recovered one fumble, 1985; rushed once for two yards, 1986; rushed once for minus two yards and recovered two fumbles, 1987.

ANDRE TOWNSEND
Defensive End-Nose Tackle—Denver Broncos
Born October 8, 1962, at Chicago, Ill.
Height, 6.03. Weight, 265.
High School—Aberdeen, Miss.
Attended University of Mississippi.

Selected by Birmingham in 1984 USFL territorial draft.
Selected by Denver in 2nd round (46th player selected) of 1984 NFL draft.
Signed by Denver Broncos, June 18, 1984.
Denver NFL, 1984 through 1988.
Games: 1984 (16), 1985 (16), 1986 (16), 1987 (12), 1988 (16). Total—76.
Pro statistics: Recovered one fumble, 1984, 1985 and 1988; recovered one fumble for seven yards and a touchdown, 1986.
Played in AFC Championship Game following 1986 and 1987 seasons.
Played in NFL Championship Game following 1986 and 1987 seasons.

GREG TOWNSEND
Linebacker-Defensive End—Los Angeles Raiders
Born November 3, 1961, at Los Angeles, Calif.
Height, 6.03. Weight, 250.
High School—Compton, Calif., Dominguez.
Attended Long Beach City College and Texas Christian University.

Selected by Oakland in 7th round (79th player selected) of 1983 USFL draft.
Selected by Los Angeles Raiders in 4th round (110th player selected) of 1983 NFL draft.
Signed by Los Angeles Raiders, July 7, 1983.
On suspended list, October 9, 1986; reinstated, October 10, 1986.
On suspended list, October 13 through October 19, 1986; activated, October 20, 1986.
Crossed picket line during players' strike, October 14, 1987.
On non-football injury list with substance abuse, August 5 through August 30, 1988; activated, August 31, 1988.
Los Angeles Raiders NFL, 1983 through 1988.
Games: 1983 (16), 1984 (16), 1985 (16), 1986 (15), 1987 (13), 1988 (16). Total—92.
Pro statistics: Recovered one fumble for 66 yards and a touchdown, 1983; recovered one fumble, 1985; credited with a safety, 1986; intercepted one pass for 86 yards and a touchdown and recovered one fumble in end zone for a touchdown, 1988.
Played in AFC Championship Game following 1983 season.
Played in NFL Championship Game following 1983 season.

STEPHEN PAUL TRAPILO
(Steve)
Guard—New Orleans Saints
Born September 20, 1964, at Boston, Mass.
Height, 6.05. Weight, 281.
High School—Boston, Mass., Boston College.
Received degree in sociology from Boston College in 1986.

Selected by New Orleans in 4th round (96th player selected) of 1987 NFL draft.
Signed by New Orleans Saints, July 27, 1987.
On injured reserve with sprained arch, September 5 through October 28, 1988; activated, October 29, 1988.
New Orleans NFL, 1987 and 1988.
Games: 1987 (11), 1988 (9). Total—20.

MARK JOSEPH TRAYNOWICZ
Name pronounced TRAY-no-witz.
Guard—Seattle Seahawks
Born November 20, 1962, at Omaha, Neb.
Height, 6.05. Weight, 280.
High School—Bellevue, Neb., West.
Received degree in civil engineering from University of Nebraska in 1985.

Selected by Houston in 1st round (9th player selected) of 1985 USFL draft.
Selected by Buffalo in 2nd round (29th player selected) of 1985 NFL draft.
Signed by Buffalo Bills, July 20, 1985.
Traded by Buffalo Bills to Philadelphia Eagles for conditional draft choice, August 23, 1988.
Released by Philadelphia Eagles, August 26, 1988; signed as free agent by Buffalo Bills, September 7, 1988.

Released by Buffalo Bills, October 10, 1988; signed as free agent by Phoenix Cardinals, November 8, 1988.
Granted unconditional free agency, February 1, 1989; signed by Seattle Seahawks, April 1, 1989.
Buffalo NFL, 1985 through 1987; Buffalo (4)-Phoenix (5) NFL, 1988.
Games: 1985 (14), 1986 (16), 1987 (11), 1988 (9). Total—50.
Pro statistics: Recovered one fumble, 1985 and 1986.

JACK FRANCIS TRUDEAU
Quarterback—Indianapolis Colts
Born September 9, 1962, at Forest Lake, Minn.
Height, 6.03. Weight, 211.
High School—Livermore, Calif., Granada.
Received degree in political science from University of Illinois in 1986.
Brother of Kevin Trudeau, pitcher in California Angels' organization.

Selected by Orlando in 1986 USFL territorial draft.
Selected by Indianapolis in 2nd round (47th player selected) of 1986 NFL draft.
Signed by Indianapolis Colts, July 31, 1986.
On injured reserve with knee injury, October 11 through remainder of 1988 season.

					—PASSING—					—RUSHING—			—TOTAL—		
Year Club	G.	Att.	Cmp.	Pct.	Gain	T.P.	P.I.	Avg.	Att.	Yds.	Avg.	TD.	TD.	Pts.	F.
1986—Indianapolis NFL	12	417	204	48.9	2225	8	18	5.34	13	21	1.6	1	1	6	*13
1987—Indianapolis NFL	10	229	128	55.9	1587	6	6	6.93	15	7	0.5	0	0	0	10
1988—Indianapolis NFL	2	34	14	41.2	158	0	3	4.65		None			0	0	0
Pro Totals—3 Years	24	680	346	50.9	3970	14	27	5.84	28	28	1.0	1	1	6	23

Quarterback Rating Points: 1986 (53.5), 1987 (75.4), 1988 (19.0). Total—59.2.
Additional pro statistics: Recovered six fumbles and fumbled 13 times for minus 15 yards, 1986; recovered two fumbles and fumbled 10 times for minus 28 yards, 1987.

ERROLL R. TUCKER
Defensive Back-Kick Returner—Buffalo Bills
Born July 6, 1964, at Pittsburgh, Pa.
Height, 5.08. Weight, 170.
High School—Lynwood, Calif.
Attended Long Beach City College and University of Utah.

Named as kick returner on THE SPORTING NEWS College All-America Team, 1985.
Selected by Pittsburgh in 5th round (122nd player selected) of 1986 NFL draft.
Selected by Baltimore in 4th round (29th player selected) of 1986 USFL draft.
Signed by Pittsburgh Steelers, July 18, 1986.
On injured reserve with fractured ankle, September 1 through entire 1986 season.
Released by Pittsburgh Steelers after failing physical, July 31, 1987; signed as free agent by Buffalo Bills, April 11, 1988.
On injured reserve with knee injury, October 29 through December 16, 1988; activated, December 17, 1988.

		–PUNT RETURNS-				—KICKOFF RET.—				—TOTAL—		
Year Club	G.	No.	Yds.	Avg.	TD.	No.	Yds.	Avg.	TD.	TD.	Pts.	F.
1988—Buffalo NFL	9	10	80	8.0	0	15	310	20.7	0	0	0	1

Played in AFC Championship Game following 1988 season.

JESSIE LLOYD TUGGLE
Linebacker—Atlanta Falcons
Born February 14, 1965, at Spalding County, Ga.
Height, 5.11. Weight, 225.
High School—Griffin, Ga.
Attended Valdosta State College.

Signed as free agent by Atlanta Falcons, May 2, 1987.
Atlanta NFL, 1987 and 1988.
Games: 1987 (12), 1988 (16). Total—28.
Pro statistics: Recovered one fumble for two yards and a touchdown, 1988.

MARK PULEMAU TUINEI
Name pronounced TWO-e-nay.
Offensive Tackle—Dallas Cowboys
Born March 31, 1960, at Nanakuli, Oahu, Haw.
Height, 6.05. Weight, 283.
High School—Honolulu, Haw., Punahou.
Attended University of California at Los Angeles and University of Hawaii.
Brother of Tom Tuinei, defensive end with Edmonton Eskimos, 1982 through 1987.

Selected by Boston in 19th round (227th player selected) of 1983 USFL draft.
Signed as free agent by Dallas Cowboys, April 28, 1983.
On injured reserve with knee injury, December 2 through remainder of 1987 season.
On injured reserve with knee injury, October 19 through remainder of 1988 season.
Dallas NFL, 1983 through 1988.
Games: 1983 (10), 1984 (16), 1985 (16), 1986 (16), 1987 (8), 1988 (5). Total—71.
Pro statistics: Returned one kickoff for no yards, recovered three fumbles and fumbled once, 1986; recovered one fumble, 1987.

WILLIE TULLIS
Cornerback—Detroit Lions
Born April 5, 1958, at Newville, Ala.
Height, 5.11. Weight, 195.
High School—Headland, Ala.
Attended University of Southern Mississippi and Troy State University.

Selected by Houston in 8th round (217th player selected) of 1981 NFL draft.
Released by Houston Oilers, September 3, 1985; signed as free agent by New Orleans Saints, September 17, 1985.
Released by New Orleans Saints, October 29, 1986; signed as free agent by Indianapolis Colts, May 11, 1987.
Granted unconditional free agency, February 1, 1989; signed by Detroit Lions, March 23, 1989.

		INTERCEPTIONS			–PUNT RETURNS–			—KICKOFF RET.—			—TOTAL—		
Year Club	G.	No.	Yds.	Avg.	TD.	No.	Yds.	Avg.	TD.	No.	Yds.	Avg.	TD.	Pts.	F.
1981—Houston NFL	16		None			2	29	14.5	0	32	779	24.3	★1	1	6	0
1982—Houston NFL	9		None				None			5	91	18.2	0	0	0	0
1983—Houston NFL	16	5	65	13.0	0		None			1	16	16.0	0	0	0	0
1984—Houston NFL	16	4	48	12.0	0		None				None			0	0	1
1985—New Orleans NFL	14	2	22	11.0	0	17	141	8.3	0	23	470	20.4	0	0	0	1
1986—New Orleans NFL	7		None			2	10	5.0	0	2	28	14.0	0	0	0	0
1987—Indianapolis NFL	12	3	0	0.0	0	4	27	6.8	0		None			0	0	0
1988—Indianapolis NFL	16	4	36	9.0	0		None				None			0	0	0
Pro Totals—8 Years	106	18	171	9.5	0	25	207	8.3	0	63	1384	22.0	1	1	6	2

Additional pro statistics: Recovered one fumble, 1984, recovered three fumbles, 1988.

THOMAS JOSEPH TUPA
(Tom)
Quarterback-Punter—Phoenix Cardinals
Born February 6, 1966, at Cleveland, O.
Height, 6.04. Weight, 220.
High School—Broadview Heights, O., Brecksville.
Attended Ohio State University.

Selected by Phoenix in 3rd round (68th player selected) of 1988 NFL draft.
Signed by Phoenix Cardinals, July 12, 1988.
Phoenix NFL, 1988.
Games: 1988 (2).
Pro statistics: Attempted six passes with four completions for 49 yards, 1988.

DANIEL ANTHONY TURK
(Dan)
Guard—Tampa Bay Buccaneers
Born June 25, 1962, at Milwaukee, Wis.
Height, 6.04. Weight, 260.
High School—Milwaukee, Wis., James Madison.
Attended Drake University and University of Wisconsin.

Selected by Jacksonville in 1985 USFL territorial draft.
USFL rights traded with rights to running back Marck Harrison and tight end Ken Whisenhunt by Jacksonville Bulls to Tampa Bay Bandits for rights to running back Cedric Jones, kicker Bobby Raymond and defensive back Eric Riley, January 3, 1985.
Selected by Pittsburgh in 4th round (101st player selected) of 1985 NFL draft.
Signed by Pittsburgh Steelers, July 19, 1985.
On injured reserve with broken wrist, September 16 through remainder of 1985 season.
Traded by Pittsburgh Steelers to Tampa Bay Buccaneers for 6th round pick in 1987 draft, April 13, 1987.
Crossed picket line during players' strike, October 14, 1987.
On injured reserve with knee injury, October 18 through November 17, 1988; activated, November 18, 1988.
Pittsburgh NFL, 1985 and 1986; Tampa Bay NFL, 1987 and 1988.
Games: 1985 (1), 1986 (16), 1987 (13), 1988 (12). Total—42.
Pro statistics: Recovered one fumble and fumbled once for minus 19 yards, 1988.

KEENA TURNER
Linebacker—San Francisco 49ers
Born October 22, 1958, at Chicago, Ill.
Height, 6.02. Weight, 219.
High School—Chicago, Ill., Vocational.
Attended Purdue University.

Selected by San Francisco in 2nd round (39th player selected) of 1980 NFL draft.
On injured reserve with knee injury, December 17 through remainder of 1987 season.
On injured reserve with pinched nerve in neck, November 19 through December 30, 1988; activated, December 31, 1988.

	—INTERCEPTIONS—					—INTERCEPTIONS—			
Year Club	G.	No.	Yds.	Avg.TD.	Year Club	G.	No.	Yds.	Avg.TD.
1980—San Francisco NFL	16	2	15	7.5 0	1986—San Francisco NFL	16	1	9	9.0 0
1981—San Francisco NFL	16	1	0	0.0 0	1987—San Francisco NFL	10	1	15	15.0 0
1982—San Francisco NFL	9		None		1988—San Francisco NFL	11	1	2	2.0 0
1983—San Francisco NFL	15		None		Pro Totals—9 Years	124	10	92	9.2 0
1984—San Francisco NFL	16	4	51	12.8 0					
1985—San Francisco NFL	15		None						

Additional pro statistics: Recovered three fumbles, 1981; recovered one fumble, 1983; returned two fumbles for 65 yards and a touchdown, 1985; recovered two fumbles, 1988.
Played in NFC Championship Game following 1981, 1983, 1984 and 1988 seasons.
Played in NFL Championship Game following 1981, 1984 and 1988 seasons.
Played in Pro Bowl (NFL All-Star Game) following 1984 season.

LONNIE TURNER
Wide Receiver—Detroit Lions
Born August 31, 1959, at Los Angeles, Calif.
Height, 5.07. Weight, 164.
High School—Compton, Calif., Centennial.
Attended Los Angeles City College and Cal Poly Pomona.

Signed by Los Angeles Express, November 8, 1982.
On developmental squad, April 10 through April 29, 1983.
Released by Los Angeles Express, April 30, 1983; signed as free agent by Oklahoma Outlaws, August 24, 1983.
Not protected in merger of Oklahoma Outlaws and Arizona Wranglers; selected by Denver Gold in USFL dispersal draft, December 6, 1984.
Released by Denver Gold, July 31, 1985; signed as free agent by New Jersey Generals, May 2, 1986.
Granted free agency when USFL suspended operations, August 7, 1986; signed as free agent replacement player by St. Louis Cardinals, September 25, 1987.
Released by St. Louis Cardinals, October 20, 1987; signed as free agent by Detroit Lions, March 15, 1989.
On developmental squad for 3 games with Los Angeles Express in 1983.
Inactive for 1 game with St. Louis Cardinals in 1987.

		PASS RECEIVING				-PUNT RETURNS-				—KICKOFF RET.—				—TOTAL—		
Year	Club	G.	P.C.	Yds.	Avg.	TD.	No.	Yds.	Avg.	TD.	No.	Yds.	Avg.	TD.	TD.	Pts.	F.
1983—Los Angeles USFL		5	3	41	13.7	0	3	9	3.0	0	7	174	24.9	0	0	0	3
1984—Oklahoma USFL		18	27	399	14.8	2	12	66	5.5	0	26	466	17.9	0	2	12	4
1985—Denver USFL		17	29	388	13.4	0			None		24	464	19.3	0	0	0	1
USFL Totals—3 Years		40	59	828	14.0	2	15	75	5.0	0	57	1104	19.4	0	2	12	8

Additional pro statistics: Recovered two fumbles, 1983; recovered four fumbles and rushed once for no yards, 1984.

ODESSA TURNER
Wide Receiver—New York Giants
Born October 12, 1964, at Monroe, La.
Height, 6.03. Weight, 205.
High School—Monroe, La., Wossman.
Attended Northwestern State (La.) University.

Selected by New York Giants in 4th round (112th player selected) of 1987 NFL draft.
Signed by New York Giants, July 27, 1987.
On injured reserve with hamstring and shoulder injuries, September 7 through October 23, 1987; activated, October 24, 1987.
On injured reserve with knee injury, November 11 through remainder of 1988 season.

		—PASS RECEIVING—			
Year	Club	G.	P.C.	Yds.	Avg.	TD.
1987—N.Y. Giants NFL		7	10	195	19.5	1
1988—N.Y. Giants NFL		4	10	128	12.8	1
Pro Totals—2 Years		11	20	323	16.2	2

THOMAS JAMES TURNER
(T. J.)
Defensive End—Miami Dolphins
Born May 16, 1963, at Lufkin, Tex.
Height, 6.04. Weight, 280.
High School—Lufkin, Tex.
Attended University of Houston.

Selected by Miami in 3rd round (81st player selected) of 1986 NFL draft.
Signed by Miami Dolphins, July 23, 1986.
Miami NFL, 1986 through 1988.
Games: 1986 (16), 1987 (12), 1988 (16). Total—44.
Pro statistics: Recovered one fumble, 1987 and 1988.

TIMOTHY G. TYRRELL
Name pronounced Tuhr-RELL.

(Tim)
Running Back—Buffalo Bills
Born February 19, 1961, at Chicago, Ill.
Height, 6.02. Weight, 215.
High School—Hoffman Estates, Ill., James B. Conant.
Attended William Rainey Harper College and Northern Illinois University.

Selected by Chicago in 1984 USFL territorial draft.
Signed as free agent by Atlanta Falcons, May 2, 1984.
Released by Atlanta Falcons, August 27, 1984; re-signed by Falcons, October 3, 1984.
Released by Atlanta Falcons, August 26, 1986; re-signed by Falcons, October 24, 1986.
Released by Atlanta Falcons, October 27, 1986; re-signed by Falcons, October 31, 1986.

Released by Atlanta Falcons, November 11, 1986; signed as free agent by Los Angeles Rams, November 13, 1986.
Crossed picket line during players' strike, October 14, 1987.
On injured reserve with hamstring injury, August 31 through September 29, 1988; activated, September 30, 1988.
Granted unconditional free agency, February 1, 1989; signed by Buffalo Bills, March 29, 1989.

		—RUSHING—			PASS RECEIVING				—TOTAL—		
Year Club	G.	Att.	Yds.	Avg.	TD.	P.C.	Yds.	Avg.	TD.	TD.	Pts.	F.
1984—Atlanta NFL	11		None				None			0	0	0
1985—Atlanta NFL	16		None				None			0	0	1
1986—Atlanta (3)-L.A. Rams (6) NFL	9		None			1	9	9.0	0	0	0	1
1987—Los Angeles Rams NFL	11	11	44	4.0	0	6	59	9.8	0	0	0	0
1988—Los Angeles Rams NFL	12		None				None			0	0	0
Pro Totals—5 Years	59	11	44	4.0	0	7	68	9.7	0	0	0	2

Additional pro statistics: Returned one kickoff for no yards and recovered three fumbles, 1984; returned one kickoff for 13 yards, 1985; returned six kickoffs for 116 yards, 1987.

RICHARD KEITH UECKER
(Known by middle name.)
Guard-Offensive Tackle—Green Bay Packers
Born June 29, 1960, at Hollywood, Fla.
Height, 6.05. Weight, 284.
High School—Hollywood, Fla., Hollywood Hills.
Attended Auburn University.

Selected by Denver in 9th round (243rd player selected) of 1982 NFL draft.
On injured reserve with Achilles tendon injury, August 14 through October 21, 1984.
Awarded on procedural waivers to Green Bay Packers, October 23, 1984.
On injured reserve with knee injury, November 2 through remainder of 1985 season.
On injured reserve with knee injury, August 22 through entire 1986 season.
Crossed picket line during players' strike, October 14, 1987.
On injured reserve with knee injury, October 31 through December 4, 1987; activated, December 5, 1987.
Denver NFL, 1982 and 1983; Green Bay NFL, 1984, 1985, 1987 and 1988.
Games: 1982 (5), 1983 (16), 1984 (6), 1985 (7), 1987 (8), 1988 (16). Total—58.
Pro statistics: Returned one kickoff for 12 yards and fumbled once, 1982; recovered one fumble, 1985; recovered two fumbles, 1988.

TERRANCE LYNN UNREIN
(Terry)
Nose Tackle—San Francisco 49ers
Born October 24, 1962, at Brighton, Colo.
Height, 6.05. Weight, 283.
High School—Fort Lupton, Colo.
Received bachelor of science degree in agricultural business
from Colorado State University in 1986.

Selected by San Diego in 3rd round (66th player selected) of 1986 NFL draft.
Signed by San Diego Chargers, July 15, 1986.
On injured reserve with knee injury, September 10 through October 10, 1986; activated, October 11, 1986.
Crossed picket line during players' strike, October 14, 1987.
Released by San Diego Chargers, August 30, 1988; signed as free agent by San Francisco 49ers, February 24, 1989.
San Diego NFL, 1986 and 1987.
Games: 1986 (12), 1987 (9). Total—21.

BENJAMIN MICHAEL UTT
(Ben)
Guard—Indianapolis Colts
Born June 13, 1959, at Richmond, Calif.
Height, 6.06. Weight, 286.
High School—Vidalia, Ga.
Received bachelor of science degree in industrial management from Georgia Tech in 1982.

Signed as free agent by Dallas Cowboys, May, 1981.
Released by Dallas Cowboys, August 14, 1981; signed as free agent by Baltimore Colts, January 18, 1982.
Franchise transferred to Indianapolis, March 31, 1984.
On injured reserve with knee and back injuries, November 4 through remainder of 1986 season.
Baltimore NFL, 1982 and 1983; Indianapolis NFL, 1984 through 1988.
Games: 1982 (9), 1983 (16), 1984 (16), 1985 (16), 1986 (9), 1987 (12), 1988 (16). Total—94.
Pro statistics: Recovered one fumble, 1984; caught one pass for minus four yards and recovered two fumbles, 1987.

IRA LYNN VALENTINE
Running Back—Tampa Bay Buccaneers
Born June 4, 1963, at Marshall, Tex.
Height, 6.01. Weight, 220.
High School—Marshall, Tex.
Attended Texas A&M University.

Selected by Houston in 12th round (314th player selected) of 1987 NFL draft.
Signed by Houston Oilers, July 22, 1987.
Released by Houston Oilers, November 7, 1987; re-signed by Oilers, November 12, 1987.
Released by Houston Oilers, August 30, 1988; signed as free agent by Tampa Bay Buccaneers, January 6, 1989.

		—————RUSHING—————				PASS RECEIVING				—TOTAL—		
Year	Club	G.	Att.	Yds.	Avg.	TD.	P.C.	Yds.	Avg.	TD.	TD.	Pts.	F.
1987—Houston NFL		7	5	10	2.0	0	2	10	5.0	0	0	0	0

Additional pro statistics: Returned one kickoff for 13 yards, 1987.

KEITH VAN HORNE
Offensive Tackle—Chicago Bears
Born November 6, 1957, at Mt. Lebanon, Pa.
Height, 6.06. Weight, 285.
High School—Fullerton, Calif.
Received bachelor of arts degree in broadcast journalism from University of Southern California.
Brother of Pete Van Horne, first baseman in Chicago Cubs' organization, 1977;
and son-in-law of Walter Mondale, former Vice-President.

Named as offensive tackle on THE SPORTING NEWS College All-America Team, 1980.
Selected by Chicago in 1st round (11th player selected) of 1981 NFL draft.
Chicago NFL, 1981 through 1988.
Games: 1981 (14), 1982 (9), 1983 (14), 1984 (14), 1985 (16), 1986 (16), 1987 (12), 1988 (15). Total—110.
Pro statistics: Recovered one fumble, 1981, 1982, 1986 and 1988.
Played in NFC Championship Game following 1984, 1985 and 1988 seasons.
Played in NFL Championship Game following 1985 season.

CLARENCE VAUGHN
Safety—Washington Redskins
Born July 17, 1964, at Chicago, Ill.
Height, 6.00. Weight, 202.
High School—Chicago, Ill., Gage Park.
Attended Northern Illinois University.

Selected by Washington in 8th round (219th player selected) of 1987 NFL draft.
Signed by Washington Redskins, July 24, 1987.
On injured reserve with ankle injury, December 5, 1987 through January 8, 1988; activated, January 9, 1988.
Washington NFL, 1987 and 1988.
Games: 1987 (5), 1988 (14). Total—19.
Played in NFC Championship Game following 1987 season.
Played in NFL Championship Game following 1987 season.

ALAN STUART VEINGRAD
Offensive Tackle-Guard—Green Bay Packers
Born July 24, 1963, at Brooklyn, N.Y.
Height, 6.05. Weight, 277.
High School—Miami, Fla., Sunset.
Received bachelor of science degree in physical education and health
from East Texas State University in 1985.

Selected by San Antonio in 11th round (163rd player selected) of 1985 USFL draft.
Signed as free agent by Tampa Bay Buccaneers, June 26, 1985.
Released by Tampa Bay Buccaneers, July 30, 1985; awarded on waivers to Houston Oilers, August 1, 1985.
Released by Houston Oilers, August 20, 1985; signed as free agent by Green Bay Packers, March 28, 1986.
On injured reserve with hip injury, August 23 through entire 1988 season.
Green Bay NFL, 1986 and 1987.
Games: 1986 (16), 1987 (11). Total—27.
Pro statistics: Recovered one fumble, 1986.

CLARENCE VERDIN
Wide Receiver—Indianapolis Colts
Born June 14, 1963, at New Orleans, La.
Height, 5.08. Weight, 160.
High School—Bourg, La., South Terrebonne.
Received bachelor of science degree in business from Southwestern Louisiana University.

Named as kick returner on THE SPORTING NEWS USFL All-Star Team, 1985.
Selected by Houston in 17th round (353rd player selected) of 1984 USFL draft.
Signed by Houston Gamblers, January 19, 1984.
On developmental squad, February 24 through March 22, 1984; activated, March 23, 1984.
Selected by Washington in 3rd round (83rd player selected) of 1984 NFL supplemental draft.
Traded with defensive backs Luther Bradley, Will Lewis, Mike Mitchell and Durwood Roquemore, defensive end Pete Catan, quarterbacks Jim Kelly and Todd Dillon, defensive tackles Tony Fitzpatrick, Van Hughes and Hosea Taylor, running back Sam Harrell, linebackers Andy Hawkins and Ladell Wills, wide receivers Richard Johnson, Scott McGhee, Gerald McNeil and Ricky Sanders, guard Rich Kehr, center Billy Kidd and offensive tackles Chris Riehm and Tommy Robison by Houston Gamblers to New Jersey Generals for past considerations, March 7, 1986.
Granted free agency when USFL suspended operations, August 7, 1986; signed by Washington Redskins, August 13, 1986.
Granted roster exemption, August 13 through August 24, 1986; activated, August 25, 1986.
On injured reserve with hamstring injury, September 1 through October 17, 1986; activated, October 18, 1986.
On injured reserve with ribs and shoulder injuries, December 9 through remainder of 1986 season.
On injured reserve with leg injury, September 7 through December 11, 1987; activated, December 12, 1987.
Traded by Washington Redskins to Indianapolis Colts for 6th round pick in 1988 draft, March 29, 1988.
On developmental squad for 4 games with Houston Gamblers in 1984.

Year Club	G.	Att.	Yds.	Avg.	TD.	P.C.	Yds.	Avg.	TD.	TD.	Pts.	F.
			RUSHING				PASS RECEIVING				TOTAL	
1984—Houston USFL	14	1	−2	−2.0	0	16	315	19.7	3	4	24	2
1985—Houston USFL	18	7	20	2.9	0	84	1004	12.0	9	12	72	0
1986—Washington NFL	8		None				None			0	0	0
1987—Washington NFL	3	1	14	14.0	0	2	62	31.0	0	0	0	0
1988—Indianapolis NFL	16	8	77	9.6	0	20	437	21.9	4	5	30	0
USFL Totals—2 Years	32	8	18	2.3	0	100	1319	13.2	12	16	96	2
NFL Totals—3 Years	27	9	91	10.1	0	22	499	22.7	4	5	30	0
Pro Totals—5 Years	59	17	109	6.4	0	122	1818	14.9	16	21	126	2

Year Club	G.	No.	Yds.	Avg.	TD.	No.	Yds.	Avg.	TD.
			PUNT RETURNS				KICKOFF RET.		
1984—Houston USFL	14		None			25	643	25.7	*1
1985—Houston USFL	18		None			28	746	*26.6	*3
1986—Washington NFL	8		None			12	240	20.0	0
1987—Washington NFL	3		None			12	244	20.3	0
1988—Indianapolis NFL	16	22	239	10.9	1	7	145	20.7	0
USFL Totals—2 Years	32	0	0	0.0	0	53	1389	26.2	4
NFL Totals—3 Years	27	22	239	10.9	1	31	629	20.3	0
Pro Totals—5 Years	59	22	239	10.9	1	84	2018	24.0	4

Additional pro statistics: Recovered four fumbles, 1984.
Member of Washington Redskins for NFL Championship Game following 1987 season; inactive.

CHRISTOPHER SEAN VERHULST
(Chris)
Tight End—Houston Oilers
Born May 16, 1966, at Sacramento, Calif.
Height, 6.02. Weight, 249.
High School—San Ramon, Calif., California.
Attended California State University at Chico.

Selected by Houston in 5th round (130th player selected) of 1988 NFL draft.
Signed by Houston Oilers, July 15, 1988.
Houston NFL, 1988.
Games: 1988 (1).

GARIN LEE VERIS
Name pronounced GARR-in VAIR-is.
Defensive End—New England Patriots
Born February 27, 1963, at Chillicothe, O.
Height, 6.04. Weight, 255.
High School—Chillicothe, O.
Attended Stanford University.

Selected by Oakland in 1985 USFL territorial draft.
Selected by New England in 2nd round (48th player selected) of 1985 NFL draft.
Signed by New England Patriots, July 25, 1985.
On injured reserve with knee injury, October 27 through December 2, 1988; activated, December 3, 1988.
New England NFL, 1985 through 1988.
Games: 1985 (16), 1986 (16), 1987 (12), 1988 (11). Total—55.
Pro statistics: Recovered two fumbles, 1985 and 1986; recovered one fumble, 1988.
Played in AFC Championship Game following 1985 season.
Played in NFL Championship Game following 1985 season.

ROGER VICK
Fullback—New York Jets
Born August 11, 1964, at Conroe, Tex.
Height, 6.03. Weight, 232.
High School—Tomball, Tex.
Attended Texas A&M University.

Selected by New York Jets in 1st round (21st player selected) of 1987 NFL draft.
Signed by New York Jets, July 21, 1987.

Year Club	G.	Att.	Yds.	Avg.	TD.	P.C.	Yds.	Avg.	TD.	TD.	Pts.	F.
			RUSHING				PASS RECEIVING				TOTAL	
1987—New York Jets NFL	12	77	257	3.3	1	13	108	8.3	0	1	6	3
1988—New York Jets NFL	16	128	540	4.2	3	19	120	6.3	0	3	18	5
Pro Totals—2 Years	28	205	797	3.9	4	32	228	7.1	0	4	24	8

DANNY VILLA
Offensive Tackle—New England Patriots
Born September 21, 1964, at Nogales, Ariz.
Height, 6.05. Weight, 305.
High School—Nogales, Ariz.
Attended Arizona State University.

Selected by New England in 5th round (113th player selected) of 1987 NFL draft.

Signed by New England Patriots, July 25, 1987.
New England NFL, 1987 and 1988.
Games: 1987 (11), 1988 (16). Total—27.
Pro statistics: Fumbled once for minus 13 yards, 1987; fumbled once for minus 39 yards, 1988.

MARK RICHARD VLASIC
Quarterback—San Diego Chargers
Born October 25, 1963, at Rochester, Pa.
Height, 6.03. Weight, 206.
High School—Monaca, Pa., Center.
Received degree in finance from University of Iowa in 1987.
Selected by San Diego in 4th round (88th player selected) of 1987 NFL draft.
Signed by San Diego Chargers, July 26, 1987.
On injured reserve with knee injury, November 23 through remainder of 1988 season.

				PASSING					RUSHING			TOTAL		
Year	Club	G.	Att.	Cmp.	Pct.	Gain	T.P.	P.I.	Avg.	Att.	Yds.	Avg.	TD.	TD.	Pts.	F.
1987—San Diego NFL		1	6	3	50.0	8	0	1	1.33		None			0	0	1
1988—San Diego NFL		2	52	25	48.1	270	1	2	5.19	2	0	0.0	0	0	0	1
Pro Totals—2 Years		3	58	28	48.3	278	1	3	4.79	2	0	0.0	0	0	0	2

Quarterback Rating Points: 1987 (16.7), 1988 (54.2). Total—46.3.
Additional pro statistics: Recovered one fumble, 1987; recovered one fumble and fumbled once for minus 10 yards, 1988.

TIMOTHY GENE VOGLER
(Tim)
Guard—Buffalo Bills
Born October 2, 1956, at Troy, O.
Height, 6.03. Weight, 285.
High School—Covington, O.
Attended Ohio State University.
Signed as free agent by Buffalo Bills, May 5, 1979.
On injured reserve with broken hand, August 28 through October 5, 1979; activated, October 6, 1979.
On injured reserve with hamstring injury, November 29 through remainder of 1980 season.
On injured reserve with knee injury, August 19 through October 17, 1986; activated, October 18, 1986.
On injured reserve with knee injury, September 7 through October 7, 1988; activated, October 8, 1988.
On injured reserve with knee injury, December 17 through remainder of 1988 season.
Buffalo NFL, 1979 through 1988.
Games: 1979 (10), 1980 (10), 1981 (14), 1982 (6), 1983 (16), 1984 (16), 1985 (14), 1986 (9), 1987 (12), 1988 (10). Total—117.
Pro statistics: Returned one kickoff for no yards, 1980; recovered one fumble, 1985; recovered two fumbles, 1987.

BRYAN J. WAGNER
Punter—Cleveland Browns
Born March 28, 1962, at Escondido, Calif.
Height, 6.02. Weight, 200.
High School—Chula Vista, Calif., Hilltop.
Attended California Lutheran College and California State University at Northridge.
Selected by Baltimore in 15th round (216th player selected) of 1985 USFL draft.
Signed as free agent by Dallas Cowboys, May 2, 1985.
Released by Dallas Cowboys, August 27, 1985; signed as free agent by New York Giants, May 10, 1986.
Released by New York Giants, August 11, 1986; signed as free agent by St. Louis Cardinals, August 19, 1986.
Released by St. Louis Cardinals, August 26, 1986; signed as free agent by Denver Broncos, May 1, 1987.
Traded with draft pick by Denver Broncos to Chicago Bears for guard Stefan Humphries, August 25, 1987.
On injured reserve with back injury, December 16, through remainder of 1987 season.
Granted unconditional free agency, February 1, 1989; signed by Cleveland Browns, March 30, 1989.

			PUNTING		
Year	Club	G.	No.	Avg.	Blk.
1987—Chicago NFL		10	36	40.6	1
1988—Chicago NFL		16	79	41.5	0
Pro Totals—2 Years		26	115	41.2	1

Additional pro statistics: Attempted one pass with one completion for three yards, rushed twice for no yards, recovered one fumble and fumbled once for minus nine yards, 1988.
Played in NFC Championship Game following 1988 season.

VAN ALLEN WAITERS
Linebacker—Cleveland Browns
Born February 27, 1965, at Coral Gables, Fla.
Height, 6.04. Weight, 240.
High School—Coral Gables, Fla.
Attended Indiana University.
Selected by Cleveland in 3rd round (77th player selected) of 1988 NFL draft.
Signed by Cleveland Browns, July 23, 1988.
Cleveland NFL, 1988.
Games: 1988 (16).

MARK CHARLES WALCZAK
Tight End—Phoenix Cardinals
Born April 26, 1962, at Rochester, N. Y.
Height, 6.06. Weight, 246.
High School—Rochester, N. Y., Greece Athena.
Attended University of Arizona.

Signed as free agent by Kansas City Chiefs, May 6, 1986.
Released by Kansas City Chiefs, August 14, 1986; signed as free agent by Indianapolis Colts, May 14, 1987.
Released by Indianapolis Colts, August 31, 1987; signed as free agent replacement player by Buffalo Bills, September 24, 1987.
Released by Buffalo Bills, October 16, 1987; signed as free agent by Indianapolis Colts, October 27, 1987.
On injured reserve with knee injury, December 23 through remainder of 1987 season.
Released by Indianapolis Colts, April 18, 1988; signed as free agent by San Diego Chargers, May 23, 1988.
Released by San Diego Chargers, June 28, 1988; signed as free agent by Phoenix Cardinals, July 18, 1988.
Buffalo (2)-Indianapolis (8) NFL, 1987; Phoenix NFL, 1988.
Games: 1987 (10), 1988 (16). Total—26.
Pro statistics: Fumbled once, 1987; recovered one fumble and fumbled once for minus 23 yards, 1988.

MARK HARTLEY WALEN
Defensive Lineman—Dallas Cowboys
Born March 10, 1963, at San Francisco, Calif.
Height, 6.05. Weight, 267.
High School—Burlingame, Calif.
Received bachelor of science degree in history
from University of California at Los Angeles in 1986.

Selected by Arizona in 1986 USFL territorial draft.
Selected by Dallas in 3rd round (74th player selected) of 1986 NFL draft.
Signed by Dallas Cowboys, August 9, 1986.
On injured reserve with broken foot, August 26 through entire 1986 season.
Dallas NFL, 1987 and 1988.
Games: 1987 (9), 1988 (15). Total—24.

HERSCHEL WALKER
Running Back—Dallas Cowboys
Born March 3, 1962, at Wrightsville, Ga.
Height, 6.01. Weight, 222.
High School—Wrightsville, Ga., Johnson County.
Received degree in criminal justice from University of Georgia in 1984.

Named THE SPORTING NEWS USFL Player of the Year, 1985.
Named as running back on THE SPORTING NEWS USFL All-Star Team, 1983 and 1985.
Heisman Trophy winner, 1982.
Named college football Player of the Year by THE SPORTING NEWS, 1982.
Named as running back on THE SPORTING NEWS College All-America Team, 1980 through 1982.
Signed by New Jersey Generals, February 22, 1983 (Generals forfeited 1st round pick in 1984 draft).
On developmental squad April 8 through April 13, 1984; activated, April 14, 1984.
Selected by Dallas in 5th round (114th player selected) of 1985 NFL draft.
Granted free agency when USFL suspended operations, August 7, 1986; signed by Dallas Cowboys, August 13, 1986.
Granted roster exemption, August 13 through August 22, 1986; activated, August 23, 1986.
On developmental squad for 1 game with New Jersey Generals in 1984.

Year Club	G.	Att.	Yds.	Avg.	TD.	P.C.	Yds.	Avg.	TD.	TD.	Pts.	F.
			—RUSHING—				PASS RECEIVING				—TOTAL—	
1983—New Jersey USFL	18	*412	*1812	4.4	*17	53	489	9.2	1	*18	†110	12
1984—New Jersey USFL	17	293	1339	4.6	16	40	528	13.2	5	*21	†128	6
1985—New Jersey USFL	18	*438	*2411	5.5	*21	37	467	12.6	1	*22	*132	9
1986—Dallas NFL	16	151	737	4.9	12	76	837	11.0	2	14	84	5
1987—Dallas NFL	12	209	891	4.3	7	60	715	11.9	1	8	48	4
1988—Dallas NFL	16	361	1514	4.2	5	53	505	9.5	2	7	42	6
USFL Totals—3 Years	53	1143	5562	4.9	54	130	1484	11.4	7	61	370	27
NFL Totals—3 Years	44	721	3142	4.4	24	189	2057	10.9	5	29	174	15
Pro Totals—6 Years	97	1864	8704	4.7	78	319	3541	11.1	12	90	544	42

†Includes one 2-point conversion.
Additional USFL statistics: Returned three kickoffs for 69 yards and recovered four fumbles, 1983; recovered two fumbles, 1984; recovered three fumbles, 1985.
Additional NFL statistics: Recovered two fumbles, 1986; recovered one fumble, 1987; recovered three fumbles, 1988.
Played in Pro Bowl (NFL All-Star Game) following 1987 and 1988 seasons.

JACKIE A. WALKER
Linebacker—New York Jets
Born November 3, 1962, at Monroe, La.
Height, 6.05. Weight, 245.
High School—Monroe, La., Carroll.
Attended Jackson State University.

Selected by Tampa Bay in 2nd round (28th player selected) of 1986 NFL draft.
Signed by Tampa Bay Buccaneers, July 22, 1986.
Granted unconditional free agency, February 1, 1989; signed by New York Jets, March 23, 1989.
Tampa Bay NFL, 1986 through 1988.
Games: 1986 (15), 1987 (12), 1988 (16). Total—43.

JEFFREY LYNN WALKER
(Jeff)
Offensive Tackle—New Orleans Saints

Born January 22, 1963, at Jonesboro, Ark.
Height, 6.04. Wright, 295.
High School—Olive Branch, Miss.
Attended Memphis State University.

Selected by Memphis in 1986 USFL territorial draft.
Selected by San Diego in 3rd round (70th player selected) of 1986 NFL draft.
Signed by San Diego Chargers, July 23, 1986.
On injured reserve with knee injury, September 7, 1987.
Traded by San Diego Chargers to Los Angeles Rams for 11th round pick in 1988 draft, September 8, 1987.
On injured reserve with knee injury, September 8 through October 24 and October 27 through remainder of 1987 season.
On injured reserve with fractured fibula, August 23 through October 17, 1988.
Released by Los Angeles Rams, October 18, 1988; signed as free agent by New Orleans Saints, November 1, 1988.
On injured reserve with leg injury, November 11 through remainder of 1988 season.
Inactive for 1 game with Los Angeles Rams in 1987.
San Diego NFL, 1986; Los Angeles Rams NFL, 1987; New Orleans NFL, 1988.
Games: 1986 (16), 1988 (1). Total—17.

KEVIN P. WALKER
Linebacker—Cincinnati Bengals

Born December 24, 1965, at Denville, N.J.
Height, 6.03. Weight, 238.
High School—West Milford, Pa.
Attended University of Maryland.

Selected by Cincinnati in 3rd round (57th player selected) of 1988 NFL draft.
Signed by Cincinnati Bengals, May 23, 1988.
On injured reserve with knee injury, October 10 through remainder of 1988 season.
Cincinnati NFL, 1988.
Games: 1988 (3).

WESLEY DARCEL WALKER
Wide Receiver—New York Jets

Born May 26, 1955, at San Bernardino, Calif.
Height, 6.00. Weight, 179.
High School—Carson, Calif.
Attended University of California.

Selected by New York Jets in 2nd round (33rd player selected) of 1977 NFL draft.
On injured reserve with knee injury, October 31 through remainder of 1979 season.
On injured reserve with thigh injury, October 11 through November 14, 1980; activated, November 15, 1980.
Placed on did not report list, August 20 through August 26, 1984.
Reported and granted roster exemption, August 27 through August 31, 1984; activated, September 1, 1984.
On injured reserve with knee injury, September 3 through October 4, 1985; activated, October 5, 1985.
On injured reserve with separated shoulder, November 11 through remainder of 1987 season.

		—PASS RECEIVING—						—PASS RECEIVING—			
Year	Club	G.	P.C.	Yds.	Avg.	TD.	Year Club	G.	P.C.	Yds.	Avg. TD.
1977—New York Jets NFL....		14	35	740	*21.1	3	1984—New York Jets NFL....	12	41	623	15.2 7
1978—New York Jets NFL....		16	48	*1169	*24.4	8	1985—New York Jets NFL....	12	34	725	21.3 5
1979—New York Jets NFL....		9	23	569	24.7	5	1986—New York Jets NFL....	16	49	1016	20.7 12
1980—New York Jets NFL....		11	18	376	20.9	1	1987—New York Jets NFL....	5	9	190	21.1 1
1981—New York Jets NFL....		13	47	770	16.4	9	1988—New York Jets NFL....	16	26	551	21.2 7
1982—New York Jets NFL....		9	39	620	15.9	6	Pro Totals—12 Years......	149	430	8217	19.1 71
1983—New York Jets NFL....		16	61	868	14.2	7					

Additional pro statistics: Rushed three times for 25 yards, 1977; fumbled twice, 1977 and 1978; rushed once for minus three yards, 1978; recovered one fumble, 1978 and 1985; rushed once for one yard, 1984; credited with a safety, 1985; fumbled once, 1985 and 1988; fumbled three times, 1986; rushed once for 12 yards, 1988.
Played in AFC Championship Game following 1982 season.
Played in Pro Bowl (NFL All-Star Game) following 1978 and 1982 seasons.

BARRON STEVEN WALLACE
(Steve)
Offensive Tackle—San Francisco 49ers

Born December 27, 1964, at Atlanta, Ga.
Height, 6.05. Weight, 276.
High School—Atlanta, Ga., Chamblee.
Attended Auburn University.

Selected by Birmingham in 1986 USFL territorial draft.
Selected by San Francisco in 4th round (101st player selected) of 1986 NFL draft.
Signed by San Francisco 49ers, July 18, 1986.
San Francisco NFL, 1986 through 1988.
Games: 1986 (16), 1987 (11), 1988 (3). Total—43.
Played in NFC Championship Game following 1988 season.
Played in NFL Championship Game following 1988 season.

RAYMOND DURYEA WALLACE
(Ray)
Running Back—Pittsburgh Steelers
Born December 3, 1963, at Indianapolis, Ind.
Height, 6.00. Weight, 230.
High School—Indianapolis, Ind., North Central.
Attended Purdue University.

Selected by Houston in 6th round (145th player selected) of 1986 NFL draft.
Signed by Houston Oilers, July 21, 1986.
On injured reserve with neck injury, August 29 through October 16, 1986; activated, October 17, 1986.
On injured reserve with ankle injury, August 29 through entire 1988 season.
Granted unconditional free agency, February 1, 1989; signed by Pittsburgh Steelers, March 15, 1989.

		—RUSHING—				PASS RECEIVING				—TOTAL—		
Year Club	G.	Att.	Yds.	Avg.	TD.	P.C.	Yds.	Avg.	TD.	TD.	Pts.	F.
1986—Houston NFL	8	52	218	4.2	3	17	177	10.4	2	5	30	1
1987—Houston NFL	12	19	102	5.4	0	7	34	4.9	0	0	0	1
Pro Totals—2 Years	20	71	320	4.5	3	24	211	8.8	2	5	30	2

Additional pro statistics: Recovered one fumble, 1987.

EVERSON COLLINS WALLS
Cornerback—Dallas Cowboys
Born December 28, 1959, at Dallas, Tex.
Height, 6.01. Weight, 194.
High School—Dallas, Tex., L.V. Berkner.
Received bachelor of arts degree in accounting from Grambling State University in 1981.
Cousin of Ralph Anderson, back with Pittsburgh Steelers and New England Patriots,
1971 through 1973; and Herkie Walls, wide receiver-kick returner with Houston Oilers and
Tampa Bay Buccaneers, 1983 through 1985 and 1987.
Established NFL record for most seasons leading league in interceptions (3).
Signed as free agent by Dallas Cowboys, May, 1981.

		—INTERCEPTIONS—			
Year Club	G.	No.	Yds.	Avg.	TD.
1981—Dallas NFL	16	*11	133	12.1	0
1982—Dallas NFL	9	*7	61	8.7	0
1983—Dallas NFL	16	4	70	17.5	0
1984—Dallas NFL	16	3	12	4.0	0
1985—Dallas NFL	16	*9	31	3.4	0
1986—Dallas NFL	16	3	46	15.3	0
1987—Dallas NFL	12	5	38	7.6	0
1988—Dallas NFL	16	2	0	0.0	0
Pro Totals—8 Years	117	44	391	8.9	0

Additional pro statistics: Recovered one fumble, 1981; fumbled once, 1982 and 1988; recovered one fumble for four yards, 1985 and 1988; returned one punt for no yards, 1988.
Played in NFC Championship Game following 1981 and 1982 seasons.
Played in Pro Bowl (NFL All-Star Game) following 1981 through 1983 and 1985 seasons.

JOSEPH FOLLMANN WALTER JR.
(Joe)
Offensive Tackle—Cincinnati Bengals
Born June 18, 1963, at Dallas, Tex.
Height, 6.06. Weight, 290.
High School—Garland, Tex., North.
Attended Texas Tech University.

Selected by Denver in 1985 USFL territorial draft.
Selected by Cincinnati in 7th round (181st player selected) of 1985 NFL draft.
Signed by Cincinnati Bengals, July 15, 1985.
On injured reserve with knee injury, December 30 through remainder of 1988 season playoffs.
Cincinnati NFL, 1985 through 1988.
Games: 1985 (14), 1986 (15), 1987 (12), 1988 (16). Total—57.
Pro statistics: Recovered two fumbles.

MICHAEL DAVID WALTER
Linebacker—San Francisco 49ers
Born November 30, 1960, at Salem, Ore.
Height, 6.03. Weight, 238.
High School—Eugene, Ore., Sheldon.
Attended University of Oregon.

Selected by Los Angeles in 20th round (240th player selected) of 1983 USFL draft.
Selected by Dallas in 2nd round (50th player selected) of 1983 NFL draft.
Signed by Dallas Cowboys, July 7, 1983.
Released by Dallas Cowboys, August 27, 1984; awarded on waivers to San Francisco 49ers, August 28, 1984.
Dallas NFL, 1983; San Francisco NFL, 1984 through 1988.
Games: 1983 (15), 1984 (16), 1985 (14), 1986 (16), 1987 (12), 1988 (16). Total—89.
Pro statistics: Intercepted one pass for no yards, 1985; recovered one fumble, 1986 and 1987; intercepted one pass for 16 yards, 1987; recovered two fumbles, 1988.

Played in NFC Championship Game following 1984 season.
Played in NFL Championship Game following 1984 season.

ALVIN EARL WALTON
Safety—Washington Redskins
Born March 14, 1964, at Riverside, Calif.
Height, 6.00. Weight, 180.
High School—Banning, Calif.
Attended Mt. San Jacinto Junior College and University of Kansas.

Selected by Washington in 3rd round (75th player selected) of 1986 NFL draft.
Signed by Washington Redskins, July 18, 1986.

			—INTERCEPTIONS—			
Year	Club	G.	No.	Yds.	Avg.	TD.
1986—Washington NFL		16	None			
1987—Washington NFL		12	3	28	9.3	0
1988—Washington NFL		16	3	54	18.0	0
Pro Totals—3 Years		44	6	82	13.7	0

Played in NFC Championship Game following 1986 and 1987 seasons.
Played in NFL Championship Game following 1987 season.

CURT WARNER
Running Back—Seattle Seahawks
Born March 18, 1961, at Wyoming, W. Va.
Height, 5.11. Weight, 205.
High School—Pineville, W. Va.
Attended Penn State University.

Selected by Philadelphia in 1983 USFL territorial draft.
Selected by Seattle in 1st round (3rd player selected) of 1983 NFL draft.
Signed by Seattle Seahawks, June 29, 1983.
On injured reserve with knee injury, September 5 through remainder of 1984 season.
Selected by Philadelphia Phillies' organization in 32nd round of free-agent draft, June 5, 1979.

			——RUSHING——				PASS RECEIVING				—TOTAL—		
Year	Club	G.	Att.	Yds.	Avg.	TD.	P.C.	Yds.	Avg.	TD.	TD.	Pts.	F.
1983—Seattle NFL		16	335	1449	4.3	13	42	325	7.7	1	14	84	6
1984—Seattle NFL		1	10	40	4.0	0	1	19	19.0	0	0	0	0
1985—Seattle NFL		16	291	1094	3.8	8	47	307	6.5	1	9	54	8
1986—Seattle NFL		16	319	1481	4.6	13	41	342	8.3	0	13	78	6
1987—Seattle NFL		12	234	985	4.2	8	17	167	9.8	2	10	60	4
1988—Seattle NFL		16	266	1025	3.9	10	22	154	7.0	2	12	72	5
Pro Totals—6 Years		77	1455	6074	4.2	52	170	1314	7.7	6	58	348	29

Additional pro statistics: Recovered two fumbles, 1983 and 1985; recovered five fumbles, 1986; recovered one fumble, 1987; recovered one fumble for minus 10 yards, 1988.
Played in AFC Championship Game following 1983 season.
Played in Pro Bowl (NFL All-Star Game) following 1983 season.
Named to play in Pro Bowl following 1986 season; replaced due to injury by Earnest Jackson.
Named to play in Pro Bowl following 1987 season; replaced due to injury by Marcus Allen.

DON WARREN
Tight End—Washington Redskins
Born May 5, 1956, at Bellingham, Wash.
Height, 6.04. Weight, 242.
High School—Covina, Calif., Royal Oak.
Attended Mt. San Antonio Junior College and San Diego State University.

Selected by Washington in 4th round (103rd player selected) of 1979 NFL draft.

		——PASS RECEIVING——						——PASS RECEIVING——			
Year	Club	G.	P.C.	Yds.	Avg.	TD.	Year Club	G.	P.C.	Yds.	Avg. TD.
1979—Washington NFL		16	26	303	11.7	0	1985—Washington NFL 16	15	163	10.9	1
1980—Washington NFL		13	31	323	10.4	0	1986—Washington NFL 16	20	164	8.2	1
1981—Washington NFL		16	29	335	11.6	1	1987—Washington NFL 12	7	43	6.1	0
1982—Washington NFL		9	27	310	11.5	0	1988—Washington NFL 14	12	112	9.3	0
1983—Washington NFL		13	20	225	11.3	2	Pro Totals—10 Years 141	205	2170	10.6	5
1984—Washington NFL		16	18	192	10.7	0					

Additional pro statistics: Recovered one fumble, 1979, 1985, 1986 and 1988; fumbled once, 1980, 1986 and 1988; rushed once for five yards, 1985.
Played in NFC Championship Game following 1982, 1983, 1986 and 1987 seasons.
Played in NFL Championship Game following 1982, 1983 and 1987 seasons.

FRANK WILLIAM WARREN III
Defensive End—New Orleans Saints
Born September 14, 1959, at Birmingham, Ala.
Height, 6.04. Weight, 290.
High School—Birmingham, Ala., Phillips.
Attended Auburn University.

Selected by New Orleans in 3rd round (57th player selected) of 1981 NFL draft.
New Orleans NFL, 1981 through 1988.

Games: 1981 (16), 1982 (9), 1983 (16), 1984 (16), 1985 (16), 1986 (16), 1987 (12), 1988 (16). Total—117.

Pro statistics: Recovered one fumble, 1981, 1983 and 1988; intercepted one pass for six yards, 1983; recovered one fumble for 50 yards and a touchdown and returned blocked field goal attempt 42 yards for a touchdown, 1985; recovered three fumbles, 1986.

BRIAN WAYNE WASHINGTON
Safety—Cleveland Browns
Born September 10, 1965, at Richmond, Va.
Height, 6.00. Weight, 210.
High School—Highland Springs, Va.
Attended University of Nebraska.

Selected by Cleveland in 10th round (272nd player selected) of 1988 NFL draft.
Signed by Cleveland Browns, July 13, 1988.

| | | | —INTERCEPTIONS— | | | |
Year Club	G.	No.	Yds.	Avg.	TD.
1988—Cleveland NFL..............	16	3	104	34.7	1

CHRIS WASHINGTON
Linebacker—San Francisco 49ers
Born March 6, 1962, at Jackson, Miss.
Height, 6.04. Weight, 240.
High School—Chicago, Ill., Percy L. Julian.
Attended Iowa State University

Selected by Washington in 3rd round (49th player selected) of 1984 USFL draft.
Selected by Tampa Bay in 6th round (142nd player selected) of 1984 NFL draft.
Signed by Tampa Bay Buccaneers, June 5, 1984.
Granted unconditional free agency, February 1, 1989; signed by San Francisco 49ers, March 7, 1989.
Tampa Bay NFL, 1984 through 1988.
Games: 1984 (16), 1985 (16), 1986 (16), 1987 (12), 1988 (16). Total—76.
Pro statistics: Recovered one fumble, 1985 and 1988; intercepted one pass for 12 yards and recovered two fumbles, 1986.

JAMES McARTHUR WASHINGTON
Safety—Los Angeles Rams
Born January 10, 1965, at Los Angeles, Calif.
Height, 6.01. Weight, 191.
High School—Los Angeles, Calif., Jordan.
Attended University of California at Los Angeles.

Selected by Los Angeles Rams in 5th round (137th player selected) of 1988 NFL draft.
Signed by Los Angeles Rams, July 12, 1988.
Los Angeles Rams NFL, 1988.
Games: 1988 (16).
Pro statistics: Intercepted one pass for seven yards, 1988.

JOHN WASHINGTON
Defensive End—New York Giants
Born February 20, 1963, at Houston, Tex.
Height, 6.04. Weight, 275.
High School—Houston, Tex., Sterling.
Attended Oklahoma State University.

Selected by New Jersey in 1986 USFL territorial draft.
Selected by New York Giants in 3rd round (73rd player selected) of 1986 NFL draft.
Signed by New York Giants, July 17, 1986.
On injured reserve with back injury, January 3 through 1986 season playoffs.
New York Giants NFL, 1986 through 1988.
Games: 1986 (16), 1987 (12), 1988 (16). Total—44.

LIONEL WASHINGTON
Cornerback—Los Angeles Raiders
Born October 21, 1960, at New Orleans, La.
Height, 6.00. Weight, 188.
High School—Lutcher, La.
Received degree in sports administration from Tulane University.

Selected by Tampa Bay in 20th round (229th player selected) of 1983 USFL draft.
Selected by St. Louis in 4th round (103rd player selected) of 1983 NFL draft.
Signed by St. Louis Cardinals, May 6, 1983.
On injured reserve with broken fibula, September 16 through November 21, 1985; activated, November 22, 1985.

—DID YOU KNOW—

That Super Bowl XXIII between San Francisco and Cincinnati was the first in which the score was tied (3-3) at halftime?

Granted free agency, February 1, 1987; re-signed by Cardinals and traded to Los Angeles Raiders for 5th round pick in 1987 draft, March 18, 1987.

Year Club	G.	No.	Yds.	Avg.TD.	
1983—St. Louis NFL	16	8	92	11.5	0
1984—St. Louis NFL	15	5	42	8.4	0
1985—St. Louis NFL	5	1	48	48.0	*1
1986—St. Louis NFL	16	2	19	9.5	0
1987—L.A. Raiders NFL	11		None		
1988—L.A. Raiders NFL	12	1	0	0.0	0
Pro Totals—6 Years	75	17	201	11.8	1

Additional pro statistics: Recovered one fumble, 1983, 1984 and 1986.

RONNIE CARROLL WASHINGTON
Linebacker—Indianapolis Colts
Born July 29, 1963, at Monroe, La.
Height, 6.01. Weight, 236.
High School—Monroe, La., Richwood.
Attended Northeast Louisiana University.
Selected by Arizona in 1st round (13th player selected) of 1985 USFL draft.
Selected by Atlanta in 8th round (215th player selected) of 1985 NFL draft.
Signed by Atlanta Falcons, July 18, 1985.
Traded with 6th round pick in 1987 draft by Atlanta Falcons to San Diego Chargers for rights to quarterback Ed Luther, August 13, 1986.
Released by San Diego Chargers, September 1, 1986; signed as free agent by Los Angeles Raiders, May 1, 1987.
Released by Los Angeles Raiders, September 7, 1987; re-signed as replacement player by Raiders, October 6, 1987.
Released by Los Angeles Raiders, December 5, 1987; re-signed by Raiders, April 22, 1988.
Released by Los Angeles Raiders, June 29, 1988; signed as free agent by Indianapolis Colts, March 29, 1989.
Atlanta NFL, 1985; Los Angeles Raiders NFL, 1987.
Games: 1985 (16), 1987 (2). Total—18.
Additional pro statistics: Returned one kickoff for no yards, 1985 and 1987; recovered one fumble and fumbled once, 1985.

ANDRE WATERS
Safety—Philadelphia Eagles
Born March 10, 1962, at Belle Glade, Fla.
Height, 5.11. Weight, 199.
High School—Pahokee, Fla.
Received degree in business administration from Cheyney State College.
Signed as free agent by Philadelphia Eagles, June 20, 1984.

		-INTERCEPTIONS-				—KICKOFF RET.—				—TOTAL—		
Year Club	G.	No.	Yds.	Avg.	TD.	No.	Yds.	Avg.	TD.	TD.	Pts.	F.
1984—Philadelphia NFL	16		None			13	319	24.5	*1	1	6	1
1985—Philadelphia NFL	16		None			4	74	18.5	0	0	0	1
1986—Philadelphia NFL	16	6	39	6.5	0		None			0	0	0
1987—Philadelphia NFL	12	3	63	21.0	0		None			0	0	0
1988—Philadelphia NFL	16	3	19	6.3	0		None			0	0	0
Pro Totals—5 Years	76	12	121	10.1	0	17	393	23.1	1	1	6	2

Additional pro statistics: Recovered one fumble, 1984 and 1985; returned one punt for 23 yards, 1985; recovered two fumbles for 81 yards, 1986; recovered two fumbles for 11 yards, 1987.

BOBBY LAWRENCE WATKINS
Cornerback—Miami Dolphins
Born May 31, 1960, at Cottonwood, Ida.
Height, 5.10. Weight, 184.
High School—Dallas, Tex., Bishop Dunne.
Attended Southwest Texas State University.
Selected by Detroit in 2nd round (42nd player selected) of 1982 NFL draft.
On injured reserve with foot injury, October 16 through remainder of 1986 season.
On injured reserve with thigh injury, October 31 through November 24, 1987; activated, November 25, 1987.
Granted unconditional free agency, February 1, 1989; signed by Miami Dolphins, March 30, 1989.

Year Club	G.	No.	Yds.	Avg.TD.	
1982—Detroit NFL	9	5	22	4.4	0
1983—Detroit NFL	16	4	48	12.0	0
1984—Detroit NFL	16	6	0	0.0	0
1985—Detroit NFL	16	5	15	3.0	0
1986—Detroit NFL	5		None		
1987—Detroit NFL	5		None		
1988—Detroit NFL	16		None		
Pro Totals—7 Years	83	20	85	4.3	0

Additional pro statistics: Recovered one fumble, 1982; recovered three fumbles for six yards and fumbled once, 1983; recovered two fumbles, 1985.

STEPHEN ROSS WATSON
(Steve)
Wide Receiver—Denver Broncos

Born May 28, 1957, at Baltimore, Md.
Height, 6.04. Weight, 195.
High School—Wilmington, Del., St. Mark's.
Received degree in parks administration from Temple University.

Signed as free agent by Denver Broncos, May 12, 1979.
Crossed picket line during players' strike, October 2, 1987.
On injured reserve with broken ribs, October 15 through December 17, 1987; activated, December 18, 1987.
On injured reserve with cracked vertebra, August 29 through entire 1988 season.

| | | —PASS RECEIVING— | | | |
Year Club	G.	P.C.	Yds.	Avg.	TD.
1979—Denver NFL	16	6	83	13.8	0
1980—Denver NFL	16	6	146	24.3	0
1981—Denver NFL	16	60	1244	20.7	*13
1982—Denver NFL	9	36	555	15.4	2
1983—Denver NFL	16	59	1133	19.2	5
1984—Denver NFL	16	69	1170	17.0	7
1985—Denver NFL	16	61	915	15.0	5
1986—Denver NFL	16	45	699	15.5	3
1987—Denver NFL	5	11	167	15.2	1
Pro Totals—9 Years	126	353	6112	17.3	36

Additional pro statistics: Returned one kickoff for five yards and recovered one fumble, 1980; rushed twice for six yards and recovered two fumbles, 1981; rushed once for minus four yards, 1982; fumbled once, 1982 and 1983; rushed three times for 17 yards, 1983.
Played in AFC Championship Game following 1986 and 1987 seasons.
Played in NFL Championship Game following 1986 and 1987 seasons.
Played in Pro Bowl (NFL All-Star Game) following 1981 season.

RANDY WATTS
Defensive End—Kansas City Chiefs

Born June 22, 1963, at Sandersville, Ga.
Height, 6.06. Weight, 279.
High School—Sandersville, Ga., Washington County.
Attended East Carolina University and Catawba College.

Selected by Kansas City in 9th round (244th player selected) of 1987 NFL draft.
Signed by Kansas City Chiefs, July 19, 1987.
Released by Kansas City Chiefs, September 7, 1987; signed as free agent replacement player by Dallas Cowboys, September 23, 1987.
Left Dallas Cowboys camp and granted roster exemption, November 11 and November 12, 1987; activated, November 13, 1987.
Released by Dallas Cowboys, November 24, 1987; re-signed by Cowboys for 1988, November 27, 1987.
Released by Dallas Cowboys, August 19, 1988; signed as free agent by Kansas City Chiefs, January 6, 1989.
Dallas NFL, 1987.
Games: 1987 (5).
Pro statistics: Recovered one fumble, 1987.

DAVID BENJAMIN WAYMER JR.
(Dave)
Cornerback—New Orleans Saints

Born July 1, 1958, at Brooklyn, N.Y.
Height, 6.01. Weight, 188.
High School—Charlotte, N.C., West.
Received bachelor of arts degree in economics from University of Notre Dame in 1980.

Selected by New Orleans in 2nd round (41st player selected) of 1980 NFL draft.

| | | —INTERCEPTIONS— | | | |
Year Club	G.	No.	Yds.	Avg.	TD.
1980—New Orleans NFL	16		None		
1981—New Orleans NFL	16	4	54	13.5	0
1982—New Orleans NFL	9		None		
1983—New Orleans NFL	16		None		
1984—New Orleans NFL	16	4	9	2.3	0
1985—New Orleans NFL	16	6	49	8.2	0
1986—New Orleans NFL	16	9	48	5.3	0
1987—New Orleans NFL	12	5	78	15.6	0
1988—New Orleans NFL	16	3	91	30.3	0
Pro Totals—9 Years	133	31	329	10.6	0

Additional pro statistics: Returned three punts for 29 yards, 1980; fumbled once, 1980, 1985 and 1988; recovered two fumbles, 1980, 1981 and 1982; recovered three fumbles, 1983; caught one pass for 13 yards, 1986; recovered one fumble, 1986 and 1988; recovered three fumbles for two yards, 1987; returned two kickoffs for 39 yards and returned blocked field goal attempt 58 yards for a touchdown, 1988.
Played in Pro Bowl (NFL All-Star Game) following 1987 season.

CLARENCE WEATHERS
Wide Receiver—Indianapolis Colts

Born January 10, 1962, at Green's Pond, S.C.
Height, 5.09. Weight, 170.
High School—Fort Pierce, Fla.
Attended Delaware State College.
Brother of Robert Weathers, running back with New England Patriots, 1982 through 1986.

Signed as free agent by New England Patriots, July 20, 1983.
On injured reserve with broken foot, August 28 through October 19, 1984; activated, October 20, 1984.
Released by New England Patriots, September 2, 1985; awarded on waivers to Cleveland Browns, September 3, 1985.
Granted unconditional free agency, February 1, 1989; signed by Indianapolis Colts, March 30, 1989.

		—PASS RECEIVING—				—PUNT RETURNS—				—TOTAL—		
Year Club	G.	P.C.	Yds.	Avg.	TD.	No.	Yds.	Avg.	TD.	TD.	Pts.	F.
1983—New England NFL	16	19	379	19.9	3	4	1	0.3	0	3	18	2
1984—New England NFL	9	8	115	14.4	2	1	7	7.0	0	2	12	0
1985—Cleveland NFL	13	16	449	28.1	3	28	218	7.8	0	3	18	3
1986—Cleveland NFL	16	9	100	11.1	0		None			0	0	0
1987—Cleveland NFL	12	11	153	13.9	2		None			2	12	0
1988—Cleveland NFL	16	29	436	15.0	1	2	10	5.0	0	1	6	2
Pro Totals—6 Years	82	92	1632	17.7	11	35	236	6.7	0	11	66	7

Additional pro statistics: Returned three kickoffs for 58 yards and rushed once for 28 yards, 1985; recovered one fumble, 1983 and 1985; returned one kickoff for 17 yards and rushed once for 18 yards, 1985.
Played in AFC Championship Game following 1986 and 1987 seasons.

MICHAEL LEWIS WEBSTER
(Mike)
Center—Kansas City Chiefs

Born March 18, 1952, at Tomahawk, Wis.
Height, 6.02. Weight, 254.
High School—Rhinelander, Wis.
Attended University of Wisconsin.

Named to THE SPORTING NEWS NFL All-Star Team, 1980, 1981 and 1983.
Named to THE SPORTING NEWS AFC All-Star Team, 1978 and 1979.
Selected by Pittsburgh in 5th round (125th player selected) of 1974 NFL draft.
On injured reserve with dislocated elbow, September 3 through October 2, 1986; activated, October 3, 1986.
Crossed picket line during players' strike, September 30, 1987.
Granted unconditional free agency, February 1, 1989; signed by Kansas City Chiefs, March 30, 1989.
Pittsburgh NFL, 1974 through 1988.
Games: 1974 (14), 1975 (14), 1976 (14), 1977 (14), 1978 (16), 1979 (16), 1980 (16), 1981 (16), 1982 (9), 1983 (16), 1984 (16), 1985 (16), 1986 (12), 1987 (15), 1988 (16). Total—220.
Pro statistics: Fumbled twice, 1976; recovered two fumbles for two yards, 1979; recovered two fumbles, 1983; recovered one fumble, 1985; fumbled twice for minus 58 yards, 1988.
Played in AFC Championship Game following 1974 through 1976, 1978, 1979 and 1984 seasons.
Played in NFL Championship Game following 1974, 1975, 1978 and 1979 seasons.
Played in Pro Bowl (NFL All-Star Game) following 1978 through 1985 and 1987 seasons.

MICHAEL WAYNE WEDDINGTON
Linebacker—Green Bay Packers

Born October 9, 1960, at Belton, Tex.
Height, 6.04. Weight, 245.
High School—Temple, Tex.
Attended University of Oklahoma.

Selected by New Jersey in 1983 USFL territorial draft.
Signed by New Jersey Generals, January 31, 1983.
On developmental squad, March 10 through May 4, 1984; activated, May 5, 1984.
On developmental squad, June 15 through June 22, 1984; activated, June 23, 1984.
Granted free agency when USFL suspended operations, August 7, 1986; signed as free agent by Green Bay Packers, August 13, 1986.
On injured reserve with shoulder injury, September 1 through December 5, 1986; activated, December 6, 1986.
On developmental squad for 9 games with New Jersey Generals in 1984.
New Jersey USFL, 1983 through 1985; Green Bay NFL, 1986 through 1988.
Games: 1983 (18), 1984 (9), 1985 (18), 1986 (3), 1987 (12), 1988 (16). Total USFL—45. Total NFL—31. Total Pro—76.
USFL statistics: Credited with six sacks for 46 yards, recovered one fumble and returned four kickoffs for 41 yards, 1983; credited with 3½ sacks for 39½ yards, 1984; credited with 2½ sacks for 23 yards and recovered two fumbles, 1985.
NFL statistics: Recovered one fumble, 1987; recovered two fumbles, 1988.

HERB DOYAN WELCH
Defensive Back—New York Giants

Born January 12, 1961, at Los Angeles, Calif.
Height, 5.11. Weight, 180.
High School—Downey, Calif., Warren.
Attended Cerritos College and University of California at Los Angeles.

Selected by Portland in 10th round (135th player selected) of 1985 USFL draft.
Selected by New York Giants in 12th round (326th player selected) of 1985 NFL draft.

Signed by New York Giants, July 9, 1985.
On injured reserve with knee injury, July 25 through entire 1988 season.

Year Club		—INTERCEPTIONS—			
	G.	No.	Yds.	Avg.	TD.
1985—N.Y. Giants NFL	16	2	8	4.0	0
1986—N.Y. Giants NFL	16	2	22	11.0	0
1987—N.Y. Giants NFL	12	2	7	3.5	0
Pro Totals—3 Years............	44	6	37	6.2	0

Additional pro statistics: Recovered one fumble for seven yards, 1986.
Played in NFC Championship Game following 1986 season.
Played in NFL Championship Game following 1986 season.

EDWARD LEE WEST III
(Ed)
Tight End—Green Bay Packers
Born August 2, 1961, at Colbert County, Ala.
Height, 6.01. Weight, 242.
High School—Leighton, Ala., Colbert County.
Attended Auburn University.

Selected by Birmingham in 1984 USFL territorial draft.
Signed as free agent by Green Bay Packers, May 3, 1984.
Released by Green Bay Packers, August 27, 1984; re-signed by Packers, August 30, 1984.

Year Club		—PASS RECEIVING—			
	G.	P.C.	Yds.	Avg.	TD.
1984—Green Bay NFL............	16	6	54	9.0	4
1985—Green Bay NFL............	16	8	95	11.9	1
1986—Green Bay NFL............	16	15	199	13.3	1
1987—Green Bay NFL............	12	19	261	13.7	1
1988—Green Bay NFL............	16	30	276	9.2	3
Pro Totals—5 Years............	76	78	885	11.3	10

Additional pro statistics: Rushed once for two yards and a touchdown, 1984; recovered one fumble, 1984 and 1986; rushed once for no yards, 1985; fumbled once, 1985 and 1988.

KENNETH MOORE WHISENHUNT
(Ken)
Tight End—Washington Redskins
Born February 28, 1962, at Atlanta, Ga.
Height, 6.03. Weight, 240.
High School—Augusta, Ga., Richmond.
Attended Georgia Tech.

Selected by Jacksonville in 1985 USFL territorial draft.
USFL rights traded with rights to running back Marck Harrison and center Dan Turk by Jacksonville Bulls to Tampa Bay Bandits for rights to kicker Bobby Raymond, running back Cedric Jones and defensive back Eric Riley, January 3, 1985.
Selected by Atlanta in 12th round (313th player selected) of 1985 NFL draft.
Signed by Atlanta Falcons, July 18, 1985.
On injured reserve with separated shoulder, December 2 through remainder of 1987 season.
Granted unconditional free agency, February 1, 1989; signed by Washington Redskins, March 8, 1989.

Year Club		—PASS RECEIVING—			
	G.	P.C.	Yds.	Avg.	TD.
1985—Atlanta NFL	16	3	48	16.0	0
1986—Atlanta NFL	16	20	184	9.2	3
1987—Atlanta NFL	7	17	145	8.5	1
1988—Atlanta NFL	16	16	174	10.9	1
Pro Totals—4 Years............	55	56	551	9.8	5

Additional pro statistics: Rushed once for three yards and returned four kickoffs for 33 yards, 1985; recovered one fumble, 1985, 1987 and 1988; rushed once for 20 yards, 1986; fumbled once, 1987 and 1988.

ADRIAN DARNELL WHITE
Safety—New York Giants
Born April 6, 1964, at Orange Park, Fla.
Height, 6.00. Weight, 200.
High School—Orange Park, Fla.
Attended University of Southern Illinois at Carbondale and University of Florida.

Selected by New York Giants in 2nd round (55th player selected) of 1987 NFL draft.
Signed by New York Giants, July 27, 1987.
On injured reserve with knee injury, August 22 through October 13, 1987; activated, October 14, 1987.
Crossed picket line during players' strike, October 14, 1987.
New York Giants NFL, 1987 and 1988.
Games: 1987 (6), 1988 (16). Total—22.
Pro statistics: Intercepted one pass for 29 yards, 1988.

LORENZO MAURICE WHITE
Running Back—Houston Oilers
Born April 12, 1966, at Hollywood, Fla.
Height, 5.11. Weight, 209.
High School—Fort Lauderdale, Fla., Dillard.
Attended Michigan State University.

Named as running back on THE SPORTING NEWS College All-America Team, 1985.
Selected by Houston in 1st round (22nd player selected) of 1988 NFL draft.
Signed by Houston Oilers, July 23, 1988.

		——RUSHING——				PASS RECEIVING				—TOTAL—		
Year	Club	G.	Att.	Yds.	Avg. TD.	P.C. Yds.	Avg. TD.			TD.	Pts.	F.
1988—Houston NFL		11	31	115	3.7 0	None				1	6	0

		KICKOFF RETURNS			
Year	Club	G.	No.	Yds.	Avg.TD.
1988—Houston NFL		11	8	196	24.5 *1

REGINALD HOWARD WHITE
(Reggie)
Defensive End—Philadelphia Eagles
Born December 19, 1961, at Chattanooga, Tenn.
Height, 6.05. Weight, 285.
High School—Chattanooga, Tenn., Howard.
Attended University of Tennessee.

Named to THE SPORTING NEWS NFL All-Star Team, 1987 and 1988.
Named as defensive end on THE SPORTING NEWS USFL All-Star Team, 1985.
Named as defensive end on THE SPORTING NEWS College All-America Team, 1983.
Selected by Memphis in 1984 USFL territorial draft.
Signed by Memphis Showboats, January 15, 1984.
On developmental squad, March 9 through March 23, 1984; activated, March 24, 1984.
Selected by Philadelphia in 1st round (4th player selected) of 1984 NFL supplemental draft.
Released by Memphis Showboats, September 19, 1985; signed by Philadelphia Eagles, September 21, 1985.
Granted roster exemption, September 21 through September 26, 1985; activated, September 27, 1985.
On developmental squad for 2 games with Memphis Showboats in 1984.
Memphis USFL, 1984 and 1985; Philadelphia NFL, 1985 through 1988.
Games: 1984 (16), 1985 USFL (18), 1985 NFL (13), 1986 (16), 1987 (12), 1988 (16). Total USFL—34. Total NFL—57. Total Pro—91.
USFL statistics: Credited with 12 sacks for 84 yards and recovered one fumble, 1984; credited with 11½ sacks for 93½ yards, credited with one safety and recovered one fumble for 20 yards and a touchdown, 1985.
NFL statistics: Recovered two fumbles, 1985 and 1988; recovered one fumble for 70 yards and a touchdown, 1987.
Played in Pro Bowl (NFL All-Star Game) following 1986 through 1988 seasons.

ROBB WHITE
Defensive End—New York Giants
Born May 26, 1965, at Aberdeen, S. D.
Height, 6.04. Weight, 270.
High School—Aberdeen, S. D., Central.
Attended University of South Dakota.

Signed as free agent by Washington Redskins, May 12, 1988.
On injured reserve with back injury, August 29 through November 16, 1988.
Released by Washington Redskins, November 17, 1988; awarded on waivers to New York Giants, November 18, 1988.
On injured reserve with back injury, December 17 through remainder of 1988 season.
New York Giants NFL, 1988.
Games: 1988 (1).

ROBERT A. WHITE
(Bob)
Center—Dallas Cowboys
Born April 9, 1963, at Fitchburg, Mass.
Height, 6.05. Weight, 273.
High School—Lunenburg, Mass.
Received bachelor of arts degree in journalism
from University of Rhode Island in 1986.

Seleted by New York Jets in 7th round (189th player selected) of 1986 NFL draft.
Signed by New York Jets, July 23, 1986.
Released by New York Jets, August 25, 1986; signed as free agent by Dallas Cowboys, March 17, 1987.
Released by Dallas Cowboys, September 7, 1987; re-signed as replacement player by Cowboys, September 23, 1987.
On injured reserve with thigh injury, August 23 through September 21, 1988; activated after clearing procedural waivers, September 23, 1988.
Dallas NFL, 1987 and 1988.
Games: 1987 (4), 1988 (12). Total—16.
Pro statistics: Fumbled twice, 1987; returned one kickoff for seven yards, 1988.

SHELDON DARNELL WHITE
Defensive Back—New York Giants
Born March 1, 1965, at Dayton, O.
Height, 5.11. Weight, 188.
High School—Dayton, O., Meadowdale.
Attended Miami University (Ohio).
Selected by New York Giants in 3rd round (62nd player selected) of 1988 NFL draft.
Signed by New York Giants, July 18, 1988.

			—INTERCEPTIONS—			
Year Club		G.	No.	Yds.	Avg.	TD.
1988—N. Y. Giants NFL.........		16	4	70	17.5	0

Additional pro statistics: Returned three kickoffs for 62 yards (20.7 avg.), 1988.

THOMAS LEON WHITE
(Known by middle name.)
Linebacker—Cincinnati Bengals
Born October 4, 1963, at San Diego, Calif.
Height, 6.02. Weight, 245.
High School—La Mesa, Calif., Helix.
Attended Brigham Young University.
Selected by Cincinnati in 5th round (123rd player selected) of 1986 NFL draft.
Signed by Cincinnati Bengals, July 20, 1986.
Cincinnati NFL, 1986 through 1988.
Games: 1986 (16), 1987 (12), 1988 (16). Total—44.
Pro statistics: Credited with a safety, 1986; recovered one fumble, 1988.
Played in AFC Championship Game following 1988 season.
Played in NFL Championship Game following 1988 season.

WILFORD DANIEL WHITE
(Danny)
Quarterback—Dallas Cowboys
Born February 9, 1952, at Mesa, Ariz.
Height, 6.03. Weight, 198.
High School—Mesa, Ariz., Westwood.
Attended Arizona State University.
Son of Wilford White, halfback with Chicago Bears, 1951 and 1952.
Selected by Dallas in 3rd round (53rd player selected) of 1974 NFL draft.
Played in World Football League with Memphis Southmen, 1974 and 1975.
Signed by Dallas Cowboys after World Football League folded, April 15, 1976.
On injured reserve with broken wrist, November 14 through remainder of 1986 season.
Crossed picket line during players' strike, September 30, 1987.
On injured reserve with knee injury, October 21 through remainder of 1988 season.
Granted unconditional free agency, February 1, 1989; did not receive qualifying offer, April 15, 1989.
Re-signed by Dallas Cowboys, May 19, 1989.
Selected by Cleveland Indians' organization in 39th round of free-agent draft, June 5, 1973.
Selected by Houston Astros' organization in secondary phase of free-agent draft, January 9, 1974.
Selected by Cleveland Indians' organization in secondary phase of free-agent draft, June 5, 1974.
Selected by Cleveland Indians' organization in secondary phase of free-agent draft, January 9, 1975.

		—PASSING—							—RUSHING—				—TOTAL—		
Year Club	G.	Att.	Cmp.	Pct.	Gain	T.P.	P.I.	Avg.	Att.	Yds.	Avg.	TD.	TD.	Pts.	F.
1974—Memphis WFL................	....	155	79	51.0	1190	11	9	7.68	24	103	4.3	0	0	0	....
1975—Memphis WFL................	....	195	104	53.3	1445	10	8	7.41	23	116	5.0	0	0	1	....
1976—Dallas NFL......................	14	20	13	65.0	213	2	2	10.65	6	17	2.8	0	0	0	0
1977—Dallas NFL......................	14	10	4	40.0	35	0	1	3.50	1	—2	—2.0	0	0	0	0
1978—Dallas NFL......................	16	34	20	58.8	215	0	1	6.32	5	7	1.4	0	0	0	2
1979—Dallas NFL......................	16	39	19	48.7	267	1	2	6.85	1	25	25.0	0	0	0	1
1980—Dallas NFL	16	436	260	59.6	3287	28	25	7.54	27	114	4.2	1	1	6	8
1981—Dallas NFL	16	391	223	57.0	3098	22	13	7.92	38	104	2.7	0	0	0	*14
1982—Dallas NFL	9	247	156	63.2	2079	16	12	8.42	17	91	5.4	0	0	0	*10
1983—Dallas NFL	16	533	334	62.7	3980	29	23	7.47	18	31	1.7	4	5	30	10
1984—Dallas NFL	14	233	126	54.1	1580	11	11	6.78	6	21	3.5	0	0	0	2
1985—Dallas NFL	14	450	267	59.3	3157	21	17	7.02	22	44	2.0	1	2	12	6
1986—Dallas NFL	7	153	95	62.1	1157	12	5	7.56	8	16	2.0	1	1	6	6
1987—Dallas NFL	11	362	215	59.4	2617	12	17	7.23	10	14	1.4	1	1	6	9
1988—Dallas NFL	3	42	29	69.0	274	1	3	6.52		None			0	0	0
WFL Totals—2 Years........	....	350	183	52.3	2635	21	17	7.53	47	219	4.7	0	0	0	....
NFL Totals—13 Years.......	166	2950	1761	59.7	21959	155	132	7.44	159	482	3.0	8	10	60	68
Pro Totals—15 Years.........	....	3300	1944	58.9	24594	176	149	7.45	206	701	3.4	8	10	60	....

NFL Quarterback Rating Points: 1976 (94.4), 1977 (10.4), 1978 (65.3), 1979 (58.6), 1980 (80.8), 1981 (87.5), 1982 (91.1), 1983 (85.6), 1984 (71.5), 1985 (80.6), 1986 (97.9), 1987 (73.2), 1988 (65.0). Total—81.8.

	—PUNTING—					—PUNTING—			
Year Club	G.	No.	Avg.	Blk.	Year Club	G.	No.	Avg.	Blk.
1974—Memphis WFL.......................	....	80	40.9	0	1977—Dallas NFL	14	80	39.6	1
1975—Memphis WFL.......................	....	41	*45.1	0	1978—Dallas NFL	16	76	40.5	1
1976—Dallas NFL	14	70	38.4	2	1979—Dallas NFL	16	76	41.7	0

Year Club	PUNTING G.	No.	Avg.	Blk.	Year Club	PUNTING G.	No.	Avg.	Blk.
1980—Dallas NFL	16	71	40.9	0	1987—Dallas NFL	11	None		
1981—Dallas NFL	16	79	40.8	0	1988—Dallas NFL	3	None		
1982—Dallas NFL	9	37	41.7	0	WFL Totals—2 Years	....	121	42.3	0
1983—Dallas NFL	16	38	40.6	1	NFL Totals—13 Years	166	610	40.3	5
1984—Dallas NFL	14	82	38.4	0	Pro Totals—15 Years	....	731	40.6	5
1985—Dallas NFL	14	1	43.0	0					
1986—Dallas NFL	7		None						

Additional WFL statistics: Scored one action point, 1975.

Additional NFL statistics: Recovered one fumble, 1977; recovered two fumbles and fumbled twice for minus eight yards, 1978; recovered one fumble for 15 yards and caught one pass for minus nine yards, 1980; recovered eight fumbles and fumbled 14 times for minus 34 yards, 1981; recovered two fumbles, 1982; caught one pass for 15 yards and a touchdown and recovered four fumbles, 1983; recovered one fumble and fumbled twice for minus three yards, 1984; caught one pass for 12 yards and a touchdown, recovered two fumbles and fumbled six times for minus six yards, 1985; recovered one fumble and fumbled six times for minus two yards, 1986; recovered three fumbles and fumbled nine times for minus seven yards, 1987.

Played in NFC Championship Game following 1977, 1978 and 1980 through 1982 seasons.

Played in NFL Championship Game following 1977 and 1978 seasons.

Played in Pro Bowl (NFL All-Star Game) following 1982 season.

WILLIAM EUGENE WHITE
Cornerback—Detroit Lions

Born February 19, 1966, at Lima, O.
Height, 5.10. Weight, 191.
High School—Lima, O.
Attended Ohio State University.

Selected by Detroit in 4th round (85th player selected) of 1988 NFL draft.
Signed by Detroit Lions, July 11, 1988.
Detroit NFL, 1988.
Games: 1988 (16).
Pro statistics: Recovered one fumble, 1988.

DAVID HAROLD WIDELL
(Name pronounced Wi-DEL.)
(Dave)
Offensive Tackle—Dallas Cowboys

Born May 14, 1965, at Hartford, Conn.
Height, 6.06. Weight, 300.
High School—Hartford, Conn., South Catholic.
Received degree in finance from Boston College in 1988.

Selected by Dallas in 4th round (94th player selected) of 1988 NFL draft.
Signed by Dallas Cowboys, July 12, 1988.
Dallas NFL, 1988.
Games: 1988 (14).
Pro statistics: Recovered one fumble, 1988.

BARRY T. WILBURN
Cornerback—Washington Redskins

Born December 9, 1963, at Memphis, Tenn.
Height, 6.03. Weight, 186.
High School—Memphis, Tenn., Melrose.
Attended University of Mississippi.

Selected by Washington in 8th round (219th player selected) of 1985 NFL draft.
Signed by Washington Redskins, July 18, 1985.
On injured reserve with knee injury, September 14 through October 28, 1988; activated, October 29, 1988.

Year Club	INTERCEPTIONS G.	No.	Yds.	Avg.	TD.
1985—Washington NFL	16	1	10	10.0	0
1986—Washington NFL	16	2	14	7.0	0
1987—Washington NFL	12	*9	135	15.0	1
1988—Washington NFL	10	4	24	6.0	0
Pro Totals—4 Years	54	16	183	11.4	1

Additional pro statistics: Recovered one fumble, 1985 and 1988; recovered two fumbles, 1986.
Played in NFC Championship Game following 1986 and 1987 seasons.
Played in NFL Championship Game following 1987 season.

STEPHEN T. WILBURN
(Steve)
Defensive End—Seattle Seahawks

Born February 25, 1961, at Chicago, Ill.
Height, 6.04. Weight, 266.
High School—Chicago, Ill., Mendel Catholic.
Attended Illinois State University.

Signed as free agent by Calgary Stampeders, June, 1983.
Released by Calgary Stampeders, August, 1985; signed as free agent by Saskatchewan Roughriders, September, 1985.
Released by Saskatchewan Roughriders, June, 1987; signed as free agent replacement player by New England Patriots, September 24, 1987.
Released by New England Patriots, October 26, 1987; re-signed by Patriots, January 27, 1988.
Released by New England Patriots, August 30, 1988; signed as free agent by Seattle Seahawks, January 5, 1989.
Calgary CFL, 1983 and 1984; Calgary (5)-Saskatchewan (4) CFL, 1985; Saskatchewan CFL, 1986; New England NFL, 1987.
Games: 1983 (11), 1984 (15), 1985 (9), 1986 (2), 1987 (3). Total CFL—37. Total Pro—40.
CFL statistics: Recovered one fumble, 1983 and 1984; intercepted one pass for no yards, 1984.

MIKE WILCHER
Linebacker—Los Angeles Rams
Born March 20, 1960, at Washington, D.C.
Height, 6.03. Weight, 240.
High School—Washington, D.C., Eastern.
Attended University of North Carolina.

Selected by Philadelphia in 1983 USFL territorial draft.
Selected by Los Angeles Rams in 2nd round (36th player selected) of 1983 NFL draft.
Signed by Los Angeles Rams NFL, June 16, 1983.
Los Angeles Rams NFL, 1983 through 1988.
Games: 1983 (15), 1984 (15), 1985 (16), 1986 (16), 1987 (12), 1988 (16). Total—90.
Pro statistics: Intercepted one pass for no yards, 1985 and 1986; intercepted one pass for 11 yards and recovered one fumble for 35 yards and a touchdown, 1987; recovered one fumble for eight yards, 1988.
Played in NFC Championship Game following 1985 season.

SOLOMON WILCOTS
Cornerback—Cincinnati Bengals
Born October 9, 1964, at Los Angeles, Calif.
Height, 5.11. Weight, 185.
High School—Riverside, Calif., Rubidoux.
Attended University of Colorado.

Selected by Cincinnati in 8th round (215th player selected) of 1987 NFL draft.
Signed by Cincinnati Bengals, July 22, 1987.
Cincinnati NFL, 1987 and 1988.
Games: 1987 (12), 1988 (16). Total—28.
Pro statistics: Intercepted one pass for 37 yards, 1987; intercepted one pass for six yards and recovered two fumbles, 1988.
Played in AFC Championship Game following 1988 season.
Played in NFL Championship Game following 1988 season.

JAMES CURTIS WILDER
Running Back—Tampa Bay Buccaneers
Born May 12, 1958, at Sikeston, Mo.
Height, 6.03. Weight, 225.
High School—Sikeston, Mo.
Attended Northeastern Oklahoma A&M and University of Missouri.

Established NFL records for most rushing attempts, season (407), 1984; most combined attempts, season (496), 1984.
Tied NFL record for most rushing attempts, game (43) vs. Green Bay Packers, September 30, 1984.
Selected by Tampa Bay in 2nd round (34th player selected) of 1981 NFL draft.
On injured reserve with broken ribs, November 15 through remainder of 1983 season.
On injured reserve with ankle injury, December 19 through remainder of 1986 season.
On injured reserve with knee injury, November 4 through remainder of 1988 season.

		—RUSHING—				PASS RECEIVING				—TOTAL—		
Year Club	G.	Att.	Yds.	Avg.	TD.	P.C.	Yds.	Avg.	TD.	TD.	Pts.	F.
1981—Tampa Bay NFL	16	107	370	3.5	4	48	507	10.6	1	5	30	3
1982—Tampa Bay NFL	9	83	324	3.9	3	53	466	8.8	1	4	24	5
1983—Tampa Bay NFL	10	161	640	4.0	4	57	380	6.7	2	6	36	4
1984—Tampa Bay NFL	16	*407	1544	3.8	13	85	685	8.1	0	13	78	10
1985—Tampa Bay NFL	16	365	1300	3.6	10	53	341	6.4	0	10	60	9
1986—Tampa Bay NFL	12	190	704	3.7	2	43	326	7.6	1	3	18	10
1987—Tampa Bay NFL	12	106	488	4.6	0	40	328	8.2	1	1	6	3
1988—Tampa Bay NFL	7	86	343	4.0	1	15	124	8.3	0	1	6	1
Pro Totals—8 Years	98	1505	5713	3.8	37	394	3157	8.0	6	43	258	42

Additional pro statistics: Returned one kickoff for 19 yards, 1981; recovered one fumble, 1981 and 1985; recovered one fumble for three yards, 1982; attempted one pass with one completion for 16 yards and a touchdown and recovered four fumbles, 1984; recovered three fumbles, 1986; recovered two fumbles, 1987.
Played in Pro Bowl (NFL All-Star Game) following 1984 season.

BRUCE ALAN WILKERSON
Guard-Offensive Tackle—Los Angeles Raiders
Born July 28, 1964, at Loudon, Tenn.
Height, 6.05. Weight, 285.
High School—Loudon, Tenn.
Attended University of Tennessee.

Selected by Los Angeles Raiders in 2nd round (52nd player selected) of 1987 NFL draft.
Signed by Los Angeles Raiders, July 10, 1987.
Crossed picket line during players' strike, October 2, 1987.
Los Angeles Raiders NFL, 1987 and 1988.
Games: 1987 (11), 1988 (16). Total—27.

GARY CLIFTON WILKINS
Tight End—Green Bay Packers
Born November 23, 1963, at West Palm Beach, Fla.
Height, 6.02. Weight, 235.
High School—West Palm Beach, Fla., Twin Lakes.
Attended Georgia Tech.

Selected by Jacksonville in 1985 USFL territorial draft.
Signed as free agent by Dallas Cowboys, May 3, 1985.
Released by Dallas Cowboys, August 16, 1985; signed as free agent by Buffalo Bills, July 19, 1986.
Released by Buffalo Bills, September 1, 1986; re-signed by Bills, September 2, 1986.
Released by Buffalo Bills, August 31, 1987; re-signed as replacement player by Bills, October 17, 1987.
Released by Buffalo Bills, November 3, 1987; signed as free agent by Atlanta Falcons for 1988, December 10, 1987.
Granted unconditional free agency, February 1, 1989; signed by Green Bay Packers, March 9, 1989.

Year Club	G.	Att.	Yds.	Avg.	TD.	P.C.	Yds.	Avg.	TD.	TD.	Pts.	F.
			RUSHING				PASS RECEIVING				—TOTAL—	
1986—Buffalo NFL	16	3	18	6.0	0	8	74	9.3	0	0	0	0
1987—Buffalo NFL	1		None				None			0	0	0
1988—Atlanta NFL	14		None			11	134	12.2	0	0	0	0
Pro Totals—3 Years	31	3	18	6.0	0	19	208	10.9	0	0	0	0

JIMMY RAY WILKS
(Jim)
Defensive End—New Orleans Saints
Born March 12, 1958, at Los Angeles, Calif.
Height, 6.05. Weight, 265.
High School—Pasadena, Calif.
Attended Pasadena Community College and San Diego State University.

Selected by New Orleans in 12th round (305th player selected) of 1981 NFL draft.
On inactive list, September 19, 1982.
New Orleans NFL, 1981 through 1988.
Games: 1981 (16), 1982 (8), 1983 (16), 1984 (16), 1985 (16), 1986 (16), 1987 (12), 1988 (16). Total—116.
Pro statistics: Recovered two fumbles, 1981; recovered one fumble, 1983, 1984 and 1988; recovered one fumble for 10 yards, 1987.

GERALD WILLIAM WILLHITE
Running Back—Denver Broncos
Born May 30, 1959, at Sacramento, Calif.
Height, 5.10. Weight, 200.
High School—Rancho Cordova, Calif., Cordova.
Attended American River Junior College and San Jose State University.

Selected by Denver in 1st round (21st player selected) of 1982 NFL draft.
On injured reserve with pulled hamstring, August 30 through October 27, 1983; activated, October 28, 1983.
On injured reserve with broken leg, October 28 through remainder of 1987 season.
On injured reserve with broken shoulder blade, December 10 through remainder of 1988 season.

Year Club	G.	Att.	Yds.	Avg.	TD.	P.C.	Yds.	Avg.	TD.	TD.	Pts.	F.
			RUSHING				PASS RECEIVING				—TOTAL—	
1982—Denver NFL	9	70	347	5.0	2	26	227	8.7	0	2	12	5
1983—Denver NFL	8	43	188	4.4	3	14	153	10.9	1	4	24	0
1984—Denver NFL	16	77	371	4.8	2	27	298	11.0	0	2	12	3
1985—Denver NFL	15	66	237	3.6	3	35	297	8.5	1	4	24	2
1986—Denver NFL	16	85	365	4.3	5	64	529	8.3	3	9	54	5
1987—Denver NFL	3	26	141	5.4	0	9	25	2.8	0	0	0	1
1988—Denver NFL	11	13	39	3.0	2	32	238	7.4	0	2	12	2
Pro Totals—7 Years	78	380	1688	4.4	17	207	1767	8.5	5	23	138	18

Year Club	G.	No.	Yds.	Avg.	TD.	No.	Yds.	Avg.	TD.
			—PUNT RETURNS—				—KICKOFF RET.—		
1982—Denver NFL	9	6	63	10.5	0	17	337	19.8	0
1983—Denver NFL	8		None				None		
1984—Denver NFL	16	20	200	10.0	0	4	109	27.3	0
1985—Denver NFL	15	16	169	10.6	0	2	40	20.0	0
1986—Denver NFL	16	42	468	11.1	1	3	35	11.7	0
1987—Denver NFL	3	4	22	5.5	0		None		
1988—Denver NFL	11	13	90	6.9	0		None		
Pro Totals—7 Years	78	101	1012	10.0	1	26	521	20.0	0

Additional pro statistics: Attempted two passes with no completions and one interception, 1982; attempted one pass with no completions, 1983 and 1987; attempted two passes with one completion for 20 yards and recovered two fumbles, 1984; attempted three passes with no completions, 1985; attempted four passes with one completion for 11 yards and recovered three fumbles, 1986; recovered one fumble, 1988.
Played in AFC Championship Game following 1986 season.
Played in NFL Championship Game following 1986 season.

BRENT DIONE WILLIAMS
Defensive End—New England Patriots
Born October 23, 1964, at Flint, Mich.
Height, 6.03. Weight, 278.
High School—Flint, Mich., Northern.
Received degree in marketing from University of Toledo in 1986.

Selected by New England in 7th round (192nd player selected) of 1986 NFL draft.
Signed by New England Patriots, July 16, 1986.
New England NFL, 1986 through 1988.
Games: 1986 (16), 1987 (12), 1988 (16). Total—44.
Pro statistics: Recovered four fumbles for 54 yards and a touchdown, 1986; recovered one fumble, 1988.

DARRYL EUGENE WILLIAMS
(Dokie)
Wide Receiver—San Diego Chargers
Born August 25, 1960, at Oceanside, Calif.
Height, 5.11. Weight, 180.
High School—Oceanside, Calif., El Camino.
Received degree in political science from University of California at Los Angeles.

Selected by Oakland in 8th round (90th player selected) of 1983 USFL draft.
Selected by Los Angeles Raiders in 5th round (138th player selected) of 1983 NFL draft.
Signed by Los Angeles Raiders, July 6, 1983.
On injured reserve with knee injury, December 17 through remainder of 1986 season.
Traded with 2nd and 4th round picks in 1988 draft by Los Angeles Raiders to San Francisco 49ers for 1st round pick in 1988 draft, April 24, 1988.
Released by San Francisco 49ers, August 26, 1988; signed as free agent by San Diego Chargers, May 11, 1989.

		PASS RECEIVING				—KICKOFF RET.—				—TOTAL—		
Year	Club	G.	P.C.	Yds.	Avg.	TD.	No.	Yds.	Avg.	TD.	TD.	Pts.	F.
1983—Los Angeles Raiders NFL		16	14	259	18.5	3	5	88	17.6	0	3	18	2
1984—Los Angeles Raiders NFL		16	22	509	23.1	4	24	621	25.9	0	4	24	0
1985—Los Angeles Raiders NFL		16	48	925	19.3	5	1	19	19.0	0	5	30	0
1986—Los Angeles Raiders NFL		15	43	843	19.6	8		None			8	48	2
1987—Los Angeles Raiders NFL		11	21	330	15.7	5	14	221	15.8	0	5	30	0
Pro Totals—5 Years		74	148	2866	19.4	25	44	949	21.6	0	25	150	4

Additional pro statistics: Rushed three times for 27 yards, 1986; recovered one fumble, 1986 and 1987.
Member of Los Angeles Raiders for AFC Championship Game following 1983 season; did not play.
Played in NFL Championship Game following 1983 season.

DOUG WILLIAMS
Offensive Tackle—Seattle Seahawks
Born October 1, 1962, at Cincinnati, O.
Height, 6.06. Weight, 295.
High School—Cincinnati, O., Moeller.
Attended Texas A&M University.

Selected by Jacksonville in 1986 USFL territorial draft.
USFL rights traded with rights to center Leonard Burton by Jacksonville Bulls to Memphis Showboats for rights to wide receiver Tim McGee, May 6, 1986.
Selected by New York Jets in 2nd round (49th player selected) of 1986 NFL draft.
Signed by New York Jets, July 27, 1986.
Released by New York Jets, August 25, 1986; awarded on waivers to Houston Oilers, August 26, 1986.
Crossed picket line during players' strike, October 14, 1987.
On injured reserve with broken leg, August 23 through entire 1988 season.
Granted unconditional free agency, February 1, 1989; signed by Seattle Seahawks, March 28, 1989.
Houston NFL, 1986 and 1987.
Games: 1986 (15), 1987 (8). Total—23.

DOUGLAS LEE WILLIAMS
(Doug)
Quarterback—Washington Redskins
Born August 9, 1955, at Zachary, La.
Height, 6.04. Weight, 220.
High School—Zachary, La., Chaneyville.
Received bachelor of science degree in education from Grambling State University in 1978.
Brother of Robert J. Williams, pitcher in Cleveland Indians' organization, 1964 and 1965.

Named as quarterback on THE SPORTING NEWS College All-America Team, 1977.
Selected by Tampa Bay in 1st round (17th player selected) of 1978 NFL draft.
Granted free agency, February 1, 1983; signed by Oklahoma Outlaws, August 8, 1983.
USFL rights traded by Boston Breakers to Oklahoma Outlaws for rights to running back Cliff Chatman and future draft pick, October 11, 1983.
On injured reserve with knee injury, June 4 through remainder of 1984 season.
Protected in merger of Oklahoma Outlaws and Arizona Wranglers, December 6, 1984.
Granted free agency when USFL suspended operations, August 7, 1986; re-signed by Tampa Bay Buccaneers and traded to Washington Redskins for 5th round pick in 1987 draft and conditional pick in 1988 draft, August 13, 1986.
Granted roster exemption, August 13 through August 22, 1986; activated, August 23, 1986.
On non-football injury list with appendectomy, September 22 through October 21, 1988; activated, October 22, 1988.

Year Club	G.	Att.	Cmp.	Pct.	Gain	T.P.	P.I.	Avg.	Att.	Yds.	Avg.	TD.	TD.	Pts.	F.
				PASSING						RUSHING				TOTAL	
1978—Tampa Bay NFL	10	194	73	37.6	1170	7	8	6.03	27	23	0.9	1	1	6	5
1979—Tampa Bay NFL	16	397	166	41.8	2448	18	24	6.17	35	119	3.4	2	2	12	2
1980—Tampa Bay NFL	16	521	254	48.8	3396	20	16	6.52	58	370	6.4	4	4	24	7
1981—Tampa Bay NFL	16	471	238	50.5	3563	19	14	7.56	48	209	4.4	4	4	24	9
1982—Tampa Bay NFL	9	307	164	53.4	2071	9	11	6.75	35	158	4.5	2	2	12	9
1984—Oklahoma USFL	15	528	261	49.4	3084	15	21	5.84	28	89	3.2	3	3	18	13
1985—Arizona USFL	17	509	271	53.2	3673	21	17	7.22	27	82	3.0	1	1	6	9
1986—Washington NFL	1	1	0	0.0	0	0	0	0.00			None		0	0	0
1987—Washington NFL	5	143	81	56.6	1156	11	5	8.08	7	9	1.3	1	1	6	3
1988—Washington NFL	11	380	213	56.1	2609	15	12	6.87	9	0	0.0	1	1	6	6
NFL Totals—8 Years	84	2414	1189	49.3	16413	99	90	6.80	219	888	4.1	15	15	90	41
USFL Totals—2 Years	32	1037	532	51.3	6757	36	38	6.52	55	171	3.1	4	4	24	22
Pro Totals—10 Years	116	3451	1721	49.9	23170	135	128	6.71	274	1059	3.9	19	19	114	63

NFL Quarterback Rating Points: 1978 (53.5), 1979 (52.6), 1980 (69.7), 1981 (76.5), 1982 (69.4), 1986 (39.6), 1987 (94.0), 1988 (77.4). Total—69.8.

USFL Quarterback Rating Points: 1984 (60.5), 1985 (76.4). Total—68.3.

Additional NFL statistics: Recovered two fumbles, 1978 and 1980; fumbled five times for minus six yards, 1978; recovered one fumble and fumbled twice for minus five yards, 1979; recovered three fumbles and fumbled nine times for minus 13 yards, 1981; recovered four fumbles, 1982.

Additional USFL statistics: Recovered seven fumbles, 1984; recovered four fumbles, 1985.

Played in NFC Championship Game following 1979 and 1987 seasons.

Member of Washington Redskins for NFC Championship Game following 1986 season; did not play.

Played in NFL Championship Game following 1987 season.

COACHING RECORD

Assistant coach, Southern University, 1985.

EDMUND SCOTT WILLIAMS

(Known by middle name.)

Fullback—Detroit Lions

Born July 21, 1962, at Charlotte, N.C.
Height, 6.02. Weight, 234.
High School—Charlotte, N.C., North Mecklenburg.
Received bachelor of arts degree in speech communications from University of Georgia in 1985.

Selected by Jacksonville in 1985 USFL territorial draft.
Selected by St. Louis in 9th round (244th player selected) of 1985 NFL draft.
Signed by St. Louis Cardinals, July 21, 1985.
Released by St. Louis Cardinals, August 19, 1985; signed as free agent by Detroit Lions, March 6, 1986.
On injured reserve with shoulder injury, November 25 through remainder of 1987 season.
On injured reserve with knee injury, August 30 through October 7, 1988; activated, October 8, 1988.

Year Club	G.	Att.	Yds.	Avg.	TD.	P.C.	Yds.	Avg.	TD.	TD.	Pts.	F.
			RUSHING				PASS RECEIVING				TOTAL	
1986—Detroit NFL	16	13	22	1.7	2	2	9	4.5	0	2	12	0
1987—Detroit NFL	5	8	29	3.6	0	4	16	4.0	1	1	6	0
1988—Detroit NFL	11	9	22	2.4	1	3	46	15.3	0	1	6	0
Pro Totals—3 Years	32	30	73	2.4	3	9	71	7.9	1	4	24	0

Additional pro statistics: Recovered one fumble, 1988.

EDWARD EUGENE WILLIAMS

(Ed)

Linebacker—New England Patriots

Born September 8, 1961, at Odessa, Tex.
Height, 6.04. Weight, 244.
High School—Odessa, Tex., Ector.
Attended University of Texas.

Selected by San Antonio in 1984 USFL territorial draft.
Selected by New England in 2nd round (43rd player selected) of 1984 NFL draft.
Signed by New England Patriots, July 13, 1984.
On injured reserve with groin injury, November 14 through remainder of 1986 season.
On injured reserve with knee injury, August 15 through entire 1988 season.
Granted unconditional free agency, February 1, 1989; did not receive qualifying offer, April 15, 1989.
Re-signed by New England Patriots, April 21, 1989.
New England NFL, 1984 through 1987.
Games: 1984 (14), 1985 (13), 1986 (8), 1987 (12). Total—47.
Pro statistics: Intercepted one pass for 51 yards and recovered two fumbles for eight yards, 1987.
Played in AFC Championship Game following 1985 season.
Played in NFL Championship Game following 1985 season.

ERIC MICHAEL WILLIAMS

Defensive End—Detroit Lions

Born February 24, 1962, at Stockton, Calif.
Height, 6.04. Weight, 286.
High School—Stockton, Calif., St. Mary's.
Attended Washington State University.
Son of Roy Williams, 2nd round selection of Detroit Lions in 1962 NFL draft.

Selected by New Jersey in 1st round (19th player selected) of 1984 USFL draft.
Selected by Detroit in 3rd round (62nd player selected) of 1984 NFL draft.
Signed by Detroit Lions, July 21, 1984.
On injured reserve with cracked cervical disc, December 4 through remainder of 1985 season.
Detroit NFL, 1984 through 1988.
Games: 1984 (12), 1985 (12), 1986 (16), 1987 (11), 1988 (16). Total—67.
Pro statistics: Recovered one fumble, 1985 and 1986; intercepted one pass for two yards, 1986.

GERALD WILLIAMS
Nose Tackle-Defensive Tackle—Pittsburgh Steelers
Born September 3, 1963, at Waycross, Ga.
Height, 6.03. Weight, 262.
High School—Valley, Ala.
Attended Auburn University.

Selected by Birmingham in 1986 USFL territorial draft.
Selected by Pittsburgh in 2nd round (36th player selected) of 1986 NFL draft.
Signed by Pittsburgh Steelers, July 25, 1986.
Crossed picket line during players' strike, October 13, 1987.
Pittsburgh NFL, 1986 through 1988.
Games: 1986 (16), 1987 (9), 1988 (16). Total—41.
Pro statistics: Recovered one fumble, 1987; recovered one fumble for one yard, 1988.

HENRY L. WILLIAMS
Wide Receiver-Kick Returner—Philadelphia Eagles
Born May 31, 1962, at Memphis, Tenn.
Height, 5.06. Weight, 185.
High School—Tunica, Miss., Rosa Fort.
Attended Northwest Mississippi Junior College and East Carolina University.

Selected by Memphis in 3rd round (36th player selected) of 1985 USFL draft.
Signed by Memphis Showboats, January 25, 1985.
On developmental squad, March 9 through March 16, 1985; activated, March 17, 1985.
Granted free agency when USFL suspended operations, August 7, 1986; signed by Edmonton Eskimos, September, 1986.
Granted free agency, March 1, 1989; signed by Philadelphia Eagles, March 22, 1989.
On developmental squad for 1 game with Memphis Showboats in 1985.

		PASS RECEIVING			-PUNT RETURNS-				—KICKOFF RET.—				—TOTAL—		
Year Club	G.	P.C.	Yds.	Avg.	TD.	No.	Yds.	Avg.	TD.	No.	Yds.	Avg.	TD.	TD.	Pts.	F.
1985—Memphis USFL	17	5	79	15.8	1	31	257	8.3	0	36	711	19.8	0	1	6	2
1986—Edmonton CFL	8	3	79	26.3	0	37	423	11.4	1	9	210	23.3	0	2	12	0
1987—Edmonton CFL	16	4	48	12.0	0	80	*951	11.9	*4	26	623	24.0	0	5	30	2
1988—Edmonton CFL	17	25	515	20.6	5	*96	*964	10.0	2	15	379	25.3	0	7	42	4
USFL Totals—1 Year	17	5	79	15.8	1	31	257	8.3	0	36	711	19.8	0	1	6	2
CFL Totals—3 Years	41	32	642	20.0	5	213	2338	11.0	7	50	1212	24.2	0	14	84	6
Pro Totals—4 Years	58	37	721	19.5	6	244	2595	10.6	7	86	1923	22.4	0	15	90	8

Additional USFL statistics: Rushed once for minus one yard, 1985.
Additional CFL statistics: Rushed twice for 49 yards and a touchdown, 1986; recovered one fumble, 1987 and 1988; scored touchdown on unsuccessful field goal return, 1987, rushed three times for minus one yard, 1988.
Played CFL Championship Game following 1987 season.

JAMES HENRY WILLIAMS
(Jimmy)
Linebacker—Detroit Lions
Born November 15, 1960, at Washington, D.C.
Height, 6.03. Weight, 230.
High School—Washington, D.C., Woodrow Wilson.
Attended University of Nebraska.
Brother of Toby Williams, nose tackle with Green Bay Packers.

Selected by Detroit in 1st round (15th player selected) of 1982 NFL draft.
On injured reserve with broken foot, December 20 through remainder of 1982 season.
Granted roster exemption, August 18 through August 21, 1986; activated, August 22, 1986.
On injured reserve with knee injury, November 11 through remainder of 1986 season.
On injured reserve with knee injury, October 15 through remainder of 1988 season.
Detroit NFL, 1982 through 1988.
Games: 1982 (6), 1983 (16), 1984 (16), 1985 (16), 1986 (10), 1987 (12), 1988 (5). Total—81.
Pro statistics: Intercepted one pass for four yards, 1982; recovered one fumble, 1983 through 1986 and 1988; intercepted two passes for 12 yards, 1986; intercepted two passes for 51 yards and recovered two fumbles, 1987; intercepted one pass for five yards, 1988.

JAMIE WILLIAMS
Tight End—San Francisco 49ers
Born February 25, 1960, at Vero Beach, Fla.
Height, 6.04. Weight, 245.
High School—Davenport, Ia., Central.
Attended University of Nebraska.

Selected by Boston in 1983 USFL territorial draft.

Selected by New York Giants in 3rd round (63rd player selected) of 1983 NFL draft.
Signed by New York Giants, June 30, 1983.
Released by New York Giants, August 29, 1983; signed as free agent by St. Louis Cardinals, September 13, 1983.
Released by St. Louis Cardinals, October 5, 1983; signed as free agent by Tampa Bay Buccaneers, January 25, 1984.
USFL rights traded by New Orleans Breakers to New Jersey Generals for past consideration, March 26, 1984.
Released by Tampa Bay Buccaneers, May 8, 1984; awarded on waivers to Houston Oilers, May 21, 1984.
Granted unconditional free agency, February 1, 1989; signed by San Francisco 49ers, March 14, 1989.

		——PASS RECEIVING——				
Year	Club	G.	P.C.	Yds.	Avg.	TD.
1983—St. Louis NFL		1		None		
1984—Houston NFL		16	41	545	13.3	3
1985—Houston NFL		16	39	444	11.4	1
1986—Houston NFL		16	22	227	10.3	1
1987—Houston NFL		12	13	158	12.2	3
1988—Houston NFL		16	6	46	7.7	0
Pro Totals—6 Years		77	121	1420	11.7	8

Additional pro statistics: Returned one kickoff for no yards and fumbled twice, 1984; recovered one fumble, 1984, 1986 and 1987; returned two kickoffs for 21 yards and fumbled once, 1985.

JARVIS ERIC WILLIAMS
Safety—Miami Dolphins
Born May 16, 1964, at Palatka, Fla.
Height, 5.11. Weight, 196.
High School—Palatka, Fla.
Attended University of Florida.

Selected by Miami in 2nd round (42nd player selected) of 1988 NFL draft.
Signed by Miami Dolphins, July 19, 1988.

			-INTERCEPTIONS-				—KICKOFF RET.—				—TOTAL—		
Year	Club	G.	No.	Yds.	Avg.	TD.	No.	Yds.	Avg.	TD.	TD.	Pts.	F.
1988—Miami NFL		16	4	62	15.5	0	8	159	19.9	0	0	0	0

Additional pro statistics: Returned three punts for 29 yards and recovered three fumbles for 26 yards, 1988.

JOEL WILLIAMS
First name pronounced Jo-EL.
Linebacker—Atlanta Falcons
Born December 13, 1956, at Miami, Fla.
Height, 6.01. Weight, 225.
High School—Miami, Fla., North.
Attended Peru College and received bachelor of business administration degree
from University of Wisconsin at LaCrosse in 1979.

Signed as free agent by Miami Dolphins, July 12, 1979.
Released by Miami Dolphins, August 27, 1979; claimed on waivers by Atlanta Falcons, August 28, 1979.
On injured reserve with knee injury, December 19 through remainder of 1981 season.
USFL rights released by Birmingham Stallions, August 16, 1983; rights awarded on waivers to Pittsburgh Maulers, August 17, 1983.
Traded by Atlanta Falcons to Philadelphia Eagles for 2nd round pick in 1984 draft, August 21, 1983.
Granted free agency, February 1, 1985; re-signed by Eagles, October 23, 1985.
Granted roster exemption, October 23 through November 3, 1985; activated, November 4, 1985.
Traded by Philadelphia Eagles to Atlanta Falcons for 5th round pick in 1986 draft, April 29, 1986.
Atlanta NFL, 1979 through 1982 and 1986 through 1988; Philadelphia NFL, 1983 through 1985.
Games: 1979 (16), 1980 (16), 1981 (10), 1982 (9), 1983 (16), 1984 (16), 1985 (7), 1986 (15), 1987 (8), 1988 (14). Total—127.
Pro statistics: Intercepted two passes for 55 yards, recovered three fumbles for 42 yards and one touchdown and credited with one safety, 1980; intercepted one pass for 25 yards and recovered two fumbles for 57 yards and a touchdown, 1981; recovered one fumble, 1982 and 1983; recovered two fumbles, 1984; intercepted two passes for 18 yards and a touchdown, 1986; recovered three fumbles for 12 yards, 1988.

JOHN L. WILLIAMS
(John L.)
Fullback—Seattle Seahawks
Born November 23, 1964, at Palatka, Fla.
Height, 5.11. Weight, 226.
High School—Palatka, Fla.
Attended University of Florida.

Selected by Tampa Bay in 1986 USFL territorial draft.
Selected by Seattle in 1st round (15th player selected) of 1986 NFL draft.
Signed by Seattle Seahawks, July 23, 1986.

			——RUSHING——				PASS RECEIVING				—TOTAL—		
Year	Club	G.	Att.	Yds.	Avg.	TD.	P.C.	Yds.	Avg.	TD.	TD.	Pts.	F.
1986—Seattle NFL		16	129	538	4.2	0	33	219	6.6	0	0	0	1
1987—Seattle NFL		12	113	500	4.4	1	38	420	11.1	3	4	24	2
1988—Seattle NFL		16	189	877	4.6	4	58	651	11.2	3	7	42	0
Pro Totals—3 Years		44	431	1915	4.4	5	129	1290	10.0	6	11	66	3

Additional pro statistic: Recovered one fumble, 1987; recovered two fumbles for minus two yards, 1988.

KEVIN J. WILLIAMS
Cornerback—San Francisco 49ers
Born November 28, 1961, at San Diego, Calif.
Height, 5.10. Weight, 174.
High School—San Diego, Calif., Crawford.
Attended San Diego City College and Iowa State University.

Selected by Los Angeles in 1st round (38th player selected) of 1985 USFL draft.
Signed as free agent by Washington Redskins, May 13, 1985.
Released by Washington Redskins, August 27, 1985; re-signed by Redskins, October 2, 1985.
Released by Washington Redskins, August 26, 1986; signed as free agent by Buffalo Bills, December 20, 1986.
On injured reserve with shoulder injury, September 1 through November 16, 1987.
Released by Buffalo Bills, November 17, 1987; signed as free agent by San Diego Chargers, March 4, 1988.
Released by San Diego Chargers, July 22, 1988; signed as free agent by Washington Redskins, September 21, 1988.
Released by Washington Redskins, October 31, 1988; signed as free agent by San Francisco 49ers, April 10, 1989.
Washington NFL, 1985 and 1988; Buffalo NFL, 1986.
Games: 1985 (12), 1986 (1), 1988 (5). Total—18.

LAWRENCE RICHARD WILLIAMS II
(Larry)
Guard—San Diego Chargers
Born July 3, 1963, at Orange, Calif.
Height, 6.05. Weight, 290.
High School—Santa Ana, Calif., Mater Dei.
Received bachelor of arts degree in American studies (journalism) and business
from University of Notre Dame in 1985.

Selected by Portland in 10th round (136th player selected) of 1985 USFL draft.
Selected by Cleveland in 10th round (259th player selected) of 1985 NFL draft.
Signed by Cleveland Browns, July 15, 1985.
On injured reserve with wrist injury, August 20 through entire 1985 season.
Granted unconditional free agency, February 1, 1989; signed by San Diego Chargers, March 7, 1989.
Cleveland NFL, 1986 through 1988.
Games: 1986 (16), 1987 (12), 1988 (14). Total—42.
Pro statistics: Recovered one fumble, 1988.
Played in AFC Championship Game following 1986 and 1987 seasons.

LEE ERIC WILLIAMS
Defensive End—San Diego Chargers
Born October 15, 1962, at Fort Lauderdale, Fla.
Height, 6.05. Weight, 271.
High School—Fort Lauderdale, Fla., Stranahan.
Received degree in business administration from Bethune-Cookman College.

Selected by Tampa Bay in 1984 USFL territorial draft.
USFL rights traded with rights to defensive tackle Dewey Forte by Tampa Bay Bandits to Los Angeles Express for draft choice, March 2, 1984.
Signed by Los Angeles Express, March 6, 1984.
Granted roster exemption, March 6 through March 15, 1984; activated, March 16, 1984.
Selected by San Diego in 1st round (6th player selected) of 1984 NFL supplemental draft.
Released by Los Angeles Express, October 20, 1984; signed by San Diego Chargers, October 22, 1984.
Granted roster exemption, October 22 through October 28, 1984; activated, October 29, 1984.
Los Angeles USFL, 1984; San Diego NFL, 1984 through 1988.
Games: 1984 USFL (14), 1984 NFL (8), 1985 (16), 1986 (16), 1987 (12), 1988 (16). Total NFL—68. Total Pro—82.
USFL statistics: Credited with 13 sacks for 92 yards, 1984.
NFL statistics: Intercepted one pass for 66 yards and a touchdown, 1984; intercepted one pass for 17 yards and recovered one fumble for two yards, 1985; recovered one fumble for six yards, 1986; credited with a safety, 1987; recovered one fumble, 1988.
Played in Pro Bowl (NFL All-Star Game) following 1988 season.

PERRY LAMAR WILLIAMS
Cornerback—New York Giants
Born May 12, 1961, at Hamlet, N.C.
Height, 6.02. Weight, 203.
High School—Hamlet, N.C., Richmond County.
Attended North Carolina State University.

Selected by Washington in 7th round (76th player selected) of 1983 USFL draft.
Selected by New York Giants in 7th round (178th player selected) of 1983 NFL draft.
Signed by New York Giants, June 13, 1983.
On injured reserve with foot injury, August 17 through entire 1983 season.
On injured reserve with pinched nerve, September 7 through October 23, 1987; activated, October 24, 1987.

Year Club	G.	No.	Yds.	Avg.	TD.
1984—N.Y. Giants NFL	16	3	7	2.3	0
1985—N.Y. Giants NFL	16	2	28	14.0	0
1986—N.Y. Giants NFL	16	4	31	7.8	0
1987—N.Y. Giants NFL	10	1	−5	−5.0	0
1988—N.Y. Giants NFL	16	1	0	0.0	0
Pro Totals—5 Years	74	11	61	5.5	0

Additional pro statistics: Recovered one fumble, 1984 and 1985; recovered two fumbles for one yard, 1987; recovered three fumbles for six yards, 1988.
Played in NFC Championship Game following 1986 season.
Played in NFL Championship Game following 1986 season.

REGINALD WILLIAMS
(Reggie)
Linebacker—Cincinnati Bengals
Born September 19, 1954, at Flint, Mich.
Height, 6.01. Weight, 228.
High School—Flint, Mich., Southwestern.
Received bachelor of arts degree in psychology from Dartmouth College.
Selected by Cincinnati in 3rd round (82nd player selected) of 1976 NFL draft.
Crossed picket line during players' strike, September 30, 1987.

Year	Club	G.	No.	Yds.	Avg.	TD.	Year	Club	G.	No.	Yds.	Avg.	TD.
			—INTERCEPTIONS—							—INTERCEPTIONS—			
1976—Cincinnati NFL		14	1	17	17.0	0	1984—Cincinnati NFL		16	2	33	16.5	0
1977—Cincinnati NFL		14	3	67	22.3	1	1985—Cincinnati NFL		16		None		
1978—Cincinnati NFL		16	1	11	11.0	0	1986—Cincinnati NFL		16		None		
1979—Cincinnati NFL		12	2	5	2.5	0	1987—Cincinnati NFL		15		None		
1980—Cincinnati NFL		14	2	8	4.0	0	1988—Cincinnati NFL		16		None		
1981—Cincinnati NFL		16	4	33	8.3	0							
1982—Cincinnati NFL		9	1	20	20.0	0	Pro Totals—13 Years		190	16	194	12.1	1
1983—Cincinnati NFL		16		None									

Additional pro statistics: Recovered blocked punt in end zone for a touchdown, recovered two fumbles, 1977, 1980 and 1987; returned one punt for no yards, 1977 and 1980; fumbled once, 1977 and 1980; recovered one fumble for 30 yards, 1978; recovered one fumble, 1979, 1980 and 1986; recovered three fumbles, 1981, recovered four fumbles and credited with one safety, 1982; recovered four fumbles for 59 yards and a touchdown, 1983; recovered four fumbles for four yards, 1985.
Played in AFC Championship Game following 1981 and 1988 seasons.
Played in NFL Championship Game following 1981 and 1988 seasons.

ROBERT COLE WILLIAMS
Cornerback—Dallas Cowboys
Born October 2, 1962, at Galveston, Tex.
Height, 5.10. Weight, 190.
High School—Galveston, Tex., Ball.
Attended Baylor University.
Signed as free agent by Washington Redskins, May 1, 1986.
Released by Washington Redskins, August 4, 1986; signed as free agent by Dallas Cowboys, April 10, 1987.
Released by Dallas Cowboys, September 7, 1987; re-signed as replacement player by Cowboys, September 23, 1987.
Dallas NFL, 1987 and 1988.
Games: 1987 (11), 1988 (16). Total—27.
Pro statistics: Recovered one fumble, 1987 and 1988; intercepted two passes for 18 yards, 1988.

TERRY WILLIAMS
Cornerback—New York Jets
Born October 14, 1965, at Homestead, Fla.
Height, 5.11. Weight, 197.
High School—Homestead, Fla., South Dade.
Attended Bethune-Cookman College.
Selected by New York Jets in 2nd round (37th player selected) of 1988 NFL draft.
Signed by New York Jets, June 3, 1988.
On injured reserve with knee injury, October 19 through December 16, 1988; activated, December 17, 1988.
New York Jets NFL, 1988.
Games: 1988 (8).

TOBIAS WILLIAMS
(Toby)
Nose Tackle—Green Bay Packers
Born November 19, 1959, at Washington, D.C.
Height, 6.04. Weight, 275.
High School—Washington, D.C., Woodrow Wilson.
Received bachelor of arts degree in criminal justice from University of Nebraska in 1983.
Brother of Jimmy Williams, linebacker with Detroit Lions.
Selected by Boston in 1983 USFL territorial draft.
Selected by New England in 10th round (265th player selected) of 1983 NFL draft.
Signed by New England Patriots, May 25, 1983.
On injured reserve with knee injury, October 18 through remainder of 1985 season.
Granted unconditional free agency, February 1, 1988; re-signed by Patriots, August 29, 1988.
Granted unconditional free agency, February 1, 1989; signed by Green Bay Packers, March 8, 1989.
New England NFL, 1983 through 1988.
Games: 1983 (16), 1984 (16), 1985 (5), 1986 (16), 1987 (12), 1988 (15). Total—80.
Pro statistics: Recovered one fumble, 1984.

WARREN WILLIAMS JR.
Running Back—Pittsburgh Steelers
Born July 29, 1965, at Fort Myers, Fla.
Height, 6.00. Weight, 202.
High School—North Fort Myers, Fla.
Attended University of Miami (Fla.).

Selected by Pittsburgh in 6th round (155th player selected) of 1988 NFL draft.
Signed by Pittsburgh Steelers, July 15, 1988.

			RUSHING			PASS RECEIVING				—TOTAL—		
Year	Club	G.	Att.	Yds.	Avg.	TD.	P.C.	Yds.	Avg.	TD.	TD.	Pts.	F.
1988—Pittsburgh NFL		15	87	409	4.7	0	11	66	6.0	1	1	6	3

Additional pro statistics: Returned one kickoff for 10 yards, 1988.

KEITH WILLIS
Defensive End—Pittsburgh Steelers
Born July 29, 1959, at Newark, N.J.
Height, 6.01. Weight, 260.
High School—Newark, N.J., Malcolm X. Shabazz.
Attended Northwestern University.

Signed as free agent by Pittsburgh Steelers, April 30, 1982.
On injured reserve with herniated disc, August 15 through entire 1988 season.
Pittsburgh NFL, 1982 through 1987.
Games: 1982 (9), 1983 (14), 1984 (16), 1985 (16), 1986 (16), 1987 (11). Total—78.
Pro statistics: Recovered one fumble, 1983 and 1984.
Played in AFC Championship Game following 1984 season.

OTIS MITCHELL WILLIS
(Mitch)
Defensive Lineman—Indianapolis Colts
Born March 16, 1962, at Dallas, Tex.
Height, 6.08. Weight, 285.
High School—Arlington, Tex., Lamar.
Received bachelor of business administration degree from Southern Methodist University in 1984.

Selected by San Antonio in 4th round (68th player selected) of 1984 USFL draft.
Selected by Los Angeles Raiders in 7th round (183rd player selected) of 1984 NFL draft.
Signed by Los Angeles Raiders, June 15, 1984.
On injured reserve with shoulder injury, August 27 through entire 1984 season.
On injured reserve with knee injury, September 7 through October 4, 1985; activated, October 5, 1985.
On injured reserve with knee injury, September 30 through October 18, 1988.
Released by Los Angeles Raiders, October 19, 1988; awarded on waivers to Atlanta Falcons, October 20, 1988.
Granted unconditional free agency, February 1, 1989; signed by Indianapolis Colts, March 14, 1989.
Los Angeles Raiders NFL, 1985 through 1987; Los Angeles Raiders (1)-Atlanta (9) NFL, 1988.
Games: 1985 (11), 1986 (16), 1987 (10), 1988 (10). Total—47.

CHARLES WADE WILSON
(Known by middle name.)
Quarterback—Minnesota Vikings
Born February 1, 1959, at Greenville, Tex.
Height, 6.03. Weight, 206.
High School—Commerce, Tex.
Attended East Texas State University.

Selected by Minnesota in 8th round (210th player selected) of 1981 NFL draft.
On inactive list, September 12, 1982.
On commissioner's exempt list, November 20 through December 7, 1982; activated, December 8, 1982.
Active for 4 games with Minnesota Vikings in 1982; did not play.

			PASSING							RUSHING				—TOTAL—		
Year	Club	G.	Att.	Cmp.	Pct.	Gain	T.P.	P.I.	Avg.	Att.	Yds.	Avg.	TD.	TD.	Pts.	F.
1981—Minnesota NFL		3	13	6	46.2	48	0	2	3.69		None			0	0	2
1983—Minnesota NFL		1	28	16	57.1	124	1	2	4.43	3	—3	—1.0	0	0	0	1
1984—Minnesota NFL		8	195	102	52.3	1019	5	11	5.23	9	30	3.3	0	0	0	2
1985—Minnesota NFL		4	60	33	55.0	404	3	3	6.73		None			0	0	0
1986—Minnesota NFL		9	143	80	55.9	1165	7	5	8.15	13	9	0.7	1	1	6	3
1987—Minnesota NFL		12	264	140	53.0	2106	14	13	*7.98	41	263	6.4	5	5	30	3
1988—Minnesota NFL		14	332	204	*61.4	2746	15	9	8.27	36	136	3.8	2	2	12	4
Pro Totals—8 Years		51	1035	581	56.1	7612	45	45	7.35	102	435	4.3	8	8	48	15

Quarterback Rating Points: 1981 (16.4), 1983 (50.3), 1984 (52.5), 1985 (71.8), 1986 (84.4), 1987 (76.7), 1988 (91.5). Total—75.9.

Additional pro statistics: Recovered one fumble, 1981; punted twice for a 38.0 average with one blocked, recovered one fumble and fumbled three times for minus two yards, 1986; fumbled three times for minus three yards, 1987; recovered four fumbles and fumbled four times for minus nine yards, 1988.
Played in NFC Championship Game following 1987 season.
Played in Pro Bowl (NFL All-Star Game) following 1988 season.

DAVID CARLTON WILSON
(Dave)
Quarterback—New Orleans Saints
Born April 27, 1959, at Anaheim, Calif.
Height, 6.03. Weight, 206.
High School—Anaheim, Calif., Katella.
Attended Fullerton Junior College and University of Illinois.

Selected by New Orleans in NFL supplementary draft, July 7, 1981; Saints forfeited 1st round pick in 1982 draft.
On injured reserve with knee injury, August 15 through entire 1982 season.
On injured reserve with elbow injury, November 15 through remainder of 1985 season.

		—————PASSING—————							—RUSHING—				—TOTAL—		
Year	Club	G.	Att.	Cmp.	Pct.	Gain	T.P.	P.I.	Avg.	Att.	Yds.	Avg.	TD.	TD.	Pts.	F.
1981—New Orleans NFL		11	159	82	51.6	1058	1	11	6.65	5	1	0.2	0	0	0	4
1983—New Orleans NFL		8	112	66	58.9	770	5	7	6.88	5	3	0.6	1	1	6	5
1984—New Orleans NFL		5	93	51	54.8	647	7	4	6.96	3	—7	—2.3	0	0	0	2
1985—New Orleans NFL		10	293	145	49.5	1843	11	15	6.29	18	7	0.4	0	0	0	6
1986—New Orleans NFL		14	342	189	55.3	2353	10	17	6.88	14	19	1.4	1	1	6	8
1987—New Orleans NFL		4	24	13	54.2	243	2	0	10.13		None			0	0	0
1988—New Orleans NFL		1	16	5	31.3	73	0	1	4.56		None			0	0	0
Pro Totals—7 Years		53	1039	551	53.0	6987	36	55	6.72	45	23	0.5	2	2	12	25

Quarterback Rating Points: 1981 (46.1), 1983 (68.7), 1984 (83.9), 1985 (60.7), 1986 (65.8), 1987 (117.2), 1988 (21.1). Total—63.8.

Additional pro statistics: Recovered three fumbles and fumbled four times for minus eight yards, 1981; recovered one fumble and fumbled six times for minus 23 yards, 1985; recovered four fumbles and fumbled eight times for minus four yards, 1986.

KARL WENDELL WILSON
Defensive End—San Diego Chargers
Born September 10, 1964, at Amite, La.
Height, 6.04. Weight, 275.
High School—Baker, La.
Received degree in general studies from Louisiana State University in 1987.

Selected by San Diego in 3rd round (59th player selected) of 1987 NFL draft.
Signed by San Diego Chargers, July 29, 1987.
On injured reserve with hamstring injury, November 3 through December 4, 1987; activated, December 5, 1987.
San Diego NFL, 1987 and 1988.
Games: 1987 (7), 1988 (13). Total—20.

MARC DOUGLAS WILSON
Quarterback—New England Patriots
Born February 15, 1957, at Bremerton, Wash.
Height, 6.06. Weight, 205.
High School—Seattle, Wash., Shorecrest.
Received bachelor of arts degree in economics from Brigham Young University in 1980.

Selected by Oakland in 1st round (15th player selected) of 1980 NFL draft.
Franchise transferred to Los Angeles, May 7, 1982.
On injured reserve with dislocated shoulder, November 7 through December 30, 1983; activated, December 31, 1983.
Crossed picket line during players' strike, September 23, 1987.
Granted free agency, February 1, 1988; Los Angeles Raiders exercised option not to re-sign, June 1, 1988.
Signed by Green Bay Packers, July 19, 1988.
Released by Green Bay Packers, August 30, 1988; signed as free agent by New England Patriots, March 23, 1989.

		—————PASSING—————							—RUSHING—				—TOTAL—		
Year	Club	G.	Att.	Cmp.	Pct.	Gain	T.P.	P.I.	Avg.	Att.	Yds.	Avg.	TD.	TD.	Pts.	F.
1980—Oakland NFL		2	5	3	60.0	31	0	0	6.20	1	3	3.0	0	0	0	0
1981—Oakland NFL		13	366	173	47.3	2311	14	19	6.31	30	147	4.9	2	2	12	8
1982—L.A. Raiders NFL		8	2	1	50.0	4	0	0	2.00		None			0	0	0
1983—L.A. Raiders NFL		10	117	67	57.3	864	8	6	7.38	13	122	9.4	0	0	0	4
1984—L.A. Raiders NFL		16	282	153	54.3	2151	15	17	7.63	30	56	1.9	1	1	6	11
1985—L.A. Raiders NFL		16	388	193	49.7	2608	16	21	6.72	24	98	4.1	2	2	12	8
1986—L.A. Raiders NFL		16	240	129	53.8	1721	12	15	7.17	14	45	3.2	0	0	0	6
1987—L.A. Raiders NFL		15	266	152	57.1	2070	12	8	7.78	17	91	5.4	0	0	0	1
Pro Totals—8 Years		96	1666	871	52.3	11760	77	86	7.06	129	562	4.4	5	5	30	38

Quarterback Rating Points: 1980 (77.9), 1981 (58.8), 1982 (56.3), 1983 (82.0), 1984 (71.7), 1985 (62.7), 1986 (67.4), 1987 (84.6). Total—68.8.

Additional pro statistics: Recovered two fumbles and fumbled eight times for minus three yards, 1981; recovered one fumble, 1983; recovered three fumbles and fumbled 11 times for minus 11 yards, 1984; recovered two fumbles and fumbled eight times for minus four yards, 1985; recovered one fumble and fumbled six times for minus 10 yards, 1986.
Played in AFC Championship Game following 1983 season.
Member of Oakland Raiders for AFC Championship Game following 1980 season; did not play.
Played in NFL Championship Game following 1983 season.
Member of Oakland Raiders for NFL Championship Game following 1980 season; did not play.

MICHAEL RUBEN WILSON
(Mike)
Wide Receiver—San Francisco 49ers
Born December 19, 1958, at Los Angeles, Calif.
Height, 6.03. Weight, 215.
High School—Carson, Calif.
Attended Washington State University.

Selected by Dallas in 9th round (246th player selected) of 1981 NFL draft.
Released by Dallas Cowboys, August 24, 1981; signed as free agent by San Francisco 49ers, August 27, 1981.
On injured reserve with broken finger, September 9 through November 19, 1982; activated, November 20, 1982.
On injured reserve with neck injury, November 21 through remainder of 1986 season.

			—PASS RECEIVING—			
Year	Club	G.	P.C.	Yds.	Avg.	TD.
1981—San Francisco NFL		16	9	125	13.9	1
1982—San Francisco NFL		6	6	80	13.3	1
1983—San Francisco NFL		15	30	433	14.4	0
1984—San Francisco NFL		13	17	245	14.4	1
1985—San Francisco NFL		16	10	165	16.5	2
1986—San Francisco NFL		11	9	104	11.6	1
1987—San Francisco NFL		11	29	450	15.5	5
1988—San Francisco NFL		16	33	405	12.3	3
Pro Totals—8 Years............		104	143	2007	14.0	14

Additional pro statistics: Returned four kickoffs for 67 yards, 1981; recovered one fumble, 1981 and 1986; fumbled once, 1983; returned one kickoff for 14 yards, 1984; returned one kickoff for 10 yards and recovered two fumbles, 1986; returned one kickoff for two yards, 1988.
Played in NFC Championship Game following 1981, 1983, 1984 and 1988 seasons.
Played in NFL Championship Game following 1981, 1984 and 1988 seasons.

OTIS RAY WILSON
Linebacker—Los Angeles Raiders
Born September 15, 1957, at New York, N.Y.
Height, 6.02. Weight, 227.
High School—Brooklyn, N.Y., Thomas Jefferson.
Attended Syracuse University and University of Louisville.

Named as linebacker on THE SPORTING NEWS College All-America Team, 1979.
Selected by Chicago in 1st round (19th player selected) of 1980 NFL draft.
On suspended list, December 2 through December 7, 1986; activated, December 8, 1986.
On injured reserve with knee injury, November 11 through December 13, 1987; activated, December 14, 1987.
On injured reserve with knee injury, August 26 through entire 1988 season.
Granted unconditional free agency, February 1, 1989; signed by Los Angeles Raiders, March 15, 1989.

			—INTERCEPTIONS—			
Year	Club	G.	No.	Yds.	Avg.	TD.
1980—Chicago NFL		16	2	4	2.0	0
1981—Chicago NFL		15		None		
1982—Chicago NFL		9	2	39	19.5	*1
1983—Chicago NFL		16	1	6	6.0	0
1984—Chicago NFL		15		None		
1985—Chicago NFL		16	3	35	11.7	*1
1986—Chicago NFL		15	2	31	15.5	0
1987—Chicago NFL		7		None		
Pro Totals—8 Years............		109	10	115	11.5	2

Additional pro statistics: Fumbled once, 1980; recovered three fumbles for 31 yards, 1981; recovered two fumbles and credited with one safety, 1985; recovered three fumbles, 1986.
Played in NFC Championship Game following 1984 and 1985 seasons.
Played in NFL Championship Game following 1985 season.
Played in Pro Bowl (NFL All-Star Game) following 1985 season.

WILLIAM MIKE WILSON
(Known by middle name.)
Offensive Tackle—Seattle Seahawks
Born May 28, 1955, at Norfolk, Va.
Height, 6.05. Weight, 274.
High School—Gainesville, Ga., Johnson.
Attended University of Georgia.

Selected by Cincinnati in 4th round (103rd player selected) of 1977 NFL draft.
Signed by Toronto Argonauts, May, 1977.
Released by Toronto Argonauts, July 6, 1978; signed by Cincinnati Bengals, July 6, 1978; activated, October 13, 1978.
Placed on physically unable to perform list with knee injury, July 6, 1978.
Traded by Cincinnati Bengals to Seattle Seahawks for 3rd round pick in 1987 draft, August 27, 1986.
Toronto CFL, 1977; Cincinnati NFL, 1978 through 1985; Seattle NFL, 1987 and 1988.
Games: 1977 (16), 1978 (9), 1979 (16), 1980 (16), 1981 (16), 1982 (9), 1983 (16), 1984 (16), 1985 (16), 1986 (16), 1987 (12), 1988 (16). Total NFL—158. Total Pro—174.
Pro statistics: Recovered one fumble, 1988.
Played in AFC Championship Game following 1981 season.
Played in NFL Championship Game following 1981 season.

SAMMY WINDER
Running Back—Denver Broncos
Born July 15, 1959, at Madison, Miss.
Height, 5.11. Weight, 203.
High School—Madison, Miss., Ridgeland.
Attended University of Southern Mississippi.

Selected by Denver in 5th round (131st player selected) of 1982 NFL draft.

		—RUSHING—			PASS RECEIVING				—TOTAL—		
Year Club	G.	Att.	Yds.	Avg. TD.	P.C.	Yds.	Avg.	TD.	TD.	Pts.	F.
1982—Denver NFL	8	67	259	3.9 1	11	83	7.5	0	1	6	1
1983—Denver NFL	14	196	757	3.9 3	23	150	6.5	0	3	18	7
1984—Denver NFL	16	296	1153	3.9 4	44	288	6.5	2	6	36	5
1985—Denver NFL	14	199	714	3.6 8	31	197	6.4	0	8	48	4
1986—Denver NFL	16	240	789	3.3 9	26	171	6.6	5	14	84	2
1987—Denver NFL	12	196	741	3.8 6	14	74	5.3	1	7	42	5
1988—Denver NFL	16	149	543	3.6 4	17	103	6.1	1	5	30	1
Pro Totals—7 Years	96	1343	4956	3.7 35	166	1066	6.4	9	44	264	25

Additional pro statistics: Recovered one fumble, 1982, 1985 and 1986; recovered two fumbles, 1984 and 1987; attempted one pass with no completions, 1985; returned one kickoff for 11 yards, 1988.
Played in AFC Championship Game following 1986 and 1987 seasons.
Played in NFL Championship Game following 1986 and 1987 seasons.
Played in Pro Bowl (NFL All-Star Game) following 1984 and 1986 seasons.

EARL WINFIELD
Wide Receiver—San Francisco 49ers
Born August 8, 1961, at Petersburg, Va.
Height, 6.00. Weight, 185.
High Schools—Dinwiddie, Va.; and Fork Union, Va., Fork Union Military.
Attended University of North Carolina.

Selected by Baltimore in 1986 USFL territorial draft.
Signed as free agent by Seattle Seahawks, May 13, 1986.
Released by Seattle Seahawks, August 18, 1986; signed as free agent by Hamilton Tiger-Cats, February 7, 1987.
Granted free agency, March 1, 1989; signed as free agent by San Francisco 49ers, March 4, 1989.

		PASS RECEIVING			-PUNT RETURNS-				—KICKOFF RET.—				—TOTAL—		
Year Club	G.	P.C.	Yds.	Avg. TD.	No.	Yds.	Avg.	TD.	No.	Yds.	Avg.	TD.	TD.	Pts.	F.
1987—Hamilton CFL	11	38	746	19.6 2	22	256	11.6	1	18	347	19.3	0	3	18	5
1988—Hamilton CFL	18	60	1213	20.2 8	74	865	11.7	*4	20	532	26.6	1	13	78	7
CFL Totals—2 Years	29	98	1959	20.0 10	96	1121	11.7	5	38	879	23.1	1	16	96	12

Additional CFL statistics: Rushed once for two yards and recovered two fumbles, 1988.

GEORGE ARTHUR WINSLOW
Punter—New Orleans Saints
Born July 28, 1963, at Philadelphia, Pa.
Height, 6.04. Weight, 205.
High School—Philadelphia, Pa., LaSalle.
Attended University of Wisconsin and received bachelor of arts degree in
communication arts from Villanova University in 1987.

Signed as free agent by Cleveland Browns, May 4, 1987.
On injured reserve with back injury, September 7 through November 6, 1987; activated, November 7, 1987.
Crossed picket line during players' strike, October 14, 1987.
On injured reserve with back injury, December 15 through remainder of 1987 season.
Released by Cleveland Browns, February 16, 1988; awarded on waivers to Buffalo Bills, February 29, 1988.
Released by Buffalo Bills, August 24, 1988; signed as free agent by New Orleans Saints, April 6, 1989.

	——PUNTING——		
Year Club	G.	No.	Avg. Blk.
1987—Cleveland NFL	5	18	34.2 0

BLAISE WINTER
Defensive Lineman—Green Bay Packers
Born January 31, 1962, at Blauvelt, N.Y.
Height, 6.03. Weight, 274.
High School—Orangeburg, N.Y., Tappan Zee.
Attended Syracuse University.

Selected by New Jersey in 1984 USFL territorial draft.
Selected by Indianapolis in 2nd round (35th player selected) of 1984 NFL draft.
Signed by Indianapolis Colts, July 27, 1984.
On injured reserve with shoulder injury, August 27 through entire 1985 season.
On injured reserve with knee injury, August 18 through October 14, 1986.
Released by Indianapolis Colts, October 15, 1986; signed as free agent by San Diego Chargers, November 24, 1986.
Released by San Diego Chargers, August 29, 1987; re-signed as replacement player by Chargers, September 28, 1987.
On injured reserve with hand injury, October 27 through remainder of 1987 season.
Traded by San Diego Chargers to Green Bay Packers for past considerations, April 28, 1988.
Indianapolis NFL, 1984; San Diego NFL, 1986 and 1987; Green Bay NFL, 1988.
Games: 1984 (16), 1986 (4), 1987 (3), 1988 (16). Total—39.
Pro statistics: Recovered one fumble, 1984; returned one kickoff for seven yards and recovered two fumbles, 1988.

FRANK MITCHELL WINTERS
Center—New York Giants
Born January 23, 1964, at Hoboken, N. J.
Height, 6.03. Weight, 290.
High School—Union City, N. J., Emerson.
Attended College of Eastern Utah and received degree in political science
administration from Western Illinois University in 1987.

Selected by Cleveland in 10th round (276th player selected) of 1987 NFL draft.
Signed by Cleveland Browns, July 25, 1987.
Granted unconditional free agency, February 1, 1989; signed by New York Giants, March 17, 1989.
Cleveland NFL, 1987 and 1988.
Games: 1987 (12), 1988 (16). Total—28.
Pro statistics: Fumbled once, 1987.
Played in AFC Championship Game following 1987 season.

MIKE WISE
Defensive End—Los Angeles Raiders
Born June 5, 1964, at Greenbrae, Calif.
Height, 6.07. Weight, 270.
High School—Novato, Calif.
Attended University of California at Davis.

Selected by Los Angeles Raiders in 4th round (85th player selected) of 1986 NFL draft.
Signed by Los Angeles Raiders, July 11, 1986.
On injured reserve with elbow injury, August 26 through October 31, 1986; activated, November 1, 1986.
On injured reserve with elbow injury, December 11 through remainder of 1986 season.
On non-football injury list with virus, September 7 through December 4, 1987; activated, December 5, 1987.
Active for 1 game with Los Angeles Raiders in 1987; did not play.
Los Angeles Raiders NFL, 1986 through 1988.
Games: 1986 (6), 1988 (16). Total—22.
Pro statistics: Recovered two fumbles, 1988.

MIKE WITHYCOMBE
Name pronounced WITH-ee-come.
Guard-Offensive Tackle—New York Jets
Born November 18, 1964, at Meridan, Miss.
Height, 6.05. Weight, 295.
High School—Lemoore, Calif.
Attended West Hills College and Fresno State University.

Selected by New York Jets in 5th round (119th player selected) of 1988 NFL draft.
Signed by New York Jets, July 12, 1988.
New York Jets NFL, 1988.
Games: 1988 (6).

JOHN STANLEY WOJCIECHOWSKI
Name pronounced Wo-ja-cow-skee.
Guard—Chicago Bears
Born July 30, 1963, at Detroit, Mich.
Height, 6.04. Weight, 270.
High School—Warren, Mich., Fitzgerald.
Received bachelor of science degree in education
from Michigan State University in 1986.

Selected by Birmingham in 1986 USFL territorial draft.
Signed as free agent by Buffalo Bills, May 6, 1986.
Released by Buffalo Bills, August 18, 1986; signed as free agent by Chicago Bears, March 10, 1987.
Released by Chicago Bears, September 7, 1987; re-signed as replacement player by Bears, September 28, 1987.
Chicago NFL, 1987 and 1988.
Games: 1987 (4), 1988 (16). Total—20.
Pro statistics: Recovered one fumble, 1987.
Member of Chicago Bears for NFC Championship Game following 1988 season; did not play.

CRAIG ALAN WOLFLEY
Offensive Tackle-Guard—Pittsburgh Steelers
Born May 19, 1958, at Buffalo, N.Y.
Height, 6.01. Weight, 272.
High School—Orchard Park, N.Y.
Received bachelor of science degree in speech communication from Syracuse University in 1980.
Brother of Ronnie Wolfley, fullback with Phoenix Cardinals;
and Dale Wolfley, guard at West Virginia University.

Selected by Pittsburgh in 5th round (138th player selected) of 1980 NFL draft.
On injured reserve with pulled hamstring, October 5 through November 18, 1984; activated, November 19, 1984.
On injured reserve with knee injury, August 19 through October 24, 1986; activated, October 25, 1986.
Pittsburgh NFL, 1980 through 1988.
Games: 1980 (16), 1981 (16), 1982 (9), 1983 (14), 1984 (9), 1985 (13), 1986 (9), 1987 (12), 1988 (16). Total—114.
Pro statistics: Recovered two fumbles, 1982; recovered one fumble, 1983 and 1985 through 1987.
Played in AFC Championship Game following 1984 season.

RONALD PAUL WOLFLEY
(Ron)
Fullback—Phoenix Cardinals

Born October 14, 1962, at Blasdel, N.Y.
Height, 6.00. Weight, 222.
High School—Hamburg, N.Y., Frontier Central.
Attended West Virginia University.
Brother of Craig Wolfley, guard with Pittsburgh Steelers;
and Dale Wolfley, guard at West Virginia University.

Selected by Birmingham in 1985 USFL territorial draft.
Selected by St. Louis in 4th round (104th player selected) of 1985 NFL draft.
Signed by St. Louis Cardinals, July 21, 1985.
Franchise transferred to Phoenix, March 15, 1988.

		—RUSHING—				PASS RECEIVING				—TOTAL—		
Year Club	G.	Att.	Yds.	Avg.	TD.	P.C.	Yds.	Avg.	TD.	TD.	Pts.	F.
1985—St. Louis NFL	16	24	64	2.7	0	2	18	9.0	0	0	0	1
1986—St. Louis NFL	16	8	19	2.4	0	2	32	16.0	0	0	0	0
1987—St. Louis NFL	12	26	87	3.3	1	8	68	8.5	0	1	6	0
1988—Phoenix NFL	16	9	43	4.8	0	2	11	5.5	0	0	0	0
Pro Totals—4 Years	60	67	213	3.2	1	14	129	9.2	0	1	6	1

		KICKOFF RETURNS			
Year Club	G.	No.	Yds.	Avg.	TD.
1985—St. Louis NFL	16	13	234	18.0	0
1986—St. Louis NFL	16	0	—6	....	0
1987—St. Louis NFL	12		None		
1988—Phoenix NFL	16		None		
Pro Totals—4 Years	60	13	228	17.5	0

Pro statistics: Recovered one fumble, 1988.
Played in Pro Bowl (NFL All-Star Game) following 1986 through 1988 seasons.

WILLIAM CHARLES WOLFORD
(Will)
Offensive Tackle—Buffalo Bills

Born May 18, 1964, at Louisville, Ky.
Height, 6.05. Weight, 276.
High School—Louisville, Ky., St. Xavier.
Attended Vanderbilt University.

Selected by Memphis in 1986 USFL territorial draft.
Selected by Buffalo in 1st round (20th player selected) of 1986 NFL draft.
Signed by Buffalo Bills, August 12, 1986.
Granted roster exemption, August 12 through August 21, 1986; activated, August 22, 1986.
Buffalo NFL, 1986 through 1988.
Games: 1986 (16), 1987 (9), 1988 (16). Total—41.
Pro statistics: Recovered one fumble, 1988.
Played in AFC Championship Game following 1988 season.

GEORGE IVORY WONSLEY
Running Back—Indianapolis Colts

Born November 23, 1960, at Moss Point, Miss.
Height, 5.10. Weight, 220.
High School—Moss Point, Miss.
Attened Mississippi State University.
Brother of Otis Wonsley, running back with Washington Redskins, 1981 through 1985;
and Nathan Wonsley, running back with Tampa Bay Buccaneers.

Selected by New Jersey in 1984 USFL territorial draft.
Selected by Indianapolis in 4th round (103rd player selected) of 1984 NFL draft.
Signed by Indianapolis Colts, May 24, 1984.

		—RUSHING—				PASS RECEIVING				—TOTAL—		
Year Club	G.	Att.	Yds.	Avg.	TD.	P.C.	Yds.	Avg.	TD.	TD.	Pts.	F.
1984—Indianapolis NFL	14	37	111	3.0	0	9	47	5.2	0	0	0	0
1985—Indianapolis NFL	16	138	716	5.2	6	30	257	8.6	0	6	36	4
1986—Indianapolis NFL	16	60	214	3.6	1	16	175	10.9	0	1	6	1
1987—Indianapolis NFL	11	18	71	3.9	1	5	48	9.6	0	1	6	1
1988—Indianapolis NFL	16	26	48	1.8	1		None			1	6	0
Pro Totals—5 Years	73	279	1160	4.2	9	60	527	8.8	0	9	54	6

Additional pro statistics: Returned four kickoffs for 52 yards, 1984; returned two kickoffs for 31 yards, 1986; returned one kickoff for 19 yards, 1987.

—DID YOU KNOW—

That four former UCLA quarterbacks started strike games on October 4, 1987? Steve Bono (UCLA '80-'84) started for Pittsburgh; Rick Neuheisel ('81-'83) started for San Diego; David Norrie ('82-'85) started for the Jets and Matt Stevens ('83-'86) started for Kansas City.

NATHAN WONSLEY JR.
Running Back—Tampa Bay Buccaneers
Born December 7, 1963, at Moss Point, Miss.
Height, 5.09. Weight, 185.
High School—Moss Point, Miss.
Attended University of Mississippi.
Brother of George Wonsley, running back with Indianapolis Colts; and Otis Wonsley,
running back with Washington Redskins, 1981 through 1985.

Selected by Birmingham in 1986 USFL territorial draft.
Signed as free agent by Tampa Bay Buccaneers, July 17, 1986.
On injured reserve with neck injury, November 10 through remainder of 1986 season.
On physically unable to perform/reserve with neck injury, July 18 through entire 1987 season.
Released by Tampa Bay Buccaneers, February 29, 1988; re-signed by Buccaneers, January 5, 1989.

		—————RUSHING—————				PASS RECEIVING				—TOTAL—		
Year	Club	G.	Att.	Yds.	Avg.	TD.	P.C.	Yds.	Avg.	TD.	TD.	Pts.	F.
1986—Tampa Bay NFL		10	73	339	4.6	3	8	57	7.1	0	3	18	2

Additional pro statistics: Returned 10 kickoffs for 208 yards (20.8 avg.) and recovered two fumbles, 1986.

KENNETH EMIL WOODARD
(Ken)
Linebacker—San Diego Chargers
Born January 22, 1960, at Detroit, Mich.
Height, 6.01. Weight, 220.
High School—Detroit, Mich., Martin Luther King.
Attended Tuskegee Institute.

Selected by Denver in 10th round (274th player selected) of 1982 NFL draft.
Traded by Denver Broncos to Pittsburgh Steelers for 10th round pick in 1988 draft, August 27, 1987.
On injured reserve with knee injury, September 18 through November 20, 1987; activated, November 21, 1987.
Traded by Pittsburgh Steelers to Indianapolis Colts for draft choice, May 5, 1988; trade voided after failing physical, May 23, 1988.
Released by Pittsburgh Steelers, June 6, 1988; signed as free agent by San Diego Chargers, August 10, 1988.
On injured reserve with knee injury, August 22 through October 26, 1988; activated after clearing procedural waivers, October 28, 1988.
Denver NFL, 1982 through 1986; Pittsburgh NFL, 1987; San Diego NFL, 1988.
Games: 1982 (9), 1983 (16), 1984 (16), 1985 (16), 1986 (16), 1987 (7), 1988 (8). Total—88.
Pro statistics: Recovered one fumble, 1983; intercepted one pass for 27 yards and a touchdown, 1984; intercepted one pass for 18 yards, 1985; recovered one fumble for 16 yards and a touchdown, 1986.
Played in AFC Championship Game following 1986 season.
Played in NFL Championship Game following 1986 season.

DENNIS EARL WOODBERRY
Cornerback—Denver Broncos
Born April 22, 1961, at Texarkana, Ark.
Height, 5.10. Weight, 180.
High School—Texarkana, Ark.
Attended Southern Arkansas University.
Cousin of Jessie Clark, fullback with Phoenix Cardinals.

Selected by Birmingham in 6th round (111th player selected) of 1984 USFL draft.
Signed by Birmingham Stallions, January 22, 1984.
Selected by Atlanta in 3rd round (63rd player selected) of 1984 NFL supplemental draft.
Granted free agency when USFL suspended operations, August 7, 1986; signed by Atlanta Falcons, August 13, 1986.
Granted roster exemption, August 13 through August 21, 1986; activated, August 22, 1986.
Released by Atlanta Falcons, September 1, 1986; re-signed by Birmingham Stallions for 1987, October 8, 1986.
Released from Birmingham Stallions contract and re-signed by Atlanta Falcons, October 27, 1986.
On developmental squad, June 23 through remainder of 1984 season.
Sold by Atlanta Falcons to Green Bay Packers, August 25, 1987.
Released by Green Bay Packers, September 7, 1987; signed as free agent replacement player by Washington Redskins, September 24, 1987.
On injured reserve with separated shoulder, August 29 through September 29, 1988; re-signed after clearing procedural waivers, October 1, 1988.
Granted unconditional free agency, February 1, 1989; signed by Denver Broncos, March 31, 1989.
On developmental squad for 1 game with Birmingham Stallions in 1984.

	—INTERCEPTIONS—			
Year Club	G.	No.	Yds.	Avg.TD.
1984—Birmingham USFL	17	7	67	9.6 0
1985—Birmingham USFL	18	5	64	12.8 0
1986—Atlanta NFL	7	2	14	7.0 0
1987—Washington NFL	12		None	
1988—Washington NFL	12		None	
USFL Totals—2 Years	35	12	131	10.9 0
NFL Totals—3 Years	31	2	14	7.0 0
Pro Totals—5 Years	66	14	145	10.4 0

Additional pro statistics: Recovered one fumble, 1987.
Played in NFC Championship Game following 1987 season.
Played in NFL Championship Game following 1987 season.

DWAYNE DONZELL WOODRUFF
Cornerback—Pittsburgh Steelers

Born February 18, 1957, at Bowling Green, Ky.
Height, 6.00. Weight, 198.
High School—New Richmond, O.
Received bachelor of science degree in commerce from University of Louisville in 1979;
and received degree from Duquesne Law School in 1988.

Selected by Pittsburgh in 6th round (161st player selected) of 1979 NFL draft.
USFL rights traded with rights to quarterback Jeff Hostetler by Pittsburgh Maulers to Arizona Wranglers for a draft pick, May 2, 1984.
On injured reserve with dislocated elbow, October 15 through November 14, 1985; activated, November 15, 1985.
On injured reserve with knee injury, August 26 through entire 1986 season.

			—INTERCEPTIONS—			
Year Club	G.	No.	Yds.	Avg.	TD.	
1979—Pittsburgh NFL............	16	1	31	31.0	0	
1980—Pittsburgh NFL............	16	1	0	0.0	0	
1981—Pittsburgh NFL............	16	1	17	17.0	0	
1982—Pittsburgh NFL............	9	5	53	10.6	0	
1983—Pittsburgh NFL............	15	3	85	28.3	0	
1984—Pittsburgh NFL............	16	5	56	11.2	1	
1985—Pittsburgh NFL............	12	5	80	16.0	0	
1987—Pittsburgh NFL............	12	5	91	18.2	1	
1988—Pittsburgh NFL............	14	4	109	27.3	1	
Pro Totals—9 Years............	126	30	522	17.4	3	

Additional pro statistics: Recovered one fumble and fumbled once, 1981; recovered one fumble for 65 yards and a touchdown, 1984.
Played in AFC Championship Game following 1979 and 1984 seasons.
Played in NFL Championship Game following 1979 season.

CHRISTOPHER WYATT WOODS
(Chris)
Wide Reciever—Cleveland Browns

Born July 19, 1962, at Birmingham, Ala.
Height, 5.11. Weight, 190.
High School—Birmingham, Ala., A. H. Parker.
Attended Auburn University.

Selected by Birmingham in 1984 USFL territorial draft.
Signed as free agent by Edmonton Eskimos, March 5, 1984.
Selected by Los Angeles Raiders in 1st round (28th player selected) of 1984 NFL supplemental draft.
Traded by Edmonton Eskimos to Toronto Argonauts, June 10, 1986.
Granted free agency, March 1, 1987; signed by Los Angeles Raiders, April 17, 1987.
On injured reserve with knee injury, September 7 through October 30, 1987; activated, October 31, 1987.
On injured reserve with knee injury, September 14 through remainder of 1988 season.
Granted unconditional free agency, February 1, 1989; signed by Cleveland Browns, March 28, 1989.

		PASS RECEIVING				–PUNT RETURNS–				—KICKOFF RET.—				—TOTAL—		
Year Club	G.	P.C.	Yds.	Avg.	TD.	No.	Yds.	Avg.	TD.	No.	Yds.	Avg.	TD.	TD.	Pts.	F.
1984—Edmonton CFL	15	38	837	22.0	6	31	303	9.8	1	18	442	24.6	0	7	42	3
1985—Edmonton CFL	13	41	779	19.0	6	36	366	10.1	0	10	239	23.9	0	6	36	1
1986—Toronto CFL.................	17	61	1163	19.1	6	64	595	9.3	0	8	152	19.0	0	6	36	1
1987—L.A. Raiders NFL........	9	1	14	14.0	0	26	189	7.3	0	3	55	18.3	0	0	0	2
1988—L.A. Raiders NFL........	2		None				None			1	20	20.0	0	0	0	0
CFL Totals—3 Years	45	140	2779	19.9	18	131	1264	9.6	1	36	833	23.1	0	19	114	5
NFL Totals—2 Years.....	11	1	14	14.0	0	26	189	7.3	0	4	75	18.8	0	0	0	2
Pro Totals—5 Years.......	56	141	2793	19.8	18	157	1453	9.3	1	40	908	22.7	0	19	114	7

Additional CFL statistics: Rushed three times for 60 yards and recovered one fumble, 1984; rushed three times for nine yards, 1985; rushed two times for 10 yards, 1986.
Additional NFL statistics: Recovered one fumble, 1987.

ELBERT WOODS
(Ickey)
Running Back—Cincinnati Bengals

Born February 28, 1966, at Fresno, Calif.
Height, 6.02. Weight, 232.
High School—Edison, Calif.
Attended University of Nevada at Las Vegas.

Selected by Cincinnati in 2nd round (31st player selected) of 1988 NFL draft.
Signed by Cincinnati Bengals, June 13, 1988.

		——RUSHING——				PASS RECEIVING				—TOTAL—		
Year Club	G.	Att.	Yds.	Avg.	TD.	P.C.	Yds.	Avg.	TD.	TD.	Pts.	F.
1988—Cincinnati NFL	16	203	1066	*5.3	15	21	199	9.5	0	15	90	8

Additional pro statistics: Recovered one fumble, 1988.
Played in AFC Championship Game following 1988 season.
Played in NFL Championship Game following 1988 season.

STANLEY ANTHONY WOODS
(Tony)
Linebacker—Seattle Seahawks
Born September 11, 1965, at Newark, N. J.
Height, 6.04. Weight, 244.
High School—South Orange, N. J., Seton Hall Prep.
Attended University of Pittsburgh.

Named as defensive lineman on THE SPORTING NEWS College All-America Team, 1986.
Selected by Seattle in 1st round (18th player selected) of 1987 NFL draft.
Signed by Seattle Seahawks, July 20, 1987.
Seattle NFL, 1987 and 1988.
Games: 1987 (12), 1988 (16). Total—28.
Pro statistics: Recovered one fumble, 1987 and 1988.

KEITH A. WOODSIDE
Running Back—Green Bay Packers
Born July 29, 1964, at Natchez, Miss.
Height, 5.11. Weight, 203.
High School—Vidalia, La.
Attended Texas A&M University.

Selected by Green Bay in 3rd round (61st player selected) of 1988 NFL draft.
Signed by Green Bay Packers, July 18, 1988.

		—RUSHING—				PASS RECEIVING			—TOTAL—		
Year Club	G.	Att.	Yds.	Avg.	TD.	P.C.	Yds.	Avg.	TD.	TD.	Pts.	F.
1988—Green Bay NFL	16	83	195	2.3	3	39	352	9.0	2	5	30	3

		KICKOFF RETURNS		
Year Club	G.	No.	Yds.	Avg.TD.
1988—Green Bay NFL	16	19	343	18.1 0

Additional pro statistics: Recovered one fumble, 1988.

RODERICK KEVIN WOODSON
(Rod)
Cornerback-Kick Returner—Pittsburgh Steelers
Born March 10, 1965, at Fort Wayne, Ind.
Height, 6.00. Weight, 202.
High School—Fort Wayne, Ind., R. Nelson Snider.
Attended Purdue University.

Named as kick returner on THE SPORTING NEWS College All-America Team, 1986.
Selected by Pittsburgh in 1st round (10th player selected) of 1987 NFL draft.
Placed on reserve/unsigned list, August 31 through October 27, 1987.
Signed by Pittsburgh Steelers, October 28, 1987.
Granted roster exemption, October 28 through November 6, 1987; activated, November 7, 1987.

		INTERCEPTIONS				-PUNT RETURNS-				—KICKOFF RET.—				—TOTAL—		
Year Club	G.	No.	Yds.	Avg.	TD.	No.	Yds.	Avg.	TD.	No.	Yds.	Avg.	TD.	TD.	Pts.	F.
1987—Pittsburgh NFL	8	1	45	45.0	1	16	135	8.4	0	13	290	22.3	0	1	6	3
1988—Pittsburgh NFL	16	4	98	24.5	0	33	281	8.5	0	37	850	23.0	*1	1	6	3
Pro Totals—2 Years	24	5	143	28.6	1	49	416	8.5	0	50	1140	22.8	1	2	12	6

Additional pro statistics: Recovered two fumbles, 1987; recovered three fumbles for two yards, 1988.

RONALD J. WOOTEN
(Ron)
Guard—New England Patriots
Born June 28, 1959, at Bourne, Mass.
Height, 6.04. Weight, 273.
High School—Kinston, N.C.
Received bachelor of science degree in chemistry
from University of North Carolina in 1982.

Selected by New England in 6th round (157th player selected) of 1981 NFL draft.
On injured reserve with back injury, August 31 through entire 1981 season.
Crossed picket line during players' strike, October 2, 1987.
New England NFL, 1982 through 1988.
Games: 1982 (9), 1983 (16), 1984 (16), 1985 (14), 1986 (16), 1987 (13), 1988 (14). Total—98.
Pro statistics: Recovered one fumble, 1986.
Played in AFC Championship Game following 1985 season.
Played in NFL Championship Game following 1985 season.

ALVIN WRIGHT
Nose Tackle—Los Angeles Rams
Born February 5, 1961, at Wedowee, Ala.
Height, 6.02. Weight, 256.
High School—Wedowee, Ala., Randolph County.
Attended Jacksonville State University.

Selected by Birmingham in 14th round (199th player selected) of 1985 USFL draft.

Signed as free agent by Los Angeles Rams, June 22, 1985.
On injured reserve with neck injury, August 27 through September 3, 1985.
Released by Los Angeles Rams, September 4, 1985; re-signed by Rams, March 9, 1986.
On injured reserve with knee injury, September 2 through October 30, 1986; activated, October 31, 1986.
Crossed picket line during players' strike, September 30, 1987.
Los Angeles Rams NFL, 1986 through 1988.
Games: 1986 (4), 1987 (15), 1988 (16). Total—35.

ERIC WRIGHT
Cornerback—San Francisco 49ers

Born April 18, 1959, at St. Louis, Mo.
Height, 6.01. Weight, 185.
High School—East St. Louis, Ill., Assumption.
Attended University of Missouri.

Named to THE SPORTING NEWS NFL All-Star Team, 1985.
Selected by San Francisco in 2nd round (40th player selected) of 1981 NFL draft.
On inactive list, September 19, 1982.
On injured reserve with pulled abdomen, December 24 through remainder of 1985 season playoffs.
On injured reserve with groin injury, September 3 through October 2, 1986; activated, October 3, 1986.
On injured reserve with groin injury, October 29 through remainder of 1986 season.
Crossed picket line during players' strike, October 7, 1987.
On injured reserve with groin injury, October 8 through remainder of 1987 season.

Year Club	G.	No.	Yds.	Avg.	TD.
1981—San Francisco NFL	16	3	26	8.7	0
1982—San Francisco NFL	7	1	31	31.0	0
1983—San Francisco NFL	16	7	*164	23.4	*2
1984—San Francisco NFL	15	2	0	0.0	0
1985—San Francisco NFL	16	1	0	0.0	0
1986—San Francisco NFL	2		None		
1987—San Francisco NFL	2		None		
1988—San Francisco NFL	15	2	—2	—1.0	0
Pro Totals—8 Years............	89	16	219	13.7	2

Additional pro statistics: Recovered two fumbles, 1981; recovered one fumble, 1983 and 1988.
Played in NFC Championship Game following 1981, 1983 and 1984 seasons.
Member of San Francisco 49ers for NFC Championship Game following 1988 season; did not play.
Played in NFL Championship Game following 1981, 1984 and 1988 seasons.
Played in Pro Bowl (NFL All-Star Game) following 1984 season.
Named to play in Pro Bowl following 1985 season; replaced due to injury by Gary Green.

FELIX CARL WRIGHT
Safety—Cleveland Browns

Born June 22, 1959, at Carthage, Mo.
Height, 6.02. Weight, 190.
High School—Carthage, Mo.
Received bachelor of science degree in physical education and history
from Drake University in 1981.
Brother of Charles Wright, defensive back with St. Louis Cardinals,
Dallas Cowboys and Tampa Bay Buccaneers, 1987 and 1988.

Signed as free agent by Houston Oilers, May 17, 1982.
Released by Houston Oilers, August 23, 1982; signed as free agent by Hamilton Tiger-Cats, October 24, 1982.
Granted free agency, March 1, 1985; signed by Cleveland Browns, May 6, 1985.

Year Club	G.	No.	Yds.	Avg.	TD.
1982—Hamilton CFL	2	2	32	16.0	0
1983—Hamilton CFL	12	6	140	23.3	1
1984—Hamilton CFL	16	7	100	14.3	1
1985—Cleveland NFL.............	16	2	11	5.5	0
1986—Cleveland NFL.............	16	3	33	11.0	0
1987—Cleveland NFL.............	12	4	152	38.0	1
1988—Cleveland NFL.............	16	5	126	25.2	0
CFL Totals—3 Years	30	15	272	18.1	2
NFL Totals—4 Years..........	60	14	322	23.0	1
Pro Totals—7 Years............	90	29	594	20.5	3

Additional CFL statistics: Returned one punt for three yards, 1982; returned seven punts for 36 yards, recovered three fumbles for 10 yards and fumbled twice, 1983; recovered two fumbles, 1984.
Additional NFL statistics: Recovered two fumbles, 1985; returned blocked punt 30 yards for a touchdown, 1986; recovered one fumble, 1986 through 1988; fumbled once, 1988.
Played in AFC Championship Game following 1986 and 1987 seasons.

JEFF DEE WRIGHT
Nose Tackle—Buffalo Bills

Born June 13, 1963, at San Bernardino, Calif.
Height, 6.02. Weight, 270.
High School—Lawrence, Kan.
Attended The University of Tulsa, Coffeyville Community College
and Central Missouri State University.

Selected by Buffalo in 8th round (213th player selected) of 1988 NFL draft.
Signed by Buffalo Bills, May 27, 1988.
Buffalo NFL, 1988.
Games: 1988 (15).
Pro statistics: Recovered one fumble, 1988.
Played in AFC Championship Game following 1988 season.

RANDALL STEVEN WRIGHT
(Randy)
Quarterback—Green Bay Packers
Born January 12, 1961, at St. Charles, Ill.
Height, 6.02. Weight, 203.
High School—St. Charles, Ill.
Received degree in communications from University of Wisconsin.

Selected by Memphis in 9th round (188th player selected) of 1984 USFL draft.
USFL rights released by Memphis Showboats, February 7, 1984.
Selected by Green Bay in 6th round (153rd player selected) of 1984 NFL draft.
Signed by Green Bay Packers, June 30, 1984.
On injured reserve with knee injury, December 12 through remainder of 1984 season.
On injured reserve with pulled groin, December 17 through remainder of 1988 season.

		PASSING							RUSHING				—TOTAL—		
Year Club	G.	Att.	Cmp.	Pct.	Gain	T.P.	P.I.	Avg.	Att.	Yds.	Avg.	TD.	TD.	Pts.	F.
1984—Green Bay NFL	8	62	27	43.5	310	2	6	5.00	8	11	1.4	0	0	0	1
1985—Green Bay NFL	5	74	39	52.7	552	2	4	7.46	8	8	1.0	0	0	0	5
1986—Green Bay NFL	16	492	263	53.5	3247	17	23	6.60	18	41	2.3	1	1	6	8
1987—Green Bay NFL	9	247	132	53.4	1507	6	11	6.10	13	70	5.4	0	0	0	3
1988—Green Bay NFL	8	244	141	57.8	1490	4	13	6.11	8	43	5.4	2	2	12	6
Pro Totals—5 Years	46	1119	602	53.8	7106	31	57	6.35	55	163	3.0	3	3	18	23

Quarterback Rating Points: 1984 (30.4), 1985 (63.6), 1986 (66.2), 1987 (61.6), 1988 (58.9). Total—61.5.
Additional pro statistics: Recovered one fumble, 1984; recovered two fumbles and fumbled five times for minus six yards, 1985; recovered three fumbles and fumbled eight times for minus four yards, 1986; recovered one fumble and fumbled three times for minus four yards, 1987; recovered three fumbles and fumbled six times for minus five yards, 1988.

STEPHEN HOUGH WRIGHT
(Steve)
Offensive Tackle—Los Angeles Raiders
Born April 8, 1959, at St. Louis, Mo.
Height, 6.06. Weight, 275.
High School—Wayzata, Minn.
Attended University of Northern Iowa.

Signed as free agent by Dallas Cowboys, May, 1981.
Traded by Dallas Cowboys to Baltimore Colts for 7th round pick in 1985 draft, August 27, 1983.
Franchise transferred to Indianapolis, March 31, 1984.
Signed by Oakland Invaders, December 1, 1984, for contract to take effect after being granted free agency, February 1, 1984.
Released by Oakland Invaders, May 28, 1986; re-signed by Indianapolis Colts, July 16, 1986.
Released by Indianapolis Colts, August 18, 1986; signed as free agent by Los Angeles Raiders, May 2, 1987.
Released by Los Angeles Raiders, September 7, 1987; re-signed as replacement player by Raiders, September 29, 1987.
On injured reserve with knee injury, December 26 through remainder of 1987 season.
Released by Los Angeles Raiders, September 2, 1988; re-signed by Raiders, September 7, 1988.
Dallas NFL, 1981 and 1982; Baltimore NFL, 1983; Indianapolis NFL, 1984; Oakland USFL, 1985; Los Angeles Raiders NFL, 1987 and 1988.
Games: 1981 (16), 1982 (9), 1983 (13), 1984 (12), 1985 (18), 1987 (9), 1988 (15). Total NFL—74. Total Pro—92.
USFL statistics: Caught one pass for two yards and a touchdown, 1985.
Played in NFC Championship Game following 1981 and 1982 seasons.
Played in USFL Championship Game following 1985 season.

DAVID MATTHEW WYMAN
Linebacker—Seattle Seahawks
Born March 31, 1964, at San Diego, Calif.
Height, 6.02. Weight, 231.
High School—Reno, Nev., Earl Wooster.
Attended Stanford University.

Named as linebacker on THE SPORTING NEWS College All-America Team, 1986.
Selected by Seattle in 2nd round (45th player selected) of 1987 NFL draft.
Signed by Seattle Seahawks, July 21, 1987.
Traded with draft choice by Seattle Seahawks to San Francisco 49ers for draft choice, November 3, 1987; trade voided after failing physical, November 4, 1987.
On injured reserve with ankle injury, December 30 through remainder of 1987 season.
Seattle NFL, 1987 and 1988.
Games: 1987 (4), 1988 (16). Total—20.
Pro statistics: Recovered two fumbles, 1988.

GEORGE ANTHONY YARNO
Center-Guard—Houston Oilers
Born August 12, 1957, at Spokane, Wash.
Height, 6.02. Weight, 270.
High Schools—Anchorage, Ala., East; and Spokane, Wash., Joel E. Ferris.
Received bachelor of arts degree in criminal justice from Washington State University in 1979.
Brother of John Yarno, center with Seattle Seahawks and Denver Gold, 1977 through 1982 and 1984.

Signed as free agent by Tampa Bay Buccanneers, May 10, 1979.
USFL rights traded by Houston Gamblers to Denver Gold for rights to defensive back John Holt and defensive end Clenzie Pierson, September 23, 1983.
Signed by Denver Gold, October 17, 1983, to contract to take effect after being granted free agency, February 1, 1984.
Released by Denver Gold, July 31, 1985; re-signed by Tampa Bay Buccaneers, August 13, 1985.
On injured reserve with knee injury, October 28 through November 28, 1985; activated, November 29, 1985.
Granted free agency, February 1, 1988; withdrew quailfying offer, May 27, 1988.
Signed by Atlanta Falcons, June 7, 1988.
Granted unconditional free agency, February 1, 1989; signed by Houston Oilers, March 29, 1989.
Tampa Bay NFL, 1979 through 1983 and 1985 through 1987; Denver USFL, 1984 and 1985; Atlanta NFL, 1988.
Games: 1979 (15), 1980 (16), 1981 (16), 1982 (9), 1983 (14), 1984 (18), 1985 USFL (18), 1985 NFL (12), 1986 (16), 1987 (11), 1988 (16). Total NFL—125. Total USFL—36. Total Pro—161.
NFL statistics: Returned one kickoff for 14 yards, 1982; kicked one extra point, 1983.
USFL statistics: Recovered two fumbles, 1984; recovered one fumble, 1985.
Played in NFC Championship Game following 1979 season.

FREDD YOUNG
Linebacker—Indianapolis Colts
Born November 14, 1961, at Dallas, Tex.
Height, 6.01. Weight, 233.
High School—Dallas, Tex., Woodrow Wilson.
Attended New Mexico State University.

Named to THE SPORTING NEWS NFL All-Star Team, 1987.
Selected by Arizona in 1984 USFL territorial draft.
Selected by Seattle in 3rd round (76th player selected) of 1984 NFL draft.
Signed by Seattle Seahawks, May 17, 1984.
Crossed picket line during players' strike, October 14, 1987.
Left Seattle Seahawks camp voluntarily, July 27, 1988; returned, August 27, 1988.
Granted roster exemption, August 27 through September 8, 1988..
Traded by Seattle Seahawks to Indianapolis Colts for 1st round picks in 1989 and 1990 drafts, September 9, 1988.
Seattle NFL, 1984 through 1987; Indianapolis NFL, 1988.
Games: 1984 (16), 1985 (16), 1986 (15), 1987 (13), 1988 (15). Total—75.
Pro statistics: Recovered one fumble for 13 yards, 1985; intercepted one pass for 50 yards and a touchdown and recovered four fumbles, 1987.
Played in Pro Bowl (NFL All-Star Game) following 1984 through 1987 seasons.

LONNIE YOUNG
Safety—Phoenix Cardinals
Born July 18, 1963, at Flint, Mich.
Height, 6.01. Weight, 182.
High School—Flint, Mich., Beecher.
Received degree in communications from Michigan State University in 1985.

Selected by New Jersey in 8th round (112th player selected) of 1985 USFL draft.
Selected by St. Louis in 12th round (325th player selected) of 1985 NFL draft.
Signed by St. Louis Cardinals, July 15, 1985.
Franchise transferred to Phoenix, March 15, 1988.
On injured reserve with torn ligaments in elbow, November 22 through remainder of 1988 season.

Year Club	G.	No.	Yds.	Avg.	TD.
1985—St. Louis NFL	16	3	0	0.0	0
1986—St. Louis NFL	13		None		
1987—St. Louis NFL	12	1	0	0.0	0
1988—Phoenix NFL	12	1	2	2.0	0
Pro Totals—4 Years	53	5	2	0.4	0

Additional pro statistics: Recovered one fumble, 1985; recovered three fumbles, 1987; recovered two fumbles, 1988.

MICHAEL DAVID YOUNG
(Mike)
Wide Receiver—Denver Broncos
Born February 21, 1962, at Hanford, Calif.
Height, 6.01. Weight, 185.
High School—Visalia, Calif., Mount Whitney.
Attended University of California at Los Angeles.

Selected by Memphis in 1985 USFL territorial draft.
Selected by Los Angeles Rams in 6th round (161st player selected) of 1985 NFL draft.
Signed by Los Angeles Rams, July 23, 1985.
Crossed picket line during players' strike, October 14, 1987.

On injured reserve with back injury, November 4 through remainder of 1988 season.
Granted unconditional free agency, February 1, 1989; signed by Denver Broncos, March 20, 1989.

Year	Club	G.	P.C.	Yds.	Avg.	TD.
				—PASS RECEIVING—		
1985—L.A. Rams NFL		15	14	157	11.2	0
1986—L.A. Rams NFL		16	15	181	12.1	3
1987—L.A. Rams NFL		12	4	56	14.0	1
1988—L.A. Rams NFL		8	2	27	13.5	0
Pro Totals—4 Years		51	35	421	12.0	4

Additional pro statistics: Fumbled once, 1985; fumbled twice, 1986.
Played in NFC Championship Game following 1985 season.

ROYNELL YOUNG
Cornerback
Born December 1, 1957, at New Orleans, La.
Height, 6.01. Weight, 185.
High School—New Orleans, La., Cohen.
Attended Alcorn State University.

Selected by Philadelphia in 1st round (23rd player selected) of 1980 NFL draft.
On injured reserve with strained abdominal muscles, October 12 through November 15, 1984; activated, November 16, 1984.
Granted free agency, February 1, 1987; re-signed by Eagles, September 16, 1987.
Granted roster exemption, September 16 and September 17, 1987; activated, September 18, 1987.
Granted unconditional free agency, February 1, 1989; released by Philadelphia Eagles, June 1, 1989.

Year	Club	G.	No.	Yds.	Avg.	TD.
				—INTERCEPTIONS—		
1980—Philadelphia NFL		16	4	27	6.8	0
1981—Philadelphia NFL		13	4	35	8.8	0
1982—Philadelphia NFL		9	4	0	0.0	0
1983—Philadelphia NFL		16	1	0	0.0	0
1984—Philadelphia NFL		7		None		
1985—Philadelphia NFL		14	1	0	0.0	0
1986—Philadelphia NFL		16	6	9	1.5	0
1987—Philadelphia NFL		11	1	30	30.0	0
1988—Philadelphia NFL		15	2	5	2.5	0
Pro Totals—9 Years		117	23	106	4.6	0

Additional pro statistics: Returned one kickoff for 18 yards and recovered two fumbles, 1983; recovered two fumbles for 20 yards, 1987.
Played in NFC Championship Game following 1980 season.
Played in NFL Championship Game following 1980 season.
Played in Pro Bowl (NFL All-Star Game) following 1981 season.

STEVE YOUNG
Quarterback—San Francisco 49ers
Born October 11, 1961, at Salt Lake City, Utah.
Height, 6.02. Weight, 200.
High School—Greenwich, Conn.
Attended Brigham Young University.

Named as quarterback on THE SPORTING NEWS College All-America Team, 1983.
Selected by Los Angeles in 1st round (10th player selected) of 1984 USFL draft.
Signed by Los Angeles Express, March 5, 1984.
Granted roster exemption, March 5, 1984; activated, March 30, 1984.
Selected by Tampa Bay in 1st round (1st player selected) of 1984 NFL supplemental draft.
On developmental squad, March 31 through April 15, 1985; activated, April 16, 1985.
Released by Los Angeles Express, September 9, 1985; signed by Tampa Bay Buccaneers, September 10, 1985.
Granted roster exemption, September 10 through September 22, 1985; activated, September 23, 1985.
Traded by Tampa Bay Buccaneers to San Francisco 49ers for 2nd and 4th round pick in 1987 draft and cash, April 24, 1987.
On developmental squad for 3 games with Los Angeles Express in 1985.

Year	Club	G.	Att.	Cmp.	Pct.	Gain	T.P.	P.I.	Avg.	Att.	Yds.	Avg.	TD.	TD.	Pts.	F.
					—PASSING—						—RUSHING—			—TOTAL—		
1984—Los Angeles USFL		12	310	179	57.7	2361	10	9	7.62	79	515	6.5	7	7	†48	7
1985—Los Angeles USFL		13	250	137	54.8	1741	6	13	6.96	56	368	6.6	2	2	12	7
1985—Tampa Bay NFL		5	138	72	52.2	935	3	8	6.78	40	233	5.8	1	1	6	4
1986—Tampa Bay NFL		14	363	195	53.7	2282	8	13	6.29	74	425	5.7	5	5	30	11
1987—San Francisco NFL		8	69	37	53.6	570	10	0	8.26	26	190	7.3	1	1	6	0
1988—San Francisco NFL		11	101	54	53.5	680	3	3	6.73	27	184	6.8	1	1	6	5
USFL Totals—2 Years		25	560	316	56.4	4102	16	22	7.33	135	883	6.5	9	9	60	14
NFL Totals—4 Years		38	671	358	53.4	4467	24	24	6.66	167	1032	6.2	8	8	48	20
Pro Totals—6 Years		63	1231	674	54.8	8569	40	46	6.96	302	1915	6.3	17	17	108	34

†Includes three 2-point conversions.
USFL Quarterback Rating Points: 1984 (80.6), 1985 (63.1). Total—73.1.
NFL Quarterback Rating Points: 1985 (56.9), 1986 (65.5), 1987 (120.8), 1988 (72.2). Total—71.3.
Additional USFL statistics: Recovered four fumbles, 1984; recovered one fumble and fumbled seven times for minus 11 yards, 1985.
Additional NFL statistics: Recovered one fumble and fumbled four times for minus one yard, 1985; recovered four

fumbles and fumbled 11 times for minus 24 yards, 1986; recovered two fumbles and fumbled five times for minus 10 yards, 1988.

Played in NFC Championship Game following 1988 season.

Member of San Francisco 49ers for NFL Championship Game following 1988 season; did not play.

THEO THOMAS YOUNG
Tight End—Buffalo Bills

Born April 25, 1965, at Newport, Ark.

Height, 6.02. Weight, 237.

High School—Newport, Ark., Remmel Park.

Attended University of Arkansas.

Selected by Pittsburgh in 12th round (317th player selected) of 1987 NFL draft.

Signed by Pittsburgh Steelers, July 26, 1987.

On injured reserve with knee injury, August 23 through October 3, 1988.

Released by Pittsburgh Steelers, October 4, 1988; signed as free agent by Buffalo Bills, January 10, 1989.

Pittsburgh NFL, 1987.

Games: 1987 (12).

Pro statistics: Caught two passes for 10 yards, 1987.

CARL AUGUST ZANDER JR.
Linebacker—Cincinnati Bengals

Born March 23, 1963, at Mendham, N.J.

Height, 6.02. Weight, 235.

High School—Mendham, N.J., West Morris.

Attended University of Tennessee.

Selected by Memphis in 1985 USFL territorial draft.

Selected by Cincinnati in 2nd round (43rd player selected) of 1985 NFL draft.

Signed by Cincinnati Bengals, July 21, 1985.

Cincinnati NFL, 1985 through 1988.

Games: 1985 (16), 1986 (16), 1987 (12), 1988 (16). Total—60.

Pro statistics: Returned one kickoff for 19 yards and recovered one fumble for 34 yards, 1985; intercepted one pass for 18 yards, 1986; recovered one fumble, 1986 and 1988; intercepted one pass for three yards, 1988.

Played in AFC Championship Game following 1988 season.

Played in NFL Championship Game following 1988 season.

LUIS FERNANDO ZENDEJAS
Placekicker—Philadelphia Eagles

Born October 22, 1961, at Mexico City, Mex.

Height, 5.09. Weight, 170.

High School—Chico, Calif., Don Antonio Lugo.

Attended Arizona State University.

Brother of Joaquin Zendejas, placekicker with New England Patriots, 1983; brother of Max Zendejas, placekicker with Washington Redskins and Green Bay Packers, 1986 through 1988; brother of Alan Zendejas, placekicker at Arizona State University; and cousin of Tony Zendejas, placekicker with Houston Oilers.

Selected by Arizona in 1985 USFL territorial draft.

Signed by Arizona Outlaws, January 24, 1985.

Released by Arizona Outlaws, June 24, 1985; signed as free agent by Atlanta Falcons, July 20, 1985.

Released by Atlanta Falcons, July 29, 1985; signed as free agent by Minnesota Vikings, March 6, 1986.

Released by Minnesota Vikings, August 21, 1986; signed as free agent by Dallas Cowboys, April 30, 1987.

Released by Dallas Cowboys, September 1, 1987; re-signed as free agent replacement player by Cowboys, September 23, 1987.

On injured reserve with ankle injury, October 27 through November 15, 1987.

Released by Dallas Cowboys, November 16, 1987; re-signed by Cowboys, July 22, 1988.

Released by Dallas Cowboys, September 14, 1988; signed as free agent by Philadelphia Eagles, September 27, 1988.

Year Club	G.	XP.	XPM.	FG.	FGA.	Pts.
1985—Arizona USFL...........	18	36	*5	24	33	108
1987—Dallas NFL	2	10	0	3	4	19
1988—Dal(2)-Phi(12) NFL.	14	35	1	20	27	95
USFL Totals—1 Year.....	18	36	5	24	33	108
NFL Totals—2 Years.....	16	45	1	23	31	114
Pro Totals—3 Years.......	34	81	6	47	64	222

—PLACE KICKING—

TONY ZENDEJAS
Placekicker—Houston Oilers

Born May 15, 1960, at Curimeo Michucan, Mexico.

Height, 5.08. Weight, 165.

High School—Chino, Calif.

Attended University of Nevada at Reno.

Cousin of Joaquin Zendejas, placekicker with New England Patriots, 1983; cousin of Max Zendejas, placekicker with Washington Redskins and Green Bay Packers, 1986 through 1988; cousin of Luis Zendejas, placekicker with Philadelphia Eagles; and cousin of Alan Zendejas, placekicker at Arizona State University.

Tied NFL record for most field goals, 50 or more yards, game (2), against San Diego Chargers, November 24, 1985.

Named as kicker on THE SPORTING NEWS USFL All-Star Team, 1984 and 1985.
Selected by Los Angeles in 5th round (90th player selected) of 1984 USFL draft.
Signed by Los Angeles Express, February 21, 1984.
Selected by Washington in 1st round (27th player selected) of 1984 NFL supplemental draft.
Granted free agency, July 1, 1985; signed by Washington Redskins, July 3, 1985.
Traded by Washington Redskins to Houston Oilers for 5th round pick in 1987 draft, August 27, 1985.
Crossed picket line during players' strike, October 14, 1987.

					—PLACE KICKING—		
Year	Club	G.	XP.	XPM.	FG.	FGA.	Pts.
1984—Los Angeles USFL...		18	33	0	21	30	96
1985—Los Angeles USFL...		18	22	1	*26	*34	100
1985—Houston NFL............		14	29	2	21	27	92
1986—Houston NFL............		15	28	1	22	27	94
1987—Houston NFL............		13	32	1	20	26	92
1988—Houston NFL............		16	48	2	22	34	114
USFL Totals—2 Years...		36	55	1	47	64	196
NFL Totals—4 Years.....		58	137	6	85	114	392
Pro Totals—6 Years.......		94	192	7	132	178	588

Additional NFL statistics: Attempted one pass with one completion for minus seven yards and recovered one fumble, 1985; punted once for 36 yards, 1986.

GARY WAYNE ZIMMERMAN
Offensive Tackle—Minnesota Vikings
Born December 13, 1961, at Fullerton, Calif.
Height, 6.06. Weight, 284.
High School—Walnut, Calif.
Attended University of Oregon.

Named to THE SPORTING NEWS NFL All-Star Team, 1987.
Named as offensive tackle on THE SPORTING NEWS USFL All-Star Team, 1984 and 1985.
Selected by Los Angeles in 2nd round (36th player selected) of 1984 USFL draft.
Signed by Los Angeles Express, February 13, 1984.
Granted roster exemption, February 13 through February 23, 1984; activated, February 24, 1984.
Selected by New York Giants in 1st round (3rd player selected) of 1984 NFL supplemental draft.
NFL rights traded by New York Giants to Minnesota Vikings for two 2nd round picks in 1986 draft, April 29, 1986.
Released by Los Angeles Express, May 19, 1986; signed by Minnesota Vikings, May 21, 1986.
Granted free agency, February 1, 1988; re-signed by Vikings, August 29, 1988.
Los Angeles USFL, 1984 and 1985; Minnesota NFL, 1986 through 1988.
Games: 1984 (17), 1985 (17), 1986 (16), 1987 (12), 1988 (16). Total USFL—34. Total NFL—44. Total Pro—78.
USFL statistics: Returned one kickoff for no yards, recovered two fumbles and fumbled once, 1984.
NFL statistics: Recovered two fumbles, 1986; recovered one fumble for four yards, 1987.
Played in NFC Championship Game following 1987 season.
Played in Pro Bowl (NFL All-Star Game) following 1987 and 1988 seasons.

JEFFREY ALAN ZIMMERMAN
(Jeff)
Guard—Dallas Cowboys
Born January 10, 1965, at Enid, Okla.
Height 6.03. Weight, 316.
High School—Orlando, Fla., Evans.
Attended University of Florida.

Named as guard on THE SPORTING NEWS College All-America Team, 1985.
Selected by Dallas in 3rd round (68th player selected) of 1987 NFL draft.
Signed by Dallas Cowboys, July 17, 1987.
On injured reserve with shoulder injury, September 23 through remainder of 1988 season.
Dallas NFL, 1987 and 1988.
Games: 1987 (11), 1988 (1). Total—12.

MICHAEL EDWARD ZORDICH
(Mike)
Safety—Phoenix Cardinals
Born October 12, 1963, at Youngstown, O.
Height, 5.11. Weight, 207.
High School—Youngstown, O., Chaney.
Received bachelor of science degree in hotel, restaurant and institutional management
from Penn State University in 1986.

Selected by Baltimore in 1986 USFL territorial draft.
Selected by San Diego in 9th round (235th player selected) of 1986 NFL draft.
Signed by San Diego Chargers, June 24, 1986.
Released by San Diego Chargers, August 22, 1986; signed as free agent by New York Jets, April 9, 1987.
Released by New York Jets, September 6, 1987; re-signed by Jets, September 14, 1987.
Granted unconditional free agency, February 1, 1989; signed by Phoenix Cardinals, March 2, 1989.
New York Jets NFL, 1987 and 1988.
Games: 1987 (10), 1988 (16). Total—26.
Pro statistics: Intercepted one pass for 35 yards and a touchdown, 1988.

ADDITIONAL PLAYER TRANSACTIONS

The following player transactions involve players in the Register occurring after May 30, 1989.

ADAMS, CURTIS—Signed as free agent by Los Angeles Raiders, May 31, 1989.

BOARD, DWAINE—Granted unconditional free agency, February 1, 1989; rights relinquished, June 15, 1989.

CLARK, BRUCE—Released by New Orleans Saints, June 15, 1989.

DeOSSIE, STEVE—Traded by Dallas Cowboys to New York Giants for draft pick, June 2, 1989.

GREGORY, TED—Released by New Orleans Saints, June 15, 1989.

JARVIS, RALPH—Released by New York Jets, May 31, 1989; awarded on waivers to Buffalo Bills, June 12, 1989.

TITENSOR, GLEN—Released by Dallas Cowboys, June 1, 1989.

TURK, DAN—Granted free agency, February 1, 1989; rights relinquished, June 6, 1989; signed by Los Angeles Raiders, June 21, 1989.

ADDITIONAL ACTIVE PLAYERS

STEVEN CHRISTOPHER BONO
(Steve)
Quarterback—San Francisco 49ers

Born May 11, 1962, at Norristown, Pa.
Height, 6.04. Weight, 215.
High School—Norristown, Pa.
Attended University of California at Los Angeles.

Selected by Memphis in 1985 USFL territorial draft.
Selected by Minnesota in 6th round (142nd player selected) of 1985 NFL draft.
Signed by Minnesota Vikings, July 10, 1985.
Released by Minnesota Vikings, October 4, 1986; re-signed by Vikings, November 19, 1986.
Released by Minnesota Vikings, December 9, 1986; signed as free agent by Pittsburgh Steelers, March 25, 1987.
Released by Pittsburgh Steelers, September 7, 1987; re-signed as replacement player by Steelers, September 24, 1987.
Granted unconditional free agency, February 1, 1989; did not receive qualifying offer, April 15, 1989.
Signed by San Francisco 49ers, June 13, 1989.

Year Club	G.	Att.	Cmp.	Pct.	Gain	T.P.	P.I.	Avg.	Att.	Yds.	Avg.	TD.	TD.	Pts.	F.
					PASSING					RUSHING				TOTAL	
1985—Minnesota NFL	1	10	1	10.0	5	0	0	0.50		None			0	0	0
1986—Minnesota NFL	1	1	1	100.0	3	0	0	3.00		None			0	0	0
1987—Pittsburgh NFL	3	74	34	45.9	438	5	2	5.92	8	27	3.4	1	1	6	5
1988—Pittsburgh NFL	2	35	10	28.6	110	1	2	3.14		None			0	0	0
Pro Totals—4 Years	7	120	46	38.3	556	6	4	4.63	8	27	3.4	1	1	6	5

Quarterback Rating Points: 1985 (39.6), 1986 (79.2), 1987 (76.3), 1988 (25.9). Total—56.2.
Additional pro statistics: Caught one pass for two yards and recovered three fumbles, 1987.

JOSE RAFAEL SEPTIEN (MICHEL)
(Known by middle name.)
Name pronounced Rah-fay-EL Sep-tee-EN.
Placekicker—Denver Broncos

Born December 12, 1953, at Mexico City, Mex.
Height, 5.10. Weight, 180.
High School—Mexico City, Mex., Colegio Vista Hernosa.
Received degree from University of Southwestern Louisiana.
Son of Carlos Septien, member of two Mexican World Cup Soccer teams.

Named to THE SPORTING NEWS NFL All-Star Team, 1981.
Selected by New Orleans in 10th round (258th player selected) of 1977 NFL draft.
Released by New Orleans Saints, August 31, 1977; signed as free agent by Los Angeles Rams, September 14, 1977.
Released by Los Angeles Rams, August 26, 1978; signed as free agent by Dallas Cowboys, August 30, 1978.
Released by Dallas Cowboys, April 15, 1987; signed as free agent by Denver Broncos, June 14, 1989.

Year Club	G.	XP.	XPM.	FG.	FGA.	Pts.	Year Club	G.	XP.	XPM.	FG.	FGA.	Pts.
		PLACE KICKING							PLACE KICKING				
1977—Los Angeles NFL	14	32	3	18	30	86	1983—Dallas NFL	16	57	2	22	27	123
1978—Dallas NFL	16	★46	1	16	26	94	1984—Dallas NFL	16	33	1	23	29	102
1979—Dallas NFL	16	40	4	19	29	97	1985—Dallas NFL	16	42	1	19	28	99
1980—Dallas NFL	16	★59	1	11	17	92	1986—Dallas NFL	16	43	0	15	21	88
1981—Dallas NFL	16	40	0	★27	35	★121	Pro Totals—10 Years	151	420	13	180	256	960
1982—Dallas NFL	9	28	0	10	14	58							

Additional pro statistics: Recovered two fumbles for 18 yards, 1980; punted two times for 31.0 average 1981.
Played in NFL Championship Game following 1978 and 1980 through 1982 seasons.
Played in NFL Championship Game following 1978 season.
Played in Pro Bowl (NFL All-Star Game) following 1981 season.

NFL Head Coaches

RAYMOND EMMETT BERRY
New England Patriots

Born February 27, 1933, at Corpus Christi, Tex.
High School—Paris, Tex.
Attended Schreiner Institute and received bachelor of arts degree from
Southern Methodist University in 1955.

Played wide receiver.
Inducted into Pro Football Hall of Fame, 1973.
Named to THE SPORTING NEWS NFL Western Conference All-Star Team, 1957 through 1960.
Selected (as future choice) by Baltimore in 20th round of 1954 NFL draft.

Year Club	G.	P.C.	Yds.	Avg.	TD.	Year Club	G.	P.C.	Yds.	Avg.	TD.
	——PASS RECEIVING——						——PASS RECEIVING——				
1955—Baltimore NFL	12	13	205	15.8	0	1962—Baltimore NFL	14	51	687	13.5	3
1956—Baltimore NFL	12	37	601	16.2	2	1963—Baltimore NFL	9	44	703	16.0	3
1957—Baltimore NFL	12	47	*800	17.0	6	1964—Baltimore NFL	12	43	663	15.4	6
1958—Baltimore NFL	12	*56	794	14.2	*9	1965—Baltimore NFL	14	58	739	12.7	7
1959—Baltimore NFL	12	*66	*959	14.5	*14	1966—Baltimore NFL	14	56	786	14.0	7
1960—Baltimore NFL	12	*74	*1298	17.5	10	1967—Baltimore NFL	7	11	167	15.2	1
1961—Baltimore NFL	12	75	873	11.6	0	Pro Totals—13 Years	154	631	9275	14.7	68

Additional pro statistics: Returned two kickoffs for 27 yards, 1955; fumbled once, 1962.
Played in NFL Championship Game following 1958, 1959 and 1964 seasons.
Played in Pro Bowl (NFL All-Star Game) following 1958, 1959, 1961, 1963 and 1964 seasons.

COACHING RECORD
Assistant coach, Dallas Cowboys NFL, 1968.
Assistant coach at University of Arkansas, 1970 through 1972.
Assistant coach, Detroit Lions NFL, 1973 through 1975.
Assistant coach, Cleveland Browns NFL, 1976 and 1977.
Assistant coach, New England Patriots NFL, 1978 through 1981.
Training camp assistant coach, Minnesota Vikings NFL, 1984.

Year Club	Pos.	W.	L.	T.
1984—New England NFL†	‡Second	4	4	0
1985—New England NFL	‡§Second	11	5	0
1986—New England NFL	‡First	11	5	0
1987—New England NFL	‡§Second	8	7	0
1988—New England NFL	‡§Second	9	7	0
Pro Totals—5 Years		43	28	0

†Replaced Ron Meyer, October 25, 1984 with 5-3 record and in third place.
‡Eastern Division (American Conference).
§Tied for position.

PLAYOFF RECORD

Year Club	W.	L.
1985—New England NFL	3	1
1986—New England NFL	0	1
Pro Totals—2 Years	3	2

1985—Won wild-card playoff game from New York Jets, 26-14; won conference playoff game from Los Angeles Raiders, 27-20; won conference championship game from Miami, 31-14; lost NFL championship game (Super Bowl XX) to Chicago, 46-10.
1986—Lost conference playoff game to Denver, 22-17.

JEROME MONAHAN BURNS
(Jerry)
Minnesota Vikings

Born January 24, 1927, at Detroit, Mich.
High School—Detroit, Mich., Catholic Central.
Received degree in physical education from University of Michigan.

COACHING RECORD
Assistant coach at University of Hawaii, 1951.
Assistant coach at Whittier College, 1952.
Head coach at St. Mary of Redford High School, Detroit, Mich., 1953.
Assistant coach at University of Iowa, 1954 through 1959.
Assistant coach, Green Bay Packers NFL, 1966 and 1967.
Assistant coach, Minnesota Vikings NFL, 1968 through 1985.

Year Club	Pos.	W.	L.	T.	Year Club	Pos.	W.	L.	T.
1961—Iowa	†‡Seventh	5	4	0	1986—Minnesota NFL	§Second	9	7	0
1962—Iowa	†‡Fifth	4	5	0	1987—Minnesota NFL	§Second	8	7	0
1963—Iowa	†Eighth	3	3	2	1988—Minnesota NFL	§Second	11	5	0
1964—Iowa	†‡Ninth	3	6	0	College Totals—5 Years		16	27	2
1965—Iowa	†Tenth	1	9	0	Pro Totals—3 Years		28	19	0

†Big 10 Conference.
‡Tied for position.
§Central Division (National Conference).

Year Club	W.	L.
1987—Minnesota NFL...	2	1
1988—Minnesota NFL...	1	1
Pro Totals—2 Years..	3	2

1987—Won wild-card playoff game from New Orleans, 44-10; won conference playoff game from San Francisco, 36-24; lost conference championship game to Washington, 17-10.
1988—Won wild-card game from Los Angeles Rams, 28-17; lost conference playoff game to San Francisco, 34-9.

FRANCIS MARION CAMPBELL
(Known by middle name.)
Atlanta Falcons
Born May 25, 1929, at Chester, S. C.
High School—Chester, S. C.
Received bachelor of science degree in education from University of Georgia.

Played defensive lineman.
Named to THE SPORTING NEWS NFL East Division All-Star Team, 1960.
Selected by San Francisco in 4th round of 1952 NFL draft.
Military service, 1952 and 1953.
Traded by San Francisco 49ers to Philadelphia Eagles for 6th round draft choice, September 20, 1956.
San Francisco NFL, 1954 and 1955; Philadelphia NFL, 1956 through 1961.
Games: 1954 (12), 1955 (11), 1956 (12), 1957 (10), 1958 (11), 1959 (12), 1960 (12), 1961 (14). Total—94.
Pro statistics: Recovered two fumbles, 1954; recovered one fumble, 1955, 1958 and 1960; intercepted one pass for no yards, 1954; intercepted one pass for one yard and fumbled once, 1956; recovered three fumbles, 1959.
Played in NFL Championship Game following 1960 season.
Played in Playoff Bowl Game following 1961 season.
Played in Pro Bowl (NFL All-Star Game) following 1960 and 1961 seasons.

COACHING RECORD
Assistant coach, Boston Patriots AFL, 1962 and 1963.
Assistant coach, Minnesota Vikings NFL, 1964 through 1966.
Assistant coach, Los Angeles Rams NFL, 1967 and 1968.
Assistant coach, Atlanta Falcons NFL, 1969 through part of 1974 and 1986.
Assistant coach, Philadelphia Eagles NFL, 1977 through 1982.

Year Club	Pos.	W.	L.	T.	Year Club	Pos.	W.	L.	T.
1974— Atlanta NFL†	‡Fourth	1	5	0	1985— Philadelphia NFL y	xFourth	6	9	0
1975— Atlanta NFL	‡Third	4	10	0	1987— Atlanta NFL	‡Fourth	3	12	0
1976— Atlanta NFL§	‡Fourth	1	4	0	1988— Atlanta NFL	‡Fourth	5	11	0
1983— Philadelphia NFL	xFifth	5	11	0	Pro Totals—8 Years.................................		31	71	1
1984— Philadelphia NFL	xFifth	6	9	1					

†Replaced Norm Van Brocklin, November 5, 1974 with 2-6 record and tied for third place.
‡Western Division (National Conference).
§Replaced by General Manager Pat Peppler, October 11, 1976.
xEastern Division (National Conference).
yReplaced by interim coach Fred Bruney, December 16, 1986.

LEON H. CARSON
(Bud)
Cleveland Browns
Born April 28, 1931, at Freeport, Pa.
High School—Freeport, Pa.
Received degree from University of North Carolina in 1952.
Served 30 months in U.S. Marines after college.

COACHING RECORD
Head coach at Scottsdale (Pa.) High School, 1955 and 1956.
Assistant coach at University of North Carolina, 1957 through 1964.
Assistant coach at University of South Carolina, 1965.
Assistant coach at Georgia Tech, 1966.
Assistant coach, Pittsburgh Steelers NFL, 1972 through 1977.
Assistant coach, Los Angeles Rams NFL, 1978 through 1981.
Assistant coach, Baltimore Colts NFL, 1982.
Assistant coach, Kansas City Chiefs NFL, 1983.
Volunteer coach at Kansas University, 1984.
Assistant coach, New York Jets NFL, 1985 through 1988.

Year Club	Pos.	W.	L.	T.
1967— Georgia Tech	†....	4	6	0
1968— Georgia Tech	†....	4	6	0
1969— Georgia Tech	†....	4	6	0
1970— Georgia Tech	†....	9	3	0
1971— Georgia Tech	†....	6	6	0
College Totals—5 Years............		27	27	0

†Independent.

COLLEGIATE BOWL GAME RECORD

Year	Club	W.	L.
1970—Georgia Tech		1	0
1971—Georgia Tech		0	1
College Totals—2 Years		1	1

1970—Won Sun Bowl from Texas Tech, 17-9.
1971—Lost Peach Bowl to Mississippi, 41-18.

MICHAEL KELLER DITKA
(Mike)
Chicago Bears
Born October 18, 1939, at Carnegie, Pa.
High School—Aliquippa, Pa.
Attended University of Pittsburgh.

Played tight end.
Inducted into Pro Football Hall of Fame, 1988.
Named as end on THE SPORTING NEWS College All-America Team, 1960.
Named NFL Rookie of the Year by THE SPORTING NEWS, 1961.
Named to THE SPORTING NEWS NFL Western Conference All-Star Team, 1961 through 1965.
Selected by Chicago in 1st round of 1961 NFL draft.
Traded by Chicago Bears to Philadelphia Eagles for quarterback Jack Concannon and a 1968 draft choice, April 26, 1967.
Traded by Philadelphia Eagles to Dallas Cowboys for receiver Dave McDaniels, January 18, 1969.

Year	Club	—PASS RECEIVING— G.	P.C.	Yds.	Avg.	TD.	Year	Club	—PASS RECEIVING— G.	P.C.	Yds.	Avg.	TD.
1961—Chicago NFL		14	56	1076	19.2	12	1968—Philadelphia NFL		11	13	111	8.5	2
1962—Chicago NFL		14	58	904	15.6	5	1969—Dallas NFL		12	17	268	15.8	3
1963—Chicago NFL		14	59	794	13.5	8	1970—Dallas NFL		14	8	98	12.3	0
1964—Chicago NFL		14	75	897	12.0	5	1971—Dallas NFL		14	30	360	12.0	1
1965—Chicago NFL		14	36	454	12.6	2	1972—Dallas NFL		14	17	198	11.6	1
1966—Chicago NFL		14	32	378	11.8	2	Pro Totals—12 Years		158	427	5812	13.6	43
1967—Philadelphia NFL		9	26	274	10.5	2							

Additional pro statistics: Recovered one fumble for a touchdown, 1962 and 1964; fumbled once, 1969; rushed twice for two yards, returned three kickoffs for 30 yards and recovered one fumble, 1971.
Played in NFC Championship Game following 1970 through 1972 seasons.
Played in NFL Championship Game following 1963, 1970 and 1971 seasons.
Played in Pro Bowl (NFL All-Star Game) following 1961 through 1965 seasons.

COACHING RECORD
Named NFL Coach of the Year by THE SPORTING NEWS, 1985.
Assistant coach, Dallas Cowboys NFL, 1973 through 1981.

Year	Club	Pos.	W.	L.	T.
1982—Chicago NFL		†‡Eleventh	3	6	0
1983—Chicago NFL		‡§Second	8	8	0
1984—Chicago NFL		§First	10	6	0
1985—Chicago NFL		§First	15	1	0
1986—Chicago NFL		§First	14	2	0
1987—Chicago NFL		§First	11	4	0
1988—Chicago NFL		§xFirst	10	4	0
Pro Totals—7 Years			71	31	0

†National Conference.
‡Tied for position.
§Central Division (National Conference).
xMissed two games due to heart attack suffered on November 1, 1988; assistant coach Vince Tobin was 2-0 during that time.

PLAYOFF RECORD

Year	Club	W.	L.
1984—Chicago NFL		1	1
1985—Chicago NFL		3	0
1986—Chicago NFL		0	1
1987—Chicago NFL		0	1
1988—Chicago NFL		1	1
Pro Totals—5 Years		5	4

1984—Won conference playoff game from Washington, 23-19; lost conference championship game to San Francisco, 23-0.
1985—Won conference playoff game from New York Giants, 21-0; won conference championship game from Los Angeles Rams, 24-0; won NFL championship game (Super Bowl XX) from New England, 46-10.
1986—Lost conference playoff game to Washington, 27-13.
1987—Lost conference playoff game to Washington, 21-17.
1988—Won conference playoff game from Philadelphia, 20-12; lost conference championship game to San Francisco, 28-3.

WAYNE HOWARD JOSEPH FONTES
Name pronounced Fonts.
Detroit Lions
Born February 2, 1940, at New Bedford, Mass.
High Schools—Wareham, Mass.; and Canton, O., McKinley.
Received bachelor's degree in biological science in 1962 and received master's degree
in administration in 1964, both from Michigan State University.
Brother of Len Fontes, graduate assistant at Eastern Michigan University, 1968; and assistant coach
with University of Dayton, 1969 through 1971; U.S. Naval Academy, 1973 through 1976;
University of Miami (Fla.), 1977 through 1979; Cleveland Browns, 1980 through 1982;
and New York Giants, 1983 through 1988; and brother of John Fontes, assistant coach with
Oregon State University, 1976 through 1979; Northwestern University, 1985;
University of Miami (Fla.), 1986; and with Louisiana State University since 1987.

Played defensive back.
Selected (as future choice) by New York Titans in 22nd round of 1961 AFL draft.
New York AFL, 1962.
Games: 1962 (9).
Pro statistics: Intercepted four passes for 145 yards (36.3 avg.) and a touchdown, 1962.

COACHING RECORD
Freshman coach at Michigan State University, 1965.
Head coach at Visitation High School, Bay City, Mich., 1966 and 1967.
Assistant coach at University of Dayton, 1968.
Assistant coach at University of Iowa, 1969 through 1971.
Assistant coach at University of Southern California, 1972 through 1975.
Assistant coach, Tampa Bay Buccaneers NFL, 1976 through 1984.
Assistant coach, Detroit Lions NFL, 1985 through November 13, 1988.

Year	Club	Pos.	W.	L.	T.
1988—Detroit†		‡§Fourth	2	3	0

†Replaced Darryl Rogers, November 14, 1988, with 2-9 record and tied for fourth place.
‡Central Division (National Conference).
§Tied for position.

JOE JACKSON GIBBS
Washington Redskins
Born November 25, 1940, at Mocksville, N. C.
High School—Sante Fe, Calif., Spring.
Attended Cerritos Junior College, received bachelor of science degree in physical education from
San Diego State University in 1964 and received master's degree from San Diego State in 1966.

COACHING RECORD
Named NFL Coach of the Year by THE SPORTING NEWS, 1982 and 1983.
Graduate assistant at San Diego State University, 1964 and 1965.
Assistant coach at San Diego State University, 1966.
Assistant coach at Florida State University, 1967 and 1968.
Assistant coach at University of Southern California, 1969 and 1970.
Assistant coach at University of Arkansas, 1971 and 1972.
Assistant coach, St. Louis Cardinals NFL, 1973 through 1977.
Assistant coach, Tampa Bay Buccaneers NFL, 1978.
Assistant coach, San Diego Chargers NFL, 1979 and 1980.

Year	Club	Pos.	W.	L.	T.
1981—Washington NFL		†Fourth	8	8	0
1982—Washington NFL		‡First	8	1	0
1983—Washington NFL		†First	14	2	0
1984—Washington NFL		†First	11	5	0
1985—Washington NFL		†§ First	10	6	0
1986—Washington NFL		†Second	12	4	0
1987—Washington NFL		†First	11	4	0
1988—Washington NFL		†§Third	7	9	0
Pro Totals—8 Years			81	39	0

†Eastern Division (National Conference).
‡National Conference.
§Tied for position.

PLAYOFF RECORD

Year	Club	W.	L.
1982—Washington NFL		4	0
1983—Washington NFL		2	1
1984—Washington NFL		0	1
1986—Washington NFL		2	1
1987—Washington NFL		3	0
Pro Totals—5 Years		11	3

1982—Won conference playoff game from Detroit, 31-7; won conference playoff game from Minnesota, 21-7; won
conference championship game from Dallas, 31-17; won NFL championship game (Super Bowl XVII) from
Miami, 27-17.
1983—Won conference playoff game from Los Angeles Rams, 51-7; won conference championship game from San
Francisco, 24-21; lost NFL championship game (Super Bowl XVIII) to Los Angeles Raiders, 38-9.
1984—Lost conference playoff game to Chicago, 23-19.

1986—Won wild-card playoff game from Los Angeles Rams, 19-7; won conference playoff game from Chicago, 27-13; lost conference championship game to New York Giants, 17-0.
1987—Won conference playoff game from Chicago, 21-17; won conference championship game from Minnesota, 17-10; won NFL championship game (Super Bowl XXII) from Denver, 42-10.

JERRY MICHAEL GLANVILLE
Houston Oilers
Born October 14, 1941, at Detroit, Mich.
High School—Reading, O.
Attended Montana State University and received bachelor of science degree from Northern Michigan University in 1964 and master's degree in art western from Western Kentucky University in 1966.

COACHING RECORD

Assistant coach at Central Catholic High School, Lima, O., 1963 and 1964.
Assistant coach at Reading High School, Reading, O., 1965.
Assistant coach at Northern Michigan University, 1966.
Assistant coach at Western Kentucky University, 1967.
Assistant coach at Georgia Tech, 1968 through 1973.
Assistant coach, Detroit Lions NFL, 1974 through 1976.
Assistant coach, Atlanta Falcons NFL, 1977 through 1982.
Assistant coach, Buffalo Bills NFL, 1983.
Assistant coach, Houston Oilers NFL, 1984 and 1985.

Year Club	Pos.	W.	L.	T.
1985—Houston NFL†	‡Fourth	0	2	0
1986—Houston NFL	‡Fourth	5	11	0
1987—Houston NFL	‡Second	9	6	0
1988—Houston NFL	‡§Second	10	6	0
Pro Totals—4 Years..............		24	25	0

†Replaced Hugh Campbell, December 9, 1985, with 5-9 record and in fifth place.
‡Central Division (American Conference).
§Tied for position.

PLAYOFF RECORD

Year Club	W.	L.
1987—Houston NFL...	1	1
1988—Houston NFL...	1	1
Pro Totals—2 Years..	2	2

1987—Won wild-card playoff game in overtime from Seattle, 23-20; lost conference playoff game to Denver, 34-10.
1988—Won wild-card playoff game from Cleveland, 24-23; lost conference playoff game to Buffalo, 17-10.

DANIEL E. HENNING
(Dan)
San Diego Chargers
Born June 21, 1942, at Bronx, N.Y.
High School—Fresh Meadows, N.Y., St. Francis Prep.
Attended College of William & Mary.

Played quarterback.
Signed as free agent by San Diego Chargers, February 19, 1964.
Released by San Diego Chargers, September 1, 1964; re-signed by Chargers, December 2, 1964.
Released by San Diego Chargers, August 2, 1965; re-signed by Chargers, July 2, 1966.
Released by San Diego Chargers, August 25, 1966; re-signed and placed on taxi squad for 1966 season.
Released by San Diego Chargers, August 29, 1967.
Active for 1 game with San Diego Chargers in 1966; did not play.
Played with Springfield, Mass., of Atlantic Coast Football League, 1964.
Played with Norfolk Neptunes of Continental Football League, 1965 and 1967.

COACHING RECORD

Assistant coach at Homer L. Ferguson High School, Newport News, Va., 1967.
Assistant coach at Florida State University, 1968 through 1970 and 1974.
Assistant coach at Virginia Tech, 1971 and 1973.
Assistant coach, Houston Oilers NFL, 1972.
Assistant coach, New York Jets NFL, 1976 through 1978.
Assistant coach, Miami Dolphins NFL, 1979 and 1980.
Assistant coach, Washington Redskins NFL, 1981, 1982, 1987 and 1988.

Year Club	Pos.	W.	L.	T.
1983—Atlanta NFL	†Fourth	7	9	0
1984—Atlanta NFL	†Fourth	4	12	0
1985—Atlanta NFL	†Fourth	4	12	0
1986—Atlanta NFL	†Third	7	8	1
Pro Totals—4 Years..............		22	41	1

†Western Division (National Conference).

JELINDO INFANTE
(Lindy)
Green Bay Packers

Born May 27, 1940, at Miami, Fla.
High School—Miami, Fla.
Received bachelor of science degree in education from University of Florida in 1964.
Selected by Cleveland in 12th round of 1963 NFL draft.
Selected by Buffalo in 11th round of 1963 AFL draft.
Signed by Buffalo Bills, 1963.
Released by Buffalo Bills, 1963; signed as free agent by Hamilton Tiger-Cats, 1963.
Released by Hamilton Tiger-Cats, 1963.
Hamilton CFL, 1963.
Games: 1963 (1).
CFL statistics: Rushed three times for 12 yards, 1963.

COACHING RECORD

Assistant coach, Miami (Fla.) High School, 1964.
Head coach at Miami (Fla.) High School, 1965.
Assistant coach at University of Florida, 1966 through 1971.
Assistant coach at Memphis State University, 1972 through 1974.
Assistant coach, Charlotte Hornets WFL, 1975.
Assistant coach at Tulane University, 1976 and 1979.
Assistant coach, New York Giants NFL, 1977 and 1978.
Assistant coach, Cincinnati Bengals NFL, 1980 through 1982.
Assistant coach, Cleveland Browns NFL, 1986 and 1987.

Year — Club	Pos.	W.	L.	T.
1984—Jacksonville USFL	†Fifth	6	12	0
1985—Jacksonville USFL	‡Sixth	9	9	0
1988—Green Bay NFL	§xFourth	4	12	0
USFL Totals—2 Years		15	21	0
NFL Totals—1 Year		4	12	0
Pro Totals—3 Years		19	33	0

†Southern Division (Eastern Conference).
‡Eastern Conference.
§Central Division (National Conference).
xTied for position.

JAMES WILLIAM JOHNSON
(Jimmy)
Dallas Cowboys

Born July 16, 1943, at Port Arthur, Tex.
High School—Port Arthur, Tex., Thomas Jefferson.
Received bachelor of arts degree in psychology from University of Arkansas in 1965.

COACHING RECORD

Assistant coach at Louisiana Tech University, 1965.
Assistant coach at Wichita State University, 1967.
Assistant coach at Iowa State University, 1968 and 1969.
Assistant coach at University of Oklahoma, 1970 through 1972.
Assistant coach at University of Arkansas, 1973 through 1976.
Assistant coach at University of Pittsburgh, 1977 and 1978.

Year — Club	Pos.	W.	L.	T.	Year — Club	Pos.	W.	L.	T.
1979—Oklahoma State	†Third	7	4	0	1985—Miami (Fla.)	x....	10	2	0
1980—Oklahoma State‡	†Fifth	3	7	1	1986—Miami (Fla.)	x....	11	1	0
1981—Oklahoma State	†§Third	7	5	0	1987—Miami (Fla.)	x....	12	0	0
1982—Oklahoma State	†Third	4	5	2	1988—Miami (Fla.)	x....	11	1	0
1983—Oklahoma State	†§Fourth	8	4	0	College Totals—10 Years		81	34	3
1984—Miami (Fla.)	x....	8	5	0					

†Big Eight Conference.
‡Oklahoma State played to a 14-14 forfeited tie vs. Kansas on October 25, 1980.
§Tied for position.
xIndependent.

COLLEGIATE BOWL GAME RECORD

Year — Club	W.	L.
1981—Oklahoma State	0	1
1983—Oklahoma State	1	0
1984—Miami (Fla.)	0	1
1985—Miami (Fla.)	0	1
1986—Miami (Fla.)	0	1
1987—Miami (Fla.)	1	0
1988—Miami (Fla.)	1	0
College Totals—7 Years	3	4

1981—Lost Independence Bowl to Texas A&M, 33-16.
1983—Won Bluebonnet Bowl from Baylor, 24-14.
1984—Lost Fiesta Bowl to UCLA, 39-37.
1985—Lost Sugar Bowl to Tennessee, 35-7.
1986—Lost Fiesta Bowl to Penn State, 14-10.
1987—Won Orange Bowl from Oklahoma, 20-14.
1988—Won Orange Bowl from Nebraska, 23-3.

CHARLES ROBERT KNOX SR.
(Chuck)
Seattle Seahawks
Born April 27, 1932, at Sewickley, Pa.
High School—Sewickley, Pa.
Received bachelor of arts degree in history from Juniata College in 1954.
Father of Chuck Knox Jr., running back at University of Arizona.

COACHING RECORD

Named NFL Coach of the Year by THE SPORTING NEWS, 1973, 1980 and 1984.
Assistant coach at Juniata College, 1954.
Assistant coach at Tyrone (Pa.) High School, 1955.
Head coach at Ellwood City (Pa.) High School, 1956 through 1958 (Won 10, Lost 16, Tied 2).
Assistant coach at Wake Forest University, 1959 and 1960.
Assistant coach at University of Kentucky, 1961 and 1962.
Assistant coach, New York Jets AFL, 1963 through 1966.
Assistant coach, Detroit Lions NFL, 1967 through 1972.

Year Club	Pos.	W.	L.	T.	Year Club	Pos.	W.	L.	T.
1973—Los Angeles NFL	†First	12	2	0	1982—Buffalo NFL	x§Eighth	4	5	0
1974—Los Angeles NFL	†First	10	4	0	1983—Seattle NFL	ySecond	9	7	0
1975—Los Angeles NFL	†First	12	2	0	1984—Seattle NFL	ySecond	12	4	0
1976—Los Angeles NFL	†First	10	3	1	1985—Seattle NFL	y§Third	8	8	0
1977—Los Angeles NFL	†First	10	4	0	1986—Seattle NFL	y§Second	10	6	0
1978—Buffalo NFL	‡§Fourth	5	11	0	1987—Seattle NFL	ySecond	9	6	0
1979—Buffalo NFL	‡Fourth	7	9	0	1988—Seattle NFL	yFirst	9	7	0
1980—Buffalo NFL	‡First	11	5	0	Pro Totals—16 Years		148	89	1
1981—Buffalo NFL	‡Third	10	6	0					

†Western Division (National Conference).
‡Eastern Division (American Conference).
§Tied for position.
xAmerican Conference.
yWestern Division (American Conference).

PLAYOFF RECORD

Year Club	W.	L.
1973—Los Angeles NFL	0	1
1974—Los Angeles NFL	1	1
1975—Los Angeles NFL	1	1
1976—Los Angeles NFL	1	1
1977—Los Angeles NFL	0	1
1980—Buffalo NFL	0	1
1981—Buffalo NFL	1	1
1983—Seattle NFL	2	1
1984—Seattle NFL	1	1
1987—Seattle NFL	0	1
1988—Seattle NFL	0	1
Pro Totals—11 Years	7	11

1973—Lost conference playoff game to Dallas, 27-16.
1974—Won conference playoff game from Washington, 19-10; lost conference championship game to Minnesota, 14-10.
1975—Won conference playoff game from St. Louis, 35-23; lost conference championship game to Dallas, 37-7.
1976—Won conference playoff game from Dallas, 14-12; lost conference championship game to Minnesota, 24-13.
1977—Lost conference playoff game to Minnesota, 14-7.
1980—Lost conference playoff game to San Diego, 20-14.
1981—Won conference playoff game from New York Jets, 31-27; lost conference playoff game to Cincinnati, 28-21.
1983—Won wild-card playoff game from Denver, 31-7; won conference playoff game from Miami, 27-20; lost conference championship game to Los Angeles Raiders, 30-14.
1984—Won wild-card playoff game from Los Angeles Raiders, 13-7; lost conference playoff game to Miami, 31-10.
1987—Lost wild-card playoff game in overtime to Houston, 23-20.
1988—Lost conference playoff game to Cincinnati, 21-13.

MARVIN DANIEL LEVY
(Marv)
Buffalo Bills
Born August 3, 1928, at Chicago, Ill.
High School—Chicago, Ill., South Shore.
Received degree from Coe College in 1950 and received master's degree
in history from Harvard University in 1951.

COACHING RECORD

Named NFL Coach of the Year by The Sporting News, 1988.
Head coach at St. Louis (Mo.) Country Day School, 1951 and 1952 (Won 13, Lost 0, Tied 1).
Assistant coach at Coe College, 1953 through 1955.
Assistant coach at University of New Mexico, 1956 and 1957.
Assistant coach, Philadelphia Eagles NFL, 1969.
Assistant coach, Los Angeles Rams NFL, 1970.
Assistant coach, Washington Redskins NFL, 1971 and 1972.

Year Club	Pos.	W.	L.	T.	Year Club	Pos.	W.	L.	T.
1958— New Mexico	†Second	7	3	0	1978— Kansas City NFL	zFifth	4	12	0
1959— New Mexico	†Third	7	3	0	1979— Kansas City NFL	zFifth	7	9	0
1960— California	‡Fourth	2	7	1	1980— Kansas City NFL	z§Third	8	8	0
1961— California	‡§Fourth	1	8	1	1981— Kansas City NFL	zThird	9	7	0
1962— California	‡Fifth	1	9	0	1982— Kansas City NFL	aEleventh	3	6	0
1963— California	‡Fourth	4	5	1	1984— Chicago USFL	bFifth	5	13	0
1964— William & Mary	x§Fourth	4	6	0	1986— Buffalo NFLc	dFourth	2	5	0
1965— William & Mary	xFirst	6	4	0	1987— Buffalo NFL	dFourth	7	8	0
1966— William & Mary	x§First	5	4	1	1988— Buffalo NFL	dFirst	12	4	0
1967— William & Mary	xFourth	5	4	1					
1968— William & Mary	x§Third	3	7	0	College Totals—11 Years		45	60	5
1973— Montreal CFL	yThird	7	6	1	NFL Totals—8 Years		52	59	0
1974— Montreal CFL	yFirst	9	5	2	CFL Totals—5 Years		43	31	4
1975— Montreal CFL	ySecond	9	7	0	USFL Totals—1 Year		5	13	0
1976— Montreal CFL	y§Third	7	8	1					
1977— Montreal CFL	yFirst	11	5	0	Pro Totals—14 Years		100	103	4

†Skyline Conference.
‡Athletic Association of Western Universities.
§Tied for position.
xSouthern Conference.
yEastern Conference.
zWestern Division (American Conference).
aAmerican Conference.
bCentral Division (Western Conference).
cReplaced Hank Bullough, November 3, 1986 with 2-7 record and in fourth place.
dEastern Division (American Conference).

PLAYOFF RECORD

Year Club	W.	L.	Year Club	W.	L.
1973—Montreal CFL	1	1	1988—Buffalo NFL	1	1
1974—Montreal CFL	2	0			
1975—Montreal CFL	2	1	CFL Totals—5 Years	7	3
1976—Montreal CFL	0	1	NFL Totals—1 Year	1	1
1977—Montreal CFL	2	0	Pro Totals—6 Years	8	4

1973—Won conference playoff game from Toronto, 32-10; lost conference championship game to Ottawa, 23-14.
1974—Won conference championship game from Ottawa, 14-4, won CFL championship game from Edmonton, 20-7.
1975—Won conference playoff game from Hamilton, 35-12; won conference championship game from Ottawa, 20-10; lost CFL championship game to Edmonton, 9-8.
1976—Lost conference playoff game to Hamilton, 23-0.
1977—Won conference championship game from Ottawa, 21-18; won CFL championship game from Edmonton, 41-6.
1988—Won conference championship game from Houston, 17-10; lost conference championship game to Cincinnati, 21-10.

RONALD SHAW MEYER
(Ron)
Indianapolis Colts

Born February 17, 1941, at Columbus, O.
High School—Westerville, O.
Received bachelor of science degree in physical education from Purdue University in 1963
and master's degree in physical education from Purdue in 1965.

COACHING RECORD

Graduate assistant coach at Purdue University, 1963.
Head coach at Penn Hill High School, Mishawaka, Ind., 1964 (Won 5, Lost 4, Tied 1).
Assistant coach at Purdue University, 1965 through 1970.
Scout for Dallas Cowboys, 1971 and 1972.

Year Club	Pos.	W.	L.	T.	Year Club	Pos.	W.	L.	T.
1973—Nevada-Las Vegas	....	8	3	0	1982—New England NFL	§Seventh	5	4	0
1974—Nevada-Las Vegas	....	12	1	0	1983—New England NFL	†xSecond	8	8	0
1975—Nevada-Las Vegas	....	7	4	0	1984—New England NFLy	xThird	5	3	0
1976—Southern Methodist	†‡Seventh	3	8	0	1986—Indianapolis NFLz	xFifth	3	0	0
1977—Southern Methodist	†‡Sixth	4	7	0	1987—Indianapolis NFL	xFirst	9	6	0
1978—Southern Methodist	†‡Sixth	4	6	1	1988—Indianapolis NFL	†xSecond	9	7	0
1979—Southern Methodist	‡Sixth	5	6	0					
1980—Southern Methodist	‡Second	8	4	0	College Totals—9 Years		61	40	1
1981—Southern Methodist	‡First	10	1	0	Pro Totals—6 Years		39	28	0

†Tied for position.
‡Southwest Conference.
§American Conference.
xEastern Division (American Conference).

zReplaced Rod Dowhower, December 1, 1986 with 0-13 record and in fifth place.

PLAYOFF RECORD

Year	Club	W.	L.
1982—New England NFL		0	1
1987—Indianapolis NFL		0	1
Pro Totals—2 Years		0	2

1982—Lost conference playoff game to Miami, 28-13.
1987—Lost conference playoff game to Cleveland, 38-21.

NCAA DIVISION II PLAYOFF RECORD

Year	Club	W.	L.
1974—Nevada-Las Vegas		1	1

1974—Nevada-Las Vegas 35, Alcorn State 22; Delaware 49, Nevada-Las Vegas 11.

COLLEGIATE BOWL GAME RECORD

Year	Club	W.	L.
1980—Southern Methodist		0	1

1980—Lost Holiday Bowl to Brigham Young, 46-45.

JAMES ERNEST MORA
(Jim)
New Orleans Saints

Born May 24, 1935, at Los Angeles, Calif.
High School—Los Angeles, Calif., University.
Received bachelor of arts degree in physical education from Occidental College
in 1957; and received master's degree in education from
University of Southern California in 1967.
Father of Jim Mora, Jr., assistant coach with San Diego Chargers.
Played in U.S. Marines at Quantico in 1957 and at Camp Lejeune in 1958 and 1959.

COACHING RECORD

Named NFL Coach of the Year by THE SPORTING NEWS, 1987.
Named THE SPORTING NEWS USFL Coach of the Year, 1984.
Assistant coach at Occidental College, 1960 through 1963.
Assistant coach at Stanford University, 1967.
Assistant coach at University of Colorado, 1968 through 1973.
Assistant coach at University of California at Los Angeles, 1974.
Assistant coach at University of Washington, 1975 through 1977.
Assistant coach, Seattle Seahawks NFL, 1978 through 1981.
Assistant coach, New England Patriots NFL, 1982.

Year	Club	Pos.	W.	L.	T.
1964—Occidental		†Third	5	4	0
1965—Occidental		†First	8	1	0
1966—Occidental		†Fourth	5	4	0
1983—Philadelphia USFL		‡First	15	3	0
1984—Philadelphia USFL		§First	16	2	0
1985—Baltimore USFL		xFourth	10	7	1
1986—New Orleans NFL		yFourth	7	9	0
1987—New Orleans NFL		ySecond	12	3	0
1988—New Orleans NFL		yzFirst	10	6	0
College Totals—3 Years			18	9	0
USFL Totals—3 Years			41	12	1
NFL Totals—3 Years			29	18	0
Pro Totals—6 Years			70	30	1

†Southern California Intercollegiate Conference.
‡Atlantic Division.
§Atlantic Division (Eastern Conference).
xEastern Conference.
yWestern Division (National Conference).
zTied for position.

PLAYOFF RECORD

Year	Club	W.	L.
1983—Philadelphia USFL		1	1
1984—Philadelphia USFL		3	0
1985—Baltimore USFL		3	0
1987—New Orleans NFL		0	1
USFL Totals—3 Years		7	1
NFL Totals—1 Year		0	1
Pro Totals—4 Years		7	2

1983—Won divisional playoff game from Chicago, 44-38 (OT); lost USFL championship game to Michigan, 24-22.
1984—Won conference playoff game from New Jersey, 28-7; won conference championship game from Birmingham, 20-10; won USFL championship game from Arizona, 23-3.
1985—Won conference playoff game from New Jersey, 20-17; won conference championship game from Birmingham, 28-14; won USFL championship game from Oakland, 28-24.
1987—Lost wild-card playoff game to Minnesota, 44-10.

CHARLES HENRY NOLL
(Chuck)
Pittsburgh Steelers

Born January 5, 1932, at Cleveland, O.
High School—Cleveland, O., Benedictine.
Received bachelor of science degree in education from University of Dayton in 1953.

Played linebacker and offensive guard.
Selected by Cleveland in 21st round of 1953 NFL draft.

Year Club	G.	INTERCEPTIONS				—KICKOFF RET.—				—TOTAL—		
		No.	Yds.	Avg.	TD.	No.	Yds.	Avg.	TD.	TD.	Pts.	F.
1953—Cleveland NFL	12		None			1	2	2.0	0	0	0	0
1954—Cleveland NFL	12		None				None			0	0	0
1955—Cleveland NFL	12	5	74	14.8	1		None			1	8	0
1956—Cleveland NFL	12	1	13	13.0	0		None			1	6	0
1957—Cleveland NFL	5		None				None			0	0	0
1958—Cleveland NFL	12		None				None			0	0	0
1959—Cleveland NFL	12	2	5	2.5	0	1	20	20.0	0	0	0	0
Pro Totals—7 Years	77	8	92	11.5	1	2	22	11.0	0	2	14	0

Additional pro statistics: Recovered two fumbles for 10 yards, 1954; credited with one safety, 1955; recovered one fumble for 39 yards and a touchdown, 1956.
Played in NFL Championship Game following 1953 through 1955 seasons.

COACHING RECORD

Assistant coach, Los Angeles Chargers AFL, 1960.
Assistant coach, San Diego Chargers AFL, 1961 through 1965.
Assistant coach, Baltimore Colts NFL, 1966 through 1968.

Year Club	Pos.	W.	L.	T.	Year Club	Pos.	W.	L.	T.
1969—Pittsburgh NFL	†Fourth	1	13	0	1980—Pittsburgh NFL	‡Third	9	7	0
1970—Pittsburgh NFL	‡Third	5	9	0	1981—Pittsburgh NFL	‡Second	8	8	0
1971—Pittsburgh NFL	‡Second	6	8	0	1982—Pittsburgh NFL	x§Fourth	6	3	0
1972—Pittsburgh NFL	‡First	11	3	0	1983—Pittsburgh NFL	‡First	10	6	0
1973—Pittsburgh NFL	†§First	10	4	0	1984—Pittsburgh NFL	‡First	9	7	0
1974—Pittsburgh NFL	‡First	10	3	1	1985—Pittsburgh NFL	‡§Second	7	9	0
1975—Pittsburgh NFL	‡First	12	2	0	1986—Pittsburgh NFL	‡Third	6	10	0
1976—Pittsburgh NFL	‡§First	10	4	0	1987—Pittsburgh NFL	‡Third	8	7	0
1977—Pittsburgh NFL	‡First	9	5	0	1988—Pittsburgh NFL	‡Fourth	5	11	0
1978—Pittsburgh NFL	‡First	14	2	0	Pro Totals—20 Years		168	125	1
1979—Pittsburgh NFL	‡First	12	4	0					

†Century Division (Eastern Conference).
‡Central Division (American Conference).
§Tied for position.
xAmerican Conference.

PLAYOFF RECORD

Year Club	W.	L.	Year Club	W.	L.
1972—Pittsburgh NFL	1	1	1978—Pittsburgh NFL	3	0
1973—Pittsburgh NFL	0	1	1979—Pittsburgh NFL	3	0
1974—Pittsburgh NFL	3	0	1982—Pittsburgh NFL	0	1
1975—Pittsburgh NFL	3	0	1983—Pittsburgh NFL	0	1
1976—Pittsburgh NFL	1	1	1984—Pittsburgh NFL	1	1
1977—Pittsburgh NFL	0	1	Pro Totals—11 Years	15	7

1972—Won conference playoff game from Oakland, 13-7; lost conference championship game to Miami, 21-17.
1973—Lost conference playoff game to Oakland, 33-14.
1974—Won conference playoff game from Buffalo, 32-14; won conference championship game from Oakland, 24-13; won NFL championship game (Super Bowl IX) from Minnesota, 16-6.
1975—Won conference playoff game from Baltimore, 28-10; won conference championship game from Oakland, 16-10; won NFL championship game (Super Bowl X) from Dallas, 21-17.
1976—Won conference playoff game from Baltimore, 40-14; lost conference championship game to Oakland, 24-7.
1977—Lost conference playoff game to Denver, 34-21.
1978—Won conference playoff game from Denver, 33-10; won conference championship game from Houston, 34-5; won NFL championship game (Super Bowl XIII) from Dallas, 35-31.
1979—Won conference playoff game from Miami, 34-14; won conference championship game from Houston, 27-13; won NFL championship game (Super Bowl XIV) from Los Angeles, 31-19.
1982—Lost conference playoff game to San Diego, 31-28.
1983—Lost conference playoff game to Los Angeles Raiders, 38-10.
1984—Won conference playoff game from Denver, 24-17; lost conference championship game to Miami, 45-28.

DUANE CHARLES PARCELLS
(Bill)
New York Giants

Born August 22, 1941, at Englewood, N.J.
High School—Oradell, N.J., River Dell.
Received bachelor of arts degree in education from Wichita State University in 1964.

COACHING RECORD

Named NFL Coach of the Year by THE SPORTING NEWS, 1986.
Assistant coach at Hastings College, 1964.

Assistant coach at Wichita State University, 1965.
Assistant coach at West Point, 1966 through 1969.
Assistant coach at Florida State University, 1970 through 1972.
Assistant coach at Vanderbilt University, 1973 and 1974.
Asstant coach at Texas Tech University, 1975 through 1977.
Assistant coach, New England Patriots NFL, 1980.
Assistant coach, New York Giants NFL, 1981 and 1982.

Year	Club	Pos.	W.	L.	T.
1978—	Air Force	....	3	8	0
1983—	New York Giants NFL	†Fifth	3	12	1
1984—	New York Giants NFL	††Second	9	7	0
1985—	New York Giants NFL	††First	10	6	0
1986—	New York Giants NFL	†First	14	2	0
1987—	New York Giants NFL	†Fifth	6	9	0
1988—	New York Giants NFL	††First	10	6	0
	College Totals—1 Year		3	8	0
	Pro Totals—6 Years		52	42	1

†Eastern Division (National Conference).
‡Tied for position.

PLAYOFF RECORD

Year	Club	W.	L.
1984—New York Giants NFL		1	1
1985—New York Giants NFL		1	1
1986—New York Giants NFL		3	0
Pro Totals—3 Years		5	2

1984—Won wild-card playoff game from Los Angeles Rams, 16-10; lost conference playoff game to San Francisco, 21-10.
1985—Won wild-card playoff game from San Francisco, 17-3; lost conference playoff game to Chicago, 21-0.
1986—Won conference playoff from San Francisco, 49-3; won conference championship from Washington, 17-0; won NFL championship game (Super Bowl XXI) from Denver, 39-20.

WALTER RAY PERKINS
(Known by middle name.)
Tampa Bay Buccaneers
Born December 6, 1941, at Mt. Olive, Miss.
High School—Petal, Miss.
Received bachelor of science degree in secondary education from University of Alabama in 1967.

Selected (as future choice) by Baltimore in 7th round of 1966 NFL draft.

Year	Club	——PASS RECEIVING——					Year	Club	——PASS RECEIVING——				
		G.	P.C.	Yds.	Avg.	TD.			G.	P.C.	Yds.	Avg.	TD.
1967—Baltimore NFL		8	16	302	18.9	2	1970—Baltimore NFL		11	10	194	19.4	1
1968—Baltimore NFL		14	15	227	15.1	1	1971—Baltimore NFL		14	24	424	17.7	4
1969—Baltimore NFL		11	28	391	14.0	3	Pro Totals—5 Years		58	93	1538	16.5	11

Additional pro statistics: Rushed three times for 36 yards, 1969; rushed twice for six yards, 1970; rushed five times for 35 yards, 1971.
Played in NFL Championship Game, 1968 and 1970.
Played in AFL-NFL Championship Game following 1968 season.

COACHING RECORD
Assistant coach at Mississippi State University, 1973.
Assistant coach, New England Patriots NFL, 1974 through 1977.
Assistant coach, San Diego Chargers NFL, 1978.

Year	Club	Pos.	W.	L.	T.
1979—	New York Giants NFL	†Fourth	6	10	0
1980—	New York Giants NFL	†Fifth	4	12	0
1981—	New York Giants NFL	†Third	9	7	0
1982—	New York Giants NFL	‡§Eighth	4	5	0
1983—	Alabama	§xThird	8	4	0
1984—	Alabama	§xSeventh	5	6	0
1985—	Alabama	§xSecond	9	2	1
1986—	Alabama	§xSecond	10	3	0
1987—	Tampa Bay NFL	§yFourth	4	11	0
1988—	Tampa Bay NFL	yThird	5	11	0
	College Totals—4 Years		32	15	1
	Pro Totals—6 Years		32	56	0

†Eastern Division (National Conference).
‡National Conference.
§Tied for position.
xSoutheastern Conference.
yCentral Division (National Conference).

PLAYOFF RECORD

Year	Club	W.	L.
1981—New York Giants NFL		1	1

1981—Won conference playoff game from Philadelphia, 27-21; lost conference playoff game to San Francisco, 38-24.

Year Club	W.	L.
1983—Alabama	1	0
1985—Alabama	1	0
1986—Alabama	1	0
College Totals—3 Years...................	3	0

1983—Won Sun Bowl from Southern Methodist, 28-7.
1985—Won Aloha Bowl from Southern California, 24-3.
1986—Won Sun Bowl from Washington, 28-6.

DANIEL EDWARD REEVES
(Dan)
Denver Broncos

Born January 19, 1944, at Rome, Ga.
High School—Americus, Ga.
Attended University of South Carolina.

Played running back.
Named to THE SPORTING NEWS NFL Eastern Conference All-Star Team, 1966.
Signed as free agent by Dallas NFL, 1965.

Year Club	G.	RUSHING Att.	Yds.	Avg.	TD.	PASS RECEIVING P.C.	Yds.	Avg.	TD.	TOTAL TD.	Pts.	F.
1965—Dallas NFL	13	33	102	3.1	2	9	210	23.3	1	3	18	0
1966—Dallas NFL	14	175	757	4.3	8	41	557	13.6	8	*16	96	6
1967—Dallas NFL	14	173	603	3.5	5	39	490	12.6	6	11	66	7
1968—Dallas NFL	4	40	178	4.5	4	7	84	12.0	1	5	30	0
1969—Dallas NFL	13	59	173	2.9	4	18	187	10.4	1	5	30	2
1970—Dallas NFL	14	35	84	2.4	2	12	140	11.7	0	2	12	4
1971—Dallas NFL	14	17	79	4.6	0	3	25	8.3	0	0	0	1
1972—Dallas NFL	14	3	14	4.7	0		None			0	0	0
Pro Totals—8 Years...................	100	535	1990	3.7	25	129	1693	13.1	17	42	252	20

Year Club	G.	PASSING Att.	Cmp.	Pct.	Gain	T.P.	P.I.	Avg.	KICKOFF RET. No.	Yds.	Avg.	TD.
1965—Dallas NFL	13	2	1	50.0	11	0	0	5.50	2	45	22.5	0
1966—Dallas NFL	14	6	3	50.0	48	0	0	8.00	3	56	18.7	0
1967—Dallas NFL	14	7	4	57.1	195	2	1	27.86		None		
1968—Dallas NFL	4	4	2	50.0	43	0	0	10.75		None		
1969—Dallas NFL	13	3	1	33.3	35	0	1	11.67		None		
1970—Dallas NFL	14	3	1	33.3	14	0	1	4.67		None		
1971—Dallas NFL	14	5	2	40.0	24	0	1	4.80		None		
1972—Dallas NFL	14	2	0	00.0	0	0	0	0.00		None		
Pro Totals—8 Years...................	100	32	14	43.8	370	2	4	11.56	5	101	20.2	0

Additional pro statistics: Returned two punts for minus one yard, 1966.
Played in NFC Championship Game following 1970 and 1971 seasons.
Played in NFL Championship Game following 1966, 1967, 1970 and 1971 seasons.

COACHING RECORD

Player-coach, Dallas Cowboys NFL, 1970 and 1971.
Assistant coach, Dallas Cowboys NFL, 1972 and 1974 through 1980.

Year Club	Pos.	W.	L.	T.
1981— Denver NFL	†‡First	10	6	0
1982— Denver NFL	§12th	2	7	0
1983— Denver NFL	†‡Second	9	7	0
1984— Denver NFL	†First	13	3	0
1985— Denver NFL	†Second	11	5	0
1986— Denver NFL	†First	11	5	0
1987— Denver NFL	†First	10	4	1
1988— Denver NFL	†Second	8	8	0
Pro Totals—8 Years...................		74	45	1

†Western Division (American Conference).
‡Tied for position.
§American Conference.

PLAYOFF RECORD

Year Club	W.	L.
1983—Denver NFL	0	1
1984—Denver NFL	0	1
1986—Denver NFL	2	1
1987—Denver NFL	2	1
Pro Totals—4 Years...................	4	4

1983—Lost wild-card playoff game to Seattle, 31-7.
1984—Lost conference playoff game to Pittsburgh, 24-17.
1986—Won conference playoff game from New England, 22-17; won conference championship game in overtime from
   Cleveland, 23-20; lost NFL championship game (Super Bowl XXI) to New York Giants, 39-20.
1987—Won conference playoff game from Houston, 34-10; won conference championship game from Cleveland, 38-33;
   lost NFL championship game (Super Bowl XXII) to Washington, 42-10.

JOHN ALEXANDER ROBINSON
Los Angeles Rams
Born July 25, 1935, at Chicago, Ill.
High School—San Mateo, Calif.
Received bachelor of science degree in education from University of Oregon in 1958.

COACHING RECORD
Assistant coach at University of Oregon, 1960 through 1971.
Assistant coach at University of Southern California, 1972 through 1974.
Assistant coach, Oakland Raiders NFL, 1975.

Year	Club	Pos.	W.	L.	T.	Year	Club	Pos.	W.	L.	T.
1976—	Southern California	†First	11	1	0	1984—	Los Angeles Rams NFL	ySecond	10	6	0
1977—	Southern California	†‡Second	8	4	0	1985—	Los Angeles Rams NFL	yFirst	11	5	0
1978—	Southern California	§First	12	1	0	1986—	Los Angeles Rams NFL	ySecond	10	6	0
1979—	Southern California	§First	11	0	1	1987—	Los Angeles Rams NFL	yThird	6	9	0
1980—	Southern California	§Third	8	2	1	1988—	Los Angeles Rams NFL	‡yFirst	10	6	0
1981—	Southern California	‡§Second	9	3	0	College Totals—7 Years			67	14	2
1982—	Southern California	§x.....	8	3	0	Pro Totals—6 Years			56	39	0
1983—	Los Angeles Rams NFL	ySecond	9	7	0						

†Pacific-8 Conference.
‡Tied for position.
§Pacific-10 Conference.
xIneligible for conference title.
yWestern Division (National Conference).

PLAYOFF RECORD

Year	Club	W.	L.
1983—	Los Angeles Rams NFL	1	1
1984—	Los Angeles Rams NFL	0	1
1985—	Los Angeles Rams NFL	1	1
1986—	Los Angeles Rams NFL	0	1
1988—	Los Angeles Rams NFL	0	1
Pro Totals—5 Years		2	5

1983—Won wild-card playoff game from Dallas, 24-17; lost conference playoff game to Washington, 51-7.
1984—Lost wild-card game to New York Giants, 16-13.
1985—Won conference playoff game from Dallas, 20-0; lost conference championship game to Chicago, 24-0.
1986—Lost wild-card playoff game to Washington, 19-7.
1988—Lost wild-card playoff game to Minnesota, 28-17.

COLLEGIATE BOWL GAME RECORD

Year	Club	W.	L.
1976—	Southern California	1	0
1977—	Southern California	1	0
1978—	Southern California	1	0
1979—	Southern California	1	0
1981—	Southern California	0	1
College Totals—5 Years		4	1

1976—Won Rose Bowl from Michigan, 14-6.
1977—Won Bluebonnet Bowl from Texas A&M, 47-28.
1978—Won Rose Bowl from Michigan, 17-10.
1979—Won Rose Bowl from Ohio State, 17-16.
1981—Lost Fiesta Bowl to Penn State, 26-10.

JAMES DAVID RYAN
(Buddy)
Philadelphia Eagles
Born February 17, 1934, at Frederick, Okla.
High School—Frederick, Okla.
Received bachelor of arts degree in education from Oklahoma State University
in 1957; and received master's degree in education
from Middle Tennessee State University in 1966.
Served in Korea.
Played on Fourth Army Championship team in Japan for two years.
Discharged as master sergeant.

COACHING RECORD
Head Coach and Athletic Director at Gainesville High School, Gainesville, Tex., 1957 through 1959.
Assistant coach at Marshall High School, Marshall, Tex., 1960.
Assistant coach at University of Buffalo, 1961 through 1965.
Assistant coach at Vanderbilt University, 1966.
Assistant coach at University of The Pacific, 1967.
Assistant coach, New York Jets NFL, 1968 through 1975.
Assistant coach, Minnesota Vikings NFL, 1976 and 1977.
Assistant coach, Chicago Bears NFL, 1978 through 1985.

Year	Club	Pos.	W.	L.	T.
1986—	Philadelphia NFL	†Fourth	5	10	1
1987—	Philadelphia NFL	†‡Second	7	8	0
1988—	Philadelphia NFL	†‡First	10	6	0
	Pro Totals—3 Years		22	24	1

†Eastern Division (National Conference).
‡Tied for position.

PLAYOFF RECORD

Year	Club	W.	L.
1988—Philadelphia NFL		0	1

1988—Lost conference playoff game to Chicago, 20-12.

MARTIN EDWARD SCHOTTENHEIMER
(Marty)
Kansas City Chiefs
Born September 23, 1943, at Canonsburg, Pa.
High School—McDonald, Pa.
Received bachelor of arts degree in English from University of Pittsburgh in 1964.
Brother of Kurt Schottenheimer, assistant coach with Kansas City Chiefs.

Played linebacker.
Selected by Buffalo in 7th round of 1965 AFL draft.
Released by Buffalo Bills and signed with Boston Patriots, 1969.
Traded by New England Patriots to Pittsburgh Steelers for offensive tackle Mike Haggerty and a draft choice,
July 10, 1971.
Released by Pittsburgh Steelers, 1971.

Year	Club	—INTERCEPTIONS— G.	No.	Yds.	Avg.	TD.	Year	Club	—INTERCEPTIONS— G.	No.	Yds.	Avg.	TD.
1965—Buffalo AFL		14			None		1970—Boston NFL		12			None	
1966—Buffalo AFL		14	1	20	20.0	0	AFL Totals—5 Years		67	6	133	22.2	1
1967—Buffalo AFL		14	3	88	29.3	1	NFL Totals—1 Year		12	0	0	0.0	0
1968—Buffalo AFL		14	1	22	22.0	0	Pro Totals—6 Years		79	6	133	22.2	1
1969—Boston AFL		11	1	3	3.0	0							

Additional pro statistics: Returned one kickoff for 13 yards, 1969; returned one kickoff for eight yards, 1970.
Played in AFL Championship Game following 1965 and 1966 seasons.
Played in AFL All-Star Game following 1965 season.

COACHING RECORD
Assistant coach, Portland Storm WFL, 1974.
Assistant coach, New York Giants NFL, 1975 through 1977.
Assistant coach, Detroit Lions NFL, 1978 and 1979.
Assistant coach, Cleveland Browns NFL, 1980 through 1984.

Year	Club	Pos.	W.	L.	T.
1984—	Cleveland NFL†	‡Third	4	4	0
1985—	Cleveland NFL	‡First	8	8	0
1986—	Cleveland NFL	‡First	12	4	0
1987—	Cleveland NFL	‡First	10	5	0
1988—	Cleveland NFL	‡§Second	10	6	0
	Pro Totals—5 Years		44	27	0

†Replaced Sam Rutigliano, October 22, 1984 with 1-7 record and in third place.
‡Central Division (American Conference).
§Tied for position.

PLAYOFF RECORD

Year	Club	W.	L.
1985—Cleveland NFL		0	1
1986—Cleveland NFL		1	1
1987—Cleveland NFL		1	1
1988—Cleveland NFL		0	1
Pro Totals—4 Years		2	4

1985—Lost conference playoff game to Miami, 24-21.
1986—Won conference playoff game in two overtimes from New York Jets, 23-20; lost conference championship game
in overtime to Denver, 23-20.
1987—Won conference playoff game from Indianapolis, 38-21; lost conference championship game to Denver, 38-33.
1988—Lost wild-card playoff game to Houston, 24-23.

GEORGE GERALD SEIFERT
San Francisco 49ers
Born January 22, 1940, at San Francisco, Calif.
High School—San Francisco, Calif., Polytechnic.
Received bachelor of science degree in zoology in 1963, and master's degree
in physical education in 1966, both from University of Utah.
Served six months in U.S. Army after college.

Graduate assistant at University of Utah, 1964.
Assistant coach at University of Iowa, 1966.
Assistant coach at University of Oregon, 1967 through 1971.
Assistant coach at Stanford University, 1972 through 1974 and 1977 through 1979.
Assistant coach, San Francisco 49ers NFL, 1980 through 1988.

Year Club	Pos.	W.	L.	T.
1965—Westminster (Utah)	†....	3	3	0
1975—Cornell	‡Eighth	1	8	0
1976—Cornell	‡§Seventh	2	7	0
College Totals—3 Years..........................		6	18	0

†Independent.
‡Ivy League.
§Tied for position.

MICHAEL EDWARD SHANAHAN
(Mike)
Los Angeles Raiders

Born August 24, 1952, at Oak Park, Ill.
High School—Franklin Park, Ill., East Leyden.
Received bachelor of science degree in physical education in 1974 and received master's degree in physical education in 1975, both from Eastern Illinois University.

COACHING RECORD

Graduate assistant at Eastern Illinois University, 1973 and 1974.
Assistant coach at University of Oklahoma, 1975 and 1976.
Assistant coach at Northern Arizona University, 1977.
Assistant coach at Eastern Illinois University, 1978.
Assistant coach at University of Minnesota, 1979.
Assistant coach at University of Florida, 1980 through 1983.
Assistant coach, Denver Broncos NFL, 1984 through 1987.

Year Club	Pos.	W.	L.	T.
1988—Los Angeles Raiders NFL	†Third	7	9	0

†Western Division (American Conference).

DONALD FRANCIS SHULA
(Don)
Miami Dolphins

Born January 4, 1930, at Painesville, O.
High School—Painesville, O., Harvey.
Received bachelor of arts degree in sociology from John Carroll University in 1951.
Father of David Shula, assistant coach with Dallas Cowboys;
and Mike Shula, assistant coach with Tampa Bay Buccaneers.

Played defensive back.
Selected by Cleveland in 9th round of 1951 NFL draft.
Traded with quarterback Harry Agganis, defensive backs Bert Rechichar and Carl Taseff, end Gern Nagler, guards Elmer Willhoite, Ed Sharkey and Art Spinney and tackles Dick Batten and Stu Sheetz by Cleveland NFL to Baltimore NFL for linebacker Tom Catlin, guard Herschel Forester, halfback John Petitbon and tackles Don Colo and Mike McCormack, March 25, 1953.
Sold by Baltimore NFL to Washington NFL, 1957.

Year Club	G.	——INTERCEPTIONS——			
		No.	Yds.	Avg.	TD.
1951—Cleveland NFL..............	12	4	23	5.8	0
1952—Cleveland NFL..............	5	None			
1953—Baltimore NFL	12	3	46	15.3	0
1954—Baltimore NFL	12	5	84	16.8	0
1955—Baltimore NFL	9	5	64	12.8	0
1956—Baltimore NFL	12	1	2	2.0	0
1957—Washington NFL	11	3	48	16.0	0
Pro Totals—7 Years...........	73	21	267	12.7	0

Additional pro statistics: Returned one kickoff for six yards, 1951; caught one pass for six yards, 1953; rushed twice for three yards, 1954; recovered two fumbles for 26 yards, 1955; recovered one fumble for six yards and returned one kickoff for no yards, 1956.
Played in NFL Championship Game following 1951 and 1952 seasons.

COACHING RECORD

Named NFL Coach of the Year by THE SPORTING NEWS, 1964, 1968, 1970 and 1972.
Assistant coach at University of Virginia, 1958.
Assistant coach at University of Kentucky, 1959.
Assistant coach, Detroit Lions NFL, 1960 through 1962.

Year	Club	Pos.	W.	L.	T.		Year	Club	Pos.	W.	L.	T.
1963—	Baltimore NFL	†Third	8	6	0		1977—	Miami NFL	§xFirst	10	4	0
1964—	Baltimore NFL	†First	12	2	0		1978—	Miami NFL	§xFirst	11	5	0
1965—	Baltimore NFL	†Second	10	3	1		1979—	Miami NFL	§First	10	6	0
1966—	Baltimore NFL	†Second	9	5	0		1980—	Miami NFL	§Third	8	8	0
1967—	Baltimore NFL	†Second	11	1	2		1981—	Miami NFL	§First	11	4	1
1968—	Baltimore NFL	‡First	13	1	0		1982—	Miami NFL	yxSecond	7	2	0
1969—	Baltimore NFL	‡Second	8	5	1		1983—	Miami NFL	§First	12	4	0
1970—	Miami NFL	§Second	10	4	0		1984—	Miami NFL	§First	14	2	0
1971—	Miami NFL	§First	10	3	1		1985—	Miami NFL	§First	12	4	0
1972—	Miami NFL	§First	14	0	0		1986—	Miami NFL	§Third	8	8	0
1973—	Miami NFL	§First	12	2	0		1987—	Miami NFL	§xSecond	8	7	0
1974—	Miami NFL	§First	11	3	0		1988—	Miami NFL	§Fifth	6	10	0
1975—	Miami NFL	§xFirst	10	4	0		Pro Totals—26 Years			261	111	6
1976—	Miami NFL	§Third	6	8	0							

†Western Conference.
‡Coastal Division (Western Conference).
§Eastern Division (American Conference).
xTied for position.
yAmerican Conference.

PLAYOFF RECORD

Year	Club	W.	L.		Year	Club	W.	L.
1964—	Baltimore NFL	0	1		1978—	Miami NFL	0	1
1965—	Baltimore NFL	1	1		1979—	Miami NFL	0	1
1966—	Baltimore NFL	1	0		1981—	Miami NFL	0	1
1968—	Baltimore NFL	2	1		1982—	Miami NFL	3	1
1970—	Miami NFL	0	1		1983—	Miami NFL	0	1
1971—	Miami NFL	2	1		1984—	Miami NFL	2	1
1972—	Miami NFL	3	0		1985—	Miami NFL	1	1
1973—	Miami NFL	3	0		Pro Totals—16 Years		18	13
1974—	Miami NFL	0	1					

1964—Lost NFL championship game to Cleveland, 27-0.
1965—Lost conference playoff game to Green Bay, 13-10; won Playoff Bowl from Dallas, 35-3.
1966—Won Playoff Bowl from Philadelphia, 20-14.
1968—Won conference playoff game from Minnesota, 24-14; won NFL championship game from Cleveland, 34-0; lost AFL-NFL playoff game (Super Bowl III) to New York Jets, 16-7.
1970—Lost conference playoff game to Oakland, 21-14.
1971—Won conference playoff game from Kansas City, 27-24; won conference playoff game from Baltimore, 21-0; lost NFL championship game (Super Bowl VI) to Dallas, 24-3.
1972—Won conference playoff game from Cleveland, 20-14; won conference championship game from Pittsburgh, 21-17; won NFL championship game (Super Bowl VII) from Washington, 14-7.
1973—Won conference playoff game from Cincinnati, 34-16; won conference championship game from Oakland, 27-10; won NFL championship game (Super Bowl VIII) from Minnesota, 24-7.
1974—Lost conference playoff game to Oakland, 28-26.
1978—Lost conference playoff game to Houston, 17-9.
1979—Lost conference playoff game to Pittsburgh, 34-14.
1981—Lost conference playoff game in overtime to San Diego, 41-38.
1982—Won conference playoff game from New England, 28-13; won conference playoff game from San Diego, 34-13; won conference championship game from New York Jets, 14-0; lost NFL championship game (Super Bowl XVII) to Washington, 27-17.
1983—Lost conference playoff game to Seattle, 27-20.
1984—Won conference playoff game from Seattle, 31-10; won conference championship game from Pittsburgh, 45-28; lost NFL championship game (Super Bowl XIX) to San Francisco, 38-16.
1985—Won conference playoff game from Cleveland, 24-21; lost conference championship game to New England, 31-14.

EUGENE CLIFTON STALLINGS
(Gene)
Phoenix Cardinals
Born March 2, 1935, at Paris, Tex.
High School—Paris, Tex.
Received bachelor of science degree in physical education from Texas A&M University in 1957.
COACHING RECORD
Student assistant coach, freshman team at Texas A&M University, 1957.
Assistant coach at University of Alabama, 1958 through 1964.
Assistant coach, Dallas Cowboys NFL, 1972 through 1985.

Year	Club	Pos.	W.	L.	T.		Year	Club	Pos.	W.	L.	T.
1965—	Texas A&M	†‡Seventh	3	7	0		1971—	Texas A&M	†Fourth	5	6	0
1966—	Texas A&M	†Fourth	4	5	1		1986—	St. Louis NFL	§Fifth	4	11	1
1967—	Texas A&M	†First	7	4	0		1987—	St. Louis NFL	‡§Second	7	8	0
1968—	Texas A&M	†‡Sixth	3	7	0		1988—	Phoenix NFL	‡§Third	7	9	0
1969—	Texas A&M	†‡Sixth	3	7	0		College Totals—7 Years			27	45	1
1970—	Texas A&M	†Eighth	2	9	0		Pro Totals—3 Years			18	28	1

†Southwest Conference.
‡Tied for position.
§Eastern Division (National Conference).

Year Club	W.	L.
1967—Texas A&M	1	0

1967—Won Cotton Bowl from Alabama, 20-16.

JOSEPH FRANK WALTON
(Joe)
New York Jets

Born December 15, 1935, at Beaver Falls, Pa.
High School—Beaver Falls, Pa.
Received bachelor of arts degree in history from University of Pittsburgh in 1957.
Son of Frank Walton, guard with Boston Redskins, 1934 and 1935;
and Washington Redskins, 1944 and 1945; assistant coach, Pittsburgh Steelers, 1946.
Played tight end.
Named end on THE SPORTING NEWS College All-America Team, 1956.
Selected by Washington in 2nd round of 1957 NFL draft.

		—PASS RECEIVING—			
Year Club	G.	P.C.	Yds.	Avg.	TD.
1957—Washington NFL	12	3	57	19.0	0
1958—Washington NFL	12	32	532	16.6	5
1959—Washington NFL	9	21	317	15.1	3
1960—Washington NFL	12	27	401	14.9	3
1961—N.Y. Giants NFL	12	36	544	15.1	2
1962—N.Y. Giants NFL	14	33	406	12.3	9
1963—N.Y. Giants NFL	12	26	371	14.3	6
Pro Totals—7 Years	83	178	2628	14.8	28

Additional pro statistics: Intercepted one pass for 55 yards, 1957; fumbled once, 1958, 1959, 1961 and 1962; recovered one fumble for four yards, 1960.

COACHING RECORD

Scout, New York Giants NFL, 1967 and 1968.
Assistant coach, New York Giants NFL, 1969 through 1973.
Assistant coach, Washington Redskins NFL, 1974 through 1980.
Assistant coach, New York Jets NFL, 1981 and 1982.

Year Club	Pos.	W.	L.	T.
1983—New York Jets NFL	†‡Fourth	7	9	0
1984—New York Jets NFL	†Third	7	9	0
1985—New York Jets NFL	†‡Second	11	5	0
1986—New York Jets NFL	†Second	10	6	0
1987—New York Jets NFL	†Fifth	6	9	0
1988—New York Jets NFL	†Fourth	8	7	1
Pro Totals—6 Years		49	45	1

†Eastern Division (American Conference).
‡Tied for position.

PLAYOFF RECORD

Year Club	W.	L.
1985—New York Jets NFL	0	1
1986—New York Jets NFL	1	1
Pro Totals—2 Years	1	2

1985—Lost wild-card playoff game to New England, 26-14.
1986—Won wild-card playoff game from Kansas City, 35-15; lost conference playoff game in two overtimes to Cleveland Browns, 23-20.

SAMUEL DAVID WYCHE
(Sam)
Cincinnati Bengals

Born January 5, 1945, at Atlanta, Ga.
High School—Atlanta, Ga., North Fulton.
Received bachelor of arts degree in business administration from Furman University
in 1966 and received master's degree from University of South Carolina.
Brother of Joseph (Bubba) Wyche, former quarterback with Saskatchewan Roughriders,
Detroit Wheels, Chicago Fire and Shreveport Steamer.
Played quarterback.
Played in Continental Football League with Wheeling Ironmen, 1966.
Signed as free agent by Cincinnati AFL, 1968.
Traded by Cincinnati Bengals to Washington Redskins for running back Henry Dyer, May 5, 1971.
Traded by Washington Redskins to Detroit Lions for quarterback Bill Cappelman, August 17, 1974.
Released by Detroit Lions, September 2, 1975; signed as free agent by St. Louis Cardinals, 1976.
Released by St. Louis Cardinals, September 23, 1976; signed as free agent by Buffalo Bills, October 26, 1976.
Member of Washington Redskins' taxi squad, 1973.
Active for 7 games with Buffalo Bills in 1976; did not play.

Year Club	G.	Att.	Cmp.	Pct.	Gain	T.P.	P.I.	Avg.	Att.	Yds.	Avg.	TD.	TD.	Pts.	F.
		PASSING							RUSHING				TOTAL		
1966—Wheeling CoFL	....	18	9	50.0	101	0	1	5.61	5	—11	—2.2	0	0	0	0
1968—Cincinnati AFL	3	55	35	63.6	494	2	2	8.98	12	74	6.2	0	0	0	2
1969—Cincinnati AFL	7	108	54	50.0	838	7	4	7.76	12	107	8.9	1	1	6	1
1970—Cincinnati NFL	13	57	26	45.6	411	3	2	7.21	19	118	6.2	2	2	12	3
1971—Washington NFL	1				None				1	4	4.0	0	0	0	0
1972—Washington NFL	7				None						None		0	0	0
1974—Detroit NFL	14	1	0	00.0	0	0	1	0.00	1	0	0.0	0	0	0	0
1976—St.L. (1)-Buf. (0) NFL	1	1	1	100.0	5	0	0	5.00			None		0	0	0
AFL Totals—2 Years	10	163	89	54.9	1332	9	6	8.17	24	181	7.5	1	1	6	3
NFL Totals—5 Years	36	59	27	45.8	416	3	3	7.05	21	122	5.8	2	2	12	3
Pro Totals—7 Years	46	222	116	52.3	1748	12	9	7.87	45	303	6.7	3	3	18	6

Additional CoFL statistics: Intercepted three passes for nine yards, 1966.
Additional AFL statistics: Caught one pass for five yards, 1968.
Additional NFL statistics: Recovered one fumble for minus one yard, 1970.
Played in NFL Championship Game following 1972 season.

COACHING RECORD

Graduate assistant at University of South Carolina, 1967.
Assistant coach, San Francisco 49ers NFL, 1979 through 1982.

Year Club	Pos.	W.	L.	T.
1983—Indiana	†‡Eighth	3	8	0
1984—Cincinnati NFL	§Second	8	8	0
1985—Cincinnati NFL	§‡Second	7	9	0
1986—Cincinnati NFL	§Second	10	6	0
1987—Cincinnati NFL	§Fourth	4	11	0
1988—Cincinnati NFL	§First	12	4	0
College Totals—1 Year		3	8	0
Pro Totals—5 Years		41	38	0

†Big Ten Conference.
‡Tied for position.
§Central Division (American Conference).

PLAYOFF RECORD

Year Club	W.	L.
1988—Cincinnati NFL	2	1

1988—Won conference playoff game from Seattle, 21-13; won conference championship game from Buffalo, 21-10; lost NFL championship game (Super Bowl XXIII) to San Francisco, 20-16.

Recently Retired Coaches

THOMAS WADE LANDRY
(Tom)

Born September 11, 1924, at Mission, Tex.
High School—Mission, Tex.
Received bachelor of business administration degree from University of Texas in 1949 and bachelor of science degree in industrial engineering from University of Houston.
Played defensive back.
Selected in 4th round from New York AAFC by New York Giants NFL in AAFC-NFL merger, 1950.

Year Club	G.	No.	Yds.	Avg.	TD.	No.	Avg.	Blk.	TD.	Pts.	F.
		INTERCEPTIONS				PUNTING			TOTAL		
1949—New York AAFC	13	1	44	44.0	0	51	44.1	★2	0	0	..
1950—New York Giants NFL	12	2	0	0.0	0	58	36.8	1	1	6	0
1951—New York Giants NFL	10	8	121	15.1	★2	15	42.5	0	3	18	0
1952—New York Giants NFL	12	8	99	12.4	1	82	41.0	1	2	12	5
1953—New York Giants NFL	12	3	55	18.3	0	44	40.3	0	0	0	1
1954—New York Giants NFL	12	8	71	8.9	0	64	42.5	0	0	0	1
1955—New York Giants NFL	12	2	14	7.0	0	★75	40.3	1	0	0	0
AAFC Totals—1 Year	13	1	44	44.0	0	51	44.1	2	0	0	..
NFL Totals—6 Years	70	31	360	11.6	3	338	40.4	3	6	36	7
Pro Totals—7 Years	83	32	404	12.6	3	389	40.9	5	6	36	..

Year Club	G.	—PUNT RETURNS— No.	Yds.	Avg.	TD.	—KICKOFF RET.— No.	Yds.	Avg.	TD.
1949—New York AAFC	13	3	52	17.3	0	2	39	19.5	0
1950—New York Giants NFL	12			None				None	
1951—New York Giants NFL	10	1	0	0.0	0	1	0	0.0	0
1952—New York Giants NFL	12	10	88	8.8	0	1	20	20.0	0
1953—New York Giants NFL	12	1	5	5.0	0	2	38	19.0	0
1954—New York Giants NFL	12			None				None	
1955—New York Giants NFL	12			None				None	
AAFC Totals—1 Year	13	3	52	17.3	0	2	39	19.5	0
NFL Totals—6 Years	70	12	93	7.8	0	4	58	14.5	0
Pro Totals—7 Years	83	15	145	9.7	0	6	97	16.2	0

Additional AAFC statistics: Rushed 29 times for 91 yards and caught six passes for 109 yards, 1949.

Additional NFL statistics: Rushed seven times for 40 yards and a touchdown, 1952; attempted 47 passes with 11 completions for 172 yards, one touchdown and seven interceptions, 1952; recovered two fumbles for 41 yards and one touchdown, 1950; recovered one fumble for nine yards and a touchdown, 1951; recovered two fumbles, 1952; recovered one fumble, 1953 and 1955; recovered two fumbles for 14 yards, 1954.

Played in Pro Bowl (NFL All-Star Game) following 1954 season.

COACHING RECORD

Named NFL Coach of the Year by THE SPORTING NEWS, 1966.
Player-coach for New York Giants NFL, 1954 and 1955.
Assistant coach, New York Giants NFL, 1956 through 1959.

Year Club	Pos.	W.	L.	T.	Year Club	Pos.	W.	L.	T.
1960—Dallas NFL	†Seventh	0	11	1	1975—Dallas NFL	ySecond	10	4	0
1961—Dallas NFL	‡Sixth	4	9	1	1976—Dallas NFL	yFirst	11	3	0
1962—Dallas NFL	‡Fifth	5	8	1	1977—Dallas NFL	yFirst	12	2	0
1963—Dallas NFL	‡Fifth	4	10	0	1978—Dallas NFL	yFirst	12	4	0
1964—Dallas NFL	‡Fifth	5	8	1	1979—Dallas NFL	y§First	11	5	0
1965—Dallas NFL	§‡Second	7	7	0	1980—Dallas NFL	y§First	12	4	0
1966—Dallas NFL	‡First	10	3	1	1981—Dallas NFL	yFirst	12	4	0
1967—Dallas NFL	xFirst	9	5	0	1982—Dallas NFL	zSecond	6	3	0
1968—Dallas NFL	xFirst	12	2	0	1983—Dallas NFL	ySecond	12	4	0
1969—Dallas NFL	xFirst	11	2	1	1984—Dallas NFL	y§Second	9	7	0
1970—Dallas NFL	yFirst	10	4	0	1985—Dallas NFL	y§First	10	6	0
1971—Dallas NFL	yFirst	11	3	0	1986—Dallas NFL	yThird	7	9	0
1972—Dallas NFL	ySecond	10	4	0	1987—Dallas NFL	§ySecond	7	8	0
1973—Dallas NFL	§yFirst	10	4	0	1988—Dallas NFL	yFifth	3	13	0
1974—Dallas NFL	yThird	8	6	0	Pro Totals—29 Years		250	162	6

†Western Conference.
‡Eastern Conference.
§Tied for position.
xCapitol Division (Eastern Conference).
yEastern Division (National Conference).
zNational Conference.

PLAYOFF RECORD

Year Club	W.	L.	Year Club	W.	L.
1965—Dallas NFL	0	1	1977—Dallas NFL	3	0
1966—Dallas NFL	0	1	1978—Dallas NFL	2	1
1967—Dallas NFL	1	1	1979—Dallas NFL	0	1
1968—Dallas NFL	1	1	1980—Dallas NFL	2	1
1969—Dallas NFL	0	2	1981—Dallas NFL	1	1
1970—Dallas NFL	2	1	1982—Dallas NFL	2	1
1971—Dallas NFL	3	0	1983—Dallas NFL	0	1
1972—Dallas NFL	1	1	1985—Dallas NFL	0	1
1973—Dallas NFL	1	1	Pro Totals—19 Years	21	18
1975—Dallas NFL	2	1			
1976—Dallas NFL	0	1			

1965—Lost Playoff Bowl to Baltimore, 35-3.
1966—Lost NFL championship game to Green Bay, 34-27.
1967—Won conference playoff game from Cleveland, 52-14; lost NFL championship game to Green Bay, 21-17.
1968—Lost conference playoff game to Cleveland, 31-20; won Playoff Bowl from Minnesota, 17-13.
1969—Lost conference playoff game to Cleveland, 38-14; lost Playoff Bowl to Los Angeles, 31-0.
1970—Won conference playoff game from Detroit, 5-0; won conference championship game from San Francisco, 17-10; lost NFL championship game (Super Bowl V) to Baltimore, 16-13.
1971—Won conference playoff game from Minnesota, 20-12; won conference championship game from San Francisco, 14-3; won NFL championship game (Super Bowl VI) from Miami, 24-3.
1972—Won conference playoff game from San Francisco, 30-28; lost conference championship game to Washington, 26-3.
1973—Won conference playoff game from Los Angeles, 27-16; lost conference championship game to Minnesota, 27-10.
1975—Won conference playoff game from Minnesota, 17-14; won conference championship game from Los Angeles, 37-7; lost NFL championship game (Super Bowl X) to Pittsburgh, 21-17.
1976—Lost conference playoff game to Los Angeles, 14-12.
1977—Won conference playoff game from Chicago, 37-7; won conference championship game from Minnesota, 23-6; won NFL championship game (Super Bowl XII) from Denver, 27-10.
1978—Won conference playoff game from Atlanta, 27-20; won conference championship game from Los Angeles, 28-0; lost NFL championship game (Super Bowl XIII) to Pittsburgh, 35-31.
1979—Lost conference playoff game to Los Angeles, 21-19.
1980—Won conference playoff game from Los Angeles, 34-13; won conference playoff game from Atlanta, 30-27; lost conference championship game to Philadelphia, 20-7.

TOM LANDRY

1981—Won conference playoff game from Tampa Bay, 38-0; lost conference championship game to San Francisco, 28-27.
1982—Won conference playoff game from Tampa Bay, 30-17; won conference playoff game from Green Bay, 37-26; lost conference championship game to Washington, 31-17.
1983—Lost wild-card playoff game to Los Angeles Rams, 24-17.
1985—Lost conference playoff game to Los Angeles Rams, 20-0.

WILLIAM ERNEST WALSH
(Bill)
Born November 30, 1931, at Los Angeles, Calif.
High School—Los Angeles, Calif., Hayward.
Attended San Mateo Junior College and received bachelor of arts degree
and master's degree in education from San Jose State in 1959.

COACHING RECORD
Named NFL Coach of the Year by THE SPORTING NEWS, 1981.
Assistant coach at Monterey Peninsula College, 1955.
Assistant coach at San Jose State University, 1956.
Head coach at Washington Union High, Fremont, Calif., 1957 through 1959.
Assistant coach at University of California, 1960 through 1962.
Assistant coach at Stanford University, 1963 through 1965.
Assistant coach, Oakland Raiders AFL, 1966.
Assistant coach, Cincinnati Bengals AFL, 1968 and 1969.
Assistant coach, Cincinnati Bengals NFL, 1970 through 1975.
Assistant coach, San Diego Chargers NFL, 1976.

Year Club	Pos.	W.	L.	T.
1967—San Jose CoFL	†Second	7	5	0
1977—Stanford	‡§Second	9	3	0
1978—Stanford	xFourth	8	4	0
1979—San Francisco NFL	yFourth	2	14	0
1980—San Francisco NFL	yThird	6	10	0
1981—San Francisco NFL	yFirst	13	3	0
1982—San Francisco NFL	z§11th	3	6	0
1983—San Francisco NFL	yFirst	10	6	0
1984—San Francisco NFL	yFirst	15	1	0
1985—San Francisco NFL	ySecond	10	6	0
1986—San Francisco NFL	yFirst	10	5	1
1987—San Francisco NFL	yFirst	13	2	0
1988—San Francisco NFL	§yFirst	10	6	0
College Totals—2 Years		17	7	0
Pro Totals—10 Years		92	59	1

†Continental League.
‡Pacific Eight Conference.
§Tied for position.
xPacific Ten Conference.
yWestern Division (National Conference).
zNational Conference.

PLAYOFF RECORD

Year Club	W.	L.
1981—San Francisco NFL	3	0
1983—San Francisco NFL	1	1
1984—San Francisco NFL	3	0
1985—San Francisco NFL	0	1
1986—San Francisco NFL	0	1
1987—San Francisco NFL	0	1
1988—San Francisco NFL	3	0
Pro Totals—7 Years	10	4

1981—Won conference playoff game from New York Giants, 38-24; won conference championship game from Dallas, 28-27; won NFL championship game (Super Bowl XVI) from Cincinnati, 26-21.
1983—Won conference playoff game from Detroit, 24-23; lost conference championship game to Washington, 24-21.
1984—Won conference playoff game from New York Giants, 21-10; won conference championship game from Chicago, 23-0; won NFL championship game (Super Bowl XIX) from Miami, 38-16.
1985—Lost wild-card playoff game to New York Giants, 17-3.
1986—Lost conference playoff game to New York Giants, 49-3.
1987—Lost conference playoff game to Minnesota, 36-24.
1988—Won conference playoff game from Minnesota, 34-9; won conference championship game from Chicago, 28-3; won NFL championship game (Super Bowl XXIII) from Cincinnati, 20-16.

COLLEGIATE BOWL GAME RECORD

Year Club	W.	L.
1977—Stanford	1	0
1978—Stanford	1	0
College Totals—2 Years	2	0

1977—Won Sun Bowl from Louisiana State, 24-14.
1978—Won Bluebonnet Bowl from Georgia, 25-22.

BILL WALSH

Recently Retired Players

DAVID ROY BUTZ
(Dave)

Born June 23, 1950, at Lafayette, Ala.
Height, 6.07. Weight, 295.
High School—Park Ridge, Ill., Maine South.
Received bachelor of science degree in physical education,
health and safety from Purdue University in 1973.
Nephew of Earl Butz, former secretary of agriculture.

Named as defensive tackle on THE SPORTING NEWS College All-America Team, 1972.
Named to THE SPORTING NEWS NFL All-Star Team, 1983.
Selected by St. Louis in 1st round (5th player selected) of 1973 NFL draft.
Played out option with St. Louis Cardinals and signed by Washington Redskins, August 5, 1975; Cardinals received three draft choices (1st round picks in 1977 and 1978 and 2nd round pick in 1979) in exchange for three draft choices (5th and 15th round picks in 1976 and 6th round pick in 1977) as compensation, September 4, 1975.
Granted unconditional free agency, February 1, 1989; did not receive qualifying offer, April 15, 1989.
St. Louis NFL, 1973 and 1974; Washington NFL, 1975 through 1988.
Games: 1973 (12), 1974 (1), 1975 (14), 1976 (14), 1977 (12), 1978 (16), 1979 (15), 1980 (16), 1981 (16), 1982 (9), 1983 (16), 1984 (15), 1985 (16), 1986 (16), 1987 (12), 1988 (16). Total—216.
Pro statistics: Returned one kickoff for 23 yards, 1973; recovered one fumble, 1973, 1976, 1982 through 1985 and 1988; intercepted one pass for three yards, 1978; intercepted one pass for 26 yards, 1981.
Played in NFC Championship Game following 1982, 1983, 1986 and 1987 seasons.
Played in NFL Championship Game following 1982, 1983 and 1987 seasons.
Played in Pro Bowl (NFL All-Star Game) following 1983 season.

HAROLD DONALD CARSON
(Harry)

Born November 26, 1953, at Florence, S. C.
Height, 6.02. Weight, 240.
High School—Florence, S. C., McClenaghan.
Received bachelor of science degree in physical education
from South Carolina State College.

Named to THE SPORTING NEWS NFL All-Star Team, 1984.
Named to THE SPORTING NEWS NFC All-Star Team, 1979.
Selected by New York Giants in 4th round (105th player selected) of 1976 NFL draft.
On injured reserve with knee injury, October 16 through November 13, 1980; activated, November 14, 1980.
On injured reserve, November 24 through remainder of 1980 season.
On injured reserve with knee injury, September 19 through October 28, 1983; activated, October 29, 1983.
On injured reserve with knee injury, November 18 through December 16, 1988; activated, December 17, 1988.
Granted unconditional free agency, February 1, 1989; did not receive qualifying offer, April 15, 1989.

Year Club	G.	No.	Yds.	Avg.	TD.
1976—N.Y. Giants NFL	12		None		
1977—N.Y. Giants NFL	14		None		
1978—N.Y. Giants NFL	16	3	86	28.7	0
1979—N.Y. Giants NFL	16	3	28	9.3	0
1980—N.Y. Giants NFL	8		None		
1981—N.Y. Giants NFL	16		None		
1982—N.Y. Giants NFL	9	1	6	6.0	0
1983—N.Y. Giants NFL	10		None		
1984—N.Y. Giants NFL	16	1	6	6.0	0
1985—N.Y. Giants NFL	16		None		
1986—N.Y. Giants NFL	16	1	20	20.0	0
1987—N.Y. Giants NFL	12		None		
1988—N.Y. Giants NFL	12	2	66	33.0	0
Pro Totals—13 Years	173	11	212	19.3	0

Additional pro statistics: Recovered one fumble, 1976 through 1978, 1980, 1984 and 1987; returned one kickoff for five yards, 1976; recovered three fumbles for 22 yards and one touchdown, 1979; recovered one fumble for two yards, 1981; caught one pass for 13 yards and a touchdown and recovered two fumbles, 1986; recovered two fumbles for 12 yards, 1988.
Played in NFC Championship Game following 1986 season.
Played in NFL Championship Game following 1986 season.
Played in Pro Bowl (NFL All-Star Game) following 1978, 1979 and 1981 through 1987 seasons.

WESLEY SANDY CHANDLER
(Wes)

Born August 22, 1956, at New Smyrna Beach, Fla.
Height, 6.00. Weight, 188.
High School—New Smyrna Beach, Fla.
Received degree in speech pathology from University of Florida.

Named as wide receiver on THE SPORTING NEWS College All-America Team, 1977.
Selected by New Orleans in 1st round (3rd player selected) of 1978 NFL draft.
Traded by New Orleans Saints to San Diego Chargers for wide receiver Aundra Thompson and 1st and 3rd round

HARRY CARSON

picks in 1982 draft, September 29, 1981.

Traded with conditional 1989 draft pick by San Diego Chargers to San Francisco 49ers for center Fred Quillan and 7th round pick in 1989 draft, June 3, 1988.

Placed on reserve/retired list, October 1 through October 6, 1988.

Released by San Francisco 49ers, October 7, 1988.

Year Club	G.	PASS RECEIVING				-PUNT RETURNS-				—KICKOFF RET.—				—TOTAL—		
		P.C.	Yds.	Avg.	TD.	No.	Yds.	Avg.	TD.	No.	Yds.	Avg.	TD.	TD.	Pts.	F.
1978—New Orleans NFL........	16	35	472	13.5	2	34	233	6.9	0	32	760	23.8	0	2	12	1
1979—New Orleans NFL........	16	65	1069	16.4	6	3	13	4.3	0	7	136	19.4	0	6	36	0
1980—New Orleans NFL........	16	65	975	15.0	6	8	36	4.5	0	None				6	36	2
1981—N.O. (4)-S.D. (12) NFL.	16	69	1142	16.6	6	5	79	15.8	0	8	125	15.6	0	6	36	1
1982—San Diego NFL	8	49	*1032	21.1	*9	None				None				9	54	0
1983—San Diego NFL	16	58	845	14.6	5	8	26	3.3	0	None				5	30	3
1984—San Diego NFL	15	52	708	13.6	6	None				None				6	36	0
1985—San Diego NFL	15	67	1199	17.9	10	None				None				10	60	1
1986—San Diego NFL	16	56	874	15.6	4	3	13	4.3	0	1	11	11.0	0	4	24	2
1987—San Diego NFL	12	39	617	15.8	2	None				None				2	12	1
1988—San Francisco NFL	4	4	33	8.3	0	6	28	4.7	0	None				0	0	0
Pro Totals—11 Years.....	150	559	8966	16.0	56	67	428	6.4	0	48	1032	21.5	0	56	336	11

Additional pro statistics: Rushed twice for 10 yards, 1978; punted eight times for 31.0 average, 1979; attempted one pass with one completion for 43 yards and recovered two fumbles, 1980; rushed once for nine yards, 1980 and 1985; recovered one fumble for 51 yards, rushed five times for minus one yard and attempted two passes with no completions, 1981; rushed five times for 32 yards, 1982; rushed twice for 25 yards and recovered one fumble, 1983; punted five times for a 33.4 average, 1986; recovered one fumble, 1987.

Played in AFC Championship Game following 1981 season.

Played in Pro Bowl (NFL All-Star Game) following 1979, 1982, 1983 and 1985 seasons.

ROBIN COLE

Born September 11, 1955, at Los Angeles, Calif.

Height, 6.02. Weight, 225.

High School—Compton, Calif.

Attended University of New Mexico.

Cousin of Willie Davis, Hall of Fame defensive end with Cleveland Browns and Green Bay Packers, 1958 through 1969.

Selected by Pittsburgh in 1st round (21st player selected) of 1977 NFL draft.

Released by Pittsburgh Steelers, August 29, 1988; awarded on waivers to New York Jets, August 31, 1988.

Pittsburgh NFL, 1977 through 1987; New York Jets NFL, 1988.

Games: 1977 (8), 1978 (16), 1979 (13), 1980 (14), 1981 (14), 1982 (9), 1983 (16), 1984 (16), 1985 (16), 1986 (16), 1987 (12), 1988 (16). Total—166.

Pro statistics: Recovered two fumbles, 1977 and 1986; recovered one fumble, 1979, 1981, 1987 and 1988; returned one kickoff for three yards, 1979; intercepted one pass for 34 yards and recovered one fumble for 14 yards, 1980; intercepted one pass for 29 yards, 1981; recovered two fumbles for 20 yards, 1983; intercepted one pass for 12 yards and recovered one fumble for eight yards, 1984; intercepted one pass for four yards and recovered three fumbles, 1985; intercepted one pass for no yards, 1987.

Played in AFC Championship Game following 1978, 1979 and 1984 seasons.

Played in NFL Championship Game following 1978 and 1979 seasons.

Played in Pro Bowl (NFL All-Star Game) following 1984 season.

JOE STANIER CRIBBS

Born January 5, 1958, at Sulligent, Ala.

Height, 5.11. Weight, 190.

High School—Sulligent, Ala.

Attended Auburn University.

Named as running back on THE SPORTING NEWS USFL All-Star Team, 1984.

Selected by Buffalo in 2nd round (29th player selected) of 1980 NFL draft.

On did not report list, August 24 through November 19, 1982; activated, November 20, 1982.

Signed by Birmingham Stallions, July 2, 1983, for contract to take affect after being granted free agency, February 1, 1984.

Granted roster exemption, February 15, 1984; activated, February 25, 1984.

On suspended list, May 9 through May 22, 1984; activated, May 23, 1984.

On developmental squad, June 3 through June 7, 1985; activated, June 8, 1985.

Released by Birmingham Stallions, October 14, 1985; re-signed by Buffalo Bills, October 11, 1985.

Granted roster exemption, October 11 through October 18, 1985; activated, October 19, 1985.

Traded by Buffalo Bills to San Francisco 49ers for 3rd round pick in 1987 draft and 5th round pick in 1988 draft, August 19, 1986.

Crossed picket line during players' strike, October 7, 1987.

Released by San Francisco 49ers, August 24, 1988; signed as free agent by Indianapolis Colts, September 2, 1988.

Released by Indianapolis Colts, September 19, 1988; signed as free agent by Miami Dolphins, September 28, 1988.

Granted unconditional free agency, February 1, 1989; did not receive qualifying offer, April 15, 1989.

On developmental squad for 1 game with Birmingham Stallions in 1985.

Year Club	G.	RUSHING				PASS RECEIVING				—TOTAL—		
		Att.	Yds.	Avg.	TD.	P.C.	Yds.	Avg.	TD.	TD.	Pts.	F.
1980—Buffalo NFL..............	16	306	1185	3.9	11	52	415	8.0	1	12	72	*16
1981—Buffalo NFL..............	15	257	1097	4.3	3	40	603	15.1	7	10	60	12
1982—Buffalo NFL..............	7	134	633	4.7	3	13	99	7.6	0	3	18	5
1983—Buffalo NFL..............	16	263	1131	4.3	3	57	524	9.2	7	10	60	6
1984—Birmingham USFL	16	*297	*1467	4.9	8	39	500	12.8	5	13	78	7
1985—Birmingham USFL	17	267	1047	3.9	7	41	287	7.0	1	8	48	3

Year Club	G.	Att.	Yds.	Avg.	TD.	P.C.	Yds.	Avg.	TD.	TD.	Pts.	F.
		——RUSHING——				PASS RECEIVING				—TOTAL—		
1985—Buffalo NFL	10	122	399	3.3	1	18	142	7.9	0	1	6	5
1986—San Francisco NFL	14	152	590	3.9	5	35	346	9.9	0	5	30	5
1987—San Francisco NFL	11	70	300	4.3	1	9	70	7.8	0	2	12	1
1988—Indianapolis (1)-Miami (12) NFL	13	5	21	4.2	0		None			0	0	1
NFL Totals—8 Years	102	1299	5356	4.1	27	224	2199	9.8	15	43	258	51
USFL Totals—2 Years	33	564	2514	4.5	15	80	787	9.8	6	21	126	10
Pro Totals—10 Years	135	1863	7870	4.2	42	304	2986	9.8	21	64	384	61

Year Club	G.	No.	Yds.	Avg.	TD.	No.	Yds.	Avg.	TD.
		—PUNT RETURNS—				—KICKOFF RET.—			
1980—Buffalo NFL	16	29	154	5.3	0	2	39	19.5	0
1981—Buffalo NFL	15		None				None		
1982—Buffalo NFL	7		None				None		
1983—Buffalo NFL	16		None				None		
1984—Birmingham USFL	16		None				None		
1985—Birmingham USFL	17		None				None		
1985—Buffalo NFL	10		None				None		
1986—San Francisco NFL	14		None				None		
1987—San Francisco NFL	11		None			13	327	25.2	1
1988—Indianapolis (1)-Miami (12) NFL	13		None			*41	863	21.0	0
NFL Totals—8 Years	102	29	154	5.3	0	56	1229	21.9	1
USFL Totals—2 Years	33	0	0	0.0	0	0	0	0.0	0
Pro Totals—10 Years	135	29	154	5.3	0	56	1229	21.9	1

Additional NFL statistics: Attempted one pass with one completion for 13 yards; recovered one fumble for minus seven yards, 1980; attempted one pass with one completion for nine yards and a touchdown, 1981; attempted one pass with one interception and recovered two fumbles, 1982; recovered one fumble, 1981, 1983, 1985 and 1986; attempted two passes with one completion for three yards, 1983.
Additional USFL statistics: Recovered one fumble, 1984 and 1985.
Played in Pro Bowl (NFL All-Star Game) following 1980 and 1983 seasons.
Named to Pro Bowl following 1981 season (replaced due to injury by Pete Johnson).

RANDALL LAUREAT CROSS
(Randy)
Born April 25, 1954, at Brooklyn, N.Y.
Height, 6.03. Weight, 265.
High School—Encino, Calif., Crespi.
Received degree in political science from University of California at Los Angeles in 1976.
Son of Dennis Cross, former television actor.

Selected by San Francisco in 2nd round (42nd player selected) of 1976 NFL draft.
On injured reserve with ankle injury, November 3 through remainder of 1978 season.
On injured reserve with knee injury, December 18 through remainder of 1985 season.
Granted unconditional free agency, February 1, 1989; did not receive qualifying offer, April 15, 1989.
San Francisco NFL, 1976 through 1988.
Games: 1976 (14), 1977 (14), 1978 (9), 1979 (16), 1980 (16), 1981 (16), 1982 (9), 1983 (16), 1984 (16), 1985, (15), 1986 (16), 1987 (12), 1988 (16). Total—185.
Pro statistics: Recovered one fumble, 1976, 1982, 1986 and 1988; fumbled once for minus 37 yards; 1977; fumbled once, 1978; recovered two fumbles, 1979.
Played in NFC Championship Game following 1981, 1983, 1984 and 1988 seasons.
Played in NFL Championship Game following 1981, 1984 and 1988 seasons.
Played in Pro Bowl (NFL All-Star Game) following 1981, 1982 and 1984 seasons.

GARY DENNIS DANIELSON
Born September 10, 1951, at Detroit, Mich.
Height, 6.02. Weight, 196.
High School—Dearborn, Mich., Divine Child.
Received bachelor of science degree in business management in 1973 and master's degree
in sports administration in 1976, both from Purdue University.
Son-in-law of George King, basketball player with Syracuse Nationals and
Cincinnati Royals, 1951-52 through 1955-56 and 1957-58.

Signed as free agent by New York Stars (WFL), 1974.
Traded by Charlotte Hornets (WFL) to Chicago Winds (WFL) for future considerations, 1975.
Signed as free agent by Detroit Lions after World Football League folded, 1976.
On injured reserve with knee injury, August 28 through entire 1979 season.
On injured reserve with broken wrist, October 8 through November 24, 1981; activated, November 25, 1981.
USFL rights traded by Michigan Panthers to Arizona Wranglers for 4th round pick in 1984 draft, April 4, 1983.
Traded by Detroit Lions to Cleveland Browns for 3rd round pick in 1986 draft, May 1, 1985.
On injured reserve with broken ankle, September 1 through entire 1986 season.
Crossed picket line during players' strike, October 14, 1987.
On injured reserve with broken ankle, September 12 through remainder of 1988 season.
Granted unconditional free agency, February 1, 1989; did not receive qualifying offer, April 15, 1989.

Year Club	G.	Att.	Cmp.	Pct.	Gain	T.P.	P.I.	Avg.	Att.	Yds.	Avg.	TD.	TD.	Pts.	F.
		——————PASSING——————							——RUSHING——				—TOTAL—		
1974—N.Y.-Char. WFL	....	60	28	46.7	305	1	0	5.08	10	51	5.1	3	3	21	....
1975—Chicago WFL	....	15	9	60.0	107	0	2	7.13		None			0	0	....
1976—Detroit NFL	1			None						None			0	0	0

Year Club	G.	Att.	Cmp.	Pct.	Gain	T.P.	P.I.	Avg.	Att.	Yds.	Avg.	TD.	TD.	Pts.	F.
					PASSING					RUSHING				TOTAL	
1977—Detroit NFL	13	100	42	42.0	445	1	5	4.45	7	62	8.9	0	0	0	0
1978—Detroit NFL	16	351	199	56.7	2294	18	17	6.54	22	93	4.2	0	0	0	5
1980—Detroit NFL	16	417	244	58.5	3223	13	11	7.73	48	232	4.8	2	2	12	11
1981—Detroit NFL	6	96	56	58.3	784	3	5	8.17	9	23	2.6	2	2	12	2
1982—Detroit NFL	8	197	100	50.8	1343	10	14	6.82	23	92	4.0	0	0	0	6
1983—Detroit NFL	10	113	59	52.2	720	7	4	6.37	6	8	1.3	0	0	0	2
1984—Detroit NFL	15	410	252	61.5	3076	17	15	7.50	41	218	5.3	3	4	24	7
1985—Cleveland NFL	8	163	97	59.5	1274	8	6	7.82	25	126	5.0	0	0	0	5
1987—Cleveland NFL	6	33	25	75.8	281	4	0	8.52	1	0	0.0	0	0	0	2
1988—Cleveland NFL	2	52	31	59.6	324	0	1	6.23	4	3	0.8	0	0	0	1
WFL Totals—2 Years	....	75	37	49.3	412	1	2	5.49	10	51	5.1	3	3	21	....
NFL Totals—11 Years	101	1932	1105	57.2	13764	81	78	7.12	186	857	4.6	7	8	48	41
Pro Totals—13 Years	....	2007	1142	56.9	14176	82	80	7.06	196	908	4.6	10	11	69	....

NFL Quarterback Rating Points: 1977 (38.1), 1978 (73.6), 1980 (82.6), 1981 (73.4), 1982 (60.3), 1983 (78.0), 1984 (83.1), 1985 (85.3), 1987 (140.3), 1988 (69.7). Total—76.8.

Additional pro statistics: Recovered one fumble, 1977, 1982 and 1983; recovered two fumbles and fumbled five times for minus 12 yards, 1978; recovered four fumbles and fumbled 11 times for minus two yards, 1980; fumbled six times for minus 11 yards, 1982; caught one pass for 22 yards and a touchdown, recovered two fumbles and fumbled seven times for minus five yards, 1984; recovered one fumble and fumbled five times for minus 17 yards, 1985; recovered two fumbles and fumbled twice for minus two yards, 1987; fumbled once for minus four yards, 1988.

Member of Cleveland Browns for AFC Championship Game following 1987 season; did not play.

ANTHONY RAY FRANKLIN
(Tony)

Born November 18, 1956, at Big Spring, Tex.
Height, 5.08. Weight, 182.
High School—Fort Worth, Tex., Arlington Heights.
Attended Texas A&M University.

Selected by Philadelphia in 3rd round (74th player) of 1979 NFL draft.
Traded by Philadelphia Eagles to New England Patriots for 6th round pick in 1985 draft, February 21, 1984.
Crossed picket line during players' strike, October 7, 1987.
Released by New England Patriots, August 24, 1988; signed as free agent by Miami Dolphins, October 19, 1988.
Released by Miami Dolphins, November 23, 1988.

Year Club	G.	XP.	XPM.	FG.	FGA.	Pts.
			PLACE KICKING			
1979—Philadelphia NFL	16	36	3	23	31	105
1980—Philadelphia NFL	16	48	0	16	31	96
1981—Philadelphia NFL	16	41	2	20	31	101
1982—Philadelphia NFL	9	23	2	6	9	41
1983—Philadelphia NFL	16	24	3	15	26	69
1984—New England NFL	16	42	0	22	28	108
1985—New England NFL	16	40	1	24	30	112
1986—New England NFL	16	44	1	*32	*41	*140
1987—New England NFL	14	37	1	15	26	82
1988—Miami NFL	5	6	1	4	11	18
Pro Totals—10 Years	140	341	14	177	264	872

Additional pro statistics: Punted once for 32 yards, 1979; punted once for 13 yards, 1981, rushed once for minus five yards, 1985.

Played in NFC Championship Game following 1980 season.
Played in AFC Championship Game following 1985 season.
Played in NFL Championship Game following 1980 and 1985 seasons.
Played in Pro Bowl (NFL All-Star Game) following 1986 season.

MARCUS D. GASTINEAU

Name pronounced GAS-tin-oh.

(Mark)

Born November 20, 1956, at Ardmore, Okla.
Height, 6.05. Weight, 255.
High School—Springerville, Ariz., Round Valley.
Attended Eastern Arizona Junior College, Arizona State University and
East Central (Okla.) University
Son of Ernie Gastineau, former professional boxer.

Named to THE SPORTING NEWS NFL All-Star Team, 1984 and 1985.
Selected by New York Jets in 2nd round (41st player selected) of 1979 NFL draft.
On injured reserve with knee injury, November 20 through December 25, 1986; activated, December 26, 1986.
Crossed picket line during players' strike, September 23, 1987.
Placed on reserve/retired list, October 22, 1988.
New York Jets NFL, 1979 through 1988.
Games: 1979 (16), 1980 (16), 1981 (16), 1982 (9), 1983 (16), 1984 (16), 1985 (16), 1986 (10), 1987 (15), 1988 (7). Total—137.

Pro statistics: Recovered two fumbles, 1981; recovered two fumbles (including one in end zone for a touchdown), 1983; recovered one fumble in end zone for a touchdown, 1984; recovered three fumbles, 1985; recovered one fumble, 1988.

Played in AFC Championship Game following 1982 season.
Played in Pro Bowl (NFL All-Star Game) following 1981 through 1985 seasons.

JOHN EDWARD HARRIS

Born June 13, 1956, at Fort Benning, Ga.
Height, 6.02. Weight, 200.
High School—Miami, Fla., Jackson.
Received bachelor of science degree in political science from Arizona State University in 1978.

Selected by Seattle in 7th round (173rd player selected) of 1978 NFL draft.
On did not report list, August 31 through September 1, 1982; activated and granted two-game roster exemption, September 2, 1982.
Activated, September 10, 1982.
Granted free agency, February 1, 1986; re-signed by Seahawks, August 31, 1986.
Granted roster exemption, August 31 and September 1, 1986.
Traded by Seattle Seahawks to Minnesota Vikings for 7th round pick in 1987 draft, September 2, 1986.
Granted roster exemption, September 2 through September 4, 1986; activated, September 5, 1986.
On injured reserve with ankle and heel injuries, October 29 through November 8, 1988; activated after clearing procedural waivers, November 10, 1988.
Granted unconditional free agency, February 1, 1989; released on waivers, April 11, 1989.

			—INTERCEPTIONS—		
Year Club	G.	No.	Yds.	Avg.	TD.
1978—Seattle NFL	16	4	65	16.3	0
1979—Seattle NFL	14	2	30	15.0	0
1980—Seattle NFL	16	6	28	4.7	0
1981—Seattle NFL	16	10	155	15.5	2
1982—Seattle NFL	9	4	33	8.3	0
1983—Seattle NFL	16	2	15	7.5	0
1984—Seattle NFL	16	6	79	13.2	0
1985—Seattle NFL	16	7	20	2.9	0
1986—Minnesota NFL	16	3	69	23.0	0
1987—Minnesota NFL	12	3	20	6.7	0
1988—Minnesota NFL	13	3	46	15.3	0
Pro Totals—11 Years	160	50	560	11.2	2

Additional pro statistics: Returned five punts for 58 yards, 1978; fumbled once, 1978, 1979 and 1981; returned eight punts for 70 yards and returned one kickoff for 21 yards, 1979; recovered one fumble, 1979, 1980, 1984 and 1987; recovered three fumbles, 1981; returned two punts for 27 yards and recovered three fumbles for 62 yards, 1983; returned one kickoff for seven yards, 1984; returned three punts for 24 yards and recovered two fumbles, 1985.
Played in AFC Championship Game following 1983 season.
Played in NFC Championship Game following 1987 season.

BRIAN DOUGLASS HOLLOWAY

Born July 25, 1959, at Omaha, Neb.
Height, 6.07. Weight, 275.
High School—Potomac, Md., Winston Churchill.
Received bachelor of arts degree in economics from Stanford University in 1981.
Son-in-law of John McKenzie, forward with Chicago Black Hawks, Detroit Red Wings, New York Rangers, Boston Bruins, Philadelphia-Vancouver Blazers, Minnesota Fighting Saints, Cincinnati Stingers and New England Whalers, 1958 through 1961 and 1963 through 1979;
and brother of Jonathan Holloway, linebacker at Stanford University.

Selected by New England in 1st round (19th player selected) of 1981 NFL draft.
Traded by New England Patriots to Los Angeles Raiders for 5th round pick in 1988 draft and 7th round pick in 1989 draft, September 1, 1987.
On injured reserve with separated shoulder, September 14 through October 18, 1988.
Released by Los Angeles Raiders, October 19, 1988.
New England NFL, 1981 through 1986; Los Angeles Raiders NFL, 1987 and 1988.
Games: 1981 (16), 1982 (9), 1983 (16), 1984 (16), 1985 (16), 1986 (15), 1987 (12), 1988 (2). Total—102.
Pro statistics: Recovered one fumble, 1981 and 1986; recovered two fumbles, 1985; caught one pass for five yards, 1986.
Played in AFC Championship Game following 1985 season.
Played in NFC Championship Game following 1985 season.
Played in Pro Bowl (NFL All-Star Game) following 1983 through 1985 seasons.

WILLIAM ARTHUR JOHNSON
(Billy White Shoes)

Born January 27, 1952, at Bouthwyn, Pa.
Height, 5.09. Weight, 170.
High School—Boothwyn, Pa., Chichester.
Received bachelor of arts degree in history from Widener College.

Established NFL record for punt return yards, career (3,317).
Tied NFL record for most touchdowns, combined returns, season (4), 1975.
Named as punt returner to THE SPORTING NEWS NFL All-Star Team, 1983.
Selected by Houston in 15th round (365th player selected) of 1974 NFL draft.
On injured reserve with knee injury, November 10 through remainder of 1978 season.
On injured reserve with knee injury, September 11 through remainder of 1979 season.
Granted free agency, February 2, 1981; signed by Montreal Alouettes, May 19, 1981.
Released by Montreal Concordes, April 15, 1982; signed as free agent by Atlanta Falcons, July 20, 1982.
On injured reserve with knee injury, October 9 through remainder of 1984 season.
On injured reserve with foot injury, August 26 through October 17, 1986; activated, October 18, 1986.
On injured reserve with foot injury, November 1 through December 12, 1986; activated, December 13, 1986.
Granted free agency with no qualifying offer, February 1, 1988; signed by Indianapolis Colts, April 27, 1988.

Released by Indianapolis Colts, July 27, 1988; signed as free agent by Washington Redskins, September 14, 1988.
Released by Washington Redskins, September 23, 1988.
Played for Philadelphia Athletics of American Professional Slo-Pitch Softball League, 1978.

Year Club	G.	Att.	Yds.	Avg.	TD.	P.C.	Yds.	Avg.	TD.	TD.	Pts.	F.
		——RUSHING——				PASS RECEIVING				—TOTAL—		
1974—Houston NFL	14	5	82	16.4	1	29	388	13.4	2	3	18	1
1975—Houston NFL	14	5	17	3.4	0	37	393	10.6	1	5	30	5
1976—Houston NFL	14	6	6	1.0	0	47	495	10.5	4	4	24	3
1977—Houston NFL	14	6	102	17.0	1	20	412	20.6	3	7	42	2
1978—Houston NFL	5		None			1	10	10.0	0	0	0	0
1979—Houston NFL	2		None			6	108	18.0	1	1	6	0
1980—Houston NFL	16	2	1	0.5	0	31	343	11.1	2	2	12	1
1981—Montreal CFL	16	1	—9	—9.0	0	65	1060	16.3	5	5	30	3
1982—Atlanta NFL	9		None			2	11	5.5	0	0	0	1
1983—Atlanta NFL	16	15	83	5.5	0	64	709	11.1	4	5	30	4
1984—Atlanta NFL	6	3	8	2.7	0	24	371	15.5	3	3	18	1
1985—Atlanta NFL	16	8	—8	—1.0	0	62	830	13.4	5	5	30	4
1986—Atlanta NFL	4	6	25	4.2	0	6	57	9.5	0	0	0	0
1987—Atlanta NFL	12		None			8	84	10.5	0	0	0	2
1988—Washington NFL	1		None				None			0	0	0
NFL Totals—14 Years	143	56	316	5.6	2	337	4211	12.5	25	35	210	24
CFL Totals—1 Year	16	1	—9	—9.0	0	65	1060	16.3	5	5	30	3
Pro Totals—15 Years	159	57	307	5.4	2	402	5271	13.1	30	40	240	27

Year Club	G.	No.	Yds.	Avg.	TD.	No.	Yds.	Avg.	TD.
		—PUNT RETURNS—				—KICKOFF RET.—			
1974—Houston NFL	14	30	409	13.6	0	29	785	27.1	0
1975—Houston NFL	14	40	612	★15.3	★3	33	798	24.2	★1
1976—Houston NFL	14	38	403	10.6	0	26	579	22.3	0
1977—Houston NFL	14	35	539	★15.4	★2	25	630	25.2	1
1978—Houston NFL	5	8	60	7.5	0	4	73	18.3	0
1979—Houston NFL	2	4	17	4.3	0	4	37	9.3	0
1980—Houston NFL	16		None				None		
1981—Montreal CFL	16	59	597	10.1	0		None		
1982—Atlanta NFL	9	24	273	11.4	0		None		
1983—Atlanta NFL	16	46	489	10.6	★1		None		
1984—Atlanta NFL	6	15	152	10.1	0	2	39	19.5	0
1985—Atlanta NFL	16	10	82	8.2	0		None		
1986—Atlanta NFL	4	8	87	10.9	0		None		
1987—Atlanta NFL	12	21	168	8.0	0		None		
1988—Washington NFL	1	3	26	8.7	0		None		
NFL Totals—14 Years	143	282	3317	11.8	6	123	2941	23.9	2
CFL Totals—1 Year	16	59	597	10.1	0	0	0	0.0	0
Pro Totals—15 Years	159	341	3914	11.5	6	123	2941	23.9	2

Additional pro statistics: Recovered one fumble, 1975 and 1976; attempted one pass with no completions and recovered two fumbles, 1983.
Played in Pro Bowl (NFL All-Star Game) following 1975, 1977 and 1983 seasons.

JOSEPH EDWARD KLECKO
(Joe)
Born October 15, 1953, at Chester, Pa.
Height, 6.03. Weight, 263.
High School—Chester, Pa., St. James.
Received bachelor of arts degree in history from Temple University in 1977.
Named to THE SPORTING NEWS NFL All-Star Team, 1981.
Selected by New York Jets in 6th round (144th player selected) of 1977 NFL draft.
On injured reserve with knee injury, November 26, 1982 through January 4, 1983; activated, January 5, 1983.
On injured reserve with knee injury, December 17 through remainder of 1986 season.
On physically unable to perform/reserve with knee injury, August 31 through November 13, 1987; activated, November 14, 1987.
Crossed picket line during players' strike, October 2, 1987.
Released by New York Jets, February 18, 1988; signed as free agent by Indianapolis Colts, April 22, 1988.
On non-football injury/active with neck injury, July 22 through July 28, 1988; passed physical, July 29, 1988.
Granted unconditional free agency, February 1, 1989; announced retirement, February 13, 1989.
Played semi-pro football with Ridley Township Green Knights, 1971 and 1972.
New York Jets NFL, 1977 through 1987; Indianapolis NFL, 1988.
Games: 1977 (13), 1978 (16), 1979 (16), 1980 (15), 1981 (16), 1982 (2), 1983 (16), 1984 (12), 1985 (16), 1986 (11), 1987 (7), 1988 (15). Total—155.
Pro statistics: Recovered one fumble, 1978, 1983, 1985, 1987 and 1988; recovered two fumbles, 1981 and 1984.
Played in AFC Championship Game following 1982 season.
Played in Pro Bowl (NFL All-Star Game) following 1981 and 1983 through 1985 seasons.

GEORGE DWIGHT MARTIN
Born February 16, 1953, at Greenville, S. C.
Height, 6.04. Weight, 255.
High School—Fairfield, Calif., Armijo.
Attended University of Oregon.
Brother of Doug Martin, defensive end with Minnesota Vikings.
Established NFL record for touchdowns by down lineman, career (6).
Selected by New York Giants in 11th round (262nd player selected) of 1975 NFL draft.

RANDY WHITE

Granted unconditional free agency, February 1, 1989; did not receive qualifying offer, April 15, 1989.
New York Giants NFL, 1975 through 1988.
Games: 1975 (14), 1976 (14), 1977 (10), 1978 (16), 1979 (16), 1980 (16), 1981 (16), 1982 (9), 1983 (14), 1984 (16), 1985 (16), 1986 (16), 1987 (12), 1988 (16). Total—201.
Pro statistics: Recovered two fumbles, 1976; intercepted one pass for 30 yards and one touchdown, 1977; recovered one fumble, 1977, 1980 and 1984 through 1986; ran 83 yards with blocked field goal for a touchdown, 1978; recovered three fumbles, 1979; caught one pass for four yards and a touchdown, 1980; recovered three fumbles for 28 yards and two touchdowns, 1981; intercepted one pass for 56 yards and a touchdown, 1985; intercepted one pass for 78 yards and a touchdown, 1986; recovered two fumbles for four yards, 1988.
Played in NFC Championship Game following 1986 season.
Played in NFL Championship Game following 1986 season.

CHARLES RAYMOND WHITE

Born January 22, 1958, at Los Angeles, Calif.
Height, 5.10. Weight, 190.
High School—San Fernando, Calif.
Attended University of Southern California.

Heisman Trophy winner, 1979.
Named to THE SPORTING NEWS NFL All-Star Team, 1987.
Named as running back on THE SPORTING NEWS College All-America Team, 1979.
Named THE SPORTING NEWS College Player of the Year, 1979.
Selected by Cleveland in 1st round (27th player selected) of 1980 NFL draft.
On injured reserve with broken ankle, August 16 through entire 1983 season.
On physically unable to perform/active with ankle injury, July 19 through August 11, 1984; activated, August 12, 1984.
On injured reserve with ankle and back injuries, November 30 through remainder of 1984 season.
Released by Cleveland Browns, June 4, 1985; signed as free agent by Los Angeles Rams, July 9, 1985.
Released by Los Angeles Rams, September 2, 1985; re-signed by Rams, September 3, 1985.
Crossed picket line during players' strike, October 1, 1987.
On non-football injury list with substance abuse, September 8 through October 3, 1988; reinstated, October 4, 1988.
Granted unconditional free agency, February 1, 1989; did not receive qualifying offer, April 15, 1989.

Year Club			—RUSHING—			PASS RECEIVING				—TOTAL—		
	G.	Att.	Yds.	Avg.	TD.	P.C.	Yds.	Avg.	TD.	TD.	Pts.	F.
1980—Cleveland NFL	14	86	279	3.2	5	17	153	9.0	1	6	36	1
1981—Cleveland NFL	16	97	342	3.5	1	27	219	8.1	0	1	6	8
1982—Cleveland NFL	9	69	259	3.8	3	34	283	8.3	0	3	18	2
1984—Cleveland NFL	10	24	62	2.6	0	5	29	5.8	0	0	0	0
1985—Los Angeles Rams NFL	16	70	310	4.4	3	1	12	12.0	0	3	18	3
1986—Los Angeles Rams NFL	16	22	126	5.7	0	1	7	7.0	0	0	0	2
1987—Los Angeles Rams NFL	15	*324	*1374	4.2	*11	23	121	5.3	0	11	66	8
1988—Los Angeles Rams NFL	12	88	323	3.7	0	6	36	6.0	0	0	0	3
Pro Totals—8 Years	108	780	3075	3.9	23	114	860	7.5	1	24	144	27

Year Club	KICKOFF RETURNS				Year Club	KICKOFF RETURNS			
	G.	No.	Yds.	Avg.TD.		G.	No.	Yds.	Avg.TD.
1980—Cleveland NFL	14	1	20	20.0 0	1986—L.A. Rams NFL	16	12	216	18.0 0
1981—Cleveland NFL	16	12	243	20.3 0	1987—L.A. Rams NFL	15	3	73	24.3 0
1982—Cleveland NFL	9			None	1988—L.A. Rams NFL	12	2	37	18.5 0
1984—Cleveland NFL	10	5	80	16.0 0	Pro Totals—8 Years	108	52	969	18.6 0
1985—L.A. Rams NFL	16	17	300	17.6 0					

Additional pro statistics: Recovered one fumble, 1980 and 1987; recovered three fumbles, 1981; returned one punt for no yards, 1985.
Played in NFC Championship Game following 1985 season.
Played in Pro Bowl (NFL All-Star Game) following 1987 season.

RANDY LEE WHITE

Born January 15, 1953, at Wilmington, Del.
Height, 6.04. Weight, 265.
High School—Wilmington, Del., Thomas McKean.
Attended University of Maryland.

Outland Trophy winner, 1974.
Named as defensive end on THE SPORTING NEWS College All-America Team, 1974.
Named to THE SPORTING NEWS NFC All-Star Team, 1978 and 1979.
Named to THE SPORTING NEWS NFL All-Star Team, 1980, 1981, 1983 and 1985.
Selected by Dallas in 1st round (2nd player selected) of 1975 NFL draft.
Placed on did not report list, August 21 through August 26, 1984.
Reported and granted roster exemption, August 27 through September 2, 1984; activated, September 3, 1984.
Crossed picket line during players' strike, September 23, 1987.
Granted unconditional free agency, February 1, 1989; did not receive qualifying offer, April 15, 1989.
Dallas NFL, 1975 through 1988.
Games: 1975 (14), 1976 (14), 1977 (14), 1978 (16), 1979 (15), 1980 (16), 1981 (16), 1982 (9), 1983 (16), 1984 (16), 1985 (16), 1986 (16), 1987 (15), 1988 (16). Total—209.
Pro statistics: Recovered two fumbles, 1975, 1977 and 1986; recovered one fumble, 1976, 1979, 1982 and 1983; returned one kickoff for 15 yards, 1978; intercepted one pass for no yards, 1987.
Played in NFC Championship Game following 1975, 1977, 1978 and 1980 through 1982 seasons.
Played in NFL Championship Game following 1975, 1977 and 1978 seasons.
Played in Pro Bowl (NFL All-Star Game) following 1977 and 1979 through 1985 seasons.
Named to play in Pro Bowl following 1978 season; replaced due to injury by Doug English.